HARRY L. RINKER

The Official® Price Guide To

COLLECTIBLES

HARRY L. RINKER

The Official® Price Guide To

COLLECTIBLES

First Edition

HOUSE OF COLLECTIBLES • NEW YORK

Copyright ©1997 by Rinker Enterprises, Inc.

Published by: House of Collectibles
201 East 50th Street
New York, New York 10022

Distributed by Ballantine Books, a division of Random House, Inc., New York, and simultaneously in Canada by Random House of Canada Limited, Toronto.

http://www.randomhouse.com

Manufactured in the United States of America

ISSN: 1094–3862

ISBN: 0–676–60106–5

Cover design by Kristine V. Mills–Noble

Cover photo by George Kerrigan

First Edition: September 1997

10 9 8 7 6 5 4 3 2 1

CONTENTS

INTRODUCTION

Welcome to the first edition of the **Harry L. Rinker The Official Price Guide to Collectibles,** my first general price guide with my name in the title. To say that I am proud of this book is an understatement. I am bursting at the seams with pride. This is the price guide I have wanted to do for years. It is my fondest hope that in time the trade will simply refer to it as **Rinker's.**

How does the **Harry L. Rinker The Official Price Guide to Collectibles** differ from other general antiques and collectibles price guides? First, it focuses on the heart of today's antiques, collectibles, and desirables market—the period between 1920 and the present. Between 80% and 85% of all the material found at auctions, flea markets, antiques malls, shops, and shows dates from this period. Further, today's collectors are primarily 20th–century collectors. Each year the percentage of individuals collecting 18th– and 19th–century material compared to the whole grows less and less. While there will always be collectors for this early material, they will need deep pocketbooks. Pre–1920 antiques are expensive. Most post–1920 antiques, collectibles, and desirables are both affordable and readily available.

Second, it is comprehensive. This book is filled with the things with which your parents, you, and your children lived and played. Nothing is missing. You will find furniture, decorative accessories, and giftware along with the traditional character and personality items, ceramics, glass, and toys. It is a complete document of the 20th–century American lifestyle.

Third, in the "Acknowledgments" in the seventh edition of *Warman's Americana & Collectibles,* I wrote: "After twelve years, *Warman's Americana & Collectibles* continues to enjoy the unique distinction of being the only general price guide devoted exclusively to things made in the 20th century. It is one of the few general price guides that has gone without formal opposition for over a decade." Without a rival, complacency develops. Publishers hate tampering with a proven winner. Complacency is not a plus in the antiques and collectibles field; and I am not a complacent person. I needed to free myself to rival myself.

Harry L. Rinker The Official Price Guide to Collectibles, a price guide to the 20th century for the 21st–century collector, is the result. Free from the restraints of *Warman's,* I created a new baby, one capable of responding more quickly to market changes and developments. It contains over one hundred categories not found in my previous book. Many categories have been restructured and reorganized. This book more accurately reflects how things are collected in today's antiques and collectibles market. And, it is just an infant. I am excited about the role that I will play in guiding its growth to maturity.

Fourth, over the years I have developed a reputation in the trade for being extremely opinionated and outspoken. I call 'em like I see 'em. I am not a member of the "if you can't say something nice, don't say anything at all" school.

As a reporter, my job is to present the facts and to interpret them. You will not find any artificial price propping in this book. If prices within a category are being manipulated or highly speculative, I spell it out. Whether you agree or not is not the issue. Unlike the good news price guides, the **Harry L. Rinker The Official Price Guide to Collectibles** is designed to make you think.

ANTIQUES, COLLECTIBLES, & DESIRABLES

Harry L. Rinker The Official Price Guide to Collectibles contains antiques, collectibles, and desirables. This being the case, why doesn't this book have a different title? The answer is twofold. When most individuals think of things made in the 20th century, they think of collectibles. People do not like to admit that objects associated with their childhood have become antiques. Further, not everyone, especially manufacturers of contemporary collectors' editions and giftware, separates collectibles and desirables into two different categories. They prefer them lumped together.

What is an antique, a collectible, and a desirable? An antique is anything made before 1945. A collectible is something made between 1945 and 1969. Antiques and collectibles have a stable secondary resale market. A desirable is something made after 1969. Desirables have a speculative secondary resale market.

As each year passes, the number of people who disagree with my definition of an antique lessens. The year 1945 is an important dividing line. Life in America in 1938 was very different than life in America in 1948. The immediate post–World War II period witnessed the arrival of the suburbs, transfer of wartime technology, e.g., injection molding, into domestic production, television, women in the work force, a global view, and, most importantly, the Baby Boomers.

Today, there are three generations of adult collectors who grew up in the post–1945 time period—those whose childhood (by my definition the period between ages 7 and 14) occurred between 1945 and 1960, between 1960 and the mid–1970s, and between the mid–1970s and the late 1980s. Half of today's population was born after 1960. All they know about John F. Kennedy is what they read in history books. They cannot answer the question: Where were you when you heard JFK was shot?

I used to define a collectible as something made between 1945 and 1962. I have now extended the end date to 1969. The reason is Rinker's Thirty–Year Rule: "For the first thirty years of anything's life, all its value is speculative." It takes thirty years to establish a viable secondary resale market. The 1960s has reached this point.

Will there come a time when I have to move the antique date forward? The answer is yes. I strongly suspect that by 2010, material from the 1950s will definitely be considered antique. However, 2010 is twelve years in the future. In the interim, a collectible remains an object made between 1945 and 1969.

America is a nation of collectors. There are more collectors than non–collectors. However, not everyone collects antiques and collectibles. Many individuals collect contemporary objects ranging from Hallmark ornaments to collectors' edition whiskey bottles. These are the desirables. It is as important to report on the market value of desirables as it is antiques and collectibles.

I do not care what someone collects. All I care about is that they collect. The joy of collecting comes from the act of collecting. I resent those who make value judgments relative to what is and is not worth collecting. I know Avon collectors who are far more caring, willing to share, and knowledgeable of the history and importance of their objects than wealthy collectors whose homes are filled with Colonial period furniture and accessories. There is no room for snobbery in today's collecting community. You will find none in this book.

Manufacturers of desirables market them as collectibles. They are not collectibles as I define the term. Desirables have not stood the test of time. Some undoubtedly will become collectibles and even eventually antiques. However, the vast majority will not. Their final resting place is more likely to be a landfill than a china cabinet or shelf.

Harry L. Rinker The Official Price Guide to Collectibles reports on objects in play, i.e., things that are currently being bought and sold actively in the secondary market. Desirables are as much in play as antiques and collectibles. Hence, they belong in this book.

ORGANIZATION

Categories: Objects are listed alphabetically by category beginning with Abingdon Pottery and ending with Yellow Ware. In the past decade, dozens of collectible subcategories, e.g., Barbie and Star Wars, have evolved as full–blown, independent collecting categories. This book's categories clearly illustrate the manner in which objects are being collected in the late 1990s.

If you have trouble locating an object, check the index. Collectibles are multifaceted, i.e., they can be assigned to more than one category. A 1949 C&O Railroad calendar

picturing Chessie and her kittens playing with a toy train would be equally at home in the Advertising Character, Calendar, Cat, Illustrator, Railroad, or Toy Train categories. Such objects have been extensively cross–referenced. Do not give up after checking your first and second classification choices. Most post–1920 objects cross over into six or more collecting categories.

Category Introduction: An object has many values. Financial is only one of them. The pleasure of owning an object and the nostalgic feelings it evokes are others.

It is a proven fact that the more that is known about an object, the more its value increases. It is for this reason that the histories found in this book are more substantial than those found in other general price guides. Every object has multiple stories attached to it—who made it, when it was made, how it was made, how it was used, why it was saved, etc. The histories answer many of these questions.

Occasionally one or two additional pieces of information—collecting tips and/or market trends—are included with the history. You will not find these insider tips in other general price guides. Yet, of all the information found in this book, these may prove to be the most valuable of all.

References: In many cases, you will find all the information you are seeking in this book. What happens when you do not? Where do you turn next? The answer is the references listed in this book.

Each reference listing contains the name of the author, complete title, edition if appropriate, publisher, and publishing date of the book. This information will enable you to purchase the book, locate it at a library, or have the location of a copy researched through interlibrary loan.

Two principal criteria—availability and quality of information, descriptions, and pricing—were used to select the books that are listed. Almost every book listed is still in print. An occasional exception was made for a seminal work in the category.

Unfortunately, the antiques and collectibles field is plagued with price guides that are nothing more than poorly done point–and–shoot priced picture books or whose prices in no way reflect true market values. They are not listed as references in this book even though they are in print.

Accuracy of information is one of the main hallmarks of this book. Nothing is gained by referencing a source that does not adhere to these same high standards. **Harry L. Rinker The Official Price Guide to Collectibles** is designed to earn your trust. Carefully selecting the references is only one example of that commitment.

David J. Maloney, Jr.'s *Maloney's Antiques & Collectibles Resource Directory,* published by Antique Trader Books, is the most important reference book, next to this one of course, in the field. Although a fourth edition is currently being prepared, do not wait to acquire a copy. Buy the third edition. You simply cannot afford to be without this book.

Periodicals and Newsletters: A list of general antiques and collectibles trade periodicals with full addresses and telephone numbers is part of this book's front matter. The periodicals and newsletters listed within a category relate specifically to that category. They are the first place to turn when looking for further information about that category.

Collectors' Clubs: Collectors' clubs play a vital role in the collecting field. They put collectors in touch with one another. Their newsletters contain information simply not found elsewhere. Their annual conventions allow for an exchange of information and objects. Their membership lists are often a who's who within the category.

Trying to keep track of the correct mailing address for a collectors' club is a full–time job. A club's address changes when its officers change. In some clubs, this occurs annually. The address provided has been checked and double–checked. Hopefully, it is current.

A few individuals and manufacturers have created collectors' clubs as sales fronts. With a few exceptions, e.g., Royal Doulton, these are not listed. The vast majority of clubs listed have an elected board of directors and operate as non–profit organizations.

Reproduction Alert: Reproductions (an exact copy of a period piece), copycats (a stylistic reproduction), fantasy items (in a shape or form that did not exist during the initial period of manufacture or licensing), and fakes (deliberately meant to deceive) are becoming a major problem within the antiques and collectibles field. It would require a book more than double the size of this one to list all the objects that fall within these categories.

Reproduction alerts have been placed throughout the book to serve as a reminder that problems exist more than to document every problem that exists. Do not assume that when no reproduction alert appears, the category is free of the problem. Assume every category has a problem. Make any object you are purchasing prove to you that it is right.

The *Antique & Collectors Reproduction News* (PO Box 12130, Des Moines, IA 50312, annual subscription $32) is a publication devoted to keeping track of current reproductions, copycats, fantasy items, and fakes. Consider subscribing.

Listings: The object descriptions and value listings are the heart and soul of this book. Listings contain the details necessary to specifically identify an object. Unlike some price guides whose listings are confined to one line, this guide sets no limit other than to provide the amount of information needed to do the job right. While this approach results in fewer listings, it raises the accuracy and comprehension level significantly. Better to be safe than sorry.

Each category's listings are only a sampling of the items found in that category. Great care has been taken to select those objects that are commonly found in the market. A few high–end objects are included to show the price range within a category. However, no price guide has value if the listed objects cannot be found or are priced so high few can afford them.

If you do not find the specific object you are seeking, look for comparable objects similar in description to the one that you own. A general price guide's role is to get you into the ballpark and up to the plate. Great care has been taken in each category to provide objects that represent a broad range of objects within a collecting category. Ideally, when looking for a comparable, you should find two or more objects that fit the bill.

The listing format is quick and easy to use. It was selected following a survey of general price guide users. Surprisingly, it allows for more listings per page than an indented system.

Auction Price Boxes: While the values provided in this price guide come from a wide variety of sources, people continually ask, "What does it sell for at auction?" A partial answer to this question is found in the Auction Prices boxes scattered throughout this book.

The assumption is that the highest values are achieved at auction. This is not the case. Dealers purchase a large percentage of objects sold at auction. This is why all auction prices are carefully evaluated and adjusted when necessary before being used in the general listings of this price guide.

Index: The index is a road map that shows you the most direct route to the information you are seeking. Take a moment and study it. Like any road map, the more you use it the more proficient you will become.

When researching your object, always start with the broadest general category. If this proves unsuccessful, try specific forms of the object and/or its manufacturer. Remember, because of their multifaceted nature, 20th–century collectibles are at home in multiple categories. Perseverance pays.

Illustrations: Great care has been taken in selecting the illustrations that appear in this book. They are not just fill. Illustrations indicate the type of object or objects commonly found in the category. They come from a variety of sources—auction houses, authors, field photography, and mail and trade catalogs.

This book provides caption information directly beside or beneath the illustration. You do not have to hunt for it in the text listings as you do in some other guides.

PRICE NOTES

The values in this book are based on an object being in very good to fine condition. This means that the object is complete and shows no visible signs of aging and wear when held at arm's length. If the value is based on a condition other than very good or fine, the precise condition is included in the descriptive listing.

Prices are designed to reflect the prices that sellers at an antiques mall or collectibles show would ask for their merchandise. When an object is collected nationally, it is possible to determine a national price consensus. Most of the objects in this book fall into that category. There are very few 20th–century collectibles whose values are regionally driven. Even racing collectibles, once collected primarily in the South, have gone national.

There are no fixed prices in the antiques and collectibles market. Value is fluid, not absolute. Price is very much of the time and moment. Change the circumstances, change the price. **Harry L. Rinker The Official Price Guide to Collectibles** is a price guide. That is all it is—a guide. It should be used to confirm, not set prices.

Must the original box or packaging accompany an object for it to be considered complete? While some would argue that the answer is yes, especially for post–1980s material, this book is based on the assumption that the box and object are two separate entities. If the price given includes the box, the presence of the box is noted in the description.

Prices represent the best judgment of the Rinker Enterprises staff after carefully reviewing all the available price source information related to the collecting category. It is not required that an object actually be sold during the past year to be listed in this book. If this policy was followed, users would have a distorted view of the market. Sales of common objects are rarely documented. A book based solely on reported prices would be far too oriented toward the middle and high ends of the market.

Instead, each category's listings have been carefully selected to reflect those objects within the category that are currently available in the antiques and collectibles market. Commonly found objects comprise the bulk of the listings. A few hard–to–find and scarce examples are included. These show the category's breadth and price range.

PRICE SOURCES

The values found in this book come from a wide variety of sources—auctions, dealers, direct sale catalogs and lists, field research, the Internet, private individuals, and trade periodicals. All prices are carefully reviewed and adjusted to reflect fair market retail value.

Several criteria are used in deciding what sources to track. All sections of the country must be represented. This is a national, not a regional, price guide. The sources must be reliable. Listings must be specific. Prices must be consistent, not only within the source but when compared to other national price sources. There must be a constant flow of information from the sources. Auctions held by collectors' clubs at their annual conventions are the one exception.

ADVISORS

I decided not to create a Board of Advisors for the first edition of this book. My reason was a selfish one. I wanted to exercise total control of the shaping of this book.

However, do not assume for one moment that I lacked or failed to seek advice from hundreds of antiques mall managers, appraisers, auctioneers, authors, dealers, private collectors, show promoters, and others during the preparation of this book. During the twenty–plus years I have been actively involved in the antiques and collectibles field, I have established a network of individuals upon whom I can call whenever a question arises. In many cases, my contacts within a collecting category are several individuals strong.

AMERICANA VERSUS INTERNATIONALISM

Americana, defined as things typical of America, is an obsolete term. It should be dropped from our collecting vocabulary.

First, the entire world is rapidly becoming Americanized. American movies, music, and television play as major a role outside as they do inside America. Burger King, Foot Locker, McDonald's, and Toys 'R Us have gone global. Barbie has a far higher worldwide recognition factor than any human personality.

Second, foreign collectors are not content to collect objects produced and licensed in their countries. America is the great mother lode of 20th–century collectibles. When African, European, Far Eastern, or South American collectors want Star Wars memorabilia, they come to America to buy. The role played by foreign buyers in the antiques and collectibles market continues to increase.

Third, thanks to the Internet, most individuals need only turn on their computers to sell and buy collectibles anywhere in the world. The Internet is not limited by international boundaries. It is turning us into world citizens no matter what our personal preferences.

Finally, many "American" goods are manufactured offshore or contain parts that were made abroad. Defining something as being distinctly American is no longer easy. We live in an age when new designs can be copied within days of their appearance. Foreign manufacturers are quick to make products that look like the American form.

Let's delete "Americana" and send it to the trash bin.

BUYER'S GUIDE, NOT A SELLER'S GUIDE

Harry L. Rinker The Official Price Guide to Collectibles is a buyer's guide. Values reflect what someone should expect to pay for an object he wishes to purchase.

This book is not a seller's guide. Do not make a mistake and assume that it is. If you have an object listed in this book and wish to sell it, expect to receive 30% to 40% of the price listed if the object is commonly found and 50% to 60% if the object is harder to find. Do not assume that a collector will pay more. In the 1990s antiques and collectibles market, collectors expect to pay what a dealer would pay for merchandise when buying privately.

Also, there is no guarantee that you will do better at auction. First, you will pay a commission for selling your goods. Second, dealers buy the vast majority of antiques and collectibles sold at auction. They certainly are not going to resell them for what they paid for them.

The method most likely to result in your selling objects for the values found in this book is to become an antiques dealer. This is not as easy as it sounds. Selling antiques and collectibles is hard work.

There is no one best way to sell antiques and collectibles. All of the above are reasonable choices. Much depends on how much time, effort, and money you wish to expend.

In the final analysis, a good price is one in which the buyer and seller are equally happy. Make as many of your purchases as possible win–win deals. Keep your focus on the object, not the buying and selling process.

COMMENTS INVITED

Every effort has been made to make this price guide useful and accurate. Your comments and suggestions, both positive and negative, are needed to make the next edition even better. Send them to: Rinker Enterprises, Inc., 5093 Vera Cruz Road, Emmaus, PA 18049.

ACKNOWLEDGMENTS

I feel somewhat akin to the Star Trek crews. Two years ago, I made a decision "to boldly go where no one has gone before." In order to explore new universes, you have to cut the ties that bind you to homeworld.

After editing fifteen editions of *Warman's Antiques and Collectibles Price Guide* and seven editions of *Warman's Americana and Collectibles,* I left to explore new frontiers. Some members of the crew remained. Those with a sense of adventure and vision welcomed the opportunity to expand their horizons. New members joined. I now command a crew I would match against any on homeworld.

Harry L. Rinker The Official Price Guide to Collectibles is the result of a shared vision, not the result of one person's dream. Three separate crews played a major role—House of Collectibles, Rinker Enterprises, and members of the trade.

Timothy J. Kochuba, general manager of House of Collectibles, immediately seized upon this book's ground–breaking vision and saw opportunity where others did not. When I began this project, I warned Tim that the gestation period of general collectibles price guides is often far longer than nine months. He did not believe me. Now, he does. It is my fondest hope that the publication and sales of this volume will reverse at least a portion of the premature aging its preparation has caused Tim. The good news is that the gestation period of subsequent editions is less than half that of the first.

Randy Ladenheim–Gil, the consummate professional publishing editor, was the team coach of this project. Publishing editors rarely receive sufficient credit for the role they play. Not in this case. Randy Ladenheim–Gil was this book's coach during the birth process. I would not have wanted anyone else in the delivery room.

Alex Klapwald provided guidance during this book's production process. Rinker Enterprises submitted the book in camera–ready pages that included text and illustrations. This represents a major step forward at Rinker Enterprises. The crew and I learned a great deal about QuarkExpress, Adobe Photoshop, scanners, and the ornery nature of computers during the past twelve months.

The leadership mantle at Rinker Enterprises now rests in the capable hands of Dana Morykan, my co–author for *Warman's Country* and *Garage Sale Manual & Price Guide.* Dana was the project manager. There is nothing she did not do, from compiling listings and values to selecting illustrations. She is responsible for the page layout. Dana took my vision and made it come alive.

Kathy Williamson temporarily joined the staff of Rinker Enterprises in the summer of 1996 to work on the fourth edition of *Price Guide to Flea Market Treasures.* She did such an excellent job I asked her to stay. Kathy's principal responsibility for this book was listings and values. She also assisted with the scanning of images.

Dena George, Dana's sister, is now a member of Rinker Enterprises. She worked on this project on an as–needed basis while working with me preparing the manuscripts for a three–book series covering dinnerware, stemware, and silverware. Once these projects were completed, she assisted in the scanning, compilation of listings and values, and final page layout corrections.

The blossoming of Nancy Butt, our reference librarian, is one of the most positive results of the recent changes at Rinker Enterprises. I regret not recognizing the hidden restraints that had been placed on Nancy. She checked the reference, periodical, newsletter, and collector club listings. Nancy was very much involved in the review and decision–making process with respect to which titles were included as references.

Virginia Reinbold manages Rinker Enterprises' finances, enabling the rest of us to devote our energies to books and other projects. Imagine a computer whiz who is over seventy. I only hope I live so rich and full a life. Richard "Cap" Schmeltzle, our jack–of–all–trades, is responsible for our work environment. Cap is an individual whose vocabulary does not include no as a response to any request for help.

Casey George's computer skills and Kristen Morykan's work with photographs and images were also valuable contributions to this book.

Finally, a general note of thanks and appreciation to those businesses and individuals in the trade who shared information and/or illustrations with me. You helped make this book possible. It is my earnest wish that you feel the same degree of pride for contributing to its success as I do for authoring it.

Rinker Enterprises, Inc.   Harry L. Rinker
5093 Vera Cruz Road   Author
Emmaus, PA 18049   August 1997

STATE OF THE MARKET REPORT

The collectibles market has fully recovered from the economic recession of the late 1980s and early 1990s. While a conservative approach still reigns supreme, there are hints that buoyant optimism, the hallmark of the mid–1980s collectibles market, is returning.

The recession slowed the collectibles market. Prices stabilized in some categories and dropped in others. The good news is that the price decline has bottomed out. Prices are gradually creeping higher in most collectibles categories. While a few categories are experiencing a major run in prices, most are keeping pace with increases in the cost of living.

The recession taught individuals involved in the collectibles market a number of valuable lessons. There is a price point above which an object will not sell. One cannot assume the sky is the limit on value. The survival rate for post–1945 collectibles is extremely high. After an initial period of collecting interest, supply can easily exceed demand. Further, there are a limited number of collectors, especially at the top, within each category. In some cases that number is in the thousands. In most cases, it is in the low to mid–hundreds.

Dealer inventory is more limited in 1997 than it was in 1987. Today dealers as well as collectors have become very cautious buyers. Dealers seek a far quicker turn around for their merchandise. They often will check with a customer regarding interest and price before purchasing an object. Direct selling has become as important as sales at antiques malls, shops, and shows.

Dealers relearned the value of second and third sales to customers. In the early 1980s, most dealers took the attitude that if you do not buy it, someone else will. This happened. The recession removed the decorator and casual buyer from the collectibles market. Remembering how they were treated by dealers in boom times, collectors extracted a modicum of revenge. They bought cautiously and selectively.

The cost of doing business rose during the recession. This was a surprise. Dealers did more shows in an effort to enhance their cash flow. They traveled greater distances. Many rented spaces in two or three antiques malls.

The recession checked the runaway inflation of the early and mid–1980s. It provided a much–needed market correction. It changed the way business was done. While painful, most of these changes were positive.

Almost ten years have passed since the recession began. Like those who lived through the Depression, the individuals who survived the recession of the late–1980s are not going to forget what happened. They plan to be prepared if it happens again.

However, there is a new generation of individuals, both collectors and dealers, in the collectibles field who were not around when the recession hit. Their market view is entirely different. They see a strong market getting stronger. Each selling season is better than the last. If they are not careful, they are going to repeat the mistakes made in the early 1980s. "Those who forget the past are condemned to repeat it."

The number of collectibles categories is increasing. Every year two to five new categories join the list. The continued growth of collectors' clubs and increase in the number of specialized book titles are the primary reasons. Americans are a nation of joiners. Collecting is always more fun when it is shared and easier to justify when there are supporting price guides. While the collectibles field has not quite reached the point where there is a price guide for everything, there are many collectibles categories, e.g., Lady's Head Planters, where the number of price guides far exceeds the need.

Perhaps it is important at this point to question whether or not there still is a general collectibles market. The collectibles market is splintering. Barbie, dolls, farm toys, military collectibles, paper, postcards, toy trains, toy soldiers, toys, and transportation memorabilia are just a few of the categories that have independent literature and show circuits. Collectors' clubs, especially those such as the Golden Glow of Christmas Past whose annual convention features a major sellers' show, contribute to the fractionalizing of the market. Unlike the antiques field where there is a sense of kinship no matter what one collects, the collector of Hopalong Cassidy memorabilia feels no camaraderie with the collector of fast food drinking glasses. In reality, given the number and diversity of the categories that fall under the collectibles umbrella, it makes more sense to think in market segments than it does of the market as a whole.

Today's collectibles market is trendy. Categories continually run hot and cold. A run of five years is a long time. In most cases, price runs end within three years. Some like the free–wheeling nature of a trendy market. They thrive on the challenge of keeping abreast of the constant changes. Traditional collectors, the vast majority even in the collectibles field, find little comfort in a market where the objects they so dearly love may lose some of their luster. Everyone prefers thinking of the objects they collect as blue chip investments.

There was an enormous growth in the public perception of collectibles as investments rather than things that are fun to own and use in the 1990s. Few can look at an object today without thinking how much it is worth. Collectibles are a very risky financial investment, far riskier than the commodities market.

In addition to an increased investment mentality, most investors want in and out in a relatively short period of time. These individuals are not investing, they are speculating. Speculative fever continues to be a major problem in the collectibles field. The media's fascination with rising prices within established categories and the desire to be the first to report on the latest collecting trend contributes heavily to this collecting fever.

In the 1980s a new player joined the collectibles team—the market manipulator. These individuals buy large quantities of objects within a single collecting category, organize a collectors' club, create a wealth of good news literature ranging from price guides to newsletters, and skillfully conduct a media blitz—all of which results in a rapid rise in prices. When market prices are at their peak, they sell. Those unsuspecting collectors who do not get out soon enough are stuck.

In the mid–1980s, the market manipulator found a fellow companion in crime, the despicable toy scalper. This is an individual who creates and capitalizes on an artificial shortage of a current–production object. Within days a $30 Holiday Barbie becomes $85. Scalpers' greed and lack of buyer patience have created the market. The buyers have the power to diffuse the situation. Do they have the intelligence?

In the early 1990s toy and other manufacturers discovered the adult collecting market. They found that adult collectors were willing to buy contemporary products that matched their collecting interests. Buy it at today's retail dollar instead of tomorrow's collecting dollar. In addition, manufacturers could create special product issues focused toward the adult collector. These carried significantly higher price points. Further, collectors often bought multiples. Collectors became speculators.

Two things happened. First, the cost to keep a collection current increased. In the case of Barbie and baseball cards, the amount exceeded $10,000. Few collectors were capable of making this commitment. Second, the secondary desirables market bubbles burst. Collectors had trouble selling their extra examples for their original purchase prices.

The result is that many collectibles collectors have stopped buying contemporary material, instead concentrating on vintage examples that are thirty years old or older. Supply is more limited; and the objects have stood the test of time. Market forces have decided what is and is not worth collecting.

Today's collectibles collectors are condition mad. MIB (mint in box) has been replaced by NFRB (never removed from the box). Individuals want thirty–, forty–, and fifty–year–old objects to appear new. This is not reality. Objects that were used show signs of wear and aging. The condition pendulum has swung too far to the right.

Because of the desire to own objects that appear in fine or better condition, many objects are being restored to assembly line new. Few restorers provide a written record of what they did. Sellers often forget to mention the restoration work or information about it becomes lost as the object passes from one owner to another. The restoration mentality of the automobile collector has spread throughout the entire collectibles field.

The 1990s saw a major increase in the number of sellers conducting trade periodical and/or catalog mail auctions. This is clearly an attempt to force up prices. Collector anger is growing. Many are refusing to participate. The auction route is not an excuse for properly pricing merchandise and offering it for direct sale to loyal customers.

When the history of the 20th–century antiques and collectibles market is written in 2050, the 1990s will be recognized as the decade that produced the profoundest changes in the market. The home computer, the Internet, and e-mail are the primary reasons. Because collectibles collectors tend to be younger than their antiques collector counterparts, they are as a group more computer literate. The Internet is loaded with collectibles shop malls and individual store sites. Some dealers are selling 75% or more of their merchandise via the Internet. Internet auctions are reality. No one knows the Internet's true potential. It is still in its infancy. If nothing else, it is going to expand the collecting market from national to international. Collecting is not a uniquely American phenomenon.

The 1990s collectibles market is a mature market. Toy categories no longer constitute over half the market. The objects we lived with are as much a part of the market as the objects we played with; 1950s furniture, decorative accessories, and textiles are hot; 1950s toys have cooled slightly. There appears to be between a fifteen– and twenty–year time lag for interest to develop in a generation's toys and household goods. At the moment, 1970s toys are hot.

Reproductions, copycats, fantasy items, and fakes plague the market. Advertising (primarily signs), ceramics (Roseville and Weller), glass (Depression to Venetian), metal (cast iron), paper (calendars, concert broadsides, and hand fans), soda pop (all brands, not just Coke), and toys (lithograph tin) are just a few of the areas of concern. Currently an effort is being made to expand the 1973 Hobby Protection Act to require permanent labeling of reproductions, copycats, and fantasy items. Lend it your support.

In summary, the future is extremely bright. While there are a few potholes in the road ahead, they are evident and can be avoided. The collectibles market is ready to move into the 21st century. Hopefully, **Harry L. Rinker The Official Price Guide to Collectibles** will help make the transition an easy one.

AUCTION HOUSES

The following auctioneers and auction companies generously supply Rinker Enterprises, Inc., with copies of their auction lists, press releases, catalogs and illustrations, and prices realized.

Action Toys
PO Box 102
Holtsville, NY 11742
(516) 563-9113
Fax: (516) 563-9182

Sanford Alderfer Auction Co.
501 Fairgrounds Road
PO Box 640
Hatfield, PA 19440
(215) 393-3000
e mail: auction@alderfercompany.com
web: http://www.alderfercompany.com

American Social History and Social
  Movements
4025 Saline Street
Pittsburgh, PA 15217
(412) 421-0903

Andre Ammelounx
PO Box 136
Palatine, IL 60078
(708) 991-5927
Fax: (708) 991-5947

Arthur Auctioneering
RD 2, Box 155
Hughesville, PA 17737
(717) 584-3697 or (800) ARTHUR 3

Aston
154 Market Street
Pittston, PA 18640
(717) 654-3090

Auction Team Köln
Breker – Die Spezialisten
Postfach 50 11 19, D-50971
Köln, Germany
Tel: 0221/38 70 49
Fax: 0221/37 48 78
Jane Herz, International Rep USA
(941) 925-0385
Fax: (941) 925-0487

Robert F. Batchelder
1 West Butler Avenue
Ambler, PA 19002
(215) 643-1430
Fax: (215) 643-6613

Butterfield & Butterfield
220 San Bruno Avenue
San Francisco, CA 94103
(415) 861-7500
Fax: (415) 861-8951

Butterfield & Butterfield
7601 Sunset Boulevard
Los Angeles, CA 90046
(213) 850-7500
Fax: (213) 850-5843

Cards From Grandma's Trunk
The Millards
PO Box 404
Northport, IN 49670
(616) 386-5351

Christie's
502 Park Avenue
New York, NY 10022
(212) 546-1000
Fax: (212) 980-8163

Christie's East
219 East 67th Street
New York, NY 10021
(212) 606-0400
Fax: (212)737-6076

Collector's Auction Services
RR 2, Box 431 Oakwood Road
Oil City, PA 16301
(814) 677-6070
Fax: (814) 677-6166

Collector's Sales and Service
PO Box 4037
Middletown, RI 02842
(401) 849-5012
Fax: (401) 846-6156

Copake Auction
Box H, 226 Route 7A
Copake, NY 12516
(518) 329-1142
Fax: (518) 329-3369

Dawson's
128 American Road
Morris Plains, NJ 07950
(973) 984-6900
Fax: (973) 984-6956

Dixie Sporting Collectibles
1206 Rama Road
Charlotte, NC 28211
(704) 364-2900
Fax: (704) 364-2322
e mail: gun1898@aol.com
web: http://www.sportauction.com

William Doyle Galleries, Inc.
175 East 87th Street
New York, NY 10128
(212) 427-2730
Fax: (212) 369-0892

Dunbars Gallery
76 Haven Street
Milford, MA 01757
(508) 634-8697 or (508) 634-TOYS
Fax: (508) 634-8698

Dunning's
755 Church Road
Elgin, IL 60123
(847) 741-3483
Fax: (847) 741-3589
web: http://www.dunnings.com

Etude Tajan
37, Rue de Mathurins 75008
Paris, France
Tel: 1-53-30-30-30
Fax: 1-53-30-30-31

Ken Farmer Auctions & Estates, LLC
105A Harrison Street
Radford, VA 24141
(540) 639-0939
Fax: (540) 639-1759
web: http://kenfarmer.com

Fink's Off The Wall Auction
108 East 7th Street
Lansdale, PA 19446
(215) 855-9732
Fax: (215) 855-6325

Frank's Antiques
Box 516
Hilliard, FL 32046
(904) 845-2870 or (904) 845-4888
Fax: (904) 845-4000

Freeman/Fine Arts Co. of Philadelphia, Inc.
1808-10 Chestnut Street
Philadelphia, PA 19103
(215) 563-9275
Fax: (215) 563-8236

Garth's Auction, Inc.
2690 Stratford Road
PO Box 369
Delaware, OH 43015
(614) 362-4771 or (614) 548-6778
Fax: (614) 363-1064

Glass–Works Auctions
PO Box 180-102 Jefferson Street
East Greenville, PA 18041
(610) 679-5849
Fax: (215) 679-3068

Morton M. Goldberg Auction Galleries
547 Baronne Street
New Orleans, LA 70113
(504) 592-2300
Fax: (504) 592-2311

Greenberg Auctions
7566 Main Street
Sykesville, MD 21784
(401) 795-7447

Marc Grobman
94 Paterson Road
Fanwood, NJ 07023-1056
(908) 322-4176
web: mgrobman@worldnet.att.net

Grogan & Co.
268 Newbury Street
Boston, MA 02116
(617) 437-9550
Fax: (617) 437-0513

Gypsyfoot Enterprises, Inc.
PO Box 5833
Helena, MT 59604
(406) 449-8076
e mail: gypsyfoot@aol.com

Hakes' Americana and Collectibles
PO Box 1444
York, PA 17405
(717) 848-1333
Fax: (7170 852-0344

Gene Harris Antique Auction Center, Inc.
203 South 18th Avenue
Marshalltown, IA 50158
(515) 752-0600
Fax: (515) 753-0226

Norman C. Heckler & Co.
Bradford Corner Road
Woodstock Valley, CT 06282
(860) 974-1634
Fax: (860) 974-2003

Leslie Hindman, Inc.
215 West Ohio Street
Chicago, IL 60610
(312) 670-0010
web: http://www.hindman.com

The Holidays Auction
4027 Brooks Hill Road
Brooks, KY 40109
(502) 955-9238
Fax: (502) 957-5027

Holzman–Caren Associates
3 Neptune Road
Poughkeepsie, NY 12601
(914) 462-1230
Fax: (914) 462-7215

International Tool Auction
Tony Morland
78 High Street
Needham Market
Suffolk, 1P6 8AW England
Tel: 01449 722992
Fax: 01449 722683

Michael Ivankovich Antiques, Inc.
PO Box 2458
Doylestown, PA 18901
(215) 345-6094
Fax: (215) 345-6692

Jackson Auction Co.
2229 Lincoln Street
Cedar Falls, IA 50613
(319) 277-2256
Fax: (319) 277-1252

James D. Julia, Inc.
PO Box 830
Fairfield, ME 04937
(207) 453-7125
Fax: (207) 453-2502

Gary Kirsner Auctions
PO Box 8807
Coral Springs, FL 33075
(954) 344-9856
Fax: (954) 344-4421

Charles E. Kirtley
PO Box 2273
Elizabeth City, NC 27906
(919) 335-1262
Fax: (919) 335-1262
e mail: ckirtley@erols.com

Henry Kurtz, Ltd.
163 Amsterdam Avenue, Suite 136
New York, NY 10023
(212) 642-5904
Fax: (212) 874-6018

Lang's Sporting Collectables, Inc.
31R Turtle Cove
Raymond, ME 04071
(207) 655-4265

Herb Latuchie Auction Gallery
2128 Front Street
Cuyahoga Falls, OH 44221
(216) 928-2844
Fax: (216) 928-2292

Los Angeles Modern Auctions
PO Box 462006
Los Angeles, CA 90046
(213) 845-9456
Fax: (213) 845-9601

Howard Lowery
3812 W Magnolia Boulevard
Burbank, CA 91505
(818) 972-9080

Mad Mike
Michael Lerner
32862 Springside Lane
Solon, OH 44139
(216) 349-3776

Majolica Auctions
Michael G Strawser
200 North Main
PO Box 332
Wolcottville, IN 46795
(219) 854-2859
Fax: (219) 854-3979

Manion's International Auction House, Inc.
PO Box 12214
Kansas City, KS 66112
(913) 299-6692
Fax: (913) 299-6792

Ted Maurer, Auctioneer
1003 Brookwood Drive
Pottstown, PA 19464
(610) 323-1573 or (610) 367-5024

Muddy River Trading Co.
Gary Metz
263 Key Lakewood Drive
Moneta, VA 24121
(540) 721-2091
Fax: (540) 721-1782

New England Auction Gallery
Box 2273
West Peabody, MA 01960
(508) 535-3140
Fax: (508) 535-7522

Nostalgia Publications, Inc.
21 South Lake Drive
Hackensack, NJ 07601
(201) 488-4536

Richard Opfer Auctioneers, Inc.
1919 Greenspring Drive
Timonium, MD 21093
(410) 252-5035
Fax: (410) 252-5863

Ron Oser Enterprises
PO Box 101
Huntingdon Valley, PA 19006
(215) 947-6575
Fax: (215) 938-7348

Pacific Book Auction Galleries
139 Townsend Street, Suite 305
San Francisco, CA 94108
(415) 989-2665
Fax: (415) 989-1664
e mail: pba@slip.net

Pettigrew Auction Co.
1645 South Tejon Street
Colorado Springs, CO 80906
(719) 633-7963

Phillips Ltd.
406 East 79th Street
New York, NY 10021
(212) 570-4830 or (800) 825-2781
Fax: (212) 570-2207

The Political Gallery
1325 North 86th Street
Indianapolis, IN 46260
(317) 257-0863
Fax: (317) 254-9167

Dennis Polk Equipment
72435 SR 15
New Paris, IN 46553
(219) 831-3555
Fax: (219) 831-5717

Postcards International
PO Box 5398
Hamden, CT 06515
(203) 248-6621
Fax: (203) 248-6628

Poster Mail Auction Co.
PO Box 133
Waterford, VA 20197
(703) 684-3656
Fax: (540) 882-4765

Provenance
PO Box 3487
Wallington, NJ 07057
(201) 779-8785
Fax: (212) 741-8756

David Rago Arts & Crafts
17 South Main Street
Lambertville, NJ 08530
(609) 397-9374
Fax: (609) 397-9374

Lloyd Ralston Toys
109 Glover Avenue
Norwalk, CT 06850
(203) 845-0033
Fax: (203) 845-0366

Red Baron's
6450 Roswell Road
Atlanta, GA 30328
(404) 252-3770
Fax: (404) 257-0268
e mail: rbarons@onramp:net

Remmey's
83 Summit Avenue
Summit, NJ 07901
(908) 273-5055
Fax: (908) 273-0171
e mail: remmeyauctiongalleries@world-
net.att.net

L. H. Selman Ltd.
761 Chestnut Street
Santa Cruz, CA 95060
(408) 427-1177
Fax: (408) 427-0111
e mail: iselman@got.net

Robert W. Skinner, Inc.
Bolton Gallery
357 Main Street
Bolton, MA 01740
(508) 779-6241
Fax: (617) 350-5429

R. M. Smythe & Co., Inc.
26 Broadway, Suite 271
New York, NY 10004-1701
(212) 983-1880

Sotheby's
1334 York Avenue
New York, NY 10021
(212) 606-7000

Steffen's Historical Militaria
PO Box 280
Newport, KY 41072
(606) 431-4499

Susanin's
Gallery 228 Merchandise Mart
Chicago, IL 60654
(312) 832-9800
Fax: (312) 832-9311
web: http://www.theauction.com

Swann Galleries, Inc.
104 East 25th Street
New York, NY 10010
(212) 254-4710

Toy Scouts
137 Casterton Avenue
Akron, OH 44303
(330) 836-0668
Fax: (330) 869-8668

Tradewinds Auctions
24 Magnolia Avenue
Manchester-by-the-Sea, MA 01944
(508) 768-3327

James A. Vanek
7031 Northeast Irving Street
Portland, OR 97213
(503) 257-8009

Victorian Images
PO Box 284
Marlton, NJ 08053
(609) 953-7711
Fax: (609) 953-7768

Tom Witte's Antiques
PO Box 399
Front Street West
Mattawan, MI 49071
(616) 668-4161

If you are an auctioneer or auction company and would like your name and address to appear on this list in subsequent editions, you can achieve this by sending copies of your auction lists, press releases, catalogs and illustrations, and prices realized to: **Rinker Enterprises, Inc., 5093 Vera Cruz Road, Emmaus, PA 18049.**

ANTIQUES & COLLECTIBLES PERIODICALS

Rinker Enterprises receives the following general and regional periodicals. Periodicals covering a specific collecting category are listed in the introductory material for that category.

NATIONAL MAGAZINES

American Collector
225 Main Street, Suite 300
Northport, NY 11768-1737
(516) 261-8337
Fax: (516) 261-8235

*Antique Trader's Collector Magazine &
Price Guide*
PO Box 1050
Dubuque, IA 52004-1050
(800) 480-0124

Antiques & Collecting Magazine
1006 South Michigan Avenue
Chicago, IL 60605
(800) 762-7576
Fax: (312) 939-0053

Collectors' Showcase
4099 McEwen Drive, Suite 350
Dallas, TX 75244-5039
(800) 477-2524

*Country Accents Collectibles, Flea Market
Finds*
GCR Publishing Group, Inc.
1700 Broadway
New York, NY 10019
(800) 955-3870

Glass Collector's Digest
PO Box 553
Marietta, OH 45750-0553
(800) 533-3433

NATIONAL NEWSPAPERS

The Antique Trader Weekly
PO Box 1050
Dubuque, IA 52004
(800) 334-7165

*Antique Week (Central and Eastern
Edition)*
27 North Jefferson Street
PO Box 90
Knightstown, IN 46148
(800) 876-5133

Collectors News
506 Second Street
PO Box 156
Grundy Center, IA 50638
(319) 824-6981 or (800) 352-8039

Maine Antique Digest
911 Main Street
PO Box 1429
Waldoboro, ME 04572
(207) 832-4888 or (207) 832-7534

Warman's Today's Collector
Krause Publications
700 East State Street
Iola, WI 54990
(715) 445-3775 Ext. 257

REGIONAL NEWSPAPERS

New England

MassBay Antiques
2 Washington Street
PO Box 192
Ipswich, MA 01938
(508) 777-7070

New England Antiques Journal
4 Church Street
PO Box 120
Ware, MA 01082
(413) 967-3505

New Hampshire Antiques Monthly
PO Box 546
Farmington, NH 03835-0546
(603) 755-4568

Unravel the Gavel
9 Hurricane Road, #1
Belmont, NH 03220
(603) 524-4281

Middle Atlantic States

American Antique Collector
PO Box 454
Murrysville, PA 15668
(412) 733-3968

Renninger's Antique Guide
PO Box 495
Lafayette Hill, PA 19444
(610) 828-4614 or (610) 825-6392

South

Cotton & Quail Antique Trail
205 East Washington Street
PO Box 326
Monticello, FL 32345
(904) 997-3880

The MidAtlantic Antiques Magazine
Henderson Newspapers, Inc.
304 South Chestnut Street
PO Box 908
Henderson, NC 27536
(919) 492-4001

*The Old News Is Good News Antiques
Gazette*
41429 West I-55 Service Road
PO Box 305
Hammond, LA 70404
(504) 429-0575

Southern Antiques
PO Drawer 1107
Decatur, GA 30031
(404) 289-0054

20th Century Folk Art News
5967 Blackberry Lane
Buford, GA 30518
(770) 932-1000
Fax: (770) 932-0506

Midwest

The American Antiquities Journal
126 East High Street
Springfield, OH 45502
(513) 322-6281
Fax: (513) 322-0294

The Antique Collector and Auction Guide
Weekly Section of Farm and Dairy
PO Box 38
Salem, OH 44460
(330) 337-3419

Auction World
101 12th Street South
Box 227
Benson, MN 56215
(800) 750-0166
Fax: (320) 843-3246

The Collector
204 South Walnut Street
Heyworth, IL 61745
(309) 473-2466
Fax: (309) 473-3610

Collectors Journal
1800 West D Street
PO Box 601
Vinton, IA 52349-0601
(319) 472-4763

Discover Mid–America
400 Grand, Suite B
Kansas City, MO 64106
(816) 474-1516 or (800) 899-9730

Great Lakes Trader
132 South Putnam
Williamstown, MI 48895
(517) 655-5621

The Old Times
PO Box 340
Maple Lake, MN 55358
(320) 963-6010 or (800) 539-1810

Yesteryear
PO Box 2
Princeton, WI 54968
(414) 787-4808

Southwest

Arizona Antique News
PO Box 26536
Phoenix, AZ 85068
(602) 943-9137

West Coast

Antique & Collectables
Kendall Communications, Inc.
500 Fensler, Suite 205
PO Box 13560
El Cajon, CA 92022
(619) 593-2930

Antique Journal
1684 Decoto Road, Suite #166
Union City, CA 94587
(510) 791-8592 or (800) 791-8592
Fax: (510) 523-5262

Antiques Today
Kruse Publishing
977 Lehigh Circle
Carson City, NV 89705
(800) 267-4602
Fax: (702) 267-4600

Old Stuff
VBM Printers, Inc.
336 North Davis
PO Box 1084
McMinnville, OR 97128
(503) 434-5386

West Coast Peddler
PO Box 5134
Whittier, CA 90607
(310) 698-1718

INTERNATIONAL NEWSPAPERS

Canada

Antique Showcase
103 Lakeshore Road, Suite 202
St. Catherine, Ontario
Canada L2N 2T6

Antiques and Collectibles Trader
PO Box 38095
550 Eglinton Avenue West
Toronto, Ontario
Canada M5N 3A8

The Upper Canadian
PO Box 653
Smiths Falls, Ontario
Canada K7A 4T6

England

Antique Trade Gazette
17 Whitcomb Street
London WC2H 7PL
England

ABBREVIATIONS

4to = 8 x 10"
8vo = 5 x 7"
12mo = 3 x 5"
ADS = autograph document signed
adv = advertising or advertisement
ALS = autograph letter signed
AOG = all over gold
AP = album page signed
AQS = autograph quotation signed
C = century
c = circa
cat = catalog
cov = cover
CS = card signed
d = depth or diameter
dec = decorated or decoration
dj = dust jacket
dwt = penny weight
DS = document signed
ed = edition
emb = embossed
ext = exterior
FDC = first day cover
FH = flat handle
folio = 12 x 16"
ftd = footed
gal = gallon
gf = gold–filled
ground = background
GW = goldware
h = height
HH = hollow handle
hp = hand painted
illus = illustrated, illustration, or illustrator
imp = impressed
int = interior
irid = iridescent
j = jewels
K = karat

l = length
lb = pound
litho = lithograph or lithographed
LS = letter signed
mfg = manufactured, manufacturer, or manufacturing
MIB = mint in box
MIP = mint in package
mkd = marked
MOC = mint on card
opal = opalescent
orig = original
oz = ounce
pat = patent
pc = piece
pcs = pcs
pg = page
pgs = pages
pkg = package or packaging
pr = pair
PS = photograph signed
pt = pint
qt = quart
rect = rectangular
sgd = signed
SP = silver plated
sq = square photo
SS = sterling silver
sq = square
ST = stainless
TLS = typed letter signed
unmkd = unmarked
unsgd = unsigned
Vol = Volume
vol = volumes
w = width
wg = white gold
yg = yellow gold
# = number

ABINGDON POTTERY

The Abingdon Sanitary Manufacturing Company began manufacturing bathroom fixtures in 1908 in Abingdon, Illinois. The company's art pottery line was introduced in 1938 and eventually consisted of over 1,000 shapes and forms decorated in nearly 150 different colors. In 1945 the company changed its name to Abingdon Potteries, Inc. The art pottery line remained in production until 1950, when fire destroyed the art pottery kiln. After the fire, the company placed its emphasis once again on plumbing fixtures. Eventually, Abingdon Potteries became Briggs Manufacturing Company, a firm noted for its sanitary fixtures.

Reference: Joe Paradis, *Abingdon Pottery Artware: 1934–1950,* Schiffer Publishing, 1997.

Collectors' Club: Abingdon Pottery Club, 210 Knox Hwy 5, Abingdon, IL 61410.

Bookends, pr, horse head, white	$ 70.00
Bookends, pr, quill, black and white	125.00
Bookends, pr, sea gull, 6" h	75.00
Bowl, oval, blue, #547	18.00
Bowl, shell, pink, #501	25.00
Candleholders, pr, #716	35.00
Console Bowl, blue	25.00
Cookie Jar, Little Bo Peep	450.00
Cookie Jar, "Choo Choo" Locomotive	175.00
Cookie Jar, Cutie Pie, blue	185.00
Cookie Jar, hippo, floral dec, white ground, #549	150.00
Cookie Jar, little girl, #693, 9½" h	50.00
Cookie Jar, little old lady, green	250.00
Cookie Jar, pineapple, #664, 10½" h	100.00
Cookie Jar, windmill	275.00
Figurine, kneeling nude holding bouquet, pink, gold trim, 10" h	175.00
Planter, fan, raised bow at base, dark green, #4844, 4¾" h, 9" l	12.00
Planter, Mexican and cactus, hand dec, #616D, 6½" h	50.00

Vase, pink matte exterior, white interior, 6⅞" h, #516, $25.00.

Vase, flattened oval shape, emb sailing ship on sides, ball column handles, blue, 7" h, #494	20.00
Vase, hourglass, 9" h	15.00
Vase, wreath, 8" h	30.00
Wall Pocket, butterfly, 9" h	65.00
Wall Pocket, cookbook, #676D	50.00
Wall Pocket, Dutch girl, 10" h	90.00

ACTION FIGURES

An action figure is a poseable plastic or diecast metal model that portrays a real or fictional character. Early action figures depicted popular television western heroes from the 1950s and were produced by Hartland. Louis Marx also included action figures in several of its playsets from the late 1950s.

Hassenfield Bros. triggered the modern action figure craze with its introduction of G.I. Joe in 1964. The following year Gilbert produced James Bond 007, The Man From U.N.C.L.E., and Honey West figures. Bonanza and Captain Action figures arrived in 1966.

In 1972 Mego introduced the first six superheroes in a series of thirty–four. Mego also established the link between action figures and the movies with its issue of Planet of the Apes and Star Trek: The Motion Picture figures. Mego's television series figures included CHiPs, Dukes of Hazzard, and Star Trek.

The success of the Star Wars figures set introduced by Kenner in 1977 prompted other toy companies to follow suit, resulting in a flooded market. Many series were unsuccessful and discontinued when initial sales did not justify the costs of further manufacture. However, unlike many collecting categories, scarcity does not necessarily equate to high value in the action figure market.

References: John Bonavita, *Mego Action Figure Toys With Values,* Schiffer Publishing, 1996; Paris and Susan Manos, *Collectible Action Figures: Identification & Value Guide, Second Edition,* Collector Books, 1996; Bill Sikora and T. N. Tumbusch, *Tomart's Encyclopedia & Price Guide to Action Figures, Book 1* (1996), *Book 2* (1996), *Book 3* (1997), Tomart Publications.

Periodicals: *Action Figure News & Review,* 556 Monroe Turnpike, Monroe, CT 06468; *Tomart's Action Figure Digest,* Tomart Publications, 3300 Encrete Ln, Dayton, OH 45439.

Collectors' Club: Classic Action Figure Collector's Club, PO Box 2095, Halesite, NY 11743.

Note: Prices listed are for figures in mint condition unless noted otherwise.

Action Boy, Captain Action, 9", Ideal, 1967, MIP	$ 375.00
Action Boy, Captain Action, 9", space suit, Ideal, 1968, MIP	825.00
Action Pilot, GI Joe, accessories, 1964, MIP	450.00
Alien, 18", Kenner, 1979	175.00
Antican, Star Trek, Galoob, MOC	160.00
Aquanaut, Adventures of GI Joe, #7910, 1969, MIP	2,000.00
Australian Jungle Fighter, GI Joe, #8205, Action Soldiers of the World, 1966, MIP	1,400.00
Batgirl, 8", Mego, 1973, MIB	300.00

The Tramp, Dick Tracy Coppers and Gangsters, Playmates Toys, 1990, MIP, $5.00.

Scotty, Star Trek, *Where No Man Has Gone Before,* Playmates Toys, mid–1990s, MOC, $8.00. Photo courtesy Playmates Toys.

Batman, World's Greatest Super Heroes, 12½", Mego, 1978, MIB **125.00**
Ben Kenobi, Star Wars, Kenner **175.00**
Black Adventurer, GI Joe, #7404, Adventure Team, accessories, 1970, MIP **250.00**
Black Soldier, GI Joe 30th Anniversary, 12", MIB **200.00**
C–3PO, Star Wars, Empire Strikes Back, Kenner, MIP **50.00**
Captain Action, 12", parachute offer on box, Ideal, 1966–68, MIP **650.00**
Catwoman, Batman Returns, Kenner, 1992–93, MIB **20.00**
Cheryl Ladd, Charlie's Angels, 8½", Hasbro, 1977 . . . . . . **35.00**
Chewbacca, Star Wars, Return of the Jedi, Kenner, MOC **55.00**
Clark Kent, Superman, 8", Mego, 1974, MIB **500.00**
Crash Dummies, Tyco, MOC **25.00**
Cylon Centurian, Battlestar Galactica, 12", Mattel, MIB **100.00**
Cyborg, Kenner Super Powers, 1986, MOC **325.00**
Darth Vader, Star Wars, Empire Strikes Back, Kenner, MIP **65.00**
Death Squad Commander, Star Wars, Empire Strikes Back, Kenner, MIP **80.00**
Diana Prince, Wonder Woman, 12", Mego, 1976, MIB **100.00**
Dick Grayson, Batman, Official World's Greatest Super Hero, Montgomery Ward exclusive, Mego, 1974, MIB **500.00**
Dick Tracy, 2½–3½", Marx, 1950s, MIB **150.00**
Dr. Evil, Captain Action, 12", Ideal, 1966–68, MIP **750.00**
Dr. Fate, Kenner Super Powers, MOC **70.00**
Eagle Eye Man of Action, GI Joe, No. 7277, 1976, MIP **125.00**
Elvis, Commemorative Jailhouse Rock, 12", Hasbro, 1993 . . . . **45.00**
F–15E Fighter Pilot, GI Joe, 12", limited edition, FAO Schwarz **135.00**
Farrah Fawcett, Charlie's Angels, 12", Mego **40.00**
French, WWF Ultimate Warrior, MOC **15.00**
Gene Simmons, KISS, Mego **200.00**

General Lando, Star Wars, MOC **100.00**
General Zod, Superman, 12½", Mego, 1978, MIB **100.00**
German Storm Trooper, GI Joe, #8100, 1966, MIP **2,000.00**
Gold Spawn, Kaybee Toys, MOC **35.00**
Gravel Gertie, Dick Tracy, 2½–3½", Marx, 1950s, MIB **150.00**
Green Lantern, Kenner Super Powers, MOC **35.00**
Han Solo, Star Wars, small head, Return of the Jedi, Kenner, MIP **125.00**
Hawkeye, M.A.S.H., Tri–Star, 1982 . . . . **18.00**
Incredible Hulk, diecast, Mego, 1979, MIB **85.00**
Incredible Hulk, super size, Toy Biz, MIB **55.00**
Japanese Soldier, GI Joe, Hasbro, 1966, MIB **1,250.00**
Jawa, Star Wars, vinyl cape, Kenner **400.00**
John Boy and Ellen, The Waltons, set, Mego, MIB **50.00**
Joker, Batman, Official World's Greatest Super Hero, Mego, 1974, MIB **150.00**
Jor–El, Superman, 12½", Mego, 1978, MIB **100.00**
Junior, Dick Tracy, 2½–3½", Marx, 1950s, MIB **150.00**
Kate Jackson, Charlie's Angels, 8½", Hasbro, 1977, MIB **50.00**
King of Cartoons, Pee–wee Herman, MOC **15.00**
Landing Signal Officer, GI Joe Action Sailor series **500.00**
Luke, Star Wars, Return of the Jedi, Kenner, MOC **175.00**
Mary Jane, Spider–Man, 12", Toy Biz, MIB **45.00**
Michael Jackson, 12", accessories, LJN, 1980s, MIB **50.00**
Mike Power Atomic Man **50.00**
Miss Yvonne, Pee–wee Herman, MOC **20.00**
Mr. Mxyzptlk, 8", mouth open, Mego, 1973, MIB **120.00**
Navy Seal, GI Joe, 12", FAO Schwarz, MIB **200.00**
Negro Adventurer, Adventures of GI Joe, 1969, MIP . . . **1,600.00**
Obi–Wan Kenobi, Star Wars, Power of the Force, Kenner, MIP **150.00**
Pee–wee Herman, with scooter, MOC **12.00**
Penguin, Batman, 5", Super Powers, Kenner, 1984, MIB **40.00**
Poison Ivy, Batman, Kenner, MOC **45.00**
Princess Leia, Star Wars, Empire Strikes Back, Kenner, MIP **250.00**

R2–D2, Star Wars, Return of the Jedi, Kenner, MIP **35.00**
Riddler, Batman, Official World's Greatest Super Hero, Mego, 1974, MIB **250.00**
Robin, Batman Returns, Kenner, 1991, MIB. **50.00**
Roy, Emergency, MOC. **35.00**
Sailor, GI Joe 30th Anniversary, 12", MIB **100.00**
Samantha, Bewitched, Ideal, MIB **500.00**
Sea Adventurer, GI Joe, #7402, accessories, 1970, MIP. **245.00**
Shazam!, World's Greatest Super Heroes, 8", Mego, 1970s, MIB **200.00**
Snaggletooth, Star Wars, blue **125.00**
Sparkle Plenty, Dick Tracy, 2¹/₂–3¹/₂", Marx, 1950s, MIB. **150.00**
Stormtrooper, Star Wars, Power of the Force, Kenner, MIP. **150.00**
Superman, 12", Mego, MIB **65.00**
Talking Action Marine, GI Joe, #7790, 1967, MIP **550.00**
Talking Action Pilot, GI Joe, #7890, Talking Adventure Pack, 1967, MIP **1,200.00**
Talking Astronaut, Adventures of GI Joe, 1969, MIP. **650.00**
Telescoping Luke, Star Wars, Kenner. **150.00**
Tusken Raider, Star Wars, Empire Strikes Back, Kenner, MIP. **80.00**
Wicked Witch, Wizard of Oz, Mego, MIB. **90.00**
Wonder Woman, 8", Mego, 1974, MIB. **275.00**
Wonder Woman, Super Powers, Kenner, 1984, MIB **20.00**
Yak Face, Star Wars, Kenner **130.00**
Zira, Planet of the Apes, Mego, 1975, MIB **150.00**
Zorak, Big Jim, 9", 1975, Mattel, MIB **65.00**

ADVERTISING

During the mid–19th century manufacturers discovered product packaging could serve multiple purposes. In addition to holding the product, it could attract the eye of potential customers, serve as a source of identification, and convey a message. The package logo also could be used effectively in pictorial advertising.

By 1880 advertising premiums such as calendars and thermometers arrived upon the scene. Diecut point–of–purchase displays, wall clocks, and signs were eagerly displayed.

Advertising continued to respond to changing opportunities and times. The advertising character was developed in the early 1900s. By the 1950s the star endorser was firmly established. Advertising became a big business as specialized firms, many headquartered in New York City, developed to meet manufacturers' needs. Today television programs frequently command well over one hundred thousand dollars a minute for commercial air time.

Many factors affect the price of an advertising collectible—the product and its manufacturer, the objects or persons used in the advertisement, the period and aesthetics of design, the designer and/or illustrator, and the form the advertisement takes. Almost every advertising item is sought by a specialized collector in one or more collectibles areas.

References: Michael Bruner, *Advertising Clocks: America's Timeless Heritage*, Schiffer Publishing, 1995; Michael Bruner, *Encyclopedia of Porcelain Enamel Advertising*, Schiffer Publishing, 1994; Douglas Collins, *America's Favorite Food: The Story of Campbell Soup Company*, Harry N. Abrams, 1994; Douglas Congdon–Martin, *America For Sale: A Collector's Guide to Antique Advertising*, Schiffer Publishing, 1991; Douglas Congdon–Martin, *Tobacco Tins: A Collector's Guide*, Schiffer Publishing, 1992; Fred Dodge, *Antique Tins: Identification & Values*, Collector Books, 1995; Ted Hake, *Hake's Guide to Advertising Collectibles*, Wallace–Homestead, Krause Publications, 1992; Sharon and Bob Huxford, *Huxford's Collectible Advertising, Second Edition* (1995), *Third Edition* (1997), Collector Books; Jerry Jankowski, *Shelf Life: Modern Package Design 1920–1945*, Chronicle Books, 1992; Jim and Vivian Karsnitz, *Oyster Cans*, Schiffer Publishing, 1993; Ray Klug, *Antique Advertising Encyclopedia, Vol. 1* (1978, 1993 value update) and *Vol. 2* (1985, 1990 value update), L–W Promotions; Norman E. Martinus and Harry L. Rinker, *Warman's Paper*, Wallace–Homestead, Krause Publications, 1994; Alice L. Muncaster and Ellen Sawyer, *The Black Cat Made Me Buy It!*, Crown Publishers, 1988; Alice L. Muncaster and Ellen Sawyer, *The Dog Made Me Buy It!*, Crown Publishers, 1990; Dawn E. Reno, *Advertising: Identification and Price Guide*, Avon Books, 1993; B. J. Summers, *Value Guide To Advertising Memorabilia*, Collector Books, 1994; David Zimmerman, *The Encyclopedia of Advertising Tins: Smalls and Samples*, published by author, 1994.

Periodicals: *The Advertising Collectors Express*, PO Box 221, Mayview, MO 64071; *Paper Collectors' Marketplace* (PCM), PO Box 128, Scandinavia, WI 54977.

Collectors' Clubs: Antique Advertising Assoc of America, PO Box 1121, Morton Grove, IL 60053; National Assoc of Paper and Advertising Collectors (P.A.C.), PO Box 500, Mt Joy, PA 17552; The Ephemera Society of America, PO Box 95, Cazenovia, NY 13035; Tin Container Collectors Assoc, PO Box 440101, Aurora, CO 80044.

REPRODUCTION ALERT

Ashtray, Ernest A. Brey, Quality Meats, Spinnerstown, PA, circular Bakelite base, center cigarette rest with adv medallion, 1955 . . . . **$ 8.00**
Ashtray, Luchow's Restaurant, ceramic, blue and white, stein in center, "Since 1882". **20.00**
Ashtray, Smith's General Store, Birdseye, IN, tin **5.00**
Beach Bag, Maxwell House Coffee, coffee can shape and image **25.00**
Blotter, F. R. Keens Co, Soda Fountain Foods, New Haven, CT, red, yellow, and black, 1931 . . . . **20.00**
Blotter, Goodrich Zipps Shoes, G. T. Foltz Department Store, Wyrheville, VA, multicolored, orange ground, c1935 . . . . **25.00**
Blotter, Morse & Rogers Shoes, celluloid button, round, black lettering, yellow ground, red and black felt, 3¹/₄" d. **15.00**
Blotter, Sunoco, Mickey and Minnie as bride and groom in convertible **25.00**
Booklet, Jell–O, Genesee Pure Food Company, Leroy, NY, multicolor cover, ©1920, 14 pgs. **20.00**
Booklet, Quaker Oats, "Travels of a Rolled Oat," 1933 Chicago World's Fair souvenir, black and white, recipes, 12 pgs. **20.00**
Box, Father John's Medicine, wood, dovetailed, stenciled lettering, 11" h, 10" w, 11" d. **25.00**
Box, Hershey Kisses, cardboard, girl giving Hershey Kiss to boy, 1930s, 7¹/₂" h, 10" w, 3" d. **7.50**

Box, Quick Mother's Oats, The Quaker Oats Company, cardboard canister, $20.00.

Box, Magnolia Brand Condensed Milk, wood, black lettering, 7 x 19 x 13"............................. 30.00

Brochure, Cushman Scotter Company, Truckster, multicolor, 1955, 24 pgs, 6 x 3³/₈".................. 5.00

Brochure, Metropolitan Life Insurance, The Metropolitan Mother Goose, color illus, 1920s 25.00

Clock, Sugardale Meats, metal body, convex glass lens, pig king on throne, working, 15¹/₂" d......... 650.00

Coloring Set, Bird's Eye, coloring book and crayons, orig General Foods premium mailer 25.00

Dispenser, Viking Snuff, dark blue ground, white lettering, red trim, "Guaranteed Fresh," 1950s, 15" h 100.00

Dispenser, Workmate Chewing Tobacco, yellow ground, green lettering and wintergreen leaves, 1950s, 15" h 65.00

Display, B-1 Lemon Lime, turquoise, white, and red, flashing colored lights behind translucent screen, "More zip in every sip!," 1960, 16 x 13 x 4" 100.00

Display, Beacon Blankets, diecut litho cardboard, multicolored, elderly man in cannonball bed pulling up blanket, "B-r-r-rrr!, Beacon Blankets Make Warm Friends," 41" h, 40" w 150.00

Display, Blony Gum, figural truck, cardboard, wood wheels, bed holds gum, 8" h, 13¹/₂" w 375.00

Display, Columbia Ring, centered diamond above twilight starry sky and suspended angel, when activated sign lights up, diamond sparkles, and angel is raised and lowered, marked "Guardian Angel Protects Columbia 'Tru-Fit' diamond rings," c1950, 12" h 225.00

Display, Elgin Watch, turquoise and pink futuristic 1950s vanity with 2 mirrors and moving watch mount, 1950s woman in ivory gown with pink sequins spins to admire herself in mirror as watchband passes through ring, c1955, 19 x 15 x 10"..... 675.00

Display, Flower Seeds, diecut cardboard, standup, purple, white, green, and black, "The Loveliest Garden can be yours easily – economically with these Flower Seeds 10¢, Plan Your Garden Now!," complete with seed packets, 41" h, 24" w 150.00

Display, Ide Shirts, cardboard, standup, well-dressed man snapping on cufflink, green ground, "New Ideas in Ide Shirts, Pre-Shrunk Collars," 1930s, 17" h, 14" w 75.00

Display, Mohawk Carpet, Indian boy standing on tree stump beating drum, "Carpet Craftsmanship from the Looms of Mohawk," c1948, 23" h 300.00

Display, Old Gold, signed Earl Christy, train with ladies in cloche hats, black waiter, businessman in fedora, and train worker all enjoying smoking Old Gold cigarettes, "quality tells the story, Not A Cough In A Carload," c1930, 32" h, 21" w 1,000.00

Display, Slinky, wholesome 1950s youngster holding Slinky, electric motor lifts and lowers one hand creating "walking" effect, with period Slinky in orig box, c1956, 16¹/₂ x 16¹/₂ x 7¹/₂" 950.00

Display, Swing's Coffee, black man seated atop Swing's Coffee box pours cup of coffee from white and red enamel coffeepot into enamel mustache cup, man moves lips, raises eyebrows, rolls eyes, and "drinks" coffee, coffee disappears into tube in cup, reappears in coffeepot, c1925, 29 x 17¹/₂ x 15¹/₂" 2,500.00

Display, Tinkertoy, electrified revolving Tinkertoy paddle wheel, c1940, 19 x 19 x 5¹/₂"............. 550.00

Display, Wyler Watch, rotating clock with round brass finish face with red plastic chapters, obverse fitted with 2 display racks for Wyler Incaflex watches, c1940, 20" h 150.00

Doll, Cream of Wheat, cloth, 1920, 18" h 150.00

Door Push, Copenhagen Tobacco, porcelain, "Made From High Grade Tobacco, Best Chew Ever Made," Art Deco design, red, white, yellow, and black, 13¹/₄" h, 3³/₄" w.......................... 300.00

Door Push, Sunbeam Bread, porcelain, dark blue ground, red and white lettering, "Reach for Sunbeam Bread," 2³/₄" h, 26¹/₂" w 100.00

Fan, Worcester Salt, Worcester Salt Company, NY, cardboard, wood stick, black and white, 12 ¹/₂" h, 9¹/₂" w 35.00

Fruit Crate Label, Doe Brand Carrots, doe, baseball, and bunch of carrots, dark blue ground, "Strictly Big League," 7 x 10", $1.00.

Flour Sack, Sleepy Eye Flour, cloth, Indian head, red and black lettering, 36" h, 16" w **225.00**

Fruit Crate Label, apples, Blewett Pass, auto on mountain road, 1940s **1.00**

Fruit Crate Label, apples, Mountain Goat, white mountain goat standing on cliff, snow–capped mountains and forest in background **2.00**

Fruit Crate Label, apricots, Brentwood Acres, 3 apricots on branch, blue ground. . . . . **.25**

Fruit Crate Label, lemons, Cutter, cutter ship in choppy seas, orange and gold sky, Oxnard, dated 1937. . . . . . **3.00**

Fruit Crate Label, oranges, Redlands Choice, shiny blue draped cloth behind large orange and blossoms, Redlands, 1938 . . . . **8.00**

Fruit Crate Label, tomatoes, Bungalow, large tomato, bungalow and grounds, Washington, 1920s, lug size **1.50**

Globe, Fellow Society of American Florists, metal frame, glass lens, red, blue, black, and yellow, "Say it with flowers," 16½" d **550.00**

Label, brooms, Skysweep, single prop biplane, dated 1931. . . . . **.50**

Letter Opener, Lincoln, Nebraska Telephone & Telegraph Silver Anniversary, logo on handle **75.00**

Match Holder, Ceresota Flour, diecut, tin, boy slicing hunk from large bread loaf, flour barrel, 5¼" h, 2½" w **125.00**

Match Safe, Laxets, litho tin, product package, "Only 5¢ Per Box, A Candy Bowel Laxative," 4¾" h, 3½" w **95.00**

Menu, Hotel Astor, NY, watercolor city scenes, 1945 . . . . . **7.50**

Menu, Mickey Mantle's Holiday Inn, c1950 . . . . **75.00**

Mirror, Arnold's Bakery, 25th Anniversary, black and white, 1923 . . . . **65.00**

Mirror, Maccabees Insurance, green, black, red, and white, 1920s **50.00**

Mirror, Revelation Tooth Powder, blue and gray, 1920s **25.00**

Pail, Ellis & Helfer H. H. Tablets Confections, tin, red ground, log cabin in center, red and black lettering, gold and black highlights, bail handle, c1940, 5¾" d, 6½" h **20.00**

Pail, Happiness Candy, rect, elephants on lid, animal circus around sides, "Happiness in Every Box," bail handle, c1925, 6" w, 3¾" d, 3¼" h **300.00**

Pail, Kid Kandy, yellow ground, black and white Jackie Coogan portrait on front, policeman chasing boy on back, bail handle, c1935, 3¼" d, 3½" h **275.00**

Pail, Miners and Puddlers Smoking Tobacco, red ground, red, black, and ivory lettering, 3 miners at center, bail handle, c1930, 6¾" h **75.00**

Pail, Pure Honey, "William Garwood Jr., Batavia NY. Copyright 1923" and "Al Root Company" at top, tin, red ground, apiary vignette, bail handle, 5 lb, 6" h, 5" w **40.00**

Pail, Sharp's Super–Kreem Toffee, Englishman wearing monocle and bowler, parrot, "Speaks for itself," bail handle, 8½" h, 7" d **165.00**

Pail, Southern Rose Shortening, red rose, bail handle. **15.00**

Paperweight, John A. Griffith & Co., Inc., Tailors' Trimmings, glass globe, flattened base, 1933 Century of Progress World's Fair souvenir, 3" d, $40.00.

Pail, Sunshine Kisses, light blue ground, yellow and orange sunrise, red, black, and yellow highlights, bail handle, c1930, 9¾" d, 7" h **65.00**

Pail, Wizard of Oz Peanut Butter, 2 lb. **50.00**

Paperweight, Crane Company 50th Anniversary, bronzed metal, 1930 . . . . **10.00**

Paperweight, Fageol Safety Coach, cast lead, 1920s bus replica, inscription both sides **20.00**

Paperweight, National Cash Registers, cast iron, painted, figural register **65.00**

Pinback Button, Big Chief White Bread, red, white, and blue, 1930s **20.00**

Pinback Button, "Ride The Green Lane Of Safety In A New 1939 Hudson," green, blue, black, and white **15.00**

Pinback Button, Pilgrim Bread and Cakes, blue, white, and orange, 1920–30 . . . . **15.00**

Pocket Knife, Purina, plastic red and white checkerboard handles with black lettering, 2 steel blades, Kutmaster, 1950s, 3" l. **25.00**

Poster, Granger Tobacco, sea captain, 1931, 30 x 42" **65.00**

Poster, Hill Brothers Fur Company, price list on back, 1928 . . . . **20.00**

Poster, International Stock Food, litho paper, cattle yard, multicolor, wood frame, 21" h, 27" w **175.00**

Poster, Ivory Soap, paper, linen back, "Ivory Soap. It Floats.," white lettering, black ground, 17" h, 56½" w **45.00**

Poster, Royal Baking Powder, product illus, 1920s, 25 x 20" **35.00**

Poster, Wings King Size Cigarettes, paper, multicolored, piper cub airplane and cigarette package, 1941, 15" h, 10" w. **85.00**

Shoe Horn, A. S. Beck Shoes, metal, 1940s. **5.00**

Seed Packet, Dodson Seed Store, Danville, IL, Harris Early Giant Pepper, 10¢, 1940s, 3¹/₄ x 5", $4.00.

Sign, ACME Quality Paint and Varnishes, diecut porcelain, 2 sided, blue, red, white, and yellow, 26" h, 27¹/₂" w 100.00

Sign, Allen's Foot Ease, diecut cardboard, young girl wearing hat and dress, feet rotate to simulate walking, 6" h, 3¹/₂" w. 10.00

Sign, Bickmore's Gall Cure, diecut cardboard, trifold standup, 3 panels with horse–drawn wagon in front of building, man with horse, and farmer and cows in pasture, 33" h, 50" w 275.00

Sign, BVD Union Suits, litho tin, man wearing union suit, black ground, "We Sell Loose Fitting Union Suits," 1920s, 13" h, 9" w 225.00

Sign, Chief Paints, painted tin, 2 sided, Indian chief wearing headdress, 12" h, 28" w. 135.00

Sign, Dromedary Dates, The Hills Bros. Company, New York City, diecut cardboard, standup, Santa holding product box, sack of toys in front, 38¹/₂" h, 18" w 125.00

Sign, DuPont Paints and Varnishes, "Brilliant Mfg. Co. Phila. PA," porcelain, flange, black and red lettering, yellow ground, black border, 16" h, 16" w 100.00

Sign, Fry's Breakfast Cocoa, J. S. Fry & Sons, Ltd., Bristol & London, porcelain, cocoa package, 21" h, 14" w 135.00

Sign, Hudson's Soap, porcelain, yellow ground, green and black bucket, "A Pail of Water With A Very Little Hudson's Goes A Very Long Way, for the People, Hudson's Soap," 20¹/₂" h, 14" w. 250.00

Sign, Kellogg's Corn Flakes, diecut cardboard, standup, young lady's head wearing bonnet, ears of corn, bowl of cereal, and cereal box, "Form No. 1–49003, Copyright 1948 by Kellogg Co. Litho in USA," 40" h, 34" w. 100.00

Sign, Knox Gelatine, Charles B. Knox Co., Johnstown, NY, diecut litho cardboard, 4 sided, cow head flanked by 2 young chefs holding molded gelatin desserts, 16" h, 15" w, 9¹/₂" d 2,250.00

Sign, Kodak Verichrome, diecut porcelain, 2 sided, multicolored, film box on diamond shaped sign, 12" h, 22" w. 350.00

Sign, Lambertville "Snag Proof" Rubber Boots & Shoes, painted metal, 2 large boots, small Charlie McCarthy figure, 4 small cartoon figures, framed, 15" h, 19¹/₂" w 775.00

Sign, Lenox Soap, porcelain, black lettering, ivory ground, 6" h, 10" w 100.00

Sign, Lictonic, emb tin, painted, yellow oval with horse holding box, "Saves Feed, Saves Money, Improves Stock, Prevents Disease," 9" h, 20" w 300.00

Sign, Morton's Salt, porcelain, rect, red and white lettering, black and white ground, red and white border, "We Sell Morton's Salt, Blocks–Barrels–Bags–Packages, The Best Grades For Every Purpose, Osage Flour & Feed Co.," 17¹/₂" h, 47¹/₂" w 250.00

Sign, New Ice Refrigerator, emb tin, red, yellow, and black ground, red and white lettering, family racing to refrigerator, "Scientific Refrigeration at low cost," 20¹/₂" h, 30" w 30.00

Sign, Old Dutch Cleanser, porcelain, cleanser can with Dutch lady, "We Sell Large Sifter Can 10¢," stamped "Ingraham Richardson," 20" h, 14" w. 475.00

Sign, Park Pollard Co. Lay or Bust Feeds, H. D. Beach Co., emb tin, chickens, c1920 . . . . 1,000.00

Sign, Pear's Soap, diecut cardboard, granny wearing bonnet scrubbing young boy, "You Dirty Boy," 17 ¹/₂" h, 14¹/₂" w 200.00

Sign, Phoenix Assurance Company, porcelain, phoenix rising from flames, blue, black, red, and white, 12" h, 18" w 200.00

Sign, Pioneer Hog Feed, tin, center circle with hog's head, "Feed Your Hogs Buttermilk For More Pork," yellow, blue, red, white, and black, 19¹/₂" h, 14" w . . . 375.00

Sign, Robbialac Paints, porcelain, Art Deco woman holding paint brush, 24" h, 16¹/₄" w. 300.00

Sign, Squire's Ham, John P. Squire & Company, Boston, tin, self–framed, oval, hog with human features, trademark logo around pig's neck, dark blue ground. 800.00

Sign, Sweet–Orr Pants Overalls Shirts, porcelain, yellow ground, blue lettering, white vignette with silhouette tug–of–war scene, framed, 28" h, 72" w 875.00

Sign, Tremont Stoves and Ranges, porcelain, flange, dark blue and white, "They Work, They Wear," 12" h, 12" w. 375.00

Sign, Waterman's Ideal Fountain Pen, porcelain, "Ideal" superimposed over globe in center, black ground, orig wood frame, 8" h, 30" w 300.00

Sign, Weight Watchers, porcelain, from old scale, black and white, silhouette of shapely woman flanked by fat woman and thin woman, "She Did Not Care" below fat and thin women, "She Watched Her Weight" below shapely woman, 9¹/₂" h, 8¹/₂" w. 400.00

Sign, Weyerhauser Balsam–Wool Blanket, porcelain, navy, turquoise, white, and orange, snow–capped cottage scene, "It Tucks In!," Veribrite Signs, 1930s, 23" h, 36" w. 315.00

Tin, Saraka for Constipation, Schering Corporation, Bloomfield, NJ, orange, 3" w, 2" d, 4⁵⁄₈" h, $5.00.

Snap Gun, Lesher's, Perkasie, PA, cardboard, red, black, and gray, 7" l, $5.00.

Store Card, Allen–A Hosiery, cardboard, standup, beautiful woman wearing red gown displaying stocking–clad legs, c1930s, 12" h, 8" w **70.00**

Store Card, Cyclone Twister Cigars, cardboard, word "Cyclone" in twister above windswept ground, 16" h, 12" w. **150.00**

Store Card, Ide Shirts, cardboard, blue ground, man with shirt draped over arm, "Eyed With Admiration, Shirts of Unusual Character," 1930s, 12" h, 9" w **55.00**

Thermometer, Clown Cigarettes, litho paper dial, black, yellow, and white, 9" d **65.00**

Thermometer, Doan's Pills, diecut wood, man holding aching back, black and white, 21" h, 5" w **275.00**

Thermometer, Hills Bros. Coffee, porcelain, old man in yellow nightgown drinking cup of coffee, white lettering, red ground, white border, "Patent No. 11324265, Beach Coshocton, O.," 21" h, 8¹⁄₂" w **550.00**

Thermometer, Jordan's Ready–To–Eat Meats, wood, enamel paint, yellow ground, black trim, stamped red lettering, c1930, 15" h **50.00**

Thermometer, Mail Pouch Tobacco, metal, dark blue ground, white lettering, "Chew Mail Pouch Tobacco, Treat Yourself to the Best," 39" h, 8¹⁄₂" w **100.00**

Thermometer, McKesson's Aspirin, porcelain, product box and bottle, 27" h, 7" w **350.00**

Thermometer, Ramon's Brownie Pills, metal, young doctor carrying satchel, "The Little Doctor Brings Happy Days," 21" h, 9" w. **275.00**

Thermometer, Sauer's Flavoring, C. F. Sauer Co, Richmond, VA, wood, painted, product image, 24" h, 6¹⁄₂" w **275.00**

Tin, Brach's Candies of Quality, square, gold ground, multicolor candies on 2 sides, factory scene other 2 sides, c1940, 5 lbs, 4¹⁄₂" sq, 10¹⁄₈" h **65.00**

Tin, Campfire Marshmallows, campfire scene **35.00**

Tin, Countess Cookies, Bond Bakers, boys playing various sports around sides, 8" h **45.00**

Tin, Forest & Stream Tobacco, fisherman, pocket size **75.00**

Tin, F. W. McNess Fine Confections, square, blue and white plaid ground, red lettering, candy dish, c1930, 4" sq, 7⁵⁄₈" h **15.00**

Tin, Grand Union Hard Candies, rect, red ground, blue bands, blue and white lettering, c1930, 5 lbs, 6" w, 8⁵⁄₈" h **30.00**

Tin, Hoadley Blood Orange Pellets, square, red ground, black and orange lettering, c1930, 5" w, 8¹⁄₂" h **50.00**

Tin, Hoyt's Selected Sweets, round, black and white checkerboard ground, boy holding candy jar, girl with hand extended, raised lettering on lid, 1920s, 5 lbs, 5" d, 9³⁄₄" h. **75.00**

Tin, Jackie Coogan Salted Nut Meats, man on elephant, black and white label, 7¹⁄₂" h, 6³⁄₄" d **30.00**

Tin, King Cole Coffee, king, key open type **20.00**

Tin, Len Wright's Chocolate Biscuits, paper label with Art Deco motif. **30.00**

Tin, Luzianne Coffee, black mammy, red ground. **50.00**

Tin, Mexene Chili Powder, devil stirring cauldron, 30 oz. **75.00**

Tin, Old Reliable Typewriter, typewriter ribbon, beavers chewing trees. **25.00**

Tin, Peerless Maid Confections, square, yellow ground, red and white candy cane striped corners, multicolor candies on 2 sides, lady with parasol other 2 sides, c1940, 5 lbs, 4¹⁄₂" sq, 10¹⁄₄" h. **45.00**

Tin, Planter's Cashews, Mr. Peanut, 4 oz, 1944 . . . . **40.00**

Tin, Sharp's Kreemy Toffee, little girl eating candy bar, "It's Alright," 7" w, 4" d, 5" h **85.00**

Tin, Sunshine Biscuit, Capitol building and cherry blossoms **75.00**

Tin, Texide Water Cured Prophylactics, litho tin, natives harvesting latex from rubber trees, 1930s, 1¹⁄₂ x 2 x ¹⁄₄". **40.00**

Tin, Tropical Brand Crystalized Ginger, black and white, shield with palm tree and alligator **20.00**

Tin, Yankee Doodle Dandy Candy, drum shape, children parading around sides, cloth strap, 1920s, 8 oz, 5⁵⁄₈" d, 2³⁄₈" h. **50.00**

Trolley Card, Beech–Nut Tomato Catsup, Beechnut Packing Co., Canojohave, NY, USA, cardboard, seated man reaching for catsup bottle, "Excuse me for reaching," multicolored, white ground, 11¹⁄₂" h, 21" w **100.00**

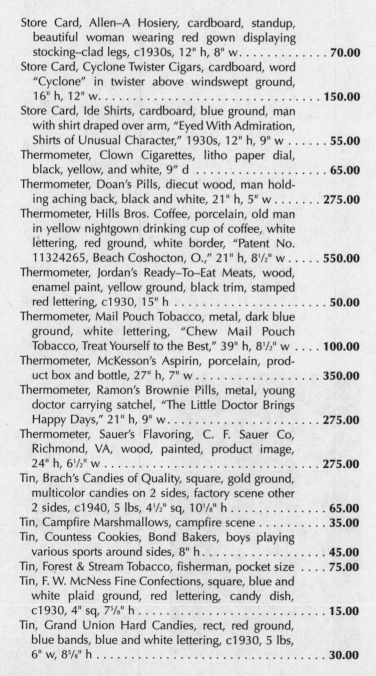

Trolley Card, Scott's Emulsion, cardboard, multicolored, boy and girl shooting marbles, c1924, 11" h, 24" w **185.00**

Trolley Card, Smith Brothers Cough Drops, cardboard, caricature men, one with cane wearing underwear and brown hat, other fully dressed wearing bowler, "...and it's just as silly to ever be without," 2 cough drop boxes, framed, 17½" h, 28" w **200.00**

Whistle, Curtiss Candy Company, Baby Ruth, litho tin, white lettering, red ground **15.00**

Whistle, Haines Shoes, plastic, orange and black, "Blow And Talk Of Haines The Shoe Wizard, Shoes For All," late 1940s. **20.00**

Whistle, Oscar Meyer, plastic, Weiner Mobile. **10.00**

Whistle, Peters Weatherbird Shoes, litho tin, yellow, 1920s **25.00**

ADVERTISING CHARACTERS

Many companies created advertising characters as a means of guaranteeing product recognition by the buying public. Consumers are more apt to purchase an item with which they are familiar and advertising characters were a surefire method of developing familiarity.

The early development of advertising characters also enabled immigrants who could not read to identify products by the colorful figures found on the packaging.

Trademarks and advertising characters are found on product labels, in magazines, as premiums, and on other types of advertising. Character subjects may be based on a real person such as Nancy Green, the original "Aunt Jemima." However, more often than not, they are comical figures, often derived from popular contemporary cartoons. Other advertising characters were designed especially to promote a specific product, like Mr. Peanut and the Campbell Kids.

References: Douglas Collins, *America's Favorite Food: The Story of Campbell Soup Company,* Harry N. Adams, 1994; Warren Dotz, *Advertising Character Collectibles: An Identification and Value Guide,* Collector Books, 1993, 1997 value update; Ted Hake, *Hake's Guide To Advertising Collectibles,* Wallace–Homestead, Krause Publications, 1992; Mary Jane Lamphier, *Zany Characters of the Ad World,* Collector Books, 1995; Norman E. Martinus and Harry L. Rinker, *Warman's Paper,* Wallace–Homestead, Krause Publications, 1994; Joan Stryker Grubaugh, *A Collector's Guide to the Gerber Baby,* published by author, 1996.

Collectors' Clubs: Charlie Tuna Collectors Club, 7812 N W Hampton Rd, Kansas City, MO 64152; R. F. Outcault Society, 103 Doubloon Drive, Slidell, LA 70461; Soup Collectors Club (Campbell Soup) 414 County Lane Ct, Wauconda, IL 60084.

REPRODUCTION ALERT

Aunt Jemima, Aunt Jemima Pancakes, tab, diecut litho tin, multicolor, Aunt Jemima's portrait, "Aunt Jemima Breakfast Club, 'Eat A Better Breakfast'," 1960s, 1½" w, 2" h. . . . . **$ 10.00**

Bud Man, Budweiser Beer, Anheuser–Busch, figure, foam rubber, red and blue costume, 1970, 17" h **75.00**

Buster Brown, Buster Brown Shoes, display, figural boy on base, plastic and cloth, small Buster Brown and Tige engaged in tug–of–war on base, 34" h **55.00**

Buster Brown, Buster Brown Shoes, rug, Buster Brown and Tige center portrait, gold ground, dark blue border with gold stars, 47" d **375.00**

Campbell's Kids, Campbell's Soup, trolley adv, multicolor, soup can and girl, dark green ground, "Campbell's Condensed Soups, 10¢," framed, 13" h, 23" w **75.00**

Charlie Tuna, Star–Kist, clock, brass, windup, "Sorry Charlie" sign hanging from fish hook beside Charlie, 1969, 6" h. **50.00**

Colonel Harland Sanders, Kentucky Fried Chicken, nodder, painted hard plastic, spring mounted bobbing head, c1960, 7½" h **85.00**

Dino Dinosaur, Sinclair Oil & Refining Corporation, ashtray, silvered metal, figural Dino in center, 1950s, 7¼" l **45.00**

Dutch Boy, Dutch Boy Paints, string holder, diecut tin, Dutch Boy painting door frame, hanging bucket string holder, American Art Sign Co, 30" h **2,000.00**

Elsie, Borden's Ice Cream, sign button, painted emb metal, Elsie head on red and white ground, ©T.B.C., 36" d **525.00**

Elsie, Borden's Milk and Cream, flange sign, double sided, Elsie head on brown and white ground, blue and white lettering, "If It's Borden's It's Got To Be Good!," 12" h, 20" w **525.00**

Exxon Tiger, water pitcher, clear glass, orange, black, and white tiger head, black lettering "Put A Tiger In Your Tank" in 8 different languages, Anchor Hocking, late 1960s, 9½" h **30.00**

Froggy, Buster Brown Shoes, mask, paper, "Froggy The Gremlin," ©1946, McConnell. **35.00**

Johnny, Philip Morris, sign, emb tin, Johnny and cigarette, yellow ground, black and red lettering, red border, Stout Sign Co, c1950s, 14" h, 27" w **300.00**

Charlie Tuna, Star–Kist Foods, lamp, plaster, stiff paper shade, c1970, 9" h, $50.00.

Nipper, RCA, salt and pepper shakers, Lenox China, "His Master's Voice" imp on base, 1930s, 3" h, price for pair, $50.00.

Jolly Green Giant, Minnesota Valley Canning Company, kite, Giant on white ground, c1970 . . . . **35.00**

Little Sprout, Minnesota Valley Canning Company, flashlight, hard plastic, figural Sprout and vegetables, 1980s, 9" h **25.00**

Mr. Bibidendum, Michelin Tires, costume, nylon and metal, pants, top, boots, sash, and head **900.00**

Mr. Bibidendum, Michelin Tires, sign, porcelain, self–framed, yellow "Michelin," running Michelin Man rolling tire, dark blue ground, white border, 32" h, 26¹/₂" w **300.00**

Nipper, sign, porcelain, oval, dog staring into music box speaker, "His Master's Voice," black ground, gold border, 18¹/₂" h, 26" w. **500.00**

Poppin' Fresh, Pillsbury, doll, cloth, stuffed, white with red, white, and blue accents, 1970s, 12" h **25.00**

Quaker Oats Man, display rack, metal, rect sign at top with Quaker man on either side, "Quaker Oats Quality Products" in red oval, 70" h, 28" w **700.00**

Red Goose, Red Goose Shoes, display, papier mâché, cardboard, metal, cloth, and wood, yellow ground, "Hey! Boys 'n Girls ask the Red Goose for a Golden Egg, Free with every purchase of a pair of Red Goose Shoes for boys and girls," figural goose, pull head forward to receive golden egg, 27" h, 22" w **225.00**

Red Goose, Red Goose Shoes, poster, paper, children and red goose outside schoolhouse, 1920 . . . . **275.00**

Reddy Kilowatt, figure, hardboard, red and cream, 10" h, 8¹/₂" w **115.00**

Reddy Kilowatt, sign, porcelain, red, white, and black, "No Trespassing, Florida Power & Light Co.," 11¹/₂" h, 15¹/₂" w. **175.00**

Speedy Relief, Alka–Seltzer, display sign, diecut cardboard, easel back, multicolor, Speedy descending steps formed from Alka–Seltzer boxes, 1950s, 2" h, 5" w, ... **150.00**

Speedy Relief, Alka–Seltzer, playing cards, commemorates Miles Laboratories' 100th anniversary, Speedy as joker, 1984. . . . . **18.00**

Squirt, sign, tin, diamond shaped, "Drink Squirt" above character holding soda bottle, "Just Call Me Squirt!," yellow ground, wood frame, 50" w, 50" h. . . . **300.00**

Sunbeam Girl, Sunbeam Batter Whipped Bread, door push, diecut porcelain, breadloaf with Sunbeam girl, multicolored, 1950s, 9" h, 18" w **275.00**

Uneeda Biscuit Boy, National Biscuit Company (Nabisco), letter opener, metal, figural boy handle, c1920, 8¹/₄" l **65.00**

AKRO AGATE

The Akro Agate Company was founded in Ohio in 1911 primarily to manufacture agate marbles. In 1914 the firm opened a large factory in Clarksburg, West Virginia.

Increasing competition in the marble industry in the 1930s prompted Akro Agate to expand. In 1936, following a major fire at the Westite factory, Akro Agate purchased many of Westite's molds. Akro Agate now boasted a large line of children's dishes, floral wares, and household accessories. The company also produced specialty glass containers for cosmetic firms, including the Mexicali cigarette jar (originally filled with Pick Wick bath salts) and a special line made for the Jean Vivaudou Company, Inc.

With its new diversity, Akro Agate prospered until the late 1940s, when competition once again forced a change. This time, the company was up against cheap imports and the production of similar products made from metals and plastics. The Clarksburg Glass Company bought the factory in 1951.

Akro Agate glass has survived the test of time because of its durability—it is thick and heavy. Transparent, opaque, and marbleized colors were produced. Most pieces are marked "Made in USA" and often include a mold number. Some pieces have a small crow in the mark. Early pieces of Akro made from Westite molds may be unmarked but were produced only in typical Akro colors and color combinations.

References: Gene Florence, *The Collectors Encyclopedia of Akro Agate Glassware, Revised Edition,* Collector Books, 1975, 1992 value update; Roger and Claudia Hardy, *The Complete Line of The Akro Agate,* published by author, 1992.

Collectors' Clubs: Akro Agate Art Assoc, PO Box 758, Salem, NH 03079; Akro Agate Collector's Club, 10 Bailey St, Clarksburg, WV 26301.

REPRODUCTION ALERT: Reproduction pieces are unmarked.

Cereal, Octagonal, pink. . . . . **$ 12.00**

Cigarette Holder, marbleized blue and white, eight sided, 2⁵/₈" h **12.00**

Creamer, Chiquita, baked–on cobalt blue **9.00**

Creamer, Interior Panel, opaque blue, large. **42.50**

Creamer, Octagonal, blue, large. **15.00**

Creamer and Sugar, J. Pressman, baked–on cobalt. **12.00**

Cup, Chiquita, opaque green **7.00**

Cup, Chiquita, transparent cobalt blue **14.00**

Cup, Concentric Ring, opaque green, small **5.00**

Cup, Concentric Ring, opaque orange, small. **10.00**

Cup, Interior Panel, red and white marbleized, small. **25.00**

Cup, Octagonal, green, large **10.00**

Cup, Stippled Band, green, large **20.00**

Cup and Saucer, Chiquita, transparent cobalt blue **17.50**

Cup and Saucer, Interior Panel, opaque pink, small. **25.00**

Cup and Saucer, Stippled Band, cobalt blue, large. **35.00**

Akro Agate, bowl, #321, lemonade and oxblood marbleized, tab handles, 9" w handle to handle, $30.00.

Cup and Saucer, Stippled Band, green, small 27.50
Demitasse Cup and Saucer, J. Pressman, green 17.50
Demitasse Cup, J. Pressman, pink 30.00
Flower Pot, Graduated Dart, orange and white mar-
    bleized 17.50
Flower Pot, Stacked Disc, blue and white marbleized 10.00
Jardiniere, Graduated Dart, bell shaped, closed han-
    dles, green and white marbleized 35.00
Lid, Octagonal, sugar, beige 10.00
Lid, Octagonal, sugar, blue 10.00
Lid, Octagonal, sugar, white 10.00
Lid, Chiquita, teapot, opaque green 10.00
Mexicali Jar, orange and white marbleized 35.00
Pitcher, Stacked Disc, opaque green, small 10.00
Plate, Concentric Ring, opaque green, small 2.50
Plate, Interior Panel, opaque green, large 7.00
Plate, Interior Panel, opaque green, small 6.00
Plate, J. Pressman, baked–on green, 3³/₄" 4.00
Plate, Octagonal, blue, large 7.50
Plate, Octagonal, green, large 5.00
Powder Jar, cov, Colonial Lady, opaque white 85.00
Saucer, Concentric Ring, opaque white, small 2.50
Saucer, Octagonal, closed handles, beige, large 3.00
Saucer, Octagonal, closed handles, white, large 3.00
Set, Octagonal, 17 pcs, closed handles, blue plates,
    teapot, creamer, and sugar lid, green cup and
    teapot lid, white saucers and sugar 100.00
Set, Octagonal, 17 pcs, closed handles, green plates
    and cups, white saucers and lids, yellow creamer
    and sugar, blue teapot 100.00
Set, Interior Panel, 21 pcs, opaque yellow, white
    teapot lid 350.00
Sugar, Chiquita, transparent cobalt blue 9.00
Table Lamp, pineapple body, blue 100.00
Teapot, Concentric Ring, blue, open, 2⁷/₈" 15.00
Teapot, Concentric Ring, opaque green, open, small 8.00
Teapot, Concentric Ring, opaque medium light blue,
    small 8.00
Teapot, Interior Panel, opaque pink, open, small 10.00
Teapot, J. Pressman, open, baked–on cobalt 10.00
Teapot, Octagonal, turquoise, large 15.00
Tumbler, Octagonal, green 10.00

ALADDIN LAMPS

Victor Samuel Johnson founded the Western Lighting Company in Kansas City, Missouri, in 1907. The company imported the for-eign–made "Practicus" lamp, forerunner and inspiration of the Aladdin lamp.

In 1908 the company incorporated, becoming the Mantle Lamp Company of America. Other changes followed. Due to deficien-cies in design of the Practicus lamp, Johnson continually strove to bring a better, more reliable and efficient lamp to the American home. In 1909, Johnson introduced the Aladdin lamp, which derived its name from the magic lamp found by Aladdin in *The Arabian Nights*. The success of the first Aladdin model, which uti-lized a new burner patented by Charles E. Wirth, enabled Johnson to establish and maintain a research and development department to further improve the Aladdin's performance.

Although the company has diversified and become as well known for its lunch boxes and vacuum bottles as its lamps, Aladdin lamps are still being manufactured today.

References: J. W. Courter, *Aladdin Collectors Manual & Price Guide #17*, published by author, 1997; J. W. Courter, *Aladdin Electric Lamps: Collectors Manual & Price Guide #2*, 1993.

Collectors' Club: The Mystic Light of the Aladdin Knights, 3995 Kelley Rd, Kevil, KY 42053.

REPRODUCTION ALERT: Tall Lincoln Drape, Short Lincoln Drape, glass and paper shades.

Note: All lamps priced with complete burners.

Model 1, parlor, polished brass . . . . $ 800.00
Model 4, student 5,500.00
Model 4, table, satin brass 300.00
Model 12, style 1230A, Crystal Vase, green alpha art
    glass, 10¹/₄" h, 1930–35 . . . . 150.00
Model 12, style 1253, floor, Verde Antique, 1930–32 . . . 175.00
Model 21C, style B–400, caboose, aluminum font 50.00
Model 23, hanging, aluminum hanger and font,
    white paper shade 50.00
Model A, style 100, table, Venetian, white, 1932–33 . . . . 100.00
Model B, hanging, flat steel frame, parchment shade 200.00
Model B, style 104, table, Colonial, clear, 1933 . . . . 100.00
Model B, style B–40, table, Washington Drape,
    green crystal, round base, 1939 . . . . 100.00
Model B, style B–60, table, Short Lincoln Drape,
    alacite, 1939 . . . . 500.00
Model B, style B–80, table, Beehive, clear, 1937–38 . . . . 100.00
Model B, style B–86, table, Quilt, green moonstone,
    1937 . . . . 300.00
Model B, style B–95, table, Queen, white moon-
    stone, oxidized bronze base, 1937–39 . . . . 375.00
Model B, style B–100, table, Corinthian, clear,
    1935–36 . . . . 80.00
Model B, style B–120, table, Majestic, white moon-
    stone, 1935–36 . . . . 375.00
Model B, style B–130, table, Orientale, ivory,
    1935–36 . . . . 50.00
Model B, style B–425, floor, ivory lacquer 200.00
Model C, hanging, aluminum hanger and font, white
    paper shade 50.00

ALUMINUM, HAND–WROUGHT

The mass production of hand–wrought aluminum decorative accessories is indebted to the inventiveness of Charles M. Hall and Paul T. Heroult. Hall of the United States and Heroult in France, working independently, simultaneously discovered an inexpensive electrolytic reduction process in 1886. Soon after, the price of aluminum dropped from $545.00 per pound to 57¢ per pound.

Aluminum ware's popularity thrived throughout the lean Depression years and into the first years of World War II, when aluminum shortages caused many factories to close. Some resumed production after the war; however, most pieces no longer originated with the artisitc craftsman—the Machine Age had arrived. By the late 1960s, decorative aluminum was no longer in fashion.

References: Dannie Woodard and Billie Wood, *Hammered Aluminum: Hand Wrought Collectibles,* published by authors, 1983, 1990 value update; Dannie A. Woodard, *Hammered Aluminum Hand Wrought Collectibles, Book Two,* Aluminum Collectors' Books, 1993.

Newsletters: *The Aluminist,* PO Box 1346, Weatherford, TX 76086; *The Continental Report,* 5128 Schultz Bridge Rd, Zionsville, PA 18092.

Ashtray, Everlast, bamboo	$ 30.00
Basket, Federal S Co, sailing ship, square knot handles, fluted edge	15.00
Beverage Set, World, pitcher and 8 tumblers, flowers, square knot handle	65.00
Bowl, Everlast, pine, 10"	15.00
Bowl, Farber, pierced frame	25.00
Bowl, Rodney Kent, tulip, floral ribbon handle, 10"	25.00
Bowl, Wendell August Forge, dogwood, 12"	75.00
Bracelet, unmarked, apple blossom, chain link	8.00
Bracelet, unmarked, cowboy on bucking bronco, chain link	35.00
Butler's Stand and Tray, Everlast	185.00
Butter, cov, Buenilum	30.00
Candle Holder, Buenilum, beaded edge, wood ball stem	10.00
Candle Holder, Everlast, side handle	15.00
Candlesticks, pr, Everlast, plain	30.00
Candy, Farberware, rose, double bowl, leaf center handle	35.00

Silent Butler, chrysanthemums, Continental Silverlook, #505, 12" l, $25.00.

Casserole Holder, Buenilum, twisted handles, loop finial, 8"	15.00
Casserole Holder, Everlast, bamboo	35.00
Casserole Holder, unmarked, rose, beaded knob, 7½"	20.00
Coaster, Wendell August Forge, turtle, 5"	2.00
Coaster Set, Buenilum, beaded edge, double loop finial, 8 coasters and caddy	15.00
Coffee Urn, Continental	150.00
Compote, Continental, wild rose, 5" h	20.00
Creamer and Sugar, Everlast	30.00
Creamer and Sugar, World	15.00
Crumber and Brush, Everlast, rose	25.00
Desk Set, Everlast, bamboo, 3 pcs, B24	30.00
Gravy Boat, Everlast, 7" l	12.00
Ice Bucket, Continental, chrysanthemum, 12 x 22"	55.00
Ice Bucket, Everlast, grapes	50.00
Ice Bucket, Everlast, rose	45.00
Ladle, Argental Cellini, 14½" l	20.00
Lazy Susan, Continental, acorns and leaf	25.00
Matchbox Holder, Palmer–Smith	65.00
Napkin Holder, Rodney Kent	25.00
Nut Dish, Everlast, bamboo, double bowl, center handle	35.00
Nut Dish, Wendell August Forge, pine	85.00
Punch Ladle, unmarked	45.00
Silent Butler, Buenilum, twisted handle	20.00
Silent Butler, Rodney Kent, ribbon handle	25.00
Tray, Arthur Armour, schooner, handles	95.00
Tray, Arthur Armour, wheat, bar handles, 6 x 14"	45.00
Tray, Everlast, folding, bamboo, center handle	65.00
Tray, Farber & Shlevin, zinnia panel, twisted handle	40.00
Wine Cooler and Stand, Everlast, grapes	250.00

AMERICAN BISQUE

The American Bisque Company, founded in Williamstown, West Virginia in 1919, was originally established for the manufacture of china head dolls. Early on the company expanded its product line to include novelties such as cookie jars and ashtrays, serving dishes, and ceramic giftware.

B. E. Allen, founder of the Sterling China Company, invested heavily in the company and eventually purchased the remaining stock. In 1982 the company changed hands, operating briefly under the name American China Company. The plant ceased operations in 1983.

American Bisque items have various markings. The trademark "Sequoia Ware" is often found on items sold in gift shops. The Berkeley trademark was used on pieces sold through chain stores. The most common mark found consists of three stacked baby blocks with the letters A, B, and C.

References: Susan and Al Bagdade, *Warman's American Pottery and Porcelain,* Wallace–Homestead, Krause Publications, 1994; Mary Jane Giacomini, *American Bisque: A Collector's Guide With Prices,* Schiffer Publishing, 1994; Lois Lehner, *Lehner's Encyclopedia of U.S. Marks on Pottery, Porcelain & Clay,* Collector Books, 1988.

Bank, Fred and Wilma Flintstone	$ 275.00
Bank, Popeye	400.00
Cookie Jar, Albert Apple	90.00

Cookie Jar, Animal Crackers, emb animals **40.00**
Cookie Jar, bear with cookie **50.00**
Cookie Jar, carousel, knob finial **50.00**
Cookie Jar, cat in basket **50.00**
Cookie Jar, churn boy **200.00**
Cookie Jar, coffeepot, brown, red flowers, bail handle **20.00**
Cookie Jar, cowboy boots, some int crazing **100.00**
Cookie Jar, Davy Crockett **350.00**
Cookie Jar, granny **125.00**
Cookie Jar, kitten and beehive, white kitten, flowers
  and bees on yellow beehive, c1958 . . . . **35.00**
Cookie Jar, lady pig **100.00**
Cookie Jar, milk can, bell in lid, "After School
  Snacks" in black **35.00**
Cookie Jar, moon rocket **280.00**
Cookie Jar, rabbit with hat **100.00**
Cookie Jar, seal on igloo **280.00**
Cookie Jar, sitting horse **150.00**
Cookie Jar, spaceship, mkd ABC **325.00**
Dinnerware, cereal bowl, Ballerina Mist, painted **5.00**
Dinnerware, dinner plate, Ballerina Mist, painted **5.00**
Lamp, Billy the Kid **175.00**
Planter, bears at tree, 5½" **15.00**
Planter, brown bear cubs, tree stump **10.00**
Planter, Dutch girl with tulips, 7½" h **15.00**
Planter, wailing kitten **20.00**
Planter, Little Davy Crockett, 5" h **45.00**
Planter, parrot, burgundy and green **15.00**
Planter, puppy, 24K gold **35.00**
Planter, pushcart man, 5⅞" h **15.00**
Planter, tugboat, 9½" h **25.00**
Salt and Pepper Shakers, pr, churn **65.00**

ANCHOR HOCKING

The Hocking Glass Company was founded in Lancaster, Ohio in 1905. Although the company originally produced hand–made items, by the 1920s the firm was manufacturing a wide variety of wares including chimneys and lantern globes, tableware, tumblers, and novelties. Hocking introduced its first line of pressed glass dinnerware in 1928. Molded etched tableware was released shortly thereafter.

Following the acquisition of several glass houses in the 1920s, Hocking began producing new glass containers. In 1937 Hocking merged with the Anchor Cap and Closure Corporation, resulting in a name change in 1939 to Anchor Hocking Glass Corporation. In 1969 the company became Anchor Hocking Corporation.

References: Gene Florence, *Collectible Glassware From The 40's, 50's, 60's, Third Edition,* Collector Books, 1996; Gene Florence, *The Collector's Encyclopedia of Depression Glass, Twelfth Edition,* Collector Books, 1996; Hazel Marie Weatherman, *Colored Glassware of the Depression Era, Book 2,* published by author, 1974, reprint available.

Additional Listings: See Depression Glass Patterns, Fire–King

Ashtray, green transparent, flared lip . . . . **$ 10.00**
Butter Dish, cov, green transparent, ribbed **85.00**
Butter Dish, cov, Block, 3 x 5" **50.00**
Canister, green transparent, smooth, metal lid, 6" h **85.00**

Coffee Canister, cov, green transparent, ribbed, clear
  glass lid **65.00**
Cookie Jar, green transparent, ribbed **50.00**
Cup, green transparent, ribbed **5.00**
Ice Bucket, clear, tab handles, black, yellow, and red
  rings **15.00**
Jar, green transparent, smooth, quart **25.00**
Juice Tumbler, pink transparent, ribbed **15.00**
Measuring Cup, green clambroth, 2 cup **130.00**
Mixing Bowl, vitrock, red dec, 10½" d **25.00**
Reamer, green transparent, ribbed **15.00**
Refrigerator Dish, cov, rect, green transparent, ribbed **20.00**
Refrigerator Dish, cov, green, 8" sq, slight roughage **20.00**
Shaker, fired–on yellow, black lettering **10.00**
Syrup, cov, green, metal top **35.00**
Water Bottle, green transparent, ribbed **25.00**

ANIMALS

The hobby of collecting objects depicting one's favorite animal has thrived for years. The more common species have enjoyed long lives of popularity. Cats, dogs, cows, horses, and pigs are examples of animals whose collectibility is well established. Their markets are so stable, in fact, that they merit separate listings of their own.

The desirability of other animals changes with the times. Many remain fashionable for only a limited period of time, or their popularity cycles, often due to marketing crazes linked to advertising.

Many animal collectors differ from other collectors in that they place little emphasis on an object's date of manufacture or its aesthetic quality. To the animal enthusiast, the only prerequisite is that the object depicts the collector's pet species.

References: Diana Callow et al., *The Charlton Price Guide To Beswick Animals, Second Edition,* The Charlton Press, 1994; Jean Dale, *The Charlton Standard Catalogue of Royal Doulton Animals,* The Charlton Press, 1994; Jean Dale, *The Charlton Standard Catalogue of Royal Doulton Beswick Storybook Figurines, Third Edition,* The Charlton Press, 1996; Lee Garmon and Dick Spencer, *Glass Animals of the Depression Era,* Collector Books, 1993; Everett Grist, *Covered Animal Dishes,* Collector Books, 1988, 1993 value update; Herbert N. Schiffer, *Collectible Rabbits,* Schiffer Publishing, 1990; Mike Schneider, *Grindley Pottery: A Menagerie,* Schiffer Publishing, 1996.

Newsletter: *Jumbo Jargon,* 1002 West 25th St, Erie, PA 16502.

Collectors' Clubs: The Frog Pond, PO Box 193, Beech Grove, IN 46107; The National Elephant Collector's Society, 380 Medford St, Somerville, MA 02145.

Antelope, bookends, pr, Frankart . . . . **$ 275.00**
Bear, bank, metal, 4½" h **20.00**
Bear, cookie jar, Smokey Bear **100.00**
Bear, figure, ceramic, tumbling, Shawnee **65.00**
Bird, bookends, pr, quail, polychrome, 5½" h **140.00**
Camel, ashtray, Whimtray, Wade Ceramics **20.00**
Donkey, doorstop, cast iron, old black paint, 11" l **200.00**
Dragon, nutcracker, brass, figural **50.00**
Duck, candy container, yellow composition, ribbon
  around neck, standing on 3" d round cardboard
  box, opens at base, Germany, 4" h **35.00**

Elephant, cigarette box, covered, green glass, Greensburg Glass Works, 2¹/₂ x 1³/₄", $65.00.

Elephant, adv trade card, Clark's ONT Spool Cotton,
  Jumbo Aesthetic, elephant walking on hind legs **5.00**
Elephant, ashtray, Occupied Japan **15.00**
Elephant, brooch, Bakelite, multicolor, movable legs,
  1930s, 1³/₄ x 2¹/₂" **25.00**
Elephant, cheese cutting board, elephant shape, cher-
  ry hardwood, 8 x 13" **85.00**
Elephant, chocolate mold, tin, 3 cavities **75.00**
Elephant, rocker blotter, amethyst glass **85.00**
Elephant, salt and pepper shakers, pr, Rosemeade **40.00**
Flying Fish, master salt, blue milk glass **125.00**
Frog, cane handle, figural, silvered white metal, inset
  glass eyes, early 1900s **50.00**
Frog, match holder, cast iron, 2 pcs, match striker
  under mouth, Pointer Stoves and Ranges adv **225.00**
Frog, paperweight, figural, cast iron **30.00**
Hippo, cookie jar, Brush **350.00**
Lion, pin dish, cov, white milk glass, 4³/₄ x 3¹/₂" **10.00**
Monkey, nutcracker, wood, figural, painted eyes **80.00**
Owl, candy container, glass, perched on branch **50.00**
Owl, cookie jar, cream, winking, Shawnee, 11" h **45.00**
Owl, creamer, milk glass **25.00**
Owl, plate, milk glass, 7¹/₂" d **35.00**
Owl, thermometer, plaster body, 6" h **75.00**
Poultry, watercolor painting, sgd "Franz Grobel"
  lower right, 13⁷/₁₆ x 18⁷/₈" **325.00**
Rabbit, bib holder, sterling silver **40.00**
Rabbit, candy container, papier mâché, Germany **55.00**
Rabbit, tape measure, metal, figural, seated **325.00**
Rooster, door knocker, old paint **125.00**
Sheep, painting, Sheeps Grazing in a Pasture, oil on
  canvas, sgd "Charles T. Phelan" lower right **1,500.00**
Sheep, pull toy, wood, fleece, and papier mâché,
  glass eyes, orig paint, 8" h **250.00**
Squirrel, figure, Red Rose Tea premium **5.00**
Squirrel, nutcracker, cast iron, figural **50.00**
Swan, master salt, white milk glass, head down,
  3¹/₄" h, 5¹/₂" l **25.00**

Turtle, cookie jar, upside down turtle, California
  Originals **50.00**
Turtle, dish, cov, figural, amber glass, shell lid **95.00**
Turtle, doorstop, figural, painted green, 8" l **85.00**
Turtle, figure, earthenware, brown, Japan, 2⁷/₈" h **1.00**

ANIMATION ART

To understand animation art, one must understand its terminology. The vocabulary involving animation cels is very specific. The difference between a master, key production, printed or publication, production, and studio background can mean thousands of dollars in value. Unfortunately, even the biggest auction houses that regularly sell animation art cannot agree.

A "cel" is an animation drawing on celluloid. The invention of the celluloid animation process is attributed to Earl Hurd. Although the technique reached perfection under animation giants such as Walt Disney and Max Fleischer, individuals such as Ub Iwerks, Walter Lantz, and Paul Terry along with studios such as Columbia, Charles Mints and Screen Gems, MGM, Paramount/Famous Studios, UPA, and Warner Brothers did pioneering work.

One second of film requires over twenty animation cels. Multiply the length of a cartoon in minutes times sixty times twenty–four in order to approximate the number of cels used in a single cartoon strip. The vast quantities of individual cels produced are mind–boggling. While Walt Disney animation cels are indisputably the most sought–after, the real bargains in the field exist elsewhere. Avoid limited edition serigraphs. A serigraph is a color print made by the silk screen process. Although it appears to be an animation cel, it is not.

References: Jeff Lotman, *Animation Art: The Early Years, 1911–1954*, Schiffer Publishing, 1995; Jeff Lotman, *Animation Art: The Later Years, 1954–1993*, Schiffer Publishing, 1996.

Periodicals: *Animation Magazine*, 4676 Admiralty Way, Suite 210, Marina Del Ray, CA 90292; *In Toon*, PO Box 487, White Plains, NY 10603.

Background Sheet, Filmation Studios, 1970s, Fat
  Albert and the Cosby Kids, tempera, framed . . . . . . **$ 850.00**
Background Sheets, pr, Hanna–Barbera Studio,
  1960s, Augie Doggie and Doggie Daddy, tempera,
  framed, 8 x 10" **1,500.00**
Gouache on Celluloid, King Features/Heinz
  Edelman, *Yellow Submarine*, 1968, John Lennon
  and Ringo Starr, 7¹/₂ x 9" **2,000.00**
Gouache on Celluloid, MGM Studios/Chuck Jones
  Productions, Disney TV show, Chip and Dale car-
  rying hobo packs, 4 x 8¹/₂", untrimmed, framed **1,500.00**
Gouache on Celluloid, Walt Disney Studio, *Mickey's
  Christmas Carol*, Mickey and Willie the Giant as
  the Ghost of Christmas Present, laminated, Disney
  seal, untrimmed, framed, 9 x 14" **1,500.00**
Gouache on Celluloid, Walt Disney Studio, 1950s,
  Donald Duck portrait, 7 x 9¹/₂", cel trimmed to 10¹/₂
  x 12", framed **1,000.00**
Gouache on Celluloid, Walt Disney Studio, *Peter
  Pan*, 1953, full–figure portrait of Michael as Indian,
  carrying teddy bear, 7 x 3" **1,000.00**

Gouache on Celluloid, Walt Disney Studio, *The Jungle Book,* full figure Baloo, unframed, 6½ x 4", cel trimmed to 10 x 12"...................... **1,000.00**

Gouache on Celluloid, on tempera background sheet, MGM Studio/Chuck Jones Productions, *Horton Hears A Who,* 1970, Horton portrait, studio notes on background, 9 x 12"................. **1,500.00**

Gouache on Celluloid, on color frame enlargement of live action film, Walt Disney Studio, *Who Framed Roger Rabbit?,* 1988, Roger cel trimmed to outline of figure, 8½ x 11½"................. **1,500.00**

AUCTION PRICES

Sotheby's, New York, Collectors' Carrousel: Animation Art, Dolls & Toys auction, December 14, 1996. Prices include a buyer's premium of 15% of the successful bid price up to and including $50,000, and 10% on any amount in excess of $50,000.

Drawing, Walt Disney Studio, *Sleeping Beauty,* 1959, Maleficent, capturing her during moment of calm, graphite on paper, full margins, image size: 9".................................... **920.00**

Gouache on Celluloid, applied to custom air-brushed studio prepared background, Touch-stone Pictures/Amblin Entertainment, *Who Framed Roger Rabbit?,* 1988, pan set–up of over 30 recognizable characters representing all eras of all cartoon studios from film's finale in which Toon Town is saved and inherited by its residents, sight: 10 x 35"........................... **17,250.00**

Gouache on Celluloid, applied to hand–prepared background, Warner Bros. Studio, *Pepe Le Pew,* c1960s, Pepe Le Pew smiles as he shrugs his shoulders and gestures with his hands, image size: 4"; sight: 8½ x 11¼".................. **920.00**

Gouache on Trimmed Celluloid, applied to air-brushed Courvoisier background, Walt Disney Studio, *Pinocchio,* 1940, Jiminy Cricket startled by curious seahorse, "Walt Disney Productions" label on back, image size: Jiminy 3½", seahorse 6"; sight: 9½ x 8"...................... **3,737.00**

APPLIANCES

The turn of the century saw the popularity of electric kitchen appliances increase to the point where most metropolitan households sported at least one of these modern conveniences. By the 1920s, innovations and improvements were occurring at a rapid pace. The variations designed for small appliances were limitless.

Some "firsts" in electrical appliances include:

1882 Patent for electric iron (H. W. Seeley [Hotpoint])
1903 Detachable cord (G. E. Iron)
1905 Toaster (Westinghouse Toaster Stove)
1909 Travel iron (G. E.)
1911 Electric frying pan (Westinghouse)
1912 Electric waffle iron (Westinghouse)
1917 Table Stove (Armstrong)
1918 Toaster/Percolator (Armstrong "Perc–O–Toaster")
1920 Heat indicator on waffle iron (Armstrong)

1920 Flip–flop toasters (all manufacturers)
1920 Mixer on permanent base (Hobart Kitchen Aid)
1920 Electric egg cooker (Hankscraft)
1923 Portable mixer (Air–O–Mix "Whip–All")
1924 Automatic iron (Westinghouse)
1924 Home malt mixer (Hamilton Beach #1)
1926 Automatic pop–up toaster (Toastmaster #1h–A–A)
1926 Steam iron (Eldec)
1937 Home coffee mill (Hobart Kitchen Aid)
1937 Automatic coffee maker (Farberware "Coffee Robot")
1937 Conveyance device toaster ("Toast–O–Lator")

References: E. Townsend Artman, *Toasters: 1909–1960,* Schiffer Publishing, 1996; Linda Campbell Franklin, *300 Years of Kitchen Collectibles, Third Edition,* Books Americana, Krause Publications, 1991; Michael J. Goldberg, *Groovy Kitchen Designs For Collectors: 1935–1965,* Schiffer Publishing, 1996; Helen Greguire, *Collector's Guide to Toasters & Accessories,* Collector Books, 1997; Diane Stoneback, *Kitchen Collectibles: The Essential Buyer's Guide,* Wallace–Homestead, Krause Publications, 1994; *Toasters and Small Kitchen Appliances: A Price Guide,* L–W Book Sales, 1995.

Newsletter: *Toasty,* PO Box 529, Temecula, CA 92593.

Collectors' Club: Electric Breakfast Club, PO Box 306, White Mills, PA 18473.

Bar–B–Q Marshmallow Toaster, Angelus–Campfire, Milwaukee, WI, flat topped, pierced pyramid top pc, base stands on loop, wire legs, rubber encased feet, flat wire forks, 3" sq, 1920s................ **$ 55.00**

Blender, Dorby Whipper, Model E, chrome motor, black Bakelite handle, off/on toggle, clear measured Vidrio glass, 1940s...................... **25.00**

Blender, Electromix Whipper, Chicago, ivory, offset metal motor housing, push–down break, filler hole in lid, measured glass base, 7½" h, 1930s........... **25.00**

Blender, Kenmore, Sears, Roebuck & Co, Chicago, Kenmore Hand Mixer, small, cream colored plastic, single 4½" beater, orig box, booklet, warranty, and hanger plate, 1940s................... **25.00**

Chafing Dish, American Beauty, American Electrical Heater Co, Detroit, MI, 3 part, nickel on copper, sealed element in base, hot water container, separate plugs, marked "fast" and "slow," black painted wood handles and knob, 1910s........... **50.00**

Coffee Maker, Porcelier Breakfast Set, Porcelier Mfg Co, Greensburg, PA, all porcelain bodies, basketweave design accents, floral transfers, silver line dec, complete set, 1930s.................... **350.00**

Coffee Maker, Royal Rochester Corp, Rochester NY, Model E610, 3 pcs, coffee set, lusterware bodies, mkd "Fraunfelter China, OH," vertically faceted alternating orange and white stripes, floral transfers... **150.00**

Food Cooker, Nesco Electric Casserole, National Enamel & Stamping Co, Inc, Milwaukee, WI, cream colored body, green enamel lid, high/low control, 3–prong plug, 9" d, early 1930s........... **25.00**

Hot Plate, Westinghouse, Mansfield, OH, round top, green porcelain metal top surrounding element, hollow legs, no control, 7½" d top, 1920s.......... **25.00**

Waffle Iron, General Electric, Cat #119W4, chrome plated, Bakelite handles, cast aluminum interior, 12" w, $35.00.

Iron, Sunbeam, Iron Master, #52, steam attachment, orig box, 2³/₄ lb chrome body, unused, 1940s 50.00

Malt Mixer, Machine Craft, Los Angeles, CA, Model B, 18³/₄" h 60.00

Popcorn Popper, White Cross, National Stamping & Electrical Co, Chicago, tin can base with heater and cord, wire basket fits into can, metal top with stirrer mounted through handle, side wooden handle, late 1910s. 30.00

Sandwich Grill, Berstead Mfg Co, Fostoria, OH and Oaksville, Ontario, Canada, Victorian Sandwich Grill, rect nickel body, permanent plates, flared legs, curved mounts, black turned handles, 10" l, 1920s 20.00

Toaster, General Mills, Minneapolis, MN, Cat #GM 5A, 2 slice pop–up chrome body, black Bakelite base, white dec sides, AC/DC, red knob, light and dark control, early 1940s 20.00

Toaster, Sunbeam, Sunbeam Corp, Chicago, IL, Art Deco design, rounded corners, rect, chrome, black Bakelite base, heat indicator light on front, fitted clear "Hostess" tray, 1936. 65.00

Waffle Iron, Coleman, Coleman Lamp & Stove Co, Wichita, KS, Art Deco style, chrome, small black and white porcelain top insert of impala, black Bakelite handles, early 1930s 50.00

ART POTTERY

Art pottery production was at an all–time high during the late 19th and early 20th centuries. At this time over one hundred companies and artisans were producing individually designed and often decorated pottery which served both utilitarian and aesthetic purposes. Artists often moved from company to company, some forming their own firms.

Condition, quality of design, beauty in glazes, and maker are the keys in buying art pottery. This category covers companies not found elsewhere in the guide.

References: Susan and Al Bagdade, *Warman's American Pottery and Porcelain*, Wallace–Homestead, Krause Publications, 1994;

Carol and Jim Carlton, *Collector's Encyclopedia of Colorado Pottery: Identification and Values,* Collector Books, 1994; Paul Evans, *Art Pottery of the United States, Second Edition,* Feingold & Lewis Publishing, 1987; Ralph and Terry Kovel, *Kovels' American Art Pottery: Collector's Guide to Makers, Marks and Factory Histories,* Crown Publishers, 1993.

Collectors' Club: American Art Pottery Assoc, PO Box 525, Cedar Hill, MO 63016.

Additional Listings: See California Faience, Cowan, Fulper, Potteries, Regional, Rookwood, Roseville, Van Briggle, and Weller.

Arthur Baggs, vase, coupe shape, hand thrown, pelicans design, glossy yellow glaze, 1925, 3¹/₂ x 3¹/₂" . . **$ 225.00**

Batchelder, ashtray, hexagonal, light blue glaze, 4¹/₂" d **150.00**

Batchelder, vase, bulging shoulder, narrow neck, clear to opaque olive green glaze, 8¹/₄" h. **200.00**

Batchelder, vase, flared shape, closed rim, mottled cobalt glossy glaze, brown ground, 5³/₄" h **275.00**

Bybee, creamer, cov, blue–green glaze, 5" h **20.00**

Bybee, vase, "Seldon Bybee" mark, dark red, 7" h. **35.00**

Clewell Art Ware, bowl, geometric design on lip, 3" h, 7" d. **500.00**

Clewell Art Ware, cider set, mkd, five 4" h mugs, 11" h pitcher **400.00**

Clewell Art Ware, vase, #254–2–6, dark green and rust brown patina, 6" h **450.00**

Clewell Art Ware, vase, #837, incised floral and leaf design, 6¹/₂" h. **800.00**

Dedham, bowl, Lotus pattern, raised fluted emb design, blue embellishments, 5¹/₂" d **700.00**

Dedham, eggcup, Grape pattern, dark blue, two blue bands above design, mkd "D.P.," 2¹/₂" h **250.00**

Dedham, pitcher, Rabbit pattern, dark blue, band on rim, marked "Dedham Pottery Registered," 5¹/₄" h **700.00**

Durant Kilns, vase, ovoid, ftd, thick mottled brown and yellow glaze, incised "Volkmar/1949," 9¹/₄ x 5". . . **650.00**

Durant Kilns, vase, spherical, ftd, matte mottled green and yellow glaze, incised "Volkmar/1931," 6¹/₂ x 6". . . **550.00**

Marblehead, bookends, pr, carved Egyptian dec, blue and semi–gloss matte glaze, mkd **600.00**

Marblehead, bud vase, gray glaze, 7" h. **275.00**

Marblehead, wall pocket, flared top, matte green glaze, 5" h, 7" w. **300.00**

Newcomb College, bowl, by Anna F. Simpson, matte glaze, carved pink morning glories and green foliage, blue ground, imp "NC/AFS/NT47/JM/212," 1924, 4¹/₂ x 6³/₄" **1,650.00**

Newcomb College, cabinet vase, by Sadie Irvine, carved pink berries, purple ground, imp "NC/SI/RV81," 1929, 2¹/₄ x 2³/₄" **1,000.00**

Newcomb College, cup and saucer, set of 4, by H. Bailey, cup with red and cream pinecones, green foliage on blue ground, saucers with green swirls on blue ground, 4" h **4,750.00**

Newcomb College, trivet, #S784, by Sadie Irvine, incised and painted white flowers, yellow centers, and green leaves and stems, dark matte blue glaze, 6" d. **875.00**

Niloak, vase, Mission Ware, marbleized swirls, brown, blue, and cream, imp mark, 9¼" h, $125.00.

Newcomb College, vase, by Anne Simpson, baluster shape, sharply carved bayou scene with oak trees and Spanish moss, tones of blue, green, and cream, imp "NC/AFS'/NL8/MJ/195," 1923, 8 x 4¾" **2,850.00**

Newcomb College, vase, by Sadie Irvine, modeled blue and yellow flowers and long green leaves, dark blue ground, imp "NC/SI/19/PL44/JM," repaired rim, 1925, 6½ x 3¼" **1,000.00**

Newcomb College, vase, by Sadie Irvine, scenic, live oak trees and Spanish moss, celadon and blue, imp "NC/SI/JM/QU75/33," 1928, 6¼ x 3¼". **1,975.00**

Newcomb College, vase, matte blue and white arched curtains, blue ground, mkd, 5½" h **1,200.00**

Niloak, bud vase, Hywood line, leaf, blue glaze, 6" h **15.00**

Niloak, candlesticks, pr, Hywood Art Pottery, double cornucopia, white, unmarked, 6¾" h **100.00**

Niloak, cornucopia, light pink, 3". **5.00**

Niloak, ewer, eagle, 9½" w **45.00**

Niloak, figure, frog **20.00**

Niloak, figure, squirrel. **20.00**

Niloak, pitcher, yellow, 3¼". **15.00**

Niloak, planter, camel, 3". **25.00**

Niloak, planter, duck, pink and white, 5" **20.00**

Niloak, planter, log, white, 7". **15.00**

Niloak, planter, rabbit, green, 3". **15.00**

Niloak, salt and pepper shakers, pr, penguin. **65.00**

Niloak, vase, maroon, handles, 7" h **15.00**

North Dakota School of Mines, bowl, by D. Kane, curled edge, brown jonquil and green leaves on soft blue ground, circular ink mark "D. Kane, 1925," 2½ x 8". **700.00**

North Dakota School of Mines, bowl, carved florals, gray–green matte, 5½" d **150.00**

North Dakota School of Mines, paperweight, "Parent's Day, 1938," deep blue, 3½" d **100.00**

North Dakota School of Mines, vase, imp rings on shoulder, matte green glaze, 6½" h **325.00**

North Dakota School of Mines, vase, by Elizabeth Bradley, incised stylized tulips under apple green glaze, c1933, 9½" h **600.00**

Overbeck, figure, southern man in pink coat and light blue pants holding hat, mkd, 4¼" h **225.00**

Overbeck, tumbler, set of 4, band of green stylized grasshoppers, light yellow ground, 4" h **1,500.00**

Paul Revere, trivet, goose on hill medallion, dark blue ground, impressed mark, 1924, 5½" d **600.00**

Paul Revere, vase, ovoid, band of green trees on satin blue–gray ground, imp circular mark, small glaze bubble on body, 1924, 6¼ x 3½". **1,425.00**

Peters and Reed/Zane, bowl, brown, green accents, 5" d, 2" h **25.00**

Peters and Reed/Zane, jardiniere, Moss Aztec, emb flowers, 10" w **75.00**

Peters and Reed/Zane, umbrella stand, marbleized finish, 17" h **300.00**

Peters and Reed/Zane, vase, hexagonal, marbleized finish, 9¼" h **75.00**

Peters and Reed/Zane, wall pocket, Egyptian, 9" h **65.00**

Pewabic, bowl, matte green glaze, high relief repeating leaves, imp "Pewabic" under maple leaves, 6¼" h, 2¾" d. **1,550.00**

Pewabic, candlestick, brown drip over brown and green ground, incised mark, 7" h **165.00**

Pewabic, vase, blue metallic glaze, pink and gold accents, 4" h **775.00**

Pisgah Forest, cameo vase, dec by Walter Stephen, white pioneering scene, dead matte gray ground, raised mark, 1953, 5½ x 3½" **250.00**

Saturday Evening Girls, bookends, pr, night scenes with owls, ink marked "S.E.G./11–21," flat chip on bottom of one, 1921, 4 x 5". **1,425.00**

Teco, coaster, Cubs, oatmeal ground, team insignia, imp mark, 4¼" d **150.00**

Wheatley, tile, emb lion, organic matte brown glaze, 7¾" sq **250.00**

AUCTION PRICES

David Rago, Antique & Auction Centre, Lambertville, New Jersey, Arts and Crafts Auction, March 16, 1997. Prices include a 10% buyer's premium.

Dedham, tea bowl, dripping mossy green glaze over rich crackled ground, blue rabbit mark, 2½ x 4½" **495.00**

Kenton Hills, ginger jar, cov, green aventurine glaze, die–stamped mark, 9½ x 6½" **440.00**

Marblehead, vase, ovoid, incised trefoil design in dark green over green speckled matte ground, incised ship mark, 5½ x 3½". **2,750.00**

Niloak, Mission ware, 3 pc console set, center bowl and pr candlesticks, bowl and one stick mkd, 10" d bowl, 8½" h candlesticks. **302.50**

North Dakota School of Mines, bowl, closed–in, dec by Margarrt Cable, meadowlarks and rushes, lime green matte finish, circular ink mark "M. Cable, Meadow Lark,155," 3¼ x 6¼" **660.00**

Pewabic, vase, ovoid, rolled rim, gold and green irid flambé glaze, imp circle mark, 6 x 4" **715.00**

ASHTRAYS

Ashtrays can be found made from every material and in any form imaginable. A popular subcategory with collectors is advertising ashtrays. Others include figural ashtrays or those produced by a particular manufacturer. It is still possible to amass an extensive collection on a limited budget. As more people quit smoking, look for ashtrays to steadily rise in price.

Reference: Nancy Wanvig, *Collector's Guide to Ashtrays: Identification & Values,* Collector Books, 1997.

Newsletter: *Ashtray Journal,* PO Box 11652, Houston, TX 77293.

Bull Dog, Art Deco, Central Die Casting and Mfg Co, $4^1/_4$ x 7"	$ 50.00
Cat, Art Deco, chrome, $7^1/_4$ x $4^1/_2$ x $2^1/_2$"	25.00
Cliff House, San Francisco, adv, shell, litho	15.00
Cowboy Hat, copper, $5^3/_4$ x 2"	10.00
Elephant, Art Deco, Hamilton, $4^1/_2$ x $1^3/_4$"	25.00
Firestone, adv, tire form	40.00
Ford, adv, diecut stainless steel, 1950s style	70.00
Glenmore Distilleries, Kentucky's Finest Whiskies adv, plaster, tan, 4" h cartoon figure, inscribed back, 1950–60, 5 x 6"	50.00
Guitar, figural, wood, $8^1/_4$ x $2^3/_4$ x $1^1/_2$"	5.00
Hanley Brewing Co, Providence, RI, adv	35.00
Horse, figural, Art Deco, 7 x $4^3/_4$ x $6^1/_4$"	40.00
Horse and Cart, milk glass, $2^1/_4$ x $4^1/_2$ x $2^1/_4$"	20.00
House of Representatives, Fostoria, 1 x $3^3/_4$ x $3^1/_8$"	20.00
Kentucky Colonel, adv	10.00
Lion, figural, Akro Agate, $7^3/_4$ x $4^1/_2$ x $3^1/_4$"	35.00
Man on Post, Japan, cast iron, 4 x $4^3/_4$"	10.00
Old Judge Coffee, adv, tin	90.00
Playing Cards, King and Ten of Diamonds, porcelain, $5^1/_2$ x 6 x $3/_4$"	15.00
Poodle, Stafford China, black, c1950s, 6 x $4^3/_4$ x $2^1/_8$"	10.00
Rockwood Boss Stoves, adv, pottery, 1946	125.00
Scottie, figural, lighter, painted cast aluminum, 6 x $1^1/_2$ x $5^1/_2$ x 4"	30.00
Seiberling Tire, Market St, Williamsport, PA, adv	18.00
Souvenir of Rhodes, butterfly center, c1930, $5^3/_4$ x $1^1/_2$"	15.00
Squirrel, Art Deco, Hamilton, cigarette holder and snuffer center, $2^3/_4$ x $5^3/_4$"	25.00
Sword, floor, $34^1/_2$ x $9^1/_2$"	50.00
Toilet Seat, Art Deco, England, 4 x $2^1/_4$"	10.00
Winston Cigarettes, adv, tin	5.00
Woman's Head, Art Deco, smoky frosted glass, $6^3/_4$ x 4"	35.00

AUTO & DRAG RACING

The earliest automobile racing occurred in Europe at the end of the 19th century. By 1910, the sport was popular in America as well. The Indianapolis 500, first held in 1911, has been run every year except for a brief interruption caused by World War II. Collectors search for both Formula 1 and NASCAR items, with pre–1945 materials the most desirable.

References: Mark Allen Baker, *Auto Racing: Memorabilia and Price Guide,* Krause Publications, 1996; James Beckett and Eddie Kelley (eds.), *Beckett Racing Price Guide and Alphabetical Checklist, Number 1,* Beckett Publications, 1996; Jack MacKenzie, *Indy 500 Buyer's Guide,* published by author [1996].

Periodicals: *Collector's World,* PO Box 562029, Charlotte, NC 28256; *Racing Collectibles Price Guide,* PO Box 608114, Orlando, FL 32860.

Collectors' Club: National Indy 500 Collectors Club, 822 22nd St, Columbus, IN 47201.

REPRODUCTION ALERT

Ashtray, Indianapolis 500, ceramic, white, black wheels, gold trim, $5^1/_4$ x $5^1/_4$ x $3/_4$"	25.00
Bottle, whiskey, 1970 Indy Race, commemorative, Jim Beam Distilling Co	15.00
Catalog, 501 Fiat and Winners 1925 Autodrome, illus, color lithos, photogravures	175.00
Cigarette Lighter, Mickey Thompson Speed Equipment, metal, chrome finish, mid–1960s, $2^1/_4$" l	20.00
Coloring Book, Hot Rod, #1313, with soap box racer cut–out, color illus, 16 black and white pgs, Abbott Publishing Co, WI, c1950, 11 x $12^3/_4$"	10.00
Dish, Indianapolis 500 souvenir, white china, red race car, red and black inscription, gold accent rim	20.00
Display, Fossil Watch Co, 3 joined replica motor oil cans, inscribed "Racer's Choice," small black and white checkered racing flag symbol, 1944, $3^1/_2$ x 7 x $9^1/_4$" h	40.00
Game, Auto Race Game, multicolored playing board, 4 metal race cars, 4 spinners, instructions on back box cov, orig box, Milton Bradley, c1925	90.00
Magazine, *Racing Pictorial,* late 1963, 48 pgs, $8^1/_2$ x 11"	10.00
Pinback Button, Indianapolis The Speedway City, yellow, red, and black, c1930s	75.00
Pit Pass Pin, 1947 Indianapolis Speedway, brass, racing car with numeral "2" above engraved serial #5342, back inscribed "Indianapolis Motor Speedway Corp./100 Mile Race/Indianapolis 1947"	75.00
Playing Cards, Indianapolis Motor Speedway design on backs	10.00
Postcard, Indy Speedway, early track image with trees in infield, full–length aerial view, postmarked 1935	10.00
Ring, Indy 500, metal, silver luster, snake ring design, 1960–70	20.00
Toy, Hot Wheels, Mattel, Snake Dragster, #5951, white, 2–pack, 1971	65.00
Trading Card, Big Time Drag, Norm Day's Car, common card, 1991	.30
Trading Card, Winston Drag Racing 24K Gold, John Force, Action Packed, common card	12.00
Tray, Indianapolis Motor Speedway, metal, bronze finish, c1950–60, $3^1/_2$ x $4^1/_2$"	40.00
Tumbler, Indy souvenir, frosted, red racing car center, 1960s, $5^1/_8$" h	10.00
Tumbler, 1964 Indianapolis Motor Speedway souvenir, gray and black speedway symbol above facsimile Tony Hulman signature, $2^1/_2$ x $4^1/_2$" h	10.00

AUTOGRAPHS

Early autograph collectors focused on signature only, often discarding the document from which it was cut. Today's collectors know that the context of the letter or document can significantly increase the autograph's value.

Standard abbreviations denoting type and size include:

ADS	Autograph Document Signed
ALS	Autograph Letter Signed
AP	Album Page Signed
AQS	Autograph Quotation Signed
CS	Card Signed
DS	Document (printed) Signed
FDC	First Day Cover
LS	Letter Signed
PS	Photograph Signed
TLS	Typed Letter Signed
Folio	12 x 16"
4to	8 x 10"
8vo	5 x 7"
12mo	3 x 5"

References: Mark Allen Baker, *All Sport Autograph Guide,* Krause Publications, 1994; Norman E. Martinus and Harry L. Rinker, *Warman's Paper,* Wallace–Homestead, Krause Publications, 1994; George Sanders, Helen Sanders, and Ralph Roberts, *The Sanders Price Guide to Autographs, 4th Edition,* Alexander Books, 1997; George Sanders, Helen Sanders and Ralph Roberts, *The Sanders Price Guide To Sports Autographs, 2nd Edition,* Alexander Books, 1997.

Periodicals: *Autograph Collector,* 510–A S Corona Mall, Corona, CA 91719; *Autograph Times,* 2303 N 44th St, #225, Phoenix, AZ 85008.

Collectors' Clubs: The Manuscript Society, 350 N Niagara St, Burbank, CA 91505; Universal Autograph Collectors Club, PO Box 6181, Washington, DC 20044.

REPRODUCTION ALERT: Forgeries abound. Signatures of many political figures, movie stars, and sports heroes are machine or secretary signed rather than by the individuals themselves. Photographic reproduction can also produce a signature resembling an original. Check all signatures using a good magnifying glass or microscope.

Ali, Muhammad, PS, color, action pose with Larry Holmes, referee talking to him, large clear gold signature, 20 x 16"	$ 300.00
Ashford, Evelyn, PS, color, 4to	15.00
Austin, Tracy, CS, 5 x 3"	5.00
Berlin, Irving, sheet music cover, blue ink signature	1,000.00
Carey, Harry, sepia, 5 x 7"	150.00
Chaplin, Charlie, CS, blue ink signature on white card, matted with magazine photo, "The Little Tramp," 11 x 16"	250.00
Cleveland, Grover, military appointment of Walker W. Joynes as second lieutenant, 1 pg oblong folio, sgd "Grover Cleveland," 16 x 21"	300.00
Cooper, Alice, album cover	60.00

Denver, Bob, "Gilligan," PS, black and white glossy, 8 x 10"	50.00
Dern, Bruce, PS, black and white glossy, 8 x 10"	10.00
Dickinson, Anna E., AQS, 4 x 3"	25.00
Duke, Charlie, Ed Mitchell, Harrison Schmidt, astronauts, FDC	125.00
Dumas, Jean Baptiste Andre, French chemist, ALS, plain paper, 5 x 8"	135.00
Durante, Jimmy, PS, sepia, western attire, 8 x 10"	25.00
Eisenhower, Dwight and Mamie, PS, black and white, matte finish, smiling after–term pose, signatures slightly brushed when signed, 8 x 10"	550.00
Elway, John, PS, color, 4to	15.00
Ferber, Edna, TLS, personal stationery, 1962, 4to	50.00
Fitzgerald, F. Scott, CS, to Paul Clute	250.00
Fromme, Lynette, Manson Family member, ALS, holograph address on back of picture postcard, "thanks for book," full signature, 1986	85.00
Garland, Judy, DS, bank check, filled in and signed, Jan 22, 1965, check included in black mat to right of close–up color photo, random glittering stars and music notes, black metallic plate with name in gold letters beneath photo, under glass, black frame, 28 x 16"	950.00
Gish, Lillian, CS, 3 x 5"	40.00
Gorbachev, Mikhail, FDC, honoring International Year of the Child, black signature, 1979	250.00
Hayes, Helen, FDC honoring D. W. Griffith, cancelled Beverly Hills, CA, 1975	30.00
Hillary, Sir Edmund, orig large ink sketch depicting expedition on Mt. Everest, white board, 10 x 8"	150.00
Holliday, Judy, PS, smiling, close–up, vertical sentiment and signature, 2 x 3"	175.00
Karloff, Boris, partly printed DS, sgd in blue ballpoint, 1965, 8 x 14"	425.00
Kelly, Walt, ADS, bank check, sgd in green ink, 1956	325.00
LaBelle, Patti, PS, black and white glossy, 8 x 10"	60.00
Lehar, Franz, PS, sepia, penned signature and 3 bars of music, 12mo	800.00
Lewis, Sinclair, TLS, thank–you note to Mrs. Barber, personal stationery, December 18, 1945, 7 x 8"	400.00
Lombardo, Victor, PS, sepia portrait, 4to	20.00
Mack, Connie, AP	150.00
Mays, Willie, 4 x 3"	10.00
Meeker, Bobby, PS, publicity, 8 x 10"	60.00
Melba, Nellie, ALS, personal stationery, photo, news article about her death, 3 pgs, 5 x 7"	85.00
Nash, Ogden, TLS, personal stationery, 1963, 4to	45.00
Nelson Family, Ozzie, Rick, Dave, and Harriet, inscribed PS, family portrait, 8 x 10"	395.00
Nutting, Wallace, LS, personal stationery, imprinted vignette of one of his works on upper center of first page, orig holograph envelope, 1941, 2 pgs	275.00
O'Connor, Sinead, PS, close–up, sgd first name only, color, 8 x 10"	75.00
Porter, Katherine Anne, TLS, plain stationery, 1958, 8 x 6"	85.00
Powell, Dick, AP	25.00
Rehnquist, William, CS, Supreme Court card	45.00
Rogers, Richard, TLS, personal stationery, 7 x 9"	40.00

Romero, Caesar, PS, debonair pose, black and white,
8 x 10" **50.00**
Staubach, Roger, CS, 5 x 3" **10.00**
Thaxter, Cilia, AQS, 30–line poem, plain paper, 5 x 7".... **60.00**
Trudeau, Gary, CS, inscribed, 5 x 3" **20.00**
Truman, Harry S., TLS, personal stationery, thank you
note, Independence, 1966, orig envelope with
printed franking **325.00**
Turner, Ted, TLS, business stationery, 4to **15.00**
Wainwright, J. M., CS, minor flaw, 5 x 3" **150.00**
Walker, Hershel, PS, color, 4to **15.00**
Weismuller, Johnny, AP, inscribed "Tarzan" **75.00**
Williams, John, AQS, large signature, white card,
10 x 7" **75.00**

AUTOMOBILES

The Antique Automobile Club of America instituted a policy whereby any motor vehicle (car, bus, motorcycle, etc.) manufactured prior to 1930 be classified as "antique." The Classic Car Club of America expanded the list, focusing on luxury models made between 1925 and 1948. The Milestone Car Society developed a similar list for cars produced between 1948 and 1964.

Some states, such as Pennsylvania, have devised a dual registration system for classifying older cars—antique and classic. Depending upon their intended use, models from the 1960s and 1970s, especially convertibles and limited production models, fall into the "classic" designation.

References: Robert H. Balderson, *The Official Price Guide to Collector Cars, Eighth Edition,* House of Collectibles, 1996; Jim Lenzke and Ken Buttolph, *1997 Standard Guide to Cars & Prices, Ninth Edition,* Krause Publications, 1996.

Periodicals: *Automobile Quarterly,* 15040 Kutztown Rd, PO Box 348, Kutztown, PA 19530; *Car Collector & Car Classics,* 1241 Canton St, Roswell, GA 30076; *Hemmings Motor News,* PO Box 100, Rt 9W, Bennington, VT 05201; *Old Cars Price Guide,* 700 E State St, Iola, WI 54990.

Collectors' Clubs: Antique Automobile Club of America, 501 W Governor Rd, PO Box 417, Hershey, PA 17033; Classic Car Club of America, 1645 Des Plaines River Rd, Ste 7, Des Plaines, IL 60018; Veteran Motor Car Club of America, PO Box 260788, Strongsville, OH 44136.

Note: Prices are for cars in good condition.

Alfa Romeo, 1960, Giulietta, Spider, convertible ... **$ 3,500.00**
Ariel Red Hunter, 1951, 500cc **3,750.00**
Austin–Healey, 1959, Sprite, roadster, 4 cyl **5,000.00**
BMW, 1958, Isetta, coupe, 1 door **1,275.00**
Buick, 1939, Roadmaster, sedan, 8 cyl **6,000.00**
Buick, 1963, Wildcat, coupe, 8 cyl **3,300.00**
Cadillac, 1954, Model 62, Coupe de Ville, 8 cyl **14,000.00**
Chandler, 1929, Model Royal 85, sedan, 8 cyl **8,200.00**
Chevrolet, 1962, Fleetside, pickup, long box **7,500.00**
Chevrolet, 1973, El Camino, pickup **4,200.00**
DeSoto, 1957, Fireflite, sedan, 8 cyl **3,000.00**
Dodge, 1947, Series WD–15, pickup, ³/₄ ton **1,250.00**
Dodge, 1949, Coronet, station wagon, 6 cyl........ **8,000.00**

Dodge, 1968, Monaco, sedan, 8 cyl **2,200.00**
Ford, 1946, Super Deluxe, convertible, 8 cyl **14,000.00**
Ford, 1959, Thunderbird, hardtop, 8 cyl **9,000.00**
Ford, 1968, Mustang, hardtop, 6 cyl **7,000.00**
General Motors, 1955, pickup, ³/₄ ton, 6 cyl........ **3,000.00**
Harley Davidson, 1960, Sportster Custom **6,000.00**
Hudson, 1933, Essex–Terraplane Series, mail delivery van **6,000.00**
Hudson, 1934, Special, coupe, 6 cyl **4,000.00**
Indian, 1939, Scout. **9,000.00**
International Harvester, 1964, Scout Series, pickup,
2–wheel drive **1,100.00**
Jaguar, 1954, Mark VII, 4 door, sedan, 6 cyl **12,000.00**
LaSalle, 1940, Model 52, coupe, 8 cyl........... **14,000.00**
Lincoln, 1955, Custom, sedan, 8 cyl **5,000.00**
Mercedes–Benz, 1933, Model 380K, sedan, 8 cyl.... **23,000.00**
Mercury, 1958, Turnpike Cruiser, hardtop, 8 cyl **6,000.00**
Oldsmobile, 1942, Model 66, station wagon, 6 cyl... **12,000.00**
Oldsmobile, 1962, Starfire, 2 door, hardtop, 8 cyl **8,000.00**
Plymouth, 1935, PJ DeLuxe, 2 door, sedan, 6 cyl **1,700.00**
Plymouth, 1964, Valiant 100, 4 door, sedan, 6 cyl **1,050.00**
Plymouth, 1970, Barracuda, convertible........... **3,400.00**
Pontiac, 1939, Deluxe 8, touring sedan, 8 cyl **4,200.00**
Pontiac, 1957, Bonneville, convertible, 8 cyl **35,000.00**
Studebaker, 1962, Daytona, 8 cyl **7,000.00**
Triumph, 1959, T20, Tiger Cub, 200cc............. **1,500.00**
Velocette, 1967, Thruxton **7,000.00**
Vincent, 1948, Black Lightning **32,000.00**
Volkswagen, 1967, Beetle, convertible, 53 hp **3,500.00**

AUTOMOBILIA

Automobilia can be broken down into three major collecting categories — parts used for restoring cars, advertising and promotional items relating to a specific make or model of car, and decorative accessories in the shape of or with an image of an automobile. Numerous subcategories also exist. Spark plugs and license plates are two examples of automobilia with reference books, collectors clubs, and periodicals dealing specifically with these fields.

References: David K. Bausch, *The Official Price Guide To Automobilia,* House of Collectibles, 1996; Bob Crisler, *License Plate Values: A Guide To Relative Prices of Collectible U.S. Auto License Plates and Their Grading, 3rd Edition,* King Publishing, 1994; David Fetherson, *Hot Rod Memorabilia & Collectibles,* Motorbooks International, 1996; John A. Gunnell, ed., *A Collector's Guide To Automobilia,* Krause Publications, 1994; Jim and Nancy Schaut, *American Automobilia: An Illustrated History and Price Guide,* Wallace–Homestead, Krause Publications, 1994.

Periodicals: *Hemmings Motor News,* PO Box 100, Rt 9W, Bennington, VT 05201; *Mobilia,* PO Box 575, Middlebury, VT 05753; *PL8S,* PO Box 222, East Texas, PA 18046.

Collectors' Clubs: Automobile License Plate Collectors Assoc, Inc, PO Box 77, Horner, WV 26372; Automobile Objects D'Art Club, 252 N 7th St, Allentown, PA 18102; Hubcap Collectors Club, PO Box 54, Buckley, MI 49620; Spark Plug Collectors of America, 4262 County Rd 121, Fulton, MO 65251.

Ashtray, tire shape, Goodrich, Silverstone .... **$ 45.00**

Spark Plug, Lodge, 2HLN, ³/₄", $5.00.

Badge, Automobile Club Martiniquais, brass, enamel,
2¹/₂" d **50.00**
Blotter, Rush Motor Truck Company, c1925 . . . . **15.00**
Brochure, Crosley, The Car of Tomorrow **15.00**
Card Game, Touring, Parker Brothers, 3rd Edition,
c1927 . . . . **45.00**
Figure, Mr Bibidendum, Michelin Man, adv, plastic,
white, 1981, 8" w, 12" h. **35.00**
Horn, Rubes, brass, bulb type, patented 1909 . . . . **125.00**
Hubcap, Buick, spun aluminum **20.00**
Instruction Manual, Volkswagen, for Sedan and
Convertible, soft cover, black and white with blue
insert, 88 pgs, 5⁵/₈ x 7⁷/₈". **15.00**
License Plate, Alabama, Disabled Veteran number
98, orange on blue. **20.00**
License Plate, Florida, commemorative, 1996
Olympic Spirit, #G388J, color Olympic rings logo
and legends **65.00**
License Plate, Hawaii, #70–408, black on silver re-
paint, 1927 . . . . **250.00**
License Plate, Pennsylvania, black on white, "City of
Allentown" over "License No." across top, "Expires
Oct. 1, 1928"across bottom, number 329 center **15.00**
Lights, Solar Model 933, pr, side, brass, patented
1909 . . . . **250.00**
Magazine, *Rod & Custom,* May, 1953. . . . . **25.00**
Magazine Tear Sheet, 1976 Buick advertisement,
Newsweek, Oct 27, 1975. **2.00**
Map, Esso, Delaware, Maryland, Virginia, West
Virginia, Baltimore's Fort McHenry, color cov,
24 panels, 1948. . . . . **5.00**
Mascot, Kissel, eagle, 1928 . . . . **65.00**
Model, 1957 Ford Rachero Sedan Pickup, Revell,
1/25th scale. **65.00**
Parking Meter, Duncan, 2–hour limit **100.00**
Patch, Automobile Association of America, cloth,
woven, red on white, Official Timer Midget Racing **15.00**
Pinback Button, Ford V8, litho tin, Scottie dog in cen-
ter, "Aye and Thrifty too!" on top, ⁷/₈" d **35.00**
Postage Stamp, US, 50th Anniversary American Auto-
mobile Association, 1952 . . . . **.15**

Postcard, 1988 Delta Royale Sedan **10.00**
Pump, Fry, early "Mae West," 5 gal **2,000.00**
Sheet Music, "See the U.S.A. in Your Chevrolet," Leon
Carr and Leo Corday, Chappel & Co, red ground,
12 conductors, radio personalities, and singers on
cover **15.00**
Spark Plug, AC Snow **10.00**
Spark Plug, Mosler Vesuvius **25.00**
Spark Plug, Norwest Tractor, ³/₄" **25.00**
Spark Plug, Stewart **5.00**
Thermometer, Buick Motor Cars, porcelain, blue,
emblem, c1915, 27" h **275.00**
Toy Truck, Hess Fuel Oils, plastic, battery operated,
includes plastic barrels and instruction sheet, 14" l,
mkd "Made in Hong Kong" and "Amerada Hess
Corporation," 14" l, MIB. **250.00**
Watch Fob, American Champion Thomas Flyer **150.00**

AUTUMN LEAF

Autumn Leaf dinnerware was manufactured by Hall China
Company and issued as a premium by the Jewel Tea Company. The
pattern was originally produced between 1933 and 1978. Many
other companies produced matching kitchen accessories in fabric,
metal, glass, and plastic.

References: Susan and Al Bagdade, *Warman's American Pottery
and Porcelain,* Wallace–Homestead, Krause Publications, 1994;
Harvey Duke, *The Official Price Guide to Pottery and Porcelain,
Eighth Edition,* House of Collectibles, 1995; C. L. Miller, *The Jewel
Tea Company: Its History and Products,* Schiffer Publishing, 1994;
Margaret and Kenn Whitmyer, *The Collector's Encyclopedia of
Hall China, Second Edition,* Collector Books, 1994, 1997 value
update.

Collectors' Club: National Autumn Leaf Collectors Club, 7346
Shamrock Dr, Indianapolis, IN 45217.

Apron, plastic . . . . **$ 500.00**
Berry Bowl **5.00**
Bowl, "Sunshine," #4. . . . . **20.00**
Bowl Cover, set, plastic **50.00**
Bread Box, tin **150.00**
Bud Vase **200.00**
Butter Dish, ¹/₄ lb **225.00**
Butter Dish, 1 lb **500.00**
Cake Plate. **25.00**
Cake Server. **550.00**
Candlesticks, pr **75.00**
Candy Dish, metal base **500.00**
Canister, coffee, tin, 4" h **35.00**
Canister, tea, tin, copper lid, 4" h **35.00**
Casserole, round, 2 qt **25.00**
Cereal Bowl **12.00**
Clock, battery operated **250.00**
Coaster **10.00**
Coffee Pot, drip **275.00**
Cookie Jar, Zeisel. **150.00**
Cream Soup **30.00**
Creamer, J–Sunshine **40.00**
Custard **7.50**

Dish Towel, cotton	40.00
Drip Jar	20.00
Dutch Oven, 5 qt	100.00
Flat Soup	25.00
Flour Sifter, tin	350.00
Fondue, set	200.00
Fruitcake Tin, tan, 7" d	10.00
Goblet, ftd, 10½ oz	60.00
Gravy Boat	25.00
Hot Pad, oval	12.00
Magnetic Holder, set	10.00
Marmalade, 3 pc	125.00
Mayonnaise, cov, underplate	50.00
Mixer Cover, plastic	45.00
Mug, conic	70.00
Napkin, 16" sq	40.00
Pickle Dish, Ruffled–D	35.00
Pie Baker	35.00
Pitcher, ice lip, Douglas	475.00
Placemat, plastic	40.00
Plate, 10" d	20.00
Plate, Ruffled–D, 6" d	5.00
Platter, melmac, 14"	20.00
Playing Cards, pinochle	160.00
Salad Bowl	20.00
Salt and Pepper Shakers, pr	25.00
Shelf Liner, 25 ft	125.00
Sherbet, Libbey, 6½ oz	55.00
Silverware, 6 pc, stainless	140.00
Skillet, 9½"	90.00
Stack Dish, 24 oz	25.00
Sugar	25.00
Tablecloth, plastic, 54" sq	140.00
Teacup	5.00
Teapot, Rayed, long spout	55.00
Thermos	325.00
Tidbit, 2 tier	75.00
Tray, metal, red border	55.00
Utility Jug	25.00
Vase	200.00

Teapot, Aladdin, gold trim, 7 cup, $75.00.

Vegetable, cov, oval	50.00
Vegetable, divided	40.00
Warmer, oval	140.00
Wastebasket	400.00

AVIATION COLLECTIBLES

Most collections relating to the field of aviation focus on one of four categories—commercial airlines, dirigibles, famous aviators, or generic images of aircraft.

Early American airlines depended on government subsidies for carrying mail. By 1930, five international and thirty–eight domestic airlines were operating in the United States. A typical passenger load was ten. After World War II, four–engine planes with a capacity of 100 or more passengers were introduced.

The jet age was launched in the 1950s. In 1955 Capitol Airlines used British–made turboprop airliners in domestic service. In 1958 National Airlines began domestic jet passenger service. The giant Boeing 747 went into operation in 1970 as part of the Pan American fleet.

References: Lynn Johnson and Michael O'Leary, *En Route: Label Art From the Golden Age of Air Travel,* Chronicle Books, 1993; Norman E. Martinus and Harry L. Rinker, *Warman's Paper,* Wallace–Homestead, Krause Publications, 1994.

Periodical: *Airliners Magazine,* 1200 NW 72nd Ave, Miami, FL 33126.

Collectors' Clubs: Aeronautica & Air Label Collectors Club, PO Box 1239, Elgin, IL 60121; World Airline Historical Society, 13739 Picarsa Dr, Jacksonville, FL 32225.

Autograph, Amelia Earhart, card, full signature, 3 x 2".	$ 175.00
Baggage Stickers, die cut, set of 10, 1940–50	40.00
Baggage Tag, plastic	2.00
Bank, Goodyear blimp, porcelain, pedestal base, 8½" l	50.00
Blotter, Bond Bread adv, P51 North American Mustang pursuit plane image, early 1940s, 6¼ x 3½"	12.00
Book, *Alone,* Richard E. Byrd, autographed, 1934	120.00
Calendar, Charles Lindberg with airplane, color, 1928	12.00
Cap, Junior Flight Captain Braniff Airways	20.00
Cap, souvenir aviator style skull cap, "We Saw The Graf Zep" on sides	125.00
Comic Book, Aviation Cadets, Street & Smith, 1943	12.00
Figure, United Airlines, 3 dimensional, Good Luck Man, 27" h	100.00
Game, Rickenbacker Ace Game–Keep Em Flying, Milton Bradley, 1945	20.00
Handkerchief, Pan American Airways, 12" sq	15.00
Key Chain Token, *Airship Akron,* Duralumin	45.00
Magazine, *Sky Lines,* Aug 1933, 8½ x 11½"	15.00
Menu, Pan Am, boat plane	2.00
Model, Air Force Rescue Boat, motorized, orig box, unassembled	50.00
Paperweight, Goodyear–Zeppelin Corp zeppelin hangar replica, "Goodyear Zeppelin" on sides, simulated side windows, 1930s	80.00

Junior Pilot's Wings, United Airlines, silvered metal, raised logo, "Future Pilot," 2" l, $12.00.

Pennant and Ribbon Badge Set, inscribed "10th Annual Miami All American Air Maneuvers Dec 2–5, 1937" 40.00
Photograph, first flight, framed, 1903, 31 x 41" 150.00
Pillow Case, Slick Airways 5.00
Pinback Button, Zeps, litho tin, airship flying through clouds, red, white, and blue, 1930s, ⅝" d 15.00
Playing Cards, Delta Air Lines, San Francisco on back 10.00
Poster, TWA to Las Vegas, 1953 .... 20.00
Program, Wright family home dedication, autographed by Orville Wright, 1938 .... 1,500.00
Punch–Out Picture Book, "Jet–O–Rama," Whitman, 1954, 10 x 14¾" 10.00
Puzzle, jigsaw, Night Bombing Over Germany, Victory Series, #315, JS Publishing Corp, color, 1943, 14½ x 21" 20.00
Salt and Pepper Shakers, set, TWA, plastic, tan, 1950s, 1 x 1¼" h 15.00
Sheet Music, *Lindy, Lindy*, black, white, and orange cov, Gilbert and Abel Baer, ©1927 .... 20.00
Shot Glass, Fly Southern logo above 1953 in yellow lettering, 2½" h 10.00
Toy, helicopter, friction, litho tin, black, white, and red with yellow and blue accents, "TWA" on side 40.00
Toy, plane, friction, litho tin, red, white, blue, and yellow, mkd USAF 60.00
Tumblers, set of 12, American Air Lines, gold stylized Golden Falcon symbol, mkd "Made in Japan," 1940s 85.00
Wings, Frontier, porcelain background, red 50.00

AVON

David H. McConnell founded the California Perfume Company in 1886. Saleswomen used a door–to–door approach for selling their wares. The first product was "Little Dot," a set of five perfumes. Following the acquisition of a new factory in Suffern, New York, in 1895, the company underwent several name changes. The trade name Avon, adopted in 1929, was derived from the similarity the Suffern landscape shared with that of Avon, England.

Reference: Bud Hastin, *Bud Hastin's Avon & C.P.C. Collector's Encyclopedia, 14th Edition*, published by author, 1995.

Newsletter: *Avon Times*, PO Box 9868, Kansas City, MO 64134.

Collectors' Club: National Assoc of Avon Collectors, Inc, PO Box 7006, Kansas City, MO 64113.

Alligator, bubble bath, plastic, green, yellow, and tan, 1978–79 .... $ 5.00

Awards and Representatives Gift, Queens Award Pin, gold colored metal, 1964, 1¼" 20.00
Christmas Bells, cologne, glass, 1979–80 .... 5.00
Dueling Pistol 1769, after shave, glass, 1973–74 .... 10.00
Kitten Little, cologne, glass, black, 1975–76 .... 5.00
Lucky Penny, lip gloss, 1976–80, 2" d 2.00
Packard Roadster, cologne, glass, amber, plastic rumble seat cap, 1970–72, 6½" l 10.00
Plate, Mother's Day, "Cherished Moments," porcelain, with stand, 1981, 5" d 10.00
Treasure Turtle, cologne, glass body, gold head, 1971–73 .... 5.00
Viking Horn, after shave, glass, amber, gold cap, 1966 .... 10.00
Wilderness Classic, cologne, deer figural, silver plated over clear glass, plastic head, 1976–77 .... 10.00
Winter's Treasure Porcelain Egg, wooden base, 1987, 3" h 15.00

BANKS

The earliest still banks were made from wood, pottery, gourds, and later, cast iron. Lithographed tin banks advertising various products and services reached their height in popularity between 1930 and 1955. The majority of these banks were miniature replicas of the products' packaging.

Inexpensive ceramic figural banks in the shape of children and animals were popular novelties during the 1960s and 1970s. The most recent variation of still banks are molded vinyl banks resembling the current favorite cartoon and movie characters.

References: Don Cranmer, *Collector's Encyclopedia: Toys–Banks*, L–W Book Sales, 1986, 1994–95 value update; Don Duer, *A Penny Saved: Still and Mechanical Banks*, Schiffer Publishing, 1993; Don Duer, *Penny Banks Around The World*, Schiffer Publishing, 1997; Andy and Susan Moore, *Penny Bank Book: Collecting Still Banks*, Schiffer Publishing, 1984, 1994 value update; Tom and Loretta Stoddard, *Ceramic Coin Banks: Identification & Value Guide*, Collector Books, 1997; Vickie Stulb, *Modern Banks*, L–W Book Sales, 1997.

Periodical: *Heuser's Quarterly Collectible Bank Newsletter*, 508 Clapson Rd, PO Box 300, West Winfield, NY 13491.

Collectors' Club: Still Bank Collectors Club of America, 4175 Millersville Rd, Indianapolis, IN 46205.

Note: All banks listed are still banks unless noted otherwise.

Admiral Appliances, adv, vinyl, George Washington figural, 1980s .... $ 20.00
Amish Man, Reynolds Toys, edition of 50, 1980 .... 130.00
Beatnik, composition, figural beatnik in blue–green outfit, yellow scarf, and red hat, foil label mkd "Ucagco Ceramics Japan," 1950s 40.00
Betsy Ross, mechanical, Ross and flag, Davidson/Imswiller, 1976 .... 2,000.00
Bob's Big Boy, adv, figural 25.00
Cabin, Book of Knowledge, orig box and documents. ... 400.00
Cash Register, Commonwealth Bank Registering and Savings, tin, green and yellow, 5 1/4" h 50.00

Clown, litho tin, clown bust figural, Chein, 1939 . . . . **75.00**
Columbia Bank, mechanical, Reynolds Toys, edition
of 25, 1984 . . . . **125.00**
Cylinder, litho tin, slots for various denominations,
1930s, 3 x 3½" **40.00**
Darth Vader, ceramic, Roman Ceramics **100.00**
Delco Radio, mechanical, 1950 Chevy Panel Truck,
#9082, Ertl. **25.00**
Dentist, Book of Knowledge, Special Medallion
Series. **350.00**
Elephant, mechanical, cast iron, Hubley, c1930,
8½" l **400.00**
Firehouse Films, 1950 Chevy Panel Truck, #9369, Ertl . . . **120.00**
Frog, mechanical, cast iron, round lattice base, paint-
ed green, red, and yellow, J. & E. Stevens, 4½" h **500.00**
Glow Worm, vinyl, Hasbro, 1986, 6" h. **25.00**
Hippopotamus, ceramic, bright green, pink and yel-
low flowers, 1960s. **15.00**
Holly Hobbie, silver plated, Japan, 6½" h **40.00**
Home Town Battery, Book of Knowledge. **250.00**
Howard Johnson's Restaurants, adv, plastic, restau-
rant replica, late 1950s, 3½" h **25.00**
Keep 'Em Sailing, Dime Register, litho tin **200.00**
Lincoln Log, tin, Penn, 1940s. **150.00**
Nabisco #1, Model A Panel, #2508 . . . . **20.00**
Owl, Book of Knowledge, head turns **275.00**
Pig, clear glass, irid highlights, textured body, 4¾" l **15.00**
Radio Flyer, adv, Mack B-61 Tractor Trailor, First
Gear, #10-1346. . . . . **120.00**
Smiley Face, ceramic, USA, 7½" h **20.00**
Statue of Liberty, cast pot metal, bronzed finish. **12.00**
Teddy and the Bear, Book of Knowledge. **300.00**
Trolley Bank, mechanical, Reynolds Toys, 1971. . . . . **350.00**
William Tell, Book of Knowledge, coin rings bell in
castle. **350.00**
Williamsburg Bank, mechanical, Reynolds Toys, edi-
tion of 35, 1991. . . . . **700.00**

Book, adv, emb cover, 1923 patent date, 3½" w, 5⅛" h, left: Quakertown National Bank, #1065; right: Bankers Utilities Co., San Francisco, #1183; price each, $25.00.

BARBER SHOP, BEAUTY SHOP & SHAVING

The neighborhood barber shop was an important social and cultural institution in the first half of the 20th century. Men and boys gathered to gossip, exchange business news, and check current fashions. With the emergence of *unisex* shops in the 1960s, the number of barber shops dropped by half in the United States. Today, most men and women patronize the same shops for services ranging from hair cuts to perms to coloring.

References: Ronald S. Barlow, *The Vanishing American Barber Shop,* Windmill Publishing, 1993; Jim Sargent, *Sargent's American Premium Guide to Pocket Knives & Razors...,* 4th Edition, Books Americana, Krause Publications, 1995.

Newsletter: *Will's Safety–Razor & Safety–Razor–Blade Newsletter,* PO Box 522, Crescent City, CA 95531.

Collectors' Club: National Shaving Mug Collectors' Assoc, 320 S Glenwood St, Allentown, PA 18104.

Barber Pole, revolving, porcelain enamel, chrome–
plated copper dome and bowl, 1935, 6 x 16" glass
cylinder, 33½" h. . . . . **$ 300.00**
Book, *Once Over Lightly,* Charles DeZemier, c1939,
270 pgs **35.00**
Bottle, Burma Shave, lotion, empty. **15.00**
Catalog, Barber Shop and Beauty Parlor Equipment,
Emil J. Paidar Co, Chicago, 20 pgs, 1932, 12 x 10" . . . **250.00**
Catalog, Hudson Beauty Shop Equipment, No. 1
Supplement, Los Angeles, CA, 8 pgs, 1936, 5¾ x
8¾" **30.00**
Catalog, Perfumers' Handbook and Catalog, Fritzsche
Brothers Inc, NY, cloth–backed printed boards,
illus, raw materials for floral waters, colognes,
powders, bath salts, hair preparations, etc, 1944,
266 pgs, 5 x 7". **22.00**
Chair, Paidar One–Level, Hydraulic Chair #409,
1925 . . . . **750.00**
Hair Curler, Westinghouse, electric, metal, black
plastic handle **25.00**
Jar, Burma Shave, empty, missing lid. **5.00**
Magazine, *Barber's Journal,* April 1936, 20 pgs,
8½ x 12" **5.00**
Matchcover, Gillette Blue Blades adv, 1930s, unused **5.00**
Razor, Eversharp Schick Injector, aqua handle, gold
plated, cardboard box, blade missing, 1940s,
2⅜ x 4⅝ x 1". **18.00**
Razor, Gem Safety Razor, gold plated, white handle,
plastic case, 1940s, 5⅛ x 2¼ x 1¼" **12.00**
Razor, Gillette Safety Razor, double edge, goldtone
metal, NRA emblem, orig leather box, blades in
orig box, 1930s **60.00**
Receipt Book, Keen Kutter, 1920s. **25.00**
Shampoo, Minipoo Dry Shampoo, 3 oz, Cosmetic
Distr, Jersey City, NJ, c1960s. **8.00**
Shaver, Noreleco Sportsman, electric, Bakelite cover,
accessories, leather case, instructions, MIB **225.00**
Shaving Cream, Burma Shave, tube **15.00**
Shaving Mug, Acme Lodge 469, 1923. . . . . **125.00**
Shaving Powder, Red Magic, red and white card-
board cylinder, 1966, 5 oz, 2 x 4¼" **8.00**

Sign, Klondike Head Rub, emb cardboard, 11 x 8³/₈", $25.00.

Sign, "Barber Shop," porcelain enamel, red, white,
  and blue, 1925, 18 x 24" **200.00**
Sign, "Beauty Parlor," 2 sided, porcelain enamel, blue
  letters, white ground, 1925, 12 x 24". **100.00**
Sign, Bicklmore Shaving Cream, 1930s, 31" h **75.00**
Sign, Burma Shave **100.00**
Toy Truck, Burma Shave, metal **50.00**

BARBIE

The first Barbie fashion dolls, patented by Mattel in 1958, arrived on toy store shelves in 1959. By 1960, Barbie was a marketing success. The development of Barbie's boyfriend, Ken, began in 1960. Many other friends, both male and female, followed. Clothing, vehicles, doll houses, and other accessories became an integral part of the line.

From September 1961 through July 1972 Mattel published a Barbie magazine. At its peak, the Barbie Fan Club was the second largest girls' organization, next to the Girl Scouts, in the nation.

Barbie sales are approaching the 100 million mark. Annual sales exceed five million units. Barbie is one of the most successful dolls in history.

References: Fashion and Accessories: Joe Blitman, *Barbie Doll & Her Mod, Mod, Mod, Mod World of Fashion*, Hobby House Press, 1996; A. Glenn Mandeville, *Doll Fashion Anthology & Price Guide, 5th Revised Edition*, Hobby House Press, 1996; Sarah Sink Eames, *Barbie Doll Fashion, Vol. I: 1959–1967* (1990, 1995 value update), *Vol II: 1968–1974* (1997), Collector Books; Rebecca Ann Rupp, *Treasury of Barbie Doll Accessories: 1961–1995*, Hobby House Press, 1996.

General: J. Michael Augustyniak, *The Barbie Doll Boom*, Collector Books, 1996; J. Michael Augustyniak, *Collector's Encyclopedia of Barbie Doll Exclusives and More: Identification & Values*, Collector Books, 1997; Sibyl DeWein and Joan Ashabraner, *The Collectors Encyclopedia of Barbie Dolls and Collectibles*, Collector Books, 1977, 1996 value update; Paris and Susan Manos, *The Wonder of Barbie: Dolls and Accessories*

1976–1986, Collector Books, 1987, 1994 value update; Paris and Susan Manos, *The World of Barbie Dolls: An Illustrated Value Guide*, Collector Books, 1983, 1994 value update; Marcie Melillo, *The Ultimate Barbie Doll Book*, Krause Publications, 1996; Lorraine Mieszala, *Collector's Guide to Barbie Doll Paper Dolls: Identification & Values*, Collector Books, 1997; Patrick C. Olds and Myrazona R. Olds, *The Barbie Doll Years: 1959–1996, Second Edition*, Collector Books, 1997; Margo Rana, *Barbie Doll Exclusively for Timeless Creations: 1986–1996, Book III*, Hobby House Press, 1997; Margo Rana, *Barbie Exclusives, Book II: Identification & Values*, Collector Books, 1996; Margo Rana, *Collector's Guide to Barbie Exclusives: Identification and Values*, Collector Books, 1995; Jane Sarasohn–Kahn, *Contemporary Barbie: Barbie Dolls 1980 and Beyond*, Antique Trader Books, 1996; Beth Summers, *A Decade of Barbie Dolls and Collectibles, 1981–1991: Identification & Values*, Collector Books, 1996; Kitturah B. Westenhouser, *The Story of Barbie*, Collector Books, 1994.

Periodicals: *Barbie Bazaar*, 5617 6th Ave, Kenosha, WI 53140; *Miller's Barbie Collector*, PO Box 8722, Spokane, WA 99203.

Collectors' Club: Barbie Doll Collectors Club International, PO Box 586, North White Plains, NY 10603.

Book, *A Very Busy Barbie*, Little Golden Book . . . . **$ 4.00**
Carrying Case, vinyl, Barbie Goes Travelin', multicol-
  ored, car and plane illus, black handle, ©1965,
  3 x 10 x 15½" **30.00**
Cassette Player, with headset microphone,
  Kiddesigns, Inc, 1993 . . . . **35.00**
Clothing, Beautiful Bride, #1698, 1967 . . . . **2,500.00**
Clothing, Campus Sweetheart, #1616 . . . . **500.00**
Clothing, Easter Parade, #971, 1959. . . . . **3,000.00**
Clothing, Enchanted Evening, #983, 1960–63 . . . . **300.00**
Clothing, Evening Splendour, #961, 1959–64 . . . . **200.00**
Clothing, Garden Tea Party, #1606, 1964, MIB **125.00**
Clothing, Picnic Set, #967, 1959–61 . . . . **200.00**
Coloring Book, Watkins–Strathmore, © Mattel 1962
  and 1963, 8 x 11" **15.00**
Diary, vinyl, glossy, One Year Diary, © Mattel 1961,
  1 x 4 x 5½" **30.00**
Display, McDonald's, Barbie and Hot Wheels, 1993 . . . . **135.00**
Doll, Black Francie **700.00**
Doll, Blossom Beautiful Barbie, MIB **285.00**
Doll, Busy Ken, MIB **70.00**
Doll, Pan American Airways Stewardess, #1678,
  1966. . . . . **2,500.00**
Doll, Ponytail Barbie, #4, brunette, swimsuit, with
  stand **475.00**
Doll, Rocker Derek, #2428, 1985, MIB. **35.00**
Doll, Sun Set Malibu Barbie, #1067, 1971–77, MIB **75.00**
Dream House, 1962 . . . . **75.00**
Dress–Up Kit, Colorforms, 1970 . . . . **40.00**
Flying Barbie Disc, Spectra Star, 1990 . . . . **5.00**
GAF Talking View–Master, Barbie's Around the World
  Trip, 1965 . . . . **100.00**
Game, Barbie's Little Sister Skipper, Mattel, 1964 . . . . . . **75.00**
High Stepper Horse, Mattel, 1994 . . . . **30.00**
Hot Wheels Barbie Camaro, First Edition, MIB **65.00**
Lawn Swing and Planter. **200.00**

Board Game, The Barbie Game, Queen of the Prom, Mattel, #450, 1960, 22 x 9¹/₄" box, $35.00.

Magazine, *Mattel Barbie Magazine,* Jan–Feb 1969,
    22 pgs 15.00
Midge Wig Wardrobe 150.00
Ornament, Hallmark, 1994, MIB 75.00
Paper Doll Book, *Skipper, Barbie's Little Sister,*
    Whitman, 1962 . . . . 70.00
Quick Curl Cara, #7291, 1974, MIB 125.00
Record Case, 1961, MIB 20.00
Sewing Cards, Colorforms, 1988 . . . . 5.00
Skipper Deluxe Dream House 275.00
Sports Car, convertible, pink, Irwin Corp, 1963 . . . . 100.00
Sunglasses, child's, orig pkg, 1978 . . . . 15.00
Telephone, Barbie Mattel–A–Phone 25.00
Thermos, litho metal, red plastic cap, full color illus,
    black ground, © Mattel, 1962, 8¹/₂" h 35.00
Video Cassette, Barbie and The Rockers–Out of This
    World, Vol 1, 1987 . . . . 30.00

BARWARE

During the late 1960s and early 1970s it became fashionable for homeowners to convert basements into family rec rooms, often equipped with bars. Most were well stocked with both utilitarian items (shot glasses and ice crushers) and decorative accessories. Objects with advertising are usually more valuable than their generic counterparts.

Reference: Stephen Visakay, *Vintage Bar Ware,* Collector Books, 1997.

Collectors' Club: International Swizzle Stick Collectors Assoc, PO Box 1117, Bellingham, WA 98227.

Additional References: See Breweriana, Cocktail Shakers, and Whiskey Bottles.

Beer Tap Handle, Genesee 12 Horse Ale, Genesee
    Brewing, Rochester, NY, red ball knob . . . . $ 30.00
Beer Tray, Indian Head Beer & Ale, Iroquois Brewing
    Co, Buffalo, NY, Indian head profile center 20.00
Coaster, Fox Head, Fox Head Brewery, Waukesha,
    WI, red, black, and yellow, 4" d 5.00
Cocktail Shaker, glass, wildflower pattern, crystal,
    chrome top, Cambridge 75.00
Cork Screw, brass, figural elephant, corkscrew tail,
    mkd "Perage England," c1930 . . . . 30.00

Ice Bucket, aluminum, hand wrought, ridged band
    handles, ring finial, Buenilum 15.00
Ice Bucket, glass, Mt. Vernon pattern, red, Cambridge 75.00
Martini Set, glass, pheasants on pitcher and glasses,
    brass stirrer 20.00
Pitcher, Wild Turkey Bourbon, white with black let-
    tering and turkey, gold trim edge and handle 65.00
Sign, Coors, 2 sided, "Open, Closed, Thank You"
    and Coors logo 10.00
Sign, Wiedemann's Beer, tin, 23 x 33" 450.00
Swizzle Stick, glass, man wearing top hat 2.00
Swizzle Stick, plastic, clear, die finial 3.00
Swizzle Stick, plastic, glitter–filled, whistle attached
    to end 50
Whiskey Glass, American pattern, crystal, Fostoria
    2¹/₂" h 10.00

BASEBALL CARDS

Baseball cards were originally issued by tobacco companies in the late 19th century. The first big producers of gum cards were Goudey Gum Company of Boston (1933–1941) and Gum, Inc. (1939). After World War II, Gum, Inc.'s successor, Bowman, was the leading manufacturer. Topps, Inc. of Brooklyn, New York, followed. Topps bought Bowman in 1956 and monopolized the field until 1981 when Fleer of Philadelphia and Donruss of Memphis challenged the market.

References: James Beckett, *The Official 1997 Price Guide to Baseball Cards, Sixteenth Edition,* House of Collectibles, 1996; James Beckett and Theo Chen (eds.), *Beckett Baseball Price Guide, Number 18,* Beckett Publications, 1996; Allan Kaye and Michael McKeever, *Baseball Card Price Guide, 1997,* Avon Books, 1996; Mark Larson (ed.), *Baseball Cards Questions & Answers,* Krause Publications, 1992; Mark Larson, *Sports Collectors Digest Minor League Baseball Card Price Guide,* Krause Publications, 1993; Mark Larson (ed.), *Sports Collectors Digest: The Sports Card Explosion,* Krause Publications, 1993; Bob Lemke (ed.), *Sportscard Counterfeit Detector, 3rd Edition,* Krause Publications, 1994.

Alan Rosen, *True Mint: Mr. Mint's Price & Investment Guide to True Mint Baseball Cards,* Krause Publications, 1994; Sports Collectors Digest, *Baseball Card Price Guide 1997, Eleventh Edition,* Krause Publications, 1997; Sports Collectors Digest, *1997 Standard Catalog of Baseball Cards, 6th Edition,* Krause Publications, 1996; Sports Collectors Digest, *101 Sportscard Investments,* Krause Publications, 1993; Sports Collectors Digest, *Premium Insert Sports Cards,* Krause Publications, 1995.

Periodicals: *Beckett Baseball Card Monthly,* 15850 Dallas Parkway, Dallas, TX 75248; *Sports Cards,* 700 E State St, Iola, WI 54990.

Bowman, 1948, #6, Yogi Berra . . . . $ 135.00
Bowman, 1948, #36, Stan Musial 200.00
Bowman, 1948, #46, Herman Wehmeier 8.00
Bowman, 1949, #36, Pee Wee Reese 45.00
Bowman, 1949, common player (37–73) 5.00
Bowman, 1949, #50, Jackie Robinson 250.00
Bowman, 1951, #165, Ted Williams 175.00
Bowman, 1951, #305, Willie Mays 825.00
Bowman, 1952, #52, Phil Rizzuto 35.00

Bowman, 1953, #109, Ken Wood 7.50
Bowman, 1953, complete set (64), black and white. 625.00
Bowman, 1954, #177, Whitey Ford 25.00
Bowman, 1955, #130, Richie Ashburn 8.00
Bowman, 1989, #12, Billy Ripken 02
Bowman, 1995, #114, Mike Bovee 10
Donruss, 1981, complete set (605) 20.00
Donruss, 1982, #405, Cal Ripken, Jr. 22.00
Donruss, 1983, #43, Mickey Mantle puzzle card,
  Hall of Fame Heroes 05
Donruss, 1984, #311, Ryne Sandberg. 7.50
Donruss, 1985, #172, Wade Boggs. 2.00
Fleer, 1923, #47, Babe Ruth. 240.00
Fleer, 1959, complete set (80) 475.00
Fleer, 1960, #47, Cy Young 2.00
Fleer, 1961–62, common player (89–154). 2.00
Fleer, 1963, #4, Brooks Robinson 20.00
Fleer, 1966, complete set (66) 110.00
Fleer, 1981, #574, Rickey Henderson 2.00
Fleer, 1982, #39, Reggie Jackson 50
Fleer, 1983, #463, Nolan Ryan. 2.00
Fleer, 1984, complete set (660) 52.00
Fleer, 1985, #371, Orel Hershiser. 1.50
Fleer, 1986, #432, Mickey Tettleton 1.00
Fleer, 1988, #276, Jose Canseco. 50
Leaf, 1948, #1, Joe DiMaggio. 525.00
Leaf, 1948, #3, Lou Gehrig 120.00
Leaf, 1960, common player (73–145) 5.00
Leaf, 1986, #103, Don Mattingly 1.50
Leaf, 1986, #260, Pete Rose. 40
Leaf, 1987, #4, Darryl Strawberry. 15
Leaf, 1988, complete set (264) 5.00
Topps, 1952, #400, Bill Dickey 150.00
Topps, 1952, common player (1–80). 10.00
Topps, 1953, #82, Mickey Mantle 600.00
Topps, 1954, #7, Ted Kluszewski 10.00
Topps, 1954, complete set (250) 2,000.00
Topps, 1956, #181, Billy Martin. 20.00
Topps, 1957, #286, Bobby Richardson 25.00

Topps, 1958, #187, Sandy Koufax. 55.00
Topps, 1959, #202, Roger Maris. 25.00
Topps, 1960, #10, Ernie Banks 10.00
Topps, 1961, #228, Yankees Team. 10.00
Topps, 1962, #387, Lou Brock 35.00
Topps, 1963, complete set (576) 1,325.00
Topps, 1976, #1, Hank Aaron 4.50
Topps, 1977, #120, Rod Carew 2.00
Topps, 1988, #700, George Brett 15
Topps, 1992, #589, Mariano Duncan 02

BASEBALL MEMORABILIA

Baseball traces its beginnings to the mid–19th century. By the turn of the century it had become America's national pastime.

The superstar has always been the key element in the game. Baseball greats were popular visitors at banquets, parades, and more recently at baseball autograph shows. Autographed items, especially those used in an actual game, command premium prices. The bigger the star, the bigger the price tag.

References: Mark Allen Baker, *Sports Collectors Digest Baseball Autograph Handbook, Second Edition,* Krause Publications, 1991; Mark Baker, *Team Baseballs: The Complete Guide to Autographed Team Baseballs,* Krause Publications, 1992; David Bushing, *Sports Equipment Price Guide,* Krause Publications, 1995; Douglas Congdon–Martin and John Kashmanian, *Baseball Treasures: Memorabilia from the National Pastime,* Schiffer Publishing, 1993; Mark Larson, *Sports Collectors Digest Complete Guide to Baseball Memorabilia, Third Edition,* Krause Publications, 1996; Mark Larson, Rick Hines, and Dave Platta (eds.), *Mickey Mantle Memorabilia,* Krause Publications, 1993; Roderick A. Malloy, *Malloy's Sports Collectibles Value Guide,* Wallace–Homestead, Krause Publications, 1993; Norman E. Martinus and Harry L. Rinker, *Warman's Paper,* Wallace–Homestead, Krause Publications, 1994; Michael McKeever, *Collecting Sports Memorabilia,* Alliance Publishers, 1996.

Periodicals: *Sports Collectors Digest,* 700 E State St, Iola, WI 54990; *Tuff Stuff,* PO Box 1637, Glen Allen, VA 23060.

Collectors' Clubs: Society for American Baseball Research, PO Box 92183, Cleveland, OH 44101–5183; The Glove Collector, 14057 Rolling Hills Ln, Dallas, TX 54210.

Baseball, Babe Ruth, sgd . . . . $ 1,300.00
Baseball, Brooklyn Dodgers, sgd, 1950. . . . . 700.00
Baseball, Roger Maris, sgd. 1,000.00
Bat, Hillerich & Bradsby, Reggie Jackson, game used,
  sgd, 1968–71 . . . . 1,800.00
Bat, Louisville Slugger, George Brett, uncracked,
  1980s 1,150.00
Bat, Louisville Slugger, P27, Robin Yount, unused,
  sgd, 1984. . . . . 350.00
Batting Glove, Rickey Henderson, Mizuno, fluores-
  cent, sgd 90.00
Batting Helmet, Wade Boggs, Boston Red Sox 800.00
Book, *Who's Who in the Major Leagues,* Speed
  Johnson, hard cov, 1933 . . . . 225.00
Bottle Cap, Coca–Cola, Tug McGraw, New York Mets,
  1967–68 . . . . 1.00

Fleer, 1963, #42,
Sandy Koufax, $90.00.

Cap, Hank Aaron, Milwaukee Brewers, blue, gold,
with "M," 1970s **1,200.00**

Cap, Mitch Williams, Chicago Cubs, "Thing" under
bill, game used **100.00**

Chair, from Wrigley Field, folding, wood, cast iron,
repainted, late 1930s **275.00**

Cup, Hank Aaron, 7–Eleven giveaway, 1973 . . . . **15.00**

Display, Reggie Candy Bar, standup, includes mail–in
promotions for Jackson autographed baseball **250.00**

Figure, Yogi Berra, blue and white uniform, Hartland,
early 1960s, 7" h **125.00**

Game, Babe Ruth's Baseball Game, Milton Bradley,
1930s **700.00**

Gumball Machine, Play Ball, keys, 1950s **135.00**

Jacket, warm–up, Orel Hershiser, Los Angeles
Dodgers **475.00**

Jersey, Johnny Bench, 1976 Cincinnati Reds, game
worn **2,500.00**

Magazine, *Sport,* Don Drysdale cov, June 1960 . . . . **10.00**

Magazine, *Sports Illustrated,* Stan Musial cov, July
1952 . . . . **35.00**

Magnet, Dwight Evans, color, Phoenix, 1989, 2 x 3" **1.00**

Movie Handbill, *Kill the Umpire,* William Bendix **15.00**

Nodder, Willie Mays **400.00**

Pants, Yogi Berra, New York Mets, sgd, 1968 . . . . **175.00**

Patch, uniform, San Francisco Giants All–Star Game,
1984 . . . . **30.00**

Pennant, Detroit Tigers, black tiger head, orange
ground, 1940s **80.00**

Photograph, Ted Williams, batting stance, 1954,
9 x 7" **90.00**

Pin, World Series, New York Yankees, threaded post,
silver, Dieges & Clust, 1941 . . . . **400.00**

Pinback Button, Jerome (Dizzy) Dean, black and
white photo, late 1940s **50.00**

Pocket Watch, New York Yankees World
Championship, Wittnauer, 1952 . . . . **1,000.00**

Poster, Pride of the Yankees, 1949, 27 x 41" **2,500.00**

Poster, Let's Go Mets, *Sports Illustrated,* 1969 . . . . **35.00**

Program, Salute to Hank Aaron, Sept 17, 1976,
Milwaukee Co Stadium, 5½" x 8½", ... **15.00**

Puzzle, ABC Wide World of Sports, Richie Allen cov,
1972, 250 pcs **50.00**

Ring, Philadelphia Phillies World Series, 1980 . . . . **2,000.00**

Shoes, Mike Schmidt, Nike spikes, sgd, game used **650.00**

Sunglasses, "Tiger Eye" Barry Bonds, flip–down **225.00**

Ticket, Pete Rose's September 11, 1985 game, sgd. **300.00**

Tobacco Pack, autographed by Buck Weaver,
unopened **850.00**

Toy, Pete Rose softball–size Wiffle Ball, with box. **45.00**

Umpire Equipment, shirt, Ted Hendry, American
League. **150.00**

Watch, Babe Ruth in center with bats over his shoulder, metal band, Exacta Time, 1949 . . . . **900.00**

BASKETBALL CARDS

Muriad cigarettes issued the first true basketball trading cards in 1911. In 1933 Goudey issued the first basketball cards found in gum packs.

The era of modern hoop basketball trading cards dates from 1948 when Bowman created the first set devoted exclusively to the sport. By the 1950s Topps, Exhibit Supply Company, Kellogg's, Wheaties, and other food manufacturers joined with Bowman in creating basketball trading cards. Collectors regard the 1957-58 Topps set as the second true modern basketball set.

Today basketball trading card sets are issued by a wide variety of manufacturers. Collectors also must contend with draft card series, special rookie cards, insert or chase cards and super premium card sets. Keeping up with contemporary issues is time consuming and expensive. As a result, many collectors focus only on pre–1990 issued cards.

References: James Beckett, *The Official 1997 Price Guide to Basketball Cards, 6th Edition,* House of Collectibles, 1997; James Beckett and Grant Sandground (eds.), *Beckett Basketball Card Price Guide, No. 5,* Beckett Publications, 1996; Sports Collectors Digest, *1997 Standard Catalog of Football, Basketball & Hockey Cards, 2nd Edition,* Krause Publications, 1996.

Fleer, 1961–62, complete set of 66 . . . . $ **500.00**

Fleer, 1973, " The Shots," #18, Free Throw **35**

Fleer, 1986–87, #11, Kareem Abdul–Jabbar **1.50**

Fleer, 1987–88, #35, Julius Erving **1.25**

Fleer, 1988–89, #43, Dennis Rodman. **5.00**

Fleer, 1992–93, #299, Scottie Pippen **05**

Fleer, 1993–94, #266, Chris Mills. **05**

Globetrotters Cocoa Puffs 28, 1971–72, complete set
of 28 . . . . **20.00**

Globetrotters Cocoa Puffs 28, 1971–72, #23,
Meadowlark Lemon **1.00**

Globetrotters Cocoa Puffs 28, 1971–72, #28, Freddie
"Curly" Neal **1.50**

Hoops, 1992–93, #337, Larry Bird, Tournament of
the Americas **05**

Hoops, 1993–94, #203, David Robinson **05**

Hoops, 1994–95, complete set of 450 . . . . **3.00**

Topps, 1957–58, #17, Bill Cousy **60.00**

Topps, 1969–70, #1, Wilt Chamberlain. **20.00**

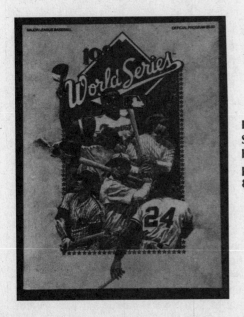

Program, 1987 World Series, color and black and white photos, 96 pgs, 8 x 11", $20.00.

Topps, 1970–71, #160, Jerry West **5.00**
Topps, 1972–73, #215, Billy Cunningham **1.00**
Topps, 1972–73, complete set of 264 . . . . **95.00**
Topps, 1981–82, #41, Darrell Griffith. **15**
Ultra, 1992–93, #27, Michael Jordan **75**
Ultra, 1993–94, #145, Charles Barkley. **05**
Ultra, 1994–95, #125, Patrick Ewing **05**
Upper Deck, 1991–92, #45, Magic Johnson **10**
Upper Deck, 1991–92, #453, Scottie Pippin. **05**
Upper Deck, 1992–93, #474, Shaquille O'Neal **25**
Upper Deck, 1993–94, complete Series 2, 255 cards **2.00**

BASKETBALL MEMORABILIA

The first basketball game was played by two opposing teams of five players each on a regulation 94 x 50′ wide court in 1891. James Naismith, physical director of the Y.M.C.A. College, Springfield, Massachusetts, originated the game. Early basketball collectibles relate to high school and college teams.

Professional basketball was played prior to World War II. However, it was not until 1949 and the founding of the United States National Basketball Association that the professional sport achieved national status. Competing leagues, franchise changes, and Olympic teams compete for collector loyalty.

References: Mark Larson, *Complete Guide to Football, Basketball & Hockey Memorabilia,* Krause Publications, 1995; Roderick Malloy, *Malloy's Sports Collectibles Value Guide: Up–To–Date Prices For Noncard Sports Memorabilia,* Attic Books, Wallace–Homestead, Krause Publications, 1993.

Cereal Box, Larry Bird, Team USA, Frosted Mini
 Wheats, 1992 . . . . **$ 20.00**
Cereal Box, Michael Jordan, Wheaties, 1989. . . . . **30.00**
Coin, NBA Champions Bulls, Enviromint, 1991. . . . . **30.00**
Figurine, Kareem Abdul–Jabbar, Kenner Starting
 Lineup, 1988. . . . . **25.00**
Figurine, Larry Bird, Kenner Starting Lineup, 1990. . . . . . **30.00**
Game, All American Basketball, Corey Games, 1941 . . . . **75.00**

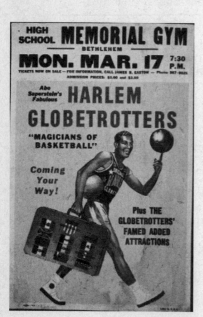

**Poster, cardboard, Harlem Globetrotters, 14 x 22",
$12.00.**

Game, Harlem Globetrotter Official Edition,
 Cadaco–Ellis, 1970s **65.00**
Jersey, Magic Johnson **5,000.00**
Magazine, *Basketball Digest,* Julius Erving, Feb 1976. . . . . **15.00**
Magazine, *Basketball Weekly,* "No War With ABA,"
 Dec 21, 1967 . . . . **5.00**
Miniature Basketball Rim and Backboard, University
 of Missouri. **25.00**
Nodder, composition, player holding basketball,
 rounded gold base, sticker inscribed "Millersville,"
 1960s, 7" h **25.00**
Poster, Billy Cunningham, Sports Illustrated, 68–71 . . . . . . **15.00**
Program, Magicians of Basketball, Harlem
 Globetrotters, 30 pgs, 1965, 8 x 10½". **15.00**
Sneakers, Wilt Chamberlain. **3,000.00**
Sticker, Pete Maravich, Topps, 1971–72 . . . . **8.00**
Ticket Stub, New York, NBA All–Star Game, 1955 . . . . **25.00**
Ticket Stub, Washington, NBA All–Star Game, 1980 . . . . . **15.00**

BAUER POTTERY

John Bauer founded the Paducah Pottery in Paducah, Kentucky in 1885. John Andrew Bauer assumed leadership of the pottery in 1898 following the death of John Bauer. In 1909 the pottery moved its operations to Los Angeles, California.

The company's award winning artware line of glazed bowls, jardinieres, and vases was introduced in 1913. Molded stoneware vases were marketed shortly thereafter.

John Andrew Bauer died in 1922, leaving control of the business to his son–in–law, Watson E. Brockmon.

In 1931 Bauer Pottery began production of its most popular line—Ring ware. Decorated in brightly colored glazes, it included over a hundred different shapes and sizes in table and kitchen lines. Ring ware proved to be Bauer's most popular and profitable pattern. Other successful dinnerware lines include Monterey (1936–1945), La Linda (1939–1959), and Brusche Contempo and Monterey Moderne (1948–1961). Increasing competition at home and abroad and a bitter strike in 1961 forced Bauer to close its doors in 1962.

References: Susan and Al Bagdade, *Warman's American Pottery and Porcelain,* Wallace–Homestead, Krause Publications, 1994; Lois Lehner, *Lehner's Encyclopedia of U.S. Marks on Pottery, Porcelain & Clay,* Collector Books, 1988; Mitch Tuchman, *Bauer: Classic American Pottery,* Chronicle Books, 1995.

Newsletters: *Bauer News,* PO Box 91279, Pasadena, CA 91109; *Bauer Quarterly,* PO Box 2524, Berkeley, CA 94702.

Brusche Contempo, dinner service, service for 4 plus
 serving pcs, pink speck. . . . . **$ 95.00**
Brusche Contempo, gravy, pink speck. **20.00**
Brusche Contempo, tea set, teapot and four #46
 mugs, spice green **45.00**
Brusche Contempo, vegetable bowl, 7½" d, indigo
 brown **20.00**
Brusche Contempo, vegetable bowl, 7½" d, pumpkin **20.00**
Gloss Pastel Kitchenware, batter bowl, yellow. **80.00**
Gloss Pastel Kitchenware, custard, gray. **18.00**
La Linda, ball jug, ice lip, gray **95.00**
La Linda, carafe, chartreuse, glossy, wood handle **20.00**

Ring, mixing bowls, nesting set of four, imp with number and "Bauer," green #12, yellow #18, cobalt blue #24, and orange–red #36, price for set, $175.00.

La Linda, cookie jar, jade **85.00**
La Linda, creamer, turquoise **20.00**
La Linda, custard, ivory, glossy **15.00**
La Linda, fruit bowl, yellow **10.00**
La Linda, plate, bread and butter, 6" d, pink **6.00**
La Linda, plate, dinner, 9" d, chartreuse **15.00**
La Linda, plate, 9½" d, ivory, glossy **10.00**
La Linda, shaker, tall, turquoise, glossy **15.00**
La Linda, teapot, 8 cup, olive green **35.00**
La Linda, tumbler, burgundy, glossy, metal handle **20.00**
La Linda, vegetable bowl, 9½" d, pink, glossy **25.00**
Monterey Moderne, butter dish, ivory **50.00**
Monterey Moderne, cake plate, pedestal base, orange **100.00**
Monterey Moderne, chop plate, 13" d, yellow **35.00**
Monterey Moderne, coffee server, 8 cup, wood handle **35.00**
Monterey Moderne, creamer and sugar, midget, orange **55.00**
Monterey Moderne, cup, green **15.00**
Monterey Moderne, cup, turquoise **20.00**
Monterey Moderne, fruit bowl, 13" d, yellow, ftd **60.00**
Monterey Moderne, pitcher, 2 quart, green **45.00**
Monterey Moderne, plate, bread and butter, 6" d, turquoise **10.00**
Monterey Moderne, plate, luncheon, 9½" d, blue **12.00**
Monterey Moderne, platter, 17" l, yellow **45.00**
Monterey Moderne, sauce boat, turquoise **45.00**
Monterey Moderne, soup bowl, 7½" d, blue **30.00**
Monterey Moderne, teapot, cov, 6 cup, yellow **65.00**
Monterey Moderne, vegetable bowl, blue, divided **45.00**
Ring, bowl, #18, orange–red **125.00**
Ring, butter dish, orange–red **150.00**
Ring, candlesticks, pr, spool, cobalt blue **300.00**
Ring, cereal bowl, ivory **115.00**
Ring, casserole, 6½" d, red–brown **50.00**
Ring, chop plate, 17" d, orange–red **225.00**
Ring, coffeepot, 8 cup **150.00**
Ring, cookie jar, cov, orange–red **125.00**
Ring, creamer and sugar, midget, yellow **55.00**

Ring, egg cup, turquoise **85.00**
Ring, mixing bowl, #36, ivory **65.00**
Ring, mug, barrel, black **450.00**
Ring, nappy, #5, black **65.00**
Ring, pickle dish **20.00**
Ring, plate, bread and butter, 6" d, burgundy **9.00**
Ring, plate, dinner, 10" d, white **20.00**
Ring, plate, salad, 7½" d, white **15.00**
Ring, punch bowl, 14" d, olive green, ftd **450.00**
Ring, ramekin, orange–red **15.00**
Ring, salt and pepper shakers, pr, jade green, low **15.00**
Ring, saucer **45.00**
Ring, soup bowl, 7½" d, burgundy **25.00**
Ring, sugar shaker, jade green **295.00**
Ring, teacup, 2 cup, burgundy **275.00**
Ring, tumbler, 6 oz, metal handle, delph blue **30.00**
Ring, vase, cylinder, 8" h **65.00**

BEATLES

Beatlemania took the country by storm in 1964, the year the Beatles appeared on The Ed Sullivan Show. Members of the Fab Four included George Harrison, John Lennon, Paul McCartney, and Ringo Starr (who replaced original drummer Pete Best in 1962). The most desirable items were produced between 1964 and 1968 and are marked "NEMS."

The group disbanded in 1970 and individual members pursued their own musical careers. John Lennon's tragic murder in New York City in 1980 invoked a new wave of interest in the group and its memorabilia.

References: Jeff Augsburger, Marty Eck, and Rick Rann, *The Beatles Memorabilia Price Guide, Third Edition,* Antique Trader Books, 1997; Perry Cox and Joe Lindsay, *The Official Price Guide To The Beatles,* House of Collectibles, 1995; Courtney McWilliams, *The Beatles, Yesterday and Tomorrow: A Collector's Guide to Beatles Memorabilia,* Schiffer Publishing, 1997.

Periodicals: *Beatlefan,* PO Box 33515, Decatur, GA 30033; *Good Day Sunshine,* 397 Edgewood Ave, New Haven, CT 06511; *Strawberry Fields Forever,* PO Box 880981, San Diego, CA 92168.

Collectors' Clubs: Beatles Connection, PO Box 1066, Pinellas Park, FL 34665; Working Class Hero Club, 3311 Niagara St, Pittsburgh, PA 15213.

REPRODUCTION ALERT: Records, picture sleeves, and album jackets have been counterfeited. Sound quality may be inferior. Printing on labels and picture jackets usually is inferior to the original. Many pieces of memorabilia also have been reproduced, often with some change in size, color, design, etc.

Bottle Stopper, composition, Ringo figural head, mkd "Ringo,"cork mkd "Achatit," c1960, 4½" h . . . . **$ 175.00**
Clothes Hanger, stiff diecut cardboard attached to white plastic hanger, George Harrison, ©Henderson/Hoggard Inc, King Features–Suba Films Ltd, 1968, 16 x 17" **60.00**
Cup, plastic, transparent, color photo of Beatles and signatures on paper insert, 4 pink lips around rim, ©Nems Enterprises, c1960, 6½" h **50.00**

Doll, Paul McCartney, molded hard plastic body, soft
vinyl head, Remco, ©1964 Nems, 4½" h **175.00**

Game, Flip Your Wig, Milton Bradley, 1964 Nems
Enterprise Ltd **75.00**

Guitar, plastic, red back, orange and maroon front,
Beatles decal, raised silver "New Beat" logo, 31" l,
orig box **500.00**

Hairbrush, soft plastic, blue, photos, facsimile signatures, and "The Beatle Brush" in relief, Genco,
c1960s, 3¾" l, orig pkg **90.00**

Lunch Box, Yellow Submarine, metal, King–Seeley,
©1968 King Features Syndicate **175.00**

Model Kit, Ringo, Revell, ©1964, unassembled, orig
box **125.00**

Pen, The Beatles Official Ballpoint Pen, silvered metal
top, plastic bottom, ©Press Initial Corp 1964, 5" l,
orig card **75.00**

Photo, color, white plastic frame, ©1964 Nems
Enterprises Ltd, mkd "Litho By Monarch, Hamilton,
Canada", 4½ x 6", price for set of 4 . . . . **125.00**

Pin, standing beetle, gold colored metal, painted
black jacket and shoes, red striped shirt, mink fur
hair, movable head and legs, playing guitar, c1960,
2" h, orig card **60.00**

Poster, "The Beatles Bulletin" fan club addresses,
1969 Summer issue, color photo, 18" sq **25.00**

Puzzle, Yellow Submarine, Jaymar, ©1968 King
Features Syndicate, orig box **75.00**

Record Case, Disk–Go–Case, plastic, purple and
pink, holds 45 rpm records, black illus and facsimile signatures, ©Charter Industries, Inc 1966
Nems Enterprises, Ltd, 7½" d, 6¾" h **100.00**

Scarf, glossy fabric, half corner design, mkd "The
Beatles, Copyright by Ramat & Co Ltd, London,
ECl," c1964, 25" sq **150.00**

Ticket, White Sox Park, Chicago, lavender, black text,
August 20, 1965, 1¼ x 4" **50.00**

Wallet, gray vinyl, folding, pinktone group photo on
one side, black facsimile signatures on other,
Standard Plastic Products, ©Rmat & Co, Ltd,
London, c1964, 3½ x 4½" **120.00**

Trading Card, Topps, 1964, 2nd Series, $2.50.

AUCTION PRICES

Sotheby's Beverly Hills, Collectors' Carrousel Rock 'n' Roll
Memorabilia, December 17, 1996. Prices include a buyer's premium of 15% of the successful bid price up to and including
$50,000, and 10% on any amount in excess of $50,000.

Bass Drum Head, Ludwig, "Ludwig, The Beatles,"
used by Ringo Starr at San Francisco Cow Palace
concert August 19, 1964, letter of provenance . . **14,950.00**

Bobbing Head Dolls, Car Mascots, Inc, 1964, hp,
wearing gray collarless suits, playing appropriate
instruments, gold colored bases with facsimile
signatures, 8" h, set of 4 . . . . **920.00**

Fan Club Card, blue pen and ink Paul McCartney
signature, matted and framed with color picture
of Beatles performing and "gold" single for
Yesterday, 17 x 20½" **345.00**

Home Movie, February 1965, Nassau, the Bahamas,
8mm, taken on family vacation where Beatles
were filming *HELP*, shows Beatles being filmed in
and around hotel pool, all 4 on bikes, and
Lennon on bike in pool, with VHS copy for easy
viewing **1,380.00**

Program and Ticket, *The Beatles Show* program matted and framed with ticket from Gaumont
Theatre, Taunton, featuring the Beatles, 13 x 17" . . . **345.00**

BELLEEK, AMERICAN

The American Belleek era spanned from the early 1880s until
1930. Several American firms manufactured porcelain wares
resembling Irish Belleek. The first was Ott and Brewer Company
of Trenton, New Jersey, from 1884 until 1893. Companies operating between 1920 and 1930 include Cook Pottery (1894–1929),
Coxon Belleek Pottery (1926–1930), Lenox, Inc. (1906–1930),
Morgan Belleek China Company (1924–1929), and Perlee, Inc.
(1920s–c1930).

Reference: Mary Frank Gaston, *American Belleek*, Collector
Books, 1984.

Bowl, green, heavy gold trim, white curled handle,
Lenox green wreath mark, 9" d . . . . **$ 90.00**

Bud Vase, Art Nouveau style florals with swirling ribbon, yellow, tan, and green, palette mark, 6" h **400.00**

Coffee Set, 3 pcs, coffeepot, creamer, and sugar
bowl, sterling silver overlay, mkd "Lenox Belleek,"
c1921 . . . . **3,500.00**

Cup and Saucer, Coxon **40.00**

Demitasse Cup, liner, gold border, sterling silver
holder with saucer, Lenox green wreath mark **60.00**

Ewer, tankard shape, green ground, 14" h **400.00**

Figure, elephant, white, Lenox green wreath mark **315.00**

Powder Box, pink, gold wheat on lid, Lenox green
wreath mark, 4 x 6" **40.00**

Salt and Pepper Shakers, pr, 1" d salt, 2" h egg shape
pepper, pink roses, Lenox green palette mark **35.00**

Soup, Coxon **100.00**

Vase, cream, gold dec, 7" h **250.00**

Vase, black spiderweb design, yellow, pink, blue and orange butterflies, pearlized ground, c1906–24, 10" h **275.00**

Vase, dancing lady with cherubs, ornate gold handles, 18" h **600.00**

BELLEEK, IRISH

Belleek is a thin, ivory–colored, almost iridescent–type porcelain. It was first made in 1857 in county Fermanagh, Ireland. Production continued until World War I, was discontinued for a period of time, and then resumed.

Shamrock is the most commonly found pattern, but many patterns were made, including Limpet, Tridacna, and Grasses. Pieces made after 1891 have the word "Ireland" or "Eire" in their mark. Some are marked "Belleek Co., Fermanagh."

The following abbreviations have been used to identify marks:

1BM   =   1st Black Mark (1863–1890)
2BM   =   2nd Black Mark (1891–1926)
3BM   =   3rd Black Mark (1926–1946)
4GM   =   4th Green Mark (1946–1955)
5GM   =   5th Green Mark (1955–1965)
6GM   =   6th Green Mark (1965–c1980)
B/GM   =   Brown/Gold Mark (1980–present)

References: Susan and Al Bagdade, *Warman's English & Continental Pottery & Porcelain, 2nd Edition,* Wallace–Homestead, Krause Publications, 1991; Richard K. Degenhardt, *Belleek: The Complete Collector's Guide and Illustrated Reference, Second Edition,* Wallace–Homestead, Krause Publications, 1993.

Collectors' Club: The Belleek Collectors' Society, 144 W Britannia St, Taunton, MA 02780.

Butter Plate, open, leaf shape, 3BM . . . . **$ 45.00**
Cake Plate, Shamrock pattern, 3BM **125.00**
Coffeepot, Limpet pattern, molded body, gilt dec handle, finial, and trim, 3BM **300.00**
Coffeepot, Shamrock pattern, basketweave gorund, twig handle, 3BM, 7" h **300.00**
Creamer and Sugar, Lily pattern, 5GM **45.00**
Creamer and Sugar, Shamrock pattern 2BM **175.00**
Creamer and Sugar, Snail pattern, pink edges and handles, 2BM **200.00**
Cup and Saucer, Limpet pattern, 3BM **85.00**
Cup and Saucer, Pinecone pattern, pink edge, 2BM **375.00**
Cup and Saucer, Shamrock pattern, 2BM, 6" d, 2" h **85.00**
Cup and Saucer, Tradacna pattern, pink trim, 2BM **60.00**
Figure, Swan, 3BM, 4¹/₂" h **35.00**
Jug, gourd shape, green accents, flared neck, loop handle, 2BM, 10" h **950.00**
Milk Pitcher, Shamrock pattern, basketweave ground, twig handle, 2GM, 6" h **85.00**
Plate, Shamrock pattern, basketweave ground, 3BM, 7" d **75.00**
Plate, Shell pattern, green tint, 3BM, 8¹/₂" d **100.00**
Plate, Shell pattern, pink trim, 1GM, 6¹/₂" d **65.00**
Spill Vase, Lily pattern, 3GM, 6¹/₂" h **80.00**
Sugar, cov, Shamrock pattern, 3BM **75.00**
Tray, Erne pattern, yellow trim, 2BM, 17¹/₂" d **600.00**

Vase, Calalily pattern, 3BM, 14" h **1,250.00**
Vase, Sunflower pattern, 3GM, 7¹/₂" h **60.00**

BESWICK

James Wright Beswick and his son, John Beswick, are well known for their ceramic figures of horses, cats, dogs, birds, and other wildlife. Produced since the 1890s, figures representing specific animal characters from children's stories, such as Winnie the Pooh and Peter Rabbit, have also been modeled. In 1969 the company was bought by Royal Doulton Tableware, Ltd.

References: Diana Callow et al., *The Charlton Standard Catalogue of Beswick Animals, Second Edition,* Charlton Press, 1996; Harvey May, *The Beswick Price Guide, Third Edition,* Francis Joseph Publications, 1995, distributed by Krause Publications.

Newsletter: *The Beswick Quarterly,* 7525 W Bernhill Rd, Spokane, WA 99208.

Additional Listings: Royal Doulton

Display Stand . . . . **$ 150.00**
Figure, American Blue Jays, blue, glossy finish, 5" h **175.00**
Figure, Courting Penguins, #1015, black and white, yellow markings, glossy finish, 5¹/₂" h **300.00**
Figure, Duck Family, #765, white, yellow beaks, glossy finish, 2¹/₄" h **80.00**
Figure, Geese, #280, pr, white, orange, glossy finish, 4" h **50.00**
Figure, Hare, running, #1024, tan, glossy finish, 5¹/₄" h **300.00**
Figure, Hippopotamus, #697, blue, glossy finish, Fun Models series, 2¹/₄" h **175.00**
Figure, Old Staffordshire Unicorn, cream, gray, and green, glossy finish, 6" h **400.00**
Figure, Turtle Doves, brown, blue, and pink, brown and green base, glossy finish, 7¹/₂" h **300.00**
Plaque, pheasant scene, 12" d **25.00**
Teapot, Peggoty, #1116, 6" h **50.00**
Vase, blue and yellow dribble glaze, pinched sides, 8" h **50.00**
Whiskey Flask, Loch Ness Monster, #2051, green, glossy finish, head stopper, 3" h **50.00**

BICYCLES & RELATED

The bicycle was introduced in America at the 1876 Centennial. Early bicycles were high wheelers with heavy iron frames and disproportionately sized wooden wheels. By 1892 wooden wheels were replaced by pneumatic air–filled tires, which were later replaced with standard rubber tires with inner tubes. The coaster brake was introduced in 1898.

Early high wheelers and safety bikes made into the 1920s and 1930s are classified as antique bicycles. Highly stylized bicycles from the 1930s and 1940s represent the transitional step to the classic period, beginning in the late 1940s and running through the end of the balloon tire era.

References: Jim Hurd, *Bicycle Blue Book,* Memory Lane Classics, 1997; Neil S. Wood, *Evolution of the Bicycle, Volume 1* (1991,

1994 value update), *Volume 2* (1994) L–W Book Sales; Jay Pridmore and Jim Hurd, *The American Bicycle,* Motorbooks International, 1995; Jay Pridmore and Jim Hurd, *Schwinn Bicycles,* Motorbooks International, 1996.

Periodicals: *Bicycle Trader,* PO Box 3324, Ashland, OR 97520; *Classic & Antique Bicycle Exchange,* 325 W Hornbeam Dr, Longwood, FL 32779; *Classic Bike News,* 5046 E Wilson Rd, Clio, MI 48420.

Collectors' Clubs: Classic Bicycle and Whizzer Club, 35769 Simon Dr, Clinton Twp, MI 48035; International Veteran Cycle Assoc, 248 Highland Dr, Findlay, OH 45840; National Pedal Vehicle Assoc, 1720 Rupert NE, Grand Rapids, MI 49505.

Alarm, Perfection	**$ 20.00**
Badge, Austrian Bike Club, enamel, brass, early 1900s	**20.00**
Bicycle, Black Phantom	**300.00**
Bicycle, Columbia, boy's, maroon and cream, whitewall tires, headlight, unrestored, c1940	**700.00**
Bicycle, Columbia 3 Star Deluxe, boy's, blue and white, c1950, 26"	**325.00**
Bicycle, Columbia Twosome Tandem, 1970	**100.00**
Bicycle, Elgin Dolly, Sears Roebuck, 1939	**1,500.00**
Bicycle, Firestone Super Cruiser, girl's, blue and white, c1947, 26"	**100.00**
Bicycle, Huffman Indian, 1948	**1,000.00**
Bicycle, Jaguar MK 4, c1958	**200.00**
Bicycle, J. C. Higgins, girl's, cream, gray, and red, c1948–50, 26"	**85.00**
Bicycle, Moulton Stoaway, 4 speed, 1964	**325.00**
Bicycle, Schwinn Debutante, girl's, pink and white, chrome, c1950, 26"	**75.00**
Bicycle, Schwinn Deluxe Stingray, boy's, metallic green, chrome fenders, whitewall tires	**165.00**
Bicycle, Schwinn Lil Chik, girl's, blue and white, c1969, 20"	**100.00**
Bicycle, Schwinn Stardust Stingray, girl's, garnet red, chrome fenders	**110.00**
Bicycle, Schwinn Tiger, 1959	**350.00**
Bicycle, Shelby Flyer, Shelby Cycle Co, Cleveland, OH, boy's, 4 rib horn tank, air flo chain guard, rd, black, and white paint, 26"	**700.00**
Bicycle, Silver King, lady's, first model, silver ray light, battery tube, aluminum fenders, c1940, orig condtion	**200.00**
Bicycle, Vrroom, 1961, 20"	**250.00**
Bicycle, Westfield Comet, c1939	**1,000.00**
Bicycle, Westfield 50th Anniversary, girl's headlight, full coverage chain guard and drop stand, c1937	**165.00**
Calendar, cardboard, Kilian and Vopel on Durkopp racing bicycles photo, 1940, 8¾ x 11"	**15.00**
Catalog, Mead Cycle Co, Chicago, IL, Bargain List No. 24, 1924 ,24 pgs, 8¼ x 10"	**25.00**
Charm, plastic, blue, world globe inside bike tire, inscribed "Arnold Schwinn & Co, Chicago" on front, "Ride The World's Cycles" on reverse, c1930s	**10.00**
Cigar Label, Royal Finish, bicycle race, Cyclist Tourist Club logo, George S. Harris & Sons, NY	**25.00**
Clock, adv, Columbia Built Bicycles Since 1877— America's First Bicycle, electric, c1950, 15"d	**350.00**
Display, Longines Watch, man riding early highwheel	**300.00**
Horn, Yoder, c1950	**8.00**
Light, Schwinn Phantom, chrome, battery operated	**70.00**
Pin, red, white, and blue, Stewart's Cycle Brake	**15.00**
Poster, National Amateur Bicycle Championships, Aug 23–24, Furman Kugler photo, 10 x 13½"	**15.00**
Stud, celluloid, metal fastener, Andrae Bicycle, "Never Disappoints"	**5.00**

AUCTION PRICES

Copake Auction, Sixth Annual Antique Bicycle Auction, April 12, 1997. Prices listed include the 10% buyer's premium.

Colson Firestone Bullnose, girl's, orig paint and Firestone whitewall tires, c1939, paint and chrome in exceptional unrestored condition	**770.00**
Colson Packard, girl's, streamlined, orig saddle, snap in "3 rib" tank, headlight, and droop rack, c1939, paint very good, chrome excellent	**440.00**
Columbia, 2–tone red, leather saddle, locking spring fork, front drum brake, Goodyear whitewalls, c1948, near mint orig condition	**1,595.00**
Elgin Blackhawk, new old stock Elgin speedometer, c1934, professionally restored	**1,925.00**
Firestone Pilot, boy's, orig red and white paint, basket, and chrome carrier, 26", excellent condition	**165.00**
Firestone Super Cruiser, girl's orig blue and white paint, c1947, poor condition	**104.50**
Schwinn Manta–Ray, boy's, 5 speed, yellow, c1969, 24", very good condition, all orig	**220.00**
Schwinn, Mini–Twinn Tandem, burnt orange, 20", new old stock condition	**1,100.00**
Schwinn, Whizzer, maroon, Stewart–Warner speedometer, orig steering lock and key, 1948, excellent condition	**6,600.00**
Silver King Monark, girl's stepped stainless steel fenders, lobdell saddle, EA headlight, 1936, excellent condition	**302.50**
Silver King Wingbar, man's stainless steel fenders, working speedometer, hex bars, tool box seat, Carlisle whitewall tires, 1938, excellent condition	**2,310.00**

BIG LITTLE BOOKS

Big Little Books is a trademark of the Whitman Publishing Company. In the 1920s Whitman issued a series of books among which were Fairy Tales, Forest Friends, and Boy Adventure. These series set the stage for Big Little Books.

The year 1933 marked Big Little Books' first appearance. Whitman experimented with ten different page lengths and eight different sizes prior to the 1940s. Many Big Little Books were remarketed as advertising premiums for companies such as Cocomalt, Kool Aid, Macy's, and others. Whitman also published a number of similar series, e.g., Big Big Books, Famous Comics, Nickel Books, Penny Books, and Wee Little Books.

In an effort to keep the line alive, Whitman introduced television characters in the Big Little Book format in the 1950s. Success was limited. Eventually, Mattel–owned Western Publishing absorbed Whitman Publishing.

References: Larry Jacobs, *Big Little Books: A Collector's Reference & Value Guide,* Collector Books, 1996; *Price Guide to Big Little Books & Better Little, Jumbo, Tiny Tales, A Fast–Action Story etc.,* L–W Books Sales, 1995.

Collectors' Club: Big Little Book Collector Club of America, PO Box 1242, Danville, CA 94526.

#715, *Houdini's Magic*	$ 40.00
#719, *Robinson Crusoe*	40.00
#725, *Big Little Mother Goose*, hard cover	900.00
#754, *Reg'lar Fellers*	25.00
#758, *Prairie Bill and the Covered Wagon*	20.00
#759, *Alice in Wonderland*	30.00
#763, *Alley Oop and Dinny*	20.00
#772, *Erik Noble and the Forty–Niners*	20.00
#1105, *Kazan in Revenge of the North*	15.00
#1106, *Ella Cinders and the Mysterious House*	30.00
#1107, *Lieutenant Commander Don Winslow U.S.N.*	25.00
#1119, *Betty Boop in Snow White*, 160 pgs, 1934	60.00
#1124, *Dickie Moore in the Little Red School House*	20.00
#1139, *Jungle Jim and the Vampire Woman*	30.00
#1146, *Chester Gump in the City of Gold*	20.00
#1172, *Tiny Tim and the Mechanical Men*	45.00
#1184, *Tailspin Tommy in the Great Air Mystery*	30.00
#1192, *The Arizona Kid on the Bandit Trail*	10.00
#1411, *Kay Darcy and the Mystery Hideout*	20.00
#1416, *Little Orphan Annie in the Movies*	45.00
#1417, *Bronc Peeler The Lone Cowboy*	10.00
#1420, *Tom Beatty Ace of the Service*	30.00
#1427, *Peggy Brown and the Runaway Auto Trailer*	20.00
#1429, *Texas Kid*	15.00
#1438, *Mary Lee and the Mystery of the Indian Beads*	20.00
#1459, *Barney Baxter in the Air With the Eagle Squadron*	10.00
#1460, *Snow White and the Seven Dwarfs*	45.00

#1480, *Coach Bernie Bierman's Brick Barton and the Winning Eleven,* $10.00.

BIG LITTLE BOOK TYPES

Today, Big Little Books is often used as a generic term that describes a host of look–alike titles from publishers such as Dell, Engel–Van Wiseman, Lynn, and Saalfield.

References: Larry Jacobs, *Big Little Books: A Collector's Reference & Value Guide,* Collector Books, 1996; *Price Guide to Big Little Books & Better Little, Jumbo, Tiny Tales, A Fast–Action Story etc.,* L–W Book Sales, 1995.

Blue Ribbon Pop–up, *Buck Rogers in the Dangerous Mission*, 1934	$ 140.00
Blue Ribbon Pop–up, *Dick Tracy, Capture of Boris Arson*, 1935	125.00
Blue Ribbon Pop–up, *Jack and the Beanstalk*, 1933	45.00
Blue Ribbon Pop–up, *Little Red Ridinghood*, 1934	75.00
Blue Ribbon Pop–up, *Popeye with the Hag of the Seven Seas*, 1935	150.00
Dell Fast–Action Story, *Black Beauty*, #1047, ©1934	40.00
Dell Fast–Action Story, *Broadway Bill*, ©1935	20.00
Dell Fast–Action Story, *Captain Marvel, The Return of the Scorpion*	55.00
Dell Fast–Action Story, *Dick Tracy and the Black-mailers*	40.00
Dell Fast–Action Story, *Dumbo the Flying Elephant*, ©1941	50.00
Dell Fast–Action Story, *Gang Busters and Guns of Law*, ©1940	32.00
Dell Fast–Action Story, *G–Man on Lightning Island*, ©1936	35.00
Dell Fast–Action Story, *Mickey Mouse, The Sheriff of Nugget Gulch*	45.00
Dell Fast–Action Story, *Minuteman*	35.00
Dell Fast–Action Story, *Smilin' Jack and the Border Bandits*, ©1941	22.00
Engle Van–Wiseman, Five Star Library, *Count of Monte Cristo, The*, #1, ©1934	25.00
Engle Van–Wiseman, Five Star Library, *Frankie Thomas in A Dog of Flanders*, #16, ©1935	15.00
Engle Van–Wiseman, Five Star Library, *Oliver Twist*, #11, ©1935	15.00
Engle Van–Wiseman, Five Star Library, *Wheels of Destiny*, #5, ©1934	18.00
Golden Press, Western Publishing, Golden Star Book, *Animals of the Little Wood*, #6080, ©1967	8.00
Golden Press, Western Publishing, Golden Star Book, *Winter Tales*, #6079, ©1955	5.00
Lynn, A Lynn Book, *Curley Harper at Lakespur*, #L19, ©1935	15.00
Lynn, A Lynn Book, *Dumb Dora & Bing Brown*, ©1936	22.00
Lynn, A Lynn Book, *Victor Hugo's Les Miserables*, #L10, ©1935	20.00
Saalfield, Jumbo Book, *Boss of the Chisholm Trail*, #1153, ©1939	15.00
Saalfield, Jumbo Book, *Joe Palooka's Great Adventure*, #1168, 1939	12.00
Saalfield, Jumbo Book, *Napoleon, Uncle Elby and Little Mary*, #1166, ©1939	25.00

Saalfield, Little Big Book, *It Happened One Night*, #1578, ©1933, soft cover **25.00**

Saalfield, Little Big Book, *Just Kids and the Mysterious Stranger*, #1324, ©1935, soft cover **25.00**

Saalfield, Little Big Book, *Little Lord Fauntleroy*, #1598, ©1936, soft cover **20.00**

Saalfield, Little Big Book, *Stan Kent Varsity Man*, #1123, ©1936 . . . . **30.00**

Saalfield, Little Big Book, *The Law of the Wild*, #1092, ©1935 . . . . **20.00**

Saalfield, Little Big Book, *West Pointers on the Gridiron*, #1121, ©1936 . . . . **20.00**

Saalfield, Little Big Book, *Will Rogers*, #1576, ©1935, soft cover **15.00**

Samuel Lowe, Swap-It Book, *Danny Meets the Cowboys*, ©1949, soft cover **5.00**

Samuel Lowe, Swap-It Book, *Little Tex Comes to XY Ranch*, ©1949, soft cover **5.00**

Samuel Lowe, Swap-It Book, *Nevada Jones, Trouble Shooter*, #582, ©1949 . . . . **5.00**

Whitman, Better Little Book, Batman, *Cheetah Caper, The*, #5771, ©1969 . . . . **10.00**

Whitman, Better Little Book, Blondie, *Papa Knows Best*, #1490, ©1945 . . . . **15.00**

Whitman, Better Little Book, *Brad Turner in Transatlantic Flight*, 1939 . . . . **25.00**

Whitman, Better Little Book, *Ellery Queen, Adventure of Last Man Club*, 341406, 1940 . . . . **35.00**

Whitman, Better Little Book, *Perry Winkle and the Rinkeydinks Get a Horse*, 1938 . . . . **20.00**

Whitman, Better Little Book, *Speed Douglas and The Mole Gang*, #1455, 1941 . . . . **30.00**

Whitman, Big Big Book, *Story of Little Orphan Annie, The*, #4054 . . . . **90.00**

Whitman, Big Big Book, *Tom Mix and the Scourge of Paradise Valley*, #4068 . . . . **30.00**

Whitman, New Better Little Book, 710 Series, *Andy Panda and Presto the Pup*, #707-10, ©1949 . . . . . **20.00**

Whitman, New Better Little Book, 710 Series, *Gene Autry and the Range War*, #714-10, 1950 . . . . **5.00**

Whitman, New Better Little Book, 710 Series, *Red Ryder Acting Sheriff*, #702-10, ©1949 . . . . **22.00**

Whitman, New Better Little Book, 710 Series, *Walt Disney's Brer Rabbit*, #704-10, 1949 . . . . **5.00**

Whitman, New Better Little Book, 710 Series, *Walt Disney's Cinderella and the Magic Wand*, #711-10, ©1950 . . . . **45.00**

Whitman, New Better Little Book, 710 Series, *Walt Disney's Donald Duck and the Mystery of the Double X*, #705-10, 1949 . . . . **10.00**

Whitman, New Better Little Book, 710 Series, *Woody Woodpecker Big Game Hunter*, #710-10, 1950 . . . . **5.00**

Whitman, Tiny Tales, *Animal Parade*, #2952, ©1959 . . . . . **12.00**

Whitman, Tiny Tales, *Hide and Seek*, #2952, ©1950 . . . . . . **8.00**

Whitman, Tiny Tales, *Steve the Steam Shovel*, #2952, ©1950 . . . . **12.00**

Whitman, Tiny Tales, *Tommy Caboose*, #2952, ©1950 . . . . **10.00**

World Syndicate, Highlights of History Series, *Pioneers of the Wild West*, J. Carroll Mansfield, ©1933, blue cover **15.00**

BING & GRONDAHL

Frederick Grondahl and brothers Meyer and Jacob Bing founded Bing & Grondahl in 1853 to create replicas of the work of the famed Danish sculptor Thorvaldsen. The company's initial success led to an expansion of its products that included elegant dinnerware, coffee services, and other tabletop products.

In 1895 Harald Bing decided to test the idea of a plate designed specifically for sale during the Christmas season. F. A. Hallin, a Danish artist, created "Behind the Frozen Window" which appeared on a limited edition of 400 plates with the words "Jule Aften" (Christmas Eve) scrolled across the bottom and decorated in the company's signature blue and white motif. While Bing & Grondahl's annual Christmas plate is its most recognized and collected product, collectors have expanded their focus to include the company's figurines, dinnerware, and other desirables.

Reference: Pat Owen, *Bing & Grondahl Christmas Plates: The First 100 Years*, Landfall Press, 1995, distributed by Viking Import House.

Bell, 1981, Christmas Peace . . . . **$ 45.00**
Bell, 1985, Christmas Eve at the Farmhouse **50.00**
Bell, 1990, Changing of the Guards **50.00**
Bell, 1992, Christmas at the Rectory **60.00**
Plate, 1920, Hare in the Snow **85.00**
Plate, 1925, The Child's Christmas **85.00**
Plate, 1927, Skating Couple **100.00**
Plate, 1931, Arrival of the Christmas Train **90.00**
Plate, 1937, Arrival of Christmas Guests **90.00**
Plate, 1943, The Ribe Cathedral **170.00**
Plate, 1944, Sorgenfri Castle **130.00**
Plate, 1945, The Old Water Mill **150.00**
Plate, 1957, Christmas Candles **170.00**
Plate, 1961, Winter Harmony **125.00**
Plate, 1964, The Fir Tree and Hare **65.00**
Plate, 1970, Pheasants in the Snow at Christmas **30.00**
Plate, 1973, Duck and Ducklings, Mother's Day **30.00**

Plate, 1969, Dog and Puppies, Mother's Day, $425.00.

Plate, 1977, Copenhagen Christmas **30.00**
Plate, 1979, White Christmas **40.00**
Plate, 1981, Hare and Young, Mother's Day **50.00**
Plate, 1983, Raccoon and Young, Mother's Day. **50.00**
Plate, 1984, Christmas Letter **60.00**
Plate, 1987, Sheep With Lambs, Mother's Day **45.00**
Plate, 1994, A Day at the Deer Park **75.00**

BLACK MEMORABILIA

Black memorabilia is a generic term covering a wide range of materials from advertising to toys that is made in the image of a black person or features an image of a black person in its artwork. The category also includes materials from the era of slavery, artistic and literary contributions by black people, Civil Rights memorabilia, and material relating to the black experience in America.

Much of the material in this category is derogatory in nature, especially pre–1960s material. In spite of or perhaps because of its subject, it is eagerly sought by both white and black collectors.

Interest in Civil Rights memorabilia has increased significantly in the past decade.

References: Douglas Congdon–Martin, *Images In Black: 150 Years of Black Collectibles,* Schiffer Publishing, 1990; Patiki Gibbs, *Black Collectibles Sold In America,* Collector Books, 1987, 1996 value update; Myla Perkins, *Black Dolls: 1820–1991,* Collector Books, 1993, 1995 value update; Myla Perkins, *Black Dolls, Book II: An Identification and Value Guide,* Collector Books, 1995; Dawn E Reno, *The Encyclopedia of Black Collectibles,* Wallace–Homestead, Krause Publications, 1996; J. P. Thompson, *Collecting Black Memorabilia: A Picture Price Guide,* L–W Book Sales, 1996; Jean Williams Turner, *Collectible Aunt Jemima,* Schiffer Publishing, 1994; Jackie Young, *Black Collectibles: Mammy and Her Friends,* Schiffer Publishing, 1988.

Collectors' Club: Black Memorabilia Collector's Assoc, 1482 Devoe Terrace, Bronx, NY 10468.

Ashtray, metal, black boy on potty, Chicago Metal
  Works, 1920s. . . . . **$ 125.00**
Bag, Plantation Coffee, cloth, Negro illus, 1930s. **5.00**
Blotter, "Green River The Whiskey Without a Head-
  ache Blots Out All Your Troubles," black man in top
  hat holding horse's bridle **15.00**
Book, *Little Black Sambo,* Saalifield, 1942. . . . . **75.00**
Book, *Uncle Tom's Cabin,* Young Folks Edition,
  Danahugh & Co. **75.00**
Bottle, Mammy's Beverage, 8" h **125.00**
Calendar, W O Strausbaugh Motor Co, 1947 . . . . **25.00**
Card Game, Snake Eyes, Selchow & Righter, 1930–57. . . . **60.00**
Cereal Box, Kellogg's Corn Flakes, Vanessa Williams **100.00**
Coffee Grinder, wood, metal handle, mkd "Made in
  Austria" on label and on handle **50.00**
Cookie Jar, Famous Amos, bisque, Treasure Craft **250.00**
Doll, celluloid, boy, nappy hair, red romper **75.00**
Doll, rubber, Louis Armstrong, Effanbee USA **125.00**
Egg Timer, seated chef **95.00**
Film, *Little Black Sambo,* orig box. **100.00**
Game, Golden Golliwog, orig envelope **50.00**
Glass, Coon Chicken Inn **25.00**
Humidor, Green River Whiskey & Tobacco **150.00**

Aunt Jemima, syrup jug, plastic, F & F Mold, 5¹⁄₂" h, $95.00.

Lunch Box, metal, Harlem Globetrotters, 1971 . . . . **60.00**
Magazine, *Ebony,* Dr. Martin Luther King and
  Coretta King cov, September 1968 . . . . **25.00**
Magazine Tear Sheet, Cream of Wheat adv, black and
  white, 1905 . . . . **10.00**
Matchbook, Dinah's Shack. **15.00**
Pancake Mold, Aunt Jemima **100.00**
Pancake Shaker, Aunt Jemima, yellow and white **100.00**
Perfume, Golliwog, medium size, orig box **250.00**
Photograph, Jesse Jackson, sgd, 1970s **50.00**
Plate, Aunt Jemima Breakfast Club, 11" d **15.00**
Plate, Coon Chicken Inn, 1940s **100.00**
Poster, Dixie Boy Firecrackers, multicolored, 28 x 18". . . . **75.00**
Salt and Pepper Shakers, pr, black and white chefs,
  mkd "Grims California," 4¹⁄₂" h **50.00**
Salt and Pepper Shakers, pr, "Peppy" and "Salty,"
  wooden, Japan, 4" h, ... **20.00**
Sheet Music, *"If You Love Your Baby, Make Goo Goo
  Eyes,"* Williams & Walker **40.00**
Sheet Music, *"Jumbo Jim,"* John Francis Gilder Band
  Orchestra. **30.00**
Sheet Music, *"Mammy's Little Coal Black Rose"* **30.00**
Sign, H. C. F. Koch & Son Dry Goods, litho on heavy
  board, round walnut frame, 12" d. **1,000.00**
Teapot, figural, native on camel, Japan, 6 x 9¹⁄₄". **125.00**
Tie Rack, pressed wood, black bellhop **80.00**

BLUE RIDGE POTTERY

The Carolina Clinchfield and Ohio Railroad, in an effort to promote industry along its right–of–way, established a pottery in Erwin, Tennessee, in 1917. J. E. Owens purchased the pottery in 1920 and changed the name to Southern Potteries. The company changed hands again within a few years, falling under the ownership of Charles W. Foreman.

By 1938 Southern Potteries was producing its famous Blue Ridge dinnerware, wares that featured hand–painted rather than decal decoration. Lena Watts, an Erwin native, designed many of the patterns. In addition, Blue Ridge made limited production patterns for a number of leading department stores.

The company experienced a highly successful period during the 1940s and early 1950s, the Golden Age of Blue Ridge. However, cheap Japanese imports and the increased use of plastic dinnerware in the mid–1950s sapped the company's market strength. Operations ceased on January 31, 1957, when stockholders decided to close the plant.

References: Susan and Al Bagdade, *Warman's American Pottery and Porcelain,* Wallace–Homestead, Krause Publications, 1994; Lois Lehner, *Lehner's Encyclopedia of U.S. Marks on Pottery, Porcelain & Clay,* Collector Books, 1988; Betty and Bill Newbound, *Encyclopedia of Blue Ridge Dinnerware,* Collector Books, 1994; Betty and Bill Newbound, *Southern Potteries, Inc.: Blue Ridge Dinnerware, Revised Third Edition,* Collector Books, 1989, 1996 value update; Frances and John Ruffin, *Blue Ridge China Today,* Schiffer Publishing, 1997.

Periodical: *The Daze,* PO Box 57, Otisville, MI 48463.

Newsletter: *National Blue Ridge Newsletter,* 144 Highland Dr, Blountville, TN 37617.

Collectors' Club: Blue Ridge Collectors Club, Rte 3, Box 161, Erwin, TN 37650.

Bonbon, Nove Rose, shell shape	$ 45.00
Butter Pat, Fruit Fantasy	15.00
Cake Plate, Chintz, maple leaf shape	50.00
Cake Plate, French Peasant, maple leaf shape	90.00
Candy Box, Calico	175.00
Celery, Chintz	20.00
Celery, Nove Rose, leaf shape	40.00
Cereal Bowl, Crab Apple, 6" d	5.00
Cereal Bowl, Ribbon Plaid	10.00
Child's Feeding Dish, Jigsaw	90.00
Chocolate Pot, French Peasant	300.00
Cigarette Set, Rooster, cov box and 4 ashtrays	180.00

Creamer, Chintz, pedestal	25.00
Creamer, Nocturne, Colonial shape, wide	15.00
Cup and Saucer, Spray	8.00
Cup and Saucer, Strawberry Sundae	5.00
Demitasse Cup and Saucer, Brittany	40.00
Demitasse Cup and Saucer, Crab Apple	30.00
Dinner Service, Cherry Bounce, 45 pcs.	200.00
Dinner Service, Quaker Apple, service for 4	150.00
Eggcup, Rock Rose	20.00
Eggcup, Sungold #2	15.00
Flat Soup, Nocturne, Colonial shape, 8" d.	15.00
Fruit Bowl, Buttercup, 6" d	10.00
Fruit Bowl, Nocturne, Colonial shape, 5¼"	5.00
Gravy Boat, Greenbriar	10.00
Gravy Boat, matching underplate, Mardi Gras	20.00
Jug, Chick	100.00
Pie Baker, Mardi Gras	25.00
Pitcher, French Peasant, 8¼" h	375.00
Plate, Christmas Tree, 10" d	70.00
Plate, Mardi Gras, 9½" d	3.00
Plate, Red Barn, 9" d	22.00
Plate, Sunflower, 10" d.	10.00
Platter, Folklore, 13½" d.	8.00
Platter, Rooster	100.00
Relish, French Peasant, leaf shape	100.00
Relish, Nove Rose, deep, shell shape	45.00
Salad Bowl, French Peasant	125.00
Salt and Pepper Shakers, pr, Rooster, toe flake	90.00
Server, French Peasant, handled	100.00
Soup Bowl, Cherries	5.00
Soup Bowl, Poinsettia, lug handle	5.00
Sugar, Rustic Plaid	5.00
Sugar, Daffodil	12.00
Teapot, Champagne Pink	100.00
Teapot, Fantasia, Skyline shape	65.00
Teapot, Yellow Nocturne	15.00
Tidbit Tray, Apple and Pear, 3 tiers	40.00
Vase, French Peasant, handled	70.00
Vase, Gladys, boot shape, 8" h	100.00
Vase, Moon Indigo	80.00

BOEHM PORCELAIN

Edward and Helen Boehm founded The Boehm Studio in 1950. It quickly became famous for its superb hand–painted, highly detailed sculptures of animals, birds, and flowers. Boehm also licensed his artwork to manufacturers of collector plates.

Boehm porcelains are included in the collections of over 130 museums and institutions throughout the world. Many U.S. presidents have used Boehm porcelains as gifts for visiting Heads of States.

Collectors' Club: Boehm Porcelain Society, PO Box 5051, Trenton, NJ 08638.

Blue Heron, #200–19	$ 375.00
Blue Jays, #466	5,000.00
California Quail, #407, pr	1,800.00
Capped Chickadee, #438, 9"	475.00
Crested Flycatcher, baby, #458C	175.00
Daisies, #3002	900.00

Plate, Briar Patch, 10½" d, $8.00.

Downy Woodpeckers, #427 . . . . **1,000.00**
Fledgling Eastern Bluebird, #442 . . . . **125.00**
Goldfinch, thistle, #457. . . . . **1,000.00**
Kingfisher, #449, 6" h. **140.00**
Oven Bird, 10" h **750.00**
Pascali Rose, #30093 . . . . **1,500.00**
Ring Neck Pheasants, #409 . . . . **850.00**
Robin, baby, #4375, 3½" h. **125.00**
Song Sparrow, #400–59 . . . . **500.00**
Tumbler Pigeons, #416 . . . . **750.00**

BOOKENDS

There was a bookend renaissance in the period between 1920 and 1950. Virtually no subject or theme was overlooked by the manufacturers of cast iron, base metal, and plaster bookends. A collection limited solely to bookends with a sailing ship motif can easily exceed 100 examples.

Theme is the most important value consideration. In most cases, the manufacturer is unknown, either because the bookends are unmarked or research information about the mark is unavailable. Be alert to basement workshop examples. Collectors prefer mass-produced examples.

References: Douglas Congdon–Martin, *Figurative Cast Iron: A Collector's Guide,* Schiffer Publishing, 1994; Robert Seecof, Donna Lee Seecof and Louis Kuritsky, *Bookend Revue,* Schiffer Publishing, 1996.

Note: All bookends are priced as pairs.

Boy With Sailboat and Dog, Frankart . . . . **$ 250.00**
Dancing Nudes, Art Deco, bronze, floral design base,
   green patina, mkd "Schroedin, Solid Bronze", 5" h . . . **180.00**
Flower Urn, soapstone. **90.00**
Geometric Design, Art Deco, black, rose, and white
   marble, 6½" h **80.00**
Golfers, Art Deco, brass, mkd "Art Brass Co. N. Y.,"
   1920s, 3¾" h, 4½" w **300.00**
Lady Godiva, crystal, K. R. Haley Glassware Co, 6" h **45.00**
Sailboats, Bronze Art, 7" h **225.00**
Scottie Dogs, metal, brass finish, Frankart, 7" h **230.00**
Setter, pointing, cast iron, black, c1920, 4½ x 7½" **120.00**
Swordfish, pressed wood **18.00**
Terriers, chrome plated, 4¼" h **100.00**
Unicorn and Lion, brass, 6" h, 5½" l **50.00**

BOOKS

Given the millions of books available, what does a collector do? The answer is specialize. Each edition of this price guide will focus on one or more specialized collecting categories.

This edition focuses on limited edition modern press and illustrated books. Values for many of these titles are determined more by the perceived value of the individuals who illustrated them than they are by the value attached to the press that printed them.

References: Allen Ahearn, *Book Collecting: A Comprehensive Guide,* G. P. Putnam's Sons, 1995; Allen and Patricia Ahearn, *Collected Books: The Guide To Values,* F. P. Putnam's Sons, 1997; *American Book Prices Current,* published annually; Ron Barlow

and Ray Reynolds, *The Insider's Guide to Old Books, Magazines, Newspapers, Trade Catalogs,* Windmill Publishing, 1995; Ian C. Ellis, *Book Finds: How to Find, Buy and Sell Used and Rare Books,* Berkley Publishing, 1996; *Huxford's Old Book Value Guide, Ninth Edition,* Collector Books, 1997; Marie Tedford and Pat Goudey, *The Official Price Guide to Old Books,* House of Collectibles, 1997; John Wade, *Tomart's Price Guide to 20th Century Books,* Tomart Publications, 1994; Nancy Wright, *Books: Identification and Price Guide,* Avon Books, 1993.

Periodicals: *AB Bookman's Weekly,* PO Box AB, Clifton, NJ 07015; *The Book Collector's Magazine,* PO Box 65166, Tucson, AZ 85728; *Book Source Monthly,* 2007 Syosett Dr, PO Box 567, Cazenovia, NY 1303.

Collectors' Club: Antiquarian Booksellers Assoc of America, 50 Rockefeller Plaza, New York, NY 10020.

Andersen, Hans Christian, *The Complete Andersen,*
   New York, 1949, translated by Jean Hersholt, illus
   by Fritz Kredel, 6 vol, 8vo, cloth–backed boards,
   sgd by Hersholt and Kredel. . . . . **$ 70.00**
Bradbury, Ray, *Fahrenheit 451,* illus by Joe Mugnaini,
   New York, 1982, tall 8vo, aluminum boards, slip-
   case, 1 of 2,000 numbered copies sgd by Bradbury
   and Mugnaini **400.00**
Carroll, Lewis, *Through the Looking–Glass and What
   Alice Found There • The Hunting of the Snark: An
   Agony in Eight Fits,* Berkeley, 1983, illus by Barry
   Moser, folio, cloth and wrappers within cloth
   chemise in publisher's cloth slipcase **260.00**
Flanner, Janet, *The Stronger Sex,* Vertes, Marcel, New
   York, 1941, 24 mounted plates by Vertes, many
   hand–colored, folio, pictorial cloth soiled, spine
   ends worn, owner's stamp on endpaper. **260.00**
Grahame, Kenneth, *The Wind in the Willows,* New
   York, 1940, mounted color plates, 4to, ¼ cloth,
   brown paper outer wrapper, slipcase, one of 2,020
   numbered copies sgd by designer Bruce Rogers. **460.00**
Hagedorn, Edward, *Ten Nudes,* San Francisco:
   Peregrine Press, 1952, 10 white–on–black etchings, folio, contents loose in cloth folder as issued,
   one of 86 numbered copies, sgd by Hagedorn. **430.00**
Hammett, Dashiell, *The Maltese Falcon,* Arion Press,
   San Francisco, 1983, numerous photographic illus,
   4to, ¼ morocco with morocco onlay of falcon on
   front cover, slipcase, one of 400 copies. **345.00**
Hawthorne, Nathaniel, *A Wonder Book,* Rackham,
   Arthur, New York, 1922, 24 full–page color illus,
   4to, later red morocco gilt, first American ed with
   Rackham illus **175.00**
Henry, O., *The Voice of the City and Other Stories,*
   illus by George Grosz, New York, 1935, 4to, cloth,
   slipcase, sgd by Grosz **230.00**
Hunter, Dard, *Paper–Making in the Classroom,*
   Peoria: Manual Arts Press, 1931, numerous photo
   illus, 8vo, cloth slightly soiled. **125.00**
Joyce, James, *Ulysses,* New York, 1935, etchings and
   illus by Henri Matisse, 4to, cloth, board slipcase
   worn, one of 1,500 numbered copies sgd by
   Matisse **3,000.00**

Maugham, Somerset, *Of Human Bondage,* New York, 1938, 16 etchings by John Sloan, 2 vol, 8vo, linen cov boards, slipcase, spines faded, ends worn **230.00**

Melville, Herman, *Moby Dick; or, the Whale,* Arion Press, San Francisco, 1979, engraved illus by Barry Moser, each sgd, folio, full blue morocco gilt, cloth slipcase, inscribed and sgd, one of 265 numbered copies sgd by Moser **1,500.00**

More, Thomas, *Utopia,* New York, 1934, illus, 8vo, vellum–backed dec boards, slipcase, sgd by designer Bruce Rogers **60.00**

Poe, Edgar Allan, *The Mask of the Red Death,* Aquarius Press, Baltimore, 1969, 16 color litho plates by Frederico Castellon, folio, 1/4 cloth, slipcase, one of 500 numbered copies sgd by Castellon **175.00**

Pyle, Howard, *Howard Pyle's Book of the American Spirit,* New York, 1923, illus by Pyle, folio, 1/4 cloth, dj chipped, 1st ed **70.00**

Sendak, Maurice, *Where the Wild Things Are,* illus by Sendak, New York, 1963, oblong 4to, pictorial boards, dj, sgd by Sendak on half–title **230.00**

Shahn, Ben, *The Alphabet of Creation,* New York: The Spiral Press, 1954, 4to, cloth, slipcase split, one of 50 copies with sgd ink drawing by Shahn **700.00**

Szyk, Arthur, *The Story of Joseph and His Brothers,* illus by Szyk, edited by Jean Jersholt, 4to, cloth, sgd by Hersholt **201.00**

Wilder, Thornton, *The Bridge of San Luis Rey,* Kent, Rockwell, New York, 1929, illus by Rockwell Kent, 4to, pictorial cloth, slipcase defective, one of 1,100 numbered copies sgd by Wilder and Kent **175.00**

BOOKS, CHILDREN'S

Although children's books date as early as the 15th century, it was the appearance of lithographed books from firms such as McLoughlin Brothers and series books for boys and girls at the turn of the 20th century that popularized the concept. The Bobbsey Twins, Nancy Drew, the Hardy Boys, and Tom Swift delighted numerous generations of readers.

The first Newberry Medal for the most distinguished children's book was issued in 1922. In 1938 the Caldecott Medal was introduced to honor the children's picture book.

Like collectors of their adult counterparts, children's book collectors specialize. Award winning books, ethnic books, first editions, mechanical books, and rag books are just a few of the specialized categories.

References: E. Lee Baumgarten (comp.), *Price Guide and Bibliographic Checklist for Children's & Illustrated Books for the Years 1880–1960, 1996 Edition,* published by author, 1995; David and Virginia Brown, *Whitman Juvenile Books: Reference & Value Guide,* Collector Books, 1997; Diane McClure Jones and Rosemary Jones, *Collector's Guide to Children's Books, 1850 to 1950: Identification & Values,* Collector Books, 1997; E. Christian Mattson and Thomas B. Davis, *A Collector's Guide to Hardcover Boys' Series Books,* published by authors, 1996; Edward S. Postal, *Price Guide & Bibliography to Children's & Illustrated Books,* M. & P. Press, 1994.

Periodicals: *Book Source Monthly,* 2007 Syossett Dr, PO Box 467, Cazenovia, NY 13035; *Mystery & Adventure Series Review,* PO Box 3488, Tucson, AZ 85722; *Yellowback Library,* PO Box 36172, Des Moines, IA 50315.

Newsletters: *The Authorized Edition Newsletter,* RR1, Box 73, Machias, ME 04654; *Martha's KidLit Newsletter,* PO Box 1488, Ames, IA 50010.

Collectors' Club: The Society of Phantom Friends, 4100 Cornelia Way, North Highlands, CA 95660.

Note: There are numerous collectors' clubs for individual authors. Consult the *Encyclopedia of Associations* at your local library for further information.

Anderson, Hans Christian, *The Nightingdale,* Nancy Ekholm Burkert illus, Harper & Row, 1965, 1st ed, dj, 33 pgs . . . . **$ 25.00**

Anglun, Joan Walsh, *A Friend Is Someone Who Likes You,* Harcourt, Brace & World, 1958, 1st ed **12.00**

Appleton, Victor, *Tom Swift Among the Fire Fighters,* Grossett & Dunlap, 1921, 214 pgs **10.00**

Blos, Joan W., *A Gathering of Days,* Scribners, 1979, 1980 Newberry Medal, 1st ed, dj, 145 pgs **20.00**

Chadwick, Lester, *Baseball Joe, Champion of the League,* Cupples & Leon, 1925, dj, 246 pgs **12.00**

Chapman, Allen, *Ralph and the Missing Mail Pouch,* Grosset & Dunlap, 1924, dj, 242 pgs **8.00**

Clyde, Geraldine, *The Jolly Jump–ups Number Book,* McLoughlin, 1950, 6 pop–ups **35.00**

De Angeli, Marguerite, *Ted and Nina Have a Happy Rainy Day,* Doubleday, 1936, 1st ed, dj **25.00**

De Jong, Meindert, *The Wheel on the School,* Maurice Sendak illus, Harper, 1954, 1st ed, dj, 298 pgs **30.00**

Deming, Richard, Whitman TV Series, *Dragnet,* Whitman, 1957, 282 pgs **3.00**

Dickey, James, *Tucky the Hunter,* Marie Angel illus, Crown, 1978, dj, 48 pgs. **15.00**

Disney, Walt, *Mickey Mouse Takes a Vacation,* Franklin Watts, puppet book, 1976 . . . . **15.00**

Dixon, F. W., Hardy Boys Series, *Secret of the Caves,* Grossett & Dunlap, 1920s **15.00**

Dixon, Franklin W., Ted Scott Series, *Following the Sun Shadow,* Grosset & Dunlap, 1932, dj, 215 pgs **5.00**

Ernest, Edward, *The Animated Circus Book,* Julian Wehr, Animateons, Saalfield, 1943 . . . . **35.00**

Garis, Howard R., *Uncle Wiggily's Fortune,* Elmer Rache illus, Platt & Munic, 1942, 186 pgs. **8.00**

Graham, Lynda, *Pinky Marie,* Ann Kirn illus, Saalfield, 1939, wraps **25.00**

Gray, William, *Dick and Jane,* Scott, Foresman, 1930, wraps, 40 pgs. **18.00**

Heinlein, Robert, *Space Cadet,* Scribner, 1948, 1st ed. . . . **45.00**

Keene, Carolyn, Nancy Drew Series, *Bungalow Mystery,* 1930 . . . . **20.00**

Lanier, Sydney, *King Arthur and His Knights of the Round Table,* 1947. . . . . **20.00**

Maybee, Bette Lou, *Barbie's Fashion Success,* Random House, 1962, 188 pgs. **10.00**

Meeker, Charles H., *Folk Tales From the Far East,* 1927 . . . **30.00**

Newberry, Clare Turlay, *Mittens,* 1936, dj **50.00**

Norton, Mary, *The Borrowers Afield,* Beth and Joe
Drush illus, Harcourt, 1955, 1st ed, dj, 193 pgs. **35.00**

O'Day, Dean, *Shirley Temple Story Book,* Corrine
and Bill Bailey illus, Saalfield, 1935, dj, 106 pgs **30.00**

Pease, Howard, *The Mystery on Telegraph Hill,*
Doubleday, 1961, 1st ed, dj, 216 pgs **12.00**

Rip Van Winkle, McLoughlin, linen cov **30.00**

Sidney, Margaret, *Five Little Peppers and How They
Grew,* Grossett & Dunlap, 1947. . . . . **20.00**

Vandegriff, Peggy, *Dy–Dee Dolls Days,* Rand
McNally, 1937. . . . . **15.00**

West, Jerry, *The Happy Hollisters and the Ice
Carnival,* Doubleday, 1958, dj, 180 pgs. **3.00**

BOTTLE OPENERS

In an age of pull–tab and twist–off tops, many younger individuals have never used a bottle opener. Figural bottle openers, primarily those made of cast iron, are the most commonly collected type. They were extremely popular from the late 1940s through the early 1960s.

Church keys, a bottle opener with a slightly down–turned "V" shaped end, have a strong following, especially when the opener's surface has some form of advertising. Wall–mounted units, especially examples with soda pop advertising, also are popular.

Collectors' Clubs: Figural Bottle Opener Collectors Club, 117 Basin Hill Rd, Duncannon, PA 17020; Just For Openers, 3712 Sunningdale Way, Durham, NC 27707.

Bear Head, cast iron, wall mount, black highlights,
John Wright Co, 3⁷/₈ x 3¹/₁₆". . . . . **$ 90.00**

Bulldog, 1947, 4" h **125.00**

Canada Goose, head extended to ground, brown and
black markings, green base, Wilton Products. **50.00**

Clown, brass, wall mount, white bowtie with red
polka dots, bald head, mkd "495, John Wright
Co," 4¹/₈ x 4". **700.00**

Cowboy, mkd "San Antonio, Texas," 4⁷/₈" h **225.00**

Daschund, brass **50.00**

DoDo Bird, cast iron, cream, black highlights, red
beak, 2³/₄" h **150.00**

Drunk, leaning against sign post, mkd "Baltimore,
MD" **10.00**

Elephant, sitting on hind legs, trunk up, mouth open,
cast iron, flat, pink, black base **80.00**

False Teeth, cast iron, wall mount, flesh gums, off
white teeth, 2³/₈" h, 3³/₈" w **100.00**

Hand, pointing finger, diecut metal, Effinger Beer adv **15.00**

Mr. Dry, cast iron, wall mount, man wearing black
top hat, red hair, blue bags under eyes, red lips,
flesh–tone face, Wilton Products, 5¹/₂" h, 3¹/₂" w. **125.00**

Pretzel, brass. **25.00**

Sea Gull, cast iron, cream, black, and gray highlights,
red beak, orange feet, gray and black stump, John
Wright Co, 3³/₁₆" h **35.00**

Sleeping Mexican, leaning on cactus, green hat, yellow serape, red shirt, green cactus, brown pants,
yellow base, Wilton Products, 2¹³/₁₆" h **225.00**

BOY SCOUTS

William D. Boyce is the father of Boy Scouting in America. Boyce was instrumental in transferring the principles of Baden-Powell's English scouting movement to the United States, merging other American boy organizations into the Scouting movement, and securing a charter from Congress for the Boy Scouts of America in 1916.

Scouting quickly spread nationwide. Manufacturers developed products to supply the movement. Department stores vied for the rights to sell Scouting equipment.

The first national jamboree in America was held in Washington, D.C., in 1937. Patch trading and collecting began in the early 1950s. The Order of the Arrow, national Scouting centers, e.g., Philmont, and local council activities continually generate new collectible materials.

Periodicals: *Fleur–de–Lis,* 5 Dawes Ct, Novato, CA 94947; *Scout Memorabilia,* PO Box 1121, Manchester, NH 03105.

Collectors' Club: National Scouting Collectors Society, 806 E Scott St, Tuscola, IL 61953.

Badge, hat, Scoutmaster's, silvered, 1st class emblem,
dark green enameled ground, 1920, ⁷/₈". . . . . **$ 35.00**

Belt Loop, brass slide, detailed image of profile of
standing Scout playing reveille on trumpet,
attached metal keychain and fob loop, c1930s **15.00**

Binoculars, Official Boy Scouts, black molded plas-
tic, carrying strap, orig box, 1950s **45.00**

Book, *Handbook for Patrol Leaders,* 1929. . . . . **20.00**

Book, *Official Boy Scout Handbook,* 9th edition **5.00**

Booklet, *Boy Scouts National Jamboree,* 106 pgs,
1937. . . . . **35.00**

Booklet, *Boy Scouts Merit Badge Series Wood-
working,* c1930s, set of 4 . . . . **12.00**

Compass, Silva, clear plastic base. **12.00**

First Aid Kit, Johnson and Johnson, green cover, New
York City, orig contents. **18.00**

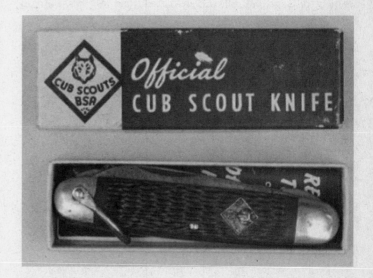

Pocketknife, Cub Scout, Camillus, blue handles, 3 blades, orig box, BSA #1885, $10.00.

Fishing Pass, National Jamboree, State of PA, 1977 . . . . 5.00
Hat, National Jamboree, 1993 . . . . 5.00
Medal, Pinewood Derby, car on medallion 2.00
Medal, Presidents Trail, Washington, DC. 5.00
Mug, National Jamboree, 1981 . . . . 5.00
Neckerchief Slide, 13th World Jamboree, blue and
   white enameled badge on brown leather slide,
   1971 . . . . 28.00
Patch, Eagle Scout rank, oval, embroidered design,
   1950s, unused 45.00
Patch, National Jamboree, design printed in full color
   on canvas, 1950, unused 30.00
Patch, New York World's Fair Service Campback,
   design embroidered on orange twill, cut edge,
   1940, unused. 45.00
Patch, Philmont Scout Ranch, Cimarron, NM, trail
   crew, arrowhead, design embroidered on twill, cut
   edge, unused 45.00
Patch, Scouting Rounds A Guy Out 2.00
Pennant, felt, orange and black, Philmont Scout
   Ranch 15.00
Pin, collar, Council Executive, silvered wreath, eagle,
   and outline, red enameled ground, ⁷/₈" d 25.00
Ring, sterling silver, silver trefoil center on black
   enamel, 1930–40 . . . . 15.00
Sleeping Bag, tan cloth, printed official seal, used 20.00
Telescope, Official Boy Scouts, 6X, aluminum and
   plastic, #1994, orig box, 1950s. 40.00
Watch Fob, scout playing bugle, crossed flags in
   background, crossed rifle and staff in foreground,
   inscribed "Boy Scout," strap, dark finish, 1¼" 75.00

BOYD CRYSTAL ART GLASS

Boyd Crystal Art Glass, Cambridge, Ohio, traces its heritage back to Bernard C. Boyd and Zackery Thomas Boyd, two glass makers who worked for a number of companies in the Cambridge area. In 1964 Elizabeth Degenhart asked Zack Boyd to assume the management of Degenhart Glass. When Zack died in 1968, Bernard assumed leadership of the company.

In 1978, Bernard C. Boyd and his son, Bernard F., purchased Degenhart Glass. Initially working with the 50 molds acquired from Degenhart, the Boyds began making pieces in a host of new colors. Eventually, John Bernard, son of Bernard F., joined the company. Today Boyd Crystal Art Glass has over 200 molds available for its use including a number of molds purchased from other glass companies such as Imperial.

The Boyds document all production molds and colors. Collectors keep track of new issues through *Boyd's Crystal Art Glass,* a newsletter published by the company (PO Box 127, 1203 Morton Ave, Cambridge, OH 43725).

Reference: *Boyd's Crystal Art Glass: The Tradition Continues,* Boyd's Crystal Art Glass, n.d.

Collectors' Club: Boyd Art Glass Collectors Guild, PO Box 52, Hatboro, PA 19040.

Bingo Deer, figurine, Azure Blue . . . . $ 10.00
Bingo Deer, figurine, Indian Orange 10.00

Hand, Carmel, $8.00.

Boyd Airplane, figurine, Classic Black. 15.00
Bull Dog Head, figurine, Ice Green 12.00
Chuckles the Clown, figurine, Baby Blue 10.00
Chuckles the Clown, figurine, Vaseline 10.00
Debbie Duck, figurine, Snow 8.00
Duck, salt, Buckeye 8.00
Duck, salt, Spinnaker Blue 8.00
Fuzzy Bear, figurine, Country Red 10.00
Fuzzy Bear, figurine, Rosewood 12.00
Grape, card holder, Classic Black Slag 8.00
Grape, card holder, Primrose 8.00
Joey, figurine, leaping pony, Persimmon 15.00
Louise, doll, Golden Delight 10.00
Louise, doll, Sunburst 15.00
Owl, figurine, Crown Tuscan 10.00
Owl, figurine, Dawn 10.00
Owl, figurine, Heather 10.00
Owl, figurine, Teal Swirl 15.00
Pooch, figurine, Confetti 20.00
Pooch, figurine, Marigold 10.00
Sammy the Squirrel, figurine, Cashmere Pink 8.00
Santa, bell, Olde Lyme 15.00
Swan, master salt, Lilac, 4½" h 15.00
Swan, master salt, Spinnaker Blue 15.00
Willie the Mouse, figurine, Christmas Willie, 1991 . . . . . . 15.00

BRASTOFF, SASCHA

In 1948, Sascha Brastoff, under the financial sponsorship of Winthrop Rockefeller, established a small pottery on Speulveda Boulevard in West Los Angeles. Brastoff's focus was that of designer. A group of skilled technicians and decorators gave life to his designs.

Brastoff was at the cutting edge of modern design. Figurines were introduced in the early 1950s to a line that included ashtrays, bowls, and vases. In 1953 a new studio was opened at 11520 West Olympic Boulevard. In 1954 production began on the first of ten fine china dinnerware lines.

Although Brastoff left the studio in 1963 as a result of nervous exhaustion, the company survived another decade thanks to the inspired leadership of plant manager Gerold Schwartz. After a period of recuperation, Brastoff pursued a career in free-lance design and marketing.

Reference: Steve Conti, A. Dewayne Bethany and Bill Seay, *Collector's Encyclopedia of Sascha Brastoff: Identification & Values,* Collector Books, 1995.

Ashtray, Aztec Jumping Horse, C21, 8" w	$ 45.00
Ashtray, Chinese, enameled, set of 3	70.00
Ashtray, Eskimo, dome, Alaska line, 6"	65.00
Ashtray, Jewel Bird, 7" l	40.00
Ashtray, log cabin, igloo shape, Alaska line	55.00
Bank, pig	275.00
Bookends, pr, horse	650.00
Bowl, Chi Chi Bird, 8" d	65.00
Bowl, Grapes, enameled dec, crazing, 20" d	50.00
Bowl, Rooftops, F45, 6 x 11"	65.00
Candle Holder, Aztec, 10" h	125.00
Figure, Kissing Horse	300.00
Figure, Owl, resin, green, 14" h	350.00
Figure, Pelican	400.00
Flowerpot, Jewel Bird, 6" h	65.00
Medallion, sun face	450.00
Pitcher, igloos, Alaska line, 10½"	95.00
Plate, fruit, 11" d	65.00
Plate, pagoda, curled lip, 12" d	85.00
Platter, rect, wavy rim with one large green and white leaf, shaded deep green ground, glossy finish, 17¾" l, 14" w	250.00
Salt and Pepper Shakers, pr, Eskimo, Alaska line	35.00
Sculpture, Nude, metal, 6" h	400.00
Switchplate, horse head design, brass, 10" h	120.00
Tile, black ground, white, rust, and gold leaves, sgd "Sascha B," 7 x 9"	100.00
Vase, Jewel Bird, F20, 6" h	40.00
Vase, Rooftops, F20, 6" h	40.00
Wall Plaque, faun mask, bronze, blue, and gold, M31, 13" h	750.00

BRAYTON LAGUNA CERAMICS

Durline E. Brayton founded Brayton Laguna, located in South Laguna Beach, California, in 1927. Hand-crafted earthenware dinnerwares were initially produced. The line soon expanded to include figurines, flowerpots, tea tiles, vases, and wall plates.

In 1938 Brayton Laguna was licensed to produce Disney figurines. Webb, Durlin's second wife, played an active role in design and management. A period of prosperity followed.

By the end of World War II, Brayton Laguna ceramics were being sold across the U.S. and abroad. In the early and mid–1960s the company fell on hard times, the result of cheap foreign imports and lack of inspired leadership. The pottery closed in 1968.

Reference: Jack Chipman, *Collector's Encyclopedia of California Pottery,* Collector Books, 1992, 1995 value update.

Canister, Provincial	$ 50.00
Cookie Jar, Swedish woman	500.00
Cookie Jar, Matilda	500.00
Creamer, calico cat	55.00
Figure, sitting clown	40.00
Figure, fighting stallions, avocado, price for pair	150.00
Figure, girl and doll	100.00
Figure, grouse	70.00

Figure, purple cow and calf, price for pair	225.00
Figure, swan	70.00
Figure, Wheezy with jump rope	75.00
Figure, zebra	70.00
Flower Holder, Sally, 6¾" h	20.00
Planter, girl and two wolfhounds, 11" h	125.00
Planter, maiden	40.00
Planter, wheelbarrow	35.00
Salt and Pepper Shakers, pr, black peasants, 5" h	28.00
Salt and Pepper Shakers, pr, calico cat with dog	45.00
Salt and Pepper Shakers, pr, granny	65.00
Vase, figural blackamoor, polychrome turban, 14" h	275.00

BREWERIANA

Breweriana is a generic term used to describe any object from advertising to giveaway premiums, from bar paraphernalia to beer cans associated with the brewing industry. Objects are divided into pre– and post–Prohibition material.

Breweries were one of the first industries established by early American settlers. Until Prohibition, the market was dominated by small to medium size local breweries. When Prohibition ended, a number of brands, e.g., Budweiser, established themselves nationwide. Advertising, distribution, and production costs plus mergers resulted in the demise of most regional breweries by the 1970s.

Imported beers arrived in America in the 1960s, often contracting with American breweries to produce their product. In the 1980s and 1990s America experienced a brewing renaissance as the number of micro-breweries continues to increase.

Collectors tend to be regional and brand loyal. Because of a strong circuit of regional Breweriana shows and national and regional clubs, objects move quickly from the general marketplace into the specialized Breweriana market.

References: George J. Baley, *Back Bar Breweriana: A Guide To Advertising Beer Statues and Beer Shelf Signs,* L–W Book Sales, 1992, 1994 value update; *Beer Cans: 1932–1975,* L–W Book Sales, 1976, 1995 value update; Herb and Helen Haydock, *The World of Beer Memorabilia,* Collector Books, 1997; Bill Mugrage, *The Official Price Guide to Beer Cans, Fifth Edition,* House of Collectibles, 1993; Gary Straub, *Collectible Beer Trays With Value Guide,* Schiffer Publishing, 1995; Robert Swinnich, *Contemporary Beer Neon Signs,* L–W Book Sales, 1994; Dale P. Van Wieren, *American Breweries II,* East Coast Breweriana Assoc, 1995.

Periodicals: *All About Beer,* 1627 Marion Ave, Durham, NC 27705; *Suds 'n' Stuff,* 4765 Galacia Way, Oceanside, CA 92056.

Collectors' Clubs: American Breweriana Assoc, Inc, PO Box 11157, Pueblo, CO 81001; East Coast Breweriana Assoc, 3712 Sunningdale Way, Durham, NC 27707; National Assoc of Breweriana Advertising, 2343 Met–To–Wee Ln, Milwaukee, WI 53226.

Ashtray, Coors, porcelain, white, 6" d	$ 5.00
Bottle, Beckers Beer, Evanston, WY	10.00
Bottle, Enterprise Brewing Co, 1qt	8.00
Can, Blatz Old Heidelberg Castle, Milwaukee, WI, cone top, 12 oz	35.00
Can, Coors, Golden, CO, flat top, 7 oz	5.00
Can, Country Club Beer, cone top	25.00

Tray, Hornung Beer, Jacob Hornung Brewing, Philadelphia, PA, 12" d, $65.00.

Can, Milwaukee's Best, Miller, Milwaukee, WI,
  pull top, 12 oz. **5.00**
Coaster, Burger Brewery, Cincinnati, OH, octagonal,
  red and green, 4" **10.00**
Coaster, Gibbons, Wilkes–Barre, PA, red and green,
  4" d **15.00**
Coaster, Ye Tavern Brew, Lafayette Brewery, Lafayette,
  IN, red, yellow, and black, 3" d **5.00**
Corkscrew, Anheuser Busch **75.00**
Display, Hamm's Beer, light–up roofed panel, picture
  changes from waterfalls to camping scenes,
  18 x 31". **375.00**
Foam Scraper, Piel's, metal, 2 dwarfs holding keg **30.00**
Globe, Miller High Life, gas globe style, 2 glass
  inserts in plastic frame **45.00**
Label, Old Mountaineer Beer, Pioneer Brewing Co,
  ½ gal. **25.00**
Label, Old Reading Cream Ale, green, 2 barkeep-
  ers above product name, 12 oz. **12.00**
Label, Old Style Brew, Schultz & Hilgers J Brewery,
  12 oz. **12.00**
Pinback Button, Miller High Life Beer, multicolored **25.00**
Poster, Schlitz Beer, festival **20.00**
Salt and Pepper Shakers, pr, Coors, wooden, barrel
  shape **40.00**
Sign, Copenhagen Castle Brand Beer, light–up,
  reverse painted glass **70.00**
Sign, Krueger Cream Ale, molded plastic, green and
  white tankard with gold lid. **35.00**
Statue, Pabst Blue Ribbon, girl's face, 1957 . . . . **175.00**
Stein, pewter, Bonn relief scenes, Besetzlich
  Geschutz, F. M. & N. Co, 8" h **40.00**
Stein, porcelain, brown and white, golfer in knickers,
  lid with porcelain inlay scene of Brooklyn Bridge,
  bottom mkd "Paris, France O'Hara Dial Co.,
  Waltham Massachusetts U.S.A.," 5" h **550.00**

Stein, stoneware, #2628, bowlers beneath trees in
  relief, inlaid lid dec with 9 pins and ball, pewter
  bowling pin thumbrest, Mettlach, 8¼" h **400.00**
Tap Handle, Hamm's Beer, chrome, ball shape, red,
  white, and gold enamel insert **50.00**
Tray, Ebling's Celebrated Beers, Ebling's Brewing,
  New York, NY, rect, factory scene **310.00**
Tray, Jacob Leinenkugel Brewery, Chippewa Falls, WI,
  founder's portrait above factory, "1867–1977,
  110th Anniversary". **20.00**

AUCTION PRICES

Fink's Off The Wall Auctions, October 1996. Prices include a
10% buyer's premium.

Clock, Iroquois Beer • Ale, International Brewery,
  2 pc, reverse glass globe, 1950s, 15 x 4". **700.70**
Horn Glasses, Michelob Beer, Anheuser–Busch, St
  Louis, MO, red painted label, 8" h, price for pair. . . . **16.50**
Necktie, Schlitz Beer, Schlitz Brewing, Milwaukee,
  WI, 1950s **18.70**
Neon Light, Bud, Anheuser–Busch, St Louis, MO,
  red light, 11 x 18" **51.70**
Sign, Ballantine Draught Beer, Ballantine Brewing,
  Newark, NJ, pressed wood, 2 glasses, "The First
  One...Suggests Another," dated 1951, 10 x 14" **27.50**
Sign, Red Top Beer, Red Top Brewing, Cincinnati,
  OH, light–up, plastic on composite backing, spin-
  ning top shape, 23 x 15 x 4". **220.00**
Statue, back bar, Schmidt's of Philadelphia Beer Ale,
  Schmidt's Brewing, Philadelphia, PA, white metal,
  painted, 9" h **42.90**
Tray, Kaier's Beer Ale Porter, Kaier Brewing,
  Mahanoy City, PA, rect, bright red, black, white,
  and gold, 13 x 10½" **130.90**

BREYER HORSES

When founded in 1943, the Breyer Molding Company of Chicago
manufactured custom designed thermoset plastics. When WWII
ended, the company shifted production to injection molded radio
and television housings. As a sideline, Breyer also produced a few
plastic animals based on designs sculpted by toolmaker Christian
Hess.

By 1958 the Breyer line contained a barnyard full of animals —
cats, cows, dogs, and horses. In 1959 the company introduced its
wood grain finish. Peter Stone headed the Breyer Animal Creations
division. By the end of the 1970s the sale of horses accounted for
more business than did the company's manufacturer of electronic
components.

Reeves International of New Jersey, a distributor of European
collectibles such as Britains and Corgi, acquired Breyer in 1984.
Manufacturing was moved to a state-of-the-art plant in New Jersey.

Periodical: *Hobby Horse News,* 5492 Tallapoosa Rd, Tallahassee,
FL 32303.

Newsletter: *The Model Horse Trader,* 143 Mercer Way, Upland,
CA 91786.

Collectors' Club: Breyer Collectors Club, PO Box 189, Pequannock, NJ 07440.

Arabian in Costume, porcelain	$ 200.00
Clydesdale Stallion, #80	30.00
Family Arabian Foal, #909, woodgrain	40.00
Family Arabian Stallion, #907, woodgrain	55.00
Jumping Horse, with stone wall, #300	36.00
Lying Foal, #165, black Appaloosa	24.00
Misty, #20, Palomino Pinto	18.00
Mustang, #87, Buckskin, semi-rearing	28.00
Pacer #46, Dark Bay	32.00
Rearing Stallion, #183, Palomino	21.00
Running Mare, #848, brown Pinto	40.00
Scratching Foal, #168, black Appaloosa	30.00
Shetland Pony, #21, black and white Pinto	21.00
Thoroughbred Mare, Stablemate series, #5030	8.00
United States Equestrian Team, #3055, classic series, set of 3	45.00

BRITISH ROYALTY COMMEMORATIVES

British royalty commemoratives fall into two distinct groups: (1) souvenir pieces purchased during a monarch's reign and (2) pieces associated with specific events such as births, coronations, investitures, jubilees, marriages, or memorials. Items associated with reigning monarchs are the most popular.

Only five monarchs have reigned since 1920 — King George V (May 6, 1910 to January 20, 1936), King Edward VIII (January 20, 1936, abdicated December 10, 1936), King George VI (December 10, 1936 to February 6, 1952), and Queen Elizabeth II (February 6, 1952 to the present).

Marriages and divorces within British royalty during the last three decades have tested the loyalty of many royalty collectors. There is only uncertainty about the long-term value of Prince Charles and Lady Diana objects.

References: Susan and Al Bagdade, *Warman's English & Continental Pottery & Porcelain, Second Edition,* Wallace–Homestead, Krause Publications, 1991; Douglas H. Flynn and Alan H. Bolton, *British Royalty Commemoratives: 19th & 20th Century Royal Events in Britain Illustrated by Commemoratives, Value Guide With Photographs,* Schiffer Publishing, 1994; Eric Knowles, *Miller's Royal Memorabilia,* Reed Consumer Books, 1994, distributed by Antique Collectors' Club.

Bell, Prince William of Wales, bone china, multicolored Windsor Castle and flowers, gold ring handle, Aynsley, 1982	$ 28.00
Box, cov, Queen Elizabeth II Coronation, orb shape, purple and gold crown finial, hp color dec, Wedgwood & Co Ltd, 1953, 5" h	95.00
Box, cov, Silver Jubilee, jasperware, heart shape, white profile portraits and dec, royal blue ground, Wedgwood, 1977	120.00
Coaster, Charles and Diana's Royal Wedding, black and white portraits, color dec, cork backing,1981, 3½" d	10.00
Coin, Charles and Diana's Royal Wedding, silver tone metal, Queen Elizabeth II reverse, 1981, 1½" d	5.00

Cup and Saucer, Prince Charles Investiture as Prince of Wales, bone china, red Welsh dragon, gold trim, Liverpool Road Pottery, 1969	45.00
Decanter, Princess Beatrice, multicolor, gold highlights, white ground, gold stopper, Wade Porcelain, 1988, 8" h	120.00
Dish, Charles and Diana's Royal Wedding, sterling silver, raised portraits and Prince of Wales' feathers, names and dates around border, 1981, 3¾" d	125.00
Goblet, Queen Elizabeth II Silver Jubilee, 1977, price for pair	250.00
Jug, Queen Elizabeth II Coronation, Royal Worcester, 1953, 4½" h	100.00
Knife, Charles and Diana's Royal Wedding, sepia portraits in gold frames, multicolor flowers, mother of pearl reverse, 2 blades, 1981	28.00
Lighter, Queen Elizabeth II Coronation, 1953, Wedgwood	375.00
Loving Cup, King Edward VIII Abdication, Spode, 1936	1,000.00
Loving Cup, miniature, Prince Henry of Wales, bone china, multicolor roses, gold highlights, Royal Crown Derby, 1984, 1¼" h, 2¼" w	85.00
Medallion, Princess Anne and Captain Mark Phillips Wedding, molded pale pink portraits, pink frame, Royal Staffordshire, 1973, 3¼" h	65.00
Mug, Prince Andrew 21st Birthday, sepia portrait, multicolor dec, gold trim, 3½" h	70.00
Mug, King George VI and Queen Elizabeth Coronation, 1937	375.00
Paperweight, Charles and Diana Royal Wedding, white sulphide portraits, cobalt blue ground, CR Albret, France, 1981, 2¾" d	270.00
Pin Tray, Elizabeth II and Philip's Canada visit, sepia portrait, 1959, 4¼" d	35.00

Candy Tin, Queen Elizabeth II, St. Lawrence Seaway opening, multicolor, George W. Horner & Co., Ltd., 5" w, $25.00.

Plaque, Queen Elizabeth II and Prince Philip Silver
   Wedding Anniversary, 1972, Wedgwood, price for
   pair **240.00**
Plate, Queen Mother's 85th Birthday, bone china,
   color portrait and dec, gold rim, limited edition of
   2,000, Coalport, 1985, 10½" d **110.00**
Platter, King George V and Queen Mary Silver
   Jubilee, 1935 . . . . **60.00**
Tea Set, Elizabeth II Coronation, 3 pcs, Queensware,
   light blue relief portrait, white ground, Wedgwood,
   1953 . . . . **295.00**
Tea Towel, Princess Anne and Captain Mark Phillips
   Wedding, blue and gold, white dec, 1973, 30 x 19" . . . **25.00**
Tin, Prince Andrew and Sarah Ferguson Wedding,
   color portraits, red ground, silver trim, 1986, 6" h **25.00**

BRUSH POTTERY

Do not confuse the Brush Pottery of Roseville, Ohio, with that of
Brush–McCoy. They are two different companies.

Brush Pottery operated between 1925 and 1982. The company
made a wide range of ceramic wares, e.g., cookie jars, garden
wares, kitchen wares, patio wares, vases, etc. It also made utilitarian wares such as redware pots.

References: Sharon and Bob Huxford, *The Collector's
Encyclopedia of Brush–McCoy Pottery,* Collector Books, 1978,
1996 value update; Martha and Steve Sanford, *The Guide to
Brush–McCoy Pottery,* published by authors, 1992; Martha and
Steve Sanford, *Sanford's Guide to Brush–McCoy Pottery, Book 2,*
published by authors, 1996.

Ashtray, brown onyx . . . . **$ 30.00**
Bird Feeder, 8 x 7½" **60.00**
Candlestick, brown onyx, 7" h **40.00**
Casserole, KolorKraft, 7" h **55.00**
Clock, Jugtime, mkd "Jugtime Novelty Art Clock,
   Made In USA, Pat. Oct. 21, 1924, Brush McCoy
   Pottery Co., Zanesville, O", 7" h **175.00**
Cookie Jar, covered wagon **650.00**
Cookie Jar, sitting hippo **400.00**
Cookie Jar, old shoe **125.00**
Cookie Jar, owl, gray **80.00**
Cookie Jar, panda bear **250.00**
Cornucopia, berries and leaves, 4 x 6" **40.00**
Cuspidor, frog, 7½" **125.00**
Decanter, blue onyx, 9" h **140.00**
Doorstop, bug, 9" l **900.00**
Eggcup, chicken **18.00**
Figure, turtle, 7" l **65.00**
Jardiniere, cameo, raised design, 10" h **250.00**
Jardiniere, Indian motif, Kolorkraft, high glossy rose **150.00**
Mug, Peter Pan **100.00**
Teapot, earthenware, ivory **35.00**
Vase, Art Vellum, 6" h **30.00**
Vase, dancing girls, 5½" h **20.00**
Vase, Dutch shoe **25.00**
Vase, oriental motif, 7½" h **40.00**
Wall Pocket, fish **70.00**
Wall Pocket, grazing horse **100.00**

BUSINESS & OFFICE MACHINES

Reference: Thomas F. Haddock, *A Collector's Guide To Personal
Computers And Pocket Calculators,* Books Americana, Krause
Publications, 1993.

A B Dick, Edison Mimeoscope . . . . **$ 300.00**
A B Dick, Edison Model 1 . . . . **175.00**
A B Dick, Edison Model 75 . . . . **22.00**
American, adding machine **25.00**
Ediphone, dictating machine **40.00**
Ediphone, saving machine **40.00**
Ediphone, transcribing machine **40.00**
F & E, International Detective Agency, check writer **25.00**
Fell & Tarrant, adding machine **70.00**
Gem, notecard duplicator **12.00**
Golden Gem, adding machine **80.00**
Instant Checkwriter **20.00**
McCaskey, account register **42.00**
Moon Hopkins/Burrroughs, accounting machine **350.00**
Remington Model 23, bookkeeping machine **350.00**
Rotary Neostyle 8–F, duplicator **45.00**
Safeguard Checkwriter **20.00**
Star, adding machine **18.00**
Sundstrand, bookkeeping machine **20.00**
Type A, Model 10, transcribing machine **50.00**
Underwood, bookkeeping machine **400.00**

CALCULATORS

Calculators were first manufactured on a commercial scale in the
mid–19th century. Production of mechanical calculators was in
full swing by 1900. Two key 20th–century technological advances
were the introduction of electric motors early in the century and
the development of the electrical–mechanical calculator in the
1960s.

The first affordable electronic integrated circuit calculator
appeared in the early 1970s. Early pocket calculators cost hundreds of dollars. By the early 1980s the price of a basic pocket
calulator was $10 or less.

Many manufacturers such as HP and Texas Instruments made
dozens of different models. The first models tend to be the most
valuable.

References: Guy Ball and Bruce Flamm, *Collector's Guide to
Pocket Calculators,* Wilson/Barnett Publishing, 1997; Thomas F.
Haddock, *A Collector's Guide to Personal Computers and Pocket
Calculators,* Books Americana, Krause Publications, 1993; W.A.C.
Mier–Jadrzejowica, *A Guide to HP Handheld Calculators and
Computers, Second Edition,* Wilson/Barnett Publishing, 1996.

Collectors Clubs: International Assoc of Calculator Collectors
(IACC), 14561 Livingston St, Tustin, CA 92780; The Oughtred
Society (Slide Rules), 2160 Middlefield Rd, Palo Alto, CA
94301.

Adler 82M, c1974 . . . . **$ 45.00**
American–1776, red LED, made for bicentennial **35.00**
Brother 408AX, c1972 . . . . **45.00**
Commodore MM1 . . . . **65.00**

Craig 4504, purple LED **35.00**
Figural, cash register, 6 x 7" **35.00**
Figural, film roll, 1991 . . . . **25.00**
Figural, tape measure **20.00**
Hewlett Packard 19C, scientific function, program-
able **100.00**
Hewlett Packard 80 . . . . **60.00**
Mathbook 806L **40.00**
Panasonic 840 . . . . **65.00**
Radio Shack EC–231, Statesman Thin **30.00**
Rockwell 10R **15.00**
Rockwell 44RD, scientific function **40.00**
Sharp EL–8016 . . . . **15.00**
Texas Instruments SR-51 . . . . **40.00**
Toshiba BC–0804B **50.00**
Toy, clown, slide–open style **20.00**
Toy, Hello Kitty, fold–open style **15.00**
Toy, Math To Go **25.00**
Unisonic 890–A **10.00**
Vista Z48AA **35.00**

1929, H. Buch, Butcher and Dealer in Fresh and Smoked Meats, color litho illus, full pad, 12 x 18¼", $30.00.

CALENDARS

The 19th–century printing revolution made calendars accessible to everyone. As the century ended, calendars were a popular form of advertising giveaway and remained so through much of the 20th century. Cheesecake calendars, now an endangered species because of societal and political correctness, enjoyed a Golden Age between 1930 and the mid–1960s.

In the 1980s, the "art" or special theme calendar arrived on the scene. Moderately expensive when purchased new, they are ignored by most calendar collectors.

Most calendars are sold today because of their subject matter, the artwork is by a famous illustrator, or the year matches the birth year of the purchaser. If the monthly pages remain attached to a calendar value increases 10% to 20%.

Reference: Norman E. Martinus and Harry L. Rinker, *Warman's Paper,* Wallace–Homestead, Krause Publications, 1994.

Collectors' Club: Calendar Collector Society, 18222 Flower Hill Way #299, Gaithersburg, MD 20879.

REPRODUCTION ALERT

1924, Pompeian Co, beautiful lady and man . . . . $ **15.00**
1928, Iroquois Brewery, profile of woman with feath-
ers and beads in hair, full pad, framed, 27½ x 13¼" . . **825.00**
1929, Star Brand Shoes, woman by stained glass win-
dow, framed **140.00**
1935, National Life & Accident Insurance Co, farm
animals playing instruments, framed, 13½ x 10½" **30.00**
1935, Royal Style Ale, Globe Brewing Co, full pad,
framed, 28 x 14" **400.00**
1940, William G. Lord Insurance, full pad, matted,
framed, 16½ x 10" **30.00**
1941, "Out In Front," Earl Moran illus, 11 x 23" **80.00**
1944, Sinclair Gasoline, 12 wildlife photos **20.00**
1946, Washington's Prayer, historical art **25.00**
1947, Gilmore Gasoline, red lion logo, 17 x 7" **20.00**
1947, Kist Beverages, 26 x 12" **70.00**

1949, Princess Elizabeth, 8½ x 4¾" **40.00**
1950, Wandering Brook Farm, outdoor scene, chil-
dren and animals **10.00**
1961, TWA, 6 sheets **15.00**

CALIFORNIA FAIENCE

William Bradgon and Chauncey Thomas first manufactured art pottery and tiles in 1916. In 1924 they named their products California Faience.

Most art pottery pieces are characterized by cast molding and a monochrome matte glaze. Some pieces did have a high gloss glaze. Plaster molds were used to make the polychrome decorated tiles. California Faience also produced a commercial floral line and made master molds for other California potteries.

The company was hard hit by the Depresssion. Bradgon bought out Thomas in the late 1930s. He sold the pottery in the early 1950s, working with the new owners until he died in 1959.

Bookends, pr, eagle, blue matte . . . . $ **675.00**
Box, raspberry tile top, cloisonné dec, 1½ x 4½ x
3½" **100.00**
Flower Holder, figural, 2 pelicans, turquoise glaze,
6" h **130.00**
Jar, cov, bulbous body, periwinkle blue gloss glaze,
incised "California Faience," 9½" h **300.00**
Potpourri Jar, oriental shape, yellow matte, incised
mark, 4½" h **225.00**
Tea Tile, flower basket pattern, matte and gloss
glazes, mounted and framed, mkd "California
Faience" **700.00**
Tile, round, stylized green dandelion leaves, red blos-
soms, sky blue ground, incised mark, 5½" d **300.00**
Trivet, blue peacock on matte ochre ground, incised
mark, 5¼" d **375.00**
Vase, maroon glaze, 9" h **500.00**
Vase, multicolored floral band, blue ground, 3" h **950.00**
Vase, fine crystalline turquoise glaze, red clay body,
imp "California Faience," 7½" h **3.00**

Vase, turquoise glaze, relief band with stylized doves,
  arrow heads, and spruce, incised mark, c1924,
  6½" h **360.00**
Vessel, gourd shape, ridged body, matte, pumpkin
  and green glaze, incised "California Faience" **525.00**

CAMARK POTTERY

Samuel Jack Carnes founded Camark Pottery, Camden, Arkansas, in 1926. The company made art pottery, earthenware, and decorative accessories. John Lessell, previously employed at Weller, and his wife were among the leading art potters working at Camark.

After Carnes sold the plant in 1966, it was run primarily as a retail operation by Mary Daniels. In January 1986 Gary and Mark Ashcraft purchased the Camark Pottery building in hopes of re–establishing a pottery at the site. At the time of the purchase, they stated they did not intend to reissue pieces using the company's old molds.

References: David Edwin Gifford, *Collector's Encyclopedia of Camark Pottery: Identification & Values,* Collector Books, 1997; Letitia Landers, *Camark Pottery: An Identification and Value Reference, Vol. 1* (1994), *Vol. 2* (1996), Colony Publishing.

Collectors' Club: Arkansas Pottery Collectors Society, PO Box 7617, Little Rock, AR 72217.

Ashtray, 5¾" . . . . **$ 10.00**
Ashtray, sunburst **15.00**
Bowl, pumpkin, small **15.00**
Casserole, chicken lid **40.00**
Figure, seated cat, 10" h. **45.00**
Figure, lion **35.00**
Figure, pointer **35.00**
Figure, tropical fish, 8½" h **50.00**
Figure, wistful kitten, 8½" h **40.00**
Flower Frog, swans **25.00**
Pitcher, bulbous, cat handle, 8½" **50.00**
Planter, elephant, 11 x 8" **60.00**
Planter, rolling pin, N1–51 . . . . **8.00**
Planter, rooster **20.00**
Vase, fluted, 7" h **30.00**
Vase, morning glory, 11" **50.00**

CAMBRIDGE GLASS

Cambridge Glass, Cambridge, Ohio, was founded in 1901. The company manufactured a wide variety of glass tablewares. After experiencing financial difficulties in 1907, Arthur J. Bennett, previously with the National Glass Company, helped reorganize the company. By the 1930s, the company had over 5,000 glass molds in inventory.

Although five different identification marks are known, not every piece of Cambridge Glass was permanently marked. Paper labels were used between 1935 and 1954.

Cambridge Glass ceased operations in 1954. Its molds were sold. Imperial Glass Company purchased some, a few wound up in private hands.

References: Gene Florence, *Elegant Glassware Of The Depression Era, Seventh Edition,* Collector Books, 1997; National Cambridge

Collectors, Inc., *The Cambridge Glass Co., Cambridge, Ohio* (reprint of 1930 catalog and supplements through 1934), Collector Books, 1976, 1997 value update; National Cambridge Collectors, Inc., *The Cambridge Glass Co., Cambridge Ohio, 1949 Thru 1953* (catalog reprint), Collector Books, 1976; 1996 value update; National Cambridge Collectors, Inc., *Colors In Cambridge Glass,* Collector Books, 1984, 1997 value update.

Periodical: *The Daze,* PO Box 57, Otisville, MI 48463.

Collectors' Club: National Cambridge Collectors, Inc, PO Box 416, Cambridge, OH 43725.

Basket, Caprice, blue, 4" h . . . . **$ 45.00**
Bonbon, Caprice, blue, ftd, 6" sq **50.00**
Bowl, Rose Point, 4 toed, handled, 3900 Line, 12" d **125.00**
Bud Vase, Rose Point, 10" h **95.00**
Butter Dish, cov, Gadroon **40.00**
Cake Plate, Caprice, crystal, ftd, 13" d **65.00**
Candlesticks, pr, Caprice, crystal, 3 light, #1338 . . . . **60.00**
Candlesticks, pr, Rose Point, 5" h **115.00**
Candy Box, cov, Apple Blossom, crystal **30.00**
Candy Dish, cov, Caprice, crystal, 3 ftd **45.00**
Champagne, Apple Blossom, yellow **25.00**
Champagne, Wildflower, crystal **30.00**
Cigarette Box, cov, Caprice, crystal, 3½ x 2½" **20.00**
Comport, Caprice, crystal, silver overlay **20.00**
Cordial, Tally Ho, red **65.00**
Corn Dish, Rose Point **60.00**
Creamer, medium, #38 . . . . **10.00**
Cruet, Deco, green, 7¾" h **75.00**
Flower Holder, Heron, crystal, 9" h **95.00**
Flower Holder, Rose Lady, amber, 8½" h **250.00**
Goblet, Cleo, pink **100.00**
Lemon Plate, Caprice, blue, handle, 5" d **25.00**
Mayonnaise and Liner, Caprice, blue, 2 handles **25.00**
Oyster Cocktail, Rose Point, tall, 4½ oz **30.00**
Plate, Caprice, blue, ftd, 11" d **75.00**
Plate, 2 handles, 11½"d, ... **110.00**
Relish, Caprice, crystal, 3 pc, 8" d **25.00**

Water Goblet, Magnolia, crystal, 6" h, $15.00.

Sherbet, Rose Point, 6 oz **30.00**
Tumbler, Caprice, ftd, crystal, 5 oz **20.00**

CAMERAS & ACCESSORIES

The development of the camera was truly international. Johann Zahn, a German monk, created the first fully portable wood box camera with a movable lens, adjustable aperture, and mirror to project the image in the early 1800s. Joseph Niepce and Louise Daguere perfected the photographic plate. Peter Von Voigtlander, an Austrian, contributed the quality lens. An industry was born.

By the late 19th century, England, France, and Germany all played major roles in the development of camera technology. America's contributions came in the area of film development and marketing.

In 1888 George Eastman introduced the Kodak No. 1, a simple box camera that revolutionized the industry. Model No. 4 was the first folding camera. The Brownie was introduced in 1900.

After World War II, the Japanese made a strong commitment to dominating the camera market. By the 1970s, they had achieved their goal.

Reference: Jim and Joan McKeown (eds.), *Price Guide To Antique And Classic Cameras, 1997–1998, 9th Edition,* Centennial Photo Service, 1997.

Periodicals: *Camera Shopper Magazine,* 313 N Quaker Ln, PO Box 37029, W Hartford, CT 06137; *Classic Camera,* PO Box 1270, New York, NY 10156.

Collectors' Clubs: American Photographic Historical Society, Inc, 1150 Avenue of the Americas, New York, NY 10036; American Society of Camera Collectors, 4918 Alcove Ave, North Hollywood, CA 91607; International Kodak Historical Society, PO Box 21, Flourtown, PA 19301; Leica Historical Society of America, 7611 Dornoch Ln, Dallas, TX 75248; Nikon Historical Society, PO Box 3213, Munster, IN 45321; The Movie Machine Society, 42 Deerhaven Dr, Nashua, NH 03060; Zeiss Historical Society, PO Box 631, Clifton, NJ 07012.

Accessory, A–B–C Darkroom Outfit, trays, glass, grad-
uates, film clips, print frame, stirring rod, and
instructions, 1940s . . . . $ **20.00**
Accessory, exposure meter, auxiliary CdS, Canon,
1965–67 . . . . **15.00**
Bag, plastic, camera shape, transparent plastic lens
and back, Leadworks, c1985 . . . . **10.00**
Book, *Amateur Carbro Colour Prints,* Viscount
Hanworth, Focal Press, London, 1950–51, 188
pgs, third edition, dj **20.00**
Book, *Guide to Kodak Retina, Retina Reflex, Signet
and Pony,* Kenneth S. Tydings, soft cov, 128 pgs,
1952 . . . . **10.00**
Booklet, *Making Titles and Editing Your Cine–Kodak
Films,* 30 pgs, 1931 . . . . **20.00**
Camera, Ansco, Rediflex **10.00**
Camera, Ansco, Readyset Royal, No. 1, folding, Antar
lens, c1926 . . . . **90.00**
Camera, Argus, Autronic, 35mm. **40.00**
Camera, Bell & Howell Inc, Stereo Colorist,
35mm, Rodenstock Trinar f3.5 lens, c1952 . . . . **145.00**

Camera, Boy Scout Kodak, folding, single lens, olive green, $60.00.

Camera, Brenda Starr Cub Reporter, black Bakelite,
127 film. **100.00**
Camera, Eastman Kodak, Brownie **25.00**
Camera, Eastman Kodak, Instamatic, 314, lever wind,
light meter, uses flash cubes, 1968–71 . . . . **15.00**
Camera, Eastman Kodak, No. 2, Folding Cartridge
Hawk–Eye **40.00**
Camera, Eastman Kodak Petite, with art decodoor
plate and colored bellows. **75.00**
Camera, Graflex, Pacemaker Crown Graphic. **125.00**
Camera, Incredible Hulk, 126 film **30.00**
Camera, Mighty Morphin Power Rangers, disposable. **15.00**
Camera, Minolta V2, 35 mm, 1958. . . . . **70.00**
Camera, Nikon, Nikkorex Zoom–8, 8mm movie
camera, fl.8 lens, zooms 8 to 32mm, manual zoom. . . . **25.00**
Sign, Kodak, Art Deco, enamel, double–sided trian-
gle, red, blue, and yellow, c1930s. **200.00**
Timer, Luxor Photo Timer, Burke & James, c1930s **10.00**
Toy, Kodak van, cast metal, enameled exterior, Model
T Ford truck, Lledo's "Models of Days Gone"
series, c1983 . . . . **15.00**

CANDLEWICK

Imperial Glass Corporation introduced its No. 400 pattern, Candlewick, in 1936. Over 650 different forms and sets are known. Although produced primarily in cyrstal (clear), other colors do exist. The pattern proved extremely popular and remained in production until Imperial closed in 1982.

After a brief period of ownership by the Lancaster–Colony Corporation and Consolidated Stores, Imperial's assets, including its molds, were sold. Various companies, groups, and individuals bought Imperial's Candlewick molds. Mirror Images of Lansing, Michigan, bought more than 200. Boyd Crystal Art Glass, Cambridge, Ohio, bought 18.

Reference: Mary M. Wetzel–Tomalka, *Candlewick: The Jewel of Imperial, Book II,* published by author, 1995.

Collectors' Club: The National Candlewick Collector's Club, 275 Milledge Terrace, Athens, GA 30606.

Teacup and Saucer, 400/35, $12.00.

Atomizer, 400/167 shaker bottoms, aqua and
   amethyst . . . . **$ 95.00**
Basket, 400/40/0, turned up sides, applied han-
   dle, 6½". **35.00**
Bowl, 400/63B, bellied, 10½" d **50.00**
Bud Vase, 400/107. . . . . **65.00**
Cake Stand, 400/103D, 11" d. **72.00**
Candleholders, pr, 400/80, 3½" h. **18.00**
Candy, cov, 400/260, 3 part **195.00**
Celery Tray, 400/105, oval, open handles, 13½" **30.00**
Decanter, 400/163, beaded foot, round stopper,
   26 oz. **200.00**
Deviled Egg Tray, 400/154 . . . . **95.00**
Goblet, 3400, 9 oz **15.00**
Ice Tub, 400/63 . . . . **85.00**
Mayonnaise Set, 400/49, 3 pc **45.00**
Mustard Jar, 400/156, 3 pc, beaded foot, notched
   beaded cover, 2-bead finial, shell bowl with
   fleur-de-lis handle, 3½" glass spoon. **30.00**
Pitcher, juice, 400/19, 40 oz **250.00**
Plate, salad, 400/5D, 8" d **8.00**
Punch Set, 400/20 bowl, twelve 400/37 cups,
   400/128B base, and 400/91 ladle **250.00**
Relish Dish, 400/268, 2 pc, oval, 8" **18.00**
Salt and Pepper Shakers, pr, 400/96, beaded foot **40.00**
Sauce Boat Set, 400/169, oval handled gravy boat,
   9" oval plate with indent. **90.00**
Tumbler, juice, 400/19, 5 oz **10.00**

CAP GUNS

The first toy cap gun was introduced in 1870. Cap guns experienced two Golden Ages: (1) the era of the cast iron cap gun from
1870 through 1900 and (2) the era of the diecast metal and plastic cap guns.

   Hubley, Kilgore, Mattel, and Nichols are among the leading
manufacturers of diecast pistols. Many diecast and plastic pistols
were sold as part of holster sets. A large number were associated
with television cowboy and detective heroes. The presence of the
original box, holster, and other accessories adds as much as 100%
to the value of the gun.

References: James L. Dundas, *Cap Guns: With Values,* Schiffer
Publishing, 1996; Jerrell Little, *Price Guide to Cowboy Cap Guns
and Guitars,* L-W Book Sales, 1996; Jim Schleyer, *Backyard
Buckaroos: Collecting Western Toy Guns,* Books Americana,
Krause Publications, 1996.

Collectors' Club: Toy Gun Collectors of America, 312 Starling
Way, Anaheim, CA 92807.

Bandolier, Winchester, leather belt, 32 metal play
   bullets, Mattel, 1950 . . . . **$ 125.00**
Big Scout, cast iron, white grips, 7½ x 3½". **100.00**
Buntline Special, Wyatt Earp, 6 x 11" **125.00**
Civil War Period Model 1861, revolver, 6 shells,
   18 bullets. **600.00**
Cowboy, gold plated, black grips, Hubley, 12 x 5¼" **200.00**
Deputy, single holster, 2¼" wide fancy belt, Kilgore. **200.00**
Forty Niner, Roy Rogers, Leslie Henry, 9" l **150.00**
Gene Autry Flying A Ranch, double leather holster
   set, two 44s, tan and black, complete with bullets,
   Leslie Henry. **600.00**
Hero, cast iron, cowboy on cast-iron grips **40.00**
Hoppy, black plastic grips, Schmidt Mfg, 1950s,
   9½" l **250.00**
Kadet Officer, target pistol, holster, shoots corks, 28
   pg Kadet handbook and ammo included, orig pkg,
   Parris Mfg Co, 5½ x 11" **50.00**
Okinawa Pistol, Monkey Division, Remco, 1964,
   13" l **35.00**
Pal, Kilgore, 5½ x 3" **10.00**
Shootin' Shell Remington Derringer, buckle gun,
   Matty's Funday Funnies, ABC TV, Mattel, 1958–59. . . . **100.00**
Smoky, gold plated, 2½ x 5½" **10.00**
Texan 38, turquoise, engraved, Hubley, 10½ x 5¼" **250.00**
Wild Bill Hickok, double leather holster set,
   2 Marsall guns, bronze grips, tan leather, felt lining . . . **500.00**
Winchester Saddle Gun, Stock No. 544, Mattel, orig
   33¾ x 6⅜ x 1½" box **500.00**

CARLTON WARE

Wiltshow and Robinson produced Staffordshire earthenware and
porcelains at the Charlton Works, Stoke-on-Trent, beginning in
the 1890s. In 1957 the company's name was changed to Carlton
Ware, Ltd.

   Black was the background color most often used on the company's wares. During the 1920s the line included pieces decorated
with Art Deco designs in brightly enameled and gilt flowers and
porcelain vases featuring luster decoration in oriental motifs.

Reference: *Collecting Carlton Ware,* Francis Joseph Publications,
1994, distributed by Krause Publications.

Collectors' Club: Carlton Ware International, PO Box 161,
Sevenoaks, Kent Tn15 6GA England.

Ashtray, oriental scene . . . . **$ 30.00**
Biscuit Jar, multicolored flowers with green leaves,
   gold accents, satin cream ground, silver-plated
   top, rim, and handle. **125.00**
Bowl, red flowers, leaf ground, 9½" l **45.00**

Bowl, stylized black tree, orange flowers, yellow
   ground. **300.00**
Bowl, swirled motif, multicolored, phoenix in flight,
   pink ground **240.00**
Dish, figural leaf, yellow, 5" l **30.00**
Jar, cov, flying ducks, multicolored flowers and reed
   base, gold rim, dog finial **200.00**
Jardiniere, oriental motif, cobalt ground, pearlized
   irid int, gold handles **145.00**
Pitcher, squat shape, green, orange, blue–green, gray,
   purple, and black bands, black handle, 3³/₄" h **130.00**
Salad Bowl, tomatoes and leaf border, ftd, 10¹/₂" d **100.00**
Sugar Shaker, green, yellow, and gold wheat design,
   orange and green top, 5" h **45.00**
Tea Service, magenta and gilt scalloped edges, mkd **225.00**
Vase, bulbous, hollyhocks and butterflies, cobalt
   ground, 6" h **210.00**
Vase, Rouge Royale, hp, oriental birds and trees,
   orange, yellow, and green, ribbed bottom, gold
   handles and trim, 5¹/₄" h **145.00**

CARNIVAL CHALKWARE

Inexpensive plaster of Paris figurines made from the 1920s through the 1960s are collected under the generic classification of carnival chalkware because they most frequently were given away as prizes at games of chance on carnival midways, amusement parks, and oceanside boardwalks. Doll and novelty companies produced them in quantity. Cost was as low as a dollar a dozen. While some pieces are marked and dated, most are not.

A wide variety of animal, character, and personality figures are found. Most are generic. Many character figures resembled famous personalities of the day, but differed enough to avoid the payment of licensing fees.

Reference: *Price Guide to Carnival Chalkware, Giveaways and Games,* L–W Book Sales, 1995.

Bag Pipe Girls, 6 x 15¹/₂" . . . . **$ 25.00**
Charlie McCarthy, 3 x 7" **30.00**

Horse, gold mica
dec, 9¹/₄" l, 11" h,
$15.00.

Chipmunk, 1945–50, 5¹/₂" h **5.00**
Clown, 1930–40, 8³/₄" h **25.00**
Drum Majorette, 15" h **20.00**
Elephant, 9 x 12" **15.00**
Gorilla, c1940, 6¹/₄" h **10.00**
Hula Girl, Indianapolis Statuary Co, 4 x 9¹/₂". **25.00**
Lamb, flat back, mkd "Rosemead Novelty Co," 7" h **5.00**
Little Sheba, hp, orig feathers, c1920s, 13" h **150.00**
Miss America, wearing bathing suit, c1940, 15" h **20.00**
Pirate Girl, 1936, 10³/₄" h **50.00**
Sailor Girl, c1940, 9" h **10.00**
Sea Hag, c1930–40 . . . . **80.00**
Ship, 9 x 10" **15.00**
Soldier, saluting flag, mkd "Luchini 1941," 14" h **65.00**
Superman, 16" h **30.00**
Wimpy, c1930–40, 8" h **45.00**

CARTOON CHARACTERS

The cartoon characters that appear in this category come from three primary sources: (1) the comic pages of the daily and Sunday newspapers, (2) movies, and (3) television. Many characters are found in more than one medium.

The comic strip was an American institution by the 1920s. Its Golden Age dates from the mid–1930s through the late 1950s. The movie cartoon came of age in the late 1930s and early 1940s as a result of the pioneers at the Disney and Warner Brothers studios. The Saturday morning television cartoon matured through the creative energies of Bill Hanna, Joe Barbera, and Jay Ward.

A successful cartoon character generates hundreds of licensed products. Most collectors focus on a single character or family of characters, e.g., Popeye, Mickey Mouse, or the Flintstones.

References: Bill Bruegman, *Cartoon Friends Of The Baby Boom Era: A Pictorial Price Guide,* Cap'n Penny Productions, 1993; Mark E. Chase and Michael J. Kelly, *Collectible Drinking Glasses,* Collector Books, 1996; Ted Hake, *Hake's Guide to Comic Character Collectibles,* Wallace–Homestead, Krause Publications, 1993; John Hervey, *Collector's Guide to Cartoon & Promotional Drinking Glasses,* L–W Book Sales, 1990, 1995 value update; L–W Books Sales, *Cartoon & Character Toys of the 50s, 60s, & 70s: Plastic & Vinyl,* L–W Book Sales, 1995, Stuart W. Wells III and Alex G. Malloy, *Comics Collectibles and Their Values,* Wallace–Homestead, Krause Publications, 1996.

Newsletter: *Frostbite Falls Far–Flung Flier* (Rocky & Bullwinkle), PO Box 39, Macedonia, OH 44056.

Collectors' Clubs: Dagwood Fan Club, 541 El Paso, Jacksonville, TX 75766; Dick Tracy Fan Club, PO Box 632, Manitou Springs, CO 80829; Official Popeye Fan Club, 1001 State St, Chester, IL 62233; Pogo Fan Club, 6908 Wentworth Ave, S Richfield, MN 55423.

Note: For additional listings see Disneyana, Hanna–Barbera, Peanuts, and Smurfs.

Alvin and The Chipmunks, hand puppet, cloth and
   vinyl, 10" h . . . . **$ 30.00**
Alvin and The Chipmunks, record, *Alvin For
   President*, 45 rpm, Liberty, 1970 . . . . **30.00**

Flintstones, banks, vinyl, 12¹/₄" h Fred, 13" h Dino and Pebbles, and 12¹/₄" h Barney and Bamm–Bamm, Homecraft Products, Vinyl Prod. Corp., 1971, $45.00 each.

Alvin and The Chipmunks, Simon, inflatable doll, plastic, Ideal, 1964, 16" h..................... $ 15.00

Andy Panda, bank, pressed cardboard, painted, 1948, 6" h...................................... 20.00

Andy Panda and His Friends, book, Story Hour series, Whitman, black and white illus, hard cov, 1949, 40 pgs.................................. 15.00

Archies, tattoo sheet and gum, Topps, 1969, 2 x 4" unopened pack.................................. 20.00

Baby Huey, hand puppet, cloth body, painted vinyl head, Gund, 1960, 10" h........................ 25.00

Beany and Cecil, game, Talk to Cecil 90.00

Beetle Bailey, Sergeant Snorkel, bank, composition, c1960, 11" h................................... 75.00

Beetle Bailey, game, The Old Time Army, Milton Bradley, 1963.................................. 35.00

Betty Boop, book, *Betty Boop in Snow White*, Whitman, Big Little Book #1119, 1934 .... 60.00

Betty Boop, alarm clock, animated, 1983, 4¹/₂" h....... 120.00

Betty Boop, mechanical valentine, stiff diecut paper, movable feather in hair controls eyes and changes message from "Don't Keep Me Waiting For Your Love, Valentine" to "Or I'll Start Looking Around, Valentine," 1940, 3¹/₂ x 4¹/₂"..................... 30.00

Blondie, book, *Blondie & Dagwood*, 1936, 92 pgs 40.00

Blondie, greeting card, "Hope Your Christmas Is Like Dagwood's Sandwich," Hallmark, 1939............. 10.00

Blondie, game, Blondie Goes to Leisureland, Westinghouse Electric Co, 1940, 8 x 11" envelope, 1940.. 35.00

Bringing Up Father, Jiggs, doll, painted composition, jointed metal ball bearing arms and legs, stuffed torso, 1920s, 7¹/₂" h.......................... 450.00

Bringing Up Father, lunch box, tin, 1930s, 6¹/₂" w...... 110.00

Bugs Bunny, nodder, composition, c1960s, 7" h........ 50.00

Bugs Bunny, cup, hard plastic, c1960s, 4" h........... 10.00

Bugs Bunny and Elmer Fudd, bank, hard plastic, talking mechanism, Janex, 1977..................... 55.00

Bullwinkle, stamp set, stamp pads, alphabet and number stamps, litho tin ink pad, Larami, 1969....... 15.00

Casper, game, Casper the Ghost Electronic Adventure Game, Tarco, 1962.................... 25.00

Casper, View–Master reel set, 3 reels, booklet, and envelope, Sawyer, 1961........................ 10.00

Chilly Willy, figure, rubber, c1950s, 6" h............. 25.00

Courageous Cat, record, TV soundtrack, *Around the World in a Daze*, Simon Says, 1962 .... 15.00

Dick Tracy, camera 35.00

Dick Tracy, jigsaw puzzle, 60 pcs, Jaymar, 1961 .... 25.00

Dick Tracy, model, plastic, 1/72 scale, police coupe, 4 H/O scale figures............................ 75.00

Dudley Do–Right, school bag, red, Dudley, Nell, and Snidely on train tracks illus, Ardee Ind, 1972, 8 x 12 x 3"................................... 75.00

Elmer Fudd, Dakin figure, plastic, swivel head, 1968, 7" h...................................... 60.00

Felix the Cat, book, *Felix on Television*, Wonder Books, color illus, hard cov, 1960, 7 x 8" 18.00

Felix the Cat, figure, wood, c1930s, 6¹/₂" h.......... 225.00

Felix the Cat, flashlight, plastic, Bantam–Lite, 1960, 4" h, MOC.................................. 35.00

Gabby Gator, frame tray puzzle, Gabby Gator conducting singing frogs, Preskool, 1963, 8 x 11"........ 10.00

George of the Jungle, game, Parker Brothers, 1968 ...... 40.00

Groovie Goolies, costume, Ben Cooper, 1962........... 50.00

Heckle and Jeckle, bagatelle, Imperial Toy, 1978, 4 x 7".................................... 8.00

Heckle and Jeckle, Little Golden Record, 45 rpm, 1958...................................... 25.00

Hector Heathcote, book, *The Minute and a Half Man*, Wonder Book, 1960, 20 pgs................. 35.00

Hector Heathcote, magic slate, wood drawing stylus, Lowe, 1964, 8 x 12"........................... 60.00

King Kong, stuffed toy, talking, plush and vinyl, Mattel, 1966, 24" h.......................... 150.00

King Leonard, board game, King Leonard and His Subjects, Milton Bradley, 1960.................... 40.00

King Leonard, coloring book, Whitman, 1961, 100 pgs, 8 x 11"................................ 25.00

Lariat Sam, Colorforms, 1962...................... 15.00

Laurel and Hardy, bank, figural Laurel, 1972, 15" h...... 15.00

Laurel and Hardy, record, *Chiller Diller Thriller*, Peter Pan, 45 rpm, 1962, 7 x 7" illus sleeve............. 12.00

Little Audrey, doll, plastic, soft vinyl painted head, red western dress, brown suede cowboy boots, gun and holster, Fillmore, 1950s, 15" h 120.00

Little Lulu, bank, painted plastic, figural, ©Western Publishing Company, Inc, Play Pal Plastics–Dell Comics, c1950s, 8" h........................... 50.00

Little Lulu, tissue box, 9" paper stand–up, Lulu in red band leader's uniform holding box of Kleenex tissues, Kimberly–Clark, 1956 .... 10.00

Mighty Hercules, board game, Hasbro, 1963 .... 985.00

Mighty Mouse, figure, vinyl and rubber, c1950s, 10" h..................................... 55.00

Mighty Mouse, sticker book, Whitman, 1967, 10 x 12"................................... 15.00

Mighty Mouse, View–Master reel set, 3 reels, booklet, 5 x 5" envelope, GAF, 1968.............. 12.00

Little Lulu, paper dolls, *Marge's Little Lulu Doll Book,* Whitman, #1970, ©1971, 6 pgs, 7¹/₄ x 15¹/₂", unused, $40.00.

Milton the Monster, board game, Milton Bradley, 1965 . . . . **40.00**

Mr. Magoo, car, litho tin, cloth top, battery operated, vinyl figure, Hubley, 1961, 9" l **250.00**

Mr. Magoo, figure, vinyl, wearing green overcoat with fur collar and hat, carrying cane, 1958, 12" h . . . **120.00**

Olive Oyl, hand puppet, cloth body, vinyl head, 10" h **25.00**

Pink Panther, figure, bendable vinyl, Bendy, 1970, 12" h **40.00**

Pink Panther, toothbrush holder, figural Pink Panther marching with drum, holds 2 toothbrushes, Avon, 1970s, 5" h, orig 4 x 6" box **15.00**

Popeye, color–by–number pencil set, Hasbro, 1950, 13 x 10" box **90.00**

Porky Pig, bank, painted metal, green base with red "Porky," ©Warner Brothers, 1940s, 4¹/₂" h **125.00**

Ricochet Rabbit and Droop Along Coyote, board game, Ideal, 1964 . . . . **295.00**

Rocky and Bullwinkle, coloring book, Whitman, 1965, 80 pgs, 8 x 11" **25.00**

Rocky and Bullwinkle, Bullwinkle, stuffed toy, talking, plush, molded vinyl face, Mattel, 1970, 18" h **75.00**

Roger Ramjet, figure, bendable rubber, AMF, 1965, 5" h **25.00**

Roger Ramjet, record, 33¹/₃ rpm, RCA, 1966 . . . . **25.00**

Space Angel, game, Transogram, 1965 . . . . **25.00**

Space Ghost, book, *Space Ghost: The Sorceress of Cyba–3,* Whitman, Big Little Book, 1968 . . . . **5.00**

Speedy Gonzales, mug, white china, c1970s, 3" h **45.00**

Sylvester, Soaky, 10" h **10.00**

Teenage Mutant Ninja Turtles, action figure, Grand Slammin' Raph, #5144, Sewer Sports All–Stars, 1991 . . . . **5.00**

Teenage Mutant Ninja Turtles, stuffed toy, plush, 13" h **20.00**

Teenage Mutant Ninja Turtles, toy, Don's Sewer Squirter, #5681, 1991 . . . . **8.00**

Tennessee Tuxedo, school bag, briefcase style, vinyl, Ardee, 1969, 12 x 10" **75.00**

Tennessee Tuxedo, Soaky, 10" h **20.00**

Underdog, harmonica, plastic, emb Underdog and Simon Bar Sinister on each side, "Have no fear...Underdog is here!," Leonardo, 1975, 8" l **15.00**

Winky Dink, Little Golden Book, Golden Press, 1956, 7 x 8" **12.00**

Yosemite Sam, lunch box, vinyl, King Seeley Thermos, 1971 . . . . **50.00**

CAT COLLECTIBLES

Unlike dog collectors who tend to collect objects picturing or portraying a single breed, cat collectors collect anything and everything with a cat image or in the shape of a cat. It makes no difference if an object is old or new, realistic or abstract. Cat collectors love it all.

The popularity of cats as a pet increased significantly in the 1980s. Rumors abound that cat owners now outnumber dog owners. The same holds true for cat collectibles. Many contemporary 1980s cat collectibles, e.g., Kliban's cats and Lowell Davis porcelains featuring cats, are experiencing strong secondary markets. Remember, this market is highly speculative. Serious cat collectors stick to vintage (pre–1965) cat collectibles that have withstood the test of time.

References: Marbena Jean Fyke, *Collectible Cats: An Identification & Value Guide* (1993, 1995 value update), *Book II* (1996), Collector Books; J. L. Lynnlee, *Purrrfection: The Cat,* Schiffer Publishing, 1990; Alice L. Muncaster and Ellen Sawyer, *The Black Cat Made Me Buy It!,* Crown Publishers, 1988; Alice Muncaster and Ellen Yanow, *The Cat Made Me Buy It,* Crown Publishers, 1984.

Collectors' Club: Cat Collectors, 33161 Wendy Dr, Sterling Hts, MI 48310.

Bank, ceramic, hp, with lock, mkd "Greatest," Japan, 1940s, 7¹/₂" h . . . . **$ 25.00**

Bank, chalk, seated full bodied cat, polychrome paint, 9¹/₂" h **200.00**

Box, brass, oval, pewter cat on lid, 1920, 5" h **40.00**

Butter Dish, ceramic, stamped "No. 52/724," 6¹/₂ x 3" **12.00**

Calendar, Chesapeake & Ohio Railway, Chessie illus, 1957 . . . . **75.00**

Can Opener, molded plastic, figural white cat handle, Hong Kong **10.00**

Candle, Kliban, different cat illus on each side **5.00**

Catalog, Fortnum's Christmas Catalogue, cat in Santa suit on cover, Fortnum & Mason, 1958 . . . . **42.00**

Checkbook Cover, plastic, Kliban illus, emb back reads "Copyright 1975 B. Kliban FG Giftware S. D. CA 92123" **8.00**

Cigar Label, Our Kitties, emb black and white cats on red rug **10.00**

Cigarette Holder and Ashtray, cast metal, 1940s, 4³/₄" h **40.00**

Cookie Jar, brown cat on coal bucket, McCoy **225.00**

Creamer, Garfield, stamped "I Love Moo Juice," Enesco, c1980s **45.00**

Creamer, Kliban, cat tail handle, Sigma Mfg, Korea **65.00**

Figure, brass, marble base, 10" h **150.00**

Figure, papier mâché, black, arched back **45.00**

Pin, sterling silver, Beau, 1½" d, $25.00.

Figure, hand–carved wood, Egyptian style, 17½" h **195.00**

Jigsaw Puzzle, Kliban, Umbrella Cat, Great American Puzzle Factory, Inc, 1980, 100 pcs, 7 x 7" **15.00**

Jigsaw Puzzle, Little Roquefont and Percy Puss, frame tray, diecut, Terrytoons, Inc, E. E. Fairchild Corp, Rochester, NY, #1600-s, c1950s, 11 x 8½" **20.00**

Kite, paper, Morris the Cat, Hi–Flier, 9–Lives Cat Food premium, "I Always Fly First Class," 29" w, 35½" h **20.00**

Mug, Kliban, ironstone, Kiln Craft, 1979–80 . . . . **5.00**

Nodder, Puss 'N' Boots, clockwork, 24" h **2,400.00**

Pin, cat face, florentined gold, rhinestone whisker tips, c1950 . . . . **20.00**

Pin Cushion, painted metal, 4" l **25.00**

Pull Toy, wood, polychrome paint, wheeled platform, 5" l **85.00**

Salt and Pepper Shakers, pr, Garfield, ceramic, "Ho Ho Ho," "Bah HumBug," Enesco, 1993 . . . . **15.00**

Salt and Pepper Shakers, pr, Jazz Cat, striped, playing piano **15.00**

Sheet Music, *I Taut I Taw a Puddy–Tat,* Sylvester and Tweety cov, Alan Livingston, Billy May, and Warren Foster **25.00**

Snow Globe, musical, yellow tabby on top of globe, 2 kittens playing with ball of yarn inside, plays *White Christmas,* Silvestri, orig box, 7" h **45.00**

Stuffed Toy, Figaro, jointed, Knickerbocker, c1930–40 . . . **650.00**

Stuffed Toy, Kitty Kat, jointed, Steiff, orig tag, c1950 . . . . **250.00**

Stuffed Toy, Sylvester, plush, Warner Brothers, ©1971, 15½" h **20.00**

Toothpick Holder, cat on cushion, glass **45.00**

CATALINA POTTERY

The Catalina Pottery, located on Santa Catalina Island, California, was founded in 1927 for the purpose of making clay building products. Decorative and functional pottery was added to the company's line in the early 1930s. A full line of color–glazed dishes was made between 1931 and 1937.

Gladding, McBean and Company bought Catalina Pottery in 1937, moved production to the mainland, and closed the island pottery. Gladding, McBean continued to use the Catalina trademark until 1947.

References: Susan and Al Bagdade, *Warman's American Pottery and Porcelain,* Wallace–Homestead, Krause Publications, 1994; Jack Chipman, *Collector's Encyclopedia of California Pottery,* Collector Books, 1992, 1995 value update; Steve and Aisha Hoefs, *Catalina Island Pottery,* published by authors, 1993.

Ashtray, bear, cream. . . . . $ 200.00
Ashtray, cowboy hat, green 100.00
Ashtray, hat, white, incised mark 145.00
Bowl, bonnet, 10½" d 225.00
Bowl, dessert, red 15.00
Candleholders, pr, #606, pedestal base, flared rim, pink. 135.00
Charger, 14" d 25.00
Coaster, yellow 20.00
Cup and Saucer, green. 38.00
Dish, shell shape, scalloped edge, white, 14" d 155.00
Figure, fish, #C253 . . . . 25.00
Head Vase, peasant girl 125.00
Nut Dish, blue. 20.00
Planter, square, green. 15.00
Plate, scalloped edge, blue, 10½" d 35.00
Platter, turquoise, 13" d 85.00
Salt and Pepper Shakers, pr, gourd shape, green 70.00
Teapot. 20.00
Tray, leaf shape, turquoise and coral 60.00
Tumbler, handled, red 35.00
Tumbler, orange, 4" h. 20.00
Vase, flared shape, red clay, blue glaze, 6" h. 120.00
Vase, handled, green, 8" h 250.00
Vase, oxblood, 5" h 75.00
Vase, Polynesian, #385, 6¾" h 250.00
Water Set, carafe and 6 tumblers, red 250.00
Wine Carafe, ivory. 115.00

CATALOGS

Trade catalogs are designed to sell products. There are three basic types of catalogs: (1) manufacturers' catalogs that are supplied primarily to distributors, (2) trade catalogs supplied to the merchant community and general public, and (3) mail–order catalogs designed for selling directly to the consumer. Montgomery Ward issued its first mail–order catalog in 1872. Sears Roebuck's came out in 1886.

A catalog revolution occurred in the 1980s with the arrival of specialized catalogs and select zip code mailing niche marketing. In the 1990s catalogs began appearing on the Internet. Many predict this will make the printed catalog obsolete by the mid–21st century. Will electronic information become collectible? In the year 2025 a paper collection may consist of nothing more than computer disks.

References: Ron Barlow and Ray Reynolds, *The Insider's Guide to Old Books, Magazines, Newspapers and Trade Catalogs,* Windmill Publishing, 1995; Norman E. Martinus and Harry L. Rinker, *Warman's Paper,* Wallace–Homestead, Krause Publications, 1994.

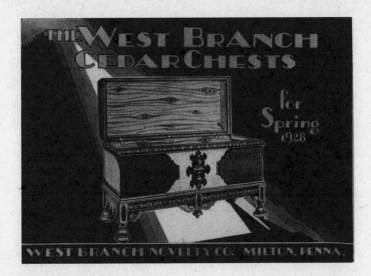

1928, The West Branch Cedar Chests, orange, black, and white, 15 pgs, 12 x 9", $30.00.

1924, Waterford Irish Crystal . . . . $ 25.00

1928, Kawneer Mfg Co, Berkeley, CA, store fronts with layouts and display frontage, 5 color sheets, 64 pgs, 8½ x 11" 50.00

1930, Revere Clock Co, Cincinnati, OH, Observatory Time, Queen Anne, Chippendale, Sheraton, Georgian, American Empire, Hepplewhite, and Modernistic periods, one clock per page in room setting, brown ink, cream paper, 8½ x 11" 70.00

1930, Tiffin Scenic Studios, Tiffin, OH, artistic scenery, draperies, velour front curtains, painted picture sets, 45 pgs, 6 x 9" 30.00

1935, Thurston Supply Co, Anoka, MN, lamps and lighting, 68 pgs, 6 x 8¾" 15.00

1937, Western Ammunition Handbook, Western Cartridge Co, East Alton, IL, illus, charts, tables of specifications, graphs, ammunition photographs, and Winchester rifles, 72 pgs 35.00

1938, Scott's Standard Postage Stamp Catalog, 1,300 pgs 12.00

1938, Emmons–Hawkins Hardware, Huntington, WV, sporting goods, 56 pgs, 8½ x 10½" 25.00

1941, Sherwin–Williams Color Styling Service, 23 pgs, 1941 . . . . 10.00

1941, Studebaker Champion, 8 pgs, 10¼ x 15½" 15.00

1944, Spiegel, Fall & Winter, 630 pgs 35.00

1945, American Chair Company Tropique Rattan Furniture, Sheboygan, WI, 16 pgs, 9 x 12" 15.00

1947, Ohio Brass Co, Mansfield, OH, insulators, 160 pgs 15.00

1949, FAO Schwarz, Christmas scene on cov, 82 pgs, 9 x 12" 50.00

1950, General Merchandise Co, Milwuakee, WI, toys, dolls, giftware, 326 pgs. 22.00

1972, Matchbox Collectors USA Edition, color illus, photos, 48 pgs, 5½ x 4" 15.00

1979, Corgi, The Mettoy Playcraft Ltd, Northampton, color illus and photos, 48 pgs, 6 x 4" 15.00

CERAMIC ARTS STUDIOS

Lawrence Rabbett and Ruben Sand founded the Ceramic Arts Studio, Madison, Wisconsin, in January 1941 for the purpose of making wheel–thrown ceramics. During World War II the company began production on a line of high–end molded figurines that were sold in jewelry stores and large department stores. The flood of cheap imported ceramics in the early 1950s led to the demise of the studio in 1955.

Reference: Mike Schneider, *Ceramic Arts Studio: Identification and Price Guide,* Schiffer Publishing, 1994.

Collectors' Club: Ceramic Arts Studio Collectors Assoc, PO Box 46, Madison, WI 53701.

Figure, Archibald the Dragon . . . . $ 185.00
Figure, Chinese girl, kneeling with fan, yellow pom–
  poms, blue coat 20.00
Figure, baby dinky skunk 25.00
Figure, cheese 15.00
Figure, frisky lamb 25.00
Figure, Gay 90's couple, pastel, price for pair 140.00
Figure, Harry, southern gentleman 50.00
Figure, panda bear, holding cub 85.00
Figure, Peter Pan and Wendy, price for pair 120.00
Figure, Pomeranian 40.00
Figure, spaniel puppy. 20.00
Figure, waterman and woman, price for pair 180.00
Figure, Wing Sang 15.00
Planter, Chinese girl. 15.00
Salt and Pepper Shakers, pr, mouse and cheese. 25.00
Salt and Pepper Shakers, pr, oriental children 40.00
Shelf Sitter, large cat 45.00
Shelf Sitter, Pete & Polly, birds, price for pair 175.00
Wall Plaque, cockatoo. 50.00
Wall Plaque, Greg & Grace, black and white, gold
  trim, price for pair 150.00

CEREAL BOXES

The first packaged, ready–to–eat breakfast cereal appeared around 1900. Until the 1930s, most advertising and packaging was targeted toward mothers. The popularity of children's radio programs and their sponsorship by cereal manufacturers, such as General Mills, Quaker, Post, and Ralston, shifted the focus to youngsters.

By the 1950s cereal premiums inside the box and cutouts on cereal box backs were a standard feature. Cereal boxes also were used to promote television shows and the personalities and characters that appeared on them. By the early 1970s, cereal manufacturers issued special promotional boxes, many of which featured local and national sports heroes.

As the 1990s come to a close, cereal box prices are highly speculative. Market manipulators are at work. Crossover collectors are paying premium prices for character and personality boxes whose long–term collectibility is uncertain.

References: Scott Bruce, *Cereal Box Bonanza: The 1950's,* Collector Books, 1995; Scott Bruce and Bill Crawford, *Cerealizing America: The Unsweetened Story of American Breakfast Cereals,* Faber and Faber, 1995.

Periodical: *Flake*, PO Box 481, Cambridge, MA 02140.

Collectors' Club: Sugar–Charged Cereal Collectors, 92B N Bedford St, Arlington, VA 22201.

Note: All boxes are in good condition.

Alpha–Bits, Post, front with classic Alpha–Bits mailman delivering his "letters," alphabet letters offer on back, 1960s . . . . **$ 225.00**

Cheerios, General Mills, Betty Crocker, Canadian, front with Air Force figure and airport offer, Cheerios Airport cutout on back, 1950s. **45.00**

Clover Farm Regular Cooking Rolled Oats, cylindrical, bee and clover flower, 1930s, 10" h **40.00**

Cocoa Puffs, General Mills, front shows aircraft carrier/jet launcher toy and cereal, aircraft carrier cutout on back, 1950s **65.00**

Corn Flakes, Kellogg's, Vanessa Williams, 1984 . . . . **45.00**

Donkey Kong Junior, baseball card pack, Ralston, 1984 . . . . **30.00**

Frosted Flakes, Kellogg's, Tony the Tiger spoon offer, 1975 . . . . **40.00**

Kix, General Mills, personalized pencil offer, 1987 . . . . . . **10.00**

OK's, Kellogg's, Snack Pack, Brawny character on front, OK information on back, 1960s **25.00**

Rice Chex, Ralston, checkerboard design, 1950s. **65.00**

Rice Krispies, Kellogg's, Canadian, Annie Oakley doll offer, French and English text, 1950s **95.00**

Rice Krispies, Kellogg's, Pop A Ball offer, 1964 . . . . **25.00**

Shreddies Whole Wheat Cereal, Nabisco, Canadian, Tom, Dick, and Harriet on colorful front, Captain Kidd's Treasure Pit treasure map offer on back, 1960s **65.00**

Sugar Corn Pops, Kellogg's, Andy Devine on his galloping horse on front, Stereo Pics of the West on back with #3 "Jingles Fights Off the Hold–Up Men," cut out and create 3–dimensional action scene, 1950s **165.00**

Wheaties, General Mills, Minnesota Twins, 1987 . . . . **10.00**

CHILDREN'S DISHES

Children's dish sets date back to the Victorian era. In the 1920s and 1930s American glass companies manufactured sets of children's dishes in their most popular patterns. Inexpensive ceramic sets came from Germany and Japan. Injection molded plastic sets first appeared in the late 1940s. By the 1950s, miniature melamine plastic sets mimmicked the family's everyday plastic service.

Most children's dish sets were designed to be used by their owners for tea and doll parties. At the moment, collecting emphasis remains on pre–war sets.

References: Doris Anderson Lechler, *Children's Glass Dishes, China and Furniture* (1983, 1991 value update), *Vol. II* (1986, 1993 value update), Collector Books; Doris Anderson Lechler, *English Toy China,* Antique Publications, 1989; Lorraine Punchard, *Playtime Pottery and Porcelain from The United Kingdom and The United States,* Schiffer Publishing, 1996; Lorraine Punchard, *Playtime Pottery and Porcelain from Europe and Asia,* Schiffer Publishing, 1996; Margaret and Kenn Whitmyer, *Collector's Encyclopedia of Children's Dishes: An Illustrated Value Guide,* Collector Books, 1993, 1995 value update.

Collectors' Club: Toy Dish Collectors, PO Box 159, Bethlehem, CT 06751.

Cake Plate, Willow Ware, open handles . . . . **$ 20.00**

Casserole, cov, Willow Ware, 4³/₄" **25.00**

Cereal Bowl, Akro Agate, fired–on red, J. Pressman **5.00**

Cereal Bowl, Pyrex, trains, blue **12.00**

Creamer, Blue Willow, 2" h **20.00**

Creamer, Cherry Blossom, Jeanette, pink, 1930s **30.00**

Creamer, Doric and Pansy, Jeanette, teal,1937–38 . . . . **35.00**

Creamer, Laurel, McKee, French ivory, red rim, 1930s **30.00**

Creamer, Phoenix Bird **20.00**

Cup, Blue Willow, 2" h **12.00**

Cup, Chiquita, Akro Agate, green **5.00**

Cup, Concentric Ring, Akro Agate, lavender **35.00**

Cup, Pyrex, circus, red. **10.00**

Cup, Pyrex, trains, blue **10.00**

Kellogg's Corn Flakes, red and black letters, white ground, c1945, 7¹/₂ x 10¹/₄ x 2³/₄", $30.00.

Tea Set, china, 9 pcs, luster finish, Japan, orig box, $45.00.

Cup and Saucer, Blue Willow. **15.00**
Cup and Saucer, graniteware, blue **30.00**
Gravy Boat, Willow Ware. **25.00**
Plate, Blue Willow, ³/₄" d **8.00**
Plate, Blue Willow, 3¹/₂" d **10.00**
Plate, Moderntone, turquoise, rust, gold, and gray. **8.00**
Plate, Pyrex, divided, circus, red. **12.00**
Platter, Blue Willow, oval, 6¹/₄ x 3¹/₄". **25.00**
Saucer, Moderntone, gray, gold **8.00**
Set, Cherry Blossom, pink, complete in orig box **375.00**
Set, E. T., pitcher, tray, sugar and creamer, and 4 cups
    and saucers, plates, and spoons, plastic, orig
    unopened box, Chilton–Globe **50.00**
Set, Jesus Loves Me Prayer Set, divided bowl, cup,
    and mug **55.00**
Set, Little Hostess Party Set, Moderntone, 14 pcs,
    pastel. **125.00**
Set, Stacked Disc, Akro Agate, 16 pcs, white creamer
    and sugar, blue cup and teapot, green plate, pink
    saucer and teapot lid **150.00**
Sugar, Chiquita, Akro Agate, transparent cobalt blue **10.00**
Sugar, cov, Blue Willow, 2³/₄" h. **22.00**
Sugar, cov, Cherry Blossom, Jeanette, delphite. **30.00**
Sugar, cov, Laurel, McKee, ivory. **35.00**
Tea Set, Homespun, Jeanette, pink, 1930–49. . . . . **250.00**
Tea Set, Nippon, 3¹/₄" teapot, creamer, sugar, 3 cups
    and saucers, 2 geese, blue bands, Sun mark **275.00**
Tea Set, tin, 11 pcs, elephants **35.00**
Teapot, cov, Blue Willow, 4" h **50.00**
Teapot, cov, Moderntone, turquoise **125.00**

CHINTZ

Chintz patterned goods owe their origin to Indian chintes, fabrics decorated with richly hued flowers and brightly plumed mythical birds that were imported to England from India in the 17th century. Although English Staffordshire potters produced chintz pattern ceramics as early as the 1820s, the golden age of chintz decorated ceramics dates from 1920 through 1940. Dozens of post–World War II patterns were made. Collectors, however, prefer pre–war examples.

This is a broad collecting category. While Chintz pattern ceramics receive the most coverage, anything from fabrics to wallpaper with a Chintz pattern has collector appeal.

References: Linda Eberle and Susan Scott, *The Charlton Standard Catalogue of Chintz, 2nd Edition,* Charlton Press, 1997; Muriel Miller, *Collecting Royal Winton Chintz,* Francis Joseph Publications, 1996, distributed by Krause Publications; Jo Anne Peterson Welsh, *Chintz Ceramics,* Schiffer Publishing, 1996.

Collectors' Club: Chintz China Collector's Club, PO Box 6126, Folsom, CA 95763.

Bonbon, Cheadle, Grimwade, Royal Winton. . . . . **$ 55.00**
Bonbon, Marina, Elijah Cotton, Lord Nelson. **45.00**
Bud Vase, Eleanor, Grimwade, Royal Winton **80.00**
Butter Dish, Cheadle, Grimwade, Royal Winton **175.00**
Cake Plate, tab handle, Rosetime, Elijah Cotton, Lord
    Nelson. **145.00**
Cake Stand, 2–tier, Chelsea, Grimwade, Royal Winton . . **200.00**

Tidbit, 2 tiers, Lefton, pink roses, gold trim, 5¹/₄" h, $55.00.

Coaster, Chelsea, Grimwade, Royal Winton **55.00**
Compote, ftd, Kinver, Grimwade, Royal Winton **200.00**
Condiment Set, Festival, Crown Ducal, AG
    Richardson. **160.00**
Creamer and Sugar, Florita, James Kent. **120.00**
Creamer and Sugar, Marina, Elijah Cotton, Lord
    Nelson. **95.00**
Egg Cup, ftd, Cheadle, Grimwade, Royal Winton **65.00**
Jam Pot, Apple Blossom, James Kent. **120.00**
Jam Pot, with liner, Rosetime, Elijah Cotton, Lord
    Nelson. **125.00**
Nut Dish, Clevedon, Grimwade, Royal Winton **60.00**
Plate, Chintz, Grimwade, Royal Winton, 9" d **75.00**
Relish, English Rose, Grimwade, Royal Winton **190.00**
Salad Bowl, chrome rim, Floral Feast, Grimwade,
    Royal Winton. **125.00**
Salt and Pepper Shakers, pr, Chintz, Grimwade, Royal
    Winton **50.00**
Sandwich Tray, Estelle, Grimwade, Royal Winton,
    10 x 6" **100.00**
Teapot, 4 cup, Eleanor, Grimwade, Royal Winton **350.00**

CHRISTMAS COLLECTIBLES

The tradition of a month–long Christmas season, beginning the day after Thanksgiving, devoted to celebration, gift–giving, and religious observance was deeply entrenched by the end of the first World War. By the 1930s retailers from small town merchants to large department stores saw Christmas season sales account for 25% and more of their annual sales volume.

Beginning in the 1960s the length of the Christmas season was extended. By the mid–1990s Christmas decorations appeared in many stores and malls the day after Halloween. Today, some Christmas catalogs arrive in mail boxes as early as September.

References: Robert Brenner, *Christmas Past, 3rd Edition,* Schiffer Publishing, 1996; Robert Brenner, *Christmas Through The Decades,* Schiffer Publishing, 1993; Jill Gallina, *Christmas Pins Past and Present,* Collector Books, 1996; George Johnson,

Christmas Ornaments, Lights & Decorations, (1987, 1995 value update), *Vol. II* (1997), *Vol. III* (1997), Collector Books; Polly and Pam Judd, *Santa Dolls & Figurines Price Guide: Antique to Contemporary, Revised,* Hobby House Press, 1994; Chris Kirk, *The Joy Of Christmas Collecting,* L–W Book Sales, 1994; Mary Morrison, *Snow Babies, Santas and Elves: Collecting Christmas Bisque Figures,* Schiffer Publishing, 1993; Margaret and Kenn Whitmyer, *Christmas Collectibles; Identification and Value Guide, Second Edition,* Collector Books, 1994, 1996 value update.

Collectors' Club: Golden Glow of Christmas Past, 6401 Winsdale St, Minneapolis, MN 55427

Advertising Trade Card, Dundee Smart Clothes, Allentown, PA, Santa with pack on back, 1941 . . . . . . **$ 4.00**
Bank, Santa sitting on chimney, chalkware, 11" h **25.00**
Bell, The Bells of St. Nicholas, electric, 1957 . . . . **100.00**
Book, *Miracle On 34th St,* Valentine Davies, Harcourt, Brace and Co, 1947 . . . . **12.00**
Book, *The Night Before Christmas,* pub by John C. Winston, Everett Shin illus, 1942 . . . . **15.00**
Candy Box, cardboard, Christmas scenes, 1930s, 3 x 5 x 1½" **5.00**
Candy Box, Fanny Farmer, litho cardboard, Santa in chimney **30.00**
Candy Box, stockings hanging over hearth, string handle, 1940–50, 3 x 5" **5.00**
Candy Cane Holder, molded cardboard, Santa holding sack over chimney, USA, late 1940s, 10" h **50.00**
Candy Container, plastic, Santa, white with black and red trim, head moves, 1960s, 4" h **5.00**
Catalog, Kirkman & Son Inc, Kirkman Products, Brooklyn, NY, "For a Merry Christmas Save Your Kirkman Coupons, They Will Bring Joy and Happiness to the Kiddies," illus, children's toys and novelties, 1920s, 8 pgs **15.00**
Chocolate Mold, Santa carrying basket, tin, double hinged, c1930 . . . . **125.00**
Clicker, Santa at fireplace, litho tin, 1930s **40.00**
Coloring Book, Santa Claus, 1950 . . . . **8.00**
Cookie Jar, Santa, mkd "Metlox Calif USA" **60.00**
Cookie Jar, Christmas tree, California Original, mkd "873" **100.00**
Cookie Jar, snowman, mkd "Made in Mexico" **35.00**
Creche, litho paper foldout, Swedish, c1930, 6" h **25.00**
Creche, pressed cardboard, 1940s **40.00**
Creche Figure, camel, celluloid, 1930s **30.00**
Figure, Santa, composition, jointed, c1930s, 16" h **300.00**
Figure, Santa, cotton, plaster face, papier mâché reindeer, cardboard sled, Japan, 1930s, 2½" h **40.00**
Greeting Card, Merry Christmas, fold out, Santa on front, trace picture inside, 1930s, 8" h **5.00**
Hooks, Grip–Its, orig price 10¢, c1930s **3.00**
Hooks, Santa's Handy Helper, USA, 1960s **2.00**
Lamp, Rudolph, E. M. C. Art, 12" h **55.00**
Lamp, Santa, plastic, red and white, electric, 1950s, 24" h **25.00**
Lamp, Santa, plastic, red flocked suit, tin back with hole for light bulb, Glo–Light Corp, Chicago, IL, 1950s, 8½" h **10.00**

Lantern, Snowman, glass, metal handle and base, 1950 . . . . **25.00**
Light Bulb, figural, Betty Boop, painted milk glass, c1940 . . . . **75.00**
Light Bulb, figural, bird, painted milk glass, 3" h **2.00**
Light Bulb, figural, boy wearing orange overalls, painted milk glass, c1940s **25.00**
Light Bulb, figural, lion wearing red jacket, blue vest, and green pants, holding pipe, painted milk glass, c1940 . . . . **45.00**
Light Bulb, figural, Santa at chimney, painted milk glass, Japan, 3" h **35.00**
Light Set, Bubble Lites, rocket ship shape, Noma **50.00**
Light Set, Japanese style houses, 1930s **80.00**
Light Set, luminous candles, 1940s **40.00**
Magazine Tear Sheet, Whitman's Candy, Christmas motif, 1934 . . . . **15.00**
Mask, Santa, 1930s **25.00**
Ornament, bear holding candy cane, felt, 3" h **2.00**
Ornament, bell, plastic, 4" h **2.00**
Ornament, Santa holding tree, glass, 1930s, 3¾" h **25.00**
Ornament, icicle, spiraled, 1950s, 14" l **20.00**
Ornament, lantern, plastic **5.00**
Ornament, reindeer, silvered glass **30.00**
Ornament, soldier, hp, c1970 . . . . **2.00**
Ornament, star, Occupied Japan **10.00**
Pinback Button, department store Santa, rim inscription, 1920s, 1¼" d **18.00**
Pinback Button, Orr's Dept Store, Santa, light green ground, black letters, 1940–50, 1½" **18.00**
Plate, Holly Hobby, Christmas 1974 . . . . **18.00**
Poster, "Buy Christmas Seals–Fight Tuberculosis," Uncle Sam carrying Christmas seals pkgs, 1926, 21 x 28" **150.00**

Light Bulb, 5–pointed star, painted and mica–coated tin with plastic points and cutout stars, Mazda, c1935, 4¼" h, $10.00.

Toy, windup, litho tin Santa with molded vinyl head, plush over tin reindeer with rubber antlers and nose, key wind, paper label "Made In Japan," 5" l, 5³/₄" h, $75.00.

Puzzle, wood, Christmas card, "Seasons Greetings," 1930 .... 20.00

Sheet Music, *All I Want For Christmas Is My Two Front Teeth,* Don Gardner, 1946 .... 2.00

Sheet Music, *Christmas Day,* Benny Davis and Ted Murry, Eddie Fisher photo on cov, 1952 .... 2.00

Sheet Music, *Rudolph the Red Nosed Reindeer,* Johnny Marks, 1949 .... 5.00

Sheet Music, *White Christmas,* Irving Berlin, 1924 .... 8.00

Telegram, Western Union, Holiday Greetings, Santa and Christmas trees, dated Dec 24, 1946 .... 12.00

Tin, Blue Bird Toffee, Santa's face and toys, litho illus, 8 sided, Henry Vincent Ltd, Worcestershire, England 40.00

Tinsel, lead, Lustre–Brite 10.00

Toy, Happy Santa, plastic and tin, cotton flannel suit, Japan, 1950s, 12" h 100.00

Toy, Santa on Tricycle, windup, litho tin tricycle, celluloid Santa, Japan, 4" l 45.00

Toy, Santa, windup, litho tin, Chein, c1930, 5¹/₂" h 95.00

Tree, aluminum, 5' h, c1950s 40.00

Tree, green cellophane needles, multicolor bubble lights, white plastic base, 1950s, 19" h 50.00

Tree, electric, white–tinted vinyl, wooden base, 1950s, 19" h 20.00

Tree Fence, wood, green, 12 sections, 44 x 66" 75.00

Tree Stand, cast iron, square, 1930s 50.00

Tree Topper, angel, hard plastic, white and gold robe, clear wings, 1950s, 10" l 20.00

Tree Topper, angel, satin skirt, braided hair, gold crown, c1950, 6" h 8.00

Tree Topper, star, tin, 5 bulbs at points, Noma, c1930 .... 25.00

CIGAR COLLECTIBLES

Cigars and cigarettes are not synonymous. Cigars have always had an aloofness about them. They were appreciated by a select group of smokers, not the masses. Cigar connoisseurs are as fanatical as wine aficionados concerning the objects of their affection.

The cigar renaissance of the early 1990s, bolstered by the auction of cigar memorabilia belonging to George Burns, has renewed collector interest in cigar collectibles. The primary focus is advertising. Prices remain stable for traditional cigar collectibles such as cutters, molds, and cigar store figures.

References: Tony Hyman, *Handbook of American Cigar Boxes,* Arnet Art Museum, 1979, 1995 value update; Norman E. Martinus and Harry L. Rinker, *Warman's Paper,* Wallace–Homestead, Krause Publications, 1994; Jerry Terranova, *Antique Cigar Cutters and Lighters,* Schiffer Publishing, 1996.

Collectors' Clubs: Cigar Label Collectors International, PO Box 66, Sharon Center, OH 44274; International Seal, Label and Cigar Band Society, 8915 E Bellevue St, Tucson, AZ 85715.

Ashtray, White Owl Cigars, blue, white, and brown, 1930s .... $ 8.00

Box, Brown Bomber, 1930s 15.00

Box, Capitol Giants, 1950s 40.00

Box, Corina Larks, 1950s 5.00

Box, Franklin Roosevelt, 1930s 45.00

Box, Ivanhoe, 1950s 10.00

Box, Lord Byron, 1950s 10.00

Box, Postmaster, 1930s 10.00

Box, Tom Moore, cardboard 5.00

Box, White Owl, cardboard 5.00

Catalog, American Electrical Nov & Mfg Co Ever Ready Portable Electric Cigar Lighters, 8 pgs, 1925 .... 30.00

Cigar, Buster Brown 7.00

Cigar Band, diecut, emb paper, red, gold, and black design, black and white Ken Maynard photo, 1930s, 1 x 3" 20.00

Cigar Box Label, Blue Bird, 1925–40 .... 75.00

Cigar Box Label, Brown Beauties, 1950s 15.00

Cigar Box Label, Co–Ed, 1940s 25.00

Cigar Box Label, Dutch Maid, 1960s 45.00

Cigar Label, Spirit of St. Louis, 6¹/₂ x 8¹/₂", $30.00.

Cigar Box Label, White House, 1930s. **12.00**
Cutter, figural, bulldog, cast iron. **45.00**
Cutter, Trick Lock Cigar Cutter, 1930s **20.00**
Jar, Dutch Masters, ceramic, 1960s. **5.00**
Jar, William Tell, plastic, 1950s. **10.00**
Key Chain, Muriel Cigars **10.00**
Label, Las Vegas Cigars, cigar crate. **5.00**
Lighter, brass, counter model **70.00**
Match Safe, Pierce's 9 Cigars **40.00**
Matchbook Holder, metal, red Muriel lady insert,
   1920s **12.00**
Pin, Tampa–Cuba Cigar Co, enameled **45.00**
Punch Board, Peter Manning Cigars adv, 1930s. **12.00**
Sign, El Wadora Cigars, tin, c1930, 24 x 36". **45.00**
Sign, Eventual 5 Cent Cigar, cardboard, red and
   green, 1920s, 7 x 20" **15.00**
Tin, Between the Acts, 1920–60. . . . . **2.00**
Tin, Dutch Masters, 1960s. **5.00**
Tin, El Producto Blunt, 1960s. **5.00**
Tin, Galleons and Admirals, 1960s. **5.00**
Tin, Gink's Stogies, 1930 . . . . **15.00**
Tin, Headline, 1950s **2.00**
Tin, Lord Baltimore, paper label, 1950s **15.00**
Tin, Muriel, 1930s. **20.00**
Tin, Optimo **5.00**
Tin, Phillies, 1920s **5.00**
Tin, Possum, 1920s **40.00**
Tin, White Owl Squires, 1970s. **2.00**
Trimmer, figural pelican. **40.00**
Vending Machine, Malkin Phillies, steel, 10¢, c1930. . . . . **75.00**

CIGARETTE COLLECTIBLES

The number of cigarette smokers grew steadily throughout the 19th century and first two decades of the 20th century. By the 1940s the cigarette was the dominant tobacco product sold in America. In the 1950s cigarette manufacturers were major periodical and television advertisers.

The Surgeon General's Report changed everything. Despite limitations on advertising and repeated non–smoking bans, the cigarette industry has proven highly resourceful in creating public exposure for its product—just watch any televised NASCAR race.

Although under attack on a number of fronts in the United States today, the cigarette industry continues to make substantial gains abroad, particularly in Asia. Surprisingly, as the anti–smoking crusade has become stronger, the interest in cigarette and cigarette-related collectibles has increased. Cigarette memorabilia, especially advertising dating between 1945 and 1960, is one of the hot collectibles of the 1990s.

References: Douglas Congdon–Martin, *Camel Cigarette Collectibles: The Early Years, 1913–1963,* Schiffer Publishing, 1996; Douglas Congdon–Martin, *Camel Cigarette Collectibles, 1964–1995,* Schiffer Publishing, 1997; Norman E. Martinus and Harry L. Rinker, *Warman's Paper,* Wallace–Homestead, Krause Publications, 1994; Murray Cards International Ltd. (comp.), *Cigarette Card Values: 1994 Catalogue of Cigarette and Other Trade Cards,* Murray Cards International, 1994; Neil Wood, *Smoking Collectibles: A Price Guide,* L–W Book Sales, 1994.

Collectors' Club: Cigarette Pack Collectors Assoc, 61 Searle St, Georgetown, MA 01833.

Ashtray, rubber tire, "I Love My Stones" glass insert,
   6 x 2" . . . . **$ 20.00**
Bottle Holder, 3–dimensional Camel Joe, vinyl head **10.00**
Brochure, Camel, "Know Your Nerves," 1934, 3 x 4". **20.00**
Camera, Parliment. **15.00**
Cigarette Case, brass collar, red and blue design on
   top, mkd "Henrietta" inside, 1930–40. . . . . **10.00**
Cigarette Pack, Domino Cigarettes, in tin, unopened **15.00**
Cigarette Rolling Machine, Bond Roller Case Co,
   1943 . . . . **5.00**
Commemorative Medal, bronze, R. J. Reynolds
   100th anniversary, 1975 . . . . **20.00**
Cooler, vinyl, Camel Joe puffing on cigarette, 1991,
   4" **10.00**
Cup, plastic, Camel Joe, 12 oz, 1980s **25.00**
Decal, Lucky Strike, full–size Lucky Green pack,
   dated 1931, 6" sq. **15.00**
Fan, Kool adv, diecut cardboard, wood handle,
   1937, 10 x 8". **30.00**
Figure, penguin, composition, Kool, black and white,
   green base, 4" h **120.00**
Magazine, *Fortune,* October, 1949, 5–pg article with
   photos, Phillip Morris comeback. **15.00**
Magazine Tear Sheet, *The Saturday Evening Post,*
   Avalon Cigarettes adv, Jan 28, 1939 . . . . **5.00**
Match Holder, tin, Kool adv, Willy the penguin, 8 x 7" . . . **15.00**
Poster, Kool, smoking penguin, c1933, 12 x 18" **35.00**
Poster, Old Gold Cigarettes, Indian maiden wearing
   headdress, holding bow and arrow, product package lower right corner, sgd by George Petty, c1940,
   31· x 43". **350.00**
Punch Board, Dixie Queen Cigarettes, unused,
   1930s, 8 x 10" **25.00**
Punch Board, Super Smokes, unused, 1940s, 13" sq **50.00**
Radio, Benson & Hedges, battery operated, MIB **20.00**
Ruler, Philip Morris Cigarettes, plastic, Johnny image,
   1940s, 2 x 6¼" **20.00**
Salt and Pepper Shakers, pr, Kool, figural penguin,
   plastic, 1950, 3½" h. **15.00**

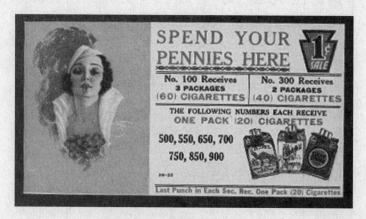

Punchboard Label, $5.00.

Sheet Music, Chesterfield Cigarettes, *A Story of Two Cigarettes,* 2 Chesterfield cigarettes resting in ashtray on cover, Mickey Stoner, Fred Jay, and Leonard K. Marker, 1945 . . . . **15.00**
Sign, Camel Cigarettes, cigarette pack, 1940s **185.00**
Sign, Kool Cigarettes, tin, penguin, 1950s **45.00**
Sign, Lucky Strike, orchestra, 1940s **125.00**
Sign, Old Gold Cigarettes, cardboard stand–up, Fred Waring and His Pennsylvanians, "Listen Every Wednesday," 18 x 24" **45.00**
Thermometer, Grads Cigarettes, porcelain, graduate, 8 x 39", 1930s **100.00**
Thermometer, Salem Cigarettes, cardboard, green and gold, emb cigarette pack **10.00**
Thermometer, Winston Cigarettes, tin, 1960s **335.00**
Tin, Lucky Strike, pocket size **35.00**
Tin, Muratti's Young Ladies Cigarettes **12.00**
Tin, Puck, yellow, blue, and red, 1920–40 . . . . **35.00**

Program, King and Franklin Circus, 1947, 8½ x 11", $15.00.

CIRCUS ITEMS

The 1920s through the 1940s marked the golden age of the tent circus. The circus trains for Ringlings and Barnum and Baily often exceeded 100 cars. The advent of television marked the beginning of the tent circus' decline. Mergers occurred. Most small circuses simply vanished. Today, the majority of circus performances occur at civic and institution auditoriums, not under the Big Top.

Most circus collectors are individuals who remember attending a circus under canvas. When this generation dies, what will be the fate of circus collectibles? Categories with crossover potential, e.g., lithographed posters, will hold collector interest. Others will vanish just as did the great circuses they document.

Reference: Norman E. Martinus and Harry L. Rinker, *Warman's Paper,* Wallace–Homestead, Krause Publications, 1994.

Collectors' Clubs: Circus Fans Assoc of America, PO Box 59710, Potomac, MD 20859; Circus Historical Society, 3477 Vienna Court, Westerville, OH 43081.

Book, *Toby Tyler or 10 Weeks With a Circus,* James Otis, Goldsmith Publishing, c1930 . . . . **$ 5.00**
Calendar, multicolored, "Season's Greetings, Helen and Karl Wallenda," 1977, 7¼ x 12¼" **10.00**
Carnival Game, bean toss, barrel with 2 caricatures of black men's heads, one above barrel, one peering through hole, 45" h, 22" w **1,000.00**
Carousel Horse, Spillman, jumper, jeweled layered trappings, fringed blanket, large single rose on breast strap, c1924, 58" l **5,500.00**
Game, Emmett Kelly's Circus, All–Fair, 1953 . . . . **45.00**
Greeting Card, multicolored, heavy paper, 1925–26 Greetings From Ringling Bros and Barnum & Bailey Combined Shows **40.00**
Magazine, *Cole Bros Circus, America's Favorite Show,* multicolored cov, 1942, 34 pages, 8¼ x11" **30.00**
Menu, Ringling Bros and Barnum & Bailey Combined, The World's Largest Amusement Institution at Home on the Nation's Birthday, Bridgeport, CT, Fourth of July, 1920, 6¼ x 9½" **25.00**

Newspaper, *Sarasota Herald–Tribune,* circus edition, Sarasota, FL, "Circus Comes To Town," March 24, 1944, 8 pgs **30.00**
Pennant, Ringling Bros and Barnum & Bailey Circus, felt, white lettering and circus scenes on brown ground, yellow trim and streamers, 1940s, 24" l **25.00**
Pinback Button, Clyde Beatty Circus, black and white photo of lion tamer Beatty and lion, blue ground, 1940s, 1¾" d **10.00**
Postcard, Ringling Bros, foldout, 1943 . . . . **20.00**
Poster, Downey Bros Big 3 Ring Circus, elephants, camels, and horses in line, aerial artist leaping overhead, audience in background, "Leaps— Revival of that Astounding and Sensational Exhibition," c1925, 41 x 27" **125.00**
Poster, Hoxie Bros Old Time Circus Land, One Mile West of Walt Disney World, multicolored view of circus grounds and big top, 20 x 27" **65.00**
Program, Ringling Bros and Barnum & Bailey Combined Shows, black and white illus, 1923 season, 14 pgs, 6¾ x 10" **30.00**
Punchout Album, Clyde Beatty & His Wild Animal Act, Fold–A–Way Toys, Will Pente, ©1935, 9 x 13" **75.00**
Ticket, Clyde Beatty–Cole Bros Combined Circus, issued by F. F. R. Brown, black and red, 1960 season, 5½ x 2", price for pair **70.00**

CLARICE CLIFF

Clarice Cliff (1899–1972) joined A. J. Wilkinson's Royal Staffordshire Pottery at Burslem, England, in the early 1910s. In 1930 she became the company's art director.

Cliff is one of England's foremost 20th century ceramic designers. Her influence covered a broad range–shapes, forms, and patterns. Her shape lines include Athens, Biarritz, Chelsea, Conical, Iris, Lynton, and Stamford. Applique, Bizarre, Crocus, Fantasque, and Ravel are among the most popular patterns.

In addition to designer shape and pattern lines, Cliff's signature also appears on a number of inexpensive dinnerware lines manufactured under the Royal Staffordshire label.

References: Susan and Al Bagdade, *Warman's English & Continental Pottery & Porcelain, 2nd Edition,* Wallace–Homestead, Krause Publications, 1991; Leonard R. Griffin and Susan Pear Meisel, *Clarice Cliff: The Bizarre Affair,* Harry N. Abrams, 1994; Pat and Howard Watson, *The Clarice Cliff Colour Price Guide,* Francis Joseph Publications, 1995, distributed by Krause Publications.

Collectors' Club: Clarice Cliff Collector's Club, Fantasque House, Tennis Dr, The Park, Nottingham, NG7 1AE, England.

REPRODUCTION ALERT: Lotus vases.

Ashtray, Tonquin pattern, Royal Staffordshire Pottery, Wilkinson, Ltd . . . . **$ 45.00**
Bone Dish, Tonquin pattern, brown transfer, 6³/₄" l **18.00**
Bowl, Bizarre Ware, Crocus pattern, orange, blue, and purple crocuses, green grass, tan band, green base, int bands of yellow, cream, and tan separated by green lines, 5³/₄" d **225.00**
Bowl, Bizarre Ware, purple and orange triangles separated by cream bands outlined in black, black base, int with green, cream, and orange bands separated by black, 7³/₄" d **750.00**
Bowl, Bizarre Ware, yellow, orange, and brown flowers, gray leaves, cream ground, yellow int with orange and brown flowers, 7³/₄" d **500.00**
Bowl, Tonquin pattern, purple, 5" d **5.00**
Bowl, Tonquin pattern, purple, 9" d **20.00**
Candlestick, Bizarre Ware, orange, blue, green, rust, and yellow geometrics, 2¹/₂" h **325.00**
Cracker Jar, Bizarre Ware, My Garden pattern, rattan handle, 9¹/₄" h **350.00**
Creamer and Sugar, Bizarre Ware, hp landscape scene with sky and gold stars, ovoid **250.00**

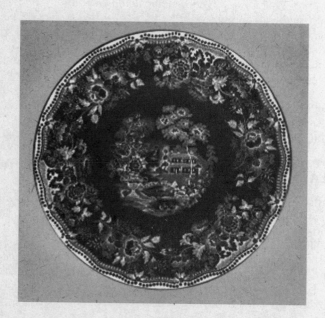

Soup Plate, Tonquin pattern, blue, 8" d, $20.00.

Dinner Service, Tonquin pattern, brown, 46 pcs, eight 10" dinner plates, 8 dessert plates, seven 6¹/₂" d salad plates, 6 cups, 8 saucers, creamer and sugar, round bowl, and oval platter **125.00**
Dish, Bizarre Ware, brown, orange, and tan stripes, cream ground, mkd "The Biarritz, Bizarre Ware," 9" l, 7³/₄" w **50.00**
Gravy Boat and Underplate, Tonquin pattern, purple **25.00**
Honey Pot, Bizarre Ware, Crocus pattern, figural bee finial **125.00**
Jug, Bizarre Ware, brown speckled ground, border of orange and yellow nasturtium with circular green leaves, 12" h **575.00**
Pitcher, Bizarre Ware, bulbous, yellow, blue, and blue floral bands, green lines, 5¹/₄" h **500.00**
Pitcher, Bizarre Ware, Delicia Pansies pattern, pink, yellow, and rose florals with brown stems on cream ground, hp green base and top, splashed green on top int, 8" h **675.00**
Pitcher, Bizarre Ware, Rhodanthe pattern, cylindrical, pastel pink, green, and yellow, 11¹/₄" h **200.00**
Plaque, Bizarre Ware, orange, yellow, and lavender flowers, 13" d **600.00**
Plate, Bizarre Ware, stylized branches, black concentric rings, 6" d **100.00**
Plate, Tonquin pattern, blue transfer, 8" d **8.00**
Plate, Tonquin pattern, pink transfer, 6¹/₂" d **5.00**
Platter, Tonquin pattern, purple transfer, 11¹/₂" l **20.00**
Platter, Tonquin pattern, red transfer, 12" l **15.00**
Sauceboat and Underplate, Tonquin pattern, brown transfer **20.00**
Soup Plate, Tonquin pattern, pink transfer, 8" d **20.00**
Sugar Bowl, cov, Bizarre Ware, ribbed, brown lines and green swag line on cream ground, 4¹/₂" h **150.00**
Sugar Shaker, Bizarre Ware, Crocus pattern, blue, orange, and purple crocuses, 5¹/₂" h **225.00**
Sugar Shaker, Bizarre Ware, orange, gold, and brown flowers, cream and yellow ground, 5" h **100.00**
Sugar Shaker, Bizarre Ware, red poppies, green, cream, and black outlines, silver top, 6¹/₄" h **650.00**
Teapot, cov, Tonquin pattern, reddish brown **100.00**
Vase, Bizarre Ware, My Garden pattern, 10¹/₂" h **1,200.00**

CLICKERS

These noisemakers were extremely popular from the early 1930s through the late 1950s. Many were distributed to adults and children as advertising premiums. Those touting a particular beer, hotel, political, or household product were meant for adults. Children delighted in receiving clickers when buying Buster Brown or Red Goose shoes. The Halloween season was responsible for more clickers than any other holiday season.

Duo–Therm, litho tin, yellow, red, and black, "Snappy Weather Ahead," c1940 . . . . **$ 20.00**
Frog, figural, Life of Party Products, Kirchhof, Newark, NJ, 3" l **5.00**
Gunther's Beer, litho tin, white and red, "The Beer That Clicks," c1930 . . . . **18.00**
Halloween, tin, orange, black, and white, 1930s **15.00**
Hirshberg's Stag Paste Paint, adv, litho tin, 1930s **20.00**

Humpty Dumpty Shoes, litho tin, multicolored,
c1930 . . . . **30.00**

Nibroc, red and black, dachshund and bone,
1940–50 . . . . **22.00**

Nixon, tin, "Click with Dick" **25.00**

Peters Weatherbird Shoes, litho tin, multicolored,
1930s, ³/₄ x 1³/₄" **25.00**

Quaker State Motor Oil, litho tin, green and white,
1930s **15.00**

Red Goose Shoes, litho tin, red goose, 1930s **25.00**

Santa, standing beside fireplace, litho tin, 1930s **40.00**

Soldier, litho tin, movable arms, mkd "Made in
Germany," 1930s **50.00**

Tastykake, Tastykake girl, 1940–50 . . . . **15.00**

Weston's Crackers, litho tin, yellow and red, c1930 . . . . . **20.00**

CLOCKS

At the moment, this collecting category is heavily dominated by
collectors of character alarm clocks, especially those dating from
the 1940s and 50s. Strong collector interest also exists for electric
and key wind novelty clocks. Clocks featuring advertising also
have a strong following.

Generic clocks, for example mass–produced Big Ben alarm
clocks, have little or no collector interest. 1920s and 30s wood-
cased mantel clocks, banjo–style wall clocks, and period 1950s
wall clocks prove the exception.

References: Hy Brown, *Comic Character Timepieces: Seven
Decades of Memories,* Schiffer Publishing, 1992; Michael Bruner,
Advertising Clocks: America's Timeless Heritage, Schiffer
Publishing, 1995.

Collectors' Club: National Assoc of Watch and Clock Collectors,
Inc, 514 Poplar St, Columbia, PA 17512.

Advertising, Diet Rite Cola, glass bubble dome cov,
black, white, and blue . . . . **$ 150.00**

Advertising, Kit Kat **30.00**

Advertising, Sylvania TV, Halolight, lights up **180.00**

Advertising, Tip Top Trailers, lights up, 1950s **150.00**

**Character,
Hopalong
Cassidy, alarm,
U.S. Time,
5¹/₂" h,
$250.00.**

Character, Cat in the Hat, windup, alarm, steel, red
enamel, ©1978, 4" d, 6" h **80.00**

Character, Charlie, Star Kist Tuna, windup, metal,
"Sorry Charlie" sign on fish hook, c1969 . . . . **65.00**

Character, Cookie Monster, Sesame Street, radio **15.00**

Character, ET, finger and chest light up when alarm
sounds, battery operated **120.00**

Character, Mickey Mouse, wall clock, red plastic
case, inset color paper photo, orig box, Elgin,
1970s **55.00**

Character, Swee' Pea and Popeye, alarm, ivory enam-
eled steel case, color illus on dial, c1968 . . . . **100.00**

Figural, television, plastic, red, black, and wood
grain, mkd "Tele–Vision," stamped "Dec 1961,"
3¹/₂ x 6 x 5" **100.00**

Figural, ship, walnut hull, chrome plated sails and
riggings, lighted portholes, United Clock Co, 1955 . . . **100.00**

Kitchen, banjo shape, New Haven Clock Co, 30" h **150.00**

CLOTHES SPRINKLERS

Although steam irons have made it unnecessary, many individuals
still sprinkle clothing before ironing. In many cases, the sprinkling
bottle is merely a soda bottle with an adaptive cap. However, in
the middle decades of the 20th century, ceramic and glass bottles
designed specifically for sprinkling were made. Many were figural, a primary reason why they have attracted collector interest.

Bottle, glass, hp Pennsylvania Dutch woman with
folk–art design . . . . **$ 35.00**

Bottle, plastic, adv **40.00**

Bottle, plastic, yellow and green, hp flower, Plas–Tex
Corp **20.00**

Cat, black, mkd "ESD," 7¹/₂" h **100.00**

Cat, Siamese, tan, marble eyes, Cardinal China Co,
8¹/₂" h **150.00**

Cat, white, orange glass eyes, mkd "Cardinal," 7¹/₂" h . . . **135.00**

Chinaman, emperor **75.00**

Chinaman, Sprinkle Plenty, yellow and green **30.00**

Chinaman, Sprinkle Plenty, head is sprinkler **125.00**

Chinaman, Sprinkle Plenty, holding sadiron **150.00**

Chinaman, white with blue trim, Cleminson Co **45.00**

Clothespin **125.00**

Dearie is Weary, yellow dress, holding iron, head is
sprinkler **225.00**

Dog, Dachshund, green coat, red bowtie, tail curled
up for handle **300.00**

Dog, Poodle, sitting up on hind legs, gray **150.00**

Dog, Poodle, sitting up on hind legs, pink **190.00**

Dutch Boy **125.00**

Dutch Girl, plastic **55.00**

Dutch Girl, wetter–downer **125.00**

Elephant, gray and pink, raised trunk **50.00**

Fireman, holding hose with sprinkler cap in front **300.00**

Kitchen Prayer Lady, Enesco Co **275.00**

Mammy, white dress with red trim **250.00**

Mary Poppins, clear glass, holding umbrella and
purse **80.00**

Mary Poppins, wearing hat and dress with striped
skirt, Cleminson **250.00**

Merry Maid, glass **100.00**

Elephants, ceramic, left: white and pink, shamrock on tummy, raised trunk. $60.00; right: happy face, fat and squatty, trunk curled up for handle, $200.00.

Merry Maid, plastic, blue, Reliance, 6½" h 20.00
Myrtle, white dress with polka–dot top, sprinkler in
  back of head, Pfaltzgraff 175.00
Rooster, long neck, plastic cap, 10" h 100.00
Sadiron, ceramic, blue flowers 50.00
Sadiron, ceramic, ivy 40.00
Sadiron, ceramic, decal of woman ironing, c1950s 50.00
Sadiron, ceramic, theme park souvenir 75.00
Sadiron, plastic, green 20.00

CLOTHING

Victorian era clothing is passé. Clothing of the flapper era has lost much of its appeal. Forget pre–1945 entirely. Today's collectors want post–1945 clothing.

1960s psychedelic era clothing is challenging 1950s clothing for front position on sellers' racks. No matter what the era, a major key to clothing's value is a design which screams a specific period. Further, collectors want clothing that is ready to wear. Older collectors still love to play "dress up."

Hollywood, television, and movie personality related and high–style fashion designer clothing is now steady fare at almost every major American auction house. Prices continue to rise. Many buyers are foreign. Paris may be center stage for the contemporary clothing market, but the American collectibles marketplace is the focus of vintage clothing sales.

References: Mark Blackburn, *Hawaiiana: The Best of Hawaiian Design*, Schiffer Publishing, 1996; Maryanne Dolan, *Vintage Clothing: 1880–1980*, 3rd Edition, Books Americana, Krause Publications, 1995; Roseanne Ettinger, *'50s Popular Fashions For Men, Women, Boys & Girls*, Schiffer Publishing, 1995; Kristina Harris, *Vintage Fashions for Women: 1920s–1940s*, Schiffer Publishing, 1996; Ellie Laubner, *Fashions of the Roaring '20s*, Schiffer Publishing, 1996; Jan Lindenberger, *Clothing & Accessories from the '40s, '50s & '60s: A Handbook and Price Guide*, Schiffer Publishing, 1996; Nancy M. Schiffer, *Hawaiian Shirt Design*, Schiffer Publishing, 1997; Diane Snyder–Haug, *Antique & Vintage Clothing: A Guide to Dating & Valuation of Women's Clothing, 1850 to 1940*, Collector Books, 1997; Sheila

Steinberg and Kate E. Dooner, *Fabulous Fifties: Designs for Modern Living*, Schiffer Publishing, 1993.

Collectors' Club: The Costume Society of America, PO Box 73, Earleville, MD 21919.

Bed Jacket, satin, pink, lavish ecru lace," B
  Altman & Co, NY," label, 1930s . . . . $ 35.00
Bush Jacket, cotton, white, bellow pockets, full belt,
  unused, 1940s 20.00
Camisole, cotton, blue, elastic waist, c1950 . . . . 15.00
Cape, Opera, blue, 1920s 95.00
Cape, satin, evening, ivory, brocade poppies, pink
  satin lining, ruffled pink and ivory silk organdy
  trim, ivory ostrich feather neck dec 200.00
Coat, mohair, mink tail clasp, c1938 . . . . 100.00
Coat, muskrat, bell shaped sleeves 50.00
Coat, fur, raccoon, full length, c1930 . . . . 125.00
Dinner Dress, chiffon, cerise print on purple, black
  lace bodice, orig taffeta slip, bolero style jacket
  with matching lace trim, c1930. . . . . 500.00
Dress, cotton, lace yoke and cuffs, cloth belt, c1929 . . . . 50.00
Dress, cotton, tucked, eyelet trimmed yoke, sleeves,
  skirt, 3½" open work, scalloped hem, 38" l 20.00
Dress, girl's, rayon, raspberry, accordion pleats 18.00
Dress, silk, floral print, multicolored, cut on bias, low
  backline, c1930 . . . . 90.00
Dress, western style, rust gabardine, white leather trim,
  c1940–50 . . . . 60.00
Dungarees, lady's, flannel lining, unused, 1950s 20.00
Evening Gown, blue velvet, rayon, V–neckline,
  puffed sleeves, c1936 . . . . 200.00
Evening Gown, moire, purple scoop neck, gathered
  front, full hip ruffle, c1940 . . . . 90.00
Evening Gown, satin, lace trim, c1938 . . . . 80.00
Evening Gown, silk, applied rhinestone front, beaded
  fringe, rhinestone belt buckle, c1926. . . . . 450.00
Jacket, wool, blue, tailored, padded shoulders, c1940 . . . . 30.00
Jacket, sequins, net, gold, long sleeves, c1935. . . . . 300.00
Nightgown, rayon, floral print, c1930–40 . . . . 90.00

Evening Dress, Hattie Carnegie, 1950s, aquamarine silk, fitted surplice front, full bubble skirt, sewn from back of shoulders with aquamarine wings faced with turquoise, size 6, labeled, $460.00. Photo courtesy William Doyle Galleries.

Pants Suit, rayon, red and white, polka dot, padded
shoulders, c1940 . . . . **50.00**

Playsuit, child's, jet pilot commander, light blue and
yellow, orig 10⅝ x 12¾ x 1½" box, Herman Iskin
& Co, Telford, PA, 1960s. **185.00**

Robe, satin, rayon, red, padded shoulders, c1940–50 . . . . **40.00**

Shirt, rayon, paisley print, multicolored, "Made in
California," label, c1950–60 . . . . **35.00**

Shirt, rayon, tropical print, "Made in Hawaii" label,
c1950–60 . . . . **45.00**

Skirt, satin, hot pink, black floral flocked designs, full,
1960s **12.00**

Stole, muskrat, "J. W. Robinson, California" label,
c1950 . . . . **120.00**

Sweater, cashmere, white, beaded, lined, c1960 . . . . **55.00**

Sweater, knit, cream, pastel floral embroidery and
beads, 1960s **45.00**

Sweater, orlon, rabbit collar, c1960–70. . . . . **60.00**

Swimsuit, wool, orig tags and box, Jantzen, 1931 . . . . **65.00**

AUCTION PRICES

William Doyle Galleries' Couture, Antique Clothing,
Accessories & Costume Jewelry, and Textiles auction,
December 5, 1996. Prices include a buyer's premium of 15%
of the successful bid price up to and including $50,000, and
10% on any amount in excess of $50,000.

Coat Dress, Christian Dior, c1950, black, white,
and charcoal wool houndstooth trimed with flat
black braid, jacket double–breasted at waist closure, skirt with 2 rows of black buttons and mock
buttonholes, size 6, labeled *Christian Dior
Paris 07825 Made in France*, very good condition . . **575.00**

Ensemble, Chanel, 1960s, single–breasted cream
wool tweed coat lined with civet pieced in banded diamond pattern, cream composition–framed
buttons centered with gilt–metal leaves, skirt of
civet edged with band of cream braid, labeled
Chanel, good condition **1,380.00**

Gentleman's Chesterfield, c1972, navy herringbone
cashmere, black velvet collar, labeled *Dunhill
Taylors New York 3/13/72*, good condition **230.00**

Maillot, Rudi Gernreich, Resort 1962, black wool
knit with triangular midriff cutout, labeled *Rudi
Gernreich for Harmon Knitwear California*, good
condition. **230.00**

Skating Costume, Abercrombie & Fitch, c1950,
black wool, short jacket fastening down front
with rhinestone centered buttons, quilted lining,
short flared skirt edged with red rickrack, both
lined with red taffeta, size 6, labeled **230.00**

CLOTHING ACCESSORIES

The fashion world has rediscovered the styles of the 1940s, 50s,
and 60s. However, the choice of accessories is limited when compared to what was available during those eras. As a result, many
modern outfits are complemented with vintage accessories.

Clothing trends abroad also impact on this market. The craze in
Mediterranean countries for American platform shoes from the
1960s has resulted in a steep rise in prices. Vintage jackets, from
bomber denim, sell better abroad than they do in the United
States.

American preferences still rest with hats and purses. Neckties
and shoes are two categories challenging these leaders.

References: Joanne Dubbs Ball and Dorothy Hehl Torem, *The Art
of Fashion Accessories,* Schiffer Publishing, 1993; Kate E. Dooner,
A Century of Handbags, Schiffer Publishing, 1993; Kate E. Dooner,
Plastic Handbags, Schiffer Publishing, 1992; Roseann Ettinger,
Handbags, Schiffer Publishing, 1992; Ellie Laubner, *Fashions of
the Roaring '20s,* Schiffer Publishing, 1996; Jan Lindenberger,
*Clothing & Accessories from the '40s, '50s & '60s: A Handbook
and Price Guide,* Schiffer Publishing, 1996; Gerald McGrath and
Janet Meana, *Fashion Buckles: Common to Classic,* Schiffer
Publishing, 1997; Peggy Anne Osborne, *Button, Button:
Identification and Price Guide, 2nd Edition,* Schiffer Publishing,
1997; Maureen Reilly and Mary Beth Detrich, *Women's Hats of
the 20th Century for Designers and Collectors,* Schiffer Publishing,
1997; Desire Smith, *Hats,* Schiffer Publishing, 1996; Debra J.
Wisniewski, *Antique & Collectible Buttons: Identification & Values,*
Collector Books, 1996.

Collectors' Club: National Button Society, 2733 Juno Place,
Akron, OH 44313.

Apron, cotton, chartreuse and gold, gold braid
trimmed patch pocket. . . . . **$ 8.00**

Apron, muslin, bib style, pre–stamped and hand–
embroidered floral design. **15.00**

Apron, organdy, bib style, fruit print **15.00**

Apron, cotton, yellow and white, rickrack trim, 1950s **5.00**

Button, oversized, alligator skin, hand stitched, brass
alligator sewn on front, c1930 . . . . **25.00**

Button, pewter, horse design front, Battersea, Ltd,
1970s **10.00**

Cummerbund, satin, black and plaid, c1940 . . . . **10.00**

Fan, paper, lacquered wooden sticks, oriental design **65.00**

Flapper Beads, blue carnival glass beads, c1920 . . . . **40.00**

Gloves, men's driving, leather, black, c1920s **25.00**

Gloves, woman's, silk, shirred, black, c1940 . . . . **15.00**

Handbag, evening, Art Deco, brocade, engraved gold
filled frame **75.00**

Handbag, alligator, baby alligator head, Cuba **45.00**

**Handbag, gold
mesh, Whiting &
Davis Co, 7" w,
$65.00.**

Handbag, beaded, red, white, and turquoise, Indian
   motif, c1920 . . . . **65.00**
Handbag, hand beaded, paisley design, silk lining,
   celluloid frame, c1920–30 . . . . **85.00**
Handbag, hand beaded, cut steel beads on black silk,
   "Made in France" label, c1925 . . . . **40.00**
Hat, Christian Dior, cloche style, brown ribbon loops,
   amber beading, 1950s **20.00**
Hat, derby, 1940s **80.00**
Hat, felt, petal–brimmed, curled feather, c1932 . . . . **25.00**
Hat, velvet, black, 1939, MIB **30.00**
Hat, woven straw, ecru, chiffon overlay, pink chiffon
   flowers, c1940 . . . . **35.00**
Muff, fur, black **20.00**
Scarf, white mesh, rectangular, lurex threads **25.00**
Shawl, silk, satin stitch embroidery, 60" sq **45.00**
Shoes, baby, leather, high top, 1930s **20.00**
Shoes, spike heel, 1950s **10.00**
Stockings, silk, rhinestone design at ankle, c1945 . . . . **25.00**

COCA–COLA

John Pemberton, a pharmacist from Atlanta, Georgia, developed the formula for Coca–Cola. However, credit for making Coca–Cola the world's leading beverage belongs to Asa G. Candler. Candler improved the formula and marketed his product aggressively.

The use of "Coke" in advertising first occurred in 1941. While Coke may have taught the world to sing, foreign collectors still prefer American Coca–Cola items over those issued in their own countries.

Reproduction and copycat items have plagued Coca–Cola collecting for the past three decades. The problem is compounded by Coca–Cola's licensing the reproduction of many of its classic products. Finally, the number of new products licensed by Coca–Cola appears to increase each year. Their sales represent a significant monetary drain of moneys previously spent in the vintage market.

References: *B. J. Summers' Guide to Coca–Cola: Identifications, Current Values, Circa Dates,* Collector Books, 1997; Gael de Courtivron, *Collectible Coca–Cola Toy Trucks: An Identification and Value Guide,* Collector Books, 1995; Steve Ebner, *Vintage Coca–Cola Machines, Vol. II, 1959–1968,* published by author, 1996; Bill McClintock, *Coca–Cola Trays,* Schiffer Publishing, 1996; Allan Petretti, *Petretti's Coca–Cola Collectibles Price Guide, 10th Edition,* Antique Trader Books, 1997; Al and Helen Wilson, *Coca–Cola: The Real Price Guide,* Schiffer Publishing, 1994.

Collectors' Clubs: Coca–Cola Collectors Club, 400 Monemar Ave, Baltimore, MD 21228; Coca–Cola Collectors Club International, PO Box 49166, Atlanta, GA 30359.

REPRODUCTION ALERT: Coca–Cola trays.

Banner, paper, "Be Really Refreshed!...Ice Cold
   Coke!," 1960s, 19 x 57" . . . . **$ 65.00**
Blotter, Dells Coca–Cola Bottling Co, 6–pack carrier
   and bottle illus, 1930s **385.00**
Bottle Opener, Starr "X," wall mount, cast metal,
   "Drink Coca–Cola," dated Apr 1925, orig box **8.00**
Bottle Opener/Corkscrew, "Coca–Cola Bottling
   Works," c1930 . . . . **50.00**

Sign, hanging, diecut cardboard, 1940, $1,350.00. Photo courtesy Muddy River Trading Co.

Calendar, full pad, 1954 . . . . **100.00**
Can, syrup, green and red paper label, 1950s **200.00**
Carrier, 6 bottle, wire, litho tin side plates, c1960 . . . . . . **150.00**
Carrier, 12 bottle, plastic, 1950s **15.00**
Clock, wood frame, 1939, 16" sq **400.00**
Coaster, cork, silk screened, "50th Anniversary,
   Fayetteville Coca–Cola Bottling Co Inc," 1950s **30.00**
Cooler, metal, red and white, "Drink Coca–Cola In
   Bottles," 1950s, large size **85.00**
Cooler, red vinyl, white lettering, 1950s **50.00**
Cup, tin, "Use This Cup For Water But Drink
   Coca–Cola In Bottles, Coca–Cola Bottling Co
   Greencastle, Ind" printed on bottom, 1930s **120.00**
Fly Swatter, metal, stamped block logo, 1930s **325.00**
Glass, diamond design, 1960 . . . . **5.00**
Golf Ball, logo, 1950s **20.00**
Opener, wall mount, metal, red enamel logo,
   1948–50 . . . . **45.00**
Paper Dolls, The Coke Crowd, Merrill, c1941 . . . . **200.00**
Pen, mechanical, tortoise shell, 1940s **30.00**
Pinback Button, "Diet Coke Just For the Taste of It,"
   1980s **2.00**
Plate, "Drink Coca–Cola, Good With Food" on rim,
   Wellsville China Co, 1940s, 6½" d **320.00**
Playing Cards, "Drink Coca–Cola in Bottles," 1939 . . . . . **200.00**
Radio, figural vending machine, 1965 . . . . **185.00**
Seltzer Bottle, "Susanville Coca–Cola Bottling Co,
   Susanville, Calif.," orange **200.00**
Sheet Music, *The Coca–Cola Girl,* Howard E. Way,
   1927 . . . . **225.00**
Sign, cardboard, Santa hushing barking dog, "When
   Friends Stop By Stock Up for the Holidays," 1960s,
   16 x 27" **45.00**
Sign, plastic, "Enjoy Coca–Cola," 1960s, 5 x 14" **45.00**
Sign, tin, "Pick Up 6 For Home Refreshment," 1950s,
   16 x 50" **300.00**
Thermometer, tin, bottle shape, 1958, 30" h **75.00**
Toy Truck, friction, Super Mini Series, 1980 . . . . **125.00**

Tray, Spring Board Girl, 1939, 13 x 10", $285.00.

Tray, Girl in the Afternoon, woman wearing yellow dress and hat, holding bottle, "Drink Coca–Cola," sgd, 1938, 10½" w, 13" h 250.00

Tray, rect, girl with ice skates sitting on log, holding bottle, "Drink Coca–Cola," 1941, 10½" w, 13" h 325.00

Waste Basket, tin, red and white, "Enjoy Coca–Cola, Enjoy Coke," 1970s 10.00

AUCTION PRICES

Gary Metz's Muddy River Trading Co. Spring Auction & Trading Convention, May 3, 1997. A buyer's premium of 15% (10% for payment by approved check or cash) was added to all successful bids. Prices do not include a buyer's premium.

Calendar, Holder, button, "Drink Coca–Cola, Sign of Good Taste, Have A Coke," 1988 Coke pad attached, light wear and scratches 525.00

Clock, light–up, round, "Drink Coca–Cola" above bottle, 1950s, 15" d, scratches, light soiling, hands may be replaced 400.00

Cooler, Westinghouse style, c1930s, 18 x 26 x 34", restored. 775.00

Sign, emb tin, rect, 1923 style bottle, "Drink Coca–Cola In Bottles, Delicious and Refreshing," 1931, 10 x 27½", minor scratches and chipping. 850.00

Sign, standing policeman, holding shield with "Slow, School Zone," back with "Drink Coca–Cola" button and bottle, 1950s, 60" h, front repainted. 900.00

Thermometer, round, "Drink Coca–Cola" and gold bottle logo, 12" d, light soiling, tiny rust areas and mildew 625.00

Toy Bus, Gray–Line, Coke logo on back, friction, ATC, Japan, 1950s–60s, 4" h, 14" l, some plastic windows on one side puched out, rear window slightly caved in, minor dents and scratches 300.00

Tray, bathing girl with glass, 1929, minor dents and surface scratches 325.00

Umbrella, stenciled, "Drink Coca–Cola, The Pause That Refreshes, Ice Cold In Bottles," c1930s, minor wear, staining, and darkening 900.00

COCKTAIL SHAKERS

The modern cocktail shaker dates from the 1920s, a result of the martini craze. As a form, it inspired designers in glass, ceramics, and metals.

Neither the Depression nor World War II hindered the sale of cocktail shakers. The 1950s was the era of the home bar and outdoor patio. The cocktail shaker played a major role in each. The arrival of the electric blender and the shift in public taste from liquor to wine in the 1960s ended the cocktail shaker's reign.

Reference: Stephen Visakay, *Vintage Bar Ware*, Collector Books, 1997.

Aluminum, black plastic base and top, West Bend patent #93,928, 1934, 11" h . . . . $ 50.00

Chrome, angular Bakelite handle, Side Car and Pink Lady recipes stamped on bottom, Forman Brothers, c1935 . . . . 75.00

Chrome, dumbbell style, red plastic top, 1930–40, 13" h, 4" d 80.00

Chrome, Holiday Cocktail Set, "Gaiety" shaker, tray, and 4 cups, Chase Brass and Copper Co, 1930s. 150.00

Chrome, teapot style, red Catalin handle, 1930s 30.00

Chrome, Tippler Tumbler, red plastic top, "Tipple Tips" booklet, West Bend Aluminum Co, ©1934 . . . . . . 45.00

Glass, recipes and sports scenes, Hazel–Atlas 10.00

Glass, litho recipes, battery operated, Swank, 1950s 25.00

Glass, red and white stripes, chrome top. 15.00

Glass, Art Deco style, glass shaker, 6 tall glasses, 5 short glasses, frosted stippled surface, multicolored bands, 1950s 60.00

Glass, white sailboats and seagulls, Hazel–Atlas, 1930s 75.00

COINS & CURRENCY

Chances are you have some old coins and currency around the house. Many individuals deposit their pocket change in a large bank or bottle on a daily basis. People who travel return home with pocket change. Most currency exchanges will not convert coinage. Millions of Americans put aside brand new one dollar silver certificate bills when America went off the silver standard.

Condition plays a critical role in determining the value of any coin or piece of currency. If your coins and currency show signs of heavy use, chances are they are worth little more than face value, even if they date prior to World War II. Circulated American silver dimes, quarters, half dollars, and dollars from before the age of sandwich coins do have a melt value ranging from two and one–half to three times face value. In some foreign countries, once a coin or currency has been withdrawn from service, it cannot be redeemed, even for face value.

The first step in valuing your coins and currency is to honestly grade them. Information about how to grade is found in the opening chapters of most reference books. Be a very tough grader. Individuals who are not serious collectors tend to overgrade.

Remember, values found in price guides are retail. Because coin and currency dealers must maintain large inventories, they pay premium prices only for extremely scarce examples.

Coins are far easier to deal with than currency, due to the fact that there are fewer variations. When researching any coin or piece of currency, the reference must match the object being researched on every point.

Allen G. Bergman and Alex G. Malloy's *Warman's Coins & Currency* (Wallace–Homestead, 1995) is a good general reference. It includes the most commonly found material. However, when detailed research is required, use one of the following:

References: American Coins: David Harper (ed.), *1997 North American Coins & Prices, 6th Edition,* Krause Publications, 1997; Thomas E. Hudgeon, Jr, (ed.), *The Official 1997 Blackbook Price Guide of U.S. Coins, 35th Edition,* House of Collectibles, 1997.

American Currency: Thomas Hudgeons, Jr, (ed.), *The Official 1997 Blackbook Price Guide to U.S. Paper Money, 29th Edition,* House of Collectibles, 1997.

Foreign Coins: Chester L. Krause and Clifford Mishler, *1998 Standard Catalog of World Coins, 1901–Present,* Krause Publications, 1997.

Foreign Currency: Colin R. Bruce II and George Cuhaj, *1997 Standard Catalog of World Paper Money: Modern Issues (1961 to Present), Volume III, 3rd Edition,* Krause Publications, 1996; Colin R. Bruce II and Neil Shafer (ed.), *Standard Catalog of World Paper Money, Specialized Issues, 7th Edition,* Krause Publications, 1996; Albert Pick, *Standard Catalog of World Paper Money: General Issues, Volume II, 8th Edition,* Krause Publications, 1997.

Periodicals: *Coin World,* PO Box 29, Sidney, OH 45365; *Coin Prices, Coins, Numismatic News,* and *World Coin News* are all publications from Krause Publication, 700 E State St, Iola, WI 54990.

COLORING BOOKS

Coloring books emerged as an independent collecting category in the early 1990s, due largely to the publication of several specialized price guides on the subject and the inclusion of the category in general price guides.

The McLoughlin Brothers were one of the first American publishers of coloring books. The Little Folks Painting Books was copyrighted in 1885. Although Binney and Smith introduced crayons in 1903, it was not until the 1930s that coloring books were crayoned rather than painted.

When Saalfied introduced its Shirley Temple coloring book in 1934, it changed a market that traditionally focused on animal, fairy tale, and military themes to one based on characters and personalities. It is for this reason that crossover collectors strongly influence the value for some titles.

Beginning in the 1970s, the number of licensed coloring books began a steady decline. If it were not for Barbie, Disney, and G.I. Joe, today's coloring book rack would consist only of generic titles, primarily because the market focuses on a younger consumer. Further, many of today's coloring books are actually activity books.

Reference: Dian Zillner, *Collectible Coloring Books,* Schiffer Publishing, 1992.

Note: Books are unused unless otherwise noted.

Animal Alphabet to Color, Merrill Publishing, 1935. . . . **$ 15.00**
Charlie Chaplin, Saalfield, 1941 . . . . **75.00**
Cracker Jack Coloring and Activity Book, Play More
   Inc, 1984. . . . . **10.00**

Lone Ranger, Whitman, 1974, unused, $15.00.

Debbie Reynolds, Whitman, 1953 . . . . **40.00**
Family Affair, cover photos, Whitman, 1968, used. **10.00**
Felix the Cat, cardboard cover, Saalfield, 1956, used. **25.00**
Gumby and Pokey, connect the dots, Whitman,
   1970, used. **15.00**
Lassie, Whitman, 1958. . . . . **20.00**
Mister Magoo, 1,001 Arabian Nights, Whitman,
   1959, used **5.00**
Nanny and the Professor, Saalfield, 1970 . . . . **15.00**
Night Before Christmas, Whitman, 1963. . . . . **10.00**
Punky Brewster, Western Publishing, 1986 . . . . **5.00**
Rin Tin Tin, Whitman, 1956, used. **15.00**
Shirley Temple My Book to Color, Saalfield, 1937 . . . . . . **100.00**
The Addams Family, includes puzzles, games, and
   cutouts, Saalfield, 1965 . . . . **60.00**
The Archies, Western Publishing, 1970. . . . . **15.00**
The Lucy Show, Golden Press, 1963. . . . . **40.00**
Tippee–Toes, Whitman, 1969 . . . . **15.00**
Uncle Wiggily, "Grandaddy Longlegs," story and
   coloring book, 10 illus stories, 1943 . . . . **10.00**
Underdog, Whitman, 1972, used **20.00**
United States Map, Whitman, 1960 . . . . **10.00**
Walt Disney's Old Yeller, ©Walt Disney Productions,
   Whitman, 1957 . . . . **15.00**
Woody Woodpecker, Chilly Willy cov, Watkins
   Strathmore, 1956, used. **15.00**

COMIC BOOKS

The modern comic book arrived on the scene in the late 1930s. Led by superheroes such as Batman and Superman, comics quickly became an integral part of growing up. Collectors classifiy comics from 1938 to the mid–1940s as "Golden Age" comics and comics from the mid–1950s through the end of the 1960s as "Silver Age" comics. The Modern Age begins in 1980 and runs to the present.

Comics experienced a renaissance in the 1960s with the introduction of the Fantastic Four and Spider–Man. A second revival occurred in the 1980s with the arrival of the independent comic.

The number of comic stores nationwide doubled. Speculation in comics as investments abounded. A period of consolidation and a bitter distribution rights fight among publishers weakened the market in the mid–1990s and burst the speculative bubble. The comic book market is in recovery as the decade ends.

References: Grant Geissman, *Collectibly MAD: The MAD and EC Collectibles Guide,* EC Publications, 1995; John Hegenberger, *Collector's Guide To Comic Books,* Wallace–Homestead, Krause Publications, 1990; Alex G. Malloy, *Comics Values Annual: 1997 Edition,* Antique Trader Books, 1997; Robert M. Overstreet, *The Overstreet Comic Book Price Guide, 27th Edition,* Avon Books, Gemstone Publishing, 1997; Robert M. Overstreet and Gary M. Carter, *The Overstreet Comic Book Grading Guide,* Avon Books, 1992; Maggie Thompson (ed.), *Marvel Comics Checklist & Price Guide, 1961–1993,* Krause Publications, 1993; Maggie Thompson and Brent Frankenhoff, *1997 Comic Book Checklist & Price Guide: 1961–Present, 3rd Edition,* Krause Publications, 1996; Jerry Weist, *Original Comic Art: Identification and Price Guide,* Avon Books, 1993.

Periodicals: *Comics Buyer's Guide,* 700 E State St, Iola, WI 54990; *Overstreet Comic Book Marketplace* and *Overstreet's Advanced Collector,* 1996 Greenspring Dr, Ste 405, Lutherville–Timonium, MD 21093.

Collectors' Club: Fawcett Collectors of America & Magazine Enterprise, Too!, 301 E Buena Vista Ave, North Augusta, SC 29841.

REPRODUCTION ALERT: Publishers often reprint popular stories. Check the fine print at the bottom of the inside cover or first page for correct titles. Also, do not confuse 10 x 13" treasury–sized "Famous First Edition" comics printed in the mid–1970s with original comic book titles.

Note: All comics listed are in fine condition.

Aquaman, DC, 1st series, #5, June 1962	$ 41.00
Aquaman, DC, Feb 1978	3.50
Archie Comics, DC, #131	8.00
Attack, Charlton, #54	20.00
Avengers, Marvel, Dec 1966	12.00

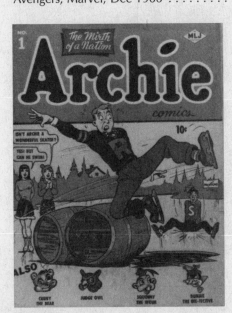

Archie Comics, MLJ, Winter 1942–43, No. 1, $1,950.00.

Bamm Bamm & Pebbles Flintstone, Gold Key, #1, Oct 1964	15.00
Baseball Comics, Will Eisner, #1, Spring 1949	180.00
Bat Masterson, Dell, #9, Nov/Jan 1961/62	20.00
Batman, DC, #63, Feb/Mar 1951	165.00
Batman, DC, Jun 1960	48.00
Batman, DC, Jun 1985	1.80
Beany and Cecil, Dell, Jan 1955	60.00
Beetle Bailey, Gold Key, #53, May 1966	3.00
Bullwinkle, Charlton, #1, July 1970	10.00
Captain America, Marvel, Jul 1971	3.00
Casper the Friendly Ghost, Harvey, #6, Dec 1958	17.50
Challengers of the Unknown, DC, Nov 1963	18.00
Chip 'N' Dale Rescue Rangers, DC	.90
Classic X–Men, Marvel, Dec 1988	1.50
Daffy Tunes Comics, Four–Star, #12, Aug 1947	16.00
Daredevil, Marvel, Feb 1972	6.00
Defenders, Marvel, May 1974	5.00
Detective Comics, DC, Mar 1961	36.00
Detective Comics, DC Sep 1968	6.00
Dexter Comics, Dearfield, #5, Jul 1949	9.00
Doc Savage, DC, Nov 1988	1.00
Donald Duck, Gladstone, Sep, 1988	1.25
Excalibur, Marvel, Nov 1988	5.00
Fantastic Adventures, Ace, Mar 1987	1.00
Fathom, Comico, May 1987	1.00
Flash, DC, Aug 1987	3.00
Fly, The, Archie/Red Circle, May 1983	.50
Freedom Fighters, DC, Apr 1976	1.50
From Beyond the Unknown, DC, Jan 1970	2.00
Further Adventures of Indiana Jones, The, Marvel, Mar 1983	.50
Futurians, Lodestone, Oct 1985	1.25
G.I. Joe: A Real American Hero, Marvel, Mar 1983	2.50
Ghost Rider, Marvel, Dec 1976	3.50
Godzilla, Marvel, Aug 1977	4.50
Godzilla, Marvel, Nov 1978	1.75
Green Hornet, Now, Dec 1989	4.25
Green Lantern, DC, Mar 1967	15.00
Green Lantern, DC, Jan 1979	1.25
Hawk and Dove, DC, Jun 1969	15.00
Hawkman, DC, May 1968	14.50
Hellblazer, DC, Feb 1988	7.00
Honeymooners, The, Triad, Aug 1989	1.25
Hot Wheels, DC, Dec 1970	11.00
Howard the Duck, Marvel, Sep 1977	1.50
Iceman, Marvel, Dec 1984	1.75
Inferior Five, The, DC, Apr 1967	33.00
Invaders, The, Marvel, Aug 1975	6.00
Invaders, The, Marvel, Aug 1978	1.75
Jemm, Son of Saturn, DC, Oct 1984	.50
Jonny Quest, Comico, Nov 1986	2.50
Karate Kid, DC, Apr 1978	.75
Kong the Untamed, DC, Jul 1975	.60
L.E.G.I.O.N., DC, May 1989	2.50
Machine Man, Marvel, Jun 1978	.75
Man From U.N.C.L.E., The, Entertainment, Feb 1987	1.00
Mars, First, Jan 1984	.75
Metamorpho, DC, Aug 1965	60.00
Miracleman, Eclipse, Aug 1985	2.50
Ms. Marvel, Marvel, May 1977	1.75

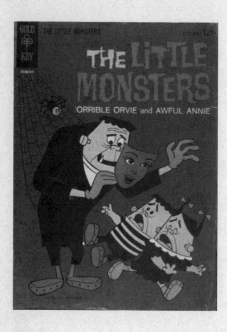

The Little Monsters, Gold Key, 1964, $5.00.

Mystery in Space, DC, Sep 1980 . . . . **3.00**
Navy Action, Atlas, #4, Feb 1955 . . . . **11.00**
Peter Parker the Spectacular Spider–Man, Marvel,
  Dec 1981 . . . . **1.75**
Phantom Stranger, DC, Feb 1970 . . . . **18.00**
Plastic Man, DC, Mar 1976 . . . . **6.00**
Popular Teen–Agers, Star, #9, Oct 1951 . . . . . . **40.00**
Real Ghostbusters, Now, Aug 1988 . . . . **1.75**
Saga of the Swamp Thing, DC, Jun 1982. . . . . **1.25**
Sea Devils, DC, Apr 1962 . . . . **55.00**
Sgt. Rock, DC, Apr 1977 . . . . **6.00**
Shadow, The, Archie, Aug 1964 . . . . **21.00**
Shazam!, DC, Mar 1974 . . . .**.50**
Shogun Warriors, Marvel, Feb 1979 . . . . **1.25**
Silver Surfer, Marvel, Sep 1970. . . . . **24.00**
Star Trek, Gold Key, May 1972 . . . . **30.00**
Star Trek, Marvel, Oct 1980 . . . . **1.25**
Star Wars, Marvel, May 1978 . . . . **3.50**
Starman, DC, Nov 1988. . . . . **1.25**
Starslayer, First, Sep 1984. . . . .**.75**
Strange Adventures, #9, Jun 1951 . . . . **420.00**
Super Friends, DC, Mar 1978. . . . . **1.00**
Superboy, DC, Jun 1960. **25.00**
Superman, DC, Jan 1961 . . . . **36.00**
Superman, DC, Apr 1984. . . . .**.50**
Teen Titans, DC, Dec 1967 . . . . **6.00**
Thing, The, Marvel, Feb 1984. . . . .**.60**
Wonder Woman, DC, Oct 1977. . . . .**.60**

COMPACTS

Cosmetic use increased significantly in the 1920s as women became liberated and started playing a major role in the business world. Compacts addressed the need created by a woman's desire to freshen her makeup on the run.

Although compacts are still made today, they experienced a Golden Age from the mid–1930s through the late 1950s. Collectors designate compacts manufactured prior to 1960 as "vintage."

Compacts are found in thousands of shapes, styles, and decorative motifs in materials ranging from precious metals to injection molded plastic. Decorative theme, construction material, manufacturer, and novelty are four major collecting themes.

References: Roseann Ettinger, *Compacts and Smoking Accessories,* Schiffer Publishing, 1991; Roselyn Gerson, *Vintage Ladies' Compacts,* Collector Books, 1996; Roselyn Gerson, *Vintage Vanity Bags and Purses: An Identification and Value Guide,* Collector Books, 1994; Laura M. Mueller, *Collector's Encyclopedia of Compacts, Carryalls & Face Powder Boxes: Identification & Values,* (1994, 1996 value update) *Vol. II* (1997), Collector Books, Lynell Schwartz, *Vintage Compacts & Beauty Accessories,* Schiffer Publishing, 1997.

Coty, figural envelope, goldtone, 1940s . . . . **$ 70.00**
Elgin, silvered, compact/music box combination,
  gilded deer, plays *Anniversary Waltz,* black carry-
  ing case, c1950s **140.00**
Evans, enamel, blue, compact/lighter/cigarette case
  combination, marcasite dec, c1930. . . . . **150.00**
Figural, Army officer's cap, plastic, khaki, 1940s **70.00**
Figural, suitcase, metal, Marine Corps insignia,
  c1940s **140.00**
Helena Rubinstein, goldtone, baroque case, black
  enameled lid, framed mirror **145.00**
Revlon, plastic, orange, turtle motif, foil label **40.00**
Ronson, Art Deco, enamel, brown and white marbe-
  lized, compact/lighter/cigarette case combination,
  c1930–40 . . . . **140.00**
Souvenir, Sesquicentennial International Exposition,
  Philadelphia, PA, silvered metal, rotating mirror,
  powder puff, George Washington, 1926, 2" d **30.00**
Souvenir, Statue of Liberty **50.00**
Volupte, "Elect Willkie President," circular, red,
  white, and blue enameled lid, inside mirror, 1940,
  3" d **40.00**
Yardley, goldtone, white enamel feather, c1940s **75.00**

Souvenir, 1936 Great Lakes Expo, $35.00.

Zell Fifth Avenue, leather, blue, sides open to bill-
   fold and coin purse, c1940 . . . . **80.00**
Ziegfield Creation, lucite photo compact, scalloped
   edges, photo slides in slot behind interior mirror,
   1940s, 4 x 4" **100.00**

CONSOLIDATED GLASS COMPANY

The Consolidated Glass Company was founded in 1893, the result of a merger between the Wallace and McAfee Company and the Fostoria Shade & Lamp Company. In the mid–1890s, the company built a new factory in Corapolis, Pennsylvania, and quickly became one of the largest lamp, globe, and shade manufacturers in the United States.

The Consolidated Glass Company began making giftware in the mid–1930s. Most collectors focus on the company's late 1920s and early 1930s product lines, e.g., Florentine, Martele, and Ruba Rombic.

Consolidated closed its operations in 1932, reopening in 1936. In 1962 Dietz Brothers acquired the company. A disastrous fire in 1963 during a labor dispute heralded the end of the company. The last glass was made in 1964.

Reference: Jack D. Wilson, *Phoenix & Consolidated Art Glass: 1926–1980,* Antique Publications, 1989.

Collectors' Club: Phoenix & Consolidated Glass Collectors' Club, PO Box 81974, Chicago, IL 60681.

Almond Dish, Ruba Rombic, smokey topaz, 3" l . . . . . **$ 250.00**
Candlestick, Catalonian, rainbow blue **75.00**
Candlestick, Martele Line, green **25.00**
Celery Tray, Florette, pink **35.00**
Cruet, Florette, pink, orig stopper **75.00**
Goblet, Martele Line, 9 oz, Russet Fruits **25.00**
Jug, Catalonian, purple **110.00**
Plate, Ruba Rombic, 10" d **80.00**
Plate, Martele Line, Bird of Paradise, pink–orchid,
   12" d **100.00**
Puff Box, Lovebirds, blue **100.00**
Snack Set, Five Fruits, yellow **40.00**
Sugar, cov, Ruba Rombic, green, 3" h **150.00**
Sugar, cov, Ruba Rombic, lavender **125.00**
Tumbler, iced tea, Catalonian Line, amethyst, ftd **25.00**
Tumbler, Martle Line, Russet Fruits, ftd, 5¾" h **30.00**
Vase, Olive, purple **170.00**

CONSTRUCTION TOYS

Childen love to build things. Modern construction toys trace their origin to the Anchor building block sets of the late 19th and early 20th centuries. A construction toy Hall of Fame includes A. C. Gilbert's Erector Set, Lego, Lincoln Logs, and Tinker Toys.

A construction set must have all its parts, instruction book(s), and period packaging to be considered complete. Collectors pay a premium for sets designed to make a specific object, e.g., a dirigible or locomotive.

Reference: Craig Shange, *Collector's Guide to Tinker Toys,* Collector Books, 1996.

Collectors' Clubs: A. C. Gilbert Heritage Society, 594 Front St, Marion, MA 02738; Girder and Panel Collectors Club (Kenner), Box 494, Bolton, MA 01740.

A. C. Gilbert, Erector, #1 . . . . **$ 60.00**
A. C. Gilbert, Erector, #4 . . . . **250.00**
A. C. Gilbert, Erector, #7, Steam Shovel **325.00**
A. C. Gilbert, Erector, #1052, Rocket Launcher **120.00**
A. C. Gilbert, Erector, #10042, Radar Scope Set **35.00**
A. C. Gilbert, Erector, #10127, Lunar Vehicle Set **95.00**
A. C. Gilbert, Erector, #10181, Action Helicopter **100.00**
A. C. Gilbert, Erector, Illumination Kit **165.00**
Bilt–E–Z, Skyscraper Building Blocks, Scott Mfg,
   Chicago, c1925 . . . . **135.00**
Elgo, American Plastic Bricks, #715, 1950s **30.00**
Halsam, American Plastic Bricks, #60 . . . . **80.00**
Kenner, #2, Girder and Panel **60.00**
Kenner, Girder and Panel Bridge and Turnpike
   Motorized Set, 1960 . . . . **125.00**
Lincoln Logs, #1A, 1920 . . . . **22.00**
Lincoln Logs, #29 . . . . **130.00**
Remco, Jumbo Construction Set, 1968 . . . . **130.00**
Riverside Construction Set, Marx, 1960s **125.00**
Tinkertoy, DeLuxe, complete, with instructions **25.00**
Tinkertoy, Double Tinkertoy, The Ten Thousand
   Wonder Builder **35.00**
Tinkertoy, Easy, complete with instructions **15.00**
Tinkertoy, Electric, with motor **55.00**
Tinkertoy, Senior, complete with instructions **35.00**
Tinkertoy, small T–style can, complete with instruc-
   tions **25.00**

COOKBOOKS

The cookbook was firmly entrentched as a basic kitchen utensil by the beginning of the 20th century. *Fannie Farmer's Cookbook* dominated during the first half of the century; *The Joy of Cooking* was the cookbook of choice of the post–1945 generations.

Betty Crocker's Cookbook, Good Housekeeping Cookbook, McCall's Cookbook, and *The Settlement Cookbook* are other million–book sellers. *Better Homes and Gardens New Cookbook* is the industry winner with 18 million copies sold. Cookbooks with printings in the hundreds of thousands and millions, e.g., the *White House Cookbook,* generally have little value except for the earliest editions.

Although some cookbooks are purchased by individuals who plan to use the recipes they contain, most are collected because of their subject matter, cover image, and use as advertising premiums. Do not hesitate to shop around for the best price and condition. The survival rate for cookbooks is exceptionally high.

References: Bob Allen, *A Guide To Collecting Cookbooks and Advertising Cookbooks,* Collector Books, 1990, 1995 value update; Mary Barile, *Cookbooks Worth Collecting,* Wallace–Homestead, Krause Publications, 1994; Linda J. Dickinson, *A Price Guide to Cookbooks and Recipe Leaflets,* Collector Books, 1990, 1997 value update.

Collectors' Blub: Cook Book Collectors Club of America, PO Box 56, St James, MO 65559.

How to get the most out of your Sunbeam Mixmaster, **1930s, $7.50.**

American Home Cook Book, The, 1932	$ **20.00**
Best From Midwest Kitchens, 1946	**5.00**
Book of Recipes, A, 1956	**25.00**
Chicago Daily News, 1930s	**10.00**
Civil War Cook Book, A, 1961	**25.00**
Down on the Farm Cook Book, 1943	**20.00**
Edith Bunker's All in the Family Cookbook, 1971	**5.00**
General Foods, 1932, 1st ed.	**10.00**
Greenwich Village Gourmet, 1949	**15.00**
Hollywood Glamor Cook Book, 1941	**25.00**
Household Searchlight Cookbook, 1943	**10.00**
How to Cook Reagan's Goose, 1984	**15.00**
How to Take a Trick a Day with Bisquick, Betty Crocker, 1935	**15.00**
Junk Food Cookbook, 1979	**5.00**
Knox Gelatine: Dainty Desserts, Candies, Salads, 1930	**5.00**
My Better Homes and Gardens Cook Book, 1930	**35.00**
New Orleans Creole Recipes, 1957	**10.00**
Our Dining Car Recipes, Southern Pacific Railroad, 1935	**15.00**
Outdoor Cooking, 1940	**20.00**
Pennsylvania Dutch Cook Book of Fine Old Recipes, 1936	**5.00**
Pillsbury's Best 1,000 Recipes, Best of the Bake Off, 1959	**25.00**
Quick and Easy Cooking with Tupperware, 1986	**10.00**
Savannah Cookbook, 1933	**15.00**
US Navy, 1944	**15.00**
Vincent Price Treasury Great Recipes, 1965, 1st ed	**35.00**

COOKIE JARS

Although cookie jars existed as a form prior to 1945, the cookie jar's Golden Age began in the late 1940s and ended in the early 1960s. Virtually every American ceramics manufacturer from Abingdon to Shawnee produced a line of cookie jars. Foreign imports were abundant.

There was a major cookie jar collecting craze in the 1980s and early 1990s that included a great deal of speculative pricing and some market manipulation. The speculative bubble is in the process of collapsing in many areas. Reproductions and high-priced contemporary jars, especially those featuring images of famous personalities such as Marilyn Monroe, also have contributed to market uncertainty. This major market shakeout is expected to continue for several more years.

References: Fred Roerig and Joyce Herndon Roerig, *Collector's Encyclopedia of Cookie Jars, Book I* (1990, 1995 value update), *Book II* (1994, 1997 value update), Collector Books; Mike Schneider, *The Complete Cookie Jar Book*, Schiffer Publishing, 1991; Ellen Supnick, *The Wonderful World of Cookie Jars*, L–W Book Sales, 1995, 1997 value update; Ermagene Westfall, *An Illustrated Value Guide To Cookie Jars*, (1983, 1997 value update), *Book II* (1993, 1997 value update), Collector Books.

Newsletter: *Cookie Jarrin'*, RR #2, Box 504, Walterboro, SC 29488.

A Little Company, Pig, 7½" h	$ **120.00**
Abingdon, Cookie Time Clock, 9" h	**125.00**
Abingdon, Money Bag	**160.00**
Abingdon, Pineapple, 10½" h	**180.00**
Abingdon, The Daisy Jar, 8" h	**100.00**
Advertising, Campbell Soup Kids, mkd "1990 Campbell Soup Company"	**90.00**
Advertising, Dreyer's Grand Ice Cream, mkd "Copyright Treasure Craft U.S.A."	**250.00**
Advertising, Green Giant Sprout, 12" h	**110.00**
Advertising, Guldens Mustard	**95.00**
Advertising, Nestle Tollhouse Cookies	**70.00**
Advertising, Oreo Cookie	**85.00**
Advertising, Pepperidge Farm	**100.00**
Advertising, Pillsbury Doughboy	**45.00**
Advertising, Pure Cane Sugar	**125.00**
Advertising, Quaker Oats, mkd "Regal China"	**165.00**
American Bisque, Beehive, kitten on lid, 11¾" h	**140.00**
American Bisque, Chick, blue, 12¼" h	**60.00**
American Bisque, Coffee Pot, pine cone dec, 9½" h	**50.00**
American Bisque, Jack–in–the–Box, 12" h	**180.00**

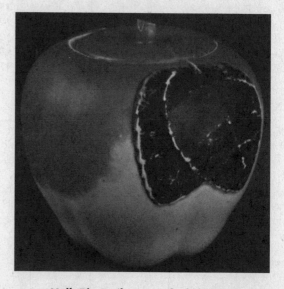

Hull, Big Apple, unmarked, $40.00.

Robinson–Ransbottom, Sheriff Pig, unmarked, 12¹/₂" h, $125.00.

American Bisque, Lamb, 11¹/₂" h 150.00
American Bisque, Liberty Bell, 9³/₄" h 250.00
American Bisque, Milk Wagon 395.00
American Bisque, Poodle, 10¹/₂" h 125.00
American Bisque, Smokey Bear, 2¹/₂" 175.00
American Bisque, Spool of Thread 35.00
American Bisque, Treasure Chest, 8³/₄" h 200.00
Brush, Brown Cow, cat finial, 8¹/₂" h 125.00
Brush, Lantern, 9¹/₂" h 70.00
Brush, Owl, 10³/₄" h 110.00
Brush, Squirrel on Log, 10³/₄" h 100.00
California Originals, Apple, 10³/₄" h 80.00
California Originals, Big Bird, 13³/₄" h 125.00
California Originals, Chipmunk, 11¹/₄ 100.00
California Originals, Fire Truck, 11¹/₄" h 225.00
California Originals, Frog, 10¹/₂" h 100.00
California Originals, Gumball Machine, 12" h 155.00
California Originals, Keystone Cop 55.00
California Originals, Liberty Bell, 10" h 70.00
California Originals, Owl, blue eyes 50.00
California Originals, Panda holding leaf 240.00
California Originals, Penguin, 12" h 110.00
California Originals, Rooster, 9" h 55.00
Clay Art, Cow with Bell, paper label 55.00
Clay Art, Toaster 60.00
DeForest, Coffee Pot, mkd "DeForest of CA Hand
    Painted" 80.00
DeForest, Monk, "Thou Shalt Not Steal" 170.00
DeForest, Parrot 200.00
Doranne, Brown Bagger, 10³/₄" h 80.00
Doranne, Dice, red and white 45.00
Doranne, Elephant, yellow, 12¹/₂" 70.00
Doranne, Hen, mkd "CJ 100" 140.00
Enesco, Garfield Playing Golf 150.00
Maddux, Squirrel, 13" h 200.00
McCoy, Black Cook Stove, 10" h 15.00
McCoy, Chipmunk, 10³/₄" h 125.00
McCoy, Fireplace, 9¹/₂" h 125.00
McCoy, Milk Can, 10" h 30.00

McCoy, Picnic Basket, 7³/₈" h 75.00
Metlox, Apple, red wine 150.00
Metlox, Barrel of Apples, 10³/₄" h 80.00
Metlox, Bear with Red Sweater 130.00
Metlox, Orange, 8³/₄" h 150.00
Metlox, Scottie Dog, white 300.00
National Potteries, Cookie Castle, mkd "Copyright
    1961 Napco Bedford OH A5286–L" 135.00
National Potteries, Winking Santa, mkd "Napco,
    Japan KX2352' 150.00
Red Wing, Barrel, rose dec, incised "Red Wing" 120.00
Red Wing, Friar Tuck, blue 100.00
Red Wing, Grapes, turquoise, 10" h 225.00
Red Wing, Pear, green, stamped "Red Wing USA" 200.00
Sierra Vista, Clown, 11" h 80.00
Sierra Vista, Rooster, mkd "Sierra Vista Ca," 12" h 80.00
Sigma, Peter Rabbit 300.00
Treasure Craft, Baseball 85.00
Treasure Craft, Bulldog 175.00
Treasure Craft, Conductor Bear 65.00
Treasure Craft, Dalmatian with Glass Bowl 65.00
Treasure Craft, Genie 100.00
Treasure Craft, Honey Bear 110.00
Treasure Craft, Old Fashioned Radio 135.00
Treasure Craft, Treasure Chest 120.00
Twin Winton, Chipmunk 120.00
Twin Winton, Cookie Safe 90.00
Twin Winton, Cow, white spots 85.00
Twin Winton, Wheelbarrow 250.00
Vandor, Cowboy 70.00
Vandor, Piano 70.00
Vandor, Radio 80.00

COOPER, SUSIE

After a brief stint as a designer at A. E. Gray & Co., Hanley Staffordshire, England, Susie Cooper founded the Susie Cooper Pottery in Burslem in 1932. There she designed ceramics that were functional in shape and decorated with bright floral and abstract designs. It was Cooper who first introduced the straight–sided "can" shape for coffeepots. Eventually Cooper was employed by the Wedgwood Group where she developed several lines of bone china tableware.

Reference: *Collecting Susie Cooper,* Francis Joseph Publications, 1994, distributed by Krause Publications.

Collectors' Club: Susie Cooper Collectors Group, PO Box 7436, London N12 7QF England.

Biscuit Barrel, Lustre Ware . . . . $ 400.00
Box, cov, Scarlet Runner Beans, yellow, orange,
    black, and brown 50.00
Candlesticks, pr, sgraffito dec 200.00
Coffeepot, Dresden Spray 150.00
Coffeepot, Lustre Ware 600.00
Cup and Saucer, Gardenia 45.00
Cup and Saucer, Lustre Ware 150.00
Fruit Bowl, hp florals 180.00
Fruit Bowl, Lustre Ware, 5" d 180.00
Jug, Paris shape 75.00

Cup and Saucer, blue ground, cream crescents, $45.00.

Meat Dish, edge dec, litho pattern	90.00
Plate, divided, man on horse dec	35.00
Plate, Dresden Spray, 5" d	20.00
Plate, hp geometric design, 10" d	300.00
Plate, Printemps, 9" d.	45.00
Plate, sgraffito dec, 8" d	60.00
Plate, The Homestead, hp landscape, 8" d	60.00
Teacup and Saucer, banded	45.00
Teapot, Swansea Spray	125.00
Tureen, cov, floral motif, yellow dotted border	200.00
Vase, Cubist	450.00

COORS POTTERY

After J. J. Herold went to work for the Western Pottery Company in Denver in 1912, Adloph Coors and the other investors in the Herold China and Pottery Company, Golden, Colorado, kept the factory open and renamed it the Golden Pottery. In 1920 the name was changed to Coors Porcelain Company.

Initially concentrating on chemical, industrial, and scientific porcelain products, the company introduced a line of household cooking ware known as "Thermo-Porcelain." Six dinnerware lines, Coorado, Golden Ivory, Golden Rainbow, Mello–Tone, Rock-Mount, and Rosebud Cook–N–Serve were added in the 1930s. Dinnerware production ceased in 1941. Although the company produced some utilitarian ware such as ashtrays, ovenware, and teapots after the war, it never resumed its dinnerware production.

References: Carol and Jim Carlton, *Collector's Encyclopedia of Colorado Pottery,* Collector Books, 1994; Robert H. Schneider, *Coors Rosebud Pottery,* published by author, 1984, 1996 value update.

Newsletter: *Coors Pottery Newsletter,* 3808 Carr Place N, Seatlle, WA 98103.

Coorado, casserole, cov, individual, maroon, 2 x 2"	$ 15.00
Coorado, casserole, cov, straight, green, medium	35.00
Coorado, custard set, 6 custards, metal holder	45.00

Coorado, dinner plate, yellow	9.00
Coorado, gravy boat, attached underplate, blue.	35.00
Coorado, pitcher, maroon	32.00
Coorado, pudding, cov, yellow.	25.00
Coorado, salt and pepper shakers, pr, green	22.00
Coorado, teapot, yellow.	175.00
Mello–Tone, bread and butter plate, yellow, 4" d.	8.00
Mello–Tone, cereal bowl, green, 6¼"	10.00
Mello–Tone, cup and saucer, blue	15.00
Mello–Tone, dinner plate, pink, 7" d.	12.00
Mello–Tone, gravy, attached underplate, green	20.00
Mello–Tone, pitcher, yellow, 2 qt	25.00
Mello–Tone, platter, oval, green, 15" l.	20.00
Mello–Tone, vegetable bowl, blue, 9" d	20.00
Rosebud, baking pan, 12¼ x 8¼ x 2¼"	20.00
Rosebud, bean pot, cov, yellow	18.00
Rosebud, bread and butter plate, rose, 6" d.	10.00
Rosebud, cake knife, maroon, yellow rosebud, 3 green leaves, 10" l.	20.00
Rosebud, cake plate, blue	30.00
Rosebud, cake plate, yellow.	18.00
Rosebud, casserole, French, orange	50.00
Rosebud, casserole, straight, rose	35.00
Rosebud, casserole, triple service, green	40.00
Rosebud, cereal bowl, yellow, 6" d.	10.00
Rosebud, cookie jar, cov, yellow	25.00
Rosebud, cream soup, blue, 4" d	12.00
Rosebud, cream soup, rose	20.00
Rosebud, cup and saucer, green.	7.50
Rosebud, custard cup, blue	9.00
Rosebud, dinner, green plate, 9½" d.	12.00
Rosebud, fruit bowl, maroon, handle, 5" d	10.00
Rosebud, honey pot, cov, maroon	20.00
Rosebud, mixing bowl, orange, handle.	24.00
Rosebud, pie baker, yellow	13.00
Rosebud, platter, ivory.	35.00
Rosebud, pudding, large, orange	60.00
Rosebud, pudding, medium, rose	30.00
Rosebud, pudding, small, rose	10.00
Rosebud, salad plate, yellow, 7" d	10.00
Rosebud, salt and pepper shakers, pr, blue	18.00
Rosebud, soup plate, green, 8" d	15.00
Rosebud, utility jar, cov, yellow	25.00
Rosebud, vase, peach, 6" h	50.00
Rosebud, vase, white, 8" h.	75.00
Rosebud, vase, yellow, rope handles, 8" h.	100.00

COUNTER CULTURE

Counter cultural collectibles are the artifacts left behind by the Beatnik and Hippie culture of the 1960s. These range from concert posters to a wealth of pinback "social cause" buttons.

Since the Age of Aquarius was primarily anti–materialistic, saving and collecting material relating to this period represents a betrayal of everything for which the culture stood.

Some collectors prefer to designate this material as psychedelic collectibles. However, the psychedelic movement was only one aspect of the much broader Counter Culture environment.

Book, *Beat, Beat, Beat,* William Brown, paperback, 1959	$ 25.00

Comic Book, *The Forty Year Old Hippie*, No. 2, Rip
Off Press, 1979 .... **8.00**

Comic Book, *Homegrown Funnies*, Kitchen Sink
Press, 1971 .... **45.00**

Comic Book, *Your Hytone Comix*, Apex Novelties,
1971 .... **35.00**

Headband, cloth, elastic band, blue and white, peace
signs and birds, c1970 .... **12.00**

Jewelry, choker, gold metal, peace signs, 15½" l **20.00**

Magazine, *Ramparts*, The Social History of the
Hippie, March, 1967 .... **40.00**

Map, Hippieville, Haight–Asbury area, San
Francisco, folding street map, 1967 .... **35.00**

Medal, Peace, emb brass, Angel of Peace waving
palm branch, text on back, 1¾" d **15.00**

Pinback Button, "Black Feminist," black and white,
1970s **15.00**

Pinback Button, Free Speech, and F.S.M., blue, white
lettering, 1964 .... **35.00**

Pinback Button, "March Against Racism Boston Dec.
14," silhouetted heads, black, gray, and white,
green rim, 1974 .... **10.00**

Pinback Button, "Schools Not War!," black, white,
and red, "May 1 March On Wash. D. C.," and
"April 29 Nat'l Day Of Student Protest" **15.00**

Pinback Button, "Stop The War," green, black lettering, 1¼" d **10.00**

Pinback Button, "Uppity Women Unite," black and
white lettering, 1970s **10.00**

Pinback Button, Yippies Convention, orange and
blue, Ying and Yang symbol, black lettering, "Youth
International Party/1972/Miami Beach/Change" **15.00**

Poster, Anti–War, "Out Now. Stop The Bombing.
March Against The War," 1970, 22 x 14" **50.00**

Poster, Rally to Free Angela Davis **45.00**

Poster, Vietnam Anti–War, black and white montage,
c1967, 23 x 27" **85.00**

Record, *Dick Gregory at Kent State*, double LP,
Poppy, 1970 .... **50.00**

Record, *San Francisco Poets*, LP, 1959 .... **65.00**

Sheet Music, *San Francisco (Be Sure to Wear Flowers
in Your Hair)*, Scott McKenzie, 1967 .... **35.00**

Switchplate Cover, cardboard, black, white peace
sign **18.00**

Ticket, Woodstock, 1969, Globe Ticket Co **100.00**

COUNTRY WESTERN

This category is primarily record driven—mainly due to the lack of products licensed by members of the Country Western communi-ty. There is not a great deal to collect.

Country Western autographed material, other paper ephemera, and costumes have attracted some collectors. Although fan clubs exist for every major singer, few stress the collecting of personal memorabilia.

Periodicals: *American Cowboy*, PO Box 12830, Wichita, KS 67277; *Country Music Reporter*, 112 Widmar Place, Clayton, CA 94517.

Newsletter: *Disc Collector*, PO Box 315, Cheswold, DE 19936.

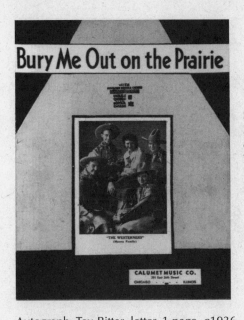

Sheet Music,
*Bury Me Out
on the Prairie,*
The Westerners
(Massey Family),
1935, $8.00.

Autograph, Tex Ritter, letter, 1 page, c1936 .... **$ 35.00**

Catalog, Ernest Tubb Record Shop issue, Nashville,
TN, 1972 .... **5.00**

Letter, Will Carter, typewritten, sgd, c1975 .... **10.00**

Lobby Card, Tex Ritter, 27 x 41" **100.00**

Lunch Box, Hee Haw, metal, 1970 .... **125.00**

Map, Nashville, TN, sgd by Roy Acuff and other performers, c1948 .... **120.00**

Membership Card, Tex Ritter Fan Club **15.00**

Paper Dolls, Hootenanny, Saalfield, #4440, punch–
out, 4 dolls, 1964, uncut **20.00**

Photograph, Crystal Gayle, 8 x 10", sgd, framed **10.00**

Photograph, Dolly Parton, 8 x 10", sgd **25.00**

Poster, Grand Old Opry, Chet Atkins **22.00**

Record, *Coal Miner's Daughter*, 45 rpm, Loretta Lynn,
1970 .... **10.00**

Record, *Ernest Tubb Sings*, 45 rpm, 1953 .... **40.00**

Record, *I Love You Because*, Leon Payne, 78 rpm,
1949 .... **10.00**

Record, *Ramblin' Man*, Hank Williams, 1960, black
label **25.00**

Record, *This Is Johnny Cash*, LP, 1969 .... **12.00**

Record, *We Only Make Believe*, Conway Twitty, 1971 .... **10.00**

Sheet Music, *Pistol Packin' Mama*, Dexter, sgd **20.00**

Sheet Music, *Wabash Cannon Ball*, Rex Griffin, 1939 ..... **8.00**

Ticket Stub, Willie Nelson concert, c1977 .... **15.00**

Wallet, inscribed "Ernest Tubb" and "Music City
USA" **25.00**

COW COLLECTIBLES

This is one of the more recent "animal" collecting categories to evolve. Cow collectors came out of the pasture in the late 1980s, the result of a shift in decorating motif preferences from ducks to cows in Country magazines.

The category is completely image driven. Few collect only a specific breed. Contemporary items are just as popular and desir-able as are vintage examples.

Newsletter: *The MOOsletter*, 240 Wahl Ave, Evans City, PA 16033.

Cookie Jar, Brush, cat finial, brown, W10, 12¹/₂" w, $125.00.

Blotter, Cow Brand Baking Soda adv, blue and white,
   c1920 . . . . **$ 10.00**
Book, *Elsie and the Looking Club*, 1946 . . . . **25.00**
Butter Stamp, turned handle, 4¹/₄" d **150.00**
Can Opener, figural head, nickel plated **45.00**
Cookie Jar, brown, pink and white ribbon around
   neck, mkd "Wm. H. Hirsch Mfg. Co." **70.00**
Cookie Jar, purple, butterfly on cow's back, mkd
   "Made in Poppytrail Calif." **70.00**
Creamer, figural, Occupied Japan **25.00**
Figure, metal, 3" h **15.00**
Game, Elsie's Milkman Game, 1963 . . . . **85.00**
Keychain Charm, brass, emb cow on award base,
   inscribed "June Daily Month Award," 1" d **15.00**
Mug, white china, Elsie dancing in daisy meadow,
   Continental Kilns, ©Borden Co, late 1930s, 3" h **50.00**
Pitcher, ceramic, white, figural **15.00**
Place Mat, Elsie **15.00**
Poster, Evaporated Milk–Pure Cow's Milk, black
   and white cows, green ground, 1940 . . . . **10.00**
Push Puppet, wood and paper, Elsie on green base,
   makes moo sound, 1950s, 5" h **210.00**
Sheet Music, *Cow Cow Boogie*, from Walter Lantz's
   Swing Symphony, Don Raye, Gen DePaul, and
   Benny Carter, 1942 . . . . **12.00**
Tee Shirt, blue, black and white cow on front, rear
   view on back, vertical lettering on front and back,
   "Vermont" **5.00**
Toy, Bossy Bell, Fisher Price **40.00**
Toy, litho tin, windup, black and white cow, Japan,
   5¹/₂" l, 4" h **40.00**

COWAN POTTERY

R. Guy Cowan's first pottery, operating between 1912 and 1917, was located on Nicholson Avenue in Lakewood, Ohio, a Cleveland suburb. When he experienced problems with his gas supply, he moved his operations to Rocky River. The move also resulted in a production switch from a red clay ceramic body to a high–fired porcelain one.

By the mid–1920s Cowan manufactured a number of commerical products including dinnerware, desk sets, and planters. In addition, he made art pottery. In 1931, just a year after establishing an artists' colony, Cowan ceased operations, one of the many victims of the Great Depression.

References: Mark Bassett and Victoria Naumann, *Cowan Pottery and the Cleveland School,* Schiffer Publishing; Ralph and Terry Kovel, *Kovels' American Art Pottery: The Collector's Guide To Makers, Marks, and Factory Histories,* Crown Publishers, 1993; Tim and Jamie Saloff, *The Collector's Encyclopedia of Cowan Pottery: Identification & Values,* Collector Books, 1994.

Bowl, irregular rectangle, shape #641, yellow ext,
   green int, c1925, 2¹/₄" h, 11" l, 8" w . . . . **$ 60.00**
Bowl, metallic glaze, mkd "587A," 7¹/₂" d, 2" h **60.00**
Bowl, shape #733–A, mark #8, white ext, pink int,
   3¹/₈" h, 7¹/₄" d **50.00**
Bowl, shape #773–A, ivory ext, green int, 4" h,
   9¹/₂" d **50.00**
Bud Vase, shape #554, pearl luster, 7" h **60.00**
Candleholders, pr, #735 . . . . **45.00**
Candlesticks, pr, blue luster **65.00**
Candlesticks, pr, gazelles, tan **150.00**
Candlesticks, pr, sea horses, green **50.00**
Candlesticks, pr, shape #782, mark #8, ivory, 3" h **65.00**
Centerpiece Bowl, flower frog, figural nude, 6¹/₂" h **175.00**
Centerpiece Bowl, mark #8, side scallops extend into
   slight handles, ivory ext, raspberry int, 9" h,
   13¹/₂" d **80.00**
Cigarette Holder, figural seahorse, ivory **50.00**
Compote, diamond shape, 7" d, 2¹/₂" h **25.00**
Compote, shape #779, pedestal, scroll feet, lemon
   ext, turquoise int, 8" h **95.00**
Compote, shape #838, mark #8, short, ivory ext,
   green int, 2" h, 6" d **30.00**
Compote, shape #848X, lime, 5" h **75.00**
Cup and Saucer, melon dec, tan glaze **30.00**
Figure, radio woman, black on cream, 9" h **4,500.00**
Flower Frog, figural nude, white, 6" h **65.00**
Flower Frog, flamingo, perforated base, white glaze,
   die–stamped mark, 6" d, 11¹/₂" h **300.00**
Flower Frog, nude dancer with scarf, 6¹/₂" h **135.00**
Paperweight, shape #d–3, mark #9, elephant, blue,
   c1930, 4⁵/₈" h **295.00**
Soap Dish, seahorses, white and pink matte, 4 x 7" **40.00**
Trivet, bust of young girl framed by flowers, scalloped
   rim, sgd, 6¹/₂" d **275.00**
Vase, Art Deco, blue luster, 10³/₄" h **145.00**
Vase, blue and green glaze, hp mushrooms, 6" h **365.00**
Vase, blue luster, 8" h **45.00**
Vase, bulbous, yellow, 6¹/₄" h, 5¹/₂" d **30.00**
Vase, classic shape, blue luster, ink stamp mark,
   7¹/₂" h **50.00**
Vase, Egyptian, blue **125.00**
Vase, fan, green with gold specks, 5" h **80.00**
Vase, fan, seahorse standard, orange luster, 7⁷/₈" h **65.00**
Vase, fan, seahorse standard, white, 7" h **85.00**
Vase, ftd, fluted, blue luster, 5¹/₂" h **95.00**
Vase, Logan, brown crystalline **150.00**
Vase, shape #649A, Logan, blue luster, 8¹/₄" h **190.00**

COWBOY HEROES

Cowboy Heroes are divided into eight major categories: (1) silent movie cowboys, (2) "B" movie cowboys, (3) "A" movie cowboys, (4) 1950s and 60s TV cowboy heroes, (5) Gene Autry, (6) Hopalong Cassidy, (7) The Lone Ranger, and (8) Roy Rogers.

Tom Mix used to be included in this list as the ninth classification. However, now that the generation who grew up watching Tom Mix movies or listening to the Ralston Straight Shooters on the radio has died, Mix collectibles, with the exception of crossover pieces such as toy guns, are depreciating rather than appreciating in value.

Do you know who William S. Hart is? There rests the problem for silent movie cowboys. They are in the final stages of the last memory roundup. "B" movie cowboys, comprising individuals such as Buck Jones, Ken Maynard, and Tim McCoy, are just down the trail. Reruns of the old "B" westerns have all but disappeared from television—out of sight, out of mind. "A" movie cowboys such as Clint Eastwood and John Wayne have cult followers, but never achieved the popularity of Gene, Hoppy, or Roy.

Currently the market is strong for 1950s and 60s television cowboy heros. The generations that watched the initial runs of Bonanza, Gunsmoke, Paladin, Rawhide, The Rifleman, and Wagon Train are at their peak earning capacities and willing to pay top dollar to buy back their childhood. Prices for common 1950s material have been stable for the past few years.

Gene, Hoppy, The Lone Ranger, and Roy are in a class by themselves. Currently, Hoppy collectibles are the hottest of the four with Roy close behind. Gene and The Lone Ranger are starting to eat dust. Look for a major collecting shift involving the collectibles of these four individuals in the next ten years.

References: Ted Hake, *Hake's Guide To Cowboy Character Collectibles: An Illustrated Price Guide Covering 50 Years of Movie & TV Cowboy Heroes,* Wallace–Homestead, Krause Publications, 1994; Robert Heide and John Gilman, *Box–Office Buckaroos,* Abbeville Press, 1989; Robert W. Philips, *Roy Rogers: A Biography, Radio History, Television Career Chronicle, Discography, Filmography, Comicography, Merchandising and Advertising History, Collectibles Description, Bibliography and Index,* McFarland & Co, 1995; Harry L. Rinker, *Hopalong Cassidy: King of the Cowboy Merchandisers,* Schiffer Publishing, 1995.

Collectors' Club: Westerns & Serials Fan Club, Rte 1 Box 103, Vernon Center, MN 56090.

Note: For information on fan clubs for individual cowboy heroes, refer to *Maloney's Antiques & Collectibles Resource Directory* by David J. Maloney, Jr., published by Antique Trader Books.

Bobby Benson, pinback button, "Bobby Benson, Special Captain," blue lettering and rope design, yellow ground, 1930s, 1¼" d . . . . **$ 35.00**

Buck Jones, Big Little Book, *Buck Jones in Ride 'Em High,* Whitman, ©1937 . . . . **25.00**

Buck Jones, guitar, made by Gibson for Sears, Roebuck & Co, c1930, 37" l **125.00**

Buck Jones, photo, black and white, "Best Wishes, Buck Jones & Silver," c1930s, 5 x 7" **15.00**

Buffalo Bill, Jr, child's outfit, 2 pc, flannel, plastic fringe trim, simulated fur, c1950s **50.00**

Gene Autry, guitar, plastic case, 16–pg song booklet, Emenee Industries, c1955, 31" h, $50.00.

Buffalo Bill, Jr, comic book, Dell, #7, February–April 1958 . . . . **8.00**

Cisco Kid, jigsaw puzzle **25.00**

Cisco Kid, postcard, Cisco and Pancho, Tip–Top Bread premium, c1953 . . . . **18.00**

Cisco Kid, program, stiff paper folder, "Cisco Kid Rodeo," Wrigley Field, Chicago, mid–July, c1950s **25.00**

Davy Crockett, cereal bowl, 5" d **25.00**

Davy Crockett, cookie jar, Brush. **125.00**

Davy Crockett, glass, frosted white, portrait on sides, Ritchey's Milk, c1950s, 5" h **35.00**

Davy Crockett, gun, plastic, flintlock, brown, silver accents, gold lettered "Davy Crockett" on side, raised pirate and ship on handle, c1955 . . . . **30.00**

Davy Crockett, playset, belt, compass, and powder horn, orig package **85.00**

Davy Crockett, sheet music, *Ballad of Davy Crockett,* Fess Parker cov, Disney **22.00**

Davy Crockett, thermos, steel, plastic cap, American Thermos, c1955–56, 8½" h **40.00**

Davy Crockett, wristwatch **15.00**

Gene Autry, book, *Gene Autry and Red Shirt,* Sandpiper, ©1951 . . . . **20.00**

Gene Autry, book, *Gene Autry Goes to the Circus,* Whitman, Tell–A–Tale series, 28 pgs, 1950, hard cover **22.00**

Gene Autry, child's galoshes, rubber, 7½" h **120.00**

Gene Autry, coloring book, 48 pgs, unused, Whitman, 1949, 11 x 15" **30.00**

Gene Autry, frame tray puzzle, Whitman, ©1953, 11½ x 15" **25.00**

Gene Autry, poster, "Melody Ranch," Wrigley's Gum, adv for "Rancho Grande," **125.00**

Gene Autry, program "The Gene Autry Show," traveling show souvenir, c1950, 8 pgs, 8½ x 11" **35.00**

Gene Autry, sheet music, *Oh Dem Golden Slippers,* ©1935 . . . . **15.00**

Gene Autry, tablet, Gene and Champion on cov, 1950s, unused, 8 x 10" **25.00**

Gene Gray, pinback button, Gray on horse, "Gene Gray, Silver King of Cowboys," blue and white, 1930s, 1³/₄" d **25.00**

Hoot Gibson, comic book, Fox Features, #5, June 1950 . . . . **40.00**

Hoot Gibson, leather holster, cartridge belt, c1930s **40.00**

Hopalong Cassidy, bank, plastic, removable hat, 4" h **30.00**

Hopalong Cassidy, bolo tie, steer head **12.00**

Hopalong Cassidy, canvas book bag, 10¹/₂ x 14" **100.00**

Hopalong Cassidy, comic book, Vol 5, #29, Mar 1949, Fawcett **55.00**

Hopalong Cassidy, fan card, color portrait, facsimile signature, 1950, 3¹/₂ x 5¹/₂" **25.00**

Hopalong Cassidy, flashlight, metal, color decal, morse code listing on barrel **50.00**

Hopalong Cassidy, hair trainer **55.00**

Hopalong Cassidy, jigsaw puzzle, set of 3, MIB **55.00**

Hopalong Cassidy, Little Golden Book, *Hopalong Cassidy and the Bar 20 Cowboy*, ©1952 . . . . **20.00**

Hopalong Cassidy, magazine, *Life*, Hoppy cov, Jun 12, 1950, 10 x 13" **20.00**

Hopalong Cassidy, playing cards, "Hopalong Canasta," Hoppy and Topper portraits on backs, Pacific Playing Card, ©1950 . . . . **85.00**

Hopalong Cassidy, poster, *Sinister Journey*, 1947 . . . . **100.00**

Hopalong Cassidy, snowdome **50.00**

Hopalong Cassidy, thermos **40.00**

John Wayne, comic book, The Cowboy Trouble Shooter, Oxydol and Dreft soap premiums, 3 x 7" **40.00**

John Wayne, frame tray puzzle, Saalfield, ©1951, 11¹/₂ x 15" **55.00**

John Wayne, record, *Ballad of the Alamo*, 45 rpm, Golden Record, ©1960 . . . . **20.00**

John Wayne, sheet music, *In Old Oklahoma*, Wayne and Dale Evans on cov, ©1943 . . . . **70.00**

Ken Maynard, cigar band, diecut paper, red, gold, and black design, black and white photo, 1930s, 1 x 3" **20.00**

Ken Maynard, lobby card, Universal, 1933, 14 x 22" **50.00**

Roy Rogers, pocket knife, Ulster, 3 blades, $75.00.

Lone Ranger, autographed photo, black and white, Clayton Moore, c1970s, 8 x 10" **35.00**

Lone Ranger, game, Legend of the Lone Ranger **12.00**

Lone Ranger, Little Golden Book, *The Lone Ranger*, Simon and Schuster, ©1956, 24 pgs **15.00**

Lone Ranger, magazine, *Golden West*, Lone Ranger cov **10.00**

Lone Ranger, model, Tonto, #183, brown plastic, 8–pg comic book, instructions, backdrop mural, Aurora Products Corp, ©1974, unopened **35.00**

Lone Ranger, pistol, brown marbleized grips, 9" l **35.00**

Lone Ranger, poster, "The Lone Ranger Wants You," 1970s **20.00**

Lone Ranger, sheet music, *Hi Yo Silver, The Lone Ranger's Song*, 1938 . . . . **80.00**

Red Ryder, bagatelle, metal, Gotham Pressed Steel Corp, c1940s **65.00**

Red Ryder, Better Little Book, *Red Ryder and Little Beaver on Hoofs of Thunder*, ©1939 . . . . **30.00**

Red Ryder, frame tray puzzle, Jaymar, ©1951, 11 x 14" **18.00**

Red Ryder, Little Beaver Archery Set, cardboard target, ©1951, 8 x 31" **25.00**

Red Ryder, poster, "Ride, Ryder, Ride!," 22 x 28" **25.00**

Rin Tin Tin, coloring book, Whitman, ©1955 . . . . **15.00**

Rin Tin Tin, game, Adventures of Rin–Tin–Tin, Transogram, ©1955 . . . . **50.00**

Rin Tin Tin, record, 33¹/₃ rpm, Columbia, ©1955 . . . . **25.00**

Roy Rogers, bandanna, red and white cloth, 17" sq **70.00**

Roy Rogers, bank, figural boot **25.00**

Roy Rogers, calendar, Nestle's Co, 1959 . . . . **165.00**

Roy Rogers, child's boots, leather, "Roy Rogers" each side, elastic pull strap, c1952, 8¹/₂" h **150.00**

Roy Rogers, coloring book, Trigger and Bullet, Whitman, #2958, 1959 . . . . **25.00**

Roy Rogers, jigsaw puzzle, Roy, Dale, and Dusty, Whitman, c1950s, 15 x 21", orig box **30.00**

Roy Rogers, paint book, Whitman, #1158, ©1948, 48 pgs, 11 x 15", unused **60.00**

Roy Rogers, playset, Roy Rogers Rodeo Ranch **100.00**

Roy Rogers, poster, "My Pal Trigger" **75.00**

Roy Rogers, pup tent, cloth, Hettrick Mfg Co **45.00**

Roy Rogers, tie, yellow **75.00**

Roy Rogers, toy telephone **40.00**

Roy Rogers, wristwatch, Happy Trails, 1985, MIB **110.00**

Tim McCoy, Big Little Book, *The Prescott Kid*, Whitman, #1152, 1935 . . . . **35.00**

Tom Mix, book, *The Fabulous Tom Mix*, Olive Stokes Mix, Eric Heath assistant, Prentice–Hall, hard cover, dj, 178 pgs, 6 x 8¹/₂" **18.00**

Hopalong Cassidy, radio, Arvin, black case, $300.00.

Tom Mix, patch, cloth, red checkerboard design, blue
T–M Bar Ranch symbol in center, Ralston premi-
um, 1933, 3" sq **70.00**
Wild Bill Hickok, gun and holster, orig box **150.00**
Wyatt Earp, Big Little Book, *Hugh O'Brian TV's Wyatt
Earp,* #1644, Whitman, 1958, 276 pgs **15.00**

CRACKER JACK

Cracker Jack arrived on the scene at the 1893 World's Columbian
Exposition in Chicago when F. W. Rueckhaim, a pop store owner,
introduced his world famous mixture of popcorn, peanuts, and
molasses. The mix was not called "Cracker Jack" until three years
later. The 1908 song, *Take Me Out to the Ball Game,* created
national recognition for Cracker Jack.

The first prize in the box appeared in 1912. In the past 85 years
plus, over 10,000 different prizes have made an appearance. New
examples are being discovered every year. Today's prizes, with the
exception of the magnifying glass, are made primarily from paper.
The Borden Company, owner of Cracker Jack, buys prizes in lots of
25 million and keeps several hundred in circulation at one time.

References: Raui Piña, *Cracker Jack Collectibles,* Schiffer
Publishing, 1995; Larry White, *Cracker Jack Toys,* Schiffer
Publishing, 1997.

Collectors' Club: Cracker Jack Collector's Assoc, 108 Central St,
Rowley, MA 01969.

Bank, tin, brass luster . . . . **$ 25.00**
Booklet, Animated Jungleland, 1928, 4 x 5" **42.00**
Booklet, Cracker Jack in Switzerland, ©1926, 4 pgs **70.00**
Box, cardboard, red, white, and blue, 1930s, 7" h **45.00**
Certificate, Cracker Jack Mystery Club, red, white,
and green, 3 x 6" **70.00**
Doll, stuffed cloth, black and white sailor outfit, black
vinyl boots, 15" h **25.00**
Flasher, cardboard, text on back, c1960, 1¼" d **5.00**
Lapel Stud, metal, wing shape, 2" l **55.00**
Mask, "Cracker Jack" on front, c1960, 8½ x 10" **18.00**
Plate, tin, silvered, c1930, 1¾" d **35.00**
Prize, clicker, aluminum, pear shape, "Noisy Cracker
Jacker Snapper" **25.00**
Prize, plastic figure, inscribed on back "Hoki, God of
Childish Mischief," 1¼" h **15.00**
Prize, spinner, plastic, multicolored **2.00**
Prize, watch, tin, 1930s, 1½" d **25.00**
Rocket Ship, plastic, green, c1950, 1½" h **10.00**
Sign, diecut cardboard, color, 7 x 11" **275.00**

Bookmark, litho tin, brown terrier, 1930s, 2¾", $20.00.

Tape Measure, Angelus Marshmallow design, c1930,
1½" d **40.00**
Toy, truck, litho tin **40.00**
Toy, wheelbarrow, litho tin, yellow and green, green
wheels, c1930 . . . . **25.00**

CRACKLE GLASS

Crackle glass, a glass–making technique that results in a multiple–fractured surface appearance, dates back to the 16th century.
Martin Bach of Durand Glass is credited with reintroducing the
concept in the late 1920s.

Crackle glass achieved widespread popularity in the late 1930s
and was produced into the 1970s. Over 500 glass companies
made crackle glass. Bischoff Glass, Blenko Glass, Hamon Glass,
Kanawha Glass, Pilgrim Glass, Rainbow Art Glass, and Vogelsong
Glass are just a few.

Collector interest in this subject began when a series of articles
appeared in trade newspapers. The publication of a major book on
the subject and the category's inclusion in general price guides
fueled the market.

References: Judy Alford, *Collecting Crackle Glass,* Schiffer
Publishing, 1997; Stan and Arlene Weitman, *Crackle Glass:
Identification and Value Guide,* Collector Books, 1996.

Collectors' Club: Crackle Glass Club, PO Box 1186, North
Massapequa, NY 11758.

Apple, crystal pink, Blenko, 3¼" h . . . . **$ 50.00**
Ashtray, amberina, 7¼" h **35.00**
Candleholder, pale sea green, Blenko, 5¼" h **50.00**
Candy Dish, amberina, Kanawha, 3" h **40.00**
Candy Dish, dark topaz, ribbed, dropover handle,
Hamon, 5½ x 2¼" **75.00**
Creamer, emerald green, dropover handle, Pilgrim,
3¾" h **35.00**
Creamer and Sugar, blue, dropover handle, Pilgrim,
3½" h **50.00**
Creamer and Sugar, gold, dropover handle, Kanawha,
3½" h **50.00**
Cruet, amber, pulled back handle, Rainbow **70.00**
Cruet, sea green, Pilgrim **40.00**
Decanter, amberina, Blenko, 1970, 8½", price for
pair **150.00**
Decanter, amberina, crackled top, Rainbow, 7¾" **85.00**
Decanter, lemon lime, Pilgrim, 6" h **100.00**
Decanter, topaz, ribbed, crystal dropover handle,
Pilgrim, 6¼" h **100.00**
Dish, green, Kanawha, 5¼ x 3" **35.00**
Glass, cream, dropover handle, 5½" h **35.00**
Glass, ruby, pinched, Hamon, 6" h **60.00**
Glass, sea green, Blenko, 5¾" h **50.00**
Glass, topaz, dropover handle, Pilgrim, 4" h **40.00**
Jug, amberina, gold dropover handle, Blenko, 8¼" h **75.00**
Jug, blue, dropover handle, Pilgrim, 4" h **30.00**
Ladle, crystal, amethyst handle, Blenko, 15" l **175.00**
Miniature Hat, amberina, Kanawha, 2" h **35.00**
Miniature Hat, olive green, Pilgrim, 3" h **35.00**
Miniature Hat, topaz, Blenko, 2¾" h **35.00**

Creamer and Sugar, vaseline, pear and leaf finial, $150.00.

Mug, amber, dropover handle, 6¼" h	25.00
Pear, sea green, Blenko, 5"	50.00
Pitcher, amberina, pulled back handle, Pilgrim, 3¾" h	30.00
Pitcher, amethyst, dropover handle, Pilgrim, 3¼" h	35.00
Pitcher, blue, 4" h	40.00
Pitcher, dark amber, dropover handle, Blenko, 17" h	100.00
Pitcher, dark amber, dropover handle, Pilgrim, 5" h	25.00
Pitcher, green, dropover handle, Pilgrim, 3½" h	35.00
Pitcher, ruby, dropover handle, Kanawha, 3¼" h	30.00
Pitcher, topaz, pulled back handle, Hamon, 3¼" h	25.00
Punch Bowl, crystal, Blenko, 11¾ x 7" w	200.00
Punch Cup, crystal, amethyst hook handle, Blenko, 2" h	40.00
Syrup Pitcher, amethyst, pulled back handle, Kanawha, 6"	60.00
Syrup Pitcher, blue, pulled back handle, Kanawha, 6"	50.00
Vase, amethyst, Pilgrim, 4" h	60.00
Vase, crystal, blue rosettes, Blenko, 7" h	75.00
Vase, fish, green, Hamon, 8¼" h	125.00
Vase, fish, topaz, Hamon, 9" h	80.00
Vase, jonquil, ftd, crimped top, Blenko, 7¼" h	100.00
Vase, olive green, double–neck, Blenko, 4" h	50.00

CREDIT CARDS & TOKENS

The charge coin, the forerunner of the credit card, first appeared in the 1890s. Each coin had a different identification number. Charge coins were made in a variety of materials from celluloid to German silver and came in two basic shapes, geometric and diecut. The form survived until the late 1950s.

Metal charge plates, similar to a G.I.'s dog tag, were issued from the 1930s through the 1950s. Paper charge cards also were used. Lamination of the cards to prolong use began in the 1940s.

The plastic credit card arrived on the scene in the late 1950s.

In the 1980s pictorial credit cards became popular. Individuals applied for credit just to get the card. The inclusion of holigrams on the card for security purposes also was introduced during the 1980s. Today institutions from airlines to universities issue credit cards, many of which feature a bonus program. Little wonder America has such a heavy credit card debt.

Reference: Lin Overholt, *The First International Credit Card Catalog, 3rd Edition,* published by author, 1995.

Collectors' Clubs: Active Token Collectors Organization, PO Box 1573, Stone Falls, SD 57101; American Credit Card Collectors Society, PO Box 2465, Midland, MI 48640; American Numismatic Assoc, 818 N Cascade Ave, Colorado Springs, CO 80903; American Vecturist Assoc, PO Box 1204, Boston, MA 02104; Token & Medal Society, Inc, 9230 SW 59th St, Miami, FL 33173.

Card, American Express, "The Money Card," green, 1970	$ 25.00
Card, AT&T, phone card, plastic	5.00
Card, Bloomingdale's, brown on white, tan border	12.00
Card, Diners Club, gray ground, Citicorp	15.00
Card, Fina, large blue "Fina," c1970s	5.00
Card, Hilton Hotels, paperboard, 1955	35.00
Card, Korvettes, personal charge plate	5.00
Card, Mastercard, pre–hologram, gold card	8.00
Card, Montgomery Ward, yellow and white, national charge–all card	8.00
Card, Sears, "Sears" in box	10.00
Card, Standard Oil, red and blue US map, 1972	15.00
Card, TWA, getaway card, couple wearing swimsuits holding hands, 1974	10.00
Card, Vickers Refining Co, lifetime courtesy card, crown over "V" logo	20.00
Token, Boggs and Buhl, Pittsburgh, PA, oval, white metal, knight's helmet between backward and regular "B"	15.00
Token, C F Massey, Rochester, MN, octagonal, white metal, ornate interlocking "C F M"	15.00
Token, Dives, Pomeroy & Stewart, Reading/Pottsville, PA, rect, white metal, initials "D F & S," thistles	15.00
Token, George B. Evans, Philadelphia, PA, diamond shape, white metal, drugs and gifts	15.00
Token, Gimble Brothers, New York City, white metal, "GB" in circle at top, "New York" at bottom	20.00
Token, Lit Brothers, Philadelphia, PA, irregular oval, white metal, "LB," date of issue	20.00
Token, Plotkin Brothers, Boston, MA, rect, white metal, lion head over shield containing "PB"	20.00
Token, R. H. Stearns, Boston, MA, oval, white metal, interlocking "R H S Co"	15.00

Card, The Playboy Club, $5.00.

CROOKSVILLE POTTERY

Founded in 1912, the Crooksville Pottery, Crooksville, Ohio, made semi–porcelain dinnerwares and utilitarian household pottery. Their decal decorated "Pantry–Bak–In" line was extremely popular in the 1930s and 40s.

The company's semi–porcelain dinnerware line was marketed as Stinhal China. Most pieces are not marked with a pattern name. Check the reference books. The company ceased operations in 1959, a victim of cheap foreign imports and the popularity of melamine plastic dinnerware.

References: Jo Cunningham, *The Collector's Encyclopedia of American Dinnerware,* Collector Books, 1982, 1995 value update; Lois Lehner, *Lehner's Encyclopedia of U.S. Marks on Pottery, Porcelain & Clay,* Collector Books, 1988; Harvey Duke, *The Official Price Guide to Pottery and Porcelain, Eighth Edition,* House of Collectibles, 1995.

Dartmouth, creamer	$ 8.00
Dartmouth, cup	5.00
Dartmouth, teapot	50.00
Dawn, bread and butter plate, 6" d	2.00
Dawn, dish 5¼" d	2.50
Euclid, batter set tray	15.00
Harmony, casserole,	25.00
Harmony, sugar	10.00
Ivora, saucer, 6" d	2.00
Ivora, teapot	30.00
Petit Point House, berry bowl	5.00
Petit Point House, cup and saucer	8.00
Petit Point House, salad plate, 7" d	5.00
Provincial Ware, gravy	15.00
Provincial Ware, platter, 11½" d	12.00
Quadro, eggcup	12.00
Quadro, vegetable bowl	12.00
Rust Bouquet, coffeepot	25.00
Rust Bouquet, pie baker	15.00
Rust Bouquet, platter, 11½" l	8.00
Silhouette, cookie jar, flat lid, rattan handle	50.00
Silhouette, creamer	12.00
Silhouette, dinner plate, 10" d	10.00
Silhouette, mixing bowl, 8" d	18.00
Silhouette, pie baker, Pantry Bak–In	20.00

Silhouette, pitcher, $20.00.

CYBIS

Boleslaw Cybis, a professor at the Academy of Fine Art in Warsaw, Poland, and his wife, Marja, came to the United States in 1939 to paint murals in the Hall of Honor at the New York's World Fair. Unable to return to Poland after war broke out, the couple remained in the United States and opened an artists' studio to create porcelain sculpture.

After a brief stint in New York, the sudio moved to Trenton, New Jersey. Sculptures were produced in a variety of themes ranging from the world of nature to elegant historical figures.

Apaloosa Colt, 1971	$ 285.00
Autumn, 1972	200.00
Bear, 1968	400.00
Buffalo, 1986	185.00
Bunny, Snowflake, 1985	75.00
Bunny Pat–a–Cake, 1977	150.00
Clarissa, 1986	195.00
Clematis with House Wren, 1969	315.00
Dapple Gray Foal, 1986	185.00
Deer Mouse in Clover, 1970	150.00
Duckling, "Baby Brother," 1962	140.00
Easter Egg Hunt, 1972	200.00
Edith, 1978	300.00
George Washington Bust, 1975	300.00
Goldilocks, 1973	325.00
Holiday Ornament, 1985	75.00
Jason, 1978	375.00
Jogger, female, 1980	425.00
Kitten, Tabitha, 1975	150.00
Lullaby, blue, 1986	160.00
Nativity Cow, 1984	200.00
Nativity Lamb, 1985	125.00
Nesting Bluebirds, 1978	250.00
Pansies, 1972	350.00
Pierre the Performing Poodle, 1986	275.00
Rebecca, 1964	345.00
Sabbath Morning, 1972	200.00
Valentine, 1985	375.00
Winter, 1972	200.00
Yellow Condesa Rose, 1980	250.00

CZECHOSLOVAKIAN WARES

The country of Czechoslovakia was created in 1918 from the Czech and Solvak regions of the old Austro–Hungarian Empire. Both regions were actively involved in the manufacture of ceramics and glass.

Czechoslovakian ceramics and glassware were imported into the United States in large numbers from the 1920s through the 1950s. Most are stamped "Made in Czechoslovakia." Pieces mirrored the styles of the day. Czechoslovakian Art Deco glass is stylish, colorful, and bright. Canister sets are one of the most popular ceramic forms.

By 1939, Czechoslovakia had fallen under the control of Germany. The country came under communist influence in 1948. Communist domination ended in 1989. On January 1, 1993, Czechoslovakia spit into two independent states, the Czech Republic and the Slovak Republic.

References: Dale and Diane Barta and Helen M. Rose, *Czechoslovakian Glass & Collectibles* (1992, 1995 value update), *Book II* (1997), Collector Books; Ruth A. Forsythe, *Made in Czechoslovakia,* Richardson Printing Corp, 1982, 1994–95 value update; Ruth A. Forsythe, *Made in Czechoslovakia, Book 2,* Antique Publications, 1993, 1995–96 value update; Diane E. Foulds, *A Guide to Czech & Slovak Glass, 2nd Edition,* published by author, 1993, 1995 value update, distributed by Antique Publications; Robert and Deborah Truitt, *Collectible Bohemian Glass: 1880–1940,* B & D Glass, 1995, distributed by Antique Publications.

Collectors' Club: Czechoslovakian Collectors Guild International, PO Box 901395, Kansas City, MO 64190.

Ashtray, blue . . . . **$ 20.00**
Bookends, pr, ram, frosted crystal **185.00**
Bowl, painted floral dec, ftd, 4¼" h **90.00**
Box, cov, mottled, 4½" h **145.00**
Candlesticks, pr, red, black enamel dec, 10½" h **170.00**
Candy Basket, yellow, black rim, crystal handle,
   6½" h **200.00**
Candy Jar, applied floral ornament, 3¾" h **85.00**
Cologne Bottle, porcelain, glossy blue, bow front,
   4" h **22.00**
Creamer, chicken, 4" h **40.00**
Figure, bird, 4⅜" h **45.00**
Figure, elephant, 4½" h **50.00**
Figure, monkey, blue, ⅞" h **40.00**
Necklace, green and white stones, metal, 7½" l **45.00**
Perfume Bottle, cranberry opalescent, Hobnail, 5½" h **85.00**
Perfume Bottle, jeweled dec, 2½" h **80.00**
Pitcher, bird and flower dec, handled, 11½" h **280.00**

Salt and Pepper Shakers, pr, Tobys, $18.00.

Plate, rooster design, green rim **10.00**
Powder Box, cov, round, yellow glass, black knob
   finial **55.00**
Salt and Pepper Shakers, pr, Mexicans **18.00**
Vase, bird and fruit dec **40.00**
Vase, mottled, petal top, 6" h **110.00**
Vase, mottled, 7¾" h **75.00**
Vase, opaque, enameled birch trees, house, and barn
   with red roof, 6" h **65.00**
Wall Pocket, woodpecker, 7¾" h **65.00**

DAIRY COLLECTIBLES

The mid–20th century was the Golden Age of the American dairy industry. Thousands of small dairies and creameries were located throughout the United States, most serving only a regional market.

Dairy cooperatives, many of which were created in the 1920s and 30s, served a broader market. Many small dairies could not compete and closed. Borden pursued a national marketing program. Elsie, The Borden Cow is one of the most widely recognized advertising characters from the 1940s and 50s.

Reference: Dana Gehman Morykan and Harry L. Rinker, *Warman's Country Antiques & Collectibles, Third Edition,* Wallace–Homestead, Krause Publications, 1996.

Newsletter: *Creamers,* PO Box 11, Lake Villa, IL 60046.

Collectors' Clubs: Cream Separator News, Rte 3, Box 189, Arcadia, WI 54612; National Assoc of Milk Bottle Collectors, Inc, 4 Ox Bow Rd, Westport, CT 06880.

Bank, Rutter Bros Dairy Products, dairy truck, plastic,
   white, red decal, c1960 . . . . **$ 40.00**
Blotter, Hood's Milk, delivery man with case of milk
   in horse–drawn wagon, multicolored, 6 x 3½",
   unused **20.00**
Booklet, *We Pull For Windsor*, Windsor Farm Dairy,
   Denver, CO, early 1930s, 18 pgs **15.00**
Box, Borden's Processed Cheese Food, wood, red and
   green logo, 1950s, 4 x 12 x 4" **20.00**
Calendar, Broad View Farm, Rochester, NH, 1927 . . . . . . **12.00**
Calendar, De Laval Cream Separators, boy building
   doghouse, mother sitting on porch watching, 1927 . . . **300.00**
Calendar, Hood's Milk, October pad, 1940 . . . . **30.00**
Clock, Old Southern Belle Dairy, girl in red dress,
   16" sq **65.00**
Container, Carnation Malted Milk, milk glass, alu-
   minum lid **140.00**
Pamphlet, "The Story of Elsie the Cow," Borden,
   c1975 . . . . **5.00**
Paperweight, Borden's Milk, milk carton shape, Elsie
   illus **20.00**
Pinback Button, Drink Aristocrat Milk, red and white,
   1930s **10.00**
Poster, Evaporated Milk–Pure Cow's Milk, black and
   white cows, green ground, 1940 . . . . **8.00**
Recipe Book, Borden's Eagle Brand, cover shows
   woman in kitchen reading cookbook, 1920s **10.00**
Recipe Book, Carnation Milk, "Teen Time Cooking
   With Carnation," 1959, 16 pgs **8.00**

DECORATIVE ACCESSORIES

Design style plays a major role in today's collecting world. The period look is back in vogue as collectors attempt to recreate the ambiance of the particular period, e.g., Art Deco or the 1950s.

This emphasis on "the look" has credited value for a wide range of tabletop decorative pieces, from stylish cigarette boxes to table lamps. Fabrics, wallpaper, and other products that cry "period" are eagerly sought.

Most of these items are being purchased for accent pieces, not as part of a collection. Buyers incorporate them in their home decor and use them. Value is as much about pizzazz as it is collectibility.

References: Tony Fusco, *Art Deco: Identification and Price Guide, 2nd Edition,* Avon Books, 1993; Mary Frank Gaston, *Collector's Guide To Art Deco, Second Edition,* Collector Books, 1997; Anne Gilbert, *40's and 50's Designs and Memorabilia: Identification and Price Guide,* Avon Books, 1993; Anne Gilbert, *60's and 70's Designs and Memorabilia: Identification and Price Guide,* Avon Books, 1994; Robert Heide and John Gilman, *Popular Art Deco: Depression Era Style and Design,* Abbeville Press, 1991; Jan Lindenberger, *Collecting the 50s & 60s, 2nd Edition,* Schiffer Publishing, 1997; Leslie Piña, *'50s & '60s Glass, Ceramics & Enamel Wares: Designed & Signed by George Briard, Sascha B., Bellaire, Higgins…,* Schiffer Publishing, 1996.

Periodical: *The Echoes Report,* PO Box 2321, Mashpee, MA 02649.

Collectors' Clubs: Chase Collectors Society, 2149 W Jibsail Loop, Mesa, AZ 85202; National Coalition of Art Deco Societies, One Murdock Terrace, Brighton, MA 02135.

Art Deco, ashtray, Holland–American Line, Dutch, silver plated, relief of house in center, 1930s–40s . . . **$ 40.00**

Art Deco, camera, #1A Gift Kodak, Walter Teague designer, metal–hinged lid with chromed–metal geometric design of rectangles and circles, enameled in brown, red, and silver, leather case, fitted black lacquered box with same design, 1930s, 4³/₈ x 8³/₄", value includes camera, case, box, and instructions **1,750.00**

Art Deco, camera, 6–20 Jiffy, Eastman Kodak, bellows camera, geometric design on case, 1935 . . . . . . **80.00**

Art Deco, candy dish, Chase Brass & Copper, 2 chrome dishes joined in center with chrome knob, chrome circular handle, 4" h, mid–1930s **100.00**

Art Deco, clock, Westclox, yellow Bakelite, flashing light and alarm, 1940s **100.00**

Art Deco, cocktail shaker, Revere Brass and Copper, chome cylindrical body, "D" handle, and dome lid, extended rod bright yellow Bakelite finial, matching yellow Bakelite spout cover, 1930s **125.00**

Art Deco, cocktail shaker set, Chase Brass & Copper, cylinder shaker, 6 matching cocktail cups with purple Bakelite foot, curved rect 2 handled tray **175.00**

Art Deco, cocktail shaker set, Farberware, chrome shaker with brown Bakelite handle, finial, and spout cover, 6 chrome cups, mkd "Farber Brothers" and "Krome Kraf" **150.00**

Art Deco, coffee service, Manning Bowman, 4 pcs (coffeepot, creamer, sugar, tray), chrome, body form with sharp, winged angles, green Bakelite handles and finials, 18" l tray **500.00**

Art Deco, desk set, American, double inkstand, pen holder, 2 letter openers, and rocking blotter, striped black and green Bakelite with chrome accents, 1920s **750.00**

Art Deco, hot and cold food server, West Bend Aluminum, penguins circle perimeter of circular server, glass liner, wooden stepped–design handles, late 1930s/early 1940s, 8¹/₂" d **85.00**

Art Deco, lamp, Chase Brass and Copper, spherical copper body, conical copper shade, brass ball finial, 8¹/₂" h **175.00**

Art Deco, magazine cover, *Vanity Fair,* Feb 1932, Miguel Covarrubia's portrayl of Greta Garbo, pointed shoulders match her pointed eyebrows **75.00**

Art Deco, picture frame, various manufacturers, chrome silver borders, painted black accent lines, 8 x 12" **45.00**

Art Deco, poster, Normandie, color photo by Nascon, ship leaving New York, tiered silver leaf frame, chrome nameplate, 19 x 33" **300.00**

Art Deco, smoking stand, top with sliding doors for smoking supplies, 3 columns leading from top to circular base,1930s, 22" h **225.00**

Modern, iron, streamlined, "General Mills," made by General Mills, black industrial plastic "V" shaped handles with appearance of oceanliner, 1930s **50.00**

Modern, iron, streamlined, "Petipoint," Waverly Tool Company, Sandusky, OH, designed by Edward Schreyer and Clifford Stevens, metal streamlined oval shape with stepped–back protruding wings motif, early 1940s **600.00**

Modern, table top radio, streamlined, Spartan, Sparks–Wittington Company, Michigan, designed by Walter Teague, round front, mirrored glass and chrome, circular dial surrounded by circle of chrome, 3 horizontal bands, 1930s **2,500.00**

1950s, flower frog, figural draped nude, ceramic, white, incised "Made in Japan," 9¹/₂" h, $15.00.

1930s, bowl, clear glass, green tone, attributed to VS, designed by Alfredo Barbinia, int dec with hot modeled fish and green swirls, unmkd, 9½" d **275.00**

1930s, figural sculpture, WPA, tortoise and hare, white and brown on blue–green base, painted on side "The Hare and the Tortoise. The race is not always to the swift. Ohio WJPA Art Project, Akron, Ohio," 4 x 9 x 6" **675.00**

1940s, compote, ftd, Barovier and Toso, iridescent clear glass, 10½" w , 4" h **75.00**

1950s, ashtray, rooftops pattern, slotted on left, light tan ground, Sasha Brastoff, 8½" l **65.00**

1950s, bust, chalkware, Indian male wearing turban, speckle dot motif fabric, flesh–tone face **50.00**

1950s, cake saver, metal, round, cover with solid red top and finial, red floral motif on white ground on sides, red rimmed base **15.00**

1950s, ceiling lamp, western motif, tapered ivory body, wagon wheel, horseshoe, and brand motif, brass mounting, frame, and finial **50.00**

1950s, clock, Herman Miller, designed by George Nelson, chrome and painted metal, 12 chromed metal rods around black painted circular works, 24" d **500.00**

1950s, figure, dolphin, Venetian glass, clear blue, unknown maker, 19¾" l **375.00**

1950s, figure, flamingo, ceramic, unknown maker, 6" h **15.00**

1950s, floor lamp, Lightolier, 3–poled, 3 red, black, and white enameled conical shades, 59" h **550.00**

1950s, floor lamp, Raak Holland, smokey glass globe housing aluminum funnel set on chrome shaft and tripod base **300.00**

1950s, hanging lamp, stacked white enameled metal circules, 17" d, 19" h **650.00**

1950s, lamp, electric, 2–masted sailing ship, tin sails, yellow ceramic body with gold accents, sea wave base **65.00**

1950s, salad bowl, glass, floral motif, bold light blue, white, and yellow 6–petal flowers **10.00**

1950s, table lamps, ceramic, blackamoors, $75.00.

1960s, vase, Art Deco style, red glass, unmkd, 12⅝" h, $15.00.

1950s, sculpture, resin, Tiki or native mask, dark chartreuse, Sascha Brastoff design, 10¼" h **100.00**

1950s, server, plastic, 3 tier, designed by Jean Cocteau, 3 coral colored dishes hinged on gold-tone metal armature that folds to display 2–sided black and gold drawing of profile faces, 11½ x 17 x 8" **400.00**

1950s, table lamps, pr, white alabaster marble ring bases, white tapered rect shades, 27" h **850.00**

1950s, wall hanging, Harris Strong, 12–tile vertical panel, woman's head in Cubist style, bright orange, ochres, blues, and whites, period frame, blue and white paper label, 19¼ x 33½" **600.00**

1950s, waste basket, oval cylinder, walking poodle holding umbrella, outline of shopping plaza in background, pink ground **25.00**

1960s, alarm clock, General Electric, plastic, pyschedelic opposing faces motif **75.00**

1960s, ashtray, Iroquois China, Peter Max design, multicolored florals **50.00**

1960s, cheese board, wood and metal, rect, Eldorado enameled metal tile insert, motif designed by Georges Briard, 8¾" sq. **20.00**

1960s, clothes hanger, Personality Hang–Ups, Framingham, MA, head with psychedelic motif in hair, four seasons theme, summer has foil glasses, price for set of 4 . . . . **80.00**

1960s, lamp, ceramic base, Metlox, Poppy Trail, Red Rooster pattern **125.00**

1960s, lava lamp, electric, blue, green, or red, 15" h, beware of recent reproductions **50.00**

1960s, motion lamp, electric, Visual Effects, rotating plastic cylinder body with alternating herringbone bands, conical metal base, 14½" h **75.00**

1960s, pitcher, ceramic, Picasso, one of 500 sgd examples, tapered body, painted and incised abstract design of woman, cream ground, 12" h **2,000.00**

1960s, poster, Peter Max Poster Corp, Dove, #20, 24 x 36" **250.00**

1960s, serving dish, rect, seated black poodle on ivory ground, Glidden Pottery **15.00**

1960s, television, Panasonic, space helmet form, tri-pod base, working condition **450.00**

1960s, wall hanging, black plastic, molded face mask, oval shape, 16 x 20" **60.00**

1960s, vase, glass, murrina, designed by Fratelli Toso, cranberry and blue murrina alternating with red petal flower murrina, 5" h **200.00**

1970s, bread box, metal, golden yellow ground, mushroom, ladybug, and butterfly motif **35.00**

1970s, clock, Sessions, plywood face, flower blossom motif, numbers 3, 6, 9, 12 in center, white hands with blue butterflies at end, flower stem extends from base **45.00**

1970s, mat, plastic, Smilie motif **15.00**

1970s, mug, Smilie, McCoy **10.00**

1970s, picture frame, plastic, Dan–Dee Import, LOVE theme, multicolored, 4¼" sq. **15.00**

1970s, pillow, inflatable plastic, flower blossom, yellow, orange, and clear, mkd "Made in Tawain" **15.00**

1970s, sculpture, glass bull, designed by Eranno Nason, solid body in iridescent glass that appears as gray or deep amethyst, paper label, 7" **275.00**

DEGENHART GLASS

John and Elizabeth Degenhart directed the operation of Crystal Art Glass, Cambridge, Ohio, from 1947 until 1978. Pressed glass novelties, such as animal covered dishes, salts, toothpicks, and paperweights were the company's principal products.

Boyd Crystal Art Glass, Cambridge, Ohio, purchased many of the company's 50 molds when operations ceased. Boyd continues to manufacture pieces from these molds, all in colors different from those used by Degenhart and most marked with a "B" in a diamond.

Collectors' Club: Friends of Degenhart, Degenhart Paperweight and Glass Museum, Inc, 65323 Highland Hills Rd, PO Box 186, Cambridge, OH 43725.

REPRODUCTION ALERT: Although most Degenhart molds were reproductions themselves, many contemporary pieces made by Kanawha, L. G. Wright, and others are nearly identical.

Animal Dish, cov, hen, dark green . . . . **$ 22.00**

Animal Dish, cov, pigeon blood **55.00**

Animal Dish, cov, robin, taffeta **55.00**

Animal Dish, cov, turkey, amethyst **55.00**

Animal Dish, cov, turkey, custard **60.00**

Basket, cobalt blue **22.00**

Bicentennial Bell, amethyst **5.00**

Bicentennial Bell, heatherbloom **18.00**

Bicentennial Bell, seafoam **12.00**

Candy Dish, cov, Wildflower, crystal **15.00**

Candy Dish, cov, Wildflower, twilight blue **25.00**

Chick, vaseline, 2" h **18.00**

Coaster, shamrock **8.00**

Creamer and Sugar, Texas, pink **45.00**

Cup Plate, Heart and Lyre, gold **18.00**

Cup Plate, Seal of Ohio, sunset **18.00**

Gypsy Pot, forest green, $20.00.

Gypsy Pot, canary **20.00**

Gypsy Pot, tomato **30.00**

Hand, amethyst **10.00**

Hand, persimmon **10.00**

Hat, Daisy and Button, opalescent **12.00**

Hat, Daisy and Button, vaseline **15.00**

Jewelry Box, Heart, fawn **18.00**

Jewelry Box, Heart, old lavender **25.00**

Mug, child's, Stork & Peacock, baby green **22.00**

Owl, bluebell **35.00**

Owl, charcoal **40.00**

Owl, ivorina **30.00**

Owl, midnight sun **30.00**

Owl, willow blue **50.00**

Paperweight, cartoon characters **175.00**

Paperweight, flower pot **85.00**

Pitcher, mini, jade **20.00**

Pooch, April green **18.00**

Pooch, royal violet **18.00**

Pooch, slag, ivory **22.00**

Priscilla, amethyst **85.00**

Priscilla, crown tuscan **70.00**

Priscilla, ivory **85.00**

Priscilla, peach **60.00**

Salt, Daisy and Button, bittersweet **15.00**

Salt, Daisy and Button, lime ice **15.00**

Salt, Pottie, milk white **10.00**

Salt, Star and Dewdrop, aqua **18.00**

Salt, Star and Dewdrop, opalescent **18.00**

Salt, Star and Dewdrop, topaz **18.00**

Salt and Pepper Shakers, pr, Birds, gun metal **20.00**

Salt and Pepper Shakers, pr, Birds, taffeta **2.00**

Slipper, Kat, sapphire **15.00**

Smoky Bear, jade green **30.00**

Tomahawk, blue green **22.00**

Tomahawk, custard maverick **55.00**

Toothpick Holder, Baby or Tramp Shoe, pearl gray **15.00**

Toothpick Holder, Beaded Oval, fog **18.00**
Toothpick Holder, Colonial Drape and Heart, amber **15.00**
Toothpick Holder, Colonial Drape and Heart, teal **22.00**
Toothpick Holder, Daisy and Button, light blue slag **25.00**
Toothpick Holder, pink **18.00**
Toothpick Holder, Forget–Me–Not, caramel **10.00**
Toothpick Holder, Forget–Me–Not, misty green **12.00**
Toothpick Holder, Forget–Me–Not, persimmon **15.00**
Toothpick Holder, Heart, amethyst **15.00**
Toothpick Holder, Heart, crystal **10.00**
Wine, Buzz Saw, honey amber **15.00**
Wine, Buzz Saw, taffeta **40.00**

DEPRESSION GLASS

Depression Glass is a generic term used to describe glassware patterns introduced and manufactured between 1920 and the early 1950s. Most of this glassware was inexpensive and machine made.

In its narrow sense, the term describes a select group of patterns identified by a group of late 1940s and early 1950s collectors as "Depression Glass." Many price guides dealing with the subject have preserved this narrow approach.

Many manufacturers did not name their patterns. The same group of individuals who determined what patterns should and should not be included in this category also assigned names to previously unidentified patterns. Disputes occurred. Hence, some patterns have more than one name.

References: Gene Florence, *Collectible Glassware from the 40's, 50's & 60's, Third Edition,* Collector Books, 1996; Gene Florence, *Elegant Glassware of the Depression Era, Seventh Edition,* Collector Books, 1997; Gene Florence, *Kitchen Glassware of the Depression Years: Identification & Values, Fifth Edition,* Collector Books, 1995; Gene Florence, *The Collector's Encyclopedia of Depression Glass, Twelfth Edition,* Collector Books, 1995; Gene Florence, *Very Rare Glassware of the Depression Years, Third Series* (1993, 1995 value update), *Fourth Series* (1995) and *Fifth Series* (1997), Collector Books; Ralph and Terry Kovel, *Kovel's Depression Glass & American Dinnerware Price List, Fifth Edition,* Crown, 1995; Carl F. Luckey: *An Identification & Value Guide To Depression Era Glassware, Third Edition,* Books Americana, Krause Publications, 1994; Naomi L. Over, *Ruby Glass of the 20th Century,* Antique Publications, 1990, 1993–94 value update; Hazel Marie Weatherman, *Colored Glassware of the Depression Era, Book 2,* published by author, 1974, available in reprint.

Periodical: *The Daze,* PO Box 57, Otisville, MI 48463.

Collectors' Clubs: National Depression Glass Assoc, PO Box 8264, Wichita, KS 67209; 20–30–40 Society, Inc, PO Box 856, La Grange, IL 60525.

REPRODUCTION ALERT: Reproductions (exact copies) of several patterns are known. In other cases, fantasy pieces have been made from period molds in non–period colors. Few of these reproductions and fantasy pieces are marked.

The Daze distributes a list of these reproductions and fantasy items. Send a self–addressed, stamped business envelope along with a request for a copy.

Adam, ashtray, 4⁵/₈", green . . . . **$ 20.00**

Adam, bowl, 4³/₄" d, pink **12.00**
Adam, bowl, cov, 9" d, pink **65.00**
Adam, cake plate, ftd, 10"d, green **25.00**
Adam, candlesticks, pr, pink **90.00**
Adam, coaster, green **20.00**
Adam, creamer, pink **25.00**
Adam, cup, pink **25.00**
Adam, dinner plate, 9" d, pink **30.00**
Adam, platter, oval, 11³/₄" d, green **30.00**
Adam, relish, 2 part, 8", green **25.00**
Adam, salad plate, 7³/₄" d, green **15.00**
Adam, salt and pepper shakers, pr, pink **75.00**
Adam, sherbet, ftd, 6", pink **30.00**
Adam, sugar, pink **40.00**
American Pioneer, bowl, handled, 5" d, amber **30.00**
American Pioneer, cup and saucer, crystal **15.00**
American Pioneer, sherbet, 4³/₄" h, green **35.00**
American Sweetheart, bowl, 9" d, monax **60.00**
American Sweetheart, bowl, 9" d, pink **40.00**
American Sweetheart, bread and butter plate, 6" d,
  monax **5.00**
American Sweetheart, bread and butter plate, 6" d,
  pink **5.00**
American Sweetheart, cereal bowl, pink **15.00**
American Sweetheart, cup and saucer, monax **12.00**
American Sweetheart, cup and saucer, pink **20.00**
American Sweetheart, platter, 13" l, pink **50.00**
American Sweetheart, vegetable, 11" l, monax **75.00**
Aunt Polly, butter, cov, iridescent **8.00**
Aunt Polly, luncheon plate, 8" d, blue **18.00**
Aunt Polly, sugar, green **25.00**
Aunt Polly, vase, ftd, 6¹/₂" h, green **28.00**
Avocado, bowl, handled, 8" d, pink **35.00**
Avocado, creamer, ftd, crystal **15.00**
Avocado, cup, ftd, pink **30.00**
Avocado, luncheon plate, 8¹/₄" d, crystal **8.00**
Avocado, salad bowl, 7¹/₂" d, green **20.00**
Avocado, tumbler, crystal **25.00**

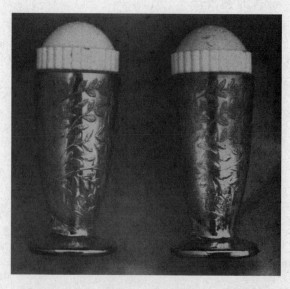

Floragold, salt and pepper shakers, pr, $45.00.

Block Optic, cereal bowl, 5¼" d, green **12.00**
Block Optic, creamer, ftd, yellow **15.00**
Block Optic, cup, green. **5.50**
Block Optic, plate, 6" d, pink. **2.50**
Block Optic, sugar, ftd, yellow **12.00**
Block Optic, tumbler, ftd, 9 oz, yellow **15.00**
Bubble, berry bowl, individual, 4" d, crystal **2.50**
Bubble, berry bowl, master, 8⅜" d, blue. **12.00**
Bubble, bread and butter plate, 6¾" d, crystal. **2.50**
Bubble, cup and saucer, blue. **5.00**
Cameo, bread and butter plate, 6" d, green. **5.00**
Cameo, cake plate, ftd, green. **20.00**
Cameo, cream soup, green. **70.00**
Cameo, creamer, 3¼" h, green. **20.00**
Cameo, cup, green **12.00**
Cameo, pitcher, 56 oz, green **50.00**
Cameo, platter, oval, green. **22.00**
Cameo, relish, 3 part, green. **22.00**
Cameo, sugar, 3¼", green **18.00**
Cameo, water goblet, green. **50.00**
Cherry Blossom, berry bowl, 4¾" d, green. **15.00**
Cherry Blossom, bowl, handled, 9" d, pink. **40.00**
Cherry Blossom, bread and butter plate, 6" d, green **5.00**
Cherry Blossom, cake plate, ftd, green **2.50**
Cherry Blossom, creamer and sugar, pink **50.00**
Cherry Blossom, cup and saucer, pink **20.00**
Cherry Blossom, dinner plate, 9" d, pink. **20.00**
Cherry Blossom, platter, 11" l, oval, green. **40.00**
Cherry Blossom, sherbet, pink **15.00**
Chinex Classic, butter, cov, ivory, rose decal **75.00**
Chinex Classic, creamer, plain ivory. **5.00**
Chinex Classic, dinner plate, 9¾" d, plain ivory **5.00**
Chinex Classic, soup bowl, 7¾" d, ivory, rose decal **20.00**
Chinex Classic, vegetable, 7" d, ivory, castle decal **30.00**
Colonial Knife & Fork, berry bowl, 4½" d, green **18.00**
Colonial Knife & Fork, bread and butter, plate, 6" d,
   crystal. **5.00**
Colonial Knife & Fork, butter, cov, crystal **40.00**
Colonial Knife & Fork, creamer, crystal. **20.00**
Colonial Knife & Fork, goblet, 5¾" d, green **25.00**
Colonial Knife & Fork, platter, oval, 12" l, green **25.00**
Colonial Knife & Fork, sherbet, ftd, 3⅜" d, pink. **10.00**
Colonial Knife & Fork, tumbler, ftd, 4" h, 5 oz, pink **30.00**
Colonial Knife & Fork, vegetable, oval, 10" l, green. **25.00**
Coronation, nappy, 6½" d, pink **8.00**
Coronation, tumbler, 5" h, 10 oz, pink **25.00**
Cubist, bowl, 6½" d, green. **18.00**
Cubist, bread and butter plate, 6" d, pink **5.00**
Cubist, candy jar, cov, pink **25.00**
Cubist, creamer, pink. **10.00**
Cubist, cup, pink. **8.00**
Cubist, powder jar, cov, green **30.00**
Cubist, saucer, pink. **5.00**
Cubist, shaker, green **15.00**
Dogwood, berry bowl, 8½", pink. **50.00**
Dogwood, cake plate, 13" d, green. **125.00**
Dogwood, creamer, 3¼", pink, thin **15.00**
Dogwood, cup, monax **35.00**
Dogwood, cup, thick, pink. **15.00**
Dogwood, cup and saucer, monax. **45.00**
Dogwood, plate, 8" d, green **8.00**

Dogwood, saucer, pink **5.00**
Dogwood, sherbet, monax. **35.00**
Dogwood, tumbler, 4" h, 10 oz, monax **40.00**
Floragold, ashtray, 4" **8.00**
Floragold, butter, cov, ¼ lb. **30.00**
Floragold, cereal bowl, 5½" d **35.00**
Floragold, cup. **8.00**
Floragold, salt and pepper shakers, pr. **45.00**
Floragold, sugar. **20.00**
Floragold, tumbler, ftd, 10 oz. **18.00**
Florentine No. 2, ashtray, 5½" d, green. **15.00**
Florentine No. 2, berry bowl, 8" d, yellow **22.00**
Florentine No. 2, butter, cov, yellow. **145.00**
Florentine No. 2, bowl, 8" d, crystal. **20.00**
Florentine No. 2, candleholder, green. **30.00**
Florentine No. 2, coaster, yellow. **12.00**
Florentine No. 2, compote, ruffled, 3½" d, crystal **12.00**
Florentine No. 2, creamer, ftd, green **12.00**
Florentine No. 2, custard, crystal **50.00**
Florentine No. 2, gravy boat, yellow. **40.00**
Florentine No. 2, parfait, ftd, 6" h, yellow. **60.00**
Florentine No. 2, relish, 3 part, 10" l, yellow. **30.00**
Florentine No. 2, salt and pepper shakers, pr, green **45.00**
Florentine No. 2, sherbet, green. **8.00**
Florentine No. 2, sugar, ftd, crystal **10.00**
Florentine No. 2, sugar, open, green. **8.00**
Florentine No. 2, vegetable, cov, 9" l, yellow **60.00**
Forest Green, bowl, 4¾" sq **5.00**
Forest Green, creamer and sugar **12.00**
Forest Green, luncheon plate, 8⅜" d. **5.00**
Forest Green, pitcher, 3 qt **30.00**
Forest Green, platter, rect, 11" l **22.00**
Forest Green, relish, 3 part, 10½" d **25.00**
Forest Green, soup bowl, 6" sq. **15.00**
Forest Green, vase, 6⅜" h **5.00**
Fortune, candy dish, cov, flat, crystal **22.50**
Fortune, cup and saucer, pink **8.00**

Mayfair/Open Rose, bowl, 11½" d, pink, $20.00.

Lace Edge, bowl, 9½" d, pink. 20.00
Lace Edge, butter, cov, pink 65.00
Lace Edge, creamer and sugar, pink 40.00
Lace Edge, cup and saucer, pink. 35.00
Lace Edge, dish, divided, oval, 12¾" l, pink 30.00
Lace Edge, salad plate, 8¼", pink. 22.00
Lace Edge, saucer, pink 20.00
Lorain, cereal bowl, 6" d, yellow 55.00
Lorain, relish, 4 part, 8" d, crystal. 20.00
Madrid, cookie jar, cov, amber. 50.00
Madrid, cup and saucer, amber 10.00
Madrid, cream soup, 4¾" d, amber 15.00
Madrid, luncheon plate, 8⅞" d, amber 8.00
Madrid, platter, 11½" d, oval, amber 22.00
Madrid, salad bowl, 8" d, amber 18.00
Madrid, tumbler, flat, 3⅞" h, 5 oz, amber 15.00
Manhattan, ashtray, round, crystal 10.00
Manhattan, candlesticks, pr, square, pink 18.00
Manhattan, candy dish, ftd, pink 12.00
Manhattan, creamer and sugar, crystal 20.00
Manhattan, dinner plate, 10¼" d, crystal. 20.00
Manhattan, fruit bowl, handled, ftd, 9½" d, crystal 40.00
Manhattan, relish, crystal, ruby inserts 55.00
Manhattan, sherbet, ftd, crystal. 12.00
Manhattan, sugar, crystal 10.00
Manhattan, wine, crystal 5.00
Mayfair/Open Rose, bowl, low, 11¾" d, blue 75.00
Mayfair/Open Rose, cake plate, ftd, pink 15.00
Mayfair/Open Rose, casserole, cov, pink. 130.00
Mayfair/Open Rose, creamer, blue 75.00
Mayfair/Open Rose, cup and saucer, pink. 30.00
Mayfair/Open Rose, demitasse cup and saucer, yel-
low 20.00
Mayfair/Open Rose, fruit bowl, scalloped rim, 12" d,
green 32.00
Mayfair/Open Rose, pitcher, 6" h, blue 135.00
Mayfair/Open Rose, sherbet, ftd, 3" h, pink. 15.00
Moderntone, berry bowl, 8" d, cobalt blue 50.00
Moderntone, bread and butter plate, 6¾" d, cobalt
blue. 15.00
Moderntone, cream soup, cobalt blue 20.00
Moderntone, creamer and sugar, amethyst 20.00
Moderntone, custard, cobalt blue. 20.00
Moderntone, platter, oval, 11" l, cobalt blue 40.00
Moderntone, salt and pepper shakers, pr, cobalt blue . . . 40.00

Console Bowl, ftd, 10½" d, ultramarine, $25.00.

Moderntone, shaker, amethyst 20.00
Moderntone, tumbler, 5 oz, cobalt blue 45.00
Old Cafe, berry bowl, 3¾" d, crystal. 2.50
Old Cafe, cup, pink. 10.00
Old Cafe, dinner plate, 10" d, crystal 25.00
Old Cafe, lamp, pink. 25.00
Old Cafe, vase, 7¼" h, pink. 15.00
Patrician, butter, cov, green 110.00
Patrician, creamer, ftd, pink 12.00
Princess, bowl, 9" d, green. 35.00
Princess, cereal bowl, 5" d, yellow 30.00
Princess, creamer, yellow. 20.00
Princess, cup, yellow. 20.00
Princess, salad plate, 8" d, green 15.00
Princess, saucer, green. 10.00
Princess, sherbet, ftd, yellow 32.00
Princess, tumbler, flat, 4" h, 9 oz, green 30.00
Princess, vegetable, oval, 10" l, green 25.00
Raindrops, berry bowl, 7½" d, green. 38.00
Raindrops, cup and saucer, green. 10.00
Raindrops, luncheon plate, 8" d, green 5.00
Raindrops, sugar, green 40.00
Raindrops, whiskey, 1⅞" h, green. 8.00
Royal Ruby, ashtray 8.00
Royal Ruby, bowl, 4¾" d 8.00
Royal Ruby, creamer and sugar. 12.00
Royal Ruby, marmalade, clear base 15.00
Royal Ruby, pitcher, 3 qt 30.00
Royal Ruby, punch bowl set, punch bowl, base, and
12 cups 100.00
Royal Ruby, salad plate, 7¾" d 5.00
Royal Ruby, soup bowl 12.00
Royal Ruby, tumbler, 13 oz 12.00
Royal Ruby, vase, 9" h 20.00
Sandwich, ashtray, amber. 5.00
Sandwich, bowl, hexagonal, 6" w, amber 8.00
Sandwich, bread and butter plate, 7" d, crystal 5.00
Sandwich, console bowl, 9" d, crystal. 15.00
Sandwich, goblet, red 48.00
Sandwich, sherbet, 3¼" h, crystal. 5.00
Sandwich, sugar, red 50.00
Sandwich, wine, red 15.00
Sharon, berry bowl, master, 8½" d, amber. 10.00

Sandwich, tray, 9¼" l, crystal, $10.00.

Sharon, candy jar, cov, amber 28.00
Sharon, cheese dish, cov, amber. 20.00
Sharon, cream soup, 5" d, green. 50.00
Sharon, creamer, ftd, green 22.00
Sharon, jam dish, 7½" d, green 45.00
Sharon, platter, oval, 12½" l, amber 20.00
Sharon, salt and pepper shakers, pr, amber 48.00
Sharon, sugar, green 48.00
Sharon, vegetable, oval, 9½" l, green 35.00
Spiral, creamer, green 8.00
Spiral, mixing bowl, 7" d, green 10.00
Spiral, platter, oval, 12" l, green 28.50
Spiral, salt and pepper shakers, pr, green 38.50
Spiral, sherbet, green 25.00
Spiral, tumbler, 5" d, green. 8.50
Swirl, candlesticks, pr, ultramarine 45.00
Swirl, cereal bowl, ultramarine. 15.00
Swirl, creamer and sugar, ultramarine. 25.00
Swirl, lug soup, ultramarine 45.00
Swirl, salad bowl, 9" d, ultramarine 22.00
Swirl, sherbet, ultramarine 20.00
Swirl, tumbler, ftd, ultramarine 42.00
Tea Room, candlesticks, pr, pink. 48.00
Tea Room, celery bowl, 8¼" d, pink. 28.00
Tea Room, finger bowl, pink 40.00
Tea Room, parfait, pink 65.00
Tea Room, relish, divided, green. 28.00
Tea Room, sundae, ruffled, ftd, pink 80.00
Tea Room, tray, rect, pink. 48.00
Tea Room, vase, straight, 9½" h, pink 68.00
Victory, bonbon, 7" d, black. 22.00
Victory, candlesticks, pr, 3" h, green 35.00
Victory, cup and saucer, black 48.00
Victory, sandwich server, center handle, amber 38.00
Victory, sherbet, green 18.00

DINNERWARE

This is a catchall category. There are hundreds of American and European dinnerware manufacturers. Several dozen have their own separate listing in this book. It is not fair to ignore the rest.

This category provides a sampling of the patterns and forms from these manufacturers. It is designed to demonstrate the wide variety of material available in the market, especially today when individuals are buying dinnerware primarily for reuse.

References: Susan and Al Bagdade, *Warman's American Pottery and Porcelain,* Wallace–Homestead, Krause Publications, 1994; Jo Cunningham, *The Best of Collectible Dinnerware,* Schiffer Publishing, 1995; Jo Cunningham, *The Collector's Encyclopedia of American Dinnerware,* Collector Books, 1982, 1995 value update; Harvey Duke, *The Official Price Guide to Pottery and Porcelain, Eighth Edition,* House of Collectibles, 1995; Joanne Jasper, *Turn of the Century American Dinnerware: 1880s to 1920s,* Collector Books, 1996; Lois Lehner, *Lehner's Encyclopedia of U.S. Marks on Pottery, Porcelain & Clay,* Collector Books, 1988; Raymonde Limoges, *American Limoges: Identification & Value Guide,* Collector Books, 1996.

American Limoges, Bermuda, cup and saucer . . . . $ 12.00
American Limoges, Bermuda, eggcup 12.00

American Limoges, Bermuda, gravy boat and under-
  plate 20.00
American Limoges, Bermuda, platter,14" l 25.00
American Limoges, Bermuda, soup bowl, flat, 8" d 8.00
American Limoges, Bermuda, sugar, cov. 10.00
American Limoges, Carolina Roses, plate, 3" sq 15.00
American Limoges, Carolina Roses, platter, 11" l 25.00
American Limoges, Charlotte, cup and saucer. 10.00
American Limoges, Charlotte, dinner plate, 10" d 12.00
American Limoges, Charlotte, gravy boat, attached
  underplate, 8" l 15.00
American Limoges, Concord, plate, 9¼" d 12.00
American Limoges, Concord, platter, 15½" l 25.00
American Limoges, Flower Shop, snack set, 9" d 25.00
American Limoges, Ideal, creamer and sugar, pink 25.00
American Limoges, Ideal, cup and saucer, pink 15.00
American Limoges, Ideal, platter, white, 11¼" l 25.00
American Limoges, Ideal, saucer, white, 6" d 6.00
American Limoges, Lorraine, dinner plate, 10" d 10.00
American Limoges, Lorraine, plate, 6¼" d 7.00
American Limoges, Monticello, plate, 7" d 7.00
American Limoges, Sundale, plate, 9" d 10.00
American Limoges, Sundale, platter, 8" l 15.00
American Limoges, Sundale, serving dish, cov, 9" d 35.00
American Limoges, Sundale Tudor Gold, platter, 11" l 25.00
American Limoges, Sundale Tudor Gold, serving
  dish, cov, handled, 9½" d 40.00
American Limoges, Trillium, cup 5.00
American Limoges, Trillium, plate, 6¼" d 7.00
American Limoges, Trillium, platter, 11" l 20.00
American Limoges, Trillium Forest Green, platter,
  11" l 20.00
American Limoges, Vermilion Buds, cup and saucer 10.00
American Limoges, Vermilion Buds, plate, 9¼" d 7.00
American Limoges, Vermilion Buds, salt and pepper
  shakers, pr. 12.00
American Limoges, Vermilion Rose, creamer. 12.00

American Limoges, Pattern #1029, teapot, 7¼" h, $28.00.

American Limoges, Vermilion Rose, cup and saucer 12.00
American Limoges, Vermilion Rose, plate, 6" d 6.00
American Limoges, Vermilion, Rose, sugar, cov. 15.00
Blair Ceramics, Bamboo, creamer. 15.00
Blair Ceramics, Bamboo, cup and saucer 20.00
Blair Ceramics, Bamboo, dinner plate, sq 12.00
Blair Ceramics, Bamboo, plate, 8" sq 8.00
Blair Ceramics, Bamboo, plate, rect 12.00
Blair Ceramics, Bamboo, onion soup bowl, cov 22.00
Blair Ceramics, Bamboo, sugar, cov 15.00
Blair Ceramics, Gay Plaid, bowl, sq 8.00
Blair Ceramics, Gay Plaid, casserole, handled, sq 32.00
Blair Ceramics, Gay Plaid, creamer 15.00
Blair Ceramics, Gay Plaid, cup and saucer 12.00
Blair Ceramics, Gay Plaid, cup and saucer, closed
    handle. 15.00
Blair Ceramics, Gay Plaid, dinner plate. 12.00
Blair Ceramics, Gay Plaid, milk pitcher. 17.00
Blair Ceramics, Gay Plaid, mug, handled 20.00
Blair Ceramics, Gay Plaid, onion soup bowl, cov 20.00
Blair Ceramics, Gay Plaid, salt and pepper shakers, pr. . . . 15.00
Blair Ceramics, Gay Plaid, sugar, cov 15.00
Blair Ceramics, Gay Plaid, tumbler. 12.00
Blair Ceramics, Gay Plaid, water pitcher, ice lip 45.00
Crown Pottery, Autumn Leaf, jug, cov 75.00
Crown Pottery, Bouquet, pie baker, 10" d 20.00
Crown Pottery, Carriage, vegetable bowl. 15.00
Crown Pottery, Poppy, plate, 9" sq 7.00
Crown Pottery, Windmill, pie baker, 10" d 20.00
Crown Pottery, Windmill, salt and pepper shakers, pr 20.00
French Saxon, Granada, bowl, 5½" d. 5.00
French Saxon, Granada, bowl, 6½" d. 7.00
French Saxon, Granada, creamer 12.00
French Saxon, Granada, cup and saucer 13.00
French Saxon, Granada, dessert plate, dark green,
    7" d. 5.00
French Saxon, Granada, dinner plate, maroon, 10" d 12.00
French Saxon, Granada, luncheon plate, chartreuse,
    9" d. 10.00
French Saxon, Granada, luncheon plate, tangerine,
    9" d. 12.00
French Saxon, Granada, shaker, ivory 10.00
French Saxon, Granada, sugar, cov, green 17.00
W. S. George, Blossoms, creamer. 10.00
W. S. George, Blossoms, cup and saucer 10.00
W. S. George, Blossoms, dinner plate, 10" d 10.00
W. S. George, Blossoms, flat soup, 8" d 10.00
W. S. George, Blossoms, sugar, cov 15.00
W. S. George, Bouquet, dinner plate, 10" d 7.00
W. S. George, Flower Rim, dinner plate, 10" d 7.00
W. S. George, Peach Blossom, plate, 8" d 6.00
W. S. George, Petalware, bowl, ivory, 5½" d 7.00
W. S. George, Petalware, cup, blue 8.00
W. S. George, Petalware, plate, dark green, 9" d 10.00
W. S. George, Petalware, plate, maroon, 9" d 10.00
W. S. George, Petalware, plate, pink, 7½" d 8.00
W. S. George, Petalware, sugar, cov, pink 12.00
W. S. George, Plain Jane, dinner plate, 10" d 7.00
W. S. George, Rainbow, bowl, deep, green, 5" d 9.00
W. S. George, Rainbow, bowl, pink, 5½" d 7.00
W. S. George, Rainbow, cup, green 8.00

W. S. George, Rainbow, egg cup, blue 17.00
W. S. George, Rainbow, saucer, yellow. 4.00
W. S. George, Roses, gravy boat, attached liner. 12.00
W. S. George, Roses, soup bowl, 8" d 7.00
W. S. George, Sailing, creamer. 8.00
W. S. George, Sailing, sugar. 8.00
W. S. George, Shortcake, coffeepot. 45.00
W. S. George, Shortcake, salt and pepper shakers, pr. . . . 20.00
Mount Clemens, California Poppy, creamer. 7.00
Mount Clemens, California Poppy, gravy boat 9.00
Mount Clemens, California Poppy, plate, 9" d 8.00
Mount Clemens, California Poppy, platter, large 12.00
Mount Clemens, California Poppy, platter, small 10.00
Mount Clemens, California Poppy, salad plate, 7" d 10.00
Mount Clemens, California Poppy, sugar. 7.00
Mount Clemens, California Poppy, vegetable dish,
    cov, handled. 20.00
Mount Clemens, Old Mexico, creamer 12.00
Mount Clemens, Old Mexico, cup 8.00
Mount Clemens, Old Mexico, plate 12.00
Mount Clemens, Old Mexico, soup bowl 10.00
Mount Clemens, Old Mexico, sugar 8.00
Mount Clemens, Old Mexico, vegetable bowl. 25.00
Mount Clemens, Petit Point Rose, creamer 8.00
Mount Clemens, Petit Point Rose, cup 5.00
Mount Clemens, Petit Point Rose, plate. 5.00
Mount Clemens, Petit Point Rose, sugar 8.00
Salem China, Basket, dessert plate, 8" sq 5.00
Salem China, Basket, saucer, 6" sq. 4.00
Salem China, Bluebird, plate, 6" d 6.00
Salem China, Bryn Mawr, dinner plate, 9" 7.00
Salem China, Goldtrim, butter pat, sq. 6.00
Salem China, Goldtrim, plate, 6" sq 4.00
Salem China, June, plate, 9" sq 5.00
Salem China, June, salad plate, 7" sq 4.00
Salem China, Mandarin Red, creamer. 10.00
Salem China, Mandarin Red, cup. 5.00

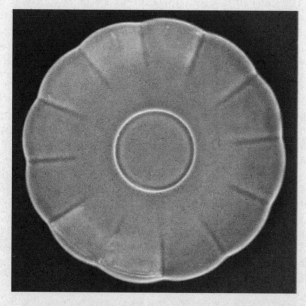

W. S. George, Petalware, saucer, light green, $4.00.

Salem China, Mandarin Red, sugar, cov **10.00**
Salem China, Maple Leaf, plate, 9" d **4.00**
Salem China, Petit Point Basket, plate, 7" d **4.00**
Salem China, Petit Point Basket, plate, 9" d **5.00**
Salem China, Petit Point Basket, shaker. **7.00**
Salem China, Rust Tulip, plate, 6" d **4.00**
Salem China, Rust Tulip, plate, 6" sq **4.00**
Salem China, Rust Tulip, plate, 7" d **4.00**
Salem China, Rust Tulip, platter **7.00**
Salem China, Sailing, bowl, triangular **7.00**
Salem China, Sailing, plate, triangular **8.00**
Salem China, Tulip, creamer. **10.00**
Salem China, Tulip, cup and saucer **7.00**
Salem China, Tulip, sugar, cov **10.00**
Salem China, Yellowridge, plate, 9" octagonal **5.00**
Steubenville Pottery, American Modern, creamer,
   seafoam green **12.00**
Steubenville Pottery, American Modern, after–dinner
   cup and saucer, golden fawn **20.00**
Steubenville Pottery, Woodfield, bowl, rust **7.00**
Steubenville Pottery, Woodfield, creamer, golden
   fawn **10.00**
Steubenville Pottery, Woodfield, salt and pepper
   shakers, pr, tropic green **15.00**
Steubenville Pottery, Woodfield, snack plate, salmon. **7.00**
Steubenville Pottery, Woodfield, snack set, white. **12.00**
Steubenville Pottery, Woodfield, sugar, cov, tropic
   green. **10.00**
Steubenville Pottery, Woodfield, teapot, cov, rust. **35.00**

DIONNE QUINTUPLETS

Annette, Cecile, Emilie, Marie, and Yvonne Dionne were born on May 28, 1934, in rural Canada between the towns of Corbeil and Callander, Ontario. Dr. Dafoe and two midwives delivered the five girls. An agreement to exhibit the babies at the Chicago World's Fair led to the passage of "An Act for the Protection of the Dionne Quintuplets" by the Canadian government.

The Dafoe Hospital, which served as visitor viewing center for thousands of people who traveled to Canada to see the Quints, was built across the street from the family home. The Quints craze lasted into the early 1940s. Hundreds of souvenir and licensed products were manufactured during that period. Emile died in August 1954 and Marie on February 27, 1970.

Collectors' Club: Dionne Quint Collectors, PO Box 2527, Woburn, MA 01888.

Book, *Dionne Quintuplets Play Mother Goose,* Dell,
   1938 . . . . **$ 30.00**
Book, *The Story of the Dionne Quintuplets,*
   Whitman, 1935, 40 pgs **45.00**
Box, Dionne Pops, Vitamin Candy Co, Providence,
   RI, 1936, 4 x 10½ x 1". **135.00**
Calendar, Harvest Days–Dionne Quintuplets, full
   pad, 1945, 10 x 7". **15.00**
Cereal Bowl, china, Marie in highchair, c1935 . . . . **20.00**
Doll, mohair wig, painted brown eyes, Madame
   Alexander, 1936, 7½" h **275.00**
Fan, diecut cardboard, "Sweethearts of the World,"
   ©1936, 8¼ x 8¾" **20.00**

Game, Line Up the Quints **30.00**
Handkerchief, linen weave cotton, 3 Quints playing,
   2 with birthday cakes, sgd "Tom Lamb," 1936–37,
   8" sq **30.00**
Magazine, *Woman's World,* Feb 1937. . . . . **15.00**
Mirror, pocket **22.00**
Paper Doll, Palmolive Soap Premium, book, five 6" h
   dolls on cov, 4 pgs uncut clothing, orig mailing
   envelope, 1937 . . . . **75.00**
Photo, girls holding identical dolls, 1935, 16 x 22". **60.00**
Playing Cards, double deck, orig cellophane and box,
   1936 . . . . **155.00**
Poster, "Today The Dionne Quints Had Quaker Oats,"
   1935, 14 x 32". **70.00**
Sheet Music, *Quintuplets' Lullaby,* tinted photo front
   cov, 6 pgs **15.00**
Spoon, set of 5 . . . . **125.00**

DISNEYANA

The Disney era began when *Steamboat Willie,* Walt Disney's first animated cartoon, appeared on theater screens in 1928. The success of Walt Disney and his studio are attributable to two major factors: (1) development of a host of cartoon characters, feature-length cartoons, and feature movies enjoyed throughout the world and (2) an aggressive marketing and licensing program.

Disneyana collecting has become highly sophisticated. 1940 and the early 1960s are major collecting watersheds. European Disney and Disney theme park collectibles are two strong growth areas within Disneyana.

Be especially price conscious when buying post–1975 Disneyana. Large amounts have been hoarded. The number of licensed products increased significantly. Disney shopping mall stores and mail–order catalog sales have significantly increased the amount of new material available. In fact, products have been created to be sold exclusively through these channels. It is for this reason that many Disneyana collectors concentrate on Disney collectibles licensed before 1965.

References: Robert Heide and John Gilman, *Disneyana: Classic Collectibles 1928–1958,* Hyperion, 1994; David Longest and Michael Stern, *The Collector's Encyclopedia of Disneyana,* Collector Books, 1992, 1996 value update; R. Michael Murray, *The Golden Age of Walt Disney Records, 1933–1988: Price Guide for Disney Fans and Record Collectors,* Antique Trader Books, 1997; Michael Stern, *Stern's Guide to Disney Collectibles, First Series* (1989, 1992 value update), *Second Series* (1990, 1995 value update), *Third Series* (1995), Collector Books; Tom Tumbusch, *Tomart's Illustrated Disneyana Catalog and Price Guide, Condensed Edition,* Tomart Publications, 1989.

Periodical: *Tomart's Disneyana Digest,* 3300 Encrete Ln, Dayton, OH 45439.

Collectors' Clubs: Mouse Club East, PO Box 3195, Wakefield, MA 01880; National Fantasy Club For Disneyana Collectors & Enthusiasts, PO Box 19212, Irvine, CA 92713; The Mouse Club, 2056 Cirone Way, San Jose, CA 95124.

Alarm Clock, windup, red case, brass bells, Mickey
   Mouse, Bradley, 1970s, 6" h . . . . **$ 55.00**

Bank, litho tin, $85.00.

Ashtray, Mickey Mouse center, gold trim 95.00

Bag, red fabric, plastic coating, Mickey Mouse each
 side, c1970, 10 x 16" 15.00

Ball, rubber, baseball design, Mickey on red ground,
 Seiberling, c1930s, 2¼" d 125.00

Bank, ceramic, Thumper, painted and glazed, incised
 "T" on back, Disney ©1940s 40.00

Bank, composition, figural house, Minnie Mouse
 standing in doorway holding broom, 1970–80, 5" h 22.50

Better Little Book, *Donald Duck and the Green
 Serpent,* Whitman, #1432, 1947 . . . . 28.00

Better Little Book, *Mickey Mouse and The Lazy Daisy
 Mystery,* Whitman, #1433, 1947 . . . . 32.00

Bookend, chalkware, Donald Duck carrying school
 books, 7" h 65.00

Bowl, plastic, Zorro, ©Disney Productions, c1960,
 5" d 18.00

Bracelet, diecut Minnie Mouse charm, brass links,
 ©Disney, c1970, 6" l 18.00

Brush, wood, black bristles, Mickey and "Mickey
 Mouse" on back, 1930s, 4" l 45.00

Candles, Mickey and 5 other characters, mkd
 "Made in Japan," ©1961, orig box, 4" h 35.00

Card Game, Mickey Mouse Old Maid 40.00

Christmas Ornaments, set of 6 balls, Mickey and
 Disney characters, orig box 150.00

Coloring Book, A Visit to Walt Disney World,
 Whitman, 1971, 8 x 11" 15.00

Comic Book, Walt Disney Presents Zorro, 907, Sept
 1967 . . . . 12.00

Doll, Dopey, cloth, Gund, 12" h. 50.00

Doll, Pinocchio, composition, Knickerbocker, c1940,
 10½" h 225.00

Drinking Glass, Doc from *Snow White and the
 Seven Dwarfs,* clear, blue illus, c1938, 4⅜" h 42.00

Figure, Bambi, vinyl, movable head and legs, orig
 bag and cardboard tag, Dakin, 1970s, 8½" h 30.00

Figure, Cinderella, porcelain, holding gold slipper,
 orig box, 1950s 110.00

Figure, Donald Duck playing accordion, bisque,
 1930s, 4" h 225.00

Figure, Lady, from *Lady and the Tramp,* painted and
 glazed, ©Walt Disney Productions, 1960s, 5" h 32.00

Figure, Mickey Mouse playing French horn, glazed
 china, Germany, 1930s, 3¼" h 325.00

Game, Davy Crockett Frontierland Game, Parker
 Brothers, ©1955 Walt Disney Productions 60.00

Game, Mickey Mouse Bowling Game, Artco
 Industries, c1980, orig box 20.00

Lamp, Dumbo, ceramic 55.00

Lamp, electric, round metal base, 3 Mickey decals
 around sides, beige ground, Soreng–Manegold Co,
 1930s, 5" d, 6½" h 75.00

Little Golden Book, *Zorro,* 1958, 9 x 12" 15.00

Lunch Box, emb steel, Mouseketeers, plastic ther-
 mos, Aladdin, 1970s 45.00

Magazine, *Mickey Mouse Magazine,* Donald Duck
 cov, 1937 . . . . 30.00

Magazine, *Walt Disney's Magazine,* Vol 4, #4, Jun
 1959 . . . . 18.00

Mug, china, Jiminy Cricket, "I've Got
 Environmentality, Every Little Bit Makes A Big
 Difference" and "Hats Off To You For Helping Out
 Environment," c1990s, 3½" h 18.00

Paint Book, Pinocchio, Collins of London, ©1940
 Disney, 48 pgs, 8¼ x 11" 80.00

Party Horn, Mickey and Minnie, cardboard, wooden
 mouthpiece, Marks Brothers 55.00

Pencil Box, Mickey and Donald skiing, Dixon 145.00

Pencil Holder, ceramic, Mickey standing beside covered barrel holder, metal and plastic sharpener,
 Enesco label, 4½" h 28.00

**Game Wheel, Walt Disney World Fun Flight Game Match Ups,
Eastern Airlines, 1980, 6¾" d, $7.50.**

Pennant, red felt, white Disneyland logo, late 1950s, 28" l **18.00**

Pin, Happy, painted wood, 1940s **22.00**

Planter, ceramic, Thumper **28.00**

Planter, painted and glazed ceramic, Peter Pan beside open treasure chest, incised "Peter Pan," ©Disney, 1950s, 4" h **72.00**

Playing Cards, Three Little Pigs, mkd "By Special Permission Walt Disney Enterprises," 1930s, orig box **80.00**

Pull Toy, Donald Duck Choo Choo, Fisher Price, c1942 .... **80.00**

Pull Toy, Mickey Mouse Puddle Jumper, Fisher Price, 1953 .... **55.00**

Puppet, Dumbo, cloth and vinyl, Gund, c1940, 10½" h .. **18.00**

Puzzle, Alice chasing White Rabbit, Jaymar, ©1950s, Walt Disney Productions, 14 x 19" **20.00**

Puzzle, Donald Duck's Diamond Jubilee, full–color photo, Hallmark Cards Inc, ©Walt Disney Productions, c1985, 18 x 23½" assembled size **15.00**

Radio, Mickey Mouse Sing Along **48.00**

Record, Pinocchio, 78 rpm, Golden Record, orange, orig jacket, ©1972 .... **12.50**

Salt and Pepper Shakers, pr, figural bells, china, white, Cinderella's castle and Tinkerbell, "Disneyland" stamped in gold on fronts, red foil "Japan" sticker, 1950s, 2½" h **40.00**

Sand Pail, litho tin, bail handle, Mickey leading parade, Ohio Art, mkd "Walt Disney Enterprises," 6" h **110.00**

Snow Dome, figural, seated Pinocchio holding clear plastic dome, mkd "Made in Hong Kong," Disney copyright, 1970s, 5" h **55.00**

Soaky, Pluto, ©Disney Productions, 1965, 8½" h **18.00**

Soap, figural, Doc, Kirk, c1939, 3½" h **25.00**

Souvenir Book, *Walt Disney Presents Fantasia*, 1940, 9½ x 12½" **50.00**

Thermos, metal, Zorro, black plastic cup, Aladdin Industries, 1960s, 6½" h **42.00**

Toothbrush, talking, Mickey Mouse **25.00**

Toy, windup, Goofy, plastic, built–in key, Marx, 1950s, 7½" h **125.00**

TV Guide, Zorro cov, 1958 .... **30.00**

Umbrella, Mickey Mouse and balloons, fabric, plastic Pluto handle **95.00**

Watering Can, Donald Duck, Ohio Art **125.00**

Wristwatch, Davy Crockett, US Time, c1950, straps replaced **55.00**

Wristwatch, Mickey Mouse, Timex, 1960s, MIB **125.00**

DOG COLLECTIBLES

Today there are over 100 breeds of dogs divided into seven classes: herding, hounds, non–sporting, sporting, terriers, toy breeds, and working dogs. The first modern dog show was held in Newcastle, England, in 1859. The recording of bloodlines soon followed.

Unlike other animal collectors, dog collectors are breed specific. A Scottie collector is highly unlikely to own a Boxer collectible. In most cases, these collections mate with the breed of dog owned by the collector. Finally, dog collectors demand that the collectibles they buy closely resemble their pet. The fact that the collectible portrays or pictures a German Shepherd is not enough. It must remind them specifically of their pooch.

Reference: Edith Butler, *Poodle Collectibles of the 50's & 60's*, L–W Book Sales, 1995.

Newsletters: *Canine Collectibles Newsletter*, 736 N Western Ave, Ste 314, Lake Forest, IL 60045; *Collectively Speaking!*, 428 Philadelphia Rd, Joppa, MD 21085.

Collectors' Club: Wee Scots, Inc, PO Box 1512, Columbus, IN 47202.

Ashtray, hunting dog, round, Stangl .... **$ 50.00**

Book, *Real Tales of Real Dogs*, A. P. Terkune, 1935 ...... **35.00**

Bookends, pr, Borzoi, Rosemeade **60.00**

Booklet, *Handling Your Hunting Dog*, Ralston Purina, 1947, 64 pgs **8.50**

Button, Scottie, Bakelite **18.00**

Catalog, Dog Furnishings, 1920 .... **30.00**

Cigarette Box, Scottie, wood, dispenses cigarettes **25.00**

Door Knocker, English Setter, bronzed metal, 4 x 5" **22.00**

Doorstop, Boston Terrier, cast iron, 8¼" h **90.00**

Doorstop, English Setter, cast iron **100.00**

Egg Timer, figural, Germany **65.00**

Figure, Boxer, reclining, Mortens Studios **55.00**

Figure, Collie, sitting, Mortens Studios **42.00**

Figure, Dachshund, German, 3½" h **20.00**

Figure, Dalmatian, Penny, Enesco **55.00**

Figure, dog holding ball, chalkware, 7" h **18.00**

Figure, Greyhounds, chalkware, American, c1920, price for pair **100.00**

Figure, lady and dog, floral trim, c1935, 11¼" h **20.00**

Hood Ornament, Bulldog, Mack Trucks **30.00**

Little Golden Book, *Rin–Tin–Tin and Rusty*, 1955 ...... **12.00**

Napkin Ring, figural dog chained to dog house, ftd base **300.00**

Nodder, Boston Terrier **15.00**

Pin, 2 Scotties, round **10.00**

Planter, bird dog, McCoy **42.00**

Rocker Blotter, Scottie, glass, jadeite, $25.00.

Powder Jar, Scottie, iridescent glass. **22.00**
Ring Holder, goldtone metal poodle in dog bed **10.00**
Salt and Pepper Shakers, pr, Bloodhound heads,
   Rosemeade **35.00**
Stuffed Toy, Dachshund, Steiff, 1950s **50.00**
Stuffed Toy, puppy, mohair, felt tongue, glass eyes,
   straw stuffing, c1920 . . . . **65.00**
Swizzle Stick, Poodle Room. **2.00**
Tie Rack, carved wood, seated Scottie, glass eyes **28.00**
Toy, Beethoven the Piano Playing Dog, plush dog,
   rubber hands, litho tin base, playing litho tin piano,
   head moves, TN, Japan, orig box, 8½" h **295.00**
Toothpick Holder, Spaniel sitting next to cup, mkd
   "Asbury Park, NJ" **20.00**
Whistle, Hush Puppy Shoes adv, figural Basset
   Hound, molded plastic, stamped "Hush Puppy" **8.00**

DOLL HOUSES & FURNISHINGS

Doll house furnishings divide into two basic types—handmade and machinemade. Handmade doll house furniture falls into the realm of miniatures. Miniatures are exact copies of their larger counterparts. Depending on the accuracy of detail, material used, and recognition of the maker, these miniatures can quickly jump into the hundreds of dollars. Miniature collectors tend to look down on machine–made material.

Petite Prince, Plastic Art Toy Corporation, Tootsietoy, and Renwal are just four of hundreds of major manufacturers of machine–made doll house furniture. Materials range from wood to injection mold-ed plastic. This furniture was meant to be used, and most surviving examples were. The period packaging and its supporting literature can double the value of a set.

References: Jean Mahan, *Doll Furniture, 1950s–1980s: Identification & Price Guide,* Hobby House Press, 1997; Margaret Towner, *Dollhouse Furniture: The Collector's Guide To Selecting and Enjoying Miniature Masterpieces,* Courage Books, Running Press, 1993; Dian Zillner, *American Dollhouses and Furniture From The 20th Century,* Schiffer Publishing, 1995.

Periodicals: *Doll Castle News,* PO Box 247, Washington, NJ 07882; *Miniature Collector,* Scott Publications, 30595 Eight Mile Rd, Livonia, MI 48152; *Nutshell News,* 21027 Crossroads Circle, PO Box 1612, Waukesha, WI 53187.

Collectors' Clubs: Dollhouse & Miniature Collectors, 9451 Lee Hwy #515, Fairfax, VA 22302; National Assoc of Miniature Enthusiasts, PO Box 69, Carmel, IN 46032.

Bathtub, metal, Tootsietoy . . . . $ **18.00**
Bed, twin, Tootsietoy, 1¼ x 3¼" **12.00**
Bed, wood, twin size, Strombecker. **8.00**
Bedroom Set, 4 pcs, plastic, bed, vanity, wardrobe,
   and mirror, c1930 . . . . **50.00**
Broom, Renwal. **40.00**
Buffet, Ideal. **15.00**
Chair, reed seat, Hitchcock **30.00**
Chair, rocking, Renwal. **10.00**
Chair, straight, wood, fabric seat, carved floral back,
   German. **15.00**
Chair, swivel, Renwal. **10.00**

Set, Nancy Forbes, Rapaport Bros, 18 pcs, $50.00.

Chair, wing, red brocade, Petite Princess. **18.00**
Chaise Lounge, Petite Princess, c1964, MIB **28.00**
Chest of Drawers, Renwal **10.00**
Coffee Table, Plasco. **8.00**
Cradle, pink, Plasco. **8.00**
Dining Room Set, 5 pcs, plastic, table and 4 chairs,
   c1945, MIB **12.00**
Dining Room Set, 8 pcs, metal, 2½" pedestal table
   and 4 matching fiddleback chairs, maroon radio,
   and 2 floor lamps, Tootsietoy **68.00**
Doghouse with Dog, Ideal. **15.00**
Doll, baby, Ideal **10.00**
Doll, boy, Renwal **20.00**
Doll, father, brown, Renwal. **30.00**
Doll, girl, bisque, swivel head, mkd "Karen #9,
   Eunice P. Tuttle," c1960 . . . . **165.00**
Doll, mother, red, Renwal **28.00**
Dollhouse, litho tin, white clapboard on multicol-
   ored stone, red roof, 2 story, 7 rooms, Marx,
   c1950s, 14 x 38" **85.00**
Dollhouse, Princess Patti, Ideal. **120.00**
Dollhouse, small, Schoenhut **275.00**
Dresser, mirror, Renwal **10.00**
Fainting Couch, green brocade, Petite Princess **22.00**
Fireplace, Renwal **18.00**
Grandfather Clock, Plasco **15.00**
Hamper, Princess Patti **10.00**
Highchair **12.50**
Hutch, Renwal **8.00**
Kitchen Set, 7 pcs, 1" scale, chestnut wood, cu
   board, table, 4 chairs, Colonial style **55.00**
Kitchen Stool, Renwal **8.00**
Kitchen Table, round, flowers, Princess Patti **30.00**
Living Room Set, 5 pcs, 5" l striped couch, wing
   chair, drop leaf table, and stool, Sheraton style **55.00**
Mantel Clock, paper dial, Renwal. **10.00**

Nursery, 9 pcs, night stand, chest, bathinette, cradle
    crib, table lamp, playpen, carriage, and highchair,
    Renwal, MIB **155.00**
Piano, bench, and metronome, Petite Princess, MIB **32.00**
Piano Stool, Ideal **5.00**
Picnic Table, Ideal **8.00**
Policeman, Renwal **40.00**
Radiator, Ideal **15.00**
Radio, floor model, Renwal **10.00**
Refrigerator, metal, Tootsietoy, c1920 . . . . **32.00**
Rolling Tea Cart, wine bottle, 3 wine cups, Princess
    Patti, MIB. **22.00**
Rug, tobacco rug, cotton, fringe, oriental rug style. **5.00**
Sideboard, Renwal. **15.00**
Sink, Renwal . . . .
Stove, metal, Tootsietoy, c1920. . . . . **30.00**
Swing, Renwal. **12.50**
Table, cast iron, red, Arcade, 3³/₄ x 6¹/₂" top, 3" h. **15.00**
Telephone, yellow, Renwal. **12.00**
Television, Plasco **20.00**
Toilet, Ideal **8.00**
Tricycle, Renwal **15.00**
Vacuum Cleaner, Renwal. **18.00**
Vanity, mirror, Plasco. **8.00**
Woodburning Stove. **12.50**
Wringer Washer, Renwal **20.00**

DOLLS

The middle decades of the 20th century witnessed a number of major changes in doll manufacture. New materials (plastic), technology (injection molding), and manufacturing location (the Far East) all played a major role in revolutionizing the industry by the mid–1960s.

Hard, then soft plastic dolls dominated the market by the mid–1950s. Barbie arrived on the scene in 1959. The Cabbage Patch doll was the marketing sensation of the 1970s.

Doll manufacturers are quick to copy any successful doll. Horsman's Dorothy looked surprisingly like Effanbee's Pastsy doll. Cosmopolitan's Ginger could easily be mistaken for Vogue's Ginny. Even with a single manufacturer, the same parts were used to make a variety of dolls. Barbie and her friends borrowed body parts from each other.

While condition has always played a major role in doll collecting, it became an obsession in the 1980s, particularly among collectors of contemporary dolls. MIB, mint–in–box, gave way to NRFB, never–removed–from–box.

The doll collecting community is currently experiencing a major transition. The number of individuals collecting late 19th– and early 20th–century French and German dolls is diminishing and the average age of the group is growing older and older. More and more collectors, especially those under the age of 45, are focusing on 1950s and 60s dolls. Many values have doubled in the past five years.

References: John Axe, *Effanbee: A Collector's Encyclopedia, 1949–Present, Second Edition,* Hobby House Press, 1994; John Axe, *Tammy and Her Family of Dolls: Identification and Price Guide,* Hobby House Press, 1995; Joe Blitman, *Francie & Her Mod, Mod, Mod, Mod World of Fashion,* Hobby House Press, 1996; Joseph Bourgeois, *Collector's Guide To Dolls In Uniform,* Collector Books, 1995; Carla Marie Cross, *Modern Doll Rarities,* Antique Trader Books, 1997; Linda Crowsey, *Madame Alexander: Collector's Dolls Price Guide #22,* Collector Books, 1997; Jan Foulke, *12th Blue Book Dolls & Values,* Hobby House Press, 1995; Dawn Herlocher, *200 Years of Dolls: Identification and Price Guide,* Antique Trader Books, 1996; Judith Izen, *Collector's Guide To Ideal Dolls: Identification & Value Guide,* Collector Books, 1994; Judith Izen and Carol Stover, *Collector's Guide to Vogue Dolls: Identification and Values,* Collector Books, 1997.

Polly Judd, *Cloth Dolls of the 1920s and 1930s,* Hobby House Press, 1990; Polly and Pam Judd, *Composition Dolls: 1909–1928, Volume II,* Hobby House Press, 1994; Polly and Pam Judd, *Composition Dolls: 1928–1955,* Hobby House Press, 1991; Polly and Pam Judd, *European Costumed Dolls,* Hobby House Press, 1994; Polly and Pam Judd, *Glamour Dolls of the 1950s & 1960s: Identification and Values, Revised Edition,* Hobby House Press, 1993; Polly and Pam Judd, *Hard Plastic Dolls I, Third Revised Edition,* Hobby House Press, 1993; Polly and Pam Judd, *Hard Plastic Dolls II, Revised,* Hobby House Press, 1994; A. Glenn Mandeville, *Alexander Dolls Collector's Price Guide, 2nd Edition,* Hobby House Press, 1995; A. Glenn Mandeville, *Doll Fashion Anthology & Price Guide, 5th Revised Edition,* Hobby House Press, 1996; A. Glenn Mandeville, *Ginny: An American Toddler Doll, 2nd Revised Edition,* Hobby House Press, 1994; A. Glenn Mandeville, *Madame Alexander Dolls Value Guide,* Hobby House Press, 1994; A. Glenn Mandeville, *Sensational '60s Doll Album,* Hobby House Press, 1996.

Marjorie A. Miller, *Nancy Ann Storybook Dolls,* Hobby House Press, 1980, available in reprint; Patsy Moyer, *Doll Values: Antique To Modern,* Collector Books, 1997; Patsy Moyer, *Modern Collectible Dolls: Identification & Value Guide,* Collector Books, 1997; Myla Perkins, *Black Dolls: 1820–1991,* Collector Books, 1993, 1995 value update; Myla Perkins, *Black Dolls, Book II, An Identification and Value Guide,* Collector Books, 1995; Susan Nettleingham Roberts and Dorothy Bunker, *The Ginny Doll Encyclopedia,* Hobby House Press, 1994; Patricia R. Smith, *Collector's Encyclopedia of Madame Alexander Dolls, 1965–1990,* Collector Books, 1991, 1997 value update; Patricia R. Smith, *Modern Collector's Dolls, Seventh Series* (1995), *Eighth Series* (1996), Collector Books; Patricia R. Smith, *Patricia Smith's Doll Values: Antique to Modern, Twelfth Edition,* Collector Books, 1996.

Periodicals: *Doll Reader,* 6405 Flank Dr, Harrisburg, PA 17112; *Dolls—The Collector's Magazine,* 170 Fifth Ave, 12th Floor, New York, NY 10010; *Doll World,* 306 E Parr Rd, Berne, IN 46711.

Collectors' Club: Cabbage Patch Kids Collectors Club, PO Box 714, Cleveland, GA 30528; Chatty Cathy Collectors Club, PO Box 140, Readington, NJ 08870; Ginny Doll Club, 305 W Beacon Rd, Lakeland, FL 33803; Ideal Toy Co Collector's Club, PO Box 623, Lexington, MA 02173; United Federation of Doll Clubs, PO Box 14146, Parkville, MO 64152.

Adams, Christine, Tiny Tots, painted oilcloth head,
    mohair wig, cloth body, "Christine Adams Tiny Tots
    Handmade Dolls" paper label, 1981, 18" h . . . . **$ 145.00**
Alexander Doll Company, Brenda Starr, hard plastic,
    jointed, blond hair, sleep eyes, 12" h **325.00**
Alexander Doll Company, Cissette, hard plastic,
    jointed, sleep eyes, 10" h **425.00**

Advertising, Campbell Kid, vinyl, 10" h, $65.00.

Alexander Doll Company, Melinda, hard plastic, swivel waist, rooted hair, sleep eyes, mkd "Alexander/1962" on head, booklet wrist tag, 16" h . . . 165.00

Allied Imported, Bride, vinyl body, rooted hair, sleep eyes, pierced ears with pearl earrings, bridal gown with lace overlay, 15" h 95.00

Allied Imported, Child, vinyl body, painted eyes, molded hair with ribbon, mkd "Allied Grand Doll Mfg Inc, 1958," and "A," 10" h 20.00

American Character, Betsy McCall, hard plastic, vinyl, socket head, rooted hair, sleep eyes, 7½" h 200.00

American Character, Cricket, plastic, bendable, painted eyes, mkd "American Character," 10" h 60.00

American Character, Eloise, cloth, yellow yarn hair, painted eyes, molded face, 16" h 275.00

American Character, Little Ricky Jr, vinyl, molded and painted hair, sleep eyes, 17" h 150.00

American Character, Sally, composition head, cloth body, 18" h 200.00

American Character, Tiny Tears, hard plastic head, vinyl body, rooted hair, sunsuit, wood and plastic bathinette, c1955, 11" h 100.00

American Character, Toni, collegiate outfit, orig booklet, 10" h 85.00

Arranbee, Angel Skin, vinyl head, stuffed magic skin body and limbs, molded and painted hair, c1954, 13" h 100.00

Arranbee, Judy, hard plastic, nylon blonde wig, braids, metal knob to wind hair back into head, open mouth, c1951, 19" h 95.00

Arranbee, Littlest Angel, hard plastic, jointed, synthetic hair, sleep eyes, 10" h 95.00

Arranbee, Nancy Lee, vinyl, socket head, stuffed vinyl body, sleep eyes, mkd "R & G," 14" h 225.00

Averill Manufacturing Company, Harriet Flanders, composition, jointed, molded hair, painted eyes, mkd "Harriet Flanders/1037," 12" h 225.00

Cameo Doll Company, Betty Boop, segmented body, composition hands, molded and painted hair,

molded and painted red swimming suit, mkd "Betty Boop/Des & Copyright by Fleischer, Studios," 12" h 650.00

Cameo Doll Company, Marcie, composition, painted hair and eyes, orig French–style outfit, molded and painted socks and shoes, 10" h 275.00

Cameo Doll Company, Pete the Pup, jointed paper label mkd "Des & Copyright by J. L. Kallus," 8" h 375.00

Cameo Doll Company, Scootles, vinyl, jointed, molded and painted hair, orig cotton dress, matching bonnet, mkd "R7234 Cameo JLK," 8" h 425.00

Cameo Doll Company, Sissy, composition, painted hair and eyes, orig printed percale dress, 12" h 225.00

Character, Archie, cloth, orange hair, printed red shirt, orange and black pants, mkd "Archie," c1960 . . . 165.00

Eegee, Child, vinyl head, wooden neck flange, latex body, molded and painted hair, sleep eyes, 14" h 60.00

Eegee, Dolly Parton, vinyl head, plastic body, jointed, painted eyes, orig gown, mkd "Dolly Parton/Eegee Co/Hong Kong" on back of head, "Goldberger Mfg Co" on back, 12" h 40.00

Effanbee, Button Nose, composition, molded and painted hair, jointed, orig blue and white dress, white apron, Dutch cap, wooden shoes, 1938, 8" h 240.00

Effanbee, Candy Kid, composition, molded and painted hair, painted eyes, jointed, orig red and white checked gingham outfit, holding stuffed monkey, 1946, 13" h 315.00

Effanbee, Dy–Dee Baby, hard rubber, attached soft rubber ears, molded and painted hair, sleep eyes, jointed, open nurser drink mouth, 9" h 225.00

Effanbee, Fluffy, vinyl, jointed, molded and painted hair, sleep eyes, 8" h 80.00

Effanbee, Half Pint, vinyl, rooted hair, jointed, 1966, 11" h 70.00

Effanbee, Happy Boy, vinyl, molded and painted hair and eyes, jointed, mkd "1960 Effanbee" on back of head and "Effanbee," 10" h 60.00

Cameo Doll Company, Scootles, 12½" h, $450.00.

Effanbee, Pun'kin, plastic, rooted hair, mkd "Effanbee/19©69," 11¹/₂" h, $200.00.

Effanbee, Harmonica Joe, cloth body, molded and painted features, sewn–on shoes, 7" h **175.00**

Effanbee, Howdy Doody, hard plastic head, cloth body, molded and painted hair, sleep eyes, orig cowboy costume with scarf, mkd "Effanbee," 19" h . . . **325.00**

Effanbee, Little Sister, composition socket head, shoulder plate, and hands, cloth body and limbs, embroidery floss hair, painted eyes, orig pink and white checkered blouse with pink skirt, 12" h **200.00**

Effanbee, Mama, cloth body, composition limbs, molded hair, sleep eyes, says "Mama," 10" h **225.00**

Effanbee, Patsy Ann, vinyl, jointed, rooted hair, sleep eyes, mkd "Effanbee Patsy Ann.1959," 15" h **200.00**

Effanbee, Precious Baby, vinyl flange neck head, cloth body, rooted hair, sleep eyes, 1969, 21" h. **90.00**

Effanbee, Sugar Plum, vinyl flange neck head, cloth body, vinyl limbs, rooted hair, 1964, 18" h **60.00**

Effanbee, Thumbkin, vinyl, cloth, rooted hair, mkd "Effanbee/1965/9500 UI," 18" h **90.00**

Fisher, Ruth E., Grand–Daughter, bisque, jointed, brown glass eyes, painted oriental features, molded socks and shoes, sleeveless dress, mkd "REF," 1939, 10" h **230.00**

Freundlich, Baby with Scale, composition, jointed, molded and painted hair and features, wearing diaper, in basket on working scale, 9¹/₂" h **200.00**

Freundlich, Goo Goo Eva, composition, cloth, mohair wig, celluloid eyes with floating disks within, orig flowered percale dress, matching bonnet, 15" h. **195.00**

Hasbro, Little Miss No Name, vinyl, hard plastic, jointed, rooted hair, plastic eyes, burlap dress, 1965, 15" h. **140.00**

Hasbro, Peace Series, vinyl, jointed, rooted hair, painted eyes, red, white, and blue pantsuit, mkd "6/Hong Kong/Hasbro/US Patented", 9" h **30.00**

Hasbro, Sweet Cookie, plastic, vinyl, rooted hair, painted eyes, freckles, dress with white pinafore with "Sweet Cookie" printed on front, 1972, 18" h **60.00**

Hasbro, That Kid, talking, plastic, vinyl, jointed, battery operated, rooted hair, sleep eyes, cotton shorts outfit, 1967, 21" h **140.00**

Horsman & Company, Ella Cinders, cloth body, movable composition limbs, molded and painted black hair, painted eyes, mkd "©/1925/M.N.S.," 18" h. **700.00**

Horsman & Company, Mary Poppins, vinyl head, plastic body, rooted hair, painted eyes, mkd "H," 12" h **45.00**

Horsman & Company, Pippi Longstocking, vinyl, cloth, rooted and braided orange hair, painted eyes, 1972, 17" h **80.00**

Horsman & Company, Poor Pitiful Pearl, vinyl head, stuffed vinyl body, rooted hair, sleep eyes, protruding ears, orig cotton dress and scarf, mkd "©1963/Wm. Steig/Horsman," 12" h **95.00**

Horsman & Company, Zodiac Baby, vinyl, jointed, rooted pink hair, black eyes, star–shaped dress and charm bracelet with zodiac signs, with "Your Individual Horoscope" booklet, mkd "Horsman Dolls Inc./1968," 6" h **15.00**

Mary Hoyer, Boy, composition, jointed, synthetic wig, sleep eyes, mkd "Original/Mary Hoyer/Doll," 14" h **525.00**

Ideal, Betsy Wetsy, composition, rubber, molded and painted hair, sleep eyes, mkd "Ideal," 11" h **150.00**

Ideal, Growing Hair Chrissy, vinyl head, plastic body, rooted hair, 17¹/₂" h **120.00**

Ideal, Judy Splinters, vinyl head, cloth body, vinyl limbs, yarn hair, painted eyes, mkd "Ideal Doll," 18" h. **200.00**

Ideal, Miss Revlon, vinyl, jointed, rooted hair, sleep eyes, 18" h. **225.00**

Ideal, Pepper, vinyl, plastic, 1963, 9¹/₄" h **30.00**

Ideal, Plassie, hard plastic head, cloth body, latex limbs, sleep eyes, mkd "P–50/Ideal/Made in U.S.A.," 17" h **165.00**

Ideal, Pos'n Pete, vinyl, plastic, 1964, 7³/₄" h. **30.00**

Ideal, Pos'n Sally, vinyl, plastic, 1965, 7³/₄" h **35.00**

Ideal, Sara Lee, black, vinyl head, cloth body, molded and painted hair, sleep eyes, mkd "Ideal Doll," 17" h **275.00**

Ideal, Saucy Walker, hard plastic, jointed, synthetic hair, sleep eyes, 15" h. **145.00**

Ideal, Thumbelina, vinyl head, cloth body, rooted hair, painted eyes, mkd "Ideal Toy Corp/©TT–19," 11" h. **60.00**

Kenner, Blythe, hard plastic head, jointed body, rooted hair, pull ring to make eyes turn color, orig "mod" style dress, high plastic boots, 12" h **50.00**

Kenner, Gabbigale, vinyl head, plastic body, jointed, rooted hair, painted eyes, pull string in chest, battery operated, orig red jumper, 18" h **55.00**

Knickerbocker, Annie, vinyl head, plastic body, rooted hair, painted eyes, orig red cotton dress with white collar, white socks, black shoes, 1982, 7" h **20.00**

Knickerbocker, Holly Hobbie, cloth, yellow yarn hair, printed features, dress and matching bonnet, 16" h **70.00**

Knickerbocker, Little House on the Prairie Child, vinyl, cloth, rooted hair, painted eyes, orig cotton dress , 12" h 35.00

Knickerbocker, Raggedy Ann, silk–screen printed face, red yarn hair, 15" h 95.00

Krueger, Pinocchio, cloth body, jointed wooden arms and legs, labeled "Authentic Walt Disney/R. G. Krueger," 15" h 475.00

Mattel, Baby Beans, talking, vinyl head, bean bag body, rooted hair, painted features, pull–string talker, 11" h. 18.00

Mattel, Baby Colleen, talking, vinyl head, cloth body, rooted hair, painted blue eyes, pull–string talker, Sears exclusive, 14" h 30.00

Mattel, Baby Go Bye Bye, vinyl head, plastic body, rooted hair, painted eyes, mkd "1968 Mattel Inc/Hong Kong," pull–string talker, 10" h 30.00

Mattel, Chatty Cathy, talking, vinyl head, plastic body, rooted hair, sleep eyes, 1962, 20" h 120.00

Mattel, Cheerful Tearful, vinyl head, plastic body, rooted hair, painted eyes, 1965, 13" h 30.00

Mattel, Cynthia, vinyl head, plastic body, rooted hair, painted features, battery operated, 20" h 60.00

Mattel, Doug Davis, Spaceman, vinyl, molded and painted hair and features, mkd "Mattel Inc/1967/Hong Kong," 6" h 45.00

Mattel, Hi Dottie, vinyl head, plastic body, vinyl left arm, plastic right arm, rooted hair, painted features, plug in left hand to connect phone, 17" h 40.00

Mattel, Julia, black, vinyl, rooted black hair, bend-able, painted eyes, mkd "1966 Mattel Inc," 11½" h . . . 240.00

Mattel, Little Kiddle, Lolli Lemon, vinyl, rooted yel-low hair, 2" h 45.00

Mattel, Miss Beasley, talking, vinyl, cloth, rooted blond hair, painted features, black plastic glasses, pull–string talker, "Mattel Miss Beasley" on cloth tag, 16" h 60.00

Nancy Ann Storybook Dolls, Nancy Ann, vinyl, jointed, rooted hair, sleep eyes with lashes, pierced ears, mkd "Nancy Ann," 10" h, $120.00.

Mattel, Shopping Sheryl, vinyl head, plastic body, jointed, rooted white hair, painted features, mag-netic right hand, 1970, 14" h 30.00

Mattel, Shrinking Violet, talking, cloth, yellow yarn hair, felt eyes, movable lids and mouth, pull–string talker, cloth label, 15" h 120.00

Mattel, Sing–A–Song, talking, vinyl head, plastic body, rooted hair, painted eyes, pull–string singer, 17" h 55.00

Mattel, Sister Small Walk, vinyl head, plastic body, rooted hair, painted eyes, molded–on socks and shoes, 11½" h 22.00

Mattel, Tippy Toes, vinyl, plastic, rooted hair, painted eyes, battery operated, rides plastic tricycle, 1967, 16" h 40.00

Mollye, Baby, vinyl, jointed, rooted hair, sleep eyes, mkd "Mollye," 9" h 75.00

Parker, Ann, Alice in Wonderland, sculptured resin, translucent, blond mohair wig, painted eyes, Sir John Tenniel–style outfit, walnut stand, mkd "Alice" on wrist tag, "English Costume Doll by Ann Parker," 8" h 275.00

Uneeda, Baby Sleep Amber, black vinyl head, arms and legs, cloth body, rooted black hair, sleep eyes, mkd "Tony Toy/1970/Made in Hong Kong," 11" h 10.00

Uneeda, Dollikins, vinyl head, hard plastic body, jointed, rooted hair, sleep eyes, pierced ears, mkd "Uneeda/25" on head, 12" h 60.00

Uneeda, Freckles, vinyl head, hard plastic body, jointed, rooted hair, jointed, orig nylon dress, 32" h . . . 120.00

Uneeda, Glamour Lady Bride Doll, vinyl head, hard plastic body, jointed, rooted hair, sleep eyes, paint-ed and real lashes, orig bride gown with lace veil, 20" h 60.00

Uneeda, Little Sophisticates, vinyl head, plastic body, vinyl arms, rooted hair, closed eyes, 8½" h 10.00

Mattel, Texaco Cheerleader, plastic, blonde hair, painted features, mkd "Hong Kong," 11½" h, $40.00.

Uneeda, Tiny Time Teens, poseable vinyl head, plastic body, rooted hair, painted features, mkd "U.D. Co. Inc./1967/ Hong Kong," 5" h 20.00

Vogue, Baby Dear, vinyl, cloth, rooted hair, painted eyes, 1960, 13" h 60.00

Vogue, Brickette, plastic body, vinyl arms and head, jointed waist, rooted hair, 18" h 45.00

Vogue, Ginny, vinyl head, plastic body, rooted hair, sleep eyes, 1963, 8" h 60.00

Vogue, Jill, hard plastic, jointed, sleep eyes, pierced ears, mkd "Vogue" on head, and "Jill/Vogue Made in U.S.A. 1957" on body, 10" h 165.00

Vogue, Li'l Imp, vinyl head, walker body, jointed, orange hair, sleep eyes, mkd "R & G" on head, 10½" h 60.00

Vogue, Littlest Angel, vinyl, rooted hair, mkd "Vogue Doll/1963" on head and back, 13" h 40.00

Vogue, Posie Pixie, vinyl head, cloth body, rooted hair, gauntlet hands, 17" h 45.00

Webster, Mary Hortence, Flapper Doll, composition, cloth, black wig, painted eyes, off–the–shoulder gown, pearl necklace, 1925, 28" h 275.00

Zeller, Fawn, Miami Miss, bisque, cloth, molded and painted hair and features, mkd "Fawn Zeller UFDC 1961," 1961, 15" h 275.00

DOORSTOPS

Prior to the 1920s, the three–dimensional, cast–metal figural doorstop reigned supreme. After 1920, the flat–back, cast–metal doorstop gained in popularity. By the late 1930s, it was the dominant form being manufactured. Basement workshop doorstops, made primarily from wood, were prevalent from the 1930s through the mid–1950s. By the 1960s the doorstop more often than not was a simple plastic wedge.

Crossover collectors have a major influence on value. Amount of surviving period paint also plays a critical role in determining value.

Beware of restrikes. Many period molds, especially those from Hubley, have survived. Manufacturers are making modern copies and painting them with the same color combinations as the period examples.

References: Jeanne Bertoia, *Doorstops: Identification and Values*, Collector Books, 1985, 1996 value update; Douglas Congdon–Martin, *Figurative Cast Iron: A Collector's Guide*, Schiffer Publishing, 1994.

Collectors' Club: Doorstop Collectors of America, 2413 Madison Ave, Vineland, NJ 08630.

Note: All listings are cast iron unless otherwise noted

Black Cat, lying on pillow, red ribbon and bow . . . . . . $ 150.00
Book, Little Miss Muffet, 7¾" h 180.00
Cat, green eyes, 10½ x 4" 40.00
Cat, lying on rug, 3 x 7" 300.00
Cinderella's Carriage, 9¾" x 19" 200.00
Clipper Ship, sgd "CJO," 5¼" h 60.00
Cornucopia and Roses, orig paint, 10¼" h 100.00
Cottage, Cape Cod style 160.00

Rose Basket, flat back, 12½ x 7", $200.00.

Dog, Cocker Spaniel, bronze, relief detail, worn green patina 165.00
Dog, German Shepherd, sitting 180.00
Dog, St Bernard, wearing keg 160.00
Dog, Wirehaired Terrier, bushes, orig paint, c1929 . . . . . 135.00
Doll on Base, 4½ x 4⅞" 115.00
Duck, white, green bush and grass, 7½" 250.00
Elephant, pulling coconut from tree, 14" 160.00
Fawn, #6, Taylor Co, 1930, 10 x 6" 350.00
Fish, molded, 6 x 5" 75.00
Fish, 3 fan-tail, orig paint, sgd "Hubley 464," 9¾" h 140.00
Flower Basket, National Foundry, 5⅞ x 5⅝" 90.00
Fraternal, Independent Order of Odd Fellows, white bird, gold chain, red base 100.00
Frog, sitting, green and yellow, 3" h 55.00
Frog, standing, 8¾ x 4" 65.00
High Heel Shoe 90.00
Horse, cast bronze, "King's Genius," Rife–Loth Corp, Waynesboro, Virginia, 1938, 11½ x 12" 45.00
House, sgd "Eastern Spec Co," 6" h 180.00
Jack, 6 x 7½" 85.00
Lion, 7 x 9½" 175.00
Ostrich, white, 8½ x 8" 325.00
Owl, red eyes 150.00
Pansy Bowl, Hubley, 7 x 6½" 140.00
Parrot, sitting on ring, 8 x 7" 120.00
Peacock, multicolored 175.00
Pelican, sitting on dock 325.00
Penguin, dressed in top hat and tails, blue vest 55.00
Pineapple, cast brass, 13" h 125.00
Poppies and Cornflowers, Hubley, 7¼" x 6½" 125.00
Rooster, black, colorful detail, 7" h 150.00
Roosting Hen, 5½ x 2½" 45.00
Santa, waving, 11 x 6" 55.00
Scottish Highlander, pedestal base, 12 x 5½" 350.00
Shoe, high–button style, 8½ x 9¾" 95.00
Uncle Sam, 16 x 8½" 45.00
Windmill, ivory, red roof, green base, 6¾" h 110.00

DRINKING GLASSES, PROMOTIONAL

The first promotional drinking glasses date from 1937 when Walt Disney licensed Libbey to manufacture a set of safety edge tumblers featuring characters from *Snow White and the Seven Dwarfs*. The set was sold in stores and used by food manufacturers for promotional product packaging. In the early 1950s Welch's sold its jelly in jars featuring Howdy Doody and his friends.

The first fast–food promotional glasses appeared in the late 1960s. Gasoline stations also found this premium concept a good trade stimulator. By the early 1980s hundreds of new glasses appeared with subject matter ranging from hit television shows and movies to local sports teams. The plastic drinking cup arrived on the scene in the late 1980s. A decade later, they have become collectible.

A never–out–of–the–box appearance is the key value component for any promotional drinking glass, whether made from glass or plastic. Regional collecting preferences affect value. Beware of hoarding. Far more examples survive in excellent to mint condition than most realize.

References: Mark Chase and Michael Kelly, *Collectible Drinking Glasses: Identification & Values,* Collector Books, 1996; John Hervey, *Collector's Guide To Cartoon & Promotional Drinking Glasses,* L–W Book Sales, 1990, 1995 value update.

Periodical: *Collector Glass News,* PO Box 308, Slippery Rock, PA 16057.

Collectors' Club: Promotional Glass Collectors Assoc, 4595 Limestone Ln, Memphis, TN 38141.

McDonald's, Garfield Characters Series, 1978, 3³/₈" h, $5.00.

A & P Peanut Butter Bicentennial Celebration, set of
    4, 1976 . . . . **$ 18.00**
Arby's, Bicentennial, Bullwinkle crossing the
    Delaware, 1976, 11 oz. **12.00**
Arby's, Yogi Bear picnic scene, plastic, snap–on
    lid, rippled straw, 4½" h **2.50**
Batman, with Robin the Boy Wonder, Zok! Crack,
    Whack!, gray and blue **15.00**
Belmont Stakes, 125th Running, 1993 . . . . **15.00**
Big Top Peanut Butter, The Band Played On, 1940–50 . . . . **10.00**
Burger Chef, Presidents Series **8.00**
Burger King, Luke Skywalker, 1977. . . . . **5.00**
Burger King, plastic, turkey with orange hat, hat–
    shaped snap–on lid, 2–finger handle **8.00**
Burger King, Where Kids Are King, set of 4, Liberty
    Bell, Patriots, Flags, Eagle & Shield **25.00**
Country Time Lemonade Flavor Drink, yellow, 6¼" h **2.50**
Dennis the Menace, plastic, yellow, molded plastic
    character head lid, straw. **5.00**
Domino's Pizza, Noid, beach chair, 1988 . . . . **5.00**
Dr Pepper, hot air balloon in clouds **2.00**
Good to the Last Drop, clear glass, 2 black illus of
    cartoon–type gas station attendants, orange ring
    bands, 1950s, 5¼" h **15.00**
Gulliver's Travels, Princess Glory, green, 1939
    Paramount, 4¾" h. **75.00**
Hardee's, Days of Thunder Racers, plastic, 1990,
    32 oz **5.00**
Holly Farms, Collectors Series, Brockway, Bullwinkle,
    1975, 16 oz. **40.00**

Indianapolis 500, 1961 Official Tony Hulman rocks
    glass, gold rim, 3¼" h. **8.00**
Jungle Book, Bagheera, blue, 6½" h **12.00**
Kentucky Derby, 1956 . . . . **55.00**
Kentucky Derby, 1964 . . . . **65.00**
Kentucky Derby, 1968 . . . . **45.00**
Kentucky Fried Chicken, bucket and balloon. **10.00**
Libbey Classics, Tom Sawyer, short **8.00**
Mobil, football, 10 different logos, price for set. **20.00**
Official Souvenir New York World's Fair, 1939 . . . . **12.50**
Pepsi, Happy Birthday Goofy, 1978 . . . . **8.00**
Pepsi, Shere Kahn, 1977 . . . . **10.00**
Pittsburgh Steelers, Superbowl XIII, Bradshaw,
    Webster, and Greenwood. **5.00**
Pizza Hut, plastic, Rogue and Gambit **2.50**
Popeye's Fried Chicken, Swee' Pea, 1979 . . . . **12.50**
Roy Rogers, Treasure Trolls. **2.00**
Taco Bell, tumbler, color changing **2.50**
Taco Villa, Beauregard **5.00**
Welch's, Archies **5.00**
Welch's, Howdy Doody, 1953, 8 oz **50.00**
Whataburger, dinosaur, plastic **5.00**
White Castle, Woozy Wizard, plastic, 5 oz. **5.00**
World Wrestling Federation, Junk Yard Dog, plastic **2.50**

DRUG STORE COLLECTIBLES

Product type, e.g., laxative, manufacturer, such as Burma Shave, and advertising display value are three standard approaches to drug store collectibles. Unlike country store collectors, whose desire it is to display their collections in a country store environment, few drug store collectors recreate a pharmacy in their home or garage.

Emphasis is primarily on products from the first two–thirds of the 20th century. Few individuals collect contemporary chain drug store, e.g., CVS, memorabilia. Dental and shaving items are two subcategories within drug store collectibles that are currently seeing values increases.

References: Al Bergevin, *Drugstore Tins & Their Prices*, Wallace–Homestead, Krause Publications, 1990; Patricia McDaniel, *Drugstore Collectibles*, Wallace–Homestead, Krause Publications, 1994.

Aftershave, Jovan Musk, 2 fl oz, clear plastic bottle, silver metal lid, silver cardboard box, includes bar of soap . . . . **$ 12.00**

Band–Aid, Charmers, Johnson & Johnson, New Brunswick, NJ, white, red, blue, yellow, and green tin, flip–top lid, red and blue letters, empty **5.00**

Bib, Playtex Bib–Smock, International Latex Corp, white, multicolored dots, clear plastic and cardboard package, 1956 . . . . **15.00**

Book, *American Drug Index*, Charles O. Wilson, Ph.D., and Tony Everett Jones, M.S., J.B. Lippincott Co, Philadelphia and Montreal, hardcover, 1957, 650 pgs **15.00**

Book, *Physicians Desk References to Pharmaceutical Specialities and Biologicals, Sixth Edition*, 1952 . . . . **15.00**

Curity Diaper Liners, Kendall Mills, Division of the Kendall Company, Walpole, MA, 6 x 1 x 14" box, contains 152 liners, 1954 . . . . **18.00**

Deodorant, Hush, The Gillette Co, Chicago, IL, made in USA, 1.35 oz white plastic container, blue, white, and yellow cardboard box, 1959 . . . . **10.00**

Display, Curity Medical Bandages & Supplies, plastic Miss Curity figure, c1950 . . . . **130.00**

Dr. Scholl's Foot Soap, tin, round, shaker top **12.00**

Electric Razor Cleaning Brushes, set of 2, wire and bristle brushes, on 5 x 3¼" yellow card, black lettering. **8.50**

Ex–Lax, sample tin, contains 2 tablets **10.00**

First Aid Packet, Johnson & Johnson, New Brunswick, NJ, contains 10 Band–Aids, gauze pads, pack of 2 Bufferin antacid tablets, and antiseptic cream, 5¾ x 5¾ x 1½" red, white, and blue box **15.00**

Flamingo Hair Net, Flamingo Products, Inc, Danville, IL, picture of woman on pink and white envelope, 1958 . . . . **5.00**

Maybelline Cream Mascara, Maybelline Co, Chicago IL, USA, clear plastic container, brush, and tube of cream on white card **12.00**

Mennen Baby Powder, tin, blue and white vertical striped paper label **30.00**

Metrecal, Mead Johnson & Co, Evansville, IN, 8 oz, gold and white can, key opener **8.00**

Pinex Wild Cherry Throat Lozenges, Pinex Co Inc, New York, NY, 10 foil–wrapped lozenges, red, white, and blue box, full **8.00**

Sweet'n–ets Sugar Sub, Rexall Drug Co, Los Angeles, Boston, St. Louis, USA, octagonal glass jar with shaker top, pink and blue label, full jar **12.00**

Tanfastic IR–9 Suntan Lotion, The Norwich Pharmaceutic Co, Norwich, NY, bottle, 3 fl oz, full **8.00**

Tooth Powder, Pepsodent Tooth Powder, Pepsodent Div, Lever Brothers Co, New York, NY, 4 oz, red, white, and blue horizontal striped tin **12.00**

Toothpaste, Colgate, Colgate–Palmolive Co, Jersey City, NJ, 3¼ oz tube, 6 x 1¼ x 1½" box with red, green, and white letters **10.00**

Toothpaste, Ipana, Bristol–Meyers Co, New York, NY, 4.6 oz tube **10.00**

Vitamins, St. Joseph Vitamins for Children, Plough Inc, clear glass bottle, 3⅝ x 1¾ x 1⅝" box, full bottle **5.00**

EASTER COLLECTIBLES

Easter collectibles are the weak sister when it comes to holiday collectibles. The number of collectors is a far cry from those of Valentine, Halloween, or Christmas memorabilia.

Focus is primarily on objects related to the secular side of this important religious holiday. Rabbit (Easter Bunny), chicken, decorated eggs, and Easter baskets head the list of desired objects. While plenty of two–dimensional material exists, most collectors focus primarily on three–dimensional objects.

Reference: H. N. Schiffer, *Collectible Rabbits*, Schiffer Publishing, 1990.

White Cloverine Brand Salve, tin, 1 oz, $10.00.

Chocolate Mold, rabbits playing drums, gang mold, tin, #26024, Anton Reich, Dresden, 10⅝" w, 6" h, $85.00.

Candy Container, rabbit, carrying basket, glass, mkd
"USA," 4½" h............................... $ 50.00
Candy Dish, egg, milk glass, hp violets and gilt script
lettering "Easter," 3 ftd........................ 25.00
Chocolate Mold, basket, tin, mkd "7166, Made in
U.S.A.," 4½" l.................................. 10.00
Chocolate Mold, chick, hatching from egg, mkd "EPP
7123," 3" h................................... 40.00
Chocolate Mold, egg, emb seashell design, tin, mkd
"727," 2" h.................................... 7.50
Chocolate Mold, girl hugging large rabbit, tin, mkd
"21889S," 7" h................................ 90.00
Chocolate Mold, hen, egg base, tin, 2¾" h.......... 10.00
Chocolate Mold, rabbit, sitting on fence, dressed,
holding basket and smoking pipe, tin, mkd "EPP
4808," 4¼" h.................................. 45.00
Chocolate Mold, rabbit, sitting, ears back, tin, mkd
"EPP 6626," 2⅞" h............................. 10.00
Chocolate Mold, rabbit, walking and carrying basket,
tin, mkd "6629," 12½" h....................... 150.00
Chocolate Mold, rabbits, sitting up, baskets on backs,
gang mold, 2 cavities, tin, mkd "REI 26944,"
9¼" h.. 50.00
Chocolate Mold, rooster, standing, tin, mkd "EPP
4689," 4½" h.................................. 40.00
Egg, celluloid, purple, Japan, 5" l................. 30.00
Figure, chick in egg, celluloid, Japan.............. 20.00
Figure, rabbit emerging from egg, composition, 6½" h.... 60.00
Figure, rabbit pushing baby buggy, hard plastic, pink,
blue trim, 7" h................................ 15.00
Ice Cream Mold, Easter lily, pewter, c1920.......... 50.00
Mask, rabbit, papier-mâché, 11" h................. 20.00
Music Box, egg, litho tin, rabbits, eggs, and chicks
dec... 15.00
Nodder, rabbit, chalkware, brown flocking, mkd
"USA," 1950s.................................. 15.00
Roly Poly, egg, rabbit holding basket on top, cellu-
loid, Japan, 1920s............................. 50.00
Roly Poly, rabbit standing on ball, purple costume,
celluloid, Japan, 4½" h......................... 25.00

Sheet Music, *Easter Parade*...................... 10.00
Toy, egg, plastic, tin chick inside, 1950s........... 40.00
Toy, hopping rabbit, tin, flocked, Japan, 5" h........ 50.00

EGGBEATERS

Kitchen collecting is becoming specialized. A new collecting category often evolves as the result of the publication of a book or for-
mation of a collectors' club. In this instance, eggbeaters became
a separate category as the result of the publication of a checklist
book on the subject.

Learn to differentiate between commonly found examples and
those eggbeaters that are scarce. Novelty and multipurpose beaters are desired. American collectors are expanding their collecting
horizons by seeking out beaters from Canada and Europe.

Reference: Don Thornton, *Beat This: The Eggbeater Chronicles*,
Off Beat Books, 1994.

A&J, metal, "Big Bingo #70", 1920s, 11" h.......... $ 25.00
A&J, metal, green wood handle, green glass pitch-
er, 1930, 12½" h.............................. 75.00
A&J, metal, white milk glass container with black
trim, 1923.................................... 60.00
Aurelius, Favorite, metal, wood handles, 11¾" h....... 30.00
Aurelius, metal, wood handles, 1926, 11½" h......... 55.00
Benson, wood handles, c1925, 12" h............... 100.00
Clipper, Archimedes type, 13" h.................. 150.00
Culinary Utilities, Keystone, Archimedes type, emb
jar, 11" h.................................... 80.00
Dover, steel handle, 9" h......................... 45.00
Edlund, plastic handle, 11¾" h.................... 18.00
EKCO, "Flint Mixer 'Rhythm Beater,'" waved blade...... 10.00
EKCO, Mary Ann, 11¼" h......................... 10.00
Ladd, Saturn, 10½" h............................ 25.00
Maynards, Bakelite handles, 13" h................. 35.00
Maynards, "Master Mixer," red plastic angled handle,
11" h.. 18.00
SJ&H, Zip Whip, white verticle plastic handle,
1950s, 13½" h................................ 50.00

**Toy, Easter Copter, windup, litho tin, plastic propeller, Japan,
6" l, 3½" h, $12.00.**

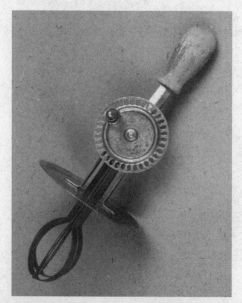

**Turner & Seymour,
Handimaid, green
wood handle, with
transparent green
2–cup pitcher,
$35.00.**

Standard Specialty, cast iron, green glass jar with tin
  screw–on lid, 12" h, 3⅞" d **75.00**
Taplin, loop handle, 5½" h. **15.00**
Taplin, metal, wood handle, 11" h **10.00**
Taplin, wood handle, 10½" h **25.00**
Turner & Seymour, Blue Whirl, wood handle, 12½" h **20.00**
Turner & Seymour, Merry Whirl, 12" h **40.00**
Turner & Seymour, Super Whirl, Bakelite handle,
  11½" h **20.00**
Ullman, cast and sheet aluminum, 10⅜" h **35.00**
Wallace, 11" h. **10.00**
Washburn, nickeled steel, green wood handle, 1936. . . . . **20.00**
Washburn, Whirlwind, metal, ivory knob, 1927,
  10½" h **25.00**

ELVIS PRESLEY

Elvis died on August 17, 1977. Or, did he? The first Elvis license material dates from the mid-1950s. Vintage Elvis dates prior to 1965.

Collectors divide Elvis material into two periods: items licensed prior to Elvis' death and those licensed by his estate, known to collectors as fantasy items. Some Elvis price guides refuse to cover fantasy pieces. Special items manufactured and marketed solely for Elvis fan club members are a third category of material and should not be overlooked.

References: Jerry Osborne, *The Official Price Guide To Elvis Presley: Records and Memorabilia,* House of Collectibles, 1994; Steve Templeton, *Elvis!: An Illustrated Guide to New and Vintage Collectibles,* Courage Books, Running Press, 1996.

Periodical: *Graceland Express,* PO Box 16508, Memphis, TN 38186.

Collectors' Club: Elvis Forever, TCB Fan Club, PO Box 1066, Pinellas Park, FL 34665.

Book, *The Elvis Presley Story,* Hillman Books,
  32 black and white photo pgs, 1960, 160 pgs . . . . . . **$ 25.00**
Booklet, *Dial E!–I Love You,* 1962. . . . . **15.00**
Catalog, Elvis RCA Victor Records, lists lps and 45s,
  3½ x 7" **20.00**
Charm Bracelet, metal link band, gold finish, ©1956
  Elvis Presley Enterprises **125.00**
Christmas Ornament, figural Elvis, Hallmark, orig
  box, 1992 . . . . **25.00**
Guitar, hard plastic, brown and white, braided strap,
  mkd "Emenee Official Elvis Presley Guitar" **400.00**
Keychain Viewer, plastic, Elvis photo inside, early
  1970s, 2" l. **15.00**
Lamp, figural, bust, 36" h **125.00**
Lobby Card, *Jail House Rock,* 1957 . . . . **50.00**
Magazine, *Elvis Monthly,* April 1961. . . . . **12.00**
Menu, Sahara Tahoe, 1970s **45.00**
Newspaper, Memphis, obituary **45.00**
Pennant, felt, red and green, center photo, 18" l **15.00**
Pillow, cotton, stuffed, blue printed portrait, "Love
  Me Tender," Personality Products Co, ©Elvis
  Presley Enterprises **250.00**

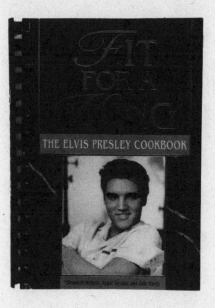

Cookbook, *Fit For A King, The Elvis Presley Cookbook,* $5.00.

Pinback Button, color photo, "Sincerely Elvis,"
  1970s, 3½" d **12.00**
Postcard, "Easter Greetings," Elivs wearing gray tuxe-
  do, red ground, 3½ x 5½" **35.00**
Poster, "Give Elvis for Christmas, RCA, 1959 . . . . **40.00**
Record, *King Creole,* RCA Victor, black label. **15.00**
Record, *Love Me Tender/Any Way You Want Me,* RCA
  Victor, 1956. . . . . **50.00**
Record Player, paper covered wood, RCA Victor, Elvis
  signature on top, 1950s, 12 x 12½ x 7" **350.00**
Salt and Pepper Shakers, pr, Elvis on TV screen **15.00**
Scarf, 1956, 32" sq **325.00**
Sheet Music, *Treat Me Nice,* 1957 . . . . **15.00**
Trading Cards, 1978, set of 66 . . . . **60.00**
Tumbler, 1970s **50.00**

AUCTION PRICES

Butterfield & Butterfield, The Elvis Presley Museum Collection, November 3, 1996. Prices include the 15% buyer's premium.

Bust, ceramic, Elvis with black hair and aqua blue
  eyes, wearing white studded jumpsuit, 18" h, with
  Elvis Presley Museum Certificate. **316.25**
Dogtag Bracelet, chrome, engraved portrait, signa-
  ture, and "Presley, Elvis – 53310761 – Type O,"
  orig chain and 2 x 8" card, 1956 Elvis Presley
  Enterprises, 1 x 1¼" dogtag, with Elvis Presley
  Museum Certificate **345.00**
Doll, wearing red jumpsuit, red and white cape,
  white belt, and gold painted TCB necklace, 11" h,
  with Elvis Presely Museum Certificate. **86.25**
Records, set of 8, 45 rpm, *From the Waist Up, Merry
  Christmas Baby, Blue Elvis, Elvis' Girls, Elvis
  Always On My Mind/Deparate Ways, Elvis Way
  Down, Elvis Moody Blue,* and *Elvis, Softly As I
  Leave You,* with Elvis Presley Museum Ceritificate . . **258.75**
Sweater, rust colored knit sleeves and collar, multi-
  colored suede front, inside label reads "Esprit by
  Campus," with certificate of authenticity from The
  Elvis Presley Museum, sgd by Joe Esposito **1,725.00**

ERTL

Fred Ertl, Sr., founded Ertl, the world's largest manufacturer of toy farm equipment, in 1945. The company has licenses from most major manufacturers. Located in Dyersville, Iowa, Ertl also manufactures a line of promotional banks, promotional trucks, and toys ranging from airplanes to trucks.

Ertl makes many of its toys in a variety of scales. It also has a line of limited edition, highly detailed models designed for direct sale to the adult collector market. When researching an Ertl toy be certain you are looking in the right scale and quality categories.

Collectors' Club: Ertl Collectors Club, PO Box 500, Dyersville, IA 52040.

Note: All toys listed are in very good condition. Banks are in mint–in–the–box condition.

Bank, 1905 Ford Delivery Van, A & W Root Beer #2, #9827, MIB	$ 35.00
Bank, 1905 Ford Delivery Van, Richard Petty #3, #9683, black, MIB	300.00
Bank, 1913 Ford Model T, Amoco, #9150, MIB	125.00
Bank, 1913 Ford Model T, Wonder Bread #1, #1660, MIB	65.00
Bank, 1917 Ford Model T, Goddyear, #9359, MIB	20.00
Bank, 1918 Ford Runabout, Champion Spark Plug #1, #9067, MIB	40.00
Bank, 1925 Kenworth Tanker, Mobil Oil, #9237, MIB	25.00
Bank, 1926 Mack Tanker, Sinclair Oil, #2119, MIB	70.00
Bank, 1926 Seagrave Fire Engine, JC Whitney, #B234, MIB	25.00
Bank, 1931 Hawkeye Tanker, Red Crown Gasoline #1, #7654, MIB	60.00
Bank, 1931 International Tanker, Pepsi, #4113, MIB	25.00
Bank, 1938 Chevy Panel Van, US Mail, #B447, MIB	30.00
Bank, 1941 Ford Tractor–Trailer, Anheuser–Busch #9, #9553, MIB	25.00
Bank, 1950 Chevy Panel Truck, Carlisle Toy Show, #2851, MIB	15.00
Bank, 1955 Chevy Cameo Pickup, Coca–Cola, #B648, MIB	30.00
Bank, 1960 Ford 4x4 Pickup, Cumberland Valley, #N288, MIB	20.00
Bank, Grumman Step Van, Bethlehem Steel #2, #3946, MIB	30.00
Box Van, Loadstar	375.00
Bulldozer, John Deere 500, with blade	75.00
Combine, John Deere 6600	100.00
Concrete Truck, Loadstar	400.00
Dump Truck, Fleetstar 10–wheel, red	125.00
Dump Truck, Fleetstar Hi-Side	140.00
Dump Truck, Loadstar	250.00
Grain Hopper	35.00
Gravity Feed Truck, International Fleetstar	250.00
Picker	50.00
Stake Truck, Loadstar, grain/cattle	200.00
Tanker, Conoco	125.00
Tanker, Mobile	70.00
Tanker, Texaco, #2	250.00
Tilt Bed, Fleetstar, green	125.00
Tilt Bed, Loadstar	180.00

Tow Truck, Loadstar	375.00
Tractor, Allis–Chalmers B-112	110.00
Tractor, Ford 8000	50.00
Trailer Truck, Mary Kay Cosmetics	125.00
Truck, GE, white	25.00

FANS, ELECTRIC

While hundreds of companies made electric fans, the market was dominated by Emerson Electric, General Electric, and Westinghouse Electric. Other collectible manufacturers include Berstead Manufacturing, Hunter-Century Gilbert, Menominee, Peerless, Robbins & Meyers, and StarRite/Eskimo.

Montgomery Ward, Sears, Singer, and Western Electric never manufactured electric fans. They put their brand names on fans made by others. Polar Cub electric fans were made for the five and dime store trade.

Electric fan collecting came of age in the 1990s. Currently, the focus is primarily on desk fans made prior to 1960. The market for large ceiling fans, with the exception of those of unusual design, is still primarily reuse.

Reference: John M. Witt, *Collector's Guide to Electric Fans,* Collector Books, 1997.

Collectors' Club: American Fan Collectors Assoc, PO Box 804, South Bend, IN 46624.

REPRODUCTION ALERT: Beware of assembled fakes. Unscrupulous individuals assemble fictitious fans by using parts from several different fans. Buy only from sellers willing to provide a money–back, no–questions–asked guarantee.

Note: All fans listed are in excellent condition

Berstead Manufacturing, Wizard, Model 45–M, 12"	$ 20.00
Century, Model 102, 12"	35.00
Century, Model 601, 10"	20.00
Emerson, Emerson B–Junior, 10"	40.00
Emerson, Model 2540–B, 8"	12.00
Emerson, Model 6250–D, 10"	30.00

Jandus, round ball motor, 12" brass blades and cage, ornate tab base, $400.00.

Emerson, Model 27048, 16" **220.00**
Emerson, Model 71666 FG, 12" **150.00**
Emerson, Model 73638, 16" **50.00**
Emerson, Model 94646–B, 12" **10.00**
Emerson, Silver Swan Pedestal, 12" **325.00**
General Electric, Model 257599 Whiz, 9" **30.00**
General Electric, Model 33X164 Quiet Fan, 10" **60.00**
General Electric, Model 34X899, 16" **40.00**
General Electric, Model 42X548, 10" **15.00**
General Electric, Model FM10V41, 10" **15.00**
General Electric, Model FM12541, 12" **20.00**
Gilbert, Model A–325, 10" **12.00**
Gilbert, Model M1384, 12" **30.00**
Knapp–Monarch, Model 3–503, 12" **30.00**
Polar Cub, Model H, 8" **20.00**
R & M, Model 5404, 10" **40.00**
R & M, Model D10–A6–01, 10" **60.00**
Sampson, "SafeFlex," Model No. 710, 10" **45.00**
Singer, "Ribbonaire," Model G–1, 6" **70.00**
Wagner, Model 5260, 10" **20.00**
Westinghouse, Model 1381675, 10" **10.00**
Westinghouse, Model 77572, 9" **20.00**

FARM COLLECTIBLES

This category includes material from barns, storage sheds, pens, and fields. It encompasses the essential items a farmer used to plant and harvest his grains and raise his livestock. Household objects are not included.

The overwhelming majority of objects that appear in this category are massproduced. By the 1920s farmers had access to these products through mail–order catalogs, farm bureaus, general stores, and regional distributors. Occasionally, a farmer would order a made–to–order implement for a special task. These survive, but in very small numbers.

Farm objects were used. In fact, collectors expect farm collectibles to have a weathered, used look. No mint-in-the-box examples in this category. However, it is a mistake to assume that junk sells. Objects must be in good enough condition to display in the home.

Advertising premiums from the manufacturers of farm equipment and supplies are included. Useful, practical premiums were issued extensively at county and state fairs and regional farm shows. Farmers showed their loyalty to a particular manufacturer by wearing hats, jackets, and other items with that manufacturer's logo on them.

Most collectors of this material tend to have a farming background. While they prefer pre–1940 material, some objects manufactured between 1945 and 1960 are attracting attention.

References: Terri Clemens, *American Family Farm Antiques,* Wallace–Homestead, Krause Publications, 1994; Jimm Moffet, *American Corn Huskers: A Patent History,* Off Beat Books, 1994; Dana Gehman Morykan and Harry L. Rinker, *Warman's Country Antiques & Collectibles, Third Edition,* Wallace–Homestead, Krause Publications, 1996; Robert Rauhauser, *Hog Oilers Plus: An Illustrated Guide,* published by author, 1996.

Periodicals: *Farm Antiques News,* 812 N Third St, Tarkio, MO 64491; *Toy Farmer,* 7496 106th Ave SE, Lamoure, ND 58458;

Tractor Classics CTM, PO Box 489, Rocanville, Saskatchewan, 20A 3L0 Canada.

Collectors' Clubs: Antique Engine, Tractor & Toy Club, 5731 Paradise Rd, Slatington, PA 18080; Farm Machinery Advertising Collectors, 10108 Tamarack Dr, Vienna, VA 22182.

Apple Picker, wire cage, wood handle . . . . **$ 25.00**
Ashtray, Gehl Farm Equipment **75.00**
Booklet, *Oliver Farm Equipment Sales*, Oliver Red
    River special threshers, 2936, 20 pgs, 8 x 9" **20.00**
Branding Iron, wrought iron, "D," 21" l **15.00**
Brochure, Vulcan Plows, multicolored **5.00**
Calendar, John Deere, 1955 . . . . **35.00**
Catalog, Gordon–Van Tine Farm Buildings, 1935,
    12 pgs **10.00**
Chicken Feeder, Full–O–Pep. **15.00**
Corn Sheller, red washed wood case, iron gears, hand
    crank, 34" h **65.00**
Cow Bell, copper. **25.00**
Cranberry Scoop, wood and tin, 18 fingers **200.00**
Cream Can, cov, Elkin's Dairy, brass nameplate, bail
    handle, 1 gal, 10" h **25.00**
Dairy Scale, Chatillon, 0–120 lbs **85.00**
Draw Knife, 8" l **15.00**
Egg Basket, splint, buttocks bottom, 2" w **75.00**
Feed Scale, Purina Feed Saver and Cow Culler adv,
    red and white checkered top, blue and cream bot-
    tom, metal pan. **100.00**
Fence Stretcher, iron **20.00**
Grain Cradle, 4 fingers, 41" l **65.00**
Grain Scale, Winchester, brass, bushel **275.00**
Hay Rake, 76" l **25.00**
Husking Tool, leather palm guard, shoestring laces **10.00**
Magazine, *Farm Journal,* Grant Wood cov, May 1939 . . . . **15.00**
Milk Can, brass nameplate, 10 gal **20.00**
Pinback Button, Pennsylvania Farm Show Exhibitor,
    Harrisburg, blue, white, and yellow, 1932, 2¼" d **12.00**
Pocket Ledger, John Deere, 1930 . . . . **7.50**
Post Hole Digger, clamshell shovels, wood handles. **30.00**
Seed Dryer, chestnut frame, pine spindles, 21 x 43". **75.00**

Nest Eggs, blown glass, 2¼ to 2¾" l, $5.00 each.

Sickle, iron blade, wood handle **20.00**
Sign, Farmer's Union, tin **25.00**
Thermometer, John Deere adv **75.00**
Weathervane, beaver, copper, 33" l. **200.00**
Weathervane, cow, copper and cast iron, full bodied,
    26" l **2,175.00**
Weathervane, flying goose, painted plywood, 42" l. . . . **1,250.00**
Wedge, log splitting, cast iron **15.00**
Windmill Weight, Crescent, Fairbanks Morse & Co,
    Chicago, IL, mkd "Eclipse B13," 10½" l **100.00**

FAST–FOOD COLLECTIBLES

McDonald's dominates the field. In fact, it has become so important that it has its own category. If you have a McDonald's fast–food collectible, look under "M."

The Howard Johnson chain, the American diner, and roadside soda and custard stands are the forerunners of the modern fast–food franchise. Suburban sprawl, television, multicar families, dual–income families, and more and more after–school activities are just a few of the post–1945 changes in society that contributed to fast food's success. Initially, meals were cheap. Today feeding a family of four can easily be a $15–plus proposition.

Each year dozens of new fast–food franchises are launched. Each year dozens of fast–food franchises fail. Collectors focus primarily on collectibles from those which have achieved national success. National fast–food chains do regional promotions. Collectors' club newsletters are the best way to keep up with these and the premiums that result.

All the major fast–food franchises have gone international. Collectors also are hopping aboard the international bandwagon. Many American collections now contain examples from abroad.

References: Ken Clee, *Kid's Meal Collectibles Update '94–'95*, published by author; Ken Clee and Susan Hufferd, *Tomart's Price Guide to Kid's Meal Collectibles (Non–McDonald's)*, Tomart Publications, 1994; Gail Pope and Keith Hammond, *Fast Food Toys*, Schiffer Publishing, 1996.

Arby's, Babar's Bucket of Fun, back–to–school, 1992. . . . **$ 5.00**
Arby's, car, molded plastic, Looney Tunes, 3½" **5.00**
Arby's, cassette tape, Classic Fairy Tales, Jack and the
    Beanstalk, 1993 . . . . **5.00**
Arby's, figure, Yosemite Sam, 1987, 2" h **4.00**
Big Boy, comic book, Adventures of the Big Boy, 1973 . . . **10.00**
Big Boy, doll, plastic, name on shirt, 1974–78, 10" h. **5.00**
Big Boy, nodder, papier mâché head, heavy base, red
    and white checkered overalls, 5" h **8.00**
Burger King, car, plastic, windup, 1979 . . . . **1.00**
Burger King, glider, styrofoam, 1978. . . . . **2.00**
Burger King, hand puppet, plastic, King, 1977 . . . . **2.00**
Burger King, whistle, green pickle **1.50**
Chuck E Cheese, bank, figural **10.00**
Dairy Queen, figure, rubber, bendable, Santa, open
    eyes, 1993. . . . . **2.50**
Dairy Queen, frame tray puzzle, Dennis the Menace
    Coloring Puzzle, 6 pcs, box of 4 crayons, golfing
    scene, 1993. . . . . **2.50**
Denny's, hand puppet, plastic, Deputy Dan, 1976 . . . . . . **1.25**
Denny's, menu, child's, 1978. . . . . **2.25**
Hardee's, doll, cloth, Gilbert Giddyup, 1971. . . . . **10.00**

Little Caesars, doll, Meatsa Meatsa Man, cloth, wearing Roman toga, slice of pizza stitched to right hand, 1990, 5" h, $8.00.

Hardee's, tumbler, Smurf illus, multicolored . . . . **.75**
Howard Johnson's, menu, ice cream cov **1.00**
Howard Johnson's, waitress doll, vinyl head and
    arms, plastic body, black painted eyes, waitress
    uniform, houndstooth check dress, apron, 11½" h **15.00**
Kentucky Fried Chicken, frisbee, plastic, red, white
    Colonel dec. **2.50**
Kentucky Fried Chicken, nodder, Colonel, 7" h **15.00**
Little Caesars, Nerf Pepperoni Flyer with wings, game
    card, 1993. . . . . **5.00**
Long John Silver's, book, *The Gingerbread Man*,
    Ladybird Well–Loved Tales, illus, 3 x 4½" **5.00**
Pizza Hut, hand puppet, latex, Land Before Time,
    Duckie, 1988. . . . . **5.00**
Pizza Hut, magic kit, Aladdin, paper tricks, instruc-
    tion book, and storage box, 1993 . . . . **5.00**
Pizza Hut, placemat, Garfield, 1992. . . . . **2.50**
Pizza Hut, puzzle, Beauty and the Beast, dance scene . . . **5.00**
Pizza Hut, sunglasses, Back to the Future, 1989 . . . . **5.00**
Roy Rogers, figure, Gumby, rubber, 6" h **5.00**
Roy Rogers, sand mold, elephant head lid, red, 1986 . . . . **5.00**
Sambo, doll, rubber, mkd "©1972 Kings Import
    Spain," 5" h **8.00**
Sambo, hand puppet, plastic, Mother Tiger with spat-
    ula in hand **1.50**
Taco Bell, comic book, Casper, Harvey Comics, 1992 . . . . **10.00**
Taco Bell, hand puppet, paper, African Wild, lion,
    1991 . . . . **2.50**
Taco Bell, shirt, Bullwinkle, mail–in offer, 1993. . . . . **5.00**
Wendy's, car, Speed Bumper, pull back, 1992 . . . . **2.50**
Wendy's, doll, cloth, 11½" h **8.00**
Wendy's, hand puppet, plastic . . . . **.75**
Wendy's, mug, ceramic, red, white, and black design,
    3⅞" h **4.00**
Wendy's, paint with water book, Black Beauty **5.00**
Wendy's, pen, Speed Writer, figural car, pull off racer
    front to reveal pen, 1991 . . . . **2.50**

FENTON GLASS

The Fenton Art Glass Company, founded by Frank L. Fenton in 1905 in Martins Ferry, Ohio, originally offered decorating services to other manufacturers. By 1907 the company had relocated to Williamstown, West Virginia, and was making its own glass.

The company's first products included carnival, chocolate, custard, and opalescent glass. Art glass and stretch glass products were introduced in the 1920s. Production of slag glass began in the 1930s. Decorating techniques ranged from acid etching to hand painting.

Through the 1970s, Fenton marked its products with a variety of paper labels. The company adopted an oval raised trademark in 1970. Recently a date code has been added to the mark.

References: Robert E. Eaton, Jr. (comp.), *Fenton Glass: The First Twenty–Five Years Comprehensive Price Guide 1995,* Glass Press, 1995; Robert E. Eaton, Jr. (comp.), *Fenton Glass: The Second Twenty–Five Years Comprehensive Price Guide 1995,* Glass Press, 1995; Fenton Art Glass Collectors of America (comp.), *Fenton Glass: The Third Twenty–Five Years Comprehensive Price Guide 1995,* Glass Press, 1995; William Heacock, *Fenton Glass: The First Twenty–Five Years,* O–Val Advertising Corp., [Antique Publications], 1978; William Heacock, *Fenton Glass: The Second Twenty–Five Years,* O–Val Advertising Corp., [Antique Publications], 1980, William Heacock, *Fenton Glass: The Third Twenty–Five Years,* O–Val Advertising Corp., [Antique Publications], 1989; James Measell (ed.), *Fenton Glass: The 1980s Decade,* Glass Press, 1996; Margaret and Kenn Whitmeyer, *Fenton Art Glass, 1907–1939: Identification and Value Guide,* Collector Books, 1996.

Periodical: *Glass Messenger,* 700 Elizabeth St, Williamstown, WV 26187.

Collectors' Clubs: Fenton Art Glass Collectors Of America, Inc, PO Box 384, Williamstown, WV 26187; National Fenton Glass Society, PO Box 4008, Marietta, OH 45750.

Bubble Optic, vase, #1359, 11½" h, coral	$ 140.00
Butterfly, bonbon, #8230, rosalene	40.00
Cactus, basket, #3439, 9" h, topaz opalescent	150.00
Cactus, compote, #3422, topaz opalescent	135.00
Cactus, vase, #3454, 5" h, topaz opalescent	30.00
Coin Dot, basket, #1437, 7" h, cranberry opalescent	80.00

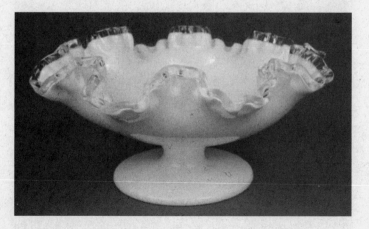

Silver Crest, low footed comport, #7329, $35.00.

Coin Dot, bowl, #1438, 8½" d, cranberry opalescent	60.00
Coin Dot, vase, #1454, 4½" h, topaz opalescent	50.00
Coin Dot, vase, #1459, 8" h, cranberry opalescent	75.00
Currier & Ives, light, #8409, crystal velvet	30.00
Grape & Cable, tobacco jar, #9188, blue marble	110.00
Hobnail, basket, oval, #3839, 12", plum opalescent	180.00
Hobnail, bonbon, #3937, 7" h, milk glass	15.00
Hobnail, candleholders, pr, #3870, cranberry opalescent	130.00
Hobnail, candy jar, ftd, #3887, green opalescent	45.00
Hobnail, nut dish, #3650, colonial amber	8.00
Hobnail, planter, #3779, 10" h, black	20.00
Hobnail, salt and pepper shakers, pr, #3602, milk glass	30.00
Hobnail, tumbler, #3947, 12 oz, cranberry opalescent	35.00
Jacqueline, vase, #9156, 6" h, pink opaline	60.00
Poppy, student lamp, #9107, 20" h, ruby	150.00
Roses, comport, #9222, colonial green	15.00
Spanish Lace, bell, #3567, decorated violets	30.00
Thumbprint, salt and pepper shakers, pr, #4409, colonial blue	35.00
Valencia, lighter, #8399, orange	15.00
Water Lily, bud vase, #8456, lavender satin	35.00
Water Lily, cake plate, #8410, 12½" d, crystal velvet	50.00

FIESTA

Homer Laughlin began production of its Fiesta line in 1936. Frederick Rhead was the designer. Concentric bands of rings were the only decorative motif besides color. Dark blue, light green, ivory, red, and yellow were the first five colors. Turquoise followed a year later.

Fiesta was restyled in 1969. Antique gold, turf green, and mango red (really the old red retitled) were introduced. These changes were not enough to save Fiesta. Production ceased in 1973.

Wishing to capitalize on the tremendous secondary market interest in Fiesta, Homer Laughlin reintroduced Fiesta in 1986. Several new colors made their appearance at that time.

Reference: Sharon and Bob Huxford, *The Collectors Encyclopedia of Fiesta with Harlequin and Riviera, Seventh Edition,* Collector Books, 1992, 1996 value update.

Collectors' Clubs: Fiesta Club of America, PO Box 15383, Loves Park, IL 61132; Fiesta Collectors Club, PO Box 361280, Strongsville, OH 44136.

Ashtray, gray	$ 65.00
Ashtray, turquoise	30.00
Cake Server, red, Kitchen Kraft	150.00
Candlesticks, pr, bulb, cobalt blue	100.00
Candlesticks, pr, bulb, red	125.00
Candlesticks, pr, tripod, cobalt blue	850.00
Candlesticks, pr, tripod, turquoise	650.00
Carafe, cobalt blue	325.00
Carafe, red	300.00
Carafe, turquoise	250.00
Casserole, cov, chartreuse	250.00
Casserole, ivory	125.00
Chop Plate, 13" d, cobalt blue	65.00

Chop Plate, 13" d, medium green 275.00
Chop Plate, 13" d, rose 50.00
Coffeepot, cov, cobalt blue 175.00
Coffeepot, cov, yellow 100.00
Compote, 12" d, green 125.00
Compote, 12" d, ivory 200.00
Creamer, ring handle, gray 30.00
Creamer, ring handle, medium green 75.00
Creamer, stick handle, turquoise 95.00
Creamer, stick handle, yellow 30.00
Cream Soup, dark green 60.00
Cream Soup, red 75.00
Cup and Saucer, cobalt blue 30.00
Cup and Saucer, green 20.00
Cup and Saucer, yellow 25.00
Demitasse Pot, red 500.00
Dessert Bowl, 6" d, ivory 30.00
Dessert Bowl, 6" d, red 40.00
Eggcup, chartreuse 125.00
Eggcup, yellow 45.00
Fork, cobalt blue, Kitchen Kraft 175.00
Fork, green, Kitchen Kraft 85.00
Fruit Bowl, 4³/₄" d, medium green 500.00
Fruit Bowl, 5¹/₂" d, chartreuse 25.00
Fruit Bowl, 4³/₄" d, dark green 25.00
Fruit Bowl, 5³/₄" d, medium green 450.00
Fruit Bowl, 11³/₄" d, yellow 325.00
Gravy Boat, green 25.00
Gravy Boat, red 65.00
Jug, 2 pt, green 55.00
Jug, 2 pt, turquoise 45.00
Jug, 3 pt, ivory 65.00
Juice Pitcher, gray 2,200.00
Juice Pitcher, yellow 55.00
Juice Tumbler, cobalt blue 45.00
Juice Tumbler, green 30.00
Juice Tumbler, ivory 45.00
Mixing Bowl, #1, green 200.00
Mixing Bowl, #1, red 225.00

Mixing Bowl, #1, turquoise 225.00
Mixing Bowl, #2, cobalt blue 175.00
Mixing Bowl, #2, yellow 95.00
Mixing Bowl, #3, cobalt blue 145.00
Mixing Bowl, #3, green 115.00
Mixing Bowl, #4, cobalt blue 175.00
Mixing Bowl, #4, green 125.00
Mixing Bowl, #4, ivory 200.00
Mixing Bowl, #4, yellow 125.00
Mixing Bowl, #5, green 175.00
Mixing Bowl, #5, turquoise 175.00
Mixing Bowl, #6, yellow 225.00
Mixing Bowl, #7, green 325.00
Mug, ivory 75.00
Nappy, 5¹/₂", chartreuse 32.00
Nappy, 5¹/₂", dark green 32.00
Nappy, 5¹/₂", medium green 110.00
Nappy, 5¹/₂", red 30.00
Nappy, 5¹/₂", rose 32.00
Nappy, 5¹/₂", turquoise 30.00
Nappy, 8¹/₂" d, ivory 35.00
Nappy, 8¹/₂" d, medium green 125.00
Onion Soup, cov, ivory 750.00
Onion Soup, cov, red 750.00
Onion Soup, cov, yellow 600.00
Pitcher, disc, chartreuse 225.00
Pitcher, disc, turquoise 100.00
Plate, bread and butter, 6" d, chartreuse 8.00
Plate, bread and butter, 6" d, gray 8.00
Plate, bread and butter, 6" d, medium green 25.00
Plate, bread and butter, 6" d, yellow 3.00
Plate, dinner, 10" d, cobalt blue 35.00
Plate, dinner, 10" d, green 20.00
Plate, dinner, 10" d, ivory 32.00
Plate, dinner, 10" d, turquoise 30.00
Plate, dinner, 10" d, yellow 20.00
Plate, grill, 12" d, red 40.00
Plate, grill, 12" d, yellow 35.00
Plate, luncheon, 9" d, chartreuse 15.00
Plate, luncheon, 9" d, gray 15.00
Plate, luncheon, 9" d, ivory 15.00
Plate, luncheon, 9" d, red 20.00
Plate, salad, 7" d, cobalt blue 8.00
Plate, salad, 7" d, ivory 9.00
Plate, salad, 7" d, medium green 35.00
Platter, medium green 110.00
Relish, cobalt blue center, green, ivory, red, and yel-
   low side dishes 350.00
Salt and Pepper Shakers, pr, light green 15.00
Salt and Pepper Shakers, pr, medium green 175.00
Sauce Boat, turquoise 30.00
Soup Plate, flat, yellow 30.00
Spoon, red, Kitchen Kraft 95.00
Stack Set, cobalt blue 35.00
Sugar, cov, individual size, yellow 125.00
Sugar, cov, ring handle, rose 35.00
Teapot, cobalt blue, large 200.00
Vase, 8" h, ivory 750.00
Vase, 10" h, ivory 975.00
Vase, 12" h, ivory 1,125.00
Water Tumbler, cobalt blue 65.00

Teapot, red, large, $200.00.

FIGURAL PLANTERS & VASES

Initially collected as a form by individuals collecting products of a specific maker, figural planters evolved as a collecting category unto itself in the mid–1990s. Figural baby planters are a major subcategory. Lady head vases command their own category.

The category is still in the process of defining itself. Most generic examples and pieces whose design and shape do not speak to a specific time period have little value. Crossover collectors, especially those seeking animal, black, and vehicle images, skew value.

References: Kathleen Deel, *Figural Planters*, Schiffer Publishing, 1996; Betty and Bill Newbound, *Collector's Encyclopedia of Figural Planter & Vases: Identification & Values*, Collector Books, 1997.

Note: Refer to specific manufacturers for additional listings.

Bud Vase, butterfly, Shawnee, #735	$ 15.00
Planter, baby and pillow, blue, Hull, #92	35.00
Planter, baby scale, McCoy	80.00
Planter, baby shoes, aqua, McCoy	12.00
Planter, bird, Sorcha Boru, 5" l	85.00
Planter, blackamoor, gold trim, Brayton Laguna	85.00
Planter, Bugs Bunny, late 1940s	75.00
Planter, bunny with carrot, matte white, McCoy	65.00
Planter, cactus and sleeping Mexican, Abingdon, #600	85.00
Planter, canoe, Red Wing	25.00
Planter, canopy bed, Sahwnee, #734	85.00
Planter, carriage, Metlox	40.00
Planter, Christmas mouse, Josef Originals	45.00
Planter, clown riding pig, McCoy	30.00
Planter, cockatoo, Maddux	40.00
Planter, cradle, pink, McCoy	25.00
Planter, dachshund, Weller, 8½" h	60.00
Planter, daffodil, Abingdon, #668D	35.00
Planter, Davy Crockett, American Bisque	40.00
Planter, deer and log, American Art Potteries	20.00
Planter, doe and fawn, Shawnee, #669	15.00

Vase, chrysanthemums, McCoy, late 1940s, 8¼" h, $10.00.

Planter, dog and cart, McCoy	30.00
Planter, dog wearing bowtie, Midwest Potteries	15.00
Planter, Donald Duck, Leeds	65.00
Planter, donkey pulling cart, Occupied Japan, 4¾" l	12.00
Planter, duck, American Art Potteries, 5½" h	15.00
Planter, duck, McCoy	40.00
Planter, duck and rabbit, Weller	60.00
Planter, duckling, Kay Finch	40.00
Planter, elephant, Camark	60.00
Planter, elephant, Hull	35.00
Planter, fawn, Brad Keeler	65.00
Planter, fish, American Art Potteries, 5" h	15.00
Planter, fish, Maddux	30.00
Planter, flamingo, Maddux	40.00
Planter, girl, Kay Finch	100.00
Planter, girl and wolfhounds, Brayton Laguna	95.00
Planter, girl at fence, Shawnee #581	7.50
Planter, girl holding kitten, De Lee Art	90.00
Planter, girl with bonnet and basket, Brayton Laguna	65.00
Planter, gondola, pink and yellow, Gonder	25.00
Planter, goose, Weller	45.00
Planter, grist mill, green, Shawnee, #769	15.00
Planter, horse head, Maddux, 12" h	30.00
Planter, kitten and yarn, yellow, Royal Copley	30.00
Planter, lady, June, Florence Ceramics	30.00
Planter, lady reading book, Hedi Schoop	60.00
Planter, lamb, Hull	45.00
Planter, lion, yellow, Midwest Potteries	15.00
Planter, love birds, Maddux	45.00
Planter, Madonna and Child, Haeger	15.00
Planter, mammy, Japan, c1930	30.00
Planter, Miss Piggy, Sigma	25.00
Planter, oriental girl, Ceramic Arts Studio	15.00
Planter, orientals carrying basket, Shawnee, #537	5.00
Planter, pheasant, Brad Keeler	75.00
Planter, piano, Shawnee, #528	20.00
Planter, poodle, Hull	95.00
Planter, puppy, Red Wing	20.00
Planter, puppy in boat, gold trim, Shawnee, #736	50.00

Planter, baby holding football, Ardco, 5½" h, $8.00.

Planter, roadster, gold trim, Shawnee, #506. . . . . 35.00
Planter, rocking chair, green, McCoy 20.00
Planter, rocking horse, pink, Shawnee, #526. . . . . 25.00
Planter, rolling pin, Camark, N1–51 . . . . 10.00
Planter, Scottie dog, Japan, 4" h 18.00
Planter, shoe, Brayton Laguna. 25.00
Planter, sprinkling can, white, rose decal, McCoy 7.50
Planter, squirrel, Rosemeade 30.00
Planter, stork and bassinet, aqua, McCoy 45.00
Planter, swan, glossy black, Maddux. 125.00
Planter, swan, Gonder, E–44. . . . . 25.00
Planter, swan, lime green, Hull, #69 . . . . 35.00
Planter, swan, McCoy 15.00
Planter, swan, Stangl, #5033, 6³/₄" h 20.00
Planter, turtle, Brush 10.00
Planter, wheelbarrow, Brayton Laguna 35.00
Planter, zebra, Occupied Japan 10.00
Vase, butterfly, McCoy, 6" h 40.00
Vase, cornucopia, green and brown, Gonder, H–14,
   10" h 25.00
Vase, cowboy boots, McCoy 40.00
Vase, doe, Rosemeade 30.00
Vase, donkey and basket, Shawnee, #722 . . . . 25.00
Vase, dove, yellow, Shawnee, #829 . . . . 30.00
Vase, fan, Pacific Clay, #3401. 25.00
Vase, fan, white, Abingdon. 20.00
Vase, flying bird, Frankoma 25.00
Vase, gazelle, Haeger, 15" h 25.00
Vase, Polynesian, Catalina, #378 . . . . 150.00
Vase, Poppet Head, Metlox 45.00
Vase, rearing stallion, Sascha Brastoff, 9¹/₂" h. 95.00
Vase, squirrel, Haeger 45.00
Vase, swan, green, McCoy, #7, 9" h 40.00
Vase, urn and leaf, pink, Gonder, H–80, 6" h 40.00

FIGURINES

Figurines played a major role in the household decorating decor between the late 1930s and the early 1960s. Those with deep pockets bought Boehm, Lladro, and Royal Doulton. The average consumer was content with generic fare, much of it inexpensive imports, or examples from a host of California figurine manufacturers such as Kay Finch and Florence ceramics.

   Animals were the most popular theme. Human forms came next. Subject matter and the ability of a piece to speak the decorative motifs of a specific time period are as important as manufacturer in determining value.

Note: Refer to specific manufacturers and animal categories for additional listings.

Angel, #4803, Kay Finch . . . . $ 90.00
Angelfish, amber, Viking, 6¹/₂" h 30.00
Bird, crystal satin, Cambridge, 2³/₄" l. 25.00
Birds, pr, #825–6, green glaze, Kay Finch 150.00
Booties, light blue, sq base, 3" h 12.00
Bucking Bronco, Royal Haeger, 13" h 150.00
Buddha, amber, Cambridge, 5¹/₂" h. 225.00
Bull, Royal Haeger, 6¹/₂" h 225.00
Cat, electric blue carnival, Fenton, 11" h 60.00
Cat, Royal Copley, 8" h 25.00

Cat, custard satin,
Fenton, #5165, $15.00.

Chickens, pr, Royal Windsor. 25.00
Choir Boy, kneeling, #211, Kay Finch, 5¹/₂" h 120.00
Cockatoo, Royal Copley, 7¹/₄" h 25.00
Cocker Spaniel, brown, black tail, Royal Haeger, 3" h 45.00
Deer on Sled, Royal Copley, 6¹/₂" h. 22.00
Donkey with Cart, blue, Royal Haeger, 3" h 15.00
Draped Lady, Cambridge, 8¹/₂" h. 60.00
Duck, caramel slag, Imperial Glass, 4¹/₂" h 40.00
Egg, #6010, Kay Finch 85.00
Egyptian Cat, mandarin orange, Royal Haeger,
   15¹/₂" h. 110.00
Elephant, caramel slag, Imperial, 4" h. 50.00
Fawn, sitting, crystal, Haley, 6" h 12.00
Fish, amber, Royal Haeger, 4" h 85.00
Girl with Goose, blue, L. E. Smith, 8" h 55.00
Greyhound, gun metal, Royal Haeger, 9" h. 50.00
Guppy, #173, Kay Finch, 1¹/₂ x 8¹/₂". 60.00
Gypsy Girl, brown and green, Royal Haeger, 16¹/₂" h. 80.00
Hen, red, green and black accents, Royal Haeger,
   11" h. 45.00
Horse, Royal Haeger, 5¹/₂" h. 35.00
Hunter, crystal, New Martinsville, 7³/₈" h 80.00
Jumping Horse, crystal, Haley, 9¹/₂ x 7¹/₂" 50.00
Leopard, chartreuse, Royal Haeger, 7³/₄" h 50.00
Madonna, crystal, Fostoria, 10" h 50.00
Mermaid, crystal, Fostoria, 11¹/₂" h 120.00
Panther, ebony, Royal Haeger, 24¹/₂ x 4³/₄". 75.00
Pelican, amber, Fostoria 40.00
Pheasant, green agate, Royal Haeger, 6" h. 30.00
Rabbit, light blue, Fostoria, 1¹/₄" h. 15.00
Rabbit, wearing flower hat, Kay Finch, 6" h. 125.00
Rooster, frosted satin, L. E. Smith, 2¹/₄" h 10.00
Scottie, crystal, Heisey, 3" h 75.00
Seal with Ball, crystal, New Martinsville, 7" h 55.00
Squirrel, frosted satin, L. E. Smith, 4¹/₂" h. 12.00
Teddy Bear, Royal Copley, 5¹/₂" h 35.00
Terrier, amethyst carnival, Imperial, 3¹/₂" h. 40.00
Terrier, #5926, orange matte glaze, Kay Finch, 6¹/₂" h . . . 125.00
Wild Goose, white matte glaze, Royal Haeger, 6¹/₂" h 15.00
Wren, Spaulding, 6¹/₄" h. 15.00

FINCH, KAY

After over a decade of ceramic studies, Kay Finch, assisted by her husband Braden, opened her commercial studio in 1939. A whimsical series of pig figurines and hand–decorated banks were the company's first successful products.

An expanded studio and showroom, located on the Pacific Coast Highway in Corona del Mar, opened on December 7,1941. The business soon had 40 employees as it produced a wide variety of items, e.g., ashtrays, bath accessories, bowls, figurines, planters, and vases. A line of dog figurines and themed items were introduced in the 1940s. Christmas plates were made from 1950 until 1962.

When Braden died in 1963, Kay Finch ceased operations. Freeman–McFarlin Potteries purchased the molds in the mid–1970s and commissioned Finch to model a new series of dog figurines. Production of these continued through the late 1970s.

References: Frances Finch Webb and Jack R. Webb, *The New Kay Finch Identification Guide,* published by authors, 1996; Devin Frick, Jean Frick and Richard Martinez, *Collectible Kay Finch,* Collector Books, 1997; Mike Nickel and Cindy Horvath, *Kay Finch: Art Pottery,* Schiffer Publishing, 1997.

Ashtray, seashell shape, #462	$ 50.00
Ashtray, swan, #4958, pink, 4½" l	50.00
Ashtray, Yorkshire illus center, #5332	50.00
Bell, #6056, white, gold, red bow, 4" h.	75.00
Cereal Bowl, #506, handled, "For a good boy"	50.00
Figure, Afghan with angel wings, #4911	150.00
Figure, Afghan, #5553	200.00
Figure, angel, #140a	125.00
Figure, bear, #5004, one eye open, other closed, 4" h	150.00
Figure, begging poodle, #5262	250.00
Figure, camel, #464, detailed design.	200.00
Figure, cat, "Jezzy," #5302	125.00
Figure, donkey, #135, dec and detailed mane	75.00
Figure, duck, #5006, white and green	75.00
Figure, girl, "PJ," #5002	125.00
Figure, lamb, standing on hind legs, #109	50.00
Figure, rabbit, "Cuddles," #4623, 11" h.	325.00

Figure, Airedale, red and black, AKC Dog Show, #4832, $200.00.

Figure, sitting elephant, #5304, black and white, 4" h	125.00
Figure, skunks, #4774 and #4775, brown and white, price for pair	300.00
Figure, squirrels, #108, brown and white, price for pair	125.00
Figure, Yorkie pups, #170 and #171, price for pair.	400.00
Mug, gold outlined holly dec	50.00
Mug, Santa Claus, #4950, white, gold, 4" h	50.00
Pin, Afghan head, gold and white, #5081	150.00
Plate, poinsettia, c1960	75.00
Plate, rooster, #4757, hp, Buffet ware	40.00
Plate, salad, #5381, vegetable designs	45.00
Salt and Pepper Shakers, pr, horse heads.	125.00
Salt and Pepper Shakers, pr, pigs, #131, floral design.	50.00
Stein, marlin handle.	150.00
Stein, Poodle handle, #5458.	125.00
Wall Plaque, eagle, #5904, white, 16" w	75.00
Wall Plaque, Santa Claus, #5373	200.00
Wall Plaque, seahorse, #5788, 16" h	75.00

FIREARMS & ACCESSORIES

Many Americans own firearms, whether a .22 plunking rifle or pistol or a 12–gauge shotgun for hunting. The vast majority were inexpensive when purchased, bought for use and not investment, and have only minor secondary value in today's market. Many firearms sold on the secondary market are purchased for reuse purposes.

Recent federal statutes have placed restrictions on the buying and selling of certain handguns and rifles on the secondary market. Check with your local police department to make certain you are in compliance with state and federal laws before attempting to sell any weapon.

Collecting interest in firearm advertising, prints, ammunition boxes, and other firearm accessories has increased significantly in the last decade. Auctioneers such as Dixie Sporting Collectibles (1206 Rama Road, Charlotte, NC 28211) and Langs (31R Turtle Cove, Raymond, ME 04071) hold several specialized catalog sales each year in this field.

References: Robert H. Balderson, *The Official Price Guide To Antique and Modern Firearms, Eighth Edition,* House of Collectibles, 1996; Robert H. Balderson, *The Official Price Guide to Collector Handguns, Fifth Edition,* House of Collectibles, 1996; Russell and Steve Quetermous, *Modern Guns Identification & Values, Eleventh Edition,* Collector Books, 1997; Ned Schwing, *Standard Catalog of Firearms, 7th Edition,* Krause Publications, 1997.

Periodicals: *Gun List,* 700 E State St, Iola, WI 54990; *Military Trader,* PO Box 1050, Dubuque, IA 52004; *The Gun Report,* PO Box 38, Aledo, IL 61231.

Note: Prices are for firearms in very good condition.

Advertising Cover, envelope, Remington UMC, color, flying turkey and 2 shells, 1930s	$ 50.00
Ammunition, Haerens Ammunitions Arsenal, 1956	15.00
Ammunition, Remington, 20 gauge, #6 shot size	15.00
Ammunition, Winchester, 45–70, 2–pc box, full, mkd "Carbine Ball Cartridges, Reloading," paper label	30.00

Target Pistol, Colt Woodsman, .22 caliber, semi–automatic, magazine, $300.00.

Ammunition, Winchester, Ranger, Super Trap Load, 20 gauge, man pointing rifle on front **100.00**

Booklet, *Colt Guns*, illus, sgd and inscribed by Joe Bodrie, "The Fastest Gun Alive," c1950, 44 pgs **30.00**

Box, Winchester, wooden shipping crate, dovetailed construction, c1920, 16½ x 11 x 33" **250.00**

Brochure, Weaver Telescope Sights, W. R. Weaver Co, El Paso, TX, sights for target and hunting rifles, illus, c1950, 10 pgs **30.00**

Calendar, The Peters Cartridge Company, color, 1930, 20 x 40". **375.00**

Catalog, Kennedy Bros Arms Co, Spring and Summer 1933, #154, fishing and hunting goods, 96 pgs **40.00**

Catalog, Colt Revolves and Automatic Pistols, Colt's Patent Fire Arms Mfg Co, Hartford, CT, 1929, 36 pgs, with price list **90.00**

Catalog, Modern Firearms and Ammunition, Remington Arms Co, New York, NY, 1923, 190 pgs . . . **100.00**

Catalog, Robert Abels Antique Firearms and Edged Weapons, #29, 1950s. **25.00**

Display, Remington Arms, heavy cardboard standup, color, 1968 . . . . **35.00**

Handgun, Beretta Cougar, semi–automatic, exposed hammer, 7–shot clip magazine, 3½" barrel, chrome finish, plastic grips, 6" l **200.00**

Handgun, Beretta Model 70S, semi–automatic, exposed hammer, 3½" barrel, fixed sight, blued finish, 2–pc wraparound plastic grip, 6¼" l **200.00**

Handgun, Beretta Tomcat 3000, semi–automatic, 7–shot magazine clip, 2½" barrel, matte finish, wood grips, 5" l **150.00**

Handgun, Colt Viper, 38 Special, 6–shot cylinder, 4" barrel, nickel finish, checkered walnut grips, 8⅝" l **180.00**

Handgun, Dan Wesson, Model 738P, 38 Special, single action, 5–shot swing–out cylinder, 2" fixed barrel, stainless steel finish, wooden grips, 6½" l **160.00**

Handgun, Ruger Standard Automatic, semi–automatic, concealed hammer, 9–shot magazine clip, Partridge–type front sight, dovetail rear, hard rubber grips, 10" l **150.00**

Handgun, Sheridan Knockabout, single action, exposed hammer, 5½" barrel, checkered plastic grips, 6¾" l **110.00**

Holster, Braeur, tooled leather, single loop, strap lined, brass snaps, for Smith & Wesson 4" revolver. . . . **200.00**

Letterhead, Laften & Taylor, Gun and Locksmith, Jacksonville, FL, orange illus, 1927 . . . . **18.00**

Poster, Remington Guns and Ammunition, 1930s **90.00**

Rifle, Browning Model 52 Ltd Edition, bolt action, adjustable trigger, 5–shot magazine, detachable box, 24" barrel, checkered high grade walnut stock, rosewood fore–end **280.00**

Rifle, Browning Model BPR, hammerless, slide action, slide release on trigger guard, blued barrel, adjustable sights, checkered walnut pistol grip stock and slide handle **150.00**

Rifle, Remington, Model 591, 5mm Remington rim fire, bolt action, 4–shot removable clip, 24" barrel, Monte Carlo plain 1 pc hardwood pistol grip and forearm **140.00**

Rifle, Winchester, Model 55, single shot, 22" barrel, wooden 1 pc semi–pistol grip **70.00**

Rifle, Winchester Western Field Model 846, semi–automatic, 15–shot tubular magazine, 18½" barrel, checkered wood 1 pc pistol grip **75.00**

Shotgun, Remington Model 17, 20 gauge, hammerless, 3–shot tubular magazine, 26–32" steel barrel **225.00**

Shotgun, Remington Model 29, 12 gauge, hammerless, slide action, 26–32" steel barrel, checkered walnut pistol grip stock. **250.00**

Shotgun, Remington Model 870 Deer Gun, 12 gauge, 26" barrel, adjustable sights **200.00**

Shotgun, Remington Model 870 Express, 20 gauge, hammerless, slide action, 4–shot tubular, checkered hardwood pistol grip stock and forearm **150.00**

Shotgun, Remington Model 870 SA Skeet, 25" barrel, skeet choke, ventilated rib, recoil pad **250.00**

Shotgun, Remington Model 870 Wingmaster Field Gun, 20 gauge, hammerless, slide action, 4–shot tubular magazine, checkered walnut pistol grip stock, matching side handle, recoil pad. **250.00**

Shotgun, Remington Model 870 Youth Gun, 20 gauge, 21" barrel, ventilated rib **175.00**

Shotgun, Remington Model 878 Automaster, 12 gauge, semi–automatic, gas operated, hammerless, 2–shot tubular magazine, 26–30" barrel, blued, plain walnut pistol grip stock and forearm **200.00**

Shotgun, Remington Peerless, 12 gauge **850.00**

Shotgun, Smith & Wesson Model 916, 12 gauge, slide action, hammerless, 5–shot tubular, 20" cylinder bore barrel, satin finish receiver, walnut semi–pistol grip stock, grooved slide handle **150.00**

Shotgun, Smith & Wesson Model 1000, 12 gauge, semi–automatic, 3–shot tubular action, engraved alloy receiver, checkered walnut pistol grip stock and forearm **275.00**

Shotgun, Smith & Wesson Model 1000 Waterfowler, 12 gauge, steel receiver, dull oil finish stock, 30" full choke barrel, Parkerized finish, camouflage sling **300.00**

Shotgun, Winchester Model, 1200 Deer, 22" barrel, rifle sights **175.00**

Shotgun, Winchester Model 1200 Skeet, 12 gauge, 26" skeet choke, ventilated rib barrel. **175.00**

Shotgun, Winchester Model 1300 Winchoke, 12 gauge, hammerless, slide action, 4–shot tubular, 26" barrel, ventilated rib, checkered walnut straight grip stock and slide handle, recoil pad. **175.00**

FIRE–KING

Fire–King is an Anchor Hocking product. Anchor Hocking resulted from the 1937 merger of the Anchor Cap Company and Hocking Glass Corporation, each of which had been involved in several previous mergers.

Oven–proof Fire–King glass was made between 1942 and 1976. It came in a variety of patterns, e.g., Alice, Fleurette, Game Bird, Honeysuckle, Laurel, Swirl, and Wheat, and body colors, e.g., azurite, forest green, jadeite, peach luster, ruby red, and white. Non–decorated utilitarian pieces also were made.

Housewives liked Fire–King because the line included matching dinnerware and ovenware. Anchor Hocking's marketing strategy included the aggressive sale of starter sets.

Anchor Hocking used two methods to mark Fire–King—a mark molded directly on the piece and an oval foil paper label.

References: Gene Florence, *Collectible Glassware From The 40's, 50's, 60's, An Illustrated Value Guide, Third Edition,* Collector Books, 1996; Gene Florence, *Kitchen Glassware of the Depression Years, Fifth Edition,* Collector Books, 1995; Gary Kilgo et al., *A Collectors Guide To Anchor Hocking's Fire–King Glassware,* K & W Collectibles Publisher, 1991; April M. Tvorak, *Fire–King, Fifth Edition,* published by author, 1997.

Newsletter: *The Fire–King News,* PO Box 473, Addison, AL 35540.

Collectors' Club: The Fire–King Collectors Club, 1161 Woodrow St, #3, Redwood City, CA 94061.

Alice, cup, white. . . . . **$ 5.00**
Alice, cup, white, blue rim. **10.00**
Alice, plate, white, red rim. **22.00**
Alice, saucer, jadeite **5.00**
Blue Mosaic, creamer **5.00**
Blue Mosaic, cup **5.00**
Blue Mosaic, dinner plate, 10" d **5.00**
Blue Mosaic, saucer **2.00**
Blue Mosaic, soup bowl. **8.00**
Blue Mosaic, vegetable bowl **8.00**

Kitchenware, batter bowl, jadeite, 7¹/₂" d, $20.00.

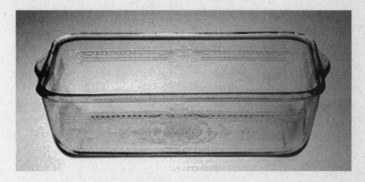

Oven Glass, deep loaf pan, sapphire blue, 9¹/₈" l, $20.00.

Bubble, bowl, 4" d. **5.00**
Bubble, creamer, white **2.50**
Bubble, fruit bowl, blue **15.00**
Bubble, grill plate, 9¹/₄" blue. **20.00**
Bubble, salad plate, 7" d, blue **5.00**
Bubble, soup bowl, blue **15.00**
Bubble, vegetable bowl, blue. **18.00**
Charm, bowl, 4³/₄" d, green **5.00**
Charm, bowl, 4³/₄" d, red **8.00**
Charm, creamer, azurite. **8.00**
Charm, cup and saucer, red **12.00**
Charm, dinner plate, 9¹/₄" d, jadeite **25.00**
Charm, luncheon plate, 8³/₈" d, green **5.50**
Charm, platter, 11 x 8", green. **25.00**
Charm, salad bowl, 7³/₈" d, green **12.50**
Charm, salad plate, 6⁵/₈" d, jadeite **5.00**
Charm, soup bowl, 6" d, jadeite **15.00**
Charm, sugar, azurite. **8.00**
Jane Ray, cereal bowl, jadeite. **15.00**
Jane Ray, cup and saucer, jadeite **4.00**
Jane Ray, dessert, jadeite **5.00**
Jane Ray, dinner plate, jadeite **8.00**
Jane Ray, vegetable, jadeite **15.00**
Kitchenware, batter bowl, white, hp floral dec **20.00**
Kitchenware, condiment set, cruet and salt and pepper shakers, Red Dots. **20.00**
Kitchenware, nested mixing bowls, beaded rim, #5, #6, and #7. . . . . **50.00**
Kitchenware, range set, grease jar, and salt and pepper shakers, Tulips **60.00**
Kitchenware, refrigerator dish, jadeite base, clear lid, 4 x 8" **17.50**
Peach Lustre, bowl, 4⁷/₈" d **4.00**
Peach Lustre, cup and saucer **6.00**
Peach Lustre, salad plate, 7¹/₂" h **2.50**
Philbe, bowl, 4³/₈" d, blue **15.00**
Philbe, casserole, cov, blue, 1 pt **15.00**
Philbe, custard cup, 5 oz, blue. **2.50**
Philbe, loaf pan, 5 x 9", blue **22.00**
Philbe, measuring cup, blue, 1 spout **15.00**
Philbe, refrigerator jar, cov, 5 x 9", blue **32.00**
Philbe, utility pan, 6¹/₂ x 10¹/₂", blue **12.00**
Shell, cereal bowl, jadeite **12.50**
Shell, fruit bowl, jadeite. **8.00**
Shell, serving bowl, luster **12.00**
Shell, soup plate, flat, jadeite **30.00**

Sunburst, pitcher, white 8.00
Sunburst, tumbler, flat, white 4.00
Swirl, cereal bowl, golden shell 5.00
Swirl, creamer and sugar, open, golden shell 5.50
Swirl, dinner plate, 9" d, pink. 8.00
Swirl, platter, golden shell 10.00
Swirl, vegetable, golden shell. 8.00
Turquoise, berry bowl, 4½" d 8.00
Turquoise, creamer 8.00
Turquoise, mug, 8 oz 12.00
Turquoise, sugar 6.00

FISHER–PRICE

Irving L. Price, a retired F. W. Woolworth executive, Herman G. Fisher, previously with Alderman–Fairchild Toy Company, and Helen M. Schelle, a former toy store owner, founded Fisher–Price Toys in 1930. The company was headquartered in East Aurora, New York. Margaret Evans Price, a writer and illustrator of children's books and wife of Irving Price, was the company's first artist and designer.

Toys made prior to 1962 are marked with a black and white rectangular logo. Plastic was introduced for the first time in 1949.

The company remained in private hands until acquired by the Quaker Oats Company in 1969.

Reference: John J. Murray and Bruce R. Fox, *Fisher–Price, 1931–1963: A Historical, Rarity, Value Guide,* Books Americana, Krause Publications, 1991.

Collectors' Club: Fisher–Price Collectors Club, 1442 N Ogden, Mesa, AZ 85205.

Note: All toys listed are in good condition.

Allie Gator, #653 . . . . $ 80.00
Baby Chick Tandem Cart, #50 . . . . 75.00
Barky Dog, #462 . . . . 95.00
Bossy Bell, #656 . . . . 30.00
Bouncing Bunny Cart, #307 . . . . 50.00
Bucky Burro, #166. . . . . 200.00
Bunny Cart, #10 . . . . 90.00
Butch the Pup, #333 . . . . 90.00
Buzzy Bee, #325 . . . . 50.00
Cackling Hen, #120. . . . . 40.00
Cement Mixer, #926. . . . . 250.00
Chatter Monk, #798. . . . . 90.00
Chick and Cart, #407. . . . . 50.00
Cookie Pig, #476. . . . . 50.00
Dizzy Donkey, #433 . . . . 90.00
Donald Duck Drum Major, #400 . . . . 200.00
Dr. Doodle, #132 . . . . 90.00
Gabby Goofies, #775. . . . . 55.00
Golden Gulch Express, #191 . . . . 90.00
Happy Helicopter, #498. . . . . 200.00
Hot Dog Wagon, #445. . . . . 200.00
Jingle Giraffe, #472 . . . . 150.00
Jolly Jumper, #450 . . . . 90.00
Katy Kackler, #140. . . . . 80.00
Leo the Drummer, #480. . . . . 200.00
Looky Chug–Chug, #220 . . . . 100.00

Timmy Turtle, #150, $90.00.

Looky Fire Truck, #7 . . . . 90.00
Merry Mousewife, #662. . . . . 50.00
Mickey Mouse Choo–Choo, #485 . . . . 95.00
Molly Moo–Moo, #190 . . . . 200.00
Mother Goose, #164 . . . . 75.00
Musical Elephant, #145 . . . . 275.00
Musical Sweeper, #100 . . . . 200.00
Nosey Pup, #445. . . . . 80.00
Perky Pot, #686 . . . . 95.00
Peter Bunny Engine, #721 . . . . 200.00
Playful Puppy, #625. . . . . 60.00
Playland Express, #192 . . . . 80.00
Pluto Pop–Up, #440 . . . . 110.00
Pony Chime, #137 . . . . 45.00
Poodle Zilo, #739 . . . . 90.00
Puffy Engine, #444 . . . . 90.00
Racing Rowboat, #730. . . . . 150.00
Roller Chimes, #123 . . . . 90.00
Safety School Bus, with figures, #983 . . . . 130.00
Shaggy Zilo, #738 . . . . 100.00
Sleep Sue, #495 . . . . 55.00
Snoopy Sniffer, #180 . . . . 120.00
Snorky Fire Engine, with figures, #169 . . . . 90.00
Sports Car, #674 . . . . 90.00
Tailspin Tabby, #400 . . . . 110.00
Tawny Tiger, #654 . . . . 95.00
Teddy Xylophone, #752 . . . . 250.00
Timber Toter, #810. . . . . 60.00
Tiny Teddy, #635 . . . . 60.00
Uncle Timmy Turtle, #125 . . . . 90.00
Walking Duck Cart, #305 . . . . 50.00

FISHING

The modern fishing lure (plug) evolved at the end of the 19th century. Wood was used primarily for the body until replaced by plastic in the mid–1930s. Hundreds of lures, many with dozens of variations, are known to exist.

As lures became more sophisticated so did reels and rods. Improvement occurred in two areas—material and mechanism.

Each improvement led to demand for more improvement. Drags and multiplying gears were added to reels. The split bamboo rod was eventually challenged by the modern graphite rod.

Serious collectors only buy examples in virtually unused condition and with their period packaging when possible. The high end of the market has become very investment focused. Many collectors are turning to licenses, paper ephemera, and secondary equipment in an effort to find affordable items within the category.

References: Ralf Coykendall, Jr., *Coykendall's Complete Guide to Sporting Collectibles,* Wallace–Homestead, Krause Publications, 1996; Carl F. Luckey, *Old Fishing Lures and Tackle: Identification and Value Guide, Fourth Edition,* Books Americana, Krause Publications, 1996; Dudley Murphy and Rick Edmisten, *Fishing Lure Collectibles: An Identification and Value Guide To The Most Collectible Antique Fishing Lures,* Collector Books, 1995; Donald J. Peterson, *Folk Art Fish Decoys,* Schiffer Publishing, 1997; Harold E. Smith, *Collector's Guide to Creek Chub Lures & Collectibles,* Collector Books, 1997; Donna Tonelli, *Top of the Line Fishing Collectibles,* Schiffer Publishing, 1997; Karl T. White, *Fishing Tackle Antiques and Collectibles,* Holli Enterprises, 1995.

Periodical: *Fishing Collectibles Magazine,* PO Box 2797, Kennebunkport, ME 04040.

Collectors' Clubs: American Fish Decoy Assoc, 624 Merritt St, Fife Lake, MI 49633; National Fishing Lure Collectors Club, 22325 B Drive S, Marshall, MI 49068; Old Reel Collectors Assoc, Inc, PO Box 2540, Weirton, WV 26062.

Catalog, Catalog of High Class Fishing Tackle, Harley–Wickham Co, London, UK, 1920, 250 pgs. . **$ 140.00**
Catalog, Parker's Fishing and Hunting Catalog, reels and rifles, 1960, 160 pgs **22.00**
Catalog, Weller Deluxe Tackle, 1963, 89 pgs, 8 x 10½" **25.00**
Creel, Adirondack style, splint, pot–bellied, pine lid with center hole, leather hinges and carrying strap, orig wood latch **150.00**
Creel, brook trout, split willow, 6" ruler attached to top, orig leather latch strap and hinges **60.00**
Creel, Brady, trout size, whole willow, leather harness and shoulder strap, canvas cover, large front pocket, 2 pouches **150.00**
Creel, Hardy, wicker, leather–edged canvas pouch on front, leather straps, fish opening at corner of lid, rubber liner, leather harness, leather and web shoulder strap **125.00**
Lure, Calkin, insect, glass, bulbous midsection, raised rings at front and back, holes for corks at ends, sgd "LBC," 2⅝" **300.00**
Lure, Heddon, #170 SOS Wounded Minnow, L–rigs, red, glass eyes, 4½" **100.00**
Lure, North Coast Minnow, green back, yellow body, glass eyes, single trailing hook, 3 belly weights, round end tail prop mkd "Pat Pen," 3" l **125.00**
Lure, Shakespeare, Revolution, aluminum, hollow, trailing feathered double hook, prop mkd "Pat Appl'd for," 3⅛" l **95.00**
Lure, green and yellow frog, double belly hook. **75.00**
Magazine, *Fly Fisherman,* 1975 . . . . **5.00**

Creel, wicker, leather trim, strap handle, buckle closure, 7½" h, 11" w, $75.00.

Poster, Canadian Pacific adv, Ewart illus, silk–screen design, hooked rainbow trout, "Canada For Game Fish," c1935, 24 x 35" **350.00**
Rod, Constable, Fine Fly, trout rod, 8 ft, 2 pc, #7 wt line, ferrule plug, orig bag **125.00**
Rod, Edwards Quadrate, Special Luxor, medium fresh water action spinning rod, 7 ft, 2 pcs, full length **55.00**
Rod, Ogden Smiths, The Warrior Rod, trout rod, 6 ft, 2 pc, 2 tip, orig bag, c1930 . . . . **200.00**

FLASHLIGHTS

The flashlight owes its origin to the search for a suitable bicycle light. The Acme Electric Lamp Company, New York, NY, manufactured the first bicycle light in 1896. Development was rapid. In 1899 Conrad Hubert filed a patent for a tubular hand-held flashlight. Two years later, Hubert had sales offices in Berlin, Chicago, London, Montreal, Paris, and Sydney.

Conrad Hubert's American Eveready company has dominated the flashlight field for the past century. National Carbon purchased the balance of the company in 1914, having bought a half–interest in it in 1906. Aurora, Chase, Franco, and Ray–O–Vac are other collectible companies.

A flashlight is actually a portable light. As such it comes in a variety of forms—candle, figural, lantern, novelty, tubular, etc. Collectors focus on flashlights from brand name companies, novelty flashlights, and character licensed flashlights.

References: L–W Book Sales, *Flashlights Price Guide,* L–W Book Sales, 1995; Stuart Schneider, *Collecting Flashlights,* Schiffer Publishing, 1997.

Newsletter: *Flashlight Newsletter,* PO Box 4095, Tustin, CA 92681.

Bond, tubular, nickel–plated brass, 2 D batteries . . . . . . **$ 18.00**
Bright Star, pen light, 2 AA batteries **8.00**

Bantam Lite, vest pocket, 1953, 3¹/₄" h, $18.00.

Burgess, vest pocket, #2, Art Deco checkerboard
 pattern, 1928 . . . . **10.00**
Burgess, tubular, metal, 1930s **15.00**
Embury, railroad, 1924 . . . . **25.00**
Eveready Masterlite, #2238, table, 2 C batteries, nick-
 el plated, opaque milk glass globe, 1935 . . . . **35.00**
Eveready Masterlite, #2354, tubular, 3 D batteries,
 1935 . . . . **25.00**
Eveready, #2602, tubular, 2 C batteries, vulcanite
 case, nickel–plated ends, small bullseye lens, 1912 . . . . **15.00**
Eveready, #2660, 2 D batteries, black painted case,
 nickel ends, beveled lens, 1924 . . . . **35.00**
Eveready Wallite, black hammer tone, oval, 1931 . . . . **30.00**
Ray–O–Vac, tubular, Sportsman, 2 D batteries,
 ribbed, 1960 . . . . **10.00**
Tiffany, 1 AA battery, sterling silver flashlight and
 chain, 1966 . . . . **50.00**

FLATWARE

Flatware refers to forks, knives, serving pieces, and spoons. There are four basic types of flatware: (1) sterling silver, (2) silver plated, (3) stainless, and (4) Dirilyte.

Sterling silver flatware has a silver content of 925 parts silver per thousand. Knives have a steel or stainless steel blade. Silver plating refers to the electroplating of a thin coating of pure silver, 1,000 parts silver per thousand, on a base metal such as brass, copper, or nickel silver. While steel only requires the addition of 13% chromium to be classified stainless, most stainless steel flatware is made from an 18/8 formula, i.e., 18% chromium for strength and stain resistance and 8% nickel for a high luster and long–lasting finish. Dirilyte is an extremely hard, solid bronze alloy developed in Sweden in the early 1900s. Although gold in color, it has no gold in it.

Most flatware is purchased by individuals seeking to replace a damaged piece or to expand an existing pattern. Prices vary widely, depending on what the seller had to pay and how he views the importance of the pattern. Prices listed below represent what a modern replacement service quotes a customer.

Abbreviations used in the listings include:

FH	Flat Handle	SS	Sterling Silver
HH	Hollow Handle	ST	Stainless Steel
SP	Silver Plated		

References: Maryanne Dolan, *American Sterling Silver Flatware, 1830's–1990's: A Collector's Identification & Value Guide,* Books Americana, Krause Publications, 1993; Tere Hagan, *Silverplated Flatware, Revised Fourth Edition,* Collector Books, 1990, 1995 value update; Richard Osterberg, *Sterling Silver Flatware for Dining Elegance,* Schiffer Publishing, 1994; Dorothy T. Rainwater, *Encyclopedia of American Silver Manufacturers, Third Edition Revised,* Schiffer Publishing, 1986; Replacements, Ltd., *Stainless Steel Flatware Identification Guide,* Replacements, Ltd.; Harry L. Rinker, *Silverware Of The 20th Century: The Top 250 Patterns,* House of Collectibles, 1997.

Dirilyte, Regal, butter serving knife, FH, 7¹/₄" . . . . **$ 25.00**
Dirilyte, Regal, cold meat fork, 8⁵/₈" **50.00**
Dirilyte, Regal, grapefruit spoon, round bowl, 7" **20.00**
Dirilyte, Regal, gravy ladle, 6³/₄" **50.00**
Dirilyte, Regal, iced tea spoon, 8³/₈" **22.00**
Dirilyte, Regal, knife, HH, Old French blade, 8" **25.00**
Dirilyte, Regal, pie/cake server, 10" **90.00**
Dirilyte, Regal, salad fork, 6¹/₄" **20.00**
Dirilyte, Regal, tablespoon, 8³/₈" **37.00**
Dirilyte, Regal, teaspoon, 6" **15.00**
Gorham, Calais, ST, butter serving knife, HH, 7" **12.00**
Gorham, Calais, ST, cold meat fork, 8³/₄" **17.00**
Gorham, Calais, ST, fork, 8" **10.00**
Gorham, Calais, ST, gravy ladle, 7" **17.00**
Gorham, Calais, ST, knife, HH, modern blade, 9¹/₄" **15.00**
Gorham, Calais, ST, salad fork, 7" **10.00**
Gorham, Calais, ST, soup spoon, oval bowl, 7" **10.00**
Gorham, Calais, ST, sugar spoon, 6¹/₈" **10.00**
Gorham, Calais, ST, tablespoon, pierced, 8³/₄" **15.00**
Gorham, Calais, ST, teaspoon, 6¹/₄" **7.00**
Gorham, Chantilly, SS, butter spreader, FH, 5⁷/₈" **30.00**
Gorham, Chantilly, SS, carving set, ST blade **130.00**
Gorham, Chantilly, SS, cocktail fork, 5¹/₂" **30.00**
Gorham, Chantilly, SS, cold meat fork, 7¹/₈" **85.00**
Gorham, Chantilly, SS, pastry server, ST bowl, 11³/₈" **45.00**
Gorham, Chantilly, SS, punch ladle, ST bowl, 14" **80.00**
Gorham, Chantilly, SS, salad fork, 6¹/₂" **50.00**
Gorham, Chantilly, SS, soup spoon, oval bowl, 7" **50.00**
Gorham, Chantilly, SS, tablespoon, pierced, 8³/₈" **115.00**
Gorham, Strasbourg, SS, bouillon spoon, round bowl,
 5" **40.00**
Gorham, Strasbourg, SS, butter spreader, HH, mod-
 ern ST blade, 6¹/₄" **30.00**
Gorham, Strasbourg, SS, cold meat fork, 8¹/₂" **115.00**
Gorham, Strasbourg, SS, gravy ladle, 7" **115.00**
Gorham, Strasbourg, SS, iced tea spoon, 7⁵/₈" **45.00**
Gorham, Strasbourg, SS, knife, HH, modern blade,
 9³/₄" **50.00**
Gorham, Strasbourg, SS, pie/cake server, ST blade,
 10¹/₂" **50.00**
Gorham, Strasbourg, SS, salad fork, 6³/₈" **50.00**
Gorham, Strasbourg, SS, tablespoon, ¹/₂" **85.00**
Gorham, Strasbourg, SS, teaspoon, 5⁷/₈" **25.00**

International, Daffodil, SP, casserole serving spoon,
SP bowl, 9" **45.00**
International, Daffodil, SP, cocktail fork, 5½" **15.00**
International, Daffodil, SP, cream soup spoon, round
bowl, 6⅝" **17.00**
International, Daffodil, SP, iced tea spoon, 7¾" **22.00**
International, Daffodil, SP, knife, HH, modern blade,
9¼" **17.00**
International, Daffodil, SP, pie server, 10¾" **70.00**
International, Daffodil, SP, salad fork, 6¾" **15.00**
International, Daffodil, SP, tablespoon, pierced, 8½" **35.00**
International, Daffodil, SP, teaspoon, 6⅛" **10.00**
International, Daffodil, SP, tomato server, flat, 7⅝" **45.00**
International, Eternally Yours, SP, cocktail fork, 5½" **15.00**
International, Eternally Yours, SP, cold meat fork, 8¾" **45.00**
International, Eternally Yours, SP, iced tea spoon, 7½" **17.00**
International, Eternally Yours, SP, knife, HH, modern
blade, 9½" **17.00**
International, Eternally Yours, SP, pie server, 10¼" **70.00**
International, Eternally Yours, SP, salad fork, 6¾" **17.00**
International, Eternally Yours, SP, soup spoon, oval
bowl, 7¼" **15.00**
International, Eternally Yours, SP, sugar spoon, 5¾" **20.00**
International, Eternally Yours, SP, tablespoon, 8⅝" **25.00**
International, Eternally Yours, SP, teaspoon, 6⅛" **10.00**
International, First Love, SP, carving set, ST blade **160.00**
International, First Love, SP, casserole serving spoon,
SP bowl, 9" **50.00**
International, First Love, SP, dessert fork, 6¼" **17.00**
International, First Love, SP, gravy ladle, 6⅛" **40.00**
International, First Love, SP, knife, HH, modern
blade, 9½" **17.00**
International, First Love, SP, pie server, 10½" **65.00**
International, First Love, SP, salad fork, 6¾" **17.00**
International, First Love, SP, sugar spoon, 6" **20.00**
International, First Love, SP, tablespoon, 8½" **25.00**
International, First Love, SP, teaspoon, 6⅛" **7.00**
International, Prelude, SS, carving fork, ST tines, 8¾" **50.00**
International, Prelude, SS, carving knife, ST blade,
11½" **50.00**

International, Prelude, SS, casserole serving spoon,
SS bowl, 9¼" **140.00**
International, Prelude, SS, cold meat fork, 7¾" **90.00**
International, Prelude, SS, demitasse spoon, 4⅛" **20.00**
International, Prelude, SS, knife, HH, New French
blade, 9½" **45.00**
International, Prelude, SS, pasta server, ST bowl,
10⅞" **40.00**
International, Prelude, SS, pickle fork, short handle,
5⅞" **35.00**
International, Prelude, SS, soup spoon, oval bowl,
6¾" **45.00**
International, Prelude, SS, tomato server, flat, 8" **95.00**
International, Remembrance, SP, butter spreader, FH,
6⅛" **10.00**
International, Remembrance, SP, cocktail fork, 5½" **10.00**
International, Remembrance, SP, demitasse spoon,
4½" **12.00**
International, Remembrance, SP, fruit spoon, 6" **12.00**
International, Remembrance, SP, gravy ladle, SP
bowl, 6⅛" **30.00**
International, Remembrance, SP, iced tea spoon, 7¾" **12.00**
International, Remembrance, SP, knife, HH, modern
blade, 9⅜" **15.00**
International, Remembrance, SP, sugar tongs, 4" **45.00**
International, Remembrance, SP, tablespoon, 8½" **20.00**
International, Remembrance, SP, teaspoon, 6⅛" **10.00**
Kirk Stieff, Repousse, SS, carving set, ST blade **130.00**
Kirk Stieff, Repousse, SS, cheese server, ST blade, 6½" **50.00**
Kirk Stieff, Repousse, SS, fork, 6¼" **50.00**
Kirk Stieff, Repousse, SS, fruit knife, SP blade, 7½" **55.00**
Kirk Stieff, Repousse, SS, fruit spoon, 6⅛" **40.00**
Kirk Stieff, Repousse, SS, gravy ladle, 7" **100.00**
Kirk Stieff, Repousse, SS, iced tea spoon, 7⅝" **40.00**
Kirk Stieff, Repousse, SS, knife, 7⅛" **45.00**
Kirk Stieff, Repousse, SS, salad fork, 6¼" **50.00**
Kirk Stieff, Repousse, SS, tablespoon, 8⅜" **85.00**
Oneida, Coronation, SP, butter serving knife, FH, 6⅞" **15.00**
Oneida, Coronation, SP, butter spreader, FH, 5½" **12.00**
Oneida, Coronation, SP, carving fork, ST tines, 9" **45.00**
Oneida, Coronation, SP, carving knife, ST blade,
11⅜" **60.00**
Oneida, Coronation, SP, dessert spoon, 6⅞" **15.00**
Oneida, Coronation, SP, gravy ladle, 7⅛" **27.00**
Oneida, Coronation, SP, knife, HH, modern blade,
9½" **15.00**
Oneida, Coronation, SP, pie fork, 5½" **15.00**
Oneida, Coronation, SP, pie server, 10¾" **45.00**
Oneida, Coronation, SP, soup spoon, oval bowl, 7¼" **12.00**
Oneida, Coronation, SP, steak knife, 9⅛" **15.00**
Oneida, Coronation, SP, sugar spoon, 6" **15.00**
Oneida, Coronation, SP, teaspoon, 6⅛" **7.00**

**International,
Prelude, SS: tea-
spoon, 6", $20.00;
knife, 9¼", $30.00;
fork, 8", $50.00;
salad fork, 6⅝",
$40.00.**

Oneida, Coronation, SP, salad fork, 6¾" l, $12.00.

Oneida, Shelley, ST, butter serving knife, HH, 6³/₄" **22.00**
Oneida, Shelley, ST, butter spreader, HH, 6¹/₂" **22.00**
Oneida, Shelley, ST, cold meat fork, 8¹/₂" **40.00**
Oneida, Shelley, ST, gravy ladle, 6³/₄" **35.00**
Oneida, Shelley, ST, knife, HH, modern blade, 9¹/₈" **25.00**
Oneida, Shelley, ST, salad fork **22.00**
Oneida, Shelley, ST, soup spoon, oval bowl, 6⁵/₈" **20.00**
Oneida, Shelley, ST, sugar spoon, 6" **22.00**
Oneida, Shelley, ST, tablespoon, pierced, 8¹/₄" **37.00**
Oneida, Shelley, ST, teaspoon **25.00**
Oneida, Venetia, ST, butter serving knife, FH, 6¹/₂" **20.00**
Oneida, Venetia, ST, fork, 6¹/₂" **17.00**
Oneida, Venetia, ST, fruit spoon, 6¹/₈" **20.00**
Oneida, Venetia, ST, gravy ladle, 8" **30.00**
Oneida, Venetia, ST, iced tea spoon, 7¹/₂" **20.00**
Oneida, Venetia, ST, knife, HH, modern blade, 9¹/₈" **20.00**
Oneida, Venetia, ST, pie server, 9⁵/₈" **40.00**
Oneida, Venetia, ST, salad fork, 6³/₄" **20.00**
Oneida, Venetia, ST, steak knife, 9¹/₈" **25.00**
Oneida, Venetia, ST, tablespoon, pierced, 8⁵/₈" **27.00**
Oneida, Venetia, ST, teaspoon, 6¹/₈" **20.00**
Reed & Barton, Francis I, SS, asparagus server, flat,
   9⁷/₈" **300.00**
Reed & Barton, Francis I, SS, cold meat fork, 7⁷/₈" **100.00**
Reed & Barton, Francis I, SS, cream sauce ladle, 5³/₄" **55.00**
Reed & Barton, Francis I, SS, gravy ladle, 6⁷/₈" **100.00**
Reed & Barton, Francis I, SS, jelly spoon, 6¹/₄" **40.00**
Reed & Barton, Francis I, SS, lasagna server, ST blade,
   10" **70.00**
Reed & Barton, Francis I, SS, soup ladle, 11¹/₂" **300.00**
Reed & Barton, Francis I, SS, teaspoon, 6" **40.00**
Reed & Barton, Francis I, SS, wedding cake knife, ST
   blade, 12⁵/₈" **55.00**
Towle, French Provincial, SS, bar knife, 8⁷/₈" **35.00**
Towle, French Provincial, SS, cheese pick, 8¹/₈" **30.00**
Towle, French Provincial, SS, cold meat fork, 8¹/₄" **90.00**
Towle, French Provincial, SS, jelly spoon, 6¹/₂" **40.00**
Towle, French Provincial, SS, knife, HH, modern
   blade, 8⁷/₈" **32.00**
Towle, French Provincial, SS, salad fork, 6³/₈" **40.00**

Towle, French Provincial, SS, salt spoon, 2¹/₂" **12.00**
Towle, French Provincial, SS, soup spoon, oval bowl,
   6¹/₂" **45.00**
Towle, French Provincial, SS, tablespoon, 8¹/₂" **80.00**
Towle, French Provincial, SS, teaspoon, 6" **25.00**
Towle, Old Master, SS, cheese knife, ST blade, 7¹/₈" **40.00**
Towle, Old Master, SS, coffee scoop, SP scoop, 4" **40.00**
Towle, Old Master, SS, fish fork, ST tines, 7⁷/₈" **40.00**
Towle, Old Master, SS, iced tea spoon, 7⁷/₈" **40.00**
Towle, Old Master, SS, knife, HH, modern blade, 8⁷/₈" **35.00**
Towle, Old Master, SS, pasta server, ST bowl, 10¹/₂" **40.00**
Towle, Old Master, SS, salad fork, 6³/₈" **35.00**
Towle, Old Master, SS, soup spoon, oval bowl, 6⁵/₈" **45.00**
Towle, Old Master, SS, steak knife, 8¹/₂" **50.00**
Towle, Old Master, SS, sugar spoon, 5⁵/₈" **30.00**
Towle, Old Master, SS, teaspoon, 6" **25.00**
Wallace, Grande Baroque, SS, bonbon spoon, 5³/₈" **60.00**
Wallace, Grande Baroque, SS, butter curler, 7" **40.00**
Wallace, Grande Baroque, SS, butter pick, 5¹/₈" **32.00**
Wallace, Grande Baroque, SS, ice tongs, 7¹/₄" **240.00**
Wallace, Grande Baroque, SS, pickle fork, short han-
   dle, 5¹/₂" **50.00**
Wallace, Grande Baroque, SS, salad fork, 6¹/₂" **45.00**
Wallace, Grande Baroque, SS, salad tongs, 8⁵/₈" **400.00**
Wallace, Grande Baroque, SS, soup spoon, oval
   bowl, 7" **55.00**
Wallace, Grande Baroque, SS, tablespoon, pierced,
   8³/₄" **120.00**
Wallace, Grande Baroque, SS, teaspoon, 6¹/₄" **35.00**
Wallace, Rose Point, SS, butter spreader, HH, pad-
   dled ST blade, 6¹/₄" **30.00**
Wallace, Rose Point, SS, cheese server, SP blade, 6¹/₄" **40.00**
Wallace, Rose Point, SS, cocktail fork, 5⁵/₈" **30.00**
Wallace, Rose Point, SS, cold meat fork, 8¹/₈" **95.00**
Wallace, Rose Point, SS, cream soup spoon, round
   bowl, 5⁷/₈" **40.00**
Wallace, Rose Point, SS, gravy ladle, 6¹/₄" **90.00**
Wallace, Rose Point, SS, lemon fork, 5¹/₂" **35.00**
Wallace, Rose Point, SS, soup ladle, 15¹/₂" **270.00**
Wallace, Rose Point, SS, soup spoon, oval bowl, 7¹/₈" **45.00**

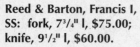

Reed & Barton, Francis I, SS: fork, 7³/₄" l, $75.00; knife, 9¹/₂" l, $60.00.

Wallace, Rose Point, SS: teaspoon, 6", $25.00; knife, 9¹/₈", $35.00; fork, 7⁵/₈", $50.00; salad fork, $35.00.

FLORENCE CERAMICS

Florence Ward of Pasedena, California, began making ceramic objects as a form of therapy in dealing with the loss of a young son. The products she produced and sold from her garage workshop provided pin money during the Second World War.

With the support of Clifford, her husband, and Clifford, Jr., their son, Florence Ward moved her ceramics business to a plant on the east side of Pasadena in 1946. Business boomed after Ward exhibited at several Los Angeles gift shows. In 1949 a state–of–the–art plant was built at 74 South San Gabriel Boulevard, Pasadena.

Florence Ceramics is best known for its figural pieces, often costumed in Colonial and Godey fashions. The company also produced birds, busts, candle holders, lamps, smoking sets, and wall pockets. Betty Davenport Ford joined the company in 1956, designing a line of bisque animal figures. Production ended after two years.

Scripto Corporation bought Florence Ceramics in 1964 following the death of Clifford Ward. Production was shifted to advertising specialty ware. Operations ceased in 1977.

Reference: Doug Fouland, *The Florence Collectibles: The Era of Elegance,* Schiffer Publishing, 1995.

Collectors' Club: Florence Collector's Club, PO Box 122, Richland, WA 99352.

Abagail, green, blue, and tan, 8½" h	$ 140.00
Amelia, brown, 9¼" h	150.00
Belle	125.00
Camille, blue, 9" h	225.00
Douglas, white	220.00
Gary, green	225.00
Grace, blue	250.00
Jeanette	150.00
Jim, gray and green, 6½" h	75.00
Karla Ballerina, matte pink	375.00
Lillian, gray	110.00
Madonna	175.00
Matalida, tan and blue	125.00
Mickey, blue	150.00

Delia, burgundy, 7¾" h, $125.00.

Sara, gray	100.00
Southern Belle, white	225.00
Wickum Boy and Girl, price for pair	250.00

FOLK ART

The definition of folk art is fluid, defined by what subcategories contemporary collectors decide are in or out at any given moment. Simply put, folk art is trendy. Edie Clark's "What Really Is Folk Art?" in the December 1986 issue of *Yankee* continues to be one of the most insightful pieces yet written on the subject.

The folk art craze struck with a vengeance in the early 1970s. Auction houses hyped folk art ranging from quilts to weathervanes as great long–term investments. Several market manipulators cornered then touted the work of contemporary artists. The speculative bubble burst in the late 1980s when the market was flooded and excellent reproductions fooled many novice buyers.

Carvings currently are one of the hottest folk art subcategories. The folk art painting market, especially for works by contemporary artists, is flat. Regional folk art, e.g., Pennsylvania German material, runs hot and cold.

Reference: Chuck and Jan Rosenak, *Contemporary American Folk Art: A Collector's Guide,* Abbeville Press, 1996.

Periodical: *20th Century Folk Art News,* 5967 Blackberry Ln, Buford, GA 30518.

Collectors' Club: Folk Art Society of America, PO Box 17041, Richmond, VA 23226.

Figural Group, dancing couple, carved and painted pine, Dave Hardy, Quakertown, Bucks County, PA, young man in blue jeans and light blue top, young lady in purple blouse and green skirt, initialed "DNH 91" on rect wood base, 11½" h	$ 125.00
Figural Group, pair of Kenya's Crowned Cranes, Saturnino Portuondo (Pucho) Odio, carved and painted with brush combs, each sgd Pucho Odio on side, 49½" h	1,850.00
Figural Group, Pyramid, Reverend Hayes, upright carving consisting of 8 units, crosshatch work, carved children, free–turning figure near center, 1 pc except for base, carved signature "W. Va. 1992 Rev. Hayes," 15" h	175.00
Figural Group, sculptor and his model, carved and painted pine, Dave Hardy, Quakertown, Bucks County, PA, sculptor carving figure from block of wood while model poses with her hands on hips, rect base, initialed and dated "DNH, '86," 10½" h	175.00
Figure, Black Bear, Garland and Minnie Adkins, carved and painted wood, 1 pc, black, white, and red, sgd "G & M Adkins 1989," 30" l, 13¾" h, 1989	345.00
Figure, cat, carved and painted wood, Paul C. Tyson, Royersford, Montgomery County, PA, stylized figure seated on its haunches with ears pricked, brown sponge–painted spots, red collar, inset glass eyes, sgd and dated "Paul Tyson, '76, #56," 8" h	925.00
Figure, cow, Linvel Barker, carved basswood and constructed, sgd and dated "1990," 13½" l, 10¾" h	375.00

Figure, lion, carved wood, Paul C. Tyson, Royersford, Montgomery County, PA, stylized figure standing foursquare with tail back, carved mane detail, inset glass eyes, sgd and dated "Paul Tyson, '76 #72," 14¼" l **1,500.00**

Figure, man, Lavell Nickoll, carved poplar, standing man with arms at sides, wearing jacket, painted in black, deep red, yellow, ochre, peach, and white, 8¾" h, 1992. . . . . **90.00**

Memory Jug, mixed media, American, tapered cylinder, strap handle, domed glass finial, encrusted with nuts, shells, sewing tools, teeth, springs, screws, and spoon, gilt ground, 11" h **300.00**

Painting, acrylic on board, Bicycle Race, Paul Lehman, Laureldale, PA, group of high–wheel bicyclers in front of merchants' building/jail, jail located at 5th and Washington, Reading, PA, sgd and dated "P. Lehman '90," 16 x 12". **125.00**

Painting, colored pencil on paper, Elephant, Gerald "Creative" DePrie, blue and gray tones, sgd on foam board mount, 23" h **95.00**

Painting, enamel and mixed media on wood, Virginia License Plate, Howard Finster, sgd and inscribed "By Howard Finster Man of Visions Hose A–12–10 March 1979," on front and on verso, extensive inscription, 1929 Virginia license plate mounted on front, "Chinaware Club" ticket on verso, painted and burnished wood frame, 27¾ x 17¼" **2,875.00**

Painting, oil on board, Blossoming Tree in a Field of Daisies, Jack Savitsky, sgd in lower right, 30 x 24" **600.00**

Painting, oil on canvas laid on board, White Washing, David Ellinger, Amish man whitewashing stone fence in front of Pennsylvania German bank barn, 22 x 18½". **4,250.00**

Painting, oil on canvasboard, Coney Island, Vestie Davis (1903–1978), children and adults walking on boardwalk, sgd and dated "Vestie E. Davis, 1977" in lower right, 15¼ x 1⅜" **2,200.00**

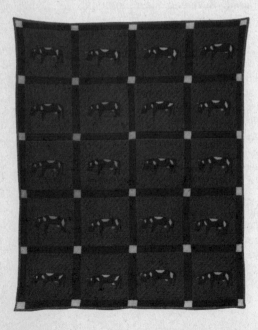

Pig Quilt, Garland and Minnie Adkins, pieced and appliquéd, olive, black, white, and peach, machine–sewn with hand quilting, black and white speckled border and reverse, 72 x 89", $330.00.

Painting, polychrome on artist board, Sacrifice of Isaac, Hugo Spencer, narrow white mat, black molded frame, titled, sgd, and dated "1989," 15¾ x 23⅞", frame 21½ x 29½" **450.00**

Painting, tempera and pen on cardboard, untitled, Sister Gertrude Morgan (1900–1980), sgd and inscribed "Sister Gertrude Morgan, Revelation" in upper left and "Battle of Armageddom (sic.)" in lower left, verso of frame mounted with photograph of artist, 12" x 9¾" **5,250.00**

Painting, tempera on cardboard, Old Fashion Mahoning Valley Country Sleigh Ride, Lamont Alfred "Old Ironsides" Pry (1921–1987), Susy the horse pulling sleigh with 5 people, titled across bottom, sgd in lower right corner, 17½ x 16". **650.00**

Painting, tempera on paper, A Pennsylvania Landscape in Snow, Hattie Brunner (1890–1982), covered bridge in foreground, farmstead in background, sgd and dated "1961," 7 x 5¼" **2,300.00**

Quilt, Tiger Quilt, Garland and Minnie Adkins, pieced and appliquéd, white, yellow, brown, red, black, and green, machine sewn with hand quilting, yellow border and reverse, maker sgd "G & M Adkins 1991," 78 x 94" **275.00**

Redware, birdhouse, Stahl Pottery, Powder Valley, PA, ovoid, incised shoulder, overhanging knob with hooded perch, inscribed "Made in Stahl's Pottery Zionsville PA for MARGARET Buchanan 11–26–38," 7¾" h **350.00**

Redware, candlestick, Isaac Stahl, Powder Valley, PA, cobalt and slip dec, molded candle socket on flaring support with incised base and circular molded drip–pan mounted with rope twist handle, inscribed "Made by I.S. Stahl / May 13–1938," 5" h . . . **575.00**

Redware, carafe, cov, Isaac Stahl, Powder Valley, PA, cobalt dec, removable hourglass–form lid with molded foot doubling as drinking cup revealing slender spout and incised shoulder, pinched ovoid body, similarly molded foot, inscribed "Made by I.S. Stahl 4–24 / 1938," 7¼" h **750.00**

Redware, plates, set of 4, Lester Breininger, Robesonia, PA, green and brown dec on yellow ground with Adam and Eve (#25), Noah's Ark (#25), Elijah (#25), and Daniel in the Lion's Den (#27), each sgd, inscribed, and dated "L.B. Breininger, Robesonia, PA," titled and dated "1970, 1971, 1972," and "1973" respectively, 9⅝" d, first of Breininger's limited edition plate series **975.00**

Sandstone, seated sheep, "Popeye" Reed, tooled and carved, incised "E. Reed," 19" l, 12¾" h **625.00**

Stoneware, Southern Pottery Face Jug, Joe Reinhardt, stoneware with swirled blue, olive, tan, and ivory glaze, blue eyes, applied features, incised heart and wavy lines at neck, imp "Joe Reinhardt Pottery, Vale, N.C. Oct93," light crazing, 10½" h **150.00**

Walking Stick, snake and lizard, Denzil Goodpaster, carved and painted, 2 coiled snakes in green and yellow extend up each side of handle, brown and ivory lizard sits on bottom half of stick below coiled snakes, carved "DG," handle 6¾" w, 35" l **125.00**

Walking Stick, woman in bikini, Earnest Patton, carved poplar, woman in dark blue bikini, black hair braided to middle of her back, sgd in ink "Earnest Patton," 39³/₄" l **150.00**

FOOD MOLDS

The earliest food molds were ceramic and cast–iron molds used for baking. Today most collectors think of food molds in terms of the cast–iron candy molds, tin chocolate molds, and pewter ice cream molds used in factories, candy shops, and drug stores throughout the first half of the 19th century. Many of these chocolate and pewter molds were imported from Germany and Holland.

A substantial collection of Jell–O and post–1960 metal and plastic molds can be assembled with a minimum of effort and expenditure. Collector interest in these items is minimal.

Beware of reproduction chocolate molds. They appeared long enough ago to have developed a patina that matches some period molds.

Cake, lamb, Griswold . . . . $ 200.00
Cake, rabbit, Griswold. 225.00
Candy, wood, 5 hearts with cross and 1 circular floral design, 15" l 325.00
Chocolate, pewter, turkey 45.00
Chocolate, tin, cowboy, clamp type 40.00
Chocolate, tin, elephant. 80.00
Chocolate, tin, hearts, book type 35.00
Chocolate, tin, rabbit, 5³/₄" h 40.00
Chocolate, tin, skeleton, 5¹/₂" h. 75.00
Chocolate, turkey, tray type, 14 x 10" 55.00
Chocolate, witch, 4 cavities 65.00
Cookie, pewter, wood back, 6 classical heads. 50.00
Cookie Board, pewter, 8 designs, wood backing 95.00
Ice Cream, castle, chess game piece, mkd "S & Co" 65.00
Ice Cream, owl, 4 pints, mkd "S & Co, #17" 275.00
Ice Cream, pewter, asparagus, 3⁵/₈" h 35.00
Ice Cream, pewter, cherub riding Easter Bunny, 4" h 35.00

Ice Cream, pewter, duck 65.00
Ice Cream, pewter, flag, 13 stars. 65.00
Ice Cream, pewter, smoking pipe 35.00
Ice Cream, rose cluster 40.00
Maple Candy, wood, fruit and foliage design, 2 part 35.00
Patty Mold, Griswold, 1937 . . . . 45.00
Pottery, ear of corn center design, yellow ware, 6" l. 50.00
Pottery, strawberries center design, 4" d 60.00
Pudding, tin and copper, oval, pineapple 70.00
Pudding, tin, cone shape, spiral design. 30.00

FOOTBALL CARDS

Although football cards originated in the 1890s, the 1948 Bowman and Leaf Gum sets mark the birth of the modern football card. Leaf only produced cards for two seasons. The last Bowman set dates from 1955.

Topps entered the field in 1950 with a college stars set. It produced a National Football League set each year between 1956 and 1963. Topps lost its National Football League license to the Philadelphia Gum Company for the 1964 season. Topps produced only American Football League cards between 1964 and 1967. Topps recovered the ball in 1968 when it once again was licensed to produce National Football League cards. It has remained undefeated ever since.

Football cards remain a weaker sister when compared to baseball cards. Many felt the collapse of the baseball market in the mid–1990s would open the door for a strong surge in the collectibility of football cards. This has not happened.

References: James Beckett, *The Official 1997 Price Guide to Football Cards, 16th Edition,* House of Collectibles, 1997; James Beckett and Dan Hitt (eds.), *Beckett Football Price Guide, No. 12,* Beckett Publications, 1995; Sports Collectors Digest, *1998 Standard Catalog of Football Cards,* Krause Publications, 1997.

Periodical: *Beckett Football Card Magazine,* 15850 Dallas Pkwy, Dallas, TX 75248; *Sports Cards,* 700 E State St, Iola, WI 54990.

Bowman, 1948, #9, Nolan Luhn . . . . $ 50.00
Bowman, 1948, #36, Bulldog Turner 95.00
Bowman, 1948, #93, Vic Sears. 50.00
Bowman, 1951, #2, Otto Graham 65.00
Bowman, 1951, #34, Sammy Baugh. 55.00
Bowman, 1951, #56, Charley Conerly 20.00
Bowman, 1952, #4, Steve Owen CO 25.00
Bowman, 1952, #36, John Lee Hancock SP 125.00
Bowman, 1955, #7, Frank Gifford 45.00
Bowman, 1955, #70, Jim Ringo 20.00
Bowman, 1955, #152, Tom Landry. 90.00
Fleer, 1960, #7, Sid Gilman CO. 8.00
Fleer, 1960, #116, Hank Stram. 10.00
Fleer, 1961, #11, Jim Brown. 60.00
Fleer, 1961, #89, Jim Taylor 15.00
Fleer, 1961, #155, Jack Kemp. 95.00
Fleer, 1963, #10, Nick Buoniconti 30.00
Fleer, 1963, #47, Len Dawson 95.00
Fleer, 1990, #209, Derrick Thomas. 15
Fleer, 1990, #311, Anthony Miller 10
Leaf, 1948, #1, Sid Luckman 80.00

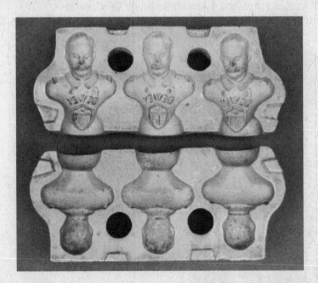

Candy, pewter, Dewey, "Dewey" and shield on chest, mkd "T. Mills & Bro., Philadelphia," #254, 3 cavities, 6¹/₄" w, $20.00.

Topps, 1960, #71, $2.30.

Leaf, 1948, #15, Charlie Justice **28.00**
Leaf, 1949, #28, Pete Pihos **15.00**
Leaf, 1949, #56, John Lujack **30.00**
Philadelphia, 1964, #30, Jim Brown **35.00**
Philadelphia, 1964, #79, Bart Starr **12.00**
Philadelphia, 1964, #161, Jim Johnson **2.50**
Philadelphia, 1966, #31, Dick Butkus **82.00**
Philadelphia, 1966, #41, Jim Brown **42.00**
Philadelphia, 1966, #114, Fran Tarkenton **15.00**
Score, 1989, #1, Joe Montana **2.00**
Score, 1989, #72, Chris Carter **1.25**
Score, 1989, #152, Andre Reed . . . . **.75**
Score, 1989, #225, Steve Largent . . . . **.50**
Score, 1990, #10, Bo Jackson . . . . **.25**
Score, 1990, #203, Reggie White . . . . **.10**
Score, 1990, #506, Heywood Jeffries . . . . **.50**
Topps, 1956, #44, Joe Schmidt **22.00**
Topps, 1956, #60, Lenny Moore **40.00**
Topps, 1956, #110, Joe Perry **10.00**
Topps, 1957, #5, Gino Marchetti **5.50**
Topps, 1957, #85, Bobby Layne **15.50**
Topps, 1957, #138, John Unitas **250.00**
Topps, 1959, #23, Bart Starr **25.50**
Topps, 1959, #140, Bobby Mitchel **20.00**
Topps, 1960, #56, Forest Gregg **15.00**
Topps, 1960, #113, Y A Tittle **10.00**
Topps, 1961, #35, Alex Karras **12.00**
Topps, 1961, #145, George Blanda **12.00**
Topps, 1964, #121, Don Maynard **12.00**
Topps, 1964, #155, Lance Alworth **18.00**
Topps, 1965, #17, Babe Parilli SP **6.50**
Topps, 1968, #65, Joe Namath **38.00**
Topps, 1970, #25, Jan Stenerud **5.00**
Topps, 1972, #35, Willie Lanier **2.00**
Topps, 1974, #105, Ahmad Rashad **10.00**
Topps, 1977, #140, Lynn Swann **5.00**
Topps, 1979, #77, Tony Dorsett **2.50**
Topps, 1981, #55, Phil Simms **1.50**
Topps, 1983, #33, Jim McMahon **3.00**
Topps, 1985, #111, Carl Banks **2.50**

FOOTBALL MEMORABILIA

Football memorabilia divides into two distinct groups, professional and collegiate, and two distinct categories, equipment and paper ephemera. Collectors of professional football memorabilia far outnumber collectors of collegiate memorabilia. Equipment collectors exceed the number of collectors of paper ephemera.

The category is heavily post–1970 driven, due to availability, and regional in nature. Collectors want game related material. Team logo material licensed for sale in sports shops has minimal to no appeal.

Reference: Roderick A. Malloy, *Malloy's Sports Collectibles Value Guide: Up–To–Date Prices For Noncard Sports Memorabilia,* Attic Books, Wallace–Homestead, Krause Publications, 1993.

Periodical: *Sports Collectors Digest,* 700 E State St, Iola, WI 54990.

Autograph, Andre Reed, 3 x 5" card . . . . **$ 8.00**
Autograph, Ricky Watters, 8 x 10" photo **8.00**
Bank, Pittsburgh Steelers, plastic, helmet shape,
    1970s, 6" h **25.00**
Book, *Super Joe, The Joe Namath Story,* paperback **15.00**
Bookends, pr, Knute Rockne, cast iron, incised
    inscription "The Rock Of Notre Dame," raised por-
    trait, c1930s **160.00**
Booklet, Gulf Football Manual, Gulf Oil premium,
    1933, 24 pgs **5.50**
Comic Book, Football Heroes, Joe Montana,
    Personality Comics **2.50**
Figure, Hershel Walker, Starting Lineup, Kenner, 1988 . . . . **20.00**
Figure, John Elway, Starting Lineup, Kenner, 1989 . . . . **30.00**
Figure, Troy Aikman, Starting Lineup, Kenner, 1990 . . . . . . **22.00**
Game, ABC Monday Night Football, Aurora, 1972 . . . . . . **40.00**
Game, NFL Strategy, Tudor Games, 1935 . . . . **65.00**
Game, Vince Lombardi's Game, Research Games,
    Inc, orig box, ©1970 . . . . **28.00**
Glass, Notre Dame University, blue and gold, Victory
    March on back, 1950s, 5¼" h **15.00**
Lighter, San Francisco 49ers Super Bowl XVI Champs,
    silvered metal and plastic **25.00**

Figure, celluloid, orange and gray, mkd "T Japan," 4¹/₂" h, $8.00.

Magazine, *Football Action,* Joe Namath cov, 1976. . . . . . . **22.00**
Magazine, *Football Digest,* 1952 . . . . **65.00**
Magazine, *Stanley Woodward's Football,* 1953 . . . . **5.00**
Nodder, Atlanta Falcons, round gold base. **25.00**
Nodder, Terry Bradshaw. **45.00**
Pencil Case, National Football League, vinyl, light
    blue, 5 x 8½". **25.00**
Pennant, felt, San Diego Chargers, helmet design,
    yellow–gold and white lettering, blue ground,
    American Football League insignia, 1960s. **20.00**
Pinback Button, National Football Conference
    Division, San Francisco and Detroit, 1983. . . . . **18.00**
Pinback Button, St. Louis Cardinals, football and car-
    dinal, black, blue, and white, 1960s **5.50**
Plate, Joe Montana, Gartlan USA, 8½" d. **42.00**
Plate, Vince Lombardi, Sports Impressions, 8½" d **55.00**
Press Pin, Super Bowl XVIII, 1984 . . . . **140.00**
Program, Illinois–Notre Dame Football Game, black
    and white photos and roster, October 9, 1937,
    20 pgs, 8 x 11". **28.00**
Program, Super Bowl XVII, Washington and Miami,
    1982 . . . . **25.00**
Puzzle, Roman Gabriel, color photo action scene,
    5½" cardboard canister, American Publishing
    Corp, ©1972, 300 pcs **20.00**
Ticket, AFC Wild Card, Houston vs Miami, 1976. . . . . . . **12.00**
Ticket, Ohio State, 1978 . . . . **2.50**
Ticket Stub, American Football League Champion-
    ship, Oakland and Houston, 1967 . . . . **28.00**
Ticket Stub, NFC Division, Minnesota and LA Rams,
    1977 . . . . **12.00**
Wrapper, Bowman's Football, waxed paper, 1954, 5
    x 6¼" **10.00**
Yearbook, Green Bay Packers, autographed by coach-
    es and players, 1974 . . . . **20.00**
Yearbook, Redskins, Joe Theisman, 1984. . . . . **8.00**

FOSTORIA

The Fostoria Glass Company broke ground for a glass factory in Fostoria, Ohio, on January 1, 1888. Within six months the factory was producing a line of glass bottles, shakers, and utilitarian wares. By 1891 Fostoria relocated to Moundsville, West Virginia.

Fostoria's stemware and tableware included a wide variety of products in crystal and colors designed to compete actively against Cambridge, Heisey, and Westmoreland. Fostoria changed with the times. When pressed and needle–etched glass fell from favor, the company turned to plate and master etchings. The role of color was increased. When teas and luncheons were replaced by brunches and cocktail parties, Fostoria added new patterns, shapes, and forms. Fostoria marketed aggressively, especially to the post–1945 bridal market.

Fostoria purchased Morgantown Glass in 1965, moving its operations to Moundsville in 1971. In 1983 Lancaster Colony Corporation purchased Fostoria. The Moundsville factory closed in 1986.

References: Gene Florence, *Elegant Glassware Of The Depression Era, Seventh Edition,* Collector Books, 1997; Ann Kerr, *Fostoria: An Identification and Value Guide of Pressed, Blown & Hand Molded Shapes,* Collector Books, 1997 value update; Ann Kerr, *Fostoria,*

Volume II: Identification & Value Guide to Etched, Carved & Cut Designs, Collector Books, 1997; Milbra Long and Emily Seate, *Fostoria Stemware: The Crystal For America,* Collector Books, 1995; Leslie Piña, *Fostoria Designer George Sakier,* Schiffer Publishing, 1996; Leslie Piña, *Fostoria: Serving the American Table 1887–1986,* Schiffer Publishing, 1995; Harry L. Rinker, *Stemware of the 20th Century: The Top 200 Patterns,* House of Collectibles, 1997.

Periodical: *The Daze,* PO Box 57, Otisville, MI 48463.

Collectors' Clubs: Fostoria Glass Collectors, Inc, PO Box 1625, Orange, CA 92668; Fostoria Glass Society of America, PO Box 826, Moundsville, WV 26041.

American, bitters bottle . . . . **$ 50.00**
American, butter dish, cov, round. **125.00**
American, coasters, set of 4 . . . . **30.00**
American, juice tumbler, 5 oz **8.00**
American, relish, oval, 3 part, 10½" **40.00**
American, salt and pepper shakers, pr **25.00**
American, vase, flared, 6" h **25.00**
Baroque, bowl, 6" sq **10.00**
Baroque, cake plate, 10" d. **12.00**
Baroque, goblet, 9 oz **15.00**
Baroque, platter, oval, 12" l **20.00**
Bellwether, goblet, 8½" h **15.00**
Bouquet, goblet. **28.00**
Bouquet, pitcher, 6⅛" h **80.00**
Buttercup, celery **40.00**
Buttercup, vase, ftd, 7" h **150.00**
Camillia, parfait, 5½ oz **22.00**
Century, bowl, handled, 5" d **15.00**
Century, candy dish, cov, ftd **48.00**
Century, mayonnaise, orig liner **30.00**
Chintz, bowl, handled, 10" d **50.00**
Chintz, celery, 11" l **45.00**
Chintz, comport, 5½" d **40.00**
Chintz, creamer, large **25.00**

American, candy dish, cov, 5½" d, crystal, $35.00.

Chintz, plate, 7½" d. **12.00**
Chintz, server, center handle **45.00**
Chintz, sherbet **12.00**
Coin, bowl, 8" d, amber. **30.00**
Coin, bud vase, amber. **30.00**
Coin, candy dish, cov, olive **35.00**
Coin, nappy, handled, 5" d, crystal **20.00**
Colony, butter, cov, ¼ lb, crystal. **50.00**
Colony, creamer and sugar, crystal **22.00**
Colony, salad plate, 7½" d, crystal **12.00**
Fairfax, bowl, 5" d, azure blue **15.00**
Fairfax, creamer, individual, azure blue. **20.00**
Fairfax, demitasse cup and saucer, azure blue. **40.00**
Fairfax, plate, 6" d, green **5.00**
Fascination, tumbler, 13 oz, burgundy **25.00**
Heather, candlesticks, pr, 4½" h **42.00**
Jamestown, goblet, 9½ oz, green **12.00**
Jamestown, sherbet, 6½ oz, amethyst **15.00**
Lafayette, ashtray, 4" d **35.00**
Mayfair, demitasse cup and saucer, yellow **25.00**
Rogene, goblet, 9 oz **20.00**
Romance, sherbet, crystal **20.00**
Royal, tumbler, ftd, 12 oz, 6" h, amber **25.00**
Trojan, bowl, ftd, 12" d **45.00**
Trojan, goblet, topaz **30.00**
Trojan, vegetable bowl, oval, topaz **60.00**
Versailles, bowl, 5½" d, yellow. **25.00**
Versailles, candlesticks, pr, 3" h, blue **55.00**
Versailles, creamer, green. **25.00**
Versailles, dinner plate, pink **80.00**
Versailles, goblet, blue. **45.00**
Versailles, ice bucket, metal handle, yellow **80.00**
Versailles, tumbler, ftd, 5¼" h, pink **30.00**
Vesper, compote, 8" d, amber. **50.00**
Vesper, cream soup, handled, amber **18.00**
Virginia, candlesticks, pr, 6" h, blue **40.00**
Willowmere, cocktail. **30.00**
Willowmere, cup and saucer **18.00**
Willowmere, relish, 3 part **40.00**
Willowmere, sugar, cov **20.00**

FRANCISCAN

Gladding, McBean and Company, Los Angeles, developed and produced the Franciscan dinnerware line in 1934. The line includes a variety of shapes, forms, and patterns. Coronado, El Patio, Metropolitan, Montecito, Padua, and Rancho are solid color dinnerware lines.

The Franciscan hand–painted, embossed patterns of Apple, Desert Rose, and Ivy dominated the secondary collecting market in the 1980s and early 1990s. Today collectors are seeking out some of the more modern Franciscan decaled patterns such as Oasis and Starburst.

References: Susan and Al Bagdade, *Warman's American Pottery and Porcelain*, Wallace–Homestead, Krause Publications, 1994; Lois Lehner, *Lehner's Encyclopedia of U.S. Marks on Pottery, Porcelain & Clay*, Collector Books, 1998; Harry L. Rinker, *Dinnerware of the 20th Century: The Top 500 Patterns*, House of Collectibles, 1997; Jeffrey B. Snyder, *Franciscan Dining Services*, Schiffer Publishing, 1997.

Apple, gravy boat, attached underplate, $60.00.

Apple, bread and butter plate, 6" d. . . . . **$ 10.00**
Apple, cereal bowl, 6" d **15.00**
Apple, compote, large **70.00**
Apple, cup and saucer, demitasse. **65.00**
Apple, dinner plate, 9½" d. **20.00**
Apple, eggcup. **20.00**
Apple, mug, 7 oz. **100.00**
Apple, platter, 14" l **45.00**
Apple, tidbit server, 2 tier. **45.00**
Coronado Swirl, bread and butter plate, 6½" d **10.00**
Coronado Swirl, chop plate, 12" d **50.00**
Coronado Swirl, cream soup, coral, satin **25.00**
Coronado Swirl, creamer and sugar, demitasse, gray,
    satin **20.00**
Coronado Swirl, dinner plate, 10½" d. **20.00**
Coronado Swirl, fruit bowl, 5" d. **15.00**
Coronado Swirl, gravy, attached underplate, yellow,
    satin **25.00**
Coronado Swirl, plate, 6" d, turquoise, glossy **5.00**
Coronado Swirl, sherbet, ftd. **20.00**
Coronado Swirl, vegetable, oval, yellow, satin. **25.00**
Desert Rose, butter pat. **18.00**
Desert Rose, cereal bowl, 6" d **15.00**
Desert Rose, chop plate, 14" d **70.00**
Desert Rose, coffee pot, cov. **100.00**
Desert Rose, cup and saucer **12.00**
Desert Rose, egg cup, single. **22.00**
Desert Rose, plate, 6½" d. **8.00**
Desert Rose, plate, 9½" d. **15.00**
Desert Rose, salt and pepper shakers, pr, rosebud **22.00**
Desert Rose, vegetable bowl, 10" divided **45.00**
Duet, bread and butter plate, 6" d **8.00**
Duet, butter dish, cov **30.00**
Duet, chop plate, 13" d **22.00**
Duet, creamer and sugar, cov. **25.00**
Duet, dinner plate, 10" d **18.00**
Duet, platter, 15" l **25.00**
Duet, salt and pepper shakers, pr **20.00**
Duet, vegetable bowl, divided **28.00**
Ivy, bread and butter plate, 6" d **10.00**
Ivy, butter dish, ¼ lb **35.00**
Ivy, cereal bowl, 7½" d **30.00**
Ivy, gravy, underplate. **12.00**

Ivy, salt and pepper shakers, pr. **35.00**
Ivy, sugar, cov **40.00**
Ivy, tumbler, Libbey, hp dec **20.00**
Starburst, ashtray, individual **25.00**
Starburst, bread and butter plate, 6" d **12.00**
Starburst, butter dish, cov **35.00**
Starburst, cup and saucer **22.00**
Starburst, dinner plate, 10" d **20.00**
Starburst, fruit bowl **18.00**
Starburst, pitcher, medium **80.00**
Starburst, platter, oval, 13" l **30.00**
Starburst, relish, triangular, divided, 6½" w **30.00**
Starburst, salt and pepper shakers, pr **65.00**
Starburst, vegetable bowl, round, divided, 8¼" d **30.00**
Trio, cup and saucer **15.00**
Trio, dinner plate, 10" d **20.00**
Trio, platter, 14" l **20.00**
Trio, saucer **8.00**
Trio, vegetable bowl, open **22.00**

FRANKART

Arthur Von Frankenberg founded Frankart, New York, New York, in the mid–1920s. The company massproduced a wide range of aquariums, ashtrays, bookends, lamps, and vases throughout the 1930s. Frankart nudes are the most desired pieces.

Frankart pieces were cast in white metal. Finishes include bronzoid, cream, French, gun metal, jap, pear green, and verde. Pieces are usually marked with "Frankart, Inc.," and a patent number or "pat. appl. for." Beware of the possibility of a mismatched ashtray when buying a standing figural.

Ashtray, caricature monkey supporting 3" d glass ash
   receiver in tail, 7" h . . . . **$ 95.00**
Ashtray, reclining Great Dane, 8½" h **155.00**
Ashtray, stylized duck with outstretched wings sup-
   porting green glass ash receiver, 5" h **100.00**
Bookends, pr, antelope **145.00**
Bookends, pr, boy with sailboat and dog **100.00**
Bookends, pr, horse heads with flowing manes, 5" h **55.00**
Bookends, pr, seated lions, stylized chip carved, 6" h . . . **125.00**
Bookends, Scottie, standing **270.00**
Incense Burner, female head on burner base, 5" h **195.00**
Lamp, 7" h, 2 nudes sitting back to back, legs out-
   stretched, 5" sq crackle glass globe **450.00**
Smoker's Set, seated nude, leaning back, geometric
   base, arms resting on removable glass cigarette
   box, 3" d removable glass ashtray at feet **295.00**
Wall Pocket, seated nude, wrought–iron metal frame-
   work, metal pan for flowers, 12" h **300.00**

FRANKOMA

John Frank, a ceramics instructor at Oklahoma University, established Frankoma in 1933. In 1938 he moved his commercial production from Norman to Sapulpa. When a fire destroyed the plant in 1939, he rebuilt immediately.

A honey–tan colored clay from Ada was used to make Frankoma pieces prior to 1954. After that date, the company switched to a red brick clay from Sapulpa. Today some clay is brought into the plant from other areas.

Fire again struck the Sapulpa plant in September 1983. By July 1984 a new plant was opened. Since the early molds were lost in the fire, new molds were designed and made.

Reference: Phyllis and Tom Bess, *Frankoma and Other Oklahoma Potteries,* Schiffer Publishing, 1995.

Collectors' Club: Frankoma Family Collectors Assoc, PO Box 32571, Oklahoma City, OK 73123.

Ashtray, Dutch shoe, #914, 6", desert gold, red clay . . . **$ 25.00**
Bowl, #45, swirled, 12", prairie green, Ada **20.00**
Bud Vase, #32, modern, prairie green, Sapulpa **12.00**
Cornucopia, #57, 7", brown satin, Sapulpa **10.00**
Flower Bowl, prairie green, Sapulpa **25.00**
Honey Jug, #833, brown satin, Sapulpa **15.00**
Lazybones, cereal bowl, #4X, brown satin, Sapulpa **5.00**
Match Holder, #89A, 1942, royal blue **40.00**
Mug, #C2, flame, Sapulpa **5.00**
Plainsman, creamer, #5A, flame **5.00**
Plainsman, dinner plate, #5F, 10½" d, desert gold **12.00**
Plainsman, salad bowl, #5X, brown satin **5.00**
Plainsman, teacup, #5CC, 5 oz, prairie green **8.00**
Vase, #23A, pedestal, brown satin, Sapulpa **8.00**
Vase, #272, ringed, brown satin, Sapulpa **8.00**
Wagon Wheel, bean pot, individual, #94U, desert
   gold, Sapulpa **40.00**
Wagon Wheel, casserole, #94V, desert gold, Sapulpa **35.00**
Wagon Wheel, creamer and sugar, #94A & B, desert
   gold, Ada **8.00**
Wagon Wheel, dinner plate, #94FL, 10" d, desert
   gold, Ada **10.00**
Wagon Wheel, fruit bowl, small, #94SX, desert gold,
   Ada **10.00**
Wagon Wheel, salad plate, #94G, 7" d, desert gold,
   Ada **10.00**
Wagon Wheel, saucer, #94E, desert gold, Ada **5.00**
Wagon Wheel, teapot, cov, #94J, 2 cup, desert gold,
   Sapulpa, no lid **10.00**

Political Mug, donkey, autumn yellow, 1975, $35.00.

FRATERNAL & SERVICE ORGANIZATIONS

Benevolent and fraternal societies from the Odd Fellows to the Knights of Columbus continued to play a major role in American life through the first two–thirds of the 20th century. Members tended to be male. Women participated through Auxiliaries. Meetings and rituals were highly secretive. Many of the policies and practices of these organizations came under attack during the Civil Rights and Women's Lib eras. Many organizations lost members and were forced to close local chapters. The decline has stabilized in the 1990s, leaving the fraternal movement but a shadow of its former self.

Local service clubs such as the Lions and Rotary established themselves as a major force in community life in the 1920s and 30s. Their golden age spanned the 1950s and 60s. Like the fraternal societies, many service clubs allowed only male members. More willing to change, most male service clubs opened their doors to the opposite sex. Female service clubs have not been as generous. Increasing workplace and family demands have cut heavily into membership. Membership has stabilized at best in most clubs. In many cases, the average age of club members is well above 50.

American Legion, cane, wood, Milwaukee, 1941 . . . . . **$ 30.00**
Benevolent & Protective Order of Elks, book,
  National Memorial, color illus, 1931 . . . . **35.00**
Independent Order of Odd Fellows, certificate, 8
  vignettes, 1927 . . . . **15.00**
Independent Order of Odd Fellows, souvenir book,
  1922 convention **30.00**
Masonic, Bible, illus, leather binding, 24k gold
  stamping, c1931, 1,200 pgs, 9½ x 11½ x 2½". **70.00**
Masonic, book, *Encyclopedia of Freemasonry,* 2 vol,
  1921 . . . . **50.00**
Masonic, book, *Short Talk Bulletin,* Masonic Service
  Assoc, 1923 . . . . **25.00**

Loyal Order of Moose, wall hanging, crochet, 24 x 23", $35.00.

Masonic, magazine, *Masonic World,* War Unity
  issue, Sep 1942 . . . . **15.00**
Masonic, tie bar, cuff links, insignia, sterling, c1940 . . . . . **65.00**
Shriner, booklet, Shrine Circus, Narragansett Park, RI,
  1940, 46 pgs **8.00**

FRUIT JARS

The canning of fruits and vegetables played a major role in the American household until the late 1950s. Canning jars were recycled year after year. Jars utilizing zinc lids and rubber–sealed metal lids are extremely common. These jars usually sell for between 50¢ and $1.00.

Do not assume the date on a jar indicates the year the jar was made. In almost every case, it is a patent date or the founding date of the company that made the jar.

References: Douglas M. Leybourne, Jr., *The Collector's Guide To Old Fruit Jars, Red Book No. 8,* published by author, 1997; Bill Schroeder, *1000 Fruit Jars: Priced and Illustrated, 5th Edition,* Collector Books, 1987, 1996 value update.

Collectors' Clubs: Ball Collectors Club, 22203 Doncaster, Riverview, MI 48192; Federation of Historical Bottle Collectors, Inc, 88 Sweetbriar Branch, Longwood, FL 32750.

Acme, pt. . . . . **$ 5.00**
Amazon Swift Seal, clear, glass lid, wire bail, qt **5.00**
Anchor Hocking Mason, clear, square, pt **2.50**
Ball, green, zinc lid, pt **2.50**
Ball Deluxe Jar, clear, glass lid, wire bail, pt **5.00**
Canadian Sure Seal, clear, smooth lip, beaded neck
  seal. **2.50**
Cleveland Fruit Juice Co, Cleveland, OH, clear,
  ground lip, glass lid, ½ gal **5.00**
Crystal Mason, clear, zinc lid, pt **10.00**
Double Safety, clear, glass lid, wire bail, ½ pt. **5.00**
Drey Ever Seal, clear **2.50**
Drey Mason, clear. **2.00**
Economy, pt, amber, cylindrical, metal lid, spring clip. **5.00**
Ermeblok, clear. **2.50**
Golden Harvest Mason 6GC, clear, cornucopia with
  fruit. **1.00**
Good House Keepers, clear, zinc lid, 2 qt. **2.50**
Harvest Time Mason, clear. **1.50**
Hormel Fine Food, clear **2.50**
Improved Corona Jar Made In Canada, clear. **2.50**
Ivanhoe, clear, metal lid, qt **5.00**
Jumbo Brand Apple Butter, patented June 24, 1930,
  smooth lip metal screw cover, painted, 10 oz **20.00**
Kerr Economy Trade Mark, clear, metal lid, clip, pt **5.00**
Kerr Self–Sealing Mason, clear, smooth lip, beaded
  neck seal, 2 pc metal lid, c1977 . . . . **40.00**
Liquid Carbonic Company, clear **2.00**
Lyon Jar, clear, cylindrical, emb "Patented Apr 10
  1900," ground mouth, qt **2.50**
Magic TM Mason, clear, cup and oz measurements
  on one side, milliliter measurements on other . . . . **.50**
Mallinger, clear. **5.00**
Mason, clear, 1776, Liberty Bell, and 1976 reverse **2.50**

Ball Ideal, clear, glass lid, wire bail, emb lettering, $2.00.

Mason, clear, wide mouth, fish emb reverse, 2 pc
metal closure. **2.50**
Metro Easi–Pak Mason, clear **2.50**
Newmark Special Extra Mason, green, metal screw
top, qt **12.00**
Pine Deluxe Jar, clear, glass lid, wire bail, emb,
machine made, pt **5.00**
Presto Fruit Jar, clear **2.00**
Pure–Food Products, clear **2.50**
Putnam, aqua **3.00**
Quick Seal, blue **2.50**
Red Mason's Patent Nov 30th 1858, aqua, zinc lid,
pt **12.00**
Regal, clear, glass lid, emb "Regal" in oval, hand-
made, qt **2.50**
Safe Seal, clear, patented July 14, 1908 . . . . **5.00**
Security Seal, clear, glass lid, wire ball, qt. **6.50**
The Weir, stoneware jar and lid, brown and white,
wire and metal clamp. **20.00**
Trademark Climax Registered, clear, smooth lip, 1/2 pt **4.00**
Tropical Canners, pt. **8.00**
Weidman Boy Brand, Cleveland, clear, glass lid, wire
bail, pt. **8.00**
Whitney Mason, aqua, smooth lip **5.00**
Woodbury Improved (monogram), aquamarine,
cylindrical, ground mouth, qt **35.00**

FRY GLASS

H. C. Fry Glass, Rochester, Pennsylvania, operated between 1901
and 1933. After an initial production period making Brilliant cut
glass, the company turned to manufacturing glass tableware.

Pearl Oven Glass, a heat–resistant opalescent colored glass, was
patented in 1922. Most pieces are marked with "Fry" and a model
number. For a two–year period, 1926–27, H. C. Fry produced
Foval, an art glass line. Its pieces are identified by their pearly
opalescent body with an applied trim of jade green or Delft blue.
Silver overlay pieces are marked "Rockwell."

Collectors' Club: H. C. Fry Glass Society, PO Box 41, Beaver, PA
15009.

REPRODUCTION ALERT: Italian reproductions of Foval, produced
in the 1970s, have a teal blue transparent trim.

Chicago, sherbet, cut glass, 4" h. . . . . **$ 75.00**
Crackle, punch cup, clear, cobalt blue ring handle **50.00**
Crackle, tumbler, green handle, 5 1/4" h **65.00**
Diamond Optic, vase, clear, azure blue trim, 7 1/2" h **150.00**
Foval, bouillon cup and saucer, blue Delft handles **75.00**
Foval, bud vase, cobalt blue foot, 10" h **130.00**
Foval, cake plate, jade green handle, ball feet, 10" d **500.00**
Foval, canape plate, cobalt blue center handle, 6 1/4" d . . . **175.00**
Foval, candlesticks, pr, cobalt blue neck and base
rings, blue threads, 9" h **275.00**
Foval, compote, 6 3/4" h, jade green stem **125.00**
Foval, creamer, blue tinted loppings, applied Delft
blue handle **155.00**
Foval, cruet, cobalt blue handle, orig stopper **120.00**
Foval, cup and saucer, cobalt blue stripe, pale blue
opaline ground **75.00**
Foval, cup and saucer, green handle. **55.00**
Foval, decanter, ftd, 9" h, applied Delft blue handle. **170.00**
Foval, goblet, opalescent bowl, pink loppings **90.00**
Foval, lemonade tumbler, Icicle, 6 1/4" h, green handle **65.00**
Foval, plate, 9 1/2" d, Delft blue rim **75.00**
Foval, teapot, cobalt blue spout, hande and knob **225.00**
Foval, toothpick holder, Delft blue handle. **75.00**
Foval, vase, jade green, rolled rim and ft, 7 1/2" h **200.00**
Foval, water pitcher, alabaster body, jade green base
and handle **300.00**
Foval, wine, Delft blue stem **160.00**
Icicle, tumbler, green handle, 5 1/4" h. **65.00**
Pearl Oven Ware, bean pot, 1 qt **40.00**
Pearl Oven Ware, butter dish, cov **75.00**
Pearl Oven Ware, casserole, cov **30.00**
Pearl Oven Ware, custard cup, 3 3/4" **8.00**
Pearl Oven Ware, grill plate, 10 1/2" d **35.00**
Pearl Oven Ware, platter, etched rim **30.00**

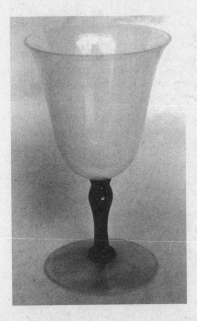

Foval, goblet, cobalt blue stem, 5 3/4" h, $125.00.

FULPER

Fulper Art Pottery was made by the American Pottery Company, Flemington, New Jersey, beginning around 1910 and ending in 1930. All pieces were molded. Pieces from the 1920s tend to be of higher quality due to less production pressures.

Pieces exhibit a strong Arts and Crafts and/or Oriental influence. Glazes differed tremendously as Fulper experimented throughout its production period.

Reference: Ralph and Terry Kovel, *Kovel's American Art Pottery: The Collector's Guide To Makers, Marks and Factory Histories,* Crown Publishers, 1993.

Collectors' Club: Stangl/Fulper Collectors Club, PO Box 64–A, Changewater, NJ 07831.

REPRODUCTION ALERT

Bowl, blue dip glaze, beige and green int, 9½" d .... **$ 225.00**
Bowl, blue green drip, 7½" d **20.00**
Bowl, #559, blue, ivory, and brown flambe glaze,
    imp mark, 11½" d **225.00**
Bud Vase, slender ovoid body, flared rim, short
    pedestal, domed, ringed ft, wisteria matte glaze,
    vertical ink mark **95.00**
Candlestick, blue green glaze, 5¼" h **60.00**
Flower Frog, mushroom shape, flambe glaze.......... **18.00**
Jar, #564, matte green glaze, 6¼" h **270.00**
Lamp, green mirror glaze, silver crystals, bronze
    base, 19" h. **250.00**
Mug, cider **55.00**
Powder Box, bisque woman holding fan............. **145.00**
Vase, aqua and yellow, mkd, 8¼" h **120.00**
Vase, handled, blue crystal glaze, oval, 6¾" h......... **80.00**
Vase, vasiform, circular ftd base, white glazed, imp
    Fulper–Stangl mark, crazing, 18" h **225.00**

AUCTION PRICES

David Rago's Arts and Crafts Auction held at the Antique & Auction Centre, Lambertville, NJ on March 16, 1997. Prices listed include a 10% buyer's premium.

Bowls, set of 6, flaring rims, leopard skin crystalline
    glaze, vertical ink racetrack marks, 2" h, 5" d **467.50**
Vase, baluster shaped, raised dots on shoulder, covered in mirrored black to copperdust crystalline
    flambe glaze, unmkd, 7 x 4½" **660.00**
Vase, bell pepper shaped, cat's eye to Chinese blue
    flambe glaze, vertical rect ink mark, 4¼ x 4¾".... **385.00**
Vase, corseted, 2 handled, copperdust crystalline to
    Flemington green flambe glaze, raised vertical
    racetrack mark, 10 x 6¾"................... **605.00**
Vase, gourd shaped, mirrored black to Flemington
    green flambe glaze, vertical rect Prang mark,
    5½ x 3"................................. **440.00**
Vase, ovoid, 2 handled, green to cobalt crystalline
    flambe glaze, incised racetrack mark and paper
    label, 7¾ x 5¾"............................ **330.00**
Vase, tapering, 2 handled, cucumber crystalline to
    cucumber matte glaze, ink racetrack mark, 13 x
    7½"................................... **1,100.00**

FURNITURE

The furniture industry experienced tremendous growth in the periods immediately following World Wars I and II as America's population ballooned and wartime advances in materials and technology were applied to furniture. Furniture was made in a variety of grades, making the latest styles available to virtually every income level.

Beginning in the 1920s, the American popular taste tended to go in two directions, Colonial Revival and upholstered furniture. Colonial Revival furniture divides into two distinct groups: (1) high style pieces that closely mirrored their historic counterparts and (2) generic forms that combined design elements from many different styles in a single piece. Large numbers of upholstered pieces utilized frames that drew their inspiration from English and European revival styles, e.g, Elizabethan and Louis XIV. Buyers with a modern bent fell briefly in love with Art Deco forms before becoming completely captivated by Streamlined Modern.

While leading designers such as Charles Eames experimented with new materials and forms prior to World War II, it was after the war that modern furniture reached the mass market. Colonial Revival gave way to an Early American craze, while upholstered furniture veered off in a sectional direction. Many trendy styles, e.g., Mediterranean, Scandinavian, and tubular, lasted less than a decade.

It was in the post–1945 period when designers shifted their focus from household furniture to office and institutional furniture. Design became truly international as English and European design studios, e.g. Memphis, replaced America as the major influence for style change.

American tastes became traditional and conservative again in the mid–1970s. Colonial Revival styles made a strong comeback. Modernism was out, except among a select few in large metropolitan areas. Today, many people desiring a modern look are buying pieces manufactured from the mid–1940s through the early 1960s.

Generic oak furniture is experiencing a revival; most forms are reproductions of earlier pieces. Upholstered sectional furniture enjoys a small, but loyal following. The Craft Revival, begun in the early 1970s, continues.

Collectors pay a premium for furniture made by a major manufacturer based on the design of an internationally recognized furniture designer. Name counts heavily, even in mass–produced furniture.

Style Chronology:

Craft Revival 1900–1940
Colonial Revival (High Style and Generic) 1915–1940
International 1920s
Art Deco 1925–1935
Streamlined Modern 1930s/early 1940s
Contemporary/Post–War Modernism ....late 1940s/early 1960s
Early American 1950s–1960s
Neo–Modernism and Pop 1960s
Craft Revival 1970s–present
Colonial Revival 1970s–present
Memphis 1980s

References: *American Manufactured Furniture, Furniture Dealers' Reference Book,* reprint by Schiffer Publishing, 1988, 1996 value update; *Fine Furniture Reproductions: 18th Century Revivals of the*

1930s and 1940s from Baker Furniture, Schiffer Publishing, 1996; Oscar Fitzgerald, *Four Centuries of American Furniture,* Wallace–Homestead, Krause Publications, 1995; Cara Greenberg, *Mid–Century Modern: Furniture of the 1950s,* Crown Publishers, 1995; Emyl Jenkin, *Emyl Jenkin's Reproduction Furniture: Antiques for the Next Generation,* Crown Publishers, 1995; David P. Lindquist and Caroline C. Warren, *Colonial Revival Furniture With Prices,* Wallace–Homestead, Krause Publications, 1993.

Leslie Piña, *Fifties Furniture,* Schiffer Publishing, 1996; Steve Rouland and Roger W. Rouland, *Heywood–Wakefield Modern Furniture,* Collector Books, 1995, 1997 value update; Robert W. and Harriett Swedberg, *Collector's Encyclopedia of American Furniture, Vol. 2,* Collector Books, 1992, 1996 value update; Robert W. and Harriett Swedberg, *Collector's Encyclopedia of American Furniture, Vol. 2,* Collector Books, 1992, 1996 value update; Robert W. and Harriett Swedberg, *Furniture of the Depression Era,* Collector Books, 1987, 1996 value update.

Art Deco, bedroom suite, burled walnut veneer and mahogany, 5 pcs, tall chest of drawers with cabinet, mirrored chest of drawers, vanity with upholstered sitting stool, double bed, all case pieces with rounded contours, circular brass pulls, round mirrors with scalloped edges, tall chest measures 40 x 21 x 56" . . . . $ 1,250.00

Art Deco, bookcase, polished aluminum, tin plates, pair of leaded glass doors, bird's eye maple back panels 58 x 17 x 65" 7,500.00

Art Deco, bureau, Marc Hand Co, New York, box format, silver tone, completely mirrored, center drawer flanked by 2 drawers, Lucite and chrome pulls, tapered legs, metal tag, 40 x 29³⁄₄ x 16¹⁄₄" 1,500.00

Art Deco, cabinet, Secessions Ltd, Chicago, wood, rect top over facet–carved cupboard doors with strong vertical and horizontal stripe motif, int drawers and cubbyholes over 2 aligned drawers set on block feet, accompanied by orig design rendering, 51 x 19¹⁄₂ x 62" 2,500.00

Art Deco, cabinet, walnut, circular inlaid wood fronts, bronze handle and back plate on carved scroll support, 36 x 18 x 40" 350.00

Art Deco, cedar chest, waterfall veneer, Lane, 1930s 200.00

Art Deco, chair, tubular chrome, from *Isle De France* ocean liner, reupholstered in plaid silk fabric, 26 x 28 x 30" 2,200.00

Art Deco, chifferobe, herringbone design waterfall veneer, arched center mirror, dropped center section, 4 deep drawers, flanked by tall cupboard doors, shaped apron, 1930s 450.00

Art Deco Style, coffee table, Kittinger, attributed to James Mont designer, Chinese motif, faux tortoise-shell top, black lacquered oval grid base, 1952, 42" d top, 14" h, 1952 . . . . 250.00

Art Deco, console table, Albert Ponteneuve, zebra-wood, rect top with scrolled ends, flip top literary display on slab supports, notched and channeled bottom dec, 47 x 13 x 28" 2,250.00

Art Deco, daybed, Jules Leleu designer, walnut, 2 high scrolling ends, rect plinth, tapering everted feet ending in scrolls, upholstered cushion and rolled pillows, 1925 . . . . 5,000.00

Art Deco, desk, box format, attributed to Donald Deskey, burlwood, fall front, full int gallery, 3 full–length drawers, brass and bronze linear pulls, 26 x 17¹⁄₂ x 40³⁄₄" 950.00

Art Deco, desk, rect form, walnut, 4 drawers, chrome–plated tube steel pulls, bent chrome tube steel support, 54 x 32 x 31" 900.00

Art Deco, living room suite, armchair and sofa, chair with barrel back, channeled bright pink velour upholstery, boldly carved arm fronts and apron, sofa with barrel back, serpentine front, 3 cushion seat, conforming upholstery, mid–1930s 3,000.00

Art Deco, sofa, Chesterfield, Michael Taylor designer, straight back, scroll over arms, upholstered in quilt-ed green floral ivory ground chintz with fringed valance and pillows, 2 seat cushions, 1930s, 105" l . 4,000.00

Art Deco, telephone table, Adler, rect top, rounded end above case with open shelves, cutout support and small drawer, 1937 . . . . 300.00

Art Deco, vanity, walnut, large round mirror, dropped center well, flanked by two 3–drawer sections, 1935 . . 350.00

Art Deco, vanity and stool, attributed to Norman Bel Geddes, yellow enameled metal and chrome, 4 drawers to right, glass shelf, free–standing circular mirror, 49 x 30¹⁄₄ x 17" 850.00

Colonial Revival, Pre–War, armchair, Chippendale style, Martha Washington, mahogany frame, worn finish, gold striped upholstery, 38" h 250.00

Colonial Revival, Pre–War, bed, Regency style, inlaid rosewood upholstered headboard, conforming footboard, shaped framework, brass inlay and mounts, double mattress size, 56" h 500.00

Colonial Revival, Pre–War, bedroom suite, generic, 5 pcs, bed, dresser, dressing table, bench, and poster bed, bed with burl walnut veneered head-board, oak broken arch pediment, center urn finial, burl walnut and oak panel on footboard, dresser with plain cut walnut veneer top and sides, 2 out-

Art Deco, desk and chair, waterfall veneer, $300.00.

Colonial Revival, drum table, Harmony House (Sears), mahogany veneer, single drawer, turned column, brass claw feet, 28" d top, 29" h, $150.00.

side shaped mirrors flank center arched and engraved mirror, arched and diamond molding on drawer fronts, dressing table with plain cut walnut veneer on top and sides, mirror shaped like dresser but larger in size, bench with turned and scrolled hardwoods, velvet upholstered sides and seat. 1,500.00

Colonial Revival, Pre–War, cabinet, generic, figured walnut veneer panels and drawer front, solid walnut back rail, 3 curly maple overlay shield designs, selected hardwood frame, bulbous turned front legs, H–stretcher base, 1920s, 38 x 14 x 65" 300.00

Colonial Revival, Pre–War, card table, Hepplewhite style, mahogany, inlaid, D–shaped top, drop leaves, minor wear, 19" w, opens to 38" w, 38" d, 31" h 500.00

Colonial Revival, Pre–War, chest of drawers, Hepplewhite style, solid mahogany, inlay on drawers and back rail, 2 small drawers over 2 long drawers, eagle brasses, 1920s, 42 x 19 x 38". 500.00

Colonial Revival, Pre–War, chifferobe, generic, burl walnut, burl mahogany, bird's eye maple, and Macassar striped ebony veneers, shaped scalloped pediment over 2 shaped doors over 2 drawers, molded cornice, int with 3 small drawers over 3 long drawers, ring–turned bulbous feet, 59 h 300.00

Colonial Revival, Pre–War, china cabinet, Chippendale style, walnut veneer breakfront, scrolled broken pediment, center urn finial, pair of glazed doors and panels, long drawer over 2 cupboard doors, 44 x 15 x 76". 850.00

Colonial Revival, Pre–War, china cabinet, generic, bird's eye maple and zebrawood veneers, marquetry on front of drawer and cabinet, oval crest with inlay and scrolled foliate motif, double arched doors with intricate mullions, shelved int, lower drawers, shaped pediment with carved center urn finials, turned reeded legs 450.00

Colonial Revival, Pre–War, desk, Chippendale style, block front, solid walnut case, walnut veneered slant front lid, fitted int with secret drawer, paw feet, 32 x 18 x 42" 750.00

Colonial Revival, Pre–War, desk, Governor Winthrop style, mahogany veneer, solid mahogany slant front, fitted int with 2 document drawers, shell–carved center door, serpentine front, 4 long drawers, brass pulls and escutcheons, 1920s. 600.00

Colonial Revival, Pre–War, desk, Jacobean style, oak, carved, 9 dovetailed drawers, applied foliage scrolls and lion heads, pullout writing surface, worn blue felt covering, rope carved legs, old soft legs, 51 x 28½ x 40¾" 750.00

Colonial Revival, Pre–War, desk, Spinet style, solid mahogany, hinged front, fitted int with drawers and pigeonholes, cylindrical reeded legs, 33 x 21 x 39" 450.00

Colonial Revival, Pre–War, dining chairs, generic, set of 6, mahogany, Cupid's bow crest, pierced splat, slip seat, cabriole legs joined by box stretcher 750.00

Colonial Revival, Pre–War, dining table, Queen Anne style, mahogany, console table shape, pullout frame, 2 shaped leaves, worn finish, 66" l extended, 39 x 30½" 750.00

Colonial Revival, Pre–War, nightstand, generic, walnut veneer, drawer over blind cupboard door, applied beaded molding around drawer, reeded trumpet legs, 5" sq top 75.00

Colonial Revival, Pre–War, Pembroke table, Hepplewhite style, Grand Rapids, plain cut mahogany veneer top and drop leaves, figured mahogany drawer front, solid base, medallion inlay, sq tapering legs, 17 x 15 x 22". 300.00

Colonial Revival, Pre–War, rocker, Windsor style, Colonial Furniture Company, Grand Rapids, MI, comb back, birch, mahogany finish, turned legs, 21 x 17 x 27½" h from seat to top of back. 250.00

Colonial Revival, Pre–War, secretary/bookcase, Governor Winthrop, bookcase with broken pediment, center urn finial, molded cornice, pair of glazed doors, shelved and fitted int with slant front, 3 graduated drawers, oval brasses, ball and claw feet, 33" w, 80" h. 1,000.00

Colonial Revival, Pre–War, secretary/bookcase, Sheraton style, Luce Furniture, Grand Rapids, MI, veneered, broken pediment with fretwork, urn finial, pair of glazed arched mullioned doors, slant front with fitted int, frieze of 2 drawers over 2 long drawers, tapered sq legs and feet. 650.00

Colonial Revival, Pre–War, settee, William and Mary style, loose cushions, turned baluster legs and stretcher, 48" l 800.00

Colonial Revival, Pre–War, sewing stand, generic, Priscilla type, painted red, dark trim, floral decal, turned rod type handle, 13 x 11 x 25". 85.00

Colonial Revival, Pre–War, sewing stand, Martha Washington style, solid mahogany, 3 drawers, shaped ends, ring–turned legs, 28 x 14 x 29". 350.00

Colonial Revival, vanity, generic, walnut, swing mirror, reeded mirror supports, stiles, and legs, 3 drawers, 2 doors, applied molding, casters, 48" w, $250.00.

Colonial Revival, Pre–War, sideboard, Chippendale style, mahogany, central bow front of 2 drawer frieze over 2 deep drawers, flanked by wine drawer, central section flanked by drawers over curved cupboard, whole raised on cabriole legs ending in ball and claw feet, 46 x 18 x 40½" **1,500.00**

Colonial Revival, Pre–War, sideboard, Federal style, Landstrom Furniture Co, mahogany, serpentine front, molded top edge, 2 drawers flanked by doors, square tapering legs, 116 x 22 x 37" **750.00**

Colonial Revival, Pre–War, side chair, Queen Anne style, walnut veneer, vase splat, slip upholstered seat, modified cabriole legs, 1920s **125.00**

Colonial Revival, Pre–War, side chair, Queen Anne style, walnut veneer slat, walnut stained hardwood frame, pressed cane seat, French legs, 1920s, 27" h **85.00**

Colonial Revival, Pre–War, smoking stand, generic, straight cut walnut veneer, rect top, figured walnut veneered door, painted William and Mary style base, 18 x 11 x 30" **150.00**

Colonial Revival, Pre–War, table, Duncan Phyfe style, drop leaf, mahogany stained and veneered, 16" l D–shaped leaves, brass casters on outswept reeded legs, 41 x 24 x 30" **350.00**

Colonial Revival, Pre–War, vanity, generic, walnut, Chippendale–style swing mirror, reeded mirror supports, mahogany veneered front, central drawer flanked by sections with small drawer over blind cupboard door, reeded trumpet feet, casters, 48" w, 20" d **250.00**

Colonial Revival, Pre–War, wing chair, Queen Anne style, Kittinger, Williamsburg reproduction, pink striped silk upholstery, 49" h **2,500.00**

Contemporary, armchair, Knoll, Jens Risom designer, blond wood reversed "U" frame with stretcher, shaped seat, adjustable seat of woven red straps, Knoll paper label, 24¾ x 26 x 29" **250.00**

Contemporary, bedroom set, Heywood Wakefield, 4 pcs, double bed, tall chest, mirrored chest, and nightstand with elevated shelves, black ink mark . . . **1,500.00**

Contemporary, bookcase, corner, Heywood Wakefield, champagne finish, 2 adjustable shelves, black ink stamp, 28 x 28 x 32¾" **350.00**

Contemporary, cabinet, Herman Miller, George Nelson designer, open front arrangement of vertical and horizontal compartments over 4 sections of drawers, 4 chrome legs, 81 x 18½ x 43" **1,750.00**

Contemporary, cabinet, Knoll, 5 drawers, marble top, oak veneer, white enameled metal legs, 37½ x 18 x 26" **475.00**

Contemporary, cabinet, Les Ateliers de Prouve, Maxeville, Nancy, Jean Prouve designer, period turquoise enameled metal ext and int with aluminum sliding door with wooden handles, 63 x 22 x 63" **12,500.00**

Contemporary, cabinet, Paul McCobb designer, mahogany, 5 drawers, 1 cabinet door, brass legs, 71¼ x 29 x 31¾" **275.00**

Contemporary, chair, LCM, Herman Miller, Charles Eames designer, molded birch plywood seat and back on chrome metal frame, 22 x 23 x 26", wear to wood **150.00**

Contemporary, chaise lounge, Knoll, Richard Schultz designer, vinyl mesh seat on white epoxy aluminum frame, 21 x 63 x 34" **500.00**

Contemporary, chest of drawers, Herman Miller, Gilbert Rhode designer, 4–drawer cabinet in Macassar striped ebony and figured maple veneer, 46 x 20 x 34" **2,750.00**

Contemporary, chest of drawers, Heywood Wakefield, Sculptura, champagne finish, die–stamp mark, 38 x 19 x 39½" **750.00**

Contemporary, children's chairs, set of 4, Knoll, white plastic–coated wire frame on black metal base, 13 x 12 x 20" **450.00**

Contemporary, china cabinet, Heywood Wakefield, 2 pcs, M593 credenza with M909 china cabinet, period wheat finish, 53 x 18 x 72" **700.00**

Contemporary, coconut chair, Herman Miller, George Nelson designer, black vinyl triangular seat, white fiberglass shell, supported by 3 chrome strut legs, 38½ x 33 x 34" **2,750.00**

Contemporary, coffee table, Knoll, Florence Knoll designer, circular walnut top on chrome base, 24" d top, 16" h **500.00**

Contemporary, desk, Winchendon Modern, Paul McCobb designer, rect top, 2 drawers to left, tapered round legs, 48 x 24 x 29" **300.00**

Contemporary, dinette set, Heywood Wakefield, Encore, 6 pcs, 4 side chairs, extension table, and shelving unit over 2–door cabinet, champagne finish, shelving unit measures 32¼ x 17½ x 64 ½", some wear to top of table and stains to cabinet doors **800.00**

Contemporary, dining chairs, set of 4, armchair and 3 side chairs, Heywood Wakefield, dog–bone back,

Contemporary, side chair, M 1554 A, Heywood–Wakefield, dog–bone back, champagne finish, striped upholstery, 1956–66, 32½" h, $125.00.

period dark green upholstered seats, wheat finish, black ink stamp **600.00**

Contemporary, dining chairs, set of 6, Plycraft, Norman Cherner designer, 2 arm and 4 side, sculpted walnut frames with walnut back and seat, armchair measures 24 x 20 x 31", refinished **2,250.00**

Contemporary, dining table, Heywood Wakefield, #5576 drop–leaf table on triple pedestal base, period wheat finish, 2 leaves, 27 x 40 x 29", some minor wear to top **475.00**

Contemporary, dining table, Johnson Furniture Co, Paul T. Frankl designer, cork top, rect top on leg supports, each having slat "V" configuration, 2 leaves, 70 x 42 x 29" **925.00**

Contemporary, dining table, Knoll, Warren Plattner designer, circular walnut veneer top on bronze finish wire base, 36" top d, 28" h **550.00**

Contemporary, dining table, Tulip, Knoll, Eero Saarinen designer, circular top, round flaring base, 54" d top, 28½" h, minor chipping to white enamel underneath table top **650.00**

Contemporary, dining table, Widdicomb, T. H. Robsjohn Gibbings designer, birch construction, rect form top, beveled sides, sculptural base, 60 x 43 x 28½" **400.00**

Contemporary, dresser, Widdicomb, T. H. Robsjohn Gibbings designer, 5 drawer, dowel pulls, silver–plated ends, 34 x 22 x 46½" **250.00**

Contemporary, dresser, Winchendon Modern, Paul McCobb designer, 6 drawer, birch construction, tapered brass pulls, tapered dowel legs, 32 x 18 x 18 . . . . **350.00**

Contemporary, egg chair, Fritz Hansen, Arne Jacobsen designer, sculptured form, period dark green wool fabric, aluminum tilt base, 32 x 29 x 42" **2,250.00**

Contemporary, egg chair and ottoman, Fritz Hansen, Arne Jacobsen designer, sculptured formed seat

and back having period rust red leather upholstery on 4–prong aluminum base, chair 42" h **4,000.00**

Contemporary, lounge chair, Atelier International, paper label, Le Corbusier designer, sgd Le Corbusier LC/4 1049, chrome tubular support structure, wooden "H" base, worn leather pad, 1968 . . . . **600.00**

Contemporary, lounge chair and ottoman, Herman Miller, Charles Eames designer, rosewood shell, black leather, sgd Herman Miller, c1970, 32 x 29 x 32½" **1,200.00**

Contemporary, love seat, Knoll, Eero Saarinen designer, new yellow–orange wool upholstery on molded base, black metal rod legs, unmkd, 61 x 33½ x 37" **1,250.00**

Contemporary, nesting tables, set of 3, Heywood Wakefield, champagne finish, each with rounded rect top, tapered legs, black ink stamp, 21 x 15 x 24" **500.00**

Contemporary, rocker, Herman Miller, Charles Eames, primary red fiberglass shell on zinc struts, birch runners, 24 x 27 x 27" **1,500.00**

Contemporary, server, Heywood Wakefield, M590, period wheat finish, 34 x 17 x 33" **675.00**

Contemporary, sling sofa, Herman Miller, George Nelson designer, 3–seat sofa upholstered in black leather with chrome frame, 87 x 33 x 29" **2,400.00**

Contemporary, sofa, Dunbar, Edward Wormley designer, period off–white upholstery, walnut frame, 84 x 29 x 29" **1,750.00**

Contemporary, sofa, Knoll, Florence Knoll designer, tufted seat and back in mauve wool fabric on stainless base, 84 x 30 x 30" **600.00**

Contemporary, stool, Sori Yanagi, butterfly, molded rosewood veneer, brass stretcher, c1956, 16" w, 16" h **1,600.00**

Craftsman, armchair, Wharton Esherick, Windsor style, 6 spindle, 2 are arm/rear leg supports, woven black leather seat, pre–1945, 22½ x 20 x 29½" **3,250.00**

Craftsman, bed, George Nakashima, large slab headboard and 2 platform boxes with joinery in contrasting woods, post–1950, king size, 80½ x 115 x 37" **6,000.00**

Craftsman, settee, carved and laminated walnut, Kavinsky, sculptured formed seat and back on abstract trunk form base, sgd, post–1950, 60 x 23 x 35" **2,000.00**

Craftsman, torchere, carved and laminated walnut, Kavinsky, flower form, reflecting light source, sgd, 71½" h **1,250.00**

Early American, commode (table), solid maple, autumn brown finish, rect top, single drawer, false front with 2 drawers over 2 drawers, shaped skirt, slightly splayed baluster turned legs, 26 x 21 x 23" **40.00**

Early American, rocker, Beacon Hill, maple frame, finished in Salem (light maple), removable cushions padded with cotton liners, mint green oval motif cotton print cover, ruffled skirt, 25 x 24 x 34" **65.00**

Early American, sofa, Chippendale style, Harmony House, upholstered in medium gold tweed fabric,

Early American, kneehole desk, Chippendale style, 9 drawers, ogee bracket feet, batwing brasses, $100.00.

2 back Serofoam plastic foam cushions with shaped tops, 2 reversible cushions on seat, padded arms and wing sides, pleated shirt, 85 x 37 x 36"..... **100.00**

International Modern, side chair, Josef Hoffmann, designer, U–form back rail above 3 cross bars continuing to shaped rect upholstered seat, 4 cylindrical legs on U–form base, first quarter 20th C **1,500.00**

International Modern, side chairs, pair, Eileen Gray designer, tan leather rect back and seat between framework formed of angular slender chromed steel supports **8,500.00**

International Modern, vanity, Herman Miller, Gilbert Rhode, 2 circular 2–drawer cabinets flanking central mirror, orig yellow lacquer, dark bands, Bakelite knobs, chrome frame, large vertical center mirror, label, 52 x 16 x 64".................... **1,750.00**

Memphis, dining table, circular top with abstract design, attached shelving on chrome and metal legs...................................... **1,250.00**

Neo–Modern, bed, Raymond Loewy and Associates DF 2000 Series Bed, mfd by CEI Paris for Dubinski Frere, designed by William Raiser, single storage cube with 2 drawers in red plastic fronts, flip–up light source **450.00**

Neo–Modern, chair, Asko Oy, Eero Aarnio Pastille chair, red glass–reinforced polyester egg form with scooped–out seat, 37" d..................... **1,000.00**

Neo–Modern, chair, Beglerian, Wendell Castle designer, distributed by Stendig, molar design, whimsical tooth forms in white glass–reinforced polyester, 33 x 30 x 25"................... **1,750.00**

Neo–Modern, chairs, set of 4, Artifort, Pierre Paulin designer, sculptured forms, vivid blue fabric upholstery, chrome disk base, 34" h **3,000.00**

Neo–Modern, coffee table, Paul Evans, sq top, block legs, covered in chrome tiles, matching ashtray, etched mark, 1960s, 48" sq top, 15" h............. **400.00**

Neo–Modern, coffee table, V Kagan style, ceramic tiles set in walnut frame, legs forming long extended arch, 69 x 14 x 19½"....................... **250.00**

Neo–Modern, lounge chair, Pierre Paulin designer, sculptured bucket form, deep recessed seat, 2 thick rect legs, purple tweed upholstery, 27 x 27½ x 32" ... **175.00**

Neo–Modern, sofa, Beglerian, Wendell Castle designer, distributed by Stendig, molar design, whimsical tooth form in white glass–reinforced polyester, 50 x 31 x 25"...................... **2,750.00**

Neo–Modern, umbrella stand, Artemide "Dedalo," designed by Emma Gismondi, thimble motif with 7 holes in top, white ABS plastic, stamped on bottom, 13½" h......................... **175.00**

1950s, chest of drawers, generic, box–like appearance, 5 identical drawers, valance skirt, block leg, 18 x 17 x 44"................................. **85.00**

1950s, desk and chair, generic, ranch style, oak, rect top, 3 center–guided dovetailed drawers to left, drawer beneath writing surface, block and ring legs to right, ox yoke hardware, chair with bowed back slats, plank seat, turned splayed front legs, double stretchers on sides, single stretchers in front, 44 x 16 x 32"....................................... **100.00**

1950s, end table, generic, stepped, walnut finished hardwood frame and legs, rect top, splayed round tapered legs, stepped–back shelf raised on 2 spindles on each end, 16 x 24 x 21".................... **50.00**

1950s, sofa, generic, Harmony House (Sears), rectilinear form, hardwood frame, walnut finished legs, orange plastic cover, spring seat base, cotton felt padded button back, welt trim, 68 x 27 x 30"....... **150.00**

1950s, bunk beds, generic, maple, ball finials on baluster turned supports, half wagon wheel motif headboards and footboards, 39" w, 68" h bunked, $250.00.

Late 1950s, sofa bed, generic, aquamarine acetate frieze uphol-stery, tapered legs with brass caps, back folds down to convert to double size bed, 89¹/₂" w, $75.00.

1950s, telephone stand, generic, wrought metal, 2 wire grill shelves, pinched paper clip–style side supports, bronze lacquer finish, 12¹/₂ x 12 x 17" **15.00**

1960s, dinette set, generic, table and 6 chairs, table with 2 leaves and high pressure plastic top in wood grain pattern, tapered black antique finished frame and legs, pillow–back chairs with vinyl plastic covers in abstract tree motif on block grid ground **150.00**

1960s, dining table, generic, high pressure plastic top in wood grain pattern, bronze–plated metal tapered block legs, 2 leaves, 42 x 84" **150.00**

Pop, chair, Studio 56 Capitello, mfd by Gurfam, painted polyurethane foam construction of Ionic capital, c1971, 44 x 52 x 30" **1,250.00**

Scandinavian, armchair, Carl Hansen, Hans Wegner designer, Windsor style, curved crest leading into arms, solid shaped slat, rect seat, round tapered legs, red lacquered finish, cane seat, leather cushion, 28" h **175.00**

Scandinavian, armchair, Fritz Hansen, Hans Wegner designer, China chair, solid rosewood construction, carved arms, single slat back, round tapered legs, leather cushion, 31¹/₂" h **650.00**

Scandinavian, chair and ottoman, Rud Rasmussens, Kare Klint designer, Safari, canvas seat with back strop arm, ash frame, label, 33" h **275.00**

Scandinavian, dining chair, Rud Rasmussens, Kare Klint designer, rust red leather seat, label, 33¹/₂" h **125.00**

Scandinavian, easy chair, Finn Juhl designer, teak construction, period yellow wood upholstered seat and back, 33" h **650.00**

Scandinavian, sofa, Frederica Stolefabrik, Borge Morgensen designer, hardwood frame, down–filled brown leather cushion upholstery, 62¹/₂ x 32 x 31" **850.00**

Scandinavian, sofa, Neils Vodder, Finn Juhl designer, upholstered, sculpted continuous seat and back, period canary yellow upholstery, 4 tapered walnut legs **2,200.00**

Scandinavian, table, low, Artek, Alvar Aalto, painted black rect top, 4 bentwood supports, refinished, 29 x 21 x 15" **150.00**

Streamline Modern, bamboo set, Paul Frankl designer, 5 pcs, two 6–banded armchairs and 2 filler chairs with brick red fabric upholstered loose pillows, corner table with mahogany top, armchair measures 28¹/₂ x 30 x 38" **1,250.00**

Streamline Modern, corner sofa, Henredon, Frank Lloyd Wright designer, tufted suede back and loose seat cushion, mahogany base with Greek key design, unmarked, 61¹/₂ x 30¹/₄ x 31" **850.00**

Streamline Modern, glider sofa, McKay, black enameled flat band steel construction, chrome plated and enameled trim, black leatherette upholstery, 80 x 30 x 31" **1,750.00**

Scandinavian, armchair, attributed to Ralph Rapson, Knoll, shaped and continuous back and seat with leather webbing, shaped arms, unsgd, 42" w, 20" d, 29¹/₂" h, $200.00.

Streamline Modern, 5–pc kitchen set, white porcelain enamel top with black trim and 2 leaves, chrome–plated legs, red artificial leather upholstery, 1940s, 40 x 25" closed size, $150.00.

Streamline Modern, living room suite, sofa and chair, blond wood arms and tapered legs, period green celadon matelasse upholstery, 1940s, 75 x 31½ x 35" sofa **1,000.00**

GAMBLING COLLECTIBLES

Gambling collectibles divide into two basic groups, those associated with gambling casinos and saloons and gaming materials designed for private "back room" use. Casino material further subdivides into actual material and equipment used on the gambling floors and advertising giveaways and premiums. The vast majority of the items in this category are associated with legalized gambling.

Gambling supply houses located throughout the country sold gambling paraphernalia to casinos, saloons, and private individuals through catalogs. Many of the items were "gaffed," meaning fixed in favor of the owner. Obviously, the general public was not meant to see these catalogs.

Legalized gambling is spreading across America. State lotteries and licensed casinos from Atlantic City to Indian reservations are being challenged by riverboat gambling. Many states have licensed off–track betting parlors.

Gaming tables and punchboards dominated the 1980s collecting market. Gambling chips are today's hot collectible.

Reference: Leonard Schneir, *Gambling Collectibles: A Sure Winner,* Schiffer Publishing, 1994.

Collectors' Club: Casino Chip & Gaming Token Collector Club, PO Box 490, Altamont, NY 12009.

Note: See Slot Machines for additional listings.

Ashtray, Bally's Grand, pressed glass, clear, maroon imprint, 4½" d . . . . **$ 2.50**
Ashtray, Hotel Tropicana, Las Vegas, pearl amber glass, curved edges, gold, aqua background imprint, 4⅛" sq **8.00**
Ashtray, Trump Taj Mahal, glass, clear, red imprint. **5.00**
Ashtray, Westerner Club, glass, clear, red on white imprint, 4¼" sq **15.00**

Catalog, Hunt & Company, Chicago, IL, blue lettering and illus, 32 pgs, 3¾ x 6", $15.00.

Bingo Cage, metal, red celluloid handle, 11 wood balls, 9 cards, ©1941, 9" h **20.00**
Book, *Confessions of a Poker Player,* by "King Jack," New York, I. Washburn, Inc, 1940, 209 pgs **25.00**
Book, *Gamblers Don't Gamble,* Michael MacDougall and J. C. Furnas, illus, 1939, 167 pgs. **35.00**
Booklet, *Gambling to Win,* 1925, 24 pgs **45.00**
Catalog, Secret Blue Book, Gambling Supply, H. C. Evans & Co, 1936, 72 pgs. **80.00**
Cigarette Lighter, Sgt. Lee, emb, poker chips and enameled aces on sides, c1945. . . . . **30.00**
Dice Board, horseshoe shaped, poker dice **195.00**
Game, Arcade Game, 1¢ draw, 5 play, counter top type, wood and metal case, orig graphics, c1930, 10 x 15 x 6" **420.00**
Playing Cards, Caesar's Palace, Las Vegas, Nevada, black and gold logos **5.00**
Playing Cards, Golden Nugget, neon marquee **8.00**
Poker Chip Caddy, Bakelite, round, brown **20.00**
Roulette Chip **2.50**

GAMES

This category deals primarily with boxed board games. While the board game dates back to Ancient Egypt and early 19th–century American examples are known, the board game first achieved widespread popularity in the period from 1890 to 1910. While games from such giants as Milton Bradley, McLoughlin Bros., and Parker Bros. were not terribly complex, their lithographed covers represented some of the finest examples of art.

After modest sales in the 1920s, board games increased in popularity in the 1930s and experienced a second golden age from the late 1940s through the mid–1960s. Television and movie licensing played a major role in board game development. As a result, crossover collectors frequently skew market values.

Generic board games such as Monopoly have little value except for the earliest editions. The same holds true for games focused on the 4 to 8 age group, e.g., Candyland, Go to the Head of the Class, etc. Generic board games dominate toy store shelves in the 1990s. Disney and a few mega–movie licensed games are the exceptions.

References: Mark Cooper, *Baseball Games: Home Versions of the National Pastime 1860s–1960s,* Schiffer Publishing, 1995; L–W Book Sales, *Board Games of the 50's, 60's, and 70's With Prices,* L–W Book Sales, 1994; Rick Polizzi, *Baby Boomer Games,* Collector Books, 1995; Desi Scarpone, *Board Games,* Schiffer Publishing, 1995; Bruce Whitehill, *Games: American Boxed Games And Their Makers, 1822–1922, With Values,* Wallace–Homestead, Krause Publications, 1992.

Periodicals: *Toy Shop,* 700 E State St, Iola, WI 54990; *Toy Trader,* PO Box 1050, Dubuque, IA 52004.

Collectors' Clubs: American Game Collectors Assoc, 49 Brooks Ave, Lewiston, ME 04240; Gamers Alliance, PO Box 197, E Meadow, NY 11554.

Note: Prices listed are for boxed games in mint condition unless otherwise noted.

Air Race Around the World, Lido Toy Co, 1950s . . . . . . **$ 12.00**

The Flying Nun, Milton Bradley, 1968, $25.00.

Alice in Wonderland, Cadaco, 1984................45.00
Autographs: Leister Game Co, 1945 ....20.00
Balloonio, Beachcraft, 1937........................55.00
Barage, Corey Games, 1941........................55.00
Barbapapa Takes a Trip, Selchow & Righter, 1977 ....12.00
Basketball, Cadaco, 1966..........................25.00
Beat the Clock, 1st ed, Lowell, 1954 ....15.00
Ben Casey MD, Transogram, 1961 ....40.00
Bionic Crisis, Parker Brothers, 1975 ....22.00
Break the Bank, 1st ed, Betty-B, 1955 ....15.00
Candid Camera, Lowell, 1963 ....20.00
Captain America, Milton Bradley, 1967 ....20.00
Chee Chow, Samuel Gabriel Sons & Co, 1939 ....45.00
Cheyenne, Milton Bradley, 1958 ....30.00
Ching Chong, Samuel Gabriel & Sons, 1937.........100.00
Chutes and Ladders, Milton Bradley, 1956 ....30.00
Combat!, Ideal, 1963..............................60.00
Confucius Say, Milton Bradley, 1937.................60.00
Cootie, Schaper,1949..............................55.00
Dark Shadows, Whitman Publishing Co, 1968 ....35.00
Dear Abby Game, Ideal, 1972 ....18.00
Deduction, Ideal, 1976 ....10.00
Dennis the Menace, Standard Toycraft, 1960..........40.00
Dick Van Dyke, Standard Toycraft, 1964 ....55.00
Domino's Pizza Delivery Game, Wortquest USA,
    Inc, 1989.....................................12.00
Don't Bug Me, Hasbro, 1967 ....12.00
Down You Go, Selchow & Righter, 1954..............25.00
Dr. Kildare, Ideal, 1962 ....25.00
Dragnet, Transogram, 1955 ....40.00
Dukes of Hazzard, Ideal, 1981......................5.00
Dune, Avalon Hill, 1979 ....12.00
Easy Money, Milton Bradley, 1936 ....25.00
Ed Wynn the Fire Chief, Selchow & Righter, 1937.......35.00
Eddie Cantor's Game, Parker Brothers, 1950s 30.00
Emergency, Milton Bradley, 1973-74 ....15.00
Fall Guy, Milton Bradley, 1982.......................5.00
Fame and Fortune, Whitman, 1962....................20.00
Fangface, Parker Brothers, 1979 ....18.00
Fantasy Island, Ideal, 1978........................15.00
Fibber McGee, Milton Bradley, 1936 ....20.00
Five Spot, Milton Bradley, 1931 ....15.00
Flapper Fortunes, The Embossing Co, 1929 ....55.00
Flinch, Flinch Card Co, 1935 ....10.00
Flintstones Game, The, Milton Bradley, 1971 ....25.00

Fonz Hanging Out at Arnolds, The, Milton Bradley,
    1978 ....15.00
Fox Hunt, E. S. Lowe, 1940s 20.00
Game of the Kennedys, Transogram, 1962 ....15.00
General Hospital, Cardinal, 1982.....................5.00
George Goebel, Highlander, 1955 ....25.00
Giant Wheel Cowboys 'N Indians Game, missing one
    cowboy playing pc, Remco,1961 ....30.00
Go For Broke, Selchow & Righter, 1965 ....30.00
Gong Show, American Publishing Corp, 1977...........8.00
Hang On Harvey, Ideal, 1969 ....35.00
Have Gun Will Travel, Parker Brothers, 1959..........45.00
Hoop-O-Loop, Wolverine Supply & Mfg Co, 1930......55.00
Hornet, Samuel Lowe Co, 1941 ....75.00
Howdy Doody's TV Game, Milton Bradley, 1950 ....55.00
Jack-Be-Nimble, Embossing Co, c1940 ....12.00
Johnny Unitas, Play Rite, 1960.....................55.00
Jungle Hunt, Rosebud Art Co, 1940s.................25.00
Kar-Zoom, Whitman, 1964 ....40.00
Kojak, Milton Bradley, 1975 ....25.00
Lassie, Whiting, 1955 ....20.00
Lone Ranger, Whiting, 1956........................65.00
Lotto, Milton Bradley, 1932 ....22.00
Macy's Pirate Treasure Hunt, Einson-Freeman
    Publishing Corp, 1942 ....60.00
Man From UNCLE, Ideal, 1965 ....25.00
Margie, Milton Bradley, 1961......................18.00
MASH, Transogram, 1975 ....20.00
Merry Milkman, Hasbro, c1955 ....75.00
Mod Squad, Remco, 1968 ....80.00
Monkeys and Coconuts, Schaper, 1965...............25.00
Monopoly, Popular Edition, Parker Brothers, separate
    board and pieces box, 1946 ....30.00
Monopoly, separate board and pieces box, box well
    worn, Parker Brothers, 1936 ....35.00
Mostly Ghostly, Cadaco Ltd, 1975 ....35.00
Movie Millions, Transogram, 1938, missing 9 cards
    and some tokens 150.00
Munsters, Hasbro, 1965 ....175.00
Mutuels, horse racing game, miniature infield, large
    metal pcs, Mutuels Inc, Los Angeles, 1938 ....225.00
Nemo, Creston Industries, 1969 ....20.00

The $64,000 Question, Lowell, quiz game, 1956, $20.00.

Newlywed Game, 1st ed, Hasbro, 1967 . . . . **25.00**
Now You See It, Milton Bradley, 1975. . . . . **15.00**
Number Please, Parker Brothers, 1961 . . . . **15.00**
Off to See the Wizard, Milton Bradley, 1968 . . . . **30.00**
Oh–Wah–Ree, Avalon Hill, 1966 . . . . **15.00**
Parcheesi, color snake charmer on 16 x 8" lid, miss-
   ing one wood disc, Selchow & Righter, 1937. . . . . **65.00**
Partridge Family, Milton Bradley, 1971 . . . . **20.00**
Password, 1st ed, Milton Bradley, 1962. . . . . **12.00**
Pathfinder, Milton Bradley, 1954. . . . . **18.00**
Perry Mason, Transogram, 1959 . . . . **35.00**
Peter Coddles Trip to New York, Parker Brothers, 1934. . . . **32.00**
Quiz Kids Own Game Box, no instructions, Parker
   Brothers, c1940 . . . . **35.00**
Ramar of the Jungle, Dexter Wayne, 1953. . . . . **30.00**
Secret of NIMH, Whitman Publishing Co, 1982 . . . . **22.00**
77 Sunset Strip, Lowell, 1960. **30.00**
$64,000 Question, missing set of diecast figures, 19
   x 10" box, Lowell, 1956 . . . . **20.00**
Snake Eyes, Selchow & Righter, 1940s **30.00**
Steve Canyon, one pc broken, Lowell, 1959 . . . . **60.00**
SWAT, Milton Bradley, 1975. . . . . **5.00**
Swayze, Milton Bradley, c1955 . . . . **45.00**
Take It and Double, 2nd series, Frederich H. Beach,
   1941 . . . . **12.00**
Tiny Tim, Parker Brothers, 1970 . . . . **25.00**
Voyage to the Bottom of the Sea, Milton Bradley,
   1964 . . . . **25.00**
Welcome Back Kotter, Ideal, 1975 . . . . **8.00**
Wicket the Ewok, Parker Brothers, 1983 . . . . **12.00**
Wild Bill Hickok, Bilt–Rite, 1956 . . . . **45.00**
Wild Kingdom, Teaching Concepts, 1977 . . . . **35.00**
Word For Word, Mattel, 1963 . . . . **10.00**
Zorro, Whitman Publishing Co, 1958 . . . . **30.00**

GAS STATION COLLECTIBLES

The company–owned, self–service, mini–mart gasoline station has been around so long that most of today's drivers no longer remember the independently owned full–service gas station where someone pumped your gas and cleaned your windshield and mechanics were available from early morning to late in the evening. Fortunately, collectors do. Many are recreating golden age, 1930s through the 1960s, versions of the independent gas station in their basements and garages.

While pump globes and oil cans remain the principal collecting focus, gasoline station advertising, uniforms, and paper ephemera have all become hot collecting subcategories in the 1990s. Road maps, especially those issued prior to the Interstate system, double in value every few years.

References: Scott Anderson, *Check The Oil,* Wallace–Homestead, Krause Publications, 1986; Mark Anderton and Sherry Mullen, *Gas Station Collectibles,* Wallace–Homestead, Krause Publications, 1994; Robert W. D. Ball, *Texaco Collectibles,* Schiffer Publishing, 1994; Scott Benjamin and Wayne Henderson, *Gas Pump Globes: Collector's Guide To Over 3,000 American Gas Globes,* Motorbooks International, 1993; Scott Benjamin and Wayne Henderson, *Oil Company Signs: A Collector's Guide,* Motorbooks International, 1995; Scott Benjamin and Wayne Henderson, *Sinclair Collectibles,* Schiffer Publishing, 1997; Mike Bruner,

Gasoline Treasures, Schiffer Publishing, 1996; Todd P. Helms, *The Conoco Collector's Bible,* Schiffer Publishing, 1995; Rick Pease, *Filling Station Collectibles,* Schiffer Publishing, 1994; Rick Pease, *Service Station Collectibles,* Schiffer Publishing, 1996; B. J. Sommers and Wayne Priddy, *Value Guide To Gas Station Memorabilia,* Collector Books, 1995; Sonya Stenzler and Rick Pease, *Gas Station Collectibles,* Schiffer Publishing, 1993; Michael Karl Witzel, *Gas Station Memories,* Motorbooks International, 1994.

Periodicals: *Hemmings Motor News,* PO Box 100, Rt 9W, Bennington, VT 05201; *Mobilia,* PO Box 575, Middlebury, VT 05753; *Petroleum Collectibles Monthly,* 411 Forest St, La Grange, OH 44050.

Collectors' Club: International Petroliana Collectors Assoc, PO Box 937, Powell, OH 43065.

Ashtray, Mobil Oil Company, attached winged horse. . . **$ 85.00**
Badge, Amoco Gasoline, Border Patrol **20.00**
Bank, Mobiloil, glass, baseball shape, winged horse **30.00**
Blotter, Red Crown Gasoline, 1930s **20.00**
Blotter, Texaco. **45.00**
Brochure, McKinley Brothers Gasoline Sales Station,
   Tours Through the Hudson Valley, 1927, 16 pgs. **10.00**
Calendar, Texaco Sky Chief, 1940. . . . . **55.00**
Can, Americo Motor Oil, 1 gal, winged "A" logo, 10" h. . . **45.00**
Can, Bison Oil, 1 qt, bison illus, 5½" h. **135.00**
Can, Blue Ribbon Cream Metal Polish, 1 gal, early
   race car image, 10¼" h **35.00**
Can, Bureau Penn Motor Oil, 2 gal. **45.00**
Can, Capitol Motor Oil, 2 gal, Capitol dome illus **12.00**
Can, Polarine Motor Oil, 5 gal, vignette with early
   touring car **110.00**
Can, Route 66 Premium Motor Oil, 2 gal **70.00**
Can, Thermo Antifreeze, 1 qt, snowman image, 5½" h. . . . **12.00**
Can, Tydol Motor Oil, 1 qt, winged "A" logo, 5½" h **12.00**
Can, Zeppelin Motor Oil, 2 gal, Zeppelin flying over
   ocean **120.00**

Bank, clear glass, "Watch Your Savings Grow With Esso" emb both sides, 43/4" h, $45.00.

Catalog, Pep Boys, 1932 . . . . 45.00

Clock, Auto–Lite, Original Service Parts, reverse painted glass, white and red ground, blue numbers, 18" d 175.00

Clock, Champion Spark Plugs. 300.00

Coin Tray, Texhoma Gasoline 45.00

Comic, *Gulf Funny Weekly,* Stan Schendel, Gulf station giveaway. 40.00

Display, Standard Oil 100.00

Display, Vedoll Oil Guide, wall mounted, 1942–50 . . . . . 55.00

Figure, vinyl, inflatable, Sinclair Dino 12.00

Gas Globe, Mobilgas Special, winged horse logo, metal body, red, 16½" d 325.00

Gas Globe, Special 175.00

Hood Ornament, fish. 50.00

Jar, Coreco Motor Oil, glass, yellow label, emb lettering, metal screw lid, 1940s, 6" h 30.00

Map, Gulf Refining Company, California, Nevada, Rand McNally, 1927 . . . . 25.00

Map, Harris Oils, Auto Trails Map, 1926. . . . . 15.00

Map, Socony Gasoline and Motor Oil, New England in Soconyland, 1929 . . . . 18.00

Map, Standard Oil, Los Angeles Street and Vicinity Maps 20.00

Map, Texaco, Quebec and the Maritime Provinces, 1927 . . . . 25.00

Motor Oil Rack, wire, 4 embossed glass bottles with metal spouts, 9" w 225.00

Pamphlet, Red Crown Gasoline Ethyl, Standard Oil Company of Indiana. 8.00

Pinback Button, AC Method Spark Plugs, donkey in tub taking shower, "Let Me Clean Your Plugs By The New AC Method". 60.00

Pinback Button, Goodyear, matte cellulloid button, yellow, blue and white design, working thermometer, maintenance record type, c1930 . . . . 25.00

Pinback Button, Linco Gasoline Oils 40.00

Pinback Button, Phillips 66 Silver Anniversary. 30.00

Pinback Button, Tydol Gasoline, oval, red, black, and white, winged logo, bright gold celluloid ground, c1920, 1" l. 20.00

Playing Cards, Mobil, double deck 25.00

Pump Nozzle, brass, 17" h 35.00

Pump Sign, Atlantic Gas, porcelain. 55.00

Pump Sign, Firestone 70.00

Pump Sign, Good Gulf. 40.00

Pump Sign, Pure Pep 65.00

Pump Sign, Sky Chief Supreme, painted metal, mkd "Made in USA 3–10–60," 18" h, 12" w 110.00

Pump Sign, Texaco Supreme. 60.00

Rack, wire, Gulf, 25½" h 50.00

Sign, Goodyear Tires, tin, Sinclair dinosaur adv 60.00

Sign, Mobil, clean restroom sign. 180.00

Sign, U.S. Tires, frosted glass, blue, yellow, and white 40.00

Station Cap, Aviation Station 125.00

Station Cap, Texaco 70.00

Thermometer, Bowes Seal Fast Radiator Chemicals, "the famous "500" line," painted metal, black, red, and white, 38½" h 110.00

Thermometer, Standard Oil, tin. 30.00

Tumblers, Fisk Tires logo, Safedge Tumblers, Libbey, 4⅝" h, price for set of 6 . . . . 45.00

GEISHA GIRL

Geisha Girl is a generic term used to describe Japanese export ceramics made between the 1880s and the present, whose decoration incorporates one or more kimono–clad Japanese ladies as part of its motif. Most collectors focus on pre–1940 ware. Geisha Girl ceramics made after 1945 are referred to as "modern" Geisha Girl.

Over one hundred different manufacturers made close to two hundred pattern variations. Elyce Litts, author of *The Collector's Encyclopedia of Geisha Girl Porcelain,* classified and named most of the patterns. Geisha Girl ceramics were made for export. As a result, forms are traditionally western. After a collecting frenzy in the 1980s, the market cooled considerably in the 1990s.

REPRODUCTION ALERT: Be alert for late 1970s and early 1980s Geisha Girl reproductions in forms ranging from ginger jars to sake sets. These contemporary pieces have red borders. Other telltale characteristics include lack of detail, very bright gold highlights, and a white porcelain body.

Czechoslovakian ceramic manufacturers also copied this ware in the 1920s. Some are marked "Czechoslovakia" or have a false Chinese mark. Many are unmarked. Decal decoration was used extensively. However, the real clue is in the faces. The faces on Czechoslovakian Geisha do not have a strong oriental look.

Bamboo Tree, teacup and saucer, Torii, Japan . . . . $ 10.00

Bamboo Tree, plate, 6" d 10.00

Bamboo Trellis, bowl, 7½" d 40.00

Bamboo Trellis, mug, 4" d 22.00

Bamboo Trellis, plate, 6½" d. 12.00

Bird Cage, cup and saucer 15.00

Bird Cage, plate, 6" d. 12.00

By Land and By Sea, cocoa set, cov chocolate pot and 5 cups and saucers 90.00

By Land and By Sea, plate, 7" d 15.00

Parasol Modern, toothpick holder, 2" h, $20.00.

Child Reaching For Butterfly, egg cup, Variation A **15.00**
Child Reaching For Butterfly, plate, 7" d, red,
Variation A **15.00**
Duck Watching B, condiment set, pine green, salt
and pepper shakers, toothpick holder, mustard pot,
and cherry blossom shape tray **50.00**
Fan A, ice cream set, red, 6 pcs **100.00**
Garden Bench, pitcher, child's, red, 2½" h, Variant N **20.00**
Ikebana in Rickshaw, bowl, 8" d **45.00**
Ikebana in Rickshaw, plate, 7¼" d **22.00**
Ikebana in Rickshaw, salt and pepper shakers, pr **20.00**
Lantern Gateway, powder jar, red **30.00**
Long–Stemmed Peony, creamer **12.00**
Long–Stemmed Peony, hair receiver **35.00**
Meeting B, creamer **25.00**
Meeting B, sake cup **15.00**
Parasol D, candlesticks, pr, red **110.00**
Porch, berry set, master and 5 individuals, scalloped
edge, red and gold, price for 6 pc set **40.00**
Porch, creamer, Torii Nippon **25.00**
Porch, teacup and saucer, cobalt blue, 2 streams of
gold lacing, gold striped handle, red–orange, mod-
ern **12.00**
River's Edge, creamer and sugar **70.00**
River's Edge, toothpick holder, mkd "Kutani" **70.00**

G.I. JOE

Hasbro Manufacturing Company introduced G.I. Joe at the February 1964 American International Toy Fair in New York. Initially, this 12–inch poseable figure was produced in only four versions, one for each branch of the military. A black G.I. Joe joined the line in 1965, followed by a talking G.I. Joe and female nurse in 1967.

Hasbro continued to refine and expand the line. The G.I. Joe Adventure Team introduced this all–American hero to civilian pursuits such as hunting and deep sea diving. The 1976 Arab oil embargo forced Hasbro to reduce G.I. Joe's size from 12 to 8 inches. Production stopped in 1977.

Hasbro reintroduced G.I. Joe in 1982 in a 3¼–inch format. Team members and villains, some current and others futuristic, changed annually. In 1994 Hasbro resumed production of the 12–inch figure, targeted primarily toward the adult collector market. Action Man, G.I. Joe's British equivalent, was marketed in the United States during the 1996 holiday season.

Collectors continue to concentrate on pre–1977 action figures. Collecting interest in accessories, especially those with period boxes, continues to grow.

References: Vincent Santelmo, *The Complete Encyclopedia To GI Joe, 2nd Edition*, Krause Publications, 1997; Vincent Santelmo, *The Official 30th Anniversary Salute To GI Joe, 1964–1994*, Krause Publications, 1994.

Periodical: *GI Joe Patrol*, PO Box 2362, Hot Springs, AR 71914.

Collectors' Club: GI Joe Collectors' Club, 12513 Birchfalls Dr, Raleigh, NC 27614.

Action Figure, Action Soldier, #7500, 1964 . . . . **$ 225.00**
Action Figure, Adventurer, Negro, #7404, MIB **295.00**

Action Figure, Airborne, 1983, ... **20.00**
Action Figure, Bazooka, 4th series, 1985 . . . . **25.00**
Action Figure, Chuckles, 6th series, 1987 . . . . **12.00**
Action Figure, Doc, 1983 . . . . **20.00**
Action Figure, Duke, 1992 . . . . **5.00**
Action Figure, Flash, 1982 . . . . **25.00**
Action Figure, Grand Slam, 1982 . . . . **5.00**
Action Figure, Grunt Infantry Trooper, 1st series, 1982 . . . . **65.00**
Action Figure, Hawk 2, 5th series, 1986 . . . . **22.00**
Action Figure, High Voltage Escape, complete, all
accessories **180.00**
Action Figure, Land Adventurer, #7401, MIB **240.00**
Action Figure, Mutt and Junkyard **12.00**
Action Figure, Night Creeper, 9th series, 1990 . . . . **8.00**
Action Figure, Race Car Driver, complete, all acces-
sories **200.00**
Action Figure, Recoil, Long–Range Recon Trooper,
1988–89 . . . . **5.00**
Action Figure, Recondo, 1984 . . . . **12.00**
Action Figure, Road Block, 3rd series, 1984 . . . . **35.00**
Action Figure, Scarlett, 1982 . . . . **40.00**
Action Figure, Sea Adventurer, #7492, MIB **250.00**
Action Figure, Sea Adventurer, kung–fu grip,
Adventure Team, 1970 . . . . **165.00**
Action Figure, Shockwave, 7th series, 1988 . . . . **12.00**
Action Figure, Snake Eyes 3, 8th series, 1989 . . . . **15.00**
Action Figure, Stalker, 1982 . . . . , ... **25.00**
Action Figure, Stalker Ranger, 2nd series, swivel
arms, 1983 . . . . **50.00**
Accessories, Airvest, orange **12.00**
Accessories, Ammo Dump **12.00**
Accessories, Battle Gear **28.00**
Accessories, boots, silver **12.50**
Accessories, Buzz Boar **10.00**
Accessories, carbine with sling **10.00**
Accessories, CLAW Cobra **10.00**
Accessories, dress outfit, Navy, complete, orig tie **80.00**
Accessories, medic bag **20.00**
Accessories, Pac Rat's Machine Gun **20.00**
Accessories, pants, Arctic Explorer **22.00**
Accessories, shirt and pants, Sailor **18.00**
Accessories, Transportable Battle Platform **70.00**

Vehicle, Hovercraft, with Cutter figure, 1984, $45.00.

Accessories, Weapon Transport. **15.00**
Dog Tag, membership **55.00**
Game, G.I. Joe Combat Infantry, MIB **150.00**
Play Set, G.I. Joe Training Center **90.00**
Play Set, Secret Mountain Outpost **75.00**
Puzzle, 221 pcs, scene #4, 1988, Mural **8.00**
Vehicle, Air Chariot **45.00**
Vehicle, Armadillo. **20.00**
Vehicle, CLAW Cobra **12.00**
Vehicle, Coastal Defender **12.00**
Vehicle, Cobra FANG **25.00**
Vehicle, Cobra Hiss, complete, orig box **65.00**
Vehicle, Desert Fox **20.00**
Vehicle, Destro's Despoiler **30.00**
Vehicle, Ferret. **25.00**
Vehicle, Night Raven, complete, orig box **50.00**
Vehicle, Persuader, with figure **22.00**
Vehicle, Rapid Fire Motorcycle, #6073–1 . . . . **30.00**
Vehicle, Rattler, complete, orig box **65.00**
Vehicle, Rhino G. P. V. **35.00**
Vehicle, Rolling Thunder **45.00**
Vehicle, SHARC, with figure **35.00**
Vehicle, Sky Sweeper. **15.00**
Vehicle, Snow Cat, complete, MIB **25.00**
Vehicle, Swamp Fire **20.00**
Vehicle, Thunder Machine **30.00**
Vehicle, USS Flagg, with figure. **210.00**
Vehicle, Vamp Attack, with figure. **80.00**
Vehicle, Water Moccasin **30.00**

GIRL SCOUTS

Juliette Gordon Low of Savannah, Georgia, began the Girl Scout movement in 1912. It grew rapidly. The 1928 Girl Scout manual suggested selling cookies to raise money. Today the annual Girl Scout cookie drive supports local troops and councils.

Overshadowed by their male counterpart, Boy Scout collectibles, Girl Scout collectibles enjoy only limited collector interest. There is a ready market for flashlights and pocket knives, primarily because they cross over into other collecting fields.

Book, *Girl Scouts at Home,* Katherine Galt,
Saalfield, 1921. . . . . **$ 12.00**
Book, *Girl Scouts at Sea Crest,* Lillian Garis, Cupples
& Leon, 1920s. **20.00**
Book, *Girl Scouts Good Turn,* Edith Lavell, Burt,
1922–25 . . . . **12.00**
Book, *Juliette Lowe and the Girl Scouts,* Choate &
Ferris, 1928 . . . . **15.00**
Book, *Lady From Savannah, The Life of Juliette Low,*
Schultz & Lawrence, Lippincott, 1st ed, 1958 . . . . **15.00**
Booklet, Girl Scouting and the Jewish Girl, 1944. . . . . . **10.00**
Calendar, 1953, full–color photo, full pad. **25.00**
Catalog, Brownie Equipment, 1950, 16 pgs. **10.00**
Catalog, Leaders Edition, 1941, 40 pgs **25.00**
Certificate, Daisy Girl Scout, vining floral border with
birds and buttterflies, Girl Scout emblem. **8.00**
Coin, 50th Anniversary, gold, 1962. . . . . **8.00**
Comic Book, Daisy Lowe of the Girl Scouts, full
color, history text, 16 pgs, ©1954 . . . . **20.00**

Girl Scout Official Compass, metal, 2" d, $20.00.

Handbook, Girl Scout Handbook, 7th ed, 1st print-
ing, 1953. . . . . **5.00**
Handbook, Intermediate, 1959. . . . . **5.00**
Handbook, Scouting For Girls, 2nd ed, 6th printing,
c1925 . . . . **10.00**
Letter, Girl Scouts of Houghton, Houghton, MI letter-
head, accepting resignation of director, orig Girl
Scout envelope, June 6, 1938 . . . . **15.00**
Magazine, *The American Girl,* June 1934, 52 pgs **8.00**
Ring, sterling silver, green enamel with emblem **25.00**
Sewing Kit, Brownies, red case, c1940 . . . . **15.00**
Sheet Music, *No Man Is an Island,* 1950. . . . . **5.00**
Thermos, metal, red, green, and white, logos and
stripes, white plastic cup, Aladdin, c1960 . . . . **40.00**

GOEBEL

Franz and William Goebel, father and son, founded the F. D. & W. Goebel Porcelain Works near Coburg, Germany, in 1879. Initially, the firm made dinnerware, utilitarian ware, and beer steins. Marx–Louis, William's son, became president in 1912. He introduced many new porcelain figurine designs and added a pottery figurine line. Franz Goebel, son of Marx–Louis, and Dr. Eugene Stocke, his uncle, assumed control of the company in 1929.

Franz Goebel is responsible for making arrangements to produce the company's famous Hummel figurines. During World War II, Goebel concentrated on the production of dinnerware. Following the war, the company exported large quantities of Hummels and other figurines. Today Goebel manufactures high quality dinnerware, limited edition collectibles, figurines, the popular Hummel figurines, and figurine series ranging from Disney characters to Friar Tuck monks.

This category includes Goebel's non–Hummel production.

Collectors' Club: Goebel Networkers, PO Box 396, Lemoyne, PA 17043.

Note: See Limited Editions and Hummel for additional listings.

Honey Pot, yellow, 5" h, $85.00.

Ashtray, figural bluebird on rim, 1974. . . . . $ 40.00
Bell, Angel with clarinet, white bisque, 1976 . . . . 8.00
Bell, Angel with french horn, white bisque, 1982 . . . . 12.00
Bell, Angel with harp, blue, 1995. . . . . 20.00
Bell, Angel with saxophone, 1980 . . . . 12.00
Bell, Angel with teddy bear, 1991. . . . . 30.00
Bell, Angel with train, white bisque, 1995. . . . . 38.00
Cookie Jar, cardinal, red robe. 150.00
Figurine, Al the Trumpet Player, Co–Boy, 1981 . . . . 45.00
Figurine, American Goldfinch, miniature, Wildlife
    Series, 1985. . . . . 85.00
Figurine, Bachelor Degree, 1970 . . . . 60.00
Figurine, Bashful, miniature, Disney, 1987 . . . . 80.00
Figurine, Bert the Soccer Player, Co–Boys Sports,
    1994. . . . . 25.00
Figurine, Blacksmith, miniature, Americana Series,
    1989 . . . . 125.00
Figurine, Boyhood Dreams, N. Rockwell, 1963. . . . . 325.00
Figurine, Brum the Lawyer, Co–Boy, 1994. . . . . 25.00
Figurine, Carl the Chef, Co–Boys Culinary, 1980. . . . . . . 40.00
Figurine, Cinderella coach with 2 horses, multicol-
    ored, c1934, 3" h, 5½" l. 325.00
Figurine, Doc the Doctor, Co–Boys Professionals,
    1980. . . . . 60.00
Figurine, God Bless You, Betsey Clark, 1972 . . . . 285.00
Figurine, Grandpa, miniature, Children's Series, 1984 . . . . 75.00
Figurine, Mothers Helper, N. Rockwell, 1963 . . . . 325.00
Figurine, She Sounds the Deep, miniature,
    Americana Series, 1983 . . . . 65.00
Figurine, The Wicked Witch, miniatures, special
    release, 1987. . . . . 75.00
Lemon Reamer, 2 pc, green and yellow body, cream
    top, brown handle, crackle finish, 1927, imp mark,
    4½" h 145.00
Ornament, Angel, 1991. . . . . 22.00
Pitcher, Boxer dog, miniature. 120.00
Planter, swan, 1969. . . . . 135.00
Salt and Pepper Shakers, pr, cowboy and cowgirl
    kissing. 55.00

GOLDSCHEIDER POTTERY

In 1885 Frederich Goldscheider founded the Goldscheider Porcelain and Majolica Factory. The firm had a factory in Pilsen and decorating shops in Carlsbad and Vienna. Regina Goldscheider and Alois Goldscheider, her brother–in–law, managed the firm from 1897 until 1918. Walter and Marcel, Regina's sons, managed the firm in the 1920s. The firm produced high–style figurines and decorative accessories during the Art Nouveau and Art Deco periods.

During World War II, the family relocated its operations to Trenton, New Jersey. When the war ended, Marcel Goldscheider moved the firm to England's Staffordshire district where it continues to make bone china figures and earthenware.

Ashtray, German Shepherd head. . . . . $ 30.00
Busts, pr, Orientals, multicolored, 8" h 50.00
Figure, cat. 25.00
Figure, chorus girl, purple skirt with flowers, Art Deco
    style, 7½" h 325.00
Figure, grazing pony 90.00
Figure, Madonna, cobalt and green, black sq base,
    5¾" h 120.00
Figure, Madonna and Child, sgd "Pierre Fumers," 7" h. . . . 80.00
Figure, peasant woman, red and yellow dress, flow-
    ers, Austria. 85.00
Figure, seated German Shepherd, mkd "Gold-
    scheider, Wein," 6" h, 9" l. 175.00
Figure, seated woman holding letter, metal stand,
    8½" h 120.00
Figure, Terrier, orange, Art Deco style, 4¾" h. 55.00
Figure, twins, Helen Diedloff, 7" h 60.00
Figure, woman holding sides of black and white lace
    dress, Art Deco style, Austria, 7½" h 250.00
Figure, Yankee Doodle Dandy 130.00
Plate, mermaid pattern, multicolored 160.00
Wall Mask, girl with yellow hair, orange lips,
    turquoise scarf, 12" h 100.00
Wall Mask, woman's face with curly brown hair, red
    lips, aqua scarf, Art Deco style, 11¼" h 190.00
Wall Mask, woman with flowing brown hair, paper
    label 325.00

GOLF COLLECTIBLES

Golf roots rest in 15th–century Scotland. Initially a game played primarily by the aristocracy and gentry, a series of innovations in club and ball design in the mid–19th century made the game accessible to everyone. By 1900, golf courses were located throughout Great Britain and the United States.

Golf collectibles divide into four basic groups: (1) golf books, (2) golf equipment, (3) items associated with a famous golfer, and (4) golf ephemera ranging from tournament programs to golf prints. Golf collecting has become highly specialized. There are several price guides to golf balls. There is even a price guide to golf tees.

References: Chuck Furjanic, *Golf Antiques: A Collector's Reference and Price Guide*, Krause Publications, 1997; John F. Hotchkiss, *Collectible Golf Balls: History and Price Guide*, Antique Trader Books, 1997; John M. Olman and Morton W. Olman, *Golf Antiques & Other Treasures of the Game, Expanded Edition,*

Market Street Press, 1993; Beverly Robb, *Collectible Golfing Novelties,* Schiffer Publishing, 1992; Shirley and Jerry Sprung, *Decorative Golf Collectibles: Collector's Information, Current Prices,* Glentiques, 1991.

Collectors' Clubs: Golf Collectors Society, PO Box 20546, Dayton, OH 45420; Logo Golf Ball Collector's Assoc, 4552 Barclay Fairway, Lake Worth, FL 33467; The Golf Club Collectors Assoc, 640 E Liberty St, Girard, OH 44420.

Ashtray, glass, Butts–N–Putts, wood and brass stand . . . **$ 25.00**
Ashtray, Art Deco figure, silver plated, mkd "Monarch Plate Brand," c1930, 6" d **155.00**
Ball, D. & M. Skull, Draper–Maynard Co, Plymouth, NH, mesh pattern, mkd "Skull & Crossbone" **75.00**
Ball, Dino Brand, Dean Martin, Pro–Tel, USA, orig box, 1970s. **40.00**
Ball, Goodyear "B," Goodyear Tire and Rubber Co, Akron, OH, mesh pattern, c1926 . . . . **125.00**
Ball, Warwick, Dunlop Sports Co, Ltd, London, mesh and dimple pattern, mkd "Warwick," c1920s. **150.00**
Ball, Whippet, A. J. Reach Co, Philadelphia, PA, mesh pattern, green ink stamped "Whippet," 8 green mesh squares around equator, c1920s **65.00**
Book, *Golfer's Cookbook,* Craft–Zavichas, The National Golf Foundation, 1984 . . . . **18.00**
Book, *Power Golf,* Ben Hogan, 1948 . . . . **22.00**
Book, *Putting Made Easy, The Mark G. Harris Method,* P. A. Vaile, 1st ed, 1935 . . . . **30.00**
Booklet, *Rules of Golf,* 1947 . . . . **15.00**
Bowl, Bob Hope Desert Classic, blue, gold trim, 1981, 11" d **40.00**
Box, Wilson Putting Disc, the Putting Instructor, 1940s **35.00**
Caddie's Badge, Plum Hollow, 1962, 2¼" d **15.00**
Club, Kroy Don, waffle face spade mashie, 1925 . . . . . . **160.00**
Club, Spalding, Ded Stop, mashie niblick, 1925 . . . . **110.00**
Coaster, plastic, The Children's Mercy Hospital Golf Classic, 1986, 4" sq **5.00**
Comic Book, The Road Runner, #8, Road Runner hitting cactus golf ball, Gold Key, 1968. . . . . **15.00**
Cookie Jar, porcelain, "Think Birdie," Taiwan, 6" h **15.00**

Cuff Links, pr, plated metal, golf ball and crossed clubs, Swank, 1960–80 . . . . **20.00**
Figurine, Sport Angel, 4" h **25.00**
Game, Tom Thumb 9–Hole Golf Game, Transogram, 1954 . . . . **30.00**
Golf Bag Tag, celluloid, "Wolfert's Roost Country Club," red, black lettering, leather strap, 1920–30, 2⅛" d **20.00**
Ice Bucket, plastic, figural golf ball, wooden ladybug finial, 11 x 8" **22.00**
Jigger, plastic, red golf bag shape, multicolored figural golf club swizzle sticks, 6" h **30.00**
Magazine, *American Golfer,* June 1932. . . . . **12.00**
Magazine, *GOLFing,* March 1952. . . . . **12.00**
Pencil, pot metal golf club head **20.00**
Pin, golf club, sterling silver, 1959 . . . . **60.00**
Pocket Watch, golf ball form, brass case, white enamel finish, Intex, mkd "17 Rubis," c1940, 1½" d **180.00**
Program, Bob Hope Classic, 1968 . . . . **20.00**
Program, Bryon Nelson Golf Classic, April 22–28, 1968, Arnold Palmer cov autograph **80.00**
Putter, Shur Line, stainless steel, brass head. **45.00**
Tee, Avon, rubber **20.00**
Tee, "Nabisco Good Luck," matchbook–style pkg **5.00**
Tee, The Reddy Tee, orig pkg, 1920s **22.00**
Tie Rack, celluloid, 1937 . . . . **25.00**
Tray, glass, Burdine's Invitational Golf Tournament, 1969, 11" d **50.00**
Tray, silver plated, Bob Hope Desert Classic, 1974, Oneida, 12½" d **50.00**

GONDER POTTERY

After a distinguished ceramic career working for American Encaustic Tiling, Cherry Art Tile, Florence Pottery, and Ohio Pottery, Lawton Gonder purchased the Zane Pottery, Zanesville, Ohio, in 1940 and renamed it Gonder Ceramic Arts. The company concentrated on art pottery and decorative accessories. Gonder hired top designers and sculptors to create his products. Gonder's glazes were innovative.

In 1946 Gonder expanded his Zanesville plant and purchased the Elgee Pottery to produce lamp bases. Elgee burned in 1954; operations were moved to Zanesville. Hurt by the flood of cheap foreign imports, Gonder sold his business in 1975 to the Allied Tile Company.

Many Gonder pieces have a double glaze and a pink interior. Most pieces are marked GONDER or GONDER USA in a variety of ways and are numbered. Some pieces were marked with a paper label.

Reference: Ron Hoopes, *The Collector's Guide and History of Gonder Pottery,* L–W Books, 1992.

Newsletter: *Gonder Collect Newsletter,* PO Box 4263, N Myrtle Beach, SC 29597.

Ashtray, #408, yellow, free form, 10" l . . . . **$ 15.00**
Candleholders, pr, E–14, lotus flower, 5" w **25.00**
Creamer and Sugar, cov, ivory ground, brown speckles and drips **15.00**
Figure, rooster, red, 21" h. **75.00**

Sheet Music, *Follow Thru,* green, black, and white, 1928, 9 x 11¾", $5.00.

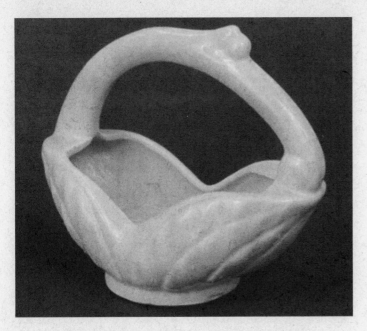

Basket, H–39, pink and gray, 8¼" w, 7" h, $35.00.

Figure, #690, 2 deer jumping over fronds, brown, Art
   Deco style, 11" h **30.00**
Figures, pr, Oriental man and woman, 14" h **80.00**
Pitcher, bulbous paneled shape, mottled yellow
   glaze, 8½" h **26.00**
Pitcher, H–73, green, 8" h **15.00**
Planter, figural gondola, yellow and pink, 13" l **30.00**
Planter, sq shape, magenta with white drip, 4½" h,
   price for pair **12.00**
Planter, swan, E–44 .... **30.00**
Television Lamp, ship, green and brown speckled,
   14" h **40.00**
Vase, chartreuse ext., pink int., 7¼" h **18.00**
Vase, H–69, leaf mold, brown shades, 8½" h **30.00**
Vase, H–80, urn with leaf shape, pink, 6" h **45.00**
Vase, H–33, ewer, brown and yellow glaze, 9" h **40.00**
Vase, H–79, tiger lily, olive green glaze, 8" h **30.00**
Vase, J–31, figural swan, green, 8" h **35.00**
Vase, pearl gray ext, pink int, 9½" h **30.00**

GOSS & CRESTED CHINA

Crested Ware is a generic term used to describe English–produced
objects, usually ceramic, that include a crest in their decorative
motif. Most were and still are sold as souvenirs. Arcadian, Carlton
China, Goss, Crafton China, Savoy China, Shelley, and Willow Art
are just a few of the English potters who made crested ware.

   The Goss China Company was founded in 1858. It was in the
1880s that Goss first began producing the now famous white
glazed souvenir pieces featuring enameled decorations and the
coats of arms of various towns and resorts. Miniature buildings followed in 1893. Cauldon Potteries purchased Goss in 1929.
Coalport China purchased the rights to Goss in 1945. Ridgway and
Adderly assumed control in 1954. Today Goss is a division of
Royal Doulton.

Collectors' Clubs: Crested Circle, 75 Cannon Grove, Fetcham,
Leatherhead, Surrey KT22 9LP England; Goss Collectors Club, 4
Khasiaberry, Walnut Tree, Milton Keynes MK7 7DP England.

Basket, Craignez Honte crest, gilt trim, center handle,
   ftd, 2⅔" h .... **$ 20.00**
Bottle, Sunderland **30.00**
Bowl, Chippenhs Ancient crest of Unity and Loyalty,
   orange, yellow, and blue, ... **10.00**
Building, Look Out House **155.00**
Building, Manx Cottage **110.00**
Creamer, City Arms London crest, white, rust, and
   gilt, 2¼" h **20.00**
Creamer, Sir William Wallace, mkd "W H Goss" **30.00**
Ewer, Arundel **25.00**
Ewer, Chichester, Roman, Beaulieu Abbey **25.00**
Figure, Margate crest, orange, turquoise, and green
   with dragons, gilt trim, reverse "To the memory of
   William Philpott and Charles Etroughton,"
   Arcadian China mark, 4" h **35.00**
Figure, swan, molded, Hastings Stoke on Trent crest,
   cobalt, gold, and orange, gilt trim, 2" h **30.00**
Hatpin Holder, Turnridge Wells crest, Shelley **55.00**
Jar, Basingstoke crest **22.00**
Jug, Litchfield, Warwick **35.00**
Lamp, Hamworthy, Reigate Poole **35.00**
Loving Cup, 3 handles, Henry of Navarre, Ramsgate,
   and Kent crests, Goss **35.00**
Mug, 1 handle, Battersea crest, Goss **20.00**
Pitcher, Cambridge **20.00**
Pitcher, Devon Oak, Warwick crest **20.00**
Pitcher, white cameo coat of arms, "Dominion of
   Canada" grape border, blue jasper ground,
   "Wedgwood England" mark, 3⅞" h **85.00**
Pot, crest of Margate, multicolored, 1⅝" h **15.00**
Pot, Roman, Painswick **25.00**
Sugar Bowl, Crest of Quebec, Wildman **12.00**
Tea Set, teapot, creamer, and sugar, New Brunswick
   coat of arms, ... **60.00**
Toothpick, St. Asaph crest, Clifton mark, 2" h **25.00**

**Pitcher, crest,
Stoke–Upon–Trent,
mkd "F. Robinson,
Victoria, porce-
lain," 2¼" h,
$20.00.**

Urn, Tewkesbury Saxon, Lizard. **28.00**
Vase, Henry of Navarre crest, 3¹/₂" h. **35.00**
Vase, Lewes Roman, Ramsgate crest. **15.00**
Wall Pocket, South End–on–Sea crest with ship, 2³/₄" h . . . **30.00**

GRANITEWARE

Graniteware is a generic term used to describe enamel–coated iron or steel kitchenware. Originating in Germany, the first American graniteware was manufactured in the 1860s. American manufacturers received a major market boost when World War I curtailed German imports.

Graniteware is still being manufactured today. Older examples tend to be heavier. Cast–iron handles date between 1870 and 1890; wood handles between 1900 and 1910.

This market experienced a major price run in the early 1990s as dealers raised their prices to agree with those published by Helen Greguire. At the moment, the category as a whole appears to be greatly overvalued.

References: Helen Greguire, *The Collector's Encyclopedia of Graniteware: Colors, Shapes & Values,* 1990, 1994 value update, *Book 2,* 1993, Collector Books; Dana Gehman Morykan and Harry L. Rinker, *Warman's Country Antiques & Collectibles, Third Edition,* Wallace–Homestead, Krause Publications, 1996.

Collectors' Club: National Graniteware Society, PO Box 10013, Cedar Rapids, IA 52410.

Berry Pail, cov, gray and black mottled, 7" d, 4³/₄" h. . . . **$ 50.00**
Bowl, blue and white mottled, 7" d **30.00**
Bowl, creamware, green trim **15.00**
Bread Loaf Pan, gray **30.00**
Bucket, aqua swirl, bail handle, 2 qt. **22.00**
Cake Pan, light blue. **25.00**
Cake Pan, gray, 10 x 14" **12.50**
Candleholder, leaf shape, red. **60.00**
Casserole, cov, cobalt blue and white swirl. **55.00**
Chamber Pot, white, blue trim **15.00**
Coffee Boiler, gray **30.00**
Coffee Boiler, cov, white, black trim, "Bisque
    Flintstone" label **70.00**
Coffeepot, black and white speckled, large **35.00**
Coffeepot, white **25.00**

Colander, gray mottled, pedestal base, 9¹/₂" d, 3³/₄" h, $20.00.

Colander, gray, pedestal base, 5" h **15.00**
Colander, gray, pedestal base, 12" d **25.00**
Cream Pail, white, red trim. **35.00**
Creamer, turquoise swirl, 5" h **15.00**
Cup, gray mottled **15.00**
Cuspidor, gray mottled, mkd "Agate Ware" **25.00**
Custard Cup, gray mottled **10.00**
Dipper, red and white **25.00**
Dishpan, gray, 5" h, 16" d **12.00**
Double Boiler, white, red trim **25.00**
Funnel, cobalt blue and white marbleized, large **50.00**
Funnel, gray, Acme **45.00**
Kettle, cov, gray mottled, 9" h, 11¹/₂" d **50.00**
Ladle, gray mottled, 12" l. **30.00**
Measure, gray, 1 cup **50.00**
Milk Can, black and white speckled, lock top, wire
    handle, 8" h. **40.00**
Milk Pan, gray, 1 qt **35.00**
Molasses Jug, white, tin lid, large **40.00**
Mold, white, fluted **45.00**
Muffin Pan, gray mottled, 9 cup **45.00**
Mug, cream, green trim **8.00**
Pie Pan, cobalt blue and white marbleized, 6" d **30.00**
Pitcher, green shaded, 6" h. **25.00**
Plate, gray, 8" d **10.00**
Roaster, cobalt blue and white mottled **25.00**
Roaster, gray mottled **65.00**
Sieve, pan style, gray **22.00**
Skimmer, gray mottled, 10" l **30.00**
Spoon, Blue Diamond Ware, long handle. **50.00**
Sugar, cov, white **50.00**
Tea Kettle, red, 1960s **55.00**
Tea Strainer, cream, circles. **45.00**
Tray, red and white swirl, 18" d **40.00**
Tube Pan, gray mottled, octagonal **45.00**
Tumbler, azure blue, orig label **40.00**
Tumbler, white, small. **12.00**
Vegetable Bowl, blue and white, oblong. **85.00**
Wash Basin, blue and white marbleized, 13¹/₂" d. **40.00**
Windsor Dipper, light blue, white wavy mottling,
    white int, riveted handle with eyelet hanger, 5" d
    bowl **80.00**

Basin, green and white swirled ext, white int, cobalt rim and riveted handles, 17¹/₂" d, 5¹/₂" h, $85.00.

GREETING CARDS

The modern greeting card originated in the middle of the 15th century in the Rhine Valley of medieval Germany. Printed new year greetings gained in popularity during the 17th and 18th centuries. Queen Victoria's interest in holiday and special occasion cards helped establish the sending of greeting cards as a regular event.

Louis Prang, a color lithography printer, was one of the first American manufacturers of greeting cards. The post–1945 era witnessed the growth of a number of card manufacturers who eventually would dominate the industry. The Hall Brothers (Joyce C., Rollie, and William), Kansas City postcard distributors and publishers, began printing greeting cards in 1910. Fred Winslow Rust established Rust Craft Company. Cincinnati's Gibson Art Co. entered the greeting card field. Arthur D. and Jane Norcross formed a mutual partnership in 1915.

Although greeting cards are collected primarily by event or occasion, a growing number of collectors seek specialized type cards, e.g., diecut or mechanical. Holiday and specialized collectors represent the principal buyers of greeting cards in the 1990s.

Birthday, Blondie and Dagwood, Hallmark, 1939 . . . . . $ **20.00**
Birthday, Superman, ©1941, Superman, Inc **55.00**
Birthday, Three Little Pigs, silver ground, Walt Disney
    Enterprises, ©1934 . . . . **25.00**
Chanukah, emb paper, gilt dec **15.00**
Christmas, Bugs Bunny, Dell Comics **40.00**
Christmas, Clint Eastwood, 1959 . . . . **25.00**
Christmas, fold–out, Santa on front, pictures to trace
    inside, 8" h **5.00**
Christmas, Jayne Mansfield, family photo, 1965 . . . . **35.00**
Christmas, Lady and The Tramp, stiff paper, orig enve-
    lope, Gibson, 1950s **18.00**
Get Well, Amos 'n Andy, black and white photo, Hall
    Brothers, 1931 . . . . **35.00**
Mother's Day, Cracker Jack, diecut, puppy, c1940 . . . . **45.00**
Thanksgiving, Happy Thanksgiving, turkey **8.00**
Thanksgiving, turkey, feather tail, 1930s **2.00**
Valentine's Day, fold–out, floral "LOVE," paper lace
    dec **20.00**

"Star light star bright first star I see tonight..."

I wished on a star for your birthday —

Birthday, bifold, Star Trek, Captain Kirk , 5³/₄ x 7³/₄" closed size, 1976, $8.00.

Valentine's Day, fold–out, girl's head in heart, flowers
    with white lace, 1940 . . . . **20.00**
Valentine's Day, mechanical, winter scene, boy on
    skis **30.00**
Valentine's Day, pop–up center, train filled with flow-
    ers and hearts, c1920 . . . . **55.00**

GRISWOLD

In the mid–1860s Matthew Griswold entered into partnership with John and Samuel Selden, his two brothers–in–law, and established a company to make butt hinges and light hardware in Erie, Pennsylvania. In 1873 the company was known as the Selden & Griswold Manufacturing Company. Matthew Griswold bought out the Selden family interests in 1884.

Fire damaged the plant in August 1895, but it was quickly repaired and placed back into operation. In 1897 the Griswold Manufacturing Company received a charter. The company moved from the old plant to the former Shaw Piano Company building, 12th and Raspberry Streets, in 1903. Numerous expansions followed.

In 1914, Marvin Griswold, one of Matthew's sons, became company president and was instrumental in making Griswold a leader in the manufacture of cast–iron cookware. He was supported in his efforts by Charles A. Massing, John Holland, and S. E. Lent of the sales staff.

Following Marvin's death in 1926, Roger Griswold, a son of Matthew Griswold, Jr., assumed the company's helm. He was responsible for the company's move into the manufacture of commercial electrical appliances. The summer of 1937 witnessed a prolonged labor stoppage when the CIO attempted to unionize the Griswold workers.

Ely Griswold, Roger's brother, assumed control following Roger's death in 1944. Ely's plans to sell the company were opposed by some family members. Ely prevailed, and the company was sold to a group of New York investors in 1946.

McGraw Edison Company, Chicago, purchased Griswold in 1957. Six months later, McGraw Edison sold the Housewares Division and the Griswold trade name to the Wagner Manufacturing Company, Griswold's major competitor. Wagner continued the company as a separate division, dropping the "Erie, Pa." designation from the trademark. Manufacturing operations moved from Erie to Sidney, Ohio, Wagner's home.

In 1959 Wagner sold Griswold to Textron, Inc., of Providence, Rhode Island, which operated the company under its subsidiary, Randall Company. In August 1969, the General Housewares Corporation acquired all rights to Griswold and Wagner. Cast–iron cookware is still made at the Sidney, Ohio, plant.

References: David G. Smith and Charles Wafford, *The Book of Griswold & Wagner: Favorite Piqua, Sidney Hollow Ware, Wapak*, Schiffer Publishing, 1995; *Griswold Cast Iron, Vol. 1* (1996), *Vol 2.* (1995), L–W Book Sales.

Newsletter: *Kettles 'n' Cookware*, Drawer B, Perrysville, NY 14129.

Collectors' Club: Griswold & Cast Iron Cookware Assoc, 54 Macon Ave, Asheville, NC 28801.

Ashtray, #570 . . . . $ **25.00**

Turk's Head Mold, #140, $200.00.

Brownie Golf Pan, #9. . . . . 175.00
Cake Mold, lamb. 85.00
Cake Mold, rabbit 275.00
Cornstick Pan, #262. . . . . 60.00
Cornstick Pan, #283. . . . . 150.00
Dutch Oven, #6, smooth top, block emblem. 175.00
Dutch Oven, #7, raised lettering, applied handle 65.00
Dutch Oven, #8, Tite Top 45.00
Dutch Oven Trivet, #9 . . . . 30.00
Egg Skillet, #53 . . . . 35.00
Gem, #16, variation 3 . . . . 65.00
Golfball Pan, pattern number only 80.00
Grill 135.00
Kettle, #8, 3 legs 45.00
Ladle, "Erie" 95.00
Muffin Pan, #8, logo 200.00
Patty Iron, #2, orig box. 40.00
Patty Mold Set, #3, with patty bowl and orig box 125.00
Popover Pan, #10. . . . . 25.00
Roaster, oval, some pitting 250.00
Scotch Bowl, "Erie," patent dates, #2 . . . . 50.00
Scocth Bowl, "Erie," patent dates, #5 . . . . 65.00
Skillet, #4, slant "Erie, Pa. USA" 35.00
Skillet, #6, block, smoke ring 100.00
Skillet, #6, slant "Erie" 40.00
Skillet, #8, slant "Erie" 45.00
Skillet, #9, block "Erie, Pa. USA," deep smooth bot-
    tom 100.00
Skillet, #11, block "Erie, Pa. USA' 195.00
Skillet, #12, big logo 95.00
Skillet, #12, small emblem, smoke ring. 35.00
Skillet Cover, #8 . . . . 35.00
Snack, #42 . . . . 55.00
Steak Plate, #849. . . . . 60.00
Wafer Iron. 225.00
Waffle Iron, #7 . . . . 60.00
Waffle Iron, #9, finger hinge. 125.00
Wheat & Corn Pan, patent number 275.00
Whole Wheat Pan, #28 . . . . 235.00

GUNDERSON

Robert Gunderson purchased the Pairpoint Corporation, Boston, Massachusetts, in the late 1930s and operated it as the Gunderson Glass Works until his death in 1952. Operating as Gunderson–Pairpoint, the company continued for only five more years.

In the 1950s, the Gunderson Glass Company produced a wide range of reproduction glassware. Its Peachblow–type art glass shades from an opaque faint pink tint to a deep rose.

Robert Bryden attempted a revival of the firm in 1970. He moved the manufacturing operations from the old Mount Washington plant in Boston back to New Bedford.

Bowl, soft blue to pink shading, 4³/₄" d . . . . $ 90.00
Cruet, 6¹/₂" h 180.00
Cup and Saucer. 125.00
Goblet 145.00
Mug, dec, satin finish, paper label, c1970. . . . . 140.00
Plate, 8" d 180.00
Sugar, ftd. 70.00
Tumbler, 4" h. 130.00
Tumbler, satin finish, 5" h. 100.00
Vase, classic shape, sq base, applied serpentine han-
    dles, 8¹/₂" h 175.00
Vase, green, 12" h 75.00
Vase, lily, 9¹/₂" h. 250.00
Wine, trumpet shaped, flared, round ft, satin finish,
    4¹/₈" h 130.00

HAEGER POTTERIES

In 1871 David H. Haeger established a brick yard on the banks of the Fox River in Dundee, Illinois. He was succeeded in 1900 by Edmund H. Haeger, his son. Edmund introduced an art pottery line in 1914. Within a short period of time, Haeger became a leading manufacturer of artware, characterized by a lustrous glaze and soft glowing pastels. The company built and operated a complete working pottery at the 1933–34 Chicago World's Fair.

The company introduced its Royal Haeger line in 1938. The Royal Haeger Lamp Company was formed in 1939, the same year the company purchased the Buckeye Pottery building in Macomb, Illinois, for the purpose of manufacturing its art line for the florist trade.

In 1954 Joseph F. Estes, Edmund's son–in–law, assumed the presidency. Nicholas Haeger Estes and Alexendria Haeger Estes, son and daughter of Joseph, continue the family tradition of providing the company's leadership.

Reference: David D. Dilley, *Haeger Potteries,* L–W Book Sales, 1997.

Ashtray, #127, gold tweed, triangular, 10¹/₄" l . . . . $ 20.00
Ashtray, #109–S, gold tweed, 7" sq. 20.00
Ashtray, #128, mandarin orange, triangular, 13¹/₄" l 10.00
Ashtray, #2145, sq leaf with acorns, green, 9³/₄" sq 15.00
Ashtray, adv, green, "A Century of Progress,
    1933–1934", 3" d. 50.00
Ashtray and Cigarette Holder, #702, mandarin
    orange, 10¹/₄" l 20.00

Bowl, #3052, aqua crystal, 1967, $20.00.

Bookends, pr, #R–638, panther planters, ebony,
c1950s **135.00**
Bookends, pr, #R718, ram heads, oxblood, 5¹/₂" h **55.00**
Bookends, pr, #R–1144, water lilies, green with white
flowers, c1952, 7¹/₂" h **60.00**
Bowl, #352, black mistique, rect, ftd, 14¹/₂" l **40.00**
Bowl, #4–112, leaf edge, green agate, 13¹/₂" l **65.00**
Bowl, #R–333, lilac, 16¹/₄" l **40.00**
Bowl, #R–442, floral relief, mauve int, mauve agate
ext, 18¹/₄" l **50.00**
Bowl, #R–1338, modern, chartreuse and ebony,
13¹/₄" l **35.00**
Candle Holders, pr, #R–304, fish, mauve agate, 4¹/₄" h . . . **50.00**
Candle Holders, pr, #R–437, leaf, ebony, 2³/₄" h **15.00**
Candle Holder/Planter, #R–458, double light, char-
treuse, c1946, 7¹/₂" l **20.00**
Candy Dish, #8044–H, 4 bowls, mandarin orange,
center handle, 8³/₄" w **20.00**
Candy Dish, #R–459, triple bowl, fish handle, blue,
c1946, 8¹/₂" l **50.00**
Compote, #3003, white ext, turquoise int, 12" l,
4¹/₂" h **25.00**
Dish, #3961, blue with black specks, c1967, 8" sq **10.00**
Figure, #612, rooster, burnt sienna, c1973, 11" h **50.00**
Figure, #R–412, standing fawn, pink, 1950, 11³/₄" h **45.00**
Figure, #R–784, elephant, chartreuse and honey,
8¹/₄" l **40.00**
Lamp, fish riding wave, yellow, 10¹/₂" h **100.00**
Planter, #508, donkey, red transparent, 9¹/₄" h **40.00**
Planter, #3910, clown jack–in–the–box, pink, 8¹/₂" h **20.00**
Table Lighter, #812–H, fish, jade crackle blue, c1960,
10" h **35.00**
Table Lighter, #889, ribbed, mandarin orange,
c1950s–60s, 3" d, 5" h **15.00**
TV Lamp, #6140, sailfish, silver spray, 9¹/₄" l **40.00**

HALL CHINA

In 1903 Robert Hall founded the Hall China Company in East
Liverpool, Ohio. Taggert Hall, his son, became president following
Robert's death in 1904. The company initially made jugs, toilet
sets, and utilitarian whiteware. Robert T. Hall's major contribution
to the firm's growth was the development of an economical, single–fire process for lead–free glazed ware.

Hall acquired a new plant in 1930. In 1933 Hall developed the
Autumn Leaf pattern as a premium for the Jewel Tea Company.
Other premium patterns include Blue Bonnett (Standard Coffee

Company), Orange Poppy (Great American Tea Company), and
Red Poppy (Grand Union Tea Company).

The company launched a decal–decorated dinnerware line in
1933. Hall's refrigerator ware was marketed to the general public
along with specific patterns and shapes manufactured for General
Electric, Hotpoint, Montgomery Ward, Sears, and Westinghouse.

Hall made a full range of products, from dinnerware to utilitarian kitchenware. Its figural teapots in the shape of Aladdin lamps,
automobiles, etc., are eagerly sought by collectors.

References: Susan and Al Bagdade, *Warman's American Pottery
and Porcelain,* Wallace–Homestead, Krause Publications, 1994;
Harvey Duke, *The Official Price Guide to Pottery and Porcelain,
Eighth Edition,* House of Collectibles, 1995; Margaret and Kenn
Whitmyer, *The Collector's Encyclopedia of Hall China, Second
Edition,* Collector Books, 1994, 1997 value update.

Newsletter: *Hall China Encore,* 317 N Pleasant St, Oberlin, OH
44074.

Collectors' Club: Hall Collector's Club, PO Box 360488,
Cleveland, OH 44136.

Carrot,casserole, radiance . . . . **$ 60.00**
Chinese Red, bean pot, #5 . . . . **160.00**
Crocus, cake plate **30.00**
Crocus, cup and saucer **20.00**
Crocus, gravy **35.00**
Crocus, mixing bowl **50.00**
Crocus, plate, 8¹/₄" d **10.00**
Crocus, plate, 10" d **35.00**
Crocus, platter, 13¹/₄" d, oval **35.00**
Crocus, teapot, banded **175.00**
Fantasy, creamer and sugar **75.00**
Heather, cup and saucer **8.00**
Heather, plate, 9" d **10.00**
Heather, tureen, cov **18.00**
Heather Rose, bowl, 6" d **8.00**
Mulberry, berry bowl, 5³/₄" l **8.00**
Mulberry, cereal bowl, 6" d **18.00**
Mulberry, salt and pepper shakers, pr **25.00**
Mulberry, vegetable bowl, open, 9" sq **25.00**
Orange Poppy, bean pot **65.00**
Orange Poppy, casserole, cov, oval, 8" l **55.00**
Orange Poppy, coffeepot, S lid **50.00**
Orange Poppy, leftover dish, loop handle **45.00**
Orange Poppy, plate, 6" d **8.00**
Orange Poppy, platter, 13" l **20.00**
Orange Poppy, sugar, cov **25.00**
Orange Poppy, teapot, Boston shape **200.00**
Orange Poppy, vegetable bowl, round **25.00**
Pastel Morning Glory, bean pot, handled **165.00**
Pastel Morning Glory, bowl, oval **40.00**
Pastel Morning Glory, creamer and sugar, D–style **60.00**
Pastel Morning Glory, plate, 6" d **8.00**
Pastel Morning Glory, plate, 7" d **18.00**
Pastel Morning Glory, plate, 9" d **40.00**
Pastel Morning Glory, soup, flat **25.00**
Red Dot, baker, individual, handled **35.00**
Red Dot, bowl, 8³/₄" d **30.00**
Red Dot, custard **22.00**
Red Poppy, cereal bowl, 6" d **20.00**

Red Poppy, cup 10.00
Red Poppy, cup and saucer 15.00
Red Poppy, custard 20.00
Red Poppy, plate, 9" d 8.00
Red Poppy, plate, 10" d 18.00
Red Poppy, soup, flat 25.00
Red Poppy, teapot, New York shape 75.00
Red Poppy, tumbler, frosted, 5¼" h 25.00
Serenade, berry bowl, 5½" d 8.00
Serenade, cup and saucer 15.00
Serenade, dinner plate, 9" d 15.00
Serenade, salad bowl, 9" d 25.00
Springtime, cup and saucer 8.00
Springtime, plate, 9" d 8.00
Springtime, platter, 13" l 20.00
Springtime, teapot 45.00
Teapot, Airflow, cobalt, gold dec 60.00
Teapot, Basket, yellow and gold 110.00
Teapot, Boston, maroon, gold dec 40.00
Teapot, Baltimore, yellow 50.00
Teapot, Cleveland, green 65.00
Teapot, Connie, celedon green 55.00
Teapot, French, brown with gold daisies, 1 cup 50.00
Teapot, Globe, turquoise, gold dec 95.00
Teapot, Hollywood, pink, gold dec 35.00
Teapot, Los Angeles, cobalt blue, 6 cup 40.00
Teapot, Manhattan, blue 65.00
Teapot, McCormick, maroon, 6 cup 40.00
Teapot, Melody, blue 65.00
Teapot, Moderne, marine, gold dec 45.00
Teapot, Murphy, light blue 85.00
Teapot, Nautilus, yellow, gold dec 70.00
Teapot, New York, emerald, gold dec 30.00
Teapot, Ohio, black and gold, 6 cup 150.00
Teapot, Parade, yellow, gold dec 30.00
Teapot, Philadelphia, ivory, gold dec, 6 cup 40.00
Teapot, Plume, pink 20.00
Teapot, Star, green, gold dec 45.00
Teapot, Teamster, yellow and gold, double spout 110.00
Teapot, Washington, marine blue, 6 cup 70.00
Tulip, cup and saucer 15.00
Tulip, fruit bowl, 5½" d 10.00
Tulip, mixing bowl, 6" d 30.00

Teapot, Los Angeles, pink, gold dec, 6 cup, $25.00.

Tulip, platter, 13¼" l, oval 45.00
Wildfire, bowl, 9" l, oval 30.00
Wildfire, gravy 35.00
Wildfire, plate, 9" d 15.00
Wildfire, salad bowl, 9" d 25.00
Wildfire, tidbit tray, 3 tiers 50.00
Wild Poppy, casserole, 9" l, oval 60.00
Wild Poppy, salt and pepper shakers, pr, handled 100.00
Windshield, gold dec 55.00

HALLMARK

After moving to Kansas City, Missouri, in 1910, Joyce C. Hall worked as a postcard jobber while attending business college. In 1913 Joyce and Rollie Hall, his brother, launched their own firm to sell Christmas cards. The line soon expanded to all types of holiday cards. In January 1913, a fire destroyed their entire stock of valentines. Undaunted, the Halls purchased a Kansas City engraving firm a year later and began printing and marketing Hallmark cards.

By 1921, the firm consisted of three Hall brothers, Joyce, Rollie, and William. Within two years, Hallmark cards were sold nationwide. Hallmark built its first plant in 1923. It introduced a line of giftwrap in 1926. The company's first national advertising took place in a 1928 issue of *The Ladies' Home Journal*.

Following World War II, Hallmark launched a major expansion. In 1948 Norman Rockwell became the first "name" artist to appear on Hallmark cards. A new nine–story building located in Kansas City was completed in 1956. Hallmark's Plans–A–Party line was introduced in 1960. Playing cards appeared a year later.

Plants in Lawrence, Leavenworth, Osage City, and Topeka, Kansas, soon joined the company's main headquarters in Kansas City. Hallmark introduced a Cookie Cutter line in early 1960s, its Keepsake Christmas Ornament line in 1973, and its Merry Miniature line in 1974.

Hallmark is a leader in preserving its company's heritage. The Hallmark Historical Collection is one of the finest company archives in America.

Red Poppy, salt and pepper shakers, pr, handled, $25.00.

Periodical: *Collectors Bulletin*, 22341 E Wells Rd, Canton, IL 61520.

Collectors' Club: Hallmark Keepsake Ornament Collectors Club, PO Box 412734, Kansas City, MO 64141.

Doll, Holiday Memories Barbie, 1995 . . . . $ 50.00
Figure, Bashful Boy With Heart, Valentine Merry
  Miniatures, 1995 . . . . 2.50
Figure, Bear in Clown Costume, Summer Merry
  Miniatures, 1995 . . . . 5.00
Figure, Bear With Surfboard, At The Beach Merry
  Miniatures, 1994 . . . . 5.00
Figure, Leprechaun, St. Patrick's Merry Miniatures, 1995 . . . 5.00
Figure, Penguin Throwing Snowball, A North Pole
  Christmas Merry Memories, 1994 . . . . 2.50
Ornament, A Heavenly Nap, 1981 . . . . 45.00
Ornament, Angel, 1973 . . . . 25.00
Ornament, Baby Sitter, 1984 . . . . 12.00
Ornament, Baby's First Christmas, photoholder, 1982 . . . . 20.00
Ornament, Bell, 1977 . . . . 45.00
Ornament, Bellringer, 1977 . . . . 40.00
Ornament, Brass Bell, 1982 . . . . 18.00
Ornament, Candle, 1977 . . . . 50.00
Ornament, Christmas Eve Surprise, 1979 . . . . 60.00
Ornament, Christmas Love, 1980 . . . . 35.00
Ornament, Currier & Ives, 1975 . . . . 45.00
Ornament, Drummer Boy, 1975 . . . . 20.00
Ornament, First Christmas Together, 1982 . . . . 20.00
Ornament, Grandparents, 1980 . . . . 45.00
Ornament, Mary Hamilton, 1979 . . . . 20.00
Ornament, Merry Santa, 1980 . . . . 15.00
Ornament, Miss Piggy and Kermit, 1982 . . . . 30.00
Ornament, Partridge in a Pear Tree, 1979 . . . . 40.00
Ornament, Peppermint Mouse, 1981 . . . . 30.00
Ornament, Raggedy Ann and Andy, 1974 . . . . 75.00
Ornament, Santa and Sleigh, 1975 . . . . 110.00
Ornament, Soldier, 1976 . . . . 90.00
Ornament, Teacher Apple, 1982 . . . . 12.00
Ornament, 25th Christmas Together, 1980 . . . . 22.00
Plate, Growing Years, Days to Remember, The Art of
  Norman Rockwell, 1994 . . . . 30.00

Ornament, Tobin Fraley Carousel, 2nd in series, 1983, $30.00.

Plate, Neighborhood Dreamer, Enchanted Garden,
  1992 . . . . **40.00**

HALLOWEEN

Halloween traces its origin to All Hallows Eve, the night before All Saints Day (November 1) when individuals supposedly returned from the dead. By the end of the 19th century, Halloween became more of secular than religious holiday. Witches with their magical abilities and aided by a bat, cat, or owl became part of the holiday's tradition. Black, the color of night and demonic influences, was countered by orange, the color of strength and endurance.

Halloween collectors divide material into pre– and post–1945 objects. Country of origin—Germany, Japan, or the United States—appears to make little difference. Image is everything. The survival rate of Halloween collectibles is extremely high. Currently, Halloween is second only to Christmas in respect to popularity among holiday collectors.

References: Dan and Pauline Campanelli, *Halloween Collectibles; A Price Guide*, L–W Books, 1995; Stuart Schneider, *Halloween In America: A Collector's Guide With Prices*, Schiffer Publishing, 1995.

Newsletters: *Boo News*, PO Box 143, Brookfield, IL 60513; *Trick or Treat Trader*, PO Box 499, Winchester, NH 03470.

Bank, skeleton in coffin, tin, Japan . . . . $ 50.00
Booklet, *Dennison Paper Costumes*, 1922 . . . . 12.50
Candle, figural black cat 10.00
Candy Box, Baby Ruth, Halloween motif 40.00
Candy Container, plastic, black cat, orange trim 5.00
Candy Container, cone, papier mâché, West
  Germany 30.00
Chocolate Mold, 4 witches, Germany 155.00
Costume, astronaut, plastic mask, boxed, Halco, 1962 . . . 55.00
Costume, Bat Masterson, boxed 45.00
Costume, bats, witches, and jack–o'–lantern design
  top, yellow and black, homemade, c1930 . . . . 55.00
Costume, California Raisin 25.00
Costume, dress, black with orange jack–o'–lanterns
  design, homemade, c1940 . . . . 70.00
Costume, First Man on the Moon, plastic mask,
  "White For Nite," Collegeville, c1969 . . . . 60.00
Costume, Ghostbusters II, cloth, plastic accessories,
  c1989 . . . . 35.00
Costume, Porky Pig, Warner Bros, orig box 30.00
Costume, skeleton, black cowl, c1940 . . . . 35.00
Costume, Tinkerbell, plastic mask, Disney, Ben
  Cooper, c1958 . . . . 40.00
Costume, Tweety Bird 20.00
Costume, Wicked Witch, Wizard of Oz, orig box 55.00
Favor, skeleton, papier–mâché head, pipe cleaner
  body, Japan, c1950, 3" h 8.00
Figure, cat, 6½" h 45.00
Figure, pumpkin, 6" h 45.00
Figure, witch, 6" h, orig hair 40.00
Game, Cat and Witch, Whitman, 1940s, MIB 50.00
Horn, vegetable design, painted pressed cardboard,
  Germany, 6½" h 65.00

Costume, Zorro, Disney, Ben Cooper, #233, $60.00.

Mask, Santa, gauze, 1930s **30.00**

Noisemaker, rattle, litho tin, ghosts and cats design,
     wooden handle, 3³/₄" d **15.00**

Party Hat, cardboard, cats dec, c1940 . . . . **5.00**

Party Plate, paper, witch with jack–o'–lantern, bats,
     black cats with green eyes, orange, black trim,
     Beach Products, c1950 . . . . **2.00**

Party Set, 4 napkins, table cover, made in USA, c1930 . . . **30.00**

Place Card, owl sitting on tree branch, moon, flying
     bat, USA, c1930 . . . . **8.00**

Punchboard Party Game, 1940s **45.00**

Salt and Pepper Shakers, pr, devils, c1930 . . . . **55.00**

Table Decoration, black cat, honeycomb base,
     c1945, 9¹/₂" h **15.00**

Table Decoration, paper scarecrow, honeycomb hay
     stack and pumpkin, c1950, 8" h **10.00**

Trick or Treat Bag, paper, Happy Halloween, litho
     pumpkin head, 1940 . . . . **20.00**

Wall Decoration, bat, paper, jointed, Beistle, c1947,
     18" w **20.00**

Wall Decoration, pumpkin man, diecut cardboard,
     jointed, 14" h **75.00**

Wall Decoration, skeleton, diecut cardboard, 1950s,
     5' h **35.00**

Wall Decoration, 2 skeletons playing musical instru-
     ments, emb diecut paper, USA, c1938, 12" h **8.00**

Wall Decoration, witch and cauldron, diecut, c1940,
     3¹/₂" h **8.00**

HANNA–BARBERA

William Denby Hanna was born on July 14, 1910, in Melrose, New Mexico. Attending college during the Depression, he studied structural engineering briefly before a lack of finances forced him to end his studies. A talent for drawing landed him a job at the Harman–Ising animation studio in 1930. Hanna worked there for seven years.

Joseph Roland Barbera was born in New York City in 1911. Although enamored with drawing, Barbera initially worked as an accountant at a law firm following his studies at the American Institute of Banking. He lost his job as a result of the Depression. After a brief stint as a magazine cartoonist, Barbera joined the Van

Beuren studio in 1932 where he helped animate and script Tom and Jerry.

The year 1937 was a magic one for Hanna and Barbera. MGM was organizing a new cartoon unit. Barbera headed west, Hanna moved across town. It was not until 1938 that Hanna and Barbera were teamed together. Their first project was Gallopin' Gals. By 1939 the two were permanently paired, devoting much of their energy to Tom and Jerry shorts. Between 1939 and 1956, they directed over 200 Tom and Jerry shorts, winning several Oscars in the process.

Twenty years after joining the MGM cartoon team, Hanna and Barbera struck out on their own. Their goal was to develop cartoons for television as well as theatrical release. The success of Huckleberry Hound and Yogi Bear paved the way for The Flintstones, one of the most successful television shows of the 1960s.

In 1966 Taft Communications purchased Hanna–Barbera Productions for a reported 26 million dollars. Hanna and Barbera continued to head the company.

Hanna–Barbera Productions has produced over 100 cartoon series and specials. In several cases, a single series produced a host of well–loved cartoon characters. Some of the most popular include Atom Ant, Auggie Doggie and Doggie Daddy, Birdman, The Flintstones, Frankenstein, Jr., Huckleberry Hound, The Jetsons, Jonny Quest, Magilla Gorilla, Peter Potamus, Penelope Pitstop, Quick Draw McGraw, Ricochet Rabbit, Ruff and Reddy, Space Ghost, Top Cat, and Yogi Bear.

References: Joseph Barbera, *My Life in 'Toons: From Flatbush to Bedrock in Under a Century,* Turner Publishing, 1994; Bill Hanna, *A Cast of Friends,* Taylor Publishing, 1996.

Atom Ant, coloring book, Watkins–Strathmore, 1965,
     8 x 10" . . . . **$ 20.00**

Atom Ant, costume, boxed, Ben Cooper, 1965 . . . . **30.00**

Atom Ant, game, Atom Ant Saves the Day,
     Transogram, 1966 . . . . **80.00**

Augie Doggie, frame tray puzzle, Whitman, 1960,
     11 x 14" **12.00**

Banana Splits, chalkboard, mounted on particle
     board, chalk, eraser, and plastic pegs, Hasbro,
     1969, 24 x 18" **30.00**

Banana Splits, game, The Banana Splits Game,
     Hasbro, 1969, 20 x 10" **45.00**

Banana Splits, Rub–Ons, 10 diecut cardboard figures,
     printed transfer sheets, stylus, Hasbro, 1969 . . . . **55.00**

Flintstones, Big Golden Book, Golden Press, 1980,
     48 pgs **20.00**

Flintstones, card game, Pre–Historic Animal Rummy,
     Ed–U–Card, 1960 . . . . **15.00**

Flintstones, coloring book, Whitman, 1980 . . . . **12.00**

Flintstones, game, Dino the Dinosaur, Transogram,
     1961 . . . . **40.00**

Flintstones, game, Flintstones Mitt–Full, Whitman,
     1962 . . . . **45.00**

Flintstones, hand puppet, Bamm–Bamm, cloth body,
     vinyl plastic head, Ideal, 1963, 12" h **25.00**

Flintstones, party place setting, 4–pc set with table-
     cloth, 16 plates, and 24 napkins, Reed, 1969 . . . . **22.00**

Flintstones, pillow case, cotton, Fred playing piano,
     Wilma, Betty, and Barney singing, c1960 . . . . **15.00**

Flintstones, poster, Welch's Fruit Drinks adv, 1962 . . . . **55.00**
Flintstones, push–button puppet, Dino, plastic, paint-
ed, jointed, Kohner, 1964 . . . . **15.00**
Funky Phantom, game, The Funky Phantom Game,
Milton Bradley, 1971 . . . . **12.00**
Huckleberry Hound, game, Huckleberry Hound
Bumps, Transogram, 1960. . . . . **30.00**
Huckleberry Hound, hand puppet, hard plastic head,
red, white, and blue cloth body, Kelloggs premium,
1960, 9" h **35.00**
Huckleberry Hound, record, 33⅓ rpm, *Huckleberry
Hound Tells Stories of Uncle Remus,* HBR, 1963 . . . . . . **20.00**
Huckleberry Hound and Yogi Bear, Big Golden Book,
Huckleberry Hound and Yogi Bear, Golden Press,
1960, 48 pgs **20.00**
Jetsons, frame tray puzzle, Whitman, 1962, 11 x 14". . . . **30.00**
Jetsons, game, Jetsons Fun Pad Game, Milton Bradley,
1963 . . . . **70.00**
Jetsons, record, 78 rpm, *Songs of the Jetsons,* Little
Golden Records, 1963 . . . . **25.00**
Jonny Quest, activity set, Pencil By Number Coloring
Set, 8 sketches, 6 colored pencils, and sharpener,
Transogram, 1965 . . . . **80.00**
Jonny Quest, game, Jonny Quest Game, Transogram,
1964 . . . . **75.00**
Lippy the Lion, Touché Turtle, and Wally Gator, cup,
plastic, paper illus of characters marching with
musical instruments sealed inside clear plastic
coating, Gothem Ind, 1964. **20.00**
Magilla Gorilla, game, Pop–Out Target Barrel Game,
Ideal, 1964 . . . . **55.00**
Mush Mouse, hand puppet, vinyl head, cloth body,
Ideal, 1964, 10" h **30.00**
Mush Mouse and Punkin' Puss Game, Ideal, 1964 . . . . . . **45.00**
Peter Potamus, game, The Peter Potamus Game,
Ideal, 1964 . . . . **85.00**
Peter Potamus, pull toy, painted molded vinyl, Peter
Potamus sitting on plastic wagon, Ideal, 1964, 5" h **45.00**
Peter Potamus, playing cards, Whitman, 1965 . . . . **20.00**

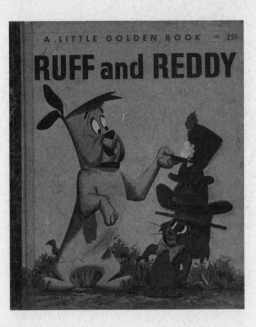

Ruff and Reddy,
**Little Golden
Book, #378,
1959, $7.50.**

Pixie and Dixie, coloring book, Whitman, 1965 . . . . **12.00**
Quick Draw McGraw, bank, figural, Knickerbocker,
1960, 10" h **20.00**
Quick Draw McGraw, stuffed toy, Sugar Smacks pre-
mium, Kelloggs, 1960, 18" h **30.00**
Ruff and Reddy, game, Ruff and Reddy at the Circus,
Transogram, 1962 . . . . **40.00**
Scooby Doo, stuffed toy, "Scooby Doo where are
you!" tag, J. S. Sutton and Sons, 1970, 14" h **40.00**
Secret Squirrel, frame tray puzzle, Whitman, 1965,
11 x 14" **15.00**
Top Cat, soaky, 1963, 10" h **20.00**
Wacky Races, jigsaw puzzle, Luke, Blabber Bear, and
Sawtooth racing scene, Whitman, 1970, 70 pcs. **18.00**
Yogi Bear, bubble pipe, plastic, 5 x 7" display card,
Transogram, 1963 . . . . **12.00**
Yogi Bear, push–button puppet, painted plastic,
jointed, Kohner, 1964, 3" h **15.00**

HARKER POTTERY

The Harker Pottery Company traces its heritage back to Benjamin Harker, Sr., who established a pottery in East Liverpool, Ohio, in 1840. The company experienced a number of reorganizations during the 19th century. The George S. Harker Company was incorporated as the Harker Pottery in 1898. In 1930 the firm moved its production facilities from East Liverpool to Chester, West Virginia.

Harker made a wide variety of household dinnerware, kitchenware, and utilitarian ware. In addition, Harker produced premium and souvenir items. Harker's kitchenwares include Bakerite (introduced in 1935), HotOven (introduced in 1926), and Sun Glow (introduced in 1937). Harker's Gadroon, a dinnerware shape line, is one of the company's best known products.

Harker's intaglio dinnerware lines included patterns by famous designers such as George Bauer, Paul Pinney, and Russel Wright. Wright's White Clover was introduced in the 1950s.

The Jeanette Glass Company purchased Harker Pottery in 1969. It made reproduction Rebekah–at–the–Well teapots and Toby jugs.

**Punkin' Puss and
Mush Mouse,
Bubble Club bubble
bath bottles, Purex
Corp, $20.00 each.**

Harker ceased operations in 1972. The plant was used by Ohio Valley Stoneware until it was destroyed by fire in 1975.

References: Susan and Al Bagdade, *Warman's American Pottery and Porcelain,* Wallace–Homestead, Krause Publications, 1994; Jo Cunningham, *The Collector's Encyclopedia Of American Dinnerware,* Collector Books, 1982, 1995 value update; Harvey Duke, *The Official Price Guide to Pottery and Porcelain, Eighth Edition,* House of Collectibles, 1995

Amy, bean pot	$ 12.00
Amy, bowl, 6¼" d	8.00
Amy, cup and saucer	12.00
Amy, pepper shaker	12.50
Amy, plate, 6¼" d	5.00
Amy, spoon	30.00
Cameoware, berry bowl	4.00
Cameoware, casserole, cov	15.00
Cameoware, cup and saucer	10.00
Cameoware, dinner plate, 10" d	10.00
Cameoware, salt and pepper shakers, pr	15.00
Colonial Lady, bread and butter plate	8.00
Colonial Lady, cereal bowl	15.00
Colonial Lady, cup and saucer	15.00
Colonial Lady, salad plate	10.00
Colonial Lady, soup bowl	22.00
Colonial Lady, vegetable bowl	25.00
Deco–Dahlia, cake lifter	30.00
Deco–Dahlia, pie baker, 9" d	20.00
Deco–Dahlia, utility plate, 12" d	20.00
Laurelton, bread and butter plate	5.00
Laurelton, creamer and sugar	22.00
Laurelton, salt and pepper shakers, pr	22.00
Laurelton, vegetable bowl	25.00
Mallow, bowl, 5" d	20.00
Mallow, plate, 8" d	15.00
Pansy, cereal bowl	15.00
Pansy, cup	15.00
Pansy, dinner plate	15.00
Pansy, salt shaker	18.00
Petit Point Rose, bowl, 8¾" d	20.00
Petit Point Rose, cake plate	15.00

Cameoware, cov jug, $18.00.

Petit Point Rose, casserole, cov, 7" d	35.00
Petit Point Rose, pie baker	15.00
Petit Point Rose, plate, 8½" d	10.00
Petit Point Rose, sugar	15.00
Red Apple, custard	10.00
Red Apple, pie server	25.00
Red Apple, spoon	30.00
Red Apple, vegetable bowl, 9" d	30.00
Rolling Pin, basket of fruits and flowers	80.00

HAVILAND CHINA

There are several different Haviland companies. It takes a detailed family tree to understand the complex family relationships that led to their creations.

David and Daniel Haviland, two brothers, were New York china importers. While on a buying trip to France in the early 1840s, David Haviland decided to remain in that country. He brought his family to Limoges where he supervised the purchase, design, and decoration of pieces sent to America. In 1852, Charles Field Haviland, David's nephew, arrived in France to learn the family business. Charles married into the Alluaud family, owner of the Casseaux works in Limoges. Charles Edward and Theodore Haviland, David's sons, entered the firm in 1864. A difference of opinion in 1891 led to the liquidation of the old firm and the establishment of several independent new ones. [Editor's note: I told you it was complicated.]

Today, Haviland generally means ceramics made at the main Casseaux works in Limoges. Charles Edward produced china under the name Haviland et Cie between 1891 and the early 1920s. Theodore Haviland's La Porcelaine Theodore Haviland was made from 1891 until 1952.

References: Harry L. Rinker, *Dinnerware of the 20th Century: The Top 500 Patterns,* House of Collectibles, 1997.

Collectors' Club: Haviland Collectors Internationale Foundation, PO Box 802462, Santa Clarita, CA 91380.

Apple Blossom, bread plate	$ 15.00
Apple Blossom, coffeepot	225.00
Apple Blossom, eggcup, double	40.00
Apple Blossom, platter, oval, 12" l	60.00
Athena, cup and saucer	45.00
Autumn Leaf, coffeepot, Haviland & Co	235.00
Autumn Leaf, platter, scalloped edge, Haviland & Co, 13¾" l	100.00
Chateaux de France, dessert plate, Theodore Haviland, 1925	7.50
Chrysantheme, dinner plate, Haviland & Co, 1970s	15.00
Eden, dinner plate, Theodore Haviland	15.00
Gold Band, butter dish, Theodore Haviland	50.00
Gold Band, creamer and sugar, Theodore Haviland, 1930	50.00
Plate, A Partridge in a Pear Tree, 1970	45.00
Plate, 5 Golden Rings, 1974	20.00
Plate, La Chasse a la Licorne, 1973, set of 6	45.00
Princess, butter pat, Haviland & Co	15.00
Princess, dinner plate, Haviland & Co, 9½" d	30.00
Rajah, bouillon cup and saucer, Theodore Haviland	25.00
Rajah, bread and butter plate, 6" d	8.00

Rosalinde, dinner plate, Theodore Haviland, 1937–56, $15.00.

Rajah, creamer and sugar, Theodore Haviland. **25.00**
Rajah, salad plate, 7" d **12.00**
Ranson, bone dish, Haviland & Co. **20.00**
Ranson, bouillon cup and saucer, 2 handled,
    Haviland & Co. **20.00**
Ranson, bread and butter plate, Haviland & Co, 5" d. **17.50**
Ranson, cup and saucer, Haviland & Co. **30.00**
Ranson, demitasse cup and saucer, Haviland & Co **25.00**
Ranson, dinner plate, Haviland & Co, 9½" d. **20.00**
Ranson, luncheon plate, Haviland & Co, 8½" d **15.00**
Ranson, salad plate, Haviland & Co, 7½" d. **20.00**
Rosalinde, bouillon cup and saucer, 2 handled,
    Theodore Haviland. **35.00**
Rosalinde, soup and underplate, applied handles,
    Theodore Haviland. **85.00**
Shalimar, bread and butter plate, Haviland & Co. **8.00**
Shalimar, cup and saucer, Haviland & Co. **15.00**
Shalimar, dinner plate, Haviland & Co **18.00**
Shalimar, salad plate, Haviland & Co **12.00**
Shalimar, soup bowl, Haviland & Co **15.00**
Springtime, creamer and cov sugar. **125.00**
Violets and Daisies, salad plate, Haviland & Co,
    c1920 . . . . **10.00**
Yale, cream soup and underplate, handled **35.00**
Yale, cup and saucer **35.00**
Yale, dinner plate, 9½" d **20.00**
Yale, platter, oval, 11½" l **45.00**

HAZEL ATLAS GLASSWARE

Hazel Atlas resulted from the 1902 merger of the Hazel Glass Company and the Atlas Glass and Metal Company, each located in Washington, Pennsylvania. The company's main offices were located in Wheeling, West Virginia.

    The company was a pioneer in automated glassware manufacture. A factory in Clarksburg, West Virginia, specialized in pressed glassware and achieved a reputation in the late 1920s as the

"World's Largest Tumbler Factory." Two factories in Zanesville, Ohio, made containers, thin–blown tumblers, and other blown ware. Washington and Wheeling plants made containers and tableware, the latter including many of the Depression era patterns for which the company is best known among collectors.

    Continental Can purchased Hazel–Atlas in 1956. Brockway Glass Company purchased the company in 1964.

References: Gene Florence, *Collectible Glassware From the 40's, 50's, 60's…, Third Edition,* Collector Books, 1996; Gene Florence, *Kitchen Glassware of the Depression Years, Fifth Edition,* Collector Books, 1995, 1997 value update.

Note: See Depression Glass for additional listings.

Cloverleaf, candy dish, green . . . . **$ 50.00**
Cloverleaf, creamer, green **15.00**
Cloverleaf, cup and saucer, green. **15.00**
Cloverleaf, dessert bowl, 4" d, pink. **15.00**
Cloverleaf, luncheon plate, 8" d, pink. **10.00**
Cloverleaf, sherbet, 3" h, pink **10.00**
Cloverleaf, sugar, ftd, 3⅝" h, green **50.00**
Cloverleaf, tumbler, 10 oz, pink **25.00**
Colonial Block, berry bowl, 4" d, pink **10.00**
Colonial Block, butter dish, pink **40.00**
Colonial Block, candy jar, cov, pink **40.00**
Colonial Block, creamer, white. **8.00**
Colonial Block, sherbet, pink **10.00**
Colonial Block, sugar, pink. **12.00**
Criss Cross, butter, 1 lb, green **60.00**
Criss Cross, lemon reamer, pink **250.00**
Criss Cross, orange reamer, pink. **195.00**
Criss Cross, refrigerator lid, cov, 4" sq, crystal **15.00**
Florentine No. 1, berry bowl, 5" d, yellow **15.00**
Florentine No. 1, cereal bowl, 6" d, pink **25.00**
Florentine No. 1, comport, ruffled, green **30.00**
Florentine No. 1, cup, yellow. **12.00**
Florentine No. 1, salad plate, 8⅞" d, yellow **15.00**
Florentine No. 1, salt and pepper shakers, pr, ftd, crystal . . **40.00**
Florentine No. 1, saucer, yellow. **5.00**
Florentine No. 1, sugar, yellow. **15.00**
Florentine No. 1, tumbler, ribbed, 9 oz, 4" h, pink **25.00**
Moderntone, cereal bowl, 6⅞" d, amethyst. **75.00**
Moderntone, cup, cobalt **12.00**
Moderntone, salad plate, 6¾" d, amethyst. **10.00**
Moderntone, saucer, amethyst **5.00**
Moderntone, sugar, cobalt **15.00**
Moderntone, tumbler, 9 oz, amethyst **30.00**

Criss Cross, butter dish, ¼ lb, 6¾" l, cobalt blue, $75.00.

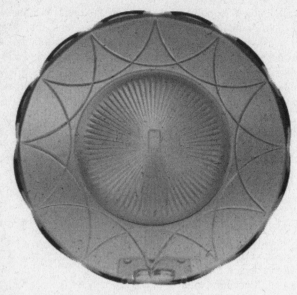

Newport, luncheon plate, 8¹/₂" d, cobalt blue, $15.00.

Newport, berry bowl, amethyst **15.00**
Newport, bowl, 4³/₄" d, amethyst **15.00**
Newport, creamer, cobalt blue **20.00**
Newport, cup, fired–on color **8.00**
Newport, cup and saucer, amethyst **20.00**
Newport, dinner plate, 9" h, cobalt blue **25.00**
Newport, luncheon plate, 8¹/₂" d, amethyst **15.00**
Newport, salt and pepper shakers, pr, cobalt blue **50.00**
Newport, salt and pepper shakers, pr, platonite white **10.00**
Newport, saucer, cobalt blue **8.00**
Newport, sherbet, 5⁷/₈" d, cobalt blue **5.50**
Newport, sugar, amethyst **15.00**
Newport, tumbler, 9 oz, amethyst. **35.00**
Ovide, berry bowl, white **10.00**
Ovide, candy dish, cov, green **25.00**
Ovide, creamer, green **5.00**
Ovide, cup, green **5.00**
Ovide, luncheon plate, 8" d, green **5.00**
Ovide, platter, dec, 11" d, white **25.00**
Ovide, salt and pepper shakers, pr, decorated white **25.00**
Ovide, sherbet, black **8.00**
Ovide, sugar, open, green **5.00**
Ovide, tumbler, decorated white **20.00**
Ribbon, berry bowl, 4" d, green **25.00**
Ribbon, candy dish, cov, green. **40.00**
Ribbon, cereal bowl, 5" d, green **30.00**
Ribbon, creamer, ftd, green **20.00**
Ribbon, cup, green **8.00**
Ribbon, luncheon plate, 8" d, black **15.00**
Ribbon, saucer, green **2.50**
Ribbon, sherbet, ftd, green **5.00**
Ribbon, sugar, ftd, green **15.00**
Roxana, bowl, golden topaz **12.00**
Roxana, cereal bowl, 6" d, yellow **18.00**
Roxana, plate, 5¹/₂" d, yellow **10.00**
Roxana, sherbet, ftd **15.00**
Roxana, tumbler, 9 oz, 4⁷/₄" h, yellow **20.00**
Royal Lace, berry bowl, 5" d, cobalt blue **50.00**

Royal Lace, console bowl, ruffled, 10" d, crystal **30.00**
Royal Lace, creamer, pink **20.00**
Royal Lace, cup and saucer, crystal **15.00**
Royal Lace, luncheon plate, 8¹/₂" d, green **25.00**
Royal Lace, sugar, crystal **25.00**
Royal Lace, vegetable bowl, oval, 11" l, pink **25.00**

HEISEY GLASS

Augustus H. Heisey, who was born in Hanover, Germany, and emigrated to the United States in 1843, began his glass industry career as a clerk with King Glass Company of Pittsburgh. In 1870, Augustus Heisey married Susan Duncan, daughter of George Duncan, owner of the Ripley Glass Company. In 1874 George Duncan deeded a one–quarter interest in his business, renamed George Duncan & Sons, to his two children, James and Susan. In 1879, two years after George Duncan's death, James Duncan and Heisey purchased George Duncan's half interest from his estate. In the 1880s Heisey applied for and obtained several design patents. In 1891 the United States Glass combine acquired George Duncan & Sons.

By 1893 Heisey had begun to formulate plans to strike out on his own. Heisey selected Newark, Ohio, as the site for his venture because of an abundant supply of natural gas, inexpensive labor, and active recruitment by the New Board of Trade. In April 1896, Heisey opened a sixteen–pot furnace in Newark. Eventually the plant would expand to three furnaces and employ over 700 people.

Early production was confined to pressed ware and bar and hotel ware. In the late 1890s, Heisey introduced colonial patterns with flutes, scallops, and panels. They were so well received that Heisey retained at least one colonial pattern in its line until the factory closed.

George Duncan Heisey, a son of Augustus H., designed the famous "Diamond H" trademark in 1900. The company registered it in 1901. By 1910 Heisey was aggressively marketing its glass through national magazines. In 1914 blown ware was first manufactured. Not content with traditional pulled stemware, the company introduced fancy pressed stemware patterns in the late 1910s.

Edgar Wilson, another son of Augustus H., became president in 1922 following Augustus' death. He was responsible for most of the colored Heisey glass. While some colored glass was made earlier, the first pastel colors and later deeper colors, e.g., cobalt and tangerine, were manufactured in quantity in the 1920s and 30s. By the time of Edgar Wilson's death in 1942, colored glassware had virtually disappeared from the market.

T. Clarence Heisey, another son of Augustus, assumed the presidency of the company. Shortages of manpower and supplies during World War II curtailed production. Many animal figures were introduced in the 1940s. An attempt was made to resurrect colored glass in the 1950s. Increasing production costs and foreign competition eventually resulted in the closing of the Heisey factory in December 1957.

The Imperial Glass Corporation of Bellaire, Ohio, bought the Heisey molds in 1958. Only a small number were kept in production, primarily those of patterns Heisey had in production when it ceased operations. Some pieces still carried the Heisey mark. In January 1968, Imperial announced it would no longer use the Heisey mark.

References: Neila Bredehoft, *The Collector's Encyclopedia of Heisey Glass, 1925–1938*, Collector Books, 1986, 1997 value update; Gene Florence, *Elegant Glassware Of The Depression Era, Seventh Edition,* Collector Books, 1997; Harry L. Rinker, *Stemware of the 20th Century: The Top 200 Patterns,* House of Collectibles, 1997.

Collectors' Club: Heisey Collectors of America, Inc, 169 W Church St, Newark, OH 43055.

Acorn, sherbet, flamingo pink	$ 20.00
Animal, goose	100.00
Animal, standing pony	70.00
Animal, Scottie dog	100.00
Animal, sparrow	80.00
Arctic, cocktail, mkd	15.00
Banded Flute, claret, clear	25.00
Banded Flute, ice cream dish	12.00
Banded Flute, oil cruet, 4 oz	45.00
Chintz, celery tray, 10" l, clear	20.00
Chintz, champagne, clear	15.00
Chintz, finger bowl, Sahara	15.00
Chintz, grapefruit, Sahara	45.00
Chintz, preserve bowl, clear, handle	20.00
Chintz, tumbler, Sahara, 10 oz	25.00
Chintz, wine, 2⅞" oz	8.00
Colonial, butter, individual	10.00
Colonial, champagne, clear	15.00
Colonial, cordial	15.00
Crystolite, ashtray with match holder, mkd	40.00
Crystolite, candleblocks, pr, 2"	15.00
Crystolite, creamer and sugar, individual, mkd	25.00
Crystolite, cup and saucer	25.00
Crystolite, custard, mkd	10.00
Crystolite, jelly, 6", mkd	18.00
Crystolite, nut dish, individual, handled	15.00
Crystolite, relish, 3 part	35.00
Crystolite, shell dish, cov	50.00
Diamond Point, ashtray, individual, mkd	10.00
Empress, celery, 13", clear	15.00
Empress, jelly, 2 handled, 6", Sahara	25.00

Empress, mint, ftd, 6", Sahara	30.00
Empress, nut dish, individual, clear	13.00
Empress, nut dish, individual, Flamingo	25.00
Empress, nut dish, individual, Moongleam	25.00
Empress, sugar, ftd, 3 handled, Sahara, mkd	32.00
Greek Key, custard	15.00
Lariat, ashtray	12.00
Lariat, creamer and sugar, individual, mkd	30.00
Lariat, goblet, 9 oz	12.00
Lariat, luncheon plate, 8", Moonglo cut	8.00
Lariat, wine, 3½ oz, Moonglo cut	14.00
Narrow Flute With Rim, nut dish, 3½", Flamingo	20.00
Narrow Flute With Rim, 3½", Moongleam	30.00
Octagon, nut dish, individual, Flamingo	25.00
Octagon, nut dish, individual, Moongleam, mkd	25.00
Old Glory, goblet, 9 oz	30.00
Old Sandwich, ashtray, individual, clear	10.00
Old Williamsburg, sherbet, low, 4½ oz	12.00
Revere, cov horseradish and underplate, gold dec, mkd	70.00
Ribbed Octagon, cream soup, 2 handled, Flamingo	15.00
Ribbed Octagon, hotel sugar, Flamingo, mkd	25.00
Ridgeleigh, custard, mkd	8.00
Ridgeleigh, jelly, oval, mkd	15.00
Ridgeleigh, nut dish, individual, divided	15.00
Sunburst, custard, mkd	18.00
Thumbprint and Panel, candlestick, 2 light, Sahara	55.00
Twist, bonbon, 2 handled, 6", Marigold, mkd	20.00
Twist, mint, 2 handled, 6", Marigold, mkd	23.00
Twist, nut dish, individual, Flamingo, mkd	20.00
Victorian, ashtray, leaf cut	30.00
Victorian, custard	10.00
Whirlpool, custard, nkd	10.00
Whirlpool, nut dish, individual, mkd	12.00

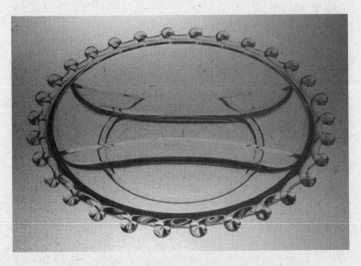

Lariat, relish, 3 section, 10" d, clear, $15.00.

HIFI EQUIPMENT

1950s and 60s Hi-Fi equipment is now collectible. Equipment wants include vacuum tube–type amplifiers, pre–amplifiers, AM–FM tuners, and receivers. Look for examples from Acrosound, Altec, Eico, Fisher, McIntosh, Marantz, and Western Electric. Some American and English record turntables and speakers are also collectible. Garrard and Thorens are two leading brand names.

Prices reflect equipment in working order. If a piece of equipment does not work, it has parts value only, usually $25 or less. Because collectors restore equipment, tubes, unused and in their period box, have value, albeit modest.

Citation II, amplifier, 120 watts, stereo, KT88 output tubes	100.00
Eico, HF–60, amplifier, 60 watts, mono, EL34 output tubes	$ 100.00
Fisher, 80AZ, amplifier, 30 watts, mono, 6L6GC tubes, narrow style chassis	50.00
Fisher, FM1000, tuner, stereo, FM only, wood case	75.00
Harmon Kardon, Citation I, pre-amplifier, stereo, tubes, wood case	50.00
Marantz, 2, amplifier, 40 watts, mono, EL34 output tubes, meter	200.00
Marantz, 10–B, tuner, stereo, tubes, AM/FM, ocilloscope display	300.00

McIntosh, MC–60, amplifier, 60 watts, mono, 6550
output tubes. **100.00**
McIntosh, MC–240, amplifier, 80 watts, stereo,
chrome chassis, 6L6GC tubes **300.00**
Telefunken 12AX7, dual triode, vacuum tube, flat
plates, made in Germany, new in box **3.00**
Thorens TD124, record turntable, 4 speeds, belt
drive, wood base **25.00**
Western Electric, 300B, vacuum tube, output, triode,
new. **12.50**

HIGGINS GLASS

Michael Higgins married Frances Stewart in 1948, the year they began experimenting with shaping and fusing glass and then decorating it with a variety of techniques ranging from enameling to gilding. By the early 1950s, they were actively involved in designing and decorating glass in their Chicago studio.

Between 1958 and 1964, the Higgins couple worked in a studio provided for them by Dearborn Glass, an industrial glass company located outside Chicago. Pieces were mass produced. A gold signature was screened on the front of each piece before the final firing. During the period with Dearborn, the Higgins developed new colors and enamels for their double–layered pieces and experimented with weaving copper wire into glass, fusing glass chips to create crystalline forms, and overlaying colors onto glass panels.

After leaving Dearborn, the Higgins established a studio at Haeger. In 1966 they re–established their own independent studio. During the late 1960s and early 1970s, the Higgins manufactured large quantities of glass plaques, often framing them in wood. In 1972 they purchased the building in Riverside, Illinois, that currently serves as their studio. Pieces made after 1972 have an engraved signature on the back. When they retire, the Higgins plan to close their studio rather than allow a successor to continue.

Reference: Donald–Brian Johnson and Leslie Piña, *Higgins: Adventures in Glass,* Schiffer Publishing, 1997.

Note: Unless stated otherwise, all pieces have a gold signature.

Ashtray, blue and gray ray, 7 x 10" . . . . **$ 45.00**
Ashtray, blue fish, 10 x 14". **80.00**
Ashtray, blue psychedelic, rolled edge, 8½" d **65.00**
Ashtray, blue waves with sand dollars, 5 x 7 . . . . **50.00**
Ashtray, jeweled sunburst, 12 x 10" **80.00**
Ashtray, orange and green psychedelic florals,
11½ x 7" **40.00**
Ashtray, orange and yellow ray, off center, 5½" d **25.00**
Ashtray, orange fish, 7 x 10". **75.00**
Bowl, blue pulled feather, 7" sq **45.00**
Bowl, blue with fried eggs, 8½" d. **85.00**
Bowl, blue with gold sunbursts, 11½" d **100.00**
Bowl, chartreuse and white stripe with gold seaweed,
6" d **45.00**
Bowl, orange spike, 8½" d **50.00**
Bowl, pink and blue amoebae, 5 cornered, 3 ftd,
8½ x 8", Stickman, etched signature **150.00**
Bowl, pink blob, 6" d **50.00**
Bowl, turquoise and black dot ray, 5 cornered, ftd,
Stickman, 8½ x 9" **95.00**

Bowl, green, orange, and blue check with bubbles, freeform, 9" h, $110.00.

Box, cov, hardwood, copper and lavender spike lid,
7½ x 4" **75.00**
Box, cov, hardwood, orange ray lid, 2 x 4" **65.00**
Charger, green spike, 17" d **135.00**
Charger, purple spike, 12½" d **100.00**
Charger, red lattice and plume, 13" d, etched Frances
"Higgins" signature **110.00**
Charger, yellow and chartreuse ray, 17" d **165.00**
Condiment, orange, green, and red rays with gold
swirl dec, 3 part, 7 x 19" **75.00**
Dish, black and gray dot ray, bowtie shape, 10" l **95.00**
Dish, blue pulled feather, 3 part, ftd, 8½" d. **80.00**
Dish, daisies, 3 part, ftd, 8½" d **110.00**
Dish, red, orange, and avocado rays, off center,
Stickman, 9 x 7". **55.00**
Plate, amber and gold pulled scroll, 6½" d, etched
signature **55.00**
Plate, blue scroll, 13½" d. **80.00**
Plate, chartreuse and white stripes with gold sea-
weed, 8½" d **55.00**
Plate, green, orange, and red fire flower, 6½" d,
etched signature. **17.50**
Plate, red and oragne spike, 7½" d **40.00**
Tray, balloons, 9" d **50.00**
Tray, balloons in smoke, off center, 14½ x 12". **160.00**
Tray, blue scroll, 10½" sq **95.00**
Tray, chartreuse and white stripe with gold seaweed,
2 part, Stickman, 7 x 14" **75.00**
Tray, keys and locks, 3½ x 7½". **40.00**
Tray, orange and green dot ray, Stickman, 5 x 10" **80.00**
Tray, red, orange, and avocado ray, gold spiral dec,
Stickman, 14 x 7". **60.00**
Tray, turquoise dot ray, divided, Stickman, 7 x 14". **75.00**
Tray, white daisy, 4½" d **25.00**
Tray, yellow and chartreuse ray, gold spiral dec,
14 x 17" **65.00**
Wall Pocket, orange and red ray, 7" h **105.00**
Wall Pocket, orange and red ray, 10" h **165.00**

HOCKEY CARDS

The first hockey cards were three cigarette sets produced between 1910 and 1913. Four candy card sets and one cigarette set were issued in the 1920s. In the 1930s Canadian chewing gum manufacturers, e.g., World Wide Gum Company, offered hockey cards as a premium.

The modern hockey card dates from the 1950s. Parkhurst issued hockey card sets between 1951 and 1964, the exception being the 1956–57 season. Topps produced its first hockey card set in 1954. Topps sets focused on players on American teams; Parkhurst focused on players on Canadian teams. Starting with the 1964–65 season, Topps issued card sets that included players from all teams in the National Hockey League. O–Pee–Chee, a producer of card sets in the 1930s, re–entered the market in 1968.

There were five major card sets for the 1990–91 season: Bowman, O–Pee–Chee Premier, Pro Set, Score, and Upper Deck. Like trading cards for other sports, current hockey card sets contain special feature cards. This is one collectible that is equally at home in either Canada or the United States.

References: James Beckett, *Beckett Hockey Card Price Guide & Alphabetical Checklist No. 6,* Beckett Publications, 1996; Sports Collectors Digest, *1997 Standard Catalog of Football, Basketball & Hockey Cards, 2nd Edition,* Krause Publications, 1996.

Periodical: *Beckett Hockey Monthly,* 15850 Dallas Pkwy, Dallas, TX 75248.

Note: Prices are for cards in excellent condition.

Donruss, 1993–94, #103, Darren McCarthy . . . . $ .15
Donruss, 1993–94, #152, Wayne Gretzky. 1.50
Donruss, 1993–94, #242, Eric Lindros 1.50
Donruss, 1994–95, #5, Mario Lemieux. 75
Donruss, 1994–95, #22, Kirk McLean 05
Donruss, 1995–96, #180, Brendan Shanahan 10
Donruss, 1995–96, #338, Patrick Roy. 50
Fleer, 1992–93, #16, Pat LaFontaine 15
Fleer, 1992–93, #126, Glenn Healy 05
Fleer, 1993–94, #334, Chris Osgood 1.50

Pro Set, 1991–92, Platinum, Series II, foil pack, 25¢.

Fleer, 1993–94, #485, Paul Kariya 2.50
Leaf, 1993–94, #117, Gilbert Dionne. 10
Leaf, 1993–94, #200, Mighty Ducks. 55
Leaf, 1994–95, #19, Alexei Yashin 10
Leaf, 1994–95, #283, Byron Dafoe. 10
Parkhurst, 1961–62, #44, Wayne Connelly 5.50
Pinnacle, 1992–93, #200, Brett Hull 50
Pinnacle, 1993–94, #263, Andrew Moog Mask. 75
Score, 1990–91, 387, Mark Pederson 05
Score Traded, 1991–92, complete set, 110 cards 2.50
Score Young Superstars, 1991–92, complete set, 40
    cards 2.50
Topps, 1961–62, #2, Ted Green 12.50
Topps, 1962–63, #33, Bobby Hull 150.00
Topps, 1963–64, #65, Rangers Team. 12.00
Topps, 1965–66, common player 2.25
Topps, 1969–70, #24, Bobby Orr 60.00
Topps, 1979–80, #83, Stanley Cup Finals 45
Topps, 1986–87, #134, Tim Kerr. 10
Upper Deck, 1990–91, #63, Jeremy Roenick 1.25
Upper Deck, 1993–94, #98, Rob Niedermayer 10

HOCKEY MEMORABILIA

Hockey memorabilia focuses primarily on material from professional hockey teams. Although the popularity of college hockey is growing rapidly and Canada's Junior Hockey is deeply entrenched, it is the professional teams that have generated almost all licensed collectibles.

Like other sports collectible categories, collecting is highly regionalized. Most collectors focus on their local teams. Even with today's National Hockey League, there is a distinct dividing line between collectors of material related to American and Canadian teams.

Superstar collecting is heavily post–1980 focused. Endorsement opportunities for early Hockey Hall of Famers were limited. Collectors want game–related material. Logo licensed merchandise for sale in sports shops has minimal or no appeal.

References: Mark K. Larson, *Complete Guide to Football, Basketball & Hockey Memorabilia,* Krause Publications, 1995; Roderick Malloy, *Malloy's Sports Collectibles Value Guide: Up–To–Date Prices for Noncard Sports Memorabilia,* Attic Books, Wallace–Homestead, Krasue Publications, 1993.

Advertising Trade Card, Victorian men playing ice
    hockey, A & P adv . . . . $ 28.00
Autograph, Bobby Hull, sgd hockey stick 145.00
Autograph, Brett Hull, sgd 8 x 10" photo 55.00
Autograph, Wayne Gretzky, sgd hockey stick 25.00
Book, *Official 1932 Field Hockey Guide,* Spaulding's
    Athletic Library 20.00
Coin, Don Marshall, Salada, 1961–62 . . . . 2.25
Coin, Pat LaFontaine, Enviromint, 1992. . . . . 32.00
Comic Book, Nolan Ryan vs Wayne Gretzky. 5.00
Equipment, hockey stick, Bobby Clarke 225.00
Figure, Bobby Hull, sgd, Gartlan USA. 265.00
Figure, Gordie Howe, sgd, Pro Sport Creations 150.00
Game, Box Hockey, Milton Bradley, 1941 . . . . 55.00
Game, National Pro Hockey, Sports Action, 1985 . . . . 40.00
Game, Sure Shot Hockey, Ideal, 1970. . . . . 25.00

Magazine Cover, *Collier's*, Dec 6, 1941, $15.00.

Jersey, Brian Leetch **70.00**
Magazine, *Hockey Digest*, Nov 1972, Bobby Orr **35.00**
Magazine, *Hockey Illustrated*, Jan 1967, Bobby Hull **18.00**
Magazine, *Sports Illustrated*, December 11, 1967,
    Bobby Orr cov **15.00**
Media Guide, Atlanta Flames, 1978–79 . . . . **6.50**
Media Guide, Flyers, 1974–75 . . . . **6.50**
Media Guide, Maple Leafs, 1977–78 . . . . **12.00**
Nodder, Canadiens, sq base, 1961–62 . . . . **65.00**
Nodder, Rangers, sq base, 1961–62 . . . . **80.00**
Plate, Guy LaFleur, sgd, D. H. Ussher Ltd, 8½" d **60.00**
Plate, Wayne Gretzky, Gartlan USA, mini **20.00**
Poster, Bobby Hull, Sports Illustrated, 1968–71 . . . . **45.00**
Poster, Derek Sanderson, Sports Illustrated, 1968–71 . . . . **12.50**
Program, Stanley Cup Playoffs, Toronto vs Detroit, 1966 . . **30.00**
Ticket Stub, NHL All–Star Game, Detroit, 1950 . . . . **48.00**
Ticket Stub, NHL All–Star Game, Philadelphia, 1992 . . . . . . **5.00**
Yearbook, Hockey News, Mario Lemieux, 1988–89 . . . . . **10.00**

HOLIDAY COLLECTIBLES

Holidays play a major role in our lives. Everyone relishes the three–day holiday weekends legislated by the federal government, e.g., the one created by merging the independent celebrations of Washington's and Lincoln's birthdays into the Presidents' Day weekend.

Holidays are religious, secular, regional, or a combination of the three. In some cases, e.g., Saint Patrick's Day, the secular celebration has completely overshadowed the religious significance of the day. Immigrants continue to transfer the holidays celebrated in their native countries to American soil.

The card and floral industries are two leading forces in the creation and support of holidays whose purpose is as much to sell merchandise as it is to honor individuals, e.g., Mother's Day and Father's Day. Although there was licensed holiday merchandise prior to 1940, licensing began to play a major role in the 1960s when Barbie, the Peanuts gang, the Smurfs, and even Star Wars characters began appearing on holiday items.

Holiday collectibles break down into three major periods: (1) pre–1940, (2) 1945 to the late 1970s, and (3) contemporary "collector" items. Crossover collectors, e.g., candy container collectors, skew the values on some items.

This is a catchall category for those holiday collectibles that do not have separate category listings. It includes Fourth of July and Thanksgiving collectibles. Look elsewhere for Christmas, Easter, Halloween, and Valentines.

Periodical: *Pyrofax Magazine*, PO Box 2010, Saratoga, CA 95070.

Newsletter: *The Phoenix* (fireworks), 44 Toner Rd, Boonton, NJ 07005.

Birthday, favor bag, litho paper, "Happy Birthday" . . . . . . **$ 5.00**
Father's Day, pinback button, blue, white, and yellow,
    c1940, 1¾" d **20.00**
Father's Day, sign, "Father's Day Special," Winchester
    Arms, 1966 . . . . **15.00**
Fourth of July, bank, Liberty Bell, white metal, wood
    closure, 7" h **120.00**
Fourth of July, bunting, red, white, and blue muslin,
    various lengths, 23" w, price per yard **8.00**
Fourth of July, lead pencil, red, white, and blue **5.00**
Fourth of July, pinback button, Fire Department of
    Forest City issue, red, white, and blue, 1930s,
    1½" d **30.00**
Fourth of July, sheet music, *Yankee Doodle Dandy*,
    James Cagney, 1931 . . . . **25.00**
George Washington's Birthday, tri–cornered hat,
    cloth cherries **35.00**
Mother's Day, pinback button, white carnation, red
    ground, white lettering, 1920s, ⅞" d **20.00**
Mother's Day, pinback button, Whitman's
    Chocolates, blue and white, 1930s **15.00**
New Year's Day, banner, "Happy New Year," paper,
    silver border, 1930 . . . . **12.00**
New Year's Day, horn, paper over cardboard, silver
    and black, 1930 . . . . **8.00**

Thanksgiving, turkey platter, Barnyard King, Johnson Brothers, 20½" l, $95.00.

New Year's Day, invitations, litho paper, Father Time,
  1930 . . . . **10.00**
New Year's Day, photograph, Times Square, NY, New
  Year's Eve, 1953 . . . . **20.00**
St. Patrick's Day, candy container, top hat, green car
  board, bisque pipe, cloth shamrock, Germany, 3" h **30.00**
St. Patrick's Day, handkerchief, linen, embroidered
  shamrock, crocheted green border **8.00**
St. Patrick's Day, sheet music, *Danny Boy*, 1940s **8.00**
St. Patrick's Day, sheet music, *When Irish Eyes Are
  Smiling*, c1930 . . . . **15.00**
Thanksgiving, book, *Thanksgiving*, Dennison, 1930 . . . . . **12.00**
Thanksgiving, candy container, composition turkey,
  metal feet, Japan **60.00**
Thanksgiving, figure, Pilgrim man and woman, co
  position, mkd "Germany," 4" h **50.00**
Thanksgiving, place card, turkey, emb cardboard,
  standup, USA, 3" h. **8.00**
Valentine's Day, banner, fabric, stenciled hearts,
  "Happy Valentine's Day," 1930s **80.00**
Valentine's Day, greeting card, fold–out, girl's head in
  heart, flowers with white lace, 1940 . . . . **20.00**
Valentine's Day, sheet music, *My Funny Valentine* **8.00**

HOMER LAUGHLIN

In 1870 Homer and Shakespeare Laughlin established two pottery kilns in East Liverpool, Ohio. Shakespeare left the company in 1879. The firm made whiteware (ironstone utilitarian products). In 1896 William Wills and a group of Pittsburgh investors, led by Marcus Aaron, purchased the Laughlin firm.

The company expanded, building two plants in Laughlin Station, Ohio, and another in Newall, West Virginia. A second plant was built in Newall in 1926. The company constantly upgraded its machinery. It was one of the first companies to use a continuous tunnel kiln, mechanical jiggering, and spray glazing.

Cooking ware, dinnerware, and kitchenware were the company's principal products. Several new dinnerware lines, including Fiesta, Harlequin, and Rhythm, went into production between 1930 and 1960. Homer Laughlin introduced a translucent tableware line in 1959.

References: Susan and Al Bagdade, *Warman's American Pottery and Porcelain,* Wallace–Homestead, Krause Publications, 1994; Jo Cunningham, *The Collector's Encyclopedia of American Dinnerware,* Collector Books, 1982, 1995 value update; Harvey Duke, *The Official Price Guide to Pottery and Porcelain, Eighth Edition,* House of Collectibles, 1995; Bob and Sharon Huxford, *The Collector's Encyclopedia of Fiesta With Harlequin and Riviera, Seventh Edition,* Collector Books, 1992; Joanne Jasper, *The Collector's Encyclopedia of Homer Laughlin China: Reference & Value Guide,* Collector Books, 1993, 1997 value update; Richard G. Racheter, *Collector's Guide to Homer Laughlin's Virginia Rose: Identification & Values,* Collector Books, 1997.

Newsletter: *The Laughlin Eagle,* 1270 63rd Terrace S, St Petersburg, FL 33705.

Dogwood, bowl, 5³/₂" d . . . . **$ 5.00**
Dogwood, plate, 9" d. **8.00**
Dogwood, vegetable, oval **10.00**

Royal Harvest, dinner plate, $6.00.

Eggshell Theme, creamer and cov sugar **25.00**
Eggshell Theme, cup and saucer **15.00**
Eggshell Theme, dinner plate **10.00**
Eggshell Theme, gravy, attached underplate **18.00**
Eggshell Theme, salad plate **7.00**
Epicure, casserole, turquoise **50.00**
Epicure, gravy, turquoise **25.00**
Harlequin, ball jug, 22 oz, gray **55.00**
Harlequin, bowl, 5¹/₂" d, red. **8.00**
Harlequin, butter, cov, maroon **100.00**
Harlequin, cereal bowl, yellow **8.00**
Harlequin, creamer, individual, yellow **12.00**
Harlequin, cup, maroon. **8.00**
Harlequin, eggcup, double, turquoise. **15.00**
Harlequin, gravy, yellow **12.00**
Harlequin, nut dish, 3 part, mauve blue **8.00**
Harlequin, plate, 6" d, maroon. **8.00**
Harlequin, plate, 7" d, rose **10.00**
Harlequin, teacup, mauve blue **20.00**
Jubilee, dinner plate, cream beige **8.00**
Jubilee, saucer, celadon green **5.00**
Kitchen Kraft, mixing bowl, 8" d. **25.00**
Kitchen Kraft, salt and pepper shakers, pr **32.00**
Mexicana, bowl, 5" d. **12.50**
Mexicana, cup and saucer **15.00**
Mexicana, plate, 7" d. **12.00**
Rhythm, plate, 7" d, maroon **5.00**
Rhythm, saucer, gray **5.00**
Rhythm, soup bowl, 8" d, harlequin yellow. **10.00**
Riviera, creamer and sugar, light green **15.00**
Riviera, cup, mauve blue **8.00**
Riviera, salt shaker, red **10.00**
Royal Harvest, bread and butter plate **4.00**
Royal Harvest, cup and saucer **8.00**
Royal Harvest, platter, oval. **12.00**
Royal Harvest, salad plate **4.00**
Royal Harvest, vegetable, round **7.50**

Virginia Rose, pickle, $10.00.

Virginia Rose, cake plate **17.50**
Virginia Rose, creamer and cov sugar **25.00**
Virginia Rose, cup and saucer **5.00**
Virginia Rose, dinner plate, 9" d **8.00**
Virginia Rose, vegetable, cov **48.00**

HORSE COLLECTIBLES

The horse arrived in America with the early explorers. Although primarily used as a means of transportation and for work in the fields and construction, the horse was a source of pride to its owner. Agricultural fairs and other events gave owners a chance to show off their prized horses.

As the 19th and early 20th century progressed, the automobile, tractor, and other transportation replaced many of the roles played by the horse. The horse still plays a vital role in western ranching and specialized farming. However, most horses bred today are for recreational use.

Objects shaped like a horse or featuring an image of a horse are everywhere. Most collectors specialize, e.g., collectors of carousel horses. Horse–related toys, especially horse–drawn cast–iron toys, are bought and sold within the toy collecting community.

Reference: Jan Lindenberger, *501 Collectible Horses: A Handbook and Price Guide,* Schiffer Publishing, 1995.

Periodicals; *Hobby Horse News,* 2053 Dyrehaven Dr, Tallahassee, FL 32311; *Just About Horses,* 14 Industrial Rd, Pequannock, NJ 07440; *TRR Pony Express,* 71 Aloha Circle, N Little Rock, AR 72120.

Newsletter: *The Model Horse Trader,* 143 Mercer Way, Upland, CA 91786.

Collectors' Club: Equine Collectors Club, PO Box 42822, Phoenix, AZ 85080.

Blanket, brown wool, cowboys and horses, 1950 . . . . **$ 100.00**
Bridle, braided leather strips, 1930s **50.00**
Calendar, Dodge Stables and Castleton Farm, 1950 . . . . . . **50.00**
Calendar, Lone Ranger and Silver, 1935 . . . . **80.00**

Catalog, DF Mangels Co, Carousel Works, Coney Island, NY, 1920, 28 pgs **210.00**
Catalog, SD Myres Saddle Co, Fine Stock Saddles, Ranch Supplies and Art Leather Goods, El Paso, TX, c1930, 80 pgs **55.00**
Cigarette Lighter, Dale Evans, horse head **20.00**
Coloring Book, Hi–Yo Silver, 1953 . . . . **25.00**
Curry Comb, stamped "Oliver Slant Tooth," 1940s **25.00**
Decanter, Appaloosa, Jim Beam, Regal China, 1974 . . . . . **30.00**
Figurine, donkey, ceramic, Hagen Renaker, 1986, 2" h **12.50**
Fruit Crate Label, Loop Loop, Washington State Apples, Indian chief on palomino **10.00**
Hat Rack, brass, horse head plaques at ends, 4 hooks **25.00**
Hobby Horse, Tom Mix, wood, wheeled platform **525.00**
Horseshoe, Hopalong Cassidy, "Good Luck," orig insert card, 1950 . . . . **25.00**
Lapel Pin, US Olympic Equestrian Team, 1988 . . . . **8.00**
Magazine, *Life,* December 22, 1952, midget horse **8.00**
Magazine, *Western Horseman,* Vol 1, #1, 1935 . . . . **18.00**
Pin, sterling silver, bar with 3 horse heads, 2½" l **20.00**
Pinback Button, horse portrait, black and white, blue ground, white border, c1940 . . . . **12.00**
Pinback Button, bucking bronco, "Let 'er Buck," red and back, white ground, 1930s **8.00**
Poster, Anheuser Busch, 50th Anniversary, Clydesdale Horses, 1933–83 . . . . **12.00**
Poster, Prescott Rodeo, Prescott, AZ, 100th Anniversary, June 30th–July 4th, 1988 . . . . **30.00**
Puzzle, Jingle Bells, horse–drawn sleigh, Strauss, 1960s **18.00**
Puzzle, Wild Horses, Jig of the Week, #5, 1933 . . . . **30.00**
Sign, Belgian Stallion, cardboard, 1935, 12 x 16" **20.00**
Snowdome, Budweiser Clydesdales, 1988 edition, MIB **45.00**
Stuffed Toy, mule, collar inscribed "One of the Twenty Mule Team," 1980 Boraxo promotion **18.00**
Tray, Genessee Twelve Horse Ale, horse team **80.00**

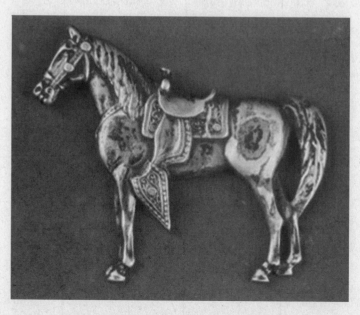

Pin, sterling silver, 2³/₄" l, 2¹/₄" h, $35.00.

HORSE RACING

Ancient chariot racing was the forerunner of modern horse racing. English kings raced horses as early as the 1600s. As a result, horse racing often is referred to as the "Sport of Kings." The English also developed the thoroughbred, descended from three stallions: Darley Arabian, Byerley Turn, and Goldophin Arabian.

Horse racing was a popular pastime in Colonial America. In the 1800s, four–mile match races were held regionally. The Saratoga Race Track dates from 1863. After reaching a record high of over 300 race tracks in America in 1897, greed and a strong anti–gambling movement reduced the number to 25 by 1908.

Horse racing enjoyed a renaissance in the period following World War I and again in the period immediately following World War II. The growth of professional sports and television viewing since the 1960s impacted negatively on the sport. Many tracks closed. Licensed off–track betting stabilized the decline. Today, with the exception of major stake races, the "Sport of Kings" finishes out of the money.

Items associated with Hall of Fame horses, e.g., Dan Patch and Man O'War, bring a premium. Do not overlook the trotters. Harness racing collectibles have much to offer.

Paper ephemera, e.g., postcards and programs, and drinking glasses are two strong areas of focus. A program was issued for the first Belmont Stakes in 1867, the first Preakness Stakes in 1873, and the first Kentucky Derby in 1875. Kentucky Derby glasses date back to 1938, Preakness glasses to 1973, Belmont glasses to 1976, and Breeders Cup glasses to 1985. Pins were introduced at the Kentucky Derby in 1973 and at other major stakes races in the 1980s.

Reference: Roderick A. Malloy, *Malloy's Sports Collectibles Value Guide: Up–To–Date Prices for Noncard Sports Memorabilia*, Attic Books, Wallace–Homestead, Krause Publications, 1993.

Collectors' Club: Sport of Kings Society, 1406 Annen Ln, Madison, WI 53711.

Book, *The American Racing Manual*, track diagrams,
    photos, and record, 1947, 978 pgs . . . . $ 20.00
Bumper Sticker, Carolina Cup, 1969. . . . . 4.00

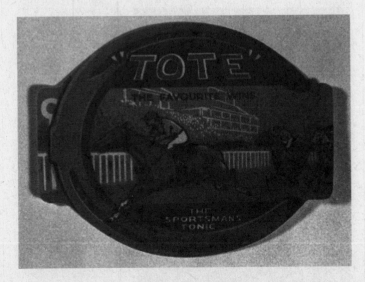

Wine Label, "Tote, The Sportsman's Tonic," 4¼" l, $3.50.

Doorstop, racehorse, Virginia Metalcrafters, 1949 . . . . . . **155.00**
Game, Derby Day, Parker Brothers, 1959 . . . . **50.00**
Game, Kentucky Derby, Racing, Whitman, 1938 . . . . **22.00**
Glass, Kentucky Derby, 1950 . . . . **90.00**
Glass, Kentucky Derby, 1964, frosted, brown horse
    head, gold inscription "Kentucky Derby/Churchill
    Downs," reverse with white lettering listing win-
    ners from 1875 to 1963, 5¼" h **30.00**
Magazine, *Sports Illustrated*, Jan 10, 1955, Santa
    Anita Horse Race **12.00**
Magazine, *TV Guide*, Jun 10–16, 1950, thoroughbred
    horse racing cov. **45.00**
Nodder, Shenandoah Downs jockey, composition,
    gold paper sticker Japan, ©1962 . . . . **55.00**
Plate, Kentucky Derby Series, Nearing Finish, Reed
    and Barton, 1972 . . . . **115.00**
Program, Arlington Park, Chicago, Jun 23, 1943 . . . . **20.00**
Program, Kentucky Derby, May 4, 1963 . . . . **22.00**
Ticket, Kentucky Derby, Saturday, May 2, 1936 . . . . **12.00**

HOT WHEELS

Automobile designer Harry Bradley, Mattel designer Howard Newman, Mattel Chairman Elliot Handler, and R & D chief Jack Ryan were the principal guiding forces in the creation of Hot Wheels. The creative process began in 1966 and culminated with the introduction of a diecast metal 16–car line in 1968.

Mattel billed Hot Wheels as the fastest metal cars in the world. Hot Wheels' low friction wheel bearings and special torsion bar suspension gave the company a competitive edge. Hot Wheels were an immediate success.

Initially cars were produced in Hong Kong and the United States. Mattel continually changed the styling and paint motif of its vehicles. Copies of modern cars were supplemented with futuristic models. Since the cars were meant to be raced, Mattel produced a variety of track sets complete with starting gates, jumping ramps, lap counters, etc.

Mattel continued to expand the line. Further, a Hot Wheels licensing program was instituted. This resulted in Hot Wheels comic books, lunch kits, etc. In the 1980s Mattel did a number of Hot Wheels promotions with McDonald's and Kellogg's. In 1993 Mattel introduced a reproduction line focused toward the adult collector market.

A recent survey indicated that Hot Wheels were the No. 2 Baby Boomer era toy, bested only by Barbie. In 1997 Mattel acquired Tyco, bringing Hot Wheels and Matchbox under one roof.

References: Bob Parker, *The Complete Book of Hot Wheels*, Schiffer Publishing, 1995; Michael Thomas Strauss, *Tomart's Price Guide to Hot Wheels, 2nd Edition*, Tomart Publications, 1997.

Newsletter: *Hot Wheels Newsletter*, 26 Madera Ave, San Carlos, CA, 94070.

Collectors' Club: Hot Wheels Collector Club, 2263 Graham Dr, Santa Rosa, CA 95404.

1153, Dodge D–50, 1980 . . . . $ 10.00
1172, CAT Bulldozer, 1980 . . . . 10.00
1699, Airport Rescue, 1981 . . . . 10.00
2013, '57 T–Bird, 1978 . . . . 10.00

2015, Packin' Pacer, 1978 . . . . **15.00**
2018, Science Friction, 1978 . . . . **10.00**
2023, Army Funny Car, 1978 . . . . **20.00**
2639, Fire Chaser, 1979. . . . . **10.00**
2853, Motocross Team, 1979 . . . . **30.00**
2855, Space Van, 1979 . . . . **40.00**
2879, Captain America, 1979. . . . . **15.00**
2882, The Thing, 1979 . . . . **25.00**
3252, '35 Classic Caddy, 1982 . . . . **10.00**
3254, Construction Crane, 1982. . . . . **10.00**
3301, Cannonade, 1981 . . . . **10.00**
3915, Formula Fever, 1983. **15.00**
5178, Bugeye, 1971 . . . . **40.00**
6000, Noodle Head, 1971 . . . . **55.00**
6007, Sweet "16", 1973. . . . . **125.00**
6020, Snorkel, 1971 . . . . **60.00**
6021, Ferrari 512S, 1972 . . . . **95.00**
6022, Side Kick, 1972 . . . . **90.00**
6169, Mercedes–Benz C111, 1972. . . . . **85.00**
6183, Pit Crew Car, 1971. . . . . **75.00**
6184, Ice "T", 1971. . . . . **50.00**
6186, Rocket–Bye–Baby, 1971 . . . . **55.00**
6192, Waste Wagon, 1971 . . . . **80.00**
6215, Custom Corvette, 1968. . . . . **60.00**
6219, Hot Heap, 1968. . . . . **20.00**
6251, Classic '31 Ford Woody, 1969 . . . . **25.00**
6262, Lotus Turbine, 1969 . . . . **20.00**
6276, Rolls–Royce Silver Shadow, 1969 . . . . **45.00**
6404, Classic Nomad, 1970. **45.00**
6412, Light By Firebird, 1970. . . . . **35.00**
6451, Ambulance, 1970 . . . . **45.00**
6453, Dump Truck, 1970. . . . . **25.00**
6466, Cockney Cab, 1971 . . . . **40.00**
6963, Police Cruiser, 1973. . . . . **80.00**
6966, Paddy Wagon, 1973 . . . . **25.00**
6974, Sand Witch, 1973 . . . . **85.00**
6975, Double Vision, 1973 . . . . **80.00**
6976, Buzz Off, 1973 . . . . **90.00**
7620, Volkswagen, 1974 . . . . **50.00**
7621, Funny Money, 1974. . . . . **35.00**
7650, Emergency Squad, 1975 . . . . **20.00**
7653, Mighty Maverick, 1975 . . . . **50.00**
7654, Warpath, 1975. . . . . **45.00**
7659, Ramblin' Wrecker, 1975 . . . . **30.00**
8240, TwinMill II, 1976 . . . . **25.00**
8259, Rodger Dodger, 1974. . . . . **45.00**
9183, Khaki Kooler, 1976 . . . . **20.00**
9240, Poison Pinto, 1976. . . . . **25.00**
9644, Second Wind, 1977 . . . . **20.00**
9648, T–Totaller, 1977 . . . . **15.00**

HULL POTTERY

In 1905 Addis E. Hull purchased the Acme Pottery Company, Crooksville, Ohio, and changed its name to the A. E. Hull Pottery Company. By 1917, Hull's lines included art pottery for gift shops and florists, kitchenware, novelties, and stoneware.

Tile production helped the company weather the economic difficulties of the Depression. Hall's Little Red Riding Hood kitchenware arrived in 1943 and remained in production until 1957.

A 1950 flood and fire destroyed the company's plant. Two years later the company returned as the Hull Pottery Company. It was during this period that Hull added a new line of high–gloss glazed ceramics and developed Floraline and Regal, its product lines for the floral industry.

The plant closed in 1986.

Hull's early stoneware is marked with an "H." Matte pieces contain pattern numbers. Series numbers identify Open Rose/Camellia pieces (100s), Iris (400s), and Wildflower (W plus a number). Many Hull pieces also are marked with a number indicating their height in inches. Pieces made after 1950, usually featuring the high–gloss glaze, are marked "hull" or "Hull" in a script signature.

References: Barbara Loveless Glick–Burke, *Collector's Guide To Hull Pottery, The Dinnerware Lines: Identification and Values,* Collector Books, 1993; Joan Gray Hull, *Hull: The Heavenly Pottery, Fifth Edition,* published by author, 1996; Brenda Roberts, *The Collectors Encyclopedia of Hull Pottery,* Collector Books, 1980, 1997 value update; Brenda Roberts, *The Companion Guide To Roberts' Ultimate Encyclopedia Of Hull Pottery,* Walsworth Publishing, 1992; Brenda Roberts, *Roberts' Ultimate Encyclopedia Of Hull Pottery,* Walsworth Publishing, 1992.

Collectors' Club: Hull Pottery Assoc, 4 Hilltop Rd, Council Bluff, IA 51503.

Blossom Flite, basket, T–4, 8½" . . . . **$ 90.00**
Blossom Flite, tea set, T–14, T–15, and T–16 . . . . **125.00**
Blossom Flite, vase, T7, handled, 10½" **55.00**
Bow–Knot, basket, B–25, 6½" **250.00**
Butterfly, bud vase, ewer shape, B1, 6¼" **25.00**
Butterfly, candy dish, B–6, 5½" **42.00**
Butterfly, sugar, B–20 . . . . **55.00**
Butterfly, vase, B–9, 9" **45.00**
Butterfly, window box, 12¾ x 4¾" **50.00**
Calla Lily, bowl, 500–32,8" **125.00**
Calla Lily, vase, 502/33, 6½" **75.00**
Capri, flower bowl, round, C–47, 5¼ x 8". **42.00**
Continental, ashtray, 8" **40.00**
Continental, planter, C–68, ftd, rect, 8½ x 4½" **25.00**

Planter, twin geese, #95, large, 1951, 7¼" h, $40.00.

Continental, vase, C–53, 8½" **42.00**
Dogwood/Wild Rose, cornucopia, 522, 4" **55.00**
Dogwood/Wild Rose, vase, 515, 8½" **55.00**
Ebbtide, twin fish vase, E–2, 7" **65.00**
Iris, bowl, 412, 4", rose **70.00**
Iris, bud vase, 410, 7½" **100.00**
Iris, vase, 407, 7" **100.00**
Magnolia, vase, H7, 6½", gloss **20.00**
Magnolia, vase, 7, 8½", matte **65.00**
Mardi Gras/Granada, vase, 47, 9" **45.00**
Mardi Gras/Granada, vase, 49, 9" **40.00**
Open Rose/Camellia, bowl, 113, low, 7" **100.00**
Open Rose/Camellia, sugar, open, 112, 5" **85.00**
Open Rose/Camellia, vase, 118, swan, 6" **85.00**
Orchid, bud vase, 306, 6¾" **45.00**
Orchid, jardiniere, 310, 6" **95.00**
Orchid, vase, 309, 8" **165.00**
Parchment and Pine, scroll planter, S–5, 10½" **85.00**
Parchment and Pine, vase, S1, 6" **20.00**
Poppy, jardiniere, 603, 4¾" **70.00**
Poppy, vase, 612, 6½" **100.00**
Rosella, creamer, R13, 5½" **55.00**
Rosella, vase, R1, 5" **40.00**
Serenade, Birds, pitcher, S–2, 6" **38.00**
Sunglow, flowerpot, 97, 5½" **38.00**
Sunglow, Kitchenware, salt and pepper, 54 . . . . **28.00**
Sunglow, vase, 91, 6½" **38.00**
Sunglow, wall pocket, 82, whisk broom, 8½" **65.00**
Thistle, vase, 51, 6½" **155.00**
Tokay/Tuscany, basket, 6, 8" **75.00**
Tokay/Tuscany, candy dish, cov, 9C, 8½" **98.00**
Tokay/Tuscany, cornucopia, 1, 6½" **32.00**
Tokay/Tuscany, vase, 4, 8¼" **25.00**
Tulip/Sueno- Tulip, jardiniere, 117–30, 5" **98.00**
Water Lily, cornucopia, L7, 6½" **75.00**
Water Lily, sugar, L20 . . . . **55.00**
Water Lily, vase, L4, 6½" **55.00**
Wild Flower, ewer, 63, 4½"" **95.00**
Wild Flower, jardiniere, 64, 4" **70.00**
Wild Flower, vase, W8, 7½" **75.00**

Woodland, cornucopia,
W5–6½, 1949–50,
$55.00.

Woodland, pitcher, W–3, 5½" **42.00**
Woodland, vase, W–8, 7½" **42.00**
Woodland, vase, W–15, double bud, 8½" **95.00**

HUMMELS

Berta Hummel, a German artist, provided the drawings that were the inspiration for W. Goebel's Hummel figurines. Berta Hummel, born in 1909 in Massing, Bavaria, Germany, enrolled at age 18 in the Academy of Fine Arts in Munich. In 1934 she entered the Convent of Siessen and became Sister Maria Innocentia.

W. Goebel, Rodental, Bavaria, produced its first Hummel figurines in 1935. John Schmid of Schmid Brothers, Randolph, Massachusetts, secured American distribution rights. When Goebel wished to distribute directly to the American market in 1967, the two companies and Berta Hummel's heirs became entangled in a lawsuit. A compromise was reached. Goebel would base its figurines on drawings made by Berta Hummel between 1934 and her death in 1964. Schmid was given the rights to produce pieces based on Hummel's pre–convent drawings.

A Hummel figurine must have the "M. I. Hummel" legend on its base and a Goebel trademark. If either is missing, the figurine is not a Goebel Hummel. Seven different trademarks are used to identify the production period of a figurine:

Trademark 1	Incised Crown Mark	.1935–1949
Trademark 2	Full Bee	.1950–1959
Trademark 3	Stylized Bee	.1957–1972
Trademark 4	Three Line Mark	.1964-1972
Trademark 5	Last Bee Mark	.1972–1980
Trademark 6	Missing Bee Mark	.1979–1990
Trademark 7	Current/New Crown Mark	.1991–Present

References: Ken Armke, *Hummel: An Illustrated Handbook and Price Guide,* Wallace–Homestead, Krause Publications, 1995; Carl F. Luckey, *Luckey's Hummel Figurines & Plates, 11th Edition,* Books Americana, 1997; Robert L. Miller, *The No. 1 Price Guide To M.I. Hummel: Figurines, Plates, More…, Sixth Edition,* Portfolio Press, 1995.

Collectors' Clubs: Hummel Collectors Club, 1261 University Dr, Yardley, PA 19067; M.I. Hummel Club, Goebel Plaza, PO Box 11, Pennington, NJ 08534.

Ashtray, Let's Sing, 114, trademark 5 . . . . $ **70.00**
Bell, In tune, 703, 1981, trademark 6 . . . . **85.00**
Figurine, Angel Trio, 238/B, trademark 4 . . . . **40.00**
Figurine, Bird Duet, 169, trademark 5 . . . . **90.00**
Figurine, Boy With Horse, 117, trademark 5 . . . . **15.00**
Figurine, Chimney Sweep, 12/2/0, trademark **80.00**
Figurine, Congratulations, 17/0, trademark 5 . . . . **40.00**
Figurine, Coquettes, 179, trademark 6 . . . . **110.00**
Figurine, Crossroads, 331, trademark 5 . . . . **90.00**
Figurine, Doctor, 127, trademark 3 . . . . **110.00**
Figurine, Farm Boy, 66, trademark 3 . . . . **168.00**
Figurine, Feeding Time, 199/0, trademark 6 . . . . **90.00**
Figurine, Flower Vendor, 381, trademark 5 . . . . **115.00**
Figurine, Friends, 136/1, trademark 5 . . . . **75.00**
Figurine, Girl With Fir Tree, 116, trademark 5 . . . . **25.00**
Figurine, Girl With Nosegay, 239/A, trademark 4 . . . . **42.00**
Figurine, Girl With Sheet Music, 389, trademark 5 . . . . . . **60.00**

Figurine, Chick Girl, 57/0, trademark 4, $85.00.

HUMMEL LOOK–ALIKES

If imitation is the most sincere form of flattery, Berta Hummel and W. Goebel should feel especially honored. Goebel's Hummel figurines have been stylistically copied by ceramic manufacturers around the world.

A Hummel look–alike is a stylistic copy of a Goebel Hummel figurine or a completely new design done in an artistic style that mimics that of Berta Hummel. It does not require much of an alteration to avoid infringing on a design patent. These copycats come from a host of Japanese firms, Herbert Dubler (House of Ars Sacra), Decorative Figures Corporation, Beswick, and Coventry Ware.

Reference: Lawrence L. Wonsch, *Hummel Copycats With Values,* Wallace–Homestead, 1987, out–of–print.

Dancing Time, 55/1556, 5½" h.	$ 38.00
Farm Chores, 44/169, 4¾" h.	15.00
Harvest Time, 8213, 5" h	28.00
Junior Doctor, U8588, 6½" h	28.00
Life on the Farm, 8394, 4½" h	18.00
Little Gardener, 8564, 6⅝" h	30.00
Little Mender, U8536, 7½" h	32.00
Picnic, boy, 55/972, 4¼" h.	15.00
Picnic, girl, 55/972, 4¼" h.	15.00
Sandy Shoes, 8248, 4⅝" base, 6⅜" h	32.00
School Time, 55/1059, 4½" h.	20.00
Sore Thumb, 55/1550, 5¾" h	20.00
Winter Time, 8218, 5" h.	22.00
Young Folks, S8515, 6" h	22.00

HUNTING

Hunting memorabilia played second fiddle to firearms and fishing collectibles until the 1980s. At that point, it came into its own as a major collecting category.

The initial focus was on hunting advertising and paper ephemera, e.g., books, calendars, and catalogs. This is a collecting category where name counts. Examples from firms such as DuPont, Peters Cartridge Company, Remington, and Winchester command premium prices.

Collectors also have identified a group of illustrators whose hunting scenes and images became highly desirable. Look for images by G. Muss Arnolt, Phillip Goodwin, Lynn Bogue Hunt, and Edmund Osthaus. Beware of the limited edition hunting prints issued in the 1970s and 80s. The secondary market is highly volatile—more will decline than rise in value over the next decade.

This category continues to expand its collecting horizons. Hunting licenses and ammunition boxes currently are two hot subcategories. Even some post–1945 decoys have joined the collectible ranks.

References: Ralf Coykendall, Jr., *Coykendall's Complete Guide to Sporting Collectibles,* Wallace–Homestead, Krause Publications, 1996; Gene and Linda Kangas, *Collector's Guide To Decoys,* Wallace–Homestead, Krause Publications, 1992; Jim and Vivian Karsnitz, *Sporting Collectibles,* Schiffer Publishing, 1992; Carl F. Luckey, *Collecting Antique Bird and Duck Calls: An Identification and Value Guide, 2nd Edition,* Books Americana, Krause

Figurine, Girl With Trumpet, 391, trademark 5	60.00
Figurine, Globe Trotter, 79, trademark 4	85.00
Figurine, Going to Grandma's, 52/0, trakemark 6	100.00
Figurine, Happy Traveler, 109, trademark 5	90.00
Figurine, Hear Ye Hear Ye, 15/0, trademark 2	60.00
Figurine, Heavenly Angel, 21/0, trademark 3	68.00
Figurine, I Brought You a Gift, 479, trademark 6, orig box	70.00
Figurine, I Wonder, 486, trademark 7, orig box	95.00
Figurine, Latest News, 184/0, trademark 5, Das Allerneuste	70.00
Figurine, Little Fiddler, 4, trademark 3.	60.00
Figurine, Little Gabriel, 32/0, trademark 1	275.00
Figurine, Little Goat Herder, 200/10, trademark 4	98.00
Figurine, Madonna, 46/0, trademark 5	25.00
Figurine, March Winds, 43, trademark 2	110.00
Figurine, Merry Wanderer, 11/2/0, trademark 3	75.00
Figurine, Nativity, Infant Jesus, 214/A, trademark 4	18.00
Figurine, On Holiday, 350, trademark 6	92.00
Figurine, Out of Danger, 56/B, trademark 2	250.00
Figurine, Playmates, 58/0, trademark 2	162.00
Figurine, She Loves Me Not, 174, trademark 6	75.00
Figurine, Signs of Spring, 203/2/0, trademark 5	78.00
Figurine, Soloist, 135, trademark 3	60.00
Figurine, Sweet Music, 186, trademark 3	85.00
Figurine, Thoughtful, 415, trademark 6	112.00
Figurine, Village Boy, 51/3/0, trademark 4	52.00
Figurine, Volunteers, 50/2/0, trademark 5	140.00
Figurine, Wash Day, 321, trademark 4	70.00
Figurine, Wayside Harmony, 111/3/0, trademark 6	65.00
Figurine, Weary Wanderer, 204, trademark 4	140.00
Figurine, Whitsuntide, 163, trademark 6	65.00
Plaque, Madonna, 48/0, trademark 4	68.00
Plaque, Standing Boy, 168, trademark 6	82.00
Plaque, Vacation Time, 125, trademark 5	110.00
Plate, Apple Tree Girl, 269, 1976, trademark 5	92.00
Plate, Ride Into Christmas, 268, 1975, trademark 5	120.00
Plate, School Girl, 273,1980, trademark 6	110.00

Publications, 1992; Bob and Beverly Strauss, *American Sporting Advertising, Volume 2*, L–W Book Sales, 1992.

Ammunition Box, Sears, Roebuck & Company, J. C. Higgins, 22 gauge, short, red, white, and blue, full box	$ 10.00
Ammunition Box, Winchester, Nublack, 10 gauge, illus of mallards in flight, 5 blanks	230.00
Book, *Game Shooting*, P. Curtis, 1927, 279 pgs	25.00
Book, *The Still Hunter*, Theodore S. Van Dyke, New York, 1943, dj	50.00
Book, *The Treasury of Hunting*, Larry Koller, New York, 1965, first edition	25.00
Box, tin, Winchester reloading tool	25.00
Calendar, Peters Cartridge Co, "Outpointed," hunter, dog, and porcupine, Goodwin, 1923	225.00
Calendar, Philip R. Goodwin illus, man on horse shooting elk, oak frame, 1930	70.00
Calendar, Winchester Arms Company, hunter holding calendar pages, 1930	325.00
Catalog, Parker Guns, green cover with flying geese, 1930, 32 pgs	80.00
Decoy, black duck, preening, nailed head, worn repaint, age cracks, 15¼" l	65.00
Decoy, bluebill drake, Saginaw Bay area, glass eyes, old repaint, 13¼" l	45.00
Decoy, brandt, William Goenne, King City, CA, branded "WRD," glass eyes, orig paint, 21" l	75.00
Decoy, Canadian goose, swimmer, Tom Humberstone, NY, glass eyes, orig paint, 27½" l	200.00
Decoy, mallard drake, Dave Hodgman, Niles, MI, carved wing detail, glass eyes, orig paint	100.00
Decoy, merganser drake, Alec Coffin, Phippsburg, ME, wood crest, orig paint, 1920s	450.00
Decoy, pintail drake, Mike Bonnet, WI, Illinois River style, glass eyes, orig paint, initialed "M.B.," 15½" l	50.00
Display, Mossberg, cardboard, stand–up, adv for 22 rifles and scopes, multicolored, c1953, 8 x 11"	25.00
Hunting License Button, California, Resident Citizen's Hunting License, no paper, 1934–35	62.00
Hunting License Button, Delaware, Resident Hunting and Trapping License, 1936	75.00
Hunting License Button, Michigan, Resident Small Game License, with paper, 1930	45.00
Hunting License Button, New Jersey, Residents' License, 1939	18.00
Hunting License Button, New York, Citizen Resident Hunting, Trapping and Fishing License, 1930	60.00
Hunting License Button, North Carolina, County Resident Hunting License, 1938–39	85.00
Keychain, "Smith & Wesson," silvered metal, miniature 6–shooter handgun, single folding knife blade, keychain loop on grip	32.00
Magazine, *Field and Stream*, 1955	12.00
Magazine, *Hunting and Fishing*, 12 issues, Jan–Dec 1933, complete set	28.00
Manual, Gentleman Beer, hunting and trapping, 1947	32.00
Paperback Book, *Lynch's Scientific Methods of Trapping*, illus, 1928, 104 pgs	15.00
Trap, coyote and fox, Verbaile	100.00
Trap, wolf, Newhouse #4½, chain and swivel	175.00

ICE CREAM COLLECTIBLES

Ice cream's origins can be traced to the Roman Emperor Nero's flavoring of frozen ice, an oriental recipe for frozen milk brought to Europe by Marco Polo, and the introduction of Italian ices to the French court of King Henry II by Catherine de Medici in the 1530s. Ice cream in its modern form arrived in the 16th century.

In 1670 the Cafe Procope in Paris introduced ice cream to the general public. An ice cream craze swept across Europe in the early 1700s. By the mid–1770s Philip Lenzi, a New York confectioner, was selling ice cream on a daily basis. George Washington and Thomas Jefferson, credited with creating Baked Alaska, were ice cream lovers.

The street ice cream vendor dates from the 1820s. In 1846 Nancy Johnson invented the hand–cranked ice cream freezer, a standard household fixture by the mid–1850s. The urban ice cream garden arrived on the scene in the middle of the 19th century.

The ice cream parlor was superseded by the drug store soda fountain in the 1920s and 30s. Improvements in the freezer portions of refrigerators, the development of efficient grocery store freezers, and the spread of chain drug stores in the 1950s, 60s, and 70s slowly lessened the role of the local drug store soda fountain.

Ice cream collectibles fall into two basic groups: (1) material from the dairy industry and (2) ice cream and soda fountain items. Beware of reproductions, reputed "warehouse" finds, and fantasy items.

Collectors' Club: The Ice Screamers, PO Box 465, Warrington, PA 18976.

Ashtray, Breyer's 90th Anniversary, 1866–1956	$ 20.00

Book, *Let's Sell Ice Cream*, Ice Cream Merchandising Institute, 1947, 9 x 11", 306 pgs **30.00**

Book, *Theory and Practice of Ice Cream Making*, Hugo Sommer, 1938 . . . . **28.00**

Booklet, *Eskimo Pie*, premiums, 1952, 2 pgs **18.00**

Box, Bing Crosby Ice Cream. **8.00**

Can, Abbott's Ice Cream, ½ gal, Amish girl, c1940 . . . . . . **15.00**

Cone Holder, Heisey Glass, individual **50.00**

Container, Chase's Ice Cream, cardboard, girl on skis, 1923 . . . . **15.00**

Dish, glass, Borden Ice Cream, Elsie portrait **30.00**

Fan, Shady Lawn Ice Cream, cardboard, 2 sided, mother and daughter eating ice cream, 9 x 9" **15.00**

Flavor Board, Borden's Ice Cream, plastic over card-board, "Elsie & Borden's...Very Big On Flavor," 26 x 13" **95.00**

Freezer, Kwik Freeze, galvanized tin, blue, paper label **55.00**

Greeting Card, Christmas, Breyer's Ice Cream, c1920. . . . **25.00**

Paper Doll, Carnation Ice Cream, doll and 3 outfits, 1950s **8.00**

Pin, Sparkle Ice Cream Dessert, aqua and white, hanger, c1940, 3½" d **22.00**

Pinback Button, Ben and Jerry's Ice Cream, black and white photo, red and white trim, 1960s **12.00**

Pinback Button, Horton's Ice Cream, blue, white, and orange, 1930s, 1" d **18.00**

Pinback Button, Skippy Ice Cream, litho, red, white, and blue, 1930s, 1⅛" d **22.00**

Pinback Button, Stewart's Ice Cream, celluloid, lamb mascot, 1940s, 2" d **20.00**

Postcard, Bodle's Ice Cream Store. **10.00**

Postcard, Carnation Ice Cream **22.00**

Poster, Lemon Flake Ice Cream, large dish of ice cream, 1945–50, 12 x 21" **28.00**

Scoop, Dover #20, nickel–plated brass, round bowl, turned wooden handle, lever–activated scraper, 1930s, 10½" l **42.00**

Scoop, Nuroll, cast aluminum, non–mechanical, 1940s **12.00**

Sheet Music, *I Scream, You Scream, We All Scream for Ice Cream*, Howard Johnson, Billy Molly, and Robert King **20.00**

Sign, Borden's Ice Cream, tin, Elsie below product name, 28 x 20" **65.00**

Sign, Breyer's Ice Cream, neon, Breyer's logo above "Ice Cream". **15.00**

Sign, Eskimo Pie 10¢, cardboard, igloo, eskimo, and polar bear, 1922 . . . . **155.00**

Sign, Gollam's Ice Cream, "The Cream Of Matchless Merit," 32 x 20" **65.00**

Sign, Home Ice Cream and Protected Milk, porcelain, white lettering, royal blue ground, 32 x 42" **95.00**

Sign, S & H Fro–Joy Ice Cream, metal, c1930, 17½ x 24" **75.00**

Spoon, "Eat Breyer's Ice Cream" **50.00**

Tray, Elmira Ice Cream, Cream Supreme, 1920s, 12½" d **250.00**

ILLUSTRATORS

Modern illustrators trace their origins to medieval manuscript illuminators and the satirical cartoonists of the 17th and 18th centuries. The mass market printing revolution of the late 19th century marked the advent of the professional illustrator.

Many illustrators listed in this category provided illustrations for books. Concentrating solely on this medium ignores the important role their art played in calendars, magazines, prints, games, jigsaw puzzles, and a host of advertising and promotional products.

Illustrator art breaks down into three major categories: (1) original art, (2) first strike prints sold as art works, and (3) commercially produced art. While the first two categories are limited, the third is not. Often images were produced in the hundreds of thousands and millions.

Magazines, more than any other medium, were responsible for introducing the illustrator to the general public. Norman Rockwell's covers for *Boy's Life* and *The Saturday Evening Post* are classics. Magazine covers remain one of the easiest and most inexpensive means of collecting illustrator art.

Throughout much of the 20th century, the artistic community looked down its nose at commercial illustrators. That attitude is completely reversed today. Collectors avidly seek the work of their favorite commercial illustrator and are engaged in extensive biographical research.

Each year the list of desirable illustrators grows. The category has reached a level of maturity where some illustrators, e.g., Maxfield Parrish, have experienced several collecting crazes. Watch for works by women illustrators. This currently is a hot subcategory.

References: Patricia L. Gibson, *R. Atkinson Fox, William M. Thompson: Identification & Price Guide,* Collectors Press, 1995; Rick and Charlotte Martin, *Vintage Illustration: Discovering America's Calendar Artists, 1900–1960,* Collectors Press, 1997; Rita C. Mortenson, *R. Atkinson Fox: His Life and Work,* L–W Book Sales, 1994; Norman I. Platnick, *Coles Phillips: A Collector's Guide,* published by author, 1997; Jo Ann Havens Wright, *The Life and Art of William McMurray Thompson, American Illustrator...,* published by author, 1995.

Newsletter: *The Illustrator Collector's News,* PO Box 1958, Sequim, WA 98382.

Sign, Purity Pasteurized Ice Cream, porcelain, 2 sided, 27" w, 27" h, $475.00.

Note: For additional listings see Nutting, Wallace; Parrish, Maxfield; and Rockwell, Norman.

Armstrong, Rolf, calendar, Beauty Parade, 1944, 6 pgs, 9 x 13" .... $ 80.00

Becker, Charlotte, calendar, Everett Ice Cream Co adv, baby with teddy bear, 1958, 26 x 14".......... 50.00

Bevens, Torre, magazine cover, sgd, *Pictorial Review,* Apr 1920................................. 22.00

Booth, Herb, print, The Home Place, unframed........ 100.00

Browne, Tom, postcard, American baseball series, green ground 10.00

Campbell, magazine cover, sgd, *The Prudential,* children fishing 20.00

Carlson, Ken, print, Rainbow Trout, unframed 75.00

Carr, Gene, postcard, St. Patrick's greeting............ 10.00

Christy, Earl F., sheet music, *I'll Love You (All Over Again),* 1920 .... 38.00

Clapsaddle, Ellen, postcard, Halloween 15.00

Cook, Arthur, print, After the Storm................. 85.00

Devorss, calendar, woman wearing bathing suit, full pad, 1938, 9 x 14"............................. 45.00

Drayton, Grace, postcard, "Could You Love A Little Girl Like Me?" 20.00

Fox, R. A., calendar, Paradise Bay, W. J. Irish Motor Co adv, 1927.................................. 20.00

Fox, R. A., calendar, The Port of Heart's Desire, 1929, 11 x 8" 45.00

Fox, R. A., print, Love's Paradise, Oct 22, 1925, 9 x 15" 40.00

Fuller, Arthur, calendar, Hercules Powder Co, A Surprise Party, 1920, 13 x 30" 130.00

Harris, magazine cover, *Collier's,* 1937.............. 8.00

Humphrey, Maud, puzzle, Parker Brothers, c1925, 15 pcs 35.00

Humphrey, Walter Beach, calendar, Hercules Powder Co adv, Stowaways, 1932, 13 x 30"............... 180.00

Hunter, Frances Tipton, magazine cover, *Saturday Evening Post,* Apr 12, 1941 .... 18.00

Kauffer, E. McKnight, poster, American Airlines–East Coast, seaman carving sailing ship, 1948, 30 x 30" ... 250.00

Kent, Rockwell, print, Climbing the Bars, transfer printed, tan paper, stamped "Oct 11, 1929," printed by George Miller, framed, 1928, 11 x 8"........ 280.00

Kettering, Charles, magazine cover, *Time,* Jan 9, 1933.... 15.00

Kuhn, Robert, print, Jaguar and Egret 145.00

Leyendecker, F. X., magazine cover, *Life,* Birds of a Feather, Feb 10, 1921......................... 40.00

Leyendecker, J. C., book, *Boy Scouts of America,* Mar 1937, 506 pgs........................... 55.00

Leyendecker, J. C., magazine cover, *Collier's,* Mar 7, 1948...................................... 15.00

Leyendecker, J. C., magazine cover, *Literary Digest,* Dec 26, 1936 .... 40.00

Leyendecker, J. C., magazine cover, *Saturday Evening Post,* Jul 4, 1925............................ 35.00

Leyendecker, J. C., magazine tear sheet, Cooper Hosiery, September 29, 1928 .... 15.00

Mucha, Alphonse, book, *Scene Painting and Bulletin Art,* emb "Salon des Cent," image on tan cov, 1927, 8 x 10½" 35.00

Armstrong, Rolf, sheet music, *I'm Forever Thinking of You,* full–color litho, 9¼ x 12¼", $35.00.

O'Neill, Rose, magazine cover, *Woman's Home Companion,* Jan 1924......................... 35.00

O'Neill, Rose, magazine tear sheet, Jell–O, 5 girls with Jell–O, 1921............................ 18.00

Petruccelli, A., magazine cover, *Fortune,* sgd, Feb 1935, 11 x 14".............................. 45.00

Phillips, Coles, magazine tear sheet, Community Plate, "Flapper Girl," full page, color, 1923 .... 12.50

Phillips, Coles, magazine tear sheet, The Apollo Chocolates, *The Saturday Evening Post,* Dec 15, 1923 .... 15.00

Sandblum, Harold, poster, Coca–Cola–Yes, bathing beauty, 1946, 11 x 27"......................... 155.00

Shepherd, Otis, poster, "Be Refreshed with Healthful Delicious Doublemint Gum," twins with sleek car, c1937, 11 x 42"............................. 220.00

Smith, James Calvert, magazine cover, *McCall's,* Nov 1921 .... 10.00

Smith, Jessie Wilcox, book, *The Princess & The Goblin,* 8 book plates, 1920 .... 45.00

Smith, Jessie Wilcox, magazine cover, *Good Housekeeping,* Jul 1922 .... 22.00

Smith, Jessie Wilcox, magazine cover, *Good Housekeeping,* May 1932, little girl aviator 15.00

Smith, Jessie Wilcox, postcard, The Lily Pool, Reinthal & Newman.......................... 22.00

Smith, Jessie Wilcox, print, The Lovers Quarrel, 10½ x 16" 20.00

Teich, Curt, postcard, jitterbug couple, C. T. Jitterbug Comics series, 1938............................ 30.00

Twelvetrees, Charles, magazine cover, *Capper's Farmer,* sgd, 1930s 15.00

Wheelan, Nister, postcard, "For My Valentine" 18.00

Whistler, James Abbott McNeill, print, The Little Pool, etching, 1961............................... 520.00

Williamson, J., magazine cover, *Saturday Evening Post,* sgd, Oct 27, 1962 .... 5.00

Wyeth, N. C., book, *Treasure Island,* 1947 .... 48.00

Wyeth, N. C., calendar, Hercules Powder Co adv, 3
men holding leashed hunting dogs and guns, 1933,
13 x 27¾" **130.00**

IMPERIAL GLASS

In 1901 a group of investors from Wheeling, West Virginia, and Bellaire, Ohio, founded the Imperial Glass Company. Bellaire had a long established glassmaking tradition. The Imperial factory was the newest of 14 glasshouses built in the city. Ed Muhleman, previously with the Crystal Glass Works of Bridgeport, Ohio, supervised construction and served as company manager. The first Imperial glass was manufactured on January 13, 1904. The company's products were mass–market directed, e.g., jelly glasses, tumblers, and assorted tableware.

Victor G. Wicke, owner of a selling agency in New York, was hired as Imperial's Secretary and Sales Manager. Imperial's success was guaranteed by one of its first orders, approximately 20 different items to be supplied to almost 500 F. W. Woolworth stores. McCrory and Kresge also became major Imperial customers.

In the decade between 1910 and 1920, machine–made glassware flooded the market. Imperial responded by introducing a number of new glassware lines. "Nuart" iridescent ware was introduced. Next came "Nucut" crystal, a pressed reproduction of English cut glass pieces. "Nucut" sold well as a premium. The Grand Union Tea Company distributed a large amount. In the 1950s, "Nucut" was reintroduced as "Collectors Crystal" and once again became very popular.

The Depression and continuing loss of market share to mass–production glass factories forced Imperial to declare bankruptcy in 1931. The plant continued to operate through court-appointed receivers. Imperial Glass Corporation, a new entity, was formed during July and August of 1931. An order from the Quaker Oats Company for a premium similar to Cape Cod helped revive the company. In 1937 Imperial launched Candlewick, its best selling line.

In 1940 Imperial acquired the Central Glass Works of Wheeling, established in 1860. It proved to be the first of a number of acquisitions, including A. H. Heisey and Company in 1958 and the Cambridge Glass Company in 1960.

In 1973, Imperial became a subsidiary of Lenox Glass Corporation. In 1981 Lenox sold the company to Arthur Lorch, a private investor living in New York, who in turn sold it to Robert Stahl, a Minneapolis, Minnesota, liquidator in 1982. In October 1982 Imperial declared bankruptcy. Consolidated–Colony, a partnership of Lancaster Colony Corporation and Consolidated International, purchased Imperial in December 1984. Most of the company's molds were sold. Maroon Enterprises of Bridgeport, Ohio, purchased the buildings and property in March 1985.

References: Margaret and Douglas Archer, *Imperial Glass: 1904–1938 Catalog,* reprint, Collector Books, 1978, 1995 value update; National Imperial Glass Collectors' Society, *Imperial Glass Encyclopedia: Volume I, A–Cane,* Antique Publications, 1995; National Imperial Glass Collectors Society, *Imperial Glass 1966 Catalog,* reprint, 1991 price guide, Antique Publications; Harry L. Rinker, *Stemware of the 20th Century: The Top 200 Patterns,* House of Collectibles, 1997.

Collectors' Club: National Imperial Glass Collectors Society, PO Box 534, Bellaire, OH 43906.

Note: See Candlewick for additional listings.

Animal Dish, cov, rabbit on nest, white milk glass,
4½" h . . . . **$ 50.00**
Ashtray, Nuart, mkd. 20.00
Basket, pressed, 10½" h 32.00
Berry Bowl, Nuart, tab handles, mkd, 4½" d 18.00
Bowl, Cape Cod, 2 part, oval, 11" d 48.00
Bowl, clear, flower and leaf design, molded star base,
6½" d 22.00
Bowl, Jewels, purple pearl green luster, mkd, 6¼" d 80.00
Bowl, Nucut, mkd, 7½" d 25.00
Cake Plate, Cape Cod, 160/67D. 30.00
Cake Salver, Cape Cod, 10" d. 42.00
Candlesticks, pr, cobalt blue luster, white vine and
leaf dec, 10½" h. 325.00
Candy Dish, cov, Jewels, pink 45.00
Cereal Bowl, Katy, blue opalescent, flared 62.00
Cheese Dish, cov, Monticello. 38.00
Compote, cov, Cape Cod 62.00
Compote, Nucut, 5½" d. 25.00
Cordial, Park Lane, amber 5.00
Cordial, Riviera, blue. 5.00
Cordial, Wakefield, amber 15.00
Creamer, Jewels, yellow luster 45.00
Creamer, Nucut. 20.00
Creamer, Pillar Flutes, light blue. 25.00
Creamer and Sugar, Flora, rose. 18.00
Cruet, Cape Cod, 4 oz. 18.00
Cup and Saucer, Pillar Flutes, light blue 25.00
Decanter, Cape Cod . . . . , ... 62.00
Fern Dish, Nucut, ftd, brass lining, mkd, 8" l. 40.00
Figure, bulldog, clear. 35.00
Figure, swan, 4½" h 20.00
Figure, tiger, jade green 18.00
Goblet, Cape Cod, red. 18.00
Hat, ruffled rim, cobalt blue luster, embedded irid
white vines and leaves, 9" w. 110.00

Plate, Cape Cod, antique blue, 8" d, $15.00.

Iced Tea Tumbler, Cape Cod, 5" h **12.00**
Juice Tumbler, Cape Cod **15.00**
Marmalade, Cape Cod **32.00**
Mayonnaise, underplate, and spoon, Monaco, amber **28.00**
Mug, red slag, robin **18.00**
Nut Dish, Design #112, clear, 5½" d **22.00**
Parfait, Cape Cod **12.00**
Pepper Mill, Cape Cod **38.00**
Pitcher, spun teal, 80 oz **100.00**
Pitcher, yellow luster, applied clear handle, 10" h **230.00**
Plate, Design #12, clear, 5½" d **18.00**
Plate, Fancy Colonial, pink, 7½" d **12.00**
Plate, Jewels, irid pale green, 8" d **48.00**
Plate, Jewels, white luster, 8" d **60.00**
Plate, Windmill, glossy, green slag, mkd **48.00**
Platter, Cape Cod, oval, 13½" l **70.00**
Rose Bowl, irid orange luster, white floral cutting,
 6" d **70.00**
Salad Bowl, Nucut, 10½" d **35.00**
Salt and Pepper Shakers, pr, Cape Cod, ftd **12.00**
Sherbet, Cape Cod, amberina **22.00**
Sugar, cov, Lace Edge, green opal **20.00**
Toothpick, ivory, orig label **22.00**
Torte Plate, Cape Cod, 13" d **38.00**
Tumbler, Buzz Star, clear **20.00**
Tumbler, Nucut, flared rim, molded star **18.00**
Vase, blue and white luster, allover swirls, white int,
 7" h **155.00**
Vase, butterscotch ground, orange luster, 8½" h **120.00**
Vase, Cape Cod, ftd, 11" h **55.00**
Vase, irid emerald green, embedded white hearts and
 vines, orange luster throat, label, 11" h **300.00**
Vase, Nuart, bulbous, irid green, 7" h **130.00**
Vase, pressed, spun red, 9" h **68.00**
Wine, Cape Cod, 3 oz **5.00**
Wine, Park Lane, amber **5.00**

INSULATORS

The development of glass and ceramic insulators resulted from a need created by the telegraph. In 1844 Ezra Cornell obtained the first insulator patent. Armstrong (1938–69), Brookfield (1865–1922), California (1912–16), Gayner (1920–22), Hemingray (1871–1919), Lynchburg (1923–25), Maydwell (1935–40), McLaughlin (1923–25), and Whitall Tatum (1920–38) are the leading insulator manufacturers.

The first insulators did not contain threads. L. A. Cauvet patented a threaded insulator in the late 1860s. Drip points were added to insulators to prevent water from accumulating and creating a short. A double skirt kept the peg or pin free of moisture.

Insulators are collected by "CD" (consolidated design) numbers as found in N. R. Woodward's *The Glass Insulator in America*. The numbers are based upon the design style of the insulator. The color, name of maker, or lettering on the insulator are not factors in assigning numbers. Thus far over 500 different design styles have been identified.

References: John and Carol McDougald, *Insulators: A History And Guide To North American Glass Pintype Insulators, Volume 1* (1990), *Volume 2* (1990), *Price Guide* (1995), published by authors; Marion and Evelyn Milholland, *Glass Insulator Reference Book, 4th Revision,* published by authors, 1976, available from C. D. Walsh (granddaughter).

Periodical: *Crown Jewels of the Wire,* PO Box 1003, St. Charles, IL 60174.

Collectors' Club: National Insulator Assoc, 1315 Old Mill Path, Broadview Heights, OH 44147.

Note: Insulators are in near mint/mint condition unless otherwise noted.

CD 102, bar/bar, dark purple . . . . **$ 18.00**
CD 102, diamond, dark amber **20.00**
CD 102, diamond, royal purple **25.00**
CD 102, star, aqua **2.00**
CD 106, PSSA, yellow, green bubbles **35.00**
CD 106.1, Duquesne, cornflower **75.00**
CD 112, star, blue **5.00**
CD 113, BGM Co, sun colored amethyst **75.00**
CD 115, McLaughlin #10, light green **8.00**
CD 115, Whitall Tatum #3, peach **5.00**
CD 121, Agee, amethyst **25.00**
CD 121, AM Tel & Tel, jade milk **8.00**
CD 121, CD & P Tel Co, light blue **20.00**
CD 121, McLaughlin #16, light lime **8.00**
CD 126.4, WE Mfg Co, lime green **45.00**
CD 133, no name #20, green **3.00**
CD 134, WGM, sun colored amethyst **65.00**
CD 142, Hemingray TS–2, carnival **25.00**
CD 145, American, light grass green **60.00**
CD 145, star, green **5.00**
CD 147, Patent Oct 8 1907, aqua **5.00**
CD 152, diamond, light green **8.00**
CD 154, Whitall Tatum, purple **20.00**
CD 154, Whitall Tatum, straw **3.00**
CD 160, McLaughlin #14, dark olive **25.00**
CD 161, California, light yellow **125.00**
CD 162, Hamilton Glass, light blue aqua **25.00**
CD 164, McLaughlin, emerald, with drips **8.00**
CD 164, star, aqua **3.00**

CD 218,
Hemingray 660,
clear, $7.00.

CD 165.1, Whitall Tatum, aqua **5.00**
CD 168, Hemingray D510, ice blue. **5.00**
CD 168, Hemingray D510, olive amber **15.00**
CD 168, Hemingray D510, red amber **25.00**
CD 168, Hemingray D510, silver carnival. **20.00**
CD 190/191, B, blue **35.00**
CD 208, Brookfield, aqua, large olive streak **20.00**
CD 218, Hemingray 660, clear **7.00**
CD 252, Lynchburg, aqua **8.00**
CD 296, #20, dark aqua **6.00**
CD 326, Pyrex #453, light carnival. **75.00**
CD 422, Agee, dark amethyst. **30.00**

IRONS

Although irons date back to the 12th century, the modern iron resulted from a series of technological advances that began in the middle of the 19th century. Until the arrival of the electric iron at the beginning of the 20th century, irons were heated by pre–heating a slug put into the iron, burning a solid fuel such as charcoal, using a liquid fuel, e.g., alcohol, gasoline, or natural gas, or drawing heat from a heated surface, such as the top of a stove.

Pre–electric irons made during the last quarter of the 19th century and first quarter of the 20th century are common. Do not overpay. High prices are reserved for novelty irons and irons from lesser known makers.

H. W. Seeley patented the first electric iron in 1882. The first iron, a General Electric with a detachable cord, dates from 1903. Westinghouse introduced the automatic iron in 1924 and Edec the steam iron in 1926. Electric irons are collected more for their body design than their historical importance or age. Check the cord and plug before attempting to use any electric iron.

Reference: David Irons, *Irons By Irons*, published by author, 1994.

Newsletter: *Iron Talk*, PO Box 68, Waelder, TX 78959.

Akron Lamp and Mfg Co, Diamond, gasoline, plated cast iron, turned wood handle . . . . **$ 30.00**
Brannon Inc, Cord–Less–Matic, black body, triple plates, Bakelite handle, non–adjusting heat indicator **30.00**
Coleman, #609–A, gas, black enameled sheet metal, gas tank and pump, 1940 . . . . **30.00**
Coleman, Instant–Lite, model 4A, gas, blue enameled sheet metal, blue painted gas tank, brass pump, tin stand **75.00**

Pyrex Silver Streak, Model 1038, electric, blue, $800.00.

Dover Mfg, Co–Ed, screw–in permanent cord, green wood handle, 2½ lbs **25.00**
Edison Electric Appliance Company, Hotpoint Model R, electric, 6½" l **22.00**
General Electric, chrome, black Bakelite handle and thumbrest **15.00**
General Electric, Moderne, 1935–36 . . . . **22.00**
General Electric/Hot Point, Calrod–A–C–Matic, nickel body, red wood handle, Bakelite thumbrest, detachable cord **18.00**
General Electric/Hot Point, Calrod Super Automatic, nickel shell, black wood handle, detachable cord **15.00**
General Mills/Betty Crocker, Tru–Heat Iron, red Bakelite knobs, black handle, side rest, steam attachment, detachable base, orig box, c1940, 3¾ lb **35.00**
Knapp Monarch, Gad–A–Bout, travel, chrome, folding cream and brown handle, heat indicator, detachable cord, brown zippered cloth bag. **15.00**
Knapp Monarch, Steem–R–Dri, chrome, steam switch, Bakelite filler cap and handle **22.00**
Kwikway Co, Kwikway Iron, nickel–clad iron, heel rest, black wood handle, detachable cord, 2½ lb **12.00**
Sun Mfg Co, gasoline, plated cast iron, turned wood grip handle attached to removable cover plate, emb casting on top, horizontal cylindrical gasoline tank at one end, "The Iron That Sizzles" **65.00**
Sunbeam, Ironmaster, red wheel control on front of black Bakelite handle, steam attachment, orig box with papers **65.00**
Universal Landers, Frary & Clark, E–909, electric, nickel plated, with stand, 7" l **35.00**
Waverly Tool Co, Petipoint, model W 410, Art Deco style, horizontal layered fins, tilt–up back sole plate, red control lever, black Bakelite handle **40.00**
Waverly Tool Co, Steam–O–Matic, electric, cast aluminum, 10½" h **75.00**
Westinghouse, Adjust–O–Matic, nickel body, black wood handle, detachable cord **12.00**

ITALIAN GLASS

Italian Glass is a generic term for glassware made in Italy from the 1920s into the early 1960s and heavily exported to the United States. Pieces range from vases with multicolored internal thick and thin filigree threads to figurals of clowns and fish.

The glass was made in Murano, the center of Italy's glass blowing industry. Beginning in the 1920s many of the firms, e.g., Seguso Vetri d'Arte, hired art directors and engaged the services of internationally known artists and designers. Venini, a firm owned by Paolo Venini, attracted designer–artists such as Fulvio Bianconi, Riccardo Licata, Tyra Lundgren (Scandinavian), Napoleone Martinuzzi, Thomas Stearns (American), and Vittorio Zechin. The 1950s was a second golden age following the flurry of high–style pieces made from the mid–1920s through the mid–1930s.

Newsletter: *Vertri: Italian Glass News*, PO Box 191, Fort Lee, NJ 07024.

Aquarium Blocks, pr, Cenedese, internally dec with hot–modeled fish and seaweed, 4¼" h, 4¾" w . . . . . **$ 275.00**

Bottle, stoppered, Venini, clear body with swirling cane dec alternating pink and white, acid stamp, 14" h 575.00

Bowl, attributed to Vamsa, designed by Alfredo Barbini, clear, internally dec with hot modeled fish and green swirls, unmkd, c1935, 4" h, 9½" w 250.00

Bowl, Barovier and Toso, conch shell, irid, c1940 9" w, 3¾" h 200.00

Bowl, Murano, amber with silver leaf inclusions, unsgd, 3" h, 7" w 35.00

Candlesticks, pr, Barovier, applied latimo grapes and gold foil, c1940, 3" d, 7½" h 575.00

Compote, ftd, attributed to Salviati, lemon–yellow, green, rim, 8¾" d, 6¾" h 275.00

Compote, ftd, controlled air bubble design with gold leaf, 6" h, 11½" d 100.00

Figure, head, Archimede Seguso, whimsical form, amber body with applied red facial devices, unsgd, c1952–56, 10" h 225.00

Figurine, Alfredo Barbini for Cenedese, bear, vetri scavo, 11" l, 5¾" h 825.00

Lamps, pr, vase shaped, gold–dust milk glass with pink circles, c1945, 31" h 715.00

Sculpture, stylized horse head, clambroth, foil label, 10¼" w, 8" h 100.00

Serving Dish, Salviati, pink and white latticino, aventurine rim, 11¼" d 300.00

Vase, attributed to Salviati, double gourds, red, 7¾" h, 4½" w 225.00

Vase, clear pink and gold foil sofiati amphora, double handles, 4" w, 6¾" h 100.00

Vase, cylindrical, clear, applied blue grape dots and white and clear caning, 4½" h, 5½" d 300.00

Vase, Enrico Capuzzo for Vistosi, dimpled cylindrical bicalmo, half clear, half latimo, c1960, paper label, 10" h, 4" d 110.00

Vase, Napoleone Martinuzzi for Venini, long flaring neck, bulbous base, linear dec with 3 applied rings at neck, unsd, 11½" h........................... 150.00

Vase, whale shaped, smoked glass, applied murrine eyes, c1920, 7¾" h, 10" w 300.00

AUCTION PRICES

Treadway Gallery, Inc., 20th Century Auction, Session Three including Art Deco, 1950s, and Modern and Italian Glass, February 16, 1997. Prices include the 10% buyer's premium.

Clessidre Timer, Venini, green basin and red basin joined incalmo, acid stamp *venini murano Italia*, 9½" h 880.00

Figure, chicken, Venini, designed by Fulvio Bianconi, opaque white body with black dec with opaque applications on black base, acid stamp *venini murano Italia*, c1950s, 7" h 3,575.00

Vase, Avem, designed by Giorgio Ferro, anse volante, deep green body with 3 pulled holes and irid surface, c1952, 11" h.................... 935.00

Vase, Barovier & Toso, deep heavy green body with fine controlled bubbles, applied clear wing handles with gold leaf, light irid overall, c1930s, 8" h .. 275.00

Vase, designed by Paolo Venini, tall teardrop form with sommerso layers of blue and pink with very fine horizontally carved surface, circular acid stamp *venini ITALY murano*, 14" h 935.00

Vase, Salir, murrina, clear, gold leaf handles and stem, applied with blue, red, green, and white band of flower murrina, c1930s, 8" h 605.00

Vase, Zecchin–Martinuzzi, designed by Napoleone Martinuzzi, opaque body created with white int and light blue ext with looping translucent blue handles and ring foot, diamond acid stamp *Made in Italy*, c1930s, 12" h 467.50

JEANNETTE GLASS

The Jeannette Glass Company, Jeannette, Pennsylvania, was founded in 1898. It originally produced hand–blown, narrow mouthed bottles. When manufacturing these style bottles no longer proved profitable, the factory was converted to semi–automatic methods and turned out wide–mouthed glass containers for food stuffs. By 1910 Jeannette Glass was producing automobile headlight lenses and glass brick, known as sidewalk tile.

The Jeannette Glass Company introduced a line of pressed table and kitchenware in the 1920s. Jeannette's popular Depression Era patterns include Adam (1932–34), Cherry Blossom (1930–39), Cube or Cubist (1929–33), Doric (1935–38), Doric and Pansy (1937–38), Floral or Poinsettia (1931–35), Hex Optic or Honeycomb (1928–32), Homespun or Fine Rib (1939–49), Iris and Iris Herringbone (1928–32, 1950s, and 1970s), Sunburst or Herringbone (late 1930s), Sunflower (1930s), Swirl or Petal Swirl (1937–38), and Windsor or Windsor Diamond (1936–46). The company also made glass candy containers for other firms and individuals during the 1920s.

In 1952 Jeannette Glass purchased the McKee Glass Corporation from the Thatcher Glass Company. This enabled the company to expand into the production of heat resistant and industrial glass.

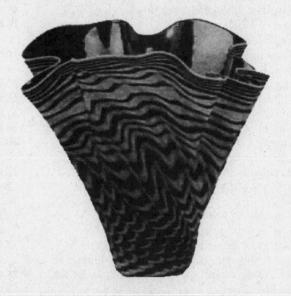

Vase, fazzoletto, marbled vetro latimo and amethyst, blue irid int, 13" h, 15" w, $225.00.

The Jeannette Glass Company experienced several periods in the post–World War II era when its stemware enjoyed a strong popularity with the American buying public. Anniversary (1947–49, late 1960s to mid–1970s), Floragold or Louisa (1950s), Harp (1954–1957), Holiday or Buttons and Bows (1947 through mid–1950s), and Shell Pink Milk Glass (1957–1959) were among the most popular patterns. The popularity of Iris was so strong it easily made the transition from pre–war to post–war pattern.

The Jeannette Glass Company ceased operations in the mid–1980s.

Reference: Gene Florence, *Collectible Glassware From the 40's, 50's, 60's..., Third Edition,* Collector Books, 1996.

Note: For additional listings see Depression Glass.

Adam, ashtray, 4⁵/₈" d, green. **$ 20.00**
Adam, bowl, 4³/₄" d, green **15.00**
Adam, bowl, 7³/₄" d, green **25.00**
Adam, cake plate, ftd, 10" d, pink **30.00**
Adam, cup, pink **25.00**
Adam, dinner plate, 9" d, green **30.00**
Adam, pitcher, sq base, pink **50.00**
Adam, platter, oval, 11³/₄" l, pink **27.00**
Adam, platter, rect, green. **30.00**
Adam, relish, divided, 8" l, pink **30.00**
Adam, saucer, pink **8.00**
Beater Bowl, metal beater, delphite **50.00**
Beater Bowl, metal beater, light jadeite. **25.00**
Canister, cov, cereal, 29 oz, black lettering, delphite **75.00**
Canister, cov, sugar, 40 oz, black lettering, delphite. **150.00**
Cherry Blossom, berry bowl, individual, 4³/₄" d, pink. **15.00**
Cherry Blossom, berry bowl, master, 8¹/₂" d, green. **40.00**
Cherry Blossom, cake plate, ftd, pink **27.00**
Cherry Blossom, creamer and cov sugar, green **50.00**
Cherry Blossom, pitcher, 42 oz, green. **60.00**
Cherry Blossom, platter, oval, 11" l, pink **40.00**
Cherry Blossom, salad plate, 7" d, green. **20.00**
Cherry Blossom, sherbet, green **17.00**
Cubist, bowl, 4¹/₂" d, green. **7.00**

Cubist, candy jar, cov, pink, $22.00.

Cubist, bowl, 6¹/₂" d, pink **12.00**
Cubist, bread and butter plate, 6" d, green **5.00**
Cubist, butter dish, cov, pink **70.00**
Cubist, candy jar, cov, green. **25.00**
Cubist, coaster, green. **7.00**
Cubist, creamer and cov sugar, large, green **35.00**
Cubist, creamer and cov sugar, large, pink **25.00**
Cubist, cup and saucer, green. **12.00**
Cubist, pitcher, pink. **250.00**
Cubist, powder jar, cov, pink **30.00**
Cubist, salt and pepper shakers, pr, green **35.00**
Cubist, sherbet, ftd, green **8.00**
Doric, berry bowl, 4¹/₂" d, delphite. **40.00**
Doric, butter dish, cov, green **85.00**
Doric, cereal bowl, 5¹/₂" d, pink **45.00**
Doric, cup, green **10.00**
Doric, relish, 4" sq, green. **10.00**
Doric, salad plate, 7" d, pink **20.00**
Doric, sherbet, ftd, delphite **7.00**
Doric, tray, handled, 10", pink **15.00**
Drip Jar, cov, delphite **55.00**
Floragold, berry bowl, 4¹/₂" d **5.00**
Floragold, bowl, ruffled, 9¹/₂" d. **10.00**
Floragold, candlesticks, pr **48.00**
Floragold, candy jar, cov **45.00**
Floragold, creamer. **10.00**
Floragold, pitcher, 64 oz **35.00**
Floragold, platter, 11¹/₄" d. **25.00**
Floragold, sherbet, ftd **13.00**
Floral, candlesticks, pr, 4", green **80.00**
Floral, cup and saucer, pink. **25.00**
Floral, refrigerator dish, cov, 5" sq, jadeite. **25.00**
Floral, salt and pepper shakers, pr, ftd, 4", green **50.00**
Floral, vegetable bowl, cov, 8" d, pink **20.00**
Harp, coaster, crystal **5.00**
Harp, cup, crystal **10.00**
Harp, saucer, crystal **5.00**
Harp, tray, rect, 2 handled, shell pink **45.00**
Harp, vase, 7¹/₂" h, crystal **15.00**
Hex Optic, bucket reamer, metal bail handle and
  stand, green **40.00**
Hex Optic, bucket reamer, metal bail handle, pink **45.00**
Iris, butter dish, cov, crystal **50.00**
Iris, candlesticks, pr, iridescent. **45.00**
Iris, demitasse cup, crystal **35.00**
Iris, dinner plate, 9" d, crystal. **40.00**
Iris, pitcher, ftd, 9¹/₂" h, iridescent. **40.00**
Iris, sandwich plate, 11³/₄" d, iridescent. **30.00**
Iris, sauce bowl, ruffled, 5" d, iridescent **25.00**
Iris, sugar, cov, iridescent **12.00**
Jennyware, mixing bowl, 10¹/₂" d, ultramarine. **40.00**
Jennyware, mixing bowls, set of 3, pink **80.00**
Jennyware, measuring cup, 1 cup, pink **35.00**
Jennyware, measuring cups, set of 4, ultramarine **125.00**
Jennyware, refrigerator dish, cov, 4¹/₂" sq, ultramarine **25.00**
Jennyware, refrigerator dish, cov, round, 70 oz, pink. **75.00**
Match Holder, delphite **45.00**
Reamer, loop handle, green **20.00**
Reamer, loop handle, small, delphite **65.00**
Reamer, tab handle, 5" d, green **15.00**

Harp, cake stand, shell pink, 1954–57, 4⁷/₈" h, $25.00.

Reamer, tab handle, 5⁷/₈" d, pink **40.00**
Reamer and pitcher, 2 cup, dark jadeite **80.00**
Salt Box, cov, round, emb "SALT" on lid, green **160.00**
Salt Box, cov, sq, jadeite **200.00**
Shaker, flour, light jadeite **15.00**
Shaker, paprika, 8 oz, delphite **50.00**
Shaker, sugar, dark jadeite **17.00**
Spice Canister, ginger, 3", jadeite **30.00**
Swirl, bread and butter plate, 6" d, ultramarine **5.00**
Swirl, butter dish, cov, pink **175.00**
Swirl, candy jar, cov, ultramarine **140.00**
Swirl, candy jar, open, 3 toed, ultramarine **15.00**
Swirl, cereal bowl, 5¼" d, delphite **15.00**
Swirl, coaster, pink **10.00**
Swirl, creamer, ftd, delphite **12.00**
Swirl, cup and saucer, ultramarine **20.00**
Swirl, dinner plate, ultramarine **15.00**
Swirl, salad plate, 8" d, delphite **10.00**
Swirl, salt and pepper shakers, pr, ultramarine **40.00**
Swirl, sandwich plate, 12" d, ultramarine **22.00**
Swirl, sherbet plate, 6½" d, pink **5.00**
Swirl, sugar, ftd, delphite **25.00**
Swirl, tumbler, 4⁵/₈" h, pink **17.00**
Swirl, vase, ftd, 8½" h, ultramarine **22.00**
Windsor, ashtray, 5³/₄" d, pink **35.00**
Windsor, cake plate, ftd, 10³/₄" d, pink **20.00**
0Windsor, cream soup bowl, 5" d, green **25.00**
Windsor, creamer, blue **65.00**
Windsor, powder jar, yellow **175.00**
Windsor, salt and pepper shakers, pr, green **50.00**
Windsor, tray, handled, 4" sq, crystal **5.00**
Windsor, tumbler, 4" h, red **55.00**
Windsor, tumbler, 5" h, pink **30.00**
Windsor, tumbler, ftd, 7¼" h, crystal **15.00**

JEWELRY

Jewelry divides into two basic groups: precious and non–precious (a.k.a., costume after 1920). This category focuses on precious jewelry. While collected, most precious jewelry is purchased to be worn or studied.

U.S. custom laws define antique jewelry as jewelry over 100 years old. Estate or Heirloom jewelry is generally assumed to be over 25 years old.

Craftsmanship, aesthetic design, scarcity, and current market worth of gemstones and the precious metal are the principal value keys. Antique and period jewelry should be set with the cut of stone prevalent at the time the piece was made. Names, manufacturer, designer, or both, also plays a major role in value.

All the major American auction houses conduct one or more sales each year of antique and estate jewelry. Even at the hammer prices, most of the lots are sold to dealers.

Be extremely cautious when buying any jewelry. Exact reproductions, copycats (stylistic reproductions), fantasies (non–period shapes and forms), and fakes abound. Also be alert for married and divorced pieces.

References: Ed Aswad and Michael Weinstein, *The Art and Mystique of Shell Cameos: Identification and Value Guide, 2nd Edition,* Books Americana, Krause Publications, 1997; Lillian Baker, *Art Nouveau & Art Deco Jewelry: An Identification & Value Guide,* Collector Books, 1981, 1997 value update; Howard L. Bell, Jr., *Cuff Jewelry: A Historical Account For Collectors and Antique Dealers,* published by author, 1994; Jeanenne Bell, *Answers to Questions About 1840–1950 Old Jewelry, Fourth Edition,* Books Americana, Krause Publications, 1996; Lodovica Rizzoli Eleuteri, *Twentieth–Century Jewelry: Art Nouveau to Modern Design,* Electa, Abbeville, 1994; Arthur Guy Kaplan, *The Official Identification and Price Guide To Antique Jewelry, Sixth Edition,* House of Collectibles, 1990, reprinted 1994; Penny Chittim Morrill and Carol A. Beck, *Mexican Silver: 20th Century Handwrought Jewelry and Metalwork,* Schiffer Publishing, 1994.

Ginger Moro, *European Designer Jewelry,* Schiffer Publishing, 1995; Dorothy T. Rainwater, *American Jewelry Manufacturers,* Schiffer Publishing, 1988; Christie Romero, *Warman's Jewelry,* Wallace–Homestead, Krause Publications, 1995; Nancy N. Schiffer, *Silver Jewelry Treasures,* Schiffer Publishing, 1993; Sheryl Gross Shatz, *What's It Made Of?: A Jewelry Materials Identification Guide, Third Edition,* published by author, 1996; Doris J. Snell, *Antique Jewelry With Prices, Second Edition,* Wallace–Homestead, Krause Publications, 1997.

Periodicals: *Auction Market Resource For Gems & Jewelry,* PO Box 7683, Rego Park, NY 11374; *Gems & Gemology,* Gemological Inst of America, 1660 Stewart St, Santa Monica, CA 90404; *Jewelers' Circular Keystone/Heritage,* PO Box 2085, Radnor, PA 19080.

Collectors' Clubs: American Society of Jewelry Historians, Box 103, 1B Quaker Ridge Rd, New Rochelle, NY 10804; National Cuff Link Society, PO Box 346, Prospect Heights, IL 60070; Society of Antique & Estate Jewelry, Ltd, 570 Seventh Ave, Ste 1900, New York, NY 10018.

Bracelet, gold, cuff, shell and pearl dec, Joseff of
   Hollywood, c1960 . . . . **$ 255.00**
Bracelet, oval medallions in gilt silver, coral beads,
   Farner, 7" l **350.00**
Bracelet, SS, filigree sterling panels with carved
   black onyx mounts, imp mark, H. Santana, 7" l **250.00**
Bracelet, SS, links spell "heavens above," imp mark,
   Flato, 8½" l **150.00**

Earring Clips, 14K yg, fluted swirls, engine–turn decorated, $375.00. Photo courtesy William Doyle Galleries.

Brooch, SS, Scandinavian, rect raised foliate and bead motif, die stamped, flat backing, mkd "925 sterling Denmark GI," c1930 . . . . 150.00

Brooch, yg, circular green jadeite disc adorned at each side with red enamel accents and small pearls. . . 625.00

Charm, SS, clown, c1950. . . . . 8.00

Charm, SS, roller skate, c1950 . . . . 8.00

Charm Bracelet, SS, military motifs, 20 charms, some with moving parts, c1940 . . . . 150.00

Cuff Links, pr, SS, mother–of–pearl, 6–gun with revolving barrel and mother–of–pearl grip, mkd "sterling," c1945 . . . . 110.00

Earrings, pr, SS, leaf shapes pave'–set with marcasites, clipbacks, mkd "sterling," c1935 . . . . 55.00

Earrings, pr, screwbacks, SS, Mexican, cutout and pierced profile of stylized face, oxidized convex backing and overlay, imp "sterling Salvador," c1955 . . . . 110.00

Earrings, pr, SS, screwbacks, shell design, Spratling, 1¹/₂" l. 150.00

Fob Pin, SS, cutout abstract design, orig black silk ribbon, imp mark, Jean Puiforcat, 4" l 150.00

Lapel Pin, SS, Budweiser 3 Million Barrel Team, inset ruby, 1941 . . . . 30.00

Necklace, 14K yg, snake chain, c1940, 16" l, ¹/₂" w 675.00

Pin, SS, abstract design with movable bead, imp mark, Rebajes, 3" l. 250.00

Pin, 14K yg, leafy vine set with 8 small diamonds, $500.00. Photo courtesy William Doyle Galleries.

Pin, SS, figural St. Peter with gate keys, imp mark, Los Castillo, 3" l 150.00

Pin and Earrings, SS, abstract design, imp marks, Miraglia, 2¹/₂" l 150.00

Ring, SS, nephrite stone, imp mark, Rabajes 250.00

Ring, yg, modified opal openwork tablet wet with rose–cut diamonds centering emerald bead 575.00

Suite, necklace and clip–on earrings, SS links, floral medallions, imp mark, McClelland & Barclay, 9" l 150.00

Suite, pin and screwback earrings, 14K red gold, budding roses 350.00

JEWELRY, COSTUME

Prior to World War I, non–precious jewelry consisted of inexpensive copies of precious jewelry. This changed in the 1920s when Coco Chanel advocated the wearing of faux jewelry as an acceptable part of haute couture. High–style fashion jewelry continued to exercise a strong influence on costume jewelry until the middle of the 20th century.

During the 1930s costume jewelry manufacture benefited from developments such as more efficient casting machines and the creation of Bakelite, one of the first entirely synthetic plastics. Material shortages during World War II promoted the increased use of ceramics and wood. Copper, plastic novelty, and rhinestone crazes marked the 1950s and 60s.

Because of this category's vastness, collectors and dealers focus on named manufacturers and designers. Understand that a maker's mark is not a guarantee of quality. Examine pieces objectively. Further, this is a very trendy category. What is in today, can be out tomorrow. Just ask anyone who collected rhinestone jewelry in the early 1980s.

References: Lillian Baker, *Fifty Years Of Collectible Fashion Jewelry: 1925–1975,* Collector Books, 1986, 1997 value update; Lillian Baker, *100 Years of Collectible Jewelry, 1850–1950,* Collector Books, 1978, 1997 value update; Lillian Baker, *Twentieth Century Fashionable Plastic Jewelry,* Collector Books, 1992, 1996 value update; Joanne Dubbs Ball, *Costume Jewelers: The Golden Age of Design, Second Edition,* Schiffer Publishing, 1997; Dee Battle and Alayne Lesser, *The Best Bakelite and Other Plastic Jewelry,* Schiffer Publishing, 1996; Vivienne Becker, *Fabulous Costume Jewelry: History of Fantasy and Fashion In Jewels,* Schiffer Publishing, 1993; Jeanenne Bell, *Answers To Questions About Old Jewelry, 1840–1950, Fourth Edition,* Books Americana, Krause Publications, 1995.

Matthew L. Burkholz and Linda Lictenberg Kaplan, *Copper Art Jewelry: A Different Luster,* Schiffer Publishing, 1992; Maryanne Dolan, *Collecting Rhinestone Jewelry, Third Edition,* Books Americana, Krause Publications, 1993; Roseann Ettinger, *Forties & Fifties Popular Jewelry,* Schiffer Publishing, 1994; Roseann Ettinger, *Popular Jewelry: 1840–1940, Second Edition,* Schiffer Publishing, 1997; Roseann Ettinger, *Popular Jewelry of the '60s, '70s & '80s,* Schiffer Publishing, 1997; Sandy Fichtner and Lynn Ann Russell, *Rainbow of Rhinestone Jewelry,* Schiffer Publishing, 1996.

Jill Gallina, *Christmas Pins: Past and Present,* Collector Books, 1996; S. Sylvia Henzel, *Collectible Costume Jewelry, Third Edition,* Krause Publications, 1997; Sibylle Jargstorf, *Baubles, Buttons and Beads: The Heritage of Bohemia,* Schiffer Publishing, 1991; Sibylle Jargstorf, *Glass in Jewelry: Hidden Artistry in Glass,* Schiffer Publishing, 1991; Lyngerda Kelley and Nancy Schiffer, *Costume*

Jewelry: The Great Pretenders, Revised Edition, Schiffer Publishing, 1996; Lyngerda Kelley and Nancy Schiffer, *Plastic Jewelry, Third Edition,* Schiffer Publishing, 1996; J. L. Lynnlee, *All That Glitters,* Schiffer Publishing, 1986, 1996 value update.

Christie Romero, *Warman's Jewelry,* Wallace–Homestead, Krause Publications, 1995; Nancy N. Schiffer, *Costume Jewelry: The Fun of Collecting,* Schiffer Publishing, 1988, 1996 value update; Nancy N. Schiffer, *Rhinestones!,* Schiffer Publishing, 1993; Cherri Simonds, *Collectible Costume Jewelry,* Collector Books, 1997; Harrice Simons Miller, *Costume Jewelry: Identification and Price Guide, Second Edition,* Avon Books, 1994; Sheryl Gross Shatz, *What's It Made Of?: A Jewelry Materials Identification Guide,* published by author, 1991; Nicholas D. Snider, *Sweetheart Jewelry and Collectibles,* Schiffer Publishing, 1995.

Bangle Bracelet, Bakelite, painted enamel, yellow, carved and painted harlequin motif, c1930 . . . . . . $ 275.00
Bangle Bracelet, plastic, lemon yellow, Monet 28.00
Bracelet, hinged brass bangle encircled with row of applied faux baroque pearls, Miriam Haskell, c1950 . . . . 125.00
Bracelet, Lucite and rhinestones, mottled opaque and translucent white, c1950 . . . . 70.00
Brooch, Bakelite, paint, yellow carved fawn, painted spots and features, c1930 . . . . 70.00
Brooch, Bakelite, yellow anchor with working compass in center, c1935 . . . . 100.00
Brooch, brass, enamel, convex–sided rect plaque, cloisonne' enameled design, overlapping vasiform shapes in shades of periwinkle blue, purple, and pink on red ground, counter–enameled reverse, c1950 . . . . 160.00
Brooch, brass, stamped, seal balancing colorless Lucite ball on nose 20.00
Brooch, carved translucent amber–colored Bakelite stylized horse's head, brass rivets at eye and mouth, C–catch, c1935 . . . . 90.00

Bracelet, gold colored metal expandable band set with colorless rhinestones, early 1940s, $75.00.

Suite, necklace and clip earrings, copper, leaf motif, paper label "Genuine Copper," 15" l necklace, $15.00.

Brooch, copper, "Starburst," inset oval mottled blue–turquoise enameled plaque, Matisse/Renoir, c1955 . . . . 85.00
Brooch, gold–plated metal, dragonfly, brushed finish, red glass eyes, Trifari, c1960 . . . . 45.00
Brooch, silver tone, blue–green irid rhinestones, Schiaparelli 255.00
Charm, yg, cat, enamel eyes 38.00
Choker, 8 fine strands, silver colored, Sarah Coventry 15.00
Clip, rhodium–plated white metal, 5–petaled flower, enameled, small rhinestone accents, Trifari, c1940. . . . 125.00
Cuff Links, pr, white metal, 2–sided octagons, circular mother–of–pearl center, blue enamel scallops, mkd "Kum–A–Part, Registered Baer & Wilde" ½" d 30.00
Earrings, pr, gold–plated white metal, faux pearls and rhinestones, elaborate pendent drops, 4" l, clips, KJL, c1965 . . . . 50.00
Earrings, pr, gold–plated white metal, 5–petal flower-heads with colorless and green rhinestones, clips, Nettie Rosenstein 15.00
Earrings, pr, thermoset plastic, light blue plastic convex oval disks, oval aurora borealis and colorless rhinestones, clips, mkd "Weiss," c1955 . . . . 60.00
Earrings, pr, domed Lucite discs, painted black surface, colorless int, set with colorless circular rhinestone clipbacks, 1⅛" d, c1955 . . . . 50.00
Hat Ornament, celluloid and metal, notched light brown triangles set with colorless rhinestone threaded pinstem, c1930 . . . . 35.00
Headband, blue celluloid cylindrical band set with blue rhinestones overlapping with ivory–colored flowerhead–shaped adjustable clasp set with blue rhinestones and ovoid pearlescent white tips, clasp mkd "pat apld for," c1920 . . . . 180.00
Necklace, black glass faceted beads, Miriam Haskell, c1950, 60" l 80.00
Necklace, crystal, double strand, Hobe 45.00

Necklace, pink glass, adjustable choker with
    prong–set links, hook and chain closure, attached
    metal tag mkd "Vendome," c1950. . . . . **155.00**
Pendant, elephant head, orig chain, Razza **25.00**
Pendant, large green stone surrounded by clear rhine-
    stone leaflets, Sarah Coventry **25.00**
Pendant, pr of stylized fish, marbled green Bakelite
    domed disks with carved and painted features,
    mounted on wood plaque with carved wood fins,
    c1940, 2½ x 3" **110.00**
Ring, Bakelite, marbled blue–green tapered dome,
    laminated black dot center, c1940 . . . . **60.00**
Suite, bracelet and earrings, multicolored stones,
    Hollycraft, dated 1950 . . . . **70.00**
Suite, bangle bracelet and earrings, plastic, hinged
    off–white bangle, front half pave'–set with black
    rhinestones, matching hoop earring clips, c1955 . . . . . **100.00**
Sweater Guard, rhinestone **30.00**
Tie Bar, fishing rod, Swank **10.00**

JOHNSON BROTHERS

Johnson Brothers was established in 1883. Three brothers, Alfred,
Frederick, and Henry Johnson, purchased the bankrupt J. W.
Pankhurst Company, a tableware manufactory in Hanley,
Staffordshire, England. Although begun on a small scale, the com-
pany prospered and expanded.

In 1896, Robert, a fourth brother, joined the firm. Robert, who
lived and worked in the United States, was assigned the task of
expanding the company's position in the American market. By
1914 Johnson Brothers owned and operated five additional factories scattered throughout Hanley, Tunstall, and Burslem.

Johnson Brothers continued to grow throughout the 1960s with
acquisitions of tableware manufacturing plants in Hamilton,
Ontario, Canada, and Croydon, Australia. Two additional English
plants were acquired in 1960 and 1965.

Johnson Brothers became part of the Wedgwood Group in 1968.

Reference: Harry L. Rinker, *Dinnerware of the 20th Century: The
Top 500 Patterns,* House of Collectibles, 1997.

Coaching Scenes, blue, bread and butter plate, 6" d . . . . **$ 5.00**
Coaching Scenes, blue, creamer and cov sugar **50.00**
Coaching Scenes, blue, cup and saucer **15.00**
Coaching Scenes, blue, dinner plate, 10" d **15.00**
Coaching Scenes, blue, platter, oval, 12" d **35.00**
Coaching Scenes, blue, vegetable bowl, oval **30.00**
Coaching Scenes, blue, vegetable bowl, round **25.00**
English Chippendale, bread and butter plate **8.00**
English Chippendale, cereal bowl, lug handle **15.00**
English Chippendale, creamer **30.00**
English Chippendale, cup and saucer **20.00**
English Chippendale, dinner plate **17.50**
English Chippendale, gravy boat. **50.00**
English Chippendale, luncheon plate **12.00**
English Chippendale, salad plate, 7½" sq **10.00**
English Chippendale, sugar, cov **30.00**
English Chippendale, vegetable, round **40.00**
Friendly Village, bread and butter plate, 6" d **3.00**
Friendly Village, butter, cov **25.00**

Coaching Scenes, blue, platter, oval, 14" l, $60.00.

Friendly Village, cereal bowl, sq **5.00**
Friendly Village, cup and saucer **10.00**
Friendly Village, dinner plate, 10" d **8.00**
Friendly Village, milk pitcher, 5½" h **30.00**
Friendly Village, relish, 8". **20.00**
Friendly Village, salt and pepper shakers, pr **28.00**
Friendly Village, teapot, cov **45.00**
Friendly Village, vegetable bowl, round **15.00**
Old Britain Castles, blue, coffeepot, cov **80.00**
Old Britain Castles, blue, cup and saucer **17.50**
Old Britain Castles, blue, dinner plate **15.00**
Old Britain Castles, blue, fruit bowl, 5⅛" **10.00**
Old Britain Castles, blue, gravy boat. **45.00**
Old Britain Castles, blue, platter, oval, 15" l **75.00**
Old Britain Castles, blue, salad plate **10.00**
Old Britain Castles, pink, berry bowl, 5" d **10.00**
Old Britain Castles, pink, bread and butter plate, 6" d **8.00**
Old Britain Castles, pink, creamer and sugar **12.00**
Old Britain Castles, pink, cup and saucer **16.00**
Old Britain Castles, pink, dinner plate, 10" d **16.00**
Old Britain Castles, pink, luncheon plate, 8¾" d **17.00**
Old Britain Castles, pink, platter, oval, 12" l **40.00**
Old Britain Castles, pink, salad plate, 7½" d **16.00**
Old Britain Castles, pink, serving tray, center handle **60.00**
Old Britain Castles, pink, vegetable bowl, 8½" sq **40.00**
Old English Countryside, brown, creamer **20.00**
Old English Countryside, brown, cup and saucer **18.00**
Old English Countryside, brown, luncheon plate **10.00**
Old English Countryside, brown, platter, oval, 12" l **35.00**
Old English Countryside, brown, sugar, cov **25.00**
Old English Countryside, brown, vegetable, cov,
    round **100.00**
Willow Blue, dinner plate **7.50**
Willow Blue, fruit bowl, 5⅛" **3.00**
Willow Blue, gravy boat and underplate **30.00**
Willow Blue, pitcher, 5½" **25.00**
Willow Blue, salt and pepper shakers, pr **28.00**
Willow Blue, teapot, cov **45.00**
Willow Blue, vegetable, oval **17.50**

JOSEF FIGURINES

When Muriel Joseph George could no longer obtain Lucite during World War II for her plastic jewelry, she used clay to fashion ceramic jewelry. George loved to model, making a wide variety of serious and whimsical figures for her own amusement.

In 1946 Muriel and her husband, Tom, made their first commercial ceramic figures in their garage. The printer misspelled Joseph, thus inadvertently creating the company's signature name Josef. Despite the company's quick growth, early 1950s cheap Japanese imitations severely undercut its market.

In 1959 Muriel, Tom, and George Good established George Imports. Production was moved to the Katayama factory in Japan in order to cut costs. Muriel created her designs in America, sent them to Japan with production instructions, and approved samples. Once again, the company enjoyed a period of prosperity.

In 1974 the company became George–Good Corporation. When Muriel Joseph George retired in 1981, George Good purchased her interest in the company. Muriel continued to do design work until 1984. In 1985 George Good sold the company to Applause, Inc.

References: Dee Harris, Jim and Kaye Whitaker, *Josef Originals: Charming Figurines with Price Guide,* Schiffer Publishing, 1994; Jim and Kaye Whitaker, *Josef Originals: A Second Look,* Schiffer Publishing, 1997.

August, Dolls of the Month, 3¼" h	$ 35.00
Austria, Little Internationals, 3½" h	35.00
Bongo, 4¼" h	45.00
Camel, 2½" h	30.00
Chinese Boy, blue hat,	45.00
Christmas Belle	35.00
Cleo	45.00
Cookie Angel, Little Commandments, 3¾" h	28.00
Deer	18.00
Elephant With Swatter	20.00
Girl with Poodle, Party Cake Toppers	28.00

December, Birthstone Dolls, 3½" h, $35.00.

Good Luck Angel	35.00
Hedy, 4¼" h	50.00
Japanese Girl, fan down, 4½" h	50.00
Jill, Nursery Rhymes, 4" h	28.00
Juliette, 5½" h	45.00
July, Birthstone Doll	22.00
Kittens Playing With Yarn	20.00
Mary Ann	35.00
Melissa	60.00
Saturday, Day of the Week	40.00
Shepherd	32.00
Sylvia, 5¾" h	45.00
Tammy, Musicale, 6" h	65.00
Teddy, 4¼" h	50.00

JUKEBOXES

A jukebox is an amplified coin–operated phonograph. The 1940s and early 1950s were its golden age, a period when bubble machines ruled every teenage hangout from dance hall to drug store. Portable radios, television's growth, and "Top 40" radio were responsible for the jukebox's decline in the 1960s.

Pre–1938 jukeboxes are made primarily of wood and resemble a phonograph or radio cabinet. Wurlitzer and Rock–Ola, whose jukeboxes often featured brightly colored plastic and animation units, made the best of the 78 rpm jukeboxes of the 1938–1948 period. The 45 rpm jukebox, made famous by the television show Happy Days, arrived on the scene in 1940 and survived until 1960. Seeburg was the principal manufacturer of these machines. Beginning in 1961, manufacturers often hid the record mechanism. These machines lack the collector appeal of their earlier counterparts.

References: Michael Adams, Jürgen Lukas, and Thomas Maschke, *Jukeboxes,* Schiffer Publishing, 1995; Jerry Ayliffe, *American Premium Guide To Jukeboxes And Slot Machines, Gumballs, Trade Stimulators, Arcade, 3rd Edition,* Books Americana, Krause Publications, 1991; Scott Wood, *A Blast From the Past Jukeboxes: A Pictorial Price Guide,* L–W Book Sales, 1992.

Periodicals: *Always Jukin',* 221 Yesler Way, Seattle, WA 98104; *Antique Amusements, Slot Machines & Jukebox Gazette,* 909 26th St NW, Washington, DC 20037; *Coin–Op Classics,* 17844 Toiyabe St, Fountain Valley, CA 92708; *Gameroom Magazine,* PO Box 41, Keyport, NJ 07735; *Jukebox Collector,* 2545 WE 60th Court, Des Moines, IA 50317.

AMI–A, 1946	$ 5,000.00
AMI–C, 1949	2,500.00
AMI G–200, 1956	2,000.00
Rock–Ola 1426, 1946	7,000.00
Rock–Ola 1428, 1948	4,500.00
Rock–Ola 1434 Super Rocket, 1951	4,500.00
Rock–Ola 1448, 1954	3,000.00
Rock–Ola 1484 Wall Mount, 1961	3,500.00
Rock–Ola Commando, 1942	10,000.00
Seeburg 100B, 1950	2,750.00
Seeburg 100C	3,000.00
Seeburg 100G	1,600.00
Seeburg 100JL	1,800.00
Seeburg 100R, 1954	3,000.00

Wurlitzer 1015, 1946, $7,500.00.

Chocolate Mold, tin, 10⁷/₈" h, $150.00.

Seeburg 147 Trash Can, 1947	3,500.00
Seeburg 148, 1948	2,750.00
Seeburg 200KS	2,200.00
Seeburg 222, 1959	3,000.00
Seeburg BNC1	1,000.00
Seeburg Colonel	1,500.00
Seeburg G, 1953	3,000.00
Seeburg H–148	500.00
Seeburg LS1	1,000.00
Seeburg Q160	1,000.00
Seeburg Regal	1,500.00
Seeburg V–200, 1955	4,000.00
Wurlitzer 41	6,000.00
Wurlitzer 61, 1938	3,500.00
Wurlitzer 750, 1940	8,500.00
Wurlitzer 1015, 1946	10,000.00
Wurlitzer 1080, 1947	8,000.00
Wurlitzer 1100, 1948	6,000.00
Wurlitzer 2000, 1956	3,500.00
Wurlitzer Victory	7,500.00

KEWPIES

Rose Cecil O'Neill (1876–1944) created the Kewpie doll. This famous nymph first appeared in the December 1909 issue of *Ladies' Home Journal*. The first doll, designed in part by Joseph L. Kallus, was marketed in 1913. Kallus owned the Cameo Doll Company; Geo. Borgfelt Company owned the Kewpie production and distribution rights.

Most of the early Kewpie items were manufactured in Germany. American and Japanese manufacturers also played a role. Composition Kewpie dolls did not arrive until after World War II.

O'Neill created a wide variety of Kewpie characters. Do not overlook Ho–Ho, Kewpie–Gal, Kewpie–Kin, Ragsy, and Scootles.

O'Neill spent the final years of her life in Bonniebrook, a town in southwest Missouri near the Bear Creek. Kewpie licensing continues, especially in the limited edition collectibles area.

Reference: Cynthia Gaskill, *The Kewpie Kompanion: A Kompendium of Kewpie Knowledge*, Gold Horse Publishing, 1994.

Collectors' Club: International Rose O'Neill Club, PO Box 668, Branson, MO 65616.

Bank, still, papier mâché	$ 50.00
Bell, brass	65.00
Book, *Sing a Song of Safety*, 1937	100.00
Child's Feeding Dish, Kewpies and alphabet border, 10" d	155.00
Chocolate Mold, tin, gang mold, 3 cavities	75.00
Crumb Tray, brass	30.00
Cup and Saucer, multicolored, sgd "Rose O'Neill Wilson"	110.00
Doll, vinyl, jointed, orig clothes, Cameo Doll Products, Port Allegheny, 14" h	70.00
Figure, bisque, 6" h, price for 3	40.00
Magazine Articles, *Ladies Home Journal*, 1925 through 1928 issues, 10 pgs	110.00
Pillowcase, "The Kewpies in the Moon," c1930, 16 x 19"	160.00
Ring, Kewpie raising one hand and kicking one foot, sterling silver, c1920s	85.00
Tin, round, 9 Kewpies; 2 on tightrope, 2 on ground, 5 clinging to rope, c1935, 5³/₄" d, 3¹/₂" h	25.00

KEYS & KEY CHAINS

People collect keys and key chains more for their novelty than any other reason. Because they are made in such quantities, few examples are rare. Most collectors specialize, focusing on a specific subject such as automobile, hotel, presentation keys ("Key to the City"), railroad, etc.

Beware of fantasy keys such as keys to the Tower of London, a *Titanic* cabin, or a Hollywood movie star's dressing room.

Collectors' Clubs: Key Collectors International, 1427 Lincoln Blvd, Santa Monica, CA 90401; License Plate Key Chain & Mini License Plate Collectors, 888 Eighth Ave, New York, NY 10019.

Key, car, Chrysler Omega, brass, 5–pc set, 1933, Yale . . **$ 18.00**
Key, door, brass, standard bow and bit, 4" l. **5.00**
Key, gate, iron, bit type, 8" l. **6.50**
Key, hotel, steel, bit type, bronze tag **3.50**
Key, jewelers, steel and brass, 5 point. **12.50**
Key, presentation, Key to the City, iron, brass plated,
    Master Lock Co, 1933 World's Fair, 2" l. **8.00**
Key, railroad, CM&ST P SIGNAL, Chicago, Milwau-
    kee & St. Paul. **12.00**
Key, ship, pin tumbler type, USN tag **2.50**
Key Chain, American Motorcycle Association, brass,
    raised image of cycle rider, worn enamel, mail
    drop guarantee on back, 1940 Gypsy Tour. **50.00**
Key Chain, Camel Cigarettes adv, silvered brass pen-
    dant trademark camel and Spanish inscription, sil-
    vered brass chain, 1930s, 1¼" d **30.00**
Key Chain, Esso Gasoline adv, gold–finished metal,
    Esso logo below slogan "Put a Tiger in Your Tank,"
    raised tiger head symbol, serial number on
    back for Happy Motoring Club, 1960s, 1⅜" d **12.00**
Key Chain, Hercules Powder Co adv, brass, rect, logo
    and company name, reverse "Fiftieth Anniversary
    1912–1962," 1¼" l. **15.00**
Key Chain, New York World's Fair, domed acrylic
    over silver and black unisphere, title, dates, flat sil-
    vered metal back, worn, 1964 . . . . **20.00**
Key Chain, Packard, metal key holder, attached metal
    ring, gold and silver shading, blue, white, and
    black enamel of convertible titled "Packard
    Panther," brass Packard logo, late 1950s **25.00**
Key Chain, Richard Nixon, 2–knife blades, white
    plastic sides, brass case, red and blue lettering
    "President Nixon. Now more than ever" **20.00**

KITCHEN COLLECTIBLES

Until recently, the kitchen was the central family focal point. It was the center for food preparation and eating, either at a table by a window or nook. Many post–1945 ranch house designs did not provide an independent dining room. Dining took place in an open space directly off the kitchen or living room.

Currently collectors are in love with the kitchen of the 1920s and 30s. A few progressive collectors are focusing on the kitchens of the 50s and 60s. Color and style are the two collecting keys. Bright blue, green, and red enamel handled utensils are in demand, not for use but to display on walls. Everything, from flatware to appliances, in Streamline Modern and Post–War Modern design styles is hot. Do not overlook wall clocks and wall decorations. There are even individuals collecting Tupperware.

References: Linda Campbell Franklin, *300 Years of Housekeeping Collectibles*, Books Americana, Krause Publications, 1992; Linda Campbell Franklin, *300 Years Of Kitchen Collectibles, Fourth Edition*, Krause Publications, 1997; Michael J. Goldberg, *Groovy Kitchen Designs for Collectors: 1935–1965*, Schiffer Publishing, 1996; Frances Johnson, *Kitchen Antiques,* Schiffer Publishing,

1996; Jan Lindenberger, *Black Memorabilia For The Kitchen: A Handbook And Price Guide,* Schiffer Publishing, 1992.

Jan Lindenberger, *Fun Kitchen Collectibles,* Schiffer Publishing, 1996; Jan Lindenberger, *The 50s and 60s Kitchen: A Collector's Handbook & Price Guide,* Schiffer Publishing, 1994; Barbara Mauzy, *The Complete Book of Kitchen Collecting,* Schiffer Publishing, 1997; C. L. Miller, *Jewel Tea Grocery Products,* Schiffer Publishing, 1996; Dana Gehman Morykan and Harry L. Rinker, *Warman's Country Antiques & Collectibles, Third Edition,* Wallace–Homestead, Krause Publications, 1996.

Ellen M. Plante, *Kitchen Collectibles: An Illustrated Price Guide,* Wallace–Homestead, Krause Publications, 1991; Diane W. Stoneback, *Kitchen Collectibles: The Essential Buyer's Guide,* Wallace–Homestead, Krause Publications, 1994; April M. Tvorak, *A History And Price Guide To Mothers–In–The–Kitchen,* published by author, 1994.

Newsletters: *Cast Iron Cookware News,* 28 Angela Ave, San Anselmo, CA 94960; *Kitchen Antiques & Collectibles News,* 3634 Laurel Ridge Dr, Harrisburg, PA 17110; *Piebirds Unlimited,* 14 Harmony School Rd, Flemington, NJ 08822.

Collectors' Clubs: Cookie Cutter Collectors Club, 1167 Teal Rd SW, Dellroy, OH 44620; Griswold & Cast–Iron Cookware Assoc, 54 Macon Ave, Asheville, NC 28801; International Society for Apple Parer Entusiasts, 3911 Morgan Center Rd, Utica, OH 43080; Jelly Jammers, 110 White Oak Dr, Butler, PA 16001.

Note: See Advertising, Appliances, Cookbooks, Cookie Jars, Egg Beaters, Fire–King, Food Molds, Fruit Jars, Graniteware, Griswold, Kitchen Glassware, Pyrex, Reamers, Wagner Ware, Yellow Ware, and individual glass and pottery categories for additional listings.

Advertising Trade Card, Briddell Cutlery Factory, 1930s . . **$ 5.00**
Apron, cotton, blue and white floral print, front
    pockets, c1940. . . . . **25.00**
Baking Pan, graniteware, blue and white swirl. **100.00**
Bean Pot, cov, orange, Jugtown Pottery **48.00**
Bean Slicer, Bean–X, blued steel blade, springs **15.00**
Blender, Drink Master Mixall, Art Deco design,
    chrome, black metal stand, 14" h **35.00**
Box, Aunt Jemima Pancake Flour, cardboard **60.00**
Bread Box, metal, Betsy Ross Moderne pattern,
    white, red trim, mkd "Roll–A–Way, E M Meder
    Co," c1930s. **20.00**
Bread Tray Cover, filet crochet, white, "Staff of Life,"
    c1925, 12½" l **8.00**

Corn Stick Pan, cast iron, unmarked, $30.00.

Broiler, Royal Master Appliance Co, Miriam, OH, 1930s **28.00**

Bun Warmer, chrome, Art Deco style, red, yellow, and green wood ball feet and finial, removable fitted wire basket, domed cover, 1930s **30.00**

Butter Mold, cast aluminum, star shape, R. Hall, c1940 . . . . **25.00**

Cake Decoration, bisque, bride and groom, sgd "Wilton," c1960, 6" h **18.00**

Calendar, A. C. Stram Groceries–URMA Brand–Green Bay, Dawn of Day print, full pad, 1930 . . . . **25.00**

Can Opener, Sharp Easy, combination can and bottle opener, knife sharpener, wood handle, iron top, Premier Mfg Co, Detroit, MI, patented 1922 . . . . **18.00**

Canner, Iron Horse Cold Pack, Rochester Can Co, tin, wood handles, wire rack and lifter, 1930s, 13¾" d **70.00**

Catalog, General Electric Company, Schenectady, NY, "Freedom," The Joy of Living Electrically–The Healthy Kitchen, refrigerators, stoves, dishwashers, etc, color illus, 1933, 28 pgs, 5½" x 8" **25.00**

Catalog, Washburn Co, kitchen utensils, 116 pgs, 1924 . . . . **55.00**

Catalog, Westinghouse All Electric Kitchens, 1936, 20 pgs, 8½" x 11" **15.00**

Cereal Bowl, plastic, Tony the Tiger, large orange paw base, 1981, 5" d **18.00**

Coffee Maker, Sunbeam Dripolator, Coffee Master, 2 pc, chrome and Bakelite, Art Deco design on side, 12½" h **25.00**

Cookbook, *Encyclopedia of Cooking*, Mary Margaret McBride, 12 vol, hard cov, 3,006 pgs **68.00**

Cookie Cutter, metal, sprinkling can, Wilton **2.75**

Cookie Cutter, plastic, arrow, hot pink, Wilton **1.50**

Cookie Cutter, plastic, gingerbread boy, blue, Betty Crocker adv **2.00**

Cookie Cutter, plastic, leprechaun, green and tan, Hallmark, 1979 . . . . **2.25**

Cookie Cutter, Strawberry Shortcake, Hallmark **12.00**

Cookie Cutter, tin, lady wearing hat and long dress, strap handle, rolled edges **40.00**

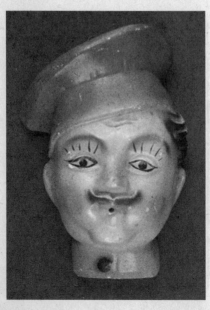

String Holder, chalk-ware, red hat, green collar, 8" h, $50.00.

Cookie Roller, tin, wire, 3 rollers, c1930, orig 2 box, Guirier **45.00**

Corn Cutter, wood, hand–forged blade, carved wood handle **15.00**

Coupon, Mirro Aluminum Bake Pan, printed, black on pale orange, 20¢ off a 55¢ bake pan, Lundt & Co, Moline, IL, 1920s, 8½" x 11" **12.00**

Cutting Board, maple, figural pig, c1930, 9 x 19" **20.00**

Deep Fryer, Betty Crocker, Model 9–A, General Mills, chrome, black Bakelite base, aluminum basket, 11 x 7" **30.00**

Egg Cooker, Hankscraft, model 599, ceramic, chrome, yellow, 1930s **20.00**

Egg Cup, ceramic, Lone Ranger, raised portrait, Lone Ranger Inc, copyright on base, c1950, 2½" h **38.00**

Flour Sifter, Miracle Electric Co, ivory metal body, blue wooden handle, decal label, 1930s **50.00**

Food Grinder, Keen Kutter, tinned cast iron, Sommons Hardware, model K110 . . . . **30.00**

French Fry Cutter, Maid of Honor, tin, stamped, 1930s **8.00**

Hot Pad, Reddy Kilowatt, red, white, and yellow, c1950, 5½" sq **35.00**

Ice Bucket, aluminum, handwrought, Canterbury Arts, hammered, double walled, rubber seal, 8" h **48.00**

Milk Bottle Cap, Christmas Seal Cap of 1939 . . . . **8.00**

Mixer, Handymix, #D–121125, Mary Dunbar, Chicago Electric Mfg Co, stand, 2 beaters, push button, 1930s, 11½" h **20.00**

Mixer, KitchenAid, Hobart Corp, cream colored body, aluminum trim, handle, and bowl, wire whisk beater, dough hook, aluminum meat grinder, 1939, 14 x 12" **55.00**

Muffin Pan, graniteware, gray, 6 muffins **25.00**

Napkin Ring, metal, lady holding stick, c1942 . . . . **18.00**

Nut Grinder, Climax, cast iron, tin, gas jar, threaded tin hopper, 1940s **15.00**

Pie Plate, orange ground, black concentric circles dec, Jugtown Pottery, 9½" d **72.00**

Playing Cards, Hotpoint All–Electric Kitchen adv, 1950s kitchen scene **20.00**

Popcorn Popper, Knapp–Monarch, Cat #12A–500B, oil, aluminum body, wire base, domed glass lid with vented sides, walnut handles, measuring cup **25.00**

Poster, Keen Kutter adv, 1950s, 15 x 22" **12.00**

Potato Ricer, Handy Things, Ludington, MI, tinned metal presser and cup, iron handles painted red, c1940, 12" l **15.00**

Reamer, 2 pcs, strawberry shape, red, green leaves and handle, Occupied Japan, 3¾" h **70.00**

Rolling Pin, maple, 14" l **30.00**

Sign, Remington adv, cardboard, "Knives that Bite," woman carving ham, full color, 1929, 7 x 10½" **35.00**

Spoon Rest, aluminum, figural black chef head with open mouth, 1930s, 4 x 6" **80.00**

Sugar, cov, 3¾" h, tobacco spit glaze, Jugtown Pottery **40.00**

Tablecloth, linen, white, printed floral and fruit dec, c1940, 56 x 66" **30.00**

Tea Kettle, Mirro, aluminum, nickel chrome domed body, Bakelite handle, 1930s, 4 qt **25.00**

Toaster, Estate Stove Co, Hamilton, OH, Model 177, nickel, sq, canted sides, pierced door rack on 4 sides turn simultaneously with one button movement, 1922 .... **80.00**

Toothpick Holder, ruby stained, Button Arches pattern, "Mother 1947' **22.00**

Toy Baking Set, Little Orphan Annie, Gold Medal Pastry Set, Transogram Toy, 1930s **80.00**

Vegetable Slicer, A & J, Binghamton, NY, wood handle, twisted wire blade, c1930, 16" l.............. **25.00**

Waffle Iron, Manning Bowman, Art Deco style, stepped Bakelite ft, drop handles, reeded edges and top, booklet, 1930s, 7" d plates, 9½" sq base **35.00**

Whipper, Sears Kenmore, cream metal dome top, clear glass bottom, dark blue Bakelite knob, 1940s **20.00**

KITCHEN GLASSWARE

Depression Glass is a confusing and limited term. Many of the patterns considered Depression Glass were in production long before 1929. It actually is a generic term for glass produced in the United States from the early 1920s through the 1960s. Further, Depression Glass patterns are only a fraction of the thousands of glass patterns and types produced during this period.

Kitchen Glassware is a catchall category for inexpensive kitchen and table glass produced during this period. Hundreds of companies made it. Hocking, Hazel Atlas, McKee, U.S. Glass, and Westmoreland are a few examples.

Kitchen glassware was used on the table and for storage. It usually has a thick body, designed to withstand heavy and daily use. Decorative motifs, often in the mold, include arches, fluting, thumbprint patterns, and ribs.

The category is dominated by storage glass items prior to 1940. Following World War II, tabletop glass prevailed. Kitchen glassware was a favored giveaway premium in the 1950s and early 1960s.

References: Gene Florence, *Kitchen Glassware of the Depression Years, Fifth Edition,* Collector Books, 1995, 1997 value update.

Newsletter: *Knife Rests of Yesterday & Today,* 4046 Graham St, Pleasanton, CA 94566.

Collectors' Club: Glass Knife Collectors Club, PO Box 342, Los Alamitos, CA 90720.

Note: For additional listings see Depression Glass, Fire–King, Pyrex, Reamers, and individual glass company categories.

Batter Bowl, large, handle .... **$ 40.00**
Batter Jug, cobalt blue, Paden City **42.00**
Bowl, Criss Cross, cobalt blue, Hazel Atlas, 7¾" d **75.00**

Canister, cov, green jadeite, Jeannette, 48 oz, 5½" h, $30.00.

Bowl, floral decal, white, McKee, 9" d **22.00**
Bowl, green, horizontal rib, Jeannette, 9¾" d **25.00**
Butter Dish, cov, Criss Cross, crystal, Hazel Atlas, 1 lb ... **18.00**
Butter Dish, cov, green transparent, ribbed, Hocking..... **80.00**
Canister, sq, Jeannette, 48 oz, 5½" h................ **30.00**
Canister, white, McKee **40.00**
Canister, yellow, McKee, 48 oz.................... **45.00**
Cheese Dish, green, Kraft....................... **25.00**
Creamer, Criss Cross, crystal, Hazel Atlas **18.00**
Cruet, pink, Hazel Atlas........................ **35.00**
Cup, Panel Optic, green, Federal **8.00**
Drawer Knob, crystal, ribbed **10.00**
Drawer Knob, peacock blue...................... **15.00**
Egg Cup, yellow transparent, Hazel Atlas **2.50**
Grease Jar, cov, Vitrock, black circles and flowers....... **40.00**
Grease Jar, yellow, Hocking **30.00**
Ice Cream Dish, Lido, pink **20.00**
Ice Pail, low, pink, bail handle **18.00**
Juice Tumbler, pink, ribbed, Hocking **15.00**
Knife, Block, crystal, 9" l, orig box **35.00**
Knife, Three Leaf, blue, Durex, 9¼" l............... **28.00**
Knife, Three Leaf, crystal, Durex, 9¼" l.............. **18.00**
Knife, Three Star, dark pink, 9½" l................. **25.00**
Mayonnaise Ladle, crystal, gold trim................ **12.00**
Measuring Cup, amber, 3 spout, handleless, 1 cup, Federal **32.00**
Measuring Cup, amber, 3 spout, 1 cup, Hazel Atlas **35.00**
Measuring Cup, crystal, Kelloggs **12.00**
Measuring Cup, crystal, 3 spout, handleless, Federal...... **8.00**
Measuring Cup, green, stippled, 2 cup **20.00**
Milk Jug, pink, Hazel Atlas...................... **18.00**
Milk Jug, cobalt blue, Paden City **35.00**
Mixing Bowl, Criss Cross, 6" d, crystal, Hazel Atlas...... **10.00**
Mixing Bowl, Jennyware, ultramarine, 6" d, Jeannette **32.00**
Mixing Bowl, pink, handle, large, US Glass **55.00**

Knife, stars and diamonds, pink, Vitex–Glas, 9⅛" l, $20.00.

Shaker, blue delphite, 6" h, $10.00.

Mixing Bowl, white, aqua kitchen utensils, Pyrex, nested set of 5 . . . . **42.00**

Mixing Bowl, Vitrock, paneled, Anchor Hocking, 10¼" d **15.00**

Mug, green, Jeannette **25.00**

Pepper Shaker, jadeite, Hocking. **20.00**

Pepper Shaker, sq, jade, McKee **15.00**

Pickle Ladle, crystal. **22.00**

Pitcher, jade, small, McKee **32.00**

Preserve Jar, Hazel Atlas. **12.00**

Punch Ladle, crystal. **28.00**

Reamer, custard, custard, emb "McK," McKee, 6" **32.00**

Reamer, green, large, Jeannette. **18.00**

Reamer, jadite, emb Sunkist **50.00**

Reamer, seville yellow, McKee **18.00**

Refrigerator Dish, cov, Criss Cross, green, Hazel Atlas, 8" sq **55.00**

Refrigerator Dish, cov, green transparent, ribbed, Hocking. **18.00**

Refrigerator Dish, cov, chalaine blue, 4 x 4", Jeannette **130.00**

Refrigerator Dish, cov, seville yellow, McKee **18.00**

Refrigerator Dish, yellow transparent, Hazel Atlas, 4½" x 5" **25.00**

Refrigerator Jar, cov, seville yellow, McKee, 10 oz **20.00**

Rolling Pin, blown, light amber **150.00**

Salad Set, fork and spoon, clear, red teardrop handles **25.00**

Salad Set, fork and spoon, pink and crystal **48.00**

Salt, Hocking, short, round, diamond, crystal **25.00**

Salt and Pepper Shakers, pr, white, green lettering, Anchor Hocking. **45.00**

Salt and Pepper Shakers, pr, white, McKee **15.00**

Sherbet, Panel Optic, green, Federal **8.00**

Soap Dish, Westite, black. **48.00**

Spice Canister, Jeanette, 3" h **25.00**

Sugar Shaker, green, Jeanette **45.00**

Towel Bar, jadeite, 17" l. **28.00**

Tumbler, Criss Cross, crystal, Hazel Atlas, 9 oz **38.00**

Tumbler, custard, McKee **10.00**

Water Bottle, cov, clear, Anchor Hocking **12.00**

Water Bottle, dark green, Owens Illinois. **20.00**

KNOWLES, EDWIN

In 1900 Edwin M. Knowles founded the Edwin M. Knowles China Company. The company's offices were located in East Liverpool, Ohio, the plant in Chester, West Virginia. From its beginnings, the company made a commitment to remaining current with technological advances. The company's products included dinnerware, kitchenware, specialties, and toilet wares.

Collectors focus primarily on the company's dinnerware. Three of its popular patterns are: Deanna (introduced 1938), a shape line featuring bright and pastel colors and decorations ranging from plaids to decals; Esquire (1956–1962), designed by Russel Wright and available in six design shapes and five colors; and Yorktown (introduced in 1936), a California patio modern shape line featuring bold solid colors or decals in patterns such as Golden Wheat or Water Lily.

In 1913 the company expanded by opening a plant in Newell, West Virginia. Harker Pottery purchased the Chester plant in 1931. Knowles continued production at the Newell plant until operations ceased in 1963.

Do not confuse Edwin M. Knowles China Company with Knowles, Taylor, and Knowles. They are two separate firms. In the 1970s the Bradford Exchange bought the rights to the Knowles name and uses it as a backstamp on some limited edition collector plates. These plates are manufactured offshore, not in America. The Knowles name is only a front for marketing purposes.

References: Susan and Al Bagdade, *Warman's American Pottery and Porcelain,* Wallace–Homestead, Krause Publications, 1994; Jo Cunningham, *The Collector's Encyclopedia of American Dinnerware,* Collector Books, 1982, 1995 value update; Harvey Duke, *The Official Identification and Price Guide to Pottery and Porcelain, Eighth Edition,* House of Collectibles, 1995; Lois Lehner, *Lehner's Encyclopedia of U.S. Marks on Pottery, Porcelain & Clay,* Collector Books, 1988.

Alice Ann, bowl, oval, 8" d . . . . **$ 12.00**

Alice Ann, butter dish **22.00**

Alice Ann, creamer **5.00**

Alice Ann, jug. **18.00**

Alice Ann, plate, 8" d. **8.00**

Alice Ann, saucer **5.00**

Arcadia, casserole **25.00**

Arcadia, plate, 6" d **2.00**

Arcadia, platter **10.00**

Arcadia, sugar. **8.00**

Beverly, bowl, oval, 9½" l **12.00**

Beverly, casserole **22.00**

Beverly, creamer **5.00**

Beverly, cup **5.00**

Beverly, eggcup, double. **12.00**

Beverly, plate, 8½" d **6.00**

Beverly, platter, 11½". **12.00**

Beverly, teapot. **30.00**

Deanna, bread and butter plate, 6" d, yellow **8.00**

Deanna, butter dish, open, dark blue **15.00**

Deanna, casserole **22.00**

Deanna, chop plate **18.00**

Deanna, coffee server, green **38.00**

Tempo, platter, rose decal, gold trim, 13³/₄" l, $12.00.

Deanna, creamer and cov sugar, red and blue stripes	45.00
Deanna, cup and saucer, yellow	12.00
Deanna, dinner plate, 10" d, dark blue	15.00
Deanna, eggcup, double, turquoise	15.00
Deanna, gravy	15.00
Deanna, lug soup, yellow	8.00
Deanna, platter, Daisies	12.00
Deanna, saucer	2.00
Deanna, vegetable bowl, 8" d, orange–red	22.00
Diana, creamer	8.00
Diana, plate, 6" d	2.00
Diana, soup bowl	15.00
Diana, sugar	10.00
Esquire, bread and butter plate, Botanica, beige ground, 6¹/₄" d	8.00
Esquire, cereal bowl, Queen Anne's Lace, white ground, 6¹/₄" d	15.00
Esquire, creamer	12.00
Esquire, cup	15.00
Esquire, cup and saucer, Snowflower	22.00
Esquire, dinner plate, Grass, blue ground, 10³/₄" d	15.00
Esquire, fruit bowl, Snowflower, 5¹/₂" d	12.00
Esquire, plate, 9" d	8.00
Esquire, platter, Queen's Anne's Lace, 13" l	25.00
Esquire, salad plate, Seeds, 8¹/₄" d	12.00
Esquire, saucer	5.00
Esquire, sugar	40.00
Esquire, vegetable bowl, divided, Seeds	70.00
Marion, creamer	8.00
Marion, vegetable bowl	15.00
Potomac, butter, open	22.00
Potomac, chop plate	15.00
Potomac, cup	8.00
Roslyn, casserole	28.00
Roslyn, saucer	2.50
Sylvin, casserole	28.00
Sylvin, sugar	12.00
Tia Juana, bowl, 9" d	15.00
Tia Juana, mixing bowl	35.00
Tia Juana, plate, 9¹/₂" d	8.00
Tia Juana, platter	15.00
Tia Juana, shaker	12.00

Tia Juana, soup, flat, 8" d	20.00
Tia Juana, stack set, Utility Ware, set of 3	20.00
Tulip, cookie jar, Utility Ware	38.00
Tulip, pie plate, Utility Ware	20.00
Williamsburg, creamer	8.00
Williamsburg, saucer	2.50
Yorktown, bread and butter plate, 6" d, yellow	8.00
Yorktown, cereal bowl, 6" d, green	8.00
Yorktown, chop plate, 10³/₄" d, burgundy	20.00
Yorktown, coaster, white	10.00
Yorktown, cup and saucer, orange–red	12.00
Yorktown, custard cup, green	10.00
Yorktown, dinner plate, Picket Fence	15.00
Yorktown, gravy boat	12.00
Yorktown, salad plate, 8" d, cadet blue	15.00
Yorktown, teapot, orange–red	55.00

KNOWLES, TAYLOR & KNOWLES

Knowles, Taylor & Knowles made ceramics in East Liverpool, Ohio, from 1854 to 1931. The firm began when Isaac Knowles and Isaac Harvey built a plant to manufacture yellowware in 1854. Knowles bought out Harvey's interest in 1856. When John W. Taylor, Knowles' son–in–law, and Homer Knowles, Knowles' son, joined the firm in 1870, it became Knowles, Taylor & Knowles.

A new plant was built and opened in 1888. In 1889 the company introduced its famed Lotus Ware, a translucent, artistically designed, superior grade of art china. In 1901 the Knowles plant included 35 kilns and employed 700 workers.

In 1929 Knowles, Taylor, Knowles joined seven other companies as part of the American China Corporation. This new company failed, one of the many victims of the Great Depression of the early 1930s.

References: Mary Frank Gaston, *Collector's Encyclopedia of Knowles, Taylor & Knowles China: Identification & Values*, Collector Books, 1996; Timothy J. Kearns, *Knowles, Taylor & Knowles: American Bone China*, Schiffer Publishing, 1994.

Basket, applied twisted rope handle	$ 35.00
Boot, incised "H," 6¹/₄" h	55.00
Bowl, applied bow and ribbon, pale red glaze, blue highlights, 6 x 5¹/₂"	45.00
Bowl, rolled rim, applied rope design handles, turquoise, 9" d	75.00
Bowl, scalloped border, applied calla lilies on side, 9" d	45.00
Bowl, scalloped border, leaf design ext, turquoise	45.00
Bowl, twisted rope handles, peach monochrome finish, 3¹/₄" x 8¹/₂"	85.00
Candle Holder, bowl form, scalloped body	30.00
Candle Holders, pr, applied bow	45.00
Creamer and Sugar, open, applied floral handle	55.00
Creamer and Sugar, open, twisted rope handle, dimple marks, peach monochrome finish	65.00
Dish, divided, applied flowers and stems center handle, blue and raspberry glazed finish	60.00
Dish, divided, applied flowers and twisted vine center handle, light green and brown glaze finish	50.00
Dish, leaf design, light blue glaze, raspberry finish, 6" d	35.00

Dish, leaf shape, 6" w **35.00**
Figure, boy with barrel on back **40.00**
Figure, lamb, applied bow around neck **35.00**
Flower Holder, diamond shaped body, floral design,
    pedestal base **90.00**
Pitcher, curved sectional body, twisted rope handle,
    sgd "Eileen 1/21/43," 6¼" h **55.00**
Planter, figural duck, 4½" h **55.00**
Rooster, 6" h, green glaze **70.00**
Sugar, open, applied floral shape handle. **55.00**
Vase, abstract overlapping line design body, incised
    "SS," 6¼" h **40.00**
Vase, applied bow design, sgd "D," 4" h **50.00**
Vase, applied flower and leaf dec, 4" h. **60.00**
Vase, applied pear and leaves dec, 5½" h **55.00**
Vase, Art Deco style, scalloped edge, leaf design,
    5¼" sq. **50.00**
Vase, incised abstract leaf design, 5½" sq **45.00**
Vase, ovoid body, round neck, mkd "H," 6" h **45.00**
Vase, scalloped neck, applied flower and stem,
    incised leaf front, turquoise. **50.00**
Wall Pocket, applied flowers, stems, and leaves,
    matte blue monochrome glaze finish. **50.00**

KOREAN WAR

The Korean War began on June 25, 1950, when North Korean troops launched an invasion across the 38th parallel into South Korea. The United Nations ordered an immediate cease–fire and withdrawal of the invading forces. On June 27 President Harry Truman ordered U.S. Forces to South Korea to help repel the North Korean invasion. The United Nations Security Council adopted a resolution for armed intervention.

The first American ground forces arrived in Korea on July 1, 1950. General Douglas MacArthur was named commander of the United Nations forces on July 8, 1950. The landing at Inchon took place on September 15, 1950. U.S. troops reached the Yalu River on the Manchurian border in late November.

On November 29, 1950, Chinese Communist troops counterattacked. Seoul was abandoned on January 4, 1951, only to be recaptured on March 21, 1951. On April 11, 1951, President Truman relieved General MacArthur of his command. General Matthew Ridgway replaced him. By early July a cease–fire had been declared, North Korean troops withdrew above the 38th parallel, and truce talks began. A stalemate was reached.

On November 29,1952, President–elect Dwight Eisenhower flew to Korea to inspect the United Nations forces. An armistice was signed at Panmunjom by the United Nations, North Korea, and Chinese delegates on July 27, 1953.

Reference: Ron Manion, *American Military Collectibles Price Guide*, Antique Trader Books, 1995.

Periodical: *Military Trader*, PO Box 1050, Dubuque, IA 52004.

Ammunition Belt, olive drab web, brass fittings, 2
    olive drab web Carlisle bandage pouches . . . . **$ 22.00**
Ammunition Magazine, 30 round, M1 Carbine, black
    painted steel **10.00**
Book, *Ten Asian Languages,* unused, 1951 . . . . **75.00**

Military Insignia, Military Government Korea, embroidered cloth, $5.00.

Book, *This Is War!*, Duncan, photos, hard cov, dj,
    1980s, 200 pgs **35.00**
Bush Jacket, tan cotton, British, 1953 . . . . **40.00**
Dog Tags, aluminum, US style, Korean characters
    and service number **22.00**
Dog Tags, USMC, pr, oval, 1/50 tetanus shot date,
    bead neckchain **72.00**
Flight Suit, nylon, olive drab, woven specification,
    diagonal zipper front, pockets, label, size 40S **35.00**
Helmet, helicopter pilot's, microphone, plug, ear-
    phones, strap, and visor, with case **100.00**
Helmet, M1, US, steel, canvas chin strap, liner **30.00**
Helmet, Navy, aviator's, model H–4, black ext,
    leather and web head restraints int, large. **50.00**
Helmet, US Paratrooper **120.00**
Lensatic Compass, folding, olive drab, mkd "US
    1952" **45.00**
Parachute, backpack style, green nylon case with
    web straps and aluminum buckles, dated Nov
    1952, Switler Parachute Mfg Co **120.00**
Patch, Army, 97th AA Honor Guard, embroidered
    cloth, 3" w. **18.00**
Patch, Army, Military Government of Korea, cloth,
    red, white, and blue swirl pattern, 2" d **65.00**
Pillowcase, souvenir, red cotton, embroidered 8th
    Army patch design center, "11th Evac Hospital
    Pusan Korea," 17 x 17". **35.00**
Rifle Case, paratrooper's, olive drab, padded, green
    case with zipper, rings, and straps. **55.00**
Scarf, souvenir, green silk, multicolored embroidered
    dragon pattern, "SEOUL KOREA 1952" above
    dragon. **15.00**
Shield, souvenir, blue cloth, paper backing, hand
    stitched, UN and Korean flags over multicolored
    dragon, "Returned From Hell, 1951 Korea 1952,"
    made in Korea, 210 mm x 180 mm. **25.00**
Spade, entrenching, folding, 1952 . . . . **20.00**
Surrender Leaflet, with attached G3 translation let-
    ters, dated 1952 . . . . **25.00**

LADY HEAD VASES

The lady head vase craze began in the early 1940s and extended through the early 1960s. They were just one of hundreds of inexpensive ceramic novelties made by American and foreign manufacturers, primarily Japanese, in the period immediately following World War II.

Leading American manufacturers include Ceramic Arts Studio, Florence Ceramics, Haeger Potteries, Hull Pottery, Betty Lou Nichols Ceramics, and Spaulding China (Royal Copley and Royal Windsor). American–based import companies include Enesco, Fitz and Floyd, International Artware Corporation (INARCO), Lefton, National Potteries Corporation (NAPCO), Norcrest China Co., Samson Import Co. (Relpo), and United China & Glass Co. (UCAGCO).

Many Japanese–produced lady head vases came from the area around the Japanese cities of Nagoya and Seto. Leading Seto manufacturers include NAPCO Airyusha, Hakuko, Akida Maruya, Katayama Sangyo KK, Marui Shokai, Goto Matsukishi Shoten, Honji Togyo, and Yamamoto.

Although designated lady head vase, the category is broadly interpreted to include all planters and vases in the shape of a human head. Clown, holiday, and character and ethnic male heads were also made. Animal heads are excluded.

References: Kathleen Cole, *The Encyclopedia of Head Vases,* Schiffer Publishing, 1996; Mike Posgay and Ian Warner, *The World of Head Vase Planters,* Antique Publications, 1992; Mary Zavada, *Lady Head Vases,* Schiffer Publishing, 1988, 1996 value update.

Collectors' Club: Head Vase Society, PO Box 83H, Scarsdale, NY 10583.

Ardco, necklace, raised gloved hand, gold highlights,
  paper label, 5³/₈" h . . . . $ 30.00
ArtMark, pierced ears, necklace, hand by face, paper
  label, 5⁷/₈" h 20.00
Glamour Girls USA, turned head, gold highlights,
  imp mark, 6¹/₄" h 20.00
Inarco, #774, earrings, hand under chin, lavender,
  mkd, 1963, 3¹/₂" h 22.50

Relpo, purple bow and dress, pearl necklace and earrings, 5¹/₂" h, $25.00.

Inarco, E–1852, Jackie Kennedy, mkd, paper label,
  5⁷/₈" h 275.00
Irice, Japan, geisha girl, short black hair, white skin,
  downcast eyes, gold eyebrows and eyelashes,
  holding white and gold fan in raised left hand, pink
  kimono, white and gold hairpiece with yellow tas-
  sel, painted fingernails, 4¹/₂" h 30.00
Japan, black woman, downcast eyes, yellow turban,
  red sarong, large gold hoop earrings, 3–strand
  pearl necklace, 5" h 35.00
Japan, plastic flower in hair, painted earrings, RB
  Japan paper label, 6" h 30.00
Japan, turned head, closed eyes, mkd, 4¹/₂" h 18.00
Napco, C32872A, painted earrings, bracelet, fingers
  on chin, mkd, paper label, 1958, 5" h 60.00
Napco, 3M2544, all white, black brows and lashes,
  turned head, paper label, Japan sticker, 5¹/₂" h 12.50
Napcoware, C794, earrings, necklace, mkd, paper
  label, 6" h 30.00
Napcoware, C7472, pearl brooch and earrings, mkd,
  paper label, 6" h 45.00
Our Own Import, necklace, paper label on shoulder,
  5¹/₈" h 25.00
Reliable Glassware and Pottery, 3088, girl, blond
  hair, blue eyes looking right, open mouth smile,
  rosy cheeks, large red hat tied with red bow
  beneath chin, holly leaves dec, red and white
  candy–striped mittens, red coat with white fur cuffs
  and gold button, 6" h 25.00
Relpo, 2031, young lady, black hat with white and
  gold ribbon tied in large bow beneath chin, black
  and white dress, bare shoulders, Sampson Import
  Co, Chicago, IL, Japan, 5¹/₂" h 20.00
Rubens, 495, earrings, gloved crossed hands beneath
  chin, mkd, 5⁵/₈" h 50.00
Rubens, 4125, ponytail, imp mark, 4³/₈" h 40.00
Stanfordware, Spanish doña, black hair, white skin,
  blue eyes, tilted head, white and gold dress, tiara,
  and mantilla, gold necklace, 6¹/₂" h 30.00

Norcrest, blue bonnet, blond hair, pink dress, paper label, 6" h, $20.00.

SunsCo, pierced ears, necklace, applied flowers,
paper label, 5" h **15.00**

Topline Imports, 50/427, hand by chin, mkd, paper
label, 5½" h **25.00**

Unknown, S569A, gloved hand by chin, pierced
brim of hat, 5" h **35.00**

Unknown, baby, blond hair, open eyes, pink cheeks,
open mouth, pink ruffled bonnet tied beneath chin,
pink dress, 5¾" h **20.00**

Unknown, graduate, straight blond hair, pink cap and
tassel, pink and white gown with gold accents, 5" h . . . **25.00**

Unknown, nurse, short blond hair, downcast eyes,
raised right hand, white cap with Red Cross
insignia, white uniform with gold accents, painted
fingernails, 5¼" h **30.00**

Unknown, white, black lashes and brows, red lips,
flowers, turned head, 5⅜" h **15.00**

LALIQUE

René Lalique (1860–1945) began his career as a designer and jewelry maker. He experimented with cire pedue (lost wax technique) and pâte–de–verre in his small atelier at Clairfontaine. Lalique's perfume flacons attracted the attention of M. Francois Coty. Coty contracted with Lalique to design and manufacture perfume bottles for the company. Initially, the bottles were made at Legras & Cie de St. Dennis. In 1909 Lalique opened a glassworks at Combs–la–Ville. Lalique acquired a larger glassworks at Wingen–sur–Moder in Alsace–Lorraine in 1921 and founded Verrerie d'Alsace René Lalique et Cie.

Although René was not involved in the actual production of the glass objects, he designed the majority of the articles manufactured by the firm. Lalique glass is lead glass that is either blown in the mold or pressed. There are also combinations of cutting and casting and some molded designs were treated with acids to produce a frosted, satiny effect. Lalique blown wares were almost all confined to stemware and large bottles. Glass made before 1945 has been found in more than ten different colors, including mauve and purple.

Early pieces were of naturalistic design—molded animals, foliage, flowers, or nudes. Later designs became stylized and reflected the angular, geometric characteristics of Art Deco. Lalique made useful household articles. He accepted commercial factory methods and mass produced his glass.

Each piece of Lalique glass is marked on the bottom or near the base. It is often marked in several places, in block letters and in script. Marks include: R. LALIQUE FRANCE (engraved and sandblasted block and script); LALIQUE FRANCE (diamond point tool, engraved, sandblasted block and script); and LALIQUE (engraved).

The "R" was deleted from the mark following the death of René Lalique in 1945. Collectors prefer pre–1945 material, feeling later pieces lack design imagination and quality workmanship.

Lalique closed its Combs–la–Ville factory in 1937. The factory at Wingen–sur–Moder was partially destroyed during World War II. Lalique made no glass between 1939 and 1946. Production resumed after the war. In 1965 Lalique made its first limited edition Christmas plate, ending the series in 1976. Marc Lalique and his daughter Marie–Claude Lalique have contributed a number of new designs. In addition, the company still produces pieces from old molds.

Reference: Robert Prescott–Walker, *Collecting Lalique Glass,* Frances Joseph Publications, 1996, distributed by Krause Publications.

Collectors' Club: Lalique Collectors Society, 400 Veterans Blvd, Carlstadt, NJ 07072.

REPRODUCTION ALERT: Beware of the Lalique engraved signature and etched mark applied to blanks made in Czechoslovakia, France, and the United States.

Atomizer, cylindrical, relief molded frieze of 6 nude
maidens holding floral garland, waisted gilt metal
mount, Le Provencal fragrance, molded "R Lalique,
Made in France," 3¾" h . . . . **$ 275.00**

Beverage Service, 45 pcs, crystal, pitcher, decanter, 3
different size wine and cordial glasses, octagonal
faceted bases, each engraved "Lalique France" **550.00**

Bookends, pr, Chrysis, clear and frosted, kneeling Art
Deco nudes raised on plinths, c1928, 6¼" h **700.00**

Bottle, cylindrical, molded butterflies, relief sgd "R
Lalique," etched "France," c1940, 5½" h **475.00**

Bowl, Actina, clear and frosted, blue opalescence,
9" d **425.00**

Bowl, Athena, clear and frosted center, designed by
Marc Claude Lalique, 8½" d **600.00**

Bowl, Coquiles, opalescent, scallop shell molded ext,
etched reverse sgd "R Lalique France N. 3204,"
5¼" d **200.00**

Bowl, Lys, opalescent, feet molded as 4 lily pads,
9¼" d **800.00**

Carafe, Tokyo, clear, handled, c1930, 6⅞" h **250.00**

Castor Set, 2 frosted bottles, matching glass hold-
er, engraved script signature, 5½" h **225.00**

Clock, Rossignols, clear and frosted, Art Deco,
c1931, 8⅛" h **4,350.00**

Figure, Chat Assis, seated cat, clear and frosted,
7½" h **500.00**

Figure, Chat Couche, crouching cat, clear and frost-
ed, designed by René Lalique, 1932, 9" l **600.00**

Figure, Danseuse, female dancer with arms up, clear
and frosted, designed by Marc Lalique, 1942,
9½" h **500.00**

Figure, nude, frosted, seated on platform disk
above black sq base, mkd "Lalique France," 3⅜" h . . . **280.00**

Figure, pan dancing with wood nymph, c1950,
5½" h **350.00**

Figure, partridge, frosted and molded, sgd "Lalique
France," set of 3 . . . . **475.00**

Figure, Pigeon Gand, clear, designed by René
Lalique, 1932, 12" h **600.00**

Paperweight, Thistle, intaglio, frosted and clear, sgd
"Lalique France" **50.00**

Perfume Bottle, Ambre, black glass, made for
D'Orsay, c1911, 5⅛" h **1,800.00**

Plate, Felix, clear and frosted, stylized petals, stenciled "R Lalique France," 13½" d **275.00**

Powder Box, cov, Emilane, circular, clear and frosted,
floral molded lid, molded "R Lalique France," 4" d **325.00**

Salad Plate, crescent, frosted molded thistle pods and
thorny branches, mkd "Lalique France," 8" d **350.00**

Scent Bottle, Coeurs, clear, frosted, 4 hearts, gilt screw cap, molded mark "R Lalique France," orig hand–stitched red leather sheath, 3³/₄" h **200.00**

Vase, Antinea, clear and applied opalescent green glass, nymphs pattern, designed by Marie Claude Lalique, c1969, 8" h **800.00**

Vase, Avalon, opalescent, gray patina, c1927 . . . . **2,185.00**

Vase, Camaret, frosted, engraved "R Lalique France, No. 1010," 5¹/₂" h **825.00**

Vase, Chevaux, charcoal gray, Art Deco, band of horses, c1930, 7³/₈" h **3,110.00**

Vase, Domremy, opalescent, green patina, thistles, c1926 . . . . **1,350.00**

Vase, Malines, opalescent, engraved "R Lalique France, No. 957," later silver rim, 4⁷/₈" h **465.00**

Vase, Mesanges, clear and frosted, birds, designed by René Lalique, 1931, 12¹/₂" h **1,200.00**

Vase, Ormeaux, clear and frosted, engraved "R Lalique France No. 984," 6⁵/₈" h **400.00**

Vase, tapering form, thistle, sgd "Lalique France," 9¹/₂" h **200.00**

Wall Sconces, pr, Lierre, clear and frosted, Art Deco, stylized ivy leaves, 13" l **2,070.00**

Wine Glasses, Alger, clear and frosted, c1935, price for 10 . . . . **500.00**

LAMPS

Kerosene lamps dominated the 19th century and first quarter of the 20th century. Thomas Edison's invention of the electric light bulb in 1879 marked the beginning of the end of the kerosene lamp era.

The 1930s was the Age of Electricity. By the end of the decade electricity was available throughout America. Manufacturers and designers responded quickly to changing styles and tastes. The arrival of the end table and television as major pieces of living room furniture presented a myriad of new design opportunities.

Most lamps are purchased for reuse, not collecting purposes. Lamps whose design speaks to a specific time period or that blend with modern decor have decorative rather than collecting value. Decorative value is significantly higher than collecting value.

With the broad lamp category, there are several lamp groups that are collected. Aladdin lamps, due primarily to an extremely strong collectors' club, are in a league of their own. Other collecting subcategories include character lamps, figural lamps, novelty, motion or revolving lamps, student lamps, Tiffany and Tiffany–style lamps, and TV lamps.

This category continues to suffer from the lack of definitive lamp research books. Most of the existing products are either catalog reprints or random point–and–shoot picture price guides. This is a field that very much needs definition.

References: *Electric Lighting of the 20s–30s, Vol. 1* (1994), *Vol. 2* (1994), L–W Book Sales; L–W Book Sales (ed.), *Better Electric Lamps of the 20's & 30's,* L–W Book Sales, 1997; L–W Book Sales (ed.), *Quality Electric Lamps: A Pictorial Price Guide,* L–W Book Sales, 1992, 1994 value update; Nadja Maril, *American Lighting: 1840–1940,* Schiffer Publishing, 1995; Leland & Crystal Payton, *Turned On: Decorative Lamps of the 'Fifties,* Abbeville Press, 1989.

Newsletter: *Light Revival,* 35 W Elm Ave, Quincy, MA 02170.

Note: See Aladdin.

Boudoir, Art Nouveau style, pink, tall tubular octagon–shaped Depression Glass era shade, emb nudes on 4 sides, sq black metal base . . . . **$ 90.00**

Character, Davy Crockett, tree, and bear ceramic base, Crockett, Indians, and fort on shade, 1950s, 16" h **185.00**

Character, Mickey Mouse, globular metal base, beige ground, 3 Mickey Mouse decals around sides, Soreng–Manegold Co, 4" d, 6¹/₂" h **80.00**

Character, Popeye, ceramic, spinach can with raised figures, King Features, 1975 . . . . **155.00**

Figural, artillery shell, brass, metal dome shade **45.00**

Figural, boat, ceramic, tin sails, c1950s **75.00**

Figural, calypso dancer, plaster, circular red shade, 1950s **25.00**

Figural, crowing rooster, ceramic, red, black, and white, circular paper shade with hex sign dec, 1950s **15.00**

Figural, elephant, ceramic, carousel beaded shade **200.00**

Figural, football player, plaster, hollow, standing next to football standard, linen over cardboard shade, WK, Japan, Sears, Roebuck, 1978, 14" h **25.00**

Figural, French poodle, ceramic, pink, circular base, pink paper shade **28.00**

Figural, lighthouse, metal, c1950–60 . . . . **120.00**

Figural, oversized light bulb, metal cage, c1960 . . . . **150.00**

Figural, panther, ceramic, black, 8¹/₂" x 6¹/₂" **22.00**

Figural, Saturn, blue Depression Glass era, circular stepped base, 1930s **65.00**

Figural, ship, ceramic, gold trim, 11 x 10¹/₂" **25.00**

Figural, Tara, Southern belle, glass, fired–on pink, matching glass parasol shade **65.00**

Floor, chrome, interlocking squares and rectangles, painted wood base, c1970, 62¹/₂" h **55.00**

Floor, white enameled steel, barbell form, pivoting circular Lucite base, c1960, 21" h **250.00**

Hall, hanging, Hobnail, amberina, ornate brass trim and fittings, 10" h **360.00**

Figural, cowboy, plaster, glass eyes, 1960s, 23¹/₂" h, $350.00.

Table, ceramic, gray, planter base, plastic Venetian blind shade, 21¹/₂" h, $75.00.

Motion, butterfly, L. A. Goodman, 1957, 9" h 50.00
Motion, Christmas Tree, 1952, 17" h 80.00
Motion, fireside toasted peanuts, glass and metal,
    Roy Stringer Co, 1930s, 15" h 275.00
Motion, forest fire, L. A. Goodman, 1956, 11" h 55.00
Motion, Mother Goose, Econolite, 1948, 11" h 70.00
Motion, mountain waterfall, L. A. Goodman, 1956,
    11" h 45.00
Table, candlestick type, brass, ribbed and fluted col-
    umn, circular dished base, orange paper shade 20.00
Table, hourglass shape, colorless glass pedestal base,
    circular white floating shade, Murano, c1960,
    21" h 100.00
Table, Medusa style, aluminum tubing, chrome, 5
    tentacles, c1960, 52" h 275.00
Torchiere, Art Deco style, circular flaring brass lamp
    over 6 wire–bound bamboo rods, circular brass
    base, Russel Wright, c1960, 64¹/₂" h 120.00

L. E. SMITH GLASS

L. E. Smith Glass began when Lewis E. Smith, a gourmet cook, needed glass jars for a mustard he planned to market. Rather than buy jars, he bought a glass factory in Mt. Pleasant, Pennsylvania, and made them himself. Smith remained active in the company from 1908 through 1911. He is credited with inventing the glass top for percolators, the modern–style juice reamer, the glass mixing bowl, and numerous other kitchen implements.

Smith sold his interest in L. E. Smith Glass in 1911. The company continued, making automobile lenses, cookware, fruit jars, kitchenware, novelties, and tableware. Black glass was a popular product in the 1920s and 30s. Giftware and tableware products remain the company's principal focus today.

Reference: Lee Garmon and Dick Spencer, *Glass Animals Of The Depression Era,* Collector Books, 1993.

Animal, cat, black, c1930 . . . . $ 25.00
Animal, cow, black, c1930 . . . . 20.00

Animal, goose, black 20.00
Animal, rearing horse, blue 35.00
Animal, rearing horse, green 40.00
Animal, reclining camel, crystal, 4¹/₂" h 55.00
Animal, reclining Scottie, black, c1930 . . . . 25.00
Animal, sparrow, head down, crystal, 1950s, 3¹/₂" h 12.00
Animal, swan, black amethyst, silver trim, 8¹/₂" l 35.00
Aquarium, ftd, green, King Fish, c1920, 7¹/₄" h 260.00
Ashtray, duck, black, 6¹/₂" l 12.00
Ashtray, elephant, black 38.00
Bon Bon, Mt. Pleasant, green, 7" 15.00
Bookends, pr, rearing horse, clear 48.00
Bowl, #77, amethyst 10.00
Bowl, Melba Green, ruffled, 10¹/₂" d 10.00
Bowl, Mt. Pleasant, cobalt, 8" sq 30.00
Cake Plate, Do–Si–Do, handled 15.00
Cake Plate, Mt. Pleasant, handled, pink, 10¹/₂" d 20.00
Candlesticks, pr, Mt. Pleasant, black 25.00
Candlesticks, pr, Romanesque, pink 15.00
Candy Dish, cov, turkey, crystal, 7¹/₄" h 35.00
Casserole, cov, Melba, oval, 9¹/₂" l 15.00
Compote, cov, Moon n' Star, amberina 38.00
Cookie Jar, cov, Amy, black 95.00
Cookie Jar, cov, black amethyst, floral dec 48.00
Cordial Tray, #381, black 10.00
Creamer, Moon n' Star, amberina 12.00
Creamer, Mt. Pleasant, pink 20.00
Creamer, Scottie, black, 5¹/₂" l 12.00
Cruet, Moon n' Star, amberina 12.00
Cup, Mt. Pleasant, pink 10.00
Cup and Saucer, Melba, pink 5.00
Fairy Lamp, Moon n' Star, ruby 32.00
Fern Dish, 3 ftd, Greek Key, black, 1930s 20.00
Fern Dish, 3 ftd, Kent, white opaque 10.00
Figure, Goose Girl, crystal, c1950, 6" h 22.00
Flower Block, By Cracky, 3" h 5.00
Grill Plate, Homestead, 9" d 8.00
Ladle, crystal 22.00
Mayonnaise, Mt. Pleasant, 3 ftd, green, 5¹/₂" 20.00
Mayonnaise, Kent 6.50
Mug, crystal, 12 oz 5.50

Vase, #432, black, crimped rim, ftd, 1930s, $15.00.

Parfait, Homestead. **8.00**
Planter, black amethyst, nude dancers on sides, mkd
  "L. E. Smith" **48.00**
Plate, Do–Si–Do **5.00**
Plate, Melba, amethyst, 6" d. **5.00**
Plate, Mt. Pleasant, handled, green, 12" d **22.00**
Salt and Pepper Shakers, pr, Dresden, white **20.00**
Salt and Pepper Shakers, pr, Mt. Pleasant, green **25.00**
Sherbet, Mt. Pleasant, green. **12.00**
Slipper, Daisy and Button, amber, 2½" h. **5.00**
Soda Glass, Soda Shop **8.00**
Sugar, cov, Do–Si–Do **8.00**
Sugar, cov, Kent. **8.00**
Sugar, cov, Moon n' Star, amberina. **15.00**
Tray, crystal, oval, 15" l **10.50**
Vase, #49, black, 6" h **12.00**
Vase, #433, black, dancing girls. **20.00**
Vase, Mt. Pleasant, amethyst, 7¼" h **25.00**
Vase, Romanesque, fan shape, black, 7¼" h **15.00**
Violet Bowl, hobnail, white opaque **8.00**
Water Goblet, Moon 'n Star, amberina . . . . `18.00`
Window Box, F. W. Woolworth **28.00**
Wine, Ruby bowl, crystal stem. **8.00**

LEFTON CHINA

George Zoltan Lefton was the driving force behind Lefton China, a china importing and marketing organization. Following World War II, Lefton, a Hungarian immigrant, began importing giftware made in the Orient into the United States.

Until the mid–1970s Japanese factories made the vast majority of Lefton China. After that date, China, Malaysia, and Taiwan became the principal supply sources.

Most Lefton pieces are identified by a fired–on trademark or a paper label. Numbers found on pieces are item identification numbers. When letters precede a number, it is a factory code, e.g., "SL" denotes Nippon Art China K.K.

References: Loretta DeLozier, *Collector's Encyclopedia of Lefton China* (1995) and *Book II* (1997), Collector Books.

Collectors' Club: National Society of Lefton Collectors, 1101 Polk St, Bedford, IA 50833.

Angel in Frame, Sunday, #6883, 4". . . . . **$ 28.00**
Angel of the Month, July, #489, 4" **25.00**
Angel of the Month, March, #3332, 4" **25.00**
Angel of the Week, Thursday, #8281, 4" **30.00**
Ashtray, gold fleur de lis, white ground, #1028 . . . . **4.00**
Bank, pig, pearl luster, #1122, 5½". **15.00**
Bud Vase, pink bisque, applied pink flowers, #1847,
  4" h **10.00**
Bust, Abraham Lincoln, #1114, 5½". **20.00**
Butter Dish, cov, Violet Chintz, #2744, ¼ lb, 6⅝" l **15.00**
Cake Set, cake plate and 6 dessert plates, fruit
  designs, #1133. . . . . **80.00**
Candy Box, egg shape, floral dec, #2209, 5½" **15.00**
Candy Box, heart shape, applied flowers, #2443, 2½". . . . **20.00**
Coffeepot, cov, Forge–Me–Not, #4174, 6 cup **40.00**
Compote, lattice edge, violets, #2330. . . . . **40.00**
Cookie Jar, cow **35.00**

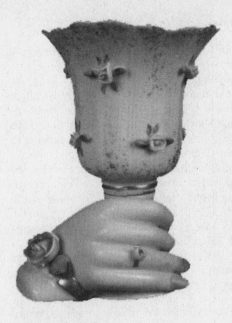

Cigarette Holder, white ground, pink flowers, gold dec, #929, 5¼" h, $50.00.

Cookie Jar, French girl **275.00**
Cookie Jar, girl's head. **125.00**
Cookie Jar, grape cluster, #3319, 7" **75.00**
Cookie Jar, lovebirds on house **165.00**
Cookie Jar, Miss Priss, kitten head, #1502, 7½" **100.00**
Cookie Jar, Scottish girl **235.00**
Creamer and Sugar, Eastern Star, #2789 . . . . **25.00**
Creamer and Sugar, holly, #29 . . . . **30.00**
Creamer and Sugar, wheat design, #20120 . . . . **15.00**
Cup and Saucer, turquoise and white, gold trim, #801. . . . **25.00**
Demitasse Cup and Saucer, blue roses, #2120 . . . . **7.50**
Figurine, colonial lady, #869 . . . . **50.00**
Figurine, kewpie, #228, 4½" **30.00**
Figurine, Madonna With Child, #2583, 6½" **35.00**
Flamingo, baby flamingo on base, #504, 5½" **60.00**
Flower Girl of the Month, #595, 4". **25.00**
Flower Girl of the Month, September, #985 . . . . **28.00**
Golden Pheasant, #1538, 7¾" **30.00**
Jam Jar, bluebird, #436 . . . . **25.00**
Kerosene Lamp, Rose Chintz, #686, 5½" **20.00**
Leaf Dish, Misty Rose, #5517. . . . . **10.00**
Owl, glass eyes, #3893, 6". **10.00**
Pin Box, cov, trunk shape, sleeping baby on lid, white
  with gold trim, #2710, 3" **10.00**
Planter, duck and blocks, #6365, 6" **15.00**
Powder Box, cov, hand finial, blue, white and gold
  bows, #90092, 4". **40.00**
Rooster, #494, 6". **30.00**
Salt and Pepper Shakers, 50th anniversary, #1955, 3" **5.00**
Salt and Pepper Shakers, Pear N Apple, #3748, 3". **7.50**
Snack Set, Brown Heritage, Fruit, #20130, 8" **17.50**
Teapot, cov, Poinsettia pattern, #4388, 6 cup, 8" h **75.00**
Teapot, cov, Rose Chintz, #660, 8¾" **80.00**
Tidbit, Green Heritage, floral, 2 tier, #1153. . . . . **40.00**
Vase, fan shape, milk white, applied pink flowers,
  #840, 6¼" **70.00**
Wall Plaque, lattice edge, rose design center, white
  ground, #6350, 8" d **15.00**
Wall Pocket, Pear N Apple, #3850, 7¼" h. **7.00**

LENOX

In 1889, Walter Scott Lenox and Jonathan Coxon, Sr., founded the Ceramic Art Company in Trenton, New Jersey. Lenox acquired sole ownership in 1894. In 1906 he formed Lenox, Inc.

Lenox gained national recognition in 1917 when President Woodrow Wilson ordered a 1,700 piece dinner service. Presidents Franklin D. Roosevelt and Harry S. Truman followed Wilson's lead in future administrations. First Lady Nancy Reagan ordered a 4,732–piece set of gold–embossed bone china from Lenox in 1981. Each raised golden seal in the center of the Reagan service plates took two and one–half to three hours to hand paint, according to Eric Poehner, the Lenox craftsman who did much of the handwork.

During the last two decades, Lenox, Inc., has expanded, acquiring Art Carved, Inc., H. Rosenthal Jewelry Corporation, Imperial Glass Corporation, and many other companies. Operating today as Lenox Brands, the company is a multimillion–dollar enterprise producing a broad range of tabletop and giftware.

References: Susan and Al Bagdade, *Warman's American Pottery and Porcelain,* Wallace–Homestead, Krause Publications, 1994; Collector's Information Bureau, *Collectibles Market Guide & Price Index, 15th Edition,* Collector's Information Bureau, 1997, distributed by Krause Publications; Harry L. Rinker, *Dinnerware of the 20th Century: The Top 500 Patterns,* House of Collectibles, 1997; Harry L. Rinker, *Stemware of the 20th Century: The Top 200 Patterns,* House of Collectibles, 1997.

Note: For additional listings see Limited Edition Collectibles.

Adrienne, bread and butter plate, 6³/₈" d	$ 15.00
Adrienne, cup and saucer	45.00
Adrienne, dinner plate, 10¹/₂" d	40.00
Adrienne, salad plate, 7⁷/₈" d	25.00
Adrienne, soup bowl, coupe shape, 7⁵/₈" d	60.00
Aristocrat, bread and butter plate, 6³/₈" d	35.00
Aristocrat, cereal bowl, coupe shape, 5³/₈" d	75.00
Aristocrat, cup and saucer, demitasse	90.00
Aristocrat, fruit bowl, 5³/₈" d	75.00
Aristocrat, salad plate, 8¹/₄" d	45.00
Belvidere, bread and butter plate, 6¹/₄" d	17.00
Belvidere, cream soup and saucer	75.00
Belvidere, dinner plate, 10⁵/₈" d	35.00
Belvidere, salad plate, 8³/₈" d	27.00
Belvidere, soup bowl, 8³/₈" d	55.00
Blue Tree, bread and butter plate, 6³/₈" d	20.00
Blue Tree, cup and saucer, ftd	55.00
Blue Tree, demitasse cup and saucer	70.00
Blue Tree, dinner plate, 10⁵/₈" d	40.00
Blue Tree, fruit bowl, 5¹/₂" d	40.00
Bowl, Art Deco, ftd, sterling silver overlay, blue glazed ground	115.00
Caribbee, bread and butter plate, 6³/₈" d	20.00
Caribbee, cup and saucer, ftd	55.00
Caribbee, dinner plate, 10⁵/₈" d	45.00
Caribbee, fruit bowl, 5¹/₂" d	45.00
Caribbee, salad plate, 8³/₈" d	30.00
Chanson, bread and butter plate, 6³/₈" d	25.00
Chanson, cup and saucer	65.00
Chanson, dinner plate, 10¹/₂" d	50.00
Chanson, luncheon plate, 9" d	45.00

Christmas Ornament, 1984, ball, crystal	50.00
Christmas Ornament, 1986, annual, china	60.00
Christmas Ornament, 1989, Christmas tree top	30.00
Dog, Labrador Retriever, Christmas dec, c1922	80.00
Essex Maroon, cup and saucer, ftd	50.00
Essex Maroon, dinner plate, 10⁵/₈" d	45.00
Essex Maroon, fruit bowl, 5¹/₂" d	45.00
Essex Maroon, luncheon plate, 9¹/₄" d	45.00
Essex Maroon, salad plate, 8³/₈" d	35.00
Eternal, bread and butter plate, 6¹/₂" d	7.00
Eternal, cup and saucer, ftd	20.00
Eternal, dinner plate, 10³/₄" d	15.00
Eternal, soup bowl, coupe, 7¹/₂" d	25.00
Eternal, sugar, cov	50.00
Eternal, vegetable bowl, oval, 10¹/₄" l	65.00
Golden Wreath, ashtray, 4³/₈" d	20.00
Golden Wreath, bread and butter plate, 6¹/₄" d	15.00
Golden Wreath, cigarette holder, 4" l	30.00
Golden Wreath, cigarette lighter	37.00
Golden Wreath, cream soup and saucer	75.00
Golden Wreath, demitasse cup and saucer	40.00
Golden Wreath, dinner plate, 10¹/₂" d	30.00
Golden Wreath, fruit bowl, 5¹/₂" d	35.00
Golden Wreath, salt shaker	55.00
Golden Wreath, soup bowl, 8¹/₄" d	40.00
Golden Wreath, sugar, cov	100.00
Harvest, cigarette box	55.00
Harvest, cigarette holder, 4" l	30.00
Harvest, cigarette lighter	37.00
Harvest, cup and saucer, ftd	35.00
Harvest, dinner plate, 10⁵/₈" d	30.00
Harvest, fruit bowl, 5⁵/₈" d	30.00
Harvest, pepper mill	65.00
Harvest, sugar, cov	75.00
Lenox Rose, bud vase, 7³/₄" h	65.00
Lenox Rose, creamer	70.00
Lenox Rose, dinner plate, 10⁵/₈" d	35.00
Lenox Rose, dish, shell shaped	55.00
Lenox Rose, powder box	90.00
Lenox Rose, salad plate, 8¹/₄" d	20.00
Lenox Rose, salt and pepper shakers, pr	70.00
Lenox Rose, sugar, cov	75.00
Pavlova, bread and butter plate, 6¹/₄" d	17.00
Pavlova, demitasse cup and saucer	60.00
Pavlova, dinner plate, 10³/₄" d	35.00
Pavlova, fruit bowl, 6³/₈" d	40.00
Rhodora, ashtray, 6¹/₄" d	27.00
Rhodora, bread and butter plate, 6¹/₄" d	20.00
Rhodora, bud vase, 8" h	75.00
Rhodora, cup and saucer, ftd	55.00
Rhodora, luncheon plate, 9¹/₈" d	40.00
Starlight, cereal bowl, coupe, 5¹/₄" d	40.00
Starlight, cup and saucer	40.00
Starlight, luncheon plate, 9" d	30.00
Starlight, teapot, cov	150.00
Wheat, ashtray, 4³/₈" d	12.00
Wheat, bud vase, 8" h	50.00
Wheat, cream soup and saucer	70.00
Wheat, demitasse cup and saucer	35.00
Wheat, hors d'oeuvre dish, 5⁷/₈" d	20.00
Wheat, pepper mill	65.00

LIBBEY GLASS

The Libbey Glass company traces its origins to the New England Glass Company, founded in 1818 in Boston. In 1888 New England Glass moved to Toledo, Ohio, to be nearer a better fuel source. The company became the Libbey Glass Company in 1892, named for the family that managed it for several decades.

Financial difficulties arising from the move ended when Libbey began producing light bulbs. The company also manufactured a brilliant cut glass line. By the 1920s, Libbey introduced an art glass line (amberina, pomona, peachblow, etc.) and a hotel and restaurant line. In 1925 Libbey acquired the Nonik Glassware Corp., a major tumbler manufacturer.

In 1933, under the direction of Douglas Nash, Libbey re–emphasized its fine glass lines. It also acquired the H. C. Fry Company. In 1935 Owen–Illinois Glass Company, Toledo, purchased Libbey Glass, then billed as the "world's largest producers of glass containers." Owen–Illinois established a separate division and continues to manufacture products using the Libbey name.

References: Bob Page and Dale Fredericksen, *A Collection of American Crystal: A Stemware Identification Guide for Glasonbury/Lotus, Libbey/Rock Sharpe & Hawkes,* Page–Fredericksen Publishing, 1995; Kenneth Wilson, *American Glass 1760–1930; The Toledo Museum of Art,* 2 vols., Hudson Hills Press and The Toledo Museum of Art, 1994.

Candlesticks, pr, Silhouette, clear candle cup, opalescent figural camel stem. . . . . $ 325.00
Cocktail, Silhouette, clear bowl, black kangaroo silhouette in stem 125.00
Compote, clear crystal bowl, fiery opalescent figural elephant stem and platform base, 7½" h, 11" d 520.00
Cordial, American Prestige, c1930 . . . . 40.00
Cordial, Golden Foliage, #8990, crystal, gold oak leaves dec, gold rim. 8.00
Cordial, Nob Hill, crystal. 8.00
Cordial, Rock Sharpe, 2010 line, crystal, 4¼" h. 30.00
Cordial, Rock Sharpe, Arctic Rose, crystal. 25.00
Cordial, Silhouette, Greyhound pattern, opalescent, 4" h 185.00
Cordial, Silver Foliage, silver leaf dec, silver rim 8.00
Cordial, 2010 line, crystal, 5¹³⁄₁₆" 18.00
Drinking Glass, Alice in Wonderland, Libbey Classics 12.00
Drinking Glass, The Wizard of Oz, Libbey Classics 28.00
Drinking Glass, Three Musketeers, Libbey Classics 12.00
Drinking Glass, Treasure Island, Libbey Classsics 12.00
Goblet, Silhouette, clear bowl, opalescent cat silhouette in stem, sgd, 7" h 140.00
Sherbet, Silhouette, clear bowl, black monkey silhouette in stem 90.00
Vase, cylindrical, light vertical ribbing, blue threaded dec, opal ground, c1933, 9" h 250.00

LIGHTERS

Although lighters for fire and firearms date back to the 17th century and earlier, the cigarette lighter (the focus of this category) did not become established until the first quarter of the 20th century. By the 1920s it enjoyed a prominent place in most American homes, even those of non–smokers who kept a lighter handy for those who did.

Well–known manufacturers include Bowers, Dunhill, Evans, Marathon, Parker, Ronson, and Zippo. Well over a thousand different manufacturers produced lighters. The principal manufacturing centers were Japan and the United States. Australia, England, France, Germany, Siam, and Switzerland also produced lighters. In fact, there was at least one lighter manufacturer in every industrialized country in the 20th century.

Collectors shy away from lighters in less than average condition. It is important that the sparking or lighting mechanism works, whether it be flint, liquid fuel, or gas. Repairing a lighter to working order is accepted among collectors.

References: James Flanagan, *Collector's Guide to Cigarette Lighters,* Collector Books, 1995; David Poore, *Zippo: The Great American Lighter,* Schiffer Publishing, 1997; Stuart Schneider and George Fischler, *Cigarette Lighters,* Schiffer Publishing, 1996; Neil S. Wood, *Collecting Cigarette Lighters* (1994) and *Vol. II* (1995), L–W Book Sales.

Collectors' Clubs: On The Lighter Side, International Lighter Collectors, 136 Circle Dr, Quitman, TX 75783; Pocket Lighter Preservation Guild & Historical Society, Inc, PO Box 1054, Addison, IL 60101.

Advertising, Coca–Cola, bottle shape, plastic, metal cap, c1953, 2½" h . . . . $ 15.00
Advertising, Lucky Strike, "L.S/M.F.T.," red, Japan, 1950s, 4³⁄₈" h. 10.00
Advertising, Philip Morris, Japan, 1960s, 2" h 10.00
Advertising, Phillips 66, Zippo 20.00
Advertising, Schwepp's, Japan, 1960s, 1³⁄₄" h. 8.00
Aurora, combination lighter/flashlight, chromium and leather, c1960, 2" h 20.00
Colibri, chromium and tortoise enamel, c1955, 1½" h 25.00
Colibri, silver, lift arm, machined design, c1937, 2½" h 75.00
Continental, chromium and enamel, floral design, mid–1950s, 2" h. 10.00

Ronson, chromium and leather, lift arm, 1937, 1⁷⁄₈" h, $30.00.

Elgin, brass and leather, early 1960s, 1³/₄" h, gift box **15.00**

Elgin, combination lighter/cigarette case, brass and imitation tortoise shell, c1940s, 3¹/₄" h. **50.00**

Evans, brass and silver plate, basketweave design, c1935, 1¹/₂" h. **30.00**

Evans, combination lighter/cigarette case, brown and yellow enameled finish, c1935, 6³/₄" h **40.00**

Evans, silver plated, machined design, c1935, 2" h **25.00**

Figural, beer stein, ceramic, Germany, c1958, 3³/₄" h **25.00**

Figural, book, striker type, metal, c1935, 1⁷/₈" h **20.00**

Figural, bottle shape, chromium, paper label, KEM, Inc, c1948, 2⁵/₈" h **25.00**

Figural, cornucopia, chromium, Evans, c1948, 4" h **18.00**

Figural, cowboy boot, metal, Evans, c1948, 5" h **20.00**

Figural, elephant, c1935, 2¹/₄" h **25.00**

Figural, horse head, brass, pull reins to light, c1945, 4³/₄" h **45.00**

Figural, ice cream cone, plastic, c1960, 3⁵/₈" h **5.00**

Figural, knight's helmet, brass, push down visor to light, c1955, 5" h **15.00**

Figural, pistol, chromium, Japan, c1950s, 1¹/₂" h **15.00**

Figural, prop plane, painted chromium, turn prop to light, c1935, 6" l **80.00**

Figural, swan, chromium, Japan, early 1960s, 3" h **10.00**

Occupied Japan, poker motif, chromium and motherofpearl, lift arm, club on both sides, c1948, 1¹/₄" h **30.00**

Penquin, chromium and leather, round, late 1950s, 2" d. **12.00**

Perfecto, chromium, c1930, 2¹/₂" h **25.00**

Ronson, Varaflame, chromium, butane, 1960s, 2³/₄" h **20.00**

Ronson, Whirlwind, chromium, c1941, 2¹/₈" h **25.00**

Scripto, Retro–Lite, plastic, butane, matchbook cover design, 1992 . . . . **2.00**

Scripto, Vu–Lighter, nude photos, clear plastic and chromium, late 1950s, 2³/₄" h **15.00**

Superfine, chromium and leather, lift arm, c1920s, 1⁷/₈" h **45.00**

Waterford, crystal, butane, faceted, c1975, 3" h **50.00**

LIMITED EDITION COLLECTIBLES

In 1895 Bing and Grondahl produced its first Christmas plate. Royal Copenhagen followed in 1908 and Rosenthal in 1910. Limited edition art prints, many copies of Old Masters, were popular in the 1920s and 30s.

In the late 1960s and extending through the early 1980s, Americans eagerly purchased large quantities of limited edition bells, eggs, mugs, ornaments, plates, and prints. Collectors series featuring the images by a single artist or honoring events, holidays, people, or places were made in ceramics, glass, metal, and a variety of other materials. Many came with a "Certificate of Authenticity," in reality a meaningless document.

Very few of these issues were truly limited. Many had production runs exceeding 100,000 units. Many individuals purchased them as investments and not because they planned to display them. The speculative limited edition bubble burst in the mid–1980s. Today, the vast majority of limited edition collectibles issued between the late 1960s and the early 1980s sell for less than 50¢ on the dollar.

Limited edition collectibles is a broad category. Not all items are numbered. In some cases, limited means produced for a relatively short period of time.

Currently, a weeding out process is occurring. Prices have stabilized or are slowly rising on a few select pieces, those that collectors have identified as desirable or whose image crosses over into other collecting categories. Shifting trends continue to affect the market, but not to the degree of a decade ago. Bargains abound for those willing to gamble on long–term growth.

References: *Collectibles Price Guide & Directory to Secondary Market Dealers, Sixth Edition,* Collectors' Information Bureau, 1996; Collector's Information Bureau, *Collectibles Market Guide & Price Index, 15th Edition,* Collector's Information Bureau, 1997, distributed by Krause Publications; Rinker Enterprises, *The Official Price Guide to Collector Plates, Sixth Edition,* House of Collectibles, 1996; Mary Sieber (ed.), *1998 Price Guide to Limited Edition Collectibles,* Krause Publications, 1997.

Periodicals: *Collector Editions,* 170 Fifth Ave, 12th Floor, New York, NY 10010; *Collector's Bulletin,* 22341 East Wells Rd, Canton, IL 61520; *Collectors Mart Magazine,* 700 E State St, Iola, WI 54990; *Plate World,* 9200 N Maryland Ave, Niles, IL 60648; *The Treasure Trunk,* PO Box 13554, Arlington, TX 76094; *White's Guide to Collecting Figures,* 8100 Three Chopt Rd, Ste 226, Richmond, VA 23229.

Note: In addition to company–sponsored collectors' clubs, there are numerous collectors' clubs for specific limited edition collectibles. Consult *Maloney's Antiques & Collectibles Resource Directory* by David J. Maloney, Jr., at your local library for further information.

Bell, Anri, Behold, wooden, 1983. . . . . $ **12.00**

Bell, Anri, Christmas, musical, 1977 . . . . **65.00**

Bell, Anri, Companions, musical, 1983 . . . . **45.00**

Bell, Anri, Lighting the Way, wooden, 1981 . . . . **15.00**

Plate, Historic Providence Mint, Vanishing American Barn, Lancaster Barn, 1983, $30.00.

Plate, Edwin M. Knowles, Rediscovered Women, Dreaming in the Attic, 1981, $15.00.

Bell, Anri, Little Drummer Boy, musical, 1980	45.00
Bell, Anri, Spreading the Word, musical, 1982	45.00
Bell, Anri, The Good Shepherd Boy, musical, 1981	45.00
Bell, Fenton Art Glass, A Chicadee Ballet, 1988	20.00
Bell, Fenton Art Glass, After the Snow, 1982	10.00
Bell, Fenton Art Glass, Anticipation, 1983	25.00
Bell, Fenton Art Glass, Christmas Eve, 1991	20.00
Bell, Fenton Art Glass, Going Home, 1980	25.00
Bell, Fenton Art Glass, Heart's Desire, 1985	25.00
Bell, Fenton Art Glass, Househunting, 1989	12.00
Bell, Fenton Art Glass, Lighthouse Point, 1983	35.00
Bell, Fenton Art Glass, Magnolia on Gold, 1994	20.00
Bell, Fenton Art Glass, Out in the Country, 1987	10.00
Bell, Fenton Art Glass, Playful Kitten, 1986	10.00
Bell, Fenton Art Glass, Precious Panda, Mother's Day Series, 1984	20.00
Bell, Fenton Art Glass, Statue of Liberty, 1986	35.00
Bell, Fenton Art Glass, Where's Mom?, Mother's Day Series, 1983	20.00
Bell, Gorham, Beguiling Buttercup, 1979	25.00
Bell, Gorham, Central Park in Winter, 1986	15.00
Bell, Gorham, Fondly Do We Remember, 1977	45.00
Bell, Gorham, Gay Blades, 1978	20.00
Bell, Gorham, Santa's Helpers, 1975	25.00
Bell, Gorham, Sweet Serenade, 1981	25.00
Bell, Gorham, The Milkmaid, 1983	25.00
Bell, Gorham, Tiny Tim, 1984	25.00
Bell, Gorham, Winter Wonderland, 1983	15.00
Bell, Gorham, Yule Logs, 1978	12.00
Bell, Gorham, Yuletide Reflections, 1985	25.00
Bell, Lenox, Carousel Horse, 1992	40.00
Bell, Lenox, Celestial Harpist, 1991	65.00
Bell, Lenox, Christmas Tree, 1990	45.00
Bell, Lenox, Dashing Through the Snow, 1986	55.00
Bell, Lenox, Holy Family Bell, 1982	45.00
Bell, Lenox, Hummingbird, 1991	45.00

Bell, Reed & Barton, Caroler, 1985	15.00
Bell, Reed & Barton, Drummer Boy, 1984	12.00
Bell, Reed & Barton, Noel, musical, 1981	40.00
Bell, Reed & Barton, Perfect Angel, 1983	12.00
Bell, Reed & Barton, The Bell Ringer, 1989	15.00
Bell, Reed & Barton, Yuletide Holiday, 1981	15.00
Bell, River Shore, Football Hero, 1977	70.00
Bell, River Shore, Grandpa's Guardian, 1991	40.00
Bell, River Shore, School Play, 1977	70.00
Bell, Schmid, Devotion For Mothers, Berta Hummel's Mother's Day Series, 1976	50.00
Bell, Schmid, Merry Mickey Claus, Disney, 1987	18.00
Bell, Schmid, Nativity, Berta Hummel, 1973	75.00
Bell, Stieff, Annual Bell, musical, 1979	45.00
Doll, Annalee Mobiltee, Abe Lincoln, 1989	120.00
Doll, Annalee Mobiltee, C. G. Bunny With Basket, 1980	125.00
Doll, Annalee Mobiltee, 22" Christmas Stocking, 1974	155.00
Doll, Annalee Mobiltee, Reindeer With Bell, 1985	55.00
Doll, Annalee Mobiltee, Santa With Mushroom, 1972	270.00
Doll, Annalee Mobiltee, Victorian Santa, 1987	200.00
Doll, Ashton–Drake, Danielle, 1991	125.00
Doll, Ashton–Drake, Jason, 1985	650.00
Doll, Ashton–Drake, Pumpkin, 1992	95.00
Doll, Gorham, Holly Hobbie, Mother's Helper, 1985	180.00
Doll, Gorham, Jessica, 1986	300.00
Doll, Gorham, Melinda, 1981	290.00
Doll, Gorham, Mlle. Yvonne, 1982	300.00
Doll, Gorham, Odette, 1985	475.00
Doll, Gorham, Robbie, 1983	300.00
Doll, Gorham, Silver Bell	200.00
Doll, Hamilton Collection, Ethel, 1988	110.00
Doll, Hamilton Collection, Heather, 1985	140.00
Doll, Hamilton Collection, Jill, 1993	100.00
Doll, Hamilton Collection, Priscilla, 1987	55.00
Doll, Sarah's Attic, Becky, 1989	125.00

Limited Edition Collector Plate, Paon (Peacock), Marie–Claude Lalique, 1970, $70.00.

Doll, Sarah's Attic, Molly, 1987 .... 35.00
Doll, Sarah's Attic, Twinkie, 1986 .... 35.00
Doll, Sarah's Attic, Victorian Emma, 1991 .... 150.00
Doll, Sarah's Attic, Willie Rag Doll, 1987 .... 35.00
Doll, Seymour Mann, Donna, 1995 .... 35.00
Doll, Seymour Mann, Elizabeth, 1995 .... 35.00
Doll, Seymour Mann, Ginny, 1990 .... 95.00
Doll, Seymour Mann, Wendy, 1985 .... 150.00
Doll, Seymour Mann, Yen Yen, 1990 .... 100.00
Eggs, Ferrandiz, 1980 .... 10.00
Eggs, Ferrandiz, 1983 .... 20.00
Eggs, Franklin Mint, porcelain, 1979 .... 40.00
Eggs, Noritake, 1972 .... 35.00
Eggs, Noritake, 1979 .... 15.00
Eggs, Wedgwood, 1977 .... 40.00
Eggs, Wedgwood, 1979 .... 20.00
Figurine, Apple of My Eye, 1984 .... 375.00
Figurine, Anri, Forever Yours, 1988 .... 250.00
Figurine, Anri, Little Nanny, 1987 .... 175.00
Figurine, Anri, Maestro Mickey, Disney, 1988 .... 175.00
Figurine, Anri, Musical Basket, 1981 .... 110.00
Figurine, Anri, Our Puppy, 1986 .... 100.00
Figurine, Anri, Peace Pipe, 1978 .... 300.00
Figurine, Anri, The Gift, 1975 .... 230.00
Figurine, Anri, Tulips For Mother, 1992 .... 275.00
Figurine, Byers' Choice Ltd, Adult Skaters, 1991 .... 45.00
Figurine, Byers' Choice Ltd, Old World Santa, 1978 .... 230.00
Figurine, Byers' Choice Ltd, Scrooge, 1984 .... 40.00
Figurine, Byers' Choice Ltd, Singing Cats 20.00
Figurine, Byers' Choice Ltd, Skating Santa, 1993 .... 65.00
Figurine, Department 56, Ceramic Car, 1980 .... 50.00
Figurine, Department 56, Hold On Tight, 1986 .... 15.00
Figurine, Department 56, Icy Igloo, 1989 .... 40.00
Figurine, Department 56, Just For You, 1991 .... 22.00
Figurine, Lenox Collections, Angels of Adoration,
  1989 .... 150.00
Figurine, Lenox Collections, Grand Tour, 1986 .... 90.00
Figurine, Lenox Collections, Great Orange Wingtip,
  1993 .... 45.00
Figurine, Lenox Collections, Rose Grosbeak, 1991 ...... 45.00
Figurine, River Shore, Gilbert, musical, 1987 .... 30.00
Figurine, River Shore, Rosecoe, red fox kit, 1979 ...... 55.00
Figurine, River Shore, Zuela, elephant, 1981 .... 65.00
Figurine, Schmid, Catnapping Too, 1984 .... 75.00
Figurine, Schmid, Right Church, Wrong Pew, 1982 ..... 85.00
Figurine, Schmid, Two's Company, 1980 .... 50.00
Mug, Bing & Grondahl, 1980 .... 30.00
Mug, Gorham, Bugs Bunny, 1981 .... 10.00
Mug, Lynell Studios, Gnome Series, Gnomelyweds,
  1983 .... 10.00
Mug, Royal Copenhagen, 1968, large 25.00
Mug, Wedgwood, Father's Day, 1977 .... 30.00
Music Box, Anri, Peter Rabbit 100.00
Music Box, Ferrandiz, Chorale 130.00
Music Box, Ferrandiz, Spring Arrivals 125.00
Music Box, Gorham, Happy Birthday 40.00
Music Box, Schmid, Paddington Bear, 1982 .... 25.00
Music Box, Schmid, Raggedy Ann, 1981 .... 20.00
Ornament, Artists of the World, De Grazia, Flower
  Boy, 1989 .... 85.00

Ornament, Artists of the World, De Grazia, Heavenly
  Flowers, 1995 .... 60.00
Ornament, Department 56, Apothecary Shop, 1986 ..... 35.00
Ornament, Department 56, Cherub on Brass Ribbon,
  1986 .... 15.00
Ornament, Department 56, Humpty Dumpty, 1985 ...... 5.00
Ornament, Department 56, Rock–A–Bye Baby,
  Snowbabies, 1990 .... 8.00
Ornament, Department 56, Swiss Chalet, 1983 .... 70.00
Ornament, Enesco, Bunny's Christmas Stocking,
  1984 .... 18.00
Ornament, Enesco, Bundled Up For the Holidays,
  1994 .... 18.00
Ornament, Enesco, Carousel Horse, 1983 .... 20.00
Ornament, Enesco, Wide Open Throttle, 1983 .... 30.00
Ornament, Gorham, Crystal, 1986 .... 30.00
Ornament, Gorham, Snowflake, sterling, 1971 .... 100.00
Ornament, Lenox, Ball, 1982 .... 70.00
Ornament, Lenox, Christmas Tree Top, 1989 .... 30.00
Ornament, Lenox, Lantern, 1993 .... 40.00
Ornament, Lenox, Starburst, 1984 .... 60.00
Ornament, Lenox, teardrop shape, 1983 .... 70.00
Ornament, Royal Doulton, Santa Bunny, 1991 .... 20.00
Ornament, Royal Doulton, Together For Christmas,
  1993 .... 20.00
Ornament, Schmid, Bah Humbug, 1995 .... 20.00
Ornament, Schmid, Church, 1986 .... 45.00
Ornament, Schmid, Mailbox, 1983 .... 60.00
Ornament, Schmid, Tree For Two, Disney, 1986 .... 18.00
Ornament, Schmid, Warm Winter Ride, 1988 .... 40.00
Ornament, Towle Silversmiths, Eleven Pipers Piping,
  1981 .... 80.00
Ornament, Towle Silversmiths, Five Golden Rings,
  1975 .... 125.00
Ornament, Towle Silversmiths, Four Calling Birds,
  1974 .... 150.00

Plate, Lynell, Burns/Young at Heart, 1982, $35.00.

Royal Copenhagen, Christmas, In The Desert, 1972, $25.00.

Ornament, Towle Silversmiths, Partridge in a Pear
Tree in a Wreath, 1991 . . . . **50.00**
Ornament, Towle Silversmiths, Two Turtle Doves,
1972 . . . . **150.00**
Plate, Anri, Alpine Mother and Child, 1973 . . . . **150.00**
Plate, Anri, Dove Girl, 1975 . . . . **150.00**
Plate, Anri, Holy Night, 1974 . . . . **100.00**
Plate, Anri, Tree of Life, 1976 . . . . **65.00**
Plate, Bad Wimpfen, 1982 . . . . **45.00**
Plate, Bareuther, Christkindlemarkt, 1969 . . . . **25.00**
Plate, Bareuther, Kapplkirche, 1968 . . . . **30.00**
Plate, Bareuther, Winter Fun, 1993 . . . . **60.00**
Plate, Berlin, Christmas in Bremen, 1974 . . . . **30.00**
Plate, Berlin, Christmas Eve in Wasserburg, 1982 . . . . . . **60.00**
Plate, Berlin, Christmas in Ramsau, 1984 . . . . **60.00**
Plate, Bing & Grondahl, Royal Hunting Castle, The
Hermitage, 1923 . . . . **60.00**
Plate, Bing & Grondahl, The Old Water Mill, 1945 . . . . . **140.00**
Plate, Bing & Grondahl, Winter Harmony, 1961 . . . . **120.00**
Plate, Franklin Mint, Hanging the Wreath, 1974 . . . . **120.00**
Plate, Franklin Mint, Under the Mistletoe, 1971 . . . . **130.00**
Plate, Haviland, Twelve Drummers Drumming, 1981 . . . . **60.00**
Plate, Haviland, Two Turtle Doves, 1971 . . . . **45.00**
Plate, Haviland & Parlon, Madonna and Child,
Murillo, 1975 . . . . **50.00**
Plate, Haviland & Parlon, Sight, 1978 . . . . **45.00**
Plate, Haviland & Parlon, The Unicorn in Captivity,
1971 . . . . **150.00**
Plate, Edwin M. Knowles, Father's Day, 1982 . . . . **40.00**
Plate, Edwin M. Knowles, Rhett, Gone With the
Wind Series, 1981 . . . . **55.00**
Plate, Lenox, Bobcats, Boehm Woodland Wildlife
Series **150.00**
Plate, Lenox, Mountain Bluebird, Boehm Bird Series,
1972 . . . . **45.00**
Plate, Reed & Barton, Decorating the Church, 1977 . . . . . **65.00**

Plate, Reed & Barton, Merry Old Santa Claus, 1979 . . . . . **70.00**
Plate, Rosenthal, Christmas By the Sea, 1935 . . . . **190.00**
Plate, Rosenthal, Christmas in the Alps, 1952 . . . . **190.00**
Plate, Rosenthal, Christmas in Wurzburg, 1974 . . . . **100.00**
Plate, Rosenthal, Winter Idyll, 1943 . . . . **300.00**
Plate, Royal Copenhagen, Christmas in the Forest,
1952 . . . . **125.00**
Plate, Royal Copenhagen, Danish Village Church,
1941 . . . . **250.00**
Plate, Royal Copenhagen, Danish Watermill, 1976 . . . . . . **25.00**
Plate, Royal Copenhagen, Mother and Child, 1931 . . . . . **100.00**
Plate, Royal Doulton, Christmas in Holland, Beswick
Christmas Series, 1976 . . . . **50.00**
Plate, Royal Doulton, Kathleen and Child, Mother
and Child Series, 1978 . . . . **100.00**
Plate, Schmid, Caroling, Disney Christmas Series,
1975 . . . . **20.00**
Plate, Schmid, Good Morning, Good Year, 1985 . . . . **165.00**
Plate, Schmid, Minnie's Surprise, Disney Mother's
Day Series, 1980 . . . . **25.00**
Plate, US Historical Society, Good Tidings of Great
Joy, Boston, 1985 . . . . **130.00**
Plate, US Historical Society, The Nativity, 1984 . . . . **150.00**
Plate, Wedgwood, Bountiful Butterfly, Calendar
Series, 1973 . . . . **15.00**
Plate, Wedgwood, St. Paul's Cathedral, Christmas
Series, 1972 . . . . **45.00**
Plate, Wedgwood, The Sewing Lesson, Mothers
Series, 1972 . . . . **25.00**

LINENS, LACE, CROCHET WORK, & OTHER EMBROIDERED HOUSEHOLD TEXTILES

Linen is now a generic term used for any household covering, e.g., bathroom, bed, kitchen, or table, made from cotton, lace, linen, man–made fibers, or silk.

Linen, a textile made from flax, originated in the Nile River Valley in ancient times. Linens experienced two golden ages, the Victorian era and the 1920s–30s. Victorian ladies prided themselves on their household linen handwork of delicate stitchery, lace insertions, fine tucking, and ruffles.

Lace divides into bobbin, embroidered, needlepoint, and machine made (also includes chemical and imitation lace). Machine–made lace dates to the first quarter of the 19th century. By 1840 technology had reached the point where machines were able to produce an imitation lace that was indistinguishable from most handmade laces.

Inexpensive mass–produced linens arrived at the turn of the century. Those women who continued to sew turned to pre–stamped embroidery kits. The popularity of bridge and formal dining in the period following World War I brought with it a renewed interest in linens. The Depression witnessed a renaissance of the 19th–century art of crochet.

Women entering the work force, casual dining from the 1950s to the present, and fast–track families reduced the emphasis placed on linens. A modest renaissance has occurred in the 1990s, largely the result of a re–emphasis on linens in Country decorating magazines and a return to more formal dining.

Today the vast majority of linens are manufactured in China, Europe, and the United States. Collectors feel modern examples lack the intricate handwork and freshness of design associated with pre–1945 linens.

References: Maryanne Dolan, *Old Lace & Linens Including Crochet: An Identification and Value Guide,* Books Americana, Krause Publications, 1989; Frances Johnson, *Collecting Antique Linens, Lace, and Needlework,* Wallace–Homestead, Krause Publications, 1991; Frances Johnson, *Collecting Household Linens,* Schiffer Publishing, 1997; Elizabeth Scofield and Peggy Zalamea, *20th Century Linens and Lace: A Guide to Identification, Care, and Prices of Household Linens,* Schiffer Publishing, 1995.

Periodical: *The Lace Collector,* PO Box 222, Plainwell, MI 49080.

Collectors' Club: International Old Lacers, PO Box 481223, Denver, CO 80248.

Bread Tray Cover, filet crochet, white, "Staff of Life," c1925, 12½" l . . . . $ 5.00
Clothespin Apron, feed bag, floral print, rounded bottom edge, 16 x 18" 10.00
Cocktail Napkins, set of 6, linen, lavender, handmade, grapes and green leaves cut work, 5 x 7" 35.00
Cocktail Napkins, set of 8, linen, white, yellow elephants appliquéd in corner, fringed edges, 8 x 8" 12.00
Crib Sheet, white muslin, blue top band, embroidered animals, matching pillowcase, 48 x 52" 40.00
Doily, cotton, embroidered, 12 x 14" 5.00
Doily, crocheted twine cotton thread, pineapple pattern, 18" d 12.00
Doily, ecru linen, painted floral and leaf design, embroidered, lace edging, 24" d 20.00
Doily, quatrefoil shape, formed filet crochet with roses, white, 24 x 24" 35.00
Doily, white cotton center, crocheted edging, 8" d 5.00
Doily, white muslin, embroidered red silk roses and green leaves, scalloped green silk floss edge, 18" d . . . 20.00
Hand Towel, white linen, embroidered orange and blue oriental designs at ends, hand–tied fringe, 18 x 24" 10.00

Antimacassar, crocheted, ecru cotton, 15½" w, $10.00.

Doily, crocheted, white cotton thread, pineapple design, 13" d, $12.00.

Handkerchief, cotton, red on white, printed bird design 22.00
Pillowcase, white muslin, embroidered, girl holding parasol surrounded by colorful flowers, 21 x 29" 12.00
Place Mats, set of 4, linen, woven red and tan checks, fringe, matching napkins, 12 x 18" 22.00
Pot Holder, white textile bag, embroidered, face on flower surrounded by leaves, 8" sq 5.00
Tablecloth, cotton, white ground, blue field with yellow and pink flowers and green leaves, 53 x 52" 20.00
Tablecloth, white linen damask, rose pattern with oval motif center, 72 x 84" 20.00
Tablecloth, white muslin, red cross–stitched floral design sides, 68 x 104" 40.00
Vanity Set, 4 pcs, white linen, royal blue embroidery of bonnet girls, 10 x 20" 30.00

LITTLE GOLDEN BOOKS

The first Little Golden Books were published in September 1942. George Duplaix and Lucile Olge of the Artist and Writers Guild, a company formed by Western Printing & Publishing in the 1930s to develop new children's books, and Albert Leventhal and Leon Shimkin of Simon & Shuster developed Little Golden Books.

The key to the success of Little Golden Books was their price, 25¢. Within the first five months, 1.5 million copies were printed. Simon & Shuster published the books, the Artists and Writers Guild produced them, and Western Printing and Lithographing printed them.

Initially books were sold primarily in book and department stores. Sales quickly spread to drug stores, supermarkets, toy stores, and variety stores. By the 10th anniversary (1952), over 182 million copies had been sold, 4 million of which came from sales of The Night Before Christmas.

The first Walt Disney title was published in 1944. Many of the titles issued in the 1950s and 60s were direct tie–ins with TV shows, TV westerns, and Saturday morning TV cartoon shows. In 1958 Western Printing and Lithographing and Pocket Books purchased the rights to Little Golden Books from Simon & Shuster. A Golden Press imprint was introduced. Eventually Western bought out Pocket Books and created Golden Press, Inc.

Little Golden Books are identified by a complex numbering system that experienced several changes over the years. Many titles have remained in print for decades. Value rests primarily in first editions, first printing examples in near mint condition. If the book contained a dust jacket or any other special feature, it must be intact for the book to have any retail market value.

References: Norman E. Martinus and Harry L. Rinker, *Warman's Paper*, Wallace–Homestead, Krause Publications, 1994; Steve Santi, *Collecting Little Golden Books, Second Edition*, Books Americana, Krause Publications, 1994.

Newsletter: *The Gold Mine Review*, PO Box 209, Hershey, PA 17033.

Collectors' Club: Golden Book Club, 19626 Ricardo Ave, Hayward, CA 94541.

Note: Prices are for books in mint condition.

A Child's Garden of Verses, #289, 1957, 24 pgs . . . . $ 5.00
A Day at the Zoo, #88, 1949, 42 pgs 8.00
Aladdin and His Magic Lamp, #371, 1959, 24 pgs 10.00
Albert's Stencil Zoo, #112, 1951, 28 pgs. 20.00
All Aboard, #152, 1952, 28 pgs 8.00
Animal Dictionary, #379, 1960, 24 pgs. 5.00
Animal Quiz, #396, 1960, 24 pgs. 5.00
Bedtime Stories, #2, 1942, 42 pgs 18.00
Brave Cowboy Bill, #93, 1950, 42 pgs 12.00
Bugs Bunny Gets a Job, #136, 1952, 28 pgs 8.00
Busy Timmy, #50, 1948, 28 pgs 12.00
Captain Kangaroo and the Panda, #278, 1951, 24 pgs 8.00
Cowboy ABC, #389, 1960, 24 pgs 8.00
Daisy Dog's Wake–Up Book, #102, 1974, 24 pgs 2.00
Doctor Dan, #399, 1960, 24 pgs 20.00
Doctor Squash, #157, 1952, 28 pgs 10.00
Fix It Please, #32, 1947, 42 pgs 15.00
Frosty the Snowman, #142, 1951, 28 pgs 6.00
Guess Who Lives Here, #60, 1949, 42 pgs 12.00
Happy Birthday, #123, 1952, 42 pgs 20.00
How to Tell Time, #285, 1957, soft cover, 24 pgs 2.00

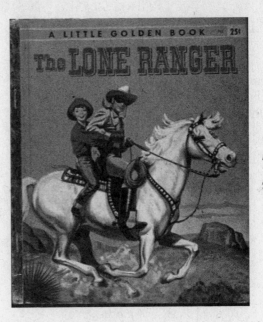

The Lone Ranger, #263, 1956, 24 pgs, $15.00.

Howdy Doody's Circus, #99, 1950, 28 pgs. 15.00
Jerry at School, #94, 1950, 28 pgs 8.00
Little Boy With a Big Horn, #100, 1950, 42 pgs. 8.00
Little Red Riding Hood, #42, 1948, 42 pgs 10.00
Machines, #455, 1961, 24 pgs 4.00
Mother Goose, #4, 1942, 42 pgs 18.00
My Baby Brother, #279, 1956, 24 pgs 15.00
My First Book, #10, 1942, 42 pgs. 15.00
My First Book of Bible Stories, #19, 1943, 42 pgs 12.00
My Home, #115, 1971, 24 pgs 2.00
Nursery Songs, #348, 1959, 24 pgs 5.00
Oscar's Book, #120, 1975, 24 pgs 2.00
Our Puppy, #56, 1948, 28 pgs 8.00
Puss in Boots, #359, 1959, 24 pgs 5.00
Robert and His New Friends, #124, 1951, 28 pgs 6.00
Rootie Kazootie, #150, 1953, 28 pgs 15.00
The Gingham's Backyard Picnic, #148, 1966, 25 pgs. 3.00
The Happy Man and His Dump Truck, #77, 1950,
  28 pgs 12.00
The Little Golden Book of Singing Games, #40, 1947,
  42 pgs 8.00
The Little Red Hen, #209, 1954, 28 pgs 5.00
The Lively Little Rabbit, #15, 1943, 42 pgs 15.00
The Rainy Day Play Book, #133, 1951, 28 pgs 6.00
The Seven Sneezes, #51, 1948, 42 pgs 12.00
The Shy Little Kitten, #23, 1946, 42 pgs 15.00
The Wonderful House, #76, 1950, 42 pgs. 10.00
This Little Piggy Counting Rhymes, #12, 1942, 42 pgs 18.00
Three Bedtime Stories, #309, 1958, 24 pgs 5.00
Thumbelina, #153, 1953, 28 pgs 8.00
Tootle, #21, 1945, 42 pgs 15.00
Top Cat, #453, 1962, 24 pgs 12.00
Toys, #22, 1945, 42 pgs. 12.00
Uncle Wiggily, #148, 1953, 28 pgs 12.00
We Like to Do Things, #62, 1949, 42 pgs 8.00
When You Were a Baby, #70, 1949, 42 pgs. 8.00
Wild Kingdom, #151, 1976, 24 pgs 3.00
Winky Dink, #266, 1956, 24 pgs 10.00
Woody Woodpecker at the Circus, #149, 1976, 24 pgs 3.00

Rin Tin Tin and Rusty, #246, 1955, 28 pgs, $12.00.

LITTLE GOLDEN BOOK TYPES

Competitors quickly rose to challenge Little Golden Books. Wonder Books, part of a publishing conglomerate that included Random House, arrived on the scene in 1946. Rand McNally published its first Elf Books in September 1947 and a Hanna–Barbera Character Series between 1975 and 1977.

Golden Press also produced variations of its successful Little Golden Book line. Giant Little Golden Books arrived in 1957, followed by the Ding Dong School Book series in 1959.

Big Golden Book, *Baby Farm Animals*, 1953, 28 pgs.... $ 5.00
Big Golden Book, *Big and Little*, 1966, 28 pgs 5.00
Big Golden Book, *Big Golden Book of Bible Stories*,
  1958, 70 pgs 12.00
Big Golden Book, *Gay Purr–ee*, 1962, 24 pgs 12.00
Big Golden Book, *I Can Count*, 1963, 28 pgs 4.50
Big Golden Book, *Nicky Goes to the Doctor*, 1972,
  Richard Scarry, 32 pgs 8.00
Big Golden Book, *Three Little Kittens*, 1942 .... 12.00
Big Little Golden Book, *Bugs Bunny and the Health
  Hog*. 1.00
Big Little Golden Book, *Little Sister*................ 1.00
DeLuxe Golden Book, *Golden Anniversary Book of
  Scouting*, 1959, 166 pgs.................... 15.00
DeLuxe Golden Book, *People and Places, Walt
  Disney's*, 1959, 176 pgs 8.00
DeLuxe Golden Book, *The Human Body, What It Is
  and How It Works*, 1959, 140 pgs............. 8.00
DeLuxe Golden Book, *Worlds of Nature, Walt
  Disney's*, 176 pgs....................... 8.00
Ding Dong School Book, *A Day Downtown With
  Daddy*, #205, 1953 .... 8.00
Ding Dong School Book, *I Decided*, #204, 1953 ...... 5.00
Giant Golden Book, *Animal Stories*, 1944, 92 pgs..... 15.00
Giant Golden Book, *Around the Year Storybook*,
  1971, 98 pgs 10.00
Giant Golden Book, *Best Word Book Ever*, 1963,
  94 pgs............................... 5.00
Giant Golden Book, *Golden Dictionary*, 1944, 94 pgs.... 10.00

Mickey Mouse Club Book, *Walt Disney's Uncle Remus*, #D6, ©1947, 42 pgs, $10.00.

Giant Little Golden Book, *This World of Ours*, #5026, 1959, 56 pgs, $20.00.

Giant Golden Book, *Mother Goose*, 1948, 96 pgs....... 20.00
Giant Golden Book, *Robinson Crusoe*, 1960, 98 pgs..... 15.00
Giant Golden Book, *The Animal's Merry Christmas*,
  1970, 68 pgs 8.00
Giant Little Golden Book, *Five Bedtime Stories*,
  1957, 56 pgs 8.00
Giant Sturdy Book, *Baby Animals*, 1952, 22 pgs 8.00
Giant Sturdy Book, *Baby's First Book*, 1955 .... 8.00
Giant Sturdy Book, *My First Counting Book*, 1956,
  22 pgs............................... 8.00
Golden Book, *About the Big Sky...*, 1978, 72 pgs 6.00
Golden Book, *Birds of the World*, 1961, 316 pgs...... 25.00
Golden Book, *Chinese Fairy Tales*, 1960, 156 pgs 20.00
Golden Book, *Funny Fingers*, 1971, 16 pgs........... 5.00
Golden Book, *Poems*, 1959, 80 pgs 5.00
Golden Book, *Rojankovsky's Wonderful Picture
  Book*, 1972, 118 pgs 18.00
Golden Forty–Niner, *Animals From All Over the
  World*, 1956, 30 pgs.................... 4.00
Golden Forty–Niner, *Bible Stories*, 1956, 28 pgs 5.00
Golden Forty–Niner, *Cowboys*, 1956, 30 pgs 6.00
Golden Funtime Book, *Birds Punch–Out Book*, 1960 .... 12.00
Golden Funtime Book, *Cars and Trucks* 2.50
Golden Funtime Book, *Charmin' Chatty Paper Dolls*,
  1964 .... 15.00
Golden Funtime Book, *Cinderella Punch–Out Book*,
  1962 .... 12.00
Golden Funtime Book, *Hokey Wolf* 6.00
Golden Funtime Book, *Little Red Riding Hood
  Stick–Um Book* 4.00
Golden Funtime Book, *Mister Magoo* 12.00
Golden Funtime Book, *Nurse Nancy Stick–Um Book* 15.00
Golden Funtime Book, *Saddle Your Pony Paper Dolls* 6.00
Golden Fuzzy Book, *The Golden Circus*, ©1950
  Simon & Schuster, 32 pgs.................. 12.00
Golden Fuzzy Book, *The White Bunny and His Magic
  Nose* 12.00
Golden Fuzzy Book, *Walt Disney's Circus*, 1944,
  32 pgs............................... 20.00

Walt Disney's Little Library, *The Cold–Blooded Penguin,* #D2, 1944, 24 pgs, $35.00.

Golden Hours Library, *Four Puppies,* 1960, 24 pgs **2.50**
Golden Hours Library, *Hop, Little Kangaroo,* 1965, 24 pgs **2.50**
Golden Hours Library, *Old MacDonald Had a Farm,* 1960, 24 pgs **2.50**
Golden Hours Library, *Rumpelstiltskin and The Princess and the Pea,* 1962, 24 pgs **2.50**
Golden Hours Library, *Tommy's Camping Adventure,* 1962, 24 pgs **2.50**
Hanna–Barbera Character Series, *Clue Club, The Case of the Missing Racehorse,* 1977 . . . . **8.00**
Hanna–Barbera Character Series, *Jabberjaw Out West, 1977* **8.00**
Hanna–Barbera Character Series, *Scooby–Doo and the Haunted Doghouse,* 1975 . . . . **10.00**
Happy Book, *I Am a Bunny,* 1963, 24 pgs **2.50**
Happy Book, *Numbers,* 1963, 24 pgs **2.50**
Junior Golden Guide, *Cats* **2.00**
Junior Golden Guide, *Snakes* **2.50**
Library of Knowledge, 7700 Series, *Butterflies and Moths,* 1958, 56 pgs **4.00**
Library of Knowledge, 7700 Series, *Indians of the Old West,* 1958, 56 pgs **5.00**
Library of Knowledge, 7700 Series, *The Moon,* 1959, 56 pgs **4.00**
Lift and Look Book, *Curious Little Kitten Plays Hide–and–Seek,* 1985, 24 pgs **2.50**
Lift and Look Book, *Poky Little Puppy and the Lost Bone,* 1985, 24 pgs **2.50**
Little Little Golden Book, *Fire Engines,* 1959, 24 pgs **1.50**
Little Little Golden Book, *We Help Mommy,* 1959, 24 pgs **1.50**
Little Silver Book, *Come Play With Me,* 1948, 24 pgs **5.00**
Little Silver Book, *Wild Animal Babies,* 1958, 24 pgs **2.00**
Look–Look Book, *Learn to Count,* 1976, 24 pgs **1.50**
Look–Look Book, *My House,* 1976, 24 pgs **1.50**
My First Learning Library, *Book of C,* 1965 . . . . **1.50**
Sandpiper Book, *Gene Autry and the Red Shirt,* 1961, 78 pgs **5.00**

Sandpiper Boo, *The Wishing Stick,* 1951, 78 pgs **1.50**
Tiny Golden Book, TG1000 Series, *Tiger Kitten's Poor, Poor Tail* **1.50**
Tiny Golden Book, TG2000 Series, *Bambi Plays Follow the Leader* **3.00**
Touch and Feel Book, *Pat the Bunny,* 1940 . . . . **5.00**
Touch and Feel Book, *Who's Baby?,* 1978, 18 pgs **2.00**
Treasury Book, *Treasury of Disney Little Golden Books,* 1978, 94 pgs **6.00**
Wonderful Worlds of Walt Disney, *Worlds of Nature* **8.00**

LITTLE RED RIDING HOOD

Design Patent #134,889, June 29,1943, for a "Design for a Cookie Jar," was granted to Louise Elizabeth Bauer of Zanesville, Ohio, and assigned to the A. E. Hull Pottery Company. This patent protected the design for Hull's Little Red Riding Hood line, produced between 1943 and 1957.

Hull and the Royal China and Novelty Company, a division of Regal China, made the blanks. Decoration was done almost exclusively at Royal China. Because the pieces were hand painted, many variations in color scheme have been discovered.

References: Harvey Duke, *The Official Identification and Price Guide to Pottery and Porcelain, Eighth Edition,* House of Collectibles, 1995.

REPRODUCTION ALERT: Be alert for Little Red Riding Hood cookie jar reproductions. The period piece measures 13" h; the Mexican reproduction is shorter.

Batter Pitcher . . . . **$ 400.00**
Butter, cov **350.00**
Canister, flour **650.00**
Cookie Jar, open basket, gold stars on apron **400.00**
Cracker Jar **575.00**
Creamer, head pour **400.00**
Creamer, top pour, tab handle **350.00**
Match Box **875.00**
Milk Pitcher **300.00**

Cookie Jar, floral apron, 13" h, $375.00.

Mustard, no spoon	250.00
Salt and Pepper Shakers, pr, 3¹⁄₄"	140.00
Salt and Pepper Shakers, pr, 5¹⁄₂"	225.00
Sugar, cov	300.00
Sugar, crawling	350.00
Teapot	375.00
Wall Pocket	450.00

LLADRO PORCELAINS

In 1951 José, Juan, and Vincente Lladró established a ceramics factory in Almacera, Spain. Each was educated at the Escuela de Artes y Oficios de San Carlos. José and Juan focused on painting and Vincente on sculpting. The Lladró brothers concentrated on the production of ceramic figurines, initially producing diminutive ceramic flowers.

In 1953 the brothers built a kiln that could produce temperatures sufficient to vitrify porcelain. With it, they began to make handled porcelain pieces in styles duplicating those of Dresden and Sevres. In 1955 they opened a shop in Valencia, and in 1958 began construction of a factory in the neighboring town of Tavernes Blanques.

In 1985 the company organized the Lladró Society, a collectors' club. Rosa Maria Lladró assumed the presidency of the Society in 1995. She, along with her sister Marie Carmen, and her cousins, Rosa and Juan Vicente, represent the second generation of the Lladró family to become involved in the business.

Reference: Collector's Information Bureau, *Collectibles Market Guide & Price Index, 15th Edition,* Collector's Information Bureau, 1997, distributed by Krause Publications.

Collectors' Club: Lladro Collectors Society, 1 Lladro Dr, Moonachie, NJ 07074.

Angel, praying, L4538G, 1969	$ 80.00
Angel With Horn, L4540M, 1969	80.00
Baby Jesus, L1388G, 1981	130.00
Bear, white, L1208G, 1972	70.00
Bearly Love, L1443G, 1983	110.00
Bird, L1053G, 1960	90.00
Boy With Dog, L4522M, 1970	145.00
Cat Nap, L5640G, 1990	135.00
Cherub, smiling, L4960G, 1977	100.00
Cow, L4680G, 1969	80.00
Ducklings, L1307G, 1974	130.00
Eskimo, L1195G, 1972	120.00
Eskimo Boy With Pet, L5238G, 1984	100.00
Flying Dove, L4550M, 1969	150.00
Flying Duck, L1263G, 1974	75.00
Friends in Flight, L2215M, 1991	170.00
Girl With Pig, L1011G, 1969	85.00
Girl With Slippers, L4523G, 1969	85.00
Joseph, L4533M, 1969	100.00
Kissing Doves, L1169M, 1971	125.00
Little Lamb, L5750G, 1991	40.00
Mary, L4534M, 1969	75.00
Monk, L2060M, 1977	130.00
Nesting Crane, L1599G, 1989	110.00
Oriental, L2057M, 1974	90.00
Pepita With Sombrero, L2140M, 1984	180.00

Pet Me, L5114G, 1982	75.00
Play With Me, L5112G, 1982	75.00
Prayerful Stitch, L2205M, 1990	175.00
Swan, wings spread, L5231G, 1984	120.00
Washing Up, L5887G, 1992	80.00

LOTTON, CHARLES

Charles Gerald Lotton (born October 21, 1935) is a contemporary glass artist. Lotton's early careers included working for Lockheed in Georgia and as a hair stylist in Chicago. In the mid–1960s he began collecting carnival glass.

Desiring to become involved in the making of glass, Lotton made a trip to the Fenton Art Glass Company in 1968. The enormity of the project temporarily discouraged him. A visit to a glass-blowing class at the Art Institute of Chicago in 1970 rekindled his dream. By the autumn of 1970 Lotton had built a small glass studio behind his house in Sauk Village, Illinois.

In June 1971 Lotton sold his first glass to C. D. Peacock, a downtown Chicago jeweler. A chance meeting with Dr. Ed McConnell during a visit to Corning, New York, resulted in a meeting with Lillian Nassau, a leading New York City art glass dealer. Paul Nassau, Lillian's son, and Lotton signed an exclusive five–year contract in 1972. Lotton leased a former lumber yard in Lansing, Illinois, to serve as his studio. In 1975 he built a new studio in Lynwood, Illinois, eventually building a glassworks behind his home in Crete, Illinois, in 1982.

By 1977 Lotton had achieved a national reputation and wanted the freedom to sell glass directly to his own distributors. Lotton glass is sold through a number of select retailers and at antiques shows. The four Lotton children, Daniel, David, John, and Rachel, are all involved with some aspect of glassmaking.

Bowl, cobalt blue, gold luster drop leaf dec, 1987	$ 225.00
Bowl, forest green drop leaf design, 1984	175.00
Bowl, seashell shape, gold King Tut design, gold ruby int	275.00
Bowl, white pulled feather design, 1985	175.00
Chalice, ftd, mandarin yellow, gold luster pulled feather design, 1980	175.00
Ornament, opal, coral pulled feather dec	35.00
Ornament, opal, yellow wave design	15.00
Paperweight, cobalt blue, blue luster King Tut design	50.00
Paperweight, cobalt blue, red multifloral dec	75.00
Paperweight, crystal, pink, blue, and white leaf and vine design	35.00
Paperweight, crystal, pink pulled feather design	40.00
Paperweight, crystal, gold ruby leaf and vine design	35.00
Paperweight, foliage green, orange morning glory blossoms design, 1983	75.00
Paperweight, iridescent cobalt blue, webbed pattern	45.00
Paperweight, mandarin red, black luster pulled feather design, 1980	75.00
Paperweight, mandarin yellow, gold luster leaf and vine dec	75.00
Paperweight, olive green, blue luster King Tut design	75.00
Paperweight, opal, sunkissed pulled drape design	75.00
Paperweight, opal, yellow and blue luster tapestry design	75.00
Sculpture, crystal, pink floral arrangement inside	375.00

Vase, cherry brown cypriot, blue luster lava draping,
  1988 . . . . **20.00**
Vase, coral, iridescent, lily pad dec, 1988. . . . . **125.00**
Vase, mandarin red, blue luster King Tut design, 1980 . . . **175.00**
Vase, miniature, mandarin yellow, blue pulled feath-
  er design **120.00**
Vase, opal, long neck, blue dec, selenium red int **350.00**
Vase, selenium red, King Tut design, 1982. . . . . **200.00**
Vase, selenium red, leaf and vine design, 1988 . . . . **125.00**
Vase, sunkissed cypriot, blue lava draping, 1978 . . . . **175.00**

LUNCH BOXES

A lunch kit is comprised of a lunch box and a thermos. Both must be present for the unit to be complete. Unfortunately, the tendency today is to separate the two units and sell them individually. Avoid buying from dealers who do this.

Although lunch kits date back to the 19th century, collectors focus on the lithographed tin lunch kits made between the mid–1930s and the late 1970s. Gender, Paeschke & Frey's 1935 Mickey Mouse lunch kit launched the modern form. The 1950s and early 1960s was the lunch kit's golden age. Hundreds of different kits were made, many featuring cartoon, movie, and television show images. Aladdin Company, Landers, Frary and Clark, Ohio Art, Thermos/King Seeley, and Universal are among the many companies who made lunch kits during the golden age.

This market went through a speculative craze that extended from the late 1970s through the early 1990s at which point the speculative bubble burst. Prices have dropped from their early 1990s high for most examples. Crossover collectors, rather than lunch kit collectors, are keeping the market alive in the late 1990s.

References: Larry Aikins, *Pictorial Price Guide To Metal Lunch Boxes & Thermoses,* L–W Book Sales, 1992, 1996 value update; Larry Aikins, *Pictorial Price Guide To Vinyl & Plastic Lunch Boxes & Thermoses,* L–W Book Sales, 1992, 1995 value update; Allen Woodall and Sean Brickell, *The Illustrated Encyclopedia of Metal Lunch Boxes,* Schiffer Publishing, 1992.

Periodical: *Paileontologist's Report,* PO Box 3255, Burbank, CA 91508.

Collectors' Club: Step Into The Ring, 829 Jacksson St Ext, Sandusky, OH 44870.

Note: Prices listed reflect boxes with thermos, both in near mint condition.

Alvin and the Chipmunks, vinyl, ©Ross Bagdasarian
  and Thermos, 1963. . . . . **$ 155.00**
Astronaut, dome, King–Seeley Thermos Co, 1963 . . . . **48.00**
Batman and Robin, Aladdin, 1967 . . . . **25.00**
Beatles, Aladdin, 1966. . . . . **85.00**
Bee Gees **20.00**
Bullwinkle, vinyl, King–Seeley Thermos Co, 1963 . . . . . . **62.00**
Cabbage Patch Kids, metal, King–Seeley Thermos Co,
  ©Original Appalachian Art Works Inc, 1983 . . . . **40.00**
Campus Queen **10.00**
Charlie's Angels Brunch Bag, vinyl, Aladdin, 1978. . . . . . . **38.00**
Davy Crockett, American Thermos Bottle Co, 1955 . . . . . **145.00**
Denver Broncos, plastic, 1980s **20.00**

Disneyland, castle, Aladdin, 1958 . . . . **50.00**
Dr. Doolittle, emb metal, Aladdin Industries, ©20th
  Century Fox Film Corp, 1967 . . . . **65.00**
Flintstones, 1964 . . . . **135.00**
Gentle Ben, 1968 . . . . **42.00**
Gremlins. **18.00**
Gunsmoke, Aladdin, 1960 . . . . **55.00**
Hogan's Heroes, dome, Aladdin, 1966 . . . . **75.00**
Jetsons, dome, Aladdin, 1965. . . . . **130.00**
King Kong **50.00**
Kiss, 1977. . . . . **38.00**
Lidsville, emb metal, Aladdin Industries, ©Sid &
  Marty Krofft Television Productions, 1971 . . . . **55.00**
Little House on the Prairie **25.00**
Mary Poppins Brunch Bag, vinyl, Aladdin, 1967 . . . . **45.00**
Miss America, 1972. . . . . **40.00**
NFL, metal, King–Seeley, ©National Football League
  Properties, Inc, 1975 . . . . **45.00**
Partridge Family. **20.00**
Peanuts, Lucy's Luncheonette **10.00**
Pebbles and Bamm–Bamm, Aladdin Industries, 1972. . . . **25.00**
Plaid, metal, American Thermos Bottle Co, c1950 . . . . . . **50.00**
Play Ball, 1969 . . . . **65.00**
Popeye, 1980s. **10.00**
Popples, Aladdin, 1986 . . . . **25.00**
Porky Pig. **150.00**
Roy Rogers and Dale Evans, American Thermos,
  c1950s **120.00**
Scooby Doo, metal, ©Hanna–Barbera Productions,
  Inc, 1973. . . . . **25.00**
Sesame Street, vinyl, Aladdin Industries, ©Children's
  Television Workshop, 1981. **55.00**
Six Million Dollar Man **10.00**
Snow White, vinyl, Aladdin, 1975 . . . . **55.00**
Space 1999, King Seeley Thermos Co, 1975 . . . . **25.00**
Strawberry Shortcake, vinyl, Aladdin Industries,
  ©American Greetings Corp, 1980 . . . . **25.00**

The Dukes of Hazzard, Aladdin, 1980, $18.00.

Transformers **6.00**
US Mail, metal, Aladdin Industries, 1970s **30.00**
Waltons, metal, Aladdin Industries, 1973 . . . . **60.00**
Wild Wild West, Aladdin Industries, 1969 . . . . **50.00**
Zorro, Aladdin Industries, 1966 . . . . **55.00**

MADE IN JAPAN

Prior to 1921, objects made in Japan were marked NIPPON or MADE IN NIPPON. After that date, objects were marked JAPAN or MADE IN JAPAN.

Although MADE IN OCCUPIED JAPAN was the primary mark used between August 1945 and April 28, 1952, some objects from this period were marked JAPAN or MADE IN JAPAN.

This is a catchall category for a wide range of ceramic, glass, and metal items made by Japanese manufacturers for export to the United States. Many were distributed by American import companies who designed the products in America, had them manufactured in Japan, and marketed them in the United States.

Reference: Carol Bess White, *Collector's Guide to Made in Japan Ceramics* (1994, 1996 value update), *Book II* (1996), Collector Books.

Note: See Occupied Japan for additional listings.

Aquarium Ornament, bisque, reclining mermaid,
   4³⁄₄" l . . . . **$ 30.00**
Aquarium Ornament, diver, orange glaze **15.00**
Ashtray, garbage can, 2 x 2¹⁄₄" **2.50**
Ashtray, metal, roulette wheel, 5" d **12.00**
Bank, cat, blue glaze, 4¹⁄₄" h **20.00**
Basket, handle, multicolored floral motif **50.00**
Bonbon, applied Canadian Mountie, brown glaze,
   inscribed "Canada," 5³⁄₄" w **10.00**
Bookends, pr, multicolored sailboats, 4³⁄₄" h **30.00**
Cache Pot, ceramic, girl and dog with toothache, 5¹⁄₂" h . . **20.00**
Chamberstick, green, black, and red glaze, 2¹⁄₂" h **15.00**
Cigarette and Match Holder, 3 black children **40.00**
Cookie Jar, Bull, mkd "Poubelle De Trole" **45.00**

Cookie Jar, Elephant, basket handle **120.00**
Cookie Jar, Hamburger, mkd "1979 Cara Creations
   Made in Japan" **150.00**
Cookie Jar, Tortoise With Top Hat **90.00**
Egg Timer, bellhop, multicolored, 2³⁄₄" h **30.00**
Figurine, 3 pc, bisque, wedding party, orig box **80.00**
Flower Frog, ceramic, white glaze, figural draped
   nude, 1950s, 9¹⁄₂" h **15.00**
Incense Burner, seated man smoking pipe, 4¹⁄₄" h **25.00**
Lighter, ceramic, African head, 8¹⁄₂" h **65.00**
Lighter, figural, lamp, pink shade, pull chain, 4 x 2" **45.00**
Lighter, figural, fire bellows, 7 x 3 x 1¹⁄₂" **25.00**
Lighter, pocket, Marxman Windproof, 1¹⁄₂" x 2¹⁄₄" **10.00**
Lighter, porcelain, flower motif, gold trim, 3¹⁄₄" h **20.00**
Napkin Ring, cat, pink glaze, 3" h **20.00**
Salt and Pepper Shakers, pr, calico cats, 3¹⁄₂" h **15.00**
Snack Set, ceramic, white and tan luster **15.00**
Toothbrush Holder, dog, brown, black, and white,
   6¹⁄₄" h **55.00**
Vase, calico hippo, 3¹⁄₄" h **20.00**
Wall Pocket, bird and bamboo, multicolored, 6¹⁄₂" h **22.00**

MAGAZINES

In the early 1700s general magazines were a major means of information for the reader. Literary magazines such as *Harper's* became popular in the 19th century. By 1900 the first photo-journal magazines appeared. Henry Luce started *Life,* the prime example, in 1932.

Magazines created for women featured "how to" articles about cooking, sewing, decorating, and child care. Many, e.g., *Harper's Bazaar* and *Vogue,* were entirely devoted to fashion and living a fashionable life. Men's magazines were directed at masculine skills of the time, such as hunting, fishing, and woodworking. "Girlie" titles became popular in the 1930s and enjoyed a golden age in the 1950s and 60s.

Popular magazines, such as *Collier's, Life, Look,* and *Saturday Evening Post,* survive in vast quantities. So do pulps. Value is driven primarily by cover image, content, and interior advertisements.

Many magazines are torn apart and the pages sold individually. The key value component for these "tear sheets" is subject matter. As a result 99% plus are purchased by crossover collectors. Except for illustrator collectors, crossover collectors care little if the tear sheet features a drawing or photograph. The most desirable tear sheets are in full color and show significant design elements.

References: Ron Barlow and Ray Reynolds, *The Insider's Guide to Old Books, Magazines, Newspapers, Trade Catalogs,* Windmill Publishing, 1995; David K. Henkel, *Magazines: Identification and Price Guide,* Avon Books, 1993; Denis C. Jackson, *Men's "Girlie" Magazines: The Only Price Guide: Newstanders, 4th Edition,* TICN, 1994; Denis C. Jackson, *Old Magazines: The Price Guide & Identification Guide, 4th Edition,* TICN, 1997; Norman E. Martinus and Harry L. Rinker, *Warman's Paper,* Wallace-Homestead, Krause Publications, 1994; *Old Magazine Price Guide,* L-W Book Sales, 1994, 1996 value update; Lee Server, *Danger Is My Business: An Illustrated History Of The Fabulous Pulp Magazines: 1896-1953,* Chronicle Books, 1993.

Teapot, ceramic, dark brown, enameled dec, 5¹⁄₂" h, $15.00.

Periodical: *PCM (Paper Collectors' Marketplace),* PO Box 128, Scandinavia, WI 54977.

Newsletter: *The Illustrator Collector's News,* PO Box 1958, Sequim, WA 98392.

All Hands, Sep 1945, End of War edition	$ 20.00
American Home	2.50
Antiques, Oct 1931	8.00
Arizona Highways, post–1960	2.50
Atlantic Monthly, 1928–1935	2.00
Bonanza, Vol #1, 1965	30.00
Building Age National Builder, 1920s	10.00
Business Week, post–1960	2.50
Charlie, June 1971, John Lennon story	5.00
Child's Life, 1930	8.00
Collier's, Jun 9, 1938	8.00
Country Music, Country Song Roundup, Feb 1966, 34 pgs	10.00
Des Moines Register Magazines, c1940s	8.00
ERA, Jun 1931	18.00
Esquire, Apr 1951	18.00
Farm Journal, Apr 1936	2.50
Farmer's Wife, Aug 1925	12.00
Fortune, 1950–1960	10.00
Girl's Companion, post–1940	2.00
Hammond Times, Walt Disney cov, Jul 1940	20.00
Harper's Monthly, 1930–1935	4.00
Highway Traveler, Greyhound, 1936	4.00
Holiday, 1950	2.50
Hot Rod, post–1960	2.50
Jack and Jill, Howdy Doody cov, 1960	15.00
Ladies' Home Journal, Marilyn Monroe cov, Jul 1973	18.00
Liberty, Jun 23, 1928	8.00
Life, Lee Harvey Oswald cov, Feb 21, 1964	22.00
Life, Beatles cov	28.00
Life, Charles Manson cov	18.00
Life, space walk cov, Jun 18, 1969	20.00
Literary Digest, 1935	1.50
Look, James Dean cov, Oct 16, 1956	20.00
Look, John F. Kennedy memorial issue, Nov 17, 1964	25.00

McCall's, 1930–1940	12.00
Modern Screen, Doris Day, Mar 1956	18.00
Movie Makers, Jun 1939	70.00
National Geographic, Jun 1926	4.00
Needlecraft, 1927	4.00
Newsweek, Mae West cov	10.00
Outdoor Life, 1932	15.00
Pictorial Review, Milwaukee Sentinel, Donald Duck and Disney characters cov, 1946	15.00
Playboy, Dec 1962	10.00
Popular Science, post–1930	2.50
Private Lives of Movie Stars, 1945	22.00
Reader's Digest, post–1930	2.50
Redbook, Apr 1925	8.00
Rolling Stone, James Dean cov, Jun 20, 1974	20.00
Saturday Evening Post, Pearl Harbor, 1923	12.00
Saturday Evening Post, Johnny Unitas cov, Dec 12, 1964	15.00
Sports Illustrated, Aug 16, 1954, 1st issue	320.00
Time, Aug 8, 1969, John Wayne cov	20.00
Town and Country, Jul 1948	38.00
TV Guide, Dark Shadows cov	32.00
TV Guide, post–1970	2.50

MARBLES

Although marbles date back to ancient times and Civil War soldiers used them as playing pieces for solitaire (a game where a marble is jumped over another marble until only one remains), the marbles found in this category are those used by children in school yards and sandlots during most of the 20th century. While terms such as shooters and peewees are part of the play vocabulary, entirely different terms are used in marble collecting.

Marbles divide into three basic types: (1) machine–made clay, glass, and mineral marbles, (2) handmade glass marbles made for use, and (3) handmade glass marbles made for display. Machine–made marbles usually sell for less than their handmade counterparts, comic strip marbles being one of the few exceptions. Watch for modern reproduction and fantasy comic strip marbles.

The Akro Agate Company, Christensen Agate Company, M. F. Christensen & Son Company, Marble King Company, Master Marble Company, Peltier Glass Company, and Vitro Agate/Gladding–Vitro Company are some of the leading manufacturers of machine–made marbles. Today, collector emphasis is on marble sets in their period packaging. This follows a similar trend in the toy train market.

Handmade marbles are collected by type—Bennington, china (glazed and painted), china (unglazed and painted), clay, end of day, Lutz, mica, sulfide, and swirl—and size. Over a dozen reproduction and fantasy sulfide marbles have appeared during the last decade.

Many contemporary studio glassblowers have made marbles, often imitating earlier styles, for sale to the adult collector market. These marbles show no signs of wear and have not been tested in the secondary resale market. Any values associated with these marbles are highly speculative.

References: Robert Block, *Marbles: Identification and Price Guide,* Schiffer Publishing, 1996; Everett Grist, *Antique and Collectible Marbles: Identification and Values, Third Edition,* Collector Books, 1992, 1996 value update; Everett Grist, *Everett Grist's Big Book of*

Saturday Evening Post, JFK memorial issue, Norman Rockwell cov, Dec 14, 1996, $30.00.

Marbles, Collector Books, 1993, 1997 value update; *Everett Grist's Machine Made and Contemporary Marbles, Second Edition,* Collector Books, 1995, 1997 value update; Dennis Webb, *Greenberg's Guide to Marbles, Second Edition,* Greenberg Books, 1994.

Collectors' Clubs: Marble Collectors Society of America, PO Box 222, Trumbull, CT 06611; National Marble Club of America, 440 Eaton Rd, Drexel Hill, PA 19026.

Akro Agate, Carnelian Agate.	$ 10.00
Akro Agate, Helmet Patch	3.00
Akro Agate, Limeade Corkscrew.	20.00
Akro Agate, Metallic stripe.	12.50
Akro Agate, Moonstone	10.00
Akro Agate, Popeye Corkscrew, green/yellow	15.00
Akro Agate, Popeye Corkscrew, red/blue.	65.00
Akro Agate, Swirl Oxblood.	22.00
Christensen Agate Company, Electric Swirl	55.00
Christensen, MF & Son Company, Slag	5.00
Marble King, Cub Scout.	5.00
Marble King, Tiger.	12.00
Marble King, White Matrix.	.25
Master Marble, Patch.	1.50
Master Marble, Sunburst, opaque.	4.00
Peltier Glass, Peerless Patch	2.50
Peltier Glass, sunset, Champion Jr, Muddy, Acme Reeler, Rainbo, Tri–color, 7–Up, Banana	1.50
Peltier Glass, 2–color Rainbo, old type	12.50
Vitro Agate/Gladding–Vitro, Blackie	.50
Vitro Agate/Gladding–Vitro, Cat's Eyes, bag of 100, c1950	40.00
Vitro Agate/Gladding–Vitro, Hybrid Catseye	2.00
Vitro Agate/Gladding–Vitro, Patch and Ribbon Transparent	.10

MARILYN MONROE

Marilyn Monroe was born Norma Jean Mortenson in Los Angeles, California, on June 1, 1926. Her movie career began in 1947 and ended in 1961. Monroe only made 29 movies, starring in 12 of them. Yet, this blond bombshell still reigns today as the greatest of the female movie stars to emerge from the Hollywood studio system of the 1950s.

Her life was filled with tragedy. Marilyn, an illegitimate child, spent her early years in a series of foster homes. She was only 16 when she married Jim Doughtery on June 19, 1942. While Jim was in the Merchant Marines, a photographer discovered Marilyn. She soon found work with the Blue Book Modeling Studio.

After a brief flirtation with the movies in 1947–48, Marilyn found herself without a contract. Her life changed dramatically after Tom Kelley's "Golden Dreams" photograph appeared in magazines and calendars across the nation in 1950. By March, Marilyn had signed a seven–year film contract with MGM.

Marilyn rocketed to fame in 1952, the result of an extensive publicity campaign. In 1953 *How to Marry a Millionaire* and *Gentlemen Prefer Blonds* turned Marilyn into a superstar. Marilyn broke with MGM in 1954 and went to New York, where she studied acting at the Actors Studio. *Bus Stop* (1956), *Some Like It Hot!* (1959), and *The Misfits* (1961) are considered among her best films.

Divorced from Doughtery, Marilyn married Joe DiMaggio in January 1951. Divorce followed in October 1954. Her marriage to Arthur Miller in June 1956 ended in 1961 following an affair with Yves Montand. The threat of mental illness and other health problems depressed Marilyn. She died on August 5, 1962, from an overdose of barbiturates.

References: Denis C. Jackson, *The Price & ID Guide to Marilyn Monroe, 3rd Edition,* TICN, 1996; Dian Zillner, *Hollywood Collectibles: The Sequel,* Schiffer Publishing, 1994.

Collectors' Club: All About Marilyn, PO Box 291176, Los Angeles, CA 90029.

Bank, battery operated, insert coin and dress blows up, 7" h.	$ 60.00
Book, *My Story by Marilyn Monroe,* Stein & Day, 1974, 141 pgs	30.00
Book, *Norma Jean, The Life of Marilyn Monroe,* dj, 1969	30.00
Book, *Will Acting Spoil Marilyn Monroe?,* Pete Martin, 1st ed, 1956, 128 pgs.	45.00
Calendar, "Golden Dreams," 1954	180.00
Calendar, full pad, 1955, 10 x 17".	30.00
Lobby Card, *The Seven Year Itch,* #8, 1955.	38.00
Magazine, *Fans Star Library*	15.00
Magazine, *Modern Man,* nude photos, 1956.	38.00
Magazine, *That Girl Marilyn!,* black and white photos, c1955, 56 pgs	20.00
Movie Poster, *Let's Make It Legal,* 20th Century Fox, 1951	150.00
Paper Dolls, Saalfield, #158610, uncut	150.00
Postcard, *Bus Stop,* French version	20.00
Poster, *Facciamo L' Amore,* 20th Century Fox.	60.00
Press Book, *Bus Stop,* Monroe cov, British promo, 96 pgs, 6 x 8"	45.00
Sheet Music, *Bus Stop,* 1956	28.00
Sheet Music, *My Heart Belongs to Daddy,* 1938	30.00
Statue, porcelain, 4" h	10.00

Magazine, *Life,* memorial issue, Aug 17, 1962, $30.00.

American Dinnerware

Homer Laughlin, Fiesta, relish tray, 10¾"d, $125.

Bauer, La Linda, creamer, glossy green, imp. "Bauer USA," 4¾"w, 3"h, $20.

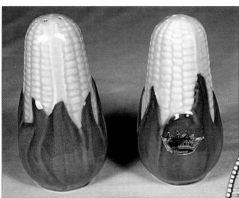

Shawnee, Corn King, salt and pepper shakers, pr., $22.

Shenango, creamer, 3½"h, $4.

Royal China, Currier & Ives, dinner plate, 10"d, $12.50.

Johnson Brothers, Coaching Scenes, dinner plate, 10"d, $20.

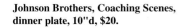

Hall China, Crocus, D-style, tidbit, platinum trim, 11½"h, $40.

Salem China, Rose-Marie, Century shape, shaker, ball, platinum trim, 3"h, $6.

Boxed Board Games

The Flintstones Stoneage Game, Transogram,
©1961 Hanna-Barbera, $32.

3 Men on a Horse, Milton Bradley, #46370, ©1936, $30.

Charlie's
Angels
Game,
Milton
Bradley,
#4721, $18.

Annie Oakley Game,
Milton Bradley, #4310,
$35.

Tru-Action Electric
Football Game,
Tudor, $40.

Dallas The Game of Empire Building Strategy, $10.

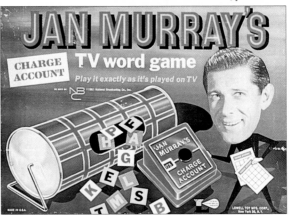

Jan Murray's
TV Word
Game,
Lowell Toy
Mfg. Co.,
©1961 NBC,
$28.

Childhood Memories

Pong, Atari, video game, $30.

American Plastic Bricks, Elgo Plastics, Inc., $15.

Noah's Ark, plastic, $25.

Water Pistol, red plastic, orig. box, $15.

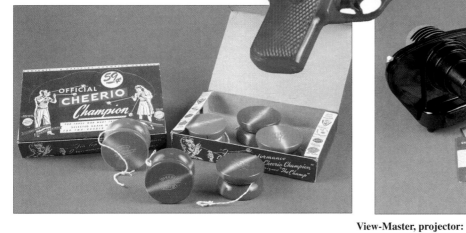

Yo-yos, Official Cheerio Champion, wood, orig. box with six yo-yos, $75.

View-Master, projector: $50; viewer with box: $15; reels: $3+.

Kitchen Set, Snow White, litho tin, 1970s, sink: $35; refrigerator: $20; stove: $35.

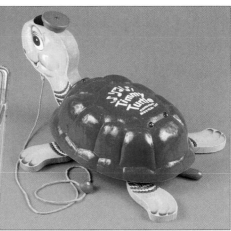

Timmy Turtle, Fisher Price, pull toy, wood and plastic, $65.

Dolls

Ideal, Snow White, 13"h, composition socket head, composition body marked "Shirley Temple 13," orig. costume, skirt printed with logo "Snow White and the Seven Dwarfs, W.D. Enterprises," $675.

Mattel, Barbie, 1961, bubble cut, $200; Red Flare outfit $100.

Nancy Ann Storybook Doll, 1947-49, $85.

Madame Alexander, Alice in Wonderland, 21"h, composition head and body, $1,200.

Cameo, 12"h, composition socket head, composition body, $250.

Buddy-Lee, 15"h, Coca-Cola outfit, $600.

Arranbee, Little Angel, 19"h, composition head, cloth body, celluloid hands, orig. costume, paper tag, $800.

Georgene, Raggedy Ann, 15"h, cloth, $300.

Fishing

Lure, Al Foss Pork Rind Minnow, metal, c. 1919, $20.

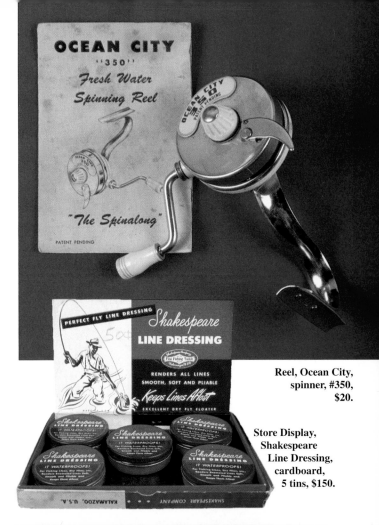

Lure, South Bend Bait Co., Bass Oreno, wood, glass eyes, $25.

Reel, Ocean City, spinner, #350, $20.

Store Display, Shakespeare Line Dressing, cardboard, 5 tins, $150.

Reel, Pflueger, Skilkast, $20.

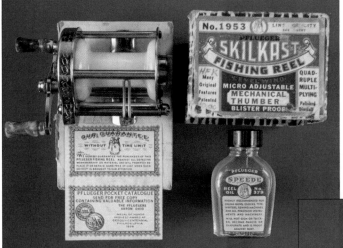

Licenses, PA, 1923, $400 (first button issue); 1946, $15; 1954, $10; 1975, $5.

Trout Net, Ed Cumings, Flint, MI, wooden, $35.

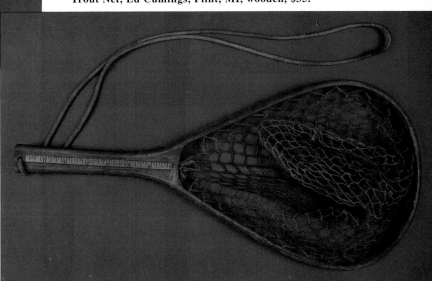

Minnow Pail, The Clipper Heater Ice Fisherman's Minnow Pail, E. L. Walstedt & Co., kerosene lamp inside, $120.

Soda Pop Collectibles

Major
Cola,
tray, 1939,
$200.

Whistle, display, 3-dimensional, cardboard,
c. 1948, 14"x17" (heavily reproduced;
repro has thin cardboard), $275.

Orange Crush,
thermometer, tin, 1930s,
12"h, $325.

Frostie, sign,
cardboard,
easel back, 1950,
13"x22", $125.

7-Up, bottle
topper, card-
board, 1946,
$50 without
bottle; $75
with bottle.

Coca-Cola, change tray,
plastic, 1960s, $175.

Pepsi-Cola, window banner,
paper, 1930s, 6½"x19½",
$200.

Nu Grape, cutout,
tin, 1940s-50s,
17"h, 5"w, $275.

TV Character Collectibles

Gumby, hand puppet, Lakeside, 1965, $25.

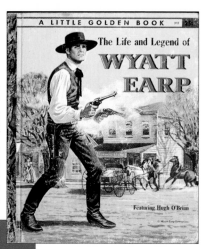

Wyatt Earp, Little Golden Book, #315, *The Life and Legend of Wyatt Earp*, featuring Hugh O'Brian, $18.

Hanna-Barbera, Sylvester & Tweety, hot water bottle, $75.

Fred Flintstone, bank, molded plastic, $35.

Julia, Colorforms dress-up kit, $18.

Masks and Envelope, 4 Star Revue, box, comic masks, sponsored by Norge, 1951, Borg-Warner Corp., $50.

Space Cadet, Golden Record, R89, *Tom Corbett Space Cadet Song and March*, ©1951 Rockhill Productions, $20.

Lone Ranger, Whitman Publishing, #2610-29, ©1953, frame tray puzzle, $25.

Batman, batmobile, Aoshing, Japan, 1966, $175.

World's Fair

1968 World's Fair, San Antonio, Jim Beam bottle, $25.

1939 World's Fair, New York, compact, $75.

1933-34 Century of Progress, Chicago, purse, mesh, enameled, $175.

1964 World's Fair, New York, bank, orig. box, $20.

1964 World's Fair, New York, ashtray, ceramic, $7.

1939 World's Fair, New York, chair, painted wood, $85.

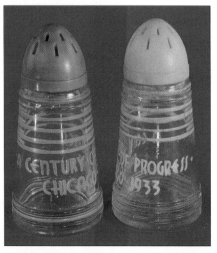

1982 World's Fair, Knoxville, beer mug, ceramic, $5.

1933-34 Century of Progress, Chicago, salt and pepper shakers, glass, plastic tops, $20.

MATCHBOX

In 1947 Leslie Smith and Rodney Smith, two unrelated Navy friends, founded Lesney (a combination of the first letters in each of their names) in London, England. Joined by John Odell, they established a factory to do die casting.

A 4¹/₂" Aveling Barford road roller was the first toy the company produced. It was quickly followed by a 4¹/₂" Caterpiller bulldozer, a 3¹/₈" Caterpillar tractor, and a 3³/₄" cement mixer. In 1953, Lesney introduced a miniature toy line packaged in a box that resembled a matchbox. The toys quickly became known as "Matchbox" toys. Moko, owned by Richard Kohnstam, marketed the toys.

The earliest Matchbox vehicles had metal wheels. These were eventually replaced with plastic wheels. In 1969 the Superfast plastic wheel was introduced. Slight variations in color and style occurred from the beginning due to paint and parts shortages. In 1956 the Models of Yesteryear series, the brainchild of John Odell, was introduced, followed in 1957 by Major Packs.

Matchbox toys arrived in the United States in 1958 and achieved widespread popularity by the early 1960s. Matchbox is a Top 5 Baby Boomer era toy. Mattel's Hot Wheels arrived on the scene in 1968, providing Matchbox with a major competitor. Matchbox revamped its models through the 1970s and added the "1–75" numbering system.

In 1982 Universal Group bought Lesney. Production was moved to the Far East to cut costs. In 1992 Tyco Toys bought Universal Group. Matchbox also introduced a line of "nostalgia" models in 1992. In 1997, Mattel, owner of Hot Wheels, Matchbox's biggest rival, acquired Tyco.

References: Dana Johnson, *Matchbox Toys: 1948–1996, Second Edition,* Collector Books, 1996; Charlie Mack, *Lesney's Matchbox Toys, Regular Wheel Years, 1947–1969,* Schiffer Publishing, 1992; Charlie Mack, *Lesney's Matchbox Toys: The Superfast Years, 1969–1982,* Schiffer Publishing, 1993; Charlie Mack, *Matchbox Toys: The Tyco Years, 1993–1994,* Schiffer Publishing, 1995; Charlie Mack, *Matchbox Toys: The Universal Years, 1982–1992,* Schiffer Publishing, 1993; Nancy Schiffer (comp.), *Matchbox Toys, Revised,* Schiffer Publishing, 1995.

Collectors' Clubs: Matchbox Collectors Club, PO Box 977, Newfield, NJ 08344; Matchbox U.S.A., 62 Saw Mill Rd, Durham, CT 06422; The Matchbox International Collectors Assoc, 574 Canewood Crescent, Waterloo, Ontario, Canada N2L5P6.

1899 London Double Decker Horse–drawn Bus, Y–12–A, Models of Yesteryear series, red body, beige driver and seats, light brown horses, 1959 . . . . $ 75.00
1899 London Double Decker Horse–drawn Bus, Y–12–A, Models of Yesteryear series, red body, pink–cream driver and seats, dark brown horses, 1959 . . . . 85.00
1903 Duke of Connaught Engine, Y–14–A, Great Western Railway, 1959 . . . . 150.00
1906 Rolls Royce Silver Ghost, Y–10–C, 1969 . . . . 35.00
1907 London E Class Tram Car, Y–3–A, 1956 . . . . 60.00
1912 Ford Model T Tanker, Y–3–D, 1982 . . . . 18.00
1912 Ford Model T Truck, Y–12–C, 1979 . . . . 25.00
1918 Crossley R.A.F. Tender, Y–13–C, 1973 . . . . 30.00

1920 Aveling Porter Steam Roller, Y–11–A, Models of Yesteryear series, green body, black roof supports, dark brown flywheel, pivoting front roller, 1958, 3" l 65.00
1926 Morris Cowley Bullnose Y–8–A, 1954 . . . . 80.00
1927 Talbot Van, Y–5–D, 1978 . . . . 25.00
1936 Jaguar SS 100, Y1C, Models of Yesteryear series, mkd "Lesney Products & Co. Ltd, Made in England," 1977, 4" l 30.00
1937 GMC Van, Y–12–D, Goblin Electric Cleaners, 1988 . . . . 20.00
1957 Chevrolet Belair Sport Convertible, DY–27, Dinky line, tan and brown seats 25.00
Allis–Chalmers Earth Scraper, K–6–A, King Size series, 1961, 5⁷/₈" l 25.00
Bedford Ambulance, 14–C, 1962, 2⁵/₈" l 20.00
Bedford Car Transporter, A–2–A, Accessory Pack #2, blue body, black decals and wheels, 1957, 6¹/₂" l 65.00
Bedford Car Transporter, A–2–A, Accessory Pack #2, red cab, gray trailer, orange decals, black plastic wheels, 1957, 6¹/₂" l 150.00
Caterpillar DW20 Earth Scraper, M–1–A, Major Pack series, mkd "Made in England No. 1 by Lesney" and "CAT DW20," 1957, 4¹/₂" l 45.00
Commer Lyons Maid Ice Cream Truck, 47–B, 1–75 series, blue body, white plastic vendor, 1963, 2⁷/₁₆" l 35.00
Coronation Coach, King and Queen, gold painted coach, 1953, small version, 4¹/₂" l 300.00
Coronation Coach, King and Queen, silver plated coach, 1953, small version, 4¹/₂" l 175.00
Double Decker London Bus, 5–A, 1–75 series, gold radiator, 1954, 2" l 60.00
Fire Station Gift Set, G–10–A, 9³/₄" l Fire Station MF–1A issued 1963, two 2¹/₂" l Merryweather Marquis Fire Engines 9C issued 1959, 2⁵/₈" l Bedford Ambulance 14–C issued 1962, 2⁵/₈" l Ford Fairlane Fire Chief car 59–B issued 1963, orig box 150.00
Ford Fairlane Fire Chief car, 59–B, 1963, 2⁵/₈" l 20.00
Ford Galaxy Police Car, 55–C, 1–75 series, white body, red bubble light, driver, 1966, 2⁷/₈" l 30.00

Massey–Harris Tractor, with fenders, 4–A, 1954, 1 5/8", $65.00.

Ford Model A Van, MB38, Champion Spark Plugs, blue, 1982, 3" l **10.00**

Ford Thames Singer Van, 59–A, 1–75 series, green, 1958, 2⅛" l **40.00**

Ford Thunderbird, 75–A, 1–75 series, 2–tone flesh and cream body, 1959, 2⅝" l **45.00**

Fowler "Big Lion" Showman's Engine, Y–9–A, 1958 ..... **80.00**

Leyland Site Office Truck, 60–C, 1–75 series, super fast wheels, 1970, 2½" l **15.00**

Massey Harris Tractor, 4–B, 175 series, attached driver, no fenders, 1⅝" l **60.00**

Mercedes 500 SL Convertible, Series III, World Class series, "Good Year" rubber tires, mirrored windows, 1991 .... **5.00**

Merryweather Marquis Fire Engine, 9–C, 1959, 2½" l **15.00**

Models of Yesteryear Gift Set, G–7, includes 1899 London Double Decker Horse–drawn Bus Y–12–A issued 1959, 1903 Duke of Connaught Engine Y–14–A from the Great Western Railway issued 1959, 1907 London E Class Tram Car Y–3–A issued 1956, 1926 Morris Cowley Bullnose Y–8–A issued 1954, and Fowler "Big Lion" Showman's Engine Y–9–A issue 1958, 1960, orig box............... **525.00**

Models of Yesteryear Limited Edition Pack Gift Set, includes 1906 Rolls Royce Silver Ghost Y–10–C issued 1969, 1912 Ford Model T Tanker Y–3–D issued 1982, 1012 Ford Model T Truck Y–12–C issued 1979, 1918 Crossley R.A.F. Tender Y–13–C issued 1973, and 1927 Talbot Van Y–5–D issued 1978, 1982, orig box **150.00**

MATCHCOVERS

Joshua Pusey, a Philadelphia lawyer who put 10 cardboard matches into a plain white board cover, is credited with inventing the matchcover. In 1892 he sold 200 to the Mendelson Opera Company, which hand–printed the cover with its advertisement.

Binghamton Match Company, Binghamton, New York, made the first machine–made matchcover for the Piso Company of Warren, Pennsylvania. Only one example survives, owned by the Diamond Match Company.

Matchcovers dating prior to the early 1930s are scarce. The modern matchcover collecting craze dates from the Chicago Century of Progress World's Fair of 1933–34. The matchcover's golden age began in the mid–1940s and extended through the early 1960s. Atlas Match, Brown and Bigelow, Crown Match, Diamond Match, Lion Match, Ohio Match, and Universal Match were manufacturers of this form of pocket advertisement.

The introduction of the throw–away lighter in the mid–1960s ended the matchcover era. Rising production costs also contributed. The per unit cost of diecut matchcovers today falls in the seven to eight cents range. Given this, matchcovers lost their appeal as a free giveaway.

The 1990s saw matchcover prices soar. The $1,000 barrier was broken. Many of these higher prices are being paid by crossover, not matchcover collectors. Trading, usually on a one for one basis, still remains the principal form of exchange among collectors.

References: Norman E. Martinus and Harry L. Rinker, *Warman's Paper,* Wallace–Homestead, Krause Publications, 1994; Bill Retskin, *the Matchcover Collector's Price Guide, 2nd Edition,* Antique Trader Books, 1997.

Collectors' Clubs: Rathkamp Matchcover Society, 2920 E 77th St, Tulsa, OK 74136; The American Matchcover Collecting Club, PO Box 18481, Asheville, NC 28814.

Air Force One, Reagan Administration .... **$ 5.00**
Albuquerque National Bank........................ **2.00**
Allied Van Lines, 1952........................... **4.00**
B & B Steak Station **3.00**
BC Telephone Company Canada **2.00**
Black Angus Motel............................... **2.00**
Bonanza Restaurant............................. **2.00**
Bowling Alleys, assorted cities **8.00**
Canada Centennial 1867–1967, Kraft Foods **5.00**
Champion Motors, Portland, ME.................. **7.00**
Chevrolet, 1952................................ **10.00**
Chevron **5.00**
Chicago Town and Tennis Club................... **3.50**
Clicks Pool Hall................................ **6.00**
Crab Orchard Brand Kentucky Straight Whiskey **7.00**
Delta Hotels and Resorts **1.00**
Enjoy Doublemint Gum, Healthful Delicious **5.00**
Gateway Diners................................ **4.00**
Gillette Blue Blades............................ **2.50**
Glamour Girl.................................. **10.00**
Goldwater for President......................... **8.00**
Hilton International Hotel, Egypt **2.00**
Holiday Inn, Alexandria, VA...................... **5.00**
Holiday Plaza, Merrillville, IN **1.50**
Hoyt's Restaurant, Yellville, AR **2.50**
JFG Coffee, 1930s.............................. **10.00**
Kennedy Space Center.......................... **1.50**
Kit Kat Ranch **10.00**
Lou's Diner, Mill Plain, CT **5.00**
McBroome's Diner, Jewett City, Conn **4.00**
Mineral Tea Room, Mineral, VA **4.00**
Pabst Blue Ribbon Beer **4.00**
Paul's Diner, Mountain Lakes, NJ **2.00**

Amusement Park, 1930s, 1½ x 3¾", $8.00.

Phillips 66. . . . . **6.00**
Playboy Club, Atlanta **10.00**
Quaker State Oil **5.00**
Radio Station WMGM **4.00**
Revelation Tooth Powder, 1930s **12.00**
Seattle Area Boy Scout Council Jamboree, Troop15,
    July 1953 . . . . **10.00**
Shell, assorted **5.00**
Snyder's Hotel and Restaurant **2.00**
Squaw Valley Lodge, 1960 Winter Olympic Games **8.00**
Starlite Room **5.00**
Stork Club, New York City **7.50**
Texas Centennial, Dallas, 1936 . . . . **15.00**
The Village Restaurant, Lancaster, PA **2.00**
Top Rail Western Entertainment, Los Angeles, CA **3.00**
Vote Bob Dole President 1988 . . . . **3.00**

MCCOY POTTERY

McCoy Pottery and Brush McCoy, a continuation of J. W. McCoy, are two separate firms. Do not confuse them. This category only includes products made by McCoy Pottery.

In 1910 Nelson McCoy, with his father's (J. W. McCoy) support, founded the Nelson McCoy Sanitary Stoneware Company, to manufacture crocks, churns, and jugs. It competed directly with Brush McCoy. Early pieces were marked on the side with a stencil of a clover within a shield with an "M" above. By the mid–1920s, the company also made molded artware in forms ranging from jardinieres to vases.

In 1933 the company became the Nelson McCoy Pottery. Products included cookware, dinnerware, floral industry ware, gardenware, kitchenware, and tableware. Early designers include Walter Bauer and Sidney Cope. The family remained active in the company's management following Nelson McCoy's death in 1945. Nelson McCoy Melick, Nelson's nephew, became president. Nelson McCoy, Jr., a fourth generation member of the family, joined the company in 1948. He was 29. A fire destroyed the plant in 1950. The family rebuilt utilizing the latest technology.

In 1967 Mount Clemens Pottery, owned by David Chase, purchased the company. Some pieces were marked "MCP" on the bottom. In 1974 Chase sold McCoy to Lancaster Colony Corporation, which added its logo to the bottom. Nelson McCoy, Jr., remained as president under the Mount Clemens and Lancaster Colony Corporation ownership until he left the firm in 1981. After being sold to Designer Accents in 1985, operations at McCoy ceased in 1990.

References: Bob Hanson, Craig Nissen, and Margaret Hanson, *McCoy Pottery: Reference & Value Guide,* Collector Books, 1997; Sharon and Bob Huxford, *The Collectors Encyclopedia of McCoy Pottery,* Collector Books, 1980, 1997 value update.

Newsletter: *Our McCoy Matters,* PO Box 14255, Parkville, MO 64152.

REPRODUCTION ALERT: Nelson McCoy Pottery Company reproduced many of its original pieces.

Ashtray, arrowhead shape, green . . . . **$ 20.00**
Ashtray, raised pheasant design center, 9" d **30.00**
Ashtray, yellow, 8" sq **20.00**

Pitcher Vase, emb daisy panels, red ext, white int, 1972, 9" h, $18.00.

Bank, eagle **38.00**
Bank, pig **45.00**
Basket, hanging, white matte glaze **30.00**
Bean Pot, Brown Drip, individual, 12 oz. **5.00**
Bookends, pr, birds, 6" h **95.00**
Canister, Brown Drip **35.00**
Centerpiece, cherub base, silver, black, 11" h **35.00**
Cereal Bowl, Brown Drip **5.00**
Cookie Jar, Basket of Eggs **70.00**
Cookie Jar, Brown Drip **20.00**
Cookie Jar, Coffee Mug **45.00**
Cookie Jar, Cookie Kettle **25.00**
Cookie Jar, Grandfather's Clock **55.00**
Cookie Jar, Panda **45.00**
Cookie Jar, Yosemite Sam **150.00**
Corn Dish, brown, 9 x 3¼" **10.00**
Creamer, Brown Drip **5.00**
Cup, Brown Drip, 8 oz **5.00**
Cuspidor, grape, brown glaze **35.00**
Custard, Brown Drip, 6 oz **5.00**
Decanter, astronaut **48.00**
Decanter, Pierce Arrow Sport Phantom **50.00**
Dog Feeder, "Man's Best Friend," brown, 7½" d **45.00**
Figure, lamb, white **25.00**
Figure, Scottie dog and cat, price for pair **45.00**
Flower Bowl, grapes **40.00**
Flower Holder, figural, elephant, coral **20.00**
Flower Holder, figural, fish, yellow **50.00**
Flower Holder, figural, swan, yellow **55.00**
Jardiniere, hobnail, pastel blue, 3½" h **25.00**
Lazy Susan, 12" d **30.00**
Mug, El Rancho, 10 oz **30.00**
Mug, gorilla, 1978 . . . . **20.00**
Pie Baker, Brown Drip, 9" d **20.00**
Pitcher, butterfly pattern, blue, 10" h **100.00**
Planter, cat face, black, 5 x 6" **25.00**
Planter, deer dec, white, 4" h **20.00**
Planter, figural, snowman, white dec, 6 x 4" **45.00**
Planter, iguana, white, 6½" h **200.00**
Planter, Liberty Bell, green, 10 x 8¼" **170.00**

Vase, emb peacocks, white, 1948, 8¼" h, $35.00.

Planter, quail. 30.00
Platter, Brown Drip, fish shape, 18" l 35.00
Salt and Pepper Shakers, pr, Pasta Corner Line. 15.00
Soup Bowl, Brown Drip. 6.00
Soup Mug, Brown Drip, double handle, 12 oz 8.00
Sprinkler, figural, turtle. 50.00
Teapot, Brown Drip, long spout, 6 cup 22.00
Vase, butterfly, blue. 45.00
Vase, figural, hand, white, 6½" h 55.00
Wall Pocket, butterfly, white, 7 x 6" 175.00
Wall Pocket, figural, violin, aqua, gold trim, 10¼" h 125.00
Wall Pocket, leaf, pink, blue, 7 x 5½". 35.00
Wall Pocket, leaves and berries, 7" h 125.00
Wall Pocket, lily bud, 8" h 150.00

MCDONALD'S

In 1948 Dick and Mac McDonald opened their first limited menu, self–service McDonald's drive–in restaurant in San Bernadino, California. They began franchising their operation as the Speedee Service System in 1952. In 1955 Ray Kroc became a franchising agent for the McDonald brothers and opened his first McDonald's restaurant in Des Plaines, Illinois.

The 100th McDonald's restaurant opened in 1959 and the 200th in 1960. In 1961 Kroc bought out the McDonald brothers and launched the All American Meal of a hamburger, french fries, and milkshake. The Golden Arches replaced the Speedee logo in 1962. The first "Ronald McDonald," Willard Scott, made his debut in Washington, D.C.'s Cherry Blossom Parade in 1963.

The Big Mac and Hot Apple Pie arrived on the scene in 1968. In 1970 "You Deserve A Break Today..." appeared for the first time. The Quarter Pounder joined the menu in 1972 and the Egg McMuffin in 1973. The Happy Meal dates from 1977. Toys were introduced in 1982.

By 1983, McDonald's had 7,000 restaurants in the United States and additional restaurants in thirty–one foreign countries. Chicken McNuggets also arrived on the menu that year. "It's a Good Time For the Great Taste of McDonald's" became the company's main advertising slogan in 1984.

In the 1990s McDonald's has continued to build new restaurants around the world. Promotional tie–ins with movies, television shows, and major toy products have proven highly successful. By 1994, the 15th anniversary of the Happy Meal, McDonald's was serving 25 million customers daily in 70 countries.

References: Gary Henriques and Audre DuVall, *McDonald's Collectibles: Identification and Value Guide*, Collector Books, 1997; Terry and Joyce Losonsky, *McDonald's Happy Meal Toys Around the World*, Schiffer Publishing, 1995; Terry and Joyce Losonsky, *McDonald's Happy Meal Toys in the U.S.A.*, Schiffer Publishing, 1995; Meredith Williams, *Tomart's Price Guide To McDonald's Happy Meal Collectibles, Revised Edition*, Tomart Publications, 1995.

Newsletter: *Collecting Tips Newsletter*, PO Box 633, Joplin, MO 64802.

Collectors' Club: McDonald's Collectors Club, 255 New Lenox Rd, Lenox, MA 01240.

Box, Aladdin's Oasis, Disney Favorites, 1987 . . . . $ 1.00
Box, Barbie, Beachfront Fun, 1992. . . . . 1.50
Box, Berenstain Bears, Barn Dance, 1987. . . . . 1.50
Box, Cat With a Mission, Garfield, 1989. . . . . 1.50
Box, Colorforms, Hamburglar/Picnic, 1986. . . . . 2.50
Box, Crayola, planets, 1988 . . . . 1.50
Box, ET Makes Friends, 1985 . . . . 2.50
Box, Friendly Skies, Windows of the World, 1991 . . . . 5.00
Box, Hot Wheels, Racers, 1991 . . . . 1.50
Box, Play Doh Place, 1985 . . . . 5.00
Box, Popoids, Octopoid, 1985 . . . . 4.00
Box, Real Ghostbusters, schoolhouse, 1987 . . . . 1.50
Drinking Glass, Captain Crook in boat, McDonald-
    land Series. 2.50
Drinking Glass, Hamburglar, McDonald's Collector
    Series 3.00
Juice Glass, frosted, golden arches 2.00
Mug, emb, smoke colored Ronald, football. 6.00
Premium, activity book, Paint It Wild, 16 pgs, 1991 . . . . . 1.50
Premium, Alvin playing electric guitar, 1991. . . . . 6.00
Premium, Bambi, 1988 . . . . 3.00
Premium, baseball, white, red stitching, McDonald's
    logo, 1990. . . . . 1.50
Premium, Beachcomber Happy Pail, Grimace, 1986. . . . . 15.00
Premium, Bicyclin' Barbie, 1994 . . . . 1.00
Premium, Big Mac Helicopter, green, 3 pcs, 1986. . . . . . . 5.00
Premium, book, *Fievel's Friends,* 1986 . . . . 2.50
Premium, book, *The Elves at the Top of the World,*
    Santa Claus The Movie, 1985 . . . . 2.50
Premium, book, *Tom and Jerry's Party,* Little Golden
    Book, 1982 . . . . 2.50
Premium, cow, Barnyard, 1986 . . . . 5.00
Premium, Dallas Cowboys trading card, Don
    Meredith, 1980 . . . . 15.00
Premium, Dino, Flintstone Kids, 1988 . . . . 6.00
Premium, Dot's Ice Cream Wagon, Animaniacs, 1994. . . . 1.50
Premium, Duck Code Quacker, orange, Duck Tales I,
    1988. . . . . 1.50
Premium, Einstein's Traveling Train, Back to the
    Future, 1992 . . . . 1.00
Premium, '55 Chevy, yellow, 1991. . . . . 2.50

Mug, Garfield Character Series, 1978, 3³/₈" h, $5.00.

Premium, Fry Kid Super Sailer, 1990 . . . . 2.00
Premium, Garfield on scooter, 1989 . . . . 1.50
Premium, Grimace Canteen, 2 pc, 1990 . . . . 1.50
Premium, Grimace in wagon, Connectibles, 1991 . . . . . . 2.50
Premium, Hamburglar stencil, orange, 4 crayons, 1987 . . . 3.00
Premium, hobby box, red, 2½ x 6 x 7½" 15.00
Premium, Ice Capades Barbie, 1991 . . . . 2.50
Premium, Lego Building Set, helicopter, yellow, 19
   pcs, 1984 . . . . 6.00
Premium, lunch box, yellow 12.00
Premium, McDonald's Funny Car, 1993 . . . . 1.00
Premium, pencil case, plastic, clear, snap closure,
   1984 . . . . 3.00
Premium, Play Doh, pink, 1985 . . . . 8.00
Premium, Romantic Bride Barbie, 1993 . . . . 1.00
Premium, Ronald toothbrush, white, red, 1985 . . . . 3.00
Premium, Soft Drink Guy, Fun With Food, 1989 . . . . 5.00
Premium, Tiny Toon Adventures flip car, Elmira pig in
   wagon, 1991 . . . . 1.50
Premium, Tonka, loader, orange, 1994 . . . . 1.00
Premium, water game, Grimace with squirting cam-
   era, purple, 1992 . . . . 12.00

MCKEE GLASS

McKee and Brothers was founded in Pittsburgh, Pennsylvania, in 1853. In 1888 the factory moved to Jeannette, Pennsylvania, named after the wife of one of the company's founders.

The company reorganized in 1903, renaming itself the McKee Glass Company. It manufactured a wide range of household and industrial glassware. McKee introduced its Glasbake line in the 1910s. Hand operations continued through the 1940s, at which point automatic machinery was introduced.

The company is best known for its crystal pressed patterns, Depression glass kitchenware, and opaque ware. Tableware lines in color were first made in the early 1920s. Many older clear pat-

terns, e.g., Aztec and Rock Crystal Flower, became available in color. Between 1923 and the late 1930s, one or more new colors was added to the line each year, e.g., orchid and ruby in 1927, Chalaine blue, Old Rose (tan), Seville yellow, Skokie green, and topaz in 1931.

The popularity of the colorful opaque ware, made between 1930 and 1940, helped the company weather the hard times of the Depression. Opaque was used on lines ranging from dinnerware to kitchenware, children's sets to Sunkist reamers. French ivory and Poudre blue were used in 1933 and 1936. Opal white, decorated and plain, was made between 1937 and 1942.

In 1951 Thatcher Glass Company purchased McKee, selling it in 1961 to the Jeannette Glass Corporation. Upon purchasing McKee, Jeannette Glass Corporation closed the manufacturing operations at its plant and moved them to the McKee factory.

References: Gene Florence, *Kitchen Glassware of the Depression Years, 6th Edition,* Collector Books, 1995, 1997 value update; Gene Florence, *Very Rare Glassware of the Depression Years, Fifth Series,* Collector Books, 1997.

Note: For additional listings see Kitchen Glassware and Reamers.

Autumn, compote, ftd, oval, Skokie green . . . . $ 45.00
Baker, oval, 5" l, Skokie green 10.00
Butter Dish, cov, 1 lb, Seville yellow 65.00
Canister, screw lid, black lettering, 48 oz, Seville
   yellow 50.00
Canister, screw lid, black lettering, 48 oz, Skokie
   green 45.00
Dots, butter dish, cov, 1 lb, blue on custard 90.00
Dots, butter dish, cov, 1 lb, red on white 35.00
Dots, canister, 28 oz, screw lid, green on custard 50.00
Dots, mixing bowl, 9" d, red on white 10.00
Eggcup, ftd, Skokie green 10.00
Flower Band, bowl, 9½" d, Skokie green 18.00
Glasbake, measure, 1 cup, white 40.00
Glasbake, measure, 2 cup, crystal 18.00
Glasbake, refregerator dish, cov, 4¼" sq, light blue 4.00
Glasbake, tea kettle, crystal 15.00
Laurel, berry bowl, 4¾" d, French ivory 6.00
Laurel, bowl, 3 ftd, green 10.00
Laurel, bowl, 9" d, Skokie green 18.00
Laurel, bowl, 11" d, green 25.00
Laurel, candlestick, pr, 4" h, jade green 30.00

Bowl, flanged rim with spout, Skokie green, 7⅛" d, $15.00

Laurel, cereal bowl, jade green 6.00
Laurel, cheese dish, cov, French ivory. 50.00
Laurel, creamer, child's, plain. 20.00
Laurel, creamer, tall, French ivory. 10.00
Laurel, cup, Poudre blue 15.00
Laurel, dinner plate, green 15.00
Laurel, luncheon plate, 9" d, Skokie green 12.00
Laurel, plate, child's, green. 15.00
Laurel, platter, oval, 10³/₄" d, green. 20.00
Laurel, salad plate, 7¹/₂" d, French ivory 8.00
Laurel, salt and pepper shakers, pr, French ivory 40.00
Laurel, saucer, green 5.00
Laurel, sherbet, Skokie green 10.00
Laurel, sugar, child's, plain. 20.00
Laurel, sugar, cov, Skokie green 12.00
Laurel, sugar, tall, white opal 10.00
Laurel, tea set, child's, 14 pcs, green. 290.00
Laurel, tumbler, flat, 9 oz, French ivory. 25.00
Laurel, vegetable, oval, 9³/₄", white opal 18.00
Measure, handle, ftd, 2 cup, Seville yellow. 25.00
Measure, handle, ftd, 4 cup, Seville yellow. 60.00
Mixing Bowl, 7¹/₂" d, Seville yellow 18.00
Range Tec, skillet, crystal . . . .
Reamer, grapefruit, Seville yellow. 175.00
Reamer, small, white 20.00
Reamer, Sunkist, Seville yellow 40.00
Refrigerator Dish, cov, 4 x 5", blue delphite 25.00
Refrigerator Dish, cov, 7¹/₄" sq, Seville yellow 35.00
Rock Crystal, bonbon, scalloped edge, red 45.00
Rock Crystal, bowl, scalloped edge, 4" d, crystal. 10.00
Rock Crystal, bread and butter plate, scalloped edge,
   6" d, red 15.00
Rock Crystal, butter dish, cov, crystal 320.00
Rock Crystal, cake stand, ftd, 2³/₄" h, crystal 30.00
Rock Crystal, candlestick, 8" h, crystal 85.00
Rock Crystal, cheese and cracker set, ruby 160.00
Rock Crystal, cocktail, ftd, 3¹/₂ oz 20.00

Salt and Pepper Shakers, pr, Roman Arches, black, range size, 4¹/₂" h, $20.00

Rock Crystal, cordial, ftd, 1 oz, crystal 35.00
Rock Crystal, creamer, ftd, 9 oz 30.00
Rock Crystal, creamer and sugar, ftd, crystal 40.00
Rock Crystal, cruet and stopper, 6 oz, crystal 75.00
Rock Crystal, cup, 7 oz, crystal 15.00
Rock Crystal, dinner plate, scalloped edge, 10¹/₂" d,
   crystal 40.00
Rock Crystal, goblet, ftd, 8 oz, crystal. 15.00
Rock Crystal, grapefruit bowl, red. 50.00
Rock Crystal, juice tumbler, clear 20.00
Rock Crystal, lamp, electric, crystal 160.00
Rock Crystal, parfait, 3¹/₂ oz, crystal 15.00
Rock Crystal, pitcher, ¹/₂ gal, crystal 100.00
Rock Crystal, relish, 2 part, crystal 25.00
Rock Crystal, relish, 6 part, crystal 35.00
Rock Crystal, salad bowl, scalloped edge, 8" d,
   crystal 35.00
Rock Crystal, salad plate, 7¹/₂" d, crystal 6.00
Rock Crystal, salt and pepper shakers, pr, crystal. 70.00
Rock Crystal, sandwich server, handle, crystal. 40.00
Rock Crystal, saucer, red 20.00
Rock Crystal, server, center handle, red. 130.00
Rock Crystal, sherbet, crystal 12.00
Rock Crystal, sugar, open, 10 oz, crystal. 10.00
Rock Crystal, sundae, ftd, 6 oz, crystal 15.00
Rock Crystal, toothpick holder, crystal 40.00
Rock Crystal, vase, 11" h, amber 80.00
Rock Crystal, vase, cornucopia, crystal 60.00
Rock Crystal, vase, ftd, 11"h, crystal 55.00
Rock Crystal, whiskey tumbler, 2¹/₂ oz, crystal. 15.00
Rock Crystal, wine, crystal 20.00
Rolling Pin, Chalaine blue 375.00
Salt and Pepper Shakers, pr, Roman arch, range size,
   custard 20.00
Tom and Jerry Set, serving bowl, 12 cups, red letters,
   white. 100.00
Water Dispenser, cov, white 100.00
Water Dispenser, screw lid, center ice compartment,
   crystal 70.00

Glasbake, casserole, individual, 6¹/₄" w, Oxydol premium, paper label, crystal, $5.00.

MEDICAL ITEMS

Doctors are the primary collectors of medical apparatus and instruments. Most collect material that relates to their medical specialty. Medical apparatus and instruments are sold by specialist dealers or auctions. This is why so little medical material is found at flea markets and antiques malls, shops, and shows.

Medical office furniture, especially large wooden storage cabinets with unusual drawer configurations, are quite popular in the general antiques marketplace. The same holds true for wall charts, ranging from the standard eye examination chart to those dealing with anatomy.

Pharmaceutical items divide into two groups: (1) material used by druggists to prepare medicines and (2) packaging associated with over–the–counter medication and medicines and pills prescribed by the doctor. There is little added value if the contents are intact. In fact, most collectors prefer that they are not.

Note: See Drug Store for additional listings.

Book, *Practical Hematological Diagnosis,* 1933 . . . . **$ 20.00**
Book, *Surgical Emergencies in Children,* 1936 . . . . **30.00**
Booklet, *Alka–Seltzer Song Book,* c1935 . . . . **4.00**
Catalog, Brewer & Co, pharmaceutical, 1938 . . . . **25.00**
Catalog, Feick Brothers Co, Pittsburgh, PA, Surgical
  Instruments, Office Equipment, Artificial Limbs,
  8th ed, hard cov, 1929, 458 pgs **65.00**
Cookbook, *Dr. Ward's Medical Co. Cookbook,* illus,
  tonics and patent medicines, c1920 . . . . **5.00**
Dental Cabinet, 3 top drawers, beveled mirror,
  drawers on bottom, orig instruments, 1926 . . . . **600.00**
Glass Eye, human size **25.00**
Poster, Health Habits, National Child Welfare
  Association, Roy Williams, 1920, 17 x 28" **40.00**
Quack Gadget, Rex Rheumatic Ring, Rex Rheumatic
  Ring Co, Hartford, Conn, USA, c1920 . . . . **65.00**
Sign, Dr Haile's Ole Injun System Tonic, color litho,
  Indian wearing headdress, "Kidney's, Liver &
  Stomach," 1940, 13 x 20" **55.00**
Sign, "Rx Sharp & Dohme's Medicinal Products are
  Standard, We Carry a Complete Line," c1930,
  12 x 25" **225.00**
Tin, Ex–Lax, sample size, 2 tablets **6.00**

MELMAC

Thermosetting plastics, principally melamine resins, were used to make plastic dinnerware. Melamine resins result from the interaction of melamine and formaldehyde. A chemical reaction creating permanent hardness occurs when thermosetting plastics are heated. Plastic dinnerware is made through a compression molding process.

The first plastic dinnerware was used in cafeterias, hospitals, restaurants, and other institutional settings. Ceramic manufacturers fought its introduction into the household tabletop market. In 1950 the Society for the Plastic Industry and the U.S. Bureau of Standards agreed upon melamine dinnerware specifications and standards ranging from size and weight to sanitation and surface or tactile qualities. Industrial designers and manufacturers used these standards to create a wide variety of plastic dinnerware.

Melmac is a trade name of American Cyanamid. Like Kleenex and Xerox, it soon became a generic term describing an entire line of products. Some of the leading manufacturers and brand names include Aztec, Boonton and Boontonware, Branchell (Color–Flyte and Royale), International Molded Products (Arrowhead and Brookpark), Mar–Crest, Prolon, Royalton, Russel Wright (made by American Cyanamid), Sears Roebuck (Harmony House, made by Plastic Masters), Spaulding and Spaulding Ware (American Plastics), Texas Ware (Plastics Manufacturing Co.), and Watertown.

Melamine dinnerware's popularity waned in the early 1960s. Repeated washing caused fading and dullness. Edges chipped, knives scratched surfaces, and foods left stains. Pieces placed too close to heat discolored or scarred. Many early 1960s designs were too delicate. Pieces actually broke. The final death blow came from inexpensive Asian and European ceramic dinnerware imported into the United States in the late 1960s and early 1970s.

Reference: Gregory R. Zimmer and Alvin Daigle, Jr., *Melmac Dinnerware,* L–W Book Sales, 1997.

Collectors' Club: Melmac Collectors Club, 6802 Glenkirk Rd, Baltimore, MD 21239.

Apollo Ware, serving bowl, brown fleck . . . . **$ 3.50**
Aztec, cup, turquoise **1.00**
Aztec, dessert bowl, gray **1.50**
Aztec, dinner plate, salmon pink **2.50**
Aztec, plate, beige, floral pattern **2.50**
Aztec, platter, mustard yellow **3.00**
Aztec, soup bowl, pink **3.50**
Aztec, sugar bowl, salmon pink **5.00**
Boonton, bowl, beige **3.00**
Boonton, butter, cov, light green **8.00**
Boonton, creamer, charcoal gray **4.00**
Boonton, dinner plate, divided, charcoal gray **3.50**
Boonton, serving bowl, tawny buff **6.00**
Boonton, sugar, cov, white **4.50**
Boontonware, cup and saucer, yellow **5.00**
Boontonware, salt and pepper, pr, powder blue **5.00**
Boontonware, serving dish, oblong, pink **4.50**
Branchell, bread and butter plate, Sweet Talk pattern **2.50**
Branchell, butter, cov, green **8.00**
Branchell, creamer, charcoal **3.00**
Branchell, dinner plate, Sweet Talk pattern **3.50**
Branchell, platter, turquoise **6.00**
Branchell, salt and pepper shakers, pr, orange **5.00**
Branchell, sugar, cov, light blue **4.50**
Branchell, tumbler, orange **8.00**
Branchell Royale, salt and pepper shakers, pr, light
  blue **6.00**
Branchell Royale, serving bowl, divided, orange **5.00**
Brookpark Arrowhead, bowl, green **3.00**
Brookpark Arrowhead, cup, white **2.00**
Brookpark Arrowhead, dinner plate, divided, yellow **3.50**
Brookpark Arrowhead, plate, red **3.00**
Brookpark Modern Design, creamer, red **3.50**
Brookpark Modern Design, salad plate, floral design **3.00**
Brookpark Modern Design, serving dish, orange **5.00**
Debonaire, bowl, white **2.50**
Debonaire, dinner plate, peach **3.50**
Debonaire, sugar, cov, red **4.50**

Flite Lane, dinner plate, green, brown flecks **2.00**
Flite Lane, cup and saucer, red–orange **1.50**
Flite Lane, serving bowl, yellow, brown flecks **3.00**
Fostoria, butter, cov, green **10.00**
Fostoria, serving bowl, divided, gray **8.00**
Harmony House, cup and saucer, green **2.00**
Harmony House, platter, Autumn Leaves pattern **5.00**
Harmony House, sugar, cov, orange **3.50**
Holiday, bread and butter, green, brown flecks **2.50**
Holiday, ice bucket, 3 pc, turquoise, brown flecks **8.00**
Holiday, serving bowl, divided, orange **5.00**
Imperial Ware, platter, speckled turquoise **6.00**
Imperial Ware, sugar, cov, yellow **4.00**
Lucent, cup and saucer, white **3.00**
Lucent, plate, Sun Petal pattern **2.50**
Mallo–Ware, dinner plate, avocado **2.50**
Mallo–Ware, gravy, beige **4.00**
Mar–Crest, plate, yellow **3.00**
Mar–crest, platter, yellow **5.00**
Monte Carlo, bowl, yellow **2.00**
Prolon, plate, Beverly pattern **2.00**
Prolon, salad bowl, ftd, orange **3.00**
Royalon, creamer, purple **3.00**
Royalon, dinner plate, Jubilee pattern **2.50**
Spaulding, dinner plate, light blue **3.00**
Spaulding, platter, yellow **5.00**
Stetson, cup and saucer, turquoise **2.00**
Stetson, platter, yellow **5.00**
Texas Ware, dinner plate, San Jacinto design **3.00**
Watertown, water pitcher, yellow **8.00**

METLOX

In 1927 T. C. Prouty and Willis, his son, established Metlox Pottery, Manhattan Beach, California, primarily for the purpose of making ceramic outdoor signs. When business declined during the Depression and T.C. died in 1931, Willis converted the plant to the production of ceramic dinnerware. California Pottery, brightly colored wares, were the company's first offering.

Between 1934 and the early 1940s, Metlox produced its Poppytrail line of kitchenware and tableware. In 1936 the company adopted the poppy, California's state flower, as its trademark.

Carl Romanelli, a designer who joined Metlox in the late 1930s, created Metlox's miniature line. Romanelli also designed the Modern Masterpiece line that included bookends, figural vases, figurines, and wall pockets.

The company shifted to war production during the early 1940s. In 1946 Willis Prouty sold Metlox to Evan Shaw, owner of the American Pottery, Los Angeles, a company under contract to Disney for ceramic figurines. Production of Disney figurines was moved to Manhattan Beach and continued until 1956; 1946 also marked the introduction of California Ivy, Metlox's first painted dinnerware. In the 1960s and 70s, Metlox made Colorstax (solid color dinnerware), cookie jars, and Poppet (stoneware flower holders and planters).

In 1958 Metlox purchased Vernon Kiln. The company's Vernon Kiln division made artware in the 1950s and 60s, American Royal Horses, and Nostalgia, a scale model carriage line.

Shaw died in 1980. His family continued the business for another decade, ending operations in 1989.

References: Susan and Al Bagdade, *Warman's American Pottery and Porcelain,* Wallace–Homestead, Krause Publications, 1994; Harvey Duke, *The Official Identification and Price Guide to Pottery and Porcelain, Eighth Edition,* House of Collectibles, 1995; Carl Gibbs, Jr., *Collector's Encyclopedia of Metlox Potteries,* Collector Books, 1995; Harry L. Rinker, *Dinnerware of the 20th Century: The Top 500 Patterns,* House of Collectibles, 1997.

Antique Grape, bread and butter plate, 6³/₈" d . . . . **$ 10.00**
Antique Grape, butter dish, cov, ¹/₄lb **60.00**
Antique Grape, cereal bowl, 7³/₈" d **15.00**
Antique Grape, coffeepot, cov **80.00**
Antique Grape, compote **80.00**
Antique Grape, creamer **25.00**
Antique Grape, dinner plate **25.00**
Antique Grape, platter, oval, 12¹/₂" l **45.00**
Antique Grape, relish, 2–part, 9" l **50.00**
Antique Grape, salt and pepper shakers, pr **30.00**
Antique Grape, sugar, cov **35.00**
Antique Grape, vegetable bowl, round, 8¹/₂" d **40.00**
California Ivy, bread and butter plate, 6¹/₂" d **8.00**
California Ivy, chop plate, 13¹/₄" d **50.00**
California Ivy, creamer **17.00**
California Ivy, cup and saucer **17.00**
California Ivy, dinner plate, 10³/₈" d **15.00**
California Ivy, gravy boat and liner **50.00**
California Ivy, pitcher, 9¹/₄" h **60.00**
California Ivy, platter, oval, 13³/₈" l **50.00**
California Ivy, serving bowl, cone shape **40.00**
California Ivy, serving bowl, round **40.00**
California Ivy, sugar, cov **25.00**
California Ivy, vegetable, divided **45.00**
California Ivy, vegetable, round, 9¹/₈" d **40.00**
California Provincial, bread tray, 9³/₄" d **75.00**
California Provincial, fruit bowl, 6" d **15.00**
California Provincial, luncheon plate, 9" d **20.00**
California Provincial, platter, oval, 11¹/₄" l **45.00**
California Provincial, salad plate, 7¹/₂" d **15.00**
California Provincial, salt and pepper shakers, pr **30.00**

La Mancha Gold, pepper shaker, 1975, $10.00.

California Provincial, tea canister **75.00**
California Provincial, vegetable bowl, rect, divided,
   8⅝" d **50.00**
California Strawberry, cereal bowl, lug, 7" d **12.00**
California Strawberry, coffee canister **35.00**
California Strawberry, coffeepot, cov. **60.00**
California Strawberry, creamer **20.00**
California Strawberry, dinner plate, 10⅜" d **17.00**
California Strawberry, mug **20.00**
California Strawberry, pitcher, 4½" h **30.00**
California Strawberry, platter, 13⅛" l **35.00**
California Strawberry, sugar, cov. **25.00**
California Strawberry, vegetable bowl, round, 8" d **30.00**
Colorstax, dinner service, 15 pcs, 4 dinner plates, 4
   salad plates, 4 mugs, and 3 cereal bowls, fern
   green. **100.00**
Della Robbia, bread and butter plate, 6½" d **7.00**
Della Robbia, butter dish, ¼ lb **70.00**
Della Robbia, creamer. **22.00**
Della Robbia, cup and saucer **17.00**
Della Robbia, fruit bowl, 6½" d **12.00**
Della Robbia, mug **20.00**
Della Robbia, platter, oval, 14½" l **45.00**
Della Robbia, salt and pepper shakers, pr **25.00**
Della Robbia, sugar, cov **32.00**
Della Robbia, teapot, cov. **100.00**
Homestead Provincial, ashtray, 4⅝" d. **15.00**
Homestead Provincial, bread and butter plate, 6½" d **10.00**
Homestead Provincial, chop plate, 12" d **60.00**
Homestead Provincial, coffeepot **90.00**
Homestead Provincial, cookie jar. **70.00**
Homestead Provincial, creamer **25.00**
Homestead Provincial, cup and saucer. **25.00**
Homestead Provincial, gravy boat **50.00**
Homestead Provincial, soup bowl, 8½" d **20.00**
Homestead Provincial, sugar, cov. **40.00**
Homestead Provincial, sugar canister **75.00**
Homestead Provincial, vegetable bowl, cov, round **75.00**
Homestead Provincial Blue, cruet set, with stand,
   #519 . . . . **100.00**
Homestead Provincial Blue, marmalade, cov **80.00**
Homestead Provincial Blue, oil cruet, stopper. **45.00**
Homestead Provincial Blue, salt and pepper shakers,
   pr, cone shape **35.00**
La Mancha Gold, cup and saucer. **10.00**
La Mancha Gold, dinner plate, 10¾" d **12.00**
La Mancha Gold, platter, oval, 11¾" l. **25.00**
La Mancha Gold, vegetable, vegetable, 8" d **25.00**
Poppytrail, Aztec, platter, oval, 13" l **45.00**
Provincial Blue, batter pitcher **75.00**
Provincial Blue, bread and butter plate. **8.00**
Provincial Blue, coaster **15.00**
Provincial Blue, cup and saucer **18.00**
Provincial Blue, dinner plate **20.00**
Provincial Blue, fruit bowl **15.00**
Provincial Blue, gravy **50.00**
Provincial Blue, platter. **40.00**
Provincial Blue, salad plate **12.50**
Provincial Blue, salt and pepper shakers, pr **25.00**
Provincial Blue, vegetable, cov. **80.00**
Provincial Blue, vegetable, open, round **40.00**

Red Rooster, dinner plate, 10" d, $15.00.

Red Rooster, bread and butter plate **5.00**
Red Rooster, bread basket **50.00**
Red Rooster, casserole, small **75.00**
Red Rooster, chop plate, 12" d **50.00**
Red Rooster, coffee carafe **100.00**
Red Rooster, cup and saucer **17.00**
Red Rooster, dinner plate, 10" d **15.00**
Red Rooster, eggcup **20.00**
Red Rooster, platter, oval, 13½" l **40.00**
Red Rooster, salad plate. **10.00**
Red Rooster, salt and pepper shakers, pr, red. **55.00**
Red Rooster, soup bowl, 8½" d **17.00**
Red Rooster, vegetable, divided **50.00**
Red Rooster, vegetable, round **40.00**

MILK BOTTLES

Hervey Thatcher is recognized as the father of the glass milk bottle. By the early 1880s glass milk bottles appeared in New York and New Jersey.

Patents are one of the best research sources for information about early milk bottles. A. V. Whiteman received a milk bottle patent as early as 1880. Patent recipients leased or sold their patents to manufacturers.

1910 to 1950 is the golden age of the glass milk bottle. Lamb Glass Company (Mt. Vernon, Ohio), Liberty Glass Company (Sapulpa, Oklahoma), Owens–Illinois Glass Company (Toledo, Ohio), and Thatcher Glass Company (New York) were leading manufacturers.

Milk bottles are collected by size: gill (quarter pint), half pint, ten ounces (third of a quart), pint, quart, half gallon (two quarts), and gallon.

Paper cartons first appeared in the early 1920s and 30s and achieved popularity after 1950. The late 1950s witnessed the arrival of plastic bottles. While a few dairies still use glass bottles today, the era has essentially ended.

References: John Tutton, *Udderly Beautiful: A Pictorial Guide to the Pyroglazed or Painted Milkbottle,* published by author, no date; John Tutton, *Udderly Delightful: Collecting Milk Bottles & Related Items,* published by author, 1994.

Newsletter: *The Udder Collectibles,* HC73 Box 1, Smithville Flats, NY 13841

Collectors' Club: National Assoc of Milk Bottle Collectors, Inc, 4 Ox Bow Rd, Westport, CT 06880.

Acme Milk Products, Junction City, KS, robust boy sitting on fence, "Grow them strong with ACME Dairy Products," round, tall, black pyroglaze, 1 qt . . . **$ 80.00**

Adam's Pasteurized Milk, Rawlins, WY, cowboy on bucking horse, "Builds 'em healthy," round, tall, red pyroglaze, 1 qt **90.00**

American Creamery, Kerrville, TX, round, tall, emb, 1 qt **45.00**

American Oyster Co, Providence, RI, round, tall, emb, 1 pt **28.00**

Arizona Creamery, Phoenix Store, V–shaped ribs on neck, round, tall, emb, 1 pt **38.00**

Bellows Falls Creamery, John T. O'Connor, VT, 1 qt **35.00**

Blue Ribbon Farms, Cloverleaf, Stockton, CA, grover, "Milk from your Courteous and Careful Grover," round, cream top, red pyroglaze, 1 qt **55.00**

Brenner's Coop, round, red pyroglaze, 1 qt **35.00**

Brighams Dairy, Burlington, VT, round, orange pyroglaze, 1 qt. **38.00**

Dairyland Creamery, Coos Bay, OR, "Pasteurized Milk & Cream," round, emb, 1/2 pt **25.00**

Dublin Coop Dairies, war slogan, 1 pt **30.00**

Enfield Dairy, Ellensburg, WA, Earl Anderson, Main 140, small child, "We help to raise them, Enfield, Milk," round, tall, orange pyroglaze, 1 qt **65.00**

Ethan Allen Creamery, Essex Jet, VT, round, orange pyroglaze, 1 qt. **35.00**

Farmers Dairy Co, Inc, baby picture, black pyroglaze, 1 pt. **17.50**

Fraim's Dairies, Wilmington, DE, Minute Man and war slogan "Buy United States War Bonds," brown pyroglaze, 1 qt. **100.00**

Gold Medal Dairy Products, Huron, SD, gold medal seal, logo, and ribbon, round, tall, red pyroglaze, 1 qt. **85.00**

Gray's Harbor Dairy Products, 1/2 pt **7.00**

Gridley Dairy Co, amethyst, base mkd "TMFGCO," 1 pt **17.50**

Hastings Springfield, VT, emb, 1 qt **25.00**

Highland Creamery Co, Reno, NV, round, tall, emb, 1 pt **45.00**

Home Owned Dairies, Salt Lake City, UT, round, tall, red pyroglaze, 1 pt. **55.00**

Klein's Dairy, Farrell, PA, man reaching for bottle on doorstep, "Pasteurized, Safe Milk, Dairy Products," round, tall, black pyroglaze, 1 pt. **25.00**

Lynthwaite Farm, Wilmington, DE, round, tall, black pyroglaze. **45.00**

Maple Dairies, Inc, Tyrone, PA, "Electropure Milk, It Whips," round, tall, cream top, emb, 1 qt **28.00**

Meadow Gold, cream top, 1 qt **25.00**

Meadow Gold, square, 1/2 gal. **12.50**

Merrills Dairy, Keesville, NY, war slogan "Think, Act, Work for Victory," orange pyroglaze, 1 qt **85.00**

Missouri Pacific Lines, slug plate, sawtooth border, round, tall, emb, 1 qt **150.00**

Monterey Bay Milk Distributors, Inc, 1/4 pt. **20.00**

Morse's Dairy, Morrisville, VT, square, green pyroglaze, 1 qt. **25.00**

Mount Mansfield, VT, square, cow skiing, green pyroglaze, 1 qt. **150.00**

Norton Dairy Co, Phoenix, AZ, safety neck ring, round, tall, emb, 1 qt **38.00**

Prices Dairy, El Paso, TX, round, tall, emb, 1 qt. **35.00**

Proctor Creamer, Proctor, VT, emb, 1 qt **35.00**

R. J. Mercure, Dairy Winooski, VT, round, orange pyroglaze, 1 qt. **55.00**

Royal Perfectly Pasteurized, "It's The Cream," 1 pt **10.00**

Rye Brothers Dairy, Billings, MT, "Pasteurized," round, emb, 1/2 pt. **25.00**

Sanitary Milk & Ice Cream Co, Morgantown, WV, "Sanitary Milk, Pasteurized–Neck Ribs," round, tall, pyroglaze, 1 qt **45.00**

Sibley Farms, Spencer, MA, round, emb, 1/2 pt. **38.00**

Spokane Bottle Exchange, Inc, round, blue pyroglaze, 1 qt. **15.00**

Star Dairy, Galveston, TX, large stars, "For Health use Pasteurized Milk," round, tall, red pyroglaze, 1 qt **125.00**

Sunrise Farm Dairy Baltic, CT, square, 2–color pyroglaze, orange sunrise front, red "Good Morning and Good Health" back, 1/2 pt. **8.00**

Sunset Farm Dairy, Woodstock, VT, square, orange pyroglaze, 1 qt. **20.00**

Sweets Dairy, Bennington, VT, round, black pyroglaze, 1 qt. **65.00**

Sycamore Farm Dairy, Rockville, MD, sycamore tree, round, tall, green pyroglaze, 1 qt **75.00**

The Dairy Farm Ice & Cold Storage Co, Ltd, Hong Kong, red pyroglaze, 1/2 pt **5.00**

UVM, Burlington, VT, round, amber pyroglaze, 1 qt **65.00**

West Coast Dairy, Everett, WA, "This bottle property of...," 1 qt **12.00**

MILK GLASS

Opaque white glass, also known as milk glass, enjoyed its greatest popularity in the period immediately prior to World War I when firms such as Atterbury, Challinor–Taylor, Flaccus, and McKee made a wide range of dinnerware, figural, household, kitchenware, and novelty forms. While the popularity of milk glass waned in the 1920s, several manufacturers continued to use milk glass, especially for kitchenware and decorative novelty items.

Milk glass enjoyed a brief renaissance extending from the early 1940s through the early 1960s. Fenton, Imperial, and Westmoreland renewed their production of milk glass. Fenton's Hobnail was first made in 1940 with its Silvercrest line introduced a few years later. Westmoreland revived Paneled Grape in the 1940s and launched Beaded Grape in the 1950s.

In 1945 John E. Kemple founded Kemple Glass Works, East Palestine, Ohio. The company only made milk glass. Kemple bought a number of the McKee molds from the Thatcher Glass Company shortly after it had purchased McKee. When fire destroyed the Kemple plant in 1956, the firm moved to Kenova, West Virginia. Its advertisements boasted, "Authentic Reproductions in Milk Glass—Made in the Original Molds." The Wheaton Company purchased Kemple's equipment and molds following the death of John Kemple in 1970.

Most milk glass offered for sale in today's market dates after 1940 and was produced by Fenton, Imperial, Kemple, and Westmoreland.

References: Everett Grist, *Covered Animal Dishes,* Collector Books, 1988, 1993 value update; Betty and Bill Newbound, *Collector's Encyclopedia of Milk Glass,* Collector Books, 1995.

Collectors' Club: National Milk Glass Collectors Society, 46 Almond Dr, Hershey, PA 17033.

Note: For additional listings see Westmoreland Glass.

Bone Dish, fish and shell, white	$ 30.00
Box, cov, couch, white, painted green	175.00
Butter Dish, cov, strawberries, white	50.00
Candle Lamp, lighthouse, blue, 6¼" h	250.00
Cardholder, terrier, white	35.00
Cigar Jar, white, cigar bundle, naturalistic painting	250.00
Compote, Jenny Lind, blue	85.00
Compote, open hand, white	35.00
Creamer, owl, white	25.00
Dish, cov, battleship *Oregon,* white	50.00
Dish, cov, chick, basketweave base, white, 5¼" l	50.00
Dish, cov, dog, blue and white, 5½" l	40.00
Dish, cov, duck, wavy base, glass eyes, white, 8" l	60.00
Dish, cov, elephant, black, 7½" l	70.00
Dish, cov, football, white, 5½" l	50.00
Dish, cov, hand and dove, white, jewelled	90.00
Dish, cov, hen on nest, basketweave base, white with blue head, 5½" l	35.00
Dish, cov, lamb, octagonal base, blue lamb, white head	45.00

Dish, cov, lion, scroll base, white	35.00
Dish, cov, owl, white	65.00
Dish, cov, rabbit on eggs, white, 4½" l	75.00
Dish, cov, salmon, white, 6" l	65.00
Dish, cov, Santa on sleigh, white	55.00
Dish, cov, swan, open neck, white, 5½" l	90.00
Dish, trunk with strap, white, 5½" l	25.00
Eggcup, kingfisher, white	10.00
Jar, cov, Scottie, pink	45.00
Lady's Shoe, blue, gold floral dec	15.00
Match Safe, Bible, blue	25.00
Match Safe, dog's head	120.00
Match Safe, hanging, elf, white	200.00
Match Safe, hanging, Indian Chief, white	60.00
Mug, bird and wheat, white	10.00
Mug, child's, duck and swan, white	20.00
Mug, child's, Liberty Bell, white, 2" h	50.00
Pickle Dish, sheaf of wheat, white	12.50
Pin Dish, cov, lion, white, 4¾ x 3½"	10.00
Pin Tray, Indian maiden with headdress, white, 7" l	45.00
Plaque, Lincoln, white, 8½ x 6¾"	125.00
Plate, Easter Bunny and egg, white, gold border	50.00
Plate, Forget–Me–Not, white, 7½" d	5.00
Plate, 3 kittens, white	15.00
Salt, master, swan, head down, white, 3¼" h, 5½" l	25.00
Salt and Pepper Shakers, pr, acorn	25.00
Sugar Bowl, cov, beehive, white	80.00
Syrup, corn cob, white, 7½" h	60.00
Toothpick, bees in basket, white	30.00
Toothpick, corset, white	85.00
Toothpick, monkey with hat, white	125.00
Tray, lion, handled, white, 5" w, 9" l	15.00
Tray, Moses in the Bulrushes, white	50.00
Trinket Box, cov, actress, white	35.00
Tumbler, actress head, white	25.00
Tureen, cov, sleigh, white, 9¼" l	40.00
Vase, corn, white, gold dec, 4¼" h	10.00

Plate, Ring & Petal, #1875, white, 8¼" d, $12.50.

AUCTION PRICES

Gene Harris Antique Auction, Inc., November 8–10, 1996. Prices include a 10% buyer's premium.

Cabbage, Portieux, blue	44.00
Cat on Drum, Portieux, blue, 4¾" d	82.50
Crawfish, finial, octagonal base, tab handles, white	220.00
Dewey, oval ribbed and collaree base, white, 5" l	137.50
Dog on Carpet, Vallerystahl	143.00
Hen on Nest, probably Flaccus, chicks on base, white, 6¼" l	165.00
Hen on Nest, Vallerystahl, basketweave base, pale amethyst, 6¾" l	77.00
Hen on Nest, Westmoreland, chocolate, 7½" l	330.00
Peep and Egg, white, 6½" h	176.00
Pekingese Dog, white	440.00
Sheep, dome cov, white	385.00
Stagecoach, white	192.50
Swan, closed neck, blue, 5½"	33.00
Turkey, white, 7" h	198.00
Turtle, finial, octagonal base, tab handles, white	209.00

MODEL KITS

Model kits break down into three basic types: (1) wood, (2) plastic, and (3) cast resin. Scratch–built wooden models, whether from magazine plans or model kits, achieved widespread popularity in the 1930s. Airplanes were the most popular form. Because of the skill levels involved, these models were built primarily by teenagers.

England's 1/72 Frog Penguin kits of the mid–1930s were the first plastic model kits. After 1945, manufacturers utilized the new plastic injection molding process developed during World War II to produce large quantities of plastic model kits. Automobile model kits quickly replaced airplanes as the market favorite.

Empire Plastics, Hawk, Linberg, Renwal, and Varney manufactured kits for the American market. They were soon joined by Airfix (English), Aurora (American), Hasegawa (Japanese), Heller (French), Marusan (Japanese), and Monogram (American).

Model kits are sold by scale with 1/48, 1/72, and 1/144 among the most common. By the 1960s, some model kit manufacturers introduced snap–together models. The 1970s oil crisis significantly reduced production. However, the market fully recovered by the mid–1980s. While vehicles still dominate model kit sales, monster and other personality kits have gained in popularity.

Resin model kits are designed for the adult market. Gruesome monsters, scantily dressed buxom women (some completely naked), and fantasy creatures abound. Many of the kits sell new at $100 or more.

Box art influences the value of a model kit, especially when the cover art is more spectacular than the assembled model. Surprisingly, collectors prefer unassembled models. If the model is assembled, its value declines by 50% or more.

References: Bill Bruegman, *Aurora: History and Price Guide, 3rd Edition,* Cap'n Penny Productions, 1996; Gordon Dutt, *Collectible Figure Kits of the 50's, 60's & 70's: Reference and Price Guide, Gordy's Kit Builders Magazine,* 1995; Rick Polizzi, *Classic Plastic Model Kits: Identification & Value Guide,* Collector Books, 1996.

Periodical: *Kit Builders Magazine,* PO Box 201, Sharon Center, OH 44274.

American Astronaut, Aurora, #409, 1967 . . . . $ 60.00
Armored Dinosaur, Prehistoric Scenes, Aurora, 1972 . . . . . 40.00
Aston Martin, James Bond, Airfix, #823, 1965 . . . . 175.00
Attack Trak, Masters of the Universe, Monogram,
    1984 . . . . 15.00
Banana Splits Banana Buggy, Aurora, 1969 . . . . 325.00
Bonanza, Revell, 1965 . . . . 150.00
Bride of Frankenstein, Horizon, 1988 . . . . 35.00
Castro, Born Losers, Parks, 1965 . . . . 125.00
Cornfield Roundup Diorama, Planet of the Apes,
    Addar, 1975 . . . . 45.00
Cro Magnon Man, Aurora, #730, 1971 . . . . 20.00
Daddy the Suburbanite, Weird–Ohs, Hawk, 1963 . . . . . . 75.00
Deputy Sheriff, Pyro, 1956 . . . . 40.00
Drag–u–la, Munsters, AMT, 1965 . . . . 200.00
Dr. Jekyll as Mr. Hyde, Monsters of the Movies,
    Aurora, 1974 . . . . 90.00
Dr. Zira, Planet of the Apes, Addar, #105, 1974 . . . . 25.00
Duke's Digger, Dukes of Hazzard, MPC, 1980 . . . . 25.00
Evil Kneivel's Sky Cycle X2, Addar, 1974 . . . . 25.00

Batman, Aurora, #467–149, 1964, $175.00.

First Lunar Landing 25th Anniversary, Monogram,
    1/48 scale 25.00
Flintstones Rock Crusher, AMT, #487, 1974 . . . . 50.00
Flipper and Sandy, Revell, 1968 . . . . 100.00
Galaxy Runner, Message From Space, Entex, 1978 . . . . . . 20.00
George Harrison, Revell, 1965 . . . . 125.00
Giant Wasp, Gigantics, MPC, 1975 . . . . 50.00
Good Ship Flounder, Dr. Doolittle, Aurora, 1967 . . . . . . 140.00
Guillotine, Aurora, 1964 . . . . 225.00
Hitler, Born Losers, Parks, 1965 . . . . 150.00
HMS Bounty, Mutiny on the Bounty, Revell, 1961 . . . . 100.00
Hulk, Aurora, Comic Scenes, #184, 1974 . . . . 75.00
Indian Warrior, Pyro, 1960 . . . . 60.00
Invisible Man, Horizon, 1988 . . . . 25.00
Jesse James, Aurora, #408, 1966 . . . . 150.00
John F. Kennedy, Aurora, 1965 . . . . 125.00
Lone Ranger, Aurora, 1972 . . . . 60.00
Mad Barber, Aurora, #455, 1972 . . . . 125.00
Mexican Señorita, Aurora, 1957 . . . . 45.00
Mondeemobile, Airfix, 1967 . . . . 240.00
Moonbus, 2001, Aurora, 1969 . . . . 350.00
Munster's Koach, AMT, 1964 . . . . 275.00
My Mother the Car, AMT, 1965 . . . . 75.00
Nutty Nose Nipper, Aurora, 1965 . . . . 175.00
Rawhide, Gil Favor, Pyro, 1958 . . . . 60.00
Robin, Comic Scenes, Aurora, 1974 . . . . 35.00
Sand Worm, Dune, Revell, 1985 . . . . 20.00
Space Taxi, Monogram, 1959 . . . . 25.00
Steel Plunkers, Frantics, Hawk, 1965 . . . . 45.00
Sunbeam Car, Get Smart, AMT, 1968 . . . . 250.00
Tarzan, Comic Series, Aurora, #181, 1974 . . . . 30.00
T–Bird, AMI, 1966 . . . . 20.00
T. J. Hooker Police Car, MPC, 1982 . . . . 15.00
Totally Fab, Frantics, Hawk, 1965 . . . . 45.00
US Infantryman, Aurora, 1956 . . . . 90.00
Vincent, Black Hole, MPC, 1982 . . . . 25.00
Wacky Woodie, Krazy Kar Kustom Kit, AMT, 1968 . . . . . . 70.00
Wyatt Earp, Pyro, 1958 . . . . 60.00
Yellow Submarine, MPC, 1968 . . . . 200.00

MONSTERS

While the two recent *Jurassic Park* movies have not created a strong interest in dinosaur collectibles, they certainly have renewed interest in monster collectibles. Monster collectibles divide into three basic groups: (1) animal monsters, (2) villainous human monsters, and (3) comedic monsters.

Animal monsters played a major role in the movies from the onset. King Kong is the best known of the pre–1945 genre. The Japanese monster epics of the 1950s introduced Godzilla, a huge reptile monster. Godzilla, his foes, and imitators are all very collectible. The 1950s also saw the introduction of a wide range of animal monsters with human characteristics, e.g., the Creature from the Black Lagoon and numerous werewolf variations.

Early film makers were well aware of the ability of film to horrify. Dracula, Frankenstein, and the Mummy have been the subjects of dozens of films. Art connoisseur that he was, it is hard to think of Vincent Price other than as one of the most formidable villains of the horror film genre.

The Addams Family and The Munsters introduced a comedic aspect to monsters. This was perpetuated by the portrayal of monsters on Saturday morning cartoon shows. The chainsaw, mentally deranged human villain movies of the 1960s to the present are a consequence of this demystification of the monster.

After a period of speculation in monster material from the mid–1980s through the early 1990s, market prices now appear to have stabilized.

Reference: Dana Cain, *Collecting Monsters of Film and TV,* Krause Publications, 1997.

Periodical: *Toy Shop,* 700 E State St, Iola, WI 54990.

Activity Book, *The Addams Family,* Saalfield
   Publishing, 1965 . . . . $ 20.00
Annual, *Castle of Frankenstein,* 1967 Monster
   Annual, Warren Publishing, c1974 . . . . 18.00
Bank, King Kong, molded plastic, hollow, black, red
   and white, A. J. Renzi Corp, c1970, 16" h 25.00
Book, *Karloff, the Man, the Monster, the Movies,* D.
   Gifford, 1973, 350 pgs 20.00

Model Kit, Godzilla, Aurora, #149, 1964, $425.00.

Book, *The Munsters and the Great Camera Caper,*
   Whitman, 1965, 212 pgs 18.00
Coloring Book, The Cool Ghoul Monster Coloring
   Book, Wanamaker, 1964, 32 pgs, unused 22.00
Comic Book, The Outer Limits, Dell, 1964–69 . . . . 5.00
Comic Book, The Twilight Zone, Dell, 1962 . . . . 5.00
Costume, Frankenstein, plastic mask, fabric 1–pc suit,
   Ben Cooper, ©1960 Universal Pictures, orig box 55.00
Costume, Godzilla, plastic mask, 1–pc suit with vinyl
   top and synthetic bottom, Ben Cooper, ©1978
   Toho Co Ltd, orig box. 30.00
Figure, Cyclops, plastic, Palmer, 1962, 3" h 55.00
Figure, Frankenstein, Marx 20.00
Figure, Vampire, hard plastic, pop–up, Multiple
   Products Corp, 1964, 5" h 18.00
Game, Creature Features, Athol–Research Co 20.00
Game, Dracula Mystery Game, Hasbro, 1963. . . . . 125.00
Game, Monster Old Maid, Milton Bradley, 1964. . . . . . . 30.00
Game, The Monster Squad Game, Milton Bradley, 1977 . . 20.00
Hand Puppet, Herman Munster, talking, vinyl head,
   cloth body, Mattel, ©1964, 12" h 145.00
Jewelry Box, Munsters, musical, MIB. 38.00
Lunch Box, King Kong, metal, light blue thermos,
   King–Seeley, ©1977 Dino De Laurentis Corp. 55.00
Magazine, *Fangoria,* 1979 . . . . 110.00
Magazine, *Monster World,* Munsters feature 48.00
Magazine, *3–D Monsers,* Vol 1, #1, Fair Publishing
   Ltd, ©1964 . . . . 30.00
Mask, Cousin Eerie, soft rubber, Warren Publications,
   c1960 . . . . 70.00
Model Kit, Dark Shadows, Barnabus Collins,
   1/2 scale, 1968 . . . . 325.00
Model Kit, Phantom of the Opera, assembled, Aurora 30.00
Movie Poster, *Munster Go Home* 55.00
Paper Dolls, The Munsters, Whitman, ©1966, 9 x 12"
   cardboard folder 50.00
Pinback Button, Creepy Magazine Fan Club, litho
   metal, color illus of Uncle Creepy, Warren
   Publishing, 1968, 2½" d 18.00
Puzzle, Dracula, APC Puzzle, cardboard container,
   ©1974 . . . . 30.00
Puzzle, Wolfman, Hasbro, orig box, 1963. . . . . 150.00
Record, *Dark Shadows,* orig music, 33⅓ rpm, Philips,
   ©1969. . . . . 8.00
Snowdome, Creature of the Black Lagoon, MIB. 18.00
Toy, Famous Monsters Candlemaking Set, plastic
   molds, orig box and instructions, Rapco, ©1974
   Universal Products 30.00

MORGANTOWN GLASS

In 1903 the Morgantown Glass Works (West Virginia), founded in 1899, changed its name to the Economy Tumbler Company which became the Economy Glass Company in 1924. It marketed its products under the "Old Morgantown" label. In 1929 the company reassumed it original name, Morgantown Glass Works.

Concentrating initially on tumblers, "Economy Tumblers—Just What The Name Implies!" was the company's slogan, Morgantown eventually expanded its product line to include household and kitchen glassware. The company also made blanks for decorating firms. Morgantown is known for several innovative design and manufacturing techniques, e.g., ornamental open stems, iridization, and application of gold, platinum, and silver decoration.

The company became a victim of the Depression, closing in 1937. In 1939 glassworkers and others associated with the company reopened it as the Morgantown Glassware Guild. In 1965 Fostoria purchased the company and continued to produce most of the Morgantown patterns and colors, marketing them under a Morgantown label. Fostoria closed the plant in 1971. In 1972 Bailey Glass Company purchased the factory and used it primarily to make lamp globes.

Reference: Gene Florence, *Elegant Glassware of the Depression Era, Seventh Edition,* Collector Books, 1997.

Collectors' Clubs: Morgantown Collectors of America, Inc, 420 First Ave NW, Plainview, MN 55964; Old Morgantown Glass Collectors' Guild, PO Box 894, Morgantown, WV 26507.

Bowl, #4355 Janice, 14K Topaz, Carlton/Madrid dec, 13" d . . . . $ 95.00
Bud Vase, #26 Catherine, jade green, enameled floral dec, crimped rim, 10" h 175.00
Bud Vase, #53 Serenade, opaque yellow, 10" h 250.00
Candleholders, pr, #81 Bravo, Thistle, 4½" h 95.00
Candleholders, pr, #9931 Florentine, Bristol blue opaque, 5½" h 65.00
Candleholders, pr, #9935 Barton, peach opaque, 5" h 75.00
Candleholders, #9962 Contessa, steel blue, 4½/½" h 50.00
Candy Jar, #63½ Lorelei, ftd, 8" h, burgundy 35.00
Candy Jar, #86½ Urn, Bristol blue opaque, crystal lid, 6" h 40.00
Champagne, #7640 Art Moderne, crystal, India black stem 60.00
Champagne, #7643 Golf Ball, Ritz blue, 5½ oz 45.00
Champagne, #7643 Golf Ball, Stiegel green, 5½ oz. 30.00
Cocktail, #7638 Avalon, Anna Rose, Peacock Optic, 3½ oz 25.00
Cocktail, #7643 Golf Ball, Spanish red, 3½ oz 40.00
Cocktail, #7678 Old English, Stiegel green, 3½ oz 30.00

Compote, #12½ Woodsfield, crystal, Nanking blue threaded rim and ft, 12" d 175.00
Cordial, #7654 Lorna, crystal, Nantucket etch, 1½ oz 55.00
Cordial, #7668 Galaxy, crystal, Mayfair etch, 1½ oz 40.00
Goblet, #7577 Venus, Anna Rose, Palm Optic, 9 oz 40.00
Goblet, #7604½ Heirloom, 14K Topaz, Adonis etch, 9 oz 60.00
Goblet, #7630 Ballerina, azure, Elizabeth etch, 10 oz 80.00
Goblet, #7638 Avalon, Venetian green, Peacock Optic, 9 oz 40.00
Goblet, #7643 Golf Ball, Ritz blue, 9 oz 55.00
Goblet, #7659 Cynthia, crystal, Sonoma etch, 10 oz 60.00
Goblet, #7690 Monroe, Golden Iris, 9 oz 70.00
Goblet, #77943½ Paragon, crystal, India black stem, 5½ oz 80.00
Ivy Bowl, #7643 Kimball, Stiegel green, crystal Golf Ball stem and ft, 4" h 70.00
Jug, #1933 Del Rey, El Mexicano Ice, 50 oz 255.00
Juice Tumbler, #196 Crinkle, India black, flat, 6 oz 30.00
Lemonade Tankard, #1962 Crinkle Line, amethyst, 64 oz 75.00
Plate, #1500 Anna Rose, Bramble Rose etch, 8½" d 35.00
Plate, #7668 Galaxy, crystal, Sear's Lace Bouquet etch, 7" d 20.00
Sherbet, #1962 Crinkle, ruby, 6 oz 25.00
Sherbet, #7640 Art Moderne, Ritz blue, crystal stem, 5½ oz 65.00
Sherbet, #7654 Lorna, crystal, meadow green stem, Nantucket etch, 5½ oz 50.00
Torte Plate, #1500 Crystal Hollywood Line, platinum and red band, 14" d 225.00
Tumbler, #7678 Old English, Spanish red, 13 oz 50.00
Tumbler, #9074 Belton, golden iris, Virginia etch, 12 oz 40.00
Vase, #1933 El Mexicano, Seaweed, 6½" h 80.00
Water Set, #20069 Melon, alabaster, Ritz blue trim, pitcher and six 11–oz tumblers 650.00
Water Tumbler, #1962 Crinkle, amberina, flat, 10 oz 70.00
Wine, #7643 Golf Ball, Ritz blue, 2½ oz 55.00
Wine, #7678 Old English, Spanish red, 3½ oz 50.00
Wine, #7690 Monroe, old amethyst, 3 oz 95.00

MORTON POTTERIES

Morton, Illinois, was home to several major potteries, all of which trace their origins to six Rapp Brothers who emigrated from Germany in 1877 and established the Morton Pottery Works.

American Art Potteries (1945–1961), Cliftwood Art Potteries (1920–1940), Midwest Potteries, the continuation of Cliftwood (1940–44), Morton Pottery Company (1922–1976), and Morton Pottery Works, also known as Morton Earthenware Company (1877–1917) were all founded and operated by Rapp descendants.

These companies produced a variety of art, household, novelty, and utilitarian pottery. Morton Pottery Company specialized in kitchenwares, novelty items, and steins. In the 1950s they made a variety of TV lamps ranging from animal figures to personality, e.g., Davy Crockett. Under contract to Sears Roebuck, they produced some of the Vincent Price National Treasures reproductions. The American Art Pottery produced a line of wares marketed through floral and gift shops.

Goblet, #7688, crystal, #795 etch, $50.00.

Reference: Doris and Burdell Hall, *Morton's Potteries: 99 Years, 1877–1976, Volume II*, L–W Book Sales, 1995

American Art Potteries, bowl, octagonal, elongated, green, yellow int, 10 x 4 x 2" . . . . $ 10.00

American Art Potteries, bud vase, blue, pink spray glaze, 8" h 10.00

American Art Potteries, creamer and sugar, stylized flowers, blue, peach spray glaze, 3" h 20.00

American Art Potteries, planter, cowboy boot, blue, pink spray glaze, 6" h 15.00

American Art Potteries, TV lamp, conch shell, purple and pink spray glaze, 7 x 10" 20.00

American Art Potteries, vase, cornucopia, gold, white int, 10½" h 12.00

American Art Potteries, wall pocket, tree stump, applied woodpecker, brown spray glaze, 5" h 18.00

Amish Pantry Ware, baking dish, 5" d 15.00

Amish Pantry Ware, creamer, 12 oz 15.00

Amish Pantry Ware, ice tea tumbler, 16 oz 15.00

Amish Pantry Ware, milk jug, 4½ pt, 5½" h. 30.00

Amish Pantry Ware, mixing bowl, 2 pt 20.00

Amish Pantry Ware, spice shaker, 5" h 15.00

Cliftwood Art Potteries, Inc, bookends, pr, elephant, blue mulberry drip glaze 80.00

Cliftwood Art Potteries, creamer, chocolate drip glaze, 4" h, 3" d 30.00

Cliftwood Art Potteries, flower insert, turtle #2, dark green glaze, 5½" l 15.00

Midwest Potteries, bird, blue, 2" h 5.00

Midwest Potteries, figurine, cocker spaniel, black gloss glaze, 6 x 4" 28.00

Midwest Potteries, figure, long–neck goose, white, yellow dec, 5¾" h 10.00

Midwest Potteries, flower bowl, 2 pc, circular, brown, yellow drip glaze, 10" d, 2½" d. 18.00

Morton Pottery, bud vase, bulbous, long neck, multi-colored, 6" h 8.00

Morton Pottery, piebird, white, multicolored wings and back, 5" h 25.00

Morton Pottery, planter, Art Deco, female bust, broad brimmed hat, matte white glaze, 7½" h 32.00

Morton Pottery, vase, cylindrical, emb crane and bamboo dec, white, 20" h 22.00

MOVIE MEMORABILIA

This movie memorabilia category includes material related to the movies themselves and the individuals who starred in them. Marilyn Monroe and Shirley Temple have their own categories, a tribute to their importance in the collecting field.

Movie collectibles divide into two basic groups, silent and sound era. With the exception of posters, material from the silent era is scarce and collected by only a small number of individuals. Most individuals under 50 would be hard pressed to name two, let alone five stars from the silent era.

An expansion of collector interest from the sound films of the 1930s through the 1950s, the period when the star system was at its zenith, to the films of the 1960s and 70s occurred during the 1990s. It is hard to think of Sophia Loren and Robert Redford as members of the AARP generation, but they are.

Prior to the 1960s movie licensing was limited. Most collectibles are tied in to media advertising and theater promotions. This changed with the blockbuster hits of the 1970s and 80s, e.g., *Star Wars* and *Superman* series. Licensing, especially in the toy sector, became an important method of generating capital for films.

Many collectors focus on a single movie personality. The number of collectors devoted to any specific star, even Clark Gable, is small. Regional association plays a major role. Many small communities still hold annual film festivals to honor those individuals who went on to fame and glory on the silver screen. The category is very generation–driven. When the generation who attended the movies associated with a specific star reaches an average age of 60+, interest in the star's memorabilia fades.

Two–dimensional material, e.g., magazines, abounds. Three–dimensional material is scarce. Pizzazz is a value factor—the greater the display potential, the higher the price.

In the 1980s movie studios and stars began selling their movie memorabilia through New York and West Coast auction houses. Many costumes broke the $1,000 barrier. Famous props, such as Dorothy's ruby glass slippers from *The Wizard of Oz*, broke the $10,000 barrier.

References: Anthony Curtis, *Lyle Film & Rock 'n' Roll Collectibles*, The Berkley Publishing Group, 1996; Tony Fusco, *Posters: Identification and Price Guide, Second Edition*, Avon Books, 1994; Ephraim Katz, *The Film Encyclopedia, Second Edition*, Harper, 1994; Norman E. Martinus and Harry L. Rinker, *Warman's Paper*, Wallace–Homestead, Krause Publications, 1994; Robert Osborne, *65 Years of The Oscar: The Official History of The Academy Awards*, Abbeville, 1994; Jay Scarfone and William Stillman, *The Wizard of Oz Collector's Treasury*, Schiffer Publishing, 1992.

Moe Wadle, *The Movie Tie–In Book: A Collector's Guide to Paperback Movie Editions*, Nostalgia Books, 1994; Jon R. Warren, *Collecting Hollywood: The Movie Poster Price Guide, Third Edition*, American Collectors Exchange, 1994; Dian Zillner, *Hollywood Collebtibles*, Schiffer Publishing, 1991; Dian Zillner, *Hollywood Collectibles: The Sequel*, Schiffer Publishing, 1994.

Periodical: *Big Reel*, PO Box 1050, Dubuque, IA 52004; *Movie Advertising Collector*, PO Box 28587, Philadelphia, PA 19149.

Morton Pottery, piebird, multicolored wings and back, 5" h, $18.00.

Note: See Animation Art, Autographs, Disneyana, Marilyn Monroe, Posters, Shirley Temple, Star Trek, and Star Wars for additional listings.

Advertisement, *Harvey Girls*, Judy Garland . . . . $ 15.00
Advertisement, *The Chase*, Peter Lorre 15.00
Afghan, *Wizard of Oz*, poster art image, 46 x 62",
   MIB. 115.00
Book, *Gone With the Wind*, Motion Picture Edition,
   1940, 392 pgs 78.00
Book, *The Emerald City of Oz*, L. Frank Baum,
   ©1932, dj 70.00
Book, Vincent Price, *Masque of the Red Death*,
   paperback, movie ed, 5 film photos on front and
   back covers, 1964 . . . . 15.00
Book, *Who's Who at MGM*, photographs, biogra-
   phies, 1940, 119 pgs 60.00
Booklet, *Ben Hur*, MGM, 1926 . . . . 18.00
Bubble Gum Cards, *Black Hole*, full–color photos,
   1979, 88 cards. 20.00
Bubble Gum Cards, *Close Encounters*, full–color
   photos, 1978, 66 cards. 20.00
Bubble Gum Cards, *Raiders of the Lost Ark*, full–color
   photos, 88 cards 20.00
Comic Book, *How the West Was Won*, Gold Key,
   1963 . . . . 6.00
Comic Book, *Moby Dick*, Dell, 1956 . . . . 10.00
Comic Book, *The Creature*, Dell, 1964. . . . . 12.00
Display, *Ghostbusters*, stand–up 32.00
Figure, Stay Puft, *Ghostbusters*, vinyl, movable head
   and arms, 6½" h. 15.00
Game, *Thunderball*, James Bond, Milton Bradley,
   1965 . . . . 70.00
Jigsaw Puzzle, *Oliver Twist*, Jaymar,1968, orig box,
   100 pcs 25.00
Lobby Cards, set of 8, *Daughter of Don Q*, Republic
   Pictures, 1946 . . . . 130.00

Lobby Card, Bob Steele, *Ambush Trail*, color, 1946, 11 x 14",
$15.00.

Matchcover, Janet Gaynor, *A Star Is Born!*, Diamond Match Co, $10.00.

Lobby Cards, set of 8, James Bond, *The Spy Who
   Loved Me*, color photos, 11 x 13" 45.00
Lobby Cards, set of 8, *Miss Tatlock's Millions*, Robert
   Stack, Dorothy Wood, framed, 1948 . . . . 42.00
Lobby Cards, set of 8, *Operation Pacific*, Warner
   Bros, 1951. . . . . 150.00
Lobby Cards, set of 8, *The Lemon Drop Kid*,
   Paramount Pictures, 1951 . . . . 100.00
Magazine, Clark Gable and Lana Turner, *Life*,
   Oct 14, 1941, *Honky Tonk* cov. 25.00
Magazine, Donna Reed, *Life*, Aug 31, 1953, *From
   Here to Eternity* feature article 15.00
Magazine, *Movie Humor*, Hollywood Girls & Gags,
   Jul 1935. . . . . 12.00
Magazine, *Picture Show Annual*, *The King and I* cov,
   1957 . . . . 25.00
Magazine, *Private Lives of Movie Stars*, Arco
   Publishing, 1945, 50 pgs 25.00
Photo, Arnold Schwarzenegger, sgd, color, scene
   from *Terminator*, 8 x 10". 80.00
Photo, Jane Russell, sgd, color, standing beside
   Marilyn Monroe, *Gentlemen Prefer Blondes*,
   8 x 10" 35.00
Pinback Buttton, *The Phantom*, celluloid, Universal
   Pictures, c1960, 3½" d 15.00
Poster, *Alice Doesn't Live Here Anymore*, 14 x 36" 45.00
Poster, *Arson Inc*, Lippert Productions, 22 x 28", 1949. . . . 32.00
Poster, Frankie Avalon, *Beach Blanket Bingo*, 22 x 22". . . . 22.00
Poster, Jack Nicholson, *Five Easy Pieces*, 14 x 36" 120.00
Poster, John Wayne, *The High and The Mighty*, 27 x
   41" 75.00
Poster, Mark Hamill, *Empire Strikes Back*, 27 x 41" 28.00
Poster, Mary Pickford, *Coquette*, United Artists, 28 x
   22", 1929. . . . . 480.00
Poster, *Raiders of the Seven Seas*, United Artist,
   1953, 27 x 41". 35.00
Pressbook, Jerry Lewis, *Don't Raise the Bridge...
   Lower the River*, 1968 . . . . 25.00
Pressbook, *Song of the South*, 1950s, 16 pgs. 75.00

Magazine, Richard Burton and Elizabeth Taylor, *Cleopatra*, April 13, 1962, complete with Post cereal baseball cards #5 Mickey Mantle and #6 Roger Maris, $175.00.

Program, *Ben Hur*, MGM. **32.00**

Prop, chariot spears, *The Ten Commandments*, metal, wood, and rubber, 1956, 3 x 7", price for pair **220.00**

Prop, head form, *Nightmare on Elm Street*, Freddie Krueger character, decomposed foam bust and molded head **450.00**

Prop, magic ticket, *Last Action Hero*, reads "ADMIT ONE" and has elephant, eye, and Indian deity illus, 1993 . . . . **170.00**

Prop, rubber knife, *Hook*, skull handle **225.00**

Record, *Guys and Dolls*, Decca, orig sleeve, 1950s. **8.00**

Sheet Music, Judy Garland, *For Me and My Gal* **10.00**

Sheet Music, Bing Crosby, *Going My Way*, Burke and Van Heusen, New York, 1944. . . . . **20.00**

Sheet Music, Judy Garland, *Over the Rainbow* **18.00**

Sheet Music, *Song of the South*, Disney **12.00**

Sheet Music, *Wizard of Oz* **22.00**

Souvenir Book, *Since You Went Away*, 1944, 9 x 12", 20 pgs **28.00**

Souvenir Book, *The Song of Bernadette*, 1944, 9 x 11½", 20 pgs **40.00**

Video, *Lt. Robin Crusoe, USN*, Walt Disney Home Video, 1966, 109 min **50.00**

Video, *Willie Wonka and the Chocolate Factory*, Warner Home Video, 1971, 95 min **30.00**

Window Card, Gary Cooper, *High Noon*, 1952. . . . . **80.00**

MOXIE

During the height of its popularity, 1920 to 1940, Moxie was distributed in approximately 36 states and even outsold Coca-Cola in many of them. It became so popular that moxie, meaning nervy, became part of the American vocabulary.

Moxie is the oldest continuously produced soft drink in the United States. It celebrated its 100th birthday in 1984. It traces its origin to a Moxie Nerve Food, a concoction developed by Dr. Augustin Thompon of Union, Maine, and first manufactured in Lowell, Massachusetts.

Moxie's fame is due largely to the promotional efforts of Frank Morton Archer, an intrepid entrepreneur endowed with a magnificent imagination. With a genius for showmanship and prophesying profits galore, Archer created an advertising campaign as famous as the soda itself.

Bottle wagons were replaced by horseless carriages. Some folks called cars "Moxies," because the first car they saw had MOXIE on its side. Archer mounted a saddled, dummy pony in the sidecar of a motorcycle and put his TNT Cowboy Outfit on the road. This was followed by his Moxiemobile, a dummy horse mounted on an automobile chassis and driven from the horse's saddle.

Scarcely an event occurred in the first half of the 20th century that Archer did not exploit. The famous World War I "I Want You For The U.S. Army" Uncle Sam poster has a striking resemblance to the Moxie man pointing at his viewers and commanding them to "Drink Moxie."

Many firms attempted to play upon the Moxie name. Hoxie, Nickletone, Noxie, Proxie, Puro, Rixie, and Toxie are just a few. Most of these spurious products were produced in limited quantities, thus making them a prime find for collectors.

Moxie is still produced today, not in New England but Georgia. However, its popularity remains strongest in the Northeast.

Collectors' Club: New England Moxie Congress, 445 Wyoming Ave, Millburn, NJ 07041.

Apron, Moxie logo, 1930s . . . . **$ 25.00**

Ashtray, ceramic, 1930s **35.00**

Bag, The Moxie Carrying Bag, boy and dog illus, 1920s. . . **15.00**

Banner, "Mad About Moxie For Thanksgiving," pilgrim holding carton at left, Indian with carton at right **30.00**

Baseball, Moxie League, 1950–60 . . . . **70.00**

Bottle Opener, "Drink Moxie," 1920s **12.00**

Can, aluminum, pull tab, Diet Moxie, Mad About Moxie, 12 oz **25.00**

Cap, Moxie logo, 1930s **30.00**

Carrier, cardboard, 2 bottle, 1940s **12.00**

Carrier, cardboard, "Original Moxie," 1940s **10.00**

Drinking Glass, flared top, "Drink Moxie" **90.00**

Fan, child sitting on man's lap, 1924, 8" **35.00**

Fan, diecut, cardboard, Moxie girl with compact, 1925, 8" **50.00**

Fan, "When the Heat Waves Go Astray Drink Moxie," 1950s **40.00**

Kite, The Moxie Flyer, 1930s **140.00**

Pocket Knife, 1930s **55.00**

Sign, cardboard, "Drink... A Nickel For Your Thirst!," bathing beauty with bottle, 1930s **325.00**

Sign, diecut cardboard, easel back, "Drink Moxie It's Always A Pleasure...... To Serve You," 1950s **45.00**

Sign, diecut cardboard, boy with dog carrying 3 pack of Moxie Teers, 1928 . . . . **300.00**

Sign, diecut cardboard, easel back, "a real thirst quencher, Drink Moxie," bottle, man holding glass, 1940s–50s, 19" h, 13" w. **55.00**

Sign, diecut cardboard, easel back, "drink Moxie for Extra Pep!," bottle and running boy and girl, c1950 . . . . **35.00**

Sign, flange, octagonal, "Drink Moxie 100%" on red button, green borders, 1920–30s, 8" w **325.00**

Syrup Jug, paper label, 1930s **90.00**

Fan, diecut cardboard, Frank Archer on front, Moxiemobile and boy on rocking horse on reverse, $75.00.

Elvis Presley, ceramic, plays "Love Me Tender," $75.00.

Thermometer, glass, round, "Drink Moxie It's Always A Pleasure......To Serve You," 1950s **90.00**
Thermometer, tin, "Old Fashioned Moxie Remember Those Days," 1970s **40.00**
Toy, bang gun, 1930s **20.00**

MUSIC BOXES

Antoine Favre, a Swiss watchmaker, made the first true music box in 1796. Early musical movements involved a tuned tooth that was plucked either by pins set in a flat wheel or by projections in the outer surface of a spring barrel. The manufacture of music boxes was largely a cottage industry until Charles Paillard established a factory in Sainte–Croix, Switzerland, in 1875.

The golden age of the music box was from 1880 to 1910. A cylinder or disc music box occupied a place of importance in many Victorian–era parlors.

The music box was far more popular in Europe than America. Most early parlor music boxes were of foreign manufacture. The radio and record player eventually replaced the parlor music box.

Although novelty music boxes date to the Victorian era, they enjoyed increased popularity following World War II. In the case of the novelty box, the musical portion is secondary to the shape of the box itself. This category focuses primarily on these novelty boxes.

Music boxes showed up everywhere, from the base of a snow globe to the rocker on a child's rocking chair. Teapots, limited edition whiskey bottles, beer steins, and modern collectibles from firms such as Enesco and Steinbach all featured music boxes. After a flood of cheap foreign imports between 1945 and the end of the 1960s, the giftware industry demanded that quality standards be raised. Contemporary music boxes are more for display than play.

Collectors' Club: Musical Box Society International, 887 Orange Ave East, St Paul, MN 55106.

Animals, Gorham, plays "Happy Birthday" **35.00**
Bank, Gorham, acrobat, plastic, green, 7½" h **18.00**
Bank, Gorham, cyclist, plastic, red, 7½" h **18.00**
Box, Santa, white, plays "Jingle Bells," 2½" h **8.00**

Children on Merry–Go–Round, wood, figures move, plays "Around the World in 80 Days", 7¾" **22.00**
Children on Seesaw, wood, figures move in time to music, 7" **20.00**
Church, mica cov wood, plays "Silent Night," 1930 . . . . . **25.00**
Clock, Mattel, plays "Hickory Dickory Dock," 1952 . . . . . **28.00**
Clown, Gorham, plastic, dome, 5½" **18.00**
Dove, figural, ceramic, 6¼" h **15.00**
Easter Egg, tin **15.00**
Kitten With Ball, ceramic, 5½" **18.00**
McDonald's Restaurant, plays "Good Times/Good Taste" theme when front door is opened, orig package **17.50**
Owl, figural, ceramic, 6" h **20.00**
Paddington Bear, Schmid, Christmas, 1981 . . . . **35.00**
Peanuts, Schmid, 30th Anniversary **18.00**
Powder Box, metal, silver, litho cov, c1940, 3½ x 4¼" **25.00**
Raggedy Ann, Schmid, 1980 . . . . **15.00**
Sesame Street's Big Bird and Snowman, Gorham, 7" h **24.00**
Snowball, glass, green wood base, Mr. and Mrs. Santa, 5" h **10.00**
Snowball, glass, green wood base, Santa and Rudolph, 5" h **10.00**
Snowball, glass, red wood base, Frosty the Snowman, 5" h **10.00**
Stein, porcelain, diamond dec, 5" h **35.00**

MUSICAL INSTRUMENTS

Most older musical instruments have far more reuse than collectible value. Instrument collecting is still largely confined to string and wind instruments dating prior to 1900. Collectors simply do not give a toot about brass instruments. The same holds true for drums unless the drum head art has collectible value.

Celebrity electric guitars is the current hot musical instrument collecting craze. They are standard offering at rock 'n roll auctions held by leading New York and West Coast auction houses. In the 1980s a number of individuals began buying guitars as investments. Prices skyrocketed. Although the market has appeared to stabilize, it should still be considered highly speculative.

From the 1890s through the 1930s, inexpensive student violins marked with a stamp or paper label featuring the name of a famous violin maker—Amati, Caspar DaSolo, Guarnerious, Maggini, Stradivarius, and Stainer are just a few examples—were sold in quantity. They were sold door to door and by Sears Roebuck. The advertisements claimed that the owner would have a violin nearly equal in quality to one made by the famous makers of the past. The cheap model sold for $2.45, the expensive model for $15. If cared for and played, these student violins have developed a wonderful, mellow tone and have a value in the $150 to $200 range. If damaged, they are $30 to $40 wall hangers.

References: S. P. Fjestad (ed.), *Blue Book of Guitar Values, Third Edition,* Blue Book Publications, 1996; Goerge Gruhn and Walter Carter, *Electric Guitars and Basses: A Photographic History,* Miller Freeman Books, GPI Books, 1994; Paul Trynka (ed.), *The Electric Guitar: An Illustrated History,* Chronicle Books, 1993.

Periodicals: *Concertina & Squeezebox,* PO Box 6706, Ithaca, NY 14851; *Vintage Guitar Magazine,* PO Box 7301, Bismarck, ND 58507.

Collectors' Club: American Musical Instrument Society, RD 3, Box 205–B, Franklin, PA 16323.

Banjo, Regina, 11" head, 18 hooks, 17 frets, peghead and fingerboard inlaid with mother–of–pearl crescent moons, double thick wood and metal rim, tone ring, metal resonator, 1920 patent date . . . . . $ 125.00
Banjo, 10" head, 11 high frets, snake skin head, aluminum hoop, fancy cutouts in aluminum resonator and armrest, torn head, c1950 . . . . 50.00
Banjo, Wondertone, S. S. Steward, walnut, marquetry inlay, 1920s 190.00
Cornet, American, Wurlitzer, silver, 6 crooks and "C" crook, orig case with accessories 300.00
Cornet, American Favorite, Pepper, Philadelphia, rose engraving on bell, orig case, mute, crook, and mouthpiece, plating worn from 2 pipes 175.00
Cornet, Carl Fisher Coronet, silver, modified shepherd's crook, orig mouthpiece, flat spring missing, no case 95.00
Cornet, Marceau & Company, solo alto, brass, flat spring, orig mouthpiece, later buttons 175.00
Cornet, Special New York Model, Franz Weber, Vienna and New York, silver, modified shepherd's crook, flat springs, gold trim, orig case and accessories, 2 mouthpieces, extra crook and lead pipe 275.00

Cornet, Standard (Vega), Boston, silver, pitch change crook, double spit, short lead pipe, mouth piece 135.00
Guitar, C. F. Martin, Model R–28, Arch Top Guitar, 18³/₄" back, 14⁷/₁₆" w bottom bout, stamped internally "C F Martin & Co Nazareth PA 67003" with "C F Martin & Co est 1833" decal, 2–pc mahogany back and sides, carved medium grain spruce top, mahogany neck, rosewood fingerboard with inlaid pearl eyes, gold–brown sunburst color finish, with case, 1937 . . . . 780.00
Harmonica, Hohner, American Ace, 10 holes, WWI biplanes or jet fighter shown on box 20.00
Harmonica, Hohner, Herb Shriner's Hoosier Boy, 10 holes, gold covers, 4" l 40.00
Harmonica, Japan, 1,000,000 $ Baby, miniature, 4 holes, cardboard box 20.00
Mandolin, 13³/₄" l back, labeled "Gibson Mandolin Style A2, Number 63752 is hereby guaranteed... Gibson Mandolin Guitar Co, Kalamazoo Mich USA," 1–pc maple back, sides similar, wide grain spruce top, body in faux ivory, laminated cedar neck with bound rosewood fingerboard with pearl eyes, with case, 1921 . . . . 600.00
Violin, Adolph Adler, Dresden, Amati copy, 2–pc back, medium to dark brown color, some edge wear, excellent condition, 1923 . . . . 350.00
Violin, Rudolph Heberlein Markneukirchen, 2–pc back with good curl, deeply carved edges, 3 repaired top cracks, good varnish, 1920 . . . . 300.00

AUCTION PRICES

Skinner, Inc's Fine Musical Instruments auction, November 10, 1996. Prices include the 15% buyer's premium.

Guitar, Model 0–28K, stamped internally and externally "C.F. Martin & Co., Nazareth, P.A., 31225," 2–pc back and sides of strongly figured koa wood with decorative inlaid center strip, top similar, with herringbone purfling, body bound in faux ivory, mahogany neck, ebony fingerboard with diamond–shaped pearl inlay, with case, 1927, 19¹/₁₆" l back 4,600.00
Guitar, Arch Top Model R–18, stamped internally "C F Martin & Co, Nazareth PA 67003" with "C F Martin & Co est 1833" decal, 2–pc mahogany back and sides, carved medium grain spruce top, mahogany neck, rosewood fingerboard with inlaid pearl eyes, gold–brown sunburst color finish, with case, 1937, 18³/₄" l back 862.50
Guitar, hollow body electric Model ES–125, Gibson Inc, Kalamazoo, stamped internally "U9330 13, ES 125," 1–pc laminated maple back, mahogany sides and neck, laminated maple top, rosewood fingerboard with pearl eyes, yellow–brown sunburst color finish, 1957, 20¹/₄" l back 632.50
Guitar, labeled "Style Guitar, Gibson Byrdland, Number A28923," 2–pc light curl maple back, similar sides, medium grain spruce top, strongly figured maple neck, bound ebony fingerboard with pearl block inlay, yellow–brown sunburst finish, orig hardshell case and Magnatone tube amplifier, 1959, 21" l back 3,565.00

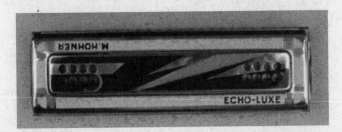

Harmonica, M. Hohner, Echo–Luxe, souvenir 1933 Century of Progress, 6⁵/₈" l, $

NAPKIN RINGS

Sterling and silver plated napkin rings were an important tabletop accessory in the pre–1940 period. Figural napkin rings from companies such as Meriden and Pairpoint were used in upper–class households. Even simple silver plated rings often contained elaborately engraved initials and/or decorative motifs.

As American dining became more casual following World War II, so did napkin rings. Plastic and wood replaced cast metal as the material of choice. Bright solid color geometric and trendy figural pieces, many mimicking the costume jewelry styles of the times, decorated the post–1945 kitchen table.

Napkins rings fell out of favor by the early 1960s. Inexpensive paper napkins and towels were a far simpler approach than washing and ironing a textile napkin ring.

Napkin rings usually were sold in sets. Full sets, especially in their period packaging, have the greatest collector appeal. Animal and Bakelite collectors have driven up the value of napkin rings that cross over into their collecting sphere.

Bakelite, red, carved . . . . $ 35.00
Bakelite, round, carved, set of 6 in orig box 75.00
Celluloid, figural bear 4.00
Celluloid, figural grapes 15.00
Celluloid, Scottie dog 15.00
Franciscan Ware, Desert Rose pattern 40.00
Metal, lady holding stick 15.00
Milk Glass, triangular. 30.00
Noritake, butterfly and flowers 20.00
Noritake, man, Art Deco design 25.00
Papier Mâché, green 4.00
Pewter, dragon. 20.00
Plastic, heart shaped, yellow 6.00
Plastic, orange, set of 4 . . . . 4.00
Silver Plated, butterfly perched on fans 100.00
Silver Plated, Dachshund, ring on back. 150.00
Silver Plated, 2 swans flanking ring. 115.00
Wood, round. 4.00

Silver Plated, cow beside ring, 2⁷/₈" h, 3¹/₄" l, $275.00.

NAZI ITEMS

Anton Drexler and Adolf Hitler founded The National Socialist German Workers Party (NSDAP) on February 24, 1920. The party advocated a 25–point plan designed to lift the German economy and government from the depths of the Depression.

When the Beer Hall Putsch failed in 1923, Hitler was sentenced to a five–year prison term. Although serving only a year, he used that time to write *Mein Kampf*, a book that became the NSDAP manifesto.

During the early 1930s the NSDAP grew from a regional party based in Southern Germany to a national party. Hitler became Reich's chancellor in the spring of 1933. Following the death of President von Hindenberg in 1934, Hitler assumed that title as well. The NSDAP virtually controlled all aspects of German life between 1934 and May 1945.

Nazi items are political items, not military items. Do not confuse the two. Although the Wehrmacht, the German military, was an independent organization, it was subject to numerous controls from the political sector. Nazi memorabilia were popular war souvenirs. Large quantities of armbands, daggers, flags, and copies of *Mein Kampf* survive in the United States.

References: Gary Kirsner, *German Military Steins: 1914 to 1945, Second Edition,* Glentiques Ltd, 1996; Ron Manion, *German Military Collectibles Price Guide,* Antique Publications, 1995.

Periodicals: *Military Collectors News,* PO Box 702073, Tulsa, OK 74170; *Military Trader,* PO Box 1050, Dubuque, IA 52004.

Badge, General Assault, silver, c1940 . . . . $ 30.00
Belt and Buckle, silver wash on brass, German
     Luftwaffe, 1942 . . . . 38.00
Book, *Hindenburg,* hp cloth, gold emb title, German
     text, 1927, 287 pgs 15.00
Dagger, Army officer's, nickel fittings, scabbard,
     orange celluloid grip, with hanger, Alcoso ACS
     Solingen 300.00
Figurine, plaster, hp, skunk body with Hitler's head,
     5" h 150.00
Hat, rabbit fur, quilted int, black ties at ear flaps, olive
     green wool body, RZM/SS, skull and eagle devices . . . 325.00
Insignia, armband, Kyffhauserbund, blue wool body,
     bevo Nazi kyffhauserbund shield, 38 x 50 mm
     bronze wreath and rayed oval badge with monu-
     ment center attached by one prong 50.00
Insignia, cap ribbon, Naval, Kriegsmarine, 56" black
     body, dark gold Gothic title 45.00
Insignia, tinnie, 1933 Hitler quote, gilt finish, reads
     "Es Wird Kunftig Nur Noch Einen Adel Geben Adel
     Der Arbeit Adolf Hitler 1933" 35.00
Magazine, *Das Banerland,* German history text, old
     train model photos, stamps, Apr–Sep, 1925, 40 pgs 15.00
Magazine, *Time,* Nazi cov, Gen Field Marshall Fedor
     Von Bock, 1942 . . . . 35.00
Newspaper, *Daily Journal–Gazette,* Nazis Open
     Aerial Battle, Aug 12, 1940. . . . . 3.00
Newspaper, *Deutsche Bug–Zeitun,* spread eagle on
     wreathed swastika in masthead, Oct 10, 1942 . . . . 25.00
Paperweight, nickel, swastika on ball mount, nickel
     base with green felt 95.00

Matchcover, striker on Hitler's backside, $25.00.

Pennant, NSDAP, triangular, painted swastika, double
  sided, 54" l, 11" h **35.00**
Plate, wood, wood burned design edges, painted
  emblem of Munich center with crest of 5 different
  cities around edge, Munich insignia crested with
  Nazi flag, 8³/₄" d. **20.00**
Postcard, black and white drawing, profile bust of
  Hitler wearing overcoat and peaked hat, unused,
  1938 . . . . **25.00**
Ring, silver, crossed swords, helmet, and swastika **55.00**
Soup Bowl, green SS Reich 1940 lettering,
  Bauscher–Weiden trademark bottom, 9" d. **130.00**
Stein, Kriegsmarine, stoneware, sailor, battleships,
  and school ship in relief, metal lid **350.00**
Stein, Reichsparteitag, pewter, Bayreuth crest, 1938. . . . . **225.00**
Stein, stoneware, eagle, swastika, and flag, plain lid **325.00**
Stein, Zur Erinnerung an die Westwallzeit, pottery,
  metal lid, c1940. . . . . **125.00**
Trench Art, airplane, aluminum, brass. **75.00**
Trousers, gray twill wool, straight leg, red doeskin
  sides, 3 slash pockets and watch pocket, 6–button
  fly, side adjustment belts, suspender fittings **625.00**

NEW MARTINSVILLE/VIKING GLASS

Mark Douglass and George Matheny, two East Liverpool, Ohio, glassmen, founded the New Martinsville Glass Manufacturing Company, New Martinsville, West Virginia, in 1901. The company made colored and plain dishes, lamps, tumblers, and a variety of other glass items. John Webb, a cousin of the famous English glass maker Thomas Webb, joined the firm in December 1901. Within a brief period of time, New Martinsville was making Muranese, a direct copy of Peachblow.

After being destroyed by a major fire in 1907, the glasshouse was rebuilt and production was resumed in 1908. Harry Barth, who eventually directed the glasshouse design, joined the firm in May 1918 as a laborer in the packing room. Barth and Ira Clarke guided the company through the difficult years of the Depression.

R. M. Rice and Carl Schultz, two New Englanders, bought New Martinsville Glass in July 1938. Barth was made general plant manager. Barth left in September 1940 to join the Optical Division of the War Production Board. He returned to the Ohio Valley ten years later and opened his own design firm creating molds for Paden City, Viking, and others.

The stockholders of the New Martinsville Glass Company changed its name to Viking Glass on June 1, 1944. Post–1945 product lines included handmade cut and etched giftware, novelties, and tableware. Most pieces were marked with a paper label reading "Viking." In 1951 Viking purchased a number of Paden City molds, including several of the Barth Art Animals. Viking also purchased several Westmoreland molds, including the 4¹/₂" and 9" dolphin candlesticks.

Viking purchased the Rainbow Art Glass Company, Huntington, West Virginia, in the early 1970s. Henry Manus, a Dutch immigrant, founded Rainbow in 1942. Rainbow made animal figurines, colored glassware, and cased, crackle, opal, and spatter decorative ware. Viking continued production of the animal figurines, retaining the "Rainbow Art" paper label.

Kenneth Dalzell, former head of the Fostoria Glass Company, purchased the Viking Glass Company in mid–1986. After closing the plant for renovations, it was reopened in October 1987. The company's name was changed to Dalzell–Viking Glass. Dalzell–Viking, using models in Viking's inventory, reintroduced animal figurines and other items, often using non–period colors.

References: Lee Garmon and Dick Spencer, *Glass Animals of the Depression Era,* Collector Books, 1993; James Jeasell, *New Martinsville Glass: 1900–1944,* Antique Publications, 1994.

Animal, chick, 1" h . . . . **$ 65.00**
Animal, eagle **70.00**
Animal, horse, oval base, 12" h **90.00**
Animal, pelican. **55.00**
Animal, piglet **65.00**
Animal, rabbit, ears back, 1" h **65.00**
Animal, rooster, 8" h **130.00**
Bookends, pr, elephant. **120.00**
Bookends, pr, sailing ships, rect block background,
  5³/₄" h **100.00**
Bookends, pr, seal with ball **140.00**
Bookends, pr, squirrel, 5¹/₄" h **130.00**
Bookends, pr, starfish, 7³/₄" h **130.00**
Bowl, swan, 10¹/₂" d, amber **35.00**
Hostmaster, cake plate, 14" d, amber **25.00**
Hostmaster, cup and saucer, ruby **15.00**
Hostmaster, goblet, 6¹/₄" h, cobalt blue **25.00**
Hostmaster, ice bowl, 5¹/₂" d, ruby **45.00**
Janice, basket, 11" h, crystal. **65.00**
Janice, bonbon, 2 handle, 6" d, 4" h, blue. **28.00**
Janice, bowl, flared, 12" d, crystal **35.00**
Janice, bowl, flower with crimps, 5¹/₂" d, crystal **18.00**
Janice, bowl, 2 handles, 9" d, blue **50.00**
Janice, candelabra, 2 light, 5" h, crystal **30.00**
Janice, celery, 11" d, crystal **15.00**
Janice, creamer, 6 oz, red **15.00**
Janice, cup, crystal **5.00**
Janice, jam jar, cov, 6" h, blue **40.00**
Janice, mayonnaise, round, crystal **10.00**
Janice, plate, 2 handle, 7" d, crystal **5.00**
Janice, platter, oval, 13" l, crystal **28.00**
Janice, salad plate, 8¹/₂" d, blue **15.00**
Janice, salt and pepper shakers, pr, red **60.00**
Janice, sugar, 6 oz, crystal **8.00**
Janice, tumbler, 12 oz, crystal **8.00**
Janice, vase, flared, 3 ftd, 8" h, crystal. **45.00**
Moondrops, ashtray, ruby. **35.00**
Moondrops, bud vase, 9¹/₄" h, cobalt **120.00**
Moondrops, butter, cov, light green. **240.00**
Moondrops, candy dish, 8" d, smoke **20.00**

Moondrops, wine, 5¹/₄" h, amethyst, $20.00.

Moondrops, celery, boat shape, 11" l, blue **25.00**
Moondrops, cordial, ³/₄ oz, blue. **32.00**
Moondrops, cordial 1 oz, amber **20.00**
Moondrops, cream soup, 4¹/₄" d, amethyst **30.00**
Moondrops, cup, crystal **8.00**
Moondrops, cup and saucer, ruby. **25.00**
Moondrops, decanter, 7³/₄" h, blue **55.00**
Moondrops, dinner plate, 9¹/₂" d, cobalt **12.00**
Moondrops, dinner plate, 9¹/₂" d, emerald green **18.00**
Moondrops, goblet, 5 oz, blue **20.00**
Moondrops, gravy, amethyst. **75.00**
Moondrops, mayonnaise, red **45.00**
Moondrops, plate, 5⁷/₈" d, blue. **8.00**
Moondrops, platter, oval, 12" d, red **30.00**
Moondrops, platter, 7¹/₈" d, blue. **10.00**
Moondrops, powder jar, 3 ftd, blue. **165.00**
Moondrops, relish, divided, 3 ftd, 8¹/₂" d, jadeite. **15.00**
Moondrops, saucer, green **3.00**
Moondrops, sherbet, 4¹/₂" h, black **12.00**
Moondrops, tumbler, 5 oz, blue **12.00**
Moondrops, whiskey, red **18.00**
Oscar, water set, tankard pitcher, 2 tumblers, amber **55.00**
Radiance, bonbon, ftd, 6" d, amber **15.00**
Radiance, bowl, flared, 10" d, amber **18.00**
Radiance, candlesticks, pr, 2 light, amber **60.00**
Radiance, celery, 10" d, amber. **15.00**
Radiance, condiment set, 4 pcs, with tray, amber **140.00**
Radiance, cruet, individual, amber **30.00**
Radiance, cup, ftd, ice blue **15.00**
Radiance, decanter, handled, stopper, cobalt blue **175.00**
Radiance, honey jar, cov, ruby **230.00**
Radiance, ladle, amber **85.00**
Radiance, luncheon plate, 8" d, amber. **8.00**
Radiance, mayonnaise, 3–pc set, amber **30.00**
Radiance, nut dish, 2 handles, 5" d, amber **10.00**
Radiance, relish, 3 part, 8" d, amber **20.00**
Radiance, salt and pepper shakers, pr, amber **40.00**
Radiance, saucer, ice blue **6.00**
Radiance, vase, flared, 12" h, amber. **45.00**

NEWSPAPERS

America's first successful newspaper was *The Boston Newsletter,* founded in 1704. The newspaper industry grew rapidly, experiencing its golden age in the early 20th century. Within the last decade, many great evening papers have ceased publication, and many local papers have been purchased by large chains.

Newspapers are collected first for their story content and second for their advertising. Volume One, Number One of any newspaper brings a premium because of its crossover value. Beware of assigning too much value to age alone; 18th–century and 19th–century newspapers with weak story content and advertising are frequently framed and used for decorative purposes.

Collecting headline edition newspapers is a popular newspaper collecting approach. Individuals like to collect newspapers related to great events that they have witnessed or that have been romanticized through the movies, television, and other media.

Saving the last edition of a newspaper has become a national fad. If the sales volume of the final issue equaled that of a daily issue, most of these papers would still be publishing. While there are collectors for the "first" of something, there are no collectors for the "last" of something. "Final" issues have little long–term value.

A newspaper must be complete and have a minimal amount of chipping and cracking to be collectible. Newsprint, commonly used after 1880, is made of wood pulp and deteriorates quickly without proper care. Pre–1880 newsprint is made from cotton and/or rag fiber and survives much better.

If only the front page of a 20th–century headline newspaper survives, value is reduced by 40% to 50%. Banner headlines, those extending across the full page, are preferred. Add a 10% to 20% premium to headline newspapers from the city where the event occurred.

Two of the most commonly reprinted papers are the January 8, 1880, *Ulster Country Gazette,* announcing the death of George Washington, and the April 15, 1865, issue of the *N.Y. Herald,* announcing Lincoln's death. If you have one of these papers, chances are you have a reprint.

References: Ron Barlow and Ray Reynolds, *The Insider's Guide to Old Books, Magazines, Newspapers, Trade Catalogs,* Windmill Publishing, 1995; Norman E. Martinus and Harry L. Rinker, *Warman's Paper,* Wallace–Homestead, Krause Publications, 1994.

Periodical: *PCM (Paper Collectors' Marketplace),* PO Box 128, Scandinavia, WI 54977.

Collectors' Club: Newspaper Collectors Society of America, PO Box 19134, Lansing, MI 48901.

1927, May 29, *St. Paul Dispatch,* Lindbergh Starts
  Paris Flight. . . . . **$ 20.00**
1929, Feb 15, *Washington Observer,* St. Valentine's
  Day Massacre **130.00**
1931, Jun 6, *Washington Observer,* Al Capone
  Indicted. **15.00**
1932, Mar 6, *St. Paul Pioneer Press,* Roosevelt Orders
  Bank Holiday. **8.00**
1933, Apr 4, *Pittsburgh Sun–Telegraph,* Akron Breaks
  To Pieces: 73 Dead **12.00**
1934, Apr 8, *Kingsport Times,* Clyde Barros Is Sought
  In Killing **15.00**

1963, Nov 23, The Indianapolis Star, President Shot By Assassin, $26.00.

1934, Jul 23, *Newport News*, Dillinger Killed **180.00**

1935, Jan 14, *St. Paul Dispatch*, Lindbergh Kidnapping Testimony **5.00**

1936, Jan 18, *Des Moines Register*, Rudyard Kipling Dies **8.00**

1938, Jun 22, *Chicago American*, Max Schmeling vs Joe Lewis **15.00**

1939, Jul 3, *Chicago Examiner*, Chamberlain Warns Britain Ready For War! **5.00**

1941, Dec 8, *Raonoke World News*, Pearl Harbor Attacked **20.00**

1941, Dec 9, *New York Herald*, Congress Votes War; 1,500 Dead In Hawaii Raid **3.00**

1944, Jun 6, *Niagara Falls Gazette*, Normandy Invasion **20.00**

1945, Jan 13, *St. Paul Pioneer Press*, Amelia Earhart Lands At Oakland **10.00**

1945, Apr 13, *New York Daily Times*, FDR Dies **30.00**

1945, Apr 25, *Oakland Tribune*, Hitler's Hideout Bombed **4.00**

1945, Aug 8, *Guinea Gold*, Atom Bomb Dropped On Japan **20.00**

1945, Aug 15, *New York Daily Times*, War With Japan Ends **15.00**

1956, Jul 27, *San Francisco Examiner*, Andrea Doria Sinks **18.00**

1958, Jun 6, *Williamsport Gazette*, Robert Kennedy Killed **15.00**

1965, Jan 21, *New York Daily News*, Johnson Takes Oath Of Office **10.00**

1969, Jul 21, *Wapakoneta Daily News*, Hometown Boy Neill Armstrong Steps On Moon **38.00**

1974, Aug 9, *New York Daily Times*, Nixon Resigns **20.00**

1977, Aug 17, *Commercial Appeal*, Memphis, TN, Elvis Presley Dies **25.00**

1979, Jun 12, *San Francisco Examiner*, John Wayne Dies **15.00**

1980, Dec 19, *San Jose News*, John Lennon Killed **12.00**

1981, Mar 31, *New York Daily Times*, Reagan Shot **60.00**

1982, Mar 7, *San Francisco Chronicle*, John Belushi Dies **10.00**

NODDERS & BOBBIN' HEADS

A nodder is a thing that nods, usually a figure's head. Today the term has been expanded to cover things that bob and sway as well as nod. Nodders were made as early as the 17th century. A nodder consists of two separate molded parts. A pin is used as the fulcrum to balance one piece on the other. A true nodder works by gravity, a counterbalance weight attached to the fulcrum located in the base piece. Eventually, electrical, frictional, mechanical, and windup mechanisms were used. While ceramic, especially bisque, nodders are the most common, nodders also were made in pressed cardboard, celluloid, ivory, metal, papier–mâché, plastic, and wood.

Most nodders are characterizations, often somewhat grotesque. Few have received immunity from the nodder designer. Buddhas, 18th–century courtiers, ethnic and professional types, cartoon figures, and animals are just a few examples.

Nodders were sold everywhere from dime stores to fine jewelry stores. Most collectors specialize, e.g., nodding salt and pepper shakers or holiday theme nodders.

A true nodder is weighted. Bobbin' heads have no weight. Their motion comes from a spring or other mechanism inside their head. While most individuals think of bobbin' heads in respect to the Beatles, Peanuts, and Sports Mascot series from the 1960s, papier–mâché cartoon and holiday figures date from the early decades of the 20th century.

Reference: Hilma R. Irtz, *Figural Nodders: Identification & Value Guide*, Collector Books, 1997.

Aloha Girl . . . . **$ 20.00**
Atlanta Braves, Brave head **120.00**
Atlanta Falcons, gold base, Merger Series, 1968 . . . . **70.00**
Auntie Blossom, bisque, Germany, c1930 . . . . **125.00**
Baltimore Colts, sq base, blue, 1962 . . . . **45.00**
Beetle Bailey **140.00**
Boston Terrier **12.00**
Bozo the Clown **230.00**
Bugs Bunny, golfing, 1990 . . . . **15.00**
Chicago White Sox, green **75.00**
Chinese Kissing **8.00**
Cincinnati Reds, ball head **140.00**
Colonel Sanders **50.00**
Davey Crockett **160.00**
Detroit Lions, silver, sq base, 1962 . . . . **55.00**
Detroit Tigers, tiger head **165.00**
Donny Osmond **75.00**
Dwight D. Eisenhower, composition, 6" h **45.00**
Florida Orange **28.00**
Georgia Tech, Berco Products, Inc **15.00**
Goofy, Disneyland/Disney World **120.00**
Green Bay Packers, gold base, Merger Series, 1968 . . . . . . **70.00**
Harold Teen, bisque, Germany, c1930 . . . . **125.00**
John Lennon **130.00**
Johnny Bench, 1992–94 . . . . **30.00**
Knott's Berry Farm, CA **65.00**
Linus **110.00**
Mammy Yokum **85.00**

Marvin the Martian, 1990 . . . . **15.00**
Nixon For President, 1960 . . . . **75.00**
Penn State, Berco Products, Inc **15.00**
Phantom of the Opera **85.00**
Reggie Jackson **35.00**
Roger Maris. **75.00**
Santa **40.00**
Seattle Supersonics, composition, figure holding bas-
  ketball, gold round base, 7" h **30.00**
Shriner **20.00**
Snoopy, Joe Cool, mini. **30.00**
Tom Seaver **45.00**
Topo Gigio **80.00**
Troy Aikman, 1992–94. . . . . **40.00**
Willie Mays, light skin **220.00**
Yogi Berra **45.00**
Yosemite Sam, 1990 . . . . **15.00**

NON–SPORT TRADING CARDS

Tobacco insert cards of the late 19th century are the historical antecedents of the modern trading (bubble gum) card. Over 500 sets, with only 25 devoted to sports, were issued between 1885 and 1894. Tobacco cards lost popularity following World War I.

In 1933 Indian Gum marketed a piece of gum and a card inside a waxed paper package, launching the era of the modern trading card. Goudey Gum and National Chicle controlled the market until the arrival of Gum, Inc., in 1936. In 1948 Bowman entered the picture, followed a year later by Topps. The Bowman–Topps rivalry continued until 1957 when Topps bought Bowman.

Although Topps enjoyed a dominant position in the baseball trading card market, Frank Fleer Company and Philadelphia Chewing Gum provided strong competition in the non–sport trading card sector in the 1960s. Eventually Donruss also became a major player in the non–sport trading card arena.

Non–sport trading cards benefited from the decline of the sport trading card in the early 1990s. Fueled by a strong comic book store market, many companies issued non–sport trading card sets covering a wide range of topics from current hit movies to pin–up girls of the past. Dozens of new issues arrived each month. As the 1990s end, the craze appears to be over. High prices, too many sets, and the introduction of chase and other gimmick cards have had a negative impact. Secondary market value for these post–1990 sets is highly speculative, a situation not likely to change within the next 10 to 15 years.

Reference: Norman E. Martinus and Harry L. Rinker, *Warman's Paper,* Wallace–Homestead, Krause Publications, 1994.

Periodicals: *Non–Sport Update,* 4019 Green St, PO Box 5858, Harrisburg, PA 17110; *The Wrapper,* 1811 Noore Ct, St Charles, IL 60174.

Collectors' Club: United States Cartophilic Society, PO Box 4020, Saint Augustine, FL 32085.

Bowman, America Salutes the FBI, 1949. . . . . $ **12.00**
Bowman, Movie Stars, 1948. . . . . **10.00**
Comic Images, Marvel Universe IV Heroic Images,
  set of 90 . . . . **12.00**
Dart, Beetlejuice, set of 100, 1990 . . . . **10.00**

Topps, Mars Attacks, card #25, front, 1962, $18.00.

Donruss, Ace Ventura: When Nature Calls, foil set, 9
  cards **35.00**
Donruss, Addams Family, 1966 . . . . **4.00**
Donruss, All Pro Skateboard, 1978. . . . .**25**
Donruss, Baseball Super Freaks I and II, 1973 . . . .**50**
Donruss, Combat, 1964. . . . . **2.00**
Donruss, Dukes of Hazzard, 1983 . . . .**30**
Donruss, Elvis, set of 66, 1978 . . . . **30.00**
Donruss, Fantastic Odd Rods, Series 1 sticker–card,
  1973 . . . . **1.50**
Donruss, King Kong, 1965 . . . . **5.00**
Donruss, Knight Rider, 1983 . . . .**25**
Donruss, M A S H, 1982 . . . .**50**
Donruss, Monkees, sepia, 1966 . . . .**25**
Eclipse, Drug Wars, set of 36, 1991 . . . . **8.00**
Eclipse, Iran Contra Scandal, set of 36, 1988 . . . . **8.00**
Fleer, Beautiful People, 1978 . . . .**50**
Fleer, Believe It or Not, 1970 . . . . **1.00**
Fleer, Cracked Magazine, 1978 . . . .**40**
Fleer, Drag Nationals, 1972 . . . . **2.00**
Fleer, Hogan's Heroes, 1965 . . . . **8.00**
Fleer, Hollywood Slap Stickers, set of 66 . . . . **20.00**
Fleer, Kustom Cars, puzzle card, 1974 . . . . **2.50**
Fleer, Three Stooges, 1959, set of 96 . . . . **650.00**
Frostick, Animal Cards, set of 44, c1930 . . . . **175.00**
Goudey Gum, Auto License Plates, 1936 . . . . **4.00**
Goudey Gum, First Column Defenders, 1940, set of
  24 . . . . **350.00**
Goudey Gum, Sky Birds, 1941, set of 24 . . . . **175.00**
Gum Inc, American Beauties, 1941 . . . . **25.00**
Gum Inc, Film Funnies, set of 24 . . . . **500.00**
Gum Inc, Lone Ranger, card 1–36, 1940. . . . . **28.00**
Hasbro, G. I. Joe, 1986 . . . .**25**
Heinz, Famous Aviators, 1939–40 . . . . **15.00**
Impel, Minnie 'n Me, set of 161 . . . . **12.00**
Johnson, Dick Tracy, card 1–96, 1930s **8.00**
Leaf, Garrison's Gorrillas, 1967 . . . . **2.00**
Lionel, Lionel Trains, 1959–60 . . . . **8.00**
Mattel, Barbie, 1990 . . . .**10**

Topps, Mars Attacks, card #25, back, 1962, $18.00.

Monogram, Monogram Models, 1970	12.00
National Licorice, African Animal Jig	15.00
Nu–Card Sales, Dinosaurs, 1961	4.00
Pacific, Andy Griffith, 110 cards, Series 1	20.00
Philly, Robert F. Kennedy, 1968	3.00
Planters, Hunted Animals, c1940`	2.50
Pro Set, Desert Storm, 1991	.10
Rosan, John F. Kennedy, 1964	1.00
SkyBox, Archie, set of 120, 1992	12.00
SkyBox, Garfield, 1992	.15
Topps, A–Team, 1983	.10
Topps, Alf, Series 1, 1987, set of 69, 8 stickers	12.00
Topps, Alien, 1969	.30
Topps, Animals of the World, 1951	4.00
Topps, Annie Album Stickers, 1982	.15
Topps, Back to the Future II, set of 88, 11 stickers	12.00
Topps, Batman, set of 44, 1966	120.00
Topps, Battle, 1965	8.00
Topps, Battlestar Galactica, 1978	.25
Topps, Bay City Rollers, 1975	1.50
Topps, Beatles, set of 60, Series I, 1964	150.00
Topps, Beverly Hillbillies, 1963	4.00
Topps, Bring 'Em Back Alive, 1950	5.00
Topps, E. T., 1982	.20
Topps, Get Smart, 1966	3.50
Topps, Indiana Jones and the Temple of Doom, 1984	.15
Topps, Jaws 2, 1978	.15
Topps, Jets, 1956	1.50
Topps, Kung Fu, 1973	1.50
Topps, Land of the Giants, 1968	35.00
Topps, Laugh–In, card 1–45, 1968	1.50
Topps, Little Shop of Horrors, 1986	.20
Topps, Lost in Space, 1966	8.00
Topps, Man on the Moon, set of 55, 1969–70	90.00
Topps, Mars Attacks, card 2–54, 1962	18.00
Topps, Master of the Universe, 1984	.10
Topps, Maya, set of 55, 1967	30.00
Upper Deck, Beauty and the Beast, 1993	.25
Weber Brothers, Animals, 1920s	2.50

NORITAKE AZALEA

Azalea is a Noritake hand–painted china pattern first produced in the early 1900s. Because the pieces are hand painted, subtle variations are common.

The Larkin Company, Buffalo, New York, used Azalea as one of its "Larkin Plan" premiums. In 1931 Larkin billed it as "Our Most Popular China." Some Azalea accessory pieces appeared in Larkin catalogs for three or four years, others for up to 19 consecutive years. Azalea decorated glass and other coordinating items were made, but never achieved the popularity of the dinnerware.

Note: All items listed are china, unless otherwise noted. For reference information and other Noritake patterns, see Noritake China.

Basket	$ 150.00
Bonbon, 6¼" d	50.00
Bouillon Cup and Saucer	25.00
Bread and Butter Plate, 6½" d	10.00
Butter Pat, 3¼" d	12.00
Butter Tub	35.00
Cake Plate, glass, hp, 10½" d	45.00
Cake Plate, handled, 9¾" d	55.00
Candlesticks, pr, glass, hp	40.00
Casserole, cov, round	125.00
Casserole, cov, round, gold finial	500.00
Celery Dish, 12½" d	45.00
Celery Dish, closed handle, 10" l	300.00
Cheese and Cracker Set, glass, hp	70.00
Creamer	20.00
Creamer, gold finial	60.00
Cup and Saucer	20.00
Demitasse Cup and Saucer	125.00
Egg Cup	55.00
Fruit Bowl, 5½" d	15.00
Fruit Bowl, glass, hp, 8½" d	55.00
Grapefruit Bowl, 4½" d	120.00
Gravy Boat	45.00
Lemon Dish	30.00
Luncheon Plate, 8½" d	20.00
Marmalade, with underplate and spoon	150.00
Mayonnaise, with underplate and ladle	475.00
Milk Jug	175.00
Mustard Jar, cov	60.00
Olive Dish, 7⅛" d	75.00
Platter, oval, 11¾" d	50.00
Platter, oval, 13⅝" d	80.00
Platter, oval, 16¼" d	425.00
Relish, oval, 8¼" l	25.00
Salad Bowl, 9½" d	50.00
Salad Plate, 7⅝" d	15.00
Salt and Pepper Shakers, pr, bulbous, 3" h	35.00
Snack Plate and Cup	45.00
Soup Bowl, 7½" d	25.00
Spoon Holder, 8" l	75.00
Sugar, cov	30.00
Sugar, cov, gold finial	75.00
Syrup, cov, with underplate	125.00
Tea Tile, 5¾" w	40.00
Teapot, cov	100.00
Teapot, cov, gold finial	450.00

Dinner Plate, 10" d, $30.00.

Toothpick Holder.	100.00
Tray, glass, hp, 10" l.	50.00
Vase, fan, ftd	125.00
Vegetable Bowl, oval, 9½" l	40.00
Vegetable Bowl, oval, 10½" l	50.00
Whipped Cream, with underplate and ladle	35.00

NORITAKE CHINA

Ichizaemon Morimura, one of the founders of Noritake, established Morimura–kumi, a Japanese exporting company located in Tokyo in 1867. An import shop was also founded in New York to sell Japanese traditional goods.

After attending the World's Fair in Paris a few years later, Morimura was inspired to open a factory to produce porcelain in Japan. He founded Nippon Toki Kaisha Ltd., the forerunner of Noritake, in Nagoya, Japan, in 1904. In 1914 Morimura produced the first white porcelain dinner plate in Japan. Production of dinner sets for export around the world became the company's main product line, and in 1932 the company produced the first bone china in Japan.

The Larkin Company, Buffalo, New York, was one of the principal distributors for Noritake China in the 1920s. The Azalea, Braircliff, Linden, Modjeska, Savory, Sheriden, and Tree in the Meadow patterns were utilized as Larkin premiums.

The factory was heavily damaged during World War II and production was greatly reduced. The company sold its china under the "Rose China" mark between 1946 and 1948 because the quality did not match that of earlier Noritake China. High quality was achieved once again by early 1949.

Noritake Company was established for selling tableware in the United States. Over the next thirty years, companies were created in Australia, Canada, the United Kingdom, Sri Lanka, Guam, the Philippines, and Ireland for the manufacture and distribution of Noritake products.

In 1956, with the introduction of a stainless steel line, Noritake began an expansion program that would eventually result in a full line of tabletop products. Crystal glassware joined the line in 1961, earthenware and stoneware dinnerware and accessories in 1971. In 1979 the company completed work on a modern new plant. The company's name was changed to Noritake Company, Ltd. in 1981.

Close to 100 different Noritake marks have been identified. Most pieces are marked with "Noritake," a wreath, "M," "N," or "Nippon."

References: Aimee Neff Alden, *Collector's Encyclopedia of Early Noritake*, Collector Books, 1995; Joan Van Patten, *Collector's Encyclopedia of Noritake* (1984, 1997 value update), *Second Series* (1994), Collector Books; Harry L. Rinker, *Dinnerware of the 20th Century: The Top 500 Patterns*, House of Collectibles, 1997.

Collectors' Club: Noritake Collectors' Society, 1237 Federal Ave East, Seattle, WA 98102.

Adagio, bread and butter plate, 6³⁄₈" d	$ 8.00
Adagio, creamer	30.00
Adagio, cup and saucer, ftd	20.00
Adagio, dinner plate, 10⁵⁄₈" d	25.00
Adagio, fruit bowl, 5½" d	12.00
Adagio, gravy boat	60.00
Adagio, platter, oval, 11½" l	55.00
Adagio, platter, oval, 13³⁄₄" l	75.00
Adagio, salad plate, 8³⁄₈" d	12.00
Adagio, salt and pepper shakers, pr	35.00
Adagio, sugar, cov	35.00
Adagio, vegetable bowl, round, 10" d	65.00
Crest, bread and butter plate, 6¼" d	8.00
Crest, casserole, cov	100.00
Crest, creamer	25.00
Crest, cup and saucer, ftd	20.00
Crest, dinner plate, 10½" d	20.00
Crest, fruit bowl, 5⁵⁄₈" d	10.00
Crest, platter, oval, 11³⁄₄" l	40.00
Crest, platter, oval, 16¹⁄₈" l	80.00
Crest, relish, 9" l	25.00
Crest, salad plate, 7½" d	10.00
Crest, soup bowl, 7½" d	20.00
Crest, sugar, cov	35.00
Crest, teapot, cov	100.00
Crest, vegetable bowl, oval, 10½" l	50.00
Crestmont, bread and butter plate, 6¼" d	5.00
Crestmont, butter dish, cov, ¼ lb	40.00
Crestmont, casserole, cov	100.00
Crestmont, cereal bowl, lug, 6³⁄₄" d	12.00
Crestmont, cream soup bowl	25.00
Crestmont, creamer	20.00
Crestmont, cup and saucer, ftd	18.00
Crestmont, demitasse cup and saucer	20.00
Crestmont, dinner plate, 10½" d	15.00
Crestmont, fruit bowl, 5⁵⁄₈" d	8.00
Crestmont, gravy boat	40.00
Crestmont, platter, oval, 11³⁄₄" l	40.00
Crestmont, platter, oval, 16¼" l	65.00
Crestmont, salad plate, 8³⁄₈" d	10.00
Crestmont, salt and pepper shakers, pr	35.00
Crestmont, sugar, cov	25.00
Crestmont, vegetable bowl, oval, 10½" l	30.00
Crestmont, vegetable bowl, oval, divided, 10¹⁄₈" l	50.00

Duetto, bread and butter plate, 6½" d. 8.00
Duetto, creamer 22.00
Duetto, cup and saucer 15.00
Duetto, dinner plate, 10½" d 20.00
Duetto, fruit bowl, 5½" d. 8.00
Duetto, gravy boat. 45.00
Duetto, platter, oval, 12⅛" l 40.00
Duetto, platter, oval, 16" l 75.00
Duetto, salad plate, 8¼" d 10.00
Duetto, soup bowl, 7½" d 12.00
Duetto, sugar, cov 30.00
Duetto, vegetable bowl, 8⅞" d. 40.00
Edgewood, bread and butter plate, 6¼" d 8.00
Edgewood, cream soup bowl 35.00
Edgewood, creamer. 30.00
Edgewood, cup and saucer, ftd. 22.00
Edgewood, dinner plate, 10½" d. 25.00
Edgewood, fruit bowl, 5⅝" d 12.00
Edgewood, platter, oval, 11¾" l 60.00
Edgewood, salad plate, 8¼" d 12.00
Edgewood, salt and pepper shakers, pr 35.00
Edgewood, sugar, cov 40.00
Edgewood, vegetable bowl, oval, 10" l 45.00
Glenwood, bread and butter plate, 6¼" d 8.00
Glenwood, casserole, cov 100.00
Glenwood, cereal bowl, lug, 6¾" d 20.00
Glenwood, cream soup and saucer. 30.00
Glenwood, creamer. 30.00
Glenwood, cup and saucer, ftd. 25.00
Glenwood, dinner plate, 10½" d 20.00
Glenwood, fruit bowl, 5¾" d 12.00
Glenwood, gravy boat 60.00
Glenwood, platter, oval, 11⅝" l 50.00
Glenwood, platter, oval, 16¼" l 90.00
Glenwood, salad plate, 8⅜" d 12.00
Glenwood, soup bowl, 7¾" d. 20.00
Glenwood, sugar, cov 40.00
Glenwood, vegetable bowl, oval, 10½" l 50.00
Glenwood, vegetable bowl, oval, divided, 10¼" l 70.00
Rothschild, bread and butter plate, 7" d 8.00
Rothschild, bud vase, 6⅞" h. 40.00
Rothschild, chop plate, 11⅜" d. 75.00
Rothschild, creamer. 30.00
Rothschild, cup and saucer 25.00
Rothschild, dinner plate, 10⅝" d 20.00
Rothschild, pie server, stainless blade 35.00
Rothschild, salad plate, 8¼" d 12.00
Rothschild, sugar, cov 40.00
Rothschild, vase, 4⅝" h 40.00
Royal Orchard, bread and butter plate, 6¾" d. 8.00
Royal Orchard, bud vase, 5" h 20.00
Royal Orchard, casserole, cov 120.00
Royal Orchard, cheese and cracker board, 8⅝" l 30.00
Royal Orchard, creamer. 32.00
Royal Orchard, cup and saucer 25.00
Royal Orchard, dinner plate, 10⅝" d 20.00
Royal Orchard, fruit bowl, 5¾" d 12.00
Royal Orchard, mug 18.00
Royal Orchard, platter, oval, 14¾" l 80.00
Royal Orchard, quiche dish, 10⅛" d. 50.00
Royal Orchard, relish. 18.00

Royal Orchard, roaster, oval, 14⅝" l 90.00
Royal Orchard, salad plate, 8½" d 12.00
Royal Orchard, salt and pepper shakers, pr 40.00
Royal Orchard, soufflé. 60.00
Royal Orchard, sugar, cov 40.00
Royal Orchard, vegetable bowl, oval, 9⅞" l 50.00

NORITAKE TREE IN THE MEADOW

Tree in the Meadow is another popular hand–painted Noritake pattern. The basic scene includes a meandering stream (usually in the foreground), a peasant cottage, and a large tree. Muted tones of brown and yellow are the principal colors.

Noritake exported the first Tree in the Meadow pieces to the United States in the early 1920s. Several different backstamps were used for marking purposes. The Larkin Company distributed the pattern in the 1920s and 30s.

Note: See Noritake for further information and additional patterns.

Bowl, 7" d. . . . . $ 25.00
Bread and Butter Plate, 6½" d 10.00
Bread Tray. 45.00
Butter Dish, cov, insert. 65.00
Cake Plate, 10" d. 40.00
Celery Dish, 12" l 35.00
Coffeepot, cov. 185.00
Condiment Set. 40.00
Creamer and Sugar, cov. 50.00
Demitasse Pot, cov 160.00
Humidor, cov 375.00
Lemon Dish, handled, 5½" d 25.00
Luncheon Plate, 8½" d. 15.00
Mayonnaise, with underplate and ladle. 30.00
Mug 100.00
Nappy. 15.00
Platter, oval, 10" l 85.00
Salt and Pepper Shakers, pr 30.00
Sugar Shaker 30.00
Syrup 50.00
Teapot, cov 100.00
Toothpick Holder, 2½" h 55.00
Vase, fan, 5¾" h 115.00
Vegetable Bowl, oval, 9¼" l 30.00

NUTCRACKERS

A bowl of nuts was a popular holiday and entertaining treat from the 1930s through the early 1960s. An individual nutcracker, a set (nutcracker and six picks), or a bowl with a central plinth to hold a nutcracker and picks was part of a hostess's serving pieces.

Lever–action cast–iron nutcrackers, often in the shape of animals, appeared in the mid–19th century. As with eggbeaters and other mechanical household devices, the nutcracker attracted the attention of hundreds of inventors between 1880 and 1950.

Nutcracker designs mirrored the popular design styles of each era. Art Deco and 1950s–era nutcrackers and sets are eagerly sought by collectors. Beginning in the 1960s, wooden nutcrackers from Germany's Erzgebirger region began flooding the American market. They were primarily decorative, not functional. Still a favorite of the giftware industry, especially as a Christmas gift, these Erzgebirger–style figurines are now being made around the world, especially in the Far East, and from a wide variety of material. Buy modern examples because you like them, not as investments. The long–term investment potential for a nutcracker made after 1980 is extremely speculative.

References: Judith Rittenhouse, *Ornamental and Figural Nutcrackers: An Identification and Value Guide,* Collector Books, 1993; James Rollband, *American Nutcrackers: A Patent History and Value Guide,* Off Beat Books, 1996.

Alligator, brass	$ 25.00
Cat, nickel–covered brass, 4½" l	45.00
Dog, cast iron, bronze finish	45.00
Eagle, brass	28.00
Fish, olive wood	20.00
Girl, wearing hoop skirt, brass, screw–type	110.00
Parrot, brass, 15½" l	15.00
Pliers Type, cast iron, Torrington	4.00
Ram, wood, carved, glass eyes, 8½" l	65.00
Rooster, brass	28.00
Squirrel, aluminum	20.00

NUTTING, WALLACE

Wallace Nutting was born in 1861 in Rockingham, Massachusetts. After his father was killed in the Civil War, Nutting moved to Maine and lived with his grandparents. He attended Harvard University from 1883 to 1886 and the Hartford Theological Seminary and Union Theological Seminary (New York) between 1886 and 1888. Park Congregational Church, St. Paul, Minnesota, was his first pastoral call.

Nutting retired from the ministry in 1904 and opened a photography studio in New York. Within a year, he moved to Southby, Connecticut and opened a larger studio. His pictures sold well. In 1907, he opened a branch office in Toronto, Canada. By 1913 Nutting's operation was located in Framingham, Massachusetts. Business boomed. At its peak, Nutting employed over 200 colorists, framers, salesmen, and support staff.

Nutting took all his own pictures. However, printing, coloring, framing, and even signing his name was the work of his employees. Over 10,000 photographs in an assortment of sizes have been identified.

In the 1920s when the sale of pictures declined, Nutting explored a host of other business opportunities, e.g., calendars, greeting cards, and silhouettes. His books, especially the States Beautiful and Furniture Treasury series (many antiques dealers used this "bible" to educate themselves about furniture design styles), and reproduction furniture were the most successful.

Wallace Nutting died on July 19, 1941. His wife continued the business. When Mrs. Nutting died in 1944, she willed the business to Ernest John Donnelly and Esther Svenson. In 1946, Svenson bought out Donnelly. In 1971 Svenson entered a nursing home and ordered the destruction of all of the Nutting glass negatives. A few were not destroyed and are in the hands of private collectors.

References: Michael Ivankovich, *Collector's Guide to Wallace Nutting Pictures: Identification & Values,* Collector Books, 1997; Michael Ivankovich, *The Alphabetical & Numerical Index to Wallace Nutting Pictures,* Diamond Press, 1988; Michael Ivankovich, *The Guide To Wallace Nutting Furniture,* Diamond Press, 1990; *Colonial Reproductions* (reprint of 1921 catalog), Diamond Press, 1992; Wallace Nutting (reprint of 1915 catalog), Diamond Press, 1987; Wallace Nutting, *Wallace Nutting General Catalog, Supreme Edition* (reprint of 1930 catalog), Schiffer Publishing, 1977; Wallace Nutting, *Windsors* (reprint of 1918 catalog), Diamond Press, 1992.

Book, *Furniture Treasury,* 1st ed	$ 50.00
Book, *Massachusetts Beautiful*	40.00
Book, *Pathways of the Puritans*	150.00
Book, *Photograph Art Secrets*	225.00
Book, *Wallace Nutting's Biography*	75.00
Chair, #390, ladderback	500.00
Chair, #464, Carver armchair	425.00
Chest, oak, single drawer	2,575.00
Print, Affectionately Yours	70.00
Print, Afternoon in Nantucket	275.00
Print, Apple Over the Brook, The	160.00
Print, Autumnal Peace	95.00
Print, Below the Arches	145.00
Print, Birthday Flowers	120.00
Print, Bridesmaid's Procession, The	130.00
Print, Canopied Road, A	75.00
Print, Children of the Sea	825.00
Print, Choosing a Bonnet	55.00
Print, Colonial Stair, A	210.00
Print, Comfort and a Cat	75.00
Print, Coming Out of Rosa, The	230.00
Print, Connecticut Blossoms	75.00
Print, Cosmos and Larkspur	550.00
Print, Drying Apples	275.00
Print, Elaborate Dinner, An	150.00
Print, Garden of Larkspur, A	120.00
Print, Grace Before Meat	375.00
Print, His Move	280.00
Print, Homestead Blossoms	225.00
Print, Into the Birchwood	120.00
Print, Knitting For Uncle Sam	100.00
Print, Listless Day, A	250.00
Print, Maid and the Mirror, The	110.00
Print, Mills at the Turn, The	350.00
Print, Model Floral Scene	70.00
Print, New Life	80.00
Print, Old Wentworth Days	110.00
Print, On the Heights	375.00
Print, Pine Landing	120.00
Print, Pitcher of Roses, A	300.00
Print, Rangley Shore, A	100.00
Print, Reeling the Yarn	55.00
Print, Southern Puritan, A	350.00
Print, Spring Fashion at Old Mill	175.00
Print, Spring Sweetness	70.00
Print, Swirling Seas	300.00
Print, Touching Tale, A	80.00
Print, Toward Purple Hills	80.00
Print, Uncle Sam Taking Leave	150.00
Print, Under the Blossoms	325.00
Print, Virginia Reel, A	110.00
Print, Washington Cherry Blossoms	55.00
Print, Wayside Inn, The	250.00

Print, Winter Welcome Home, The **425.00**
Silhouette, girl playing piano, 7 x 8" **75.00**
Silhouettes, pr, John Alden and Priscilla **125.00**
Tavern Table, pine top, turned maple legs, block
    branded signature **1,250.00**

NUTTING–LIKE PHOTOGRAPHS

The commercial success of Wallace Nutting's hand–colored, framed photographs spawned a series of imitators. David Davidson (1881–1967), Charles Higgins (1867–1930), Charles Sawyer (born 1904) and his Sawyer Picture Company, and Fred Thompson (1844–1923) are only a few of the dozens of individuals and businesses that attempted to ride Nutting's coattails.

Most of these photographers followed the same procedure as Nutting. They took their own photographs, usually with a glass plate camera. Upon returning to the studio, prints were made on special platinum paper. Substitute paper was used during World War I. Each picture was titled and numbered, usually by the photographer. A model picture was colored. Colorists then finished the remainder of the prints. Finally, the print was matted, titled, signed, and sold.

Reference: Michael Ivankovich, *The Guide To Wallace Nutting–Like Photographers of the Early 20th Century,* Diamond Press, 1991.

Davidson, David, A Puritan Lady, 12 x 16" .... **$ 75.00**
Davidson, David, Diadem Aisle, 10 x 12" **50.00**
Davidson, David, Echo Lake, 8 x 10" **65.00**
Davidson, David, Prize Pewter, 12 x 16" **45.00**
Davidson, David, The Barefoot Boy, 9 x 16" **195.00**
Davidson, David, The Rambler Rose, 12 x 16 .... **170.00**
Davidson, David, The Village Maiden, 14 x 17" **180.00**
Davidson, David, Wisteria, 13 x 16" **95.00**
Davidson, David, Ye Olden Tyme, 13 x 16" **300.00**
Higgins, Charles, A Rocky Shore, 8 x 14" **55.00**
Higgins, Charles, Apple Blossom Lane, 8 x 12" **35.00**
Higgins, Charles, By the Fireplace, 11 x 14" **125.00**
Higgins, Charles, Untitled Interior, 7 x 9" **35.00**
Higgins, Charles, Untitled Seascape, 7 x 11" **65.00**
Sawyer, Charles H. and Harold B., Autumn Glory,
    9 x 12" **50.00**
Sawyer, Charles H. and Harold B., Autumn Glory, A
    Rock Garden, Cape Cod, 16 x 20" **165.00**
Sawyer, Charles H. and Harold B., Autumn Glory,
    Chapel, San Juan Capistrano, 13 x 16" **155.00**
Sawyer, Charles H. and Harold B., Autumn Glory,
    Joseph Lincoln's Garden, 16 x 20" **185.00**
Sawyer, Charles H. and Harold B., Autumn Glory,
    Lafayette Slides, 13 x 15" **90.00**
Sawyer, Charles H. and Harold B., Autumn Glory,
    Surf at Pinnacle Rock, 13 x 20" **90.00**
Sawyer, Charles H. and Harold B., Camel's Hump,
    7 x 9" **35.00**
Sawyer, Charles H. and Harold B., Gateway to the
    Adirondacks, 13 x 20" **155.00**
Sawyer, Charles H. and Harold B., Sunset on the
    Kennebec, 12 x 20" **70.00**
Sawyer, Charles H. and Harold B., The Old Man of
    the Mountains, 11 x 14" **45.00**

Thompson, Fred, Bridal Blossoms, 8 x 15" **60.00**
Thompson, Fred, Covered Bridge, 9 x 12 .... **75.00**
Thompson, Fred, Fireside Fancies, 11 x 14" **85.00**
Thompson, Fred, Old Mill Dam, 9 x 12" **25.00**
Thompson, Fred, Pine Grove, 14 x 17" **40.00**
Thompson, Fred, Sailing Ship, 8 x 10" **240.00**
Thompson, Fred, Senitnels, 6 x 12" **25.00**
Thompson, Fred, Spinning Days, 14 x 17" **95.00**

OCCUPIED JAPAN

America occupied Japan from August 1945 until April 28,1952. World War II devastated the Japanese economy. The Japanese ceramics industry was one of the first to be revitalized. Thousands of inexpensive figurines and knickknacks were exported to the United States and elsewhere in the late 1940s and 1950s.

Not all products made in Japan between 1946 and April 1952 are marked "Made in Occupied Japan" or "Occupied Japan." Some pieces simply were marked "Japan" or "Made in Japan." However, collectors of Occupied Japan material insist that "Occupied" be found in the mark for an item to be considered a true Occupied Japan collectible.

Initially, collectors focused almost exclusively on ceramic items. Today, Occupied Japan collectors are looking for any items marked "Occupied Japan." Women's handbags, textiles, and toys are just a few examples.

Beware of Occupied Japan reproductions, copycats, fantasy pieces, and fakes. Period marks tend to be underglaze. They will not scratch off. Rubber–stamped fake marks will. The marks on recent reproductions are excellent. Shape, form, color, and aging characteristics are now the primary means of distinguishing period pieces form later examples.

Reference: Florence Archambault, *Occupied Japan For Collectors,* Schiffer Publishing, 1992; Gene Florence, *The Collector's Encyclopedia Of Occupied Japan Collectibles, First Series* (1976), *Second Series* (1979), *Third Series* (1987), *Fourth Series* (1990), *Fifth Series* (1992), (1996 value update for series I–V), Collector Books; Anthony Marsella, *Toys From Occupied Japan,* Schiffer Publishing, 1995; Lynette Palmer, *Collecting Occupied Japan,* Schiffer Publishing, 1997.

Collectors' Club: The Occupied Japan Club, 29 Freeborn St, Newport, RI 02840.

Ashtray, metal, black boy smoking cigar, spring–
    loaded head, 4³/₄" h .... **$ 50.00**
Ashtray, reticulated border with roaring dragon motif,
    clear view depicts life and times of silkworm,
    5⁵/₈" d **35.00**
Bowl, cov, ceramic, Capodimonte style, double han-
    dled, wooded scene with winged cherubs **20.00**
Box, cov, hen on nest **50.00**
Box, cov, inlaid dog motif **15.00**
Cigarette Dispenser, inlaid wood, mechanical,
    spring–operated sliding drawer dispenses cigarette
    into bird's beak **55.00**
Cigarette Lighter, metal, figural cowboy, head flips
    back, 4" h **25.00**
Clock, bisque, double figure, colonial dancing cou-
    ple atop floral–encrusted case, 10¹/₂" h **250.00**

Teapot, Spring Violets pattern, mkd on bottom "Spring Violets, Rossetti, Chicago, U.S.A., Hand Printed, Made in Occupied Japan," 5½" h, 8" w, $25.00.

Crumber and Scoop, emb metal 10.00
Demitasse Set, coffeepot, sugar bowl, creamer, saucer, and 3 cups, translated script "Black like the devil, hot like hell, pure like an angel, sweet like love: Recipe of Rareecand" 40.00
Figure, bisque, ballerina, 5½" h 40.00
Figure, bisque, black shoeshine boy, 5¾" h 40.00
Figure, metal, cowboy on rearing horse, 3¾" h 15.00
Figure, porcelain, lady, lavender and yellow dress 20.00
Finger Bowl, porcelain, winged cherub and raspberry motif, 5¾" 30.00
Flower Frog, ceramic, underplate, green crown motif 30.00
Grouping, porcelain, Chinese couple, woman playing stringed instrument, man peacefully watching while smoking pipe, 4½" h, 5¾" l 30.00
Harmonica, metal, butterfly shape 25.00
Honey Pot, porcelain, black Mammy, head lifts off, spoon as tongue, holding spoon and frying pan, 4½" h 35.00
Incense Burner, porcelain, cobalt blue, floral dec, gold trim 20.00
Lamp, ceramic, colonial couple, gentleman with guitar, lady holding floral bouquet, floral emb base, 13½" h 25.00
Lantern, owl motif, 4½" h 35.00
Nativity Scene, bisque, Baby Jesus, cradle, animals, Wise Men, orig box 195.00
Necklace, plastic, figural charms, sports motif, 25" l 75.00
Nodder, papier mâché, sitting rabbit 35.00
Nut Dish, metal, floral border, 6" d 15.00
Planter, ceramic, figural rabbit 12.50
Planter, porcelain, figural shoe, floral dec 20.00
Plate, silvered metal, pierced scalloped rim, 4½" d 15.00
Purse, lady's, faux pearl dec 50.00
Rolling Pin, wood 45.00
Salt and Pepper Shakers, pr, coffeepots, cobalt blue glass, red Bakelite handles, metal tray, orig box 25.00

Salt and Pepper Shakers, pr, porcelain, black chefs 30.00
Tape Measure, celluloid, pig, 2⅜" 45.00
Tea Set, ceramic, teapot, creamer, and cov sugar, base mkd "Sango China, Made in Occupied Japan" 30.00
Toby Mug, grinning man, large white teeth, black bowtie, green cap, 5½" h 50.00
Toy, celluloid boy on tin tricycle, windup 70.00
Toy, celluloid, windup, dancing couple, 5" h 40.00
Toy, celluloid, windup, South Seas native, grass skirt, 6" h 50.00
Toy, tin, windup, car, "Baby Pontiac," orig box 65.00
Toy, windup, hopping dog 25.00
Tray, papier mâché, rect, floral dec, 10½" l 50.00
Vase, bisque, figural, 3 maidens with flowing skirts, 6½" h 65.00
Vase, bisque, figural, young lady and scrolled cornucopia, 10" h 65.00
Vase, ceramic, figural, boy reading book, Hummel type, 5¼" h 25.00
Wall Pocket, ceramic, colonial couple with baskets hanging out window 30.00
Wall Pocket, ceramic, Dutch Girl, 7¼" h 12.50
Wall Pocket, porcelain, lady with hat, Art Deco style, 5" h 35.00
Wall Pockets, porcelain, 1 large and 3 small, flying geese 25.00

OCEAN LINER COLLECTIBLES

This category is devoted to collectibles from the era of the diesel–powered ocean liner, whose golden age dates between 1910 and the mid–1950s. These floating palaces were a city unto themselves.

The category is dominated by legendary companies, e.g., Cunard and Holland–American, and ships, e.g., *Queen Elizabeth* and *Queen Elizabeth II*. Many World War II servicemen and women have fond memories of traveling overseas on a fabulous ocean liner after being pressed into military service.

Collectors focus primarily on pre–1960 material. Shipboard stores sold a wide range of souvenirs. Printed menus, daily newspapers, and postcards are popular. The category is very much fame driven—the more famous, the more value.

References: Karl D. Spence, *How To Identify and Price Ocean Liner Collectibles,* published by author, 1991; Karl D. Spence, *Oceanliner Collectibles* (1992), *Vol. 2* (1996), published by author, James Steele, *Queen Mary,* Phaidon, 1995.

Booklet, *Britannic,* Mar 1955, first–class deck plans, color photos, 12 pgs, 9 x 12" . . . . $ 20.00
Booklet, *Cunard,* Sep 1953, 23 pgs 12.00
Booklet, *Independence,* American Export Lines, itinerary and deck plan inserts, 1966 Gala Springtime Cruise 22.00
Booklet, White Star Line Sailing List, 1933 . . . . 40.00
Candy Container, litho tin, full–color *Queen Mary* illus on lid, 1930s 50.00
Cruise Book, *Scythia,* 1929 . . . . 32.00
Deck Plan, *MV Westerdam,* multicolored, 1950 . . . . 18.00
Deck Plan, *SS Hamburg,* fold out, 1930 . . . . 38.00
Deck Plan, *SS Manhattan,* 10 pgs 50.00

Dish, *Queen Mary,* Cunard Line, ceramic, oval, color portrait, gold edge, Staffordshire, 5" l. **38.00**

Letter Card, *Cunard RMS Queen Mary,* fold–out, color illus, 1930s **20.00**

Log Extract, *Aurana,* Quebec to London, Cunard Line, 1938 . . . . **8.00**

Magazine, *Life,* Aug 6, 1956, *Andrea Doria Sinks* **12.00**

Menu, *Bremen,* Welcome Aboard First Class Dinner Menu, Jul 17, 1936 . . . . **28.00**

Menu, *Liberte,* Dec 10, 1956, 4 pgs **75.00**

Menu, *RMS Queen Mary,* dinner, Jun 7, 1936 . . . . **18.00**

Menu, *RMS Samaria,* Cunard Line, 1938 . . . . **8.00**

Menu, *SS Lurline,* March 1960 . . . . **18.00**

Menu, *SS Oakwood,* American Export Lines, Christmas 1939 . . . . **5.00**

Menu, Statendam, farewell dinner, Jul 23, 1935, Frans Hals on cov, ship on back cov **10.00**

Newspaper, *RMS Queen Mary, Ocean Time,* Jun 6, 1936 . . . . **18.00**

Pamphlet, Ward Line, New York and Cuba Mail Steamship Co, 1926, 24 pgs **15.00**

Paper Ephemera, *RMS Maureta Seas,* West Indies, loose–leaf activity schedules and menus, Feb 18 through Mar 8, 1954 . . . . **45.00**

Passenger List, *RMS Aquitania,* color illus **55.00**

Pinback Button, Carnival Cruises **4.00**

Postcard, *Andrea Doria,* multicolored **20.00**

Postcard, Cosulich Lines, 1929 . . . . **20.00**

Poster, *Queen Mary,* docking at Southampton, sepia tone, c1938, 20 x 30" **130.00**

Program, *Queen of Bermuda,* Feb 7, 1959 . . . . **18.00**

Schedule, Cunard Lines, Programme of Events, embarkation notice, stationery, 1929 . . . . **20.00**

Stationery, *Queen Mary,* Cunard Line, notepaper, envelope, color portrait, line and ship name, 5 x 7" **12.00**

Tie Clasp, *Queen Mary,* Cunard Line, goldtone, red, white, and blue enameled ship **18.00**

Tin, Bremen Coffee, *Bremen* at Sea on front panel, litho tin, 1930s **50.00**

Toy, *Rigby's Book of Model Ships,* punch–out, unused, 1953 . . . . **55.00**

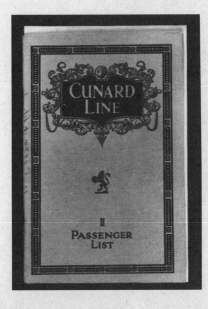

Passenger List, *R.M.S. Aquitania,* Cunard Line, sailing from Southampton to New York via Cherbourg, Saturday, June 20, 1925, 32 pgs, 5 x 7½", $30.00.

PADEN CITY GLASS

The Paden City Glass Manufacturing Company, Paden City, West Virginia, was founded in 1916. David Fisher, formerly president and general manager of the New Martinsville Glass Company, headed the company. When he died in 1933, Sam Fisher, David's son, assumed the presidency.

Initially the company produced pressed lamps, tableware, and vases. Later the company expanded its lines to include hotel and restaurant glassware. The company also acted as a jobber, doing mold work for other glass companies.

Color was one of Paden City's strong points. It offered a wide range of colored glasswares, e.g., amber (three shades), blue (two shades), cherigo (pale pink), dark green, ebony (opaque black), mulberry (deep amethyst), and opal. Thus far over 35 etchings have been identified as being done at Paden City.

In 1949 Paden City purchased the fully–automated American Glass Company, continuing production of ashtrays, containers, and novelties. The American Glass acquisition proved disastrous. Paden City Glass ceased operations in 1951.

Reference: Dick Spencer, *Glass Animals Of The Depression Era,* Collector Books, 1993

Animal, Chinese Pheasant, crystal . . . . **$ 70.00**

Animal, Cottontail Rabbit, crystal **68.00**

Animal, Pony, 11½" h **95.00**

Animal, Squirrel, log base **48.00**

Berry Bowl, Crows Foot, 5¼" sq, amber **8.00**

Bowl, ftd, Orchid, 10" d, black **90.00**

Bowl, Largo, handled, 11¼" d, ruby **22.00**

Bowl, Sunset, ftd, 9" d, amber **38.00**

Cake Stand, Ardith, ftd, 11½" d, yellow, cherry etch **55.00**

Cake Stand, Crows Foot, 12" d, ruby **72.00**

Candlesticks, pr, low, cheriglo **25.00**

Candlesticks, pr, Orchid, 5¾" h, red **100.00**

Candy, cov, Crows Foot, crystal, gold–encrusted flowers **15.00**

Candy, cov, 3 sections, Mrs B, ruby, gold filigree trim **48.00**

Champagne, Popeye and Olive, ruby **12.00**

Cocktail Set, frosted ice bucket and 4 ftd glasses, Hotcha Glade etch **45.00**

Cocktail Shaker, Party Line, ruby **22.00**

Compote, Crows Foot, 7" d, 6¾" h, ruby **48.00**

Console Bowl, Ardith, 12" d, yellow **38.00**

Console Bowl, Largo, crystal, sterling trim **38.00**

Cordial, Cupid **15.00**

Creamer, ftd, Cupid **22.00**

Creamer, Orchid, cobalt blue **45.00**

Cup, Penny Line, amethyst **5.00**

Cup and Saucer, Crows Foot, sq, amber **8.00**

Decanter, Ardith, oval, orig stopper, 5¾" h **90.00**

Dinner Plate, Crows Foot, 9" d, amber **12.00**

Goblet, Cupid **18.00**

Goblet, Penny Line **10.00**

Ice Bucket, Orchid, 6" h, cobalt blue **45.00**

Iced Tea Tumbler, Popeye and Olive, 5" h, ruby **15.00**

Mayonnaise Set, 2 pc, Secrets, crystal **18.00**

Plate, Black Forest, 7½" d **48.00**

Plate, Cupid, 10" d, green **18.00**

Plate, Largo, 12" d, crystal, sterling rim **18.00**
Plate, Orchid, 8½" sq, red **42.00**
Plate, Popeye and Olive, 12" d, ruby **22.00**
Reamer, Party Line, frosted turquoise, metal reamer
    top **90.00**
Relish, 3 part, Sunset, amber **18.00**
Salad Plate, Crows Foot, 6" sq, amber **3.00**
Salt and Pepper Shakers, pr, Penny Line, cobalt blue,
    flat base **50.00**
Sandwich Tray, Amy, chrome handles **18.00**
Serving Plate, 11¼" d, Gazebo etch **40.00**
Sherbet, Peacock Reverse **22.00**
Sherbet, Penny Line, amethyst **4.00**
Sugar, Orchid, red **45.00**
Sugar, Peacock Reverse, 2¾" h, yellow **38.00**
Sugar, cov, Wotta Line, ruby **6.00**
Tray, Penny Line, flat base, 3½" h, amethyst **5.00**
Tumbler, Peacock Reverse, ruby **35.00**
Tumbler, Penny Line, 5¼" h, amethyst **8.00**
Vase, Black Forest, 6½" h, pink **40.00**
Vase, Crows Foot, 10" h, white milk glass, floral dec **65.00**
Vase, Lela Bird, eliptical, 8¼" h, green **80.00**
Vase, Orchid, 10" h, yellow **35.00**

PADEN CITY POTTERY

Paden City Pottery, located near Sisterville, West Virginia, was founded in September 1914. The company manufactured high quality, semi–porcelain dinnerware. The quality of Paden City's decals was such that their ware often was assumed to be hand painted.

The company's Shenandoah Ware shape line was made with six different applied patterns. Sears Roebuck featured Paden City's Naturtium pattern in the 1940s. Bak–Serv, a 1930s kitchenware line, was produced in solid colors and with decal patterns. Paden City also made Caliente, a line of single–color glazed ware introduced in 1936. Russel Wright designed the company's Highlight pattern, manufactured in five different colors between 1951 and 1952.

Paden City Pottery ceased operation in November 1963. Pieces are found with a variety of backstamps.

Reference: Harvey Duke, *The Official Price Guide to Pottery & Porcelain, Eighth Edition,* House of Collectibles, 1995.

Bak–Serv, carafe, ceramic lid, wooden handle . . . . **$ 25.00**
Bak–Serv, custard **5.00**
Bak–Serv, jug, ftd **15.00**
Blue Willow, chop plate, 12¾" d **15.00**
Blue Willow, cup **5.00**
Blue Willow, plate, 9" d **10.00**
Blue Willow, platter, 10" l **12.00**
Blue Willow, saucer **1.50**
Caliente, casserole, cov, cobalt **10.00**
Caliente, dinner plate, cobalt **4.00**
Caliente, mixing bowl, 9⅛" d **18.00**
Caliente, pitcher, orange **20.00**
Caliente, salad bowl, 10" d **20.00**
Caliente, serving plate, 13" d, tangerine **20.00**
Caliente, teapot, blue **28.00**
Elite, chop plate, 12¾" d **15.00**

Elite, creamer **5.00**
Elite, cup **4.00**
Elite, gravy **12.00**
Elite, plate, 9¼" d **8.00**
Far East, creamer **5.00**
Far East, soup bowl **5.00**
Highlight, bread and butter plate **8.00**
Highlight, creamer **18.00**
Highlight, platter, oval **35.00**
Highlight, saucer **8.00**
Highlight, vegetable bowl, oval **35.00**
Ivy, cup and saucer **2.50**
Jonquil, creamer and sugar **10.00**
Jonquil, teapot **12.00**
Manhattan, casserole **20.00**
Manhattan, creamer **4.00**
Manhattan, gravy **12.00**
Manhattan, plate, 9" d **8.00**
Manhattan, saucer **1.50**
Modern Orchid, cup and saucer **5.00**
New Virginia, casserole **20.00**
New Virginia, cup **5.00**
New Virginia, dinner plate **10.00**
New Virginia, gravy **12.00**
New Virginia, salad plate **4.00**
New Virginia, teapot **25.00**
Papoco, casserole **20.00**
Papoco, creamer **5.00**
Papoco, plate, 9¾" d **8.00**
Papoco, saucer **1.00**
Patio, berry bowl **3.00**
Patio, bowl, oval **8.00**
Patio, casserole, cov **15.00**
Patio, platter, oval **10.00**
Poppy, cup and saucer **4.00**
Poppy, teapot **12.00**
Regina, casserole, cov **20.00**
Regina, cup **5.00**

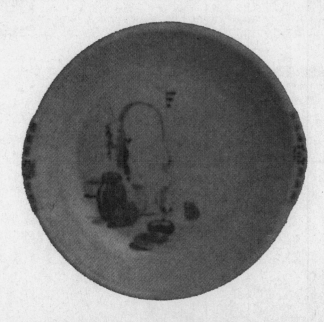

Patio, Shell–Krest shape, bowl, $8.00.

Regina, plate, 10" d 10.00
Regina, saucer. 1.00
Regina, soup bowl, 8" d. 10.00
Regina, sugar 8.00
Regina, vegetable bowl, oval, 9" l. 10.00
Sally Paden, casserole 20.00
Sally Paden, creamer 4.00
Sally Paden, cup 5.00
Sally Paden, plate, 9¼" d 8.00
Sally Paden, platter, 11½" l. . . . . . \ 10.00
Shell Crest, casserole, ftd 30.00
Shell Crest, creamer. 5.00
Shell Crest, cup. 6.00
Shell Crest, gravy. 15.00
Shell Crest, plate, 8½" d. 6.00
Shell Crest, plate, 10½" d 12.00
Shell Crest, platter, 16½" l 25.00
Shell Crest, saucer. 2.00
Shell Crest, shaker, pr 12.00
Shell Crest, sugar. 10.00
Spinning Wheel, cup and saucer 5.00
Spinning Wheel, fruit bowl 4.00

PAINT BY NUMBER SETS

Paint By Number sets achieved widespread popularity in the early 1950s. They claimed to turn rank amateurs into accomplished painters overnight. Virtually every generic scene, from a winter landscape to horse and clown portraits, was reduced to an outlined canvas with each section having a number that corresponded to one of the paints that came with the set.

Craft House Corporation (Toledo, Ohio), Craft Master (Toledo, Ohio, a division of General Mills), and Standard Toykraft (New York, New York) were among the leading manufacturers. Hassenfeld Brothers (Hasbro) did a number of licensed sets, e.g., Popeye and Superman.

Contemporary licensed paint by number sets, sometimes employing acrylic crayons rather than paint, can be found in today's toy stores. Rose Art Industries makes many of them.

Alvin and the Chipmunks, Hasbro, 1959 . . . . $ 75.00
Banana Splits Paint By Number 'N Frame Set, Hasbro,
    1969. . . . . 75.00
Beatles, John Lennon, Artistic Creations 250.00
Crusader Rabbit, 13 x 19" box 45.00
Dick Tracy Oil Paint Set, Hasbro, 1967 . . . . 80.00
Farm Scenes, #12905, Oil Paint by Number Set,
    New Artist 2, Craft Master, 1972 . . . . 10.00
Fess Parker Oil Paint by Number Set, 1964 . . . . 35.00
Green Hornet, Hasbro, 1966 . . . . 90.00
Howdy Doody, acrylic, Art Award, 1976. . . . . 25.00
Land of the Giants, Hasbro, 1969. . . . . 50.00
Rin Tin Tin, four 9¼ x 12" sheets, watercolor tablets,
    orig box, Transogram, 1956 . . . . 60.00
Show Folk, #759, Oil Paint by Number Set, Craft
    House 15.00
Space Traveler, 8 fluorescent color paints, brush,
    instructions, Craft Master 35.00
Superman, Stardust, "Touch of Velvet Art," Hasbro. 35.00
Tom Sawyer, Standard Toykraft 20.00

Popeye Oil Painting By Number T.V. Edition, Hasbro, 5 pictures, 12 paints, $75.00.

PAIRPOINT

The Pairpoint Manufacturing Company, a silver plating firm, was founded in New Bedford, Massachusetts, in 1880. In 1894 Pairpoint merged with Mount Washington Glass Company and became Pairpoint Corporation. The company produced a wide range of glass products, often encased in silver–plated holders or frames.

The Pairpoint Corporation fell upon hard times during the Depression. In 1938 the Kenner Salvage Company purchased Pairpoint, selling it in 1939 to Isaac N. Babbitt. Babbitt reorganized the company and named it the Gundersen Glass Works. Robert Gundersen, a master glass blower at Pairpoint, guided the new company.

When Gundersen died in 1952, Edwin V. Babbitt, president of National Pairpoint Company, a manufacturer of aluminum windows, chemical ordinance, glass, and toys, purchased Gundersen Glass Works and renamed it Gundersen–Pairpoint Glass Works. The company made a full line of plain and engraved lead crystal.

In 1957 old equipment and a decline in sales forced a closure. Robert Bryden, a chemist who joined Gundersen–Pairpoint in 1950, was assigned the task of moving the plant from New Bedford to Wareham, Massachusetts. An attempt at reorganization by a group of glassmen failed. The Wareham plant closed in February 1958.

Desiring to fill existing orders, Bryden leased facilities in Spain and moved Pairpoint there. In 1968 Bryden, along with a group of Scottish glassworks, returned to Massachusetts with plans to revive glass production in America. In 1970 Pairpoint opened a new, two–pot factory in Sagamore, Massachusetts.

When Bryden retired in 1988, Robert Bancroft bought the company. Production of lead crystal glass continues.

Reference: John A. Shumann III, *The Collector's Encyclopedia of American Art Glass,* Collector Books, 1988, 1996 value update.

Collectors' Club: Pairpoint Cup Plate Collectors, Box 52D, East Weymouth, MA 02189.

Vase, trumpet shape, ruby, clear paperweight base, Gunderson–Pairpoint, 7" h, $75.00.

Bowl, cov, peppermint stick, satin, clear, overlay rose
   rim cut to clear stripes, engraved, 8" d, 6½" h . . . . . **$ 100.00**
Bud Vase, amethyst, clear bubble ball connector, orig
   label, 5½" h **100.00**
Calling Card Receiver, clear bubble ball connected to
   base, engraved floral dec, 5" d **110.00**
Champagne, Flambo, crystal, 5⅛" h **40.00**
Cologne Bottle, ribbed, pointed stopper, 7⅛" h **80.00**
Compote, amber, engraved floral design, 6" d **70.00**
Cornucopia, ruby, clear sq base **125.00**
Dresser Jar, cov, clear green ground, clear finial, cran-
   berry cov, orig label, 4" h **110.00**
Hat, red ground, white spatter, controlled bubbles,
   paper label, 4¼" h **65.00**
Jack–in–the–Pulpit Vase, ruby, enameled bird on
   pine bough, 7¾" h **155.00**
Perfume Bottle, crystal, controlled bubbles, 5½" h **55.00**
Pitcher, amberina, applied ruby handle, 8½" h **165.00**
Punch Cup, cylindrical, flared rim, low foot, vaseline,
   engraved grapes **32.00**
Salt, master, clear, controlled bubbles **80.00**
Tumbler, clear ground, black and white polar bear
   dec, 5¼" h **70.00**

PAPER DOLLS

European jumping jacks (pantins) are the forerunners of the paper doll. By the 19th century, boxed sets and diecut sheets of paper dolls ranging in subject matter from opera stars to generic themes were widely available. England's Raphael Tuck and Sons produced ornate paper doll series in the 1880s.

Paper dolls were used as advertising and promotional premiums. *Good Housekeeping, Ladies' Home Journal,* and *McCall's* are just a few of the magazines that included paper doll pages as part of their monthly fare. Children's magazines, such as *Jack and Jill,* also featured paper doll pages.

The first paper doll books appeared in the 1920s. Lowe, Merrill, Saalfield, and Whitman were leading publishers. These inexpensive stiffboard covered books became extremely popular. Celebrity paper dolls first appeared in the 1940s. Entertainment personalities from movies, radio, and television were the primary focus.

The growth of television and the arrival of Barbie ended the reign of the paper doll book. While still being made today, most stores do not carry more than four or five titles. Those titles that are published usually have a cartoon, celebrity, or political theme.

Most paper dolls are collected in uncut books, sheets, or boxed sets. Cut sets are priced at 50% of an uncut set if all dolls, clothing, and accessories are present.

Many paper doll books have been reprinted. An identical reprint is just slightly lower in value. If the dolls have been redrawn, the price is reduced significantly.

References: Norman E. Martinus and Harry L. Rinker, *Warman's Paper,* Wallace–Homestead, Krause Publications, 1994; Lorraine Mieszala, *Collector's Guide to Barbie Doll Paper Dolls: Identification & Values,* Collector Books, 1997; Mary Young, *Tomart's Price Guide To Lowe and Whitman Paper Dolls,* Tomart Publications, 1993.

Newsletter: *Paper Doll News,* PO Box 807, Vivian, LA 71082.

Collectors' Club: Original Paper Doll Artist Guild, PO Box 14, Kingsfield, ME 04947.

Note: Prices listed are for books and sets in unused condition.

Airline Stewardess, 4913, Lowe, 1957 . . . . **$ 25.00**
Alive–Like Baby Elizabeth, 2750, Lowe, 1963 . . . . **20.00**
Archies Girls, 2764, Lowe, 1964 . . . . **35.00**
Baby Alive, 4398, Whitman 1973` **5.00**
Baby Sister, 920, Whitman, 1929 . . . . **50.00**
Barbie Country Camper and Paper Dolls, 4347,
   Whitman, 1973 . . . . **15.00**
Beauty Contest, 1026, Lowe, 1941 . . . . **65.00**
Blondie, 967, Whitman, 1948 . . . . **75.00**
Bob Hope, Dorothy Lamour, 976, Whitman, 1942 . . . . . **150.00**
Career Girls, 973, Whitman, 1944 . . . . **40.00**
Carol Linley, autographed, Whitman, 1960 . . . . **55.00**
Cowboys and Cowgirls, 1286, Lowe, 1950 . . . . **18.00**
Deanna Durbin, 3480, Merrill, 1940 . . . . **170.00**

Tricia Paper Doll, Artcraft, 1970, 6 pgs, 8¼ x 12¼", $25.00.

Welcome Back Kotter Sweathogs Paper Doll Set, "Magic Touch" clothes, The Toy Factory, #108, 1977, $30.00.

Dollies Go 'Round the World, 2714, Lowe, 1971	6.00
Doris Day, 1179, Whitman, 1954	75.00
Double Date, 962, Whitman, 1949	35.00
Girls in the War, 1028, Lowe, 1943	65.00
Gone With the Wind, 3404, Merrill, c1940	250.00
Henry and Henrietta Paper Dolls for Tiny Tots, Saalfield, 1938	50.00
Here's the Bride, 1948, Whitman, 1960	25.00
Hot Looks, 1541, Whitman, 1988	2.00
Janet Leigh Cutouts and Coloring, 2554, Merrill	45.00
Judy Garland, 980, Whitman, 1941	100.00
Kathy, 9986, Lowe, 1962	35.00
Kewpie–Kin Paper Dolls, Artcraft, 1967	40.00
Little Girls, 2784, Lowe, 1969	5.00
Little Orphan Annie, 9338, Whitman, 1934	150.00
Majorette Paper Dolls, Saalfield, 1957	6.00
Malibu Skipper, 1952, Whitman, 1973	10.00
Margaret O'Brien, 970, Whitman, 1944	75.00
Mary and Her Toys, 523, Lowe, 1943	18.00
Moon Dreamers, 1542, Whitman, 1987	2.00
Movie Stars Paper Dolls, 905, Whitman, 1931	150.00
Patti Page, 2406, Lowe, 1957	50.00
Peter Rabbit, 955, Whitman, 1939–40	65.00
Playhouse Dolls, Stephens Co, 1949	15.00
Playtime Fashions, 135, Stephens Publishing, 1946	8.00
Popeye, 980, Whitman, 1937	200.00
Punky Brewster, 1532, Whitman, 1986	2.50
Sally and Dick, Bob and Jean, 1023, Lowe, 1940	35.00
Shirley Temple Masquerade Costumes, 1787, Saalfield, 1940	185.00
Sonja Henie, Merrill, 1940	75.00
Teen Time Dolls, 4401, Whitman, 1959	15.00
The Bobbsey Twins, 1254, Lowe, 1952	45.00
The Honeymooners, 2560, Lowe, 1956	100.00
TV Tap Stars, 990, Lowe, 1952	20.00
Walt Disney's Cinderella, 1545, Whitman, 1989	2.00
Wedding Bell, 4375, Whitman, 1971	12.00
Wedding Party, Saalfield, 1951	10.00
Your Own Quintuplets, 275, Burton Playthings, 1935	25.00

PAPER EPHEMERA

This is a catchall category for a number of paper collecting categories that do not appear elsewhere in this book. Maurice Richards, author of *Collecting Paper Ephemera,* defines ephemera as the "minor transient documents of everyday life," i.e., material destined for the wastebasket but never quite making it.

Ephemera collecting has a distinguished history, tracing its origins back to English pioneers such as John Bagford (1650–1716), Samuel Pepys (1633–1703), and John Seldon (1584–1654). The Museum of the City of New York and the Wadsworth Athenaeum, Hartford, Connecticut, are two American museums with outstanding ephemera collections. The libraries at Harvard and Yale also have superior collections.

It is wrong to think of ephemera only in terms of paper objects, e.g., billhead, bookplates, documents, tickets, etc. Many three–dimensional items also have a transient quality to them. Advertising tins and pinback buttons are two examples.

References: Norman E. Martinus and Harry L. Rinker, *Warman's Paper,* Wallace–Homestead, Krause Publications, 1994; Gordon T. McClelland and Jay T. Last, *Fruit Box Labels,* Hillcrest Press, 1995; Craig A. Tuttle, *An Ounce of Preservation: A Guide to the Care of Papers and Photographs,* Rainbow Books, 1995; Gene Utz, *Collecting Paper: A Collector's Identification & Value Guide,* Books Americana, Krause Publications, 1993.

Periodical: *Bank Note Reporter,* 700 E State St, Iola, WI 54990; *PCM (Paper Collectors' Marketplace),* PO Box 128, Scandinavia, WI 54977.

Collectors' Clubs: Bond and Share Society, 26 Broadway at Bowling Green, Rm 200, New York, NY 10004; National Assoc of Paper & Advertising Collectors, PO Box 500, Mount Joy, PA 17552; Society of Antique Label Collectors, PO Box 412, Rapid City, SD 57709; The Citrus Label Society, 131 Miramonte Dr, Newberry Springs, CA 92365; The Ephemera Society of America, Inc, PO Box 95, Cazenovia, NY 13035.

Note: For additional listings see Advertising, Autographs, Cigar Collectibles, Photographs, and Postcards.

Blotter, Arm & Hammer Baking Soda, black and white, 1920s, 4 x 9¼"	$ 12.00
Blotter, Caroid Throat Medicine, 1920s	6.00

Blotter, Amoco adv, J. C. Leyendecker illus, red and black, 1941, $35.00.

Booklet, *The Dutch Boy's Hobby*, **child's paint book and paints, 1926, 12 pgs, $10.00.**

Blotter, Firestone Bicycle Tires, blue, orange, black, and white, 1920s, 3 x 5¼" **15.00**

Blotter, Jersey Cream, children illus, 1920s, 4 x 9". **4.00**

Blotter, Levi's, color illus, unused, 1970s, 2¾ x 6⅓" **22.00**

Blotter, Medusa Cement, printed color, 1925, 3½ x 6". **5.00**

Blotter, Nash Auto, 1928, 5 x 9" **5.00**

Blotter, Rolf Armstrong illus, nude blond woman sitting by pond, ©Brown & Bigelow, 1935, 3½ x 6" **25.00**

Blotter, Sunoco, Mickey and Minnie Mouse wearing bride and groom outfits, sitting in convertible **28.00**

Booklet, *A Calendar of Desserts*, General Foods, 1940s, 48 pgs **6.00**

Booklet, *Hartford Trial Range*, Hartford Electric Light Co, 1930s, 12 pgs **4.00**

Booklet, *San Francisco Railroad*, Golden Gate, 1940s **5.00**

Booklet, *The Art of Ventriloquism*, Johnson Smith & Co, Detroit, 1930s, 32 pgs **10.00**

Booklet, *The Meat Packing Industry in America*, Swift & Co, 1937, 108 pgs **6.00**

Booklet, *Triumph Herald 12/50 Model*, Leyland Motor Corp, 1950, 8 pgs **12.00**

Booklet, *Yosemite Park*, National Park Services, 1933, 62 pgs **12.00**

Calling Card, El West Delight, 1933, 3 x 4". **2.00**

Check, Carter's Warehouse, Plains Mercantile Co, sgd by Rosalyn S. Carter, 1968 . . . . **22.00**

Check, Coca-Cola Bottling Co, Newark, OH, canceled Art Deco log, 1949 . . . . **12.00**

Check, First National Bank of Nevada, filled in and sgd Tyrus R. Cobb, cancellation mark, 1945 . . . . **110.00**

Check, Hudson Trust Co, NY, sgd by Enrico Caruso, 1920 . . . . **45.00**

Check, sgd by George Burns **28.00**

Document, bill of sale, Bentley Auto, 1926. . . . . **3.00**

Document, stock certificate, ABC Brewing Corp, 1934 . . . . **12.00**

Label, American Airlines **8.00**

Label, Forest City Lima Beans, 1920s **2.00**

Label, Forest City Sweet Potatoes, 1920s. **2.50**

Label, Hotel De Coronado, 1930s **5.00**

Label, Lone Star Beer, 1940s . . . . **.50**

Label, Miracle, genie holding tray with 3 oranges, 1928, Plancentia **5.00**

Label, Old Mission, Spanish mission scene, mission bells, green grapes, 1920s . . . . **.50**

Label, Palm Springs Soda, silver Art Deco design, black and gold ground, 1935 . . . . **.50**

Label, Rooseville Belle. . . . . **.50**

Label, Skysweep Broom, 1931 . . . . **.75**

Label, Uncle Jake's Nickel Seegar, 1925 . . . . **3.00**

Label, Uncle Remus Syrup, 1924 . . . . **8.50**

Letterhead, Mack International Motor Truck Corp, Fire Engine Div, 300th Anniversary of Volunteer Fireman, color, 1948 . . . . **28.00**

Letterhead, United States Cigar Co, York, PA, 1933 . . . . **8.50**

Letterhead, Winchester Repeating Arms Co, New Haven, CT, black and white, used, 1929 . . . . **12.00**

License, archery, Pennsylvania, issued to Warren Rex Shoff, Pittsburgh, 1952 . . . . **6.00**

License, hunting, Junior Hunter, waterproof tagboard, blue, black letters and numbers, 1963. . . . . **8.00**

License, marriage, William Yeakel to Julia Lazor, Old Zionsville United Church of Christ, Zionsville, PA, Lehigh County, September 25, 1954 . . . . **6.50**

License, trapping, non-resident, white, black ink-stamped year, red letters and numbers, 1951. . . . . . **12.00**

Manuscript, play, *The Dump*, Everett Shinn, typed carbon copy, 1931, 39 pgs **28.00**

Map, Alaska, geological map of Chitna River Valley and surrounding areas, 1939, 29 x 53" **18.00**

Map, Wisconsin Fun Map, Wisconsin Conservation Dept, 1936, 24 x 28" **10.00**

Menu, Lehigh Valley Railroad, dinner, tugboat photo cov, 1950–60. . . . . **5.50**

Label, Ritz Lemon Soda, yellow and black, 3½ x 4¼", $3.00.

Menu, Sevilla Biltmore, Havana, Cuba, 1930 . . . . **6.00**
Program, An Evening With Procol Harem, 1973, 8 pgs . . . **28.00**
Program, Army–Navy 1955 Official Program, Philadelphia, Nov 26, 1955 . . . . **10.00**
Program, Johnny Mathis, color photo cov, c1970, 10 x 13" **12.00**
Ticket, Cab Calloway and His Cotton Club Orchestra, 1935 . . . . **15.00**
Ticket, Jack Dempsey vs Tom Gibbons, World's Heavyweight Championship, O'Toole County American Legion, Shelby, MT, ringside, 3–part ticket, July 4, 1923 . . . . **52.00**

PAPERBACK BOOKS

The mass–market paperback, the subject of this collecting category, arrived on the scene in 1938. Selling between 15¢ and 25¢, the concept was an instant success. World War II gave paperback book sales a tremendous boost. Hundreds of publishers rushed into the marketplace.

Paperback books are found in a variety of size formats and page counts. Some came with dust jackets or in boxed sets. Price is a key factor in dating paperback books. Many collectors focus on titles that sold initially for 75¢ or less.

The mid–1940s through the end of the 1950s was the golden age of paperback books. Titles are identified by their lurid, colorful, highly graphic covers, a continuation of the pulp era covers.

Most collections are assembled around one or more unifying themes, e.g., author, cover artist, fictional genre, or publisher.

Hugh collections still enter the market on a regular basis. Further, many paperbacks were printed on inexpensive pulp paper that has turned brown and brittle over time. Although books in excellent condition are difficult to find, they are available. Do not buy into a dealer's argument that his high asking price for a paperback in poor condition is valid because excellent examples are not available. Tell him you read otherwise in this paperback.

References: Norman E. Martinus and Harry L. Rinker, *Warman's Paper,* Wallace–Homestead, Krause Publishing, 1994; Dawn E. Reno, *Collecting Romance Novels,* Alliance Publishers, 1995; Lee Server, *Over My Dead Body: The Sensational Age of the American Paperback: 1945–1955,* Chronicle Books, 1994; Moe Wadle, *The Movie Tie–In Book: A Collector's Guide to Paperback Movie Editions,* Nostalgia Books, 1994.

Periodical: *Paperback Parade,* PO Box 209, Brooklyn, NY 11228.

Addams, Charles, *Drawn and Quartered,* Pocket Book, 1964 . . . . **$ 6.50**
Anderson, Poul, *Brain Wave,* Ballantine Books, 1954. . . . . . . **6.50**
Christie, Agatha, *Murder at the Vicarage,* Dell, 1961 . . . . . . **3.00**
Dean, Dudley, *The Diehards,* Gold Medal, 1956. . . . . **5.00**
Delany, Samuel R., *Einstein Intersection,* Ace, 1967. . . . . . **12.00**
De Marco, Carl, *Woman on a String,* Midwood. **4.50**
Dickson, Gordon R., *Time Storm* Bantam, 1979 . . . . **3.00**
Doyle, Arthur Conan, *Lost World,* Harlequin, 1953 . . . . . . **55.00**
Eden, Dorothy, *Whistle For the Crows,* Ace, 1963 . . . . **4.50**
Ellson, Hal, *Rock,* Ballantine, 1955. . . . . **15.00**
Falk, Lee, *Island of Dogs,* Avon, 1975. . . . . **8.00**
Farrell, Henry, *Whatever Happened to Baby Jane?,* Avon, 1960 . . . . **6.50**

Ferguson, Margaret, *Sign of the Ram,* Bantam, 1948 . . . . . . **3.00**
Fielding, William J., *Strange Superstitions and Magical,* PB Library, 1966. . . . . **4.00**
Flint, Kenneth C., *Dark Druid,* Bantam, 1987 . . . . **22.00**
Follett, Ken, *Paper Money,* Signet, 1987 . . . . **2.50**
Foran, Tom, *Twisted Ones,* Beacon, 1963 . . . . **18.00**
Gaddis, Peggy, *Intruders in Eden,* Belmont Books, 1966 . . . . **2.50**
Garth, David, *Appointment With Danger,* Popular, 1948 . . . . **12.00**
Goldman, William, *Great Waldo Pepper,* Dell, 1975 . . . . . . **1.50**
Goodis, David, *Cassidy's Girl,* Gold Medal, 1955 . . . . **18.00**
Goulart, Ron, *Hawkeye,* Award, 1972. . . . . **6.00**
Hamilton, Donald, *Ambushers,* Gold Medal, 1963 . . . . **3.00**
Hamilton, Edmond, *Haunted Stars,* Pyramid, 1963 . . . . . . **5.00**
Haycock, Ernest, *Long Storm,* Bantam, 1950. . . . . **3.00**
Howard, Robert E., *Moon of Skulls,* Centaur, 1969 . . . . . . **6.00**
Hunter, Evan, *Vanishing Ladies,* Perma, 1957. . . . . **18.00**
Jakes, John I., *Barbarian,* Avon, 1959 . . . . **18.00**
Ketchum, Hank, *In This Corner...Dennis the Menace,* Crest, 1959 . . . . **5.00**
King, Stephen, *Salem's Lot,* Signet, 1978. . . . . **6.00**
Kipling, Rudyard, *Captain Courageous,* Bantam, 1946 . . . . **3.00**
Knight, Adam, *Murder For Madame,* Signet, 1952. . . . . **8.00**
Krepps, Robert W., *Stagecoach,* Gold Medal, 1967 . . . . **4.50**
Kurtzman, Harvey, *The Mad Reader,* Ballantine, 1954 . . . . **10.00**
Kyle, Robert, *Ben Gates Is Hot,* Dell, 1964 . . . . **3.00**
Lamb, Harold, *Babur the Tiger,* Bantam, 1964. . . . . **2.00**
Lariar, Lawrence, *He Died Laughing,* Boardman **6.00**
Larrick, Nancy, *Parent's Guide to Children's Reading,* Cardinal, 1964. . . . . **3.00**
Marlowe, Stephen, *Killers Are My Meat,* Gold Medal, 1957 . . . . **6.00**
Moravia, Alberto, *The Wayward Wife,* Ace, 1968 . . . . **2.00**
Neumann, Alfred, *Strange Conquest,* Ballantine, 1954. . . . . **3.50**
Okazi, Milton K., *Case of the Deadly Kiss,* Gold Medal, 1957 . . . . **6.00**
Rabe, Peter, *Mission For Vengeance,* Gold Medal, 1958. . . . **7.00**

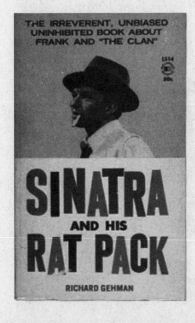

Richard Gehman, *Sinatra and His Rat Pack,* Belmont Books, 1961, $7.00.

Robinson, Ray, *Baseball Stars of 1961*, Pyramid **2.50**
Snyder, Leonard, *The Velvet Whip*, Berkley, 1955 . . . . **3.75**
Williams, Charles, *Talk of the Town*, Dell, 1958 . . . . **4.00**

PAPERWEIGHTS

The paperweights found in this category divide into three basic types: (1) advertising paperweights, (2) souvenir or commemorative paperweights, and (3) contemporary glass paperweights. Advertising paperweights, made from a variety of materials, were popular giveaway premiums between 1920 and the late 1950s. Cast–iron figural paperweights are the most eagerly sought.

Souvenir paperweights are valued more as regional than paperweight collectibles. Most were cheaply made. Many are nothing more than a round plastic disk with information stenciled on the top or a colored photograph applied to the bottom. No wonder collector interest is limited.

Paperweights enjoyed a renaissance in the 1970s and 80s. Baccarat, Perthshire, and Saint Louis are leading contemporary manufacturers. Many studio glassmarkers, e.g. Ray and Bob Banford, Paul Stankard, and Victor Trabucco, also make paperweights.

References: Monika Flemming and Peter Pommerencke, *Paperweights of the World,* Schiffer Publishing, 1994; John D. Hawley, *The Glass Menagerie: A Study of Silhouette Canes in Antique Paperweights,* Paperweight Press, 1995; Paul Hollister, Jr., *The Encyclopedia of Glass Paperweights,* Paperweight Press, 1969; Sibylle Jargstorf, *Paperweights,* Schiffer Publishing, 1991; Lawrence H. Selman, *All About Paperweights,* Paperweight Press, 1992.

Collectors' Clubs: International Paperweight Society, 761 Chestnut St, Santa Cruz, CA 95060; Paperweight Collectors Assoc, Inc, PO Box 1263, Betsville, MD 20704.

Advertising, ABCO Electronics, NJ, aircraft supplies, celluloid over glass and metal, maroon lettering and airplane, buff ground, 1930s, 3½" d . . . . **$ 28.00**
Advertising, Bell Telephone System, replica bell, dark blue glass, gold lettering, 1920s, 3½" d, 3" h **48.00**

Limited Edition, D'Albret, sulphide, Mark Twain cameo on sunburst–cut aquamarine ground, 7 and 1 faceting, sgd, acid–etched insignia, 2⁷⁄₈" d, $143.00.

Photo courtesy
L. H. Selman Ltd.

Advertising, Chicago Cubs, metal, baseball on sq base, silver luster, blue lettering, inscribed "Glassenhart & Mayerhofer," c1920. . . . . **225.00**
Advertising, Dutch Boy Paint, white metal, figural Dutch Boy, c1930 . . . . **75.00**
Advertising, Twenty One, nightclub, metal figural jockey, china base, gold inscription, 1950 . . . . **75.00**
Commemorative, Edward VIII 1937 Coronation, black and white portrait, 4¼" l **22.00**
Commemorative, John F. Kennedy, sulphide overlay, cobalt blue over white, Baccarat, 3" w **120.00**
Limited Edition, Drew Ebelhare, egg shape, abstract colored glass, cobalt blue, orange, yellow, pink, green aventurine, white, sgd, dated 1992, 3¼" h **75.00**
Limited Edition, D' Albret, Prince Charles sulphide, front view cameo of prince in full regalia, translucent purple ground, base inscribed "H R H Prince Charles," diamond–cut top and side facets, acid–etched insignia,1970, 2⁷⁄₈" d **75.00**
Limited Edition, sulphide marble, 3–dimensional, Mary and lamb, crystal, 1¾" d **60.00**

AUCTION PRICES

L. H. Selman Ltd. Spring 1997 Price Guide & Mail Auction, April 24, 1997. Prices for these limited edition paperweights include a 10% buyer's premium.

Baccarat, Gridel dancing devil patterned millefiori, large dancing devil silhouette cane surrounded by star–shaped arrangement of complex canes in red, pink, yellow, blue, green, and white on translucent blue–over–opaque white ground, 17 other Gridel silhouette canes composed around edge, signature/date cane, acid–etched Baccarat insignia, 1977, 3³⁄₁₆" d **495.00**
Chris Buzzini, azalea bouquet, 3 red azaleas with yellow stamens, yellow wildflowers with black stamens, blue bellflowers and buds, entwined stems, signature/date cane, sgd and dated, 1987, 3¹⁄₁₆" d **825.00**
Josh Simpson, floral, large pink and amethyst blossom with millefiori center and opalescent stem, floating over abstract world created from opalescent blue, black, and yellow glass, sgd, 3" d **303.00**
Ken Rosenfeld, yellow thistles, 3 vibrant yellow tufts on stems with spiky green leaves, sgd and dated, signature cane, 1991, 3¼" d **660.00**
Parabelle, close concentric millefiori, central yellow pansy cane surrounded by complex edelweiss and cog canes in pink, royal blue, tangerine, olive, and white, translucent dark green ground, signature/date cane, 1989, 2¹³⁄₁₆" d **440.00**
Perthshire, miniature Damson plum, 3 dark purple plums on stems with green leaves over grid–cut ground, circular top facet and 2 rows of circular side facets, sgd, 1977, 2" d **176.00**
Randall Grubb, Pink Ladies, pair of pink lilies on stalk with 3 buds and slender green leaves, sgd and dated, signature cane, 1994, 3¹⁄₈" d **330.00**
Steuben Glass, magnum air bubble, hundreds of evenly spaced bubbles in large crystal globe, bubbles get smaller toward top, acid–etched signature, chip on base, 4⁵⁄₁₆" d **275.00**

PARRISH, MAXFIELD

Maxfield Parrish was born in Philadelphia on July 25, 1870. Originally named Frederick Parrish, he later adopted his mother's maiden name, Maxfield, as his middle name. As a youth, he made several trips abroad with his parents.

Parrish received his academic training at Haverford College and the Pennsylvania Academy of Fine Arts, and spent a brief period as a pupil of Howard Pyle at Drexel. Parrish's first art exhibit was held at the Philadelphia Art Club in 1893.

His first magazine cover appeared on an 1895 issue of *Harper's Bazaar*. He soon was receiving commissions from *Century Magazine, Collier's, Ladies' Home Journal, Life,* and *Scribners*. In 1897 Parrish was elected to the Society of American Artists.

Parrish established a studio, The Oaks, in Cornish, New Hampshire. Constantly plagued with recurring bouts of tuberculosis, Parrish painted a large number of works for advertisements, book illustrations, and calendars. He frequently interrupted his work for travel, both within the United States and abroad. He is best known for the work he did between 1900 and 1940.

He married and had three sons and a daughter. He continually was recognized for his contributions to architecture and painting. Parrish died on March 30, 1966.

References: Erwin Flacks, *The Maxfield Parrish Identification & Price Guide, Second Edition*, Collectors Press, 1995; *Maxfield Parrish: A Price Guide*, L–W Book Sales, 1993, 1996 value update.

Book, *Emerald Storybook,* Duffield, 1924 . . . . $ 75.00
Book, *Maxfield Parrish: The Early Years*, Paul Skeeters,
   1973, dj 250.00
Booklet, *1939 World's Fair*, New Hampshire Exhibit,
   5 x 6" 75.00
Calendar, Autumn Afternoon, full pad, 1956, 17 x 10" . . . 125.00
Calendar, Cadmus Sowing the Dragon's Teeth, 1923 . . . . 130.00
Magazine Cover, *You and Your Work*, Tranquility,
   May 13, 1944 . . . . 45.00
Magazine Cover, *Youth's Companion*, Jan 3, 1924,
   Jell–O adv 55.00
Poster, "Buy Products Not Advertised On Our
   Roadside," 1939 . . . . 600.00
Print, Dreaming, 1928, 6 x 10" 175.00
Print, The Lute Players, 1924, 6 x 10" 125.00
Print, White Birch, 1931, 9 x 11¼" 100.00
Program, Cohan & Harris Theatre, 1920s 130.00
Puzzle, Daybreak, 1970s 22.00
Puzzle, The Broadmoor, 1940s 75.00
Recipe Booklet, Jell–O, color illus, 1924, 6½ x 4¼" 65.00

PATRIOTIC COLLECTIBLES

Columbia and the Goddess of Liberty, the eagle, the flag and its representations, the Liberty Bell, the Statue of Liberty, and Uncle Sam are important symbols of American patriotism. Today they are most prevalent during national holidays, such as Memorial Day and the Fourth of July, and centennial celebrations. They often appear subtley in print advertising and television commercials.

Uncle Sam enjoys his greatest popularity during wartime. He became a national symbol during the Civil War. His modern day appearance resulted from drawings by Thomas Nast in Harper's Weekly and portraits by the artist, James Montgomery Flagg. Uncle Sam played a major role in military recruiting during World Wars I and II.

The anti–American sentiment created by the Vietnam War and increased emphasis on global thinking has diminished the importance of these patriotic symbols in the eyes of some. Hopefully, it will not take another major war to restore these individuals' pride.

Reference: Gerald E. Czulewicz, Sr., *The Foremost Guide To Uncle Sam Collectibles*, Collector Books, 1995.

Collectors' Club: Statue of Liberty Collectors' Club, 26601 Bernwood Rd, Cleveland, OH 44122.

Advertising Display, Uncle Sam cardboard cutout,
   OshKosh B'Gosh adv, 1942, 45 x 27" . . . . $ 500.00
Bandanna, flag, wreath with 36 stars, silk, 22 x 25" 110.00
Bank, Liberty Bell, pot metal and wood, brown, mkd
   "USA, 1947," 4½" h 30.00
Bookmark, US Capitol, brass 25.00
Bowl, US Capitol in relief, Syroco Wood, oval 12.00
Catalog, Detra Flag Company, #24, New York and Los
   Angeles, 1941, 6½ x 9" 100.00
Comic Book, Captain America's Bicentennial Battles,
   Vol 1, #1, Marvel Comics Group, 1976 . . . . 20.00
Cookie Cutter, eagle, tin, 6½" l 85.00
Creamer, Uncle Sam, Royal Winton, c1920 . . . . 75.00
Dresser Scarf, embroidered top hat, c1940 . . . . 10.00
Flag, 48 stars, nylon, 4 x 5" 85.00
Game, Heroes of America, Games of the Nations
   Series, Paul Educational Games, box with flag illus,
   1920s 25.00
Jigsaw Puzzle, hound dog dressed as Uncle Sam,
   Wolverine World–Wide, 19 x 12¾" 10.00
Magazine Tear Sheet, "Greyhound Presents A Great
   New Super–Coach," Uncle Sam waving at bus,
   1939 . . . . 15.00

Pillow Cover, silk, 48–star flag, "Tennessee Maneuvers – 1944" and poem to Mother and Dad in shield, red and blue flocking, white ground, red fringed border, 17½" sq, $25.00.

Souvenir, Statue of Liberty, gold colored metal, 4¹/₂" h, $8.00.

PEANUTS

In 1950 Charles M. Schulz launched Peanuts, a comic strip about kids and a beagle named Snoopy. Charlie Brown, Lucy, Linus, and the Peanuts gang have become a national institution. The Peanuts gang has been featured in over 60 television specials, translated in over a dozen languages.

Charles M. Schulz Creative Associates and United Features Syndicate have pursued an aggressive licensing program. Almost no aspect of a child's life has escaped the licensing process.

Given this, why is the number of Peanuts collectors relatively small? The reason is that the strip's humor is targeted primarily toward adults. Children do not actively follow it during the formative years, i.e., ages seven to fourteen, that influence their adult collecting.

Reference: Jan Lindenberger, *The Unauthorized Guide to Snoopy Collectibles,* Schiffer Publishing, 1997.

Bank, Snoopy lying on flowered egg, ceramic, Determined, #1503, 1970s . . . . **$ 28.00**

Banner, Lucy, "For A Nickel I Can Cure Anything," Determined, 1971 . . . . **8.00**

Bell, Snoopy and the Beaglescouts, Schmid, orig box, 1984 . . . . **25.00**

Book, *Happiness Is a Warm Puppy,* Charles M. Schulz, Determined, Lucy hugging Snoopy cov, hard cover, 1962 . . . . **3.50**

Book, *It's Good to Have a Friend,* Charles M. Schulz, pop–up, Hallmark, #400HEC36, 1972 . . . . **35.00**

Book, *Peanuts,* Charles M. Schulz, Peppermint Patty taking picture of Schroeder and Snoopy on piano cov, Charlie Brown frowning, Rinehart & Co, 1952 . . . . . **5.00**

Bookends, pr, Snoopy dressed as tennis player, ceramic, Butterfly, #1000 1301, 1979, 5" h **32.00**

Box, cov, Snoopy finial, porcelain, heart shaped **25.00**

Bubble Bath, figural Lucy wearing red dress and beanie, Avon **8.00**

Cake Decoration, edible, Snoopy as Flying Ace, 10 candle holders, 6 Woodstocks, "Happy Birthday," Hallmark **10.00**

Doll, Peppermint Patty, cloth, green and white shirt, black pants, removable outfit, Ideal, #1413–4, 1976 . . . . **18.00**

Doll, Snoopy, plush, felt eyes, eyebrows, and nose, red paper tag, Determined, #835, 1971, 12" h **18.00**

Figure, Charlie Brown, hp, Determined, 1969, 6" h **25.00**

Game, Peanuts, Selchow & Righter, 1959 . . . . **45.00**

Lunch Box, Schroeder playing piano surrounded by Peanuts gang one side, baseball illus other side, white vinyl, plastic thermos, King Seeley, #6168/3, 1973 . . . . **32.00**

Magazine, *Newsweek,* December 27, 1971, Peanuts Gang cov, "Good Grief, $150 Million" article **8.00**

Matchcover, Snoopy, 1961 Ford Falcon adv **5.00**

Music Box, Flying Ace Snoopy on doghouse, wood, Schmid **85.00**

Ornament, Snoopy carrying red and white striped candy cane, Determined, 1975 . . . . **8.00**

Paper Dolls, Snoopy, 10 outfits, Determined, #274, 1976 . . . . **28.00**

Match Cover, The United States Secret Service Treasury Department, "Beware of Counterfeits, Know Your Money," Diamond Match Co, c1948 . . . . **1.50**

Mug, ceramic, Sam the Olympic Eagle mascot front, Los Angeles Olympic Games, Papel, 1980 L. A. Olympic Committee. **5.00**

Paper Doll, Uncle Sam's Little Helpers Paper Dolls, Ann Kovach, 1943 . . . . **15.00**

Pinback Button, Good Teeth, Cincinnati Schools dental care program, red, white, and blue, 1930s, 1" d **15.00**

Pinback Button, Philadelphia Sesqui–Centennial, 1776–1926, gold, red, white, and blue, small red, white, and blue flag, yellow and blue ribbon, ⁷/₈" d **12.00**

Planter, figural, top hat, molded poly–ceramic, red, white, and blue, Ruben's Originals, 1974 . . . . **10.00**

Postcard, bust of Uncle Sam front, story of Samuel Wilson on back, Yankee Colour Corp, 1966. . . . . **10.00**

Postcard, Independence Hall, Philadelphia, sepia **5.00**

Scrapbook, simulated leather, green and gold, emb Uncle Sam behind ship's wheel, 11¹/₂ x 15¹/₄", c1945 . . . . **45.00**

Sheet Music, *Any Bonds Today,* National Defense program, theme song, Uncle Sam cov, ©1941, 6 pgs, 9 x 12" **18.00**

Sheet Music, *Father of the Land We Love,* George M. Cohan, 1931 . . . . **8.00**

Sign, "Protect Your Hands with Yankee Doodle Gloves and Mittens," cardboard, Galena Glove & Mitten Co, Dubuque, Iowa, c1940 . . . . **50.00**

Stickers, "Patriotic Decorations," die cut, gummed seals, red, white, and blue, cardboard packet, 10 of orig 25 seals, Dennison, c1925. . . . . **18.00**

Tie Slide, Statue of Liberty, Boy Scout, emb brass, detailed raised Statue, scroll banner at base, c1930, 1¹/₄ x 2" **22.00**

Watch Fob, silvered brass, raised portrait of Uncle Sam and IOOF Grand Lodge of NY State symbol, 1946 convention, Troy, NY, ·1¹/₂ x 1¹/₂" **25.00**

Drinking Glass, McDonald's premium, Camp Snoopy, "Civilization Is Overrated!," 1983, $2.00.

Patch, Snoopy on roller skates, "Jamming," Determined, 1970, 3" d 3.00

Plate, Peanuts in Concert, Schmid, 1983 . . . . 28.00

Plate, Woodstock's Christmas, Schmid, orig box, 1976 . . . 28.00

Pull Toy, Snoopy 12.00

Radio, figural Snoopy, plastic, Determined, #351, 1975 . . . . 18.00

Scissors, Joe Cool, red plastic 10.00

Toothbrush, Snoopy on doghouse stand, plastic, battery operated, Kenner, #30301, 1972 . . . . 42.00

Toy, Snoopy chef flips food, windup, orig box, 1958 . . . . 45.00

Trophy, Snoopy looking in mirror, plastic, "You're The Fairest One Of All," 10.00

Wall Plaque, Charlie Brown hugging Snoopy, "Have You Hugged Your Dog Today?," Hallmark, #DE8053, 3 x 4½" 10.00

Watch, dancing Snoopy, silver case, red face, red band, Timex, 1976 . . . . 30.00

Wind Chimes, figural Woodstock and Snoopy on doghouse, plastic, metal chimes, Aviva, orig box, 1973 . . . . 32.00

PEDAL CARS

Pedal car is a generic term used to describe any pedal toy. Automobiles were only one form. There are also pedal airplanes, fire engines, motorcycles, and tractors.

By the mid–1910s pedal cars resembling their full–sized counterparts were being made. Buick, Dodge, Overland, and Packard are just a few examples. American National, Garton, Gendron, Steelcraft, and Toledo Wheel were the five principal pedal car manufacturers in the 1920s and 30s. Ertl, Garton, and Murray made pedal cars in the post–1945 period. Many mail–order catalogs, e.g., Sears, Roebuck, sold pedal cars. Several television shows issued pedal car licenses during the mid–1950s and 60s.

Pedal car collecting is serious business in the 1990s. The $10,000 barrier has been broken. Many pedal cars are being stripped down and completely restored to look as though they just came off the assembly line. Some feel this emphasis, especially when it destroys surviving paint, goes too far.

References: *Evolution of the Pedal Car, Vol. 1* (1989, 1996 value update), *Vol. 2* (1990, 1997 value update), *Vol. 3* (1992), *Vol. 4* (1993, 1997 value update), L–W Book Sales; Andrew G. Gurka, *Pedal Car Restoration and Price Guide,* Krause Publications, 1996;

Newsletter: *The Wheel Goods Trader,* PO Box 435, Fraser, MI 48026.

Boat, red, Murray, 1960s . . . . **$ 500.00**

Buick, black and white, Steelcraft, 1941 . . . . **1,250.00**

Cadillac 8, red, black and yellow trim, Gendron, 1923 . . . . **3,000.00**

Camaro, gold, red and white trim, Murray, 1969 . . . . . . **450.00**

Cannonball Express, red, 27" l **300.00**

City Fire Dept, red and white, jet–flow drive, Murray, 1952 . . . . **650.00**

Dump Truck #742, yellow and black, Murray, 1950s, 46" l **600.00**

F.D. Pumper #7, red and white, AMF, 1955 . . . . **850.00**

Ford Country Squire Station Wagon, 2–tone green, Murray, 1956 . . . . **600.00**

Ford Mustang, red and white, AMF, 1965 . . . . **750.00**

Hot Rod, yellow, red trim, chain drive, Garton, 1950s . . . **800.00**

Navy Fighter Plane, Murray, 1945 . . . . **1,500.00**

Packard, #6, red, black and yellow trim, 1925 . . . . **3,000.00**

Plymouth Strato–Flite Auto, blue and white, 1957 . . . . **1,000.00**

Pontiac G–Man Cruiser, green and white, Steelcraft, 1936 . . . . **800.00**

Race Car, BMC Special, BMC, 1947 . . . . **650.00**

Race Car, dark blue, yellow trim, Garton, 1950s **650.00**

Race Car, Eureka, c1940, 51" l **600.00**

Service Truck, green and white, Murray, 1948 . . . . **750.00**

Sports Car, blue, whitewall tires, red steering wheel, AMF, 1960s **550.00**

Station Wagon, burgundy, white trim, Murray, 1946 . . . . **750.00**

Comet Happi–Time Sports Car, turquoise, red and white trim, 1959, 36" l, $500.00.

Station Wagon, burgundy, wood trim, Garton, 1949 . . . **1,500.00**
Super Sonic Jet, Model K–900, red and gray, Murray,
 1952 . . . . **500.00**
Thunderbolt, red, white trim **750.00**
Tow Wrecker, black and white, AMF, 1955 . . . . **800.00**
Tractor, Allis–Chalmers, red, 1950s **250.00**
Tractor, Ford 8000, blue, white trim, 1968 . . . . **150.00**
US Mail Truck #7, red, white, and blue, AMF, 1955 . . . . . **900.00**

PENNANTS

Felt pennants were popular souvenirs from the 1920s through the end of the 1950s. College sports pennants decorated the walls of dormitory rooms during this period. Pennants graced the radio antenna of hot rods and street rods. A pennant served as a pleasant reminder of a trip to the mountains, shore, or an historic site.

The majority of commercial pennants were stenciled. Once a pennant's paint cracks and starts to fall off, its value is gone. Handmade pennants, some exhibiting talented design and sewing work, are common.

Baseball Hall of Fame, green, white inscription, yel-
 low trim, 1950s, 11" l . . . . **$ 22.00**
Captain Marvel, blue felt, 1944–47 . . . . **85.00**
Cleveland Indians, red felt, white lettering, c1950 . . . . . . **18.00**
Derby Day, red felt, white lettering, red and white
 design with pink accents, 1939, 18" l **18.00**
Elvis, blue felt, yellow design and lettering, black and
 white photo, white "Love, Elvis" signature,
 c1960, 29" l **42.00**
First Man on Moon, felt, red and white, blue trim,
 29" l **18.00**
John F. Kennedy, felt, red, white, and blue, "In
 Memory Of," 3 x 5½" color photo, and inaugural
 quote "Ask Not...," hangs vertically, 11½" h **15.00**
New York Mets, blue, white and orange inscriptions
 and designs, late 1960s, 29½" l **18.00**
1933 Chicago World's Fair, red felt, white lettering,
 "Electrical Building" image, yellow felt end trim
 streamers **15.00**
Pee Wee Reese, white felt, red portrait and signature,
 1950s **45.00**
Philmont Scout Ranch, orange felt, black lettering **15.00**
Playboy PMOC, gold felt, white lettering and crest,
 1960s, 29" l **12.00**

23rd Annual Gypsy Tour, 100 Mile, 1939 Championship, red felt, white lettering, 23" l, $380.00. Photo courtesy Dunbar's Gallery.

Roy Rogers, red felt, white inscription and Roy on
 Trigger, "Many Happy Trails, Roy Rogers and
 Trigger," late 1940s, 27" l **50.00**
10th Annual Miami All American Air Maneuvers, Dec
 . 2–5, 1937, green felt, yellow lettering, 16½ x 33" **35.00**

PENNSBURY POTTERY

In 1950 Henry Below, a ceramic engineer and mold maker, and Lee Below, a ceramic designer and modeler, founded Pennsbury Pottery. The pottery was located near Morrisville, Pennsylvania, the location of William Penn's estate, Pennsbury.

Henry and Lee Below previously worked for Stangl. Therefore, it is no surprise that many forms, manufacturing techniques, and motifs are similar to those used at Stangl. A series of bird figurines were Pennsbury's first products.

Although Pennsbury is best known for its pieces with a brown wash background, other background colors were used. In addition to Christmas plates (1960–70), commemorative pieces, novelties, and special order pieces, Pennsbury made several dinnerware lines, most reflecting the strong German heritage of eastern Pennsylvania. Amish, Black Rooster, Eagle, Folkart, Harvest, Hex, Quartet Red Barn, and Red Rooster are a few examples.

The company employed local housewives and young ladies. Many of these decorators initialed their work or added the initials of the piece's designer. At its peak in 1963, Pennsbury had 46 employees. Cheap foreign imports impacted negatively on sales by the late 1960s.

Henry Below died on December 21, 1959, leaving the pottery in trust to his wife, Lee, and their three children. Lee Below died on December 12, 1968. Attempts to continue operations proved unsuccessful. The company filed for bankruptcy in October 1970 and the property was auctioned in December. The pottery and its supporting buildings were destroyed by fire on May 18, 1971.

References: Harvey Duke, *The Official Price Guide to Pottery and Porcelain, Eighth Edition,* House of Collectibles, 1995; Lucile Henzke, *Pennsbury Pottery,* Schiffer Publishing, 1990; Dana Gehman Morykan and Harry L. Rinker, *Warman's Country Antiques & Collectibles, Third Edition,* Wallace–Homestead, Krause Publications, 1996; Mike Schneider, *Stangl and Pennsbury Birds: Identification and Price Guide,* Schiffer Publishing, 1994.

REPRODUCTION ALERT: Some Pennsbury pieces (many with Pennsbury markings) have been reproduced from original molds purchased by Lewis Brothers Pottery in Trenton, New Jersey. Glen View in Langhorne, Pennsylvania, marketed the 1970s Angel Christmas plate with Pennsbury markings and continued the Christmas plate line into the 1970s. Lenape Products, a division of Pennington, bought Glen View in 1975 and continued making products with a Pennsbury feel.

Amish, ashtray, 5" d . . . . **$ 25.00**
Amish, coffee mug, 3¼" h **30.00**
Amish, creamer and sugar, cov, 4" h **70.00**
Amish, plate, 8" d **60.00**
Amish, salt and pepper shakers, pr **35.00**
Ashtray, commemorative, "The Solebury National
 Bank of New Hope Pa," 5" d **30.00**
Ashtray, "Outen the light," 5" d **30.00**
Barber Shop Quartet, coaster, 5" d **30.00**

Barber Shop Quartet, coffee mug, 3¼" h 35.00
Barber Shop Quartet, pitcher, 7¼" h 90.00
Black Rooster, casserole, cov, 10¼ x 8¼" 100.00
Black Rooster, coffeepot, 8" h 90.00
Black Rooster, dinner plate, 10" d 35.00
Black Rooster, pie plate, 10" d 35.00
Black Rooster, plaque, 4" d 30.00
Black Rooster, tile, 6" sq 30.00
Black Rooster, tray, 7½ x 5" 35.00
Black Rooster, vinegar and oil, pr 150.00
Blue Dowry, dinner plate, 10" d 35.00
Delft Toleware, bowl, 9" d 45.00
Delft Toleware, candlestick, 3¾" h 40.00
Delft Toleware, mug, 4½" h 35.00
Delft Toleware, pitcher, 5" h 55.00
Eagle, beer mug, 5" h 30.00
Eagle, cigarette box, 3½ x 5" 40.00
Eagle, coffee mug, 3¼" h 25.00
Eagle, desk basket, 5" h 50.00
Eagle, pitcher, 5¼" h 60.00
Eagle, plate, 8" d 50.00
Eagle, pretzel bowl, 12 x 8" 90.00
Farm Scene, plaque, 6" d 50.00
Fisherman, beer mug, 5" h 50.00
Fisherman, coasters, 4½" d, price for set of 4 . . . . . . 100.00
Fisherman, plaque, 5" d 30.00
Folkart, butter dish, 5 x 4" 45.00
Folkart, pie plate, 9" d 50.00
Gay Ninety, beer mug, 5" h 40.00
Gay Ninety, plaque, oval, 5" l 35.00
Gay Ninety, pretzel bowl, 12 x 8" 90.00
Harvest, plate, 11" d 80.00
Hex, bowl, 9" d 40.00
Hex, butter dish, 5 x 4" 50.00
Hex, candy dish, heart shaped, 6" l 35.00
Hex, coffee mug, sgd "L.B." 25.00
Hex, cup and saucer 30.00
Hex, pitcher, 6¼" h 65.00
Hex Star, ashtray, 8" d 40.00
Kissing Over Cow, plaque, 6" d 50.00
Mother Serving Pie, pie plate, 9" d 85.00

Mother Serving Pie, plaque, sgd "K," 6" d 35.00
Pennsylvania Hex, coffeepot 50.00
Pennsylvania Hex, cup and saucer 30.00
Plaque, commemorative, "Iron Horse Ramble" and
  "Reading Railroad 1960," 7¼ x 5¼" 55.00
Plaque, commemorative, "Pop's half et already," mkd
  "NFBPWC Philadelphia, PA 1960," 4" d 30.00
Plaque, "Such Schmootzers," 4" d 30.00
Red Barn, coffee mug, 3¼" h 30.00
Red Barn, pitcher, 6¼" h 100.00
Red Barn, plate, 8" d 75.00
Red Rooster, butter dish, cov, 5 x 4" 45.00
Red Rooster, candleholder, 5" h 40.00
Red Rooster, chip and dip 90.00
Red Rooster, cigarette box, 5 x 4" 40.00
Red Rooster, coffeepot, cov, 6" h 50.00
Red Rooster, compote, ftd, 5" d 40.00
Red Rooster, creamer and sugar, pr, 4" h 50.00
Red Rooster, dinner plate, 10" d 35.00
Red Rooster, egg cup, 4" h 22.00
Red Rooster, mug, 5" h 35.00
Red Rooster, pie plate, 9" d 40.00
Red Rooster, relish tray, 5 part, 14½ x 11½" 90.00
Red Rooster, salt and pepper shakers, pr, 2½" h 25.00
Red Rooster, teapot 60.00
Red Rooster, tray, 7½ x 5" 30.00
Red Rooster, wall pocket, 6½" sq 45.00
Toleware, plaque, brown, 5 x 7" 40.00
Tray, "Laurel Ridge," 8½ x 4¼" 40.00
Treetops Christmas Plate, 1962 . . . . 45.00
Tulip, candleholder, 5" d 40.00
Tulip, pitcher, 4" h 40.00
Two Birds Over Heart, cake stand, 11" d 80.00
Two Birds Over Heart, plate, 11" d 80.00
Two Women Under Tree, desk basket, 5" h 50.00

PENS & PENCILS

Fountains pens are far more collectible than mechanical pencils. While a few individuals are beginning to collect ballpoint pens, most are valued by collectors more for their advertising than historical importance. Defects, e.g., dents, mechanical damage, missing parts, or scratches, cause a rapid decline in value. Surprisingly, engraved initials, a monogram, or name has little impact on value.

Lewis Waterman developed the fountain pen in the 1880s. Parker, Sheaffer, and Wahl–Eversharp refined the product. Conklin, Eversharp, Moore, Parker, Sheaffer, Wahl, and Waterman were leading manufacturers. Reynolds introduction of the ballpoint pen in late 1945 signaled the end for the nib fountain pen.

Sampson Mordan patented the mechanical pencil in 1822. Early mechanical pencils used a slide action mechanism. It was eventually replaced by a spiral mechanism. Wahl–Eversharp developed the automatic "click" mechanism used on pens as well as pencils.

Fountain pen values rose dramatically from the late 1970s through the early 1990s. Many of these values were speculative. The speculative bubble burst in the mid–1990s. Today, prices are extremely stable with common fountain pens a very difficult sell.

References: George Fischler and Stuart Schneider, *Fountain Pens and Pencils,* Schiffer Publishing, 1990; Regina Martini, *Pens & Pencils: A Collector's Handbook,* Schiffer Publishing, 1996; Stuart

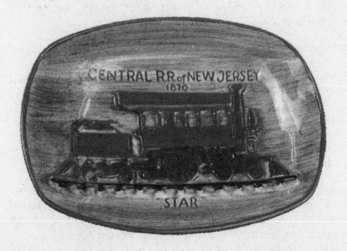

Plaque, commemorative, Central R.R. of New Jersey, _Star,_ 1870, 7⅞" l, $50.00.

Schneider and George Fischler, *The Illustrated Guide To Antique Writing Instruments, Second Edition,* Schiffer Publishing, 1997.

Periodical: *Pen World Magazine,* PO Box 6007, Kingwood, TX 77325.

Collectors' Clubs: American Pencil Collectors Society, 2222 S Millwood, Wichita, KS 67213; Pen Collectors of America, PO Box 821449, Houston, TX 77282.

Pen, Durabilt Ribbon, black pearl marbleized, gold–filled trim, lever filled, 1930	$ 50.00
Pen, Gold Medal, blue marbleized, gold–filled trim, lever filled, 1934	225.00
Pen, Grieshaber #016, Ambassador, burgundy, gold–filled trim, lever filled, 1929	250.00
Pen, maroon, stainless steel cap, chrome–plated trim, 1950	32.00
Pen, Parker, Blue Diamond Vacumatic, gold pearl stripes, 1940	90.00
Pen, Parker, Hopalong Cassidy, black plastic and silvered metal, 3–D plastic portrait, c1950, 6" l	50.00
Pen, Parker, Parkette, red, nickel silver cap, chromium–plated trim, lever filled, 1951	20.00
Pen, Sheaffer's, emerald pearl stripes, 1939	60.00
Pen, Sheaffer's, #74TR Lifetime, black, gold–filled trim, lever filled, 1928	150.00
Pen, Wahl–Eversharp Gold Seal Doric, black, gold–filled trim, lever filled, 1931	300.00
Pen, Waterman, Corinth Taperite, blue, chrome cap, gold–filled trim, lever filled, 1949	50.00
Pen, Waterman, Ideal #452, SS, 1925	150.00
Pen/Pencil Combination, Diamond Medal Diplomat, black and green pearl marbleized, gold–filled trim, lever filled, 1932	350.00
Pen/Pencil Combination, Sheaffer's, 5–30, black, gold–filled trim, lever filled, 1936	225.00
Pencil, mechanical, American Foundry and Mfg Co, St. Louis, MO, red, white, and blue, 1950s	50.00
Pencil, mechanical, Kendall Oil adv, "The 2000 Mile OIl," metal and plastic	15.00
Pencil, mechanical, Secretary Pen Co, Elsie, ©Borden Co, 1930–40, 5" l	60.00
Pencil, "Remember Pearl Harbor, United We Stand, We Will Win," red, white, and blue plastic, local business sponsor adv, 5" l	65.00
Pencil, repeating, Eversharp, dark blue, gold–filled trim, 1941	50.00

Pens, top: Gold Medal #636, black, gold–filled trim, lever filled, 1937, $75.00; bottom: Gold Medal #437, marbleized vein gray pearl, gold–filled trim, lever filled, 1937, $85.00.

Pencil, mechanical, Eagle Pencil Co #1025, 1939 New York World's Fair souvenir, wood, orig box, $40.00.

PEPSI–COLA

Caleb D. Bradham, a pharmacist and drug store owner in New Bern, North Carolina, developed "Brad's Drink," a soda mix, in the mid–1890s. By 1898, Brad's Drink had become Pepsi–Cola. By 1902 Bradham was promoting Pepsi–Cola on a full–time basis. Two years later he sold his first franchise.

In 1910 the Pepsi–Cola network consisted of 250 bottlers in 24 states. Investing in the sugar market, Pepsi–Cola found itself in deep financial difficulties when the market collapsed immediately following World War I. Roy Megargel, a Wall Street financier, rescued and guided the company out of its difficulties. Pepsi–Cola also survived a second bankruptcy in 1931.

In 1933 Pepsi–Cola's fortunes soared when the company doubled its bottle size and held its price to a nickel. Walter Mack (1938 to 1951) provided the leadership that enabled Pepsi to challenge Coca–Cola for the number one spot in the soda market. "Pepsi–Cola Hits The Spot, Twelve Full Ounces That's A Lot" was one of the most popular advertising jingles of the 1950s.

Pepsi Co., a division of Beatrice, enjoys a worldwide reputation, outselling Cola–Cola in a number of foreign countries. This is one reason why many foreign buyers have an interest in Pepsi–Cola memorabilia.

Beware of a wide range of Pepsi–Cola reproductions, copycats, fantasy items, and fakes. The 1970s Pepsi and Pete pillow, a Pepsi double bed quilt, and a 12" high ceramic statute of a woman holding a glass of Pepsi are a few examples.

Collectors place little secondary market value on contemporary licensed products.

References: James C. Ayers, *Pepsi–Cola Bottles Collectors Guide,* RJM Enterprises, 1995; Everette and Mary Lloyd, *Pepsi–Cola Collectibles,* Schiffer Publishing, 1993; Bill Vehling and Michael Hunt, *Pepsi–Cola Collectibles, Vol. 1* (1990, 1993 value update), *Vol. 2* (1990, 1992 value update), and *Vol. 3* (1993, 1995 value update), L–W Book Sales.

Collectors' Club: Pepsi–Cola Collectors Club, PO Box 1275, Covina, CA 91722.

Apron, 1940s	$ 35.00
Bank, composition, 1940, 3 x 3½"	110.00
Blotter, "Sip Ahoy!," 1941	90.00
Booklet, *Hospitality Recipes Out of a Pepsi–Cola Bottle,* 1940s	20.00
Bottle, 1958, 20" h	155.00
Calendar, 1948, winter scene, 15 x 20"	55.00

Clock, light up, yellow face, 1950s, $325.00.

Calendar, 1954, woman with hands on hips, 13 x 16".... **90.00**
Can, aluminum, lift tab, "Seasons Greetings" **5.00**
Can, first space flight commemorative, Jul 1995 .... **20.00**
Carrier, cardboard, 1951 .... **20.00**
Carrier, metal, 1950......................... **35.00**
Carrier, wood, 1951......................... **40.00**
Clock, glass face, "Drink Pepsi Cola Ice Cold," 1951,
    15" d **185.00**
Clock, plastic, counter top, light up, "Please Pay
    Cashier," 1970s **50.00**
Cooler, vinyl, 2–bottle carrier, opener, 1950s **60.00**
Cup Holder, Bakelite, cone shape, 1943............. **85.00**
Dart Board, 14 x 18" **85.00**
Dispenser, musical "Jingle Pump," 1948 .... **235.00**
Glass, 10 oz, 1940s **10.00**
Jigsaw Puzzle, 1970s............................ **8.00**
Kite, Mary Poppins **90.00**
Letterhead, Pepsi Cola Bottling Company, Jackson,
    Tennessee, 1940s **10.00**
Lighter, figural bottle, 1941 .... **25.00**
Magazine Tear Sheet, Lizabeth Scott holding bottle,
    1940s **15.00**
Matchcover, "Bigger And Better" **10.00**
Menu Board, cardboard, "Pepsi–Cola Order Of The
    Day," 1945, 13 x 20" **275.00**
Menu Board, tin, "Drink Pepsi–Cola 12 Ounces 5¢,"
    1939, 20 x 30"........................... **200.00**
Pencil Clip, 1950s................................ **4.00**
Radio, figural bottle, Bakelite, orig decals, 1947,
    24" h **280.00**
Radio, transistor, 1950s, 6³⁄₄" h **140.00**
Ruler, wood, c1930............................... **8.00**
Salt and Pepper Shakers, pr, ceramic, 1940........... **185.00**
Sign, diecut cardboard, Santa holding Pepsi bottle,
    Norman Rockwell art, 1970s, 18" h **70.00**
Sign, cardboard, "Now At Our Fountain Pepsi Cola
    Big 10 oz Glass," 1940, 6 x 11" **60.00**
Sign, cardboard, "Think young...say Pepsi please,"
    man and woman holding bottle and darts, 1960s,
    25 x 37" **80.00**

Sign, paper, "Drink Pepsi Ice Cold," 1940s, 20 x 65".... **110.00**
Soda Jerk Cap, canvas, c1940 .... **45.00**
Syrup Can, metal, "Bigger And Better Pepsi–Cola
    Nickel Drink – Worth A Dime," 1930s, 5 gal **85.00**
Toy, dispenser, plastic **30.00**
Toy, truck, tin and plastic, 1970s, 3¹⁄₂" l **10.00**
Tray, Coney Island scene, 1955, 12" d **30.00**
Watch, Waltham, 1950s........................ **120.00**

AUCTION PRICES

Gary Metz's Muddy River Trading Co. Spring Auction & Trading Convention, May 3, 1997.

Bottle Display, diecut cardboard, "Pepsi–Cola
    Double Size, 5¢," 1930s, with refilled and
    recapped 1930s Pepsi bottle.................. **650.00**
Cash Register Topper, cardboard, "Purity...
    Pepsi–Cola...In The Big, Big Bottle" on front,
    identifying counterfeit currency on back, red,
    white, and blue, late 1930s/early 1940s, ... **550.00**
Dispenser, counter top, probably mfg by Multiplex,
    1950s **525.00**
Door Handle, "Enjoy Pepsi–Cola, Bigger, Better,"
    dark blue, red, and white, c1940s.............. **145.00**
Sign, button, celluloid, "Ice Cold Pepsi–Cola Sold
    Here," red, white, and blue, late 1930s/early
    1940s, 9" d **425.00**
Sign, silk screen and decals on glass, wood base,
    bottle cap, "20¢, 10¢," 1950s–60s **210.00**
Thermometer, porcelain, rect, bottle, blue ground,
    white rim, late 1930s/early 1940s, 16" h........ **400.00**

PERFUME BOTTLES

Perfume manufacturers discovered that packaging, especially the bottle, is almost as important a selling factor for a perfume as its scent. Coty contracted with Lalique to produce exquisitely designed bottles for many of its perfumes. Many Czechoslovakian perfume bottles manufactured between the 1920s and 1960s are architectural miniatures reflecting the very best in the design styles of the eras.

A perfume bottle is a bottle with a stopper, often elongated, that serves as an applicator. A cologne bottle is usually larger than a perfume bottle. Its stopper also serves as an applicator. An atomizer is a bottle with a spray mechanism.

After a period of speculation and rapidly escalating prices in the 1980s and early 1990s, perfume bottle prices have stabilized, especially for common and middle range examples. Large countertop display bottles enjoyed a brief speculative price run in the early 1990s. They are tough sells today, largely because most collectors consider them overvalued.

References: Joanne Dubbs Ball and Dorothy Hehl Torem, *Commercial Fragrance Bottles,* Schiffer Publishing, 1993; Glinda Bowman, *Miniature Perfume Bottles,* Schiffer Publishing, 1994; Jacquelyne Jones–North, *Commercial Perfume Bottles, Third Edition,* Schiffer Publishing, 1996; Tirza True Latimer, *The Perfume Atomizer: An Object With Atmosphere,* Schiffer Publishing, 1991; Jeri Lyn Ringblum, *A Collector's Handbook of Miniature Perfume Bottles: Minis, Mates and More,* Schiffer Publishing, 1996.

Collectos' Clubs: International Perfume Bottle Assoc, PO Box 529, Vienna, VA 22180; Mini–Scents, 7 St John's Rd, West Hollywood, CA 90069.

Atomizer, black amethyst, art glass, goldstone spider web dec, no bulb, DeVilbiss . . . . $ 80.00

Atomizer, gold ground, enameled floral dec, clear blue glass stemmed base, Czechoslovakian 125.00

Atomizer, lavender transparent, Czechoslovakian, 3½" h 40.00

Atomizer, pale blue, enameled pink rose, yellow base, Czechoslovakian, 6" h 120.00

Atomizer, red, mottled colors, Czechoslovakian, 7½" h 65.00

Atomizer, stippled gold, opaque jade, orig silk–lined box, Cambridge 135.00

Atomizer, sapphire blue, gold flowers, leaves, and swirls, melon ribbed body, orig gold top and bulb, Moser, 4½" h 250.00

Atomizer, yellow, blue band, white enamel dec, Czechoslovakian, 6" h 40.00

Cologne, amber, Czechoslovakian, 4¼" h 55.00

Cologne, applied vertical cranberry ribbing, elaborate flower form cranberry and clear stopper, Pairpoint, 8" h 110.00

Cologne, blue transparent, stopper, Czechoslovakian, 3½" h 85.00

Cologne, chintz, paperweight stopper, Nash Glass 225.00

Cologne, clear, panel cut, matching stopper, Baccarat 75.00

Cologne, cobalt blue overlay, thousand eye, faceted base, matching stopper, 4½" h 110.00

Cologne, sterling silver overlay, clear ground 150.00

Perfume, amethyst, stopper with dancing girl throwing flowers dec, Czechoslovakian, 3½" h 175.00

Perfume, clear ribbed, blue cut fan stopper, Czechoslovakian 5¼" h, ... 130.00

Perfume, cranberry, white enameled girl dec, clear ball stopper, Mary Gregory, 4⅝" h 165.00

Perfume, crystal, brass and jewel ornamentation stopper, Czechoslovakian, 2¼" h 75.00

Perfume, crystal, brass and jewel top with dangling beads, Czechoslovakian, 2¼" h 80.00

Perfume, molded and frosted, gray, acid–stamped "Baccarat/France," 6⅜" h 635.00

Perfume, pink, stopper, Czechoslovakian, 3½" h 80.00

Perfume, Sirenes, frosted mermaids with traces of gray patine, molded signature on base, no cov, Rene Lalique, 5½" h 250.00

Scent, flattened globe form, silver hinged rim and screw cap mkd "Black, Starr & Frost," Agate, 3" h 250.00

Scent, ivory, carved, figural, woman, holding basket of flowers in one hand, fan in other, polychrome dec, Japanese, 3¾" h 85.00

Scent, ivory, carved, gourd shape, miniature, Oriental, 1½" h 65.00

Scent, multicolored jewels, enameled top, Czechoslovakian 100.00

Scent, opalescent, blown, cast pewter lid 165.00

Vinaigrette, cut glass, cobalt blue, yellow flashing, sterling overlay, emb sterling cap, 3⅞" h 125.00

PEZ

Eduard Haas, an Austrian food manufacturer, developed the PEZ formula in 1927. He added peppermint (Pffefferminz in German) oil to a candy formula, pressed it into small rectangular pellets, and sold it as an adult breath mint and a cigarette substitute.

World War II halted the production of PEZ. When it reappeared in the late 1940s it was packaged in a rectangular dispenser. An initial foray into the United States market in 1952 was only modestly successful. Evaluating the situation, Haas added fruit flavors and novelty dispensers, thus enabling PEZ to make a major impact on the children's candy market.

Because the company carefully guards its design and production records, information regarding the first appearance of a particular dispenser and dispenser variations is open to interpretation. PEZ Candy, Inc., is located in Connecticut. A second, independent company with distribution rights to the rest of the world, including Canada, is located in Linz, Austria. Although the two cooperate, it is common for each company to issue dispensers with different heads or the same dispenser in different packaging.

There are three basic types of dispensers—generic, licensed, and seasonal. New dispensers appear regularly. Further, the company is quite willing to modify an existing design. The Mickey Mouse dispenser has gone through at least a dozen changes.

Pez has been made in Austria (current), Czechoslovakia (closed), Germany (closed), Hungary (current), Mexico (closed), United States (current), and Yugoslavia (current). Plants in Austria, China, Hong Kong, Hungary, and Slovenia make dispensers.

References: Richard Geary, *More PEZ For Collectors,* Schiffer Publishing, 1995; Richard Geary, *PEZ Collectibles,* Schiffer Publishing, 1994; David Welch, *Collecting Pez,* Bubba Scrubba Publications, 1994.

Newsletter: *PEZ Collector's News,* PO Box 124, Sea Cliff, NY 11579.

Atomizer, Baccarat, amethyst panels, clear cut daisies, acid–etched mark, 5⅞" h, $110.00.

Angel, with feet . . . . $ 25.00
Annie, 1970s 20.00
Barney Bear, 1980s 10.00

Baseball Glove, 1960s 100.00
Blob Octopus, 1960s 70.00
Boy With Hat, Pez Pal, 1960–79 . . . . 10.00
Bugs Bunny, with feet, 1979 . . . . 6.00
Bullwinkle, 1960s 150.00
Captain America, black, visor 50.00
Cat, derby 40.00
Charlie Brown 5.00
Clown, with collar 40.00
Cockatoo, Kooky Zoo, 1970s 10.00
Cool Cat 40.00
Crocodile, Kooky Zoo, 1970s 30.00
Dalmatian 20.00
Dead Head Dr. Skull, 1960s 1.00
Dog, Merry Melody Maker 20.00
Dumbo, blue head, with feet 20.00
Easter Bunny, color variation, entirely in pink, test
    mold bunny, 1990 . . . . 120.00
Elephant, aqua hair 170.00
Foghorn Leghorn 20.00
Fozzie Bear, Sesame Street 1.00
Goofy, removable nose and teeth 35.00
Happy Bear, 1970s 10.00
Icee Bear, with feet 8.00
Incredible Hulk, Super Heroes, 1970s 5.00
Indian Brave, dark face 150.00
Lamb 1.00
Li'l Bad Wolf, Disney, 1960s 5.00
Mama Giraffe, 1970s 20.00
Monkey, Merry Melody Maker 15.00
Moo Moo Cow, Kooky Zoo, 1960s 20.00
Mowgli, with feet 15.00
Mr. Ugly Scrooge, 1960s 1.00
Orange, crazy fruit, 1970s 40.00
Panda, Merry Melody Maker 5.00
Peter Pez 5.00
Pinocchio, 1950s 12.00
Pirate 40.00
Policeman 20.00
Pony, orange 65.00

Practical Pig, Disney, 1960s 10.00
Raven, Kooky Zoo, 1970s 10.00
Road Runner 5.00
Robot, blue, c1950, 3½" h 75.00
Rudolph the Red–Nosed Reindeer, 1960s 5.00
Silver Glow 10.00
Snowman 10.00
Space Gun, red, 1980s 55.00
Speedy Gonzalez 10.00
Thor, Super Heroes, 1970s 60.00
Truck, cab #1, single rear axle, 1960s 10.00
Whistle, 1980s 2.00
Winnie the Pooh 20.00
Zorro, with logo 50.00

PFALTZGRAFF

Pfaltzgraff is named after a famous Rhine River castle, still standing today, in the Pfalz region of Germany. In 1811 George Pfaltzgraff, a German immigrant potter, began producing salt-glazed stoneware in York, Pennsylvania.

The Pfaltzgraff Pottery Company initially produced stoneware storage crocks and jugs. When the demand for stoneware diminished, the company shifted its production to animal and poultry feeders and red clay flower pots. The production focus changed again in the late 1940s and early 1950s as the company produced more and more household products, including its first dinnerware line, and giftwares.

In 1964 the company became The Pfaltzgraff Company. Over the next 15 years, Pfaltzgraff expanded via construction of a new manufacturing plant and distribution center at Thomasville, North Carolina, the purchase of the Stangl Pottery of Trenton, New Jersey, and the acquisition of factories in Dover, Aspers, and Bendersville, Pennsylvania. Retail stores were opened in York County, Pennsylvania; Flemington, New Jersey; and Fairfax, Virginia.

References: Susan and Al Bagdade, *Warman's American Pottery and Porcelain,* Wallace–Homestead, Krause Publications, 1994; Harvey Duke, *The Official Price Guide to Pottery and Porcelain, Eighth Edition,* House of Collectibles, 1995; Harry L. Rinker, *Dinnerware of the 20th Century: The Top 500 Patterns,* House of Collectibles, 1997.

America, baker, rect, 14⅛" l . . . . $ 30.00
America, cereal bowl, 5⅝" d 6.00
America, creamer and sugar, cov 22.00
America, cup and saucer 5.00
America, dinner plate 7.00
America, salad plate 4.00
Christmas Heirloom, creamer and sugar, cov 22.00
Christmas Heirloom, cup and saucer 8.00
Christmas Heirloom, dinner plate 8.00
Christmas Heirloom, salt and pepper shakers, pr 12.00
Gourmet, ashtray, 9¼" d 5.00
Gourmet, cereal bowl, 5⅝" d 4.00
Gourmet, creamer and sugar, cov 15.00
Gourmet, cup and saucer 6.00
Gourmet, dinner plate 7.00
Gourmet, mug 3.00
Gourmet, salad plate, 6⅞" d 5.00
Gourmet, tray, 14⅝" l 17.00

Left: Tweety Bird, 4¾" h, Austria, $10.00; right: Sylvester, 4¼" h, Hong Kong, $10.00.

Yorktowne, dinner plate, 10¹/₄" d, $4.00.

Gourmet, vegetable bowl, oval, divided, 12³/₈" l **12.00**
Heritage, baker, rect, 14³/₈" l **10.00**
Heritage, creamer and sugar, cov **18.00**
Heritage, cup and saucer **7.00**
Heritage, dinner plate, 10³/₈" d **5.00**
Heritage, gravy boat and underplate **13.00**
Heritage, mug, 4¹/₄" h **5.00**
Heritage, platter, oval, 12" l **10.00**
Heritage, salad bowl, 9⁷/₈" d **12.00**
Heritage, salad plate, 6³/₄" d **4.00**
Heritage, salt and pepper shakers, pr **12.00**
Heritage, soup bowl, 8⁵/₈" d **8.00**
Heritage, vegetable bowl 7" d **9.00**
Village, butter dish, cov, ¼ lb **15.00**
Village, creamer **10.00**
Village, cup and saucer **8.00**
Village, dinner plate **8.00**
Village, platter, oval, 14¹/₈" l **12.00**
Village, salad plate, 7" d **4.00**
Village, sugar, cov **12.00**
Windsong, bread and butter plate **6.00**
Windsong, cup and saucer **10.00**
Windsong, dinner plate **12.00**
Yorktowne, cup and saucer **4.00**
Yorktowne, luncheon plate, 8¹/₂" d **4.00**
Yorktowne, platter, 12" d **7.00**
Yorktowne, salad plate, 7" d **2.50**
Yorktowne, salt and pepper shakers, pr **7.00**
Yorktowne, soup bowl, 6" d **2.00**

PHOENIX BIRD CHINA

Phoenix Bird pattern ware was extremely popular in the United States in the period between World War I and World War II. The pattern features a Phoenix Bird facing back over its left wing, its chest spotted, and wings spread upward. Although blue and white is the dominant color scheme, pieces have been found in celedon (green).

Phoenix Bird was manufactured through hand painting and using the transfer process. Pieces with a cloud and mountain bor-

der are the most common. Pieces with a heart–like border are known as HO–O for identification purposes.

There are a number of Phoenix Bird pattern variations: (1) Firebird with its downward tail, (2) Flying Dragon typified by six Chinese characters and a pinwheel–like design, (3) Flying Turkey with no spots on its chest and one wing only partially visible, (4) Howo with no feet and a peony–like flower, and (5) Twin Phoenix with two birds facing each other.

Phoenix Bird china was available in a wide variety of markets, e.g., five and dime stores, mail–order catalogs, wholesale catalogs, and retail stores. Grocery stores, magazines, and others used select pieces as premiums.

Phoenix Bird pieces are found with a variety of marks. Most manufacturers trademarked their pieces during the 1920s and 30s. Unfortunately, World War II destroyed the records that would identify many of these marks.

Myott & Son, an English firm, used the Phoenix Bird to decorate a line of earthenware products in the 1930s. Japanese Phoenix Bird is porcelain. Beginning in the 1970s many new pieces of Phoenix Bird arrived on the market. The shapes are more modern, the blues more brilliant, and most lack an identifying backstamp.

References: Joan Collett Oates, *Phoenix Bird Chinaware, Book 1* (1984), *Book II* (1985), *Book III* (1986), *Book 4* (1989), 1996 value update, published by author.

Collectors' Club: Phoenix Bird Collectors of America, 685 S Washington, Constantine, MI 49042.

After Dinner Cup and Saucer, unmkd, c1930s . . . . **$ 18.00**
Berry Bowl, HO–O, mkd "Made in Japan," 5¹/₂" d **25.00**
Breakfast Plate, English **35.00**
Butter Dish, cov, handled, mkd "Made in Japan,"
  8³/₈" d, 4" h **85.00**
Buttermilk Pitcher, thumb–lug on handle, mkd
  "Japan," 6³/₈" h **80.00**
Cake Tray, mkd "Japan," 9⁷/₈" d **60.00**

Sugar, cov, $35.00.

Children's Playtime Cake Tray, mkd "Made in Japan,"
   6¼" d **35.00**
Creamer and Sugar, cov, mkd "Maruta" and "Made in
   Occupied Japan," 1945–52 . . . . **35.00**
Dinner Plate, 9¾" d **50.00**
Luncheon Plate, unmkd, 8⅜" d **35.00**
Platter, HO–O, unmkd, 15 x 10¾" **125.00**
Teapot, cov, indented shoulder and handle, mkd
   "Made in Japan," 5½" h, 8" w **55.00**
Teapot, cov, Q–shaped handle, mkd "M" and
   "Japan," 4" h, 8" w **70.00**
Teapot, cov, thumb–lug on handle, mkd "Made in
   Japan," 4½" h, 9" w **70.00**
Vegetable Dish, oval, birds on sides of dish, mkd "M"
   and "Made in Japan," 7⅝ x 6" **35.00**

Vase, pale green frosted ground, relief molded berries and branches, 9½" h, $130.00.

PHOENIX GLASS

In 1880 Andrew Howard founded the Phoenix Glass Company in Phillispburg (later Monaca), Pennsylvania, to manufacture glass tubes for the new electrical wires in houses. Phoenix bought J. A. Bergun, Charles Challinor's decorating business, in 1882. A year later Phoenix signed a contract with Joseph Webb to produce Victorian art glass.

Phoenix began producing light bulbs in the early 1890s. In 1893 Phoenix and General Electric collaborated on an exhibit at the Columbian Exposition.

Phoenix glass experienced four major fires during the course of its history—1884, 1895, 1964, and 1978. Each time the company rebuilt.

In 1933 the company introduced its Reuben and Sculptured lines. Phoenix acquired the Co–Operative Flint molds in 1937. Using these molds, Phoenix began manufacturing Early American, a pressed milk glass line in 1938.

In 1970 Anchor Hocking acquired Phoenix Glass. The construction of Phoenix's new plant coincided with the company's 100th anniversary in 1980. In 1987 Newell Corporation acquired Anchor Hocking.

Reference: Jack D. Wilson, *Phoenix & Consolidated Art Glass, 1926–1980*, Antique Publications, 1989.

Collectors' Club: Phoenix & Consolidated Glass Collectors, PO Box 81974, Chicago, IL 60681.

Ashtray, triangular, white ground, relief molded pray-
   ing mantis . . . . **$ 40.00**
Cigarette Box, cov, blue ground, sculptured white
   flowers, 4½" d, 3½" h **70.00**
Dish, cov, oval, amber ground, sculptured lotus blos-
   soms and dragonflies, 8½" l **90.00**
Pitcher, green and gold, relief molded water lilies **400.00**
Planter, white ground, relief molded green lion,
   3¼" h **80.00**
Plate, yellow ground, relief molded dancing nudes,
   8¼" d **60.00**
Plate, frosted and clear ground, relief molded cher-
   ries, 8½" d **50.00**
Tumbler, yellow ground, relief molded dancing nudes **35.00**
Vase, cream ground, relief molded pink owls, 6" h **85.00**
Vase, white ground, relief molded gilted roses, 9½" h . . . **120.00**

PHOTOGRAPHS

The earliest attempts to project images involved the camera obscura, a device known to the Greeks and Romans. The Scientific Revolution of the 17th century, especially in chemistry, paved the way for capturing images on plate and film.

In 1830 J. M. Daugerre of France patented a process consisting of covering a copper plate with silver salts, sandwiching the plate between glass for protection, and exposing the plate to light and mercury vapors to imprint the image. The process produced Daguerreotypes.

Fox Talbot of Britain patented the method for making paper negatives and prints (calotypes) in 1841. Frederick Scott Archer introduced the wet collodion process in 1851. Dr. Maddox developed dry plates in 1871. When George Eastman produced roll film in 1888, the photographic industry reached maturity.

Cartes de visite (calling card) photographs, roughly measuring 2¼" x 3¼", were patented in France in 1854, flourished from 1857 to 1910, and survived into the 1920s. In 1866 the cabinet card, roughly measuring 4" x 5" and mounted on a 4½" x 6" card, first appeared in England. The format quickly spread to the United States. It was the preferred form by the 1890s.

The family photo album with its head and shoulder images of the larger nucleated family, was second only to the Bible in importance to late 19th and early 20th century families. As Kodak and other inexpensive cameras gained in popularity, the family photograph album shifted to one filled with pictures taken on family vacations and outings. The principal problem with family album photographs is that the vast majority are unidentified as to person, place, or time. As a result, the image value is minimal.

Americans, especially those living between 1920 and 1940, loved photographs. Professional photographers produced and sold "art" folios. Two post–1945 developments produced profound changes. The 35mm "slide" camera and home video equipment decreased the importance of the photographic print. One positive development was the lowering of the cost of color prints to the point where they are cheaper today than black and white prints.

Before discarding box after box of family photographic prints, check them carefully. A photograph showing a child playing with a toy, riding a bicycle or in a vehicle, or dressed in a costume or an adult at work, in military garb, or shopping in a store has value. Value is modest, often only a few dollars. Collectors primarily want black and white. Since color prints and slides deteriorate over time, most collectors will not purchase them.

References: Norman E. Martinus and Harry L. Rinker, *Warman's Paper,* Wallace–Homestead, Krause Publications, 1994; Susan Theran, *Prints, Posters & Photographs: Identification and Price Guide,* Avon Books, 1993.

Collectors' Clubs: American Photographic Historical Society, 1150 Avenue of the Americas, New York, NY 10036; The Photographic Historical Society, PO Box 39563, Rochester, NY 14604.

Note: Refer to Nutting–Like Photographs for additional listings.

American Girl in Italy, stamp signature beneath image lower right, titled and dated in pencil on reverse, photographer Ruth Orkin estate stamp on reverse, 1952, 11 x 14"........................ $ 575.00
Armistice Day Celebration, parade float, black and white, 1931, 8 x 10"............................ 30.00
Bette Davis, 1931, 11 x 14"........................ 125.00
Boris Karloff, 1932, 11 x 14"...................... 300.00
Boy with American Flag, carte de visite............. 15.00
Chinese Children, one holding flower, other holding ABC Book of Birds, San Francisco, studio portrait, orig stand–up mount, c1925, 6 x 4"............. 30.00
Citizen Kane, black and white still, RKO, 1941, 8 x 10".. 75.00
Downtown Louisville Kentucky Flood, 1937, 3½ x 5½"...................................... 10.00
Greta Garbo and Charles Bickford, *Anna Christie,* black and white still, MGM, 1930................ 25.00
Indianapolis Motor Speedway, black and white, 1961.... 10.00
James Arness, scene from *Gunsmoke,* black and white, wire service photo, 1966................ 15.00
Lon Chaney, smiling, c1920s...................... 35.00
Man with Motorcycle, 1943....................... 8.00

Peter Miles and Wayde Preston, *Colt .45 "The Escape,"* Warner Bros., black and white still, 8 x 10", $20.00.

Minstrel Group, black face, Chicago, 1920s, 8 x 14"..... 85.00
Mountain Climber, carte de visite.................... 4.00
1946 Chevrolet Sedan, two children in foreground....... 2.50
Portrait of Matisse, chromogenic print, Gisele Freund, photographer's inked signature and chopmark on recto, copyright handstamp on verso, 1940s, printed later, 15¾ x 11¾"........................ 425.00
President Kennedy and daughter Caroline, July 1963, wire service photo.............................. 18.00
Priest, wearing religious garb, carte de visite........... 5.00
Radio Studio, int. view, close–up of equipment, man at microphone, and engineer, black and white, 1920s, 11 x 7".............................. 20.00
Rudolph Valentino, *The Eagle,* black and white still, 1925, 8 x 10"............................... 35.00
Seed Store, int. view with Ferry Seed Co display racks and salespeople, 1920, 5 x 7"................. 10.00
Steamer, *De Grasse,* San Francisco, 1930s, 6 x 9"...... 15.00
Supermarket, int. view, 1950s, 8 x 10".............. 15.00
Tony Orlando and Charro, publicity photo, CBS, 1974..................................... 3.50
Wedding Portrait, bride and bride's maid, bride's veil spread on floor, 1930, 9½ x 7"............... 20.00
Wedding Portrait, bride and groom with best man and bridesmaid, studio portrait, 1935.............. 5.00
Woman on Motorcycle, sepia tones, c1920, 5 x 7"...... 35.00

Child on Riding Toy, black and white, 1920s, 2¾ x 4½", $6.00.

PICKARD CHINA

In 1894 Willard Pickard founded Pickard China. The company began operations in Chicago. Until 1938, the company was a decorating firm, it did not manufacture the ceramics it decorated. Blanks were bought from foreign manufacturers, primarily French prior to World War I and German after the war.

Its fame is due primarily to its painted and gold decorated dinnerware. Most of Pickard's early decorators were trained at Chicago's famed Art Institute. The company's reputation for quality soon attracted top ceramic painters from around the world. Many artists signed their work. Edward S. Challinor, noted for his bird, floral, fruit, and scenic designs, began working at Pickard in 1902 and remained with the company until his death in 1952.

By 1908 Pickard offered more than 1,000 shapes and designs. In 1911 the company introduced gold–encrusted and gold–etched china. Bordure Antique, Deserted Garden, Encrusted Linear, Honeysuckle, and Italian Garden are a few of the company's most popular patterns.

In the early 1930s Pickard began conducting experiments in ceramic manufacturing. In 1938 the company opened its own pottery in Antioch, Illinois. Pickard made china for the Navy during World War II. Decal patterns were introduced after the war. Aurora, Botany, Bouquet, Camillia, Challinor Rose, Chinese Seasons, and Field Flowers are a few examples. Production of hand painted ware decreased after Challinor's death in 1952.

Pickard entered the limited edition bell and plate market in 1970. The company introduced its first Christmas plate in 1976. In 1977 the U.S. Department of State selected Pickard to manufacture the official china services used at embassies and diplomatic missions around the world.

In 1988 Henry A. "Pete" Pickard, the third generation of Pickard management, served as Pickard's president. At that time, the company was the only American china company still managed by its founding family.

References: Susan and Al Bagdade, *Warman's American Pottery and Porcelain,* Wallace–Homestead, Krause Publications, 1994; Alan B. Reed, *Collector's Encyclopedia of Pickard China with Additional Section on Other Chicago China Studios,* Collector Books, 1995.

Collectors' Club: Pickard Collectors Club, 300 E Grove St, Bloomington, IL 61701.

Note: AOG stands for "all over gold."

Bonbon, handled, Daisy AOG, unsgd, late 1920s, 4" sq . . . . **$ 50.00**
Bonbon, pedestal base, Rose medallion on Morning Glory AOG, sgd "Marker," early 1920s, 6" d **250.00**

Cake Plate, scenic, gold rim and handles, sgd "Marker," gold mark, $300.00.

Cake Plate, handled, Golden Pheasant, sgd "E. Challinor," early 1920s, 10" d **375.00**
Dish, perforated handles, encrusted AOG, black border with flower sprays, sgd "Rean," late 1920s, 6¾" d **100.00**
Flower Frog, figural scarf dancer, AOG, unsgd, 1930s, 6" h **160.00**
Mayonnaise Dish, flower shaped, with underplate and ladle, Rose and Daisy AOG, unsgd, 1930s, 6¼" d **140.00**
Nut Cup, hexagonal, blue ext., gold int., unsgd, 1930s, 3" w **70.00**
Nut Dish, 3 part, center perforated handle, Rose and Daisy AOG, unsgd, 1930s, 6¼" d **40.00**
Service Plate, scenic with gold scrolled border, sgd "C. Marker," late 1920s, 10¾" d **350.00**
Vase, Pheasant medallion on white, sgd "E. Challinor," early 1920s **500.00**
Vase, Rose medallion on Morning Glory AOG, sgd "C. Marker," early 1920s, 8" h **300.00**

PICTURE FRAMES

Until the early 1990s most picture frames were sold at auction in boxed lots. This is no longer true. Collectors discovered that picture frames are an excellent indication of changing design styles and that the manufacturing quality of many picture frames, whether handmade or mass produced, was quite high.

Some New York art galleries mounted frame exhibits in an attempt to convince the public that the ornate gilded frames of the late 19th century and early 20th century were objects of art. Prices in the thousands of dollars were common. Most of these so–called objects of art were mass produced.

Frame divide into two basic groups, those designed for use on the wall and those that sit on a tabletop surface. Tabletop frames are the "hot" portion of the market in the late 1990s. Beware of placing too much credence in the prices on frames associated with a licensed movie or television character. Crossover collectors are the group forcing these value upward.

Acrylic, glass inserts . . . . **$ 20.00**
Brass, Art Deco, half circle projection on two sides, easel back, 6 x 8" **100.00**
Brass, Art Nouveau, two oval openings, easel back, 7 x 12" **125.00**
Brass, plain, 2¾ x 3½" **10.00**
Cast Iron, Art Nouveau, oval, gilded, folding stand, openwork scrolls and leaves, 10½ x 8" **50.00**
Celluloid, four–way easel back, 1950s, 8 x 10" **55.00**
Curly Maple, refinished, 16¾ x 20½" **90.00**
Gesso, pine framework, oval, acorns and leaves, gilded inner edge, mahogany stained **65.00**
Glass, beveled, Art Deco, etched floral and leaf design, c1940s, 14½ x 17" **95.00**
Golden Oak, molded, 14¼ x 17½" **20.00**
Mahogany, deep well, black inner edge, 12½ x 15" **40.00**
Mahogany, laminated, folk art pyramid dec, old varnish finish, 9 x 12¾" **45.00**
Rosewood Veneer, beveled, 7⅝ x 8¾" **50.00**
Silver Plated, rough textured finish, 2" wide border, 9¾ x 17½" **100.00**

Tramp Art, rect, chip carved, diamond shape projec-
tions on each corner, 1915, 17¼ x 19½" **45.00**
Walnut, chip carved edge, applied hearts, 16 x 19½" **50.00**
Wood and Glass, Art Deco, black and white diagonal
stripe design **75.00**

PIG COLLECTIBLES

Austrian, English, and German produced bisque and hand painted glazed ceramic pig figurines and planters were popular souvenirs and fair prizes at the turn of the century. So many early banks were in the shape of a pig that "Piggy Bank" became a generic term for a child's bank in the early 20th century.

As an important food source, the pig was featured prominently in farm advertising. Warner Brothers' Porky Pig and Walt Disney's The Three Little Pigs are among the most recognized cartoon characters of the mid–20th century.

A pig collecting craze swept across America in the late 1970s and early 1980s, eventually displaced by cow mania.

Three German bisque pig figurines have been reproduced—a pig by an outhouse, a pig playing a piano, and a pig poking his head out of a large purse. Their darker green color distinguishes them from period pieces. Playmates' 1989 Barnyard Commandos toy series featured the R.A.M.S. versus the P.O.R.K.S. (Platoon of Rebel Killer Swine). It was not the pig's finest hour.

Note: Shawnee Pottery produced Smiley Pig and Winnie Pig kitchen accessories, figural pigs with various decorative motifs.

Ashtray, one pig bowling, one watching, pink with
green, 5" w . . . . **$ 90.00**
Ashtray, two pigs peering into old fashioned Victrola,
4½" w **70.00**
Bank, china, Royal Copley **65.00**
Bank, Porky Pig, plastic **25.00**
Bank, souvenir of Danville, IL, front pink pig sticking
out of bank, back end sticking out other end, gold
pig, yellow pouch, 3½" h **50.00**
Basket, pink pig poking out of basket, orange seal **45.00**
Comic Book, Porky Pig, Whitman, #1408, 1942 . . . . **25.00**

**Cookie Jar/Bank,
Smiley Pig, butterscotch
bottom, Shawnee, #60,
$200.00.**

Figure, pink pig in canoe **75.00**
Figure, Porky Pig, carnival chalk, painted, 1940s, 11" h . . . **38.00**
Figure, two little pigs in caboose **75.00**
Figure, two pigs playing table tennis, "Patience" **85.00**
Figure, two pigs riding in automobile **55.00**
Figure, washtub with pig **55.00**
Gravy, two light pink pigs swinging, porcelain,
English, 4" w **50.00**
Matchsafe, pink pig poking head through fence **60.00**
Pillow, figural **15.00**
Salt and Pepper Shakers, pr, figural, one pig playing
accordion, other playing saxophone, glazed and
painted, mkd "Japan," c1930, 4" h **45.00**
Salt, open, three little pigs around water trough, 2½" h . . . **50.00**
Tape Measure, figural, celluloid **25.00**
Toothpick Holder, pig with mug in hand leaning on
fence, 3" h **55.00**
Toothpick Holder, two little pigs in front of egg, 2¼" h . . . **50.00**

PINBACK BUTTONS

The invention of celluloid made the production of expensive pinback buttons possible. Celluloid lapel pins were used in the 1888 presidential campaign. Some celluloid advertising pieces appeared in the 1890s. In 1896 Whitehead & Hoag Company, Newark, New Jersey, obtained the first button patent.

The period from 1896 through the early 1920s is the golden age of the celluloid pinback button. Hundreds of different manufactures made thousands of different buttons. Bastian Brothers, C. J. Bainbridge Badges and Buttons, St. Louis Button Company, Western Badge and Novelty Company, and Whitehead & Hoag were among the leading manufacturers.

J. Lynch Company of Chicago introduced the first lithograph tin pinback buttons during World War I. Although lithograph buttons could be printed in multiple colors, the process did not produced the wide color range found in celluloid buttons. This mattered little. Lithograph tin buttons were much less costly to produce.

The lithograph tin pinback button played a major role in political campaigns from the early 1930s through the 1980s.

**Bank, plaster, hp features
and floral dec, incised
"©ABCo," 8⁵⁄₈" h, $15.00.**

Advertising lithograph tin buttons became larger. Social cause buttons were dominant in the 1960s, colorful rock group buttons in the 1970s.

As the cost of lithograph tin pinback buttons rose, their popularity diminished. Today pinback buttons are sold primarily by greeting card manufacturers and retail gift shops.

Big Horn Coal, mountain ram emerging from coal
lump, black and white, c1930 . . . . **$ 12.00**

Canal Days, Manayunk, PA, May 17, 1980, blue
ground, photo of canal passing under railroad **5.00**

Golden Guernsey Products, gold and yellow, black
inscriptions, 1930s **12.00**

I'm From Pennsylvania, red and white litho band at
center, blue lettering for PA visitor to Century of
Progress World's Fair, 1933 . . . . **10.00**

IGA Booster Club, red, white, and blue, pink eagle
logo, 1" d **15.00**

Jimmy Carter, "Trust Me," Carter caricature, color,
4" d **12.00**

Joe Di Maggio, black and white portrait, c1940 . . . . **35.00**

Kennedy, "Let's Back Jack," litho, red, white, and
blue, 3½" d **15.00**

King Kong, black and white portrait, red building **15.00**

Mandan Brand Top Hat Turkey, 1930s **20.00**

Mr Pikle Keeps Your Weight Right, red, white, and
green, 1946 . . . . **20.00**

Mr Zip, red, white, and blue, yellow US mailbag,
1960 . . . . **8.00**

Nabisco Shredded Wheat, Top O' The Morning, red
on white, c1940, 1¼" d **22.00**

Nixon, red, white, and blue, photo center, 3½" d **10.00**

Orr's, Santa's Good Behavior Award, red, green,
white **15.00**

Packard–Bell Radio and Televisions, dark red and
white, late 1940s, 2½" d **40.00**

Penn State Homecoming, blue lettering, white
ground, 1978 . . . . **4.00**

Quackenbush's Toyland Santa, red, green, fleshtone **12.00**

Borden's, Uncle Don's Ice Cream Club, red, white, and black, $15.00.

The Constitutionalists, No Third Term, red, white, and blue, ⁷⁄₈" d, $15.00.

Rally Round The Budweiser, white lettering, turquoise
ground, c1970 . . . . **3.00**

Red Cross Macaroni, red, white, and blue, 1930s,
1½" d **28.00**

Red Goose Club Member, brown and yellow, 1930s,
1³⁄₈" d **22.00**

Ronald Reagan, "Reagan For Governor," red, white,
and blue, Reagan photo center, 3½" d **12.00**

Roy Rogers King Of The Cowboys, black and white
portrait, red scarf and hat, 1¾" d **75.00**

Royal Typewriter Co, silvered metal, dark green
enameled symbol, inscribed "Royal, Accuracy
First," 1930s **12.00**

Saint Paul Victory Carnival, 1946 . . . . **15.00**

Santa Portrait, white ground, 1930–40 . . . . **12.00**

Soul Brother, day–glo pink on black, late 1960s **8.00**

Turkey From Henry Ballard's Flock, multicolored,
1½" d **50.00**

TWA Getaway USA '71, brown silhouette of sun-
bathers on white ground **5.00**

Welcome Home POW's, white, blue ground, 1970s **8.00**

Westinghouse Electric & Manufacturing Company,
service award, brass, blue enameled, logo and
inscription, 1930s **12.00**

PINBALL MACHINES

The introduction of Gottlieb's "Baffle Ball" in 1931 marked the beginning of the modern pinball machine era. The Depression turned out to be plus in promoting the popularity of the pinball machine. People were not afraid to invest a nickel for a little fun.

Pre–1940 pinball machines typically had production runs of 25,000 to 50,000 machines. After 1945 production runs fell within the 500 to 2,000 range with an occasional machine reaching 10,000. Some scholars suggest that over 200 manufacturers made over 10,000 models, a result of a machine's high attrition rate.

Several companies released a new model every three weeks during the 1950s.

The pinball machine advanced technologically. The first electric machine appeared in 1933. Bumpers were added in 1936. Flippers arrived in 1947, kicking rubbers in 1950, score totalizers in 1950, multiple player machines in 1954, and solid state electronics in 1977.

Chicago, home to Bally, Gottlieb, and Williams, was the center of pinball manufacture. Machines by D. Gottlieb are considered the best of the pinballs, primarily because of their superior play and graphics.

The entire pinball machine was collected through the mid–1980s. More recently, collecting back glasses has become popular. Manufacturers were not concerned with longevity when making these glasses. Flaking paint is a restoration nightmare.

References: Richard M. Bueschel, *Collector's Guide to Vintage Coin Machines*, Schiffer Publishing, 1995; Heirbert Eiden and Jürgen Lukas, *Pinball Machines*, Schiffer Publishing, 1992; Bill Kurtz, *Arcade Treasures*, Schiffer Publishing, 1994.

Periodicals: *Coin Drop International*, 5815 W 52nd Ave, Denver, CO 80212; *Coin–Op Classics*, 17844 Toiyabe St, Fountain Valley, CA 92708; *PinGame Journal,* 31937 Olde Franklin Dr, Farmington Hills, MI 48334.

Bally, Airway, 1933	$ 320.00
Bally, Coney Island, 1951	350.00
Bally, Harlem Globetrotters, electronic, 1979	300.00
Bally, Lost World, electronic, 1978	350.00
Bally, Moon Shot, 19633	275.00
Bally, Nip–It, 1973	230.00
Bally, Nudgy, electric shaker, 1947	420.00
Bally, Rock Makers, 1968	250.00
Bally, Xenon, electronic, 1980	425.00
Chicago Coin, Spinball, 1948	180.00
Exhibit, Big Parade, 1941	200.00
Genco, Black Gold, replay, 1949	350.00
Genco, Cargo, 1937	375.00
Gottlieb, Aquarius, 1970	325.00

Gottlieb, Sinbad, 1978, $325.00.

Gottlieb, Atlantis, 1975	350.00
Gottlieb, Cow Poke, 1965	475.00
Gottlieb, Daily Races, 1936	375.00
Gottlieb, Duette, replay, first 2–player, 1955	340.00
Gottlieb, Gigi, 1963	380.00
Gottlieb, King of Dinosaurs, 1967	380.00
Gottlieb, Relay, 1934	280.00
Gottlieb, Roller Coaster, 1971	330.00
Gottlieb, Royal Guard, 1968	310.00
Gottlieb, Spin–A–Card, 1969	320.00
Mills Novelty Co, Official, 1932	355.00
Pacific Amusement, Lite–A–Lite, 1934	340.00
Rock–Ola, Flash, 1935	325.00
Rock–Ola, Juggle Ball, countertop, 1932	300.00
United, ABC, first bingo, 1951	410.00
Williams, Army Navy, 1953	310.00
Williams, Firepower, electronic	455.00
Williams, Gusher, 1958	380.00
Williams, Olympic Hockey, 1972	275.00
Williams, Palooka, 1964	300.00
Williams, Touchdown, animated	255.00
Williams, Travel Time, 1973	230.00
Williams, Yanks, baseball, animated, 1948	310.00

PIN–UP ART

Should Charles Dana Gibson, creator of the Gibson Girl in the early 1900s, be credited with creating the first pin–up girl? The answer is no. The Gibson Girl showed little or no flesh. What Gibson did create was the glamour girl, a concept captured by other illustrators of the period, e.g., Howard Chandler Christy, Coles Phillips, and Charles Sheldon.

The minimally clad beauty owes her origin to 1920s film magazines such as *Film Fun* and *Real Screen* whose front covers showed women with a fair amount of exposed skin. Artists such a Cardwell Higgins, George Petty, and Charles Sheldon continued to refine the concept through the 1930s. Petty's first gatefold appeared in *Esquire* in 1939.

Pin–up art reached its zenith in the 1940s. Joyce Ballantyne, Billy DeVorss, Gillete Elvgren, Earl Moran, and Alberto Vargas (the "s" was dropped at Esquire's request) were among the leading artists of the period. Their pin–up girls appeared everywhere— blotters, calendars, jigsaw puzzles, matchcovers, magazine covers, posters, punchboards, etc.

The reign of the pin–up girl ended in the early 1960s when the photograph replaced the artist sketch as the preferred illustration for magazines.

References: Denis C. Jackson, *The Price & ID Guide to Pin–Ups & Glamour Art*, TICN, 1996; Charles G. Martignette and Louis K. Meisel, *The Great American Pin–Up*, Taschen, 1996.

Periodical: *Glamour Girls: Then and Now*, PO Box 34501, Washington, DC 20043.

Newsletter: *The Illustrator Collector's News*, PO Box 1958, Sequim, WA 98382.

Blotter, Bubble Girl, 1950s, 4 x 9"	$ 4.00
Booklet, World's Smallest Pin–up Book, 16 fold–out photos of nude nymphs, vinyl bound, 1955–60	5.50

Calendar, 1933, Earl Moran, woman wearing orange bathing suit, full pad, 1933, 10 x 17" **70.00**

Calendar, 1938, DeVorss, woman wearing bathing suit, full pad, 9 x 14" **42.00**

Calendar, 1940, Petty, monthly Old Gold Cigarettes adv, Petty girl, 1940 . . . . **90.00**

Calendar, 1941, Earl Moran, Out In Front, full pad, 11 x 23" **80.00**

Calendar, 1942, *Esquire*, Varga Girl, plastic spiral binding, horizontal format, verses by Phil Stack, 12 pgs **90.00**

Calendar, 1944, Petty, A Good Hook–Up, full pad, 15 x 8" **62.00**

Calendar, 1946, DeVorss, Jeanne, full pad, 16 x 33" **95.00**

Calendar, 1947, Rolf Armstrong, See You Soon, salesman's sample, September pad, 11 x 23" **45.00**

Calendar, 1948, Willie Pogony, Gone With The Wind, nude at seaside with one foot on inflatable horse, black Scottie looking on, 12 x 19" **75.00**

Calendar, 1950, Medcalf, sgd, Ditzler Paint Auto Body adv, blonde with Scottie dog splashing foot in ocean, Dec only, 14 x 45" **55.00**

Calendar, 1954, Petty Girl, vertical format, verses, 8¼ x 11", 12 pgs **62.00**

Calendar, 1956, MacPherson, color drawing, 9½ x 12½" **38.00**

Calendar, 1959, Rolf Armstrong, So Nice, "Season's Greetings," pad cover, strawberry blonde wearing pink sunsuit **22.00**

Calendar Top, Elvgren, Double Exposure, woman with towel, pad missing, 16 x 20" **60.00**

Calendar Yearbook, 1945, Varga **130.00**

Date Book, Esquire color cov, spiral binding, full color pin–up photos, George Hurrell, ©1943, 5 x 7" . . . **42.00**

Folder, Albine Calendar And Novelty Co, Chicago, IL, 12 pin–up art calendar tops, 1948 . . . . **20.00**

Magazine, *Hollywood Tales*, Vol. 1, #36, full color art, 1930s, 24 pgs **32.00**

Magazine, *Movieland Pin–Ups*, Anita Ekberg cov, 1955 . . . . **20.00**

Note Pad, 1944 calendar on back, 3 x 4½" **8.00**

Playing Cards, Gorgeous Girls, Creative Playing Card Co, full color art, orig box, c1950 . . . . **75.00**

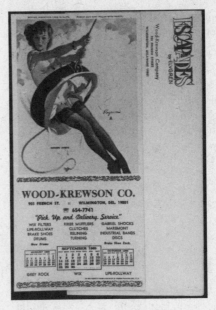

Calendar, 1969, Elvgren, Swingin' Sweeti, folding punch–out, orig envelope, September pad, 4¾ x 10", $15.00.

Playing Cards, Royal Flushes, nudes, large size, orig box **12.00**

Postcard, Earl Moran, Sheer Nonsense, undivided back, printed color, 1940s **12.00**

Poster, Raleigh Tobacco, beautiful brunette, full color, 1939–41 . . . . **16.00**

Print, Rolf Armstrong, brunette in bibbed shorts and yellow shirt, matted and framed, 11 x 14" **32.00**

Print, John La Gatta, The Ziegfield Girl of 1941, 9 x 12" **8.50**

Print, woman sitting on red bench, mkd "Copr C Moss 1947 Litho in USA" **50.00**

Print, Vargas, *Esquire*, Phil Stack verse, WWII, matted, framed, 11 x 14" **65.00**

Program, Vargas, Skating Vanities of 1947, blonde roller skater wearing pink outfit, 8 x 11" **35.00**

PLANTERS PEANUTS

In 1906 Amedeo Obici, known as a peanut specialist, and Mario Peruzzi founded the Planters Nut and Chocolate Company, Wilkes–Barre, Pennsylvania. Initially, the company sold Spanish salted red skins priced at 10¢ a pound.

Planter's fame is based on two things: (1) its whole white, blanched peanut and (2) Mr. Peanut. The Mr. Peanut trademark evolved from a 1916 contest. A young Italian boy submittred a rough sketch of a monocled Peanut figure. Hundreds of Mr. Peanut advertising and promotional items have been issued.

In 1913 Planters built a plant in Suffolk, Virginia. Plants in San Francisco (1921) and Toronto, Canada (1925), followed. In addition to selling its products to wholesalers, Planters opened a chain of stores across the country.

Standard Brands, a division of Nabisco, bought Planters in 1961. When R. J. R. Nabisco was purchased in 1988, the new owners closed the San Francisco and Toronto plants. In 1994 a totally new facility was opened in Suffolk. With the exception of the Peanut Store in Suffolk, all the former peanut stores are either closed or privately owned.

Blotter, Rolf Armstrong, Brown & Bigelow adv, $10.00.

Reference: Jan Lindenberger, *Planters Peanut Collectibles Since 1961: A Handbook and Price Guide,* Schiffer Publishing, 1995.

Collectors' Club: Peanut Pals, PO Box 4465, Huntsville, AL 35815.

Advertising Trade Card, wild animals, c1935, 2 x 2½" . . . $ 4.00
Bank, tin, Planters Sweet N Crunchy Peanuts 5.00
Baseball Cap, cotton, mesh back, Mr Peanut logo 4.00
Beach Ball, blue and yellow, 1974 . . . . 5.00
Beach Towel, cotton, Mr Peanut, 1980s, 56 x 30" 15.00
Belt, leather, Planters logo, 1960s. 25.00
Book, *Mr Peanut's Book of Magic,* 1970s 8.00
Book, *Mr Peanut,* Mr Peanut crossing finish line
   cov, 1970s. 10.00
Book, *Smokey Bear Finds A Friend,* Mr Peanut and
   Smokey cov, 1971 . . . . 8.00
Box, Planters Tavern Nuts, 1970s 10.00
Coaster, leather, logo 15.00
Coloring Book, Mr Peanut & Smokey the Bear, 1973 . . . . . 15.00
Costume, Mr Peanut, plastic mask, cloth outfit 20.00
Display, cardboard, Mr Peanut in nut shell canoe, girl
   with parasol, 1920s, 6 x 9" 450.00
Doll, cloth, Mr Peanut, 1970s 5.00
Ice Cream Scoop, set, metal, orig box, 1985 . . . . 18.00
Jar, yellow, blue, red, and white silk screened design,
   Anchor Hocking, 1966. . . . . 30.00
Key Chain, leather, metal Mr Peanut insert, 2½" h 8.00
Lunch Tote, vinyl, Mr Peanut, days of the week,
   8½ x 10½". 10.00
Manual, *Plant Rules,* Planters Peanuts, Suffolk,
   VA, 1960s 8.00
Matchcover, Planters Dry Roasted, 1970s 18.00
Mug, pewter, Armetale, 5" h. 15.00
Mug, plastic, yellow and white Mr Peanut illus, blue
   ground, white rim and handle, 1978. . . . . 5.00
Neck Tie, clip-on, silver, Mr Peanut logo 8.00
Paint Book, Colorful Story of Peanuts as Told by Mr
   Peanut, 1957, 28 pgs 32.00

Mug, blue plastic, $5.00.

Peanut Butter Maker, plastic, figural Mr. Peanut,
   attachments, orig box, 1976, 12½" h. 18.00
Pencil Holder, green plastic, Mr Peanut Pencil Pack,
   1968 . . . . 40.00
Pennant, felt, Mr Peanut, Ocean City, NJ. 25.00
Planter, plastic, blue, tin-shaped 20.00
Poster, Mr Peanut, 1980 Winter Olympics, 18 x 26" 8.50
Purse, child's, "I'm A Little Peanut," 1970s. 20.00
Radio, figural Mr Peanut, 10¼" h, 1979 . . . . 25.00
Sign, cardboard, 1939 World's Fair. 15.00
Sign, metal, "Planters The Name for Quality!,"
   24 x 12½" 45.00
Tie Pin, enameled Mr Peanut, 1970s. 10.00
Tote Bag, cloth, blue, yellow trim, 18" l 10.00
Travel Mug, insulated, plastic holder, 1994 . . . . 3.00
Tray, metal, square, "Planters Temptation Beyond
   Endurance" 12.00
Volley Ball, rubber, Kick 'n Throw, 1970s, 6½" d 18.00
Waste Basket, metal, Mr Peanut, yellow and white
   lettering, green ground, 1968 . . . . 10.00

PLASTICS

Webster's Ninth New Collegiate Dictionary defines plastic as "any of numerous organic, synthetic, or processed materials that are mostly thermoplastic or thermosetting polymers of high molecular weight and that can be molded, cast, extruded, drawn, or laminated into objects, films, or filaments." There are hundreds of different natural, semisynthetic, and synthetic plastics known.

Collectors focus on three basic plastic types: celluloid, Bakelite, and melamine. Celluloid, made from cellulose nitrate and camphor, is a thin, tough, flammable material. It was used in the late 1880s and through the first four decades of the 20th century to make a wide range of objects from toilet articles to toys. Celluloid's ability to mimic other materials, e.g., amber, ivory, and tortoise shell, made it extremely popular.

In 1913 L. H. Baekeland invented Bakelite, a synthetic resinous material made from formaldehyde and phenol. It proved to be a viable substitute for celluloid and rubber. Easily died and molded,

Bookmark, diecut cardboard, souvenir 1939 New York World's Fair, yellow, black, and white, 6½" h, $20.00.

Bakelite found multiple uses from radio cases to jewelry. Often it was a secondary element, e.g., it was commonly used for handles.

Although injection molding was developed prior to World War II, its major impact occurred during and after the war. Many new plastics, e.g., melamine, were developed to take advantage of this new technology. The 1950s through the 1960s was the golden age of plastic. It was found everywhere, from the furniture in which one sat to the dashboard of a car.

This is a catchall category. It includes objects made from plastic that do not quite fit into other collecting categories.

References: Shirley Dunn, *Celluloid Collectibles Identification & Value Guide,* Collector Books, 1996; Michael J. Goldberg, *Collectible Plastic Kitchenware and Dinnerware: 1935–1965,* Schiffer Publishing, 1995; Bill Hanlon, *Plastic Toys: Dimestore Dreams of the '40s & '50s,* Schiffer Publishing, 1993; Jan Lindenberger, *More Plastics for Collectors: A Handbook & Price Guide,* Schiffer Publishing, 1996; Lyndi Stewart McNulty, *Wallace–Homestead Price Guide To Plastic Collectibles,* Wallace–Homestead, Krause Publications, 1987, 1992 value update; Holly Wahlberg, *Everyday Elegance: 1950s Plastic Design,* Schiffer Publishing, 1994.

Note: For additional listings see Costume Jewelry and Melmac.

Bakelite, ashtray, horse logo, Davies adv . . . . $ 20.00
Bakelite, cigarette box, medallion center with man
   on horse, Art Deco lines, 3 x 4" 25.00
Bakelite, clock, Telechron, black, octagonal 38.00
Bakelite, corn cob holders, orig box 30.00
Bakelite, flashlight, swivel head 20.00
Bakelite, game, Mah–jongg 125.00
Bakelite, bangle bracelet, wide 65.00
Bakelite, brooch, Life Preserver, green 30.00
Bakelite, earrings, pr, hoops, yellow 25.00
Bakelite, link bracelet, orange 135.00
Bakelite, necklace, circles, red, ... 120.00
Bakelite, necklace, fruit, multicolored 95.00
Bakelite, necklace, red heart, celluloid chain 220.00

Bakelite, record player, RCA Victor, Model 45–EY–2, dark brown, 10⁵/₈" w, 8¹/₄" h, $45.00.

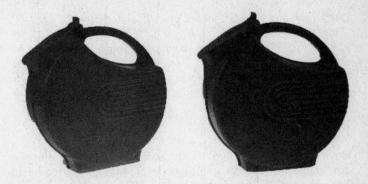

Plastic, refrigerator jugs, Art Deco style, Burrite, The Burroughs Co, Los Angeles, CA, #123, medium green and red, 8¹/₄" h, $5.00 each.

Bakelite, pin, boot 60.00
Bakelite, pin, brown cat 55.00
Bakelite, child's flatware, knife, fork, and spoon, but-
   terscotch handles, price for set 20.00
Bakelite, pencil sharpener, figural Donald Duck 60.00
Bakelite, radio, RCA Victor, police band 65.00
Bakelite, thermometer, key shape, Wildwood, NJ
   souvenir 10.00
Bakelite, tip tray, red 8.00
Catalin, alarm clock, General Electric 50.00
Catalin, radio, Crosley, brown 30.00
Catalin, salt and pepper shakers, pr, rose shape, metal
   mounts 40.00
Celluloid, calculator, mechanical disk, calculates
   costs of gasoline ranging from 34¢ to 44¢ per gal-
   lon, American Art Works, c1940 . . . . 30.00
Celluloid, charm, pig in green overalls, pink cap,
   holding gray trowel, brass loops, Japan, early
   1930s 32.00
Celluloid, folding comb, Art Deco style, cream and
   black 25.00
Celluloid, cuticle cutter, ivory and cream 3.00
Celluloid, bride and groom dolls, Kewpie type, crepe
   paper clothes, 3¹/₄" h, price for pair 42.00
Celluloid, doll, Pammi, part vinyl, orig polyester
   clothes and hat, Effanbee, 1966, 14" h 175.00
Celluloid, magnet, Scotties, black and white, price for
   pair 15.00
Celluloid, rattle, duck shape 12.00
Celluloid, salt and pepper shakers, pr, figural sky-
   scrapers, black and red 25.00
Celluloid, steak knives, ivory handles, set of 6 . . . . 25.00
Celluloid, tape measure, figural lion 30.00
Celluloid, doll, black boy, jointed, 8" h 90.00
Celluloid, toy, hawaiian dancer, windup, 8¹/₂" h 125.00
Plastic, bank, First Federal Savings and Loan 5.00
Plastic, bread box, red and white 20.00
Plastic, canister set, red, white name, Lustro–Ware,
   price for set of 4 . . . . 20.00
Plastic, clock, red case, white insert 10.00
Plastic, clothes sprinkler, mkd "USA Plastic" 8.00

Plastic, salt and pepper shakers, pr, red, white letter-
ing, Lustro–Ware **12.00**
Plastic, shot glasses, painted flamingoes and palm
trees, price for set of 4 . . . . **15.00**
Plastic, silverware tray, pink flecked **5.00**
Plastic, toy, roly–poly, Dutch girl **55.00**

PLAYBOY

Hugh M. Hefner launched the first issue of *Playboy*, featuring the
now famous calendar photograph of Marilyn Monroe, in
December 1953. There was no cover date. Hefner was not certain
the concept would work. *Playboy* grew at a phenomenal rate.

In the early 1960s, Hefner authored "The Playboy Philosophy,"
a series of editorial statements underlining his deep concern for
the rights of the individual in a free society. Hefner founded The
Playboy Foundation as the action arm of this philosophy.

During the 1960s and 70s, Hefner opened a series of Playboy
Clubs, launched several foreign editions, operated several gam-
bling casinos, and organized a Hollywood production company.
Playboy went public in 1971 and was listed on the New York and
Pacific stock exchanges. *Oui* was launched in October 1972.

After four years as a corporate vice president and three as a
member of the Board of Directors, Christie Hefner became president of Playboy Enterprises in 1982. In November 1982 The
Playboy Channel began. In the mid–1980s more than 60 companies were licensed to market products bearing the Playboy,
Playmate, and Rabbit Head trademarks.

Reference: Denis C. Jackson, *The Price & ID Guide to Playboy
Magazines, 3rd Edition,* TICN, 1997.

Collectors' Club: Playboy Collectors Assoc, PO Box 653,
Phillipsburg, MO 65722.

Ashtray, clear, emb rabbit head . . . . **$ 5.00**
Ashtray, clear, Playboy Hotel & Casino, Atlantic City,
1980s **12.00**
Bar Set, 4 pcs, sterling silver, box **25.00**

Cake Pan, aluminum, Stock No. 2105–3025, orig paper label, Wilton, 10¼" w, 15" h, $10.00.

Jigsaw Puzzle, Playboy Playmate Puzzle, American Publishing Co, AP110, 1967, $15.00.

Belt Buckle, round, gold, rabbit head **10.00**
Book, *Playboy Jazz Festival*, hard cov, 1959 . . . . **15.00**
Book, *Twelfth Anniversary Playboy Reader,* hard cov,
1966, 874 pgs **25.00**
Calendar, 1964, spiral bound, 8½" x 12½" **25.00**
Calendar, 1969, desk type, easel back, unused, orig
envelope, 6 x 8" **25.00**
Calendar, 1973, spiral bound, monthly glossy color
Playmate photos, 8¼" x 12½" **20.00**
Car Air Freshener, Playboy logo, black and white **2.00**
Credit Card, The Playboy Club **5.00**
Cup and Saucer, early 1960s **20.00**
Frisbee, 1970s **10.00**
Hand Puppet, Playboy Rabbit, plush. **150.00**
Lighter, chromium, black enameled panels with
white rabbit logo, 2½" h. **45.00**
Magazine, 1957 . . . . **5.00**
Magazine, 1966 . . . . **3.00**
Magazine, 1980 . . . . **3.00**
Matches, wooden, boxed, 1961 . . . . **5.00**
Mug, aluminum, engraved rabbit head, glass bottom,
early 1960s, 5" h **5.00**
Mug, black glass, Femlin in gold, Play club in circu-
lar, 1960s, 6" h **5.00**
Mug, ceramic, black, white rabbit logo. **5.00**
Mug, Thermo–Serv, black, white rabbit head, 6¼" h **5.00**
Playing Cards, Playmate, open and complete, 1971–73 . . . **20.00**
Puzzle, 1967, Miss October, Majken Haugedal, card-
board canister **40.00**
Puzzle, 1970, blonde Playmate centerfold on white
airbag cushion, red carpeting, cardboard canister **28.00**
Puzzle, 1972, Annie Fanny. **50.00**
Puzzle, 1973, Marilyn Monroe. **25.00**
Swizzle Stick, black and white **1.00**
Swizzle Stick, transparent color **3.00**
Wine Glass, long stem, small rabbit head logo **10.00**

PLAYING CARDS

The Chinese are credited with inventing playing cards. However, their approach differs from the traditional European set. Chinese playing cards have four sets of three suits.

The first European playing cards, Swiss in origin, date from 14th century. Shortly thereafter, Tarot cards appeared in Italy. The European playing card concept of four suits quickly spread around the world. Only China and Korea proved immune to the European influence.

Pips (suit signs) vary from country to country. Italian and Spanish cards use clubs, coins, cups, and swords instead of clubs, diamond, hearts, and spades. Court cards also differ. Not every country uses the king, queen, and jack.

Playing cards came to America with the colonists. They were European in origin. The first American playing cards did not arrive on the scene until after the American Revolution. Caleb Bartlett (New York), Thomas Crehore (Dorchester, Massachusetts), David Felt (New York), the Ford (Foord) family (Milton, Massachusetts), and Amos and Daniel Whitney printed some of the first playing cards made in America. A. Dougherty, The New York Consolidated Card Company, and the United States Playing Card Company were the leading American manufacturers of playing cards. U.S. Playing Card introduced its Bicycle Brand in 1885. American card manufacturers are credited with introducing the classic joker, slick finish for shuffling, standard size, and upper corner indexes.

Card collectors specialize. Advertising, children's card games, miniature decks, novelty decks, and souvenir decks are just a few examples. Some collectors only collect one type of card, e.g., jokers. Although play is the primary focus of most playing cards, cards also have been used for fortune telling, instruction, e.g., World War II airplane spotting, and aiding travelers, e.g., a language set. These sets also appeal to collectors.

Always count the cards to make certain you are buying complete decks. American poker decks have 52 cards plus one or two jokers, a pinochle decks have 48 cards, and Tarot decks 78 cards.

Reference: Norman E. Martinus and Harry L. Rinker, *Warman's Paper,* Wallace–Homestead, Krause Publication, 1994.

Collectors' Clubs: Chicago Playing Card Collectors, 1559 West Platt Blvd, Chicago, IL 60626; 52 Plus Joker, 204 Gorham Ave, Hamden, CT 06514; International Playing Card Society, 3570 Delaware Common, Indianapolis, IN 46220.

Note: Prices are for complete poker decks in mint condition.

AAA Welding, monkey . . . . $ 4.00
Ajax Auto Co, Chicago 5.00
Avis 4.00
B F Goodrich 4.00
Belmont Laundry 4.00
Boomtown Wild West, red and white 4.00
Bring Home the Blue Seal Bread, Fred!, man pushing
    shopping cart 3.00
Budweiser 6.00
Camel Cigarettes 4.00
Capital Bakers, the Aristocrat of Breads, loaf of bread 4.00
Caribbean Cruise Lines 12.00
Cedarcrest Realty Company 4.00
Continental Motors 6.00
Coricidin D 12.00

Prosser's Drug Store, Hellertown, PA, pinochle deck, orig box, $4.00.

Delta Air Lines, San Francisco 5.00
Disneyland, Cinderella's castle 4.00
Dolly Madison Ice Cream, red, white, and blue, yel-
    low ground 3.00
Donegal, The Sport Shirt You Live In, brown and
    white 4.00
Dorney Park, Allentown, PA 4.00
Eckerd Drug Stores, black and white 3.00
Eureka Vacuum Cleaner Co, eagle, black, gold, and
    white 3.00
Firestone, red and white 3.00
Ford GT 8.00
Gatorade, red, white, and green 4.00
Genuine Auto Parts, red, white, and blue 4.00
Grandma's Cake, Lantz Bros Baking Co, St Louis,
    MO, woman with parasol 3.00
Kennedy Space Center, Florida 6.00
Kiddie Kookies with Arrowroot 5.00
Krauss' Tasty Meats, pig, red, gold, and white 5.00
Lone Star Beer 6.50
Marlboro 5.00
Mayflower, green and white 4.00
Merchants National Bank & Trust, Indianapolis 4.00
Merit Cigarettes 4.50
Michelob 6.00
Narragansett Lager Beer 6.50
Norwalk 5 Ply Tire, tire 5.50
Overseas National Airways 5.00
Ozark Flies Your Way, Colorado 8.00
Pan American World Airways 6.00
Quick–Way Truck Shovel Co, Denver, Colorado 4.00
Rock River Motors 5.00
Round Lake Centennial Farmers State Bank, Round
    Lake, Minn, 1882–1982 . . . . 6.00
S S Milwaukee Clipper, ocean liner 10.00
Sea World, 1978 . . . . 6.00
The Baltimore Storage Co 2.50
TWA 10.00

Rust–Oleum, poker deck, Brown & Bigelow, orig box, $7.50.

Vantage Cigarettes **4.00**
Washington Monument, Washington, DC **5.00**
Western Airlines **6.00**
Westinghouse, appliance **4.00**
Wild Animal Park, San Diego **5.00**
Winston Rodeo Awards, man riding bucking bronco,
    red, white, and black **15.00**

POCKET KNIVES

Archaeologists have found figural folding knives in Roman excavations. Technically, they are not pocket knives because the pocket had not yet become a standard fixture on garments.

In 1742 Benjamin Huntsman, an English clockmaker from Sheffield, invented a reliable spring steel. Sheffield cutlery manufacturers used it for knife blades and the blades in their finer cutlery items.

The mass production of cheap pocket knives, known as penny knives, occurred in France in the early 1770s. However, most knives were handmade until the middle of the 19th century. It was during the 19th century that standard pocket knife patterns emerged, e.g., Bowie knife, dirk, etc.

American manufacturers such as Samuel Mason and C. W. Platts of the Northfield Knife Company, began making pocket knives in the 1840s. Numerous design, manufacturing, and marketing advances occurred. Collectors consider the period between the 1880s and 1940 as the pocket knife's golden age. American knife manufacturers received favorable tariff protection beginning in the 1890s. Before 1940, the best factory folding knives were actually handmade in a wide variety of designs and with the best material available.

The period between 1945 and the early 1960s is considered a dark age. Many pre–war manufacturers went out of business. A renaissance occurred in the 1970s as individual knife craftsmen began making pocket knives that were more for collecting and display than use. Bob Hayes, Jess Horn, Ron Lake, Jimmy Lile, Paul Pehlmann, Robert Ogg, and Barry Wood were leaders in the craftsman revival. Recently, collector and limited edition knives have flooded the market.

Pocket knives divide into three main groups: (1) utilitarian and functional knives, (2) advertising, character, and other promotional knives, and (3) craftsman knives. Alcas, Case, Colonial, Ka–Bar, Queen, Remington, Schrade, and Winchester are the best known manufacturers of the first group. Aerial Cutlery, Canton Cutlery, Golden Rule Cutlery, Imperial Knife Company, and Novelty Cutlery made many of the knives in the second group.

References: Jacob N. Jarrett, *Price Guide To Pocket Knives, 1890–1970*, L–W Books, 1993, 1995 value update; Bernard Levine, *Levine's Guide To Knives and Their Values, 4th Edition*, Krause Publications, 1997; C. Houston Price, *The Official Price Guide To Collector Knives, Eleventh Edition*, House of Collectibles, 1996; Roy Ritchie and Ron Stewart, *The Standard Knife Collector's Guide, 3rd Edition*, Collector Books, 1997; Jim Sargent, *Sargent's American Premium Guide To Pocket Knives & Razors, Identification and Values, 4th Edition*, Books Americana, Krause Publications, 1995; J. Bruce Voyles, *The International Blade Collectors Association Price Guide to Antique Knives, 2nd Edition*, Krause Publications, 1995.

Periodical: *Blade Magazine*, 700 E State St, Iola, WI 54990.

Collectors' Club: The National Knife Collectors Assoc, PO Box 21070, Chattanooga, TN 37421.

Note: Prices are for pocket knives in mint condition.

Advertising, Gulf . . . . **$ 30.00**
Advertising, St Paul Girl, nickel and silver, 4" l **35.00**
Bulldog, Congress, tobacco etching, celluloid han-
    dle, leaf shield, 3⅞" l **70.00**
Bulldog, Gunstock Jack, pit bull etching, brown bone
    handle, 3½" l **100.00**
Bulldog, Muskrat, dog and coon etching, celluloid
    handle, raccoon shield, 3⅞" l **75.00**
Bulldog, Serpentine Stockman, Oktoberfest etching,
    celluloid handle, beer stein shield, 3⅜" l **50.00**
Bulldog, Stockman, pit bull etching, celluloid handle,
    3¾" l **70.00**
Case, 2137SS, Sodbuster Jr, black composition,
    1970–71 . . . . **35.00**
Case, 2165, Folding Hunter, black composition han-
    dle, 1984 . . . . **60.00**

Camillus, Whittler, Boy Scouts, white handles, 3 blades, BSA #1047, $15.00.

Case, 4100, Melon Tester, white composition handle,
1960–65 . . . . **90.00**
Case, 6292, Texas Jack, bone handle, 1970s, 4" l **30.00**
Case, 6294, Equal End Jack, bone handle, 1940–65 . . . . **175.00**
Case, 6318SS, Premium Stock, bone handle **20.00**
Case, 6333, Baby Premium Stock, Delrin handle. **20.00**
Case, 13031R, electrician's, walnut handle, 3³/₄" l **35.00**
Case, 22087, Serpentine Jack, black composition
handle, 1970s **15.00**
Case, 62087, Serpentine Jack, bone handle,
1965–70 . . . . **20.00**
Case, watch fob, pearl handle **200.00**
Cattaraugus Cutlery, 2586, scout/utility, 2 blade **115.00**
Cattaraugus Cutlery, 10101, florist's, 1 blade **60.00**
Cattaraugus Cutlery, 22119, Dogleg Jack, two blade. **85.00**
Cattaraugus Cutlery, 22772, Equal End Jack, two blade. . . **60.00**
Character, Dick Tracy, blue and white, 2 blades,
3¹/₄" l **115.00**
Character, Tom Mix and Tony, celluloid, black and
white, 3" l **32.00**
Ka–Bar, 2307, lobster, stag handle **65.00**
Ka–Bar, 6233¹/₂, Barlow, Delrin handle, 3¹/₄" l **80.00**
Ka–Bar, 22107, hunter's, folding, stag handle, 5¹/₄" l **75.00**
Ka–Bar, 42027S, office, imitation ivory handle, 3¹/₂" l **80.00**
Ka–Bar, 52217, sailor's, celluloid handle, 4¹/₂" l **30.00**
Ka–Bar, 61103, Bowtie, bone handle **65.00**
Ka–Bar, T–29, fish, celluloid handle, 5" l **50.00**
Remington, R1085, Jack, pyremite handle. **70.00**
Remington, RC090, Barlow, black bone handle. **90.00**
Schrade, 744SS, Senator, sterling handle **240.00**
Schrade, 7434G, Senator Pen, pearl pyralin handle **50.00**
Schrade, 7604W, Lobster Pen, ivory celluloid han-
dle, 2¹/₄" l. **40.00**
Shapleigh IS445, Hardware, Maize, cocobolo han-
dle, 4¹/₈" l. **60.00**
Winchester, 1608, Jack, cocobolo handle, 3¹/₂" l **70.00**
Winchester, 2059, Senator Pen, celluloid handle, 3¹/₈" l . . . **85.00**
Winchester, 2094, Tear Drop Jack, celluloid handle,
3¹/₂" l. **190.00**

POLITICAL & CAMPAIGN

Campaign items are those objects issued during a campaign. While the vast majority of collectors concentrate on material from presidential campaigns, there are collectors who focus on regional and statewide races.

Political items are those objects associated with an individual once they have achieved office. In reality, the category is broadly interpreted to include any object associated with the office winner, before, after, and during his tenure.

Collectors prefer three–dimensional items over two–dimensional material. Material associated with those who won is more desirable than that associated with individuals who lost. While there are third party collectors, their number is small.

The period from the late 1890s through the mid–1960s is the golden age of political and campaign material. Today candidates spend most of their money on television advertising. The 1996 presidential election was noteworthy for its lack of political collectibles. Today one has to make a significant contribution to a candidate to obtain a button or bumper sticker.

Political and campaign item collectors were one of the first specialty collector groups to organize. As a result, large hoards of post–1970 material exist. This is why most collectors concentrate on material dating prior to the 1970s.

Reference: Ted Hake, *Hake's Guide to Presidential Campaign Collectibles,* Wallace–Homestead, Krause Publications, 1992.

Newsletter: *The Political Bandwagon,* PO Box 348, Leola, PA 17540.

Collectors' Club: American Political Items Collectors, PO Box 340339, San Antonio, TX 78234.

REPRODUCTION ALERT: Campaign buttons have been widely reproduced. Examine the curl for evidence of modern identification marks having been scratched out. The backs of most early buttons were bare or had a paper label. Beware of any button with a painted back. Buttons made prior to 1896 were celluloid. Any lithograph button from an election earlier than 1896 is incorrect. Celluloid buttons need a collar since they are made in a sandwich fashion. Lithograph buttons have a one–piece construction.

Carter, James E., bank, figural smiling peanut, beige
vinyl, 1976, 5" d, 11¹/₂" h . . . . **$ 18.00**
Carter, James E., inaugural license plate, "District of
Columbia, Inauguration 1977" **15.00**
Carter/Mondale, bandanna, white and green, 1980,
28" sq **25.00**
Coolidge, Calvin, Coolidge home souvenir pitcher,
blue and white glazed ceramic, c1930s, 4¹/₂ x 6
x 6" **35.00**
Coolidge, Calvin, fan, cardboard, red, white, and
blue, Coolidge portrait, "Keep Cool–idge," ice
cream adv reverse, 1924 . . . . **150.00**
Cox, James M., lapel stud, white metal, 1920, 1" d **25.00**
Cox, James M., stickpin, round, red celluloid, white
"Jim Cox," ³/₄" h **60.00**
Davis, John W., biography, "Biography and Record of
John W. Davis, Democratic Nominee for
President," 1924, 32 pgs, 3¹/₂ x 9" **50.00**

John F. Kennedy, pinback button, black and white portrait, white lettering, red, white, and blue ground, $10.00.

Dewey, Thomas E., necktie, blue ground, white
Dewey portrait, U.S. Capitol, and "Dewey in '48" 35.00

Dewey, Thomas E., pin, brown plastic, "Dewey" on
bar with elephant below, 1944, 1½ x 1½" 15.00

Eisenhower, Dwight D., adv card, black and white,
Zippo Eisenhower cigarette lighter, "Ike Lights Your
Way," c1956, 3½ x6½" 30.00

Eisenhower, Dwight D., inauguration medal, brass,
"Dwight David Eisenhower MCMLIII," 2¾" d 18.00

Eisenhower/Nixon, tab, red, white, and blue litho,
"Ike – Dick – They're For You," c1956 .... 3.00

Ford, Gerald R., pinback button, tan, brown, black,
and white, caricatures of Ford in white hat and
Reagan in black hat, "Shoot Out At Kansas City, I
Was There 1976, Republican National Convention," 2¼" d 10.00

Ford/Dole, pinback button, jugate, multicolor,
"Ford–Dole In '76," 4" d 6.00

Goldwater, Barry M., tin, white, gold, and green,
"Gold Water – The Right Drink For The Conservative Taste," 1964, 5"h 12.00

Goldwater, Barry M., bank, white plastic, blue portrait, red name, 1964, 1½ x 3" 28.00

Goldwater/Miller, pinback button, jugate, black,
white, red, and blue litho, "The Winning Team,
Goldwater/Miller," 1964, 1⅜" d 5.00

Harding, Warren G., stickpin, silvered brass, gray
and white photo, 1920, 3" l 65.00

Harding/Coolidge, pinback button, jugate, brown-
tone, 1920, ⅞" d 1,500.00

Hoover, Herbert, bandanna, red, white, and blue,
1932, 17 x 18" 55.00

Hoover, Herbert, convention brochure, jugate cover,
"Republican Party Platform 1932," 24 pgs 25.00

Hoover and Wife, clothing buttons, pr, celluloid covered color portraits, brass rims, c1932, 1½" d 100.00

Hoover/Curtis, pin, jugate, rect, black, white, red,
and blue, 1928, 1½" l 75.00

Al Smith, booklet, *National Life Magazine,* Vol. 1, No. 1, 1928, 45 pgs, 8⅜ x 10½", $25.00.

Humphrey/Muskie, bank, figural donkey, cast iron,
painted silver, "Humphrey Muskie 68," 1½ x 4½
x 4" 32.00

Johnson, Lyndon B., bank, white plastic, blue portrait,
red name, 1964, 1½ x 3" 12.00

Johnson, Lyndon B., pennant, felt, red, white, and
blue, 5½" black and white photo, "Win With
Johnson," 1964, 11 x 30" 15.00

Johnson, Lyndon B., pin, brass, state of Texas with
raised "LBJ," 1964, 1" 10.00

Kennedy, John F., clip-on bowtie, white fabric, hp
"I'm For Kennedy," 1960, 4½ x 6½" 75.00

Kennedy, John F., memorial button, celluloid, black
and white, "In Memory Of Our Beloved President,"
1963, 7" d 15.00

Kennedy, Robert, mug, white china, red and blue
dec, caricature portrait, "Bobby For President,"
1968, 4" h 32.00

Kennedy/Johnson, inaugural invitation, gold emb
inaugural seal, 4 blank pgs inside, Jan 20, 1961,
8½ x 11" 40.00

La Follette/Wheeler, pinback button, jugate, black
and white, 1924, ⅞" d 400.00

Landon, Alfred M., fan, cardboard, brown and yellow, Landon portrait, "Landon For President,"
1936, 8½" h 38.00

Landon/Knox/GOP, pinback button, jugate, brown,
white, and yellow, sunflower petal background,
1936, ⅞" d 25.00

McGovern/Shriver, bank, cardboard and tin canister,
white ground, black and gray print, "Small Change
for Big Changes," 1972, 5½" h 20.00

Nixon, Richard M., doll, soft vinyl plastic, dark tan
and fleshtone, black suit, arms raised in classic victory pose, c1972, 4" h 22.00

Nixon, Richard M., mechanical bank, figural ele-
phant, cast iron, white, raised red letters, "Vote
Right, Nixon Agnew in '72, Better The Second Time
Around," 3 x 7 x 4½" 130.00

Franklin Delano Roosevelt, fan, diecut litho card-board, Boyd School, Washington, DC adv on reverse, 7½ x 10½", $25.00.

Nixon/Agnew, bank, figural elephant, cast iron, painted silver, "Nixon Agnew 68," 2½" h. **32.00**

Nixon/Agnew, wristwatch, Nixon and Agnew caricatures wearing striped prison uniforms, "Watch Them Doing Time For You," c1974 . . . . **110.00**

Nixon/Lodge, gardening gloves, pr, yellow, "I'm Working For Nixon And Lodge," 1960, 10" l **22.00**

Reagan, Ronald, yo–yo, metal, black and gray celluloid sides, "President Ronald Reagan, Inauguration Jan. 20, 21, 1985," 1985, 2½" d **15.00**

Roosevelt, Franklin Delano, bank, white metal, dark bronze finish, "F.D. Roosevelt," c1940, 2 x 3 x 4½" **45.00**

Roosevelt, Franklin Delano, lapel pin, mechanical, brown and beige litho, when string is pulled donkey kicks elephant, "Kick Out Depression With A Democratic Vote," 1932, 2½" d. **65.00**

Roosevelt, Franklin Delano, mug, figural head, blue ceramic, "3rd Term," 1940, 3 x 4 x 4". **50.00**

Roosevelt/Garner, pinback button, jugate, red, white, and blue, 1936, 1¼" d **45.00**

Roosevelt/Wallace, program, brown, red, white, and blue, jugate cover, "Official Inaugural Program," 1941, 56 pgs **55.00**

Smith, Alfred E., handkerchief, 2½" oval black and white photo, 1928, 11" sq **45.00**

Smith, Alfred E., pipe, carved portrait, yellow celluloid stem, 1928, 2 x 3". **200.00**

Smith & Robinson, pin, shield shape, brass, red, white, and blue enamel dec, "You Know Me Al," 1928, 1" h. **90.00**

Stevenson, Adlai E., brochure, "Veterans for Stevenson," Bill Mauldin cartoon illus, c1956, 4 pgs, 4 x 7" **18.00**

Stevenson, Adlai E., tie tack, brass, "Adlai," 1952, 1¼" l **10.00**

Stevenson/Sparkman, pinback button, jugate, black, white, red, and blue, 1952, 3½" d. **75.00**

Truman, Harry S., clothing button, black and white photo, green fabric rim, 1948, 1" d **90.00**

Truman, Harry S., necktie, blue ground, white Truman, U.S. Capitol, and "Truman in '48" **60.00**

Truman/Barkley, tab, blue and white litho, 1948 . . . . **20.00**

Willkie, pinback button, red, white, and blue, 1" w, $12.00.

Wallace, George C., wristwatch, red, white, and blue dial, Wallace caricature wearing boxing trunks and gloves, "George C. Wallace Original," 1970 . . . . **100.00**

Willkie, Wendell, handkerchief, red, white, and blue, "We Want Willkie," 1940, 12" sq **50.00**

Willkie, Wendell, pin, gold, red, white, and blue dec, eagle holding banner with "Willkie," 1940, 1½ x 1½". **22.00**

PORCELIER PORCELAIN

The Porcelier Manufacturing Company was incorporated on October 14, 1926, with business offices in Pittsburgh, Pennsylvania, and a manufacturing plant in East Liverpool, Ohio. In 1930 Porcelier purchased the vacant plant of the American China Company in South Greensburg, Westmoreland County, Pennsylvania.

Initially, Porcelier produced light fixtures. Electrical kitchen appliances were added by the mid–1930s. Some credit Porcelier with making the first all–ceramic electrical appliances. In the course of its history, Porcelier made over 100 patterns of kitchenware and over 100 different light fixtures.

Sears Roebuck and Company and Montgomery Ward were among Porcelier's biggest customers. As such many of their products appear with brand names such as Heatmaster and Harmony House.

The company was unionized in the late 1930s, remaining a union shop until it closed. In March 1954 Pittsburgh Plate Glass Industries bought the Porcelier plant and adjacent land. The company was dissolved in the summer of 1954.

Reference: Susan E. Grindberg, *Collector's Guide to Porcelier China*, Collector Books, 1996.

Collectors' Club: Porcelier Collectors Club, 21 Tamarac Swamp Rd, Wallingford, CT 06492.

Antique Rose Deco, creamer . . . . **$ 6.00**
Barock–Colonial, pretzel jar, gold. **85.00**
Barock–Colonial, sugar canister, #2016, gold **25.00**
Barock–Colonial, teapot, #2011, red. **30.00**
Basketweave Cameo, casserole, cov, 8½" d **45.00**
Basketweave Wild Flowers, creamer. **8.00**
Basketweave Wild Flowers, spaghetti bowl **75.00**
Basketweave Wild Flowers, sugar. **8.00**
Beehive Crisscross, ball jug **60.00**
Black–Eyed Susan, electric percolator **65.00**
Cattail, creamer. **7.50**
Double Floral, creamer. **8.00**
Double Floral, teapot, 8 cup **25.00**
Field Flowers, sugar. **8.00**
Flamingo, creamer. **6.00**
Fleur–de–Lis, creamer **8.00**
Floral Panel, sugar **8.00**
Flower Pot, creamer. **10.00**
Golden Fuchia Platinum, creamer **12.00**
Golden Wheat, electric percolator, 120 . . . . **60.00**
Hearth, creamer **6.00**
Hearth, pot, 2 cup **20.00**
Lavender Bluebell, creamer **4.00**
Lavender Bluebell, sugar **4.00**

Leaf and Shadow, electric percolator, short handle 75.00
Leaf and Shadow, teapot, green trim, 4 cup 22.00
Mexican, ball jug 70.00
Mexican, sugar 8.00
Nautical, creamer 12.00
Nautical, teapot, 8 cup 25.00
1939 New York World's Fair, ashtray 100.00
1939 New York World's Fair, sugar 80.00
Orange Poppy, creamer 8.00
Orange Poppy, electric percolator 60.00
Oriental Deco, salt and pepper shakers, pr 22.00
Rope Bow, sugar 6.00
Scalloped Wild Flowers, creamer 10.00
Scalloped Wild Flowers, sugar 10.00
Scalloped Wild Flowers, teapot, 6 cup 35.00
Silhouette, creamer 8.00
Silhouette, tray, #2611, wood 40.00
Starflower, electric percolator, #120 . . . . 60.00
Tulips, creamer 12.00
White Flower Platinum, creamer 4.00

POSTCARDS

In 1869 the Austrian government, following a proposal by Dr. Emanuel Herrmann, introduced the first government–issued postcard. The postal card concept quickly spread across Europe, arriving in the United States in 1873.

The period from 1898 until 1918 is considered the golden age of postcards. English, e.g. Raphael Tuck, and German, e.g., Paul Finkenrath (Berlin, "BFP–Germany) publishes produced most of the cards during the golden age. Detroit Publishing and John Winsch were leading American publishers.

The postcard collecting mania that engulfed Americans ended at the beginning of World War I. Although greeting cards replace many postcards on sales racks, the postcard survived. Linen cards dominated the period between 1930 and the end of the 1940s. Chromolithograph cards were popular in the 1950s and 60s. Postcards experienced a brief renaissance in the 1970s and 80s with the introduction of the continental size format (4" x 6") and the use of contemporary designs.

Are the stamps on postcards valuable? The answer is no 99.9% of the time. If you have doubts, consult a philatelic price guide. A postcard's postmark may be an added value factor. There are individuals who collect obscure postmarks.

Collectors divide postcards into two main categories: topics and view cards. Value is closely linked to scarcity. Big city cards, cards from popular tourist attractions, and ordinary holiday cards have minimal value.

Keep your eye open for "real" photo postcards. These are photographs printed on postcard stock. They are a completely separate postcard collecting category.

References: Diane Allmen, *The Official Price Guide to Postcards,* House of Collectibles, 1990; J. L. Mashburn, *Black Americana: A Century of History Preserved on Postcards,* Colonial Houe, 1996; J. L. Mashburn, *Fantasy Postcards,* Colonial House, 1996; J. L. Mashburn, *The Artist–Signed Postcard Price Guide,* Colonial House, 1993; J. L. Mashburn, *The Postcard Price Guide: A Comprehensive Listing, Third Edition,* Colonial House, 1997; J. L. Mashburn, *The Super Rare Postcards of Harrison Fisher with Price Guide,* Colonial House, 1992; Susan Brown Nicholson, *The*

Encyclopedia of Antique Postcards, Wallace–Homestead, Krause Publications, 1994; Robert Ward, *Investment Guide To North American Real Photo Postcards,* Antique Paper Guide, 1991; Jane Wood, *The Collectors' Guide To Post Cards,* L–W Books, 1984, 1997 value update.

Periodicals: *Barr's Post Card News,* 70 S Sixth St, Lansing, IA 52151; *Postcard Collector,* PO Box 1050, Dubuque, IA 52004.

Collectors' Clubs: Deltiologists of America, PO Box 8, Norwood, PA 19074; Postcard History Society, PO Box 1765, Manassas, VA 22110.

Note: *Barr's Post Card News* and the *Postcard Collector* publish lists of over fifty regional clubs in the United States and Canada. Prices listed are for postcards in excellent condition.

All Woman Band, Marion Miller Orchestra, 1943 . . . . . $ 10.00
Amelia Earhart, christening of *Essex Terraplane,* 1932 . . . . 85.00
Balloon Races at Indiana Speedway, c1920 . . . . 10.00
Barnum & Bailey Circus, 1920–40 . . . . 15.00
Bob Lemon, Cleveland Indians, sgd, 1950s 10.00
Bowling Alley, int view 15.00
Century of Progress, 1932 . . . . 5.00
Cheerios Kid and Donald Duck, Huey, Louie, and
  Disneyland, black and white, Cheerios premium,
  1957 . . . . 12.00
Chevrolet Auto, 1938–41 . . . . 8.00
Child Wearing Costume, holding flowers, c1920 . . . . 12.00
Coney Island 5.00
Elvis, "Easter Greetings," Elvis wearing gray tux, red
  ground, unused 35.00
Firestone Tires, 1939 . . . . 4.00
Ford Exhibit, Cycle of Progress, 1939 . . . . 3.00
Fred Astaire 5.00
Girl In Cart, 1934 . . . . 6.00
Girl Sitting on Bench, wearing clown costume, 1923 . . . . 12.00
Graf Zeppelin, postmarked "Stuttgart, 1933" 10.00
Havelock, Nebraska, downtown view with trolley 8.00
Heinz Ocean Pier, Atlantic City, Sun Parlor 8.00
Indian Woman and 3 Children, holding ornate
  bags, Toppenish, Wash, c1824 . . . . 12.00
James Dean 8.00
Judy Garland 8.00

Chesapeake and Ohio Canal, linen, $2.00.

Child with Pumpkin, "Hallowe'en Greetings, Ellen Clapsaddle, artist sgd, $10.00.

ers and galleries. Editions Sagot in Paris offered posters for sale featuring the art of Toulouse–Lautrec.

Posters were an inexpensive advertising form. Publishers, circuses, theaters and theater acts, automobile and bicycle manufacturers, the movie industry, and the travel industry are only a few of the many business that utilized the poster. Posters played a major role during World War I and II.

Scarce is a term that must be used very carefully when referring to posters. Print runs into the millions are known. Yet, most were destroyed. The poster collecting community was relatively small and heavily art focused until the 1970s.

Carefully check the date mark on movie posters. An "R," usually located in the lower right corner near the border in the white area, followed by slash and the date denotes a later release of a movie. These posters generally are not as valuable as posters associated with the initial release.

References: Tony Fusco, *Posters: identification and Price Guide, Second Edition,* Avon Books, 1994; Susan Theran, *Prints, Posters & Photographs: Identification and Price Guide,* Avon Books, 1993.

Leap Year	5.00
Lone Ranger, Gimbals at New York World's Fair	6.00
Marathon Auto,1950s	6.00
Maytag Kitchen Washers	6.00
McDonald's	5.00
Men, wearing native dress in front of tepee, dog drawn sled, late 1920s	10.00
Mercedes Benz, set of 6, 2 black and white, 4 color, unused, 1956	25.00
National League Baseball Park, Toledo, Ohio, c1920	5.00
Native American Indian	3.00
New York World's Fair, Trylon and Perisphere, gold, orange, and indigo, 1939	5.00
New York World's Fair, 1964	15.00
Olympics, Paris, French, swimming, sgd, 1924	50.00
Pine Camp Hotel Cottages, Vandosta, Georgia	5.00
Plymouth Auto, 1939–41	10.00
Pontiac, 1933, 2–door sedan	6.00
Railroad, depot scene	8.00
Shirley Temple, scene from *Captain January,* glossy sepia picture, unused, 1936	12.00
Solar Eclipse	10.00
Statue of Liberty, Hold–to–Light, 1986	3.50
Texas Ranger, horseback	5.00
Tupperware	3.00
Win With Wilkie, real photo, 1940	60.00

POSTERS

The printed broadside, often with one or more block illustrations, is the ancestor of the poster as we know it today. The full color poster arrived on the scene in the 1880s, the result of the lithographic printing revolution. Posters by Courier and Strobridge are considered some of the finest examples of American lithography ever printed. Philadelphia was the center of the poster printing industry in America prior to 1945.

Almost from its inception, collectors were fascinated with this colorful art form. Before long printers began overprinting their commercial runs and selling the extra posters through print deal-

American Airlines, Aloha Hawaii, E. McKnight Kauffer, 1953, 27 x 41"	$ 270.00
Annie Get Your Gun, 1950, 14 x 36"	55.00
Be Refreshed with Healthful Delicious Doublemint Gum, twins with sleek car, Otis Shephard, c1937, 11 x 42"	190.00
Beach Blanket Bingo, Frankie Avalon, 22" sq	22.00
Cincinnati Kid, 1965, 22 x 28"	42.00
Dirty Dozen, Lee Marvin, 27 x 41"	15.00
Empire Strikes Back, Mark Hamill, 27 x 41"	28.00
Evening Standard—Best of All for Sport, c1950, 20 x 30"	75.00
Fidass Sporting Goods, F Romoli, 1962 Italian soccer player, 29 x 52"	310.00
Hasten the Homecoming—Buy Victory Bonds, color, Norman Rockwell illus, 1945, 29 x 20"	35.00
Healthy & Happy, color, c1940, 21 x 17"	20.00
I Married An Angel, Nelson Eddy, Jeanette MacDonald, MGM, 1942	85.00
Kodak, monotone photo of young lady in beret, jacket, and necktie, self framed, c1920, 17 x 26"	185.00
Let Freedom Ring, Nelson Eddy, Virginia Bruce, MGM, 1939	65.00
Life Begins At Forty, Will Rogers, Rochelle Hudson, Fox, 1935	225.00
Life with Father, 1947, 14 x 36"	85.00
Little Rascals, Fish Hooky, 1952, 41 x 27"	130.00
Los Angeles—American Airlines, DC7 flying over LA nightscape, Fred Ludikens, c1954, 30 x 39"	340.00
Mercedes Benz, showroom poster, blue, brown, red, black, and yellow, white ground, futuristic race car against ghostly logo, 1955, 23 x 33"	975.00
Mission Orange Soda, Everybody's Choice, 1940–50, 20 x 26¼"	45.00
Mouse Cleaning, Tom and Jerry, MGM, 1948	325.00
Mr Broadway, 1933	185.00
Niagara, Marilyn Monroe, 22 x 28"	575.00
Pit And The Pendulum, Vincent Price, John Kerr, 1961	25.00
Play Misty For Me, Clint Eastwood, Jessica Walter, Donna Mills, Universal, 1971	15.00

Frogs, **horror movie, Ray Milland, Sam Elliott, American International, 1972, $25.00.**

Pony Express, Charlton Heston, Rhonda Fleming, Paramount, 1953 . . . . **15.00**

Raiders of The Seven Seas, United Artists, 1953, 27 x 41" **32.00**

Requiem For A Heavyweight, Anthony Quinn, Jackie Gleason, Columbia, 1962 . . . . **12.00**

Rooster Cogburn, John Wayne **42.00**

Sgt. Preston and Yukon King, Contest Winner Award, 1950, 16 x 22" **200.00**

State Fair, 1962, 22 x 28" **12.00**

The New Oakland All American Six, showroom poster, 1929, 26 x 38" **220.00**

TWA, Along The Way of TWA—California Yosemite National Park, deep tint color photo panoramic view of park, c1947, 35 x 28" **120.00**

Use Virginia Dare Double Strength Extracts, smiling housewife making cookies, c1925, 21 x 28" **170.00**

POTTERIES, REGIONAL

There were thousands of pottery factories scattered across the United States. Many existed only for a brief period of time.

Recent scholarship by individuals such as Phyllis and Tom Bess on the Oklahoma potteries, and Carol and Jim Carlton on Colorado pottery, Jack Chipman on California pottery, and Darlene Dommel on the Dakota potteries have demonstrated how rich America's ceramic heritage is. This is only the tip of the iceberg.

This is a catchall category for all those companies that have not reached a strong enough collecting status to deserve their own category. Eventually, some will achieve this level. Collectors collect what they know. Thanks to today's scholarship, collectors are learning more and more.

References: California: Jack Chipman, *Collector's Encyclopedia of California Pottery,* Collector Books, 1992, 1995 value update; Michael Schneider, *California Potteries: The Complete Book,* Schiffer Publishing, 1995; Bernice Stamper, *Vallona Starr Ceramics,* Schiffer Publishing, 1995.

Colorado: Carol and Jim Carlton, *Collector's Encyclopedia of Colorado Pottery: Identification and Values,* Collector Books, 1994; North Dakota: Darlene Hurst Dommel, *Collector's Encyclopedia of the Dakota Potteries: Identification & Values,* Collector Books, 1996; Oklahoma: Phyllis and Tom Bess, *Frankoma and Other Oklahoma Potteries,* Schiffer Publishing, 1995.

Collectors' Clubs: Minnesota: Nemadji Pottery Collectors Club, 200 Old Co. Rd. 8, Moose Lake, MN 55767; North Dakota: North Dakota Pottery Collectors Society, PO Box 14, Beach, ND 58621.

California, Cleminsons, pie bird, 4½" h . . . . **$ 8.00**

California, Cleminsons, plate, crowing rooster center 9½" d **5.00**

California, Cleminsons, spoon rest, gray, gold, and purple leaf design, 8½" l **8.00**

California, Cleminsons, wall pocket, chef, 7¼" h **15.00**

California, Freeman–McFarlin, figure, cat, woodtone, 12½" h **15.00**

California, Freeman–McFarlin, figure, giraffe, woodtone, crackle glaze, 11" h **25.00**

California, Freeman–McFarlin, vase, orange glaze, paper label, 11¼" h **12.00**

California, Hagen–Renaker, figure, Arabian stallion, 9 x 11¼" **90.00**

California, Hagen–Renaker, figure, Chihuahua puppy, Pedigree Dogs Line, label reads "Hagen–Renaker, Carmencita, 1953" 2" h **35.00**

California, Hagen–Renaker, figure, squirrel, "Peggy," 4¼ x 4" **20.00**

California, Hagen–Renaker, figure, 3 bears, c1950, 2" h papa bear **25.00**

California, Hagen–Renaker, wall plaque, prancing horses, 15 x 22" **65.00**

California, Haldeman, bowl, flared, Chinese style, yellow and white blended glaze, 3½ x 10" **15.00**

California, Haldeman, bud vase, triple, white, 6½" h **12.00**

California, Haldeman, candle holder, green glaze, 1½ x 4½" **4.50**

California, Haldeman, figure, dancing lady, #402, 7" h **15.00**

California, Haldeman, figure, monkey, dressed as bellboy, c1943, 2¾" h **25.00**

California, Haldeman, flower bowl, applied roses, 9½ x 11¼" l **15.00**

California, Keeler, figure, begging cocker spaniel, 6" h, mkd "Brad Keeler #735" **10.00**

California, Keeler, figure, blue jay, mkd "Brad Keeler #735," 9¼" h **15.00**

California, Keeler, figure, flamingo, 7½" h, mkd "Brad Keeler #3" **25.00**

California, Manker, bowl, egg shape, green and blue blended glaze, 3¼" h **25.00**

California, Manker, cup and saucer, leaf shape **30.00**

California, Manker, plate, leaf shape, c1947, 7½" d **25.00**

California, Manker, vase, pink and blue drip glaze, 7¼" h **50.00**

California, Manker, vase, cylindrical, citron green and dove gray blended glaze, 8" h **50.00**

California, Pacific, baking dish, delphinium blue, clip-on wood handle, 8¾" d **35.00**

California, Pacific, coaster, Hostess Ware, 4" d **2.00**
California, Pacific, eggcup **12.00**
California, Pacific, pitcher, Hostess Ware, 2 qt. **28.00**
California, Pacific, plate, divided, bunny border, c1934, 9" d **35.00**
California, Pacific, plate, spiral design. **8.00**
California, Pacific, teapot, ftd, jade green **55.00**
California, Pacific, tumbler, 4" h **8.00**
California, Pacific, vase, bird motif, c1939, 8¼" h **18.00**
California, Pierce, figure, penguin, black and white, stamped "Howard Pierce," c1953, 7" h **20.00**
California, Pierce, figure, pigeon, 7½" h **12.00**
California, Pacific, figures, giraffe, brown agate, 10½" h, price for pair **30.00**
California, Pierce, figure, quail, stamped "Howard Pierce," price for 3 . . . . **40.00**
California, Pierce, vase, mottled green glaze, 7¼" h **15.00**
California, Roselane, bowl, pedestal, square, Chinese Modern, 2½ x 6¼" **10.00**
California, Roselane, figure, Bali dancer, 11" h **18.00**
California, Roselane, figure, boy with dog, 5½" h **4.50**
California, Roselane, figure, fawn, brown and white, plastic eyes, c1965. . . . . **2.50**
California, Roselane, figure, elephant, brown luster glaze, wood base, Roselane logo burned into base, 8" h **65.00**
California, Santa Anita, dinner plate, Bird Of Paradise, Flowers Of Hawaii Line, 10½" d **6.00**
California, Twin Winton, pitcher, Open Range Line **28.00**
California, Twin Winton, salt and pepper shakers, pr, Hillbilly Line **5.00**
California, Twin Winton, tankard, man–shaped handle, Hillbilly Line **12.00**
California, Weil, vase, sailor boy, c1943, 10¾" h **15.00**
California, Will–George/The Claysmiths, figure, cardinal on branch, 12" h **28.00**
California, Will–George/The Claysmiths, tray, rooster **15.00**
California, Winfield, plate, hp geranium, 8½" d **10.00**
California, Winfield, salad plate, blue and white, 7½" sq **6.00**
California, Ynez, figure, Jennifer, lace trim, c1946, 5½" h **12.00**
Colorado, Broadmoor, bean pot **65.00**
Colorado, Broadmoor, cornucopia, blue and mauve glaze, 6" h **35.00**
Colorado, Broadmoor, figure, squirrel, 2" h, stamped. **35.00**
Colorado, Broadmoor, paperweight, scarab design, turquoise **65.00**
Colorado, Broadmoor, planter, turquoise, 18" h **110.00**
Colorado, Broadmoor, urn, handled, turquoise, 7" h **35.00**
Colorado, Broadmoor, vase, handled, sgd "Eric Hellman," 8" h **110.00**
Colorado, Denver White, bowl, gray, 6 x 8" **135.00**
Colorado, Denver White, creamer, pine cone dec **45.00**
Colorado, Denver White, vase, pine cone dec, sgd "Stabler," 6" h **110.00**
Colorado, Denver White, vase, 10" h, mountains and deer, sgd "Skiff" **290.00**
Colorado, Indian Hills, wedding jug, blue **35.00**
Colorado, Johnson, ashtray, leaf design **35.00**
Colorado, Johnson, bowl, brown swirl design, 8" d **55.00**

Colorado, Loveland, condiment tray, applied deer, 10" d **6.00**
Colorado, salt and pepper shakers, pr, 3" h **6.00**
Colorado, Loveland, tray, 10" l **15.00**
Colorado, Loveland, vase, floral design, 6" h **35.00**
Colorado, Rocky Mountain, figures, doe and buck, price for pair **25.00**
Colorado, Rocky Mountain, figure, poodle, 10" h **15.00**
Colorado, Rocky Mountain, pitcher **15.00**
Colorado, Rocky Mountain, teapot **20.00**
Colorado, Morrison, vase, blue matte glaze, 8" h **40.00**
Colorado, Hopkins, figure, tree with branch and birds, 12" h **65.00**
Colorado, McKinnell, bowl, brown and blue, 8" d **35.00**
Colorado, McKinnell, wall plaque, marbelized design, 10" d **65.00**
North Dakota, Dickinson Clay Products, ashtray, marine blue glaze, white flowing overglaze, 4¼" d **28.00**
North Dakota, Dickinson Clay Products, paperweight, shield shape, red, 2¾" h **28.00**
North Dakota, Dickinson Clay Products, salt and pepper shakers, pr, black, 2" h **15.00**
North Dakota, Dickinson Clay Products, vase, orange, gold and black overglaze, 4" h **35.00**
North Dakota, Dickinson Clay Products, water pitcher, blue mottled glaze, 8" h **135.00**
North Dakota, Messer, bell, "Merry Christmas," green and white, 1½" h **185.00**
North Dakota, Messer, figure, prairie dog, 2¼" h **85.00**
North Dakota, Pine Ridge, hanging basket, geometric design, Woody, 5 x 7½" **235.00**
North Dakota, Pine Ridge, pitcher, bulbous, green and brown, 5" h **40.00**
North Dakota, Pine Ridge, plate, geometric star, 7" d **185.00**
North Dakota, Pine Ridge, salt and pepper shakers, pr, geometric star **65.00**
North Dakota, Pine Ridge, vase, geometric sgraffito design, light green, 4¼" h **110.00**
North Dakota, Rushmore, ashtray, relief pine cone motif, blue, 4½" l **65.00**
North Dakota, Rushmore, bowl, turquoise int, orange uranium glaze ext, sgd "Ivan Houser 41," 7½" d **110.00**
North Dakota, Rushmore, figure, cowboy hat, brown gloss glaze, 2¼ x 5¼" **25.00**
North Dakota, Rushmore, pitcher, orange swirl design, 7" h **110.00**
North Dakota, Rushmore, trivet, Art Deco style, floral design, mint green **110.00**
North Dakota, Rushmore, vase, concentric rings, blue, 3½" h **25.00**
North Dakota, University Of North Dakota, ashtray, fish shape, mkd "UND Flossie MC" **85.00**
North Dakota, University Of North Dakota, bowl, rose color, 3¾ x 5¾" **135.00**
North Dakota, University Of North Dakota, bowl, sgraffito mule design, 3¾ x 5¾" **380.00**
North Dakota, University Of North Dakota, creamer, emb floral design, 3½" h **135.00**
North Dakota, University Of North Dakota, figure, horse, turquoise, 6" h **180.00**

North Dakota, University Of North Dakota, paper-
weight, figural coyote, blue, 3" h **65.00**

North Dakota, University Of North Dakota, pitcher,
white, oxcart motif, 4¹/₂" h **285.00**

North Dakota, University Of North Dakota, vase,
relief wheat shocks, 4¹/₂" h **365.00**

North Dakota, University Of North Dakota, wall
plaque, oxen pulling covered wagon, 5" d **225.00**

North Dakota, WPA Ceramics, cereal bowl, 2 x 5¹/₄" **18.00**

North Dakota, WPA Ceramics, paperweight, Native
American Indian design, mkd "BK WPA 1936" **85.00**

North Dakota, WPA Ceramics, strawberry jar,
turquoise, 6" h **235.00**

North Dakota, WPA Ceramics, tumbler, yellow int,
turquoise ext, 4" h **25.00**

North Dakota, WPA Ceramics, vase, sgraffito wheat
design, 5" h **325.00**

Oklahoma, Cherokee Pottery, bowl, 8 different ani-
mals, 12" d **12.00**

Oklahoma, Creek Pottery, bank, Indian head one
side, buffalo nickel other, 7¹/₂" h **10.00**

Oklahoma, Creek Pottery, eggcup, figural duck, red,
3¹/₂" h **3.00**

Oklahoma, Gracetone Pottery, bowl, pedestal, gun-
metal finish, 6" h **12.00**

Oklahoma, Gracetone Pottery, figure, English setter,
cinnamon, 5¹/₂" l **160.00**

Oklahoma, Gracetone Pottery, pitcher, black, 3 qt **30.00**

Oklahoma, Gracetone Pottery, salt and pepper shak-
ers, pr, pink champagne finish **10.00**

Oklahoma, Hammat Originals, ashtray, figural foot,
green, dated 1951, 9" l **18.00**

Oklahoma, Hammat Originals, ashtray, nubian bust,
bottom reads "Property Of The Tulsa Club," 6¹/₂" h **40.00**

Oklahoma, Hammat Originals, bowl, conch shell,
5" d **15.00**

Oklahoma, Hammat Originals, cigarette rest **6.00**

Oklahoma, Hammat Originals, figure, monkey, 10" h **55.00**

Oklahoma, Hammat Originals, hors d'oeuvre tray,
figural cowboy hat, bottom reads "Copyright 1953
Hammat Originals," 13" d **35.00**

Oklahoma, Hammat Originals, mug, figural
coconut, 7 oz **3.50**

Oklahoma, Hammat Originals, platter, Sportsman
Series, 12¹/₂" l **35.00**

Oklahoma, Hammat Originals, tumbler, western
motif, 4¹/₂" h **12.00**

Oklahoma, National Youth Administration Pottery,
salt and pepper shakers, pr, orange, 2¹/₂" h **10.00**

Oklahoma, Sequoyah Pottery, ashtray, 5" d **30.00**

Oklahoma, Sequoyah Pottery, figure, kneeling pot-
ters, red, 6" h **65.00**

Oklahoma, Sequoyah Pottery, pitcher, thunderbird
dec, green, beige, 3¹/₂" h **20.00**

Oklahoma, Sequoyah Pottery, pitcher, frog handle,
red, 5" h **65.00**

Oklahoma, Sequoyah Pottery, planter, 5¹/₂" h **75.00**

Oklahoma, Sequoyah Pottery, urn, red, 10" h **160.00**

Oklahoma, Sequoyah Pottery, vase, red, 4¹/₄" h **55.00**

Oklahoma, Synar Ceramics, basket, aqua int, wood-
pine ext, 7¹/₂" h **10.00**

Oklahoma, Synar Ceramics, bowl, aqua int, wood-
pine ext **10.00**

Oklahoma, Synar Ceramics, figure, cannibal 4¹/₂" h **15.00**

Oklahoma, Synar Ceramics, vase, wheat design,
10" h **10.00**

Oklahoma, Tamac Pottery, ashtray, "Oklahoma,"
raspberry **8.00**

Oklahoma, Tamac Pottery, spoon rest, raspberry, "For
My Stirring Spoon," 6" h **5.00**

Oklahoma, Tamac Pottery, vase, frosty pine, 4¹/₂" h **10.00**

Oklahoma, Winart Pottery, chip n' dip plate, persim-
mon, frost, 13" d **10.00**

Oklahoma, Winart Pottery, juice tumbler, persim-
mon, frost, 7 oz **3.00**

Oklahoma, Winart Pottery, lazy susan, persimmon,
frost, 16" d **22.00**

Oklahoma, Winart Pottery, pitcher, chartreuse,
brown, 6" h **3.50**

Oklahoma, Winart Pottery, teapot, individual, brown,
frost, 12 oz **10.00**

Oklahoma, Winart Pottery, tidbit tray, 2–tier, pink,
frost rim, 10" d **18.00**

PRECIOUS MOMENTS

During a visit to the Los Angeles Gift Show in 1978, Eugene
Freeman, president of Enesco, saw some cards and posters featuring the drawings of Samuel J. Butcher. Initially Butcher and Bill
Biel, his partner in Jonathan and David, were not thrilled with the
idea of having Butcher's art transformed into three–dimensional
form. However, after seeing a prototype sculpted by Yashei Fojioka
of Japan, Butcher and Biel agreed.

Initially 21 pieces were made. Early figures are darker in color
than those made today. Pieces produced between 1978 and 1984
and licensed by Jonathan & David Company have smaller heads
than pieces relicensed by the Samuel J. Butcher Company and
Precious Moments. Jonathan & David ceased operating in 1988.

The Enesco Precious Moments Club began in 1981. In 1989,
Butcher opened the Precious Moments Chapel in Carthage,
Missouri. In 1995 Goebel introduced hand painted bronze minia-
tures. The year 1995 is also saw Enesco launch its Century Circle
Retailers, a group of 35 retailers selling a limited edition line of
Precious Moments material.

References: Collector's Information Bureau, *Collectibles market
Guide & Price Index, 15th Edition,* Collector's Information Bureau,
1997, distributed by Krause Publications; Rosie Wells (ed.), *Rosie's
Secondary Market Price Guide for Enesco's precious Moments
Collection, 14th Edition,* Rosie Wells Enterprises, 1996.

Periodical: *Collectors' Bulletin,* 22341 E Wells Rd, Canton, IL
61520.

Bell, But The Greatest Of These Is Love, 1992 . . . . **$ 30.00**

Bell, God Sent His Love, 1985 . . . . **35.00**

Bell, I'll Play My Drum For Him, 1982 . . . . **65.00**

Bell, Jesus Is Born, 1981 . . . . **40.00**

Bell, Jesus Loves Me, 1981 . . . . **40.00**

Bell, One Upon A Holy Night, 1990 . . . . **30.00**

Bell, Prayer Changes Things, 1981 . . . . **45.00**

Bell, Surrounded With Joy, 1983 . . . . **60.00**

Figurine, Peace On Earth...Anyway, #183342, 1996, original price $32.50.

Bell, Wishing You A Cozy Christmas, 1986 . . . . **40.00**
Doll, Connie, 1986, 12" h **230.00**
Doll, Debbie, 1981, 18" h **230.00**
Doll, Mikey, 1981, 18" h **165.00**
Doll, Summer's Joy, 1990 . . . . **140.00**
Doll, Tammy, 1981, 18" h **475.00**
Doll, Timmy, 1984, 12" h **75.00**
Doll, You Have Touched So Many Hearts, 1991 . . . . **80.00**
Figurine, Birds Of A Feather Collect Together, 1986 . . . . . . **30.00**
Figurine, Blessings From My House To Yours, 1983 . . . . . . **65.00**
Figurine, Bridesmaid, 1984 . . . . **15.00**
Figurine, But Love Goes On Forever, 1981 . . . . **120.00**
Figurine, Christmas Is A Time To Share, musical, 1979 . . . **130.00**
Figurine, Crown Him Lord Of All, 1980 . . . . **50.00**
Figurine, Dawn's Early Light, 1983 . . . . **55.00**
Figurine, Eggs Over Easy, 1980. **65.00**
Figurine, God Blessed Our Years Together With So
    Much Love And Happiness, 1984 . . . . **40.00**
Figurine, God Understands, 1979. . . . . **75.00**
Figurine, Hello, Lord, It's Me Again, 1981 . . . . **365.00**
Figurine, January, 1988 . . . . **30.00**
Figurine, Jesus Is The Light That Shines, 1983 . . . . **40.00**
Figurine, Join In On The Blessings, 1984 . . . . **40.00**
Figurine, Let Us Call The Club To Order, 1983 . . . . **40.00**
Figurine, Loving You Dear Valentine, 1987 . . . . **25.00**
Figurine, Our Club Can't Be Beat, 1986 . . . . **75.00**
Figurine, Sending You A Rainbow, 1983 . . . . **45.00**
Figurine, Sharing Our Season Together, 1983. . . . . **110.00**
Figurine, Sharing The Good News Together, 1991 . . . . **20.00**
Figurine, Silent Knight, musical, 1980. . . . . **210.00**
Figurine, Smile, God Loves You, 1982. . . . . **140.00**
Figurine, The Hand That Rocks The Future, musical,
    1980. . . . . **45.00**
Figurine, The Lord Bless You And Keep You, 1980 . . . . **35.00**
Figurine, To Thee With Love, 1980 . . . . **50.00**
Figurine, Trust In The Lord To The Finish, 1984 . . . . **35.00**
Figurine, Unto Us A Child Is Born, 1979. . . . . **75.00**
Figurine, Walking By Faith, 1980 . . . . **60.00**

Figurine, Unto Us A Child Is Born, musical, 1979 . . . . **85.00**
Figurine, You Will Always Be My Choice, 1989 . . . . **20.00**
Figurine, You're Worth Your Weight In Gold, 1983 . . . . **20.00**
Ornament, Baby's First Christmas, 1981 . . . . **35.00**
Ornament, But Love Goes On Forever, 1981 . . . . **65.00**
Ornament, Camel, Donkey, & Cow, 3 pc set, 1982 . . . . . . **45.00**
Ornament, Come Let Us Adore Him, 4 pc set, 1981 . . . . **100.00**
Ornament, 15 Years Tweet Music Together, 1993 . . . . **15.00**
Ornament, Glide Through The Holidays, 1990 . . . . **15.00**
Ornament, Let Heaven And Nature Sing, 1983 . . . . **15.00**
Ornament, Let The Heavens Rejoice, 1981 . . . . **185.00**
Ornament, Love Is Kind, 1984 . . . . **20.00**
Ornament, Love Rescued Me, 1986 . . . . **12.00**
Ornament, May God Bless You With A Perfect
    Holiday Season, 1984 . . . . **10.00**
Ornament, Mouse With Cheese, 1982 . . . . **80.00**
Ornament, O Come All Ye Faithful, 1983 . . . . **45.00**
Ornament, Our First Christmas Together, 1982 . . . . **15.00**
Ornament, Peace On Earth. **20.00**
Ornament, The First Noel, 1982 . . . . **55.00**
Ornament, The Magic Starts With You, 1992 . . . . **20.00**
Ornament, The Purr–fect Grandma, 1983 . . . . **12.00**
Ornament, The Purr–fect Grandpa, 1983. . . . . **12.00**
Ornament, To A Special Dad, 1983 . . . . **20.00**
Ornament, To My Forever Friend, 1988. . . . . **12.00**
Ornament, Unicorn, 1982 . . . . **30.00**
Ornament, Unto Us A child Is Born, 1981 . . . . **35.00**
Ornament, Waddle I Do Without You, 1987 . . . . **12.00**
Plate, Blessings From Me To Thee, 1991 . . . . **45.00**
Plate, But The Greatest Of These Is Love, 1992 . . . . **45.00**
Plate, Christmastime Is For Sharing, 1983 . . . . **50.00**
Plate, Come Let Us Adore Him, 1981 . . . . **35.00**
Plate, I'll Play My Drum For Him, 1982 . . . . **80.00**
Plate, Love One Another, 1985. **55.00**
Plate, Let Heaven and Nature Sing, 1982 . . . . **30.00**
Plate, Love Is Kind, 1984 . . . . **30.00**
Plate, Make A Joyful Noise, 1982 . . . . **30.00**
Plate, The Lord Bless You And Keep You, 1981. . . . . **30.00**
Plate, Unto Us A Child Is Born, 1984 . . . . **30.00**
Plate, Mother Sew Deer, 1981 . . . . **40.00**
Plate, Winter's Song, 1986 . . . . **45.00**
Plate, Wishing You A Yummy Christmas, 1990. . . . . **40.00**

PREMIUMS

A premium is an object given free or at a reduced value with the purchase of a product or service. Premiums divide into two groups: (1) point of purchase (you obtain your premium when you make the purchase) or (2) proof of purchase (you send proof of purchase, often box labels or seals, to a distribution point which then sends the premium to you).

Premiums are generational. The sixty–something and seventy–something generations think of radio premiums. The fifty–something, forty–something, and older thirty–something generations identify with cereal and radio premiums. The twenty–something and modern–somethings collect fast food premiums.

A relatively small number of premiums were made of paper. Collectors place a premium on three–dimensional premiums. However, many of these premiums arrived in paper containers and envelopes and contained paper instruction sheets. A premium is considered complete only if it has its period packaging and all the units that came with it.

Ovaltine's offer of a "Little Orphan Annie" music sheet was one of the earliest radio premiums. Jack Armstrong, Lone Ranger, and Tom Mix premiums soon followed. By the middle of the 1930s every child eagerly awaited the phrase "Now, an important word from our sponsor" with pad in hand, ready to write down the address of the latest premium offer. Thousands of radio premiums were offered in the 1930s, 40s, and 50s.

Cereal manufacturers found that the simple fact that a premium was included in the box, even if it was unrelated to a specific radio or television show, was enough of an incentive to stimulate extra sales. Cereal premiums flourished in the post–1945 period. Although television premiums were offered, they never matched in numbers those offered over the radio.

The arrival of the fast food restaurant and eventual competition between chains led to the use of premiums to attract customers. Many premiums were tied to television shows and movies. Although not a premium, fast food packaging has also attracted the interest of collectors.

Not all premiums originated via cereal boxes, fast food chains, radio, or television. Local and national food manufacturers and merchants used premiums to attract customers. Cracker Jack is the most obvious example.

References: Scott Bruce, *Cereal Box Bonanza: The 1950's,* Collector Books, 1995; *Hake's Price Guide to Character Toy Premiums: Including Comic, Cereal, TV, Movies, Radio & Related Store Bought Items,* Gemstone Publishing, 1996; Jim Harmon, *Radio & TV Premiums: Value and History From Tom Mix to Space Patrol,* Krause Publications, 1997; Robert M. Overstreet, *Overstreet Premium Ring Price Guide, Second Edition,* Gemstone Publishing, 1996; Tom Tumbusch, *Tomart's Price Guide To Radio Premiums and Cereal Box Collectibles,* Wallace–Homestead, Krause Publications, 1991.

Periodical: *Box Top Bonanza,* 3403 46th Ave, Moline, IL 61265; *Flake,* PO Box 481, Cambridge, MA 02140.

Note: See Cracker Jack, Fast Food Collectibles, and McDonald's for additional listings.

REPRODUCTION ALERT

Amos 'n Andy, cardboard stand–up figure set, Pepsodent, 1930 . . . . $ 25.00
Archies, *Jingle–Jangle,* 33⅓ rpm record, Post, 1968–70 . . . . 5.00
Around The World In 80 Days, book, Crest Tooth-paste, hard cover, 1978 . . . . 8.00
Aunt Jenny's Real Life Stories, recipe book, Aunt Jennie's Recipe Book–12 Pies Husbands Like Best, Lever Brothers, 1952 . . . . 8.00
Bachelor's Children, fan newsletter, Wonder Bread, c1945 . . . . 12.00
Banana Splits, Bingo puppet, plastic, Kellogg's, 1969 . . . . . 10.00
Blondie, game, Blondie Goes To Leisureland, Westinghouse, 1940. . . . . 18.00
Bob Hope, book, *They Got Me Covered,* Pepsodent, 1941. . . . . 10.00
Bob Hope, poster, Popsicle contest, 8 x 20", 1961 . . . . . . 30.00
Boo Berry, poster and figural monster crayons, General Mills, 1988 . . . . 20.00

Breakfast Club, tab, litho, Aunt Jemima, 1960s 5.00
Buck Rogers, Solar System Map, Cocomalt, 1933, 18 x 25". 250.00
Bullwinkle, plate, white plastic, Bullwinkle jumping off diving board with Cheerios kid watching, General Mills, 8" d. 25.00
Cap'n Crunch, figure, vinyl, Quaker, 1971, 8" h 35.00
Cap'n Crunch, toy, plastic, sea cycle and Cap'n Crunch and Seadog figures, rubber band powered, orig mailing box, unused, Quaker, 1960s 60.00
Captain Midnight, badge, Mysto–Magic weather for-casting flight wings, Skelly Oil Co, 1939 . . . . 12.00
Captain Midnight, insignia shoulder patch 35.00
Captain Midnight, key–o–matic code–o–graph 45.00
Captain Midnight, Mystery Dial Code–O–Graph brass decoder, 1941 . . . . 30.00
Captain Midnight, ring, brass, sliding secret compart-ment, 1942 . . . . 75.00
Captain Tim Healy, booklet, *Spies I Have Known,* photos, Ivory Soap, 1936 . . . . 15.00
Chandu The Magician, magic trick, Chinese coin on string, mailer envelope, Beech–Nut Gum, 1930s 30.00
Chandu The Magician, magic slate, wood stylus marker, 1930s 55.00
Charlie McCarthy, figure, cardboard, Mortimer Snerd, c1938 . . . . 50.00
Charlie McCarthy, ring, brass, McCarthy bust, 1940. . . . . 150.00
Charlie McCarthy, spoon 10.00
Cheerios Kid and Donald Duck, Huey, Louie, and Disneyland, postcard, black and white, General Mills Cheerios, 1957, 3½ x 6". 10.00
Chick Carter, club card, "Chick Carter Inner Circle," 1944 . . . . 15.00
Choo Choo Cherry, cloth pillow, Pillsbury, 1970 . . . . 15.00
Chug A Lug, mug, plastic, Pillsbury, 1969 . . . . 12.00
Cisco Kid, mask, paper, Pancho, 1949 . . . . 15.00
Cisco Kid, membership kit, "The Cisco Kids Book of Famous Western Brands," includes 2 certificates, manual, application, and "Cattle Brand" card, 1950s 75.00
Cisco Kid, pinback button, "Safety Club Member," c1948 . . . . 30.00

Little Orphan Annie, mug, ceramic, Ovaltine, $50.00.

Cisco Kid, ring, name appears on each side, c1940s **100.00**

Cisco Kid, tumbler, plastic, Leatherwood Dairy, 1950s. . . . **18.00**

Counterspy, activity book, Junior Counterspy fun and game book, 1951 . . . . **15.00**

Death Valley Days, book, *Death Valley Days,* 1931 . . . . **5.00**

Death Valley Days, radio script, "The World's Biggest Job," for April 11 episode, cover folder, envelope, 1935 . . . . **10.00**

Death Valley Days, Old Ranger's Seed Packets **15.00**

Dick Tracy, Air Detective Brass Wings Badge, 1938 . . . . . **30.00**

Dick Tracy, badge, brass, "Second Year Member," 1939 . . . **25.00**

Dick Tracy, booklet, Secret Detective Methods and Magic Tricks, Quaker, 1939 . . . . **35.00**

Dick Tracy, club manual, 1938 . . . . **65.00**

Dick Tracy, game book, Hatful Of Fun!, 1940s **15.00**

Dick Tracy, pocketknife, celluloid grips, Imperial Co, 1930s **55.00**

Dick Tracy, rubber band gun **22.00**

Dizzy Dean, booklet, "Let me send you these valuable prizes...free!, 1935 . . . . **15.00**

Dizzy Dean, charm, brass, figural, baseball, 1935 . . . . **12.00**

Dizzy Dean, pin, brass, figural, bat, 1935 . . . . **15.00**

Don Winslow of the Navy, badge, silvered brass, Ensign/Squadron of Peace, 1939 . . . . **300.00**

Don Winslow of the Navy, periscope, cardboard, slanted mirrors on each end, 1939 . . . . **50.00**

Don Winslow of the Navy, rubber stamp **30.00**

Eddie Cantor, booklet, How to Make a Quack–Quack, Chase & Sanborn, 1932 . . . . **22.00**

Ed Wynn, mask, cardboard, Texaco Fire Chief, c1933 . . . . **25.00**

Eddie Cantor, ink blotter, 1934 . . . . **5.00**

Felix The Cat, ring, litho tin, Post, 1949 . . . . **25.00**

Fibber McGee and Molly, Molly spinner top, wood peg, Johnson's Wax Polishes, 1936 . . . . **65.00**

Flintstones, Fred and Barney figures, ceramic, Post, 1990, price for pair **5.00**

Frosted Flakes, spoon, sterling silver, Kellogg's, 1983 . . . . . . **5.00**

Fury's Western Roundup Party Kit, paper, 8 punch–out sheets, Borden's, c1955 . . . . **25.00**

Gabby Hayes, hat, black felt, Quaker, 1951 . . . . **30.00**

Gene Autry, pinback button, photo, Sunbeam Bread c1950 . . . . **12.00**

Ghostbusters, Ectomobile, diecast, 2 rolls of Fuji film, carded, 1988 . . . . **45.00**

Gulliver's Travels, booklet, Macy's, 1939 . . . . **25.00**

His Nibs, compass ring, carded, Nabisco, 1947 . . . . **25.00**

Huckleberry Hound, figure, plastic, removable head with secret storage space, Kellogg's, 1960s **30.00**

Huckleberry Hound, pinback button, "Huck Hound for President," Kellogg's, 1960, 3" d. **15.00**

Jack Armstrong, explorer telescope, cardboard, map, glass lense, 1938 . . . . **10.00**

Jack Armstrong, secret whistling ring, brass, Egyptian symbols on side, 1937 . . . . **45.00**

Jack Armstrong, Sky Ranger plane, 1940 . . . . **55.00**

Jack Pearl, Baron Munchasen map of Radioland, 19 x 24" **55.00**

Jean LaFoote, bank, vinyl, Quaker, 1972 . . . . **30.00**

Jimmie Allen, aviator cap, felt, 1934 . . . . **40.00**

Jimmie Allen, postcard, Log Cabin Bread, c1934 . . . . **15.00**

Jimmie Allen, ring, brass, J. A. Cadets, Canadian issue, 1930s **100.00**

Jimmie Allen, whistle, brass **48.00**

Joe Corntassel, photo, Ovaltine and R. O. A., orig mailer, 1930 . . . . **48.00**

Joe E. Brown Club, booklet, You Said a Mouthful, Meier's Bread, 1944 . . . . **22.00**

Joe E. Brown Club, membership ring **50.00**

Joe DiMaggio, Sports Club membership card, M & M Candy, 1940s **30.00**

Keds, ring, "U.S. Keds," silvered brass, c1962 . . . . **55.00**

Kellogg's, ring, brass, 1949 . . . . **25.00**

Kellogg's, Space Satellite Launcher Set, 1956 . . . . **200.00**

Kool–Aid, Treasure Hunt brass ring, 1930s **110.00**

Linus The Lion, activity book, Post, 1964 . . . . **25.00**

Little Lulu, mask, Kleenex, 1952 . . . . **25.00**

Little Orphan Annie, comic book, *The Adventures Of Little Orphan Annie, Quaker,* 1941 . . . . **18.00**

Little Orphan Annie, bandanna, 1934 . . . . **38.00**

Little Orphan Annie, club manual, 1938 . . . . **25.00**

Little Orphan Annie, doll, oilcloth, 1930s **100.00**

Little Orphan Annie, Miracle Compass Sun–Watch, 1938 . . . . **25.00**

Little Orphan Annie, photo, Ann Gillis, Little Orphan Annie portrayer, c1938 . . . . **25.00**

Little Orphan Annie, sheet music, *Little Orphan Annie's Song,* Ovaltine, 1931 . . . . **18.00**

Lone Ranger, badge, enameled brass, inscribed "Chief Scout," and "Lone Ranger Safety Scout/Silvercup," 1934 . . . . **100.00**

Lone Ranger, bat–o–ball, Pure Oil, 1938 . . . . **35.00**

Lone Ranger, mask, cardboard, 1938 . . . . **40.00**

Lone Ranger, newspaper, *Lone Ranger Roundup,* Vol. 1, Bond Bread, Aug 1939 . . . . **55.00**

Lone Ranger, photo, sgd "Your Friend, The Lone Ranger," Bond Bread, c1940 . . . . **20.00**

Lone Wolf Tribe, necklace, Tribe Arrowhead **18.00**

Lone Wolf Tribe, tom tom **12.00**

Straight Arrow, Injun–uity Manual, Book 3, cardboard, green lettering, Nabisco, 3⁷/₈" w, 7³/₈" h, 1951, $10.00.

Lucky Charms, Cocoa Puffs, Franken Berry, Trix, Count Chocula, and Boo Berry, card game, 2 decks with cereal characters, complete with mailer, General Mills, 1981 . . . . **10.00**

Lum and Abner, decanter, aluminum lid, Horlick's Malted Milk, c1936 . . . . **45.00**

Lum and Abner, Horlick malted maker **60.00**

Lum and Abner, 1936 family almanac **5.00**

Magic Pup, ring, magnetized pup's head, Ralson Wheat Chex, 1951 . . . . **65.00**

Major Jet, bookley, *Major Jet's Magic Paint Set #1,* General Mills, 1954 . . . . **10.00**

Mickey and Minnie Mouse, ink blotter, cardboard, Mickey and Minnie as bride and groom driving in car, Sunoco, 1939 . . . . **30.00**

Mickey Mouse, Big Little Book, *Mickey Mouse The Mail Pilot,* American Oil Co, 1933 . . . . **45.00**

Mickey Mouse, comic book, *Mickey And Goofy Explore The Universe Of Energy,* Exxon, 1985 . . . . **1.50**

Mickey Mouse, spoon, Post, 1930s **10.00**

Mickey Mouse Club, Magic Manual, Mars Candy, 1950s **12.00**

Mickey Mouse Club, record, *Mousketeer Record,* 78 rpm, sleeve, General Mills, 1956 . . . . **12.00**

Mickey Mouse Club, ring, aluminum, Pillsbury, 1950s **12.50**

Mickey Mouse Explorers, coloring book, Kroger Food Stores, 1965 . . . . **10.00**

Mighty Mouse, Merry–Pack, punch–out sheets, Post, Alpha Bits, c1956 . . . . **60.00**

Monkees, record, *The Monkees,* cereal box cut–out, Kellogg's, c1970 . . . . **5.00**

Mr. Magoo, figural badge, metal, G. E. Lightbulbs **10.00**

Munchy, spoon attachment, vinyl, Nabisco, 1959 . . . . . . **18.00**

Muttley, Wacky Races Bi–Plane, Muttley, missing one wing support, Kellogg's, 1969 . . . . **50.00**

Ogg, figure, Kellogg's Rice Krispies, 1970 . . . . **30.00**

One Man's Family, Barbour family scrapbook, 1946 . . . . . . **8.00**

One Man's Family, Teddy Barbour's diary, 1937 . . . . **15.00**

Our Gang, activity booklet, *Our Gang Fun Kit,* mask–like photos, "Eagles Club" rules, Morton's Salt, 1937 . . . . **40.00**

Pep, beanie, felt, orange and white, Kellogg's, 1943 . . . . . **25.00**

Peter Pan, coloring book, Peter Pan Peanut Butter, 1963 . . . . **8.00**

Pillsbury Dough Boy, cloth doll, Pillsbury, 1970s **8.00**

Pink Panther, RPX race car, Pink Panther Cereal, 1973 . . . . **60.00**

Popeye, comic gum folder, Tattoo Gum, 1933 . . . . **10.00**

Popsicle, ring, plastic, figural cowboy boot, 1951 . . . . **30.00**

Popsicle Pete, "Mystery Box With Mystery Prize," Popsicle, c1940s, empty **12.00**

Post, bowl and mug set, instructions, mailer, 1954 . . . . . . **35.00**

Quake and Quisp, comic book, *Adventures of Quake And Quisp,* Quaker, 1965 . . . . **5.00**

Quaker, mug, plastic, c1950 . . . . **8.00**

Quisp, card game, Space Match, Quaker, 1968 . . . . **25.00**

Quisp, doll, cloth, Quaker, 1965 . . . . **30.00**

Quisp, flying saucer, plastic, battery operated, Quaker, 1966 . . . . **285.00**

Quisp, meteorite ring, Quaker, 1960s **55.00**

Quisp, smoke gun, plastic, Quaker, 1960s **80.00**

Reddy Kilowatt, glow–in–the–dark figure, plastic, 1961 . . . . **55.00**

Rin–Tin–Tin, bagatelle, Bead In Hole Game, Nabisco, 1956 . . . . **15.00**

Rin–Tin–Tin, booklet, *What Every Dog Should Know,* Ken–L–Ration, c1931 . . . . **15.00**

Rin–Tin–Tin, peel–off stickers, Nabisco, 1958 . . . . **3.00**

Rin–Tin–Tin, ring, plastic, Nabisco, 1955 . . . . **12.00**

Rin–Tin–Tin, Wonda–Scope, Nabisco **25.00**

Roger Wilco, magni–ray ring, brass, paper insert under hinged cover, Power House Candy, 1948 . . . . . . **35.00**

Roy Rogers, pin, Post Grape Nut Flakes, 1953 . . . . **5.00**

Roy Rogers, record, *Roy Rogers Ranch,* cardboard, Post, 1955 . . . . **45.00**

Seckatary Hawkins, fair and square spinner, 1932 . . . . . . **22.00**

Sgt. Preston, record, record, Challenge of the Yukon/Maple Leaf Forever, 45 rpm **2.50**

Sgt. Preston, signal flashlight **25.00**

Skippy, compass **15.00**

Skippy, secret code folder **18.00**

Sky King, stamping kit **30.00**

Smilin' Jack, ring, litho tin, Post Raisin Bran, 1948 . . . . . . **10.00**

Snoopy, clip–on badge, plastic, Millbrook Bread, 1970 . . . . **2.50**

Space Ranger, pinback button, litho, Rocky Jones illus, Johnston Cookies, c1954 . . . . **12.00**

Speedy Alka–Seltzer, figural pin, enameled brass, c1950s . . . . **$ 25.00**

Squadron Of Peace, membership card, Kellogg's Wheat Krispies, 1939 . . . . **18.00**

Star Wars, character stick–ons, Lucky Charms, General Mills, 1977 . . . . **8.00**

Sugar Crisp, paint–by–number set, Post, 1954 . . . . **30.00**

Sugar Crisp, puppet, Post, 1953 . . . . **10.00**

Sundial Shoes, ring, brass, plastic dome top over sundial, 1950 . . . . **35.00**

Taystee Bread, New Magic Tricks sheet, c1940 . . . . **25.00**

The Shadow, Shadow Club rubber stamp **30.00**

Tony the Tiger, bank, figural, plastic, Kellogg's, 1967 . . . . **30.00**

Tony the Tiger, inflatable toy, figural, vinyl, 1953 . . . . **10.00**

Tony the Tiger, radio, figural, plastic, Kellogg's, 1980 . . . . **10.00**

Toucan Sam, secret decoder, plastic, Toucan Sam, Kellogg's, 1983 . . . . **5.00**

Trix Rabbit, pinback button, litho, "No! Trix Are For Kids!," General Mills, 1970s **5.00**

Wheaties Rare Rock Collection, General Mills, $25.00.

Trix Rabbit, puppet, cloth and vinyl, General Mills,
    1960s, 12" h **30.00**
Uncle Don, booklet, Terry and Ted on the Trail of the
    Secret Formula, 1930s **8.00**
Veronica Lake, pinback button, litho, Quaker Puffed
    Wheat & Rice, 1948.............................. **5.00**
Voodoo Eye Pendant, metal, envelope, Wheato–
    Nuts, 1930s **80.00**
Wonder Bread, ring, plastic, c1970s................ **5.00**
Yogi Bear, eraser, Kellogg's, 1960s, 2" h **20.00**
Young Forty–Niners, Captain Sam's wagon punch–out
    folder, cardboard, 19 x 37".................... **45.00**
Young Forty–Niners, United States Adventure Map,
    20 x 31", c 1932 .... **45.00**

PSYCHEDELIC

Psychedelic collectibles describes a group of objects made during the 1960s an 70s that are highly innovative in their use of colors and design. American Indian tribal art, the artworks of Toulouse Lautrec and Alphonse Mucha, the color reversal approach of Joseph Albers, dancer Loie Fuller's diaphanous material, late 19th century graphics, paisley fabrics, and quilts are just a few of the objects and techniques that are the roots of psychedelic design.

The period is marked by eclecticism, not unity—there were no limits on design. Psychedelic artists and manufacturers drew heavily on new technologies, e.g., inflatable plastic furniture. Coverings such as polyester and vinyl were heavily used.

Peter Max is the most famous designer associated with the psychedelic era. His artwork graced hundreds of different objects. Although mass produced, some items are hard to find.

References: Eric King, *The Collector's Guide to Psychedelic Rock Concert Posters, Postcards and Handbills,* Svaha Press, 1996; Susanne White, *Psychedelic Collectibles of the 1960s & 1970s: An Illustrated price Guide,* Wallace–Homestead, 1990, out–of–print.

Ashtray, Peter Max design, multicolored, Iroquois
    China, Syracuse, NY, 10" d .... **$ 48.00**
Belt, cloth, leather fringed ends, green, orange, light
    green, and gold design, c1968 .... **8.00**
Belt, leather, American Indian, psychedelic enam–
    el–bead design, c1960 .... **40.00**
Book, *Get On Down,* Mick Farren, Futura
    Publications and Dempsey & Squires, Great
    Britain, 1977 .... **28.00**
Book, *Steal This Book,* Abbe Hoffman, Pirate
    Editions, New York, c1971 .... **30.00**
Clock, peace sign motif, blue, green, white, and yel–
    low, Westclox **55.00**
Clothing, caftan, cotton, "Dashiki" olive, maroon,
    rust, and yellow African motif, c1970 .... **160.00**
Clothing, dress, Flower Fantasy, paper, pink, green,
    yellow, and white, Hallmark, Kansas City, MO,
    c1969 .... **18.00**
Clothing, mini dress, cotton, orange, blue, yellow,
    pink, and green print, 1969–70................ **32.00**
Comic Book, The Forty Year Old Hippie, #2, The Rip
    Off Press, Inc, 1979 .... **5.50**
Curtain, beaded, plastic, yellow, brown, and orange,
    60 x 36" per section, c1969 .... **70.00**

Poster, Allman Brothers, green, reprint, $20.00.

Headband, cloth, elastic band, blue and white, peace
    signs and birds, c1970 .... **10.00**
Jewelry, choker, white, green, black, and yellow,
    metal peace charm............................ **10.00**
Jewelry, pin, set of four, metal, enamel, Peter Max
    design, paper label, c1970 .... **140.00**
Jewelry, pin, SS, "LOVE" **40.00**
Magazine, *Freak Out USA,* February, 1967 .... **15.00**
Necktie, Peter Max design, multicolored............ **48.00**
Paperweight, letters form word LOVE **10.00**
Pillow, Peter Max design, needlepoint, orange, black,
    red, blue, purple, white, green, and yellow butte
    fly design, c1972 .... **65.00**
Plate, 8¼" d, Peter Max design, dark smoked glass,
    enamel paint design **65.00**
Poster, Bob Dylan, Milton Glazer, artist, blue, green,
    white, brown, pink, and orange **185.00**
Poster, Psychedelic Shop–Jook Savage Art Show, Rick
    Griffin, artist, white and black, 14 x 20" **100.00**
Poster, The Print Mint, pink, white, and maroon, 15½
    x 20³⁄₈", c1966................................ **225.00**
Puzzle, Flower Power, Optical–Popticals, pop art
    design, Saalfield, ©1969...................... **15.00**
Scarf, silk, white, bright yellow, purple, blue, and
    green, large butterfly illus. center, Seagram's and 7
    Up logos surrounded by flower border, c1970....... **40.00**
Shoes, suede, platform style, multicolored **135.00**

PUNCHBOARDS

Punchboards are self–contained games of chance that are made of pressed paper and contain holes with a coded ticket inside each hole. After paying an agreed upon amount, the player uses a "punch" to extract the ticket of his choice. Cost to play ranged from 1¢ to $1.00.

Animal and fruit symbols, cards, dominos, and words were used as well as numbers to indicate prizes. While some punchboards had no printing, most contained elaborate letters and a picture or two.

Punchboards initially paid the winner in cash. In an effort to appease the anti–gambling crowd, some punchboards paid off in cameras, candy, cigar, cigarettes, clocks, jewelry, radios, sporting goods, toys, etc.

The 1920s through the 1950s was the golden age of the punchboard. An endless variety of punchboard were made. Many had catchy names, e.g., Break the Bank, or featured pin–up girls, e.g., Take It Off. Negative publicity resulting from the movie *The Flim Flam Man* hurt the punchboard industry.

Value rests with unpunched boards. Most boards still sell between $15 and $30. Some board have broken through the $100 barrier.

Reference: Norman E. Martinus and Harry L. Rinker, *Warman's Paper,* Wallace–Homestead, Krause Publications, 1994.

Big Bills, 25¢ punch	$ 20.00
Block Buster, double jackpot, cash payout, 5¢ per punch	20.00
Charlie Ten Spots	12.00
Delicious Cherries	12.00
Dixie Queen Cigarettes, 10 color tickets	10.00
Gas with a Punch, old pump and car	15.00
Hearts Desire, heart shape, 10 x 10"	25.00
Hit A Buck	5.00
Joe's Special Prize, cash board with name, 25¢	20.00
Lucky Coins	20.00
Lulu Belle	8.50
Musical Cigarettes	12.50
Nickel Fins, 1,000 holes with seals	15.00
Off We Go!, 5¢, play for packs of cigarettes	15.00
Pep and Beauty, 2¢, green	15.00
Prize Pots, red head girl, 50¢	65.00
Section Play, 25¢ cash board	10.50
Sports Push Cards, baseball, basketball, football	5.50
Sunshine Special	15.00
Tip Top Charley	15.50
Win A Buck	6.00
Your Pick, money seals, 10¢	32.00

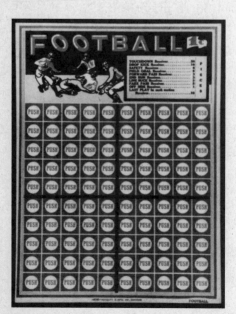

Football, 1¢, 1930s, 7¼ x 10", $20.00.

PURINTON POTTERY

Bernard Purinton founded Purinton Pottery, Wellsville, Ohio, in 1936. The company produced dinnerware and special order pieces. In 1940, Peter Underwood, president of Knox Glass Company, was instrumental in convincing Purinton to move to Shippenville, Pennsylvania. Ironically, the company's two–cup premium teapot made for the McCormick Tea Company, rolled off the assembly line at the brand new Shippenville plant on December 7, 1941.

Dorothy Purinton and William H. Blair, her brother, were the company's principal designers. Dorothy designed Maywood, Plaid, and several Pennsylvania German theme lines. Blair is responsible for Apple and Intaglio.

Purinton hand painted its wares. Because of this, variations with a pattern are common. Purinton made a complete dinnerware service including accessory pieces for each of its patterns.

The company utilized an open stock marketing approach. Purinton products were sold nationwide. Some were exported.

In 1958 the company ceased operations, reopened briefly, and then closed for good in 1959. Cheap foreign imports were the principal reason for the company's demise.

Reference: Susan Morris, *Purinton Pottery: An Identification & Value Guide,* Collector Books, 1994.

Newsletter: *Purinton Pastimes,* PO Box 9294, Arlington, VA 22219.

Apple, butter dish, 6½" l	$ 65.00
Apple, candy dish, 2 part, center loop handle, 6¼" h	50.00
Apple, covered dish, oval, 9" l	70.00
Apple, fruit bowl, scalloped border, 12' d	45.00
Apple, grill platter, 12" d	50.00
Apple, jug, 5¾" h	50.00
Apple, roll tray, rect, 11" l	37.00
Apple, snack set	25.00
Apple, tumbler, 5" h	22.00
Fruit, creamer and covered sugar	40.00
Fruit, cup and saucer	12.00
Fruit, dinner plate, 9¾" d	22.00
Fruit, relish, 3 part, 10" d	60.00
Fruit, salt and pepper shakers, jug–style, 2½" h	20.00
Fruit, sugar canister, red or blue trim, 9" h	70.00
Fruit, teapot, 5" h	60.00
Heather Plaid, coffee canister, square, 7½" h	45.00
Heather Plaid, creamer and covered sugar	50.00
Heather Plaid, grease jar, cov, 5½" h	65.00
Heather Plaid, jug planter, 6½" h	45.00
Heather Plaid, mug, 4" h	27.00
Heather Plaid, platter, oval, 12" l	35.00
Heather Plaid, wall pocket, 3½" h	35.00
Intaglio, bean pot, 3¾" h	50.00
Intaglio, chop plate, 12" d	27.00
Intaglio, cookie jar, oval–shaped, 9½" h	75.00
Intaglio, jam and jelly dish, 5½" l	45.00
Intaglio, vegetable dish, divided, 10½" l	35.00
Normandy Plaid, chop plate, 12" d	27.00
Normandy Plaid, cookie jar, oval–shaped, 9½" h	65.00
Normandy Plaid, dessert bowl, 4" d	10.00
Normandy Plaid, spaghetti bowl, oval, 14½" l	60.00
Normandy Plaid, tumbler, 5" h	22.00

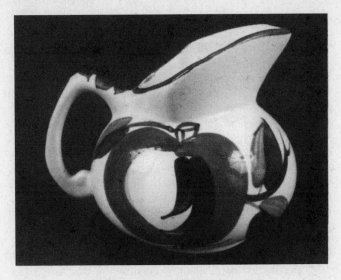

Apple, creamer, 4¹/₂" h, $15.00.

Normandy Plaid, vegetable dish, 8¹/₂" d **22.00**
Turquoise, baker, 7" d **32.00**
Turquoise, butter dish, 6¹/₂" l. **75.00**
Turquoise, fruit bowl, 12" d **45.00**

PUZZLES

Puzzles divide into two groups: (1) jigsaw and (2) mechanical. American and English collectors focus primarily on jigsaw puzzles. European collectors love mechanical puzzles.

The jigsaw puzzle first appeared in the mid–18th century Europe. John Silbury, a London map maker, offered dissected map jigsaw puzzles for sale by the early 1760s. The first jigsaw puzzles in America were English and European imports and designed primarily for use by children.

Samuel L. Hill, W. and S. B. Ives, and McLoughlin Brothers are American manufacturers who made jigsaw puzzles prior to 1860. However, it was not until the end of the 19th century that the jigsaw puzzle gained a foothold among the children of America.

Puzzles designed specifically for adults first appeared in the late 1890s and first decades of the 20th century. Children and adult puzzles have existed side by side ever since. Adult puzzles were responsible for two 20th century puzzle crazes: 1908–09 and 1932–33.

Prior to the mid–1920s, the vast majority of jigsaw puzzles were cut using wood for the adult market and composition board for the children's market. In the 1920s the diecut, cardboard jigsaw puzzle evolved. By the jigsaw puzzles craze of 1932–33, it was the dominant medium.

Jigsaw puzzle interest has cycled between peaks and valleys several times since 1933. Mini–revivals occurred during World War II and in the mid–1960s when Springbok entered the American market.

Puzzles are often difficult to date. Some puzzles, such as Milton Bradley's Smashed Up Locomotive, were produced for decades. The most popular prints were kept in inventory or reproduced as needed, often by several different manufacturers. Thus, the date when a puzzle was made is often years later than the date or copyright on the print or box. Avoid puzzles whose manufacturer can-

not be determined, unless the puzzle has especially attractive graphics or craftsmanship.

The number of jigsaw puzzle collectors has grown dramatically in the past two decades. Current collectors appear to be concentrating their efforts on wooden and diecut cardboard puzzles made before 1945, a few specialty areas, e.g., advertising and World War II, and turn of the century juvenile puzzles. Diecut cardboard puzzles in excess of 500 pieces remain primarily garage sale items. Some collector interest exists for early Springbok puzzles.

Mechanical puzzles have solid pieces that must be manipulated by one's hands to find a solution. Although some are made into a picture (the standard definition of a jigsaw puzzle), most are not.

Collectors divide mechanical puzzles into put–together puzzles, take–apart puzzles, interlocking solid puzzles, disentanglement puzzles, sequential movement puzzles, vanish puzzles, impossible object puzzles, and folding puzzles.

References: *Dexterity Games and Other Hand–Held Puzzles,* L–W Books Sales, 1995; Norman E. Martinus and Harry L. Rinker, *Warman's Paper,* Wallace–Homestead, Krause Publications, 1994.

Collectors' Clubs: American Game Collectors Assoc, 49 Brooks Ave, Lewiston, ME 04240; national Puzzler's League, PO Box 82289, Portland, OR 97282.

Jigsaw, adv, diecut cardboard, Campfire or Angelus Marshmallows, #1 in series of 4, Fishing Boats, tied at wharf, 48 pcs, 9³/₄ x 6 ³/₄", paper envelope. . . . . . . **$ 10.00**
Jigsaw, adv, diecut cardboard, Curtis Candy Company, Singing in the Rain Jig Saw Puzzle, 2–sided, front shows boy and girl under umbrella, reverse shows 1¢ candies produced by Curtis, 5⁵/₈ x 7¹/₂", paper envelope **30.00**
Jigsaw, adv, diecut cardboard, Heinz 57 Varieties, shows children playing store with all 57 products displayed on shelf, 10¹/₈ x 12", paper envelope **60.00**
Jigsaw, adv, diecut cardboard, The Kolynos Company, The Hunt, English fox hunting party arriving at Rosello Inn, illus by J. R. Óllé, © Brandt & Brandt, 1932, 104 pcs, 10 x 8", paper envelope measuring 10⁵/₈ x 8¹/₂", only adv is return address of company on envelope. **12.00**
Jigsaw, adv, diecut cardboard, New England Coke, Winter Sports, skiers and sledders on mountain slope overlooking village in distance, P. O. Palinstram illus, imprinted for Consolidation Coal Co., Portsmouth, NH, 48 pcs, 10⁷/₁₆ x 7³/₁₆", paper envelope measuring 10⁹/₁₆ x 7⁷/₁₆", insert entitled "The Camera Sees Fire," 4 panels, 13⁹/₁₆ x 6¹/₄" open, promotion pc for New England Coke, includes instruction on how to effectively stoke coal furnace. **60.00**
Jigsaw, adv, diecut cardboard, Pacific Coast Borax Co., Hauling 20 Mule Team Borax Out of Death Valley, 20 mule head figural pcs, 10³/₄ x 8¹/₄", paper envelope, newsprint cartoon insert (deduct $10 if insert is missing). **40.00**
Jigsaw, adv, diecut cardboard, Pacific Coast Borax Co., Hauling 20 Mule Team Borax Out of Death Valley, no figural pcs, 10³/₄ x 8¹/₂", paper envelope, cartoon insert (deduct $10 if insert is missing) **25.00**

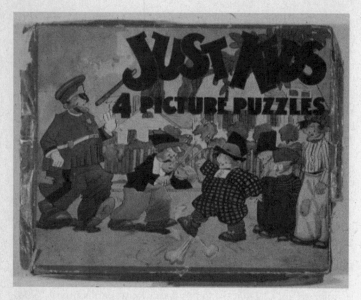

Jigsaw, Saalfield Publishing Co., #910, Just Kids Picture Puzzles, 4 puzzle set, each puzzle approx. 9³/₄ x 8", guide picture for 1 puzzle on front of box, $60.00.

Jigsaw, adv, diecut cardboard, Richfield Golden Gasoline/Richlube Motor Oil, Goofy Golf Jig–Saw Puzzle, #2 in series of 6, In Hawaii—And How!, 49 pcs, 7 x 9", paper envelope, front of envelope contains golf lesson by Alex Morrison **40.00**

Jigsaw, adv, diecut cardboard, Scott's Emulsion Cod Liver Oil, The Harbor at Balstad, Lofoten Islands, Norway; Site of Scott & Bowne's Cod Liver Oil Refinery, central figure of fisherman carrying large cod, sign adv product across figure, abstract harbor, village, mountain scene in background, 60 pcs, 7 figural pcs spelling SCOTT'S, 13¹/₄ x 10¹/₂", mkd "PRINTED IN U.S.A.," packaging missing **40.00**

Jigsaw, adv, diecut cardboard, Sloan's Liniment, Aerial View of Sing Sing Prison, includes portion of town of Ossining, insert of Warden Lewis E. Lawes in upper right corner, 104 pcs, 10 x 8", paper envelope, 10¹/₂ x 8¹/₂", no mention of puzzle on envelope, only return address for Sloan's Liniment **35.00**

Jigsaw, adv, diecut cardboard, Standard Oil Company of Ohio, Radio Jigsaw Puzzle #3, A Bully time in Spain, double sided, obverse shows Lena fighting bull in Spanish bull ring, reverse with head and shoulder portrait of Gene and Glenn, 252 pcs, 14¹/₂ x 11", adv sheet with guide picture, cardboard box **25.00**

Jigsaw, diecut cardboard, adult, Ballyhoo Magazines, Ballyhoo, No Nudes is Bad Nudes, 333 pcs, 10¹/₂ x 15¹/₂", 1930s, cardboard box **40.00**

Jigsaw, diecut cardboard, adult, Milton Bradley, Piccadilly Picture Puzzle, #81, On the Loire, over 200 pcs, 1930s, box with blue on white ground **10.00**

Jigsaw, diecut cardboard, adult, Consolidated Paper Box, Big 10 Perfect Picture Puzzle, #1010, Millstream in Winter, over 250 pcs, approx 13¹/₂ x 10", late 1930s, box **8.00**

Jigsaw, diecut cardboard, adult, Consolidated Paper Box, Perfect Picture Puzzle, #2016, #211 Cool and Silence, over 450 pcs, small guide picture on box **5.00**

Jigsaw, diecut cardboard, adult, Einson-Freeman, Every Week Jig–Saw Puzzle, #17, Abraham Lincoln, Ray Morgan illus, 10⁵/₈ x 14¹/₂", period box. . . . **25.00**

Jigsaw, diecut cardboard, adult, Harter Publishing Company, Cleveland, Ohio, #H–131, Series III, #4, Fishin' and Wishin', over 200 pcs, approx 15 x 11", green tone box **10.00**

Jigsaw, diecut cardboard, adult, Jaymar Specialty Company, Hobby Jigs Saws, Grizzly Bear, over 300 pcs, approx 14 x 22", small guide picture, box in treasure chest format, green ground **10.00**

Jigsaw, diecut cardboard, adult, Movie Cut-Up, Peabody, MA, Movie Cut–Up #7, Bitter Tea of General Yen, over 225 pcs, 9⁷/₈ x 13¹/₈", period box **35.00**

Jigsaw, diecut cardboard, adult, J. Pressman & Co., Victory Picture Puzzle, #20, Flying Fortresses Bombing Enemy Base, over 375 pcs, 19¹/₄ x 15¹/₄", c1945, guide picture on box **35.00**

Jigsaw, diecut cardboard, adult, Regent Specialties, De Luxe Picture Puzzle, Snow Capped Peaks, approx 400 pcs, approx 20 x 16", 1930s, period orange box **15.00**

Jigsaw, diecut cardboard, adult, Upson Company, TUCO Picture Puzzle, Quietude, over 200 pcs, approx 16 x 12", period box **8.00**

Jigsaw, diecut cardboard, adult, Viking Manufacturing Co, Picture Puzzle Weekly, Series A–4, Lions at Sunset, 13⁷/₈ x 10", box **17.50**

Jigsaw, diecut cardboard, children, Built Rite Sta–N–Place Inlaid Puzzle, frame tray, #1129, Dagwood and children rush out the door while Blondie watches, 13¹/₂ x 10⁵/₈", early 1960s **20.00**

Jigsaw, diecut cardboard, children, Consolidated Paper Box Co., Big 4 Circus Puzzles Jig–Saw Type, 3 puzzle set, Set #1, each puzzle 9 x 6³/₄", c1930–40s **18.00**

Jigsaw, diecut cardboard, children, E. E. Fairchild, #162, Weird–ohs Picture Puzzle, Freddy Flameout: The Way Out Jet Jockey, 1 of series of 4, 108 pcs, approx 15 x 10¹/₂", guide picture on box **20.00**

Jigsaw, diecut cardboard, children, HG Toys, #465–02, Happy Days Featuring "The Fonz," 150 pcs, approx 14 x 10", guide photograph on box. **10.00**

Jigsaw, diecut cardboard, children, Jaymar, Bedtime Story Picture Puzzle, Puss In Boots, guide picture on box, c1950s **10.00**

Jigsaw, diecut cardboard, children, Milton Bradley, #4318, Dr. Kildare Jigsaw Puzzle, #2, We are going to call him Jimmy, over 600 pcs, includes 14 x 12" color portrait for framing, guide picture on box, 1962 copyright. **22.50**

Jigsaw, diecut cardboard, children, Milton Bradley, #4691–1, James Bond 007 Jigsaw Puzzle, Thunderball, #1, Spectre's Surprise, over 600 pcs, approx 24 x 14", portion of puzzle pictured on box cover **35.00**

Jigsaw, diecut cardboard, children, Saalfield Publishing Co., #567, Kitty–Cat Picture Puzzle

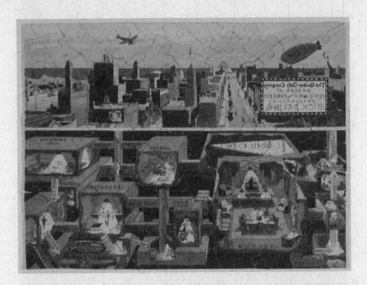

Jigsaw, diecut cardboard, adv, Quaker Oats, "The Quaker Oats Company, Makers of Puffed Wheat and Puffed Rice, Presenting Dick Daring," 100 pcs, 12 x 8³/₄", paper insert showing identical scene, paper envelope, $40.00.

box, 6 puzzle set, Fern Biesel Peat illus, each puzzle approx 7⅞ x 9⅞", guide picture for 1 puzzle on box lid. **50.00**

Jigsaw, diecut cardboard, children, Whitman Publishing, Series 302, Authorized Jr. Jigsaw Puzzle, Hugh O'Brian As Wyatt Earp, 63 pcs, guide picture on box. **20.00**

Jigsaw, diecut cardboard, children, Whitman Publishing, #3932, Edgar Bergen's Charlie McCarthy Picture Puzzles, 2 puzzle set, approx 7¼ x 10", 1938 copyright. **35.00**

Jigsaw, diecut cardboard, children, Whitman Publishing, #4427, frame tray, Wagon Train, drawing of wagon master and scout hunting buffalo, 11³/₈ x 14¹/₂", 1961 copyright **22.50**

Jigsaw, diecut cardboard, children, Whitman Publishing, #4457, frame tray, Hanna–Barbera Top Cat, Top Cat sits in trash can sipping milk from bottle on porch while policeman looks on, 11³/₈ x 14¹/₈", 1961 copyright. **20.00**

Jigsaw, ephemera, broadside, University Distributing Co., Jig of the Week #22, Boyhood of Sir Walter Raleigh, paper, 14 x 10³/₄" **20.00**

Jigsaw, ephemera, catalog, Parker Brothers Autumn List 1913 Famous Pastime Puzzles, double sided sheet, 9 x 15¹/₂", fold marks (folded twice in thirds) **15.00**

Jigsaw, ephemera, magazine, Future, #10, May 1979, space station jigsaw puzzle theme on cover. **10.00**

Jigsaw, hand cut, composition board, children, McLoughlin Bros., The Young Blue Jackets, set of 2, United States Cruiser Columbia, 18 pcs, 10 x 6", and United States Cruiser San Francisco, 15 pcs, 9 x 6¹/₂", box lithography shows 3 sailors around naval gun, pre–1915. . . . . **350.00**

Jigsaw, hand cut, composition board, children, Milton Bradley, Smashed Up Locomotive, 9 x 7", wooden box, pre–1915. . . . . **300.00**

Jigsaw, wood, Reid S. Baker, Washington, D.C., Indian Summer, corn stalks in foreground, farmstead in background, Enneking illus, 158 pcs, 9³/₄ x 7³/₄", box measures 6¹/₄ x 6¹/₄ x 1¹/₂", paper label with rental information. **20.00**

Jigsaw, wood, R. W. Bliss, Wallaston, MA, The Arab Raiding Party, A. D. Schreyer illus of armed horsemen riding at dusk, 153 pcs, 12 x 9", black and orange box, early 20th C **30.00**

Jigsaw, wood, Hanks Puzzle Shop, Conway, NH, A Colonial Sweetheart, portrait of Dutch colonial woman with vase of flowers, J. Van Vredand illus, 538 pcs, 16 x 20", period box. **65.00**

Jigsaw, wood, Madmar Interlox Puzzle, Spoils of War, Prussian Officer enjoying leisurely evening of music and relaxation in European parlor, 755 pcs, 20 x 16", period box **85.00**

Jigsaw, wood, Milton Bradley, Premier Jigsaw Puzzle, Port of Heart's Desire, kneeling mother holding daughter, 168 pcs, 8 x 10", period box **25.00**

Jigsaw, wood, Parker Brothers, A Shady Pathway, lake country scene with shepherd and sheep, 350 pcs, 36 figural pcs, 17 x 11", period box, late 1930s. **45.00**

Jigsaw, wood, Parker Brothers, Pastime Picture Puzzle, Master of the House, H. M. Brett illus, portrait of family with infant at table, 183 pcs, 19 figural pcs, 13 x 9", c1920s **30.00**

Jigsaw, wood, Picture Puzzle Exchange, Boston, The First Note of the Bell, colonial Philadelphia scene of christening of Liberty Bell, 196 pcs, 14 x 10", period box, 1916 . . . . **32.50**

Jigsaw, diecut cardboard, Whitman, No. 4429, Series No. 302, untitled, Francis Tipton Hunter illus, $10.00.

Jigsaw, wood, Straus, Joseph K., Guardians of Liberty, World War II scene of battleship and planes passing Statue of Liberty, T. J. Slaughter illustration, 482 pcs, 16 x 20", period box, mid–1940s **35.00**

Jigsaw, wood, unknown cutter, My Little Girl, elderly host introducing marriageable–age daughter to young huntsman, 323 pcs, 14 x 10" **40.00**

Jigsaw, wood, unknown cutter, The Birth of Our Country, Benjamin Franklin, colonial hearthside scene, Hy Hintermeister illus, 80 pcs, 13 x 9", c1920 . . . . **25.00**

Skill, checkerboard, diecut cardboard, The Famous and Baffling Checker Board Puzzle, The Vasen Company, Davenport, IA, 14 pcs, content puzzle, solutions must be submitted by March 1, 1927, box measures 4¹/₈" sq **10.00**

Skill, head and tail puzzle, A–Treat Bottle Co., Allentown, PA, A–Treat Mystery Puzzle, 9 pcs, A–Treat bottles on different colored grounds, puzzle measures 7⁹/₁₆ x 7⁹/₁₆", different adv on the back of each pc, paper envelope, 3¹/₈ x 5¹/₂" **12.00**

Skill, letter dissection puzzle, Royal Typewriter Company, New York, NY, The "R" Puzzle, 7 pcs, Royal logo on the front of pcs, paper envelope, 4¹/₂ x 3" **20.00**

Skill, sliced or dissected puzzle, Pratt Food Co., Philadelphia, PA, dealer rubber stamp for W. D. Wilder, Laurenceville, NY, Pratt's Cut Up Puzzle (2 Puzzles in 1), double sided, obverse shows group of animals laughing and making sarcastic remarks to a gentleman attempting to get them to eat "Imitation Food," light green ground (another version has dark yellow ground), reverse contains series of slogan advertisements, puzzle measures 9 x 6¹/₄", paper envelope measures 6¹/₈ x 4⁵/₈" **25.00**

PYREX

The origins of Corning Glass begin with Amory Houghton and the Bay State Glass Company, East Cambridge, Massachusetts, founded in 1851. In 1854 Houghton established the Union Glass Company, a leading producer of consumer and specialty glass, in Sommerville, Massachusetts. In 1864 Houghton purchased the Brooklyn Flint Glass Works and moved it to Sommerville. Fuel and other costs necessitated a move.

In 1868 Houghton moved his company to Corning, New York, and renamed it the Corning Flint Glass Works. After an initial period focused on the production of tabletop glassware, the company's main product became hand–blown glass light bulbs. In 1908 Dr. Eugene C. Sullivan established a research laboratory at Corning. Dr. William C. Taylor, a young chemist graduate from the Massachusetts Institute of Technology, joined Sullivan that same year.

In the early 1910s Sullivan and Taylor developed Nonex, a heat resistant glass. Dr. Jesse T. Littleton joined Corning around 1912 and began experiments on glass suitable for baking vessels. Littleton's wife was asked to try baking with the cut off bottom of some experimental glass jars. Mrs. Littleton found the glass cooking vessel lowered cooking time, ingredients did not stick, and the flavor of the food did not remain after washing.

Corning Glass created a consumer products business in 1915, launching a 12–piece Pyrex line. Although a brand name, Pyrex has become a generic term describing any heat–resistant glass kitchenware. In 1920 Corning granted Fry Glass Company, Rochester, Pennsylvania, a license to produce Pyrex cooking glass under its Fry Oven Glass label. The 200–inch glass disk for the Hale telescope at the California Institute of Technology is one of the most famous uses for Pyrex.

Pyrex divides into three principal collecting categories: (1) clear or crystal, made since 1915, (2) Flameware, made between 1936 and 1979, a slightly different composition capable of withstanding open–flame, stovetop cooking, and (3) colored opal or fired–on color Pyrex, an opaque glass introduced in 1974.

Pyrex was only made at four plants: (1) the Main Plant "A" Factory Main (1915–1983) in Corning, (2) Charleroi (1946 to the present), Pennsylvania, (3) Greenville (1973 to present), Ohio, and (4) the Main Factory "B" Factory (1936–40, 1948–1979).

Reference: Susan Tobier Rogove and Marcie Buan Steinhauer, *Pyrex By Corning: A Collector's Guide,* Antique Publications, 1993.

Baker, open, Gold Acorn, 1¹/₂ qt. . . . . $ **12.50**
Baking Dish, cov, oval, 10" l **10.00**
Baking Dish, individual, fluted, 9¹/₂ oz. **4.50**
Bowl, clear, 3 qt. **10.00**
Bowl, Hostess, blue int, black ext, 1¹/₂ qt. **18.00**
Bowl, set, Bluebelle, 1¹/₂ pt., 1¹/₂ qt., 2¹/₂ qt. **20.00**
Cake Dish, clear, 8¹/₂" sq.. . . . . **8.00**
Calendar, 1932, Pyrex Ovenware for Baking and Serving **6.50**
Casserole, cov, Blue Stripe
Casserole, cov, Constellation, 1¹/₂ qt. **12.50**
Casserole, cov, Daisy, 1¹/₂ qt. **12.50**
Casserole, cov, Deluxe Buffet Server, double warmer, 2¹/₂ qt **20.00**
Casserole, cov, Flamingo, 2 qt.. . . . . **12.50**
Casserole, cov, Golden Honeysuckle, 2¹/₂ qt.. . . . . **20.00**
Casserole, cov, Golden Wreath, 2¹/₂qt. **20.00**
Casserole, cov, Gooseberry, 1¹/₂ pt.. . . . . **8.00**
Casserole, cov, Medallion, candle warmer, 2¹/₂"\ qt. **20.00**
Casserole, cov, Rich Colonial Brown, 1¹/₂ qt.. . . . . **15.00**

Nesting Bowls, #404 yellow, #403 green, #402 red, and #401 blue, price for set, $30.00.

Casserole, cov, Snowflake, 2½ qt. . . . .
   3.50 Casserole, cov, Town & Country, 1½ qt. **12.50**
Casserole, cov, Zodiac, 2½ qt. **20.00**
Casserole, individual, round, 8 oz. **4.00**
Casserole, oval, 1 qt. **6.00**
Chip and Dip, 1½ pt. **6.00**
Cook Book, *Be a Better Cook with Pyrexware–Good
   Things to Eat*, 1947 . . . . **5.00**
Cook Book, *Getting the Most Out of Food*, 1931 . . . . **8.00**
Custard Cup, fluted, clear, 6½ oz. **3.50**
Loaf Pan, clear, 1½ qt. **8.00**
Measuring Bowl, clear, 1½ pt. **3.00**
Measuring Cup, clear, 2–spout, 1 cup. **8.00**
Measuring Cup, clear, 16 oz **6.00**
Measuring Bowl, clear, 1½ qt. **6.00**
Measuring Bowl, clear, 3 qt. **10.00**
Nesting Bowl, #401, Orange Dot **4.00**
Nesting Bowl, #402, Sandalwood Rainbow stripes **6.50**
Nesting Bowl, #403, Terra **8.00**
Nesting Bowl, #441, Butterprint Cinderella. **5.00**
Pie Plate, hexagonal, clear, 9" **6.00**
Pie Plate, fluted, clear, 11" d **12.00**
Platter, clear, oval, 13" l **8.00**
Ramekin, yellow, 12 oz. **4.00**
Refrigerator and Oven Dish, set, turquoise **28.00**
Refrigerator Dish, #501, Early American, 1½ cup **4.00**
Serving Dish, Bluebelle, 1½ qt. **15.50**
Serving Dish, Butterprint, oven, freezer, 1¼ qt **10.00**
Serving Dish, cov, Royal, 1½ qt **15.00**
Serving Dish, cov, Snowflake, oven, freezer, 2 qt. **15.00**
Teapot, round, sq. handle, 4 cup **70.00**
Utility Dish, mounter, oval, 10" l **18.00**
Vegetable Dish, divided, round **10.00**

QUILTS

Basically, a quilt consists of a layer of padding sandwiched between two layers of fabric that is then stitched to hold the sandwich together. Changes and advances in quilting occur primarily in appliqué and patchwork techniques and fabric patterns.

In the 18th century, quilting was used for garments. Although out of fashion in large urban areas by the beginning of the 19th century, quilted clothing remained popular in rural areas until the beginning of the 20th century.

Quilted curtains and bedcovers enjoyed widespread popularity by the 18th century. Lap quilts and covers were common during the Victorian era. World War I had a negative effect on quilting as women worked in factories during wartime. A quilting revival occurred in the late 1920s and 1930s. World War II ended this quilting renaissance.

A quilt exhibition at the Cooper Hewitt Museum in New York in 1971 reawakened interest in historic quilts and revitalized the art of quilt making. Many of today's contemporary quilts are done as works of art, never intended to grace the top of a bed.

Beginning in the 1920s, most patchwork quilts are made using silk screened fabrics. Cherry Basket, Dresden Plate, Grandmother's Flower Garden, Nursery Rhyme blocks, and Sunbonnet Babies were popular quilt patterns of the 1920–30s period.

Reference: Liz Greenbacker and Kathleen Barach, *Quilts: Identification and Price Guide*, Avon Books, 1992.

Periodical: *Quilters Newsletter*, PO Box 4101, Golden, CO 80401.

Collectors' Club: American Quilter's Society, PO Box 3290, Paducah, KY 42001; The National Quilting Assoc, Inc, PO Box 393, Ellicott City, MD 21043.

Alphabet, pieced, pink, embroidered letters, 35 x 50" . **$ 380.00**
Baby Blocks, pieced, blue, outline quilting of blocks,
   36 x 45". **115.00**
Bow Tie, pieced, geometric quilting, Mennonite,
   unused, 61 x 78". **250.00**
Broken Star, pieced, pink, yellow, multicolored
   prints, 108 x 90" **80.00**
Carnations, appliqued, red, blue on white, embroi-
   dered accents on flowers, 80 x 92" **165.00**
Crazy Quilt, pieced, flannel, multicolored, 54 x 72" **50.00**
Eagle and Flowers, appliqued, central eagle in shield
   surrounded by vining flowers, vining floral border,
   solid red and teal, yellow, calico, 79 x 93" **475.00**
Embroidered, white ground, red embroidered squares
   with animals, people, flowers, and nursery rhymes,
   76 x 82". **140.00**
Four–Point Stars, pieced, 5 stars, red, multicolored
   print, yellow ground, machine quilted scroll pat-
   tern, 72 x 80". **185.00**
Flower Urns, appliqued, 4 floral wreaths in red, gold-
   enrod, and teal green, red and green border stripes,
   red binding, feather quilted border, blue quilting
   pattern, machine and hand sewn, hand quilted,
   71 x 73". **385.00**
Fruit Basket and Butterflies, appliqued, red and pink,
   white muslin ground, red stripe around border,
   70 x 80" **65.00**
Ice Cream Cones, appliqued, strawberry, tan, and
   white, 30 x 40" **235.00**

Star, pieced, cotton, pink, red, yellow, and ivory, prints and solids, 71 x 69", $425.00.

Indiana Puzzle, pieced, medium blue on blue and white calico, machine quilted, 67½ x 85" **100.00**

Lemoyne Star, pieced, multicolored, feather stitch embroidery around stars, 68 x 68" **65.00**

Lightning Zig Zag, pieced, red and blue fabrics with white polka dots, back has 3 wide bars of alternating blue and green print, 68 x 84" **175.00**

Log Cabin, pieced, black and white, red, large logs, 70 x 80" **35.00**

Monkey Wrench, pieced, calico, 90 yellow squares with black wrench on blue ground, black border, brown and white homespun backing, worn and faded, 68 x 74" **100.00**

Nine Patch, pieced, multicolored print squares, red and green calico grid, 75 x 85" **195.00**

Ocean Waves, pieced, multicolored print, 1930s, 86 x 70" **65.00**

Panels, pieced, 9 stars in grid in center surrounded by 2 rows of stars and diamonds panels, pink, yellow, and blue calico with zig zag and sawtooth grids in solid red, goldenrod, and green, worn and frayed, 81 x83" **195.00**

Pinwheel, pieced, yellow, green, black, and pink, pink border, floral print backing, 70 x 70" **175.00**

Sailboats, pieced, pastel, pink and lavender double border, embroidered, 77 x96" **110.00**

School House Blocks, pieced, brown, rust, blue, and tan, tan muslin sashing and border, 70 x 84" **80.00**

Star, pieced, central star surrounded by smaller stars, pink, orange, blue, yellow, and pastel prints and solids on yellow ground, small stars machine sewn, 75 x 75". **110.00**

RADIO CHARACTERS & PERSONALITIES

Radio's golden age began in the 1920s and extended through the 1950s. Listening to the radio kept the housewife company during the day. Many families gathered around the radio in the evening to listen to a favorite program. American Movie Classics' Remember WENN television show provides an accurate portrayal of the early days of radio.

Classic radio characters such as Amos and Andy, the Great Gildersleeve, Molly Goldberg, and Fibber McGee and Molly were as real as one's next door neighbors. Radio personalities such as Gracie Allen and George Burns, Jack Benny, and Arthur Godfrey, became as famous and well–known as movie stars. When Don McNeill launched his Charter Breakfast Club Membership drive in the spring of 1944, he received 875,000 membership applications the first week. Many movie and music stars, e.g., Gene Autry, began their careers on the radio.

Sponsors and manufacturers provided a wide variety of material ranging from cookbooks to photographs directed toward the adult audience. Magazines devoted exclusively to radio appeared on newsstand racks.

When collecting radio material, do not overlook objects relating to the shows themselves. Props, publicity kits, and scripts are a few examples. Many Big Little Book titles focused on radio shows.

Television hurt, but it did not kill radio. The car radio plays a major role in one's daily commute. Many individuals still listen to

sporting events. The future for Country, Golden Oldies, and Talk radio remains bright.

References: Jon D. Swartz and Robert C. Reinehr, *Handbook of Old–Time Radio: A Comprehensive Guide to Golden Age Radio Listening and Collecting,* Scarecrow Press, 1993.

Periodical: *Old Time Radio Digest,* 4114 Montgomery Rd, Cincinnati, OH 45212.

Newsletter: *Friends of Old Time Radio,* PO Box 4321, Hamden, CT 06514.

Collectors' Clubs: North America Radio Archives, 134 Vincewood Dr, Nicholasville, KY 40356; Old Time Radio Club, 100 Harvey Dr, Lancaster, NY 14086; Oldtime Radio Show Collectors Assoc, 45 Barry St, Sudbury, Ontario P3B 3H6 Canada; Radio Collectors of America, 8 Ardsley Circle, Brockton, MA 02402; Society To Preserve & Encourage Radio Drama, Variety & Comedy, PO Box 7177, Van Nuys, CA 91409.

Note: For additional listings see Premiums.

Amos 'n Andy, booklet, *All about Amos 'n Andy,* scripts, photos, 1929, 128 pgs . . . . **$ 48.00**

Amos 'n Andy, game, Acrobat Ring and Disk **100.00**

Amos 'n Andy, game, Card Party, M. Davis Co, 1938. . . . . **70.00**

Amos 'n Andy, poster, Campbell Soups adv, 13 x 20". **50.00**

Amos 'n Andy, sheet music, *Check 'N Double Check,* 1931 . . . . **15.00**

Charlie McCarthy, bank, composition, McCarthy and Edgar Bergen, c1940 . . . . **50.00**

Charlie McCarthy, contest postcard, 1944. . . . . **15.00**

Charlie McCarthy, doll, celluloid, Effanbee, c1938 . . . . . . **45.00**

Don McNeill's Breakfast Club, membership card. **8.00**

Don McNeill's Breakfast Club, membership folder. **10.00**

Don McNeill's Breakfast Club, *The 1954 Breakfast Club Yearbook,* spiral bound. **10.00**

Don Winslow, bank, Uncle Earnest Saver Club, oval, paper label, photo and cartoon illus, Greenwich Savings Bank, New York City, 1930s, 2¼" h **40.00**

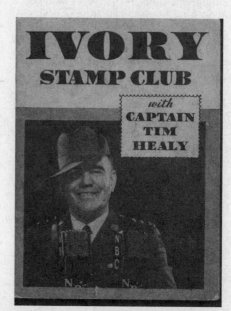

Captain Tim Healy, Ivory Stamp Club of the Air, stamp album, 1930s, 6¾ x 9⅜", $30.00.

Don McNeill, book, *Don's Other Life...,* by Kay McNeill, 8 x 9¼", $20.00.

Don Winslow, salt and pepper shakers, pr, Winslow and Red Pennington, 1940s 35.00
Ed Wynn, figure, wood, jointed, c1935. ...... 45.00
Ed Wynn, game, Ed Wynn, The Fire Chief, Selchow & Righter, c1937 ...... 25.00
Eddie Cantor, Big Little Book, *Eddie Cantor In An Hour With You,* Whitman #774, 1934 ...... 32.00
Eddie Cantor, pinback button, litho, "For President Eddie Cantor Great in '48" 10.00
Eddie Cantor, store sign, "Strike me pink if I don't think new Pebeco is Swell," 12 x 19" 45.00
Fibber McGee, game, The Merry Game of Fibber McGee and the Wistful Vista Mystery, Milton Bradley, 1940. ...... 25.00
Fibber McGee, photo, cast members, 1930s 20.00
Fibber McGee, sign, cardboard, Johnson Glo–Coat Floor Polish, 8 x 14". 50.00
Jack Benny, money clip, metal, gold luster, Friars luncheon souvenir, c1950s 20.00
Jack Benny, play money, "Buck Henry Rides Again," Cameo Theater, Aug 25–26, 1939 ...... 15.00
Jack Pearl, book, *Jack Pearl as Detective Baron Munchausen,* Goldsmith Co, 1934 ...... 15.00
Jimmie Allen, model, Thunderbolt, orig box, 1930s, 19" l, 24" wingspan 100.00
Jimmie Allen, photo, cast from movie *The Sky Parade,* 1936 ...... 40.00
Kate Smith, menu, A & P, 8 pgs 5.00
Little Orphan Annie, Big Little Book, *Little Orphan Annie and Sandy,* Whitman, #716, 1933 ...... 38.00
Little Orphan Annie, booklet, Official 1936 Secrets For Silver Star Member, Radio Orpan Annie's Secret Society–Strictly Confidential #47447 ...... 20.00
Little Orphan Annie, cup, plastic, Beetleware, 1933 ...... 20.00
Little Orphan Annie, photo, "Mitzi Green as Little Orphan Annie," 1932 ...... 30.00
Little Orphan Annie, pinback button, litho, "In Person at Kennedy Center," 1980s 15.00

Little Orphan Annie, sheet music, *Little Orphan Annie's Song,* Annie and Sandy on cov, compliments of Ovaltine & Radio's Orphan Annie, 1931 ...... 22.00
Little Orphan Annie, stove, child's, 1930s 55.00
Major Bowes, gong alarm clock, Ingersoll, 1930s 80.00
Major Bowes, postcard, 1930s 5.00
Quiz Kids, game, Parker Brothers, 1940 ...... 12.00
Sgt. Preston, coloring book, Whitman, 32 pgs. 22.00
Skippy, figure, bisque, movable arms, no base, 1930s 70.00
The Shadow, book, *The Living Shadow,* Maxwell Grant, c1931 ...... 8.50
The Shadow, game, Milton Bradley, 1994 ...... 15.00
The Shadow, matchbook cover, diecut hinged inside tab lowers to expose jail cell view, 1940s 45.00
The Shadow, photo, unmasked, 1930s 70.00

RADIOS

Marconi, who designed and perfected the transmission and reception instruments that permitted the sending of electrical messages without the use of direct communication, is considered the father of radio. By the end of the 1890s, the Marconi "Wireless" was being used for ship–to–shore communications.

A number of significant technological developments took place rapidly, e.g., DeForest's invention of the vacuum tube. By the mid–1920s the cost and quality of radios had reached a point where they were within the budget of most American households. The radio was transformed from a black box with knobs, dials, and a messy battery to a piece of stylized console furniture.

The tabletop radio arrived on the scene in the 1930s. Cathedral and Tombstone are two popular case shapes. Continued miniaturization marked radio production in the 1930s.

Miniature tubes and increased sound quality were two byproducts of radio research work done during World War II. The arrival of FM and the use of injection molded plastics for cases attracted more and more people to radio.

Although the transistor was invented in 1927, it was not until the post–1945 period that it was used heavily in the production of radios. Today transistor radios is a major subcategory of radio collection. The transistor also made possible the novelty radio, another popular collecting subcategory.

The value of any radio is directly related to is playability. If components, parts, or tubes are missing or if the radio needs minor repairs, its value is lowered by 50% or more. Parts are readily available to restore radios. In fact, the collecting of radio accessories, ephemera, and parts is increasing.

References: John H. Bryant and Harold N. Cones, *The Zenith Trans–Oceanic: The Royalty of Radios,* Schiffer Publishing, 1995, Marty Bunis and Robert F. Breed, *Collector's Guide To Novelty Radios,* Collector Books, 1995, Marty and Sue Bunis, *Collector's Guide To Antique Radios, Fourth Edition,* Collector Books, 1997, Marty and Sue Bunis, *Collector's Guide To Transistor Radios, Second Edition,* Collector Books, 1996; Chuck Dachis, *Radios By Hallicrafters,* Schiffer Publishing, 1996; David and Betty Johnson, *Guide To Old Radios: Pointers, Pictures, And Prices, Second Edition,* Wallace–Homestead, Krause Publications, 1995; David R. Lane and Robert A. Lane, *Transistor Radios: A Collector's Encyclopedia and Price Guide,* Wallace–Homestead, Krause Publications, 1994; Ron Ramirez, *Philco Radio: 1928–1942,* Schiffer Publishing, 1993; Scott Wood (ed.), *Evolution of the*

Radio, Vol. 1 (1991, 1994 value update), *Vol. 2* (1993), L–W Books Sales.

Periodicals: Antique Radio Classified, *PO Box 802, Carlisle, MA 01741; Radio Age,* PO Box 1362, Wahington Grove, MD20880; *The Horn Speaker,* PO Box 1193, Mabank, TX 75147.

Collectors' Clubs: Antique Radio Club of America, 300 Washington Trails, Washington, PA 15301; Antique Wireless Assoc, 59 Main St, Bloomfield, NY 14469.

Admiral, #5A32, circular clock face and dial, plain
  front panel, brown, 1952 . . . . $ **20.00**
Admiral, #6T02, rect Bakelite tabletop, molded grill
  louvers, white, 1946. . . . . **20.00**
Admiral, #8C2, Clipper, transistor. **5.00**
Admiral, #33–F5, portable, 5–tube, cloth covering,
  1940 . . . . **10.00**
Arvin, #657–T, "Sleeptimer," clock radio, square face,
  green, 1952 . . . . **15.00**
Bulova, #715, transistor, leatherette covering, top
  handle **10.00**
Channel Master, #6502, transistor, chrome front **5.00**
Emerson, #368, console, elongated dial, push but-
  tons,1940 . . . . **40.00**
Emerson, #656, portable, semicircular grill, front
  dial, maroon, 1950 . . . . **25.00**
Emerson, #899, Mercury, transistor. **35.00**
General Electric, #422, plastic, AM, 1951. . . . . **10.00**
General Electric, #J–62, wooden, square, tabletop,
  jewelry box style, side handles, 1940 . . . . **40.00**
General Electric, #LB–702, portable, suitcase style,
  brown leatherette covering, 1941 . . . . **10.00**
General Electric, #P725, transistor, plastic, metal
  front grill **25.00**
Motorola, #X11, transistor, metal front, oval window,
  logo. **25.00**
Novelty, Avon Skin–So–Soft **12.00**
Novelty, baseball, figural, plastic, white **12.00**
Novelty, Batman, figural, plastic. **55.00**
Novelty, dollar bill, figural **10.00**

RCA, #96–X–1, table model, white plastic, Art Deco style, AC, 1939, 11 x 7¹/₄ x 7¹/₂", $200.00.

Novelty, gas pump, figural, Sunoco **5.00**
Novelty, hamburger, figural **10.00**
Novelty, Little Sprout, figural **25.00**
Novelty, Mickey Mouse, figural **20.00**
Novelty, owl, figural **30.00**
Novelty, Pepsi Can, figural **15.00**
Novelty, Popeye, figural **55.00**
Novelty, Seagram's Cooler, figural. **10.00**
Philco, #T–4, transistor, large tuner dial, black and
  white **50.00**
RCA, #1X591, Gladwin, tabletop, Bakelite **25.00**
RCA, #45W9, AM/FM, veneered doors, pullout 45
  rpm phono, 1950. . . . . **65.00**
RCA, #8BX6, portable, aluminum and Bakelite, 1948 . . . . **40.00**
Sharp, #TR–182, transistor, front metal grill. **75.00**
Silvertone, #211, transistor. **15.00**
Stromberg–Carlson, #1101–HB, Dynamatic, table-
  top, white painted bakelite, 1946 . . . . **55.00**
Sylvania, #4P14, transistor **40.00**
Sylvania, #548, plastic, clock radio, square face,
  1957 . . . . **10.00**
Sylvania, #1202, Twilighter, tabletop, polystyrene,
  round front dial, backlighted pierced–metal grill,
  1957 . . . . **35.00**
Toshiba, #6TP–31, transistor, chrome front **55.00**
Westinghouse, #RS21P, Escort, transistor. **10.00**
Westinghouse, #523T4, Star Value, tabletop, plastic,
  square, oversized knob, 1955 . . . . **10.00**

RAILROADIANA

The Delaware and Hudson Canal Company Stourbridge Lion, the first steam powered locomotive in America, was used to haul coal from the mine head to the canal shipping wharves. When the Commonwealth of Pennsylvania commissioned William Strickland to study the state's transportation's need in the mid–1820s, Strickland recommended building railroads instead of canals. Pennsylvania failed to heed this sound advice.

Novelty, Coca–Cola bottle, figural, illuminated interior, 1933, 24" h, $8,800.00. Photo courtesy Muddy River Trading Company.

Canals and railroads competed head to head for right of ways in the 1830s. By the early 1840s, the railroad was the clear victor. The Civil War showed the importance and value of railroads. Immediately following the war, America went on a railroad building spree. The transcontinental railroad was completed. Robber barons such as Gould and Vanderbilt created huge financial fortunes from their railroad activities. A period of mergers occurred as the 19th century came to a close.

The period from the 1880s through the end of World War II is considered the golden age of railroads. The Interstate Highway system, a car in every garage, and the growing importance of air transportation ended the steel highway's dominance. Poor management and a bloated labor force added to the decline.

In the 1970s the Federal Government became actively involved in railroad management through Amtrak and Conrail. Thousands of miles of track were abandoned. Passenger service, except for a few key corridors, disappeared. Mergers continued into the 1990s. Even Conrail became a victim of consolidation.

References: Susan and Al Bagdade, *Warman's American Pottery and Porcelain,* Wallace–Homestead, Krause Publications, 1994; Stanley L. Baker, *Railroad Collectibles: An Illustrated Value Guide,* 4th Edition, Collector Books, 1990, 1996 value update; Richard C. Barrett, *The Illustrated Encyclopedia of Railroad Lighting, Volume 1: The Railroad Lantern,* Railroad Research Publications, 1994; Richard W. Luckin, *Butter Pat World: Transportation Collector's Guide Book,* RK Publishing, 1995.

Collectors' Clubs: Key, Lock and Lantern, Inc, 3 Berkeley Heights Park, Bloomfield, NJ 07003; Railroadiana Collectors Assoc, Inc, 795 Aspen Dr, Buffalo Grove, IL 60089; Railroadiana Collectors Assoc, PO Box 8051, Rowland Hts, CA 91748; Railway and Locomotive Historical Society, PO Box 1418, Westford, MA 01886; Twentieth Century Railroad Club, 329 W 18th St, Ste 902, Chicago, IL 60616.

Napkin, Chessie, paper, blue on white, 1960s, 4 x 8¹/₂" folded size, $8.00.

Album, The Western Pacific RR, Feather Canyon Route, Salt Lake City to San Francisco Bay, 1923	$ 38.00
Ashtray, Chesapeake & Ohio, white, outer blue band, inner yellow pinstripe, black Chessie kitten logo at center, Syracuse, 4" d	75.00
Badge, police sergeant, Penn Central RR, brass, lacquered, stamped "1969–1976"	75.00
Book, *History of Burlington Route,* Overton, NY, 1st ed, 1965	32.00
Book, *History of Pennsylvania RR, 1846–1946*	65.00
Booklet, *Claremont–The Great Terminal of the World's Great Port,* Lehigh Valley, c1920, 7 x 10"	20.00
Booklet, *The Erie Limited,* Jun 1929	18.00
Brochure, Pennsylvania Railroad, 1943, 48 pgs	8.00
Calendar, C&O, 1960	5.00
Calendar, D&RGW, 1944, 15 x 26"	10.00
Calendar, GN Railroad, 1934	50.00
Calendar, NYC, 1923	265.00
Calendar, Pittsburgh Promotes Progress, 1954, 4 pgs	25.00
Calendar, Union Pacific Railroad, 1960	12.00
Catalog, American Steel & Wire Co, Chicago, IL, railroad bonding of rails and tracks, 1928, 167 pgs, 6 x 9"	22.00
Catalog, Pullman Coach Co, 1920	15.00

Coaster, Amtrak, white ground, red and blue logo, blue border	.50
Dinner Plate, New York Central, 9" d	45.00
Handkerchief, cotton, C&O, Chessie, Peake, and kittens in corners and center, multicolored, white ground, 14 x 14¹/₂"	25.00
Ink Blotter, Norfolk & Western, multicolored wharf scene, 3³/₄ x 9"	5.00
Key, CNR–Mitchell, Canada, solid barrel, caboose, Canada, 4" l	15.00
Lantern, Soo Line, etched red globe, 1925	85.00
Lantern Globe, NYC Lines	25.00
Lighter, C&NW, stainless steel, red and black logo, Zippo	18.00
Lock, GNRY, 11939	12.00
Luggage Sticker, C&O, red and white, sleepy kitten, "Sleep like a Kitten," 2¹/₂" d	4.00
Magazine, *Burlington Bulletin,* 1962, 7 pgs, 9 x 12"	4.00
Magazine, *Great Northern Goat,* Vol. 7, #4, Apr 1930, Special Edition	4.00
Magazine, *Railway Conductor,* Roosevelt cov, May 1945	5.00
Magazine, *Saturday Evening Post,* "A Night on Troop Train," Norman Rockwell illus, 2 pgs of sketches, May 8, 1943	50.00
Magazine, *The Railroad Trainman,* Vol. 47, #2, Feb 1930	1.50
Manual, Pennsylvania Railroad Manual of Instructions to Railroad Conductors, Ticket Collectors & Baggagemen, 1945, 120 pgs	8.00
Map, Rock Island, 1923	6.00
Map, UP, Military map of the U.S., Union Pacific Railroad, dated 1950	5.00
Medal, bronze, Rock Island 70th Anniversary, 1¹/₄" d	25.00
Memo Pad, Burlington Route, logo, red and black, 4 x 7¹/₄"	1.50
Menu, Canadian Pacific Railroad, 1928	5.50
Menu, Great Northern, 1944	12.00

Mug, "BN Burlington Northern, Transportation Needs You Back," 5½" h **6.00**

Napkin, Rock Island Railroad, linen, acorn and leaves border, dated 3–62, 20" sq **15.00**

Napkin, Rock Island, paper, black logo, "Route of the Rockets" **1.00**

Pamphlet, Burlington Route, The Cody Road to Yellowstone Park, color, 1931 . . . . **10.00**

Pass, Great Northern Railway Co, goat logo, 1950 . . . . **4.00**

Pen, Soo Line, black, 4 gold stripes at clip, box logo and lettering in gold, Wings, USA **6.00**

Pencil, CGW, gold printing on green **2.50**

Pinback Button, B of LF&E–Lodge 814, celluloid, 1920 . . . . **8.00**

Pinback Button, Rock Island, celluloid, 1959 . . . . **15.50**

Pinback Button, Northern Pacific Railway, 1964, 1¾" d **6.00**

Platter, AT & SF, Griffon, 1924, 10" d **130.00**

Playing Cards, D&RGW, 1930s **25.00**

Playing Cards, Great Northern, c1930 . . . . **35.00**

Playing Cards, New York Central Line, 1932 . . . . **35.00**

Postcard, L&N Railroad, 1952 . . . . **2.50**

Postcard, Pennsylvania Railroad, 1926 . . . . **5.00**

Poster, cardboard, "Travel in Pullman Safety and Comfort to Your Favorite Winter Resort," 1936 . . . . **30.00**

Rule Book, Northern Pacific Railway, 1922 . . . . **8.00**

Rule Book, WCF&N RR, 1947 . . . . **40.00**

Ruler, Alton and Southern Railroad, aluminum, "The St. Louis Gateway's Speed Belt" in center, 1937 calendar on back **15.00**

Ruler, Rock Island, white, plastic, red and black lettering, 6" l **2.50**

Sheet Music, *Dream Train*, Guy Lombardo on cov, 1928 . . . . **3.50**

Sheet Music, *Hail to the Baltimore & Ohio*, engraved B & O engine, 1927 . . . . **22.00**

Sheet Music, *I've Been Working on the Railroad*, Calumet Music Co, Chicago, man waving to train, 1935 . . . . **6.00**

Sign, Railway Express Agency, 1950s, 14 x 14" **115.00**

Sign, Western Union Telegraph and Cable Blanks, white lettering, blue ground, 1930s, 3 x 9½" **45.00**

Stock Certificate, Chicago, Saint Paul, Minneapolis, and Omaha Railway Co, 20 shares, 2 trains in landscapes vignettes, brown border, 1922 . . . . **10.00**

Stock Certificate, Erie Railroad Co, 1950s **8.00**

Stock Certificate, Gulf Mobile and Northern Railroad Co, 100 shares, 1929 . . . . **10.00**

Stock Certificate, Philadelphia Railroad Co, State of PA, woman vignette, 1980 . . . . **6.00**

Stock Certificate, Western Railroad, train station and locomotive vignette, 1955 . . . . **10.00**

Tablecloth, Rock Island Railroad, linen, acorn and leaves border, 57 x 63½" **35.00**

Ticket, Boston & Maine RR, 1947 . . . . **5.50**

Ticket, Southern Pacific Lines, Railroad Boosters, Ojai–Ventura County Railway Trip, 1939 . . . . **12.00**

Ticket Booklet, Burlington Route, carbonized, blue cov with logo and streamline Zephyr, unused, 1960s **3.50**

Ticket Booklet, Chicago, Milwaukee, St. Paul, and Pacific Railroad, carbonized, Milwaukee Road Super Dome car cov, 1955 . . . . **2.50**

Time Table, Baltimore & Ohio Railroad, Apr 26, 1936 . . . . . **4.00**

Time Table, Burlington Northern, Oct 25, 1970 . . . . **1.50**

Time Table, Chesapeake & Ohio RR, passenger train, 1964 . . . . **5.00**

Time Table, Great Northern Railway, Apr, May, Jun, 1948 . . . . **5.00**

Time Table, Pennsylvania Railroad System, Chicago, St Louis, Pittsburgh, black and white, 1923 . . . . **10.00**

Time Table, Union Pacific Railroad, 1937, 48 pgs, 8 x 9" **15.00**

Token, B & ORR, aluminum, Lincoln penny inserted in center, obverse "Baltimore & Ohio Railroad Century of Progress, Chicago, 1933" **10.00**

REAMERS

A reamer is a device used to extract juice from fruits. Reamers are collected primarily by composition, i.e., ceramic, glass, and metal. In an attempt to bring order to reamer collecting, Ken and Linda Ricketts and Mary Walker assigned reamers an identification number. These numbers are used by most collectors.

There are two basic types of reamers: (1) hand operated and (2) mechanical. Reamers were extremely popular in the period between World War I and II. Only a few were made in the post–1945 period, a result of the popularity of frozen juice concentrates and prepackaged fruit juices.

In the early 1980s Edna Barnes reproduced a number of old reamers from molds belonging to the Jenkins Glass Company and Imperial Glass Company. These reproductions are marked with a "B" in a circle.

Reference: Gene Florence, *Kitchen Glassware of the Depression Years, Fifth Edition,* Collector Books, 1995.

Collectors' Club: National Reamer Collectors Assoc, 47 Midline Ct, Gaithersburg, MD 20878.

Ade–O–Matic Genuine, green glass, 9" h . . . . **$ 38.00**

Anchor Hocking, glass, orange, green transparent, loop handle, $20.00.

Japan, ceramic, 2 pcs, $35.00.

Anchor Hocking, glass, lime green, pouring spout,
6¼" d **20.00**

Austria, ceramic, white, pink flowers, green trim,
2¾" h **40.00**

Czechoslovakia, ceramic, 2 pcs, orange shape, white,
green leaves, mkd "Erphila," 6" h **32.00**

England, ceramic, 2 pcs, orange shape, orange body,
green leaves, 3¾" h **25.00**

Fenton, glass, transparent green, pointed cone, tab
handle.. **85.00**

Fry, glass, opal, pouring spout, 6⁵⁄₁₆" d **45.00**

Gem Squeezer, aluminum, 2 pcs, crank handle, table
model **10.00**

Germany, ceramic, scrolling flow blue dec, white
ground, 3½" d **55.00**

Handy Andy, aluminum, table type, crank, red base,
10½" h **18.00**

Hazel Atlas, glass, Crisscross pattern, large, clear **10.00**

Hazel Atlas, glass, Crisscross pattern, cobalt blue **245.00**

Hazel Atlas, glass, Crisscross pattern, large, green **18.00**

Hazel Atlas, glass, Crisscross pattern, lemon, pink...... **285.00**

Hazel Atlas, glass, green transparent, tab handle........ **35.00**

Hong Kong, stainless steel, 2 pcs, flat, 2½" h **8.00**

Japan, ceramic, baby's, orange, blue on white, 4½" d **30.00**

Japan, ceramic, lemon, yellow, white flowers, green
leaves, 4¾" d **40.00**

Jeanette, glass, small, delphite blue.................. **125.00**

Kwicky Juicer, aluminum, pan style, Quam–Nichols
Co... **6.50**

Limoges, ceramic, scalloped, orange and pearl luster,
brown handle, 5¼" d **115.00**

McCoy, ceramic, green, 1948, 8" d.................. **42.00**

McKee, glass, French ivory......................... **45.00**

McKee, glass, green, 1948 .... **20.00**

Nasco–Royal, metal, scissor type **6.50**

Occupied Japan, ceranuc, 2 pcs, strawberry shape,
red, green handle and leaves, mkd, 3¾" h **65.00**

Presto Juicer, metal stand, porcelain juicer **58.00**

Red Wing, ceramic, gray, red, and blue, 6¼" d **300.00**

Universal, ceramic, 2 pcs, lavender lillies, green
leaves, silver trim, 9" h **145.00**

Wagner Ware, cast aluminum, skillet shape, 2 spouts,
6" d **20.00**

Wearever, aluminum, 6" h **5.00**

Zippy, hand crank cone, Wolverine Products, Detroit,
Mi **60.00**

RECORDS

Thomas Edison is credited with the invention of the phonograph as well as the light bulb. In 1877 Edison demonstrated a phonograph he designed that played wax cylinder records. Although patenting his phonograph in 1878, Edison did not pursue the concept, preferring instead to concentrate on further development of the light bulb.

Alexander Graham Bell, a friend of Edison and inventor of the telephone, created the graphaphone. By the end of the 1880s, Bell was successfully marketing his graphaphone. Bell's, Edison's, and other early phonographs utilized a hand crank mechanism to provide movement to the cylinder.

Emile Berliner developed the flat disk phonograph in 1900. In less than a year, the United States Gramophone Company, eventually RCA, was successfully marketing it. Discs replaced cylinders as the most popular record form by the end of the decade.

Initially records were played at a speed of 78 revolutions per minute (rpm). 45 rpm records became the dominant form in the late 1940s and 50s, eventually begin replaced by the 33⅓ rpm format. Most phonographs, more frequently referred to as record players in the post–1945 period, could play 33⅓, 45, and 78 rpm records The arrival of the compact disc with its quality sound and need for a totally new player in the early 1980s made the turntable obsolete.

Most records have relatively little value, especially those without their dust jackets or album covers. The more popular a song title, the less likely it is to have value. Many records were released in several different pressings. Do your homework to find out exactly what pressing you own. If a record is scratched or warped, its value disappears.

References: Perry Cox and Joe Lindsay, *The Official Price Guide to the Beatles: Records and Memorabilia,* House of Collectibles, 1995; Les Docks, *American Premium Record Guide, 1900–1965: Identification and Value Guide to 78s, 45s and Lps, Fifth Edition,* Books Americana, Krause Publications, 1997; Anthony J. Gribin and Matthew M. Schiff, *Doo–Wop: The Forgotten Third of Rock 'n' Roll,* Krause Publications, 1992; Fred Heggeness, *Goldmine Country Western Record & CD Price Guide,* Krause Publications, 1996; Fred Heggeness, *Goldmine's Promo Record & CD Price Guide,* Krause Publications, 1995; Ron Lofman, *Goldmine's Celebrity Vocals,* Krause Publications, 1994; Vito R. Marino and Anthony C. Furfero, *The Official Price Guide To Frank Sinatra Records and CDs,* House of Collectibles, 1993.

Tim Neely, *Goldmine Christmas Record Price Guide,* Krause Publications, 1997; Tim Neely, *Goldmine Price Guide to Alternative Records,* Krause Publications, 1996; Tim Neely (ed.), *Goldmine Price Guide to 45 RPM Records,* Krause Publications, 1996; Tim Neely and Dave Thompson, *Goldmine British Invasion Price Guide,* Krause Publications, 1997; Jerry Osborne, *Rockin' Records, 18th Edition,* Antique Trader Books, 1997; Jerry Osborne, *The Official Price Guide to Country Music,* House of Collectibles,

Elvis' Christmas Album, RCA Victor, LPM–1951, $25.00.

1996; Jerry Osborne, *The Official Price Guide To Movie/TV Soudtracks & Original Cast Albums, Second Edition,* House of Collectibles, 1997; Jerry Osborne, *The Official Price Guide To Records, Twelfth Edition,* House of Collectibles, 1997.

Ronald L. Smith, Goldmine's Comedy Record Price Guide, Krause Publications, 1996; Neal Umphred, *Goldmine's Price Guide To Collectible Jazz Albums, 1949–1969, 2nd Edition,* Krause Publications, 1994, Neal Umphred, *Goldmine's Price Guide To Collectible Record Albums, 5th Edition,* Krause Publications, 1996.

Periodicals: *DISCoveries Magazine,* PO Box 1050, Dubuque, IA 52004; *Goldmine,* 700 E State St, Iola, WI 54990.

Collectors' Clubs: Assoc of Independent Record Collectors, PO Box 222, Northford, CT 06472; International Assoc of Jazz Record Collectors, PO Box 75155, Tampa, FL 33605.

Note: For additional listings see Beatles, Elvis Presley, and Rock 'n' Roll.

Advertising, Chevrolet, Ben Cartwright, *Musical Message* . . . . **$ 10.00**
Advertising, Travelers Insurance Co, *Triumph of Man,* New York World's Fair **8.50**
Archie Campbell, *Make Friends with Archie Campbell,* Starday, SLP–162, 1962 . . . . **8.00**
Beach Bums, *Ballad of the Yellow Beret,* 1961 . . . . **30.00**
Bill Cosby, *I Started Out as a Child,* orig sleeve **15.00**
Bing Crosby, *Hits From Musical Comedies,* Decca, DL–5000, 1949 . . . . **12.00**
Chuck Berry, *Chuck Berry Twist,* Chess, LP–1465, 1962. . . **28.00**
Dick Van Dyke, *Songs I Like,* Command, R–860, 1963 . . . . **6.00**
Don Adams, *The Detective,* Roulette, R–25317, 1966 . . . . . **5.00**
Dr. Feelgood & The Interns, *OKeh,* OKM–12101, 1962 . . . **18.00**
Elvis Presley, *Elvis Is Back!,* sticker, RCA Victor, LPM–2231, 1960 . . . . **45.00**

Gene Autry, *Merry Christmas,* Columbia, CL–2547, 1950 . . . . **45.00**
Jack Webb, *Dragnet–The Christmas Story,* RCA Victor, LPM–3199, 1954 . . . . **45.00**
Lee Dorsey, *Ride Your Pony,* Amy, 8010, 1966 . . . . **8.00**
Lenny Bruce, *The Sick Humor of Lenny Bruce,* Fantasy, 7003, 1959 . . . . **10.00**
Let's Polka **12.50**
Madame X, soundtrack, Decca, 1966 . . . . **15.00**
Mel Blanc, *Party Panic,* Capitol, H–436, 1953 . . . . **25.00**
Muhammad Ali & Frank Sinatra, *Ali and His Gang Fight Tooth Decay,* promotional issue **15.00**
Odetta, *Odetta and Larry,* Fantasy, 3–15, 1955 . . . . **12.00**
Paul McCartney & Wings, *The Family Way,* sound-track, London, M–76007, 1967 . . . . **20.00**
Pearl Bailey, *I'm With You,* Coral, CRL–56078, 1953 . . . . **12.00**
Peter Sellers, *The Bobo,* soundtrack, Warner Bros., W–1711, 1967 . . . . **10.00**
Petula Clark, *Uptown With Petula Clark,* Imperial, LP–9281, 1965 . . . . **5.00**
Porter Wagoner & The Wagonmasters, *A Slice of Life– Songs Happy 'n Sad,* RCA Victor, LSP–2447, 1962 . . . . . **10.00**
Ricky Nelson, *Ricky Sings Again,* Imperial, LP–12090, 1962 . . . . **45.00**
The Addams Family, soundtrack, RCA Victor, 1964 . . . . . . **25.00**
The Andrews Sisters, *Tropical Songs,* Decca, DL– 5065, 1950 . . . . **10.00**
The Archies, *This Is Love,* Kirshner, KES–110, 1971 . . . . **5.00**
The Banana Splits, *We're The Banana Splits,* Decca, DL–75075, 1969 . . . . **55.00**
The Chipmunks, *Sing Again with The Chipmunks,* Liberty, LST–7159, 1961 . . . . **8.00**
The Crew Cuts, *The Crew Cuts on the Campus,* Mercury, MG–25200, 1956 . . . . **18.00**
The Maguire Sisters, *Children's Holiday,* Coral, CRL– 57097, 1956 . . . . **8.00**
The Mills Brothers, *Barber Shop Ballads,* Decca, DL–5051, 1950 . . . . **12.00**
Tommy Boyce & Bobby Hart, *Test Patterns,* A&M, LP–126, 1967 . . . . **5.00**
Vic Damone, *Song Hits,* Mercury, MG–25054, 1950 . . . . . **10.00**

RED WING POTTERY

The Red Wing Stoneware Company, Minnesota Stoneware Company (1883–1906), and North Star Stoneware Company (1892–96) were located in Red Wing, Minnesota. David Hallem founded the Red Wing Stoneware Company in 1868. By the 1880s Red Wing was the largest American producer of stoneware storage vessels.

In 1894 the Union Stoneware Company was established as a selling agency for Minnesota, North Star, and Red Wing. Minnesota and Red Wing bought out North Star in 1896. In 1906 production was merged into one location and the Red Wing Union Stoneware Company created. The company made stoneware until introducing an art pottery line in the 1920s. During the 1930s Red Wing created several popular lines of hand painted dinnerware that were sold through department stores, gift stamp redemption centers, and Sears.

In 1936 the company became Red Wing Potteries, Inc. Stoneware production ended in 1947. In the early 1960s the company began producing hotel and restaurant china. Financial difficulties that began in the 1950s continued. Red Wing ceased operations in 1967.

References: Dan and Gail DePasquale and Larry Peterson, *Red Wing Collectibles,* Collector Books, 1985, 1995 value update; B. L. Dollen, *Red Wing Art Pottery: Identification & Value Guide,* Collector Books, 1997; Harvey Duke, *The Official Price Guide to Pottery and Porcelain, Eighth Edition,* House of Collectibles, 1995; Ray Reiss, *Red Wing Art Pottery: Including Pottery Made for RumRill,* Property, 1996.

Collectors' Clubs: Red Wing Collectors Society, PO Box 184, Galesburg, IL 61402; The RumRill Society, PO Box 2161, Hudson, OH 44236.

Fondoso, Gypsy Trail line, teapot, pastel green, 7½" h, $40.00.

Ash Receiver, donkey	$ 75.00
Ash Receiver, pelican	75.00
Bob White, beverage server, stopper	85.00
Bob White, butter warmer, cov, stick handle	80.00
Bob White, casserole, 2 qt	30.00
Bob White, cookie jar	45.00
Bob White, creamer	25.00
Bob White, cup	3.00
Bob White, Lazy Susan, stand	90.00
Bob White, mug	65.00
Bob White, platter, 13" l	80.00
Bob White, salad bowl, 12" d	75.00
Bob White, saucer	2.50
Bob White, soup bowl	15.00
Bob White, sugar	25.00
Bob White, teapot	110.00
Bob White, tumbler	90.00
Bob White, vegetable bowl, divided	20.00
Bob White, water jar, base, 2 gal	500.00
Chevron, ashtray, 4" d	10.00
Chevron, bud vase, kettle, 3" h	15.00
Chevron, coffeepot	50.00
Chevron, drip jar	25.00
Chevron, jug, 32 oz	25.00
Chevron, plate, 8" d	5.00
Chevron, platter, oval, 12"l	12.00
Chevron, saucer	3.50
Chevron, sugar	20.00
Console Set, #1365, 3 pcs, crackle glaze, royal blue, black candlesticks, Oriental woman carrying bamboo baskets on shoulders	160.00
Cookie Jar, chef, figural, brown	90.00
Cookie Jar, King of Hearts with Bag of Tarts, figural, white	310.00
Cookie Jar, dancing peasants, figural	35.00
Country Garden, dinner plate, 10½" d	12.00
Country Garden, gravy	20.00
Country Garden, salad plate, 8" d	8.00
Figure, cowboy, hp	165.00
Figure, girl with flower, hp, 8½" h	140.00
Figure, man with accordion, solid color	50.00
Figure, Oriental goddess, solid color	40.00
Figure, Woman with Tambourine, hp	140.00

Fondoso, creamer, small	8.00
Fondoso, mixing bowl, 8" d	20.00
Fondoso, plate, 6½" d	5.00
Fondoso, syrup jug	30.00
Fruit Service, casserole, large, pineapple	35.00
Fruit Service, cookie jar, bananas	100.00
Fruit Service, marmalade, apple	25.00
Fruit Service, salad bowl, individual, apple	10.00
Fruit Service, salad bowl, large, pear	20.00
Iris, bowl, 5½" d	8.00
Iris, creamer	4.50
Labriego, casserole, French, oval, small	30.00
Labriego, creamer	15.00
Labriego, mug	20.00
Labriego, sugar	25.00
Labriego, water jug	30.00
Lute Song, bowl, 8" d	12.00
Lute Song, celery, 16" l	12.00
Lute Song, creamer	8.00
Lute Song, vegetable bowl, divided	18.00
Magnolia, cup	4.00
Magnolia, cup and saucer	6.50
Magnolia, salad plate, 7" d	4.00
Magnolia, saucer	1.50
Magnolia, vase, ivory, brown, handle, 7" h	25.00
Merrileaf, celery, 15" l	28.00
Planter, banjo, 15" h, black and white	35.00
Planter, dachshund	50.00
Planter, guitar	35.00
Planter, rabbit	30.00
Planter, swan	15.00
Planter, violin, 14½" h	35.00
Reed, egg dish, shirred	8.00
Reed, mixing bowl, 8" d	20.00
Reed, pie baker, 9" d	15.00
Reed, ramekin, small	5.00
Reed, tea cup	10.00
Round Up, bread tray, rectangular, 24"	185.00
Round Up, butter, ¼ lb	145.00
Round Up, casserole, 2 qt	145.00

Smart Set, creamer, 7" h, $25.00.

Round Up, creamer 40.00
Round Up, gravy, cov, stick handle. 90.00
Round Up, plate, 10½" d, chuckwagon 55.00
Round Up, platter, 13" l 40.00
Round Up, salad bowl, 10½" d 80.00
Round Up, teapot 190.00
Round Up, vegetable bowl, divided 65.00
Smart Set, beverage server, stopper 165.00
Smart Set, butter warmer, cov, stick handle 35.00
Smart Set, casserole, 4 qt 65.00
Smart Set, cocktail tray. 25.00
Smart Set, cruets, pr, stopper, stand. 165.00
Smart Set, cup 10.00
Smart Set, jug, 60 oz 75.00
Smart Set, lazy susan, 5 pcs, carrier, tray 140.00
Smart Set, pepper mill 90.00
Smart Set, plate, 7½" d 8.00
Smart Set, relish, 3 part 55.00
Smart Set, salad bowl, 10½" d 85.00
Tampico, beverage server, cov 75.00
Tampico, cake plate, ruffled edge 35.00
Tampico, cereal bowl 8.00
Tampico, creamer 15.00
Tampico, fruit dish 5.00
Tampico, jug, 2 qt 75.00
Tampico, mug 50.00
Tampico, nut bowl, 5 part 75.00
Tampico, plate, 8½" d 6.50
Tampico, relish 20.00
Tampico, salad bowl, 12" d 75.00
Tampico, sugar 15.00
Tampico, teapot. 90.00
Town and Country, ashtray. 8.00
Town & Country, cruet, stopper 50.00
Town & Country, cup. 8.00
Town & Country, plate, 8" d 10.00
Village Green/Brown, baking dish, cov, 12" d 8.00
Village Green/Brown, casserole, 1 qt 15.00
Village Green/Brown, salad bowl, 12" d 35.00

REGAL CHINA

Regal China Corporation, Antioch, Illinois, was established in 1938. In the 1940s, Regal was purchased by Royal China and Novelty Company, a distribution and sales organization. Royal used Regal to make the ceramic products that is sold.

Ruth Van Tellingen Bendel designed Snuggle Hugs in the shape of bears, bunnies, pigs, etc., in 1948. He also designed cookie jars, other figurines, and salt and pepper shaker sets.

Regal did large amounts of decorating for other firms, e.g., Hull's Red Riding Hood pieces. Regal has not sold to the retail trade since 1968, continuing to operate on a contract basis only. In 1976 it produced a cookie jar for Quaker Oat in 1976. 1983 products include a milk pitcher for Ovaltine and a ship decanter and coffee mugs for Old Spice. Regal currently is a wholly owned subsidiary of Jim Beam Distilleries.

Reference; Harvey Duke, *The Official Price Guide to Pottery and Porcelain, Eighth Edition,* House of Collectibles, 1995.

Alice In Wonderland, creamer, White Rabbit . . . . $ 385.00
Alice In Wonderland, shaker, pr, Alice, white, gold 485.00
Old MacDonald, canister, cereal medium 210.00
Old MacDonald, canister, flour, medium 200.00
Old MacDonald, canister, popcorn, large 285.00
Old MacDonald, canister, pretzels, large 285.00
Old MacDonald, canister, sugar, medium 200.00
Old MacDonald, cookie jar, barn 315.00
Old MacDonald, creamer, rooster 85.00
Old MacDonald, jar, cinnamon 90.00
Old MacDonald, jar, ginger 90.00
Old MacDonald, jar, nutmeg 85.00
Old MacDonald, shaker, pr, boy and girl 75.00
Old MacDonald, shaker, pr, flour sack, emb sheep 140.00
Old MacDonald, teapot, duck head on lid 285.00
Peek–A–Boos, shaker, small, white, red. 265.00
Peek–A–Boos, shaker, large, white, gold 435.00
Snuggle Hugs, bear, brown, pink 15.00
Snuggle Hugs, bear, pink 15.00
Snuggle Hugs, boy/dog, white 65.00
Snuggle Hugs, bunny, green 15.00
Snuggle Hugs, bunny, yellow, painted clothes 45.00
Snuggle Hugs, Dutch girl/boy, white 25.00
Snuggle Hugs, Mary/lamb, yellow, black tail 45.00
Snuggle Hugs, mermaid/sailor, tan mermaid, white
   sailor 115.00

ROBOTS

Although there are robot toys dating before 1940, this category covers robot toys that arrived in the American market in the post–1945 period. Most were of Japanese manufacture. Robot toys of the late 1940s and early 1950s were friction or wind–up powered. Many of these lithographed tin beauties were made from recycled material.

By the mid–1950s, most robots were battery powered. Japanese manufacturers produced several hundred models. Model variations are common, the result of manufacturers freely interchanging parts. Plastic replaced lithographed tin as the material of choice in the late 1960s, due in part to a United States government requirement that sharp edges of toys be softened.

Robot models responded to changing Space Age motifs. The Japanese Atomic Robot Man, made between 1948 and 1949, heralded the arrival of the Atomic age. Movies, such as *Destination Moon* (1950) and *Forbidden Planet* (1956) featuring Robbie the Robot, provided the inspiration for robot toys in the early and mid–1950s. Space theme television programs, e.g., *Lost in Space* (1965–1968), played a similar role in the 1960s. Ideal and Marx entered the toy robot market in the late 1960s.

Markings can be confusing. Many of the marks are those of importers and/or distributors, not manufacturers. Cragston is an importer, not a maker. Reproductions and fantasy items are a major problem in the late 1990s. Because of the high desirability and secondary market cost of robots such as Mr. Atomic ($10,000+), modern copies costing between $250 and $750 new are being made. Inexpensive Chinese and Taiwanese fantasy toy robots, i.e., shapes that never existed historically, are flooding the market.

Reference: Maxine A. Pinsky, *Marx Toys: Robots, Space, Comic & TV Characters,* Schiffer Publishing, 1996.

Mighty Robot, litho tin and plastic, battery operated, flashing lights, mystery action, Yoshiya, 1955–60, 12" h, $1,870.00.   Photo courtesy Sotheby's.

Acrobat Robot, plastic body, litho tin chestplate, battery operated, orig box, Yonezawa, Japan, 1960s, 9³/₄" h . . . . **$ 285.00**

Astronaut Robot, metal and plastic, battery operated, Japan, 1960, 12" h **1,500.00**

Astronaut Robot, metal and plastic, battery operated, Cragstan, Japan, c1960, 13" h **800.00**

Blazer Superhero Robot, tin, red, yellow, black, and blue, plastic arms, windup, orig box, Bullmark, 1960s **170.00**

Dalek, plastic, battery operated, red body, black base, orig box, Marx, 6½" h **185.00**

Ding–A–Lings, fireman, plastic, Topper Corp, 1970s, Electric Robot and Son, plastic, battery operated, 5½" h **50.00**

Excavator Robot, S–H Company, 1960s. **145.00**

Japanese Robot Warrior, plastic, walks forward, ST, 1960s **75.00**

Lost In Space Robot, battery operated, Masuyada, 1985, 22" h **115.00**

Mechanical Walking Spaceman, metal and plastic, battery operated, Linemar, Japan, 7" h **2,500.00**

Mighty Robot, tin, windup, sparkling chest, walks **90.00**

Monster Robot, space helmet reveals growling lighted dragon, walks **90.00**

Mr. Atom, plastic, battery operated, orig box, Advance Toy, West Haven, CT, 18" h **700.00**

Mr. Smash, silver body, red head, plastic antennae, windup, Marx, 1970s, 5" h **90.00**

Planet Robot, tin and plastic, windup, orig box, KO, Japan, 9" h **285.00**

R–35, tin, remote control, battery operated, plastic battery box, Marx, 1950s, 8" h **185.00**

Robby The Robot, windup, Masudaya, 1985, 4" h **18.00**

Robot, tin, windup, Linemar, 1950s, 6" h **475.00**

Robot ST1, silvered tin, key wind, orig box, West Germany, 7½" h **500.00**

Rock 'Em Sock 'Em Robots, game, plastic, red, blue, lever controlled, orig box, Marx, 1964, 30 x 12½" h **90.00**

Rom, plastic, 3 attachments and instruction sheet, Parker Brothers, 1979, 13" h **50.00**

Smoking Spaceman, tin, battery operated, Linemar, 1950s, 12" h **1,800.00**

Spaceman Robot, metal litho, blue and red, windup, Yonezawa, Japan, 8" h **700.00**

Spaceman Robot, plastic, windup, ray guns, fish bowl helmet, 1953, 12" h **135.00**

Super Hero Robot, litho tin, vinyl head, ST, 1960s. **120.00**

Television Spaceman, tin, battery operated, orig box, Alps, Japan, 11" h **725.00**

Video Robot and Dinosaur, tin and plastic, battery operated, orig box, Japan, 11" h **675.00**

V.I.N.C.E.N.T., plastic, gray, windup, Marx, 1980, 3½" h **12.00**

X–27 Explorer, metal litho, blue and red, battery operated, Yonezawa, Japan, c1950, 8½" h **700.00**

AUCTION PRICES

Sotheby's Tin Toy Robot Collection sale held November 7, 1996. Prices include a 15% buyer's premium.

Earth Man, astronaut type, litho tin, yellow, walks, lifts gun with lighting barrel and fires, wears oxygen tank with telescoping antenna, Normura, 1950s, 9½" h **977.00**

Mars King, litho tin, battery operated, dark silver, screen in torso, missing treads, orig box, Horikawa, 1960s, 9¼" h **460.00**

Mr. Mercury, scarce version, tin and plastic, , remote battery operated, light blue, bends and picks up objects, control room at helmet visor, electric light on helmet, Yonezawa/Linemar, 1955–60s, 13" h **1,150.00**

Star Strider, battery operated, astronaut walks forward, body rotates as guns fire from chest, Japanese, 1970s, 12½" h **172.00**

Venus Robot, red and black plastic, clockwork mechanism, Yoshiya, 1965–70, 5½" h **316.00**

ROCK 'N' ROLL

This is a broad category covering the full spectrum of rock 'n' roll from Chubby Checker to Sex Pistols. The category is heavily personality–driven with The Beatles and Elvis (see separate categories The Beatles and Elvis) leading the pack. Eddie Cochran, Bill Haley, Buddy Holly, and Gene Vincent are among the popular 1950s rock 'n' roll stars. David Bowie, The Rolling Stones and The Who are favorites among those collecting rock 'n' roll memorabilia from the 1960s and 70s. 1980s stars include Phil Collins, Dire Straits, Boy George, Michael Jackson, The Police, and U2.

In spite of its outward appearance, the field tends to be traditionalist. Material from short–lived new wave or punk groups of the 1970s, e.g., The Damned and Generation X, do not appear to be attracting large numbers of collectors.

Collectors are specializing. Memorabilia from the girl groups of the late 1950s and early 1960s has become hot. The field is trendy. Autographs, guitars, and stage costumes are three categories that have gotten hot, cooled off, and show signs of resurgence. Hard Rock Cafés have spread around the world, creating an international interest in this topic. The top end of this market is documented by the values received at rock 'n' roll auctions held in London, Los Angeles, and New York.

References: Mark A. Baker, *Goldmine Price Guide to Rock 'N' Roll Memorabilia,* Krause Publications, 1997; David K. Henkel, *The Official Price Guide to Rock and Roll,* House of Collectibles, 1992; Eric King, *The Collector's Guide to Psychedelic Rock Concert Posters, Postcards and Handbills,* Svaha Press, 1996; Karen and John Lesniewski, *Kiss Collectibles: Identification and Price Guide,* Avon Books, 1993.

Collectors' Club: Kissaholics, PO Box 22334, Nashville, TN 37202.

REPRODUCTION ALERT: Records, picture sleeves, and album jackets, especially for the Beatles, have been counterfeited. Sound may be inferior. Printing on labels and picture jackets usually is inferior to the original. Many pieces of memorabilia also have been reproduced, often with some change in size, color, and design.

Note: See Beatles, Elvis Presley, Psychedelic, and Records for additional listings.

Beatles, coloring book, Saalfield, 1964 . . . . $ 35.00
Beatles, trading card, black and white, Topps, 1964 . . . . . . 2.00
Bee Gees, scrapbook, 9 x 12", 34 pgs. 12.00
Blondie, magazine, Penthouse, Debbie Harry cov, Feb 1980 . . . . 6.00
Bobby Sherman, lunch box, metal, color photos and illus, metal thermos, white plastic cup, King Seeley, ©1972 Bobby Sherman Enterprises Ltd 55.00
Brenda Lee, necklace, gold chain with cultured pearl pendant, mounted on orig sealed card designed like a record, ©Brenda Lee, 1950–60 . . . . 38.00
Buddy Holly, record, *Peggy Sue/Everyday,* Coral, 61885 . . . 8.00
Chubby Checker, record, *The Class,* 78 rpm, Parkway 40.00
Dave Clark Five, program, Dave Clark Five Show, Arthur Kimbrell Presents, English, 1964 . . . . 40.00
Derek & The Dominos, concert flyer, McFarlim Auditorium, bright red, white, and blue, 1969 . . . . . . 170.00

Genesis, record album, *Foxtrot,* 33¹/₃ rpm, $10.00.

Dick Clark, pinback button, litho tin, black and white photo, dark green ground, 3" d 10.00
Dick Clark, record case, cardboard, red, white plastic handle, full color photo, white paper label with facsimile signature, c1950, 5 x 8 x 8" 70.00
Dick Clark, yearbook, *New Dick Clark Yearbook,* 1958 . . . 30.00
Duane Eddy, record, *Ring Of Fire/Bobbie,* paper slip cover, Jamie label, 1961, 7 x 7" 12.00
Elvis Presley, tab, litho tin, I Love Elvis, blue and gold lettering, silver ground, 1970, 2" d 20.00
Everly Brothers, sheet music, *So It Always Will Be,* pink tone photo on front cover, ©1963, 9 x 12" 8.00
Fats Domino, photo, color, seated at piano, 10 x 8" 25.00
Frank Zappa, album cover, sgd, *Joe's Garage/Act I,* framed, 13" sq 550.00
Grateful Dead, poster, Grateful Dead Fan Club, black and white photo, gold and blue ground, "The Golden Road To Unlimited Devotion," late 1960s, 14 x 20" 45.00
Grateful Dead, record, 33¹/₃ rpm, *Sampler For Deadheads,* Garcia photo on label reverse, ©1974 . . . . 50.00
Hermans Hermits, record, *Best of Herman's Hermits,* MGM, DT–90613, 1965 . . . . 6.00
James Gang, poster, cardboard, Oct 2, 1971 at Curtis Hixong Hall, Tampa, FL, "Wanted" poster design, 14 x 22" 20.00
Jerry Garcia, photograph, color, blue felt tip pen signature 285.00
Jerry Lee Lewis, record, *Whole Lot of Shakin' Going On/It'll Be Me,* 45 rpm, Sun, 1956 . . . . 20.00
Jimmi Hendrix, hanger, cardboard, black and white photo both sides, punch–out center, mkd "Manufactured Exclusively By Sunders Enterprises, Jimmi Hendrix," 15 x 17" 165.00
Kiss, book, *Kiss: The Real Story,* Peggy Tomarkin 10.00
Kiss, buckle, brass 8.00
Kiss, game, Kiss On Tour, MIB 25.00

Kiss, makeup kit, Kiss Your Face, 1st ed, unopened **20.00**
Michael Jackson, record, *Thriller,* Epic, HE–48112, 1982 . . . . **10.00**
Monkees, magazine, *16 Magazine,* Vol 8, #9, Feb 1967, Monkees and other performers, 68 pgs **10.00**
Monkees, puppet, Mickey Dolenz, plastic torso, movable arms, molded vinyl head, brown curly hair, ©1970, 5" h **12.00**
Monkees, record, *A Barrel Full of Monkees,* 2 record set, Colgems, SCOS–1001, 1971 . . . . **28.00**
Moody Blues, poster, Apr 1, 1970 concert, Terrace Ballroom, Salt Lake City, UT, 18½ x 25½" **50.00**
New Kids On The Block, coloring book, Golden, 1990 . . . . **2.00**
New Kids On The Block, game, Milton Bradley, 1990 . . . . . **3.00**
Osmonds, lunch box, litho metal, thermos, unused, ©1973 . . . . **20.00**
Paul McCartney, photo, color, sgd, inscribed "cheers!" with caricature face, matted, framed, 20 x 16" **625.00**
Queen, album, *A Day At The Race,* sgd **750.00**
Ricky Nelson, record, *Rick Is 21,* Imperial, LP–9125, 1961 . . . . **10.00**
Rod Stewart, book, *A Biography in Words and Pictures,* Richard Cromelin, 1976, 56 pgs **8.00**
Rod Stewart, calendar, 1985, spiral bound, 12 color photos,12 x 16" **8.00**
Rod Stewart, program, Blondes Have More Fun, world tour 1978–79, 96 pgs **10.00**
Rolling Stones, book, *Rolling Stones Pixerama Foldbook,* 12 glossy photos, 1964 . . . . **22.00**
Rolling Stones, magazine, *Life,* Stones cov, 1971 . . . . **8.00**
Sam Cooke and Clyde McPhatter, concert program, large fold open page from 1958 "Biggest Show of Stars" concert, sgd near images in ink and pencil by Sam Cooke, The Everly Brothers, and Clyde McPhatter, matted and framed, 16 x 20" **575.00**

Simon & Garfunkel, poster, album insert, black and white had photo, outline body with full color bridge and sunset scene, ©1968 Columbia Records, 22 x 33" **12.00**
Sonny & Cher, doll, Sonny, orig box, Mego, 1976, 12" h **30.00**
Sonny & Cher, record, *Look At Us,* Atco, 33–177, 1965 . . . . **4.00**
Sonny & Cher, TV Guide cover, 1972 . . . . **6.00**
The Doors, poster, white logo, green bottom border, Doors Production Corp, ©1968, 24 x 36" **20.00**
Woodstock, pin, Woodstock 69, enameled brass, white dove on blue guitar central design, red background, 1½" **25.00**
Yard Birds, poster, paper, 1967 concert at Civic Auditorium, Santa Monica, 14½ x 23½" **65.00**
ZZ Top, mirror, 6 x 6" **3.00**

ROCKWELL, NORMAN

Norman Rockwell was born on February 3, 1894. His first professional drawing appeared in *Tell Me Why Stories,* a children's book. Rockwell was 18 at the time. Rockwell is best know for his magazine covers, the most recognized appearing on *Boy's Life* and the *Saturday Evening Post* (over 320 covers). Advertising, books, and calendars are only a few of the additional areas where his artwork appeared. His artistic legacy includes more than 2,000 paintings.

Rockwell is one of America's foremost genre painters. He specialized in capturing a moment in the life of the average American. His approach ranged from serious to humorous, from social commentary to inspirational. He used those he knew for inspiration. His subjects ranged from New England villagers to presidents.

Rockwell's artwork continues to be heavily reproduced. Do not confuse contemporary with period pieces. His estate continues to license the use of his images. Buy modern collectibles for display and enjoyment. Their long term value is minimal.

Reference: Denis C. Jackson, *The Norman Rockwell Identification And Value Guide To: Magazines, Posters, Calendars, Books, 2nd Edition,* TICN, 1985.

Collectors' Club: Rockwell Society of America, PO Box 705, Ardsley, NY 10502.

REPRODUCTION ALERT

Note: For additional listings see Limited Edition Collectibles.

Bell, Lovers, Gorham, 1982 . . . . **$ 30.00**
Bell, Ben Franklin Bicentennial, Dave Grosman, 1976 . . . . **30.00**
Book, *My Life as an Illustrator,* Rockwell, 1960 . . . . **18.00**
Book, *Norman Rockwell Collectibles Value Guide,* Mary Moline, Rumbleseat Press, 1978, 150 pgs **8.00**
Calendar, 1941, boy and dog, Hercules Powder Company adv, 13 x 30¼" **180.00**
Calendar, 1946, John Morrell & Co, Tom Sawyer **55.00**
Calendar, 1948, Boy Scouts, Men of Tomorrow **70.00**
Catalog, Sears, Roebuck & Co, 1932 . . . . **60.00**
Catalog, Winchester Western Sporting Arms, 1966 . . . . . . **35.00**
Figurine, A Daily Prayer, Lynell Studios, 1981 . . . . **30.00**
Figurine, Bedtime, Rockwell Museum, 1978 . . . . **50.00**

The Doors, puzzle, black and white photo, 10 x 8", $15.00.

Plate, First Day of School, Touch of Rockwell series, Rockwell Museum, 1984, $15.00.

Figurine, Jolly Coachman, Gorham, 1982 . . . . **50.00**
Figurine, No Swimming, Dave Grossman Designs, Inc, 1973 . . . . **45.00**
Ignot, Charles Dickens, 1977 . . . . **50.00**
Ignot, Spirit of Scouting, Franklin Mint, 1972, price for set of 12 . . . . **275.00**
Magazine, *American Artist,* illus cov, 1976 . . . . **22.00**
Magazine, *Life,* June 1, 1945 . . . . **55.00**
Magazine, *Saturday Evening Post,* January 29, 1921, cover and full pg ads **32.00**
Magazine Cover, *American Boy,* April 1920 . . . . **30.00**
Magazine Cover, *Boys Life,* February 1947 . . . . **45.00**
Magazine Cover, *Boys Life,* June 1957 . . . . **45.00**
Magazine Cover, *Country Gentleman,* March 18, 1922 . . . **45.00**
Magazine Cover, *Family Circle,* December 1967, Santa Claus **10.00**
Magazine Cover, *Jack & Jill,* December 1974 . . . . **5.00**
Magazine Cover, *Literary Digest,* May 8, 1920 . . . . **22.00**
Magazine Cover, *Look,* July 14, 1964 . . . . **10.00**
Magazine Cover, *Parents,* May 1951 . . . . **10.00**
Magazine Cover, *Saturday Evening Post,* July 31, 1920 . . . **65.00**
Magazine Cover, *Saturday Evening Post,* March 12, 1955 . **20.00**
Magazine Cover, *Saturday Evening Post,* September 12, 1963, John F Kennedy **15.00**
Magazine Tear Sheet, *Country Gentleman,* Jell-o adv, 1922 . . . . **22.00**
Magazine Tear Sheet, *Good Housekeeping,* article, Rockwell story, 1929 . . . . **10.00**
Plate, Boy Scout, Our Heritage, Gorham, 1975 . . . . **55.00**
Plate, Leapfrog, Dave Grossman Designs, Annual Series, 1979 . . . . **50.00**
Plate, Santa's Helpers, Gorham, Christmas Series, 1979 . . . **22.00**
Plate, Scotty Gets His Tree, Rockwell Society, Christmas Series, 1974 . . . . **155.00**
Plate, Snow Queen, Lynell Studios, Christmas, 1979 . . . . . **32.00**
Plate, The Carolers, Franklin Mint, 1972 . . . . **160.00**

Plate, Toy Maker, Rockwell Society, Heritage Series, 1977 . . . . **250.00**
Plate, Whitewashing Fence, Dave Grossman Designs, Tom Sawyer Series, 1976 . . . . **75.00**
Playing Cards, Four Seasons, unopened, orig box **10.00**
Post Card, sgd, Fish Tires adv **22.00**
Poster, Maxwell House Coffee, 1931–32 . . . . **325.00**
Stein, Pensive Pals, Gorham **35.00**
Stein, Fishin' Pals, Rockwell Museum **70.00**
Stein, The Music Lesson, Rockwell Museum **85.00**

ROOKWOOD

In 1880 Cincinnatian Maria Longworth Nichols established Rookwood, a pottery named after her father's estate. She and a number of other Cincinnati society women designed and produced the first forms and decorative motifs.

In 1881 Albert Valentien became the first full–time decorator. He was quickly joined by others, e.g., Laura Fry, most of whom marked the pieces on which they worked with their initials. W.W. Taylor became manager in 1883 and president in 1890 when Nichols retired.

Rookwood pieces are separated by ware, glaze, and decoration. Standard Ware was produced by applying an underglaze slip painting (fish, native flowers, fruit, portraits, etc.) to a white or yellow clay body and then glazing the entire piece with a glossy, yellow–tinted glaze. Standard Ware was extremely popular in the 1880s and 90s.

When faced with heavy competition from firms such as J. B. Owens and Roseville, Rookwood sent many of its artisans to Europe for training. In 1904 Stanley Burt developed Vellum ware, a glaze that was a cross between high–glaze and matte glaze. By 1905 a matte glaze replaced the company's high–glazed wares. Ombroso, a matte–glaze line, was introduced in 1910 to mark the company's 30th anniversary. In 1915 the company introduced a soft porcelain line featuring gloss and matte glazes.

By the early 1930s, the company was experiencing financial difficulties. The company filed for bankruptcy in 1941. Walter and Marge Schott and a group of investors bought the company. A shortage of supplies during World War II forced the Schotts to transfer ownership to the Institution Divi Thomae Foundation of the Roman Catholic Archdiocese of Cincinnati in 1941. Sperti, Inc., operated the company for the Archdiocese. By the end of the 1940s the company was again experiencing financial difficulties.

In 1954 Edgar Heltman took over, shifting production to commercial ware and accessory pieces. Production ceased briefly in 1955. In 1956 James Smith bought the company from Sperti. Herschede Hall Clock Company bought Rookwood in 1959, moved its operations to Starksville, Missouri, and finally ceased operations for good in 1967.

Rookwood pieces are well marked. Many have five different marking symbols: (1) clay or body mark, (2) size mark, (3) decorator mark, (4) date mark, and (5) factory mark.

References: Susan and Al Bagdade, *Warman's American Pottery and Porcelain,* Wallace–Homestead, Krause Publications, 1994; Anita J. Ellis, *Rookwood Pottery: The Glaze Lines,* Schiffer Publishing, 1995; Ralph and Terry Kovel, *Kovels' American Art Pottery: The Collector's Guide To Makers, marks and Factory Histories,* Crown Publishers, 1993; L–W Book Sales (ed.), *A Price Guide To Rookwood,* L–W Book Sales, 1993.

Collectors' Club: American Art Pottery Assoc, PO Box 525, Cedar Hill, MO 63016.

Bookends, pr, elephants, charcoal gray, 1925 . . . . $ 400.00

Bookends, pr, elephants, white glaze, shape #2444C, 1931, 5³/₄" h 285.00

Bookends, pr, rook on berried branches, tand and dusky blue, semi–matte glaze, Helen McDonald, 1925 . . . . 350.00

Bookends, pr, shape #2275, William P. McDonald, 1943, 5¹/₂" h 250.00

Box, rect, molded head, animals, scrolls, flowers, and leaves, matte green glaze, 1929, 4" l, 2⁵/₈" w 150.00

Box, triangular, ftd, abstract molded dec, triangular finial, powder blue, high gloss glaze, Louise Abel, 1932, 5¹/₄" h 225.00

Ewer, rose jar form, fruiting vines, mustard yellow, wax matte glaze, Catherine Covaleno, 1925, 8¹/₄" h . . . 600.00

Flower Holder, rook on stump, blue, shape #2710, c1928, 6¹/₂" h 100.00

Inkwell, sphinx, figural, molded pen tray, variegated straw colors, gray matte glaze, Louise Abel, 1920, 8¹/₂" l, 8¹/₄" w, 9" h 250.00

Jar, low relief medial band of stylized flowers, basketweave pattern on bottom band, high gloss white glaze, brown and blue underglaze, 1946 . . . . 225.00

Paperweight, elephant, figural, matte olive glaze, 1930, 4" h 250.00

Plaque, rook on branch, incised "Rookwood," green glaze, c1925, 4¹/₄" h, 8¹/₂" w 1,350.00

Plaque, sailboats in harbor, blue, pink, yellow, and peach, Edward Hurley, 1942, 9³/₄" l, 7³/₄" h 5,500.00

Plaque, woodland river scene, Fred Rothenbusch, 1922, 8" h, 6" w 2,750.00

Rose Jar, powder pink, plum blossoms around shoulder, E. T. Hurley, 1925, 5¹/₂" h 350.00

Trivet, southern belle wearing hoop skirt, parasol, pastel colors, 1921, 5¹/₂" sq 225.00

Vase, iris and wisteria, Carl Schmidt, 14¹/₂" h, $41,800.00.
Photo courtesy David Rago Auctions.

Vase, apple blossoms, cream petals, tan pollen details, pink buds, green leaves, blue–gray outlines, light blue–green ground, Lenore Asbury, shape #2746, 1928, 9¹/₂" h 1,425.00

Vase, baluster form, round foot, multicolor matte glaze, Jens Jensen, 1930, 5¹/₂" h 600.00

Vase, bleeding hearts, pale pink, blue, and green, vellum glaze, baluster form, Edward Diers, 1931, 6³/₄" h 800.00

Vase, mistletoe garland, gray, blue, and white, pale blue berries, pale green and blue shaded ground, blue int rim, Ed Kiers, 1922, 5³/₈" h 475.00

Vase, molded classical women, deep mauve ext., turquoise int, flared mouth, tapering toward foot, Louise Abel, c1930, 13" h 200.00

Vase, multicolored lilies, vellum glaze, Lenore Asbury, 1928, 6" h 1,250.00

Vase, pond and landscape, blue, green, and pale yellow, E. T. Hurley, 1921, 14¹/₈" h 2,650.00

Vase, red and yellow peony, green leaves, pink–blue ground, wax matte glaze, shape #1369C, Elizabeth N. Lincoln, 1928, 11¹/₄" h 1,000.00

Vase, red and yellow tulips, green leaves, blue outlines, dusty rose ground, wax matte glaze, shape #932E, 1925, 8" h 525.00

Vase, stylized floral dec, olive green over red, pink, and yellow flowers, blue outline, lavender ground, Elizabeth N. Lincoln, 1929, 4³/₄" h 400.00

Vase, stylized floral dec, teal green, deep rose, and brown, blue outline, wax matte glaze, deep rose rim, shoulder with mustard highlights, W. E. Hentschel, 1921, 5¹/₄" h 450.00

Vase, sunset and landscape, red, blue, green, and yellow, E. T. Hurley, 1938, 10⁵/₈" h 3,225.00

Vase, underglazed wide band of stylized white flowers, red accents, stylized green leaves, high glaze, shape #614B, Elizabeth Barrett, 1935, 14¹/₂" h 825.00

Ashtray, rook, reddish–brown, $125.00.

ROSE BOWLS

A rose bowl is a small round or ovoid shaped bowl with a crimped, petaled, pinched, or scalloped opening at its top. It served as a container for fragrant potpourri or rose pedals.

Rose bowls are found in a wide variety of material with glass being the most common. A favorite giftware accessory, rose bowls often incorporate the best design qualities and materials of their era. Rose bowls are found in virtually every type of art glass.

The popularity of rose bowls extended from the second half of the Victorian era through the 1950s. The form is still made today.

Collectors' Club: Rose Bowl Collectors, 1111 Delps Rd, Danielsville, PA 18038.

Acid Etched, enameled purple violets, gold stems and trim, Mont Joye	$ 150.00
Amberina, Diamond Quilted, tricorn rim, 3 applied amber reeded feet	550.00
Amberina, Hobnail, 6" h	275.00
Amethyst, squatty, enameled dec, fluted top	100.00
Blue Opalescent, Opalescent Open, pedestal base	50.00
Blue Opalescent, Opalescent Stripe	100.00
Burmese, hp roses, Fenton	70.00
Carnival, amethyst, Hobnail	450.00
Carnival, amethyst, scalloped design	275.00
Cranberry, Coin Spot, 3 loop top	200.00
Cranberry, lacy enameled dec, Baccarat	150.00
Cranberry Opalescent, Coin Dot, large	95.00
Cranberry Opalescent, Coin Dot, small	65.00
Cranberry Opalescent, enameled forget–me–nots	75.00
Cranberry Opalescent, Fancy Fantails	75.00
Cranberry Opalescent, Hobnail, Fenton	130.00
Crystal, gold enameling	95.00
Crystal, Scalloped Six Points, George Duncan Sons & Co.	50.00
Crystal, Torpedo, Thompson	85.00
Custard, Beaded Cable	65.00

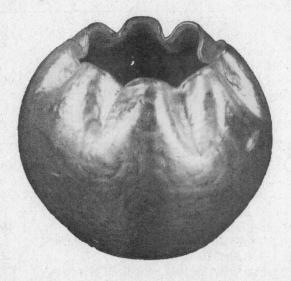

Verre de Soie, iridescent, pebbled surface, 4³/₄" h, $125.00.

Frosted, enameled intertwining yellow and green geometric Art Deco design	60.00
Green Opalescent, Beaded Drape	50.00
Green Opalescent, Beatty Honeycomb, Fenton	30.00
Green Opalescent, white opalescent swirl, collar	50.00
Green Overlay, cut to clear, X's around top and bottom, long vertical oval cuts around middle	100.00
Green Satin, cabbage leaf form, crimped edge, 3⁷/₈" h	100.00
Green Satin, Shell and Seaweed, gold enameling	200.00
Olive Green Satin, molded roses, smooth rim	85.00
Orange Iridescent, Honeycomb	350.00
Multicolor Spatter	60.00
Peach Satin, tall, enameled and hp flowers	300.00
Pink and Yellow Spatter, tall	65.00
Pink Satin, Maize	140.00
Pink Satin, stenciled and hp cherubs	150.00
Pink Stretch, melon ribbed	50.00
Robin's Egg Blue, cased, applied crystal swag trim, crystal rosettes, scroll feet, white int	265.00
Ruby Flashed, Deer and Castle, Bohemian	250.00
Ruby Flashed, Eureka, National	80.00
Ruby Flashed, Heart with Thumbprint, Tarentum Glass	100.00
Ruby Flashed, Red Block	75.00
Spangled, cased deep rose, heavy mica coral branch design, white int, 8 crimp top	125.00
Turquoise Satin	110.00
Yellow Satin, enameled red berries, pale orange leaves and branches, 8 large ribbed swirls, Mount Washington	150.00
Yellow Satin, stenciled Victorian lady's portrait	125.00
Yellow Satin, swirl design, floral enameling	150.00

ROSEMEADE

Rosemeade's origins began with Laura Taylor, a North Dakota studio potter who demonstrated her skills at the North Dakota Building at the 1939 New York World's Fair. Robert J. Hughes, president of the Greater North Dakota Association and owner of the Globe–Gazette Printing Company and Gift Shop in Wahpeton, saw Taylor's demonstration.

In 1940 Hughes organized the Wahpeton Pottery Company. Laura Taylor, a partner, was secretary/treasurer. The company's initial machinery was purchased from the defunct Dickinson Clay Products Company. The company's products were marketed under the trade name Rosemeade in honor of Rosemeade Township, Taylor's birthplace. Vera Gethman and Taylor were the company's two principal designers. Glaze development fell under the watchful eye of Howard Lewis and Taylor.

Initially, Rosemeade was marketed in North and South Dakota, Minnesota, and Wisconsin. Eventually the market expanded to include most of the United States and several foreign countries. The company produced a wide range of objects from commemorative and souvenir pieces to household and kitchenware, e.g., salt and pepper shakers. In the early 1950s, the company employed 27, had a daily production of approximately 1,400 pieces, and offered between 200 and 250 different forms.

In 1953 the Wahpeton Pottery Company became Rosemeade Potteries. Howard Lewis left Rosemeade in 1956, replaced by Joe McLaughlin, who previously worked for Red Wing Potteries.

Dish, wheat, gold, 6³/₄" l, $75.00.

McLaughlin began importing some clay from Kentucky, introduced decal decoration, and incorporated the artistic designs of Les Kouba into the line.

Laura Taylor died in 1959. The company continued operating until 1961. Cheap Japanese copies made from molds cast from Rosemeade pieces and a new minimum wage law contributed to the company's closing. The salesroom remained open until 1964.

References: Darlene Hurst Dommel, *Collector's Encyclopedia of the Dakota Potteries: Identification & Values,* Collector Books, 1996; Harvey Duke, *The Official Price Guide to Pottery and Porcelain, Eighth Edition,* House of Collectibles, 1995.

Ashtray, gopher, 5" d, "Gopher State Minnesota"	$ 135.00
Ashtray, pony, large	110.00
Ashtray, United States shape	160.00
Bank, panda	285.00
Bank, rhinoceros	285.00
Bell, flamingo	80.00
Bookend, bear, 4" h	185.00
Bowl, viking ship, medium	85.00
Candle Holder, bird	15.00
Candle Holder, heart shape	25.00
Casserole, chicken	185.00
Creamer, turkey	40.00
Dish, cov, turkey	65.00
Figure, bear	25.00
Figure, chicken	30.00
Figure, dog, 2³/₄" h	65.00
Figure, goose, 4" h	65.00
Figure, lamb	85.00
Figure, mule, 5" h	85.00
Figure, penguin, price for pair	25.00
Figure, pony, 4" h	110.00
Figure, rabbit, 3" h	15.00
Figure, skunk	10.00
Figure, zebra	65.00
Jam Jar, barrel shape	45.00
Incense Burner, log cabin	65.00

Pin, blackbird	30.00
Pin, fish	30.00
Pin, horse head	30.00
Pin, squirrel	30.00
Pitcher, yellow and brown swirl design, 3¹/₄" h	110.00
Planter, bird, 6¹/₂" h	15.00
Planter, deer, 8" h	40.00
Planter, grapes	25.00
Planter, mule, 5" h	110.00
Planter, swan, 4³/₄" h	40.00
Planter, watering can	30.00
Plate, mouse	40.00
Plaque, dove	85.00
Plaque, mallard drake, 5¹/₄" h	85.00
Salt and Pepper Shakers, pr, figural, cat, 3¹/₂" h	45.00
Salt and Pepper Shakers, pr, figural, flamingos, 2¹/₂" h	55.00
Salt and Pepper Shakers, pr, figural, quail, 3¹/₂" h	55.00
Spoon Rest, bat	65.00
Spoon Rest, cocker spaniel	65.00
Spoon Rest, elephant	40.00
Spoon Rest, flying pheasant, 5¹/₂" l	45.00
Spoon Rest, ladyslipper	25.00
Spoon Rest, tulip, 5¹/₂" ;	40.00
Tea Bell, 3³/₄" h, figural, tulip, Art Nouveau style, yellow	110.00
Television Lamp, Palomino, 9¹/₂" h	450.00
Tidbit Tray, pheasant	40.00
Tidbit Tray, turkey	65.00
Vase, 7" h, wheat design	50.00
Vase, 9¹/₂" h, green	70.00
Wall Pocket, 5" h, deer	40.00
Wall Vase, 5¹/₂" h, Egyptian design	140.00

ROSEVILLE POTTERY

George Young purchased the J. B. Owens Pottery, renaming it the Roseville Pottery, in 1892. Cooking utensils, cuspidors, flowerpots, and umbrella stands were among the company's earliest products. Around the turn of the century, Roseville purchased the Midland Pottery plant in Roseville (1898), moved the company's main office to Zanesville, Ohio, bought Peters and Reed, and acquired the Muskingum Stoneware plant (1901).

Ross Purdy developed Roseville's Rozane, the company's first artware line. Rozane evolved into a general term used to describe all the company's art or prestige lines. Rozane features a high-gloss glaze of dark, blended colors over an underglaze slip painting ranging from American Indians to nature studies.

Roseville introduced dozens of different lines, e.g., Azurean (1902) featuring blue and white underglaze decorations on a blue ground, Mongol (1904) with its high-gloss oxblood color, and Woodland (1905) capturing naturalistic flower images.

John Herold established Roseville's commercial artware department in 1903. Artware included dresser sets, juvenile ware, tea sets, smoker sets, and steins. Harry Rhead replaced his brother Frederick Rhead as art director in 1908. Aztec, Donatello, and Pauleo are a few of Harry Rhead's contributions. Artware dominated Roseville production until the late 1910s.

Roseville closed two of its factories in 1910. Fire destroyed another in 1917. In 1918 Russell Young replaced his father as manager; Frank Ferrel replaced Harry Rhead as art director. Ferrel shifted the company's production into industrial artware. Dogwood, Pine Cone, and Sylvan are just three of the 80 plus new lines introduced under Ferrel's direction.

In 1932 the firm became Roseville Pottery, Inc. The company experienced a major slump in sales following World War II. New industrial artware lines, e.g., Artwood and Maywood, and Raymor (1952) an oven–to–tabletop dinnerware line, failed to halt the decline. Mosaic Tile Company bought the Roseville plant in 1954. Production of Roseville ceased.

References: Virginia Buxton, *Roseville Pottery For Love...Or Money,* Tymbre Hill Publishing, 1996; Sharon and Bob Huxford, *The Collectors Encyclopedia Of Roseville Pottery, First Series* (1976, 1997 value update), *Second Series* (1980, 1997 value update), Collector Books; Ralph and Terry Kovel, *Kovel's American Art Pottery: The Collector's Guide To Makers, Marks and Factory Histories,* Crown Publishers, 1993; Randall B. Monsen, *Collectors' Compendium of Roseville Pottery and Price Guide, Vol. 1,* Monsen and Baer, 1995.

Collectors' Clubs: American Art Pottery Assoc, PO Box 525, Cedar Hill, MO 63016; Roseville's of the Past, PO Box 656, Clarcona, FL 32710.

REPRODUCTION ALERT: Cheap reproduction Roseville pieces are currently surfacing at auctions and flea markets. Distinguishing characteristics include glaze colors and crude decorative techniques.

Ashtray, Imperial II, blue	$ 250.00
Basket, Bittersweet, #810–10	175.00
Basket, Columbine, handled, yellow flowers, green leaves, blue ground, raised mrk, 12¼ x 10¼"	450.00
Basket, Lustre, tall pointed handle, black label, 8 x 5"	90.00
Basket, Montacello, brown, #632	550.00
Basket, Silhouette	135.00
Bookends, pr, Gardenia	165.00
Bookends, pr, Pinecone, brown	200.00
Bowl, Apple Blossom, green, #326–6	125.00

Basket, Snowberry, blue, 8" h, $125.00.

Candy Dish, Zephyr Lily, sienna tan, #4736, 2½" h, $45.00.

Bowl, Baneda	175.00
Bowl, Ferella, 12" d	700.00
Bowl, Florentine, 7" d	75.00
Bowl, Pinecone, brown, #278–4	225.00
Bud Vases, pr, Pinecone, twig handles, circular bases, golden brown, imp mark, 7½ x 5"	375.00
Candleholder, Clematis, brown, #1154–2	50.00
Candleholder, Tourmaline, dark pink and turquoise	100.00
Candleholders, pr, Cherry Blossom, 2 handled, yellow and white flowers, cream and brown ground, silver label, 4¼ x 4¾"	450.00
Candleholders, pr, Rosecraft, hexagonal, orange dec, brown ground, 8½ x 5"	550.00
Candleholders, pr, White Rose	75.00
Console Bowl, Ferella, oval, yellow and green stylized flowers, brown ground, reticulated rim, 5½ x 12½"	700.00
Console Bowl, Freesia, brown, #568–12	100.00
Console Bowl, Pinecone, brown, 11" d	300.00
Console Bowl, Topeo, oval, pink and green raised design, blue–green ground, silver label, 4 x 13"	100.00
Console Set, Calla Lily, 7" d bowl, pr candleholders	100.00
Console Set, Columbine, blue, 10" d bowl, pr 2½" h candleholders	175.00
Cornucopia, Bleeding Heart, green, #141–6	85.00
Cornucopia, Peony, tan, #171–8	125.00
Creamer and Sugar, Zephyr Lily, blue	100.00
Dish, cov, Volpatto, ftd, fluted sides, satin white, silver label, 4¾ x 5¼"	275.00
Ewer, Clematis, #18–15	300.00
Ewer, Freesia, blue, #19–6	125.00
Ewer, Fuschia, handled, green leaves, brown flowers, brown and green ground, foil label, imp mark, 10½ x 5"	275.00
Floor Vase, Carnelian II, futuristic stacked form, mottled blue–green matte glaze, 16 x 11"	2,400.00
Floor Vase, Freesia, 2 handled, purple flowers, green leaves, brown and green ground, silver label, 15½ x 7"	2,500.00
Floor Vase, Zephyr Lily, yellow flowers, green leaves, blue ground, raised mrk, 18" h	850.00
Flower Pot, Poppy, green, matching underplate	250.00
Hanging Basket, Mostique, yellow and green spade–shaped flowers, pebbled gray ground, 6½ x 6½"	350.00

Jardiniere and Pedestal, Baneda, orange fruit and yellow flowers on blue band, speckled pink ground, 24½ x 11".. 2,500.00

Jardiniere and Pedestal, Dahlrose, green 500.00

Jardiniere and Pedestal, Rozane, pink and yellow roses, ivory honeycomb ground, 29 x 14" 450.00

Pitcher, Colonial, blue stripes, glossy cream ground, 8¼" h 50.00

Pitcher, Holland, 6½" h 225.00

Planter, Magnolia, #388–6 .... 115.00

Planter, Poppy, blue............................... 50.00

Planter, Vista, round, yellow, green, and pink flowers, green and lavender ground, mkd "249–6," 3½ x 7" ... 150.00

Urn, Florentine, brown, #463–5 .... 85.00

Vase, Cherry Blossom, 2 handled, 5" h 225.00

Vase, Ferella, 2 handled, bulbous, stylized red and green flowers, burgundy ground, reticulated rim, 5½ x 6½".. 550.00

Vase, Foxglove, pink, #54–15...................... 350.00

Vase, Fuschia, green, #895–7 .... 300.00

Vase, Futura, balloon shape, yellow, pink, blue, and green circles, deep blue ground, unmkd, 8½ x 6¾".. 1,300.00

Vase, Ixia, #855–7 .... 75.00

Vase, Jonquil, squatty, 4" h 125.00

Vase, Jonquil, stovepipe neck, bulbous base, 2 handled, white and amber blossoms, orange–brown ground, 9½" h 450.00

Vase, Luffa, 2 handled, ivory and green leaves, ivory and brown blossoms, rust and green ground, gold decal, 12¼ x 7¼"............................. 700.00

Vase, Magnolia, blue, #185–8 .... 150.00

Vase, Peony, tan, #171–19 .... 100.00

Vase, Pinecone, blue, #840–7 .... 185.00

Vase, Poppy, pink, #873–9........................ 250.00

Vase, Primrose, #760–6 .... 100.00

Vase, Rosecraft, black, 5½" h 50.00

Vaee, Rozane, pansies, 5" h 150.00

Vase, Tourmaline, blue............................ 85.00

Vase, White Rose, #994–18 .... 700.00

Vase, Clematis, brown, 108–8", $95.00.

Vase, Windsor, spherical, 2 handled, green fern, orange ground, 7½ x 7¾"..................... 400.00

Wall Pocket, Bittersweet, green................... 300.00

Wall Pocket, Carnelian I, pink and blue 175.00

Wall Pocket, Cosmos, blue....................... 375.00

Wall Pocket, Imperial II, triple, frothy green glaze, burnt–orange ground, 7½ x 9" 600.00

Wall Pocket, Lotus, burgundy..................... 150.00

Window Box, Dahlrose, rect, yellow flowers, green leaves, brown ground, orig liner, 6¼ x 16" 450.00

ROYAL CHINA

Although the Royal China Company purchased the former E. H. Sebring Company (Sebring, Ohio) plant in 1933, extensive renovation delayed production of the first ware until 1934. Initially, Royal China produced mainly overglaze decal ware. Kenneth Doyle's underglaze stamping machine, developed for Royal China in 1948, revolutionized the dinnerware industry. This allowed the inexpensive production of underglaze ware. By 1950 Royal China eliminated its decal ware.

Royal China produced a wide range of dinnerware lines. Bluebell (1940s), Colonial Homestead (early 1950s, sold by Sears in the 1960s), Currier and Ives (1949/50, designed border and adapted center by Gordon Parker), Old Curiosity Shop (a Parker design), and Blue and Pink Willow Ware (1940s) are among the most popular. Patterns with a series varied from year to year. Shapes within a series were not always identical. Royal Oven Ware was introduced in the 1940s.

In 1964 Royal China purchased the French–Saxon China Company, operating it as a wholly owned subsidiary. The Jeannette Corporation acquired the company in 1969. Jeannette also purchased Harker Pottery in 1969, with management for Harker provided by Royal China until Harker closed in 1972. In 1970 fire destroyed Royal China's Sebring, Ohio, plant. Jeannette moved Royal China's operations to the French–Saxon plant, also located in Sebring, Ohio.

The company changed hands several times in the 1970s and 80s, being purchased by the Coca–Cola Bottling Company (1976), J. Corporation of Boston (1981), and Nordic Capitol of New York (1984). Each owner continued to manufacture ware under the Royal China brand name. Operations ceased in 1986.

References: Eldon R. Aupperle, *A Collector's Guide For Currier & Ives Dinnerware,* published by quthor, 1996; Susan and Al Bagdade, *Warman's American Pottery and Porcelain,* Wallace–Homestead, Krause Publications, 1994; Harvey Duke, *The Official Price Guide to Pottery and Porcelain, Eighth Edition,* House of Collectibles, 1995.

Collectors' Club: C & I Dinnerware Collectors, 29470 Saxon Rd, Toulon, IL 61483

Colonial Homestead, bread and butter plate.......... $ 2.50

Colonial Homestead, cake plate, tab handles 15.00

Colonial Homestead, cereal bowl, 6¼" d 7.00

Colonial Homestead, chop plate, 12" d.............. 20.00

Colonial Homestead, creamer and sugar, cov 18.00

Colonial Homestead, dinner plate 4.00

Colonial Homestead, fruit bowl, 5½" d.............. 4.00

Colonial Homestead, gravy, with underplate........... 25.00

Currier & Ives, fruit bowl, 5 1/2" d, $3.00.

Colonial Homestead, luncheon plate	3.00
Colonial Homestead, salad plate, 7" d	2.50
Colonial Homestead, salt and pepper shakers, pr	15.00
Colonial Homestead, soup bowl, flat	8.00
Colonial Homestead, teapot, cov	50.00
Currier & Ives, ashtray	10.00
Currier & Ives, baker	15.00
Currier & Ives, bread and butter plate, 6" d	3.00
Currier & Ives, cake plate, 10" d	25.00
Currier & Ives, casserole, cov	80.00
Currier & Ives, cereal bowl, 6 1/2" d	6.00
Currier & Ives, chop plate, 12" d	25.00
Currier & Ives, creamer	10.00
Currier & Ives, creamer and sugar, cov	20.00
Currier & Ives, cup and saucer	4.00
Currier & Ives, dinner plate, 10 1/2" d	5.00
Currier & Ives, gravy, with underplate	25.00
Currier & Ives, luncheon plate, 9" d	15.00
Currier & Ives, plate, 11 1/4" d	20.00
Currier & Ives, platter, oval, 13"	30.00
Currier & Ives, salad plate, 7 1/4" d	8.00
Currier & Ives, salt and pepper shakers, pr	20.00
Currier & Ives, saucer	1.00
Currier & Ives, soup bowl, flat, 8 1/2" d	12.00
Currier & Ives, sugar, cov	12.00
Currier & Ives, teapot	125.00
Currier & Ives, vegetable bowl, 9" d	20.00
Memory Lane, bread and butter plate, 6" d	3.00
Memory Lane, cake plate, handled	15.00
Memory Lane, chop plate	25.00
Memory Lane, creamer and sugar	18.00
Memory Lane, cup and saucer	6.00
Memory Lane, dinner plate	6.00
Memory Lane, fruit bowl	4.00
Memory Lane, gravy, with underplate	20.00
Memory Lane, luncheon plate, 9" d	7.00

Memory Lane, platter	35.00
Memory Lane, salad plate, 7" d	6.00
Memory Lane, soup bowl, flat	8.00
Memory Lane, vegetable bowl, 9" d	20.00
Memory Lane, vegetable bowl, 10" d	25.00
Old Curiosity Shop, bowl, 9 1/4" d	20.00
Old Curiosity Shop, bread and butter plate	3.00
Old Curiosity Shop, cake plate, 2 handles, 10" d	20.00
Old Curiosity Shop, casserole, cov	60.00
Old Cruiosity Shop, cereal bowl, tab handles	10.00
Old Curiosity Shop, creamer	8.00
Old Curiosity Shop, cup and saucer	5.00
Old Curiosity Shop, dinner plate	4.00
Old Curiosity Shop, fruit bowl	4.00
Old Curiosity Shop, gravy	15.00
Old Curiosity Shop, platter, oval, handled, 10" l	15.00
Old Curiosity Shop, soup bowl, flat	7.00
Old Curiosity Shop, sugar, cov	12.00
Old Curiosity Shop, teapot	60.00
Old Curiosity Shop, vegetable bowl, 10" d	25.00

ROYAL COPENHAGEN

In the mid–18th century, Europe's royal families competed with each other to see who would be the first to develop a porcelain formula. The Danish King hired Louis Fournier, a renowned French sculptor and chemist. His experiments were unsuccessful. In 1772 Franz Heinrich Muller, a Danish pharmacist and chemist, discovered a formula for hard paste porcelain.

Muller submitted his samples to the Queen Dowager, Juliane Marie. She was so delighted that she christened his firm "The Danish Porcelain Factory." Although founded privately in 1775 as the Danish Porcelain Factory, the Danish monarchy fully controlled the firm by 1779. Three wavy lines were chosen as the firm's trademark to symbolize the seafaring tradition of the Danes.

Blue Fluted, the company's most famous dinnerware pattern, was introduced in 1780. Production of Royal Copenhagen's Flora Danica, a dinnerware service featuring native plants of Denmark, began around 1790. It remains in the possession of the Danish royal family. A modern version is available for sale to the public.

Although there was strong public acceptance of Royal Copenhagen's accessory pieces, figurines, and vases during the first half of the 19th century, the company proved a drain on the Danish monarchy's finances. In 1867 A. Falch purchased the company under the condition that he be allowed to retain the use of "Royal" in the firm's title. Falch sold the company to Philip Schou in 1882.

In 1885 Arnold Krog, an architect, became art director of Royal Copenhagen and developed underglaze painting. Only one color is used. Shading is achieved by varying the thickness of the pigment layers and firing the painted plate at a high temperature, 2,640 degrees Fahrenheit. Krog revitalized the company. In 1902 Dalgas became art director. He introduced the blue and white Christmas Plate series that was introduced in 1908.

Today the Royal Copenhagen Group also includes Bing and Grondahl. The firm is noted for its extensive dinnerware and giftware lines.

Reference: Susan and Al Bagdade, *Warman's English & Continental Pottery & Porcelain, Second Edition,* Wallace–Homestead, Krause Publications, 1991.

Vase, green and black dec, gold highlights, crackle ground, 8¼" h, $375.00.

Figure, two girls, native Scandinavian dress, plinth
base, labeled "piter or trein dirchans, #12105" .... $ 365.00
Plate, A Peaceful Motif, 1945 . . . . 350.00
Plate, Aabenraa marketplace, 1921. . . . . 65.00
Plate, American Mother, Mother's Day Series, 1971 . . . . 120.00
Plate, An Outing With Mother, 1980. . . . . 30.00
Plate, Bird In Nest, Mother's Day Series, 1975. . . . . 45.00
Plate, Christianshavn, 1925 . . . . 100.00
Plate, Christmas In The Forest, 1952 . . . . 165.00
Plate, Christmas Night, 1959 . . . . 165.00
Plate, Frederiksberg Gardens, 1932. . . . . 100.00
Plate, Fishing Boats, 1930 . . . . 125.00
Plate, Greenland Scenery, 1978 . . . . 20.00
Plate, Hare In Winter, 1971 . . . . 15.00
Plate, Kronborg Castle, 1935 . . . . 210.00
Plate, Main Street Copenhagen, 1937 . . . . 210.00
Plate, Merry Christmas, 1983 . . . . 55.00
Plate, Our Lady's Cathedral, 1949. . . . . 110.00
Plate, Sailing Ship, 1924 . . . . 125.00
Plate, The Children's Hour, Mother's Day Series, 1982 . . . . 40.00
Plate, The Good Shepherd, 1940 . . . . 425.00
Plate, The Little Mermaid, 1962 . . . . 225.00
Plate, The Stag, 1960 . . . . 125.00
Plate, The Twins, Mother's Day Series, 1977 . . . . 45.00
Plate, Train Homeward Bound, 1973 . . . . 15.00
Plate, Training Ship, 1961. . . . . 125.00
Plate, Winter Birds, 1987 . . . . 55.00
Vase, lace pattern, blue and white, 1935, 2¾" h 85.00
Vase, lace pattern, blue and white, 1926, 5¼" h 45.00

ROYAL COPLEY

Royal Copley and Royal Windsor are tradenames of the Spaulding China Company. Royal Copley, representing approximately 85% of all Spaulding production, was sold through chain stores such as Grants, Kresges, Murphys, and Woolworth along with an occasional gift or department store. Royal Windsor items were sold to the florist trade.

Spaulding China, Sebring, Ohio, began in 1942. Initially located in the abandoned plant of the Alliance Vitreous China Company, Spaulding eventually acquired and renovated the Sebring Rubber Company plant. Morris Feinberg served as president; James G. Eardley as plant manager.

Initially a straight tunnel kiln and a low–temperature decorating kiln were used for decal and gold decorated wares. In 1948 the tunnel kiln was replaced by a continuous circular kiln. Daily production was 18,000 pieces.

The company deliberately chose names that had an English air to them, e.g., Spaulding not Spalding. Royal Copley and Royal Windsor were chosen because they sounded regal and fine. Even marketing terms such as Crown Assortment and Oxford Assortment continued this English theme. The company's motto was "Gift Shop Merchandise at Chain Store Prices." Pieces were marked with a paper label.

Birds, ducks, piggy banks, Oriental boy and girl wall pockets, and roosters were among Royal Copley's biggest sellers. The small birds originally retailed for 25¢.

Cheap Japanese imports and labor difficulties plagued Spaulding throughout the post–war period. In 1957 Morris Feinberg retired, contracting with nearby China Craft to fill Spaulding's remaining orders. Initially Spaudling was sold to a Mr. Shiffman, who made small sinks for mobile homes. After being closed for several years, Eugene Meskil, of Holiday Designs, bought the plant. The company made accessories, canisters, cookie jars, and teapots. Richard C. Durstein of Pittsburgh bought the plant in 1982.

Reference: Mike Schneider, *Royal Copley: Identification and Price Guide,* Schiffer Publishing, 1995.

Newsletter: *The Copley Courier,* 1639 N Catalina St, Burbank, CA 91505.

Ashtray, leaf and bird, 5½" d . . . . $ 20.00
Bank, pig wearing bow tie, 7½" h. 40.00
Bank, rooster, 7½" h 50.00
Bank, teddy bear, 7½" h. 60.00
Creamer, leaf design, handled, green stamp on base 20.00

Vase, black floral leaf and stem, pink ground, 6 3/4" h, $15.00.

Figure, cockatoo, 7¼" h, paper label **30.00**
Figure, cocker spaniel, 6" h **15.00**
Figure, deer on sled, 6½" h **25.00**
Figure, lark, 5" h **8.00**
Figure, oriental girl, 7½" h **15.00**
Figure, parrot, 5" h, yellow. **12.00**
Figure, rooster, 8" h, white, green base **50.00**
Figure, swallow, 8" h **20.00**
Figure, warbler, 5" h **12.00**
Lamp, colonial gentleman, orig shade **40.00**
Lamp, dancing girl, orig shade, metal base **40.00**
Pitcher, 6¼" h, floral decal, two handles, gold stamp
   on bottom **10.00**
Pitcher, 8" h, daffodil, yellow and pink **32.00**
Pitcher, 8" h, floral elegance, greens stamp on bottom **25.00**
Pitcher, 8" h, pink floral design, blue ground. **30.00**
Pitcher, 8" h, pome fruit, light blue, green stamp on
   bottom. **35.00**
Planter, 3¼ x 6", coach, green stamp on bottom **16.00**
Planter, 4 x 7", ivory dec, paper label **12.00**
Planter, 4½" h, pink dogwood design **8.00**
Planter, 5" h, cocker spaniel head. **10.00**
Planter, 5" h, sitting mallard **20.00**
Planter, 5¼" h, hummingbird **30.00**
Planter, 5½" h, pony **12.00**
Planter, 5½" h, wide brimmed hat with bow **25.00**
Planter, 6" h, elephant on yellow ball **25.00**
Planter, 6½" h, apple and finch **18.00**
Planter, 6½" h, kitten and book **25.00**
Planter, 6½" h, ram head **20.00**
Planter, 7" h, girl with pigtails. **20.00**
Planter, 7" h, oriental girl and wheelbarrow, paper label . . **25.00**
Planter, 7" h, white prancing poodle **25.00**
Planter, 7½" h, girl wearing wide brim hat **30.00**
Planter, 7¾" h, dog and mail box **18.00**
Planter, 7½" h, teddy bear with concertina **65.00**
Planter, 8" h, angel **25.00**
Planter, 8" h. kitten in basket **65.00**
Planter, 8" h, rooster and wheelbarrow, paper label **55.00**
Planter, 8" h, teddy bear. **40.00**

Vase, fish, cylindrical, green and brown, gold highlights, 8" h, $20.00.

Planter, 8¼" h, kitten with ball of yarn **25.00**
Vase, 5½" h, stylized leaf design, paper label **8.00**
Vase, 6½" h, ftd, bow design **12.00**
Vase, 7" h, fish, cylindrical. **18.00**
Vase, 7" h, floral decal, paper label **12.00**
Vase, 7" h, ftd, ivory dec, paper label **10.00**
Vase, 8¼" h, cornucopia, gold trim. **20.00**
Vase, 8v h, trailing leaf and vine. **15.00**

ROYAL DOULTON

In 1815 John Doulton founded the Doulton Lambeth Pottery in Lambeth, London. Utilitarian salt glazed stoneware was the company's product. The firm was known as Doulton and Watts between 1820 and 1853. Henry Doulton, John's second son, joined the firm in 1835. He introduced steam power to the plant. The company produced a wide range of products from bottles and spirit flasks to architectural terra cotta and sanitary ware.

A connection was formed between the Lambeth School of Art and Doulton in the early 1870s. By 1885 over 250 artists, including Arthur and Hannah Barlow and George Tinsworth, were working at Doulton. In 1887 Henry Doulton was knighted by Queen Victoria for his achievements in the ceramic arts.

Henry Doulton acquired the Niles Street pottery in Burslem, Staffordshire in 1877, changing the name to Doulton & Co. in 1882. This plant made high quality porcelain and inexpensive earthenware tableware. Charles Noke joined the firm in 1889, becoming one its most famous designers. Noke introduced Rouge Flambé. In 1901 King Edward VII granted the Royal Warrant of appointment to Doulton. "Royal" has appeared on the company's ware since that date.

Whereas production increased at the Burslem plant during the 20th century, it decreased at the Lambeth plant. By 1925 only 24 artists were employed, one of whom was Leslie Harradine, noted for his famed Dickens' characters. Commemorative wares were produced at Lambeth in the 1920s and 30s. Agnete Hoy, famous for her cat figures, worked at Lambeth between 1951 and 1956. Production at the Lambeth plant ended in 1956.

Although Royal Doulton made a full line of tabletop ware, it is best know for its figurines, character and toby jugs, and series ware. Almost all Doulton's figurines were made at Burslem. The HN numbers, named for Harry Nixon, were introduced in 1913. HN numbers were chronological until 1949 after which each modeler received a block of numbers. Noke introduced the first character jugs in 1934. Noke also created series ware, a line that utilizes a standard blank decorated with a wide range of scenes.

Today the Royal Doulton Group includes John Beswick, Colclough, Webb Corbett, Minton, Paragon, Ridgway, Royal Adderley, Royal Albert, and Royal Crown Derby. It is the largest manufacturer of ceramic products in the United Kingdom.

References: Susan and Al Bagdade, *Warman's English & Continental Pottery & Porcelain, 2nd Edition* Wallace–Homestead, Krause Publications, 1991; Jean Dale, *The Charlton Standard Catalogue of Royal Doulton Animals,* Charlton Press, 1994; Jean Dale, *The Charlton Standard Catalogue of Royal Doulton Beswick Figurines, Fifth Edition,* Charlton Press, 1996; Jean Dale, *The Charlton Standard Catalogue of Royal Doulton Beswick Storybook Figurines, Third Edition,* Charlton Press, 1996; Jean Dale, *The Charlton Standard Catalogue of Royal Doulton Beswick Jugs, Fourth Edition,* Charlton Press, 1997; Harry L. Rinker, *Dinnerware* *of the 20th Century: The Top 500 Patterns,* House of Collectibles, 1997.

Periodical: *Doulton Divvy,* PO Box 2434, Joliet, IL 60434.

Collectors' Clubs: Royal Doulton International Collectors Club, PO Box 6705, Somerset, NJ 08873; Royal Doulton International Collectors Club, 850 Progress Ave, Scarborough Ontario M1H 3C4 Canada.

Character Mug, Beefeater, D6251, 2¼" h	$ 50.00
Character Mug, Gone Away, D6545, 2½" h.	60.00
Character Mug, John Doulton, D6656, 4½" h	70.00
Character Mug, John Peel, 2¼" h	50.00
Character Mug, Sam Weller, 3⅜" h.	50.00
Character Mug, Tam O'Shanter, 2¼" h	50.00
Character Mug, Tony Weller, 2¼" h	50.00
Character Mug, Trapper, 3¾" h.	60.00
Figure, Balloon Man, HN1954, 7¼" h.	110.00
Figure, Biddy Penny Farthing, HN1843, 8½" h	130.00
Figure, Blue Beard, HN2105, 10" h	350.00
Figure, Boatman, HN2417, 6¾" h.	135.00
Figure, Captain, HN2260, 9⅜" h	300.00
Figure, Captain Coo, HN2889, 8" h	235.00
Figure, China Repairer, HN2943, 6¾" h	125.00
Figure, Crouching Lion, HN2641, 10⅛" h, 17" l	775.00
Figure, Doctor, HN2858, 7½" h	110.00
Figure, Elegance, HN2264, 7¼" h.	100.00
Figure, Falstaff, HN3236, 4⅛" h	40.00
Figure, Falstaff, HN2054, 7" h	115.00
Figure, helmsman, HN2499, 9½" h	175.00
Figure, Jester, HN2016, 9⅝" h	150.00
Figure, Lobster Man, HN2317, 7¼" h	120.00
Figure, Mask Seller, HN2103, 8⅜" h.	175.00
Figure, Officer of the Line, HN2733, 9¼" h.	150.00
Figure, Old Balloon Seller, HN2129, 3⅝" h.	110.00
Figure, Old Balloon Seller, HN1315, 7½" h.	115.00
Figure, Old King, HN2134, 10" h	475.00
Figure, Omar Khayyam, HN2247, 6¼" h.	140.00
Figure, Potter, HN1493, 7" h	225.00

Figure, Autumn Breezes, HN1954, $115.00.

Figure, Pride & Joy, HN2945, 7" h	195.00
Figure, Prized Possessions, HN2942, 7" h	345.00
Figure, Robin Hood, HN2733, 7¾" h	125.00
Figure, Rumpelstiltskin, HN3025, 8¼" h	130.00
Figure, Sailors Holiday, HN2442, 6⅜" h	150.00
Figure, Schoolmarm, HN2223, 6½" h.	195.00
Figure, Sleepy Darling, HN2953, 7¼" h	130.00
Figure, Song of the Sea, HN2729, 7½" h.	160.00
Figure, Springtime, HN3033, 8" h.	195.00
Figure, St. George, HN2051, 7⅜" h	300.00
Figure, Stop Press, HN2683, 7⅝" h.	95.00
Figure, Tuppence a Bag, HN2320, 5⅜" h	120.00
Figure, Union Jack, HN6407, 2⅜" h.	130.00
Figure, Votes for Women, HN2816, 10" h	200.00
Figure, Wizard, HN2877, 9⅝" h.	160.00
Miramont, bread and butter plate, 6½" d	15.00
Miramont, creamer	35.00
Miramont, cup and saucer, ftd	30.00
Miramont, dinner plate	25.00
Miramont, individual casserole, 4⅜" d	40.00
Miramont, platter, oval, 13¼" l	75.00
Miramont, sugar, cov	50.00
Old Colony, bread and butter plate, 6½" d	10.00
Old Colony, cream soup and saucer	45.00
Old Colony, creamer	30.00
Old Colony, cup and saucer, ftd	25.00
Old Colony, dinner plate, 10⅝" d.	25.00
Old Colony, salad plate, 8" d	18.00
Old Colony, sugar, cov.	50.00
Old Colony, vegetable bowl, oval	50.00

SALT & PEPPER SHAKERS

The salt and pepper shaker emerged during the latter half of the Victorian era. Fine ceramic and glass shakers slowly replaced individual and master salts. Major American art glass manufacturers such as Mt. Washington made salt and pepper shakers. Large pattern glass services, e.g., Daisy and Button, included the form. These early shakers were documented by Arthur G. Peterson in *Glass Salt Shakers: 1,000 Patterns* (Wallace–Homestead, 1970).

Although pre–World War I figural salt shakers do exist, e.g., Royal Bayreuth's lobster and tomato sets, the figural salt and pepper shaker gained in popularity during the 1920s and 30s, reaching its zenith in the 1940s and 50s. By the 1960s, inexpensive plastic salt and pepper shakes had replace their ceramic and glass counterparts.

Salt and pepper shaker collectors specialize. Salt and pepper shakers that included mechanical devices to loosen salt were popular in the 1960s and 70s. Depression era glass sets also enjoyed strong collector interest during that period. Currently, figural salt and pepper shakers are hot, having experienced a 100 percent price increase during the past five years.

References: Gideon Bosker and Lena Lencer, *Salt and Pepper Shakers: Identification and Price Guide,* Avon Books, 1994; Larry Carey and Sylvia Tompkins, *Salt and Pepper: Over 1001 Shakers,* Schiffer Publishing, 1994; Larry Carey and Sylvia Tompkins, *1002 Salt and Pepper Shakers,* Schiffer Publishing, 1995; Larry Carey and Sylvia Thompkins, *1003 Salt & Pepper Shakers,* Schiffer Publishing, 1997; Melva Davern, *The Collector's Encyclopedia of Salt & Pepper Shakers: Figural And Novelty, Second Series,*

Collector Books, 1990, 1995 value update; Helene Guarnaccia, *Salt & Pepper Shakers, Vol. 1* (1985, 1996 value update), *Vol. II* (1989, 1993 value update), *Vol. III* (1991, 1995 value update), *Vol. IV* (1993, 1997 value update), Collector Books; Mike Schneider, *The Complete Salt and Pepper Shaker Book,* Schiffer Publishing, 1993.

Collectors' Club: Novelty Salt & Pepper Shakers Club, PO Box 3617, Lantana, FL 33465.

Note: All shakers listed are ceramic unless noted otherwise. Prices are for sets. For additional listings refer to Depression Glass and individual ceramics and glass manufacturer's categories.

Alcatraz Convicts	$ 40.00
Amish Couple, painted white metal	6.00
Art Deco Woman, holding two hat boxes	95.00
Bananas, yellow and tan	9.00
Bed and Pillow, black and white	15.00
Bears, black and white	15.00
Begging Dog and Blue Bow	15.00
Black Cats and Fishbowls	150.00
Black Chef and Maid, chalkware, 2½" h	40.00
Black Lady's Heads	70.00
Black Leapfrogging Kids	75.00
Black Natives, baskets on heads	25.00
Black Porter and Suitcase	70.00
Boy and Dog, brown, Van Telligen	65.00
Bride and Groom inCar	45.00
Bud Man, blue shoes	20.00
Cactus, Rosemeade	15.00
Camels, monkeys on backs, nodders	85.00
Cat, winking, Enesco	15.00
Cat and Fiddle	40.00
Cat Head, Lefton	25.00
Caveman and Cavewoman	15.00
Chickens, Rosemeade	25.00
Christmas Trees	20.00
Colonial Couple, Erphila, Czechoslovakia	25.00
Conestoga Wagons, brown and black, white tops	10.00
Cows, purple	15.00
Deer, nodders	65.00

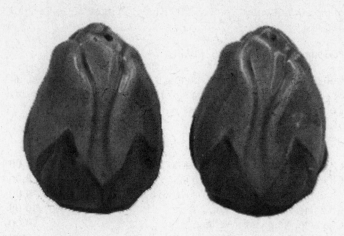

Rosebuds, Desert Rose pattern, Franciscan, $22.00.

Dickens Couple, Beswick	25.00
Donkey and Tipped Cart	15.00
Dutch Boy and Girl, Shawnee	60.00
Dutch Couple, large size	25.00
Elephants, gray, blue trim, trunks form letter "S" or "P," ceramic Arts Studios	35.00
Esso Pumps	30.00
Farmer Pigs, Shawnee	50.00
Firestone Tires	55.00
Fish, Rosemeade	35.00
Flamingos	15.00
Flying Saucers	45.00
Fred Flintstone and Barney Rubble	55.00
Frogs, sitting on lily pad, bulging eyes, 1 brown, 1 green	15.00
Ghosts	20.00
Greyhound Buses	75.00
Hammer and Nail	15.00
Hillbillies in Barrels	15.00
Humpty Dumpty, Regal	175.00
Jonah and the Whale, black	85.00
Johah and the Whale, white	75.00
Kangaroo Mother and Baby	20.00
Kangaroos, nodders	95.00
Kellogg's Snap and Pop	65.00
Kip's Big Boy	55.00
Lenny, Lenox	165.00
Lobster, red, green base, claws held above head attached by springs	25.00
Marilyn Monroe and Cake	35.00
Mickey and Minnie Mouse, on park bench	195.00
Milk Cans, Shawnee	45.00
Miss Priss, Lefton	30.00
Mixmaster, plastic, 1950s	25.00
Mona Lisa and Picture Frame	25.00
Monkey and Palm Tree	20.00
Native with Banjo and Palm Tree	55.00
Pears	15.00
Penguins, black, white, and orange, 1930s	25.00
Pillsbury Dough Boy	35.00
Pillsbury Dough Boy and Poppy, hard plastic, 1974	60.00
Pixies, blue outfits, yellow hair	15.00

Dogs, pink ground, green and red spots, 1 winking, 1 laughing, Japan, 2³/₄" h, $15.00.

Prairie Dogs, Rosemeade **40.00**
Rooster and Hen, Germany **25.00**
Rotisserie, plastic **200.00**
Sailor and Bo Peep, Shawnee **45.00**
Sailor and Mermaid, huggies **225.00**
Sandman **95.00**
Schmoos, Red Wing **100.00**
Sea Lions **15.00**
Skulls, nodders **90.00**
Skunks, Rosemeade **45.00**
Smiley Pig, Shawnee, large **135.00**
Smokey Bear **100.00**
Sneezy and Bashful **40.00**
Squirrel, brown **8.00**
Surfer Boy and Surfboard **60.00**
surfer Girl and Surfboard **200.00**
Tasmanian Devil **35.00**
Telephone and Directory, black phone, white book **15.00**
Turkeys, multicolored **15.00**
Westinghouse Washer and Dryer **30.00**
Wrestlers, 1 held in body slam position over other
    wrestler's head **25.00**

SAND PAILS

Sand pails is one of a growing list of children's lithographed tin and plastic toy collecting categories gaining in popularity with collectors. Children's paint sets is another.

Pre–1900 tin sand pails were japanned, a technique involving layers of paint with a final lacquer coating. Lithographed printed tin sand pails arrived on the scene in the first two decades of the 20th century.

The golden age of lithographed tin sand pails began in the late 1930s and extended into the 1960s. After World War II, the four leading manufacturers were J. Chein & Co., T. Cohn, The Ohio Art Company, and U.S. Metal Toy Manufacturing. Character–licensed pails arrived on the scene in the late 1940s and early 1950s. By the mid–1960s, almost all sand pails were made of plastic.

Many sand pails were sold as sets. Sets could include sand molds, a sifter, spade, and/or sprinkling can.

Reference: Carole and Richard Smyth, *Sand Pails & Other Sand Toys,* published by authors, 1996.

Apex Tire and Rubber, splattered paint design, rubber,
    4¼" h . . . . **$ 35.00**
Charms Co, Hansel, Gretel and Wicked Witch, 3" h **130.00**
Kirchhoff, children and dogs on beach, 4" h **110.00**
Ohio Art, banjo player and farm animals, paper label
    reads "Fenstermacher 59 cents" **45.00**
Ohio Art, boy riding sea horse, 4¼" h **110.00**
Ohio Art, children and dog at beach, 4¼" h **110.00**
Ohio Art, children picking strawberries, 7¾" h **125.00**
Ohio Art, clowns and dog, 4¼" h **110.00**
Ohio Art, cowboy and Indian, 4¼" h **85.00**
Ohio Art, Donald Duck, 3" h **210.00**
Ohio Art, "FIRE" on both sides, white letters, red
    ground, 5¼" h **65.00**
Ohio Art, Mexican children playing musical instru-
    ments, 4¼" h **45.00**

T. Cohn, children playing instruments, patriotic motif, red, white, and blue, $85.00.

Stover Candies, Hershey, PA, ducks, geese, frogs, and
    fish playing by pond, 3" h **110.00**
T. Cohn, animals and birds wearing clothing, 3½" h **85.00**
T. Cohn, children bathing animals, 4¼" h **85.00**
T. Cohn, children playing with garden sprinkler,
    4¼" h **80.00**
T. Cohn, farmer, horse and cart, 7½" h **135.00**
J. Chein & Co, nursery rhymes, red, white, and blue,
    5¼" h **85.00**
J. Chein & Co, Three Little Pigs, 3½" h **110.00**
U.S. Metal Toy Mfg Co, children riding carousel ani-
    mals, 7½" h **110.00**

SCHOOP, HEDI

Hedi Schoop, born in Switzerland in 1906, was educated at Vienna's Kunstgewerbeschule and Berlin's Reimann Institute. In the early 1930s she and her husband, Frederick Hollander, a well–known composer, emigrated to America.

After arriving in Los Angeles, Schoop began making and marketing a line of plaster of Paris dolls dressed in contemporary fashions. Discovered by a representative of Barker Brothers, she was advised to scrap the textile clothing and do figures that were entirely ceramic.

Hedi's mother financed a plant located at 10852 Burbank Boulevard in North Hollywood. Schoop employed many displaced European actors, dancers, and musicians as decorators. She designed the vast majority of figurines produced by her studio. Figures ranged from Asian and European couples to animals. Forms ranged from ashtrays and covered boxes to vases and wall plaques.

In 1942 the company became Hedi Schoop Art Creations. Business was strong in the late 1940s and early 1950s. The company introduced a line of TV lamps in the mid–1950s. A disastrous fire ended production in 1958. Schoop did not rebuild. Instead, she worked as a free lance designer for several other Los Angeles area firms. She retired permanently from the ceramics business in the 1960s, devoting her time after that to painting.

References: Jack Chipman, *Collector's Encyclopedia of California Pottery,* Collector Books, 1992, 1995 value update; Mike Schneider, *California Potteries; The Complete Book,* Schiffer Publishing, 1995.

Ashtray, duck, 5 x 6 1/2" . . . . $ 35.00
Candle Holder, mermaid, c1950, 13½" h 125.00
Figure, clown playing cello, mkd, c1943, 12½" h 80.00
Figure, Debutante, 12½" h 50.00
Figure, girl with ponytail and flower basket wearing
   white and pink dress and walking black and white
   collie, 9½" h 95.00
Figurine, Josephine, holding bowl, mkd, c1943, 13" h. . . . 75.00
Figure, Margie, 12" h 75.00
Figure, Repose, woman holding bowl, 1949 . . . . 95.00
Figures, pr, French peasant couple, 13" h 195.00
Figures, pr, man and woman carrying carrying urns,
   green and gold, 12"h 75.00
Figures, pr, Siamese dancers, tinted bisque, gold
   overglaze, mkd, 1947, 14½" man, 14" woman. 100.00
Heads, pr, Chinese man and woman, c1950s 65.00
Lamp, Colbert, woman holding 2 baskets, c1940,
   11½" h 125.00
Planter, hobby horse 40.00
Tray, King of Diamonds 45.00
Tray, Queen of Hearts 45.00
Vase, crowing rooster, gold overglaze, c1949, 12" h 50.00

SEBASTIAN MINIATURES

Sebastian Miniatures, hand painted, lightly glazed figurines, are the creation of Prescott W. Baston (1909–1984). He received his training at the Vesper George School of Art in Boston in the late 1920s. Although sculpting figures as early as 1938, Baston organized the Sebastian Miniature Company in 1940. Production initially was located in Marblehead, Massachusetts, eventually moving to Hudson, Massachusetts.

Sebastian Miniatures range in size from three to four inches. Production was limited. Characters from literature and history, scenes from family life, and children are just a few series designed by this creative artist. Baston also produced special commission advertising and souvenir figurines (exceeding 100 in number). Over 900 different figures have been documented.

Pewter miniatures were introduced in 1969. In 1976, the Lance Corporation produced 100 of Baston's most popular designs for national distribution.

Prescott Baston died on May 25, 1984. His son, Woody, continued in his father's footsteps. The Sebastian Collectors Society plays a far greater role in determining secondary market pricing than normally expected from a collectors' club.

Reference: Collector's Information Bureau, *Collectibles market Gruide & Price Indes, 15th Edition,* Collector's Information Bureau, 1997, distributed by Krause Publications.

Collectors' Club: The Sebastian Exchange Collector Assoc, PO Box 10905, Lancaster, PA 17605.

Abraham Lincoln, seated . . . . $ 125.00
Aunt Betzy Trotwood, marblehead label 60.00
Barkis, 1946 . . . . 55.00

Lobsterman, Marblehead paper label, $85.00.

Benjamin Franklin Printing Press. 65.00
Betsy Ross, #129 . . . . 85.00
Cleopatra, version I, 1950–62. . . . . 200.00
Clown, sgd "Hudson" 100.00
Colonial Lacemaker, blue label 30.00
Daniel Boone, 1940–45. . . . . 150.00
Davy Crockett, #249 . . . . 225.00
1850 Baby Buggy 90.00
Evangeline, #12. . . . . 125.00
Gabriel, #11 . . . . 135.00
Gathering Tulips. 125.00
George and Martha Washington, price for pair 110.00
George Washington, cannon, sgd, 1947 . . . . 80.00
Gibson Girl, #316–A 90.00
Henry Hudson, #311 . . . . 175.00
In The Candy Store, Necco, Hudson 175.00
John Smith and Pocahontas, Marblehead mark, price
   for pair 200.00
Kennel Fresh, ashtray, #239 . . . . 300.00
Little George, #350–A, American National Bank,
   Nashville, TN, 1966 . . . . 225.00
Manager 50.00
Mark Twain, #315 . . . . 100.00
Parade Rest, #216 . . . . 100.00
Paul Bunyan, red hat 250.00
Peggotty, #52–A. 85.00
Raphael's Madonna 20.00
Sampling the Stew. 60.00
Santa Claus, 1980 . . . . 80.00
Santa Girl, lamppost, sgd 65.00
Shaker Man, #1. . . . . 150.00
St. Joan of Arc, bronzed 275.00
Stagecoach 80.00
The Doctor, green,Marblehead label 110.00
The Pilgrim, 1947 . . . . 65.00
Thomas Jefferson, #124 . . . . 85.00
Town Crier 25.00
Uncle Sam, green label 45.00
Victorian Couple, Marblehead label 50.00

SEWING COLLECTIBLES

The ability to sew and to sew well was considered a basic household skill in the 18th century, 19th century, and first two–thirds of the 20th century. In addition to utilitarian sewing, many individuals sewed for pleasure, producing a wide range of works from samplers to elaborately embroidered table coverings.

The number of sewing implements, some practical and some whimsical, multiplied during the Victorian era. Crochet hooks, pincushions, and tape measures were among the new forms. Metals, including gold and silver, were used. Thimbles were a popular courting and anniversary gift. Sewing birds attached to the edge of the table helped the sewer keep fabric taught.

As America became more mobile, the sewing industry responded. Many advertisers used needle threaders, tape measures, and sewing kits as premiums. A match cover–like sewing kit became a popular feature in hotels and motels in the post–1945 era. While collectors eagerly seek sewing items made of celluloid, they have shown little interest thus far for post–1960 plastic sewing items.

References: *Advertising & Figural Tape Measures,* L–W Book Sales, 1995; Elizabeth Arbittier et al., *Collecting Figural Tape Measures,* Schiffer Publishing, 1995, Averil Mathias, *Antique and Collectible Thimbles and Accessories,* Collector Books, 1986, 1995 value update, Wayne Muller, *Darn It!, The History and Romance of Darners,* L–W Book Sales, 1995; Gay Ann Rogers, *An Illustrated History of Needlework Tools,* Needlework Unlimited, 1983, 1989 Price Guide; Glenda Thomas, *Toy and Miniature Sewing Machines* (1995) *Book II* (1997), Collector Books; Helen Lester Thompson, *Sewing Tools & Trinkets: Collector's Identification & Value Guide,* Collector Books, 1997; Estelle Zalkin, *Zalkin's Handbook Of Thimbles & Sewing Implements,* Warman Publishing Co, 1988, distributed by Krause Publications.

Collectors' Clubs: International Sewing Machine Collectors Society, 1000 E Charleston Blvd, Las Vegas, NV 89104; Toy Stitchers, 623 Santa Florita Ave, Millbrae, CA 94030.

Note: See Thimbles for additional listings.

Book, *The Singer Drawing Book For Young Artists,* 1930	$ 8.50
Booklet, *How to Make Children's Clothes,* Singer, 1930	8.00
Button, celluloid, polychrome, aviator and plane	.38
Button, celluloid, black, metal center strip, 1¼ x 2"	.35
Button, wood, brass rim, 1¼" d	.50
Embroidery Hoop, wood, round, handmade, 16" d	6.00
Footstool, hinged lid, sewing compartment, Queen Anne style, c1925	40.00
Magazine, *Needlecraft,* 1939	1.50
Magazine, *Woman's Circle,* Christmas issue, 1966	4.50
Needle and Pin Case, Bakelite, penguin, black and white, 3" l	6.50
Needle and Pin Case, celluloid, silver overlay design, sc1920	12.00
Needle and Pin Case, polished metal, snap top, c1920	20.00
Needle and Pin Case, suede folder, cross stitch dec, wool pgs, c1920	6.50
Needle Book, Happy Home, paper, gold eye needles and threader, c1920, 6 x 3½"	20.00

Needle Book, Fashion Quality Needle Book, 115 needles, Japan, 1950s, 6¾ x 4¼", $5.00.

Ornament, "Sew Christmasy," #58820, Enesco, 1992–94	15.00
Pamphlet, *How to Make Children's Clothes, The Modern Singer Way,* Singer Service Library #3, 1928	5.00
Pincushion, apple, metal, gold color finish, c1950	5.00
Pincushion, doll, Art Deco style, Japan, 2¾" h	28.00
Pincushion, heart, metal, gold finish	5.00
Pincushion, ladies shoe, copperwash metal, c1920	20.00
Pincushion, Liberty Bell, glazed pottery, Bicentennial souvenir, 1976	3.50
Pincushion, tomato, satin	6.50
Scissors, polished steel, blade mkd "Chicago Mail Order Co, Eversham Forged Steel USA," c1930, 8" l	6.00
Scissors, polished steel, embroidery, Germany, c1930, 3½" l	6.00
Scissors, sterling silver, miniature, England, 1" l	45.00
Sewing Kit, celluloid, mkd "Genova, Hotel Britannia," c1920	55.00
Sewing Kit, J. P. Coats, 6 spools of thread, aluminum thimble, 2 needles, c1930	20.00
Sewing Kit, leather, tan, snap closure, painted metal ends, needle pocket for thread and thimble, "Compliments of Hartsfield thru out California," c1940	25.00
Sewing Kit, Tiffany and Co, cylindrical, needles and 3 thread winders, tassel dec lid, c1920	185.00
Sewing Machine, Singer, Art Deco walnut cabinet, gold and red dec, oak attachment box, c1920	185.00
Sewing Machine, Singer Automatic, black, gold geometric design, treadle base	135.00
Sewing Machine, Singer Featherweight, cast metal, portable, gold design, attachments, needles, bobbins, and instruction book, c1935	450.00
Tape Measure, celluloid, hen and chicks, Japan, c1920	55.00
Tape Measure, celluloid, pig, mkd "Occupied Japan," c1947	25.00
Toy Sewing Machine, Casige, metal, blue and white, wood base, battery operated	40.00

Toy Sewing Machine, Elna Junior, musical, plays *Blue Danube Waltz*, Switzerland, c1956 . . . . **35.00**
Toy Sewing Machine, Singer Sewhandy, Model 20, cast metal, shiny black finish, nickel plated sewing plate, gear driven black spiral handwheel, painted black presser foot, 1950s, 6½"h **90.00**
Toy Sewing Machine, Vulcan Junior, metal, hand operated, Made in England, c1950–60 . . . . **55.00**
Toy Sewing Machine, Vulcan Minor, metal, red, manually operated, Made in England, 1960s **55.00**

SHAWNEE POTTERY

Addis E. Hull, Jr., Robert C. Shilling, and a group of investors established the Shawnee Pottery Company, Zanesville, Ohio, in 1937. It was named for an Indian tribe that lived in the area.

Shawnee manufactured inexpensive, high–quality kitchen and utilitarian earthenware. The company perfected a bisque drying method that enabled decorating and glazing to be achieved in a single firing. In the late 1930s and early 1940s, Shawnee supplied products to large chain stores such as Kresge, Kress, Sears, and Woolworth. Valencia, a dinnerware and kitchenware line, was created for Sears.

Robert Ganz joined Shawnee as a designer in 1938, creating some of the company's most popular cookie jars, e.g., Puss 'n Boots and Smiley. Designer Robert Heckman arrived in 1945 and was responsible for the King Corn line and numerous pieces featuring a Pennsylvania German motif.

Hull left Shawnee in 1950. A flooded market resulted in economic difficulties. In 1954 John Bonistall became president and shifted production from kitchenware to decorative accessories. He created the Kenwood Ceramics division to market the remaining kitchenware products. Chantilly, Cameo, Elegance, Fernwood, Petit Point, and Touché are several art lines introduced in the late 1950s. The company prospered in the late 1950s.

A decision was made to cease operations in 1961. Bonistall purchased Shawnee's molds and established Terrace Ceramics, Marietta, Ohio.

References: Pam Curran, *Shawnee Pottery,* Schiffer Publishing, 1995, Jim and Bev Mangus, *Shawnee Pottery: An Identification and Value Guide,* Collector Books, 1994, 1996 value update; Mark Supnick, *Collecting Shawnee Pottery: A Pictorial Reference And Price Guide,* L–W Book Sales, 1989, 1996 value update; Duane and Janice Vanderbilt, *The Collector's Guide To Shawnee Pottery,* Collector Books, 1992, 1996 value update.

Collectors' Club: Shawnee Pottery Collectors Club, PO Box 713, New Smyrna Beach, FL 32170.

Casserole, King Corn . . . . **$ 65.00**
Cookie Jar, elephant, white. **100.00**
Cookie Jar, King Corn. **225.00**
Cookie Jar, Mugsey **450.00**
Cookie Jar, Mugsey, gold trim **800.00**
Cookie Jar, Puss 'n Boots, gold trim **400.00**
Cookie Jar, Smiley Pig, cloverbud **450.00**
Cookie Jar, Smiley Pig, shamrock **300.00**
Creamer, elephant **40.00**
Creamer, elephant, gold trim **275.00**
Creamer, Puss 'n Boots. **65.00**

Planter, puppy and shoe, burgundy, $25.00.

Creamer, Puss 'n Boots, gold trim **200.00**
Creamer, Smiley Pig, cloverbud **150.00**
Cup and Saucer, King Corn **65.00**
Grease Jar, White Corn, gold **150.00**
Pitcher, chanticleer **85.00**
Pitcher, Little Bo Peep **125.00**
Pitcher, Smiley Pig, cloverbud **350.00**
Planter, bear and wagon. **90.00**
Planter, bird and cup, #502 . . . . **12.00**
Planter, boy and chicken, #645 . . . . **18.00**
Planter, boy at high stump, #532 . . . . **8.00**
Planter, boy with wheelbarrow, #750 . . . . **15.00**
Planter, Buddha, #524 . . . . **15.00**
Planter, butterfly, #524. . . . . **15.00**
Planter, canopy bed, #734 . . . . **95.00**
Planter, chick and cart, #720 . . . . **50.00**
Planter, children on shoe **14.00**
Planter, clown, #607 . . . . **35.00**
Planter, coal bucket. **12.00**
Planter, cockatiel, #522 . . . . **10.00**
Planter, cocker spaniel and doghouse. **25.00**
Planter conestoga wagon, bronze, #733 . . . . **50.00**
Planter, cradle, yellow **10.00**
Planter, doe and fawn, #669. . . . . **15.00**
Planter, donkey with basket, #722 . . . . **25.00**
Planter, elf shoe, white, gold trim, #765 . . . . **15.00**
Planter, flying goose, #707. . . . . **15.00**
Planter, giraffe, #521 . . . . **25.00**
Planter, girl with basket of flowers, #616. . . . . **15.00**
Planter, grist mill, green, #769 . . . . **14.00**
Planter, horse with hat and cart **22.00**
Planter, JoJo, #607. . . . . **22.00**
Planter, man with pushcart, #621 . . . . **15.00**
Planter, Oriental girl with mandolin, #576 . . . . **14.00**
Planter, 2 coolies carrying basket, #537 . . . . **5.00**
Planter, piano, green, #528 . . . . **15.00**
Planter, poodle on bicycle, #712 . . . . **38.00**
Planter, pushcart, #J544P **30.00**
Planter, rabbit at stump, green, #606 . . . . **9.00**
Planter, ram, #515 . . . . **18.00**
Planter, roadster, gold trim, #506 . . . . **36.00**

Teapot, Granny Anne, 8¹/₂" h, $75.00.

Planter, rocking horse, pink, #526	**22.00**
Planter, rooster, #503	**18.00**
Planter, skunk, pink, #512	**28.00**
Planter, squirrel pulling acorn, #713	**40.00**
Planter, 2 gazelles, #613	**15.00**
Planter, wheelbarrow, emb flower	**15.00**
Planter, windmill, blue, #715	**20.00**
Salt and Pepper Shakers, pr, chanticleer, small	**45.00**
Salt and Pepper Shakers, pr, Farmer Pig.	**35.00**
Salt and Pepper Shakers, pr, flower pots	**20.00**
Salt and Pepper Shakers, pr, fruit, small, gold trim	**40.00**
Salt and Pepper Shakers, pr, owl	**20.00**
Salt and Pepper Shakers, pr, watering cans	**25.00**
Salt and Pepper Shakers, pr, White Corn, large, gold trim.	**150.00**
Sugar Bowl, cov, King Corn	**25.00**
Sugar Shaker, White Corn, gold trim	**150.00**
Teapot, elephant	**250.00**
Teapot, emb rose, gold trim	**35.00**
Teapot, Heart Flower	**65.00**
Teapot, King Corn, individual	**250.00**
Teapot, yellow, 10 oz.	**60.00**
Vase, burlap, green, 9" h	**12.00**
Vase, dove, yellow, #829	**30.00**
Vase, swan, yellow, gold trim	**35.00**
Wall Pocket, wheat	**35.00**

SHEET MUSIC

Printed sheet music, especially piano scores, became popular in the early 19th century. Covers featured elaborately engraved lettering and highly inspirational, e.g., military, or romantic prints. Favorite songs frequently were bound into an album.

Sheet music is collected primarily for its cover art, followed by type of music, composer, and printer. The late 1880s through the early 1950s is considered the golden age of sheet music cover art. Every conceivable theme, current fad, moral, political, and social topic was illustrated. Leading illustrators, such as Rolf Armstrong,

lent their talents to sheet music covers just as they did to magazine covers.

Covers frequently featured a picture of the singer, group, or orchestra responsible for introducing the song to the public. Photographic covers followed the times. Radio stars, movie stars, and television stars appeared on sheet music covers to promote their show or latest screen epic.

Sheet music's popularity is closely related to the popularity of piano playing. When interest in piano playing declined in the 1950s, sheet music covers no longer exhibited the artistic and design creativity of former times. Collector interest in post–1960s sheet music, with the exception of TV show themes and rock 'n' roll sheets, is minimal.

The vast majority of sheet music is worth between $1.00 and $3.00, provided it is in near mint condition. In spite of this, many dealers now ask an average $5.00 to $10.00 per sheet for mundane titles. Part of the reason for this discrepancy in pricing is the crossover influence of subject collectors. These collectors have little patience with the hunt. Not realizing how easy it is to find copies, they pay high prices and fuel the unrealistic expectations of the general dealer.

Further complicating the picture is the inaccurate, highly manipulative pricing in the Guiheen and Pafik guide. The book has been roundly criticized, and rightly so, within the sheet music collecting community.

References: Debbie Dillon, *Collectors Guide To Sheet Music*, L–W Book Promotions, 1988, 1995 value update; Marie Reine A. Pafik and Anna Marie Guiheen, *The Sheet Music Reference and Price Guide, Second Edition*, Collector Books, 1995; Marion Short, *The Gold in Your Piano Bench*, Schiffer Publishing, 1997.

Newsletter: *Sheet Music Exchange*, PO Box 2114, Key West, FL 33045.

Collectors' Clubs: National Music Society, 1597 Fair Park Ave, Los Angeles, CA 90041; New York Sheet Music Society, PO Box 1214, Great Neck, NY 11023; Remember That Song, 5623 N 64th Ave, Glendale, AZ 85301; Sonneck Society for American Music & Music in America, PO Box 476, Canton, MA 02021.

Love Walke In, Goldwyn Follies, c1938, $10.00.

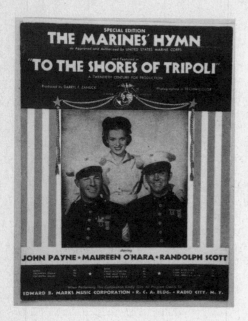

*The Marines'
Hymn,* Twentieth
Century Fox, John
Payne, Maureen
O'Hara, and
Randolph Scott cov,
$5.00.

All's Fair In Love And War, 1936 . . . . **$ 3.50**
Always, Irving Berlin, 1925 . . . . **3.50**
An Apple Blossom Wedding, 1947 . . . . **2.50**
Auf Wiedershe'n, Sweetheart, 1951 . . . . **3.50**
Band Played On, 1926 . . . . **6.00**
Beautiful Girls, 1933 . . . . **3.50**
Bill, Oscar Hammerstein II and Jerome Kern, 1927 . . . . **5.00**
Blue Hawaii, Leo Robin, and Ralph Rainger, 1937 . . . . **3.50**
By The Light Of The Silvery Moon, 1932 . . . . **8.00**
By The Time I Get To Phoenix, Jim Webb, Glen
    Campbell photo cov, 1967 . . . . **2.50**
Chim Chim Cher–ee, Mary Poppins, Richard and
    Robert Sherman, 1963 . . . . **6.00**
Cry, Baby, Cry, Remus Harris, 1938 . . . . **2.00**
Day By Day, Sammy Cahn, Axel Stordahl, and Paul
    Weston, Bing Crosby cov photo, 1945 . . . . **3.00**
Fuzzy Wuzzy, 1944 . . . . **3.50**
Georgie, Howard Johnson and Walter Donaldson,
    1922 . . . . **3.50**
God Bless This Child, Billie Holiday photo cov, 1951 . . . . . **2.50**
Goodnight Sweetheart, Rudy Vallee photo cov, 1931 . . . . . **6.50**
Hawaiian Wedding Song, Andy Williams photo
cov, 1948 . . . . **2.00**
Heart And Soul, Frank Loesser and Hoagy
    Carmichael, 1938 . . . . **3.50**
Hello Dolly, Jerry Herman, 1963 . . . . **3.50**
Home On The Range, Andrew Fuller, 1932 . . . . **3.50**
I Left My Heart In San Francisco **8.00**
I Want To Hold Your Hand, 1978 . . . . **18.00**
I'll Be With You In Apple Blossom Time, Andrews
    Sisters photo cov, 1920 . . . . **3.50**
I'll Walk Alone, Sammy Cahn and Jule Styne, 1944 . . . . . . **3.50**
Impossible, 1946 . . . . **3.50**
It May As Well Be Spring, Richard and Oscar
    Hammerstein II, 1945 . . . . **3.50**
It's On, It's Off, Coslow and Siegel, 1937 . . . . **6.00**
I've Got A Feeling I'm Falling, 1929 . . . . **3.50**
I've Got You Under My Skin, Cole Porter, 1936 . . . . **8.00**
Just A Prayer Away, Bing Crosby photo cov, 1944 . . . . **2.50**

Kiss Me Kate, Cole Porter, 1948 . . . . **4.00**
Lady Of Spain, 1944 . . . . **2.00**
Laura, Johnny Mercer and David Raskin, 1945 . . . . **4.50**
Let It Snow, Sammy Cahn and Jule Styne, 1945 . . . . **2.50**
Let Me In, Bob Merrill, 1951 . . . . **3.00**
Love Me Tender, W. W. Fosdick and George Paulton,
    Elvis Presley photo cov, 1956 . . . . **20.00**
Mad About Him, Sad Without Him, How Can I Be
    Glad Without Him Blues, Larry Markes and Dick
    Charles, 1944 . . . . **4.50**
Make Room For The Joy, Hal David and Burt
    Bacharach, 1958 . . . . **8.00**
Mary Had A Little Lamb, Symes and Maine, 1936 . . . . **4.50**
Maybe I Love You Too Much, Irving Berlin, 1933 . . . . **8.00**
Memories Are Made Of This, Dean Martin photo cov **2.50**
Moon River, Benton Ley and Lee David, 1949 . . . . **2.50**
She'll Be Coming Round The Mountain, 1935 . . . . **4.00**
Tonight, Stephen Sondheim and Leonard Bernstein,
    1957 . . . . **4.50**
Where The Boys Are, Greenfield and Sedaka, 1960 . . . . . . **4.50**

SHELLEY CHINA

Members of the Shelley family have manufactured ceramics in England's Staffordshire district since the middle of the 18th century. In 1872 Joseph Shelley and James Wileman formed Wileman & Co. Percy, Joseph's son, joined the firm in 1881. Percy hired designers and artists, significantly upgrading the company's product line.

Rowland Morris created Dainty White, the company's most successful popular dinnerware shape, around 1900. Frederick Rhead, trained at Minton, introduced Intarsio, Pastello, Primitif, Spano-Lustra, and Urbato series ware. Although officially Wileman & Co., the company's mark consisted of the Shelley family name enclosed in a shield.

Walter Slater, also trained at Minton, joined the firm. He adapted Intarsio to include Art Nouveau motifs, created Cloisello and Flamboyant ware, and introduced bone china production. Shelley dinnerware exported to America was well received.

The company began making crest ware, miniature, and Parian busts following World War I. The company's fine china was known as "Eggshell." In 1925 Wileman & Co. became Shelley. Hild Cowham and Mabel Atwell's nursery ware proved highly popular in the 1920s and 30s. However, it was teawares that really added luster to Shelley's reputation. The Queen Anne octagonal shape is one of the best known.

Earthernware production ceased after World War II. Shelly concentrated on dinnerware. In 1966 Allied English Potteries acquired Shelley. It became part of the Doulton Group in 1971.

Reference: Robert Prescott Walker, *Collecting Shelley Pottery,* Francis Joseph Publications, 1997, distributed by Krause Publications.

Collectors' Club: National Shelley China Club, PO Box 580, Chokoloskee, FL 33925.

Begonia, creamer and sugar . . . . **$ 40.00**
Begonia, cup and saucer, demitasse, 16 flutes **52.00**
Begonia, nappy, 6 flutes **38.00**
Begonia, plate, Westminster Abbey, 8 d **35.00**

Blue Rock, creamer and sugar, 6 flutes **52.00**
Blue Rock, cup and saucer. **45.00**
Bridal Rose, plate, 6" d **25.00**
Blue Rock, snack set **55.00**
Campanula, snack set **55.00**
Charm 5, creamer and sugar **60.00**
Crochet, candy dish, white, blue trim, 4½" d **35.00**
Crochet, plate, 8" d **30.00**
Dainty White, cup and saucer, gold, oversized **50.00**
Dainty White, eggcup, gold **35.00**
Dainty White, mug and saucer. **42.00**
Dainty White, plate, 6" d **32.00**
Forget–Me–Nots, plate, 5" d **35.00**
Lily of the Valley, cup and saucer, 14 flutes **45.00**
Lily of the Valley, sugar, individual **28.00**
Pansy, candy dish, 4" l **40.00**
Pansy, demitasse cup and saucer **65.00**
Pansy, plate, 5" d **35.00**
Pink Charm, cup and saucer **45.00**
Primrose, creamer and sugar, 6 flutes **45.00**
Primrose, eggcup, 6 flutes **62.00**
Rock Garden, creamer and sugar **72.00**
Rose, candy dish, 4" l **40.00**
Rose, demitasse cup and saucer **65.00**
Violets, demitasse cup and saucer, 16 flutes **60.00**
Wildflower, cup and saucer **60.00**
Wildflower, demitasse cup and saucer **70.00**
Wildflower, plate, 7" d **35.00**

SILVER, PLATED & STERLING

Sterling silver contains 925 parts of silver per 1,000. The remaining 75 parts consist of additional metals, primarily copper, that add strength and hardness to the silver. Silver plate, developed in England in the late 1860s, is achieved through electrolysis. A thin layer of silver is added to a base metal, usually britannia (an alloy of antimony, copper, and tin), copper, or white metal (an alloy of bismuth, copper, lead, and tin).

Silver plated ware achieved great popularity in the period between 1880 and 1915. Alvin, Gorham, International Silver Company (the result of a series of mergers), Oneida, Reed & Barton, William Rogers, and Wallace are among the principal manufacturers.

Silverware can be divided into three distinct categories: (1) flatware, (2) hollowware, and (3) giftware. This category includes hollowware and giftware. Currently silverware collecting is enjoying a number of renaissances. Silver plated pieces from the late Victorian era, especially small accessories such as napkin rings, benefited from the Victorian revival of the 1980s. The return to more formal dining has created renewed interest in tabletop accessory pieces.

References: Nancy Gluck, *The Grosvenor Pattern of Silverplate,* Silver Season, 1996; Tere Hagan, *Silverplated Flatware: An Identification & Value Guide, Revised 4th Edition,* Collector Books, 1990, 1995 value update; Penny Chittim Morrill and Carole A. Berk, *Mexican Silver 205h Century Handwrought Jewelry & Metalwork,* Schiffer Publishing, 1994; Richart Osterberg, *Sterling Silver Flatware for Dining Elegance,* Schiffer Publishing, 1994; Dorothy T. Rainwater, *Encyclopedia of American Silver Manufacturers, 3rd Edition,* Schiffer Publishing, 1986; Harry L.

Rinker, *Silverware of the 20th Century: The Top 250 Patterns,* House of Collectibles, 1997.

Note: See Flatware for additional silverware listings.

Bowl, sterling, Georg Jensen, Model #296A, oval, ftd, articulated grape cluster handles, grape clusters around base, inscription under base, 65 troy oz, 1933. . . . . $ **6,600.00**
Bowl, sterling, Urouhart, chased hunt scene, racing scene, floral scrolls, spreading foot, 29 troy oz, c1935, 9" d **2,530.00**
Box, silver plate, collar button, ftd, 2½" w **25.00**
Butter Dish, cov, silver plate, rolltop, engraved **60.00**
Candlesticks, pr, silver plate, repoussé scenes and figures, c1920 . . . . **150.00**
Candlesticks, pr, sterling, Gorham, Colonial Revival style, weighted, 1926, 11¾" h. **750.00**
Centerpiece, silver plate, 3 dolphin supports, engraved trefoil base with winged lion feet, large cut–glass bowl **275.00**
Clock, silver plate, Birmingham, Art Deco, circular shape, guilloche–enameled black and white wit applied marcasite dec, 1931 . . . . **100.00**
Charger, silver plate, wide chased band of fruit, foliage, and scrolls, larel border, 161/2" d **175.00**
Cocktail Shaker, silver plate, novelty, bell shape, engraved reeded bands. **225.00**
Coffee Set, sterling, J. C. Boardman and Son, coffeepot, creamer, and open sugar, Colonial Revival style, 30 troy oz, mid–1900s, price for set **425.00**
Coffee/Tea Set, sterling, Crichton & Co, Ltd, Queen Anne style, coffeepot, teapot, creamer, sugar, and waste bowl, globular, molded handle, 71 troy oz, c1933, price for set **1825.00**
Coffee/Tea Set, sterling, Gorham, Plymouth pattern, coffeepot, teapot, creamer, cov sugar, waste bowl, and waiter, 182 troy oz, 20th C, price for set **2,760.00**
Compact, silver plate, La Mode, heart shape. **60.00**
Desk Bell, silver plate, windup, open filigree skirt, top knob **85.00**

Compote, sterling, ruffled top, gadrooned and pierced border, weighted base, L. & C. Mayers Company, 1937, 6" h, 6¼" d, $

Meat Dish, silver plate, Rogers Bros., well and tree, 18" l, $150.00.

Egg Cruet, silver plate, 4 cups, circular, scroll legs, gadrooned domed cover with wood button finial..... **100.00**

Hatpin, silver plate, tennis racquet shape **25.00**

Hot Water Kettle and Stand, sterling, Hunt and Roshell Ltd, pear shape, engraved foliage, stand has shell feet, 44 troy oz, c1934, 13" h **875.00**

Ice Bucket, silver plate rim and handle, cut glass bucket, 7" h **90.00**

Matchsafe, silver plate, textured pattern **40.00**

Picture Frame, sterling, Chester, enameled front, multicolored pansies and leaves, easel back, 1921 ...... **325.00**

Sugar Caster, sterling, Crichton & Co, Ltd, Elizabeth II pattern, baluster, gadrooned detail, 19 troy oz, 1953, 8³⁄₈" h.................................... **425.00**

Tray, silver plate, oval, pierced border with floral swags, 24" l **350.00**

Tray, sterling, rect cross section with molded cavetto corners, engraved foliage, and border of medallions, scroll legs, stepped pad feet, mkd "R C," 214 troy oz, c1928, 27¹⁄₂" l....................... **4,400.00**

Watch Holder, silver plate, figural child and dog **275.00**

Water Pitcher, silver plate, Classical style, scroll handles, circular base, 28 troy oz, c1920, 10" h **380.00**

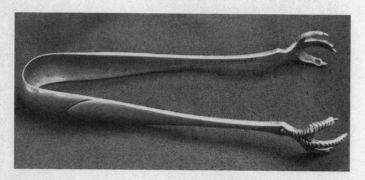

Sugar Tongs, sterling claw ends, c1920, 5" l, $115.00.

SLOT CARS

Abe Shikes, Joseph Giammarino, and a group of silent partners founded Aurora Plastics Corporation in March 1950. Initially, Aurora was a contract molding shop with much of its production devoted to novelty jewelry and plastic clothes hangers.

In 1952 the silent partners withdrew, and the company reorganized. Aurora introduced a line of plastic model airplane kits in the fall of 1952. It was also during this period that John Cuomo joined the firm. Cuomo served as Aurora's spokesperson to advertisers, distributors, and retailers.

In December 1953, Aurora moved into a new plant in West Hempstead, Long Island, New York. Shortly thereafter Aurora began making a line of hobby craft products, e.g., Coppersmith kits and crystal radio kits. In 1960 Aurora purchased K& B Allyn, a California manufacturer of gas–powered airplane motors.

Derek Brand is credited with the development of the HO slot car. Carl Robinette, head of Carfco, sold Brand's concept to Mettoy, a British firm famed for its Corgi Toys. An initial launch by Mettoy's Playcraft Division was unsuccessful. However, Shikes and Giammarino attended the Brighton Toy Fair where the toy was first shown. They applied for an American license.

Aurora launched the electric powered slot car in 1960. They were built at the West Hempstead and Downey, California, plants. Slot cars were an overnight success, helped by extended television appearances on NBC's *Today* and *Jack Paar Show*.

In 1961 Kellogg's Corn Flakes packages contained a slot car racing set offer. Additional cars, track items, and racing accessories soon were made available. From the beginning, slot cars were noted for their detailed model body styles, i.e., they looked like the real thing. By 1962 slot car mania had swept the country. An attempt to introduce a 1/48 scale car failed.

The slot car's golden age extends from 1962 through the mid–1970s. New models, other successful new scales, and track sets and accessories appeared on a regular basis However, by the mid–1970s, many of the Aurora slot car innovators no longer worked for Aurora. The company changed hands several times during the 1970s and 80s. By the 1980s, Tyco assumed the leadership role in the slot car field.

References: John A. Clark, *HO Slot Car Identification and Price Guide*, L–W Book Sales, 1995; Thomas Graham, *Greenberg's Guide to Aurora Slot Cars*, Greenberg Books, 1995.

Aurora, AFX, Grand Am Funny Car, white, red, blue ... **$ 15.00**

Aurora, AFX Flamethrower, Flamethrower Porsche 917, yellow, blue **10.00**

Aurora, Cigarbox, Stingray, off–white **15.00**

Aurora, Cigarbox, Toronado, turquoise **15.00**

Aurora, Dragster, 1957 Chevy Nomad, orange **30.00**

Aurora, Flashback, Mako Shark, metallic orange, silver stripe **15.00**

Aurora, Flashback,Toronado, metallic purple, silver stripe **15.00**

Aurora, Screecher, Super Chief, white, red flames **10.00**

Aurora, Speedline, AC Cobra, lavender, silver **15.00**

Aurora, Speedline, Ferrari Berlinetta, red and silver **15.00**

Aurora, Speedline, Stingray, purple chrome............ **15.00**

Aurora, Super Speedster, Pontiac Firebird **20.00**

Aurora, Riviera, light red, silver **15.00**

Aurora, The Wild One, Sand Van Dune Buggy, pink, white **30.00**

Aurora, The Wild One, Wild Camaro, white, blue **40.00**

Aurora, Thunderjet Flamethrower, Flamethrower Chaparral 2F, white **20.00**

Aurora, Ultra 5, Shadow Can–Am "A," black, orange, yellow, and white. **25.00**

Aurora, Vibrator, 1960 Thunderbird hardtop, green, black **65.00**

Aurora, Vibrator, 1962 Ford Galaxie 500 hardtop, white, red, and black **65.00**

Aurora, Vibrator, Jaguar XK140 Convertible, white, tan . . . **50.00**

Aurora, Xlerator, Willys Gasser, red, black, and yellow . . . **40.00**

Eldon, Pontiac Bonneville, white **40.00**

Strombecker, Cheetah **28.00**

Tyco, Autoworld Carrera, white, red, white, and blue stripes **8.00**

Tyco, Blazer, black, red **6.50**

Tyco, Javelin, red, white, and blue **10.00**

Tyco, Lamborghini, red **8.00**

Tyco, Turbo Firebird, black, gold **8.00**

Tyco, Z–28 Camaro #7, red, white, and blue **8.00**

Tyco, 1957 Chevy, red, orange and yellow stripes **15.00**

SLOT MACHINES

In 1905 Charles Frey of San Francisco invented the first three–reel slot machine, known as the Liberty Bell. An example survives at the Liberty Bell Saloon, an establishment owned by Frey's grandson in Reno, Nevada.

Although the Mills Novelty Company copyrighted the famous fruit symbols in 1910, they were quickly copied by other manufacturers. They are still one of the most popular slot machine symbols. The jackpot was added in 1928.

Early slot machines featured wooden cabinets. The first cast iron cabinets appeared in the mid–1910s. Aluminum fronts arrived in the early 1920s. Mechanical improvements, such as variations in coin entry and detection of slugs, occurred during the 1930s. Additional security devices to prevent cheating and tampering were added in the 1940s. The 1950s marked the introduction of electricity, for operation as well as illumination.

The 1920s and 30s is the golden age of slot machines. Machines featured elaborate castings, ornate decoration, and numerous gimmicks. Caille, Jennings, Mill, Pace, and Watling are among the leading manufacturers.

References: Jerry Ayliff, *American Premium Guide To Jukeboxes and Slot Machines, Third Edition,* Books Americana, Krause Publications, 1991; Richard M. Bueschel, *Collector's Guide To Vintage Coin Machines,* Schiffer Publishing, 1995; Richard M. Bueschel, *Lemons, Cherries and Bell–Fruit–Gum: Illustrated History of Automatic Payout Slot Machines,* Royal Ben Books, 1995; Marshal Fey, *Slot Machines: A Pictorial History of the First 100 Years, Fourth Edition,* published by author.

Periodicals: *Antique Amusements, Slot Machines & Jukebox Gazette,* 909 26th St NW, Washington, DC 20037; *Coin Drop International,* 5815 W 52nd Ave, Denver, CO 80212; *Coin–Op Classics,* 17844 Toiyabe St, Fountain Valley, CA 92708; *Loose Change,* 1515 S Commerce St, Las Vegas, NV 89102.

Baker's Pacers, horse racing, 5¢, floor model, wood case, 7 coin slots correspond to colors of racing horses, payoff drawer, Baker, 1930s, 40" w . . . . . . **$ 1,600.00**

Bantam, 3 reel, jackpot vendor front, Pace, 1932 . . . . . **1,500.00**

Blue Seal, gooseneck, twin jackpot, Watling, 1930. . . . **1,000.00**

Bones, countertop, spinning disks roll dice for craps, Buckley, c1937 . . . . **4,000.00**

Cadet, circular jackpot, Caille, c1938. . . . . **900.00**

Challenger Console, 5¢ and 25¢, silkscreened glass panels, Jennings, c1946. . . . . **1,200.00**

Comet, 5¢, 3 fruit reels, oak case, cast iron front, Pace, c1935, 25" h **1,725.00**

Commander Streamline, yellow cast, Caille, 1930s. . . . **1,000.00**

Diamond Front, escalator, Mills, 1940 . . . . **1,000.00**

Duchess, 3 reel, front vendor, candy displayed behind windows flanking jackpot, Jennings, c1934 . . **2,000.00**

Extraordinary, 10¢, 3 fruit reels, cast aluminum case, jackpot, Mills, 24" h **9,250.00**

Four Star Chief, Jennings, 1936 . . . . **1,250.00**

Futurity Bell, 5¢, 3 reel, Mills, 1936. . . . . **1,500.00**

Governor, tic–tac–toe, Indian head above jackpot, Jennings, 1948 . . . . **850.00**

Groetchen Columbia, club handle, small reels, coins travel in circle behind coin head, Caille, 1934. . . . . . . **250.00**

Gumball Vendor, 1¢, gooseneck, gumball vendors flanking twin jackpots, Watling, c1921 . . . . **1,750.00**

High Top, jackpot, Mills, 1947–62 . . . . **1,100.00**

Little Duke, 1¢, 3 reel, painted cast aluminum Art Deco style case, Jennings, c1935 . . . . **1,150.00**

Mystery Castle, Mills, 1933 . . . . **1,200.00**

Pointsettia, 5¢, 3 fruit reels, operator's bell, cast front, jackpot, Mills, c1924, 25" h **1,600.00**

QT, 5¢, 3 reel, bell, brown cast front, cigarette symbols, win table, side handle, Mills, c1944, 18" h **1,600.00**

Roman Head, 5¢, 3 reel, silent golden bell, cast iron front, Mills, c1932, 26" h **2,000.00**

Silent FOK, 5¢, cast iron, 2 columns, fortune reels, jackpot, Mills, c1932, 26" h **1,725.00**

Silver Moon, Jennings, 1941 . . . . **1,000.00**

Groetchen Yankee, 1¢, 3–reel, red, $350.00.

Sportsman, golf ball vendor, Jennings, 1937 . . . . **2,750.00**
Standard Chief, chromium finish, Jennings, 1948 . . . . . **1,000.00**
Sun Chief, Indian bust, illuminated side panels,
 Jennings, c1948. . . . . **1,750.00**
Superior, center coin slot above award card, cast
 metal case with nude and scrollwork Caille, c1938. . **1,750.00**
Treasury, 5¢, , 3 reel, cast front, twin jackpot,
 Watling, c1936, 24" h **3,200.00**
Vest Pocket, 5¢, 3 reel, blue painted metal case with
 front coin slot, top display, Mills, c1939, 8" h **250.00**
Victory Mint, center pull handle, Caille, c1924 . . . . . . **2,750.00**

SMURFS

Pierro "Peyo" Culliford, a Belgian cartoonist, created the Smurfs. Smurfs have a human appearance, are "three apples high," and blue in color. The name Smurf is a shortening of Schtroumpf, a French colloquialism meaning "watchamacallit." Over 100 different Smurf characters are known.

The Smurfs first appeared as a comic strip. Soon the strips were collected into books and line of toys licensed. In 1965 Schleich, a German firm, began marketing a line of two-inch high, PVC Smurf figures. A full collection numbers in the hundreds, the results of numerous decorating variations and discontinued markings. The first Smurf figures arrived in the United States in 1979.

After appearing in the movie, Smurfs and the Magic Flute in 1975, Smurfs secured a permanent place in the collecting field when Hanna-Barbera launched its Smurf Saturday morning cartoon show in 1981.

The Smurfs popularity remains strong. Currently, dozens of Smurf products are available for sale in retail stores. When buying any Smurf item, make certain to date it correctly. Avoid over paying for recent production items.

Reference: Jan Lindenberger, *Smurf Collectibles: A Handbook & Price Guide,* Schiffer Publishing, 1996.

Collectors' Club: Smurf Collectors' Club International, 24 Cabot Rd W, Massapequa, NY 11758.

Activity Book, *Smurfing Sing Song and Fun Book,* Hal
 Leonard Publishing, 1981. . . . . $ **2.50**
Alarm Clock, metal, 1980s. **25.00**
Banner, plastic, "Happy Smurfday," Unique, 64 x 9" **3.00**
Birthday Candle, Grandpa Smurf holding #4. . . . . **2.00**
Book, *A Smurf Picnic,* pop–up, Random House, 1982. . . . . **4.00**
Book, *Baby Smurf's First Words,* soft cover, 1984 . . . . **2.00**
Book, *Billy Baker's Sniffy Book,* spiral, hardback,
 Random House, 1982 . . . . **2.00**
Book, *Smurf on the Grow,* Little Pops, 1982 . . . . **3.00**
Book, *The Astrosmurf,* soft cover, 1978. . . . . **5.00**
Book, *The Smurfic Games,* soft cover, 1975 . . . . **10.00**
Car, metal, blue, Gargamel driver, Ertl, 1982. . . . . **18.00**
Christmas Stocking, felt, "Have a Smurfette
 Christmas," 17" l **3.00**
Coloring Book, *Smurfs and More Smurfs,* A Learn–to–
 Read Coloring Book, Happy House, 1983. . . . . **2.00**
Comic Book, *Smurfs,* Vol 1, #3142, Feb 3, 1982,
 Marvel Comics. **2.50**
Costume, Smurfette, plastic **12.00**

Doll, Baby Smurf, plush, cotton, outstretched arms,
 12" h **5.00**
Doll, Brainy Smurf, plush, cotton, orig clothes, 1984. . . . . **3.00**
Doll, Smurfette, rubber, synthetic hair, Hong Kong,
 5" h **3.00**
Figure, Artist Smurf, #20045. **2.50**
Figure, Bowler Smurf, #20051 . . . . **2.50**
Figure, Flower Smurf, #20019 . . . . **5.00**
Figure, Gargamel, #20232 . . . . **3.50**
Figure, Grandpa Smurf, #20226 . . . . **3.00**
Figure, Jonah Smurf, #20498 . . . . **3.00**
Figure, Mechanic Smurf, #20012 . . . . **5.00**
Figure, Postman Smurf, #20031 . . . . **3.50**
Figure, Singing Smurf, #20038 . . . . **3.00**
Figure, Skier Smurf, #20091 . . . . **4.00**
Figure, Smurfette, #20034 . . . . **3.00**
Figure, Trumpet Player Smurf, #20072 . . . . **15.00**
Game, Smurf Spin–a–Round Game, Milton Bradley,
 1983 . . . . **12.00**
Game, The Smurf Card Game, Milton Bradley, 1982 . . . . . **8.00**
Lunch Box, plastic, no thermos, 1980s **10.00**
Mug, "Happy Birthday" **4.00**
Mug, "Sporty Smurf" **5.00**
Napkin, paper, "Happy Smurfday" **3.00**
Plate, set of 8, plastic coated plastic, "Happy
 Smurfday" **2.50**
Puzzle, cardboard, Track and Field, 100 pcs, 16 x 11". **4.00**
Puzzle, Rhyming Match–Ups, Playskool, 1982 . . . . **8.00**
Puzzle, Smurfs Turnabout Puzzle, Milton Bradley **2.50**
Puzzle, wood, Smurf carrying buckets, 10 pcs,
 Playskool, 1982 . . . . **5.00**
Radio, plastic, transistor, Hong Kong, 1982, 5 x 3" **25.00**
Record Player, plays 45 and 33 rpm records, Vanity
 Fair, 1982 . . . . **50.00**
Tablecloth, paper, Christmas theme, Unique Ind,
 Philadelphia, PA, 1982. . . . . **3.00**
Thermos, plastic, square, Smurfette with flower, yel-
 low ground, white lid, King Seeley **10.00**
Toy, Ball Darts, velcro board and balls **10.00**
Toy, camera, plastic, Ilko Co, 1982. . . . . **8.00**
Toy, Smurf Around, plastic, 18 x 12" **20.00**
Toy, spinning top, metal, 10" d **12.00**
Whistle, plastic, figural Gargamel, Helm, 1980s **5.00**

SNACK SETS

A snack set consists of two pieces, an underplate with a reservoir for a cup and a cup. Although glass snack sets are the most commonly found, they also were made in a variety of other materials ranging from ceramics to plastic.

Although dating back as early as the 1920s, the snack set achieved its greatest popularity in the 1950s and 60s. Snack sets were ideal for informal, i.e. patio, entertaining. Guests balanced them on their knees or laps.

Most snack sets were sold in services consisting of four cups and four plates. Collectors pay a slight premium for a service of four sets still housed in their period box.

Some snack sets have become quite expensive, not because they are snack sets but because of their crossover value. Some chintz snack sets exceed $250.

Newsletter: *Snack Set Searchers,* PO Box 158, Hallock, MN 56728.

Note: Prices are for snack sets consisting of one cup and one plate.

Anchor Hocking, Blue Mosaic, white milk glass ...... **$ 10.00**
Anchor Hocking, Classic, crystal **1.00**
Anchor Hocking, Classic, white milk glass **7.00**
Anchor Hocking, Fleurette, white milk glass **4.00**
Anchor Hocking, Golden Veil, white milk glass **5.00**
anchor Hocking, Primrose, white milk glass **8.00**
Anchor Hocking, Sandwidge, crystal **12.00**
Anchor Hocking, Soreno, avocado green **2.00**
Anchor Hocking, iridized crystal **3.00**
Anchor Hocking, Blair, Gay Plaid, hp **35.00**
Federal, Blossom, white milk glass **5.00**
Federal, Crystal Leaf, crystal **1.00**
Federal, Crystal Leaf, crystal, silver floral overlay **4.00**
Federal, Hawaiian Leaf, crystal **2.00**
Federal, Yorktown, amber **3.00**
Hazel Atlas, Crystal Daisy, crystal **3.00**
Hazel Atlas, Simplicity, crystal **1.00**
Hazel Atlas, Simplicity, crystal, hp tulip by "Gay Fad
    Studios" **10.00**
Indiana, King's Crown, amber **6.00**
Indiana, King's Crown, avocado green **6.00**
Indiana, Smartset, white milk glass **3.00**
Indiana, Sunbrust, amber **6.00**
Indiana, Sunburst, crystal **4.00**
Jeannette, Button & Daisy, amber **3.00**
Jeannette, Button & Daisy, avocado green **3.00**
Jeannette, Feather, shell pink milk glass **10.00**
Laurel China, Rose Petal, Japan **6.00**
Lefton, Golden Pine Cone **12.00**
Lefton, Golden Wheat **10.00**
Lefton, Silver Wheat **10.00**
Nasco Products, Delcoronado, Japan **4.00**
Noritake, oval, pink, orange, and gray floral dec **12.00**
Purinton, chartreuse, hp **35.00**
Royal Sealy, rose design, Japan **8.00**
Stangl, Orchard Song **26.00**
Steubenville, Woodfield, chartreuse **5.00**

SNOW BABIES

Snow babies, also known as sugar dolls, are small bisque figurines whose bodies are spattered with glitter sand, thus giving them the appearance of being coated in snow. Most are German or Japanese in origin and date between 1900 and 1940.

The exact origin of these figurines is unknown. The favored theory is that they were developed to honor Admiral Peary's daughter, Marie, born in Greenland on September 12, 1893. The Eskimos named the baby "Ah–Poo–Mickaninny," meaning snow baby. However, it is far more likely they were copied from traditional German sugar candy Christmas ornaments.

Babies, children at play, and Santa Claus are the most commonly found snow forms. Animal figures, such as bears, also are know.

Cramer & Co., Nurenberg, Germany, exported most snow babies to the United States. German bakery suppliers in New York,

Milwaukee, and Philadelphia, Schall & Company, B. Schackman, Sears, and Westphalia Imports were major American suppliers.

Some estimate that over 1,000 snow baby figurines were made. Many collections number in the hundreds. Snow babies also appeared on postcards and in advertising. Do not overlook snow baby paper items.

Reference: Mary Morrison, *Snow Babies, Santas, and Elves: Collecting Christmas Bisque Figures,* Schiffer Publishing, 1993.

Baby, crawling with red baby on back .... **$ 165.00**
Baby, holding ball over seals nose **120.00**
Baby, inside igloo, polar bear on top **110.00**
Baby, lying on stomach **50.00**
Baby, pulling sled carrying penguins................. **110.00**
Baby, sitting in sled being pulled by reindeer **110.00**
Baby, wearing gold suit, sitting on white sled, gilded,
    1 1/4" h **95.00**
Boy, ice skating, Japan **20.00**
Boy, skier, carrying poles, 4" h **10.00**
Child, pulling sled, Germany **110.00**
Children, beside brick bell arch, 1 blowing horn,
    other pulling rope, Germany...................... **75.00**
Girl, striding in winter coat carrying leaf **12.00**
Girl, wearing red skirt, sitting on snowball **125.00**
Girl, with ski poles, incised "Japan" **12.00**
Music Box, baby wearing pale yellow snowsuit, out-
    stretched arms, snowy scarf, Department 56, 7" h **650.00**
Three Babies, in pyramid form, yellow, red, and white. .. **165.00**
Three Children, singing dressed in Dickensian
    clothes, Germany, 1 3/4" h **20.00**
Three Children, standing around snowman, 1 1/4" h **135.00**
Two Babies, carrying brown bear **185.00**
Two Babies, hugging, 1 3/4" h....................... **10.00**
Two Babies, on red sled, Germany **85.00**
Two Babies, planting American flag atop globe, 3 1/4" h .. **185.00**
Two Children, sliding down brick wedge **130.00**

Bear, on skis, 2" h, $75.00.

SNOW GLOBES

Snow globes originated in Europe in the mid–18th century. Manufacturing was primarily a cottage industry. In 1878 seven different French firms marketed snow globes, along with firms in Austria, Czechoslovakia, Germany, and Poland.

Constantly gaining in popularity during the later decades of the Victorian era and the first three decades of the 20th century, the snow globe became extremely popular in the 1930s and early 1940s. Although the first American snow globe patent dates from the late 1920s, most of the snow globes sold in the 1930s were imported from Germany and Japan. These globes consisted primarily of a round ball on a ceramic or plastic base.

William M. Snyder founded Atlas Crystal Works, first located in Trenton, New Jersey, and later Covington, Tennessee, in the early 1940s to fill the snow globe void created by World War II. Driss Company of Chicago and Progressive Products of Union, New Jersey, were American firms making snow globes in the post–war period. Driss manufactured a series based on four popular characters (Davy Crockett, Frosty the Snowman, The Lone Ranger, and Rudoph the Red Nosed Reindeer); Progressive made advertising and award products.

The plastic domed snow globe arrived on the scene in the early 1950s. Initially German in origin, the concept was quickly copied by Japanese manufacturers. After a period of decline in the late 1960s and 70s, a snow globe renaissance occurred in the 1980s, the result of snow globes designed for the giftware market.

Reference: Nancy McMichael, *Snowdomes*, Abbeville Press, 1990.

Collectors' Club: Snowdome Collectors Club, PO Box 53262, Washington, DC 20009.

Note: Snow globes listed are plastic unless stated otherwise.

Figural, Santa Claus, holding deer across shoulders, $18.00.

Advertising, Abbeville Press	$ 15.00
Advertising, Atlantic Scaffold and Ladder Co, Art Deco landscape, oil filled, c1950	70.00
Advertising, Coca–Cola, woman holding bottle of Coke	15.00
Angel Sitting on Concorde Jet, mkd "fabrique en Chine"	25.00
Ashtray, Florida, pink shell–shaped ashtray with flamigos in globe	45.00
Australia, kangaroo and koala bear	18.00
Bottle Resting on Side, London, castle	15.00
Calendar Base, Hearst Castle, California, orange base	22.00
Calendar Base, Six Flags over Georgia, red base	20.00
Character, Cookie Monster, mkd "Jim Henson Productions	10.00
Character, Marilyn Monroe, large glass globe	35.00
Character, Snoopy, Willits, 1966	20.00
Chicago Bears, football, goal post, and helmet	8.00
Donald Duck Holding Skis, glass globe, wood base	10.00
Dutch Wonderland, Lancaster, PA, castle and swans	10.00
Easter, bunnies with Easter eggs, egg–shaped globe	8.00
Elvis, singing into microphone, rect, figure moves back and forth in front of Graceland mansion panel, Graceland plaque, 1970s	15.00
Figural, apple, "#1 Teacher"	10.00
Figural, baby bottle, "It's a Boy"	8.00
Figural, bell, child sledding	10.00
Figural, box, snow+covered house and trees, ribbon bow on top	15.00
Figural, Christmas tree, dome in center of tree	25.00
Figural, coffeepot, child inside	15.00
Figural, Halloween witch,"Best Witches"	18.00
Figural, seated Pinocchio holding dome, mkd "©Walt Disney Productions"	100.00
Figural, snowman, ceramic, dome is bottom ball of snowman	22.00
Flintstones, Fred, Pebbles, Bam Bam, and Dino in front of "Bedrock City" gateway, Hanna Barbera Productions, Inc, 1975	25.00
Kanssas, pine tree and buffalo	10.00
Key Chain, flamingo, ³⁄₄" w	10.00
Minnie Mouse, black and white, Bully, Walt Disney Co, 1977	18.00
Lone Ranger, glass globe, green or red base	75.00
Los Angeles Lakers, basketball and backboard	8.00
Paul Bunyan and Babe	15.00
Pen Holder, advertising globe, HeHart Co	45.00
Pencil Sharpener Base, Niagara Falls, Canada	12.00
Pink Panther, plastic dome, skating around Inspector Clouseau, 1980s	10.00
Ring Toss Game, Gulf Shores, red lobster standing with claws upright, rings land on claws	8.00
Salt and Pepper, pr, Niagara Falls, figural TV's, pink and blue	25.00
Salt and Pepper, pr, Seattle Space Needle, tall domes	20.00
Salt Lake City, mountains and skyline	10.00
Santa Claus, pull string activates snow	10.00
Santa Claus and Gnomes on Sled, large glass globe, ornate metal base, music box plays *Santa Claus is Coming to Town*, Mercuries, USA	30.00
Snow White in Glass Globe, base in dwarfs' house, music box plays *Some Day My Prince Will Come*, Walt Disney Co	40.00
Star Trek, glass dome, U.S.S. Enterprise, Willits	55.00
Yosemite Sam, "Congratulations!"	8.00

SOAKIES

Soakies, plastic figural character bubble bath bottles, were developed to entice children into the bathtub. Soakies, now a generic term for all plastic bubble bath bottles, originates from "Soaky," a product of the Colgate Palmolive Company.

Colgate Palmolive licensed numerous popular characters, e.g., Rocky and Bullwinkle, Felix the Cat, and Universal Monsters. Colgate Palmolive's success was soon copied, e.g., Purex's Bubble Club. Purex licensed the popular Hanna–Barbera characters. Avon, DuCair Bioessence, Koscot, Lander Company, and Stephen Reiley are other companies who have produced Soakies.

Soakies arrived on the scene in the early 1960s and have remained in production since. Most are 10″ high. Over a hundred different Soakies have been produced. Many are found in two or more variations, e.g., there are five versions of Bullwinkle.

Baby Louie, 10" h	$ 20.00
Bambi, 10" h	20.00
Bamm–Bamm, 10" h	30.00
Bozo the Clown, 10" h	25.00
Bugs Bunny, 10" h	15.00
Bullwinkle, 11" h	24.00
Cecil, 8" h	35.00
Cement Truck, 10" h	25.00
Cinderella, 10" h	15.00
Creature From the Black Lagoon, 10" h	60.00
Deputy Dawg, 8½" h	25.00
Elmer Fudd, 9" h	20.00
Fire Engine, hose gun, 10" h	30.00
Frankenstein, 10" h	125.00
Goofy, 10" h	15.00
Huckleberry Hound, 10" h	24.00
Mighty Mouse, 10" h	35.00
Mr. Jinx, 10" h	30.00
Mr. Magoo, 10" h	20.00
Mummy, 10" h	65.00
Musky Muskrat, 10" h	25.00
Pebbles Flintstone, 10" h	30.00
Pinocchio, 10" h	15.00
Pluto, 10" h	15.00
Popeye, 10" h	20.00
Porky Pig, 10" h	20.00
Punkin Puss, 11½" h	75.00
Santa, 10" h	15.00
Simon Chipmunk, 10" h	20.00
Smokey Bear, 10" h	18.00
Snagglepuss, 9" h	50.00
Snow White, 10" h	25.00
Speedy Gonzales, 10" h	18.00
Spouty Whale, 10" h	35.00
Sylvester Cat, 10" h	20.00
Tennessee Tuxedo, 10" h	30.00
Thumper, 10" h	25.00
Top Cat, 10" h	20.00
Touché Turtle, 10" h	32.00
Tweety Bird, 10" h	25.00
Wendy Witch, 10" h	40.00
Woody Woodpecker, 10" h	15.00
Yakki Doodle, 6" h	25.00
Yogi Bear, 10" h	25.00

Felix the Cat, 10″ h, $32.00.

SODA POP COLLECTIBLES

Coca–Cola is king of the hill. Pepsi is a distant second. Moxie is treated separately just because it has moxie. However, there are thousands of soda brands, ranging from regional to national, that continue to attract collector interest.

Many early soda brands were made by adding carbonated water to medical formulas. The local soda fountain, dominant from the late 1880s through the 1950s, dispensed ice cream, floats, and carbonated drinks ranging from Coca–Cola to beverages such as phosphates and rickies. However, it was not until the 1920s that Americans became enamored with buying soda in a bottle to consume at their leisure.

Tens of thousands of local bottling plants sprang up across America. Almost every community had one, producing flavors ranging from cream to root beer. Some brands achieved multistate and national popularity, e.g., Grapette and Hires.

Capitalizing on the increased consumption of soda pop during World War II, regional and national soda manufacturers launched a major advertising blitz in the late 1940s and early 1950s. From elaborate cardboard signs to numerous promotional premiums, the soda industry was determined to make its influence felt.

The soda bubble burst in the early 1970s. Most local and regional bottling plants ceased operations or were purchased by larger corporations. A few national brands survived and dominate the market. At the moment, there is no evidence that bottled soda will experience a micro–renaissance like that currently enjoyed by micro–brewed beer.

Collectors prefer to collect dark, caramel–colored soda. Although there are some wonderful pieces associated with 7–Up and ginger ales, collectors want little to do with clear soda memorabilia.

Collectors' Clubs: Dr. Pepper 10–2–4 Collectors Club, PO Box 153221, Irving, TX 75015; National Pop Can Collectors, PO Box 7862, Rockford, IL 61126.

Note: For additional listings refer to Coca–Cola, Moxie, and Pepsi–Cola.

Apron, Dr. Pepper, 1940s........................ $ 45.00
Ashtray, 7–Up, "Fresh up with Seven–Up It Likes
    You," 5½" d................................... 20.00
Blotter, Canada Dry, 1930s...................... 12.00
Booklet, *Mountain Dew, Hillbilly Game Book*, 1960s 6.50
Booklet, *Nehi*, 1929........................... 8.00
Booklet, *7–UP Likes You*, 1950s 5.00
Bottle, Canada Dry, miniature 15.00
Bottle, Dad's, miniature 30.00
Bottle, Frostie, miniature 10.00
Bottle, Hires, miniature 15.00
Bottle, 7–Up, miniature 45.00
Bottle Bag, Hires, 1940s........................ 20.00
Bottle Bag, Orange Crush, "Trick or Treat," 1960s 12.00
Bottle Cap, Cherry Smash 2.00
Bottle Cap, Dr. Pepper......................... 2.00
Bottle Cap, Kist Grapefruit 4.00
Bottle Cap, Mason's Root Beer 3.50
Bottle Cap, Orange–Crush 7.00
Bottle Cap, Whistle 2.50
Bottle Opener, Kist, 1950s 5.00
Box, Sweetheart Straws, 1940s................... 40.00
Calendar, Dr. Pepper, Jan 1937, woman wearing
    gown holding bottle, clock face background 785.00
Calendar, Kist, 1930s, woman standing next to life–
    size bottle, no pad 215.00
Calendar, Mission Orange, Dec 1953, woman talking
    on telephone 55.00
Can, Fanta, Disney series, aluminum, lift tab, foreign 8.50
Can, Fresca, aluminum, pull tab................... 6.00
Can, Nehi Orange, Happy Days series, aluminum, lift
    tab 7.00
Can, Old Fashioned Ma's Root Beer, steel, cone top 40.00

Thermometer, Sun Crest, c1940s, 7 x 16", $120.00.

Carrier, Donald Duck, ©Walt Disney Productions,
    1950s 80.00
Carrier, Frostie, cardboard, 1950s.................. 8.50
Carrier, Kist, cardboard, 1950s..................... 6.50
Carrier, Nehi, wire, 1930s........................ 90.00
Cup, Yoo–Hoo, plastic, Yogi Berra.................. 15.00
Dispenser, Cherry Smash, glass, Bakelite, 1930s 150.00
Dispenser, Tan Gee Orange, metal, 1930s............. 185.00
Doll, vinyl, 7–Up, Fresh–Up Freddie, 9" h........... 265.00
Fan, Dr. Pepper, 1960 Texas State Fair.............. 80.00
Fan, Pal Bottling Company 15.00
Fan, RC Cola, 1940s 40.00
Game, Skill Dice, Dr. Pepper, 1943 .... 285.00
Glass, Canada Dry, set of 6, 1939 World's Fair,
    applied color label......................... 45.00
Glass, Cas Cola, applied color label 25.00
Glass, Fanta, applied color label.................. 10.00
Label, Grape Smash.............................. 10.00
Letterhead, Dr. Sweet's, envelope, 1923 .... 20.00
Magazine Tear Sheet, Orange–Crush, 1930s 10.00
Magazine Tear Sheet, RC, Shirley Temple photo,
    1940s 22.00
Matchbook, 7–UP 8.00
Matchbook, Nehi................................ 15.50
Menu Board, Kayo, "Tops In Taste Kayo The Real
    Chocolate Flavor," 1950s, 13 x 27" 90.00
Menu Board, Orange–Crush, "Ask for Orange–Crush
    Carbonated Beverage," scoreboard scene, 1940s,
    23 x 36" 85.00
Mug, A&W, applied color label 8.50
Napkin, Dr. Pepper, 1930s....................... 40.00
Needle Case, Nu Grape, 1930s 45.00
Notebook, Chero–Cola, 1920...................... 35.00
Paddle Ball, Dr. Pepper, 1950s................... 30.00
Pocketknife, Pop Kola, 1950s 40.00
Postcard, Royal Crown Cola, 1950s 4.00
Postcard, Spur, 1940s........................... 3.00
Puzzle, Cleo Cola, 1930s 45.00

Left: Door push, Mission Orange, heavily emb, $120.00; Right: Sign, Royal Crown Cola, diecut emb tin, c1940s, 16 x 58", $300.00.

Serving Tray, Frank's, flamingos in water scene,
1950s, 13 x 18" **40.00**
Serving Tray, 7–Up, 1950s, 12½" d **115.00**
Sign, Canada Dry, "Thirsty? Go Steady With Ginger,"
cardboard, 1950s, 16 x 28" **35.00**
Sign, Donald Duck Cola, cardboard cutout, 1950s,
20 x 26" **175.00**
Sign, Hires, "Hires to You!, Tune To Good Taste,"
cardboard, 1950s, 12 x 18" **55.00**
Sign, Lime Crush, "like limes? drink Lime–Crush,"
cardboard, Norman Rockwell illus, 1930s, 9 x 12" . . . **535.00**
Sign, Nu–Grape, cartoon figure pushing wheelbar-
row with bottle inside behind man with gardening
tools, cardboard, wood frame, 1950 . . . . **115.00**
Sign, Pal, girl and boy with dog, "Pals Drink Pal Ade,"
cardboard, 1950s, 11 x 18" **40.00**
Soda Jerk Cap, Orange–Crush, 1939 . . . . **20.00**
Syrup Jug, Dr. Pepper, paper label **115.00**
Syrup Jug, Hires, paper label, 1940 . . . . **75.00**
Syrup Jug, 7–Up, green, paper label, 1950s **25.00**

AUCTION PRICES

Collectors Auction Services, November 2nd, 1996.

Bottle Opener, Canada Dry, metal, wall mount, gray
and red raised lettering, Starr X Brown Co, 3¼" h,
2¾" w **50.00**
Bottle Opener, Dr. Pepper, hand held, aluminum,
diecut, lion's head shape, Crown T & D Co,
Chicago, IL, 3" l **85.00**
Clock, Dr. Pepper, illuminated, plastic and metal,
bottle cap shape, white ground, black hands and
numerals, red Dr. Pepper label and numerals 10,
2, and 4, 11½" d **135.00**
Clock, Nu Grape, salesman's sample, electric, rect,
bottle image, glass front, metal body and clock
face, Swinhart Products, IN, 8" h, 6½" w, 2¾" d . . . **135.00**
Cooler, Whistle, metal, Whistle logo decal, "Thirsty?
Just Whistle," red ground, 2 bail handles, Progress
Refrigerator Co, Louisville, KY, 11¾" h, 17½" w,
8" d **160.00**
Dispenser, Howel's Orange–Julep, ceramic, ball
shaped, adv both sides, 15½" h **2,100.00**
Menu Board, Teem, rect, emb painted tin, bottle and
"Enjoy Teem a Lemon–Lime Drink," 22" h, 26" w . . . **20.00**
Sign, Grapette, flange, painted metal, oval, "Drink
Grapette Soda," 13½" h, 18" w **230.00**
Sign, Natural Chilean Soda, flange, rect, painted
metal, black man's face, "Yassuh!—Uncle
Natchel," 15" h, 22" w **150.00**
Sign, Nesbitt's Orange, button, tin over cardboard,
self–framed, professor with bottle at blackboard,
"Don't Say orange Say Sesbitt's, a soft drink made
from real Oranges," c1950, 9¼" d **65.00**
Sign, Nichol Kola, rect, painted emb tin, red, white,
and black, marching drum major, "Drink Nichol
Kola, 5¢, Vitamin B1 added, America's taste sen-
sation," 28" h, 20" w **75.00**
Sign, Nu Grape, painted emb tin, yellow ground,
hand holding bottle, "Drink NuGrape, Demand It
In This Bottle," 36" h, 14" w **250.00**
Thermometer, Wishing Well Orange, tin,
self–framed, bottle, "Drink Wishing Well
Orange," c1961, 40½" h, 10½" w **195.00**

SOUVENIRS

A novelty ceramic or glass object with a transfer featuring a historical or natural landmark with an identifying name was a popular keepsake in the period preceding World War I. Commemorative pieces include plates issued during anniversary celebrations and store premiums, many of which featured calendars. Souvenirs tend to be from carnivals, fairs, popular tourist attractions and hotels, and world's fairs.

The souvenir spoon arrived on the scene in the late 1880s. In the 1920s the demitasse spoon replaced the teaspoon as the favored size. The souvenir spoon craze finally ended in the 1950s, albeit the form can still be found today.

Plastic souvenir items dominate the post–World War II period. Many pieces were generic with only the name of the town, site, or state changed from one piece to another. In the late 1960s ceramic commemorative plates enjoyed a renaissance.

The vast majority of items sold in today's souvenir shops have nothing on them to indicate their origin. Souvenir shops are gift shops, designed to appeal to the universal taste of the buyer. T-shirts are the one major exception.

References: Dorothy T. Rainwater and Donna H. Felger, *American Spoons, Souvenir and Historical,* Everybodys Press, Schiffer Publishing, 1977; Dorothy T. Rainwater and Donna H. Felger, *Spoons From Around The World,* Schiffer Publishing, 1992.

Periodical: *Souvenir Building Collector,* 25 Falls Rd, Roxbury, CT 06783.

Newsletter: *Antique Souvenir Collectors News,* Box 562, Great Barrington, MA 01230.

Collectors' Clubs: American Spoon Collectors, 4922 State Line, Kansas City, MO 64133; Souvenir Spoon Collectors of America, 8200 Boulevard East, North Bergen, NJ 07047; The Scoop Club, 84 Oak Ave, Shelton, CT 06484.

Note: See Advertising, British Royal Commemoratives, Postcards, and World's Fair for additional listings.

Ashtray, Florida, brass, state shape, emb tourist sites . . . **$ 12.00**
Ashtray, Niagara Falls, blue and white jasperware,
mkd "Occupied Japan" **25.00**
Ashtray, Seattle Space Needle, potmetal **10.00**
Ashtray, Washington Monument **15.00**
Bank, Capitol, Washington DC **40.00**
Bank, Easton National Bank, Easton, PA, copper fin-
ish, 3¾" w **65.00**
Bank, Statue of Liberty, potmetal **40.00**
Booklet, *Yosemite Visitor's Guide,* 32 color photos **8.00**
Building, Alamo, San Antonio, TX, 4" w **15.00**
Building, Bunker Hill Monument, Boston, MA, cop-
per finish **12.00**
Building, Eiffel Tower, Paris, silver finish, 1" w **7.00**
Building, Empire State Building, NY, potmetal, 3" h **65.00**
Building, Woolworth Building, New York City, NY,
4" h **25.00**
Card Folder, Yellowstone Park, 1928 . . . . **5.00**
Compact, Empire State Building, Art Deco motif **35.00**
Compact, Statue of Liberty **50.00**
Creamer, St. James, MN **25.00**

Cup, Bicentennial **10.00**

Cup, Hotel Richmond, Richmond, VA, made in Germany **15.00**

Cup, New Orleans. **12.00**

Cup, Niagara Falls, Czechoslovakian **18.00**

Cup and Saucer, Santa Fe capital building, made in Austria. **22.00**

Cup and Saucer, Virginia capital building, ceramic stand **12.00**

Dresser Tray, Portland Hotel, white milk glass **30.00**

Fan, hand held, Cypress Garden. **7.00**

Fan, hand held, Yosemite National Park. **15.00**

Figure, Alaskan Eskimo, porcelain, 6" h. **18.00**

Figure, Statue of Liberty, potmetal, 9½" h **8.00**

Incense Burner, Alder Planetarium, Chicago, IL, copper finish, 3" h **40.00**

Ink Blotter, Yellowstone Park, metal. **35.00**

Letter Opener, Niagara Falls, American side, sterling silver **21.00**

Match Box, Niagara Falls, sterling. **100.00**

Mug, Joilet High School, Joilet, IL, china. **18.00**

Paperweight, Harrisburg, PA Senate House of Assembly, rect **85.00**

Paperweight, Kraft International Headquarters, Chicago, IL, silvered lead, A. C. Rehberger, 3⅛" h **74.00**

Pencil Box, Alaska, pyrography of Eskimo totem pole **15.00**

Pin, New York City, enameled **20.00**

Pinback Button, Detroit, lighthouse, "Where Life Is Worth Living" **45.00**

Pinback Button, Grand Island Fair, laughing devil **60.00**

Pitcher, Arkansas capital building, state seal **8.00**

Pitcher, Beverly, MA **35.00**

Pitcher, Statue of Liberty. **20.00**

Plate, City Meat Market, Leonardsville, KS, sheep **35.00**

Plate, Clark House, Lexington, MA, square **12.00**

Plate, Florida. **6.00**

Plate, Hot Springs, Arkansas Observation Tower **12.00**

View Card, Los Angeles, color, 12–card foldout, 1930s, 6 x 4¼", $4.00.

Plate, Idaho. **6.00**

Plate, Lookout Mountain **10.00**

Plate, Ocean Pier and Fun Chase, Wildwood, NJ, lattice trim. **8.00**

Plate, Rhode Island, scenic center, 22K gold border **20.00**

Plate, Statue of Liberty, NY, Enco Gold **12.00**

Postcard, Hawaii, hula dancer photo **15.00**

Postcard, 1952 Tournament of Roses, folding **7.00**

Program, Lawn Tennis Championship of U.S., Forest Hills, NY, Sep 1929 . . . . **45.00**

Program, Walt Disney's Snow White Radio City, Jan 1935 . . . . **35.00**

Ring, Yellowstone Park, brass, enameled bear **15.00**

Salt and Pepper Shakers, pr, alcasar de Segovia emblem, Limoges. **30.00**

Spoon, Algiers, sterling. **20.00**

Spoon, Alma **30.00**

Spoon, Bangor, ME, sterling **12.00**

Spoon, Battleship *Maine* **10.00**

Spoon, Brooklyn Bridge, "New York," sterling **35.00**

Spoon, Canton, MS, sterling. **12.00**

Spoon, Checolah, OK, sterling **20.00**

Spoon, Clear Lake, IA **35.00**

Spoon, Colorado, sterling. **12.00**

Spoon, Detroit, cutout handle, sterling **18.00**

Spoon, Helen, silver plated **20.00**

Spoon, Logan College, Russellville, KY **20.00**

Spoon, Mackinac Lake, sterling **30.00**

Spoon, Niagara Falls, sterling **17.00**

Spoon, Pike's Peak, Manitou, CO, cutout handle, sterling **18.00**

Tea Set, Niagara Falls, hp scenic transfers, Stadler **125.00**

Thermometer, Havoline Tower, 1933 Chicago World's Fair, plastic, marble base, 4⅝" h **20.00**

Tray, Alabama, metal **30.00**

Tray, City Hall, Philadelphia, PA, cobalt lattice sides, made in Germany **20.00**

Tray, Grand Canyon National Park, metal **30.00**

Tray, Lake George, NY, metal **8.00**

Plate, University of Chicago, Ida Noyes Hall, mkd "Copeland Spode, England," 1931, 10½" d, $30.00.

Tray, Plymouth, MA, metal **30.00**
Tumbler, Bicentennial Celebration, 1776–1976 . . . . **7.00**
Tumbler, Pearl Harbor **10.00**
Vase, Camp Lake View, Lake City, MN **12.00**
Vase, Florida, ftd **6.00**
Wall Pocket, Hamburg, Germany, heart shaped,
    scenic, hp **30.00**

SPACE ADVENTURERS, FICTIONAL

Philip Francis Nowland and John F. Dille launched *Buck Rogers 2429 A.D.* in January 1929. While not the first fictional space adventurers, Buck, Wilma Deering, Dr. Huer, and Killer Kane are among the best known. Cocomalt and Cream of Wheat are only two of the many companies that issued Buck Rogers premiums. The late 1930s was the golden age of this famous space explorer. Buck Rogers in the 25th Century, a television program airing on NBC between September 1979 and April 1981 starring Gil Gerard, created a renewed interest in Buck. Alas, by the end of the 1980s Buck's star had faded once again.

Flash Gordon was Buck Rogers' main rival in the 1930s. Although a popular cartoon strip, Flash came to life through the movie serials starring Buster Crabbe as Flash Gordon. The 1940s was Flash's golden age. A second generation became hooked on Flash when the movie serials were repeated dozens of times on television in the late 1940s and 50s.

Americans were enamored by space in the early 1950s. Television responded with Captain Video and His Video Rangers (Dumont Network, June 1949 to April 1955), Flash Gordon (syndicated, 39 episodes, 1953–54, Flash played by Steve Holland), Rocky Jones Space Ranger (syndicated, 1953; NBC, February–April 1954), Space Patrol (ABC, September 1950 to February 1955), and Tom Corbett, Space Cadet (CBS, October 1950 to September 1952; ABC January 1951 to September 1952; NBC, July to September 1951 and December 1954 to June 1955; Dumont, August 1953 to May 1954).

A second generation of space adventure television series were launched in the 1960s and 70s. These include Battlestar Galactica (ABC, September 1978 to August 1979), Lost in Space (CBS, September 1965 to September 1968), and Star Trek (September 1966 to September 1969). The continuation of the Star Trek saga with Star Trek: The Next Generation, Deep Space Nine, and Star Trek: Voyager along with Babylon 5 has kept the legend of the space adventurer alive on television.

Although there have been a host of space movies, e.g. the *Alien* series, the success of the initial *Star Wars* trilogy has relegated them all to a secondary status. *Star Wars* collectibles are also in a world by themselves. They have their own separate category.

This category does not include two groups of fictional space adventurers material. The first is books, paperbacks, and pulps unless they relate to the above characters or television shows. Material from Saturday morning cartoon shows involving space adventurers, e.g., Flash Gordon, is also excluded.

Note: See Star Trek and Star Wars for additional listings.

Alien, costume, Ben Cooper . . . . **$ 25.00**
Alien, egg puzzle **10.00**
Battlestar Galactica, action figure, Cylon, Mattel,
    1978, 12" h **18.00**
Battlestar Galactica, book, *The Living Legend*, #6 . . . . **2.00**

Battlestar Galactica, game, Milton Bradley, 1976 . . . . **18.00**
Battlestar Galactica, lunch box, Aladdin, 1979 . . . . **15.00**
The Black Hole, figure, Dr. Durant **20.00**
The Black Hole, puzzle, Maximillian and Dr.
    Reinhardt, Western Publishing **6.00**
Buck Rogers, Big Little Book, *Buck Rogers in the City
    Below the Sea* **35.00**
Buck Rogers, book, *Buck Rogers Origin*, Kellogg's,
    1933 . . . . **100.00**
Buck Rogers, book, *Stranger Adventures in the Spider
    Ship*, pop-up, Pleasure Books, 1935 . . . . **200.00**
Buck Rogers, booklet, *Buck Rogers Twenty–Fifth
    Century Presents A Century Of Progress*, stiff paper,
    folder holds pencil and table with Automatic Soap
    Flakes adv cov, Chicago World's Fair giveaway **120.00**
Buck Rogers, disintegrator pistol, Cream of Wheat
    premium **145.00**
Buck Rogers, game, Transogram, 1965 . . . . **55.00**
Buck Rogers, paddle ball, "Comet Socker," Lee–Tex
    Products Co **75.00**
Buck Rogers, paint book, #679, Whitman, 1935 . . . . **60.00**
Buck Rogers, photo, Buck and Wilma in Grand
    Canyon, Cocomalt **75.00**
Buck Rogers, Planet Venus coloring map, 1931 . . . . **85.00**
Captain Video, game, Milton Bradley, 1950s **135.00**
Captain Video, goggles **50.00**
Close Encounters of the Third Kind, magazine,
    Science Fantasy **4.00**
Close Encounters of the Third Kind, pinback button,
    "A Close Encounter" **2.00**
Close Encounter of the Third Kind, UFO sighting
    map, Skywatchers Club premium **4.50**
Dune, book, *Heretics of Dune*, hardcover **5.00**
Dune, toy, Sand Roller **15.00**
Flash Gordon, action figure, Dale, Mego, 1976 . . . . **25.00**
Flash Gordon, action figure, Dr. Zarkov, Mego, 1976 . . . . **20.00**
Flash Gordon, bank, metal, rocket **22.00**
Flash Gordon, Better Little Books, *The Ice World of
    Mongo*, Whitman, 1942 . . . . **40.00**
Flash Gordon, book, *The Space Circus*, paperback,
    Avon, 1974 . . . . **3.00**
Flash Gordon, Dixie lid, "Buster Crabbe Starring in
    the Universal Chapter Play Flash Gordon," sepia
    photo, c1936, 2¹/₄" d **18.00**
Lost in Space, comic book, Gold Key **20.00**
Lost in Space, costume, Ben Cooper, unused, 1965 . . . . . . **75.00**
Lost in Space, game, Milton Bradley, 1965 . . . . **55.00**
Lost in Space, helmet and gun set, Remco, 1967 . . . . . . **300.00**
Lost in Space, lunch box, metal, dome shape, King
    Seeley, 1966 . . . . **300.00**
Lost in Space, puzzle, frame tray, Milton Bradley, 1966 . . . **25.00**
Lost in Space, writing tablet, cov with June Lockhart
    as Maureen Robinson wearing silver flight uniform,
    unused, 8 x 10" **25.00**
Matt Mason, Unitred Space Vehicle, toes 1–man
    space bubble, orig box, Mattel, 1968 . . . . **32.00**
Planet of the Apes, action figure, Cornelius, Mego **30.00**
Planet of the Apes, book, *Beneath the Planet of the
    Apes* **1.00**
Planet of the Apes, figure, plaster, Zira, Tuscany
    Statues, 1973 . . . . **30.00**

Tom Corbett, Space Cadet, record album, *Tom Corbett Space Cadet Song and March,* Golden Record, R89, 1951, $20.00.

Planet of the Apes, puzzle, General Aldo, cylinder
  package..**10.00**
Rocky Jones, pinback button, "Rocky Jones, Space
  Ranger, Silvercup Bread," c1953....................**18.00**
Space: 1999, action figure, Dr. Russell, Mattel.........**20.00**
Space: 1999, book, Moon Odyssey......................**1.50**
Space: 1999, game, Milton Bradley, 1976..............**15.00**
Space: 1999, lunch box, King Seeley...................**20.00**
Space: 1999, Stun Gun flashlight......................**20.00**
Space: 1999, utility belt..............................**18.00**
Space: 1999, View–Master Pack, 1975.................**8.00**
Space Patrol, membership card.......................**25.00**
Space Patrol, periscope.............................**150.00**
Tom Corbett, Space Cadet, book, *Stand by for Mars,*
  Grosset & Dunlap.................................**18.00**
Tom Corbett, Space Cadet, coloring book, Saalfield,
  1952..**40.00**
Tom Corbett, Space Cadet, lunch box, Aladdin.........**40.00**
Tom Corbett, Space Cadet, record, Golden Record,
  1951..**25.00**
Tom Corbett, Space Cadet, ring, insignia..............**18.00**
Tom Corbett, Space Cadet, view master reel, set of 3.....**45.00**
Tom Corbett, Space Cadet, wrist compass.............**45.00**

SPACE EXPLORATION

Man's landing on the moon on July 12, 1969, marked the culmination of the first step of a real– life space odyssey that began with short orbital flights around the earth. The current joint efforts of nations of the world to build a manned spaced station is a continuation of that journey.

Collector interest in artifacts relating to the manned space program began in the early 1980s. After a brief fascination with autographed material, collectors quickly moved to three–dimensional objects.

The collapse of the Soviet Union coupled with Russia's and several cosmonauts' need for capital has resulted in the sale of space memorabilia by several leading auction houses around the world. Everything from capsules to space suits are available for purchase.

This category focuses primarily on material associated with manned space flight. Collector interest in material from unmanned flights is extremely limited.

Reference: Stuart Schneider, *Collecting The Space Race,* Schiffer Publishing, 1993.

Collectors' Club: Society for the Advancement of Space Activities, PO Box 192, Kents Hill, ME 04349.

Bank, astronaut, painted plastic, c1972.............**$ 30.00**
Bank, moon shape, plaster, "Save your pennies for a
  trip to the moon," c1960..........................**40.00**
Bank, *Sputnik,* litho tin, satellite shape, c1959.........**125.00**
Book, *First On The Moon,* Neil Armstrong, Michael
  Collins, and Edwin E. Aldrin Jr., 1970..............**52.00**
Comic Book, Space Adventures, July 1962............**20.00**
Costume, astronaut, Ben Cooper.....................**40.00**
Greeting Card, "Hail Columbia," Hallmark, 1981........**5.50**
Jigsaw Puzzle, Astronauts, *Apollo 1*.................**22.00**
Magazine, *Newsweek,* Apr 27, 1981.................**5.00**
Medal, commemorative, sterling silver, astronaut
  descending from landing module onto moon,
  "One Small Step" inscription, reverse with moon
  plaque, acrylic case, 1½" d........................**32.00**
Medallion, commemorative, First *Gemini* Space
  Walk, 1965......................................**75.00**
Newspaper, *Daily News,* May 25, 1962, "Great Scott"....**25.00**
Newspaper, *New York Times,* Jul 21, 1969, "Men
  Walk On Moon".................................**20.00**
Patch, Space Shuttle, *Columbia,* 1981................**8.00**
Pen, titanium, commemorating man landing on
  moon, Parker, 1970..............................**325.00**
Pennant, felt, Cape Kennedy, rocket taking off, 1965.....**50.00**
Pennant, felt, Kennedy Space Center, FL, white letter-
  ing, red ground, 1968............................**40.00**
Pennant, felt, U.S. Victory in Space, yellow on black
  ground..**50.00**
Photo, Crippen and Young holding replica rocket,
  sgd, 1981.......................................**60.00**
Photo, Gordon Cooper, sgd, 1961...................**125.00**
Pin, lapel, enameled, honoring Russia's Yuri Gagarin's
  flight, Apr 12, 1961..............................**40.00**
Pinback Button, "America's First Orbital Space Man
  Astronaut John Glenn"...........................**30.00**
Pinback Button, *Challenger 7,* black and white photo,
  purple ground, 3" d..............................**8.00**
Pinback Button, 3–dimensional, men planting flag on
  moon, Earth in background, c1969.................**30.00**
Plaque, plaster, Flight of *Apollo 11,* Jul 1969, 15" d......**85.00**
Poster, Space Shuttle, Postal Service issue, 1981........**20.00**
Press Kit, Space Shuttle Saga *Columbia,* 1981..........**6.00**
Press Pass, ABC News, Space Shuttle *Columbia,* 1981....**70.00**
Record, *Go! Colonel Glenn in Orbit,* 33 rpm, 1962......**40.00**
Record and Book Set, *To The Moon,* 33 rpm, *Time–
  Life,* 1969.......................................**40.00**
Rug, First Man on the Moon, 1969, 37 x 20"..........**145.00**

Spoon, *Apollo 8,* engraved astronauts' names and flight date, detailed design on handle, Kleps Arts, Holland, 4½" l **8.50**

Stamp, commemorative, return of *Apollo 11,* 1969 . . . . . . **20.00**

Tickets, Farewell *Gemini* Party, Dec 10, 1966 . . . . **15.00**

Whiskey Bottle, commemorative, *Apollo 14,* blue irid glass, emb portraits 1 side, emblem other side, Wheaton Ltd Edition, Great American Series, 1971, 8½" d **25.00**

Wine Bottles, pr, Space Shuttle Red and Space Shuttle White, Bully Hill Vineyards, 1982 . . . . **55.00**

SPACE TOYS

Space toys divide into three basic groups: (1) astronauts and space-men, (2) spacecraft (capsules, flying saucers, rockets, and satel-lites), and (3) tanks and vehicles. Robots are excluded. They have reached the level of independent collecting status.

The toy industry, especially the Japanese, responded quickly to the growing worldwide interest in manned space flight. The first lithographed tin, friction, and key–wound toys arrived on the market in the late 1940s. Toys became increasingly sophisticated during the 1950s. More action was added. The number of parts that lit up or made sounds increased. By the end of the 1950s, the battery–operated space toy was dominant.

Initially used as a supplemental material, plastic became the principal construction material by the early 1970s. Production also shifted from Japan to China and Taiwan, a move that collectors view as having cheapened the toys. The decline in public interest in the space program in the mid–1970s also led to a decline in the production of space toys. Most collectors focus on space toys made prior to 1970.

The period box is an essential component of value, often adding 25 to 40 percent to the toy's value. The artwork on the box often is more impressive than the toy itself. Further, the box may contain information about the name of the toy, manufacturer, and/or distributor not found on the toy itself.

References: Dennis Way Nicholson (comp.), *The Gerry Anderson Memorabilia Guide,* Cooee Concepts Pty, 1994; Maxine A. Pinsky, *Marx Toys: Robots, Space, Comic, Disney & TV Characters,* Schiffer Publishing, 1996; Stuart Schneider, *Collecting The Space Race,* Schiffer Publishing, 1993.

Note: For additional listings see Robots, Space Adventurers, Star Trek, and Star Wars.

Astro Base, motorized, plastic, orig box, Ideal, 20" h, 8" d . . . . **$ 75.00**

Atomic Disintegrator, cap pistol, silvered metal, red plastic grips, orig box, Hubley, 7½" l **175.00**

Cosmic Ray Gun, plastic, red, blue, and amber, transparent barrel, sparking, orig box, Ranger Steel Products, 1950s, 8" l **40.00**

Docking Rocket, battery operated, tin and plastic rocket and capsule, revolving radar, lights, orig box and inserts, Daiya, Japan, 16" l **50.00**

Electric Rainbow Top, battery operated, litho tin, planets and stars dec, lights up, orig box, Haji, Japan, 7½" d **125.00**

Flying Spaceman, #617, friction, litho tin, orig box, Bandai, Japan, 12" l, 5¾" h, $8,000.00.

Electronic Space Gun, plastic, transparent dual telescopic sights, color rays, high speed atom smasher twirls, atomic sound waves, orig box, Remco, 9" l **125.00**

Flying Jeep, friction, litho tin and plastic, orig box, Asahitoy, Japan, 8½" l **100.00**

Interplanetary Spaceship Atom Rocket–15, battery operated, litho tin and plastic, orig instructions and box, Yone, Japan, 1970s, 13" h **150.00**

King Flying Saucer, battery operated, litho tin and plastic, mkd "Space Patroler," flashing lights, space sound, turning action simulates space flight, orig box, KO, Japan, 7½" d **125.00**

Magic Color Moon Express, battery operated, tin and plastic, non–stop action, spacenoise, light display, orig box, Daysran, Taiwan, 14" l **55.00**

Man Made Satellite, friction, litho tin, spring antennae, red, dog head image at each window, orig box, Yonezawa, Japan, 7" l **250.00**

Mars Gun, friction, litho tin, transparent red plastic insert windows, sparking, siren noise, orig box, 9" l . . . **100.00**

Moon City, battery operated, plastic *Apollo* moon shuttle travels around lunar command posts, blinking lights, orig 15 x 17½" box, Cragstan, Japan **60.00**

Moon Orbiter, battery operated, plastic and tin, space vehicle moves along magnet rail track, orig 9 x 11" box, Yonezawa, Japan **325.00**

NASA *Columbia* Space Ship, battery operated, tin and plastic, space vehicle rolls forward, bump–and–go action, stops, canopy opens, tin astronaut floats through space, space noise, lights up, orig box, Spain, 14 x 9½" **120.00**

NASA Space Shuttle *Challenger* and Flying Jet Plane, battery operated, tin and plastic, 1/175 scale, taxies, takes off, flies, and lands, toy removed from market following *Challenger* crash, orig box, Taiwan, 16" wing span **195.00**

New Space Capsule, battery operated, tin and plastic *Apollo* capsule with graphic int and NASA markings, mystery action, stop–and–go action, opening-hatch, tin astronaut, orig box and inserts, SH, Japan, 9½" l **85.00**

Project Mercury Recovery Set, helicopter, space capsule, and astronaut, orig box, Marx, 1961 . . . . **75.00**

Robert the Robot and His Remote Control Bulldozer, plastic, battery–operated light, trigger gun with cranking directional controls, seated red and silver robot works gears, blue and yellow bulldozer with red treads, orig box, Ideal, 9" l **2,000.00**

Rocket Fighter, windup, litho tin, rocketship and pilot, sparking action, space noise, rolls forward, Marx, 12" l **225.00**

Space Bus, friction, litho tin, astronauts, capsules, planets, rockets, and comets dec, destination plate reads "Space," Robbie robot image on roof, clear plastic window inserts, orig box, Usagayi, Japan, 14½" l **1,500.00**

Space Gun, #8, tin, sparking action, gray, red lettering, 7¾" l, 5" h **30.00**

Space Helmet With Radar Goggles, copper metallic swirled plastic with day–glo orange trim, helmet top shaped as rocketship, yellow and green goggles, orig box with inserts, Banner Plastics, 1950s **600.00**

Space Patrol Fire Bird, battery operated, litho tin rocket, mystery action, blinking light, clear plastic dome over litho tin astronaut, orig box, MT, Japan, 14" l **600.00**

Space Patrol Round Rocket, windup, litho tin, raised pilot's helmet in cockpit, orig box, Asahitoy, Japan, 5½" l **175.00**

Space Patrol Super Cycle, friction, litho tin motorcycle, sparking action, rotating radar, working compass, green rubber figure with bubble helmet, orig box, Bandai, Japan, 14" l **3,750.00**

Space Patrol Walkie Talkie, battery operated, plastic microphones, orig 6 x 9½" box, J. & L. Randall, England, 1955 . . . . **150.00**

Space Patrol 2019 Flying Saucer, #758, battery operated, litho tin and plastic, Y, Japan, 8" d, 6" h, orig box, $150.00.

Space Pilot X–Ray Gun, friction, plastic, gold, simulated satellite openings, 2 sounds, flashing barrel, orig box, KO, Japan, 8½" l **95.00**

Space Port Planetary Cruiser Patrol, litho tin hangar, 10½" l plastic spaceship, 6 hard plastic spacemen, 3" h plastic "boiler plate" type robot, Pyro, 1950s **400.00**

Space Station, battery operated, tin, red, mystery action, blinking lights, space noise, revolving plastic antenna, 3–dimensional tin figures and furniture, NASA markings, orig box, SH, Japan, 9¼" h, 11½" d **1,500.00**

Space Super Jet Gun, litho tin, transparent green barrel, sparking light, sound, orig box, KO, Japan, 9½" l **75.00**

Super Sonic SpeedsterRocket Racer, friction, litho tin, sparking, orig box and cardboard insert, Modern Toys, Japan, 6½" l **350.00**

XZ–7 Space Ship, friction, litho tin, spinning overhead rotor, orig box, ST, Japan, 6½" l **60.00**

SPORTING COLLECTIBLES

This catchall category includes memorabilia from those sports, from bowling to swimming, that do not have separate categories, e.g., baseball, basketball, football, hockey, etc. The listings include amateur and professional material. Today, this line is blurred. Amateurs have access to and use the same equipment available to professionals.

Sports memorabilia has attracted collector interest for two reasons. First, collectors grew tired of flat two–dimensional trading cards. They want three–dimensional material, especially items specifically used to play the sport. Second, decorators began creating sports theme restaurants and bars in the 1980s and have continued the trend through the 1990s. Collectors were amazed at the variety of material that was available.

When buying any game–related object, obtain a written provenance. Beware of sports autographs. The FBI reports that forgeries are as high as 70 percent and more in some sports categories. The only way to make certain the signature is authentic is to see the person sign it. One hot area in the late 1990s is trophies.

References: Mark Allen Baker, *Sports Collectors Digest Complete Guide to Boxing Collectibles*, Krause Publications, 1995; Roderick A. Malloy, *Malloy's Sports Collectibles Value Guide, Up–To–Date Prices For Noncard Sports Memorabilia*, Attic Books, Wallace–Homestead, Krause Publications, 1994.

Periodical: *Boxing Collectors Newsletter*, 3316 Luallen Dr, Carrollton, TX 75007.

Collectors' Clubs: Boxiana & Pugilistica Collectors International, PO Box 83135, Portland, OR 97203; Olympian Collector's Club, 1386 5th St, Schenectady, NY 12303.

Note: For additional listings see Auto & Drag Racing, Baseball Cards, Baseball Memorabilia, Basketball Cards, Basketball Memorabilia, Football Cards, Football Memorabilia, Golf Collectibles, Hockey Cards, Hockey Memorabilia, Horse Racing, Hunting, and Tennis Collectibles.

Bowling, game, Bowlem, Parker Brothers, 1930s . . . . . $ **20.00**

Bowling, game, Donald Duck Pins and Bowling Game, Pressman, 1950s 45.00

Bowling, magazine, *Sports Illustrated,* March 28, 1955, Steve Nagy. 8.50

Boxing, autograph, Evander Holyfield. 5.00

Boxing, autograph, George Foreman, sgd 8 x 10" photo 30.00

Boxing, figurine, Muhammad Ali, Salvino Sports Legend 250.00

Boxing, game, Championship Fight Game, Frankie Goodman, 1940s 45.00

Boxing, game, Kellogg's Boxing Game, Kellogg's premium, 1936 .... 40.00

Boxing, game, Knockout, Scarne Games, 1937 ...... 70.00

Boxing, pin, Muhammad Ali, "Sting Like a Bee," 3½" d 12.00

Boxing, program, Ken Norton/Muhammad Ali, Mar 31, 1973. .... 50.00

Cycling, game, The Bike Race Game, Master Toy Co, 1930s 45.00

Gymnastics, autograph, Bart Conner, sgd 8 x 10" photo 18.00

Gymnastics, autograph, Olga Korbut 8.00

Ice Skating, autograph, Dorothy Hamill 10.00

Sailing, game, Clipper Race, Gabriel, 1930s 85.00

Sailing, magazine cover, *Sports Illustrated,* Sep 6, 1954 .... 10.00

Scuba Diving, magazine cover, *Sports Illustrated,* Aug 11, 1958. .... 3.50

Skiing, game, Ski Gammon, American Publishing Corp, 1962 .... 5.00

Skiing, game, Walt Disney's Ski Jump Target Game, American Toy Works, c1930 .... 235.00

Skiing, program, Winter Olympics, Lake Placid, NY, 1932 .... 45.00

Sky Diving, magazine cover, *Sports Illustrated,* Dec 24, 1962, double issue 4.00

Soccer, figurine, Pat Bonner, Kenner Starting Lineup, 1989 .... 30.00

Swimming, autograph, Janet Evans, sgd 8 x 10" photo 15.00

Swimming, autograph, Mark Spitz 2.50

Tennis, autograph, Billie Jean King 8.00

Tennis, game, Tennis, Parker Brothers, 1975 .... 5.00

Wrestling, poster, Pat "Crusher" O'Hara vs Luke Graham and midgets Diamond Jim Brady vs Vincent Garabaldi, cardboard, black and white, 14 x 22", $25.00.

Tennis, magazine cover, *Sports Illustrated,* Billie Jean King, Jul 16, 1973 .... 3.00

Tennis, magazine cover, *Sports Illustrated,* World Tennis Crisis, Jul 10, 1961 .... 4.00

Track and Field, autograph, Florence Griffith Joyner 2.50

Track and Field, comic book, True Comics, Track & Field, Apr 1941, Parents' Magazine Press. 65.00

Track and Field, game, Cross Country Marathon Game, Rosebud Art Co, 1930s 65.00

Wrestling, autogaph, Andre the Giant, sgd 8 x 10" photo 40.00

Wrestling, comic book, WWF Battlemania, WWF Action, Valiant. 1.50

Wrestling, game, Verne Gagne World Champion Wrestling, Gardner, 1950 .... 85.00

STAMPS

Stamp collecting as a hobby was extremely popular throughout the middle decades of the 20th century. After a speculation period in the 1960s and 70s, when stamps became an investment commodity, the bubble burst in the 1980s. Middle– and low–end stamps experienced major price declines. To its credit, Scott Publishing adjusted the prices within its guides to reflect true market sales. Since this meant reducing the value for many stamps, the results sent shock waves through the market.

Stamp collecting is still in a period of recovery. Many question whether stamp collecting will ever recover its former popularity. Today's market is almost exclusively adult–driven. Investment continues to be the dominant collecting motivation. The overall feeling within the market is positive. Attendance is up at stamp shows. Modestly priced stamps are selling strongly. Interest in foreign issues is rising.

Condition, scarcity, and desirability (popularity) are the three pricing keys. Before researching the value of any stamps, carefully read the front matter of the book you are using, especially information relating to catalog values, grade, and condition. Make cer-

Boxing, ticket, World's Heavyweight Championship Fight, Dempsey vs Gibbons, Shelby, MT, $50 ringside, Jul 4, 1923, 7 x 2¾", $50.00.

tain you understand the condition grade being used for pricing. Most stamp collectors want examples graded at very fine or above.

Book values are retail value. Valuable stamps are far easier to sell than lesser valued stamps. Expect to have to discount commonly found stamps by 60 to 70 percent when selling them. If you have recently issued United States stamps, it may make far more sense to use them for postage than to try to sell them on the secondary market.

Most catalogs provide values for the stamp unused and used (canceled). In some cases, the postmark and/or cancellation may have more value than the stamp.

The five–volume *Scott 1998 Standard Postage Stamp Catalogue* (Scott Publishing Co., 911 Vandemark Road, Sidney, OH 45365) is the basic reference work used by most collectors to determine the values of their collections. Volume 1 contains information about United States stamps. If the collection you are evaluating only contains United States stamps, also consult Marc Hudgeons' *The Official 1997 Blackbook Price Guide of United States Postage Stamps, Nineteenth Edition* (House of Collectibles, 1996).

Over the past few years, numerous advertisements from the International Collectors Society have appeared in newspapers and magazines offering stamp series featuring pictures of prominent movie, music, and sports personalities issued by countries such as Grenada. These stamps are being printed specifically for sale to unknowledgeable collectors who believe they are purchasing a bargain and long–term collectible. Nothing is further from the truth. They are not the "Hot New Collectible" claimed by the International Collectors Society. Both philatelic and regular collectors are shunning these stamps now and will do so in the future.

Periodicals: *Scott Stamp Monthly*, Box 828, Sidney, OH 45365; *Stamp Collector*, 700 E State St, Iola, WI 54990; *Stamps*, 85 Canisteo St, Hornell, NY 14843.

Collectors' Clubs: American Philatelic Society, PO Box 8000, State College, PA 16803; International Stamp Collectors Society, PO Box 854, Van Nuys, CA 91408.

Note: David J. Maloney, Jr.'s *Maloney's Antique & Collectibles Resource Directory* (found at your local library) contains the names of many specialized collectors' clubs.

STANGL

Stangl Pottery is a continuation of Fulper Pottery. In the 1880s Edward, George W., and William Fulper, three brothers, operated a pottery in Flemington, New Jersey. In 1910 Johann Martin Stangl joined Fulper, working as a chemist and plant manager. Stangl left Fulper to work for Haeger Potteries in 1914, returning to Fulper in 1920 as general manager. In 1926 Fulper purchased the Anchor Pottery, a dinnerware manufacturer, in Trenton, New Jersey. After a fire destroyed the Flemington plant in 1929, all production was moved temporarily to Trenton. The Flemington plant was rebuilt.

Johann Martin Stangl became Fulper's president following the death of William Fulper in 1928. In 1929 Stangl purchased Fulper. Stangl continued to produce some pieces under the Fulper trademark until around 1955. Stangl made inexpensive artware, dinnerware, and utilitarian ware. By the end of the 1930s, production was concentrated primarily at the Trenton facility. The Flemington plant served as a sales outlet and demonstration facility.

In 1940 Stangl introduced a line of bird figurines, inspired by images from Audubon prints. Auguste Jacob designed and created the models for the birds. Initially, twelve birds were produced. During World War II demand was so great that between 40 and 60 decorators were employed to keep up with demand. Some body-work was contracted out to other manufacturers. A few out–of–production birds were reissued between 1972 and 1977. These are clearly dated on the bottom. When production ceased in 1978, over a hundred different shapes and varieties had been made.

More than 50 dinnerware patterns, e.g., Indian Summer and Maize–Ware, were introduced between 1942 and 1968. Antique Gold was an extremely popular 1950s dinnerware line.

Fire destroyed the Trenton plant on August 25, 1965. It was rebuilt and back in production by May 1966. Johann Martin Stangl died in 1972. Frank Wheaton, Jr., Millville, New Jersey, bought Stangl, selling it to Pfaltzgraff Pottery in 1978. Pfaltzgraff ended production, using the salesroom in Flemington as an outlet store for Pfaltzgraff products.

References: Susan and Al Bagdade, *Warman's American Pottery and Porcelain,* Wallace–Homestead, Krause Publications, 1994; Harvey Duke, *The Official Identification And Price Guide To Pottery And Porcelain, Eighth Edition,* House of Collectibles, 1995; Harvey Duke, *Stangl Pottery,* Wallace–Homestead, Krause Publications, 1992; Mike Schneider, *Stangl and Pennsbury Birds,* Schiffer Publishing, 1994.

Collectors' Club: Stangl/Fulper Collectors Club, PO Box 64–A, Changewater, NJ 07831.

Amber Glo, butter dish	$ 25.00
Amber Glo, casserole, 6" d	15.00
Amber Glo, cereal bowl, 5½" d	5.00
Amber Glo, chop plate, 12½" d	15.00
Amber Glo, salad bowl, 12" d	30.00
Amber Glo, vegetable bowl, divided	25.00
Americana, chop plate, 12" d	20.00
Americana, creamer	4.00
Americana, plate, 10" d	6.00
Americana, salad bowl, 10" d	25.00
Americana, sugar, open, individual	6.00
Americana, vegetable bowl, oval, 8" l	15.00
Apple Delight, cereal bowl, 5½" d	10.00
Apple Delight, chop plate, 12¼" d	20.00
Apple Delight, salad bowl, 10" d	30.00
Apple Delight, saucer	2.00
Bella Rosa, bread and butter plate, 6" d	4.00
Bella Rosa, casserole, individual, stick handle	12.00
Bella Rosa, fruit dish, 5½" d	8.00
Bella Rosa, server, center handle	6.50
Bird, #3250 A, Duck, standing, green, 3¼" h	50.00
Bird, #3250 D, Duck, gazing, mauve, 3¾" h	50.00
Bird, #3250 E, Duck, drinking, 1¾" h	50.00
Bird, #3274, Penguin, 6" h	385.00
Bird, #3275, Turkey, 3½" h	375.00
Bird, #3286, Hen, 3¼" h	30.00
Bird, #3401 D, Wren, 8" h, price for pair	110.00
Bird, #3405 D, Cockatoo, 9½" h, price for pair	40.00
Bird, #3406 S, Kingfisher, 3½" h	40.00
Bird, #3408, Bird of Paradise, 5½" h	65.00
Bird, #3447, Yellow Warbler, 5" h	55.00

Bird, #3457, Cerulean Warbler, 4¼" h 45.00
Bird, #3585, Rufous Humming Bird, 3" h 35.00
Bird, #3592, Titmouse, 2½" h 40.00
Bird, #3752 D, Red–Headed Woodpecker, 7¾" h,
    price for pair 140.00
Bird, #3812, Chestnut–sided Warbler, 4" h 65.00
Bird, #3849, Goldfinch, 4" h 65.00
Blueberry, casserole, 8" d 70.00
Blueberry, coffee pot, 4 cup 45.00
Blueberry, creamer, individual 10.00
Blueberry, plate, 10" d 15.00
Blueberry, salad bowl, 10" d 35.00
Chicory, casserole, 8" d 22.00
Chicory, chop plate, 12½" d 25.00
Chicory, creamer, old style 6.00
Chicory, plate, 9" d 8.00
Chicory, salad bowl, 10" d 35.00
Colonial, creamer 6.50
Colonial, cup 5.00
Colonial, salad bowl, 8" d 15.00
Country Garden, cereal bowl, 5½" d 10.00
Country Garden, chop plate, 12½" d 35.00
Country Garden, coffee warmer 18.00
Country Garden, cup 10.00
Country Garden, platter, oval, 14¾" d 40.00
Country Life, eggcup, Chick 40.00
Country Life, fruit dish, Pony, 5½" d 70.00
Country Life, plate, Rooster, 10" d 120.00
Country Life, shaker, Duckling 30.00
Fruit, bean pot, 2 handles 75.00
Fruit, cake stand 20.00
Fruit, mixing bowl, 4" d 10.00
Fruit, plate, 7" d 6.00
Fruit, platter, oval, 14¾" d 40.00
Fruit, salad bowl, 11" d 50.00
Fruit, server, 2 tier 25.00
Garden Flower, casserole, Balloon Flower, 8" d 50.00
Garden Flower, cereal bowl, Morning Glory, 5½" d 12.00
Garden Flower, creamer, individual, Rose 12.00
Garden Flower, plate, Tiger Lily, 9" d 10.00
Garden Flower, saucer, Leaves 3.50
Garden Flower, teapot, Sunflower 45.00
Golden Harvest, casserole, 6" d 15.00
Golden Harvest, coffee pot, 2 cup 25.00
Golden Harvest, creamer 5.00
Golden Harvest, plate, 9" d 8.00
Golden Harvest, sugar 10.00
Golden Harvest, vegetable bowl, cov, 8" d 40.00
Lyric, creamer 12.00
Lyric, cup 10.00
Lyric, mug, 2 cup 30.00
Lyric, plate, 6" d 5.00
Lyric, salad bowl, 10" d 35.00
Lyric, saucer 3.50
Lyric, sugar 15.00
Orchard Song, fruit bowl, 5½" d 8.00
Orchard Song, server, 2 tiers 18.00
Rooster, cake stand 30.00
Rooster, cereal bowl, 5½" d 15.00
Rooster, cup 12.00
Rooster, pitcher, 1 pint 20.00

Garden Flower, dinner plate, Sunflower, 11" d, $20.00.

Rooster, plate, 10" d 25.00
Rooster, saucer 5.00
Stoby Mug, #1681, Archie 185.00
Stoby Mug, #1676, Chief 235.00
Stoby Mug, #1673, Grand 215.00
Thistle, casserole, 6" d 20.00
Thistle, chop plate, 14½" d 35.00
Thistle, coffee pot, individual 40.00
Thistle, creamer, individual 10.00
Thistle, cup 5.00
Thistle, plate, 9" d 10.00
Thistle, salad bowl, 12" d 45.00
Town and Country, bowl, blue, 26 oz 30.00
Town and Country, creamer, blue 15.00
Town and Country, ladle 20.00
Town and Country, plate, 6" d, blue 6.00
Tulip, casserole, 8" d 40.00
Tulip, salad bowl, 11" d 45.00
Tulip, vegetable bowl, divided, round, 10" d 35.00
Wild Rose, casserole, 8" d 45.00
Wild Rose, creamer 15.00
Wild Rose, cruet 30.00
Wild Rose, eggcup 10.00
Wild Rose, pitcher, 6 oz 10.00
Wild Rose, plate, 10" d 12.00
Wild Rose, salad bowl 12" d 50.00

STAR TREK

Gene Roddenberry is the creative genius behind *Star Trek*. Desilu Company worked with Roddenberry to develop the Star Trek pilot. NBC turned down the first pilot episode in February 1965. Jeff Hunter starred as Captain Kirk. A second pilot was ordered. Hunter was unavailable. William Shatner was hired to play Captain Kirk. The second pilot, submitted to NBC in January 1966, was accepted and the series ordered.

Star Trek appeared on TV beginning in September 1966 and ending on June 3, 1969. The show's initial success was modest. NBC reversed a decision to cancel the show in 1968 when fans rose in protest. However, a move to Friday evenings in its final season spelled doom for the show in the ratings war.

NBC syndicated Star Trek. By 1978 it had been translated in 42 languages and shown in 51 countries. Over 125 stations carried it in the United States. There were more than 350 local fan clubs.

The first Star Trek convention was held in 1972, drawing 3,000 fans. A dispute arose between the professional and fan managers of the convention which resulted in two separate conventions in 1974. Before long, dozens of individuals were organizing Star Trek conventions around the country.

In 1979 Paramount released *Star Trek: The Motion Picture*. Its success led to additional films and television series starring the crew of the *Enterprise*. In September 1987 *Star Trek: The Next Generation* was launched. *Deep Space Nine* and *Star Trek: Voyager* followed. The *Generations* movie appeared in 1994 and *First Contact* in 1996.

References: Sue Cornwell and Mike Kott, *Star Trek Collectibles, Fourth Edition*, House of Collectibles, 1996; Christine Gentry and Sally Gibson–Sowns, *Greenberg's Guide to Star Trek Collectibles, Vol. 1* (1991), *Vol. 2* (1992), *Vol. 3* (1992), Greenberg Books, Kalmbach Books; Jerry B. Snyder, *A Trekker's Guide to Collectibles With Values*, Schiffer Publishing, 1996.

Collectors' Clubs: International Federation of Trekkers, PO Box 3123, Lorain, OH 44052; Starfleet, PO Box 24052, Belleville, IL 62223; Star Trek: The Official Fan Club, PO Box 111000, Aurora, CO 80011.

Action Figure, Kirk, belt buckle, phaser, Star Trek: The
   Motion Picture, 1979, Mego, 12" h . . . . $ 45.00
Action Figure, Klingon, Star Trek: The Motion Picture,
   1979, Mego, 12" h 80.00
Action Figure, Spock, phaser, Star Trek III: The Search
   For Spock, Ertl, 1984, 3³/₄" h 15.00
Activity Book, Star Trek Action Toy Book, James
   Razzi, Random House, 1976 . . . . 15.00
Bank, hard vinyl, Captain Kirk, Play Pal, 1975, 11" h 75.00
Bank, plastic, Mr. Spock, Play Pal, 1975, 12" h 85.00
Book, *City on the Edge of Forever*, Fotonovel #1,
   Bantam, 1977 . . . . 10.00
Book, *I Am Not Spock*, Leonard Nimoy, Celestial
   Arts, 1975 . . . . 12.00
Book, *The Making Of Star Trek II*, Stephen Whitfield
   and Gene Roddenberry, Ballantine, 1968 . . . . 20.00
Book, *The Truth Machine*, C. Cerf and S. Lerner,
   Random House, 1977 . . . . 10.00
Book, *Trillions of Trilligs*, pop–up, Random House,
   1977, hardback 10.00
Brush and Comb Set, 6 x 3" brush, color transfer,
   clear plastic box, Gabil, 1977 . . . . 35.00
Buckle, Kirk and Spock, brass, enamel trim, 1979 . . . . 10.00
Calendar, 1973, color television stills, Lincoln
   Enterprises 15.00
Calendar, 1976, Kirk and Spock cov, color stills
   inside, Ballantine Books, 1976 . . . . 40.00
Clock, wall, red 20th Anniversary logo, white ground,
   Official Star Trek Fan Club, 1986. . . . . 35.00

Birthday Card, punch–out Captain Kirk, Random House, 1976, 5 x 10" folded size, $15.00.

Coloring Book, The Uncharted World, Parkes Run
   Publishing, 1978 . . . . 6.00
Comic Book, Issue #2, Gold Key Comics, 1967–79 . . . . . . 85.00
Cookie Jar, *U.S.S. Enterprise* NCC–1701–A, Pfaltzgraff 30.00
Costume, knit, gold, Star Fleet Uniforms, 1970s 25.00
Costume, Klingon, Ben Cooper, 1975 . . . . 15.00
Costume, Spock, Collegeville, 1967 . . . . 25.00
Flashlight, phaser shape, battery operated,
   Azrak–Hamway, 1976 . . . . 25.00
Game, pinball, plastic, Azrak–Hamway, 12" 55.00
Game, Star Trek Game, Hasbro, 1974. . . . . 85.00
Game, Star Trek: The Motion Picture, Milton Bradley,
   1979 . . . . 85.00
Glass, *U.S.S. Enterprise* color illus, Dr. Pepper, 6¹/₄" h 75.00
Greeting Card, birthday, Kirk and Spock, "Fire all
   phasers...Fire all photon torpedoes...What the
   heck. It's your Birthday!," California Dreamers,
   1985 . . . . 2.00
Jacket, lightweight, silver Star Trek: The Motion
   Picture insignia, D. D. Bean & Sons, 1979. . . . . 75.00
Jigsaw Puzzle, Star Trek: The Motion Picture, 551 pcs,
   Aviva, 1979, 18 x 24". 25.00
Keychain, *Enterprise*, oval blue background, Aviva,
   1979 . . . . 3.50
Lunch Box, plastic, rectangular, Aladdin, 1978 . . . . 65.00
Mirror, metal, black and white crew photo on back,
   2 x 3", 1966. . . . . 3.50
Mobile, *Starship Enterprise*, paper, orig envelope. 35.00
Mug, ceramic, molded and glazed Kirk face ext, blue
   int, film logo on back, Image Products, 6" h 165.00
Pennant, felt, "Paramount Pictures Star Trek
   Adventure, Universal Studios Tour," multicolored,
   Enterprise and planet, 9 x 12¹/₂" 10.00
Plate, Beam Us Down Scotty, Hamilton/Ernst, 1986,
   8¹/₂" d 45.00
Playing Cards, Star Trek: The Motion Picture, Aviva,
   1979 . . . . 20.00
Program, 1973 International Convention. 60.00
Trading Cards, complete set of 88, 1979 . . . . 35.00

STAR WARS

Star Wars: A New Hope, George Lucas' 1977 movie epic, changed the history of film making. Unable to buy the rights to make Flash Gordon, Lucas decided to write his own fantasy adventure. After being turned down by Universal, Lucas received support from Twentieth Century Fox.

Luke Skywalker, Princess Leia, Hans Solo, Chewbacca, Ben (Obi–Wan) Kenobi, Darth Vadar, R2–D2, and C–3PO have become cultural icons. Their adventures in the *Star Wars* trilogy that includes *The Empire Strikes Back* (1980) and *The Return of the Jedi* (1983) were as eagerly followed throughout their 20th anniversary re–release in 1997 as they were when they first appeared on the silver screen.

Much of the success of the *Star Wars* trilogy is credited to the special effects created by Lucas' Industrial Light and Magic Company. John Williams' score and Ben Burtt's sound effects also contributed. Twentieth Century Fox granted a broad license to the Kenner Toy Company of Cincinnati. Approximately 80% of *Star Wars* merchandise sold in Canada and the United States is made by Kenner. Almost every Kenner product was available in England, Europe, and other English–speaking countries through Palitoy of London.

The *Star Wars* trilogy actually is Chapters IV, V, and VI of a nine–part saga. Filming of Chapter I currently is underway. Fans eagerly await seeing what Lucas has in store for them next in "A Long Time Ago In a Galaxy Far Far Away..."

The logo on the box is a good dating tool. Licensing rights associated with the release of *Star Wars* was retained by Twentieth Century Fox. Lucasfilm Ltd. owns the licensing rights to the sequels and regained the right to the *Stars War* name before releasing *The Empire Strikes Back.*

In January 1987 Star Tours opened at Disneyland in California. Additional *Star Wars* theme rides are located at Tokyo Disneyland and Disney–MGM Studio Tour at Walt Disney World.

Reference: Stephen J. Sansweet, *Star Wars: From Concept to Screen to Collectible,* Chronicle Books, 1992.

Collectors' Club: Star Wars Collectors Club, 20201 Burnt Tree Ln, Walnut, CA 91789.

Action Figure, Chewbacca, Kenner, MIP . . . . $ 60.00
Action Figure, Darth Vader, Kenner, MIP 40.00
Action Figure, Luke Skywalker X–wing Pilot, Kenner, 1978–79, MIP 60.00
Action Figure, Princess Leia Organa, Kenner, 1977–79, MIP 30.00
Activity Book, Luke Skywalker's Activity Book, Random House 8.00
Alarm Clock, C–3PO and R2–D2, talking, Bradley, 1980 . . . . 30.00
Alarm Clock, Star Wars/Empire Strikes Back, talking, Bradley Time 40.00
Bank, ceramic, R2–D2 . . . . 30.00
Bookmark, #3, Princess Lela, Random House 6.00
Bowl, 16 oz, Deka Plastics 8.00
Buckle, brass, oval, Darth Vader bust 20.00
Bumper Sticker, Star Wars 10th Anniversary Convention, gold foil 1.50
Cake Pan, R2–D2, Wilton 12.00
Calendar, 1978, Star Wars 10.00

Card Game, Ewoks Paw Pals, Parker Brothers 4.00
Coloring Book, Return of the Jedi: The Max Rebo Band, Kenner 2.50
Comic Book, Star Wars Annual, #1, Marvel, 1979 . . . . 2.50
Doll, plush, Princess Kneesaa, Kenner, 1979 . . . . 15.00
Figurine, Jabba the Hutt, Sigma 40.00
Figurine, Luke Skywalker, Sigma 20.00
Greeting Card, C–3PO and R2–D2 Christmas shopping, 1978 . . . . 10.00
Hat, Yoda, with ears 15.00
Jacket, windbreaker, quilted, red, white trim, "Darth Vader Lives" patch 10.00
Jewelry, earrings, C–3PO, clip–on 8.00
Keychain, metal, Star Wars: Stormtrooper, Weingeroff Enterprises 8.00
Lunch Box, plastic, red, Darth Vader and Droids 25.00
Mask, Darth Vader helmet, Don Post Studios, 1977 . . . . . . 90.00
Mask, plastic, Chewbacca, Ben Cooper 5.00
Mask, rubber, Yoda, Ben Cooper 15.00
Model, plastic, Luke Skywalker's X–wing fighter 25.00
Music Box, Wicket and Kneesaa, Sigma 45.00
Paint By Number Set, Ewoks: Wicket and Baga 10.00
Paperweight, plastic, Darth Vader hologram, Third Dimension Arts 25.00
Patch, cloth, Brotherhood of Jedi Knights, 3½" d 10.00
Play–Doh Set, Attack the Death Star, Kenner 30.00
Playset, Death Star Space Station, Kenner, complete 65.00
Record, *Star Wars Original Soundtrack: John Williams and London Symphony,* 2 records, 2 sleeves, liner note insert, poster, 20th Century Records 20.00
Storage Case, vinyl, Star Wars 8.00
Switch Plate Cover, Darth Vader Switcheroo, Kenner 20.00
Tankard, Chewbacca, California Originals, 1977–78 . . . . . 50.00
Toothbrush, Empire Strikes Back, battery operated, Kenner 30.00
Toy, Han Solo Laser Pistol, 1977 . . . . 50.00
Toy, Talking R2–D2, radio–controlled, Kenner 55.00
Underwear, Chewbacca, Underoos 12.00
Wallet, vinyl, Droids 10.00
Watch, digital, black Star Wars logo, silver face plate, black vinyl band, R2–D2 and Darth Vader on opposite sides, Texas Instruments 65.00

Playset, Creature Cantina Action Playset, #39120, Kenner, 14¼" l, 8" w, 3½" h, MIP, $50.00.

STEIFF

Giegen on the Benz, Bad Wurtemburg, Germany, is the birthplace and home of Steiff. In the 1880s, Margarette Steiff, a clothing manufacturer, made animal–theme pincushions for her nephews and their friends. Fritz, Margarette's brother, took some to a county fair and sold them all. In 1893 an agent representing Steiff appeared at the Leipzig Toy Fair.

It was Margarette's nephew, Richard, who suggested Steiff make a small bear with movable head and joints. The bear appears for the first time in Steiff's 1903 catalog. The bear was an instant success. An American buyer ordered 3,000 of them. It was first called the "teddy" bear in the 1908 catalog.

In 1905 the famous "button in the ear" was added to Steiff toys. The first buttons were small tin circles with the name in raised block letters. The familiar script logo was introduced in 1932, about the same time a shiny, possibly chrome, button was first used. Brass ear buttons date after 1980.

The earliest Steiff toys were made entirely of felt. Mohair plush was not used until 1903. When fabrics were in scarce supply in World War I and World War II, other materials were used. None proved successful.

By 1903–04 the Steiff catalog included several character dolls. The speedway monkey on wooden wheels and information touting prizes won at the 1904 St. Louis World's Fair and the 1910 Brussels's World Fair appeared in the 1913 catalog. Character dolls were discontinued in the mid–1910s. Cardboard tags were added to the chests of animals in the late 1920s. Teddy Babies were introduced in 1929.

Steiff's popularity increased tremendously following World War II. A line of miniatures was introduced. After a period of uncertainty in the 1970s, due in part to currency fluctuation, Steiff enjoyed a renaissance when it introduced its 1980 Limited Edition "Papa" Centennial Bear. More than 5,000 were sold in the United States. Steiff collectors organized. A series of other limited edition pieces followed. Many credit the sale of the "Papa" Bear with creating the teddy bear craze that swept across America in the 1980s.

References: Jurgen and Marianne Cieslik, *Button In Ear: The History of Teddy Bear and His Friends,* distributed by Theriault's, 1989; Margaret Fox Mandel, *Teddy Bears and Steiff Animals* (1984, 1997 value update), *Second Series* (1987, 1996 value update), Collector Books; Margaret Fox Mandel, *Teddy Bears, Annalee Animals & Steiff Animals, Third Series,* Collector Books, 1990, 1996 value update; Linda Mullins, *Teddy Bear & Friends Price Guide, Fourth Edition,* Hobby House Press, 1993; Christel and Rolf Pistorius, *Steiff: Sensational Teddy Bear, Animals & Dolls,* Hobby House Press, 1991.

Collectors' Clubs: Steiff Club USA, 225 Fifth Ave, Ste 1033, New York, NY 10010; Steiff Collectors Club, PO Box 798, Holland, OH 43528.

Note: Refer to Stuffed Toys and Teddy Bears for listings on other stuffed animals.

Bat, 2 pc, 1960 . . . . **$ 200.00**
Bulldog, mohair, 1960s, 6" h. **40.00**
Camel, raised script button, 1950s, 11" h **200.00**
Cat, mohair, green plastic eyes, jointed head and
    legs, c1950, 5¼" h. **50.00**

Lion, growler, ear button, 62" l, 36" h, $550.00.

Chimpanzee, dark brown mohair, tan felt face, ears,
    hands, and feet, 1950s, 9⅝" h seated **115.00**
Dachshund, black and brown wool, fully jointed,
    black shoe button eyes, embroidered nose, mouth,
    and claws, c1930, 18" l including tail **350.00**
Donkey, plush, glass eyes, ear button, 1960s, 8" h. **60.00**
Elephant, gray mohair, plastic tusks, red felt blanket
    and bells, 1959–60, 7" h. **150.00**
Fox Terrier, white mohair, black and brown markings,
    6½" h **75.00**
Frog, mohair, 1950s, 4" h. **60.00**
Goat, frosted brown mohair, black felt horns,
    1950–60, 6" h **75.00**
Groundhog, mohair, 1950s, 5" h **50.00**
Hen, gold and black spotted feathers, yellow plush
    head, felt tail, black button eyes, c1949, 7" h **75.00**
Koala Bear, mohair, glass eyes, ear button, 1960s,
    8" h. **85.00**
Lamb, pul toy, curly mohair coat, glass eyes, felt face
    and legs, steel frame and wheels, missing ear but-
    ton, c1920, 20" l, 15¾" h **750.00**
Mickey Mouse, felt, applied leatherette eyes, painted
    features, green shorts, yellow gloves, orange shoes,
    ear button tag, and tail missing, 1930s, 5" h **800.00**
Mickey Mouse, velveteen, applied leatherette eyes,
    painted features, red shorts, yellow gloves, ginger
    shoes, ear button, tag, and tail missing, 1930s, 7" h . **1,150.00**
Opossum, Joggi, 5" l **45.00**
Pekingese, Pinky, mohair, 1960s, 6" l **50.00**
Squirrel, blonde mohair, fully jointed, black steel
    eyes with felt backing, emroidered nose, mouth,
    and claws, excelsior stuffing, 1920, 7½" h. **400.00**
Squirrel, rust–tipped mohair, fully jointed, ear button,
    1930s, 9" h **300.00**
Teddy Bear, blonde mohair, fully jointed, black bead
    eyes, embroidered nose and mouth, 3⅞" h **225.00**
Teddy Bear, long gold mohair, fully jointed, glass
    eyes, embroidered nose, mouth, and claws, felt
    pads, straw stuffing, ear button missing, 1950s,
    19½" h **500.00**

STEMWARE

Stemware refers to all drinking vessels, i.e. champagne glasses, cordials, footed and flat iced tea and juice glasses, water goblets, tumblers, etc. There are two basic types of stemware: (1) soda–based glass and (2) lead– or flint–based glass, also known as crystal.

Early glass was made from a soda–based formula, which was costly and therefore available only to the rich. In the mid–19th century, a soda–lime glass was perfected, which was lighter and less expensive, but lacked the clarity and brilliance of crystal glass. This advance made glassware available to the common man.

The pricipal ingredients of crystal are silica (sand), litharge (a fused lead monoxide), and potash or potassium carbonate. The exact formula differs from manufacturer to manufacturer and is a closely guarded secret. Crystal can be plain or decorated, hand blown or machine made. Its association with fine quality is assumed.

There are three basic methods used to make glass—free blown, mold blown, or pressed. Furthermore, stemware can be decorated in a variety of ways. It may be cut or etched, or the bowl, stem or both may be made of colored glass. The varieties are as endless as the manufacturers. A few of the most noteable manufacturers include Baccarat, Fostoria, Lenox, Orrefors, and Waterford.

References: Harry L. Rinker, *Stemware of the 20th Century: The Top 200 Patterns,* House of Collectibles, 1997.

Note: See individual manufacturer's categories for additional listings.

Baccarat, Capri, champagne, 5¼" h	$ 30.00
Baccarat, Capri, claret, 6" h	40.00
Baccarat, Capri, cordial, 3⅝" h	35.00
Baccarat, Capri, water goblet, 7¼" h	35.00
Baccarat, Massena, claret, 6⅜" h	70.00
Baccarat, Massena, fluted champagne, 8½" h	75.00
Baccarat, Massena, old fashioned, 3⅝" h	60.00
Baccarat, Massena, water goblet, high, 7½" h	80.00
Baccarat, Massena, water goblet, low, 7" h	70.00
Cambridge, Statuesque, brandy, royal blue bowl, 6" h	125.00
Cambridge, Statuesque, champagne, royal blue bowl, 7¼" h	125.00
Cambridge, Statuesque, claret, royal blue bowl 7⅝" h	125.00
Cambridge, Statuesque, cordial, royal blue bowl, 5¾" h	450.00
Cambridge, Statuesque, cocktail, round royal blue bowl, 6⅜" h	100.00
Cambridge, Statuesque, cocktail, tulip–shaped royal blue bowl, 6½" h	425.00
Cambridge, Statuesque, cocktail, v–shaped royal blue bowl, 6⅜" h	400.00
Cambridge, Statuesque, hock, royal blue bowl, 7¾" h	350.00
Cambridge, Statuesque, sauterne, royal blue bowl, 6½" h	325.00
Cambridge, Statuesque, water goblet, royal blue bowl, 9½" h	150.00
Cambridge, Statuesque, wine, royal blue bowl, 6½" h	250.00

Duncan & Miller, Canterbury, champagne, 4¼" h	8.00
Duncan & Miller, Canterbury, claret, 5" h	15.00
Duncan & Miller, Canterbury, cocktail, 4¼" h	8.00
Duncan & Miller, Canterbury, cordial	10.00
Duncan & Miller, Canterbury, iced tea, ftd, 6¼" h	10.00
Duncan & Miller, Canterbury, juice, ftd, 4¼" h	8.00
Duncan & Miller, Canterbury, old fashioned, 3¼" h	7.00
Duncan & Miller, Canterbury, oyster cocktail, 4" h	8.00
Duncan & Miller, Canterbury, tumbler, 3¾" h	5.00
Duncan & Miller, Canterbury, tumbler, 6¼" h	8.00
Duncan & Miller, Canterbury, water goblet, 6" h	8.00
Duncan & Miller, Canterbury, wine	15.00
Duncan & Miller, Teardrop, champagne, 5" h	15.00
Duncan & Miller, Teardrop, cocktail, 4½" h	15.00
Duncan & Miller, Teardrop, iced tea, ftd, 6" h	17.00
Duncan & Miller, Teardrop, juice, ftd, 4" h	12.00
Duncan & Miller, Teardrop, sherbet, 2¼" h	12.00
Duncan & Miller, Teardrop, tumbler, ftd, 5" h	12.00
Duncan & Miller, Teardrop, water goblet, 7¼" h	15.00
Gorham, Florentine, champagne, 5⅜" h	30.00
Gorham, Florentine, fluted champagne, 8½" h	38.00
Gorham, Florentine, iced tea, ftd	35.00
Gorham, Florentine, water goblet	35.00
Gorham, Florentine, wine	38.00
Gorham, King Edward, brandy	20.00
Gorham, King Edward, fluted champagne, 7⅜" h	18.00
Gorham, King Edward, iced tea, ftd, 7⅛" h	18.00
Gorham, King Edward, water goblet, 7⅛" h	15.00
Gorham, King Edward, wine, 6" h	18.00
Lenox, Antique, champagne, blue, 5" h	10.00
Lenox, Antique, champagne, clear, 5" h	15.00
Lenox, Antique, highball, clear, 5" h	17.00
Lenox, Antique, iced tea, blue, 6⅝" h	12.00
Lenox, Antique, iced tea, clear, 6¾" h	17.00
Lenox, Antique, juice, clear, 6" h	15.00
Lenox, Antique, old fashioned, clear, 3⅜" h	17.00
Lenox, Antique, water goblet, blue, 6¾" h	12.00
Lenox, Antique, water goblet, clear, 6¾" h	15.00
Lenox, Antique, wine, blue, 5" h	12.00
Lenox, Antique, wine, clear, 5" h	17.00
Lenox, Blue Mist, champagne, 5" h	8.00
Lenox, Blue Mist, fluted champagne	10.00
Lenox, Blue Mist, iced tea, 6⅜" h	12.00
Lenox, Blue Mist, water goblet, 7⅛" h	12.00
Lenox, Blue Mist, wine, 6¼" h	12.00
Lenox, Castle Garden, champagne	22.00
Lenox, Castle Garden, fluted champagne	25.00
Lenox, Castle Garden, iced tea, 6⅝" h	25.00
Lenox, Castle Garden, water goblet, 7⅝" h	22.00
Lenox, Castle Garden, wine, 6¾" h	25.00
Lenox, Moonspun, champagne	22.00
Lenox, Moonspun, fluted champagne, 7⅝" h	25.00
Lenox, Moonspun, iced tea, 6¼" h	25.00
Lenox, Moonspun, water goblet, 7⅛" h	20.00
Lenox, Moonspun, wine, 6⅜" h	22.00
Lenox, Windswept, champagne	12.00
Lenox, Windswept, fluted champagne, 9½" h	12.00
Lenox, Windswept, highball, 6" h	8.00
Lenox, Windswept, iced tea, 8¼" h	15.00
Lenox, Windswept, water goblet, 8⅝" h	12.00
Mikasa, Versailles, champagne, 6" h	17.00

Orrefors, Illusion, fluted champagne,
8¹/₂" h, $18.00.

Mikasa, Versailles, fluted champagne **17.00**
Mikasa, Versailles, cordial, 5¹/₄" h **15.00**
Mikasa, Versialles, iced tea, 7" h **20.00**
Mikasa, Versailles, old fashioned, 3¹/₂" h **17.00**
Mikasa, Versailles, water goblet, 8" h **17.00**
Mikasa, Versailles, wine, 71/8" h **20.00**
Orrefors, Illusion, champagne, 5¹/₄" h **15.00**
Orrefors, Illusion, claret, 7¹/₄" h **18.00**
Orrefors, Illusion, cordial, 5" h **15.00**
Orrefors, Illusion, iced tea, ftd, 9³/₈" h **18.00**
Orrefors, Illusion, wine, 6¹/₂" h **17.00**
Orrefors, Rhapsody, champagne, clear, 5³/₈" h **15.00**
Orrefors, Rhapsody, champagne, smoke, 5³/₈" h **12.00**
Orrefors, Rhapsody, claret, clear, 6" h **20.00**
Orrefors, Rhapsody, claret, smoke, 6" h. **17.00**
Orrefors, Rhapsody, cocktail, smoke, 4¹/₈" h **12.00**
Orrefors, Rhapsody, cordial, clear, 4¹/₄" h **17.00**
Orrefors, Rhapsody, cordial, smoke, 4¹/₄" h **12.00**
Orrefors, Rhapsody, double old fashioned, smoke, 3¹/₂" h . **12.00**
Orrefors, Rhapsody, iced tea, clear **20.00**
Orrefors, Rhapsody, iced tea, smoke **18.00**
Orrefors, Rhapsody, old fashioned, smoke, 3¹/₄" h **12.00**
Orrefors, Rhapsody, sherry, smoke, 5" h **12.00**
Orrefors, Rhapsody, water goblet, clear, 7¹/₄" h **20.00**
Orrefors, Rhapsody, water coblet, smoke, 7³/₈" h **17.00**
Orrefors, Rhapsody, wine, clear, 5¹/₄" h **17.00**

STEUBEN GLASS

After a distinguished career as a glass designer and educator in
England, Frederick Carder (1863–1963) and Thomas Hawkes,
president of T. G. Hawkes and Company, founded the Steuben
Glass Works in 1903. Initially Steuben made blanks for Hawkes.
The company also made Art Nouveau ornamental and colored
glass. Steuben Glass had trouble securing raw materials during
World War I. In 1918 Corning purchased Steuben Glass from
Carder and Hawkes. Carder became art director at Corning.

Carder created one innovative design after another, some
remaining in production for less than a year. Aurene, an iridescent

glassware produced between 1904 and 1930, Jade Glass, Rouge
Flambé, and a host of transparent colored glass ranging from
Bristol Yellow to Wisteria are only a few of Carder's contributions.

Steuben experienced numerous financial difficulties in the
1920s, reorganizing several times. When Corning threatened to
close its Steuben division, Arthur Houghton, Jr., led the move to
save it. Steuben Glass Incorporated was established. John Monteith
Gates became director of design. He hired Sidney Waugh, a sculptor, as the principal designer. All earlier glass formulas were abandoned. The company concentrated on producing crystal products.

Although retiring in 1933, Carder continued to work privately at
a studio at Steuben. He conducted glass experiments and produced several Art Deco pieces. Carder closed his workshop in
1959.

In 1937 Steuben produced the first in a series of crystal pieces
featuring engraved designs from famous artists such as Thomas
Benton, Salvador Dali, Henri Matisse, Isamu Noguchi, and Grant
Wood. Although production was cut back during World War II,
Steuben emerged in the post–war period as a major manufacturer
of crystal products from presentation pieces to utilitarian wares
such as cocktail shakers and decanters. The company's first crystal
animals were introduced in 1949. Special series incorporating the
works of Asian and British painters and a group of 31 Collector's
pieces, each an interpretation of a poem commissioned by
Steuben, were produced during the 1950s and 60s.

Reference: Kenneth Wilson, *American Glass 1760–1930: The
Toledo Museum of Art,* 2 vols., Hudson Hills Press and The Toledo
Museum of Art, 1994.

Basket, Aurene, cobalt blue, folded rim, berry prunts
  on handle, 11" h . . . . **$ 1,850.00**
Bowl, Nedra, etched Art Deco floral design, textured
  etched ground, Carder, 8¹/₄" d **1,275.00**
Bowl and Underplate, Celeste blue, optic ridged and
  smooth, fleur de lis design, price for set of 18 . . . . . . **1,000.00**
Cake Plate, Calcite Aurene, gold, iridescent, applied
  rope twist center handle, 11¹/₂" d **700.00**
Center Bowl, Calcite, Aurene int, blue, cupped
  pedestal foot, 14" d **700.00**
Center Bowl, Calcite, Aurene int, gold, flared rim,
  12" d **450.00**
Cologne, aurene, blue, conical form, cone stopper
  with dauber, 9³/₄" h **1,375.00**
Compote, Calcite, blue Aurene int, inward curved
  rim, 6¹/₄" h, 6" d **525.00**
Console Set, Jade, 3 pcs, 7³/₄" d compote with
  alabaster stem, 14¹/₄" h candlesticks with applied
  accoutrements, fleur de lis marks, Carder **1,500.00**
Fruit Bowl, Aurene, gold, cupped foot, mkd
  "Steuben," 19" d **200.00**
Goblet, Oriental Poppy, Optic Rib, opal and pink,
  green stem and disk foot, 8" h **1,000.00**
Lamp, Aurene, iridescent gold, domed shade with
  scalloped edge mkd "F. Carder Aurene," matching
  base, 21" h **3,325.00**
Lamp, Jade, vase shaped, green, etched chrysanthe-
  mum blossoms and leaves, lappet border, 2 gilt
  metal socket fittings, 22" h **1,275.00**
Posy Vase, Aurene, gold, iridescent platinum ruffled
  rim, mkd "Aurene 162," 3³/₈" h **425.00**

Vase, spiral design, fleur de lis mark, 11½" h, $275.00.

Bonds and stocks help spread financial risk. The New York Stock Exchange was founded in the late 18th century.

In the middle of the 19th century, engraving firms such as the American Bank Note Company and Rawdon, Wright & Hatch created a wide variety of financial instruments ranging from bank notes to stock certificates. Most featured one or more ornately engraved vignettes. While some generic vignettes were used repeatedly, vignettes often provided a detailed picture of a manufacturing plant or facility, product, or location associated with the company.

Stocks and bonds are collected primarily for their subject matter, e.g., automobile, mining, railroad, public utilities, etc. Date is a value factor. Pre–1850 stocks and bonds command the highest price provided they have nice vignettes. Stocks and bonds issued between 1850 and 1915 tend to be more valuable than those issued after 1920.

Before paying top dollar attempt to ascertain how many examples of the certificate you are buying have survived. The survival rate is higher than most realize. Unused stock and bond certificates are less desirable than issued certificates. Finally, check the signatures on all pre–1915 stocks. Many important personages served as company presidents.

References: Norman E. Martinus and Harry L. Rinker, *Warman's Paper*, Wallace–Homestead, Krause Publications, 1994; Gene Utz, *Collecting Paper: A Collector's Identification & Value Guide*, Books Americana, 1993.

Periodical: *Bank Note Reporter*, 700 E State St, Iola, WI 54990.

Collectors' Club: Bond and Share Society, 26 Broadway at Bowling Green, Rm 200, New York, NY 10004.

Sculpture, cat, crystal, engraved eyes, Heritage series, #8102, Donald Pollard design, mkd "Steuben," 8½" h 475.00
Sculpture, sailboat, crystal, prismatic enhancements, #8570, Peter Aldridge design, 1980s, 6¼" h 300.00
Sculpture, shooting star, crystal, faceted, stepped slate and brushed metal display base, orig velvet–lined red leather case, #1130, David Dowler design, 5¼" h. 975.00
Sherbet and Underplate, Oriental Poppy, Optic Rib, opal and pink, green foot, 2¼" h sherbet, 8¼" d plate 575.00
Vase, Aurene, gold, bulbous squat form, orange tone iridescence, 3 pulled elongated oval handles, mkd "Aurene 2706," 4" h 1,150.00
Vase, Aurene, blue, 10–ribbed flared body, green striped base, mkd "Steuben," 5⅜" h 650.00
Vase, Aurene, gold, trumpet form, flared rim, 10 ribs, mkd "Steuben," 5½" h 500.00
Vase, Aurene, blue, hexagonal angular body, disk base, mkd "Steuben Aurene 6241," 8" h 700.00
Vase, Jade, green and alabaster, applied disk and folded edge base, fleur de lis mark, 6¼" h 250.00
Vase, Oriental Poppy, Optic Rib, opalescent pink, satin iridescent finish, Carder, 7" h 1,850.00

STOCKS & BONDS

A stock certificate is a financial document that shows the amount of capital on a per share basis that the owner has invested in a company. Gain is achieved through dividends and an increase in unit value. A bond is an interest bearing certificate of public or private indebtedness. The interest is generally paid on a fixed schedule with the principal being repaid when the bond is due.

Joint stock companies were used to finance world exploration in the 16th, 17th, and 18th centuries. Several American colonies received financial backing from joint stock companies.

Aviation Corp, engraved, U.S. map vignette, 1940s .... $ 12.00
Belt RR & Stock Yard, black and white, vignette of train at station, 1930s 20.00
Black Mountain Railroad, Kentucky Short Line Railroad, $1,000 gold bond, 40 coupons, blue border, 1921 .... 30.00
Chicago & Eastern Illinois Railway, engraved, green, vignette of large old train, 1924 .... 12.00
Cincinnati, New Orleans & Texas Pacific RR, gray, ornate, 1920s 20.00
Commonwealth & Southern Corp, engraved, blue, vignette of man and seated woman looking out over industiral factories, 1934 .... 3.50
Corona Typewriter Co, blue border, early typewriter vignette, 1920s 40.00
Denver & Rio Grande Western RR, engraved, orange, $1,000 bond, coupons, vignette of 2 trains at station, 1924 .... 125.00
Glenmore Productions, Inc, brown border, eagle vignette, issued to and sgd by Billy Rose, 1948–50 ... 165.00
Green Bay & Western RR, engraved, brown, vignette of man on horseback watching train crossing bridge, 1920s 20.00
Gulf, Mobile & Ohio RR, engraved, blue, train vignette 7.00
Key System Transit Co, San Francisco, orange, large, vignette of seated lady and shield, 1920s 165.00
Lexington Union Station Co, Kentucky, brown, c1920s–30s 12.00

Market Street Railway, San Francisco, engraved, vignette of eagle perched on rock, 1920s **10.00**

Missouri, Kansas & Texas RR, vignette of surveyor and train at station, 1920s. **20.00**

National City Bank of New York, engraved, olive, vignette of man, Indian, and shield, 1929 . . . . **15.00**

New Orleans Great Northern RR, engraved, blue, 1933 . . . . **28.00**

New York Railways Corp, engraved, pink, trolley car vignette, 1920–35 . . . . **18.00**

Pan Motor Co, green, 3 vignettes including Pan automobile, 1921 . . . . **265.00**

Pennsylvania–Ohio Electric, engraved, green, vignette of standing goddess, generator, and trolley car, 1920s **8.00**

Philadelphia Traction Co, engraved, gray, vignette of trolleys and city scene, 1920s. **30.00**

Philip Morris, Inc, coupons, orange, seated woman vignette, 1959 . . . . **25.00**

Seatrain Lines, Inc, engraved, vignette of man, company symbol, and 2 world globes **3.50**

Southern Railway Co, engraved, purple, vignette of trains and industrial complex, 1920s–30s **40.00**

Sunnyside Lead–Silver Mining Co, Nevada, orange, eagle vignette, 1928. . . . . **20.00**

Tom Reed Gold Mines, Arizona, brown, 3 mining vignettes, 1920s **20.00**

Virginia Transit Co, engraved, green, 1940s. **15.00**

Western Apex Mining, Oatman, AZ, orange, seated woman vignette, 1920s **25.00**

STUFFED TOYS

The bear is only one of dozens of animals that have been made into stuffed toys. In fact, Margarette Steiff's first stuffed toy was not a bear but an elephant. The stuffed toy animal was a toy/department store fixture by the early 1920s.

Many companies, e.g., Ideal and Knickerbocker, competed with Steiff for market share. In the period following World War II, stuffed toys became a favorite prize of games of chance found in carnivals, fairs, and vacation spots. Most of these stuffed toys were inexpensive imports from China and Taiwan.

Many characters from Disney animated cartoons, e.g., *Jungle Book* and *The Lion King,* appear as stuffed toys. A major collection could be assembled focusing solely on Disney licensed products. The 1970s stuffed toys of R. Dakin Company, San Francisco, are a modern favorite among collectors.

The current Beanie Baby craze has focused interest on the miniature stuffed toy. As with any popular craze, the market already is flooded with Beanie Baby imitations. The Beanie Baby market is highly speculative. Expect a major price collapse in a relatively short period of time.

References: Dee Hockenberry, *Collectible German Animals Value Guide: 1948–1968,* Hobby House Press, 1988; Carol J. Smith, *Identification & Price Guide To Winnie The Pooh Collectibles, I* (1994), *II* (1996), Hobby House Press.

Note: See Steiff and Teddy Bears for additional listings.

Dr. Seuss, The Cat in the Hat, Coleco, plush, 1983, 25" h, $20.00.

Alvin the Chipmunk, Knickerbocker, vinyl head, 1963, 13½" h. . . . . **$ 30.00**

Bugs Bunny, Mattel, talking, gray and white, molded vinyl face and hands, pull–string, 1962, 27" h **75.00**

Bullwinkle, Mattel, talking, plastic head and antlers, 1972, 11" h **25.00**

Casper, Knickerbocker, musical, blue vest and cap, 1960, 11" h **25.00**

Casper, Mattel, talking, hard plastic face, pull–string, 1961, 15" h **125.00**

Cecil, Mattel, posable, green, blue eyelashes and tail fins, moving eyes, 1961, 24" l. **30.00**

Curious George, Knickerbocker, talking, red shirt and cap, 16" h **20.00**

Deputy Dawg, Ideal, soft vinyl head, black plastic hat, metal badge, 1960s, 14" h **55.00**

Dr. Seuss Hedwig Bird, Mattel, talking, molded vinyl beak, pull–string, 1970, 14" l **75.00**

King Kong, Mattel, talking, vinyl Bobby Bond figure, 1966, 24" h **125.00**

Magilla Gorilla, Ideal, posable, soft vinyl face, 1964, 8" h **35.00**

Pixie and Dixie, Knickerbocker, pair, vests, bowties, and whiskers, 1960, 10" h **50.00**

Porky Pig, Mattel, talking, vinyl head, jacket, cap, and bowtie, 1960s, 17" h **45.00**

Quick Draw McGraw, Knickerbocker, soft vinyl face, red cowboy hat, polka dot neckerchief, plastic gun belt, c1960, 16" h **100.00**

Reddy, Knickerbocker, hard plastic face, red collar with "Reddy" in white, 1960, 15" h. **75.00**

Rin Tin Tin, Smile Novelty Toy Co, rubber head, plastic collar, 1959, 4 x 7 x11". **75.00**

Scooby Doo, J. S. Sutton and Sons, orange and brown, 1970, 14"h. **25.00**

Tazmanian Devil, Mighty Star Ltd, Montreal, brown and gray, 1971, 13" h **20.00**

Rajah, Disney's *Aladdin* movie, Mattel, $10.00.

Woody Woodpecker, Mattel, talking, vinyl head, corduroy body, felt hands and feet, 1960s, 18" h **75.00**
Yogi Bear, Knickerbocker, vinyl face, 1959, 10" h **25.00**

SUPER HEROES

Early super heroes such as Batman and Superman were individuals who possessed extraordinary strength and/or cunning, yet led normal lives as private citizens. These super heroes dominated the world of comic books, movie serials, newspaper cartoon strips, radio, and television from the late 1930s through the end of the 1950s. Captain Marvel, Captain Midnight, The Green Lantern, and Wonder Woman are other leading examples of the genre.

The 1960s introduced a new form of super hero, the mutant. The Fantastic Four (Mr. Fantastic, The Human Torch, The Invisible Girl, and The Thing) initiated an era that included a host of characters ranging from the members of the Justice League of America to The Hulk. Spiderman is perhaps the best known of this group. Most mutant super heroes are found only in comic books. A few such as The Hulk and Spiderman achieved fame on television.

In the 1990s comic book storytellers and movie directors began blurring the line between these two distinct groups of super heroes. The death of Superman and his resurrection as a person more attune with the mutant super heroes and the dark approach of the Batman movies are two classic examples.

Super heroes are a popular product license. Collectors prefer three–dimensional objects over two–dimensional material. Carefully research an object's date. Age as a value factor plays a greater role in this category than it does in other collectibles categories.

Reference: Bill Bruegman, *Superhero Collectibles: A Pictorial Price Guide*, Toy Scouts, 1996.

Collectors' Clubs: Air Heroes Fan Club, 19205 Seneca Ridge Club, Gaithersburg, MD 20879; Batman TV Series Fan Club, PO Box 107, Venice, CA 90291; Captain Action Collectors Club, PO Box 2095, Halesite, NY 11743.

Note: For additional listings see Action Figures, Comic Books, and Model Kits.

Aquaman, game, Justic League of America, Hasbro, 1967 . . . . **$ 175.00**
Aquaman, Halloween costume, Ben Cooper, 1967 . . . . . **200.00**
Aquaman, jigsaw puzzle, Whitman, 1967 . . . . **40.00**
Batman, Batcave, Mego, 1980 . . . . **35.00**
Batman, Batchute, CDC, 1966 . . . . **38.00**
Batman, mask, rubber, full head, ©DC Comics 1989, 21" h **45.00**
Batman, night light, plastic, figural, Snapit, ©National Periodical Publication 1966 . . . . **25.00**
Batman, pinball game, plastic and litho tin, Marx, ©National Periodical Publications, 1966, 10 x 21½ x 1" **100.00**
Batman, Robin doll, Mego, 1974, 7½" h **10.00**
Batman, sponge, blue Batman, yellow ground, ©National Periodical Publications, 1966, 5" d **20.00**
Batman, stationery, bond paper, purple bat symbol and trim, yellow ground, purple "Bat Mail" symbol on envelopes, 5 sheets and envelopes, c1966 . . . . . **20.00**
Captain America, badge, Sentinels of Liberty **325.00**
Captain America, coloring book, Whitman, 1966 . . . . . . **35.00**
Captain America, hand puppet, molded soft vinyl head, Imperial Toy Corp, ©Marvel Comics Group 1978 . . . . **15.00**
Captain America, iron–on transfer, Kirby Art, 1960s **10.00**
Captain Marvel, cereal bowl, plastic, white, "Captain Marvel, Shazam!," 1973 . . . . **30.00**
Captain Marvel, drinking glass, "Shazam," Pepsi Collector Series, 1978 . . . . **10.00**
Captain Marvel, iron–on transfer, "Shazam!," color, 1972–73, 8 x 10" **12.00**
Captain Marvel, jigsaw puzzle, Captain Marvel Rides the Engine of Doom, Fawcett Publications, 1941, 13 x 18" **150.00**
Captain Marvel, Little Golden Book, *A Circus Adventure*, Western Publishing, 1977 . . . . **5.00**
Captain Marvel, pencil clip, silvered brass, cream ground, red and blue portrait, "Captain Marvel, Shazam!," 1940s **75.00**

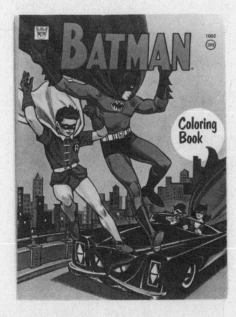

Batman, coloring book, Whitman, unused, 1974, 8 x 11", $18.00.

Captain Marvel, pennant, felt **100.00**

Captain Marvel, postcard, secret message, blue, dip in water to reveal message, 1940s, 3 x 5½" **75.00**

Captain Midnight, decoder, premium **85.00**

Captain Midnight, Flight Commander ring, eagle and shield on brass bands, wing and propeller design top, mkd "Captain Midnight Super code 3," c1940 . . . **175.00**

Captain Midnight, shoulder patch **40.00**

Captain Midnight, stamp album, Air Heroes, Skelly Oil premium **25.00**

Captain Midnight, whistle, plastic, dark blue, logo, code wheel, "Captain Midnight's SS 1947" **75.00**

Fantastic Four, drinking glass, 7–Eleven promo, 1977, 5½" h **10.00**

Flash, game, Justice League of America, Hasbro, 1967 . . . . **300.00**

Flash, ring, flasher, running and punching villain, 1960s **25.00**

Green Hornet, book, *Case of the Disappearing Doctor,* Whitman TV Edition series, 1966, 225 pgs. **10.00**

Green Hornet, coloring book, Watkins–Strathmore, ©1966, 8 x 11" **30.00**

Green Hornet, fork and spoon, silvered metal, lettering and Hornet on handle, Imeprial, c1966 . . . . **25.00**

Green Hornet, mug, white, color illus, 1966 . . . . **35.00**

Green Hornet, pinback button, © 1966 Greenway Productions, 4" d **50.00**

Green Hornet, record album, *The Horn Meets The Hornet,* Al Hirt, orig jacket **25.00**

Green Hornet, secret print putty, print book, and magic print paper, Colorforms, ©1966 . . . . **65.00**

Green Hornet, T–shirt, Hornet logo, 1966 . . . . **40.00**

Green Lantern, magazine, *Comic Crusader,* #10, Green Lantern cov, 1970 . . . . **30.00**

Incredible Hulk, gum card pack, 7 photo cards, 1 sticker, Lou Ferrigno photo wrapper, unopened, Topps, 1979 . . . . **8.00**

Incredible Hulk, paperback book, black and white reprints of early Hulk comics, 1966, 5 x 7" **18.00**

Incredible Hulk, poster, Marvel Comics, color, Jack Kirby illus, 1966, 28 x 42" **50.00**

Incredible Hulk, record album, 4 stories, Neal Admas cover art, Peter Pan, 1978 . . . . **8.00**

Marvel Comics Superheroes, lunch box, no thermos, Aladdin, 1976 . . . . **10.00**

Phantom, coloring book, Ottenheimer, 1965 . . . . . . **45.00**

Phantom, Halloween costume, Collegeville, 1956 . . . . . . **200.00**

Spiderman, bicycle siren, plastic, red and yellow, Empire Toys, ©Marvel Comics, 1978, 4" h **40.00**

Spiderman, doll, Knickerbocker, ©Marvel Comics, 1978, 20" h **20.00**

Spiderman, mask, Reed, 1978, 8 x 10", set of 4 . . . . **12.00**

Spiderman, paperback book, *The Amazing Spiderman Collector's Album,* Lancer Books, 1966, 4 x 7" **13.00**

Spiderman, poster puzzle, Aurora, 1974, 34 x 40 . . . . **8.00**

Supergirl, book, *The Supergirl Storybook,* G. P. Putnam's Sons, movie photos, 1984 . . . . **3.00**

Superheroes, postcard book, DC Comics, 1981 . . . . **10.00**

Superman, bank, dime register, metal, red, yellow, and blue, 1940s, 2 1/2" sq **85.00**

Wonder Woman, Peter Pan, book and record set, Wonder Woman vs The War God *and* Amazons From Space, *1977, 33⅓ rpm, 16 pgs, $15.00.*

Superman, drinking glass, "Superman in Action," ©National Periodical Publications, 1964, 4¼" h **50.00**

Superman, fork **20.00**

Superman, greeting card, Superman & Friends, 1978, set of 48 . . . . **50.00**

Superman, gym bag, vinyl, yellow and blue, red Superman and logo, DC Comics, 1971 . . . . **50.00**

Superman, hair brush, wood, red, white, and blue decal, 1940s, 2½ x 4½" **75.00**

Superman, hand puppet, Ideal, 1965 . . . . **30.00**

Superman, jigsaw puzzle, Superman surrounded by Brainiacs, Whitman, 1964 . . . . **30.00**

Superman, model, assembled and painted, MPC, 1984 . . . . **15.00**

Superman, paint book, *Superman to the Rescue,* Western Publishing, ©1980 DC Comics, 24 pgs **15.00**

Superman, pencil case, yellow vinyl, zipper closure, red and blue illus and logo, Standard Plastic Products, ©National Periodical Publications, 1966, 3½ x 8" **60.00**

Superman, pillow case, flying Superman saving Lois Lane, 1966 . . . . **40.00**

Superman, record player, 1978 . . . . **65.00**

Wonder Woman, card game, Russell's Mfg Co, 1977, 40 cards, 10 different illus, orig box **12.00**

Wonder Woman, planter, ceramic, 1978 . . . . **15.00**

Wonder Woman, Queen Hippolyte doll, Mego, 1976, 12" h **80.00**

Wonder Woman, wall hanging, pressed cardboard, color photo, 6½ x 9" **10.00**

Wonder Woman, wristwatch, gold–colored case, Dabs, © DC Comics, 1977 . . . . **75.00**

SWANKYSWIGS

Swankyswigs refer to decorated glass containers used as packaging for Kraft Cheese that doubled as kitchen juice glasses once the cheese was consumed. The earliest Swankyswigs date from the 1930s. They proved extremely popular during the Depression, adding a touch of brightness to the kitchen table and helping people forget the difficult times.

Initially designs were hand stenciled. Eventually machines were developed to apply the decoration. Kraft test marketed designs. As a result, some designs are very difficult to find. Unfortunately, Kraft does not have a list of all the designs it produced.

Production was discontinued briefly during World War II when the paint used for decoration was needed for the war effort. Cornflower No. 2 or Posy (1947), Forget–Me–Not (1948), and Tulip No. 3 (195) are several of the new patterns included after World War II ended. Bicentennial Tulip (1975) was the last Swankyswig pattern.

Beware of Swankyswig imitators dating from the 1970s and early 1980s. These come from other companies, including at least one Canadian firm. Cherry, Diamond over Triangle, Rooster's Head, Sportsman series, and Wildlife series are a few of the later themes. In order to be considered a Swankyswig, the glass has to be a Kraft product.

References: Gene Florence, *Collectible Glassware From The 40's, 50's, 60's: An Illustrated Value Guide, Third Edition,* Collector Books, 1996; Jan Warner, *Swankyswigs, A Pattern Guide Checklist, Revised,* The Daze, 1988, 1992 value update.

Collectors' Club: Swankyswig Club, 201 Alvena, Wichita, KS 67203.

Antique #1, blue, 1954	$ 3.00
Atlantic City, cobalt, 5" h	25.00
Bands, white, blue, blue, white, 1933	3.00
Bicentennial, yellow, 1938 type tulip, 1975	8.00
Bustling Betsy, brown, 1953	3.00
Carnival, fired–on orange, 1939	5.00
Checkerboard, white and blue, 1936	18.00
Circles, red, 1934	4.00
Daisy, red, green, white	3.00
Dots and Circles, green	3.50
Forget–Me–Not, yellow, 1948	3.00
Kiddie Kup, bird and elephant, red	2.00
Kiddie Kup, black, 1956	3.00
Lily of the Valley, red and black	10.00
Posy Pattern, jonquil, 1941	4.00
Posy Pattern, cornflower #2, light blue, 1947	3.00

Forget–Me–Not, royal blue, 1948, $3.00.

Sailboat #2, red, 1936	8.50
Stars, green, 1935	4.00
Stars, red, 1935	4.00
Tavern, silver	12.00
Texas Centennial, blue, 1936	8.50
Tulip #3, red, 1950	3.00
Tulips, bachelor's button, 1955	3.00
Tulips, blue, 1937	5.00

SWAROVSKI CRYSTAL

Daniel Swarovski founded D. Swarovski & Co. in Georgenthal, Bohemia, in 1895. Daniel learned the art of crystal production from his father and was instrumental in developing precise, automatic crystal cutting methods utilizing the water power found in the Tyrol region. Initially the company produced high quality abrasives, crystal stones for the costume jewelry industry, and optical items. The company continues to produce several accessory and jewelry lines including the inexpensive Savvy line and the high-end Daniel Swarovski boutique collection.

In 1977 Swarovski introduced a line of collectible figurines and desk items. A crystal mouse and a spiny crystal hedgehog were the first two figurines. Swarovski figurines have a 30 plus percent lead content. In 1987 the International Swarovski Collectors Society was formed. Swarovski produces an annual figurine available only to Society members. Every three years a new theme is introduced, e.g., "Mother and Child," three annual figures featuring a mother sea mammal and her offspring.

Initially Swarovski crystal figurines were marked with a block-style SC. In 1989 Swarovski began using a mark that included a swan. Swarovski was included in the mark on larger pieces. Pieces made for the Swarovski Collectors Society are marked with an SCS logo, the initials of the designer, and the year. The first SCS logo included an edelweiss flower above the SCS.

Regional issues are common. Some items were produced in two versions, one for Europe and one for the United States. Many items featuring a metal trim are available in either rhodium (white metal) or gold.

A Swarovski figurine is considered incomplete on the secondary market if it does not include its period box, product identification sticker, and any period paper work. Society items should be accompanied by a certificate of authenticity.

Today the Daniel Swarovski Corporation is headquartered in Zurich, Switzerland. Production and design is based in Wattens, Austria. Swarovski has manufacturing facilities in 11 countries, including a plant in Cranston, Rhode Island. The company employs more than 8,000 people worldwide.

Be alert to Swarovski imitations. These have a lower lead content, often contain flaws in the crystal, and lack the Swarovski logo.

Reference: Tom and Jane Warner, *Warner's Blue Ribbon Book on Swarovski Silver Crystal,* published by authors, 1994, revised 1995.

Periodical: *Swan Seekers News,* 9740 Campo Rd, Ste 134, Spring Valley, CA 91977.

Angel, 7475NR000009, retired 1/1/94	$ 125.00
Annual Edition, turtledoves #3, DO1X891, retired 12/31/89	850.00

Apple, Sparkling Fruit, 7476NR000001, retired
    12/31/96 . . . . **220.00**
Ashtray, 7461NR100, retired 1/1/91 . . . . **300.00**
Automobile, old timer, 7473NR000001, retired
    1/1/96 . . . . **195.00**
Bee, gold, 7553NR100, retired 1/1/89 . . . . **1,680.00**
Birthday Cake, SCS 003–0169678, retired 12/31/93 . . . . **140.00**
Blowfish, Under Water, large, 7644NR41, retired
    1/1/92 . . . . **150.00**
Butterfly, mini, 7671NR30, retired 1/1/89 . . . . **105.00**
Candleholder, global, large, 7600NR134, retired
    1/1/91 . . . . **90.00**
Candleholder, snowflake, 7600NR101, retired 1/1/82 . . . **130.00**
Chicken, mini, 7651NR20, retired, 1/1/89 . . . . **65.00**
Christmas Ornament, 1992, retired 12/31/92 . . . . **90.00**
Crystal City, town hall, 7474NR000027, retired
    12/31/94 . . . . **180.00**
Dumbo, 1988 special edition, large tusks and ears,
    7640NR35V5, retired 1/1/89 . . . . **4,200.00**
Frog, clear eyes, 7642NR48C, retired 1/1/92 . . . . **360.00**
Hedgehog, large, 7630NR50, retired 12/1/87 . . . . **155.00**
Lighter, 7500NR050, retired 1/1/82 . . . . **2,000.00**
Mallard, 7647NR80, retired, 12/31/94 . . . . **180.00**
Mouse, medium, 7631NR40, retired 1/1/89 . . . . **85.00**
Paperweight, atomic VM, 7454NR60087, retired
    7/1/85 . . . . **1,750.00**
Paperweight, 30mm round, 7404NR30, retired
    1/1/83 . . . . **90.00**
Partridge, 7625NR50, retired, 1/1/91 . . . . **150.00**
Penguin, Trimlite, medium, 72113 . . . . **300.00**
Pineapple, Sparkling Fruit, rhodium, large,
    7507NR105002, retired 1/1/87 . . . . **425.00**
Sali With Accordion, Julia's World, 9540NR000032,
    retired 1/1/91 . . . . **80.00**
Unicorn, Trimlite, 52501 . . . . **125.00**
Vase, Apple Blossom, ER1, Ebeling and Reuss **80.00**
Vase, 7511NR70, retired 1/1/91 . . . . **145.00**

SYRACUSE CHINA

Syracuse China traces its origins to W. H. Farrar who established a pottery in Syracuse, New York, in 1841. The plant moved from Genessee Street to Fayette Street in 1855 and operated as the Empire Pottery. The Empire Pottery became the Onondaga Pottery Company after a reorganization in 1871, retaining that name until 1966 when the company became the Syracuse China Company. Few noticed the change because Onondaga Pottery had marketed its dinnerware under a Syracuse China brand name since as early as 1879.

Onondaga introduced a high–fired, semi–vitreous ware in the mid–1880s that was guaranteed against crackling and crazing. In 1888 James Pass introduced Imperial Geddo, a translucent, vitrified china. By the early 1890s, the company offered a full line of fine china ware.

Onondaga made commercial as well as household china. In 1921 a new plant, devoted exclusively to commercial production, was opened. In 1959 Onondaga Pottery acquired Vandesca–Syracuse, Joliette, Quebec, Canada, a producer of vitrified hotel china. In 1984 Syracuse China absorbed the Mayer China Company.

After manufacturing fine dinnerware for 99 years, Syracuse China discontinued its household china line in 1970, devoting its production efforts exclusively to airline, commercial, hotel, and restaurant china.

References: Susan and Al Bagdade, *Warman's American Pottery and Porcelain,* Wallace–Homestead, Krause Publications, 1994; Harry L. Rinker, *Dinnerware of the 20th Century: The Top 500 Patterns,* House of Collectibles, 1997.

Bracelet, berry bowl, 5" d . . . . $ **10.00**
Barcelet, bread and butter plate, 6¼" d **5.00**
Bracelet, cream soup and saucer **25.00**
Bracelet, creamer **25.00**
Bracelet, cup and saucer, ftd **18.00**
Bracelet, dinner plate, 9¾" d **12.00**
Bracelet, luncheon plate, 9" d **10.00**
Bracelet, platter, oval, 14" l **40.00**
Bracelet, sugar bowl, cov **30.00**
Bracelet, vegetable bowl, oval, 10¼" l **35.00**
Coralbel, bread and butter plate, 6¼" d **5.00**
Coralbel, cake plate, handled, 10⅞" d **30.00**
Coralbel, cereal bowl, 6⅜" d **15.00**
Coralbel, chop plate, 12½" d **35.00**
Coralbel, dinner plate, 10¼" d **12.00**
Coralbel, gravy boat, attached underplate **35.00**
Coralbel, platter, 12¼" d **30.00**
Coralbel, salad plate, 8" d **8.00**
Coralbel, teapot **60.00**
Coralbel, vegetable bowl, 9" d **30.00**
Minuet, bread and butter plate, 6¼" d **8.00**
Minuet, cream soup bowl **25.00**
Minuet, creamer **20.00**
Minuet, dinner plate, 10⅝" d **15.00**
Minuet, gravy boat, attached underplate **60.00**
Minuet, platter, 16" d **65.00**
Minuet, soup bowl, 7⅝" d **18.00**
Minuet, sugar bowl, cov **30.00**
Stansbury, berry bowl, 5⅛" d **15.00**
Stansbury, bread and butter plate, 6½" d **5.00**
Stansbury, cereal bowl, 5" d **10.00**
Stansbury, creamer **15.00**
Stansbury, cup and saucer, ftd **20.00**
Stansbury, dinner plate, 10⅜" d **18.00**
Stansbury, gravy boat, attached underplate **45.00**
Stansbury, platter, 12⅛" d **30.00**
Stansbury, salad lpate, 8" d **12.00**
Stansbury, soup bowl, 8" d **12.00**
Stansbury, sugar, cov **20.00**
Stansbury, vegetable bowl, oval, 10⅝" l **30.00**

TAYLOR SMITH, & TAYLOR

Around 1900 Joseph G. Lee, W. L. Smith, John N. Taylor, W. L. Taylor, and Homer J. Taylor founded the firm that eventually became Taylor Smith, & Taylor. The Taylors purchased Lee's interests in 1903, only to sell their interests to the Smiths in 1906. The company's plant was located in Chester, West Virginia, the corporate offices in East Liverpool, Ohio.

Taylor Smith, & Taylor made a wide range of plain and painted semi–porcelain wares, e.g., dinnerware, hotel and restaurant ware, and toilet sets. Lu–Ray (introduced in 1930), Pebbleford, and Vistosa are three of the company's most popular dinnerware shapes. In the 1960s a line of cooking and oven ware was produced. Special commission work ranged from dinnerware premiums for Mother's Oats to Gigi and Holly Hobbie plates for American Greetings Corp.

Anchor Hocking purchased Taylor Smith, & Taylor in 1973. The plant closed in January 1982, the result of a depressed dinnerware market.

References: Susan and Al Bagdade, *Warman's American Pottery and Porcelain,* Wallace–Homestead, 1994; Harvey Duke, *The Official Identification and Price Guide to Pottery and Porcelain, Eighth Edition,* House of Collectibles, 1995; Kathy and Bill Meehan, *Collector's Guide To Lu–Ray Pastels: Identification and Values,* Collector Books, 1995.

Beverly, creamer	$ 5.00
Beverly, plate, 6¼" d	2.00
Beverly, platter, oval, 11½" l	10.00
Garland, cup	5.00
Garland, plate, 7" d	4.00
Garland, saucer	2.00
Golden Button, bread and butter plate	2.50
Golden Button, creamer	2.50
Golden Button, cup and saucer	5.00
Golden Button, platter, oval	3.00
Golden Button, salt and pepper shakers, pr	8.00
Golden Button, vegetable, cov	20.00
Laurel, casserole	20.00
Laurel, plate, 8½" d	4.00
Laurel, saucer	1.50
Laurel, sugar	8.00
Lu–Ray, bowl, 36's, windsor blue	22.00
Lu–Ray, bread and butter plate, 6" d, pink	4.00
Lu–Ray, chop plate, 14" d, surf green	20.00
Lu–Ray, cup, chatham gray	12.00
Lu–Ray, cup and saucer, demitasse, chatham gray	20.00
Lu–Ray, dinner plate, 10" d, persian cream	12.50
Lu–Ray, dinner service, 64 pcs	200.00
Lu–Ray, eggcup, persian cream	12.00
Lu–Ray, epergne, blue	95.00
Lu–Ray, grill plate, yellow	25.00
Lu–Ray, juice pitcher, windsor blue	35.00
Lu–Ray, nappy, pink	15.00
Lu–Ray, pitcher, ftd, sharon pink	60.00
Lu–Ray, plate, 8" d, sharon pink	15.00
Lu–Ray, plate, 8" d, windsor blue	12.50
Lu–Ray, plate, 9" d, sharon pink	8.00
Lu–Ray, platter, 12" l, surf green	10.00
Lu–Ray, relish, green	25.00
Lu–Ray, salad bowl, surf green	40.00
Lu–Ray, salt and pepper shakers, pr, Michigan decal	12.50
Lu–Ray, sugar, cov, demitasse, windsor blue	18.00
Lu–Ray, soup, flat, persian cream	15.00
Lu–Ray, soup, tab handles, sharon pink	18.00
Lu–Ray, teapot, sharon pink	50.00
Lu–Ray, vegetable dish, cov, oval, 10" l, windsor blue	12.50
Lu–Ray, water pitcher, pink	50.00
Marvel, cup	4.00
Marvel, eggcup	10.00
Marvel, salad bowl, 9½" d	15.00
Marvel, vegetable bowl, oval, 9¼" l	10.00
Paramount, butter pat	6.00
Paramount, casserole, ftd, rattan handle, 11 x 8¼"	20.00
Paramount, cup	4.00
Paramount, plate, 8" d	4.00
Pastoral, cup	4.00
Pastoral, saucer	1.50
Pebbleford, butter, ¼ lb	20.00
Pebbleford, casserole	20.00
Pebbleford, plate, 10" d	10.00
Pebbleford, vegetable bowl, divided	15.00
Petit Point Bouquet, cake plate, 11" d, tab handled	10.00
Petit Point Bouquet, dinner plate	6.00
Petit Point Bouquet, platter, 12½" d, tab handled	12.00
Plymouth, casserole	20.00
Plymouth, chop plate, lug, 12¼"	12.00
Plymouth, sugar	8.00
Taverne, bowl, 36's	20.00
Vistosa, bowl, 8" d, mango red	65.00
Vistosa, gravy boat, cobalt blue	150.00
Vistosa, jug, mango red	20.00
Vistosa, teacup, cobalt blue	8.00
Vistosa, teapot, red	80.00
Vogue, casserole	20.00
Vogue, creamer	4.00
Vogue, plate, 10" d	10.00

Golden Button, Ever Yours shape, dinner plate, 10¼" d, $3.50.

TEAPOTS

Collecting by form, e.g., teapots, was extremely popular in the 1940s and 1950s. It fell completely out of favor in the 1970s and 1980s. A small, but dedicated group of teapot collectors kept collecting interest alive. Today, the teapot is enjoying a collecting renaissance.

Tea drinking was firmly established in England and its American colonies by the middle of the 18th century. The earliest teapots were modeled after their Far Eastern ancestors. Teapot shapes and decorative motifs kept pace with the ceramic and new design styles of the 19th century. The whimsical, figural teapot was around from the start.

Teapots were a common product of American ceramic, glass, and metal manufacturers. The "Rebekah at the Well" teapot appeared in the mid–1850s. Hall China of East Liverpool, Ohio, was one of the leading teapot manufacturers of the 1920s and 30s. Figural teapots were extremely popular in the 1930s. The first etched Pyrex teapot was made in the late 1930s.

Teapots divide into formal, kitchenware, figural, and children's ware. While ceramic teapots are the most common, teapots were made in a host of other materials such as glass, pewter, silver, etc. Shape followed by decoration, then manufacturer and/or country of origin are the value keys.

References: Tina M. Carter, *Teapots: The Collectors' Guide to Selecting, Identifying and Displaying New and Vintage Teapots,* Running Press, Courage Books, 1995; Garth Clark, *The Eccentric Teapot: 400 Years of Invention,* Abbeville Press, 1989.

Periodical: *Tea Talk,* PO Box 860, Sausalito, CA 94966.

Note: All teapots listed are ceramic.

Beswick, Peggoty, #1116, 6" h	$ 45.00
Clarice Cliff, souvenir, "Greetings from Canada," tepee shape, spout is Indian, handle is totem pole, c1950, 5⁷⁄₈" h	150.00
Cortendorf, Germany, cat, beckoning pose, black and white, green eyes and ribbon, 6 cup	50.00
Czechoslovakia, figural Dutch girl, hp, blue dress, holding basket of flowers	95.00
Dartmouth Potteries, England, commemorative, coronation, dark brown profile of Queen Elizabeth, crown finial, 5" h	125.00
England, porcelain, red and blue sprigs, 6" h	100.00
Germany, souvenir, U.S. Capitol, Washington, DC, square, scenic, gold trim, 4½" h	20.00
Hall, Airflow, orange, 6 cup	100.00
Hall, Albany, brown with gold	70.00
Hall, Basket, canary with gold	110.00
Hall, Benjamin, Celedon green	80.00
Hall, Birdcage, maroon with gold, 6 cup	200.00
Hall, Boston, Addison gray	20.00
Hall, Connie, Celedon green	55.00
Hall, Doughnut, cobalt blue	160.00
Hall, French, pale blue, 1 cup	25.00
Hall, Globe, light green and gold, dripless, 6 cup	80.00
Hall, Hallcraft, Holiday pattern, red and black on white, Eva Zeisel	60.00
Hall, Manhattan, blue	65.00
Hall, Murphy, light blue	85.00
Hall, Newport, pink with floral decal, 5 cup	50.00
Hall, New York, black, 2 cup	25.00
Hall, Ohio, black with gold, 6 cup	150.00
Hall, Philadelphia, pink with gold	45.00
Hall, Plume, pink	20.00
Hall, Rhythm, canary with gold, 6 cup	110.00
Hall, Royal, ivory	150.00
Hall, Star, pale blue, 6 cup	90.00
Hall, Starlight, canary	25.00

Hall, French drip, stock brown, 5" h, 8" w, $65.00.

Hall, Sundial, canary with gold	125.00
Hall, Surfside, emerald with gold, 6 cup	175.00
Haviland, pine cone design, gold trim, 10½" h	25.00
Japan, musical, oval, 6 cup	10.00
Japan, whimsical man, nose is spout, pastel pink, blue, and yellow, c1930	25.00
Lefton, Bluebird, bright blue, 6 cup	30.00
Occupied Japan, Dragonware, raised dragon and coralene dec, gold trim, 6 cup	30.00
Price Kensington, England, Cottage Ware, Ye Olde Cottage	35.00
Royal Canadian Art Potter, Hamilton, Canada, dripless, brown, hp flowers	30.00
Royal Copenhagen, blue and white flowers and leaves design, acorn finial, 10" h	65.00
Royal Doulton, Gold Lace pattern, H4989, 9½" h	100.00
Sessions, Clock pattern, plastic	45.00
Shelley China, Wildflower pattern, 4½" h	125.00
Torquay, sailboat scene, "Take a Cup of Tea Its Very Refreshing," 4½" h	95.00
Treasurecraft, Bunny, 1990s	25.00
U.S. Zone, Germany, figural cat, black, ivory, and gray, tail handle, paw spout, 9" h	50.00
Victoria Carlsbad, Austria, floral, 5" h	35.00
Wade, England, Scotsman, nose is spout, cap is lid, brown	40.00

TEDDY BEARS

The teddy bear, named for President Theodore Roosevelt, arrived on the scene in late 1902 or early 1903. The Ideal Toy Corporation (American) and Margarette Steiff (German) are among the earliest firms to include a bear in their stuffed toy lines.

Early teddy bears are identified by the humps in their backs, elongated muzzles, jointed limbs, mohair bodies (some exceptions), glass or pinback eyes, and black shoe buttons. Stuffing materials include excelsior, the most popular, Kapoka, and wood–wool. Elongated limbs, oversized feet, felt paws, and a black embroidered nose and mouth are other indicators of a quality early bear.

Teddy bear manufacturers closely copied each other. Once the manufacturer's identification label or marking is lost, a common situation for well–loved bears, it is impossible to tell one maker's bear from another.

America went teddy bear crazy in the 1980s. A strong secondary market for older bears developed. Many stuffed (plush) toy manufacturers reintroduced teddy bears to their line. Dozens of teddy bear hand–crafted artisans marketed their creations. Some examples sold in the hundreds of dollars.

The speculative fever of the 1980s has subsided. Sale of the hand–crafted artisan bears on the secondary market has met with mixed results. While the market is still strong enough to support its own literature, magazines, and show circuit, the number of collectors has diminished. Those that remain are extremely passionate about their favorite collectible.

References: Pauline Cockrill, *Teddy Bear Encyclopedia,* Dorling Kindersley, 1993, distributed by Hobby House Press; Dee Hockenberry, *The Big Bear Book,* Schiffer Publishing, 1996; Margaret Fox Mandel, *Teddy Bears And Steiff Animals, First Series* (1984, 1997 value update), *Second Series* (1987, 1996 value update), Collector Books; Margaret Fox Mandel, *Teddy Bears, Annalee Animals & Steiff Animals, Third Series,* Collector Books, 1990, 1996 value update; Linda Mullins, *American Teddy Bear Encyclopedia,* Hobby House Press, 1995; Linda Mullins, *Teddy Bear & Friends Price Guide, 4th Edition,* Hobby House Press, 1993; Linda Mullins, *Teddy Bears Past & Present, Vol. II,* Hobby House Press, 1992; Jesse Murray, *Teddy Bear Figurines Price Guide,* Hobby House Press, 1996; Cynthia Powell, *Collector's Guide To Miniature Teddy Bears: Identification & Values,* Collector Books, 1994; Carol J. Smith, *Identification & Price Guide To Winnie The Pooh Collectibles,* Hobby House Press, 1994.

Periodicals: *National Doll & Teddy Bear Collector,* PO Box 4032, Portland, OR 97208; *Teddy Bear And Friends,* 6405 Flank Dr, Harrisburg, PA 17112; *Teddy Bear Review,* 170 Fifth Ave, New York, NY 10010.

Collectors' Clubs: Good Bears of the World, PO Box 13097, Toledo, OH 43613; Winnie The Pooh Collectors Club, 468 W Alpine #40, Upland, CA 91786.

Note: See Steiff and Stuffed Toys for additional listings.

Chad Valley, mohair, gold, jointed, excelsior and
   kapok stuffing, glass eyes, label sewn into side
   seam, c1930, 22" h . . . . $ 500.00
Character Novelty Co, synthetic plush, cinnamon,
   plastic eyes, label sewn in ear, c1960, 15" h 60.00
Clemens, mohair, beige, short mohair inset snout,
   glass eyes, metal tag, c1950, 16" h 275.00
Crisly, mohair, beige, jointed, kapok stuffing, glass
   eyes, paper tag attached to chest, c1960, 22" h 325.00
Gund, Cubbie Bear, acrylic plush, dark brown, soft
   vinyl molded face, painted eyes, wearing dress and
   shoes, removable apron, label sewn in leg seam,
   c1950, 13" h 85.00
Ideal Toy Co, Musical Clown Bear, synthetic plush,
   cinnamon colored body, paw pads and ear linings,
   molded soft vinyl face, plastic eyes, white pants
   with brown and yellow spots, yellow felt hat, label
   sewn in shoulder seam, c1950, 15" h 135.00

Knickerbocker, mohair, brown, jointed, flat face,
   20" h **100.00**
Knickerbocker, mohair, brown, jointed, inset snout,
   floss nose and mouth, felt pads, windup music box,
   1950s, 14" h **175.00**
North American Bear Co, Vanderbear Family, Fluffy,
   1983, 12" h **28.00**
North American Bear Co, Very Important Bear,
   William Shakesbear, 1981–88 . . . . **400.00**
Petz, mohair, gold tipped with reddish–brown, short
   blonde mohair inset snout, jointed, excelsior stuffing, glass eyes, milk glass button fastened to
   chest, label sewn in arm seam, c1940, 19" h **650.00**
Schuco Toy Co, Acrobat Bear, short mohair, pale
   beige over metal body, jointed arms and legs, black
   metal eyes, bear does somersaults when arms are
   wound, c1960, 5½" h **750.00**
Unidentified Maker, long mohair, cinnamon, jointed,
   excelsior and kapok stuffing, straight arms and
   legs, embroidered nose and mouth, flannel pads,
   glass eyes, 1920s, 14½" h, moth damage, fiber loss . . . **125.00**
Unidentified Maker, long mohair, gold, short gold
   mohair inset snout, wide–set glass eyes, American,
   c1930, 19" h **325.00**
Unidentified Maker, long mohair, gold, velveteen
   paw pads, glass eyes, British, c1930, 21" h **500.00**
Unidentified Maker, long mohair, yellow, jointed,
   kapok stuffing, embroidered nose and mouth, felt
   pads, glass eyes, blue and white knitted overalls,
   British, 1930s, 17" h **200.00**
Unidentified Maker, mohair, blonde, jointed, excel-
   sior stuffing, embroidered nose, mouth, felt pads,
   glass eyes, remnants of rayon label sewn in arm
   seam, German, mid–20th C, 9½" h, some moth
   damage **400.00**
Unidentified Maker, mohair, yellow, jointed, excel-
   sior stuffing, embroidered nose and mouth, long
   oval body, short curved arms, straight legs, glass
   eyes, pink and white knitted sweater, probably
   American, early 1920s, 19" h, fiber loss and repairs . . . **325.00**

Unidentified Maker, short mohair, gold, jointed, straw stuffing, growler, embroidered nose and mouth, c1925, 20" h, $500.00.

TELEPHONES & RELATED MEMORABILIA

Until the mid–1990s, telephone collecting centered primarily on candlestick telephones and single, double, and triple wall–mounted, oak case telephones. Avant–garde collectors concentrated on colored, rotary–dial telephones from the Art Deco period. The Automatic Telephone Company (General Telephone) and Western Electric (Bell System) were the two principal manufacturers of this later group. Kellogg, Leich, and Stromberg Carlson also made colored case telephones.

Recently collector interest has increased in three new areas: (1) the desk sets of the late 1930s and 40s, typified by Western Electric Model 302 A–G dial cradle telephone (1937–1954 and designated the "Perry Mason" phone by collectors), (2) colored plastic phones of the 1950s and 60s, e.g., the Princess, and (3) figural telephones, popular in the late 1970s and throughout the 1980s.

References: Kate Dooner, *Telephones: Antique to Modern,* Schiffer Publishing, 1992; Kate Dooner, *Telephone Collecting: Seven Decades of Design,* Schiffer Publishing, 1993; Richard D. Mountjoy, *One Hundred Years of Bell Telephone,* Schiffer Publishing, 1995.

Collectors' Clubs: Antique Telephone Collectors Assoc, PO Box 94, Abilene, KS 67410; Telephone Collectors International, 19 N Cherry Dr, Oswego, IL 60543.

Keychain, princess phone, pink . . . . $ 5.00
Magazine, *Telephony,* 1955. 50
Novelty, Banana Splits Talking Telephone, plastic,
    battery operated, payphone style, interchangeable
    records, Hasbro, 1969 . . . . 75.00
Novelty, Snoopy and Woodstock, telephone lamp,
    plastic wood–grained base, red platform, touch-
    tone, Comdial/American Telecommunications, Inc,
    c1980 . . . . 150.00
Paperweight, Bell System, New York Telephone
    Company, figural, bell, glass, dark blue, gold let-
    tering, c1920, 3¼" h 70.00
Payphone, credit card slot, c1975, 21" h. 150.00
Payphone, GTE Automatic Electric, Model 120–A,
    "semi post pay," 21 x 6" 125.00
Payphone, Model 23J, metal, Gray Manufacturing
    Company, Gray Telephone Pay Station Company,
    Hartford, 10½ x 6" 100.00
Payphone, 10 button, touch–tone, c1960s. 100.00
Pencil, lead, Bell Telephone, Auto Point 25.00
Sign, Indiana Telephone Co, 2–sided, porcelain,
    black and white, "Indiana Telephone Corporation,
    Local & Long Distance Service," late 1940s, 18" sq 75.00
Sign, New England Telephone & Telegraph System,
    square, early roped "Local and Long Distance
    Telephone" bell in center of Bell Systems circle,
    blue and white, 11" sq 80.00
Telephone, advertising, Sparkle, Crest Toothpaste,
    10½" h 40.00
Telephone, AT&T Experimental Phone, clear bulbous
    shape, red base, rotary dial, c1960s 200.00
Telephone, Federal Tel & Tel Company, Grab–a–
    Phone, 8 x 10" 150.00
Telephone, Stromberg–Carlson, dial upright desk
    stand, c1920s. 125.00

Telephone, Western Electric, Model 102, oval base,
    black, c1928–29 . . . . 100.00
Telephone, Western Electric, Model 202, red, c1935. . . . . 50.00
Telephone, Western Electric, Model 292, oval base,
    black, c1930 . . . . 90.00
Telephone, Western Electric, Model 300, desk style. 50.00
Telephone, Western Electric, Model 354, wall set, F1
    handset, 1950–54 . . . . 50.00
Telephone, Western Electric, Model 500, clear plastic 55.00
Telephone, Western Electric, railroad dial upright
    desk stand, c1920–30. . . . . 150.00
Telephone, Western Electric, Trimline, c1968 . . . . 25.00
Toy, Smurf–A–Ring, plastic, Hg Toys Inc, 1982 . . . . 15.00

TELEVISION CHARACTERS & PERSONALITIES

Television programming is only 50 years old. Prior to World War II, television viewing was largely centered in the New York market. In 1946 the first network was established, linking WNBT, NBC's New York station, with Schenectady and Philadelphia.

Networks were organized, and programming ordered. By 1949 Americans were purchasing televisions at the rate of 100,000 units a week. In 1955 one–third of all American homes had a television. In the mid–1980s virtually every home included one or more sets. Over 4,000 different shows and series have appeared.

Thanks to William Boyd's successful licensing of Hopalong Cassidy in 1949/50, the television industry discovered the financial potential of licensed products. The 1950s and 60s are the golden age of television licensing. Many early space and western programs licensed over 50 different products. The vast majority of the licensed products were directed toward the infant and juvenile markets.

Television licensing fell off significantly in the 1970s and 80s, the result of increased adult programming, higher fees, and demands by stars for a portion of the licensing fees. Most television shows have no licensed products. The Star Trek series, a few professional sports, such as wrestling, quiz shows, and Saturday morning cartoon shows are the exceptions.

Do not overlook television literature. Regional guides and early copies of *TV Guide,* first issued nationally on April 3, 1953, are highly desired. While most are collected for their cover art, do not forget to check the inside stories.

Television star autographs is a popular subcollecting category.

References: Paul Anderson, *The Davy Crockett Craze: A Look at the 1950's Phenomenon and Davy Crockett Collectibles,* R & G Productions, 1996; Tim Brooks and Earle Marsh, *The Complete Directory to Prime Time Network and Cable TV Shows: 1946 – Present, Sixth Edition,* Ballantine Books, 1995; Greg Davis and Bill Morgan, *Collector's Guide to TV Memorabilia: 1960s & 1970s,* Collector Books, 1996; Ted Hake, *Hake's Guide To TV Collectibles,* Wallace–Homestead, Krause Publications, 1990; Jack Koch, *Howdy Doody: Collector's Reference and Trivia Guide,* Collector Books, 1996; Cynthia Boris Liljeblad, *TV Toys and The Shows That Inspired Them,* Krause Publications, 1996; Norman E. Martinus and Harry L. Rinker, *Warman's Paper,* Wallace–Homestead, Krause Publications, 1994; Vincent Terrace, *Encyclopedia Of Television—Series, Pilots, And Specials, 1937–1973,* 3 Vol, Zoetrope, 1986; Ric Wyman, *For The Love Of Lucy: The Complete Guide For Collectors* *and Fans,* Chronicle Books, 1995; Alan Young, *Mister Ed and Me,* St. Martin's Press, 1994; Dian Zillner, *Collectible Television Memorabilia,* Schiffer Publishing, 1996.

Periodical: *Big Reel,* PO Box 1050, Dubuque, IA 52004.

Note: See Autographs, Cartoon Characters, Coloring Books, Comic Books, Cowboy Heroes, Hanna–Barbera, Games, Little Golden Books, Lunch Boxes, Pez, Smurfs, Space Adventurers, Star Trek, and Super Heroes for additional listings.

Addams Family, card game, Milton Bradley, 1965 . . . . . $ 32.00
Addams Family, coloring book, Saalfield, 1965 . . . . 10.00
Ben Casey, game, Ben Casey M. D., Transogram,
   1961 . . . . 30.00
Ben Casey, nodder, composition, 6½" h 70.00
Beverly Hillbillies, frame tray puzzle, Milton Bradley,
   1963 . . . . 20.00
Beverly Hillbillies, game, The Beverly Hillbillies
   Set Back Card Game, Milton Bradley, 1963 . . . . 25.00
Bewitched, game, Bewitched, Game Gems, 1965 . . . . . . 75.00
Bewitched, paper dolls, Samantha, 2 clothing sheets,
   plastic wand, Magic Wand, 1965 . . . . 55.00
Bionic Woman, lunch box, emb steel, plastic
   thermos, Aladdin, c1977 . . . . 30.00
Bionic Woman, model, The Bionic Woman Repair
   Kit, plastic, MTC, 1976 . . . . 20.00
Bonanza, coloring book, Saalfield, #4535, 1965 . . . . . . 12.00
Bonanza, movie viewer, 2 films, K–Kids series, 1961 . . . . 45.00
Bozo the Clown, Larry Harmon's Bozo's pocket
   watch, plastic, metal hands, 4 x 6" display bag with
   header card, Japan 12.00
Bozo the Clown, record, *Bozo Has a Party,* 78 rpm,
   20–pg booklet, Capitol, 1952 . . . . 18.00
Brady Bunch, frame tray puzzle, Whitman, 1972 . . . . 15.00
Captain Kangaroo, game, The Game of Captain
   Kangaroo, Milton Bradley, 1956 . . . . 22.00
Captain Kangaroo, thermos, steel, King Seeley, 1964 . . . . 28.00
Car 54, Where Are You?, coloring book, Whitman,
   #1157, 1962 . . . . 40.00

Bonanza, cup, litho tin, 2¾" h, $ 22.00.

Beverly Hillbillies, book, *The Saga of Wildcat Creek,* by Doris Schroeder, Whitman Publishing, hard cover, 1963, 212 pgs, 5¾ x 7¾", $15.00.

Car 54, Where Are You?, comic book, Dell, #1257,
   Mar–May 1962 . . . . 20.00
Car 54, Where Are You?, game, Allison, 1962 . . . . 85.00
Charlie's Angels, game, Cheryl Ladd cov, Milton
   Bradley, 1965 . . . . 15.00
Charlie's Angels, paper doll, Jill, Toy Factory, c1977 . . . . 22.00
Dennis the Menace, frame tray puzzle, Whitman,
   1960 . . . . 15.00
Dennis the Menace, record, 33⅓ rpm, Colpix, 1960s 25.00
Dobie Gillis, bobbing head, composition, 7" h 110.00
Donna Reed Show, *TV Guide,* Jun 29, 1963, Reed
   and Betz cov 25.00
Dr. Kildare, Dr. Kildare's Thumpy–The Heartbeat
   Stethoscope, Amson Industries, c1960 . . . . 35.00
Dr. Kildare, game, Dr. Kildare Medical Game For the
   Young, Ideal, 1962 . . . . 25.00
Dr. Kildare, paper dolls, Dr. Kildare and Nurse
   Susan, Collins, 1965 . . . . 35.00
Dr. Who, postcard, Patrick Troughton color photo,
   blue marker autograph, "Best Wishes Patrick
   Troughton" 38.00
Ed Sullivan, autograph, 7 x 9" black and white photo 55.00
Ed Sullivan, magazine cover, *TV World,* Apr 1956 . . . . . . 12.00
Ed Sullivan, nodder, Topo Gigio, ceramic, 5½" h 50.00
F Troop, coloring book, Saalfield, #9560, 1966 . . . . 18.00
F Troop, comic book, Dell, #6, 1967 . . . . 10.00
Family Affair, Buffy doll, talking, red and white dress,
   Mattel, 1967 . . . . 35.00
Family Affair, coloring book, Western/Whitman, 1969 . . . . 5.00
Family Affair, game, The Family Affair Game,
   Whitman, 1971 . . . . 15.00
Family Affair, paper dolls, Buffy & Jody, Whitman,
   1970 . . . . 12.00
Flying Nun, game, Flying Nun Marble Maze Game,
   Hasbro, 1967 . . . . 55.00
Gabby Hayes Show, book, *Gabby Hayes Tall Tales
   For Little Folks,* diecut cardboard pcs make 17"
   Hayes figure, 6 outfit changes, Jack–in–the–Box
   series, Samuel Lowe, 1954 . . . . 35.00

Howdy Doody, child's shoe bag, red plastic, yellow and black dec, 14¹/₂" h, $40.00.

Gabby Hayes, frame tray puzzle, Kagran, c1950s **22.00**
Get Smart, game, Get Smart Exploding Time Bomb
  Game, Ideal, 1965 . . . . **25.00**
Get Smart, lunch box, metal, King Seeley, 1966 . . . . **45.00**
Gilligan's Island, tablet, Alan Hale and Bob Denver
  cov photo, c1965 . . . . **25.00**
Gomer Pyle, U.S.M.C., lunch box, steel, embossed,
  Aladdin, 1966 . . . . **65.00**
Green Acres, tablet, Eddie Albert and Eva Gabor cov
  photo, 8 x 10", c1966 . . . . **12.00**
Green Hornet, trading cards, Donruss, 1966, com-
  plete set of 44 . . . . **150.00**
Green Hornet, *TV Guide*, Oct 29, 1966, cov photo,
  3-pg article **25.00**
Hardy Boys, model, Hardy Boys' Van, plastic, Revell
  Plastics, c1977–78 . . . . **25.00**
Hawaii Five–O, book, *Hawaii Five–O/The Octopus
  Caper,* hard cover, Whitman, 1971, 212 pgs **15.00**
Hogan's Heroes, record, *Hogan's Heroes Sing the
  Best of World War II,* 33¹/₃ rpm, Sunset label,
  Liberty Records **30.00**
Howdy Doody, bank, figural, black base **30.00**
Howdy Doody, hand puppet, vinyl head, red and
  white checkered cloth body, Bob Smith, c1950,
  8¹/₂" h **30.00**
Howdy Doody, lunch box, plastic, red, NBC, c1970 . . . . **60.00**
Howdy Doody, marionette, wood, composition head,
  cloth outfit, Peter Puppet Playthings, 15" h **120.00**
Howdy Doody, watch, silvered metal case, green
  vinyl straps, Bob Smith, c1950, 1¹/₄" d face **155.00**
I Dream of Jeannie, doll, hard plastic body, soft
  vinyl head, blonde rooted hair, sleep eyes,
  Libby, 1966 . . . . **155.00**
I Love Lucy, *Lucy's Notebook,* Lucy's menus, recipes,
  and entertaining tips, c1957–60, soft cover, 44 pgs,
  6 x 9" **30.00**
Jackie Gleason Show, *TV Digest,* Jan 3, 1953, cov
  photo, 2-pg article **22.00**

Johnny Carson, tablet, cov photo, blue ground with
  silver stars, 8 x 10" **15.00**
Julia, coloring book, Saalfield, #9523, 1968 . . . . **18.00**
Kojak, action figure, hard plastic, orig outfit, minia-
  ture glasses, cigar, lollipops, and holster, Excel Toy
  Corp, 1976, 8" h **35.00**
Kojak, game, Kojak The Stake Out Detective Game,
  Milton Bradley, 1975 . . . . **20.00**
Kukla, Fran, and Ollie, record, *Burr Tillstrom's Kukla,
  Fran, and Ollie,* 45 rpm, RCA Victor, c1950,
  2 record set **45.00**
Kung Fu, lunch box, steel, plastic thermos, King
  Seeley, 1974 . . . . **50.00**
Milton Berle Show, *TV Guide,* Vol. 5, #21, May
  23–29, 1952, Berle cov photo and article **30.00**
Monkees, book, *The Monkees Go Mod,* Popular
  Library, 1967 . . . . **5.00**
Monkees, game, Hey! Hey! The Monkees Game,
  Transogram, 1967 . . . . **30.00**
Monkees, jigsaw puzzle, 1967, 340 pcs, 17 x 11" **20.00**
Mr. Ed, comic book, Mister Ed the Talking
  Horse, #260, 16 pgs, 1964 . . . . **20.00**
Mr. Ed, game, Mister Ed the Talking Horse Game,
  Parker Brothers, 1962 . . . . **45.00**
Mr. Peepers, book, *Mr. Peepers,* soft cover, Simon &
  Schuster, 1955, 248 pgs **25.00**
Mr. Peepers, school bag and game kit, bag, slate,
  report cards, attendance sheets, stencils, chalk,
  pencil, paint, eraser, and lotto, bingo and word
  game, Pressman Toys, 1955, 9 x 13" vinyl **45.00**
Perry Mason, comic book, Dell, #2, Oct–Dec 1964 . . . . . **10.00**
Perry Mason, game, Perry Mason Case of the Missing
  Suspect Game, Transogram, 1959 . . . . **40.00**
Pinky Lee Show, game, Pinky Lee Game Time,
  Pressman, 1950s **35.00**
Pinky Lee Show, serving tray, litho tin, c1954, 10¹/₂ x
  14¹/₂" **25.00**
Rootie Kazootie, card game, Rootie Kazootie Word
  Game, Ed–U–Cards, 1953, 36 cards **12.00**

Huckleberry Hound, Yogi Bear, Quick Draw McGraw, and T.V. Friends, waste basket, litho tin, 1960s, $35.00.

Rootie Kazootie, hand puppet, vinyl head, cloth
body, 11" h **30.00**

Sergeant Preston of the Yukon, coloring book,
Treasure Books, 1957, 52 pgs **18.00**

Shari Lewis Show, doll, Lamb Chop, stuffed, plush,
vinyl plastic head, Ideal **55.00**

Shari Lewis, game, Shari Lewis Party Game, Lowell
Toys, 1962 .... **30.00**

Six Million Dollar Man, lunch box, emb steel,
plastic thermos, Aladdin, 1974 .... **40.00**

Starsky & Hutch, action figure, Huggy Bear, plastic,
8" h **18.00**

Starsky & Hutch, book, *Starsky & Hutch*, soft cover,
Golden All–Star Book, 1977, 36 pgs **10.00**

Tarzan, game, Tarzan to the Rescue, Milton Bradley,
1977 .... **25.00**

Today, game, Today With Dave Garroway, Athletic
Products, 1950s **50.00**

Waltons, game, The Waltons, Milton Bradley, 1974 ..... **10.00**

Welcome Back Kotter, model, Sweathogs Dream
Machine, 1/25 scale, Sweathog figures, MPC, 1976 .... **28.00**

Wild, Wild West, book, *The Wild, Wild West*, paperback, Robert Conrad cov photo, Signet, Jan 1966 ..... **30.00**

TELEVISION LAMPS

"You will go blind if you watch television in the dark" was a common warning in the early 1950s. American lamp manufacturers responded by creating lamps designed to sit atop the television set and provide the correct amount of indirect lighting necessary to preserve the viewer's eyesight.

The need was simple. The solutions were imaginative and of questionable taste in more than a few cases. Motifs ranged from leaping gazelles to a prancing horse with a clock in the middle of his body graced by a red Venetian blind, pagoda–like shade.

Most television lamps were ceramic and back lit. Lane and Company (Van Nuys, CA), Hedi Schoop (North Hollywood, CA), and Tower Craftsmen (Red Bank, NJ) are three manufacturers of television lamps.

Accordion, ceramic, translucent, ivory, "Lawrence
Welk," gold trim and lettering .... **$ 65.00**

Angel Fish, antique, black spots, foil label, Royal
Haeger, 5¼" d base, 13¾" h **80.00**

Fish, ceramic, white, round metal base **20.00**

Flamingos, ceramic, pink, black, and white, planter
base, Lane & Co, 1957 .... **50.00**

Gazelle, planter base, ebony cascade, Royal Haeger,
25½" h **110.00**

Greyhound, planter base, brown, Royal Haeger,
11½" l **80.00**

Horse Head, 12 x 10¾" **25.00**

Island Girl, leaning against palm tree, ceramic, green,
screen background **40.00**

Lighthouse and Cottage, multicolored **35.00**

Mallards in Flight, ceramic, Maddux **45.00**

Panther, ceramic, black, 8½ x 6½" **20.00**

Panther, ceramic, ebony and turquoise, Royal Haeger,
13¼ x 5⅞" **70.00**

Poodle, chalkware, 1950s **40.00**

Gondola, ceramic, Premco Mfg, IL, 1954, 16" l, 7" h, $25.00.

Prancing Horse, ceramic, chartreuse and honey, foil
label, Royal Haeger, 11½" l **40.00**

Sailfish, silver spray, Royal Haeger, 19¼" l **45.00**

Ship, gold trim, 11 x 10½" **20.00**

Two Deer, abstract, oxblood and white, Royal
Haeger, 5½" h **175.00**

Two Race Horses, ceramic, black, green foliate base **40.00**

TELEVISIONS

Television sets are divided into three groups: (1) mechanical era sets, 1925 to 1932, (2) pre–World War II sets, 1938–1941, and (3) post–1946 sets. Mechanical era sets, also known as radiovisors, were used in conjunction with the radio. Braird, Daven, Insuline Corporation, Jenkins, Pioneer, Rawls, and See–All were a few of the early manufacturers. Reception was limited to the Chicago and New York area.

The electronic picture tube was introduced in 1938. The smaller the tube, the older the set is a good general rule. Early electric sets provided for a maximum of five channels, 1 through 5.

Many sets made prior to 1941 combined the television with a multi–band radio. Fewer than 20,000 sets were produced. Many of the sets were sold in kit form. The Albany/Schnectady/Troy, Philadelphia, and Los Angeles areas joined Chicago and New York as television markets.

Production of television sets significantly increased following World War II. Channels 6 to 13 were added between 1946 and 1948. Channel 1 was dropped in 1949, replaced with V.H.F. channels 2 through 13. The U.H.F. band was added in 1953.

Collectors' interest focuses primarily on the black and white sets from the 1940s and 1950s. There is some interest in color sets made prior to 1955. Brand and model number are essential to researching value. Cabinet condition also is critical to value, sometimes more important than whether or not the set is operational. Sets made after 1960 have more reuse than collectible value.

Reference: Scott Wood (ed.), *Classic TVs With Price Guide: Pre–War thru 1950s,* L–W Book Sales, 1992, 1997 value update.

Periodical: *Radio Age,* PO Box 1362, Washington Grove, MD 20880.

Admiral, 20X122, console, Bakelite, 1948, 10"
screen .... $ 210.00

Admiral 22X12, console, Bakelite, square speaker
grill, 1949, 12" screen 30.00

Andrea, CO–VK12, double doors conceal tuner at
right of screen, pull–out phono below, 1948, 12"
screen 80.00

Arvin, 9218, console, screen above 2 knobs, 1953,
21" screen 15.00

Bendix, 325M8, TV upper right, phono and radio
upper left, speaker and storage space below, 10"
screen 55.00

CBS–Columbia, U22C05, console, UHF, 1955 .... 30.00

CBS–Columbia, tabletop, 1955, 21" screen 30.00

Crosley, F–17TOL, tabletop, square, 3 large knobs,
17" screen 15.00

Crosley, 9–407, tabletop, metal mesh around screen,
tuner control and window right of screen, 12"
screen 70.00

Du–Mont, RA–101, Plymouth, console, double
doors, 1946 .... 50.00

Emerson, 585, pull–out phono, double doors front of
screen, 10" screen 80.00

Emerson, 631, tabletop, rounded top, porthole–look
screen, 16" screen 70.00

General Electric, 12T1, tabletop, wooden, square
cabinet, screen above 4 knobs, 12" screen 25.00

General Electric, 835, tabletop, metal mesh grill, 10"
screen 55.00

General Electric, Hotpoint, tabletop, painted metal,
top handle, c1950 .... 30.00

Hallicrafters, 715, tabletop, Bakelite, 12" screen 80.00

JVC, 3240, Video Sphere, oval plastic front screen
cov, chain on top, 1972 .... 110.00

Motorola, 19CK2, console, color, 1955, 19" screen 310.00

Motorola, VK–101, console, 13 channels, AM/FM
radio, 1948, 10" screen 130.00

Panasonic, TR–005, Flying Saucer, silver, oval shape,
metal tripod, 1972 .... 180.00

Philco, 4660, Miss America, console, swivel, pop–up
controls 110.00

Philco, 49–1280, wooden, double doors, 12" screen 55.00

Philco, 51–T1871, console, 4 knobs, drop–down
phonograph, 20" screen 20.00

RCA, 4T101, tabletop, 14" screen 20.00

RCA, 8–PT–7010, portable, metal, folding plastic top
handle, 8" screen 40.00

RCA, 9T246, tabletop, metal, grill around screen,
imitation mahogany finish, 10" screen 30.00

Stromberg–Carlson, TC–125–HM, tabletop, wooden,
porthole–look screen, 4 knobs, wooden top cover,
12" screen 130.00

Sylvania, 14P101, Holiday, metal, side controls,
1957 .... 30.00

Sylvania, 21C534, Sylouette, colonial–style wooden
base 150.00

Westinghouse, H–196, tabletop, wooden, 10" screen 90.00

Westinghouse, H–626, tabletop, tuner lower right,
16" screen 50.00

Westinghouse, 17T247, portable, painted metal, top
handle, 17" screen 30.00

TEMPLE, SHIRLEY

Born on April 23, 1928, in Santa Monica, California, Shirley Temple was the most successful child movie star of all time. She was discovered by movie scout Charles Lamont while attending dance class at the Meglin Dance Studios in Los Angeles. Fox Film's *Stand Up and Cheer* (1934) was her first starring role. She made a total of twelve pictures that year.

Gertrude George, Shirley's mother, played a major role in creating Shirley's image and directing her licensing program. Requests for endorsements and licenses were immediate. The Ideal Novelty and Toy Company manufactured seven different size (11", 13", 15", 18", 20", 25", and 27") all–composition Shirley Temple dolls between 1934 and the late 1930s. Hundreds of products were endorsed or licensed.

By 1935 Temple was the number one box office star, a spot she retained through 1938. In 1940 Temple starred in *The Blue Bird* and *Young People,* her last films for Fox. She immediately signed a $100,000 a year contract with MGM and starred in *Kathleen* in 1941, her first teenage/adult movie role. Shirley married for the first time in 1945. She retired from films in 1950, the same year she divorced her husband and married Charles Black.

In 1957 Shirley was host of the *Shirley Temple Storybook.* Ideal introduced five sizes (12", 15", 17", 19", and 36") of vinyl Shirley Temple dolls that same year. Numerous other Shirley Temple products were licensed.

In the 1960s Shirley Temple Black became active in Republican politics. After serving as a U.S. Delegate to the United Nations and Ambassador to Ghana, she became Chief of Protocol in Washington. Her final government service was as Ambassador to Czechoslovakia in 1989.

References: Edward R. Pardella, *Shirley Temple Dolls And Fashion: A Collector's Guide To The World's Darling,* Schiffer Publishing, 1992; Dian Zillner, *Hollywood Collectibles: The Sequel,* Schiffer Publishing, 1994.

Olympic, TV–104, table model, wood case, Bakelite knobs, 1948, 10" screen, $125.00.

Creamer, glass, cobalt blue, 1938, 4 1/2" h, $30.00.

Bank, celluloid, white, picture mounted on top,
  c1936, 2" sq . . . . $ 75.00
Book, *Littlest Rebel,* Edward Peple, 1935 . . . . 50.00
Book, *Shirley Temple Through The Day,* Saalfield,
  1946 . . . . 12.00
Candy Mold 25.00
Cereal Bowl 40.00
Clothes Hanger, cardboard, blue, 1930s 10.50
Coloring Book, Saalfield, #1735, hardcover, 1935 . . . . . . 40.00
Doll, Curly Top, composition, orig clothes and box,
  1935, 16" h 150.00
Fan, R Cola adv, "I'll Be Seeing You" 25.00
Game, The Little Colonel, Selchow & Righter, orig
  box, 1935 . . . . 70.00
Lobby Card, *Adventure in Baltimore,* RKO, 1949 . . . . . . 12.50
Magazine, *Photoplay,* Sep 1939, Temple cov 12.00
Magazine, *This Week of Milwaukee Sentinel,*
  Dec 28, 1941 . . . . 5.00
Movie Still, *Little Miss Marker,* Paramount Films,
  1934, 8 x 10" 22.00
Paper Doll, Saalfield, #1765, life-size, 1936 . . . . 90.00
Paper Doll, Shirley Temple Christmas Book, Saalfield,
  #1770, 1937 . . . . 55.00
Pocket Mirror, celluloid, brown photo, pale pink
  ground, 1¾" d 45.00
Postcard, *Captain January* scene, glossy sepia picture,
  unused, 1936, 3½ x 5½" 15.00
Ring, celluloid, red, white, and black, diecut Shirley
  head, Japan 25.00
Sewing Cards, Saalfield, 6 black and white cards,
  yarn, 1936, 5 x 7" box 45.00
Sheet Music, *Animal Crackers In My Soup,* 1935 . . . . . . 20.00
Sheet Music, *Goodnight My Love,* 1936 . . . . 20.00
Sheet Music, *Good Ship Lollipop,* 1934 . . . . 12.50
Souvenir Book, Tournament of Roses Parade, Temple
  as Grand Marshal, 1939, 32 pgs, 9 x 12" 25.00

TENNIS COLLECTIBLES

The game of tennis originated in France in the 12th century. Until the 19th century, it was played primarily by royalty and the wealthy on indoor courts. The invention of the lawnmower in 1830 and the India rubber ball in the 1850s led to the development of lawn tennis.

Tennis came to America in the mid–1870s. After a tennis craze in the 1880s, the sport went into a decline. International play, i.e. Wimbledon and the Davis Cup, led to a revival in the early 1900s. The period from 1919 to 1940 is viewed by many tennis scholars as the sport's golden age.

Tennis collectibles divide into two basic periods: (1) pre–1945 and (2) post–1945. Collector interest in post–1945 material is minimal. There are three basic groups of tennis collectibles: (1) items associated with play, e.g., balls, ball cans, rackets, and fashions, (2) paper ephemera ranging from books to photographs, and (3) objects decorated with a tennis image or in a tennis shape. Because tennis collecting is in its infancy, some areas remain highly affordable, e.g., rackets. Others already are in the middle of a price run, e.g., tennis ball cans.

Reference: Jeanne Cherry, *Tennis Antiques & Collectibles,* Amaryllis Press, 1995.

Collectors' Club: The Tennis Collectors Society, Guildhall Orchard, Great Bromley, Colchester, CO7 7TU U.K.

Ball Can, Bancroft, Winner, black, gold, and white . . . . $ 25.00
Ball Can, Dunlop, Vinnie Richards, red, white, and
  black, dome lid 20.00
Ball Can, Spalding, Pancho Gonzales, red or blue 20.00
Ball Can, Voit, green and white, dome lid 25.00
Ball Can, Wilson, blue, white, and gold, 12 balls 100.00
Cigarette Card, Helen Jacobs, color, Ogden's
  Cigarettes, 1936 . . . . 8.00
Game, Set Point, Tennis Strategy Game, SV
  Productions, 1971 . . . . 30.00
Magazine, *American Lawn Tennis,* 1920s 5.00

Ball Cans, left: Dunlop, Vinnie Richards, U.S.A., flat lid, $45.00; left center: Dunlop, Vinnie Richards, U.S.A., dome lid, $20.00; right center: Bancroft, Winner, England, flat lid, no solder spot, $25.00; right: Bancroft, Winner, U.S.A., dome lid, $20.00.

Magazine, *Sports Illustrated,* Jul 15, 1974, Jimmy
Connors and Chris Evert **7.50**

Pinback Button, U.S. Open Tennis Championship,
celluloid, 1975 championships, 2⅛" **10.00**

Playing Cards, Arzy's Tennis Shop, Beverly Hills adv,
black and white tennis player and banner logo,
white ground, gold and red border **5.50**

Program, Wimbledon, All England Lawn Tennis Club,
1950s **4.00**

Racquet, Dayton, wood handle, steel head, wire
strings, no breaks, trademark decal on handle,
1930s **15.00**

Racquet, Prince Classic, aluminum, green throat
piece, 1960s **7.50**

Racquet, Winchester, wood handle, trademark decal,
c1930s **40.00**

THIMBLES

Although Americans imported most of their thimbles in the 18th
century and the early part of the 19th century, advertisements for
American–made gold, pinchbeck, and silver thimbles appeared in
1790s New York and Philadelphia newspapers. By the middle of
the 19th century, the American thimble industry was able to produce finely worked thimbles.

Precious metal, e.g., gold and silver, thimbles were restricted to
the upper class. Utilitarian thimbles were made of brass or steel. In
1880 William Halsey patented a process to make celluloid thimbles. Aluminum thimbles made their appearance in the second
quarter of the 20th century.

A thimble was one of the few gifts considered appropriate for an
unmarried man to give to a lady. Many of these fancy thimbles
show little wear, possibly a result of both inappropriate sizing and
the desire to preseve the memento.

Advertising thimbles featuring the name of a merchant, manufacturer, or product were popular between 1920 and the
mid–1950s. Early examples are made from celluloid or aluminum.
Plastic was the popular post–war medium. The first political thimbles appeared in 1920, shortly after the amendment to the
Constitution giving women the right to vote was ratified. They
proved to be popular campaign giveaways through the early
1960s.

References: Averil Mathis, *Antique and Collectible Thimbles and
Accessories,* Collector Books, 1986, 1995 value update; Gay Ann
Rogers, *Price Guide Keyed To American Silver Thimbles,*
Needlework Unlimited, 1989; Estelle Zalkin, *Zalkin's Handbook
Of Thimbles & Sewing Implements,* Warman Publishing, 1988, dis-
tributed by Krause Publications.

Periodical: *Thimbletter,* 93 Walnut Hill Rd, Newton Highlands,
MA 02161.

Collectors' Clubs: Empire State Thimble Collectors, 8289
Northgate Dr, Rome, NY 13440; The Thimble Guild, PO Box
381807, Duncanville, TX 75138; Thimble Collectors International,
6411 Montego Bay Rd, Louisville, KY 40228.

Note: For additional sewing listings refer to Sewing Items.

Brass, cloisonné design, China . . . . **$ 10.00**

Brass, "Golden Egg," etched egg holder and thimble,
22K gold plated, velvet int, West Germany, c1985 . . . . **385.00**

Brass, plain band **3.00**

Copper, "Are you a Digitabulus?" **15.00**

Copper, blue stone top, Germany, 1920s **40.00**

Enameled Metal, flower spray, "Bicentennial 1976,"
Betsy Ross and U.S. flag, Holland **40.00**

Glass, crystal, bell shape, octagonal, 2" h **10.00**

Glass, crystal, enameled blue and white cornflower,
1" h **5.00**

Glass, spun crystal, hummingbird and blossom finial,
gold trim **10.00**

Glass, spun crystal, yellow saxophone finial **8.00**

Gold, plain band **75.00**

Gold, semi–precious stones on band **200.00**

Ivory, modern scrimshaw **20.00**

Mexican Silver, abalone and mother–of–pearl inlay,
c1980 . . . . **12.00**

Plastic, "Re–elect d'Alesandro for Mayor '86" **1.50**

Plastic, 2–colors, red top **2.00**

Porcelain, modern, hp, Meissen, German **125.00**

Sterling Silver, American Quilter's Society, Paducah,
Kentucky, limited edition, Simons Brothers, 1986. . . . . . **55.00**

Sterling Silver, 1933 Chicago World's Fair souvenir **150.00**

Sterling Silver, enameled band **75.00**

Sterling Silver, flowers in high relief **35.00**

Sterling Silver, Palm Beach souvenir **150.00**

Sterling Silver, Queen's mark, "Silver Jubilee of ER II,"
Birmingham, England, 1077 . . . . **90.00**

TIFFANY

Charles L. Tiffany and John B. Young founded Tiffany & Young, a
stationery and gift store, in 1837. Tiffany & Young offered a wide
variety of goods ranging from desks to umbrellas. They purchased
most of the silverware they sold from John C. Moore, a firm founded in 1827 and located in New York. In 1841 Tiffany & Young
became Tiffany, Young & Ellis. The name was changed to Tiffany &
Company in 1853.

In 1852 Tiffany insisted that its silver comply with the English
sterling silver standard of 925/1000. Charles Lewis Tiffany was one
of the leaders in the fight that resulted in the federal government
adopting this standard, passing a 1906 statute that set 925/1000 as
the minimum requirement for articles marked "sterling."

During the 1850s Tiffany & Company produced some electroplated wares. Production increased significantly following the
Civil War. Tiffany marked its electroplated wares with a variety of
marks ranging from the company name to more complex marks
similar to those found on Tiffany silver. The manufacture of electroplated ware ended in 1931.

Tiffany achieved international recognition in 1867 when its
designs won the coveted gold medal for silver craftsmanship at the
Paris Exposition Universelle. This recognition resulted in Tiffany
becoming the silversmith and goldsmith to 17 crown heads of
Europe.

Tiffany incorporated as Tiffany & Co., Inc., in 1868. It was also
in 1868 that Tiffany acquired the Moore silverware factory and
made Edward C. Moore, son of John Moore, a director. Edward
Moore became head of Tiffany's silver studio. The studio became
America's first school of design. Moore encouraged apprentices to

observe and sketch nature, a theme that dominated many Tiffany designs in the last half of the 19th century. Beginning in 1868, Tiffany silverware was marked with "Tiffany & Co." and the letter "M." When Edward C. Moore died in 1891, the company continued marking its silverware with the initial of its incumbent president until the practice was discontinued in 1965.

It was Tiffany's jewelry, especially its botanical brooches and use of semi–precious gemstones, that captured the world's attention at the Paris Exposition Universelle in 1878. Louis Comfort Tiffany, son of Charles Tiffany, became the company's first Design Director. Under his leadership, the company manufactured a wealth of Art Nouveau objects, especially jewelry and lamps.

Recognized as one of the world's most respected sources of diamonds and other jewelry, Tiffany craftsmanship extends to a broad range of items including fine china, clocks, flatware, leather goods, perfume, scarves, silver, stationery, and watches. Tiffany opened its New York Corporate Division 1960. The Vince Lombardi Trophy for the National Football League Super Bowl Championship is one of its most famous commissions. Thus far, Tiffany has established ten additional corporate sales offices with more scheduled to open in the future.

References: John A. Shuman III, *The Collector's Encyclopedia of American Art Glass,* Collector Books, 1988, 1996 value update; Moise S. Steeg, Jr., *Tiffany Favrile Art Glass,* Schiffer Publishing, 1997; Kenneth Wilson, *American Glass 1760–1930: The Toledo Museum of Art,* 2 vols., Hudson Hills Press and The Toledo Museum of Art, 1994.

REPRODUCTION ALERT: Brass belt buckles and badges marked "Tiffany" have been widely reproduced.

Bonbon, glass, engraved gold irid, intaglio cut leaf border on lustrous golden amber bowl with 3 applied shell feet, inscribed "L. C. Tiffany–Favrile," 4³/₄" d, 3³/₄" h . . . . $ 850.00
Bookends, pr, gilt bronze, Buddha, oval, coppery patina, monogram, inscribed 11–23–31, mkd "Tiffany Studios New York 1025". 360.00

Lamp, table, green, red, and yellow striated leaded glass segments arranged in bellflower pattern, oil font, shaded green cased to white favrile glass ribbed base, 16" d shade, 20¹/₂" h, $20,000.00.

Sherbet, favrile glass, pulled feather design bowl, ftd, inscribed "L. C. T.," $850.00.

Bowl, glass, cased green, 10 ribbed, transparent pale green jar form with iridized gold int, inscribed "L. C. T. H1802," stained, 2¹/₂" h, 4¹/₂" d 300.00
Bowl, glass, opal and blue pastel flower bowl, bright cornflower blue rolled rim on white opal bowl internally decorated in Tiffany's molded herringbone leaf design, unsgd, 2³/₄" h, 7¹/₄" d, ... 900.00
Candleholders, pr, glass, gold irid, flared stretched and flattened bobéche rims on pedestaled candlecups, base inscribed "L. C. Tiffany–Favrile 1927," 1 restored foot, 4" h 550.00
Candlestick, glass, gold irid, twisted, heavy walled amber stick with 10 prominent swirled ribs on shaft, fine gold luster, inscribed "L. C. T.," and labeled, 6³/₄" h 400.00
Compote, glass, blue irid optic 10–rib scalloped bowl on tapered stem above folded foot, lustrous purple–blue surface overall, inscribed "L. C. T. Favrile 1710," gold foil label, 6" h, 6¹/₄" d 1,035.00
Compote, glass, gold irid, ruffled floriform amber bowl raised on cupped pedestal foot, inscribed "L. C. Tiffany Favrile 3472," 2³/₄" h, 9¹/₄" d 630.00
Compote, glass, purple irid, flared bowl raised on baluster stem with disk foot, bright purple lustrous color stretched at edges, base inscribed "L. C. Tiffany Inc. Favrile 1710," 4¹/₂" h, 8" d 860.00
Goblets, set of 6, glass, gold irid, delicate transparent amber stemmed wines with gold irid luster, inscribed "L. C. T." and "N8639, N8623, 8630, 8642," 5" h, 3¹/₂" d 970.00
Lamp, boudoir, dome–shaped amber cased to opal shade, subtle irid surface, gold Favrile baluster–form lamp, leaf–form lamp inclusions, lightly engraved outlines, glass foot inscribed "L. C. Tiffany Favrile," 15" h, 8" d 1,210.00
Lamp, floor, counterbalance, gold doré finish, bulbed 5 ftd base, adjustable ball lever socket, sgd "Tiffany Studios" on foot, 54" h 825.00
Lamp, table, Lily, 3 green pulled feather on opal lily blossom shades, sgd "L C. T.," squat–form 320 base, dark patina, candleholder lappet base, rewired, new sockets, 1 shade cracked, 9" h 1,100.00

Lamp Base, bronze, fluid, urn style, quatraform, oil canister and base mkd "Tiffany Studios New York 2993," 8" h **275.00**

Picture Frame, bronze, Chinese, broad dark alligatored finish, imp "Tiffany Studios New York 1761," 6³⁄₄ x 9" **385.00**

Pot, cast bronze, deeply molded frieze of robed men standing before classical architectural elements, mkd "S113, Tiffany Studios, From the Antique, 1607," 4³⁄₄" d, 3³⁄₄" h **470.00**

Vase, glass, cobalt blue ribbed, bulbed oval chimney form with 16 subtle vertical ribs, dark translucent blue, inscribed "L. C. T. Favrile," 9" h **900.00**

Vase, glass, millefiore favrile glass, lustrous gold oval body with green heart–shaped leaves on amber vines overall, further dec by subtle blossom form–millefiore canes, inscribed "L. C. Tiffany Favrile 4927G," 5" h **1,150.00**

TIFFIN GLASS

J. Beatty and Sons built a large glass works in Tiffin, Ohio, in 1888. In 1892 Tiffin Glass Company became part of the U.S. Glass Company, a combine based in Pittsburgh, Pennsylvania. The Tiffin plant was designated as factory "R."

Initially, factory "R" made only pressed tumblers and barware. By the early 1900s, production had expanded to lighter weight stemware and brilliant cut glass. The 1910s saw the product line expanded further with the addition of blown, cut, and etched dinnerware and stemware patterns in crystal and color.

Tiffin billed itself as "America's Prestige Crystal...within reach of the limited budget." During the Depression, Tiffin made hundreds of patterns, its output twice that of Cambridge and A. H. Heisey. Tiffin purchased Heisey blanks to meet its production requirements. The company's famed "Lady Stems" were made between 1939 and 1956.

Tiffin's profits carried many other plants in the U.S. Glass Company. Several plants making inexpensive glassware were closed or sold during the Depression. In 1937 the main office of the U.S. Glass Company moved from Pittsburgh to the Tiffin factory in Steubenville.

In 1938 C. W. Carlson, Sr. became president of the U.S. Glass Company. Under his leadership and that of his son, C. W. Carlson, Jr., Tiffin was rejuvenated. New shapes and colors were added to the Tiffin line. Swedish–trained craftsmen were responsible for the hand–blown, hand–crafted Swedish line introduced in 1940.

By 1951 Tiffin was the only U.S. Glass plant remaining in operation. U.S. Glass Company purchased Duncan & Miller in 1955 and moved some of the company's molds and glassmakers to Steubenville. New Duncan patterns by Tiffin included Countess and Wistaria.

The early 1960s proved very difficult for the U.S. Glass Company. It declared bankruptcy in 1962 and closed the Tiffin factory. Production resumed under the name "Tiffin Art Glass Corporation," a firm created by C. W. Carlson, Jr., and several former Tiffin employees. Tiffin Art Glass produced high quality, etched stemware and glass accent pieces. The company also offered a pattern matching program, annually manufacturing retired patterns. The phrase "Tiffin Is Forever" was used to promote this program.

Tiffin purchased the molds and equipment of the T. G. Hawkes Cut Glass Company, Corning, New York, in 1964. Hawkes' Delft Diamond and Laurel were continued in production.

Continental Can purchased the Tiffin factory in 1966, selling it in 1968 to the Interpace Corporation, a holding company of Franciscan china. Interpace kept many Tiffin patterns in production including Palais Versailles. In addition, Madeira, made in colors identified as Blue, Citron, Cornsilk, Ice, Plum, Olive, and Smoke, was created to coordinate with Franciscan dinnerware patterns.

Tiffin was sold once again in 1980, this time to Towle Silversmiths. Towle began importing blanks from Eastern Europe. In 1984 Towle closed the Tiffin factory and donated the land and buildings to the city of Tiffin. Jim Maxwell, a former Tiffin glass cutter, bought the Tiffin molds and equipment. The Tiffin trademark is now a registered trademark of Maxwell Crystal, Inc. In 1992 Maxwell placed four Hawkes and Tiffin patterns back into production.

Reference: Fred Bickenheuser, *Tiffin Glassmasters, Book I* (1979, 1994–95 value update), *Book II* (1981, 1994–95 value update), *Book III* (1985), Glassmasters Publications; Bob Page and Dale Fredericksen, *Tiffin Is Forever, A Stemware Identification Guide,* Page–Fredericksen, 1994; Leslie Piña, *Tiffin Glass: 1914–1940,* Schiffer Publishing, 1997; Harry L. Rinker, *Stemware of the 20th Century: The Top 200 Patterns,* House of Collectibles, 1997.

Adam, champagne, pink . . . . **$ 35.00**

Black Satin, candlesticks, pr, #15328, 8" h **50.00**

Black Satin, compote, twisted stem, hp cockatoos, sprays of green leaves, white enamel dots, 10" d, 5³⁄₄" h **170.00**

Black Satin, vase, gold dec, 7³⁄₄" h **80.00**

Cadena, bowl, yellow, handled, 6" d **25.00**

Cadena, console bowl, 12" d **30.00**

Cadena, cream soup bowl, pink **35.00**

Cadena, creamer, yellow **40.00**

Cadena, mayonnaise set, 3 pcs **35.00**

Cadena, plate, yellow, 6" d **12.00**

Cadena, sugar, cov, yellow **28.00**

Classic, champagne, crystal, platinum band, $25.00.

Canterbury, iced tea tumbler, ftd, citron	20.00
Cerice, bell	80.00
Cerice, creamer and sugar, crystal, matching tray	100.00
Cerice, juice tumbler, #071	22.00
Cerice, mayonnaise set, 3 pcs	35.00
Cerice, plate, 8" d	18.00
Cerice, sugar, cov	30.00
Cerice, sundae	25.00
Cherokee Rose, bud vase, 8" h	50.00
Cherokee Rose, celery, 10½" l	40.00
Cherokee Rose, champagne, #17399	25.00
Cherokee Rose, finger bowl	25.00
Cherokee Rose, mayonnaise set, 3 pcs	45.00
Cherokee Rose, relish, 3 part, 12½" d	50.00
Cherokee Rose, sherbet, #17403	25.00
Cherokee Rose, table bell	70.00
Chinese Modern, sugar, cov	18.00
Classic, juice tumbler, 3½" h	40.00
Classic, wine, pink	52.00
Empire, plate, twilight, 8" d	22.00
Flanders, bowl, pink	55.00
Flanders, cup and saucer, blown, yellow	70.00
Flanders, decanter, yellow	230.00
Flanders, oyster cocktail, crystal	18.00
Flanders, plate, pink, 8" d	20.00
Flanders, tumbler, ftd, pink	40.00
Fontaine, champagne, pink	35.00
Fontaine, cup and saucer, blown, twilight	130.00
Fontaine, goblet, pink	45.00
Fontaine, sundae, green	30.00
Fuschia, ashtray	25.00
Fuchsia, cake plate, 10½" d	55.00
Fuchsia, claret, #15083	25.00
Fuchsia, iced tea tumbler, ftd, #15083	32.00
Fuchsia, salt and pepper shakers, pr	100.00
June Night, champagne	22.00
June Night, claret	38.00
June Night, cocktail	25.00
June Night, creamer	25.00
June Night, iced tea tumbler, ftd	35.00
June Night, sherry, #17403, 2 oz	50.00
June Night, sugar, cov	22.00
June Night, wine, #17403	38.00
Juno, candlesticks, pr, #348, green	35.00
Juno, server, server, center handle, pink	80.00
Juno, sugar, cov, yellow	25.00
Le Fleure, cup and saucer, yellow	50.00
Le Fleure, plate, yellow, 7¼" d	20.00
Leige, cocktail, #17467	20.00
Rambling Rose, goblet	25.00
Rosalind, cup and saucer, blown, yellow	40.00
Twilight, bowl, ftd, wishbone, 6½" d	80.00
Twilight, cornucopia, 9¼" l	100.00
Twilight, plate, 8" d	25.00
Wistaria, champagne, 4½"	25.00
Wistaria, claret	25.00
Wistaria, cordial	38.00
Wistaria, iced tea	32.00
Wistaria, juice, 5½"	28.00
Wistaria, oyster cocktail	25.00
Wistaria, parfait	32.00

TOOLS

Tools divide into hand tools and power tools. Power tools divide into hand and bench models. Many craftsmen made their own tools during the 18th century and early part of the 19th century. As a result, tools exhibited a wide variety of shapes and forms.

Mass–produced tools arrived on the scene in the mid–19th century. Stanley manufactured its first tools in 1854. Craftsman and handyman now had access to the same tool. Sales distribution through hardware stores, mail–order catalogs such as Sears, Roebuck, and automobile stores such as Pep Boys contributed to universal equality among tool users.

From the 1920s through the end of the 1950s, the basement workshop was a standard fixture in many homes. Manufacturers quickly developed hand and machine tools for this specific market. The do–it–yourself, fix–it–yourself attitude of the late 1940s through the 1960s resulted in strong tool sales.

Tool collectors collect primarily by brand or tool type. Most focus on tools made before 1940. Quality is critical. Most collectors want nothing to do with cheap foreign imports. Interest is building in power tools and some specialized tool groups, e.g., Snap–on–Tools.

References: Ronald S. Barlow, *The Anique Tool Collector's Guide to Value, Third Edition,* Windmill Publishing, 1991; Terri Clemens, *American Family Farm Antiques,* Wallace–Homestead, Krause Publications, 1994; Herbert P. Kean and Emil S. Pollak, *A Price Guide To Antique Tools,* Astragal Press, 1992; Herbert P. Kean and Emil S. Pollak, *Collecting Antique Tools,* Astragal Press, 1990; Kathryn McNerney, *Antique Tools, Our American Heritage,* Collector Books, 1979, 1996 value update; Emil and Martyl Pollak, *A Guide To American Wooden Planes and Their Makers, Third Edition* The Astragal Press, 1994; R. A. Salaman, *Dictionary of Tools,* Charles Scribner's Sons, 1974; John Walter, *Antique & Collectible Stanley Tools: A Guide To Identity and Value,* Tool Merchants, 1990; Jack P. Wood, *Town–Country Old Tools and Locks, Keys and Closures,* L–W Books, 1990, 1995 value update.

Collectors' Clubs: Early American Industries Assoc, PO Box 143, Delmar, NY 12054; Early American Industries–West, 8476 West Way Dr, La Jolla, CA 92038; Tool Group of Canada, 7 Tottenham Rd, Ontario MC3 2J3 Canada.

Axe, Keen Kutter, hand, 3" blade	$ 25.00
Axe, Winchester, diamond edge broad axe	60.00
Carpenter's Rule, Stanley, hardwood, steel trim, painted finish, 4 fold, 2 ft	20.00
Chisel, Stanley, #25, Everlasting Chisel, steel shank, hickory handle, lacquered finish	15.00
Dowel Jig, Stanley, cast iron, nickel–plated finish	20.00
Drill, Stanley, hand, cast–iron frame, hardwood handles, japanned finish, 12" l	20.00
Gauge, #374 butt marker, plastic case, 4" w	8.00
Hammer, Stanley, #100, "Golden Hammer of Merit," velvet–lined box, presentation plaque	130.00
Hammer, Winchester, claw	40.00
Hammer, Keen Kutter	25.00
Level, lignum vitae and brass, unusual rotating brass cov protects level's vial, 12" l	12.50
Pattern Maker's Block, Stanley, #9, late adjuster, new side handle, type "AA" mark on iron, S & W Hart	950.00

Pulley Block, iron hook, wood block and wheel, 10¼" h, $35.00.

Plane, Stanley, #2 Smooth Plane, type "BB" mark on
 iron, cleaned and lightly repainted 175.00
Plane, Stanley, #6 Fore Plane, type "20," blue finish 45.00
Plane, Stanley, #8C Jointer Plane, type "17", orig
 box, unused. 350.00
Plane, Stanley, #9 Patternmaker's Block Plane, late
 adjuster, new side handle, type "AA" mark on iron,
 S & W Hart 950.00
Plane, Stanley, #1104 Victor Smooth Plane, gray
 frame, red frog, stained red handle and knob, orig
 box 100.00
Plane, Stanley, #S18 Steel Block Plane, S & W Hart
 trademark, type "AA" on cutter, small owner's initials "W. N." stamped on both sides 135.00
Plumb Bob, Berger, C. L. & Sons, Boston, MA, brass,
 surveyor's, 3" l 55.00
Rule, Esborn Lumber Corp, New York, NY, advertising
 hook rule, with lumber scales, reverse imprinted
 with company advertising, 24" l 65.00
Rule, Winchester, #9532, 4–fold boxwood caliper,
 brass arch hinge, 1 ft l 40.00
Rule and Level, Stanley, #38½, machinist's bench
 level, "Sweetheart" trademark, 4" l 65.00
Saw, Keen Kutter, hand, #816, applewood handle. 55.00
Saw, Stanley, bead saw, steel blade, hardwood han-
 dle, orange enamel finish, 10" l. 25.00
Saw, Winchester, hand. 35.00
Screwdriver, Keen Kutter, Blue Brand, steel, hard-
 wood handle, rosewood finish, nickel–plated steel
 ferrule 20.00
Screwdriver, Stanley, steel blade, hardwood handle,
 nickel–plated finish, 8" l. 25.00
Screwdriver, Winchester, #7160, 1½" l 35.00
Socket Chisel, Stanley, steel shank, hickory handle,
 lacquered finish 10.00
Tool Cabinet, Stanley, 32 tools, oak cabinet, lac-
 quered finish, 29" l. 150.00
Tool Tray, pine, sq nail construction, cutout handle,
 well worn, refinished, 29⅑" l, 12" w, 8½" h. 45.00

Wrench, H & E Wrench Co, New Bedford, MA, pipe,
 metal. 45.00
Wrench, Keen Kutter, #93, pocket, 4" l 12.00
Wrench, Stanley, tire bolt, cast iron, rosewood knob,
 16" l 225.00
Wrench, Winchester, monkey wrench, wooden han-
 dle, 6" l 50.00

TOOTHPICK HOLDERS

The toothpick holder became an important tabletop accessory during the Victorian era. Many dinnerware, stemware, and silverware
services included a toothpick holder. While glass toothpick holders are most common, examples in bisque, earthenware, plastic,
porcelain, silver plate, silver, and other materials are easily found.

Toothpick holders remained popular household accessories
through the end of the 1950s. They still are a common fixture on
restaurant checkout counters. In fact, restaurant size toothpicks
and individual silver–plated toothpicks are two underappreciated
subcategories. Today, one is more likely to find the family toothpick holder inside a kitchen cabinet than on the table. Daily brush-
ing and water jets have relegated the toothpick to occasional rather
than daily use.

When is a toothpick holder not a toothpick holder? When it is a
match holder, miniature spoon holder for a toy table setting, a salt
shaker with a ground off top, a small rose bowl, shot glass, an individual open sugar, a vase, or a whimsy. A toothpick is designed to
hold toothpicks. Toothpicks have a flat bottom and allow enough
of the toothpick to extend above the top so one can be extracted
with no problem. If the toothpicks do not extend above the top or
stand erect, chances are the object is not a toothpick holder.

References: Neila and Tom Bredehoft, *Findlay Toothpick Holders*,
Cherry Hill Publications, 1995; William Heacock, *Encyclopedia of
Victorian Colored Pattern Glass, Book 1, Toothpick Holders From
A To Z, Second Edition,* Antique Publications, 1976, 1992 value
update; National Toothpick Holders Collectors Society, *Toothpick
Holders: China, Glass, and Metal,* Antique Publications, 1992.

Collector's Club: National Toothpick Holders Collectors Society,
1224 Spring Valley Ln, West Chester, PA 19380.

Art Glass, custard, souvenir, Belvedere, IL. . . . . $ 35.00
Art Glass, purple slag, figural, boot. 50.00
Bisque, cat wearing coachman's outfit, barrel, figural 55.00
Bisque, Geisha, blue rim, 2½" h. 15.00
Brass, top hat, umbrella 20.00
Ceramic, blue–faced dog, multicolored glaze, Japan,
 3¼" h 20.00
Ceramic, man with cart, multicolored glaze, shiny
 finish, Japan. 25.00
Ceramic, donkey pulling cart, Occupied Japan 7.50
Ceramic, top hat, sunset hunting dog scene, green
 and cream ground, cobalt blue band. 40.00
Glass, amber, frosted, Gonterman swirl. 150.00
Glass, custard, argonaut shell 375.00
Glass, 3– fruits, Jenkins Glass 45.00
Glass, shoe, gold, 1972 . . . . 10.00
Majolica, figural, mouse with ear of corn 135.00
Milk Glass, white, barrel, metal hoops 25.00

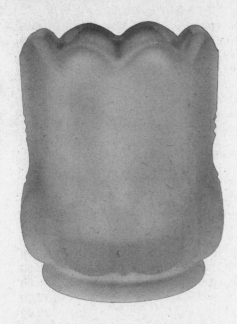

Glass, frosted, Michigan–type pattern, Degenhart, 2⁵/₈" h, $10.00.

Milk Glass, white, horseshoe and clover **22.00**
Milk Glass, white, pansy, 3 handles, Kemple **35.00**
Milk Glass, white, scrolled shell, goofus dec **12.00**
Milk Glass, white, Spirit of '76, bottom reads "N. T.
    H. C. S," and "St. Louis, MO" in outside ring, "Aug
    1978" in center **15.00**
Pattern Glass, Beatty Rib, blue opalescent **50.00**
Pattern Glass, Box in Box, green, gold dec **80.00**
Pattern Glass, Button Arches, ruby stained, "Mother,
    1947" **20.00**
Pattern Glass, Continental, Heisey **45.00**
Pattern Glass, Daisy and Button, blue **70.00**
Pattern Glass, Delft Diamond, ftd base **25.00**
Pattern Glass, Feather, clear **65.00**
Pattern Glass, Hobb's Hobnail, vaseline **20.00**
Pattern Glass, Iowa, clear **25.00**
Pattern Glass, Melon, opalescent **50.00**
Pattern Glass, Minnesota **45.00**

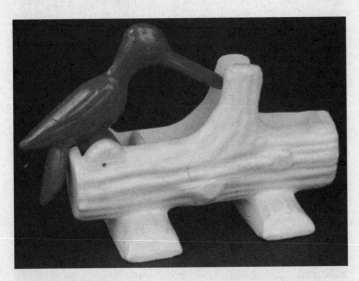

Plastic, white log, red woodpecker with pronged beak picks up toothpicks, 4¹/₂" l, 2¹/₂" h, $10.00.

Pattern Glass, Rising Sun **35.00**
Pattern Glass, Swinger, clear and ruby **22.00**
Pattern Glass, Windows, cranberry opalescent **45.00**
Silver Plate, cat and bucket **65.00**
Silver Plate, chick emerging from egg, feet on branch,
    square base, mkd "Hartford" **70.00**
Silver Plate, rooster, engraved "Picks," 2" h **50.00**
Wood, beaver, painted features, broad tail, hollowed
    out trunk **5.00**

TORQUAY POTTERY

Pottery manufacturing came to the Torquay district of South Devon, England, in the 1870s following G. J. Allen's discovery of a red terra–cotta potting clay in 1869. Allen organized the Watcombe Pottery, producing a wealth of art pottery terra–cotta products ranging from busts and plaques to garden ornaments and vases. Classical forms and decorative motifs were used as was enamel decoration.

In 1875 Dr. Gillow founded the Torquay Terra–Cotta Company. Its products were similar to those of Watcombe Pottery. It closed in 1905, only to be reopened by Enoch Staddon in 1908. Staddon produced pottery rather than terra–cotta ware.

John Philips established the Aller Vale Pottery in 1881. The company specialized in souvenir pieces. Designs were painted on pieces with a thick colored slip that contrasted with the color of the ground slip coat. This "motto" ware achieved widespread popularity by 1900. In 1902 Aller Vale and Watcombe merged and became Royal Aller Vale and Watcombe Art Potteries. The new company produced commemorative and motto ware.

Burton, Daison, and Longpark pottery are examples of numerous small companies that sprang up in the Torquay District and made wares similar to that produced by Aller Vale and Watcombe. Longpark, the last of these companies, closed in 1957. When Royal Aller Vale and Watcombe closed in 1962, the era of red pottery production in Torquay ended.

Collectors' Club: Torquay Pottery Collectors Society, PO Box 373, Schoolcraft, MI 49087.

Bowl, cottage, "May the Hinges of Friendship Never
    Go Rusty," 4¹/₄" d . . . . **$ 50.00**
Cake Stand, fruit, "He is Well Paid Who is Well
    Satisfied," 9" d **100.00**
Condiment Set, cottage, "Actions Speak Louder Than
    Words" salt, "Good Examples Are Best Sermons"
    pepper, and "Speak Little Speak Well" sugar **40.00**
Creamer, cottage, "Put a Stout Heart to a Steep Hill,"
    2¹/₄" h **35.00**
Eggcup and Saucer, cottage, "Fine Words Will Not
    Fill," 3" h **40.00**
Jam Jar, sailboat scene, "Southsea, Be Aisy With Tha
    Jam," stamped "Longpark Torquay, England," 4³/₄" h **50.00**
Pitcher, cottage, "Good Morning, Never Say Die Up
    Man and Try," 4¹/₂" h **70.00**
Plate, black cockerel, "From Durham Tis Deeds Alone
    Must Win the Prize," 5" d **60.00**
Plate, cottage, "Home Well and Have Well," mkd
    Royal Watcombe Pottery, 5" d **45.00**
Plate, cottage, "Better To Sit Still Than Rise To Fall,"
    Watcombe Torquay mark, 6¹/₂" d **50.00**

Pot, story house, "If You Can't Fly Climb," 3½" h **35.00**
Sugar Bowl, snow cottage, "Take a Little Sugar,"
    Watcombe Torquay mark, 1¾" h **45.00**
Tray, cottage, "A Stitch in Time Saves Nine," 5" l **35.00**

TOY SOLDIERS

Toy soldiers divide into two main groups: (1) two–dimensional, primarily paper soldiers and (2) three–dimensional soldiers. Stand–up toy soldiers, made by applying a printed image to a composition or wooden cutout, and used for bowling or shooting sets, bridge the gap between the two categories. Three–dimensional soldiers were made in a wide variety of material, e.g., composition, lead, pewter, plastic, tin, etc.

The earliest toy soldiers were paper soldiers, often printed in sheets that were cut apart for play. Hilperts of Nuremberg, Germany, introduced the first three–dimensional toy soldiers near the end of the 18th century. Blondel (French), Britains (English), Courtenay (English), Gerbeau (French), Gottschalk (Swiss), Mignot (French), and Wehrli (Swiss) are leading 19th–century toy soldier manufacturers.

While Britains and Mignot are the leading manufacturers of 20th–century toy soldiers, other companies, such as Blenheim, Elastolin/Lineol, Heyde, and S.A.E., did impact on the market. Mignot acquired Cuperly, Blondel, and Gerbeau, a combine that had previously purchased the French firm of Lucotte. Mignot offered models of more than 20,000 different soldiers in the 1950s. Britains introduced its first hollow–cast figures in 1893. Many of their figures had movable arms. Britains quality is the standard by which collectors judge all other mass–produced figures.

The American dime store soldier arrived on the scene in the 1930s and remained popular through the early 1950s. Auburn Rubber, Barclay, Grey Iron, and Manoil are the four leading manufacturers. All–Nu, American Alloy, American Soldier Co., Beton, Ideal, Jones, Lincoln Log, Miller, Playwood Plastic Soljertoys, Tommy Toy, Tootsietoy, and Warren are other American companies who made lead, plastic, or rubber soldiers.

Barclay and Manoil dominated the market primarily because of their realistic castings and originality of poses. Pre–1941 Barclay soldiers have helmets that are glued or clipped on.

Toy soldier is a generic term. The category includes animal, civilian, holiday, and western figures in addition to military figures. Military figures are preferred over civilian figures.

There are two toy soldier markets—children and adult. Children play with the soldier. So do adults, but in an entirely different way. Adults use the soldiers to create mock battle scenes, some involving thousands of figures. These platform battlegrounds and dioramas are often elaborate and highly authentic.

Recently adult collectors have been speculating heavily in limited production toy soldiers made by a small group of toy soldier craftsman. Others are buying unpainted castings and painting them. The result is an increased variety of material on the market. Make certain you know exactly what you are buying.

Toy soldier collectors place a premium of 20 to 40 percent on set boxes. Beware of repainted pieces. Undocumented touch–up is a major problem in the market.

References: Norman Joplin, *The Great Book Of Hollow–Cast Figures,* New Cavendish Books, 1992; Norman Joplin, *Toy Soldiers,* Running Press, Courage Books, 1994; Henry I. Kurtz and Burtt R. Ehrlich, *The Art Of The Toy Soldier,* Abbeville Press, 1987;

Richard O'Brien, *Collecting American–Made Toy Soldiers: Identification and Value Guide, No. 3,* Books Americana, Krause Publications, 1997; James Opie, *Collecting Toy Soldiers,* Pincushion Press, 1992; Edward Ryan, *Paper Soldiers: The Illustrated History of Printed Paper Armies of the 18th, 19th & 20th Centuries,* Golden Age Editions, 1995, distributed by P.E.I. International; Joe Wallis, *Armies of the World, Britains Ltd. Lead Soldiers 1925–1941,* published by author, 1993.

Periodical: *Military Trader,* PO Box 1050, Dubuque, IA 52004.

Collectors' Clubs: American Model Soldier Society, 1528 El Camino Real, San Carlos, CA 94070; Miniature Figure Collectors of America, 102 St. Paul's Rd, Ardmore, PA 19003; Toy Soldier Collectors Of America, 5340 40th Ave N, St Petersburg, FL 33710.

All–Nu Paper Soldiers, jeep and 3 soldiers, c1942 . . . . . . **$ 5.00**
All–Nu Paper Soldiers, tank and 3 soldiers, c1942 . . . . **7.00**
Auburn Rubber, grenade thrower **18.00**
Auburn Rubber, machine gunner, kneeling **12.00**
Auburn Rubber, motorcyclist **30.00**
Auburn Rubber, soldier, kneeling with binoculars **15.00**
Authenticast, Russian Infantry **65.00**
Barclay, anti–aircraft gunner, standing, pre–WWII **15.00**
Barclay, bugler, tin helmet, pre–WWII **15.00**
Barclay, cook, holding roast, pre–WWII **12.00**
Barclay, doctor, carrying bag, pre–WWII **15.00**
Barclay, flag bearer, pot helmet, post–WWII **15.00**
Barclay, machine gunner, prone, pot helmet,
    post–WWII **15.00**
Barclay, parachutist, landing, pre–WWII **25.00**
Barclay, pilot, standing, pre–WWII **18.00**
Barclay, sailor, marching, pre–WWII **20.00**
Barclay, signalman with flags, pre–WWII **20.00**
Barclay, soldier, standing at attention, tin hat,
    pre–WWII **15.00**
Barclay, stretcher bearer, pre–WWII **15.00**
Barclay, wireless operator, tin hat, pre–WWII **30.00**
Blenheim, #B2, Coldstream Guards Colors, 1812,
    orig box **120.00**
Blenheim, #B17, Royal Marines, 1923, orig box **75.00**
Blenheim, #C13, 17th Lancers, 1879, orig box **150.00**
Britains, #44, 2nd Dragoon Guards, The Queen's
    Bays, c1940, orig Whisstock box **100.00**
Britains, #48, Egyptian Camel Corps, orig box **80.00**
Britains, #136, Russian Cossacks, orig box **175.00**
Britains, #138, French Cuirassiers, orig box **150.00**

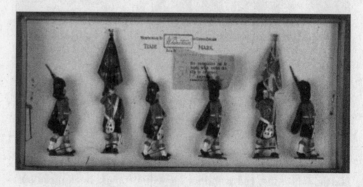

Britains, #2111, Black Watch Colour Party, c1958, $325.00.

Manoil, aviator holding bomb, #85, mkd "USA," post–WWII, 2½", $25.00.

Britains, #201, Officers of the General Staff. 125.00
Britains, #1343, The Royal Horse Guards, c1940, orig "Armies of the World" box 140.00
Britains, #2009, Belgian Grenadier Regiment, orig box 125.00
Britains, #2028, Red Army Cavalry, orig box 200.00
Britains, #2035, Swedish Life Guard, tied in orig box . . . 200.00
Britains, #9291, Arabs of the Desert on Horses, orig box 85.00
Britains, #9402, State Open Road Landau, tied in orig box 325.00
Built–Rite, Army Camp, #16, 1936 . . . . 75.00
Built–Rite, Army Raider's Victory Unit, paper, 28 pcs 75.00
Built–Rite, Fort and Soldier Set 175.00
Built–Rite, Navy Battle Fleet and Coast Artillery Gun, #60 . . . . 50.00
Elastolin/Lineol, flak gunner, kneeling with shell 40.00
Elastolin/Lineol, medic, walking, carrying pack with red cross 35.00
Elastolin/Lineol, staff officer, pointing, with field glasses 35.00
Heyde, French Ambulance Unit, orig box 275.00
Heyde, WWI German Infantry 95.00
Manoil, aircraft spotter, post–WWII, mkd "USA," 2½" 25.00
Manoil, bomb thrower, 3 grenades, pre–WWII 15.00
Manoil, cannon loader, pre–WWII 15.00
Manoil, flag bearer, pre–WWII 18.00
Manoil, grenade thrower, post–WWII, mkd "USA," 2½" 25.00
Manoil, machine gunner, prone, pre–WWII 15.00
Manoil, navy gunner, white, firing deck gun, pre–WWII 35.00
Manoil, observer with binoculars, post–WWII, mkd "USA," 2½" 28.00
Manoil, radio operator, standing, pre–WWII 35.00
Manoil, sharpshooter, camouflage, prone, pre–WWII 20.00
Manoil, soldier, charging with bayonet, pre–WWII 28.00
Manoil, soldier with bazooka, post–WWII 20.00

Manoil, soldier with gas mask and flare gun, pre–WWII 20.00
Manoil, soldier with mine detector, post–WWII 30.00
Manoil, soldier, wounded, pre–WWII 15.00
Manoil, soldier, writing letter, pre–WWII 50.00
Manoil, tommy gunner, standing, post–WWII 25.00
Mignot, Austrian Infantry, 1805, tied in orig box 225.00
Mignot, Band of Napoleon's Imperial Guard, 1812 . . . . 350.00
Mignot, Bengal Lancers, 1890–1914, tied in orig box . . . 300.00
Mignot, Drum Majors of the Empire, orig boxes 475.00
Mignot, French Napoleonic Skirmishers of the 17th Line Regiment, 1809, orig box, c1965 . . . . 85.00
Mignot, French Touraine Regiment, 1750, orig box 200.00
Mignot, French Volunteer Infantry, 1790, orig box, c1950 . . . . 225.00
Mignot, Infantry of King Louis XIV, c1950, orig box 400.00
Mignot, Polish Lancers, 1812, orig box 250.00
Mignot, Spanish Hussars, 1805, orig box 275.00
Militia Models, Gatling Gun Team of 3rd London Rifles, orig box 95.00
Militia Models, The Pipes and Drums of 1st Battalion Royal Irish Rangers, orig box 125.00
Nostalgia, Kaffrarian Rifles, 1910, orig box 125.00
Nostalgia, New South Wales Irish Rifles, 1900, orig box 95.00
S.A.E., #1358, Royal Horse Guards, 1945, orig box 50.00
S.A.E., #3310, 1st Bengal Lancers, orig box 115.00

TOY TRAIN ACCESSORIES

Toy train accessories and boxed train sets are two of the hottest toy train collecting categories in the 1990s. Toy train accessories divide into two main groups: (1) those made by toy train manufacturers and (2) those made by others. Many of the latter were in kit form.

As with toy trains, toy train accessories are sized by gauge. An HO building on a Lionel train platform appears very much out of place. O and S gauge accessories are the most desired. The period box adds 15 to 25 percent to the value.

Bachmann Brothers, a manufacturer of eyeglasses, produced its first plastic train accessory, a picket fence, in 1949. A log cabin followed in 1950. By the mid–1950s Bachmann's Plasticville O/S gauge buildings were found on the vast majority of America's toy train platforms. An HO line was introduced in 1955, an N gauge line in 1968. Plasticville houses are marked with a "BB" on a banner in a circle.

Bachmann ended a challenge to its market supremacy by Unlimited Plastics' Littletown when it acquired the company in 1956. Bachmann carefully stores its Plasticville dies, giving it the ability to put any model back into production when sufficient demand occurs.

References: Frank C. Hare, *Plasticville, 3rd Edition*, Kalmbach, 1993; Alan Stewart, *Greenberg's Guide To Lionel Trains, 1945–1969, Vol VI: Accessories*, Kalmbach, 1994.

Accessory Set, 10 pcs, clock, telegraph poles, crossing gate, crossing signal, sign, and double semaphore, Ives, 1930–32 . . . . $ 60.00
Automatic Crossing Gate, 0–77, Lionel, 1923–39 . . . . 25.00

Portal Gantry Crane, #282, swinging boom with electro magnet, Lionel, 1954, 10¹/₂" h, $95.00.

Automatic Gateman, HO–145, Lionel, 1959 . . . . 40.00
Bank, Plasticville 15.00
Bell Danger Signal, 584, S gauge, American Flyer 18.00
Billboard, Plasticville 1.50
Bridge, 91, O gauge, Ives 20.00
Coal Elevator, 96, manual control, Lionel, 1938–40 . . . . 110.00
Colonial Mansion, Plasticville 15.00
Country Church, Plasticville 5.00
Covered Bridge, Plasticville 8.00
Crossing Gate, plastic, Marx, 8¹/₄" l. 05
Diner Kit, Plasticville 25.00
Direction Controller, 88, Lionel, 1933 . . . . 3.00
Eureka Diner, 275, S gauge, American Flyer 40.00
Fence and Gate, 12 pcs, Plasticville 3.50
Figure, conductor, #552, Lionel, 1932 . . . . 18.00
Figure Set, 32 pcs, plastic, Lionel, 1959 . . . . 10.00
Flashing Signal, 79, cream or aluminum, Lionel,
    1928–42 . . . . 75.00
Flag Pole, 89, O gauge, Lionel 30.00
Freight Shed, 155, ivory base, grey roof, Lionel,
    1930–39 . . . . 200.00
Freight Station, Plasticville 20.00
Gas Station, Plasticville 15.00
Lamp Post, 35, gray or silver, Lionel, 1940 . . . . 20.00
Lamp Post, 54, double light, dark green, Lionel 45.00
Lamp Post, electric, boulevard type, green base, sig-
    nal bulb, Ives, 1931–32 . . . . 75.00
Lamp Post, lighted, Marx 5.50
Lamp Post, twin bulbs, stamped steel, Marx 6.00
Log Cabin, rustic fence and tree, Plasticville 12.00
Low Bridge Sign, 75, Lionel, 1921 . . . . 40.00
Newstand with whistle, 118, Lionel, 1958 . . . . 50.00
Passenger Station, #88 lamp brackets, tin chimney,
    Ives, 1924–28 . . . . 100.00
Passenger Station, Plasticville 20.00
Post Office, Plasticville 18.00
Railroad Signal Bridge, Plasticville 5.50
Railroad Station, plastic, Marx 12.00

Railroad Work Car, Plasticville 22.00
Road Signs, Plasticville 20.00
Semaphore, 107–S, Ives, 1907–30 . . . . 15.00
Signal Set, 3 pcs, plastic, Marx 1.50
Street Accessories, 15 pcs, Plasticville. 28.00
Suburban Home, #912, Lionel, 1932 . . . . 400.00
Supermarket, small, Plasticville 8.00
Switch Tower, Plasticville 8.00
Telegraph Pole, 85, Lionel 12.00
Telegraph Pole, 1564, Ives, 1931–32 . . . . 45.00
Telephone Booth, Plasticville 5.00
Town Hall, Plasticville 15.00
Traffic Crossing Signal, 83, red base, Lionel 175.00
Truss Bridge, S gauge, American Flyer. 5.00
Tunnel, HO–119, Lionel, 1959. . . . . 8.50
Union Station, Plasticville 20.00
Warning Bell, 69, Lionel, 1921–35 . . . . 30.00
Water Tank, O gauge, American Flyer 40.00
Water Tank, Plasticville 5.00
Water Tower, 93, green, Lionel, 1932 . . . . 25.00
Well, Plasticville 5.00
Whistle Controller, 65, Lionel, 1935 . . . . 8.00
Whistle Station, 48W, litho building, Lionel, 1937–42 . . . . 15.00
Whistle Unit, remote control, American Flyer 25.00

TOY TRAINS

Cast–iron push and windup trains, some running on tracks and some not, typified the pre–1920 period. The mid–1920s through the late 1950s is the golden age of toy trains. American Flyer, Ives, and Lionel produced electric model trains that featured highly detailed castings and markings. Inexpensive lithographed tin windup train sets made by firms ranging from Marx to unknown Japanese manufacturers made during the 1930s through the 1960s hardly dented the toy train market. A slow conversion to plastic occurred within the toy train industry in the late 1950s and early 1960s. Most collectors shun plastic like the plague.

Toy trains divide into mass–produced trains and scratch–built trains. This category only includes mass–produced trains.

Trains are collected first by company and second by gauge. Lionel is king of the hill, followed by American Flyer. As a result, O, O27, and S are the three most popular gauges among collectors. Collector interest in HO gauge trains has increased significantly in the past five years. Many toy train auctions now include HO trains among their offerings. Interest is minimal in N gauge.

The 1990s witnessed several major shifts in collecting emphasis. First, post–World War II replaced pre–World War II trains as the hot chronological collecting period. Pre–1945 prices have stabilized. In the case of cast–iron trains, some decline has been noted. Second, accessories and sets are the hot post–1945 collecting areas. Prices on most engines and rolling stock have stabilized. Third, the speculative bubble in mass–produced trains of the 1970s and 1980s, e.g., LBG, has burst. With some exceptions, most of these trains are selling below their initial retail cost on the secondary market. Fourth, adult collectors currently are investing heavily in limited edition reproductions and special model issues. These pieces have not been strongly tested on the secondary market. Fifth, there are initial signs of a growing collector interest in HO material, primarily the better grade German trains, and inexpensive lithographed tin windup trains.

References: General: *Greenberg's Pocket Price Guide, Lionel Trains, 1901–1996, 16th Edition,* Kalmbach, 1996; *Greenberg's Pocket Price Guide: Marx Trains, 5th Edition,* Kalmbach, 1995; *Greenberg's Pocket Price Guide, American Flyer S Gauge, 12th Edition,* Kalmbach, 1996; Richard O'Brien, *Collecting Toy Trains: Identification and Value Guide, No. 4,* Krause Publishing, 1997; Bob Roth, *Greenberg's Pocket Price Guide, LGB, 1968–1996, Third Edition,* Kalmbach, 1996.

American Flyer: Greenberg Books, three volume set.

Lionel: Greenberg Books, four volumes dealing with Lionel trains made between 1901 and 1942, seven volumes covering the 1945 to 1969 period. and two volumes for the 1970 to 1991 period. Also check Lionel Book Committee, Train Collectors Association, *Lionel Trains: Standard of the World, 1900–1943, Second Edition,* Train Collectors Association, 1989.

Miscellaneous: Greenberg Books has one or more price guides for Athearn, Kusan, Ives, Marx, and Varney.

Note: For a complete list of toy train titles from Greenberg Books, a division of Kalmbach Publishing Co., write PO Box 986, Waukesha, WI 53187, and request a copy of their latest catalog. If you are a serious collector, also ask to be put on their mailing list.

Periodicals: *Classic Toy Trains,* PO Box 1612, Waukesha, WI 53187; *LGB Telegram,* 5630 Plainview Rd, Harrisburg, PA 17111; *Lionel Collector Series Marketmaker,* Trainmaster, PO Box 1499, Gainesville, FL 32602.

Collectors' Clubs: American Flyer Collectors Club, PO Box 13269, Pittsburgh, PA 15234; LGB Model Railroad Club, PO Box 15835, Montour, PA 15244; Lionel Collectors Club of America, PO Box 479, LaSalle, IL 61301; Marklin Club—North America, PO Box 51559, New Berlin, WI 53141; The National Model Railroad Assoc, 4121 Cromwell Rd, Chattanooga, TN 37421; The Toy Train Operating Society, 25 W Walnut St, Ste 308, Pasadena, CA 91103; Train Collector's Assoc, PO Box 248, Strasburg, PA 17579.

American Flyer, S gauge, baggage car, #30, yellow, 1959–60 . . . . $ 55.00
American Flyer, S gauge, box car, #807, Rio Grande, white, 1957 . . . . 15.00
American Flyer, S gauge, caboose, #638, red, 1949–53 . . . . 5.00
American Flyer, S gauge, coal dump car, #719, maroon, 1950–54 . . . . 35.00
American Flyer, S gauge, crane car, #24562, Industrial Brownhoist, 1961–66 . . . . 12.00
American Flyer, S gauge, flatcar, #928, New Haven, log load, 1954 . . . . 12.00
American Flyer, S gauge, gondola, #911, black, 1955–57 . . . . 12.00
American Flyer, S gauge, locomotive, steam, #285, C&NW, Pacific, 1952 . . . . 30.00
American Flyer, S gauge, locomotive, steam, #L2002, Casey Jones, 1963 . . . . 20.00
American Flyer, S gauge, locomotive, steam, #325AC, New York Central, Hudson, 1950 . . . . 45.00
American Flyer, S gauge, observation, #954, Grand Canyon, 1953–56. . . . . 60.00
American Flyer, S gauge, stock car, #24077, Northern Pacific, red, 1959–62 . . . . 75.00

American Flyer, S gauge, caboose, #630, ³/₁₆" scale, red, 6" l, orig box, $15.00.

American Flyer, S gauge, tank car, #958, Mobilgas, red, 1957. . . . . 25.00
Buddy L, ballast car, #1008, black, 1928–31, 23" l 700.00
Buddy L, flatcar, , #1006, black, 1926–31 . . . . 475.00
Buddy L, gondola, #54, red 75.00
Buddy L, locomotive, #51, dark green 295.00
Dorfan, baggage car, #492, green maroon, brass trim 40.00
Dorfan, box car, #517953, orange, brown, O gauge 20.00
Dorfan, caboose, #5 . . . . 40.00
Dorfan, caboose, #600, narrow gauge 25.00
Dorfan, coach, #493, Seattle 35.00
Dorfan, engine, #3919, orange, wide gauge 340.00
Dorfan, locomotive, electric, #3931, green 550.00
Dorfan, observation car, #773, orange, black, people in windows 70.00
Ives, baggage car, #70, tin roof, sliding center door, door at each end of side, 1923–25 . . . . 45.00
Ives, buffet, #130, 1930 . . . . 75.00
Ives, caboose, #67, red–orange tin litho, green roof, yellow lettering, 1929–30 . . . . 50.00
Ives, cattle car, #1678, green litho body, sliding door, 1931–32 . . . . 35.00
Ives, drawing room car, #129, The Ives Railway Lines, green steel litho, grey roof, 1918–24 . . . . 85.00
Ives, gondola, #1512, blue tin body, 1931–32. . . . . 50.00
Ives, gravel car, #63, grey litho, 1930 . . . . 45.00
Ives, livestock car, #20–193, orange, red roof, 1930 . . . . 100.00
Ives, locomotive, #6, cast iron, diecast wheels, stamped "Ives No. 6" beneath, 1926–28 . . . . 100.00
Ives, locomotive, #1506, mechanical, black tin body, die cast wheels, 1931–32 . . . . 130.00
Ives, locomotive, #1661, black tin body, red trim, diecast wheels, 1932 . . . . 110.00
Ives, locomotive, #1694, box cab electric, maroon roof, brass trim, diecast wheels, headlights on each end, 1932 . . . . 500.00
Ives, merchandise car, #192, painted yellow body, double sliding doors, 1930 . . . . 100.00

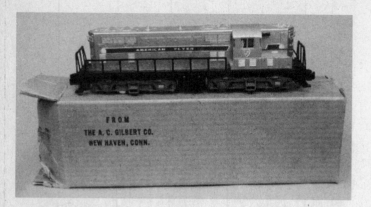

American Flyer, GP–7 road switcher, #370, silver, blue and yellow decals, 10" l, orig shipping carton, $80.00.

Ives, parlor car, #62, "The Ives Railway Lines" above
   windows, "62 Parlor Car" below, 1924–30 . . . . **95.00**

Ives, tank car, orange body, "190" and "Texas Oil"
   lettering, 1923–28 . . . . **100.00**

Lionel, baggage car, #310, 1926. . . . . **65.00**

Lionel, box car, #2954, 1940–42 . . . . **145.00**

Lionel, caboose, #217, orange, maroon **120.00**

Lionel, caboose, #1007, 1948 . . . . **3.50**

Lionel, caboose, #2817, red body and roof, 1938 . . . . . . **40.00**

Lionel, coach, #617, black and chrome, 1935 . . . . **30.00**

Lionel, coach, #637, 1936–39 . . . . **55.00**

Lionel, flatcar, #2651, bright green, lumber load, 1938 . . . **20.00**

Lionel, flatcar, #3330, operating submarine kit,
   1960–61 . . . . **50.00**

Lionel, gondola, #812, 1926 . . . . **30.00**

Lionel, hopper and dump car, #0016, South Pacific,
   1938–42 . . . . **60.00**

Lionel, locomotive, steam, #201, 1940 . . . . **350.00**

Lionel, locomotive, #204, Alco Diesel AA, 1957 . . . . . . **50.00**

Lionel, locomotive, electric, #248, red, orange, dark
   green, and olive, 1926–32 . . . . **65.00**

Lionel, locomotive, #614, diesel SW2, Alaska–027,
   blue, yellow structure on roof, 1959–60 . . . . **80.00**

Lionel, locomotive, #HO–055, M. & St. L switcher,
   1961 . . . . **40.00**

Lionel, lumber car, #3651, black frame, nickel stakes,
   logs and bin, 1939 . . . . **15.00**

Lionel, refrigerator car, #2814R, white body, brown
   roof, 1938 . . . . **200.00**

Lionel, savings bank car, "Cities Service" **15.00**

Lionel, tank car, #2465, Sunoco, 1946 . . . . **8.50**

Lionel, trolley, #60, yellow, red roof, blue lettering,
   1955–58 . . . . **65.00**

Marx, box car, #817, Colorado & Southern, tin, 4
   wheels, yellow, black lettering **12.00**

Marx, caboose, #234, plastic, 8 wheels, olive drab,
   white "USA" lettering **25.00**

Marx, flatcar, #2824, plastic, 8 wheels, olive drab,
   missile launcher, white lettering **15.00**

Marx, gondola, tin, Joy Line, mkd "Bunny Express" **60.00**

Marx, locomotive, diesel, #54, tin litho, red, yellow,
   and black, yellow and white lettering **30.00**

Marx, locomotive, #90, Lumar Lines, streamlined
   steam, tin litho, black, blue, yellow lettering **30.00**

Marx, tank car, #652, Shell, tin litho, 8 wheels,
   orange, red lettering, $^3/_{16}$ scale. **8.00**

Strombecker, wood, 6 pcs, 1930s **75.00**

Tootsie Toy, Akana Midnight Flyer, #5015, boxed set,
   1929 . . . . **200.00**

Tootsie Toy, Midnight Flyer, #7001, boxed set **120.00**

Tootsie Toy, Pennsylvania RR Passenger Train, #5850,
   boxed set. **140.00**

Tootsie Toy, Santa Fe RR Passenger Train, #5851,
   boxed set. **150.00**

TOYS

Toys drive the 20th–century collectibles market. They are the first objects from a chronological time period to be collected. The standards for condition, scarcity, and desirability established by the toy community are now being universally applied throughout the antiques marketplace.

The toy market of the 1990s is highly sophisticated. In fact, some question if there is a single toy market any longer. Many categories within the toy market (action figures, dolls, GI Joe, Hot Wheels, Matchbox, toy trains, etc.) have broken away and become independent collecting categories. This category covers manufacturers and toy types still located within the general toy category.

Toys divide basically into three chronological periods: (1) pre–World War I, (2) 1920 to 1940, and (3) post–1945. Toys made between 1940 and 1945 are considered "war toys" and collected separately. While the post–1945 period is still viewed as a whole by most collectors, some are beginning to suggest it should be broken into two parts with 1980 as the dividing line.

Currently, the post–1945 period is the hot period among toy collectors. Prices for pre–1920 cast–iron and penny toys are stable and, in some cases, in decline. Pressed steel dominates vehicle collecting with a small cadre of collectors beginning to look at plastic. Diecast toys, the darlings of the 1970s and 80s, have lost some of their luster.

Vehicles remain the toy of choice among collectors aged 35 and above. Young collectors are focusing on action figures and licensed toys.

With so many toys of the post–1945 era of Far Eastern origin, the national collecting prejudice for toys made in one's own country has diminished. What it is rather than where it was made is the key today. One result is a lowering of quality standards for more recently issued toys. The pre–1960s toy market remains heavily quality–driven.

Because so many collectors collect the toys with which they grew up, many have begun to ask: what is going to happen to these toys when the generation that grew up with them dies? There are many subcategories within the toy market where interest has not passed from one generation to another. The concept of a "one generation" collectible is well worth considering.

The contemporary toy market is cursed by two groups of individuals—toy speculators and toy scalpers—whose activities badly distort pricing reality. Toy speculators hoard toys, thus upsetting the traditional supply and demand cycle. Toy scalpers created artificial shortages for modern toys. They accept no financial or moral responsibility for their actions when the speculative bubble they created bursts. And, it always does.

References: General: Sharon and Bob Huxford (eds.), *Schroeder's Collectible Toys: Antique to Modern Price Guide, Third Edition,* Collector Books, 1997; Sharon Korbeck (ed.), *Toys & Prices, 4th Edition,* Krause Publications, 1996; Richard O'Brien, *Collecting Toys: A Collectors Identification and Value Guide, 8th Edition,* Krause Publications, 1997.

Generational: Bill Bruegman, *Toys of the Sixties,* Cap'n Penny Productions, 1991; Tom Frey, *Toy Bop: Kid Classics of the 50's & 60's,* Fuzzy Dice Productions, 1994; Robin Sommer, *I Had One Of Those: Toys of Our Generation,* Crescent Books, 1992.

Juvenile: Joe Johnson and Dana McGuinn, *Toys That Talk: Over 300 Pullstring Dolls & Toys—1960s to Today,* Firefly Publishing, 1992; *Price Guide to Pull Toys,* L–W Book Sales, 1996; *Tops and Yo–Yos and Other Spinning Toys,* L–W Book Sales, 1995.

Lithograph Tin: Lisa Kerr, *American Tin–Litho Toys,* Collectors Press, 1995; Maxine A. Pinsky, *Greenberg's Guide to Marx Toys, Vol. I* (1988) and *Vol. II* (1990), Greenberg Publishing.

Miscellaneous: David Gould and Donna Crevar–Donaldson, *Occupied Japan Toys With Prices,* L–W Book Sales, 1993; Jay Horowitz, *Marx Western Playsets: The Authorized Guide,* Greenberg Publishing, 1992; Don Hultzman, *Collecting Battery Toys: A Reference, Rarity, and Value Guide,* Books Americana, Krause Publications, 1994; Anthony Marsella, *Toys From Occupied Japan,* Schiffer Publishing, 1995; Jack Matthews, *Toys Go To War: World War II Military Toys, Games, Puzzles & Books,* Pictorial Histories Publishing, 1994.

Plastic: Bill Hanlon, *Plastic Toys: Dimestore Dreams of the '40s & '50s,* Schiffer Publishing, 1993.

Vehicles: John Clark, *HO Slot Car Identification and Price Guide,* L–W Book Sales, 1995; Edward Force, *Corgi Toys,* Schiffer Publishing, 1984, 1991 value update; Edward Force, *Dinky Toys,* Schiffer Publishing, 1988, 1992 value update; Edward Force, *Solido Toys,* Schiffer Publishing, 1993; Joe and Sharon Freed, *Collector's Guide to American Transportation Toys, 1895–1941,* Freedom Press, 1995; Sally Gibson–Downs and Christine Gentry, *Motorcycle Toys: Antique and Contemporary,* Collector Books, 1995; Dana Johnson, *Collector's Guide to Diecast Toys & Scale Models,* Collector Books, 1996; Douglas P. Kelley, *The Die Cast Price Guide Post–War: 1946 to Present,* Antique Trader Books, 1997; Raymond R. Klein, *Greenberg's Guide to Tootsietoys, 1945–1969,* Greenberg Publishing, 1993; Richard O'Brien, *Collecting Toy Cars & Trucks: Identification and Value Guide, 2nd Edition,* Krause Publications, 1997; John Ramsay's *Catalogue of British Diecast Model Toys, Sixth Edition,* Swapmeet Publications, 1995; David Richter, *Collector's Guide to Tootsietoys, Second Edition,* Collector Books, 1996; Ron Smith, *Collecting Toy Airplanes: An Identification & Value Guide,* Books Americana, Krause Publications, 1995.

Periodicals: *Antique Toy World,* PO Box 34509, Chicago, IL 60634; *Collecting Toys,* PO Box 437, Waupaca, WI 54981; *Model and Toy Collector Magazine,* PO Box 347240, Cleveland, OH 44134; *Toy Farmer,* 7496 106th Ave, SE, Lamoure, ND 58458; *Toy Shop,* 700 E State St, Iola, WI 54490; *Toy Trader,* PO Box 1050, Dubuque, IA 52003; *U.S. Toy Collector Magazine,* PO Box 4244, Missoula, MT 59806.

Collectors' Clubs: Antique Toy Collectors of America, Two Wall Street, 13th Floor, New York, NY 10005; Canadian Toy Collectors Society, 91 Rylander Blvd, Unit 7, Ste 245, Scarborough, Ontario M1B 5M5.

Note: For additional toy listings see Action Figures, Barbie, Bicycles, Breyer Horses, Cap Guns, Cartoon Characters, Coloring Books, Construction Toys, Cowboy Heroes, Disneyana, Dolls, Ertl, Fisher–Price, Games, GI Joe, Hot Wheels, Matchbox, Model Kits, Monsters, Occupied Japan, Paint By Number Sets, Pedal Cars, Premiums, Puzzles, Radio Characters and Personalities, Robots, Sand Pails, Slot Cars, Space Adventurers, Space Toys, Star Trek, Star Wars, Steiff, Stuffed Toys, Super Heroes, Teddy Bears, Television Characters & Personalities, Toy Soldiers, Toy Trains, and View–Master.

Alps, Antique Gooney Car, battery operated, 4 actions, 1960s, 9" l	$ 80.00
Alps, Arthur A–Go–Go, battery operated, detachable cymbals and drum set, 1960s, 10" h	250.00
Alps, Balloon Blowing Monkey, battery operated, 11⅛" h	125.00
Alps, Lambo, magnetic trunk and light, trailer, 2 tin logs, 1950s, 16" l	275.00
Arcade, Allis–Chambers tractor and trailer, #2650, 1936, 13" l	180.00
Arcade, army tank, #3960, shoots, 1941, 4" l	80.00
Arcade, Austin delivery truck, #173, 1932, 3¾" l	60.00
Arcade, Chevrolet sedan, #1170X, 1934	60.00
Arcade, farm mower, #4210X, 1939, 4" l	70.00
Arcade, racer, #1457, 5¾" l	70.00
Arcade, wrecker, #1503X, 4¾" l	95.00
Avalon, Weaving Loom, 18" wooden loom, instruction booklet, 1970s	20.00
Bandai, Auto–Top Ferrari Convertible, 1960s, 11" l	500.00
Bandai, B50 Airplane, friction, litho tin, 7½" l	45.00
Bandai, King Size Fire Engine, battery operated, 12½" l	175.00
Bandai, white knob wind–up, Pink Panther, 1981	10.00
Big Bang Cannon, #10W, 9" l	60.00
Big Bang Cannon, #12F, 16⅜" l	80.00
Buddy L, army tank, wood, 1943, 13" l	95.00
Buddy L, Buick, plastic, 5⅜" l	6.00
Buddy L, sand loader, #230, 1925–31	175.00
Buddy L, Sit–N–Ride Dump Truck, steering wheel, removable seat, 1956–57	100.00
Buddy L, wrecker, Emergency Towing Rider, #903, 1949, 33" l	110.00
Chein, army drummer, plunger activated, 1930s, 7" h	140.00
Chein, bear with hat, pants, shirt, and bowtie, c1938	65.00
Chein, chicken pulling wheelbarrow, 6 x 3½"	60.00
Chein, Col–R–Tone Top, #99, musical, clear polystyrene bell shape, color metal discs, suction cup stand, 1956–57	45.00

Asahi, Japan, race car, battery operated, plastic, 8½" l, $85.00.

Hess, Box Trailer, 1975, $350.00.

Chein, frog man, mechanical, 1950s, 11" l **100.00**
Chein, handstand clown, 1940s, 6" h **60.00**
Chein, Marine, hand on belt, 1950s, 6" h **130.00**
Chein, Playland Merry–Go–Round, 9½" h **375.00**
Chein, *Spirit of St. Louis* Airplane, 8" l **275.00**
Chein, toy town helicopter, 13" l **75.00**
Chein, walking penguin, 5" h **120.00**
Corgi, Austin Police Minivan, #448, 1964–67 . . . . **65.00**
Corgi, Chevrolet Impala Fire Chief, #439, 1963–77 . . . . . **50.00**
Corgi, Commer Military Ambulance, #354, 1964–66 . . . . . **85.00**
Corgi, Country Farm Set, #4–B, 1974–75 . . . . **50.00**
Corgi, Giant Daktari Set, #14–B, 1969–73 . . . . **120.00**
Corgi, Jean Richard Circus Set, #48, 1978–81 . . . . **175.00**
Corgi, Mercedes–Benz 300SL Coupe, #304 . . . . **65.00**
Corgi, Military Set, 360, #17–B, 1975–80 . . . . **65.00**
Courtland, Black Diamond coal truck, mechanical,
  #5100 . . . . **175.00**
Courtland, circus elephant and African lions cart,
  #400, 11⅝" l **275.00**
Courtland, City Meat Market delivery sedan, #4000 . . . . **100.00**
Courtland, dump truck, mechanical, #1600, 7" l **120.00**
Courtland, Easter rabbit and trailer, #200 . . . . **110.00**
Courtland, farm tractor with scraper, #6000 . . . . **120.00**
Courtland, fire chief car with siren, mechanical,
  #7000 . . . . **150.00**
Courtland, fire patrol No. 2 truck, mechanical, #1300 . . . **150.00**
Courtland, hook and ladder tractor trailer, mechani-
  cal, #2100, 13" l **120.00**
Courtland, ice cream truck, mechanical, #1300, 9" l **175.00**
Courtland, lawn mower, mechanical, #21 . . . . **65.00**
Courtland, Rocking R Ranch See–Saw, mechanical,
  #8000 . . . . **140.00**
Daisy, BB gun, double barrel, Model 21, plastic,
  painted finish, 1968 . . . . **200.00**
Daisy, BB gun, Red Ryder, #94, plastic stock, painted
  finish, 1955 . . . . **30.00**
Daisy, Paper Popper, #901, figural submachine gun shoots
  paper,1962–63 . . . .
Dinky, Austin Devon, #151 . . . . **22.00**
Dinky, Beach Buggy, #227 . . . . **20.00**
Dinky, Euclid truck, #97 . . . . **12.50**
Dinky, Ferrari racer, #23h **20.00**
Dinky, Fordson truck, #30r **50.00**
Dinky, Hudson Hornet sedan, #174 . . . . **65.00**
Dinky, Leyland tractor, #308 . . . . **30.00**
Dinky, Rolls Royce Phantom V, #198 . . . . **35.00**
Dinky, Rover, #36d **100.00**
Dinky, Triumph Vitesse, #134 . . . . **28.00**
Duncan, yo–yo, Batman and Robin, butterfly, 1978 . . . . . **20.00**

Eldon Mfg, Navy Cargo Plane, #902, nose opens to
  unload jeep, armored car and rocket launcher,
  22" l, 1956–57 . . . . **65.00**
Ely Mfg, Key Baby Grand Piano, #8200C, 20 keys,
  mella–tone chimes, play–by–color chart, 1956–57 . . . . **30.00**
Gabriel, Box of Crafts, #T419, clay, leather, foil,
  muslin, pipe cleaners, yarn, and instructions,
  1956–57 . . . . **20.00**
Galoob, white knob windup, Mity Machines, bull-
  dozer, 1984 . . . . **5.50**
General Molds and Plastics, MG Sports Car, battery
  operated, remote control steering wheel, 1956–57 . . . . **75.00**
Gerber, Swiss Bells, polyethylene bells, multicolored,
  vinyl band, 1956–57 . . . . **30.00**
Gilbert, Chemistry Set, #12131, complete **50.00**
Gilbert, Gemcraft Rock Tumbler, electric, includes
  polishing compounds, pellets, and instruction
  booklet, 1970s **35.00**
Gilbert, Mysto Magic, magic cards, coins, acces-
  sories, and instruction booklet, 1938 . . . . **40.00**
Gilbert, Tool Chest, #L–5, 1956–57 . . . . **25.00**
Gilbert, Which–Lane Chicane Race Set, #19075,
  American Flyer, Auto–Rama **75.00**
Gilbert, Zoom Microscope, #13094, electric,
  triple–turret, and lab equipment **35.00**
Gong Bell Mfg, Zebra Rider, revolving spiral striped
  legs, rubber wheels, 19" h, 1950s **30.00**
HAJI, Japan, Mansei Toy Company, galloping horse,
  windup, litho tin, cowboy rider holds pistol, 8" l **90.00**
Hasbro, catalog, 1975 . . . . **35.00**
Hasbro, Junior Miss Knitting Kit, #1564, vinyl case,
  8 balls of yarn, sewing accessories, and instruction
  book, 1956–57 . . . . **20.00**
Hasbro, Magnetic Letters, magnetic plastic letters,
  litho faced board, 12 x 15" **15.00**
Hasbro, Mr. and Mrs. Potato Head, #2054, plastic
  figural fruits and vegetable pcs, c1960 . . . . **45.00**
Hasbro, Young Doctor Hasbro, #1361, miniature
  instruments, carrying case, snap closure **20.00**

**Irwin, Walking
Bear, #622,
windup, brown
plastic body, fabric
costume, orig box,
5¼" l, 4½" h,
$175.00.**

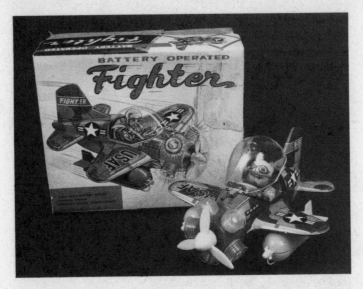

KO, Japan, F–50 Fighter, battery operated, litho tin and plastic, stop–and–go action, orig box, 11" l, 6" h, $150.00.

Hess, Split Window Tanker, 1972 . . . . 375.00
Hess, Tanker Truck, 1968 . . . . 650.00
Hess, Tank Truck Bank, 1984 . . . . 85.00
Hubley, auto, diecast, black plastic wheels 15.00
Hubley, Bell Telephone truck, 12½" l 85.00
Hubley, Chevrolet 1932 Coupe Kit 30.00
Hubley, Chevrolet 1932 Phaeton Kit 30.00
Hubley, crash car, white rubber tires, 4¾" l 120.00
Hubley, fire truck, 5" l 130.00
Hubley, Ford Model A Town Car Kit 40.00
Hubley, Harley–Davidson Motorcycle, white rubber
    wheels, with policeman, 5½" l 300.00
Hubley, hook and ladder, #463 . . . . 35.00
Hubley, Jaguar Roadster, 9" l 65.00
Hubley, ladder truck, c1930, 10" l 125.00
Hubley, motorcycle, Kiddietoy, plastic, 5" l 18.00
Hubley, Navy Fighter–Bomber, transparent sliding
    cockpit bubble, folding wings, retractable landing
    gear, revolving propeller, 1956–57 . . . . 50.00
Hubley, racer, #2241, 7½" l 65.00
Hubley, sedan, 2–door, rubber wheels, c1938, 3½" l 80.00
Ideal, Astrobase, motorized, 1960s, 20" h 150.00
Ideal, Car Wash, #3031, jeep, deluxe sedan, 1950s 100.00
Ideal, catalog, 1973 . . . . 15.00
Ideal, Fire Boat, #4714, shoots water, moving lifeboat
    and anchor, siren, 1956–57 . . . . 125.00
Ideal, MC Sports Car, #4054, plastic, orig box 135.00
Ideal, National Trailways Bus, #3093, plastic, open-
    ing and closing door and luggage compartment,
    10" l 150.00
Ideal, Poky Little Puppy, #4304, plastic, crank handle
    and Poky recites from Little Golden Book story-
    book, orig box, 7½" h 125.00
Ideal, Power Speed Boat, #4040, plastic, windup,
    21" l 175.00
Ideal, Racer Pull Toy, #4501, plastic, litho cardboard
    cylinder, 16" l 25.00

Ideal, XP–600 Fix–It Convertible, #3062, plastic, bat-
    tery operated, opening hood and trunk, diecast
    tools, working headlights and horn 150.00
Imperial, white knob windup, Mini–Tools, circular
    saw, 1988 . . . . 2.50
Irwin, Self–Steering Electronic Wonder Car, #1423,
    battery operated, convertible, 1950s 40.00
James Industries, Slinky Worm, 1956–57 . . . . 15.00
Japan, Buick Station Wagon, tin, battery operat-
    ed, 1954, 8" l 85.00
Japan, Cadillac 60, friction, tin, 1961, 9" l 100.00
Japan, Chrysler car, battery operated, 1958, 13" l 325.00
Japan, WWII Fighter Plane, friction, litho tin, 14½" l 95.00
KA, Japan, US Army Air Fighter, litho tin, friction,
    plastic propellers, orig box, 8" l 115.00
Kamar, Bucky the Basset Hound, battery operated,
    plush, collar, leash, 17" l, c1975 . . . . 20.00
Kenner, Give–A–Show Projector, #502, battery oper-
    ated, 112 color slides of Huck, Yogi, Quick Draw
    and friends, 1962–63 . . . . 40.00
Kenner, Home Workshop, #1010, motorized, plastic
    lumber, 7 power tools, paints, adhesive, and
    instruction booklet, 1962–63 . . . . 30.00
Kenner, Lincoln Logs, #1C 70.00
Kilgore, bus, plastic, 4" l 22.00
Kilgore, dump truck, c1930, 7" l 200.00
Kilgore, police car, plastic, 1937, 4" l 22.00
Kilgore, taxi, plastic, 4" l 20.00
Knickerbocker, Dragnet Target Game, styrene cork
    target, 2 dart guns, and target, 1955–56 . . . . 40.00
Lindstrom, steam roller, #181, mechanical, 12" l 60.00
Linemar, Anti–Aircraft Unit No. 1, 1950s, 12½" l 175.00
Linemar, Army Radio Jeep J1490, 1950s, 7¼" l 125.00
Linemar, Bubbling Bull, battery operated, 8" h 100.00
Marusan, Japan, Cadillac, tin, battery operated,
    1950, 11" l 425.00
Marx, airplane, #90 . . . . 120.00
Marx, ambulance, with siren, 14½" l 375.00
Marx, Armored Attack Set, jeep, tank, plastic figures,
    1960s 200.00
Marx, Army staff car, #W601158, flasher and siren,
    11" l 125.00

M, Japan, jeep, friction, litho tin, swivelling gunner, 6" l, 3" h, $75.00.

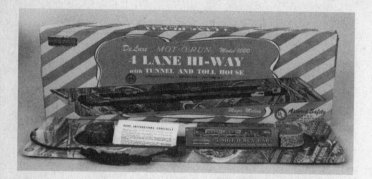

Marx, DeLuxe Mot–O–Run 4 Lane Hi–Way, Model 1000, electric, litho tin, 5 vehicles, orig box, 1949, 27" l, $150.00.

Marx, bear cyclist, 6" l	175.00
Marx, Be–Bop "The Jivin' Jigger," 10" l	225.00
Marx, Big Lizzie Car	165.00
Marx, bomber, 2 engine, camouflaged	135.00
Marx, bulldozer climbing tractor, 10½" l	175.00
Marx, Busy Parking Station, 1930s, 2" tin race car, 17" l	250.00
Marx, catalog, 1930s, 36 pgs	250.00
Marx, Dora Dipsy Car, plastic nodder, 5½" l	125.00
Marx, Flying Fortress 2095, 1940s	300.00
Marx, Gee Whiz Auto Racer, set of 4 cars, 2" l	500.00
Marx, G–Man Sparkling Machine Gun, revolving turret, 1938, 22" l	65.00
Marx, George the Drummer Boy, moving eyes, 9" h	175.00
Marx, Helicopter Skyport, 2 plastic copters, 9 x 11"	120.00
Marx, Jolly Joe Jeep, plastic helmet, 6" l	240.00
Marx, Looping Plane, #382	250.00
Marx, Police Patrol, motorcycle with sidecar	300.00
Marx, ramp walker, Chilly Willy on sled	20.00
Marx, ramp walker, Fred Flintstone and Barney Rubble	35.00
Mattel, Musical Man on the Flying Trapeze, plastic clown, turn crank, litho tin trapeze base, plays title tune, orig box, 1953	100.00
Mattel, Wizzer Gyrating Top, plastic, 1975	6.00
Metalcraft, Bordens Milk Truck	275.00
Metalcraft, delivery truck van, steel, 11" l	250.00
Metalcraft, Kroger Food Express, 11" l	275.00
Metalcraft, Steam Shovel	100.00
Midgetoy, 4–in–1 Truck Set, diecast	35.00
Midgetoy, MG Sports Car, diecast	8.00
Milton Bradley, Magi Paint, finger paint, powder, 6 colors, paper, water pan, and instructions	15.00
Montgomery Ward, catalog, Christmas, 1941–65	75.00
Nomura, Buick, friction, 11" l	100.00
Nomura, Dodge Yellow Cab, friction, 12" l	125.00
Nomura, Ford Airplane, friction, litho tin, 15" l	70.00
Nomura, F–11 Jet Fighter, friction, litho tin, engine noise, 11" l	150.00
Nomura, Mercedes Benz 300SL, battery operated, 11" l	125.00
Nylint, Custom Camper, #5300, 12½" l	95.00
Nylint, Guided Missile Carrier, #2800	85.00
Nylint, Scootcycle, #800, windup, 7¼" l	250.00

Nylint, Tournahauler, #1700, 1953–56	75.00
Occupied Japan, boy drummer, tin and celluloid, 6" h	225.00
Occupied Japan, Crawling Tortoise, tin and celluloid, 5" l	250.00
Occupied Japan, Skier, tin and celluloid, orig box	240.00
Occupied Japan, Tumbling Monkey, celluloid, orig box	90.00
Ohio Art, Astroray Gun, #562, flashlight gun, target, and 6 rubber tipped darts, 1962–63	30.00
Ohio Art, Fido's Musical Dog House, 8" h	45.00
Ohio Art, Realistic Farm Set, #197, 16" l, 7" h	95.00
Ohio Art, Shooting Gallery, circus, key wind	60.00
Ohio Art, Sparkling Stove, #133, 9–pc utensil set, mechanical motor, 1955–56	35.00
Ohio Art, spinning top, race car theme, tin and wood	20.00
Ohio Art, washtub, litho tin, metal and wood scrubboard	20.00
Playskool, Big, Big Tool Bench, wooden bench, plastic tools, 1970s	15.00
Playskool, Clean–Up Truck, plastic, red and white, blue lettering, sponge, removable truck body becomes bucket, 1970s, 15 x 6 x 8⅞"	20.00
Playskool, peg desk, molded plastic seat, tubular steel legs, blackboard, chalk, eraser, silk–screened alphabet, 36–pc magnetic letter set, 1970s	35.00
Remco, Electronic Mobile Loudspeaker Truck, long–beam searchlight, electronic switches, microphone, and loudspeaker, 1955–56	50.00
Remco, Telecom Interphone System, #900, battery operated, 2 telephones and wire, 1956–57	40.00
Remco, Transistor Radio Kit, #107, electronic, headphones, 1956–57	35.00
Sanyo, Japan, Continental III, car, friction, tin, plastic steering wheel and front windshield, orig box, 1950s, 9" l	150.00
Schuco, Clown Juggler, #965, 5" h	350.00
Schuco, Dalli 1011, tin car, plastic driver, 6½" l	195.00
Schuco, Latso 3042, truck, 1950s	75.00
Schuco, Magico Car and Garage, 1950s	150.00
Schuco, Micro Racer 1041, 4" l	75.00
Schuco, Porsche Formel II–1037, 4½" l	95.00
Schuco, Station Car 3118, 4½" l	75.00
Schuco, Varianto Electro 3112u, truck, 4¼" l	95.00
Spiegel, catalog, Christmas, 1966–70	65.00

Sun Rubber, truck, red and yellow, 4¾" l, $30.00.

SSS, Japan, Cadillac Fleetwood, tin, friction, 1961, 22" l 125.00
Structo, Aerial Fire Truck 125.00
Structo, camper, cloth top, 12" l 30.00
Structo, communications center truck, 21" l 85.00
Structo, gasoline truck, #912, 13" l 90.00
Structo, Guided Missile Launching Truck, metal truck, plastic accessories, rubber tires 65.00
Structo, sand loader, c1928 .... 50.00
Structo, steam shovel, 16" l 65.00
Structo, Toyland Garage Wrecker 60.00
Structo, Toyand Oil Co truck 145.00
Sun Rubber, 1936 White Bus, #520, 4¼" l 25.00
Sun Rubber, 1940 Dodge, 4–door sedan, #12001, 4½" l 25.00
Sun Rubber, Texaco tank truck 45.00
Taiyo, Japan, Chevrolet Camaro Rusher, battery oper- ated, tin, 1971, 9½" l 15.00
Tomy, white knob windup, Bathtubbies, swimming whale, 1983 .... 3.00
Tomy, white knob windup, Pac Man, blinky ghost, red, 1982 .... 12.00
Tonka, Carnation Milk delivery truck, #750 .... 200.00
Tonka, crane and clam, #150, 24" l 100.00
Tonka, hydraulic dump truck, #20, 1961 .... 75.00
Tonka, logger semi, #575, wood flat bed, 1953 .... 175.00
Tonka, sand loader set, loader and dump truck, 1956, #994 .... 110.00
Tonka, steam shovel deluxe, #100, 1949, 22" l 95.00
Tonka, utility hauler, #175, 1950, 12" l 125.00
Tonka, wrecker truck, #250, 12½" l 125.00
Tootsietoy, Aero–Dawn Seaplane, blue, green, or red, 1952–46 .... 30.00
Tootsietoy, Army Searchlight Trailer, metal, chrome reflector, olive drab, rubber tires, 1958–60, 4" l 25.00

Tootsietoy, submarine, metal and plastic, black body, red deck, gray conning tower, $75.00.

Tootsietoy, Army Set, 2 U.S. Army planes, Waco bomber, 2 miniature bombers, tank, armored car, 2 Mack supply trucks, Graham Army ambulance, and 2 field cannons, 1942–46, 4" 475.00
Tootsietoy, Bi–Wing Seaplane, #4650, 1926 .... 45.00
Tootsietoy, cannon, self–propelled 15mm Howitzer, 1950s 25.00
Tootsietoy, Cutlass Army Jet, F7U3 Vought Cutlass, olive drab, wing and large fins on each side, 2 red, white, and blue star decals on top of each wing, rubber tires, 1958–60, 3½" wingspan 20.00
Tootsietoy, Fighter Plane, 1942–46, 5" wing span 65.00
Tootsietoy, Fleet Set, 9 miniature battleships, assorted colors, 1942–46 .... 65.00
Tootsietoy, International Army Ambulance, green or tan, Red Cross symbol on roof, rubber tires, 1949, 4" l 30.00
Tootsietoy, Navy Set, submarine, destroyer, cruiser, battleship, carrier and transport, 1942–46 .... 85.00
Tootsietoy, 1924 Buick Touring Car, #4641, 1925, 3" l 85.00
Tootsietoy, 1924 Federal Delivery Van, #4630, 1924 ... 85.00
Tootsietoy, 1926 Fageol Bus Safety Coach, #4651, 1927 .... 45.00
Tootsietoy, 1955 Ford Army Tanker, olive drab, 3" l ... 15.00
Tootsietoy, tractor 15.00
Toplay, Giraffe, windup, litho tin, bounces beach ball, 9" h 135.00
Toplay, Mustang Swinger, battery operated, litho tin, orig box, 10" l 80.00
Tudor, Disney Character Xylophone, #135, multicol- ored, color–keyed music book, 1962–63 .... 35.00
Unique Art, Bombo the Monk, 2 pc, 5½" l monkey, 9½" h tree, c1930 .... 125.00
Unique Art, Daredevil Motor Cop, 1940s, 8½" l 250.00
Unique Art, Gerite the Galloping Goose, 9½" l 160.00
Unique Art, Hillbilly Express, 3 pcs, tin locomotive, 1930s 100.00
Wolverine, Acrobatic Monkeys, #810 .... 250.00
Wolverine, Farm Wagon, plastic, 1950s, 10" l 30.00
Wolverine, Mechanical Man on the Flying Trapee, 8½" h 140.00
Wolverine, stove, #600, steel, oven shelf, clicking control knobs, steel spring oven door, 27¾" h 40.00
Wolverine, Zilotone, 6 interchangeable records, c1930 .... 350.00

TN, Japan, Wash–O–Matic washing machine, battery operated, tin and plastic, rubber hose, orig box, 5¾" h, $65.00.

Wyandotte, Man on the Flying Trapeze, windup, litho tin, 1930s, 9" h, $250.00.

Wyandotte, Cadillac station wagon, #1007, metal, 21" l **200.00**

Wyandotte, cannon, shoots marbles, 14" l **50.00**

Wyandotte, double–barrel pop gun, steel barrel, walnut stock, shoulder strap, 1956–57 . . . . **40.00**

Wyandotte, dump truck, 12½" l **65.00**

Wyandotte, musical children's spinning top, tin and wood. **25.00**

Wyandotte, Pickway Pastures truck **120.00**

Wyandotte, Rider Fire Truck, metal, steering wheel, bicycle type seat, siren, and searchlight, 31" l **145.00**

TRANSPORTATION

America is a highly mobile society. America's expansion and growth is linked to its transportation system, whether road, canal, rail, or sky. Few communities have escaped the impact of one or more transportation systems. As a result, transportation memorabilia has a strong regional collecting base.

Further, collectors are fascinated with anything relating to transportation vehicles and systems. This is a catchall category for those transportation categories, e.g., bus, canal, and trolley, not found elsewhere in the book.

Reference: Alex Roggero and Tony Beadle, *Greyhound: A Pictorial Tribute to an American Icon*, Motorbooks International, 1995.

Collectors' Clubs: Bus History Assoc, 965 McEwan, Windsor, Ontario N9B 2G1; Central Electric Railfans' Assoc, PO Box 503, Chicago, IL 60690; International Bus Collectors Club, 1518 "C" Trailee Dr, Charleston, SC 29407; Motor Bus Society, PO Box 251, New Brunswick, NJ 07653.

Note: For additional listings see Automobiles, Automobilia, Aviation Collectibles, Bicycles, Ocean Liner Collectibles, and Railroad Collectibles.

Ashtray, Pennsbury Pottery, Lehigh Canal boat at dock, camelback bridge in background, "The Solebury National Bank of New Hope Pa" adv premium, green, gray, and brown, light brown ground, 5" d . . . . **$ 22.50**

Bond, Arkansas Highway Bond, $10,000, State House vignette, green border, 1931. . . . . **12.00**

Bond, New York City Rapid Transit, $1,000, orange, Indian engraving, 1961. . . . . **8.00**

Book, *High–Water Cargo*, Edith M. Doran, New Brunswick, NJ, Rutgers University Press, 1850s life along the Delaware and Raritan Canal, illus by Forrest Orr, hard cover, orig dj, 1950 and 1965, 224 pgs **22.00**

Book, *Motorbus Transportation*, 4–vol set, illus, 1930 . . . . **20.00**

Book, *The Delaware Canal: A Picture Story*, Robert J. McClellan, New Brunswick, NJ, Rutgers University Press, hard cover, dj, 1967, 112 pgs **18.00**

Book, *The Galley Guide: A Purely Humanitarian Work, Planned Out of Consideration For the Digestive Apparatus of Those Who Cruise–The Thing, After All, Upon Which Success or Failure Largely Depends*, Alex W. Moffat, Motor Boat Publishing, NY, 1923, 145 pgs **22.00**

Book, *Trolley Car Treasury*, Frank Rowsome, 300+ photos, dj, 1946, 200 pgs. **32.00**

Brochure, Cruising With Safety, sailboat and motorboat photos, glossy stiff covs, 3rd ed, 1947, 76 pgs **10.50**

Brochure, Greyhound Bus, foldout, route maps, bus pictures, 1930s **12.00**

Calendar, 1949, Rapid Transit, Moses King, photos **22.00**

Medal, commemorative, 100th Anniversary of Hamburg Savings and Trust Company, 1872–1972, bronze, obverse shows bank building, reverse shows mules pulling canal boat, orig pkg, 1½" d **10.50**

Pinback Button, Canal Days Badge, Manayunk, PA, May 17, 1980, blue ground, canal beneath railroad bridge photo, 3⅛" x 2⅛" **4.50**

Trolley Ticket, commemorates Aug 15, 1914 Panama Canal opening, ticket good Aug 9–15, 1937, 3½ x 2", $8.00.

Poster, The Greyhound Lines, streamlined Greyhound bus shooting down southern road amid plantation house and trees, leaping greyhound dog in foreground, Walt Brownson, c1938, 20 x 20" **55.00**

Schedule, Travel by Motor Coach Richmond Fredericksburg, Washington, blue and white, 1927 . . . . . **8.50**

Sheet Music, *A Sailboat in the Moonlight,* Carmen Lombardo and John Jacob Loeb, Guy Lombardo cov photo, 1937 . . . . **6.00**

Sheet Music, *Travelin' Man,* Jerry Fuller, 1961 . . . . **5.50**

Stock Certificate, Boston Elevated Railway Co, 1929 . . . . . . **8.50**

Stock Certificate, Philadelphia Transportation Company, angel vignette, brown border, 1948 . . . . **5.50**

TROLLS

Trolls originated in Scandinavian folklore. These supernatural beings have been around for centuries. Identified by their generally ugly appearance, trolls traditionally have long noses, often with warts, completely unmanageable hair, four fingers on each hand, and tails. They are dirty and smelly. Considered extremely selfish, trolls are in constant conflict with humans. An occasional good troll provides little compensation for this largely bad community.

Scandinavians believe that treating a troll with kindness, in spite of his appearance or disposition, will lead to good luck. As a result, most homes contain one or more troll figures.

In the late 1950s Helena and Martii Kuuskoski, a Finnish couple, began marketing cloth troll dolls. Thomas Dam, a Danish woodcarver, also started selling troll figurines. A troll craze developed. By the early 1960s, Dam–designed trolls were being produced in Denmark, New Zealand, and the United States (Hialeah, Florida).

Dozens of manufacturers, many failing to permanently mark their products, hopped aboard the troll bandwagon. Dam filed a copyright infringement suit against Scandia House Enterprises, a division of Royalty Designs of Florida. The court ruled that the troll image was in the public domain. Eventually Dam signed an agreement with Scandia House to distribute his designs in America. Troll collectors take a negative approach to cheap foreign troll imports from Hong Kong and Japan.

A second major troll craze occurred in the early 1990s. Thomas Dam trolls were distributed by EFS Marketing Associates during this period under the Norfin trademark. Ace Novelty, Applause Toys, Russ Berrie & Company, and Uneeda Doll Company also manufactured troll lines. China and Korea replaced Hong Kong and Japan as the source for inexpensive, often unmarked trolls.

References: Debra Clark, *Troll: Identification & Price Guide,* Hobby House Press, 1993; Pat Peterson, *Collector's Guide To Trolls: Identification & Values,* Collector Books, 1995.

Periodicals: *Troll Monthly,* 216 Washington St, Canton, MA 02021; *Trollin',* PO Box 601292, Sacramento, CA 95860.

Collectors' Club: Norfin Fan Club, 585 Washington St, Canton, MA 02021.

Bank, cowgirl, molded, brown accents, red hair, head turns, Creative Mfg, 1978, 8½" h . . . . **$ 20.00**

Bank, girl wearing yellow raincoat, red hair, blue eyes, mkd "Made in Denmark Thomas Dam," 7" h **30.00**

Book, *It's A Dam Dam World,* Hal Goodman and Larry Klein, hard cover, ©1965 . . . . **10.00**

Brochure, Dam Things, front shows orig sales brochure featuring Dam Things dolls, back lists prices and order information **15.00**

Case, molded plastic, 3–D cave scene with waterfall, Ideal **25.00**

Cookie Cutter, aluminum, mail–in offer, 3½" h **20.00**

Costume, Wishnik holding balloon, Ben Cooper, 1965 . . . . **45.00**

Doll, frontier, red fringed outfit, brown moccasins and coonskin cap, yellow hair, brown eyes, Russ, 4" h **5.00**

Doll, Hula Girl, plastic lei, fringe skirt, Dam, 6" h **10.00**

Doll, Laugh–In Wishnik, Sock-it-to-me costume, white hair, red eyes, mkd "Uneeda Wishnik TM Patent No. D–190–918," 6" h **40.00**

Doll, Playboy Bunny, felt costume, yellow hair, blue eyes, mkd "Thomas Dam" on back, 5½" h, ... **35.00**

Doll, Wishnik, double–nik clown, red and white flannel costume, red and blue hair, white shoes, mkd "Uneeda" **40.00**

Doll, Wishnik, groom, white hair, gray eyes, orig outfit, mkd "Uneeda Wishnik Patent No. D190–918" **25.00**

Doll, Wishnik, naked troll, blonde hair, amber eyes, mkd "Uneeda Doll Co Inc, 19©64" on head, 5" h **10.00**

Doll, Wishnik, salt and pepper hair, mkd with Uneeda horseshoes on both feet, 3" h **8.00**

Marionette, Terry Troll, stuffed body, vinyl head, painted features, peach hair, mkd "Knickerbocker 19©64 Japan," 11" h **50.00**

Nodder, Chicago Cubs, molded vinyl body, blue cap, red hair, brown eyes, mkd "Russ©MLB 1992 China," 8½" h **6.00**

Nodder, Lucky Nik, bright red hair, brown eyes, green pedestal base, white lettering, mkd "Japan," 5" h **25.00**

Pattern, McCall's, #7589, uncut **8.00**

Pencil Topper, yellow hair, green eyes, green felt dress, green bow in hair, mkd "S. H. E. 1964" **10.00**

Play Set, Troll Party, scenic playground, Marx **45.00**

Troll House, plastic, log shape, clear front window, mkd "1966 Mattel" **35.00**

TYPEWRITERS

E. Remington & Son's Sholes & Glidden typewriter, introduced in 1874, was the first commercially produced typewriter in the United States. The keyboard consisted only of capital letters. Remington received national exposure for its typewriter by exhibiting it at the 1876 Centennial in Philadelphia. Samuel Clemens (Mark Twain) purchased one of the first models.

The earliest typewriters are known as blind models, i.e., the carriage had to be lifted away from the machine to see what had been written. Five major manufacturers joined forces in 1893 to form the Union Typewriter Company. Their monopoly was soon challenged by L. C. Smith & Brothers and the Underwood Typewriter Company. These companies led the field in typewriter innovation in the pre–1940 period.

Electric typewriters, e.g., the Blickenderfer and Cahill electric, appeared briefly in the 1900s. It was not until the 1930s that IBM introduced the first commercially successful electric typewriter. IBM introduced its ball typewriter in 1981. The electric typewriter replaced the manual typewriter by the late 1960s, only to lose its market position to the home computer in the late 1980s. In July 1995, the Smith Corona Corporation declared bankruptcy.

Advanced typewriter collectors focus primarily on pre–1920 models. Post–1920 typewriters with unusual features are the exception. The keyboard is a good barometer. If the letter placement, i.e., QWERTY, is the same as a modern typewriter or computer keyboard, chances are strong the machine has little value.

Europe, particularly Germany, is the center of typewriter collecting. The number of American collectors remains small. Far more typewriters are purchased for their decorative/conversation value than for their collecting value.

References: Michael Adler, *Antique Typewriters: From Creed to QWERTY,* Schiffer Publishing, 1997; Darryl Rehr, *Antique Typewriters & Office Collectibles,* Collector Books, 1997.

Periodicals: *Ribbon Tin News,* 28 The Green, Watertown, CT 06795; *The Typewriter Exchange,* 2125 Mount Vernon St, Philadelphia, PA 19130.

Collectors' Club: Early Typewriter Collectors Assoc, 2591 Military Ave, Los Angeles, CA 90064.

Booklet, *The Typewriter, A Short History,* Zellers, 1873–1948	$ 8.00
Brochure, Oliver Co, Chicago, IL, foldout, New Model 9 Typewriter, 1922, 8½ x 10½" opened	8.50
Ribbon Tin, Cavilier	7.00
Ribbon Tin, Hallmark	5.00
Ribbon Tin, M and M	6.00
Ribbon Tin, Midnight	5.00
Ribbon Tin, Osborn	5.00
Ribbon Tin, Plenty Copy	5.00
Ribbon Tin, Remtico	8.00
Ribbon Tin, Type Bar, round	5.00
Toy, Berwin, gold, raised keyboard, 74 metal characters, 1960s	50.00
Toy, Western Stamping Co, standard keyboard, individual key operation, shift keys, 1950s	40.00
Typewriter, Corona, fold–up model, 3–row keyboard, black, orig case	35.00
Typewriter, IBM, Selectric, electric, interchangeable ball type face	25.00
Typewriter, Remington, portable, 1929	30.00
Typewriter, Underwood, #25, orig wood case, 1929	80.00

UNIVERSAL POTTERY

In 1926 the Atlas China Company (Niles, Ohio) and the Globe Pottery Company (Cambridge, Ohio), both owned by A. O. C. Ahrendts, were consolidated and renamed the Atlas Globe China Company. Financial pressures resulted in another reorganization in the early 1930s. The factory in Niles closed. Globe was liquidated, its assets becoming part of the Oxford Pottery, also owned by Ahrendts.

In 1934 the company became Universal Pottery. Universal made baking dishes, a fine grade of semi–porcelain dinnerware, and utilitarian kitchenware. Laurella was introduced in the mid–1930s.

Upico, one of Universal's most popular shape lines, was designed by Walter Kail Titze in 1937. Cattail was heavily advertised in *Needlecraft Magazine* in the 1940s. It also sold well through Sears, Roebuck under its Harmony House brand. Sears developed a line of accessories, to complement the pattern. Ballerina and Calico Fruit were other popular 1940s dinnerware patterns. Permacel, a detergent–resistant decal that remained bright, was a strong selling point of the company's dinnerware lines.

Tile manufacturing was introduced in 1956, and the company became The Oxford Tile Company. It continued to make dinnerware until 1960. Universal Promotions distributed Universal. It subcontracted with Hull, Homer Laughlin, and Taylor, Smith & Taylor to continue manufacturing Universal patterned pieces with a Universal backstamp into the 1960s. When Oxford Tile ceased operations in 1976, it marked the end of ceramic production in Cambridge.

References: Susan and Al Bagdade, *Warman's American Pottery and Porcelain,* Wallace–Homestead, Krause Publications, 1994; Harvey Duke, *The Official Identification and Price Guide to Pottery and Porcelain, Eighth Edition,* House of Collectibles, 1995.

Ballerina Mist, canister set, 3 pcs, light aqua with cream, silver trim lids	$ 20.00
Bittersweet, creamer	15.00
Bittersweet, grease jar, cov	20.00
Bittersweet, mixing bowl	32.00
Bittersweet, platter	30.00
Bittersweet, salad bowl	35.00
Bittersweet, salad plate, 7" d	12.00
Bittersweet, stack set	35.00
Calico Fruit, bread and butter plate, 6" d	4.00
Calico Fruit, chop plate, 11½" d	25.00
Calico Fruit, cookie jar, cov	50.00
Calico Fruit, creamer	10.00
Calico Fruit, cup and saucer	12.00
Calico Fruit, dinner plate	10.00
Calico Fruit, jug, cov	50.00
Calico Fruit, milk pitcher	30.00

Calico Fruit, platter, 11½" l, $25.00.

Calico Fruit, salt and pepper shakers, pr	18.00
Calico Fruit, soup, tab handle	8.00
Calico Fruit, stack set, 3 pcs	60.00
Cattail, bowl, 7½" d	20.00
Cattail, bowl, 8¾"	32.00
Cattail, bread and butter plate	4.00
Cattail, butter, cov	42.00
Cattail, cake lifter	20.00
Cattail, casserole, cov, 8¼" d	18.00
Cattail, creamer and sugar	25.00
Cattail, cup and saucer	10.00
Cattail, dinner plate, 9" d	8.00
Cattail, fork	25.00
Cattail, fruit bowl, individual	5.00
Cattail, gravy boat	25.00
Cattail, milk pitcher	22.00
Cattail, pie baker	20.00
Cattail, platter, large	20.00
Cattail, platter, small	18.00
Cattail, range set, 5 pcs	45.00
Cattail, refrigerator dish, cov	15.00
Cattail, refrigerator jug	20.00
Cattail, salad bowl	20.00
Cattail, salad plate	3.00
Cattail, salad spoon	20.00
Cattail, salt and pepper shakers, pr	20.00
Cattail, saucer	3.00
Cattail, soup bowl	5.00
Cattail, spoon	25.00
Cattail, sugar, cov	12.00
Cattail, teacup	3.00
Cattail, teapot	35.00
Cattail, tea set, 4 pcs	50.00
Cattail, utility jug, cork stopper	45.00
Cattail, vegetable bowl	15.00
Cottage Garden, dinner plate	8.00
Largo, bowl, small	4.00
Largo, bread and butter plate, 6" d	4.00
Largo, creamer and sugar	18.00
Largo, luncheon plate, sq	8.00
Largo, pie baker	12.00
Largo, salt and pepper shakers, pr	10.00
Largo, utility bowl, cov	10.00
Rambler Rose, gravy	10.00
Rambler Rose, milk pitcher	24.00
Rambler Rose, salad plate	8.00
Rambler Rose, salt and pepper shakers, pr	18.00
Rambler Rose, soup, flat	7.00
Three Red Roses, bowl, 9¾" d	15.00
Three Red Roses, casserole, cov, tab handles, 4¼" d	18.00
Three Red Roses, casserole, cov, tab handles, 5¼" d	20.00
Three Red Roses, casserole, cov, tab handles, 6" d	25.00
Three Red Roses, casserole, cov, tab handles, 8½" d	28.00
Three Red Roses, pie plate	15.00
Three Red Roses, soup, flat	12.00
Woodvine, bowl, 5¼" d	7.00
Woodvine, creamer and sugar, cov	20.00
Woodvine, milk pitcher, 6½" h	40.00
Woodvine, mixing bowl, 4" d	20.00
Woodvine, mixing bowl, 7½" d	25.00

U.S. GLASS

United States Glass resulted from the merger of 18 different glass companies in 1891. The company's headquarters were in Pittsburgh. Plants were scattered throughout Indiana, Ohio, Pennsylvania, and West Virginia.

Most plants continued to manufacture the same products that they made before the merger. Older trademarks and pattern names were retained. Some new shapes and patterns used a U.S. Glass trademark. New plants were built in Gas City, Indiana, and Tiffin, Ohio. The Gas City plant made machine–made dinnerware, kitchenware, and tabletop items in colors that included amber, black, canary, green, and pink. The Tiffin plant made delicate pressed dinnerware and blown stemware in crystal and a host of other colors. Pieces ranged from plain to patterns featuring cutting and/or etching. U.S. Glass' main decorating facility was in Pittsburgh.

During the first three decades of the 20th century, several plants closed, the result of strikes, organizational mismanagement, and/or economic difficulties. In 1938, following the appointment of C. W. Carlson, Sr., as president, the corporate headquarters moved from Pittsburgh to Tiffin. Only the Pittsburgh and Tiffin plants were still operating. Carlson, along with C. W. Carlson, Jr., his son, revived the company by adding several new shapes and colors to the line. The company prospered until the late 1950s.

By 1951 all production was located in Tiffin. U.S. Glass bought the Duncan and Miller molds in 1955. Some former Duncan and Miller employees moved to Tiffin. U.S. Glass created a Duncan and Miller Division.

C. W. Carlson, Sr., retired in 1959. U.S. Glass profits declined. In 1962 U.S. Glass was in bankruptcy. Production resumed when C. W. Carlson, Jr. and some former Tiffin workers founded Tiffin Art Glass Corporation.

Reference: Gene Florence, *Collector's Encyclopedia of Depression Glass, 12th Edition,* Collector Books, 1996.

Aunt Polly, berry bowl, blue, 7⅞" d	$ 30.00
Aunt Polly, butter, cov, blue	200.00
Aunt Polly, candy, cov, blue	50.00
Aunt Polly, candy, ftd, 2 handled, green	20.00
Aunt Polly, creamer, green	22.00
Aunt Polly, luncheon plate, 8" d	15.00
Aunt Polly, sherbet, ftd, green	7.50
Aunt Polly, salt and pepper shakers, pr, blue	200.00
Aunt Polly, sugar, blue	32.00
Aunt Polly, tumbler, blue, 8 oz, 3⅝" h	25.00
Cherryberry, berry bowl, individual, crystal, 4" d	6.50
Cherryberry, bowl, green, 6½" d	18.00
Cherryberry, butter, cov, crystal	140.00
Cherryberry, coaster, crystal	8.00
Cherryberry, creamer, small, crystal	12.00
Cherryberry, fruit bowl, 3 legs, green, 10½" d	75.00
Cherryberry, pickle dish, oval, crystal, 8¼" l	8.00
Cherryberry, pitcher, crystal, 7¾" h	155.00
Cherryberry, salad plate, crystal, 7½" d	7.00
Cherryberry, sherbet, green	7.50
Cherryberry, sugar, small, pink	18.00
Cherryberry, tumbler, flat, green, 9 oz, 4²⁄₄" h	22.00
Floral and Diamond Band, berry bowl, pink, 4½" d	6.50
Floral and Diamond Band, butter, cov, pink	125.00

Floral and Diamond Band, compote, green, 5½" h **15.00**
Floral and Diamond Band, creamer, pink, 4¾" h. **15.50**
Floral and Diamond Band, luncheon plate, pink, 8" d **35.00**
Floral and Diamond Band, sugar, 5¼" h, pink. **12.00**
Flower Garden With Butterflies, creamer, pink **65.00**
Flower Garden With Butterflies, plate, 7" d, crystal **15.00**
Flower Garden With Butterflies, sandwich server,
    center handle, amber **45.00**
Flower Garden With Butterflies, saucer, pink. **25.00**
Flower Garden With Butterflies, tumbler, amber,
    7½ oz **170.00**
Flower Garden With Butterflies, vase, green, 10½" h **120.00**
Primo, bowl, 4½" d, yellow **12.00**
Primo, cake plate, 3 ftd, green, 10" d **20.00**
Primo, creamer, yellow **10.00**
Primo, dinner plate, green, 10" d **15.00**
Primo, grill plate, yellow, 10" d **12.00**
Primo, saucer, green **2.50**
Primo, sugar, yellow **10.00**
Strawberry, berry bowl, pink, 4" d **6.00**
Strawberry, butter, cov, pink **140.00**
Strawberry, compote, crystal, 5¾" h **12.00**
Strawberry, pickle dish, oval, crystal, 8¼" l **8.00**
Strawberry, pitcher, crystal, 7¾" h **150.00**
Strawberry, sherbet plate, pink, 6" d **5.00**
Strawberry, sugar, open, crystal. **10.00**
U.S. Swirl, butter, cov, pink **100.00**
U.S. Swirl, candy, cov, 2 handled, pink. **30.00**
U.S. Swirl, creamer, green **12.00**
U.S. Swirl, salad plate, green, 7⅞" d. **5.00**
U.S. Swirl, sherbet plate, pink, 6⅛" d **2.00**
U.S. Swirl, tumbler, 8 oz, 3⅝" h **8.00**
U.S. Swirl, vase, green, 6½" h **15.00**

VALENTINES

Valentine collectors divide valentines into four major chronological time periods: (1) 1740–1840, the handmade valentine era, (2) 1840–1915, the Victorian era, (3) 1920–1940, and (4) post–1945. Most collectors completely ignore the last period. American collectors concentrate exclusively on American, English, and Continental examples.

Handmade valentines were often laboriously wrought containing decorative motifs ranging from pen work and watercolor to cutouts and pin pricks. Some involved intricate folds and had verses in the form of a rebus. Most early examples originated in New England and the Mid–Atlantic states with those associated with the Pennsylvania Germans constituting a unique subgroup.

The lithographed valentine arrived on the scene in 1840 and was dominant until the 1860s. Esther Howland is credited with introducing the lace valentine in America, a form that proved extremely popular during the last half of the 19th century. A. J. Fisher, McLoughlin Brothers, and George C. Whitney & Company competed with Howland. The comic valentine, also known as the Penny Dreadful, arrived on the scene in the 1840s.

The valentine experienced several major changes in the early decades of the 20th century. Fold or pull out, lithograph novelty, mechanical action, and postcard valentines replaced lacy valentines as the preferred form. Die–cut cards became common. Chromolithography brightened the color scheme.

The candy, card, flower, and giftware industry hopped aboard the valentine bandwagon big time following 1920. Elementary schools introduced valentine exchanges when inexpensive mass-produced valentine packs became available. Many companies and stars, e.g., Disney and William Boyd (Hopalong Cassidy), licensed their images for valentine use.

Valentine collectors specialize. Many 20th–century valentines, especially post–1945 examples, are purchased by crossover collectors more interested in the card's subject matter than the fact that it is a valentine. Valentine survival rate is high. Never assume any post–1920 valentine is in short supply.

References: Robert Brenner, *Valentine Treasury: A Century of Valentine Cards,* Schiffer Publishing, 1997; Dan and Pauline Campanelli, *Romantic Valentines,* L–W Book Sales, 1996.

Collectors' Club: National Valentine Collectors Assoc, Box 1404, Santa Ana, CA 92702.

Decoration, heart and arrow, #V524, set of 6, cardboard, cut–out, Dennison, Framingham, MA, 1920–30 . . . . **$ 7.50**
Greeting Card, "A Valentine Message," curly haired child putting valentine in mailbox, die–cut, folded, c1930s, 3 x 4" **4.00**
Greeting Card, "Best Valentine Wishes," woman wearing winter clothes reading card, c1920 . . . . **1.75**
Greeting Card, "Cupid's Temple of Love," honeycomb, c1928 . . . . **15.50**
Greeting Card, "Hello! Be My Valentine?," honeycomb, boy and girl talking on phone, Germany, Carrington Card Co, c1930 . . . . **15.00**
Greeting Card, "Hoping I will be a Purr–fectly good Valentine," mechanical, kitten in basket rolls eyes as mouse bobs back and forth, c1930, 5 x 7" **8.00**
Greeting Card, "I Hope I Can Catch Your Heart, Dear Valentine," mechanical, girl sitting on ground, boy standing with arms up looking at 2 squirrels in tree, Germany, 1930s. **25.00**

Greeting Card, folding, teacher's valentine, 1960s, 4³⁄₈ x 5³⁄₈", $1.00.

Greeting Card, mechanical, arm moves, Germany, 4 x 6⅛", $4.00.

Greeting Card, "Loving Greetings," honeycomb, cut–out hearts, cherub holding floral strand, Beistle, 1930s 35.00

Greeting Card, "Reflecting my Love for You," mechanical, girl looking at herself in mirror, arm moves up and down, Carrington Co, Chicago, IL, c1930–1940, 4 x 6" 4.50

Greeting Card, "To My Love," honeycomb, easel back, Saxony, c1920–30, 6 x 8" 25.00

Greeting Card, "To My Valentine," fold–out, airplane with passengers, floral dec wings, Germany, 1920–30, 9 x 5" 75.00

Greeting Card, "To My Valentine, Squirrels go for nuts In a great big way, I go nuts for you more every day," honeycomb heart being pushed by squirrel, Germany, c1930 . . . . 10.00

Greeting Card, "We'll be just like Cinderella and the Prince if you will be my Valentine," Germany, c1930 . . . . 4.50

Postcard, "Be My Valentine," girl wearing purple dress, holding bouquet of roses, gold heart and verse background, Whitney, USA, 1930s 1.50

Postcard, "Love's Greeting," boy and girl, sgd "Ellen H. Clapsaddle," 1922 . . . . 5.50

Postcard, "Love's Greetings, My heart is light, my heart is free, my sweetheart is bright, she'll ever love me," 1924 . . . . 3.00

VAN BRIGGLE POTTERY

After a highly successful career at Rookwood, where he successfully copied the Ming dynasty matte glaze, Artus Van Briggle moved to Colorado Springs, Colorado, and established the Van Briggle Pottery Company in 1900. Van Briggle continued his glaze experiments at Colorado College.

Shortly after arriving in Colorado, Van Briggle married Anne Gregory, an artist who worked with him. His pottery won numerous awards including one from the 1903 Paris Exhibition. Artus Van Briggle died in 1904.

Anne became president of Van Briggle Pottery, reorganized the company, and built a new plant. Van Briggle produced a wide range of products including art pottery, garden pottery, novelty items, and utilitarian ware such as decorative tiles. Artware pieces produced between 1901 and 1912 are recognized for the high quality of their design and glaze. Van Briggle's Lorelei vase is a classic.

Anne remarried in 1908. A reorganization in 1910 produced the Van Briggle Pottery and Tile Company. By 1912 the pottery was leased to Edwin DeForest Curtis who in turn sold it to Charles B. Lansing in 1915. The plant was destroyed by fire in 1919. Lansing sold the company to I. F. and J. H. Lewis in 1920 who renamed the company Van Briggle Art Pottery.

The company survived a major flood in 1935. In 1953, Van Briggle purchased the Midland Terminal Railroad roundhouse for use as an auxiliary plant.

Kenneth Stevenson acquired the company in 1969. He continued the production of art pottery, introducing some new designs and glazes. Upon his death in 1990, Bertha (his wife) and Craig (his son) continued production.

The Stevensons use a mark that is extremely close to the interlocking "AA" mark used by Artus and Anne. Because they also make the same shapes and glazes, novice collectors frequently confuse newly made ware for older pieces. Because the Stevensons only selectively release their wholesale list, discovering what older shapes and glazes are in current production is difficult.

All pieces had the "AA" mark and "Van Briggle" prior to 1907. These marks also were used occasionally during the 1910s and 20s. "Colorado Springs" or an abbreviation often appears on pieces made after 1920. Some early pieces were dated. Value rises considerably when a date mark is present.

References: Susan and Al Bagdade, *Warman's American Pottery and Porcelain*, Wallace–Homestead, Krause Publications, 1994; Carol and Jim Carlton, *Colorado Pottery*, Collector Books, 1994; Richard Sasicki and Josie Fania, *Collector's Encyclopedia of Van Briggle Art Pottery*, Collector Books, 1993, 1995 value update.

Collectors' Club: American Art Pottery Assoc, PO Box 525, Cedar Hill, MO 63016.

REPRODUCTION ALERT: Van Briggle pottery is still being produced today. Modern glazes include Midnight (black), Moonglo (off–white), Russet, and Turquoise Ming.

Ashtray, kneeling Hopi maiden grinding corn, turquoise, 6½" w . . . . $ 75.00

Bookends, pr, Pug dog, mulberry, 1920s 175.00

Bowl, Lotus, white, with flower frog 45.00

Bowl, moth pattern, purple 50.00

Bowl, mulberry, #903D, with flower frog, 1920s 250.00

Bowl, Persian Rose Leaf, 8½" d, 4¾" h 150.00

Bust, child reading book, 6½" h 50.00

Cowboy Hat, turquoise and dark blue, 5½" w 125.00

Creamer, melon ribbed body, turquoise, #291, 1970s 15.00

Creamer, Sweetheart, 2–tone blue 50.00

Ewer, turquoise, #71, c1955 . . . . 30.00

Figurine, cat, brown, 1950s, 15" h 90.00

Lamp, bird, white, no shade 85.00

Lamp, butterfly 150.00

Lamp, Damsel of Damascus, c1950 . . . . 250.00

Vase, 2–tone blue, handled, #774, c1925, $200.00.

Lamp, wishing well, Persian Rose, orig shade **275.00**
Night Light, owl, mulberry **400.00**
Paperweight, rabbit, maroon, c1925, 3" d **125.00**
Planter, conch shell, blue, #325, 9" l **55.00**
Rose Bowl, foliate rim, turquoise, 5" d **50.00**
Vase, baluster turned, blue, c1960 . . . . **75.00**
Vase, blue, #645, 1920s, 5" h **150.00**
Vase, Dragonfly, blue **95.00**
Vase, mulberry, c1925, #841 . . . . **120.00**
Vase, mulberry, #838, 1920, 6" h **125.00**
Vase, 2–tone blue, #859, 1922, 6" h **120.00**

VENDING MACHINES

Today's vending machines with their wide merchandise selections and change–making abilities are a far cry from the globe–type gumball machines of the 1920s. Choice not chance is the order of the day.

Vending machines were silent salesmen. They worked 24 hours a day. Thomas Adams of Adams Gum is created with popularizing the vending machine. In 1888 his Tutti–Frutti gum machines were placed on elevated train platforms in New York City. The wedding of the gumball and vending machine occurred around 1910.

Leading vending machine manufacturers from its golden age, 1920 through the end of the 1950s, include Ad–Lee Novelty, Bluebird Products, Columbus Vending, Northwestern, Pulver, Volkmann, Stollwerck and Co., and Victor Vending. Figural machines and those incorporating unusual mechanical action are among the most desirable.

Today's vending machine collectors collect either globe–type machines or lithograph tin counter top models dating prior to 1960. While period paint is considered a added value factor, retention of period decals and labels and workability are the main value keys. Since the average life of many vending machines is measured in decades, collectors expect machines to be touched up or repainted.

Vending machines are collected either by type or by material dispensed. Crossover collectors, e.g., gum collectors, can skew pricing.

References: Richard M. Bueschel, *Collector's Guide To Vintage Coin Machines*, Schiffer Publishing, 1995; Bill Enes, *Silent Salesmen: An Encyclopedia of Collectible Gum, Candy & Nut Machines*, published by author, 1987; Bill Enes, *Silent Salesman Too: The Encyclopedia of Collectible Vending Machines*, published by author, 1995.

Newsletter: *Around The Vending Wheel*, 5417 Costana Ave, Lakewood, CA 90712.

Candy, Wilbur–Suchard Chocolate, cast iron, Art Deco motif, 4 columns, L. Miles, c1930, 16½" h . . . **$ 225.00**
Cigar, Malkin Phillies, 10¢, steel, c1930 . . . . **85.00**
Cigarette, Cent–A–Smoke, Marshall Supply Co, c1930, 9" h **325.00**
Cigarette, Rowe Mfg, 15¢, 6 column, glass and metal, c1935 . . . . **250.00**
Cigarette, Wilson Mfg, Lucky Strike, 1¢, dispenses single cigarette, c1931 . . . . **800.00**
Comb, Advance, Model #4, 10¢, c1950 . . . . **50.00**
Condom, Harmon Mfg, 25¢, c1962 . . . . **75.00**
Gum, Advance, metal, c1925 . . . . **75.00**
Gum, Dugreiner, Adams, 4 column, stainless case, c1934 . . . . **75.00**
Gum, Kayum, Beechnut, metal cast, c1947 . . . . **200.00**
Gum, Penny King, 1930s **100.00**
Gum, Pulver, Too Choos and Joy Mint, red porcelain case, c1930 . . . . **400.00**
Gum Ball, Atlas, aluminum case, c1950 . . . . **90.00**
Gum Ball, Ford, 1¢, chrome case, c1947 . . . . **50.00**
Gum Ball, Masters, #2, aluminum and porcelain case, c1925 . . . . **200.00**
Gum Ball, Penny King, chrome case, Art Deco motif, 4 sections, c1935 . . . . **575.00**
Gum Ball, Victor Topper, plastic top, c1950 . . . . **45.00**
Lotion, Jergens, National Dispenser, 1¢, c1938 . . . . **50.00**
Match, Kelley Mfg, 1¢, c1920 . . . . **200.00**
Match, Morrell Vending, aluminum front, c1927, 19½" h **250.00**
Peanut, Acorn, Oak Mfg, c1947 . . . . **40.00**
Peanut, Hot Nuts, Cebco Products, cast aluminum case, c1930 . . . . **175.00**
Peanut, Hot Nuts, C. D. Stover, flashing red glass bullseye in base, c1933, 16" h **350.00**
Peanut, In The Bag Co, O. D. Jennings, glass globe, c1934, 19" h **500.00**
Peanut, Mity Mite, R. H. Osbrink Mfg, glass barrel shaped globe, octagonal aluminum base, c1934, 11" h **500.00**
Peanut, Silver King Hot Nut, aluminum, flashing ruby hobnail glass dome, c1947, 15½" h **250.00**
Pen, Victor Vending, 25¢, revolving, c1950 . . . . **225.00**
Pencil, Library Booster Pencils, Parker Pencil Co, aluminum, c1927, 11" h **250.00**
Perfume, Perfumatic, Mercury Tool, c1950 . . . . **225.00**
Postage Stamp, Postage Stamp Machine Co, 5¢ and 10¢, c1948 . . . . **45.00**
Postage Stamp, Bushnell, flashing glass globe, 3 windows, 27" h **275.00**
Postage Stamp, U.S. Postage Stamps, Anderson Die & Model Co, cast iron, c1920, 13" h **225.00**

VERNON KILNS

In 1912 George Poxon, related to England's Wade potting family and a pottery chemist, arrived in California and established Poxon China in Vernon, California. Workers were recruited from England's Staffordshire district and East Liverpool, Ohio. Initially the company made tiles. Following World War I production shifted to earthenware dishes and hotel and restaurant ware. In 1928 George Poxon turned the company over to his wife Judith and her brother James Furlong. The company was renamed Vernon China.

In 1931 Faye G. Bennison bought Vernon China, appointed himself president and general manager, and changed the name to Vernon Kilns. Initially the company produced decal ware utilizing older Vernon China/Paxon shapes. A destructive earthquake in 1933 shattered most of the company's inventory and did extensive damage to the kilns. This proved a blessing in disguise as Vernon Kilns introduced numerous new shapes, e.g., Montecito, and pattern lines. Art ware also was introduced, remaining in production until 1937.

Vernon Kilns products divide into three main groups: (1) art ware, (2) dinnerware, and (3) specialty ware. Jane Bennison, Bennison's daughter, Diane May Hamilton de Causse, and Genevieve Bartlett Hamilton Montgomery designed the art ware pieces. Harry Bird designed a dinnerware line for the art group.

Vernon Kilns worked with a number of famous artists to design dinnerware motifs and patterns. The list includes Jean Goodwin Ames, Don Blanding, Allen F. Brewer, Jr., Cavett, Paul L. Davidson, Till Goodan, Royal Hickman, Elliott House, Rockwell Kent, Orpha Klinker, Robert Mayokok, Sharon Merrill, Janice Pettee, and Gale Turnbull. On October 10, 1940, Vernon Kilns signed a contract with Walt Disney Productions to make figures of the characters from *Dumbo, Fantasia,* and *The Reluctant Dragon.* Specialty transfer print ware was introduced in the 1930s. The late 1940s and early 1950s saw the production of hundreds of different commemorative patterns ranging from the University of Notre Dame to General Douglas MacArthur. Series included Moby Dick and Our America.

The Coronada shape line was introduced in 1938, Melinda in 1942, San Marino in the mid–1940s, and Anytime, designed by Elliott House, in 1955. Hand–painted Organdie in its many variations and Brown–Eyed Susan were popular patterns.

Faye Bennison retired in 1955, succeeded by Edward Fischer. Cheap foreign imports and labor costs seriously affected the company. In January 1958 a decision was made to close the company. Metlox Potteries, Manhattan Beach, California, bought the molds, modified some, and continued production of Anytime, Barkwood, Brown–Eyed Susan, Organdie, Sherwood, and Tickled Pink for a year. Although the Vernon Kilns plant closed, the corporation remained alive until it was legally dissolved in 1969.

References: Susan and Al Bagdade, *Warman's American Pottery and Porcelain,* Wallace–Homestead, Krause Publications, 1994; Harvey Duke, *The Official Price Guide to Pottery and Porcelain, Eighth Edition,* House of Collectibles, 1995; Maxine Feek Nelson, *Collectible Vernon Kilns,* Collector Books, 1994.

Periodical: *Vernon Views,* PO Box 945, Scottsdale, AZ 85252.

Anytime, chowder . . . . $ 11.00
Anytime, pitcher, streamline, 2 qt 35.00
Anytime, relish, divided 25.00
Anytime, tumbler 28.00

Arcadia, bread and butter plate 6.00
Arcadia, cup and saucer 10.00
Arcadia, gravy 22.00
Arcadia, dinner plate 12.00
Arcadia, lug chowder 12.00
Arcadia, luncheon plate 12.00
Arcadia, vegetable bowl, round 15.00
Bell–Aire, creamer 12.00
Bell–Aire, cup and saucer 12.00
Bell–Aire, dinner plate 12.00
Bell–Aire, gravy 22.00
Bell–Aire, platter 15.00
Bell–Aire, salt and pepper shakers, pr 20.00
Bell–Aire, sugar, cov 14.00
Bell–Aire, tumbler 20.00
Brown Eyed Susan, bread and butter plate 2.50
Brown Eyed Susan, creamer, ice lip 6.00
Brown Eyed Susan, cup and saucer 6.00
Brown Eyed Susan, dinner plate, 9¾" 6.00
Brown Eyed Susan, salad plate 4.00
Brown Eyed Susan, salt and pepper shakers, pr 10.00
Camelia, chop plate, 14" 35.00
Camelia, cup and saucer 12.00
Camelia, dinner plate 12.00
Camelia, fruit bowl 10.00
Camelia, soup, flat 15.00
Camelia, sugar, cov 18.00
Country Cousins, cereal bowl, lug handle, 6" 4.00
Country Cousins, creamer 4.00
Country Cousins, cup and saucer 10.00
Country Cousins, dinner plate, 10" d 8.00
Country Cousins, fruit bowl, 5½" 2.50
Country Cousins, mug 7.50
Country Cousins, salad plate, 7½" 2.50
Early California, creamer, ice lip, pink 2.50
Early California, cup and saucer, dark blue 4.00
Early California, dinner plate, 10½", turquoise 4.00
Early California, fruit bowl, 5½", brown 2.50
Gingham, bread and butter plate 2.50

Brown–Eyed Susan, dinner plate, 10¼" d, $7.50

Gingham, bulb jug, 1 pt. 25.00
Gingham, bulb jug, 1 qt. 35.00
Gingham, butter, cov 45.00
Gingham, casserole, cov 45.00
Gingham, chicken pot pie, cov. 30.00
Gingham, chop plate, 12" 12.50
Gingham, chowder 11.00
Gingham, coaster 30.00
Gingham, coffee carafe 40.00
Gingham, cup 4.00
Gingham, dinner plate, 9³/₄" d 8.00
Gingham, eggcup 25.00
Gingham, gravy, round 12.00
Gingham, pitcher, streamline, 2 qt 35.00
Gingham, platter, oval, 14¹/₄" l 15.00
Gingham, salad bowl, individual 20.00
Gingham, salad plate, 7¹/₂" 4.00
Gingham, salt and pepper shakers, pr 10.00
Gingham, soup, flat 13.00
Gingham, teapot 55.00
Gingham, tumbler 28.00
Heavenly Days, butter, cov. 15.00
Heavenly Days, cup. 2.50
Heavenly Days, dinner plate, 10" d 4.00
Heavenly Days, tumbler. 28.00
Heavenly Days, vegetable, 7¹/₂" 6.00
Homespun, bread and butter plate 2.50
Homespun, butter, cov. 45.00
Homespun, butter pat 30.00
Homespun, chop plate, 12¹/₄" 15.00
Homespun, chowder 11.00
Homespun, coaster 30.00
Homespun, coffee carafe 40.00
Homespun, dinner plate, 9¹/₂" 6.00
Homespun, eggcup 25.00
Homespun, pitcher, streamline, 2 qt 35.00
Homespun, plate, 6¹/₂" 5.00
Homespun, plate, 9¹/₂" d 9.00

Homespun, salt and pepper shakers, pr 15.00
Homespun, saucer. 2.00
Homespun, syrup 55.00
Homespun, teapot 55.00
Homespun, tumbler. 28.00
Mexican, cup and saucer. 4.00
Mexicana, gravy, round 8.00
Mexicana, tumbler, 14 oz 7.50
Organdie, bulb jug, 1 pt 25.00
Organdie, bulb jug, 1 qt 35.00
Organdie, butter, cov. 45.00
Organdie, casserole, cov 45.00
Organdie, chicken pot pie, cov 30.00
Organdie, coffee carafe 40.00
Organdie, eggcup 25.00
Organdie, pitcher, streamline, 2 qt 35.00
Organdie, soup, flat. 13.00
Organdie, tumbler 28.00
Raffia, bread and butter plate. 5.00
Raffia, cup and saucer 9.00
Raffia, eggcup 18.00
Raffia, pitcher 2 qt. 45.00
Raffia, tumbler. 20.00
Tam O'Shanter, butter pat. 30.00
Tam O'Shanter, casserole, cov 45.00
Tam O'Shanter, chicken pot pie, cov 30.00
Tam O'Shanter, coaster 30.00
Tam O'Shanter, coffee carafe 40.00
Tam O'Shanter, eggcup 25.00
Tam O'Shanter, salad bowl, individual 20.00
Tam O'Shanter, soup, flat. 13.00
Tam O'Shanter, teapot 55.00
Tam O'Shanter, tumbler 28.00

VIETNAM WAR

The Vietnam War divided America. As a result, there are two groups of Vietnam War collectibles, anti–war demonstration and military.

Following the withdrawal of the French from Indo–China, destabilization in the area continued. In the early 1960s American military advisors were in South Vietnam assisting the country's military. In May 1962 President Kennedy sent 1,800 U.S. Marines to Thailand to protect it from a possible invasion by communist forces from Laos. On June 16, 1962 two U.S. Army officers were killed north of Saigon. On November 1, 1963, the government of President Diem was overthrown by South Vietnamese armed forces. America recognized the new government on November 7, 1963.

America increased its military and economic assistance to South Vietnam in 1964. Vietnam casualties mounted during 1965 and protests began. By the end of 1966, the United States had 400,000 troops in South Vietnam. The casualty count was over 6,600 killed and 37,500 wounded. Nguyen Van Thieu was elected president in 1967 amid charges of election fraud. Dissent continued to mount, reaching a fever pitch in the late 1960s and 70s. Lyndon Johnson declined to run for another term. North Vietnam launched the Tet offensive on January 30, 1968.

Although Nixon reduced the U.S. troop commitment in 1969, major anti–war demonstrations took place in October and

Homespun, tidbit, 2 tiers, metal center handle, 10" h, $30.00.

November. America continued to disengage from Vietnam. By December 1971 American troop strength dropped to 184,000. On March 30, 1972, North Vietnam moved into South Vietnam across the DMZ and from Cambodia.

A peace agreement was signed on January 22, 1973. It proved ineffective. The South Vietnamese government fell to the North in 1975. America's presence in Vietnam ended. President Ford offered amnesty to deserters and draft evaders in September 1974. A general pardon was issued in 1977.

References: Ray Bows, *Vietnam Military Lore 1959–1973... Another Way to Remember,* Bows & Sons, 1988; Ron Manion, *American Military Collectibles,* Antique Trader Books, 1995.

Army Aviator Jungle Jacket, poplin, olive drab, hand–embroidered insignia, patch on left shoulder, senior pilot and paratrooper wings, hand–embroidered name tape . . . . **$ 40.00**

Ashtray, souvenir, black, mother–of–pearl inlay in form of flowers, brass inner tray, 6" d **25.00**

Beret, wool, green, black leather sweatband, black cotton lining, tie in rear, dated 1971 . . . . **85.00**

Book, *Frontline–The Commands of Wm. Chase,* autographed 1st ed, 1975, 228 pgs **38.00**

Book, *Vietnam II 3D Brigade,* 82nd Airborne Division Jan to Dec 1969, hard cover, 140 pgs **35.00**

Bracelet, POW, names **25.00**

Cigarette Lighter, "CO A 1st," engraved "CO A 1st, ENGR BN, QUANLOI, VIETNAM, 66–67–68" **40.00**

Cloth Insignia, Army Airborne, eagle in jumpsuit, "1st Brigade" at bottom, 4" d **55.00**

Cloth Insignia, Army 101st Airborne Division, black cotton, machine embroidered design, cloth back **25.00**

Cloth Insignia, Filthy Five Flying Death, black twill, spade shaped, embroidered design, 5" d **45.00**

Crossbow, wood, bamboo, Vietnamese **325.00**

Duffel Bag, canvas, olive drab, web straps, mkd "US," dated 1972 . . . . **25.00**

Grenade, olive drab, iron body, plug, handle, and safety ring, dated 1968 . . . . **20.00**

Helmet, helicopter aviator's, blue ext with gold and white pattern, dark blue star over each ear, center pull visor with cov, boom mike, and earpiece **235.00**

Helmet Bag, nylon, olive drab, zipper, handles, dated 1974 . . . . **45.00**

Jungle Boots, black leather body, olive drab canvas uppers, cleated soles, lace fronts, size 10XN, dated 1968 . . . . **20.00**

Manual, *Army Model UH–1D/H Helicopters,* Department of Army, 1971, 300 pgs **30.00**

Medal, Air Force Commendation, parade ribbon and lapel bar, orig case **20.00**

Medal, Vietnam Service, Japanese–made **20.00**

Medical Kit, nylon, pouch type, plastic inside container, belt clips, complete **35.00**

Metal Insignia, Airborne Para Wing, 1½" l **35.00**

Newspaper, headline, 1973, "Vietnam Peace Pacts Signed" **12.00**

Patch, green B–52 in center, "Peace Hell, Bomb Hanoi" border, 4" d **20.00**

Pinback Button, "March on Washington, San Francisco April 24, Out Now, NPAC," 1971, 1⅝" d **20.00**

Plaque, commemorative Navy NC–4, rect, wood and brass, May 10, 1969 . . . . **25.00**

Poster, "Out Now. Stop the Bombing, March Against the War," Student Mobilization Committee, Berkeley, CA, 1970, 22 x 14" **50.00**

Poster, "Know Your Enemy," 1967 MACV Command, color, 16 x 25" **220.00**

Record, *Dick Gregory at Kent State,* 2–record set, Poppy, 1970, May 4, 1970 Kent State shooting account **50.00**

Trench Art, urn, made from brass 105 mm shell, fluted top, inscribed **25.00**

VIEW–MASTER

William Gruber, a Portland, Oregon, piano tuner, and Harold Graves, president of Sawyer's, a Portland photo–finishing and postcard company, were the two principals behind View–Master. On January 20, 1939, a patent was filed for a special stereoscope utilizing a card with seven pairs of views. Sawyer, Inc., manufactured and sold View–Master products.

The Model A viewer, with its flip front opening and straight viewing barrels, was introduced in 1939. It was replaced by an improved Model B viewer in 1943. The more familiar Model C square viewer arrived in 1946 and remained in production for eleven years.

By 1941 there were more than 1,000 View–Master sales outlets. During World War II, View–Master made special training reels for the United States Navy and Army Air Corps. View–Master's golden years were 1945 to 1960. Hundreds of new reels appeared. The three–pack set was introduced.

In 1966 General Aniline and Film Corporation (GAF) purchased Sawyer's. GAF introduced new projects and the 3–D talking View–Master. Arnold Thaler purchased View–Master in 1980, only to sell it to Ideal. When Tyco acquired Ideal, View–Master was part of the purchase. Today, the View–Master brand name is owned by Mattel, the result of its purchase of Tyco in 1997.

Reference: John Waldsmith, *Stereo Views: An Illustrated History and Price Guide,* Wallace–Homestead, Krause Publications, 1991.

Collectors' Club: National Stereoscopic Assoc, PO Box 14801, Columbus, OH 43214.

Camera, Personal 3–D, custom film cutter . . . . **$ 175.00**

Camera, Mark II, film cutter **200.00**

Projector, S–1, brown metal, single lens, carrying case **50.00**

Projector, Sawyer's, plastic, single lens **10.00**

Projector, Stereomatic 500, 3–dimensional, two lenses, carrying case **250.00**

Reel, Alpine Wild Flowers, Sawyer's **12.50**

Reel, Amazing Spider–Man, GAF #H–11 . . . . **15.00**

Reel, Balance of Nature, Ecology, GAF #B–686 . . . . **25.00**

Reel, Batman, GAF #B–492 . . . . **20.00**

Reel, Boys Town, NE, #SP–9062, 1951 . . . . **1.00**

Reel, Brady Bunch, 1974 . . . . **45.00**

Reel, Buck Rogers, GAF #L–15 . . . . **15.00**

Reel, Buckaroo Banzai, GAF #4056 . . . . **5.00**
Reel, Butterflies of North America, GAF #B–610 . . . . **10.00**
Reel, Colonial Williamsburg, VA, #181 . . . . **10.00**
Reel, Cowboy Stars, 1950s **20.00**
Reel, Euphorbiacease, #C–18, 1945 . . . . **8.00**
Reel, Family Affair, 1969 . . . . **50.00**
Reel, Golden Gate Exposition, Flowers and Land-
    scaping, #58 . . . . **15.00**
Reel, Hawaiian Hula Dancers, #62. . . . . **3.00**
Reel, Hot Springs National Park, AR, #299 . . . . **1.00**
Reel, Island of Kuai, HI, #72 . . . . **6.00**
Reel, Jack and the Beanstalk, #FT–3, 1951 . . . . **1.00**
Reel, Kings Canyon National Park, CA, #118 . . . . **2.00**
Reel, Land of the Giants, 1968 . . . . **70.00**
Reel, La Plata, Argentina, #667 . . . . **5.00**
Reel, Lassie, Look Homeward, Sawyer #B–480 . . . . **25.00**
Reel, Laugh–In, GAF #B–497 . . . . **28.00**
Reel, Lone Ranger, GAF reissue **40.00**
Reel, M*A*S*H, 1978 . . . . **24.00**
Reel, Mission Impossible, 1968 . . . . **55.00**
Reel, MOD Squad **45.00**
Reel, Morphology of Succulents, #C–1 . . . . **8.00**
Reel, Mount Vernon, VA, #76 . . . . **10.00**
Reel, Movie Stars, Holywood III, #742 . . . . **15.00**
Reel, People of the Nile Valley, Egypt, #3308, 1950 . . . . . . **3.00**
Reel, Prehistoric Cliff Dwellers of Mesa Verde, CO,
    #9055, 1950 . . . . **5.00**
Reel, Puss 'N Boots, GAF #B–320. . . . . **20.00**
Reel, Reno, Biggest Little City in the World, #14 . . . . **8.00**
Reel, Roy Rogers **45.00**
Reel, Seven Wonders of the World, Sawyer #B–901 . . . . . **12.00**
Reel, The Inauguration of President Dwight D.
    Eisenhower, #400, 1953 . . . . **10.00**
Reel, Tom and Jerry in The Cat Trapper, #810, 1951. . . . . . **2.00**
Reel, Washington, DC, #137 . . . . **3.00**
Reel Set, Arlington National Cemetery, A–818,
    Edition A **6.00**
Reel Set, Archie, 1975 . . . . **30.00**
Reel Set, Barbie's Great American Photo Race,
    #B–576 . . . . **10.00**
Reel Set, Christmas Carol, #FT–31A, B, and C. **3.00**

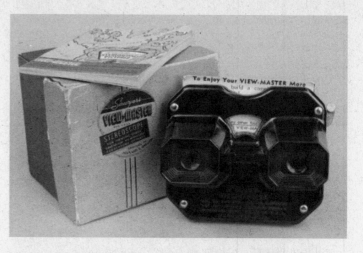

Viewer, Sawyer's De Luxe Steroscope, black Bakelite, brown and silver box, instruction card, and catalog, 1948, 4¹/₄" w, $25.00.

Reel Set, Cowboy Star Adventures, #946, 951, and
    956 . . . . **10.00**
Reel Set, Dale Evans, Queen of the West, #944–A, B,
    and C **25.00**
Reel Set, Disneyland, Fantasyland **18.00**
Reel Set, Disney World, Tomorrowland, #H–19. . . . . **5.00**
Reel Set, Dracula, 1976. . . . . **21.00**
Reel Set, Dr. Shrinker and the Wonderbug, Kroft
    Supershow #1 . . . . **30.00**
Reel Set, Frankenstein, 1976 . . . . **20.00**
Reel Set, Grand Tour of Asia, B–215 . . . . **15.00**
Reel Set, Grizzly Adams, 1976. **23.00**
Reel Set, Happy Days, The Not Making of a President **21.00**
Reel Set, Harlem Globetrotters, 1977 . . . . **25.00**
Reel Set, Historic Philadelphia, A–635, Edition A **12.00**
Reel Set, James Bond, Moonraker, 1979 . . . . **31.00**
Reel Set, Jetsons, 1981. . . . . **21.00**
Reel Set, Los Angeles, CA, #A–181, Edition B **6.00**
Reel Set, Mark Twain's Huckleberry Finn, #B–343 . . . . . . **30.00**
Reel Set, Mork and Mindy, 1979 . . . . **18.00**
Reel Set, Six Million Dollar Man, 1974. . . . . **30.00**
Reel Set, Thailand, GAF #J–32 . . . . **6.00**
Reel Set, The Rookies, #BB–452 . . . . **10.00**
Reel Set, U.N.C.L.E., 1965 . . . . **35.00**
Viewer, Model C, black Bakelite, light attachment,
    1946–56 . . . . **25.00**
Viewer, Model D, focus, orig box **85.00**
Viewer, Model F, illuminated, dark brown plastic **20.00**
Viewer, Model H, illuminated, GAF logo, 1967–81 . . . . . . **15.00**

WADE CERAMICS

In 1958 A. J. Wade, George Wade and Son, Wade Heath & Co., and Wade (Ulster) combined, formed The Wade Group of Potteries, and went public.

George Wade and Son, located at the Manchester Pottery in Burslem, is the best known of the group. Prior to World War I, the company made industrial ceramics, concentrating heavily on the

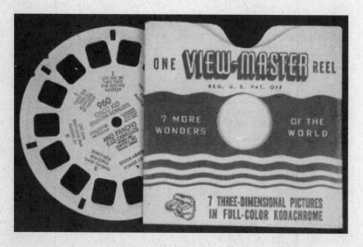

Reel, Cisco Kid and Pancho, Sawyer #960, $5.00.

needs of the textile industry. After the war, the company made insulators for the electrical industry.

A. J. Wade, George's brother, established a firm to market glazed tiles and faience fireplace surrounds. A. J. Wade became a partner in Wade, Heath & Co., a manufacturer of Rockingham jugs, teapots, etc. In 1935 Colonel G. A. Wade, a son of George Wade, gained control of A. J. Wade's two companies upon his death. Previously, in 1926/28, Col. Wade assumed control of George Wade and Son.

In the late 1920s, George Wade and Son introduced a line of moderately priced figurines. They did so well, the company added a line of animals. Faust Lang did a number of the designs. Production of these figurines ceased during World War II when the company directed its production to wartime necessities.

In 1938 Wade, Heath & Co. acquired the Royal Victoria Pottery. A line of tableware was introduced. A license was acquired from Disney to produce character figurines. Although heavily devoted to wartime production in the early 1940s, the company did manufacture a line of utilitarian dinnerware and tea ware.

In 1950 Wade (Ulster) was established. Located in Portadown, Northern Ireland, the company produced industrial ceramics.

The ceramic giftware industry went into decline in the 1960s. The Wade Group focused on industrial production. When the giftware industry revived in the 1970s, The Wade Group returned to the market. Wade Heath & Co. devotes its efforts to commission and special contract orders, serving a large number of clients ranging from breweries to tobacco companies. In 1969 Wade (PDM) was established within The Wade Group to deal with the design and marketing of promotional items. This new group works with glass, plastic, and tin, in addition to ceramics.

Wade is best known in the United States through its Red Rose Tea premiums. These are made by George Wade & Son. Different sets are made for the American and Canadian market. Some figures are based on figures in the "Whimsies" line. Do not confuse the two. Whimsies are slightly larger.

References: Pat Murray, *The Charlton Standard Catalogue of Wade: Vol. One, General Issues, Second Edition,* Charlton Press, 1996; Pat Murray, *The Charlton Standard Catalogue of Wade: Volume Two, Decorative Ware, Second Edition,* Charlton Press, 1996; Pat Murray, *The Charlton Standard Catalogue of Wade Whimsical Collectables, Third Edition,* Charlton Press, 1996; Ian Warner and Mike Posgay, *The World of Wade, Collectable Porcelain and Pottery* (1988, 1993 value update), *Book 2* (1995) Antique Publications.

Collectors' Club: Wade Watch, 8199 Pierson Ct, Arvada, CO 80005.

Bank, fawn, brown, orange–brown patches	$ 60.00
Bank, kennel and puppy	30.00
Bank, Percy the Small Engine	115.00
Butter Dish, cobbler, blue hat, yellow dish	20.00
Candle Holder, angel, sitting, green dress, yellow hair	110.00
Candle Holder, panda, Disney Lights series, 1960s	50.00
Cigarette Box, lid mkd "Capt. Kidd 1698"	30.00
Dish, angel, standing, green dress, brown hair	65.00
Dish, mare and colt, brown horses, black dish	50.00
Dish, "Remember? Broadway"	10.00
Dish, Royal Canadian Mounted Police	6.00
Figure, angel, yellow dress, brown hair	85.00

Figure, baby giraffe, sleeping	10.00
Figure, bear cup, Red Rose Tea premium	5.00
Figure, cockatoo	30.00
Figure, hippo, sleeping baby	4.00
Figure, Irish comical pig	45.00
Figure, Irish Setter, lying down	10.00
Figure, lion, Red Rose Tea premium	6.00
Figure, llama	15.00
Figure, otter, Red Rose Tea premium	3.00
Figure, poodle, brown, white	30.00
Figure, squirrel, Red Rose Tea premium	5.00
Figure, St. Bernard, St. Bruno Tobacco premium	20.00
Figure, turtle, souvenir, shell mkd "Devil's Hole, Bermuda"	20.00
Figure, wild boar, Red Rose Tea premium	2.00
Jug, Gothic Ware	85.00
Lamp, Gilbey's Gin Wine Barrel, Scotch	30.00
Pin Tray, tailor, blue hat, gray trousers	10.00
Pipe Rest, German Shepherd	25.00
Pitcher, advertising, White Label Dewar's Scotch Whiskey	28.00
Plate, Grape dec	18.00
Tankard, barrel	15.00
Trinket Box, treasure chest	50.00
Vase, cream ground, multicolored flowers	80.00
Vase, Viking, mottled green	60.00
Wall Pocket, Gothic Ware, yellow	50.00
Wall Plate, post office, "Please write soon"	12.00

WAGNER WARE

In 1891 Milton M. and Bernard P. Wagner, two brothers, established the Wagner Manufacturing Company in Sidney, Ohio. William, a third brother, soon wished to join the company. In order to add a line of skillets, Milton and Bernard purchased the Sidney Hollow Ware Foundry in 1903, placing William in charge. Finding the two companies in direct competition, Sidney Hollow Ware was sold and William bought into the main company as a partner. Louis, a fourth brother, joined the company a short time later.

Wagner Manufacturing made brass casting and cast–iron hollow ware, some of which was nickel plated. Wagner was one of the first companies to make aluminum cookware. The line included cake and ice cream molds, coffeepots, percolators, pitchers, scoops, spoons, and teapots. The company won numerous awards for its aluminum products between 1900 and 1940.

Several generations of Wagners were involved in the company management as individuals died and passed on their stock interests to their sons. In 1953 Philip Wagner, one of Milton Wagner's sons, was serving as president. He made it known he wanted to sell the company. Cable Wagner, William Wagner's son, purchased the Wagner Hotel Company. Randall Company of Cincinnati, Ohio, purchased the balance.

In 1957 Randall's Wagner Division purchased the Griswold Cookware line from McGraw Edison. Textron of Providence, Rhode Island, acquired the Randall Company in 1959. Textron's Wagner Division acquired the Durham Manufacturing Company of Muncie, Indiana, a manufacturer of casual leisure furniture for household use. In 1969, Textron sold its household line to General Housewares Corporation, a holding company. The sale included all patent and trademark rights for Griswold and Wagner.

Reference: David G. Smith and Charles Wafford, *The Book of Griswold & Wagner: Favorite Piqua, Sidney Hollow Ware, Wapak,* Schiffer Publishing, 1995.

Baking Pan, #1508	$ 250.00
Breadstick, EE	50.00
Bundt Pan, B, mkd	250.00
Corn Bread Skillet, USA	25.00
Corn Bread Stick Pan, B	50.00
Dutch Oven, #7, 4 ring	50.00
French Roll, D, logo	85.00
Gem Pan, D	60.00
Griddle, #7, oval, "Wagner"	75.00
Griddle, #7, round	35.00
Griddle, #9, round	35.00
Lid, #5	195.00
Lid, #11 Dutch Oven, 4 ring	45.00
Muffin, F, 12 cup	70.00
Muffin, R, 8 cup	70.00
Muffin, Turk's head, 6 cup	275.00
Muffin, Turk's head, 12 cup	250.00
Roaster, #7, oval	325.00
Roaster, #9, oval, 5–ring lid, pattern #1289	275.00
Scotch Bowl, #2, "Wagner"	35.00
Skillet, #2, smooth bottom, stylized logo	50.00
Skillet, #4, pattern #1054	75.00
Skillet, #4, script logo, smoke ring	65.00
Skillet, #5, pattern #1055	20.00
Skillet, #7, pattern #1067	125.00
Skillet, #7, "Wagner"	30.00
Skillet, #9, pattern #1069	50.00
Skillet, #10, pattern #1070	75.00
Skillet, #12, "Wagner"	90.00
Skillet, #13	200.00
Skillet, #1403, 5 star	125.00
Vienna Roll, 6 cup	125.00
Waffle Iron, #8, high base	50.00
Waffle Iron, #9, low base	55.00

WALGREEN

Charles R. Walgreen established the first Walgreen's in Chicago, Illinois, around 1900. A Walgreen has headed the company ever since. The company continues to expand. Today there are more than 2,000 stores coast to coast.

There are many different Walgreen brand products—cosmetics, drugs, soda fountain items, toys, etc. In the 1950s, Walgreen's was the largest drugstore operation with soda fountains in the United States. They sold more ice cream, malts, and sundaes than any other retailer.

Do not overlook Walgreen souvenirs, such as those handed out at the company's exhibit at the 1933/34 Chicago World's Fair. Walgreen advertising is also highly desirable.

Bottle, Child's Witch Hazel, paper label, 1928, 16 oz, 8" h	$ 18.00
Bottle, Gay Cologne, Leon Laraine, Art Deco style, green and white, 1941, 6 oz, 6" h	22.00
Bottle, Olafin Cod Liver Oil, paper label, 1935, 16 oz, 8" h	12.00

First Aid Kit, tin, 1942, 3¹/₂ x 8 x 4¹/₂", $35.00.

Bottle, Union Drug Alcohol, paper label, 1930, 16 oz, 7" h	12.00
Box, Peau–Doux Shaving Cream, yellow, red, and black, orig 4 oz tube, 1938, 7¹/₂" h	15.00
Canister, Powdered Alum, cardboard, Walgreen Labs, vertical cylinder, orange and blue, 1920, 3 oz, 4" h	22.00
Canister, Salted Peanuts, tin, vertical cylinder, orange, cream, and black, 16 oz, 1935, 4¹/₂" h	35.00
Canister, Triomphe Bath Powder, cardboard, Carrel, cream and pink, 1940, 6 oz, 14" d	20.00
Clock, soda fountain type, white and green adv insert above clock face, 1940	150.00
Dinner Plate, white, 1940, 6¹/₂" d	15.00
Dosage Glass, white letters, 1930, 4oz	25.00
Jar, ointment, Union Drug, white glass, paper label, orange and blue, 1935, 3 oz, 2¹/₂" h	16.00
Menu Holder, black, 1935, 1¹/₂ x 3¹/₂"	75.00
Mug, white and maroon lettering, 1950, 3¹/₂ x 4" h	12.00
Playing Cards, Peau–Doux brand adv, green and black, 2–deck set, 1935	20.00
Pocket Mirror, Green Bay store opening, 1938	60.00
Sign, Malted Milk, blackboard, 1938, 45 x 25 x 3"	400.00
Straw Holder, white china, 4" w base, 3¹/₂" h	50.00
Tin, All Purpose Talc, vertical oval, litho, blue and cream, 1934, 6" h	18.00
Tin, Golden Crown Tennis Balls, sleeve of 3 cylinders, 1938, 8" h	75.00
Tin, Lady Charlotte Chocolates, colonial scenes, cream ground, 1940, 2¹/₂ x 4 x 7¹/₂"	25.00
Tin, Peau–Doux Brand, Styptic Powder, vertical oval, litho, yellow and red, 1938, 1¹/₂ x 2³/₄" h	45.00
Tin, Quick–Strip Bandages, 1940, 1 x 2¹/₄ x 3¹/₂"	12.00
Tin, Walgreen Brand, aspirin, rect flat, orange and brown, 1938, 24 tablets	22.00
Tin, Walgreen Brand, Malted Milk, litho tin, 1935, 25 lb, 13 x 9¹/₂ x 9¹/₂"	125.00
Toiletry Kit, includes talc, styptic powder, and shaving cream, red box, 1938	125.00
Toy, Walgreen cash register bank, litho tin, red, gray, and blue, Linemar, 2¹/₂" h	40.00

Toy, Walgreen Ice Cream truck, litho tin, white, blue
    letters, Linemar, 1950, 20½ x 7 x 4" **200.00**
World's Fair Souvenir, bracelet, copper, Walgreen
    building. **45.00**
World's Fair Souvenir, drink shaker, Art Deco style,
    aluminum, black letters, 1933–34, 11" h **75.00**
World's Fair Souvenir, napkin, auto dealership adv,
    lists Walgreen store locations at Fair, 4½" sq **15.00**

WALL POCKETS

People were accustomed to hanging things on a wall, e.g., clothing on pegs, match holders, etc. It was a logical step to create a flower vase that could be hung on a wall. The earliest American wall pockets were made by folk potters in Virginia's Shenandoah Valley. Purchasers used them to hold the large matches of the time as well as flowers.

The funeral industry used glass vases with spike or spade–shaped ends in the latter part of the 19th century. Glass automobile vases date from the 1910s and 1920s.

The flower wall pocket became a standard household form in the 1920s and remained popular through the end of the 1940s. Flowers could be fresh, dried, or artificial.

Abingdon Potteries, Rookwood, Roseville, and Weller are considered the premier quality ceramic wall pocket manufacturers. California Cleminson, Hull, McCoy, Shawnee, and Spaulding (Royal Copley) are a few of the other companies making ceramic wall pockets. All were challenged for market share by inexpensive Japanese and later Far Eastern imports. Ceramic wall pockets from Czechoslovakia, England, and Italy are viewed more favorably by collectors. Imperial, Jeannette, McKee, and Tiffin are among the American glass firms that made wall pockets.

When the post–war Modern design styles became popular, wall pockets were out. The wall pocket regained some of its former popularity in the 1960s and 1970s. Import companies, such as ENESCO, included wall pockets in their catalogs. These new examples stimulated interest in collecting older ones.

References: Marvin and Joy Gibson, *Collectors Guide to Wall Pockets: Affordable & Others*, L–W Book Sales, 1994; Joy and Marvin Gibson, *Collector's Guide to Wall Pockets: Book II*, L–W Book Sales, 1997; Betty and Bill Newbound, *Collector's Encyclopedia of Wall Pockets: Identification and Values*, Collector Books, 1996; Fredda Perkins, *Wall Pockets of the Past*, Collector Books, 1996.

Collectors' Club: Wall Pocket Collectors Club, 1356 Takiti, St. Louis, MO 63128.

Abingdon, butterfly, #610. . . . . **$ 65.00**
Abingdon, calla lily **30.00**
Abingdon, Cookbook, #676D **45.00**
Abingdon, Morning Glory, #377. . . . . **40.00**
American Art Pottery, tree stump and woodpecker. **15.00**
Brayton Laguna, blackamoor holding planter above
    head, 2 pcs **200.00**
Brush, boxer **85.00**
Brush, bucking horse **135.00**
Brush, fish. **75.00**
Brush, flying duck **75.00**
Brush, grazing horse **100.00**

Japan, blue luster band, orange, blue, and yellow flowers, green leaves, white ground, 5½" h, $40.00.

California Arts, conch shell, yellow. **15.00**
Ceramic Arts Studio, cockatoo **50.00**
Ceramic Arts Studio, Zor and Zorina, pr **65.00**
Cleminson, clock. **15.00**
Czechoslovakia, parrot. **50.00**
Dee Lee, de Stinker **30.00**
Frankoma, acorn, brown, #190. . . . . **15.00**
Frankoma, cowboy boot, blue, #133 . . . . **18.00**
Germany, parrot, #10151–2 . . . . **60.00**
Gilner, grapes **28.00**
Haeger, flower, blue. **12.00**
Haeger, grapes, R–745 . . . . **20.00**
Hollywood Ceramics, trivet **25.00**
Hull, Bow Knot, cup and saucer, B–24, 6" **245.00**
Hull, Bow Knot, pitcher, B–26, 6". **245.00**
Hull, Bow Knot, whisk broom **200.00**
Japan, dust pan, green **10.00**
Japan, girl's head, paper label. **25.00**
Japan, rolling pin, "Home Sweet Home" **12.00**
Japan, spice rack, "Nutmeg, Pepper, Cinnamon, Salt" **15.00**
Jeannette, clear glass, Anniversary pattern **35.00**
Kay Finch, lady **50.00**
Lefton, elf, green **75.00**
McCoy, apple, 1953 . . . . **40.00**
McCoy, bellows, green. **75.00**
McCoy, flower, rustic glaze, 1946. . . . . **15.00**
McCoy, mailbox, blue, 1951 . . . . **45.00**
McCoy, turtles **40.00**
McCoy, umbrella, yellow, 1955 . . . . **18.00**
McCoy, viloin, turquoise, 1957 . . . . **30.00**
Metlox, Homestead Provincial **45.00**
Morton, harp, floral dec **15.00**
Morton, Mary Quite Contrary, red dress, blue apron **12.00**
Morton, parrot on grapes **20.00**
Morton, teapot, red apple **15.00**
Morton, violin, 2 notes, price for pair **30.00**
Nicodemus, double cornucopia, incised **350.00**
Niloak, Bouquet, brown. **45.00**
Noritake, lusterware, red roses **85.00**

Northwood, carnival glass, marigold, Woodpecker
  pattern **100.00**
Occupied Japan, violin **15.00**
Red Wing, guitar **35.00**
Red Wing, violins, turquoise, price for pair **150.00**
Roseville, Apple Blossom, green **300.00**
Roseville, Florentine, 12½" **250.00**
Roseville, Snowberry, green **200.00**
Royal Copley, apple **15.00**
Royal Copley, cocker spaniel head **18.00**
Royal Copley, mill **70.00**
Shawnee, birds at birdhouse **25.00**
Shawnee, bird on cornucopia, peach **20.00**
Shawnee, fern **35.00**
Shawnee, wheat **40.00**
Stangl, Cosmos, green, #2091, 1937 . . . . **45.00**
Treasure Craft, elf at well **15.00**
Weller, Woodcraft, owl in tree **400.00**

WALLACE CHINA

The Wallace China Company, Vernon, California, was founded around 1931. The company made vitrified, plain and transfer printed wares for the hotel, institution, and restaurant markets. Willow ware in blue, brown, green, and red transfers was produced during the 1930s and 1940s.

After turning Poxon China, which eventually became Vernon Kilns, over to his wife and her brother in 1928, George Poxon pursued a number of different careers, one of which involved helping Wallace China establish its manufacturing facilities. Poxon also shared some of his shape and pattern designs.

Wallace China is best known for its Westward Ho houseware line, the result of a 1943 commission from the M. C. Wentz Company of Pasadena. Wentz wanted restaurant barbecue ware. Till Goodan, a well–known western artist, created three patterns: Boots and Saddles, Pioneer Trails, and Rodeo. His name is incorporated in most designs. A three–piece Little Buckaroo Chuck set for children and the El Rancho and Longhorn dinnerware patterns also were designed by Goodan.

In 1959 Shenango China Company acquired Wallace China. Wallace China operated as a wholly owned subsidiary until 1964 when all production ceased.

References: Jack Chipman, *Collector's Encyclopedia of California Pottery,* Collector Books, 1992, 1995 value update; Harvey Duke, *The Official Price Guide to Pottery and Porcelain, Eighth Edition,* House of Collectibles, 1995.

Boots and Saddle, ashtray . . . . $ **40.00**
Boots and Saddle, cup and saucer **40.00**
Boots and Saddle, plate, 9" d **30.00**
Boots and Saddle, plate, 10½" d **35.00**
Boots and Saddle, shakers, pr **75.00**
Boots and Saddle, sugar **45.00**
Chuckwagon, bowl, 6¾" d **12.00**
Chuckwagon, plate, 6¼" d **35.00**
Davy Crockett, ashtray **45.00**
Desert Ware, dinner plate, 9" d **10.00**
El Rancho, bowl 4¾" d **20.00**
El Rancho, gravy **60.00**
El Rancho, jam jar, cov, undertray **80.00**

El Rancho, pitcher, "Last Frontier Village, Las Vegas,
  Nevada" adv **265.00**
El Rancho, plate, 6" d **40.00**
El Rancho, plate, 9½" d **70.00**
Hibiscus, dinner plate **8.00**
Kit Carson, ashtray, 5½" d **40.00**
Kit Carson, cereal bowl **20.00**
Mark Twain, ashtray **40.00**
Pioneer, bowl, 9" d **90.00**
Pioneer, chop plate, 13" d **95.00**
Pioneer, creamer and sugar, cov **90.00**
Pioneer, vegetable bowl, round **90.00**
Rodeo, bowl, 5¼" d **60.00**
Rodeo, bread and butter plate **25.00**
Rodeo, chop plate **80.00**
Rodeo, creamer **15.00**
Rodeo, cup, 7½ oz **35.00**
Rodeo, plate, 9" d **70.00**
Rodeo, salt and pepper **55.00**
Rodeo, saucer **12.00**
Rodeo, vegetable bowl **45.00**

WATCHES

Watches divide into three main collecting categories: (1) character licensed, (2) pocket, and (3) wrist. Character licensed watches arrived on the scene in the late 1930s. Although some character pocket watches are known, the vast majority are the wrist variety. Collectors divide character watches into two types: (a) stem wound and (b) battery operated. Because they are relatively inexpensive to make, battery–operated licensed watches are frequently used as premiums by fast food companies.

Pocket watches date back to the 17th century. They were the timepiece of choice in the early part of the 20th century, remaining popular through the early 1930s. Pocket watches are collected by size (18/0 to 20), number of jewels in the movement, open or closed (hunter) face, case decoration, and case composition. Railroad watches generally are 16 to 18 in size, have a minimum of 17 jewels, and adjust to at least five positions. Double check to make certain the movement is period and has not been switched, a common practice.

A wristwatch is a small watch that is attached to a bracelet or strap, is worn around the wrist, and allows the reading of the time at a glance. Although the first wristwatches appeared in the 1850s, it was not until the 1920s that the wristwatch achieved mass popularity. Hundreds of American, German, and Swiss companies entered the market. Quality ranged from Rolex to Timex. Again, collectors divide the category into two groups: (a) stem wound and (b) battery operated.

Make certain you understand the quality level of any wristwatch you plan to buy. Further, many lady's wristwatches are placed in settings with precious and semi–precious stones. Take the time to know how much of the value is in the setting and how much is in the watch.

In the early 1990s a speculative Swatch watch collecting craze occurred. The bubble burst in the late 1990s. Prices have fallen sharply. The craze had a strong international flavor.

Watch collecting as a whole enjoys one of the strongest international markets. On this level, brand name is the name of the game. Watches are bought primarily as investments, not for use.

References: Hy Brown with Nancy Thomas, *Comic Character Timepieces: Seven Decades of Memories,* Schiffer Publishing, 1992; Gisbert L. Brunner and Christian Pfeiffer–Belli, *Wristwatches,* Schiffer Publishing, 1993; Edward Faber and Stewart Unger, *American Wristwatches: Five Decades of Style and Design, Revised,* Schiffer Publishing, 1997; Helmut Kahlert, Richard Mühe, and Gisbert L. Brunner, *Wristwatches: History of a Century's Development,* Schiffer Publishing, 1986; Cooksey Shugart and Richard E. Gilbert, *Complete Price Guide to Watches, 17th Edition,* Cooksey Shugart Publications, 1997.

Periodical: *International Wrist Watch,* 26 6th St, Ste 514, Stamford, CT 06905.

Collectors' Club: National Assoc of Watch & Clock Collectors, 514 Poplar St, Columbia, PA 17512.

Pocket Watch, character, Betty Boop, Ingraham, 1934, MIB . . . . $ 500.00
Pocket Watch, character, Charlie McCarthy, Gilbert, 1938, MIB 500.00
Pocket Watch, character, Hopalong Cassidy, U.S. Time, 1950, MIB 250.00
Pocket Watch, character, Roy Rogers, Bradley, 1959, MIB 175.00
Pocket Watch, character, Superman, Bradley, 1959, MIB 250.00
Pocket Watch, Longines, gold–filled, open face, c1930 . . . . 30.00
Wristwatch, Alpha, 17 jewels, chronograph, stainless steel, c1950s 140.00
Wristwatch, character, Barbie, turquoise leather straps, ©1971 . . . . 100.00
Wristwatch, character, Dale Evans, Ingraham, western style leather straps with silvered metal fittings, ©1951, orig display box 175.00
Wristwatch, character, Gerald Ford caricature, Trying Times, Ltd, orig textured black leather straps, 1974 . . . . 75.00

Wristwatch, character, Mickey Mouse, Ingersoll, leather straps with Mickey charms, 1930s, $250.00.

Wristwatch, character, King Kong, Fossil, orig cardboard box, pewter Kong figure, ©1994 RKO Pictures, 7" d litho tin movie reel tin 65.00
Wristwatch, character, Lucy Van Pelt, Peanuts, United Features Syndicate, Inc, full figure Lucy wearing yellow dress, white straps, 1952 copyright on face, c1970 . . . . 40.00
Wristwatch, character, Mickey Mouse, plastic figure, orig box, US Time, 1958 . . . . 200.00
Wristwatch, character, Nightmare Before Christmas, Timex, black and white plastic and vinyl, 3–D dial with digital display, ©1993 Touchstone Pictures, MIP 25.00
Wristwatch, character, Orphan Annie, orig box, New Haven Clock Co, 1935 . . . . 180.00
Wristwatch, character, Pappy Parker, drooping moustache hands, black vinyl leatherette straps, c1970s 75.00
Wristwatch, character, Spiro Agnes caricature, waving flag with 1 hand, "V" sign with other, orig red suede straps, c1972 . . . . 75.00
Wristwatch, character, Superman, missing one strap, not running, ©1968 National Periodical Pub 30.00
Wristwatch, character, Tom Mix, Mix face and "It's Ralston Time!!," orig straps, Ralston cereal premium, 1982–83 . . . . 175.00
Wristwatch, character, X–Men, "The Famous First Cover From 1963," orig spacecraft box and trading card 175.00
Wristwatch, Elgin, 17 jewels, gold filled, curved 60.00
Wristwatch, Hamilton, electric, Titan II, gold filled 110.00
Wristwatch, Longines, 17 jewels, gold jewel settings, flared case, c1950 . . . . 140.00
Wristwatch, Rolex, Air King, 25 jewels, stainless steel, c1962 . . . . 390.00
Wristwatch, Swatch, Coral Reef, Tri–Color Racer 110.00
Wristwatch, Swatch, Granita Di Fruta, Banana 110.00
Wristwatch, Swatch, Memphis, Miss Channel 100.00
Wristwatch, Zenith, 36 jewels, chronograph, auto wind, stainless steel, c1969 . . . . 190.00

Pocket Watch, Waltham, Colonial, open face, 10K yellow gold filled, 17 jewels, 1937, $65.00.

WATERFORD CRYSTAL

Waterford Crystal, Waterford, County Waterford, Ireland, traces its lineage to a crystal manufacturing business established by George and William Penrose in 1783. Although this initial effort to manufacture crystal and other glassware in Waterford only lasted 68 years, the items produced enjoyed an unequaled reputation that survives to the present.

The end of the flint glass production in Dublin around 1893 marked the demise of almost three centuries of glassmaking in Ireland. In 1902 sand from Muckish in Donegal was brought to the Cork Exhibition where London glass–blowers used a small furnace and made drinking glasses cut in an "early Waterford style." This attempt to create an interest in reviving glassmaking in Ireland failed.

In 1947, almost 50 years later, a small glass factory was established in Ballytuckle, a suburb of Waterford, located approximately one and one–half miles from the site of the Penrose glasshouse on the western edge of the city. Apprentices were trained by immigrant European craftsmen displaced by World War II.

The management of Waterford Crystal dedicated its efforts to matching the purity of color, inspired design, and the highest quality levels of 18th– and 19th–century Waterford glass. Capturing the brilliance of the traditional, deeply incised cutting patterns of earlier Waterford pieces provided an additional challenge.

Waterford Crystal continued to grow and prosper, eventually moving to a 40–acre site in Johnstown, near the center of Waterford. In the early 1980s computer technology improved the accuracy of the raw materials mix, known in the crystal industry as the batch. Improvements in furnace design and diamond cutting wheels enabled Waterford craftsmen to create exciting new intricate glass patterns. Two additional plants in County Waterford helped the company meet its manufacturing requirements.

Waterford Crystal stemware consists of essentially twelve stem shapes with a variety of cutting patterns that extends the range to over 30 suites. Some of the most popular stemware patterns have been adapted for giftware, providing an opportunity to acquire matching bowls, vases, and other accessories. In addition to producing stemware, giftware, and lighting, Waterford Crystal also executes hundreds of commissioned pieces. All Waterford Crystal can be identified by the distinctive "Waterford" signature on the base.

Reference: Harry L. Rinker, *Stemware of the 20th Century: The Top 200 Patterns,* House of Collectibles, 1997.

Alana, brandy, 5⅛" h	$ 50.00
Alana, decanter, 10¾" h	200.00
Alana, fluted champagne, 7⅜" h	40.00
Alana, jug, 5¼" h	100.00
Alana, plate, 6" d	25.00
Alana, plate, 8" d	30.00
Alana, tumbler, 3½" h	40.00
Alana, water goblet, 7" h	40.00
Araglin, cordial	40.00
Araglin, iced tea, ftd	45.00
Araglin, water goblet	35.00
Ashling, decanter, 13¼" h	225.00
Ashling, plate, 6" d	30.00
Ashling, plate, 8" d	35.00
Ashling, saucer champagne, 4⅛" h	45.00

Colleen, left: water goblet, 5¼" h, $50.00; right: fluted champagne, 7⅜" h, $55.00

Ashling, wine glass	50.00
Castlemaine, cordial, 4⅝" h	30.00
Castlemaine, fluted champagne, 8⅜" h	35.00
Castlemaine, old fashioned, 3½" h	35.00
Castlemaine, water goblet, 7⅞" h	35.00
Clare, cocktail, 4" h	55.00
Clare, decanter, wine	225.00
Clare, finger bowl	90.00
Clare, jug	150.00
Clare, plate, 6" d	40.00
Clare, plate, 8" d	50.00
Clare, tumbler	55.00
Clare, wine glass	65.00
Colleen, ashtray, 3½" d	35.00
Colleen, brandy, 5" h	60.00
Colleen, compote, 4½" h	130.00
Colleen, decanter, 13¼" h	225.00
Colleen, finger bowl, 4" d	75.00
Colleen, iced tea, ftd, 6⅜" h	60.00
Colleen, jug, 5½" h	150.00
Colleen, plate, 6" d	30.00
Colleen, plate, 8" d	35.00
Curraghmore, decanter, wine	225.00
Curraghmore, finger bowl	75.00
Curraghmore, juice, ftd	60.00
Curraghmore, plate, 6" d	40.00
Curraghmore, plate, 8" d	50.00
Curraghmore, saucer champagne, 5½" h	65.00
Curraghmore, tumbler, 4½" d	55.00
Curraghmore, wine glass, 6¼" h	65.00
Glenmore, cocktail, 4¼" h	50.00
Glenmore, cordial, 3¾" h	40.00
Glenmore, decanter, spirit	200.00
Glenmore, finger bowl	70.00
Glenmore, fluted champagne	55.00
Glenmore, old fashioned, 3½" d	55.00
Glenmore, plate, 6" d	30.00
Glenmore, plate, 8" d	35.00
Glenmore, water goblet, 7" h	70.00

Kildare, cordial, 4" h **30.00**
Kildare, creamer, 3⅞" h **55.00**
Kildare, decanter **175.00**
Kildare, iced tea, ftd **45.00**
Kildare, juice **40.00**
Kildare, saucer champagne **35.00**
Kildare, tumbler **40.00**
Lismore, biscuit barrel, 6¾" h **150.00**
Lismore, bowl, 5" d **80.00**
Lismore, bowl, 7" d **90.00**
Lismore, compote, 4½" h **130.00**
Lismore, decanter, 9½" h **210.00**
Lismore, finger bowl **70.00**
Lismore, iced tea, ftd, 6⅜" h **50.00**
Lismore, jug, 6¼" h **150.00**
Lismore, juice, ftd, 4" h **40.00**
Lismore, old fashioned, 3⅜" h **35.00**
Lismore, plate, 6" d **25.00**
Lismore, plate, 8" d **30.00**
Lismore, salt shaker, 3⅞" h **45.00**
Lismore, sherbet, ftd, 3" h **50.00**
Lismore, shot glass **30.00**
Lismore, tumbler, 5⅛" h **35.00**
Lismore, water goblet, 6⅞" h **35.00**
Lismore, wine glass **35.00**

WATT POTTERY

In 1886 W. J. Watt founded the Brilliant Stoneware Company in Rose Farm, Ohio. The company made salt–glazed utilitarian stoneware. Watt sold his business in 1897. Between 1903 and 1921 Watt worked for the Ransbottom Brothers Pottery in Ironspot, Ohio. The Ransbottoms were Watt's brothers–in–law.

In 1921 Watt purchased the Globe Stoneware Company in Crooksville, Ohio, renaming it the Watt Pottery Company. Joining Watt were Harry and Thomas, his two sons, C. L. Dawson, his son–in–law, Marion Watt, his daughter, and several other relatives. Watt made stoneware containers between 1922 and 1935.

In response to changing cooking and other kitchen trends in the 1930s, Watt introduced a line of kitchenware designed to withstand high oven temperatures. The line included bean pots, covered casseroles, cookie jars, pie plates, pitchers, salt and pepper shakers, etc. A continuous tunnel kiln was constructed. Production exceeded 15,000 pieces per day.

During the 1940s Watt kitchenware was rather plain with decoration limited to a white and/or blue band. The mid–1940s' Kla-Ham'rd series featured pieces dipped in a brown glaze.

Watt's Wild Rose pattern, known to collectors as Raised Pansy, was introduced in 1950. Production difficulties resulted in a second pattern design, marketed as Rio Rose but called Cut Leaf Pansy by collectors. Eventually Watt hired professional artists to assist in the creation of designs.

Watt introduced new patterns each year during the 1950s. Although Watt sold patterns under specific pattern names, collectors group them in a single category, e.g., Starflower covers Moonflower and Silhouette. Watt introduced its Apple series in 1952, producing pieces for approximately ten years. Several variations were produced. The Tulip and Cherry series appeared in the mid–1950s. Rooster was introduced in 1955. The Morning Glory series arrived in the late 1950s followed by the Autumn Foliage

series in 1959. New lines introduced in the 1960s, e.g., the Kathy Kale series, met with only limited sales success.

Watt made advertising and special commission ware. Pieces marked Esmond, Heirloom, Orchard Ware, Peedeeco, and R–F Spaghetti may have Watt backstamps. Watt was not distributed nationally—50% of the company's products were sold in New York and New England, 25% in the greater Chicago area, and the balance throughout the midwestern and northeastern states. Safeway did distribute some Watt in the southern and western states.

On October 4, 1965, fire destroyed the Watt Pottery Company factory and warehouse. Production never resumed.

References: Sue and Dave Morris, *Watt Pottery: An Identification and Value Guide,* Collector Books, 1993, 1996 value update; Dennis Thompson and W. Bryce Watt, *Watt Pottery: A Collector's Reference with Price Guide,* Schiffer Publishing, 1994.

Collectors' Club: Watt Pottery Collectors USA, Box 26067, Fairview Park, OH 44126.

Apple, baker, open, #96 . . . . **$ 100.00**
Apple, casserole, cov, #19 . . . . **200.00**
Apple, chop plate, #49 . . . . **300.00**
Apple, creamer, #62 . . . . **110.00**
Apple, mug, #121 . . . . **225.00**
Apple, nappy, cov, #05 . . . . **325.00**
Apple, pie plate **150.00**
Apple, pitcher, #15 . . . . **100.00**
Apple, pitcher, #16, 3 leaf **135.00**
Apple, pitcher, #17, ice lip **185.00**
Apple, platter, #31 . . . . **500.00**
Apple, salad bowl, #73 . . . . **85.00**
Commemorative, grease jar, 1995 . . . . **150.00**
Commemorative, sugar, Green Apple, 1995 . . . . **150.00**
Double Apple, baker, cov, wire stand, #96 . . . . **400.00**
Double Apple, dip bowl, #120 . . . . **250.00**
Double Apple, Nappy, #05 . . . . **125.00**
Double Apple, salad bowl, #73 . . . . **175.00**
Dutch Tulip, creamer, #62 . . . . **350.00**
Dutch Tulip, pitcher, #15 . . . . **225.00**

Open Apple, mixing bowl, #7, $125.00.

Tear Drop, bean pot, cov, #76, $125.00.

Open Apple, creamer, #62	1,500.00
Pansy, cup, large	85.00
Pansy, snack set	135.00
Pumpkin, casserole, #8, loops	40.00
Rooster, bowl, cov, #05, PA Dutch Days adv	400.00
Rooster, ice bucket, cov	300.00
Starflower, bowl, #5, 5 petal	50.00
Starflower, casserole, cov, tab handle, #18, 4 petal	125.00
Starflower, cookie jar, #21	200.00
Starflower, drip bowl, #120	100.00
Starflower, grease jar, #47	400.00
Starflower, ice bucket, #59, 5 petal	250.00
Starflower, mixing bowl, #8	50.00
Starflower, pitcher, #15	100.00
Starflower, platter, silhouette, 15" l	100.00
Starflower, salt and pepper shakers, pr, #117 and #118, 4 petal	225.00
Tear Drop, canister, #72	450.00
Tear Drop, mixing bowl, ribbed, #7	50.00
Tear Drop, nappy, cov, #05	300.00
Tear Drop, refrigerator jug, #69	500.00
Tear Drop, salt and pepper shakers, pr	300.00
Tulip, creamer, #62	250.00
Tulip, mixing bowl, #65	150.00
Tulip, pitcher, #16	200.00

WEDGWOOD

In 1759 Josiah Wedgwood established a pottery near Stoke–on–Trent at the former Ivy House works in Burslem, England. By 1761, Wedgwood had perfected a superior quality inexpensive clear–glazed creamware which proved to be very successful.

Wedgwood moved his pottery from the Ivy House to the larger Brick House works in Burslem in 1764. In 1766, upon being appointed "Potter to Her Majesty" by Queen Charlotte,

Wedgwood named his creamware "Queen's ware". The Brick House works remained in production until 1772.

Wedgwood built a new factory in Etruria in 1769, the same year he formed a partnership with Thomas Bentley. Wedgwood's most famous set of Queen's ware, the 1,000 piece "Frog" Service created for Catherine the Great, Empress of Russia, was produced at the Etruria factory in 1774.

By the late 1700s, the Wedgwood product line included black basalt, creamware, jasper, pearlware, and redware. Moonlight luster was made from 1805 to 1815. Bone China was produced from 1812 to 1822, and revived in 1878. Fairyland luster was introduced in 1915. The last luster pieces were made in 1932.

In 1906 Wedgwood established a museum at its Etruria pottery. A new factory was built at nearby Barlaston in 1940. The museum was moved to Barlaston and expanded. The Etruria works was closed in 1950.

During the 1960s and 1970s Wedgwood acquired many English potteries, including William Adams & Sons, Coalport, Susie Cooper, Crown Staffordshire, Johnson Brothers, Mason's Ironstone, J. & G. Meakin, Midwinter Companies, Precision Studios and Royal Tuscan. In 1969 Wedgwood acquired King's Lynn Glass, renaming it Wedgwood Glass. The acquisition of Galway Crystal Company of Galway, Erie, followed in 1974.

In 1986 Waterford and Wedgwood merged. The Wedgwood Group, now a division of Waterford Wedgwood, consists of six major divisions: Wedgwood, Coalport, Johnson Brothers, Mason's Ironstone, Wedgwood Hotelware, and Wedgwood Jewellery. The Wedgwood Group is one of the largest tabletop manufacturers in the world. It is a public company comprising eight factories and employing 5,500 people in the United Kingdom and overseas.

References: Susan and Al Bagdade, *Warman's English & Continental Pottery & Porcelain, Second Edition,* Wallace–Homestead, Krause Publications, 1991; Robin Reilly, *Wedgwood: The New Illustrated Dictionary, Revised,* Antique Collectors' Club, 1995; Harry L. Rinker, *Dinnerware of the 20th Century: The Top 500 Patterns,* House of Collectibles, 1997; Harry L. Rinker, *Stemware of the 20th Century: The Top 200 Patterns,* House of Collectibles, 1997.

Collectors' Club: The Wedgwood Society, The Roman Villa, Rockbourne, Fordingbridge, Hants, SP6 3PG, England.

Appledore, bread and butter plate, 6" d	$ 15.00
Appledore, chop plate, 13¼" d	100.00
Appledore, cream soup and saucer, 4⅝" d	45.00
Appledore, creamer	38.00
Appledore, cup and saucer, ftd	30.00
Appledore, dinner plate, 10¾" d	32.00
Appledore, fruit bowl, 5⅛" d	20.00
Appledore, gravy boat, attached underplate	105.00
Appledore, luncheon plate, 9" d	25.00
Appledore, platter, oval, 14⅛" l	115.00
Appledore, salad plate, 8" d	18.00
Appledore, soup bowl, 9" d	38.00
Appledore, sugar, cov, ftd	50.00
Appledore, vegetable bowl, oval, 9¾" l	65.00
Basalt, candlesticks, pr, Triton, modeled as part human, part fish, holding sconce formed as shell, imp mark, 1974, 11" h	825.00
Basalt, figure, bulldog, 4½" l	325.00

Basalt, figure, crow, 4½" h **375.00**

Basalt, figure, kingfisher, by Ernest Light, 8" h **550.00**

Basalt, figure, titled "Skills of the Nation–The Potter,"
Colin Melbourne, #146 from limited edition of
1,000, imp and printed marks, c1980, 9½" h **440.00**

Basalt, tumbler, engine turned, inscribed below base
"A.L.G. 3.2.23," imp mark, 1923, 4" h. **115.00**

Cavendish, bread and butter plate, 6" d **12.00**

Cavendish, cake plate, sq, handled, 11⅛" d **55.00**

Cavendish, cereal bowl, 6⅛" d **18.00**

Cavendish, chop plate, 13½" d **70.00**

Cavendish, coffeepot, cov **100.00**

Cavendish, creamer, 3¾" h **35.00**

Cavendish, cup and saucer, ftd **28.00**

Cavendish, dessert plate, 7" d **12.00**

Cavendish, fruit bowl, 5" d **18.00**

Cavendish, luncheon plate, 9" d **20.00**

Cavendish, salad plate, 8⅛" d **15.00**

Cavendish, soup tureen and underplate, cov **250.00**

Cavendish, vegetable bowl, cov **130.00**

Cream Color on Lavender, chop plate, 12¾" d **85.00**

Cream Color on Lavender, coffeepot, cov **100.00**

Cream Color on Lavender, cream soup and saucer **45.00**

Cream Color on Lavender, creamer. **35.00**

Cream Color on Lavender, cup and saucer, ftd **28.00**

Cream Color on Lavender, demitasse cup and saucer **25.00**

Cream Color on Lavender, dinner plate, 10½" d **30.00**

Cream Color on Lavender, luncheon plate, 9¼" d **25.00**

Cream Color on Lavender, platter, oval, 14⅜" l **100.00**

Cream Color on Lavender, salad plate, 8⅛" d **15.00**

Cream Color on Lavender, soup bowl, 8⅛" d **28.00**

Cream Color on Lavender, sugar, cov **40.00**

Florentine Black, ashtray, 4½" d **12.00**

Florentine Black, bread and butter plate, 6⅛" d **10.00**

Florentine Black, cereal bowl, 6⅛" d **30.00**

Florentine Black, cigarette holder, 2⅜" l **25.00**

Florentine Black, cup and saucer, ftd **28.00**

Florentine Black, dinner plate, 10¾" d **25.00**

Florentine Black, fruit bowl, 5" d **30.00**

Florentine Black, gravy boat and underplate **85.00**

Florentine Black, luncheon plate, 9" d **22.00**

Florentine Black, platter, oval, 14¼" l **100.00**

Florentine Black, salad bowl, 8" d **90.00**

Florentine Black, salad plate, 8" d. **15.00**

Florentine Black, sugar, cov **45.00**

Florentine Black, teapot, cov **100.00**

Jasper, cache pot, scrolled feet, olive green dip, white
classical relief, imp mark, c1920, 6" d **400.00**

Jasper, cache pot, yellow dip, black classical relief,
white jasper liner, imp mark, c1930 . . . . **500.00**

Jasper, commemorative plate, Arkansas statehood
centennial, 1836–1936, 10½" d **35.00**

Jasper, jardiniere, crimson dip, white classical relief,
imp mark, c1920, 7" h. **1,100.00**

Jasper, pitcher, yellow dip, white classical relief, imp
marks, 6" h **775.00**

Jasper, potpourri, cov, dark blue dip, white classical
relief, imp mark, 4¾" w **300.00**

Jasper, spill vases, pr, yellow dip, black classical
relief, imp mark, 5⅝" h **525.00**

Jasper, tea set, 3 pcs, yellow dip, white classical
relief, imp mark, 4¾" h teapot **550.00**

Jasper, vase, dark blue dip, white upright leaves and
flower stalks, flower garlands with ram's head in
rasied work around sides, mkd "Wedgwood,"
5¾" h, 2¾" d **175.00**

Jasper, vase, cov, black dip, engine turned, Bacchus
head handle, acorn finial, imp mark, c1963, 8" h **650.00**

Luster, butterfly, Melba bowl, butterflies on mother–of–pearl ext, orange luster int, pattern Z4832,
printed mark, c1920, 8" d. **550.00**

Luster, dragon, cup, 3 handles, blue ext, gilt reptiles,
eggshell int with central dragon, printed mark,
c1920, 2" h **275.00**

Luster, dragon, vase, mottled blue ext, shape 2355,
pattern Z4829, printed mark, c1920, 8¾" h **450.00**

Luster, Fairyland, bowl, Woodland Elves VIII, toad-
stool design ext, Fairy in Cage int, printed marks,
c1925, 8⅞" d **3,000.00**

Luster, hummingbird, Melba cup, mottled blue ext,
orange int, printed mark, c1920, 3¼" h **275.00**

Majesty, bud vase, 7½" h **30.00**

Majesty, iced tea, 8¾" h. **40.00**

Majesty, water goblet, 8⅞" h **40.00**

Majesty, wine glass **35.00**

Runnymede Dark Blue, bread and butter plate, 6" d **8.00**

Runnymede Dark Blue, cereal bowl, 6" d **38.00**

Runnymede Dark Blue, creamer, 2⅜" h **35.00**

Runnymede Dark Blue, dinner plate, 10¾" d **22.00**

Runnymede Dark Blue, fruit bowl, 5" d **30.00**

Runnymede Dark Blue, gravy boat and underplate **110.00**

Runnymede Dark Blue, platter, oval, 15⅜" l **125.00**

Runnymede Dark Blue, salad plate, 8⅛" d **12.00**

Runnymede Dark Blue, soup bowl, 8⅞" d **38.00**

Runnymede Dark Blue, vegetable bowl, cov. **160.00**

Runnymede Dark Blue, vegetable bowl, oval, 7⅞" l **75.00**

Sovereign, brandy glass **25.00**

Sovereign, cordial **40.00**

Cavendish, dinner plate, 10¾" d, $22.00.

Jasper, pitcher, light blue dip, white classical relief, #36, imp "Wedgwood, Made in England, 1951," 4³/₄" h, $75.00.

Sovereign, highball glass **45.00**
Sovereign, saucer champagne **40.00**
Sovereign, water goblet **50.00**
Sovereign, wine glass. **42.00**

WELLER

Samuel Augutus Weller established the Weller Pottery Company, in Fultonham, Ohio, in 1872. In 1888, Weller moved his plant operations to a frame building on Pierce Street in Zanesville. By 1890 a new plant (Putnam, Plant #1) was built. Products included hanging baskets, jardinieres and pedestals, umbrella stands, and vases.

During a visit to the 1893 Columbian Exposition in Chicago, Weller saw Lonhuda ware. He bought the Lonhuda Pottery and brought William Long, its owner, to Zanesville to supervise production at Weller. After a disastrous fire in May 1895, Weller rebuilt. When Long resigned in 1896, Weller introduced Louwelsa Weller, based on Long's glaze formula.

Weller did not hesitate to hire the best talent available. Ruth Axline, Charles Chilcote, Henri Gellée, and Jacques Sicard are examples. Charles Upjohn became head of the decorating department in 1895 and shortly thereafter introduced Second Line Dickensware. Weller purchased the American Encaustic Tiling Company plant (Marietta Street, Plant #2) in 1899. Cook ware, flower pots, and sanitary ware lines were produced.

By 1900 Weller enjoyed a virtual monopoly on mass–produced art pottery. The company's 1905 catalog included Art Nouveau, Aurelian, Dickensware, Eocean, Floretta, Golbrogreen, Hunter, Jap Birdimal, Louwelsa, Monochrome, Oriental, Perfecto, Pictorial, and Sicardo. In 1904 Karl Kappes replaced Upjohn as head of the decorating department. By 1907 Weller was exporting large amounts of pottery to England, Germany, and Russia.

In the 1910s Japanese potteries made almost exact copies of Weller products that sold in the American market for half the cost. Weller increased its production of ware for the floral and garden industries to offset the financial losses. Edwin L. Pickens, Weller's brother–in–law, became head of the art department around 1909.

Weller purchased the Zanesville Art Pottery (Ceramic Avenue, Plant #3) in 1920. Weller Pottery incorporated in 1920. Henry Weller, Samuel's nephew, became president in 1925. He installed a continuous kiln and began advertising heavily in popular magazines. A fire on July 29, 1927 destroyed the Ceramic Avenue plant. It was quickly rebuilt. As a result of economic difficulties due to the Depression, Henry Weller consolidated the three plants into one, Plant #3.

Several new lines, many designed by Rudolph Lorber, were introduced in the late 1920s. A 1928 price list included art pottery lines such as Alvin, Flemish, Forest, Glendale, Hudson, Ivory, Malta, Roma, Veletone, and Woodcraft, cookware, and utilitarian ware. Beer mugs, cookware, garden ware, and vases helped Weller get through the Depression. In 1933 Lorber introduced Neiska, Seneca, and Ting.

Frederic Weller, Weller's son–in–law, became president in 1932. A year later he divorced his wife and left the company. He received the rights to reproduced Zona dinnerware, which he took to Gladding, McBean, as part of the divorce settlement. Irvin Smith, another Weller son–in–law, became president. He was succeeded by Walter Hughes in 1937.

Although Weller enjoyed large profits during World War II, increased competition, especially from abroad, cost of materials, and labor spelled doom for Weller. Bouquet and Cameo, lines that were cheap and inexpensive to make, could not stem the tide.

In 1945 Essex Wire Corporation leased space in the Weller factory. By 1947 Essex Wire bought the controlling stock of the company. The factory closed in 1948.

References: Sharon and Bob Huxford, *The Collectors Encyclopedia of Weller Pottery,* Collector Books, 1979, 1996 value update; Ralph and Terry Kovel, *Kovels' American Art Pottery: The Collector's Guide to Makers, Marks and Factory Histories,* Crown Publishers, 1993.

Collectors' Club: American Art Pottery Assoc, PO Box 525, Cedar Hill, MO 63016.

Ashtray, Woodcraft, 3" d. . . . . **$ 75.00**
Basket, Camoe, blue, 7¹/₂" **25.00**
Basket, Flemish, 3¹/₂" **30.00**
Basket, Florenzo, 5¹/₂" **75.00**
Basket, Forest Basket **200.00**
Basket, Wild Rose, peach, 6" d. **50.00**
Bowl, Bonito, underplate **125.00**
Bowl, Cornish, light orange, 7¹/₄" d **75.00**
Bowl, Florala, 8" d. **165.00**
Bowl, Sunflower **250.00**
Candlesticks, pr, Glendale **175.00**
Compote, Bonito, 4" h. **60.00**
Console Bowl, Hobnail **75.00**
Console Bowl, Silvertone, with flower frog **475.00**
Console Bowl, Sydonia, 17 x 6" **100.00**
Console Set, Blossom, bowl and 2 candlesticks. **60.00**
Cornucopia, Lido, mauve. **50.00**
Cornucopia, Softone, light blue, 10" d **25.00**
Cornucopia, Wild Rose, peach and green **45.00**
Ewer, Barcelona Ware, orig label **250.00**
Ewer, Dickensware. **450.00**
Flask, Order of Moose **100.00**
Hanging Basket, creamware. **125.00**
Hanging Basket, Flemish **100.00**
Hanging Basket, Forest, 10" d. **250.00**
Hanging Basket, Scenic Green **100.00**

Jardiniere, Evergreen, small 75.00
Jardiniere, Forest, brown int, 11½" 950.00
Jardiniere, Louwelsa, orange, brown, green, and
    gold, 9" 130.00
Jardiniere, Roma, cat chasing canary 200.00
Jug, Louwelsa, hexagonal, pansies, #521C 100.00
Lamp, Blue Ware, 10½" 250.00
Mug, Claywood, star flowers 65.00
Mug, Etna, grapes, 6" h 100.00
Mug, Louwelsa, raspberries, 6" h 200.00
Pitcher, Bouquet, ruffled top, lavender flower, sgd
    "M," 6" h. 40.00
Pitcher, Marvo, 8" h 160.00
Pitcher, Zona, pink. 150.00
Pitcher, Zona, prancing duck 185.00
Planter, Burntwood, Knifewood mold swan, 5" h,
    6" w 150.00
Planter, dachshund, 8½" h 65.00
Teapot, pumpkin, 6" h 125.00
Toothpick Holder, Coppertone, frog, figural. 325.00
Vase, Alvin, 7½" h 125.00
Vase, Baldwin, 5½" h. 75.00
Vase, Baldin, 7" h 95.00
Vase, caramel marbleized, 10" h 110.00
Vase, Chengtu, orange, 7" h 75.00
Vase, Cloudburst, green, 4½" h 150.00
Vase, Cornish, brown, 10" h 150.00
Vase, Drapery, blue, 8" h 50.00
Vase, Eocean, 8" h. 300.00
Vase, Etna, 2 handled, 9" h 350.00
Vase, Forest, fan shape, 8" h 140.00
Vase, Glendale, 8" h 400.00
Vase, Goldenglow, ftd, 7" h 150.00
Vase, Greenbriar, 8" h 135.00
Vase, Ivory, unmkd, 10" h 85.00
Vase, Louwelsa, Nasturtium, jug shape, sgd "D.L.B.,"
    5½" h 235.00
Vase, Marvo, fan shape 85.00
Vase, Neiska, #11, 7" h 85.00
Vase, Panella, blue. 50.00

Vase, Warwick, half kiln ink
stamp, c1925, 9½" h, $90.00.

Vase, Sicard, 6" h. 700.00
Vase, Silvertone, 7" h, 7" w 300.00
Vase, Turkis, 4" h 80.00
Vase, Woodcraft, sgd 150.00
Wall Pocket, Glendale 225.00
Wall Pocket, oak leaf, brown 200.00
Wall Pocket, owl 175.00
Wall Pocket, squirrel 135.00
Wall Pocket, Wood Rose 85.00
Window Box, Wood Rose 100.00

AUCTION PRICES

David Rago's Roseville/Zanesville Pottery Auction, closing date
January 31, 1997. Prices include the 10% buyer's premium.

Bowl, Coppertone, with frog, incised "Weller
    Pottery," 4 x 11" 990.00
Hanging Baskets, pr, Klyro, with liners, short line
    from firing next to 1 hole, both with "Weller
    Ware" glaze stamp, 3¼ x 7" 357.50
Table Lamp, Louwelsa, horse's head on brown and
    green ground, marble base, shallow scratches to
    surface, 32½" h. 1,100.00
Vase, Chengtu, tall, ink kiln mark, 12¾ x 4¾" 412.50
Vase, Coppertone, amphora shaped, 2 handled,
    glaze nick to 1 handle, script mark, 8½ x 8½" 330.00
Vase, Coppertone, corseted, unmkd, 9 x 5" 302.50
Vase, Glendale, 2 parakeets in polychrome, unmkd,
    8¾ x 4½" 825.00
Vase, Hudson, by Hester Pillsbury, pink and yellow
    wild roses, shaded green to pink ground, artist sgd
    "HP, Weller" in script, 6¼ x 3½" 605.00
Vase, Sicard, bullet shaped, gold Art Nouveau flow-
    ers on burgundy luster ground, sgd "Weller
    Sicard," 9½ x 4¼" 440.00
Vase, Suevo, bulbous, unmkd, 4½ x 4¾" 192.50
Vases, pr, Greora, 2 handled, imp mark, 7¼ x 6¼" . . . 385.00
Vessel, Lonhuda, 3 handled, 3 ftd, green dogwood
    dec, die–stamped "Weller," artist cipher, 7 x 3" 220.00
Vessel, Sicard, acorn shaped, stylized mistletoe dec,
    burgundy ground, abrasion to rim, "Weller
    Sicard" in script, 4 x 3¾" 495.00

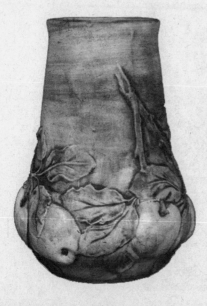

Vase, Baldin, incised
"Weller," 11" h,
$250.00.

WESTERN COLLECTIBLES

This category divides into three parts: (1) items associated with working cowboys and cowgirls such as horse tack, wagon trail memorabilia, everyday work clothes, dress duds, and rodeo memorabilia; (2) material related to the western dude ranch, and (3) objects shaped like or portraying images associated with the American West. It does not include items associated with literary, movie, and television characters.

The taming and settling of the American western frontier is an established part of America's romantic folklore. Between the 1840s and 1890s hundreds of thousands of individuals emigrated to the Great Plains, Southwest, California Coast, and Northwest. Gold and silver rushes saw towns grow up and disappear overnight. Railroads offered sweetheart land deals to attract individuals to settle along their right–of–way and subsequently alter the course of cattle trails. Resistance by the American Indian proved futile.

Although the Western frontier was declared non–existent by the 1890s, much remained to be done. Great cattle ranches continue to survive today. Midwest granaries supply much of the nation's food needs. Today the cowboy is as likely to drive a pickup truck as ride a horse.

The dude ranch arrived on the scene in the 1920s. After declining somewhat in the late 1930s, a dude ranch renewal occurred in the 1950s. Dude ranch clothing differed significantly from that worn by working cowboys and cowgirls.

Americans went western crazy in the 1950s, partially the result of the dominance of the TV western. Western maple furniture was found in living rooms, dens, and children's bedrooms. Western motifs from riders on bucking horses to Mexicans taking siestas beneath cactus decorated everything from dinnerware to linens. The western revival of the early 1990s reawakened collector interest in this western motif material from the 1950s. As the decade ends, the craze seems to be abating, largely the result of high prices asked by dealers for commonly found items.

References: Judy Crandall, *Cowgirls: Early Images and Collectibles,* Schiffer Publishing, 1994; Michael Friedman, *Cowboy Culture: The Last Frontier of American Antiques,* Schiffer Publishing, 1992; Dan and Sebie Hutchins, *Old Cowboy Saddles & Spurs: Identifying The Craftsmen Who Made Them, Sixth Annual,* Horse Feathers Publishing, 1996.

Collectors' Club: National Bit, Spur & Saddle Collectors Assoc, PO Box 3098, Colorado Springs, CO 80934.

Ashtray, covered wagon, hp, c1950 . . . . $ 22.00
Badge, Sheriff, Lancaster County, NE, eagle top, photo accompanies with Sheriff Miles Holloway, 1942 . . . . 175.00
Better Little Book, *2–Gun Montana,* 1939 . . . . 8.50
Book, *Apache Gold and Yanqui Silver,* Frank J. Dobie, New York, illus by Tom Lea, 1939, 384 pgs 25.00
Book, *"Boots & Saddles,"* or, *Life in Dakota With General Custer,* Elizabeth Custer, Norman, University of Oklahoma Press, map and illus, part of Western Frontier Library series, dj, 1961, 280 pgs . . . 15.00
Book, *Lives & Legends of Buffalo Bill,* Don Russell, 1st edition, maps and illus, dj, 1960, 514 pgs 50.00
Book, *The Colorado Range Cattle Industry,* Ora Peake, 1st edition, maps and illus, orig cloth, top page edges gilt, 1937, 357 pgs 150.00

Bridle Rosettes, Anti Horse Thief Assoc, pr 250.00
Catalog, Leroy Shane Novelties, Authentic Western Merchandise, Indian Craft, Hit Toys, 1949, 48 pgs 12.00
Check, Wells Fargo, San Francisco, ornate, 1972, 7¾ x 3" 65.00
Lobby Sheet, The Tall Texan 8.00
Magazine Article, *TV Guide,* Paladin, May 10, 1958, cov with full–color photo of Richard Boone. 10.00
Photo, cowboys roping and branding cattle on prairie, c1920, 6 x 4" 22.50
Photo, group on horseback descending canyon trail, guide wearing 10–gallon hat and kerchief, black and white, dated 1925, 7 x 5". 10.00
Photo, movie still, *The Culpepper Cattle Co,* 20th Century Fox, 1972, 8 x 10". 8.00
Pin, Sam Houston, Texas, ribbon, 1936. . . . . 85.00
Poster, Jubilee Trail 100.00
Poster, *Winchester '73,* starring Jimmy Stewart 100.00
Print, Northern Pacific North Coast, "Montana Roundup," orig shipping tube 100.00
Program, Tuscon, AZ Rodeo, February 1939, illus, large format, folding map, 36 pgs 20.00
Program, World's Championship Rodeo, 1941, Gene Autry photo 10.00
Radio Premium Kit, "Wild West Rodeo," General Electric, red, white, and blue envelope, punchout sheets, 1952, 15 x 16" 25.00
Restaurant China, chili bowl, 5" d, Tepco Western Traveller, Wells Fargo 18.00
Restaurant China, cup and saucer, Wellsville Cowboys . . . 12.00
Restaurant China, fruit bowl, 4¾" d, Tepco Western Traveller, Wells Fargo 15.00
Riata, rawhide 165.00
Rope, horsehair 40.00
Scrapbook, Southwestern postcards, snapshots, and other travel ephemera, 1940s–50 . . . . 50.00
Scrapbook, Western and Hillbilly Stars, 1952, 52 pgs 15.00
Sheet Music, *Home on the Range,* Andrew Fuller, 1932 . . . . 5.00

Label, Hot Brand California Vegetables, Western Packing Co., 7 x 10", $1.00.

Stockman's Saddle, John M. Drake, Nocona, TX, 1920s, $650.00.

Sheet Music, *The Utah Trail,* Bob Palmer and Tex
 Ritter, 1928 . . . . **6.00**
Timetable, Nevada Pony Express, 1960 Centennial
 Re–Run, offset litho, framed, 22 x 14" **75.00**

WESTMORELAND GLASS

Westmoreland, Jeannette, Pennsylvania, traces its history to the East Liverpool Specialty Glass Company and the influence of Major George Irwin. Irwin was instrumental in moving the company from East Liverpool, Ohio, to Jeannette, Pennsylvania, to take advantage of the large natural gas reserves in the area. Specialty Glass, a new Pennsylvania Company, was established in 1888. When the company ran out of money in 1889, Charles H. and George R. West put up $40,000 for 53% of the company's stock. The name was changed to Westmoreland Specialty Company.

Initially Westmoreland made candy containers and a number of other glass containers. In 1910 the company introduced its Keystone line of tableware. Charles West had opposed the move into tableware production, and the brothers split in 1920. George West continued with the Westmoreland Specialty Company, changing its name in 1924 to the Westmoreland Glass Company.

Westmoreland made decorative wares and colonial era reproductions, e.g., dolphin pedestal forms, in the 1920s. Color, introduced to the tableware lines in the early 1930s, was virtually gone by the mid–1930s. Amber, black, and ruby colors were introduced in the 1950s in an attempt to bolster the line.

In 1937 Charles West retired and J. H. Brainard assumed the company's helm. Phillip and Walter Brainard, J. H.'s two sons, joined the firm in 1940. In an effort to cut costs, all cutting and engraving work was eliminated in the 1940s. Grinding and polishing of glass ceased in 1957. No new molds were made until the milk glass surge in the early and mid–1950s.

The milk glass boom was over by 1958. While continuing to produce large quantities of milk glass in the 1960s, Westmoreland expanded its product line to include crystal tableware and colored items. The effort was unsuccessful. Attempts to introduce color into the milk glass line also proved disappointing. The company kept its doors open, albeit barely, by appealing to the bridal trade.

In the search for capital, an on–site gift shop was opened on April 12, 1962. The shop produced a steady cash flow. Shortly after the shop opened, Westmoreland began selling seconds. Another valuable source of cash was found.

By 1980 J. H. Brainard was searching for a buyer for the company. After turning down a proposal from a group of company employees, Brainard sold Westmoreland to David Grossman, a St. Louis–based distributor and importer, best known for his Norman Rockwell Collectibles series. Operations ceased on January 8, 1984. Most of the molds, glass, historic information, catalogs, and furniture were sold at auction.

References: Lorraine Kovar, *Westmoreland Glass, 1950–1984,* Antique Publications, 1991; Lorraine Kovar, *Westmoreland Glass, 1950–1984, Volume II,* Antique Publications, 1991; Chas West Wilson, *Westmoreland Glass,* Collector Books, 1996.

Collectors' Clubs: National Westmoreland Glass Collectors Club, PO Box 625, Irwin, PA 15642; Westmoreland Glass Society, 4809 420th St SE, Iowa City, IA 52240.

American Hobnail, butter, cov, lilac opalescent, 5½". . . **$ 60.00**
American Hobnail, compote, crimped rim, ftd,
 brandywine blue opalescent, 6½" **45.00**
American Hobnail, cruet, brandywine blue opales-
 cent, 2 oz **45.00**
American Hobnail, mint compote, double crimped,
 ftd, lilac opalescent, 5" **25.00**
Beaded Grape, ashtray, square, laurel green, 6½" **25.00**
Beaded Grape, bowl, cov, flared, ftd, laurel green, 5" **40.00**
Beaded Grape, bowl, square, flared, ftd, milk glass,
 7" **18.00**
Beaded Grape, creamer, square, milk glass **12.00**
Colonial, ashtray, round, purple marble, 5" **30.00**
Colonial, creamer, flat, laurel green **25.00**
Colonial, jack–in–the–pulpit vase, flame, 6½" h **38.00**
Colonial, vase, ftd, green mist **30.00**
Colonial, water goblet, ftd, crystal **15.00**
Dolphin, Line #1049, candlesticks, pr, hexagonal
 base, almond, 9" h **100.00**

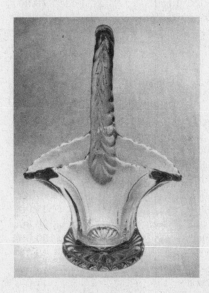

Basket, vaseline, 7" h, $20.00.

Fan & File, Line #299, child's creamer, milk glass, 1950s, 2¹/₂" h, $12.00.

Dolphin, Line #1049, serving tray, center handle, crystal mist **40.00**
Doric, bowl, cupped, ftd, golden sunset, 10" **28.00**
Doric, bowl, oval, crimped, flame, 12" **45.00**
Doric, cake salver, ftd, dark blue mist, 11" **35.00**
Doric, candlesticks, pr, amber, 4¹/₂" **25.00**
English Hobnail, ashtray, square, ruby, 4¹/₂" **30.00**
English Hobnail, basket, pink pastel, 9" h **40.00**
English Hobnail, bowl, rolled edge, green, 10³/₄" **45.00**
English Hobnail, bowl, bell shape, amber, 9¹/₂" **32.00**
English Hobnail, tidbit, 2 tier, center handle, brandy-wine blue **60.00**
Fruits, Line #81, punch set, bowl, base, 12 cups, and ladle, milk glass **275.00**
Lotus, bowl, cupped, flame, 9" **45.00**
Lotus, compote, green, 8¹/₄" d, 6" h **40.00**
Lotus, candlesticks, pr, apricot mist, 3¹/₂" **30.00**
Lotus, vase, ftd, pink mist, 10" **20.00**
Lotus, salt and pepper shakers, pr, pink **35.00**
Maple Leaf, bowl, crimped, ftd, blue pastel, 10" d, 5¹/₂" h **45.00**
Maple Leaf, chocolate box, cov, round, flat, blue pastel, 6¹/₂" d, 3³/₄" h **30.00**
Maple Leaf, compote, ruffled, cirmped, green mist, 7¹/₂" **25.00**
Old Quilt, candy dish, cov, ftd, golden sunset **40.00**
Old Quilt, cigarette box, cov, milk glass, 5 x 4" **35.00**
Old Quilt, cruet, stopper, crystal, 6 oz **45.00**
Old Quilt, pitcher, honey carnival, 3 pt, 8¹/₂" h **20.00**
Old Quilt, sugar, cov, milk glass, 6¹/₂" h **25.00**
Old Quilt, water goblet, ftd, golden sunset, 8 oz **20.00**
Paneled Grape, cake salver, brandywine blue, 12" d **100.00**
Paneled Grape, cup and saucer, milk glass **30.00**
Paneled Grape, mayonnaise, 3 pcs, crystal **35.00**
Paneled Grape, pitcher, ftd, crystal, 1 qt **40.00**
Paneled Grape, luncheon plate, laurel green, 8¹/₂" d **30.00**

Paneled Grape, dinner plate, milk glass, 10¹/₂" d **45.00**
Paneled Grape, water goblet, ftd, brandywine blue, 8 oz **25.00**
Paneled Grape, water goblet, ftd, crystal, 8 oz. **15.00**
Sawtooth, bowl, flared, ftd, golden sunset, 12" **75.00**
Sawtooth, bowl, cov, ftd, almond, 9" d, 14" h **135.00**
Waterford, fairy lite, ftd, 2 pcs, ruby stained crystal **30.00**

WHISKEY BOTTLES, COLLECTIBLE

This market has fallen on hard times. The speculative bubble burst in the mid–1980s. Prices did not stabilize, they totally collapsed for most examples. Most manufacturers, distributors, and collectors' clubs have disappeared. Today more bottles are purchased for their crossover theme, e.g., Elvis or golf, than they are for their importance as collectors' special editions whiskey bottles. Although often priced higher by sellers, the vast majority of bottles really sell for less than $10, provided a buyer can be found at all.

The Jim Beam Distillery offered its first set of novelty (collectors' special edition) bottles during the 1953 Christmas season. Over a hundred other distillers, e.g., Ezra Brooks, Cyrus Noble, Grenadier, Hoffman, Lionstone, McCormick, Old Fitzgerald, Ski Country, and Wild Turkey followed suit. Jon–Sol, a dealer, distributed his own line of bottles.

The early 1970s was the golden age of collectors' special edition whiskey bottles. Several distillers offered miniature series. By the late 1970s the market was saturated. Most distillers returned to the basic bottle package.

The argument still rages as to whether or not a bottle is worth more with its seal unbroken. Check the liquor laws in your state. Most states strictly prohibit selling liquor without a license. Value has always centered on the theme of the bottle. The liquor inside has never affected value. As a result, an empty bottle has the same value as a full one.

References: Ralph and Terry Kovel, *The Kovels' Bottle Price List, Tenth Edition,* Crown Publishers, 1996; Jim Megura, *The Official Price Guide to Bottles, Eleventh Edition,* House of Collectibles, 1991; Michael Polak, *Bottles: Identification and Price Guide,* Avon Books, 1994.

Collectors' Clubs: National Ski Country Bottle Club, 1224 Washington Ave, Golden, CO 80401.

Double Springs, Missouri, Bicentennial series . . . . $ **18.00**
Double Springs, Rolls Royce, car series, 1971 . . . . **40.00**
Ezra Brooks, Alabama Bicentennial, 1976 . . . . **14.00**
Ezra Brooks, Arizona, 1969 . . . . **8.00**
Ezra Brooks, Big Daddy Lounge, 1969 . . . . **6.00**
Ezra Brooks, Ceremonial Indian, 1970 . . . . **18.00**
Ezra Brooks, Christmas decanter, 1966 . . . . **8.00**
Ezra Brooks, Harolds Club Dice, 1968 . . . . **12.00**
Ezra Brooks, Trail Bike Rider, 1972 . . . . **12.00**
Ezra Brooks, Vermont Skier, 1972 . . . . **12.00**
Ezra Brooks, Whitetail Deer, 1947 . . . . **24.00**
Grenadier, Fire Chief, 1973 . . . . **85.00**
Grenadier, Soldier, Civil War series, miniature, 1975 . . . . **20.00**
Japanese, Kikukawa, Haru **6.00**
Jim Beam, AC Spark Plug, 1977 . . . . **25.00**
Jim Beam, Alaska 1958, star shape **55.00**
Jim Beam, antique clock **40.00**

Jim Beam, State Series, Arizona, 1968, $8.00.

Jim Beam, antique telephone, 1978 . . . . 55.00
Jim Beam, Armanetti vase, 1968. . . . . 6.00
Jim Beam, baseball, 100 anniversary commemorative, 1969 . . . . 18.00
Jim Beam, Bing Crosby National Pro–Am, 1970 . . . . 6.00
Jim Beam, Bob Hope Desert Classic, 1974 . . . . 10.00
Jim Beam, Boys Town of Italy 8.00
Jim Beam, Bonded Gold 6.00
Jim Beam, flower basket, 1962. . . . . 32.00
Jim Beam, Ponderosa, 1969 . . . . 5.00
Jim Beam, Statue of Liberty, 1975 . . . . 12.00
Jim Beam, Volkswagen, 1977 . . . . 50.00
J. W. Dant, Paul Bunyan. 6.00
J. W. Dant, Reverse Eagle. 8.00
J. W. Dant, Ruffed Grouse 7.00
J. W. Dant, Washington Crossing Delaware. 7.00
Kentucky Gentlemen, Frontiersman, 1969. . . . . 15.00
Kentucky Gentlemen, Pink Lady, 1969 . . . . 32.00
Kentucky Gentlemen, Union Army Sergeant 12.00
Lionstone, Blacksmith 30.00
Lionstone, Bluejay, bird series, 1972–74 . . . . 25.00
Lionstone, Calamity Jane 22.00
Lionstone, Highway Robber 20.00
Lionstone, Mallard Duck 40.00
Lionstone, Riverboat Captain 15.00
Luxardo, Apothecary Jar, 1960 . . . . 20.00
Luxardo, Calypso Girl, 1962 . . . . 22.00
Luxardo, Eagle, 1970. . . . . 45.00
Luxardo, Gambia princess, 1961 . . . . 10.00
McCormick, Arizona Wildcats 25.00
McCormick, Buffalo Bill, 1979 . . . . 75.00
McCormick, Canadian Goose, miniature, bird series 20.00
McCormick, Packard, car series, 1937 . . . . 30.00
McCormick, Pocahontas 35.00
McCormick, Tom T. Hall, western series, 1980 . . . . 40.00
Old Fitzgerald, Colonial decanter, 1969 . . . . 5.00
Old Fitzgerald, Hillbilly, pint, 1969 . . . . 15.00
Old Fitzgerald, Old Cabin Still decanter, 1958 . . . . 20.00
Ski Country, Bobcat Family, miniature. 20.00

WICKER

Extremely popular in the late 19th century, wicker fell from grace briefly in the early 1910s, regained its popularity in the 1920s, vanished completely by the 1930s, and enjoyed a renaissance in the 1960s and 70s, only to disappear in the mid–1980s.

Wicker is not made from wicker. Wicker is a generic term used to describe woven objects made from cane, fiber, dried grasses, rattan, reed, rush, or willow. Wicker as a term was not used until the early 20th century. While most individuals think of wicker primarily in terms of furniture, it was used for a wide range of materials from baskets to window boxes.

Cyrus Wakefield and his Wakefield Rattan Company, South Reading, Massachusetts, introduced wicker furniture to America. A few years prior to his death in 1873, Wakefield was selling rattan to Levi Heywood, founder of Heywood Brothers Company in Gardner, Massachusetts. Gardner A. Watkins, a Heywood employee, invented a loom that could weave cane into continuous sheets and an automatic channeling machine which cut grooves in a wooden seat. As a result, many hand–caners lost their jobs. Heywood Brothers prospered.

Wakefield and Heywood were fierce competitors in the wicker furniture market through the 1870s, 80s, and 90s. In 1897 the two firms merged, creating the Heywood Brothers and Wakefield Company. The company had a virtual monopoly on the wicker furniture market until the 1920s.

Heywood–Wakefield continually changed the design of its furniture to conform with current design styles. When ornate Victorian designs became passé in the late 1890s, the firm made wicker in Mission styles. Although not as well received as the Victorian wicker, Mission wicker kept the company profitable.

In 1917 Marshall B. Lloyd of Menominee, Michigan, invented a machine that twisted chemically treated paper that in turn could be woven by his Lloyd loom. Lloyd's art fiber furniture featuring a closely woven style gained rapid acceptance. In 1921 Heywood Brothers and Wakefield Company, now officially Heywood–Wakefield, purchased Lloyd Manufacturing.

The wicker market collapsed in the 1930s. Heywood–Wakefield shifted to the manufacture of metal and wood furniture. In 1979 Heywood–Wakefield stopped production of wood furniture at its Gardner, Massachusetts, plant. Today the company makes metal furniture for auditoriums and schools at its Menominee facility.

Heywood–Wakefield was only one of many American companies making wicker objects. Chittenden–Eastman Company (Burlington, Iowa), High Point Bending and Chair Company (Silver City, North Carolina), and Joseph P. McHugh & Company (New York, NY) are other companies which manufactured wicker furniture. Montgomery Ward and Sears, Roebuck sold wicker since the 1880s. Most was inexpensively made by outside suppliers, e.g., G. W. Randall & Company (Grand Rapids, Michigan), who supplied Sears, Roebuck.

Collectors have little interest in post–1930 wicker. Its only value is as secondhand furniture. Use form, e.g., coffee tables and end tables, and weave, loosely done, to identify post–1930 wicker.

Reference: Tim Scott, *Fine Wicker Furniture: 1870–1930*, Schiffer Publishing, 1990.

Armchair, white, diamond design woven into back and sides . . . . $ 475.00
Basket, natural, tin insert 85.00

Parlor Set, sofa (missing from photo), table, rocker, and armchair, Fogle, $1,000.00.

Bassinet, white, golding hood, wooden wheels, rubber tires 350.00
Butler's Tray, natural, lift–off glass top, turned wood legs 200.00
Cake Stand, cov, natural, openwork design 175.00
Candlestick Holders, natural, 5" h 75.00
Carriage, white, close weave design, diamond pattern on sides, wire wheels, rubber tires 210.00
Chair, natural, rolled arms, multicolored diamond pattern on back 360.00
Coat Rack, child's, white, tight weave base, gessoed roses on base and pole, wooden hooks, 28" h 250.00
Coat Rack, white, wrapped columns 310.00
Cradle, white, open weave design, cushioned bottom, crescent lattice work under cradle, ball feet 810.00
Crib, white, open weave design, floral design on headboard and footboard, wrapped legs 655.00
Desk, dark brown, oak top, woven shelf, wrapped legs 460.00
Desk, white, 2 woven shelves on each side 455.00
Desk, white, wooden top, wrapped legs, 1 drawer 560.00
End Table, white, stained oak top, wrapped legs, open weave skirt, and woven shelf 260.00
Fernery, white, 2 tight weave handles 240.00
High Chair, doll's, white, pine frame, woven backrest, 27" h 225.00
Inkwell Holder, green, scalloped reed trim, wooden base 175.00
Lamp, floor, white, pagoda shaped shade 450.00
Lamp, floor, natural, dark stained circular design on base, brass finial 325.00
Lamp, table, natural, orig silk fringe 210.00
Lingerie Chest, natural, 6 drawers, tight weave design, cane and gesso 655.00
Lounge Chair, white, Bar Harbor, flat woven arms, footrest, and ball feet 655.00
Night Stand, white, lift–off shelf reveals bottom hamper, machine made 200.00
Plant Stand, natural, square bottom shelf, 46" l 225.00
Plant Stand, white, square, turned wood framework 150.00
Planter, natural, tightly woven design, wrapped legs 185.00
Porch Swing, white, machine made wickerwork fiber, metal framework under seat, 4 ft l 625.00

Rocking Chair, child's, white, wing back design, diamond pattern 210.00
Rocking Chair, white, orig tie–on back pad and seat cushion, hand–woven reed seat 350.00
Scale, natural, open weave design 110.00
Sewing Basket, white, wrapped circular handles, ball feet 175.00
Side Chair, natural, braided construction 150.00
Table, natural, oak top, wooden shelf 260.00
Tea Cart, light blue, tight weave design, leaf pattern on sides, woven shelf, wrapped legs, lift out tray 610.00
Tea Cart, natural, 2 shelves, braided edges, wrapped legs 355.00
Telephone Chair, white, tight weave design, oak side shelf, storage shelf below 675.00
Vanity and Chair, white, oval–shaped desk 700.00

WILLOW WARE

Willow ware is a pattern based upon a Chinese legend. A wealthy father wishes his daughter to marry a man he has chosen. Instead, she runs off with a young lover. The couple is pursued by a group of assassins (or the father or bridegroom–to–be depending on who you believe). Escaping to a pagoda on an island, the gods take pity on the young lovers, turning them into a pair of turtle doves so they can be together forever. This story provides the key decorative elements of the Willow pattern—a willow tree, two pagodas (one for the father, the other on the island for the lovers), a fence, three individuals crossing a bridge to the island, and two birds.

As early as the 1830s, over 200 British pottery manufacturers made pieces featuring a variation of the Willow pattern. Johnson Brothers (Wedgwood Group), Royal Doulton, and Wedgwood are still manufacturing pieces of Willow ware.

By 1900 American, Dutch, French, German, Irish, and Swedish ceramic manufacturers had copied the pattern. Buffalo China introduced its Willow ware in 1905. Homer Laughlin and Royal China produced vast quantities for the household market; Shenango did the same for the hotel and restaurant market.

The Japanese also copied the Willow pattern. Noritake produced its first pieces in 1902. Pieces bearing the NKT Co., Maruta, and Moriyama are among those most highly desired by collectors. Willow was one of the most popular patterns made during the "Occupied Japan" period.

Although found primarily in blue, Willow ware also was produced in black, brown, green, mulberry, pink, red, and polychrome. Collectors prefer blue. As a result, harder–to–find colors often sell for less. The maker is the key to value. Collectors place a premium on ware made by manufacturers with a reputation for quality, e.g., Wedgwood.

References: Leslie Bockol, *Willow Ware,* Schiffer Publishing, 1995; Mary Frank Gaston, *Blue Willow: An Identification & Value Guide, Revised Second Edition,* Collector Books, 1990, 1996 value update.

Newsletter: *The Willow Word,* PO Box 13382, Arlington, TX 76094.

Collectors' Club: International Willow Collectors, 836 Moss Hill, Ashland, OH 44805.

REPRODUCTION ALERT: The Scio Pottery, located in Scio, Ohio, is currently producing a Willow pattern. These poor–quality pieces are unmarked. A wall plaque (plate) made in China is also being produced. It is marked "BLUE WILLOW" and impressed "Made in China."

Note: All pieces listed are blue unless noted otherwise.

Allerton, dinner plate, 10" d . . . . $ 25.00
Booths, cup and saucer 30.00
Buffalo Pottery, cup and saucer 25.00
Buffalo Pottery, chop plate, 13" d 85.00
Churchill, bread and butter plate 8.00
Churchill, butter dish, cov, ¼ lb 30.00
Churchill, cereal bowl, 6" d 8.00
Churchill, chop plate, 12¾" d 25.00
Churchill, coffeepot, cov 50.00
Churchill, creamer 15.00
Churchill, cup and saucer 10.00
Churchill, dinner plate, 10⅜" d 8.00
Churchill, gravy boat 30.00
Churchill, mug 8.00
Churchill, platter, oval, 14½" d 50.00
Churchill, salad plate, 8⅛" d 8.00
Churchill, salt and pepper shakers, pr 20.00
Churchill, soup bowl, 8" d 10.00
Churchill, vegetable bowl, 8⅞" d 15.00
Coalport, ginger jar, cov 70.00
Hazel Atlas Glass Co, sugar, cov, 4½" h, red 20.00
Homer Laughlin Co, berry bowl, small 6.00
Homer Laughlin Co, bread and butter plate 5.00
Homer Laughlin Co, creamer 12.00
Homer Laughlin Co, cup and saucer 10.00
Homer Laughlin Co, cup and saucer, jumbo 30.00
Homer Laughlin Co, custard cup, 3" h 15.00
Homer Laughlin Co, gravy boat, 7¼" l 20.00
Homer Laughlin Co, platter, oval, 12" l 25.00
Homer Laughlin Co, soup bowl, 8¼" d 12.00
Homer Laughlin Co, sugar, cov 15.00
Homer Laughlin Co, teapot, cov 45.00

Homer Laughlin Co, vegetable bowl, 9" d 12.00
Homer Laughlin Co, vegetable bowl, oval, 9" l 12.00
Japan, berry bowl, small, pink 5.00
Japanese, cup and saucer, decal inside cup, pink 25.00
Johnson Bros, bread and butter plate, 6¼" d 5.00
Johnson Bros, butter dish, cov, 1/4 lb 50.00
Johnson Bros, cake plate and server 55.00
Johnson Bros, cereal bowl, 6⅛" d 8.00
Johnson Bros, chop plate, 12" d 40.00
Johnson Bros, coffeepot, cov 70.00
Johnson Bros, creamer, 2⅞" h 20.00
Johnson Bros, creamer, 6" h, pink 75.00
Johnson Bros, cup and saucer 10.00
Johnson Bros, dinner plate, 10¼" d 15.00
Johnson Bros, fruit bowl, 5⅛" d 5.00
Johnson Bros, gravy boat and underplate 45.00
Johnson Bros, luncheon plate, 8¾" d 10.00
Johnson Bros, mug 12.00
Johnson Bros, oatmeal bowl, 5½" d 15.00
Johnson Bros, pie server, stainless blade 20.00
Johnson Bros, pitcher, 5½" h 35.00
Johnson Bros, platter, oval, 12" l 25.00
Johnson Bros, platter, oval, 14" l 35.00
Johnson Bros, platter, oval, 14½" l, pink 85.00
Johnson Bros, salad plate, 7⅞" d 8.00
Johnson Bros, salt and pepper shakers, pr 35.00
Johnson Bros, soup bowl, flat, 8⅛" d 10.00
Johnson Bros, sugar bowl, cov, 2½" h 30.00
Johnson Bros, teapot, cov 60.00
Johnson Bros, teapot, cov, pink 85.00
Johnson Bros, tumbler, 4⅛" h 8.00
Johnson Bros, vegetable bowl, cov 75.00
Johnson Bros, vegetable bowl, oval, 9" l 22.00
Jones and Sons, A. B., relish, 9½" sq 75.00
Maling, C. T., sherbet dish, 3½" h 45.00
Mason's, bowl, 9" d 45.00
McNichol China, grill plate, 9½" d 20.00
North Staffordshire Pottery Co, Ltd, teapot, cov 65.00
Royal China Co, ashtray, 5½" d 10.00
Royal China Co, bread and butter plate 5.00
Royal China Co, cake plate, tab handles 15.00
Royal China Co, casserole 25.00
Royal China Co, chop plate, 12¼" d 20.00
Royal China Co, chop plate, 13½" d 22.00
Royal China Co, creamer and sugar 20.00
Royal China Co, cup and saucer 8.00
Royal China Co, dinner plate, 9" d 8.00
Royal China Co, gravy boat and ladle 25.00
Royal China Co, grill plate, 10½" d 12.00
Royal China Co, salad plate 4.00
Royal China Co, salt and pepper shakers, pr, pink 20.00
Royal China Co, server, 2–tier 20.00
Royal China Co, server, 3–tier 30.00
Royal China Co, shaker, handled 10.00
Royal China Co, soup bowl, 8½" d 10.00
Royal China Co, teapot, cov 40.00
Royal China Co, vegetable bowl, 9" d, pink 15.00
Royal China Co, vegetable bowl, 10" d 15.00
Royal Doulton, bread and butter plate, 7" d 15.00
Royal Doulton, cake plate, 11" d 55.00
Royal Doulton, cereal bowl, 6¼" d 35.00

Venton/Steventon, vegetable bowl, 9½" l, 7½" w, $35.00.

Royal Doulton, creamer **55.00**
Royal Doulton, cup and saucer **30.00**
Royal Doulton, demitasse cup and saucer **30.00**
Royal Doulton, dinner plate, 10½" d **25.00**
Royal Doulton, fruit bowl, 5¼" d **25.00**
Royal Doulton, gravy boat and underplate **140.00**
Royal Doulton, luncheon plate, 10" d **35.00**
Royal Doulton, mug **25.00**
Royal Doulton, platter, oval, 13½" l **120.00**
Royal Doulton, platter, oval, 16¼" l **150.00**
Royal Doulton, soup bowl, flat, 8¾" d **30.00**
Royal Doulton, sugar bowl, cov **100.00**
Royal Doulton, vegetable bowl, oval, 10⅜" d **85.00**
Shenango, bread and butter plate **12.00**
Shenango, cadelabra and 2 side dishes, 11" h, price
    for set **200.00**
Shenango, cereal bowl **20.00**
Shenango, compote, 3" h, 6" d **50.00**
Shenango, creamer, individual, 2½" h **35.00**
Shenango, cup and saucer **15.00**
Shenango, dessert bowl **15.00**
Shenango, dinner plate **20.00**
Shenango, fruit bowl **12.00**
Shenango, gravy boat, 6" l **50.00**
Shenango, grill plate, 10" d **20.00**
Shenango, match safe, 2" h **75.00**
Shenango, mustard pot, 2½" h **50.00**
Shenango, relish, 5–part, 9½" d **40.00**
Shenango, soup bowl, 9" d **25.00**
Shenango, vegetable bowl **25.00**
Unmarked, creamer, 2½" h **12.00**
Unmarked, tray, 19" d **30.00**
Venton/Steventon, creamer, pink **15.00**
Venton/Steventon, dinner plate, 10" d, pink **12.00**
Venton/Steventon, soup plate, 7" d, pink **12.00**

WORLD WAR II

World War II collectibles are divided into two basic groups, Allied versus Axis and military versus home front. During the recent 50th World War II anniversary celebrations, home front material received as much attention as military material.

By the late 1930s the European nations were engaged in a massive arms race. Using the Depression as a spring board, Adolph Hitler and the National Socialists gained political power in Germany in the mid–1930s. Bitter over the peace terms of World War I, Hitler developed a concept of a Third Reich and began an aggressive unification and expansion program.

The roots of the Second World War are found in the Far East, not Europe. Japan's invasions of China and Korea and the world's failure to react encouraged Hitler. In 1939 Germany launched a blitzkrieg invasion of Poland. Although technically remaining neutral, America provided as much support as it could to the Allies.

America entered the war on December 7, 1941, following the Japanese attack on Pearl Harbor. There were four main theaters—Western, Eastern, Mediterranean, and Pacific. The entire world, either directly or indirectly, was involved in World War II in the period between 1942 and 1945. Neutral countries faced tremendous pressure from both sides.

The tide of battle turned in the Pacific with the Battle of Midway and the invasion of Guadalcanal in 1942. In 1943 the surrender of General von Arnim in Tunisia and the invasion of Italy put Allied forces in command in the Mediterranean theater. The year 1943 also marked the end of the siege of Stalingrad and the recapture of Kiev. Allied forces regained the offensive in the Western theater on June 6, 1944, D–Day.

Germany surrendered on May 7, 1945. After atomic bombs were dropped on Hiroshima (August 6) and Nagasaki (August 9), Japan surrendered on August 14, 1945.

It is incorrect to assume military collectibles are war–driven. Many armed forces fighting in 1939, 1940, and 1941 used equipment left over from World War I. During the Korean Conflict, many military units used large quantities of World War II equipment. This is why provenance (ownership) plays a critical role in determining the value of a military collectible.

Further, beware of the large quantity of Russian material that is flooding the collecting market now that the Iron Curtain has fallen. Much of this material is of recent production and hastily made.

References: Stan Cohen, *V For Victory: America's Home Front During World War II,* Pictorial Histories Publishing, 1991; Stanley Cohen, *To Win the War: Home Front Memorabilia of World War II,* Mortorbooks International, 1995; Robert Heide and John Gilman, *Home Front America: Popular Culture of the World War II Era,* Chronicle Books, 1995; Jon A. Maguire, *Silver Wings, Pinks & Greens: Uniforms, Wings, & Insignia of USAAF Airmen in World War II,* Schiffer Publishing, 1994; Ron Manion, *American Military Collectibles Price Guide,* Antique Trader Books, 1995; Jack Matthews, *Toys Go To War: World War II Military Toys, Games, Puzzles & Books,* Pictorial Histories Publishing, 1994; Sydney B. Vernon, *Vernon's Collector's Guide to Orders, Medals, and Decorations, 3rd Revised Edition,* published by author, 1995.

Periodicals: *Military Collector Magazine,* PO Box 245, Lyon Station, PA 19536; *Military Collectors' News,* PO Box 702073, Tulsa, OK 74170; *Military Trader,* PO Box 1050, Dubuque, IA 52004.

Collectors' Clubs: American Society of Military Insignia Collectors, 526 Lafayette Ave, Palmerton, PA 18701; Orders and Medals Society of America, PO Box 484, Glassboro, NJ 08028.

Note: For additional listings see Nazi Items.

Aircraft Clock, 8–day, black dial, black Bakelite body,
    Elgin . . . . **$ 75.00**
Aircraft Oxygen Indicator Gauge, orig carton **8.00**
Aviator's Scarf, white rayon, stamped black "Army Air
    Forces" on one side **35.00**
Bank, litho tin, drum shape, "Remember Pearl
    Harbor," Ohio Art, 2¼" h **175.00**
Banner, window, relative in service, red, white, and
    blue, star center, black wood post, gold cord,
    11 x 15" **25.00**
Bayonet, 18" l, no scabbard **22.00**
Blotter, insignia guide, color, 1942, 4 x 9" **8.00**
Book, *World War II in Headlines and Pictures,*
    Philadelphia, *Evening Bulletin,* soft cover, 1956,
    10½ x 14" **35.00**

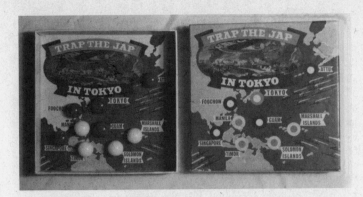

Game, Trap The Jap, marble puzzle, Modern Novelties, Cleveland, OH, 4¹/₂" sq, $15.00.

Booklet, *War Birds of the U. S. A.*, Hart, Schaffner, and Marx Clothes premium, 24 pgs **75.00**

Bracelet, souvenir, Army, 8th Air Force, nickel–plated brass band, incised short wing 8th Air Force patch design center, "England–ETO–1945–USAF" on band, inside inscribed "With Love" **45.00**

Candy Dish, officer's visor cap shape, removable crown **20.00**

Cartridge Belt, USMC, olive drab web, black metal buckle **15.00**

Cigarette Case, aluminum, engraved int and ext, Army emblem and initials "PE" and star in cigarette chamber **55.00**

Figurine, Hitler as skunk, plaster, black and white, red mouthline accents, 5¹/₂" h **175.00**

Handkerchief, silk, "11th Airborne Division/188th Paraglider Infantry/the Philippines/1945," printed airborne wing in center, colored trim **18.00**

Helmet, British, liner, chin strap, netting **40.00**

Identification Bracelet, gilt, Navy pilot wing in center, reinforced links **40.00**

Jacket, United States, bomber type, issue wool, Army **25.00**

Letter Opener, figural propeller, 3D, "Keep 'Em Buying–WSAN Allentown, Penna" **22.00**

Magazine, *Time,* Apr 6, 1942, WWII coverage **28.00**

Magazine, *War Stories From the Front,* 1944 . . . . **15.00**

Mail Cover, Anti–Axis, 2 envelopes, 1 depicting Hitler in blue with red lettered inscription, other has black and white Nazi and Japanese vultures under 1944 date above caption "The Last Quarter, They're In A Huddle," postmarked Aug 1944 . . . . **50.00**

Matchbook, Remember Pearl Harbor **5.00**

Medal, Purple Heart, ribbon bar, lapel device, cased **45.00**

Mess Tin, British, 2 pc, 1 with steel wire folding handle, mkd, dated, broad arrow **30.00**

Mortar Shell, German, 80mm, deactivated, lightly rusted **25.00**

Newspaper, *Deutsche Bug–Zeitung,* Nazi, Oct 10, 1942, large spread eagle on wreathed swastika in masthead **20.00**

Newspaper, *New York Daily Mirror,* "Hitler Dead, Nazi Radio Claims," Wednesday, May 2, 1945 . . . . **50.00**

Newspaper, *Scranton PA Tribune,* "Tokyo Bombed By Allies," Saturday, Apr 18, 1942 . . . . **50.00**

Officer's ID Card, mug shot photo in center, finger prints on 1 side, date on other, serial number printed on outside of card, official emb seal over lapping photo, issued to 2nd Lieutenant in Signal Corps, Nov 20, 1942 . . . . **22.00**

Photo Album, American Navy, 1953, 49th Seabee Battalion, large company photo, names, autographs, photos **140.00**

Pin, enamel, French Paratrooper, symbols of vertical sword behind winged parachute, 3 entwined red, white, and blue rings beneath parachute, gold luster accents, inscribed "Honneur Et Patrie" **50.00**

Pin, leather, "Remember Pearl Harbor," die–cut, brown, red, white, and blue Uncle Sam illus, white lettering **50.00**

Plaque, Army Quartermaster's, brass, wheel showing 13 stars, crossed sword, and key, spread winged eagle at top, 12" d **38.00**

Postcard, anti–axis, black and white card depicting newspaper with small rectangular opening at center on gummed paper for placement of serviceman photo, headlines are Anti–Axis **50.00**

Poster, "Help Buy This Gun By Buying Stamps Or Bonds," GI manning anti–aircraft gun, sgd "Jos Popa," 36 x 47" **20.00**

Poster, "Mine Eyes Have Seen The Glory," Women Army Corps, color graphics, shadow profiles of GI's in combat and woman in Army uniform looking up, WAC, Women's Army Corps, and emblem on sides, 20 x 30" **95.00**

Poster, "Think American, Our Hearts, Heads, and Hands are United," marines, sailors, and workers standing before huge draped American Flag, silver ground, 1944, 20 x 27" **300.00**

Propaganda Leaflet, Hans Frank photo below quotes from Roosevelt's speech about war crimes, gummed back, written in Polish, 1943, 9¹/₂ x 6¹/₂" **50.00**

Sheet Music, *Anchors Away,* Charles A. Zimmerman, 1942 . . . . **5.00**

Army–Navy Insignia Guide, mechanical wheel with branch insignia, cardboard, 1942, 4 x 5¹/₂", $20.00

Sheet Music, *Remember Pearl Harbor*, Don Reid and
Sammy Kaye, 1942 . . . . **10.00**

Sheet Music, *We'll Always Remember Pearl Harbor*,
Alfred Bryan, Willie Raskin and Gerald Marks,
1941 . . . . **15.00**

Streamer, white silk, black embroidered "Combat
Infantry Regiment," 4' l. **22.00**

Sweetheart Locket, heart shaped, gold finish, Eagle,
globe, and anchor on front **18.00**

Sweetheart Pin, Army Air Force, pinback, stamped
polished metal, fighter with Army Air Force stars
on wing. **20.00**

Sweetheart Pin, Navy, visor cap design, simulated
mother–of–pearl, mini USN anchor appliqué. **25.00**

Sweetheart Ring, SS, Lieutenant Colonel's leaf. **30.00**

Sweetheart Wing, Army Air Force, pilot style, pinback, gilded center disc, army emblem surrounded
by jewel chips **20.00**

Tray, Navy Submarine Remembrance, wooden frame
and handles, black and white litho of submarine,
glass front, 15 x 21" **25.00**

Trench Art, ashtray, brass, made from 105 mm shell,
4 rifles rounds act as center pedestals, 50–caliber
round center dec, 2" h **35.00**

Trench Art, lighter, made from German 25 mm round **38.00**

Tumbler, set of 8, "V" for Victory decal, red, white,
and blue, double gold band at top **45.00**

Window Sticker, "Home of a Marine," red, yellow,
and white, Jun 19, 1943, 4 x 8¹⁄" **15.00**

WORLD'S FAIRS & EXPOSITIONS

World's Fairs trace their origins to the great 19th century trading fairs of Sturbridge, England, and Nizhni Novgorod, Russia. The 1851 London Crystal Palace Exhibition is considered the first modern World's Fair. Forty nations participated in the 13,937 exhibits, half of which were from Great Britain. Five of America's 534 exhibits won a prize for originality of design. Charles Goodyear's vulcanized rubber boots and Cyrus McCormick's reaper were two of them.

The 1853 New York Crystal Palace Exhibition was America's first World's Fair. It featured 4,685 exhibitions, approximately half of which were from the United States. A Colt revolver and repeating rifle were one of the exhibit's highlights.

Several World's Fairs were held each decade during the 19th century. For example, there were four World's Fairs in the 1870s—Vienna (1873), Philadelphia (1876), Paris (1878), and Sydney (1879). In 1928 an international convention was called to regulate the scheduling and method of conducting World's Fairs. Thirty–nine nations signed a Paris agreement creating the Bureau of International Expositions to limit the frequency of World's Fairs and define the rights and obligations of organizers and participants. The Bureau meets biannually.

World's Fairs divide into two basic types: (1) universal and (2) special category. The 1939/40 New York World's Fair and the 1967 Montreal Expo are examples of universal World's Fairs. Spokane's 1974 Expo and Transpo '86 in Vancouver were special category World's Fairs. BIF rules stipulate that one universal fair can be held every ten years, special category fairs can be held every two years but in different countries.

Most World's Fair material pictures a building, logo, or mascot. Often the name of the fair is missing. Manufacturers assume individuals will recognize the image. Collectors should familiarize themselves with the main buildings and special features of each World's Fair and Exposition.

There were thousands of local, regional, state, and national fairs and exhibitions that were not World's Fairs. This material is collected at the local level. It is shunned by most World's Fair collectors. Further, World's Fair collecting is very nationalistic. American collectors concentrate primarily on World's Fairs held in America.

Periodical: *World's Fair*, PO Box 339, Corte Madera, CA 94976.

Collectors' Club: World's Fair Collectors' Society, PO Box 20806, Sarasota, FL 34276.

1926, Philadelphia Sesquicentennial Exposition, pin,
die–cut, bronze colored, Liberty Bell inscribed
with "1776" inside horseshoe. . . . . **$ 15.00**

1926, Philadelphia Sesquicentennial Exposition,
postcard, "Greetings to you from Philadlephia, The
Sesqui Centennial," Liberty Bell, garland, and
shields, divided back with blue Sesqui Centennial
seal, unused. **18.00**

1933/34, Chicago Exposition, book, *A Century of
Progress Official Book of Views*, soft cover, color
illus of fair buildings and scenes, ©1933 Reuben
Donnelly Corp, 64 pgs, 9 x 12". **20.00**

1933/34, Chicago Exposition, bookmark, celluloid,
hot pink design, black fair symbol, 1½" d holder
attached to 4" bookmark. **15.00**

1933/34, Chicago Exposition, elongated coin,
"American Indian Villages, Chicago World's Fair". **25.00**

1933/34, Chicago Exposition, medal, bronze luster,
"Research/Industry 1833–1933," "A Century of
Progress International Exposition–Chicago 1933"
inscribed on back rim. **25.00**

1933/34, Chicago Exposition, pinback button, "A
Century of Progress," black and silver **28.00**

1933/34, Chicago Exposition, mesh purse, silver frame, green and white enameled front with "1934 World's Fair Chicago," white enameled back, 4" w, 6¹⁄₂" h with handle, $125.00.

1933/34, Chicago Exposition, thermometer, round, enameled steel, "Chicago World's Fair, Fort Dearborn," 3³/₈" d. **30.00**

1935, California Pacific Internaional Exposition, San Diego, "National Parks of the West," Standard Oil premium, black and white photos by western photographers, orig mailing envelope, 16 pgs, 5 x 8". **5.00**

1936, Cleveland, Great Lakes Exposition, bank, waxed cardboard milk carton, red and blue design on white ground, Dairymens Milk Co, Cleveland sponsors, 3¹/₂" h **38.00**

1936, Texas Centennial Exposition, drinking glass, clear, dark blue official seal, reverse with dark blue cowboy on rearing horse, 3¹/₂" h **28.00**

1939, Golden Gate Exposition, San Francisco, California, comb, amber plastic, pocket size, emb gold–tone metal case with center brass medallion **35.00**

1939, Golden Gate Exposition, San Francisco, California, drinking glass, "California Building" **18.00**

1939, New York World's Fair, appreciation certificate, "Hotel Chesterfield," parchment–like paper, Fair logo with gold accent at top, facsimile signature of hotel president and mayor of New York City at bottom, 9¹/₄ x 13³/₄" **20.00**

1939, New York World's Fair, ashtray, metal, dark finish, inscribed "Strikalite," 3 x 3³/₄ x 4¹/₂" **55.00**

1939, New York World's Fair, catalog, Stoeger's Catalog and Handbook of Arms and Ammunition, Jubilee issue. **155.00**

1939, New York World's Fair, drinking glass, amusement area, parachute jump, Libbey **15.00**

1939, New York World's Fair, soda fountain glass, Lagoon of the Nations, Libbey **15.00**

1939, New York World's Fair, drinking glass, "Official Souvenir New York World's Fair, 1939," Canada Dry promotion. **15.00**

1939, New York World's Fair, drinking glass, textile building exhibit **18.00**

1939, New York World's Fair, map, fairgrounds and New York City, Trylon and Perisphere, 20 x 28" **28.00**

1939, New York World's Fair, pin, Bakelite, yellow, metal stickpin, blue glass orb on front center, "New York World's Fair" over Theme Center, mkd "molded in the F. J. Stokes automatic press" **75.00**

1939, New York World's Fair, pinback button, blue, white, and orange, 1³/₄" d **75.00**

1939, New York World's Fair, pocket knife, steel, 2–blade, pearl–like handles, Theme Center in blue. . . . **100.00**

1939, New York World's Fair, postcard, Chase & Sanborn Coffee marionettes, color, 3¹/₄ x 5¹/₂" **10.00**

1939, New York World's Fair, poster, "Go By All Means, World's Fair of 1940," stylized image of family riding high wheel bicycle, scooter, and running to Fair, S. Ekmar, 13 x 20" **100.00**

1939, New York World's Fair, salt and pepper shaker, 1 pc, teardrop shaped base, orange and blue, gold Fair inscription, 3³/₄" h **35.00**

1939, New York World's Fair, playing cards, Perisphere and Trylon, red border **22.00**

1939, New York World's Fair, timetable, Around the Grounds, Greyhound NYC transit **10.00**

1939, New York World's Fair, radio, RCA Victor, table model, dark brown syroco and wood case, molded front with Trylon and Perisphere, 9 x 6 x 6", $85.00.

1940, New York World's Fair, brochure, "Largest Model Railroad in the World," fold–out, black, white, red accents, 6¹/₂ x 10". **12.00**

1940, New York World's Fair, guide book, soft cover, full–color cov, black and white photos, fold–out map, 5¹/₄ x 8". **15.00**

1940, New York World's Fair, patch, felt, dark blue Trylon and Perisphere and "1940" date, orange ground, 3 x 3" **22.00**

1962, Seattle, Century 21 Exposition, iced tea tumbler, frosted, United States Science Pavilion **5.00**

1962, Seattle, Century 21 Exposition, serving tray, litho tin, dark blue, Space Needle, Monorail, Science Pavilion, and Coliseum, 11" d **15.00**

1964, New York World's Fair, bank, ceramic, girl and boy with balloons on one side, fair scene on reverse. **65.00**

1964, New York World's Fair, employee badge, celluloid, "American Express," blue, black, and white **50.00**

1964, New York World's Fair, iced tea tumbler, frosted, Hall of Science. **5.00**

1964, New York World's Fair, juice glass, sponsored by U.S. Steel. **8.00**

1964, New York World's Fair, nodder, composition, Unisphere, blue and white, "1964–New York World's Fair–1965" decal on base, 4" h **35.00**

1964, New York World's Fair, plate, milk glass, Unisphere, Swiss Sky Ride, Monorail, and exhibit buildings, Anchor Hocking, 10" d **18.00**

1964, New York World's Fair, salt and pepper shakers, pr, ceramic, figural Unisphere, blue and white, orig foil sticker **12.00**

1964, New York World's Fair, snow dome, white oval plastic base, int image of Unisphere and stylized images of skyscraper with blue night sky and small fireworks bursts **60.00**

1964, New York World's Fair, tray, plastic, oval, raised fair attractions, 10¹/₂ x 11¹/₂" **42.00**

1962, Seattle, Century 21 Exposition, orange and brown, "Seattle World's Fair," mkd "Made in Seattle Wash, House of Porcelain," 5 x 4¹/₂", $8.00.

1967, Montreal Exposition, lapel pin, brass, repeated
motif around edge, threaded post fastener **12.00**
1976, Philadelphia Bicentennial, alarm clock, metal,
windup, Declaration of Independence on dial,
dark copper–bronze finish, "Commemorative
Series Registered Edition" on back **45.00**
1982, Knoxville World's Fair, sailor cap, black and
white inscription on brim **5.50**

WRIGHT, RUSSEL

Russel Wright (1904–1976) is one of the most important industrial designers of the 20th century. He received his artistic training at the Cincinnati Art Academy under the direction of Frank Duveneck and in New York, in part under the watchful eye of Norman Bel Geddes for whom he designed stage sets. While in New York, Wright met and married Mary Small Einstein.

In 1930 Wright was making masks of stage and political personalities, e.g., Greta Garbo and Herbert Hoover. A year later he was selling aluminum and pewter objects from a small studio on East 53rd Street. It was also during this period that he introduced his Circus Animals series. Suffering financially in 1933 and 1934, Wright's life changed for the better when Americans fell in love with aluminum.

In 1936 he joined with his wife Mary and Irving Richards to form the Raymor Company. Wright designed exclusively for Raymor for five years, after which time he sold his interests to Richards and formed Russel Wright Associates. In 1951 Wright spelled out his design philosophy in his book, *Guide To Easier Living.*

Wright designs appeared in a wide range of mediums from wood to metal. Acme Lamps Company, American Cyanide (plastic dinnerware), Chase Brass and Copper, Conant Ball (furniture), General Electric, Heywood–Wakefield (a 60–piece furniture line), Hull Cutlery (flatware), Imperial Glass, Klise Woodworking Company, National Silver (flatware), Mutual Sunset Lamp

Company, Old Hickory Furniture, Old Morgantown, and the Stratton Furniture Company are some the companies that made products based upon Wright's designs.

Russel Wright designed several major dinnerware lines: American Modern for Steubenville (1939–1959), Iroquois Casual for Iroquois China (1946–1960s), Highlight for Paden City (1948) a solid color institutional line for Sterling China (1949), White Clover for Harker (1951), and the oriental–inspired Esquire shape for Knowles (1955). In addition, he designed an art pottery line for Bauer.

In 1983 the Hudson River Museum, Yonkers, New York, mounted a major exhibition of Wright's designs. Russel Wright's papers are available for research at the George Ahrents Research Library at Syracuse University.

References: Susan and Al Bagdade, *Warman's American Pottery and Porcelain,* Wallace–Homestead, Krause Publications, 1994; Ann Kerr, *The Collector's Encyclopedia of Russel Wright Designs, Second Edition,* Collector Books, 1997.

Aluminumware, bowl	$ 50.00
Aluminumware, gravy	150.00
Aluminumware, tidbit tray	75.00
American Modern, bread and butter plate, gray	6.00
American Modern, casserole, stick handle, chartreuse, 8"	32.00
American Modern, chop plate, white	75.00
American Modern, coaster, coral, gold imprint "Ohio State Auto Assn. 1902–1952," Steubenville backstamp	65.00
American Modern, creamer, coral	12.00
American Modern, creamer, gray	9.00
American Modern, demitasse cup and saucer, coral	24.00
American Modern, demitasse cup and saucer, seafoam	24.00
American Modern, demitasse cup and saucer, white	48.00
American Modern, dinner plate, cedar brown	12.00
American Modern, dinner plate, gray	10.00
American Modern, gravy liner, coral	14.00
American Modern, gravy liner, gray	12.00
American Modern, platter, rect, chartreuse	20.00
American Modern, platter, rect, gray	20.00
American Modern, relish, divided, seafoam	225.00
American Modern, salad bowl, coral	70.00
American Modern, salad bowl, seafoam	95.00
American Modern, sugar, coral	12.00
American Modern, vegetable bowl, open, coral	18.00
Harker White Clover, ashtray, clock face, adv, charcoal gray	150.00
Harker White Clover, dinner plate, 10" d	18.00
Harker, White Clover, salt and pepper shakers, pr, meadow green	40.00
Harker White Clover, vegetable dish, cov, 8¹/₄"	50.00
Iroquois Casual, bread and butter plate, ice blue	5.00
Iroquois Casual, bread and butter plate, nutmeg	5.00
Iroquois Casual, bread and butter plate, pink sherbet	5.00
Iroquois Casual, bread and butter plate, white	4.00
Iroquois Casual, butte, nutmeg	45.00
Iroquois Casual, carafe, charcoal	125.00
Iroquois Casual, casserole, divided, ice blue, 10" d	70.00
Iroquois Casual, casserole, 2 qt, avocado	30.00

Harker White Clover, vases, left: $30.00; right: $20.00.

Iroquois Casual, cereal, white **8.00**
Iroquois Casual, creamer, stacking, lemon. **12.00**
Iroquois Casual, creamer and sugar, stacking,
  avocado. **24.00**
Iroquois Casual, creamer and sugar, stacking,
  charcoal **34.00**
Iroquois Casual, creamer and sugar, stacking, ice
  blue. **24.00**
Iroquois Casual, creamer and sugar, stacking, pink **24.00**
Iroquois Casual, cup and saucer, gray **15.00**
Iroquois Casual, cup and saucer, ice blue **10.00**
Iroquois Casual, cup and saucer, pink sherbet **10.00**
Iroquois Casual, cup and saucer, white **15.00**
Iroquois Casual, dinner plate, avocado **9.00**
Iroquois Casual, dinner plate, gray **12.00**
Iroquois Casual, dinner plate, ice blue **10.00**
Iroquois Casual, dinner plate, pink sherbet **10.00**
Iroquois Casual, dinner plate, white **9.00**
Iroquois Casual, fruit bowl, gray **8.00**
Iroquois Casual, fruit bowl, ice blue **5.00**
Iroquois Casual, pitcher, cov, white. **150.00**
Iroquois Casual, platter, oval, ice blue, 14½" l **30.00**
Iroquois Casual, platter, oval, oyster, 14½" l **45.00**
Iroquois Casual, saucer, pink **5.00**
Iroquois Casual, sugar, stacking, ice blue **20.00**
Iroquois Casual, sugar, stacking, lettuce **20.00**
Iroquois Casual, teacup and saucer, apricot **15.00**
Iroquois Casual, teacup and saucer, pink **15.00**
Iroquois Casual, vegetable, divided, apricot **40.00**
Iroquois Casual, vegetable, divided, avocado **35.00**
Iroquois Casual, vegetable, divided, parsley **40.00**
Iroquois Casual, vegetable, divided, pink **40.00**
Iroquois Casual, vegetable, open, nutmeg, 8" d **20.00**
Iroquois Casual, vegetable, open, pink, 8" d **20.00**
Iroquois Casual, vegetable, open, lemon, 10" d **35.00**
Iroquois Casual, vegetable, open, parsley, 10" d **40.00**

Iroquois Casual Redesigned, cereal, white **8.00**
Iroquois Casual Redesigned, creamer, ice blue **11.00**
Iroquois Casual Redesigned, cup and saucer, pink. **10.00**
Iroquois Casual Redesigned, cup and saucer, white **10.00**
Pinch, Highlight Line, dinner fork, stainless steel,
  brushed satin finish **35.00**
Pinch, Highlight Line, salad fork, stainless steel,
  brushed satin finish **32.00**
Pinch, Highlight Line, soup spoon, stainless steel,
  brushed satin finish **38.00**
Pinch, Highlight Line, teaspoon, stainless steel,
  brushed satin finish **32.00**
Sterling, dinner plate, pink. **12.00**
Sterling, platter, oval, ivy green, 7½" l **22.00**
Sterling, platter, oval, suede gray, 13½" l **35.00**
Sterling, salad plate, cedar brown, 7½" d **8.00**
Sterling, salad plate, pink, 7½" d **8.00**

YARD–LONG PHOTOGRAPHS & PRINTS

Yard–long is a generic term used to refer to photographs and prints that measure approximately 36 inches in length. The format can be horizontal or vertical.

The yard–long print arrived on the scene in the first quarter of the 20th century, experiencing a period of popularity in the late 1910s and early 1920s. Most were premiums, issued by such diverse companies as Pompeian Beauty and Pabst Brewing's Malt Extract. Some came with calendars and were distributed by a wide range of merchants. Some had titles such as "A Yard of Kittens" or "A Yard of Roses." Always check the back. Many yard–long prints have elaborately printed advertisements on their back.

Yard–long prints are one of the many forms that show the amazing capabilities of American lithographers. Brett Litho, Jos. Hoover & Sons, J. Ottmann, and The Osborne Company are a few of the American lithographers who produced yard–long prints.

Yard–long photographs also were popular in the 1910s and 20s. The form survived until the early 1950s. Graduation pictures, especially military units, banquet photographs, and touring groups are the most commonly found. Many have faded from their original black and white to a sepia tone. Unless stopped, this fading will continue until the picture is lost.

Reference: Keagy and Rhoden, *Yard–Long Prints, Book III*, published by authors, 1995.

Calendar, Harvest Moon, sgd by Frank H. Desch,
  John Clay and Company Live Stock Commission
  adv, 1922. . . . . **$ 375.00**
Calendar, Honeymooning in Venice, sgd by
  Gene Pressler, Pompeian Beauty adv, 1922 . . . . **225.00**
Calendar, woman holding bouquet of roses, sgd Earl
  Christy left corner, George Peterman, Bell Plaine,
  Iowa adv, 1928 . . . . **375.00**
Calendar, woman wearing black dress and white
  stole, Selz Good Shoes, G. B. Aschenbrener,
  Fairfield, Wisconsin adv, 1922 . . . . **375.00**
Calendar, woman wearing black sleeveless gown
  with yellow shawl, E. R. Christen & Co adv, 1921 . . . . **375.00**
Calendar, woman wearing red coat with umbrella sit-
  ting on rail, John Clay and Company Live Stock
  Commission adv, 1924 . . . . **375.00**

Photograph, choral society. **35.00**
Photograph, civic organization banquet **35.00**
Photograph, family reunion **30.00**
Photograph, military company grouping **60.00**
Photograph, military graduation **35.00**
Photograph, scenic, panoramic, Grand Canyon. **35.00**
Photograph, school graduation class. **20.00**
Photograph, theater group **45.00**
Photograph, tourist group. **30.00**
Print, Absence Cannot Hearts Divide, sgd
　　Marguerite Clark, Pompeian Beauty adv, 1921. . . . . . **225.00**
Print, A Yard of Youth, F. L. Martini, 1927 . . . . **175.00**
Print, Alluring, sgd Bradshaw Krandall, Pompeian
　　Beauty adv, 1928 . . . . **175.00**
Print, Beauty Gained Is Love Retained, Pompeian
　　Beauty adv, 1925 . . . . **145.00**
Print, Butterick Pattern Lady, Butterick Transfers adv,
　　1930 . . . . **425.00**
Print, Irrestible, sgd by Clement Donshea, Pompeian
　　Art Panel, 1930 . . . . **275.00**
Print, Sweetest Story Ever Told, Pompeian Beauty adv,
　　1920 . . . . **75.00**
Print, The Bride, sgd by Rolf Armstrong, Pompeian
　　Beauty adv, 1927 . . . . **225.00**
Print, woman wearing gold–colored robe, Selz Good
　　Shoes, Peterman's Shoe Store adv, 1927 . . . . **325.00**

YELLOW WARE

Because it was made from a finer clay, yellow ware is sturdier than redware and less dense than stoneware. Most pieces are fired twice, the second firing necessary to harden the alkaline–based glaze of flint, kaolin, and white lead.

The greatest period of yellow ware production occurred in the last half of the 19th century. By 1900 Americans favored white bodied ware over yellow ware. Although no longer playing a major role in the utilitarian household ceramic market, some yellow ware forms, such as mixing bowls and cake molds, were made into the 1950s by firms such as J. A. Bauer, Brush Pottery, Morton Pottery, Pfaltzgraff Pottery, Red Wing, and Weller.

Bowl, blue and brown sponging, mkd "Red Wing
　　Saffron Ware," 9³/₄" d . . . . **$ 45.00**
Bowl, blue and brown sponging, 8³/₈" d, 4¹/₄" h **75.00**
Bowl, brown sponging, oval, 8³/₄" l. **30.00**
Bowl, brown stripes, white slip, 8" d **75.00**
Bowl, mkd "Sharpe's Warranted Fire Proof," 13" d,
　　3³/₈" h **75.00**
Canning Jar, barrel shaped, 7" h **100.00**
Canning Jar, cov, tan and white stripes, 6" h, 8" d **35.00**
Casserole, cov, brown sponging, 7¹/₄" d. **50.00**
Creamer, brown and green sponging, 4¹/₂" h **75.00**
Creamer, molded tavern scenes, brown Rockingham
　　glaze, 4¹/₄" h **20.00**
Crock, brown bands, 5¹/₂" h **35.00**
Custard Cup, brown sponging **10.00**
Food Mold, corn, oval **90.00**

Mixing Bowls, nesting set of 6, continuous molded design of girl watering flowers outside window, $350.00.

Food Mold, pinwheel. **100.00**
Food Mold, rabbit, 8" l. **125.00**
Food Mold, Turk's head, brown sponging, 9" d **110.00**
Ladle, 7¹/₂" l. **25.00**
Milk Pan, 11¹/₂" d. **60.00**
Mixing Bowl, blue and white stripes, mkd
　　"Warranted Fire Proof," 12¹/₄" d, 5³/₄" h **80.00**
Mixing Bowl, blue band, molded rim, 22¹/₂" d. **85.00**
Mixing Bowl, brown and white stripes, 13³/₄" d **35.00**
Mixing Bowl, brown stripes, 15¹/₂" d, 6¹/₂" h **75.00**
Mixing Bowl, molded bark pattern, 6¹/₄" d, 3¹/₂" h **30.00**
Mixing Bowls, nesting set of 4, white band, 10" to
　　14" d. **275.00**
Mixing Bowls, nesting set of 3, brown and green spat-
　　ter, molded rims, 7" to 9¹/₂" d **175.00**
Mixing Bowls, nesting set of 3, brown and white
　　stripes **110.00**
Mug, brown and white stripes, ribbed handle **35.00**
Nappy, 8" d. **100.00**
Pie Funnel, 2¹/₄" h **125.00**
Pie Plate, molded rim, mkd "Oven Serve," 9" d. **60.00**
Pitcher, brown and green drip glaze, molded ribs,
　　5⁵/₈" h **30.00**
Pitcher, brown band, darker brown stripes, 8¹/₂" h **200.00**
Pitcher, brown Rockingham glaze, 4¹/₂" h **75.00**
Pitcher, blue spotted glaze, molded shoulder and
　　neck, 6¹/₄" h. **40.00**
Pitcher, transfer labeled "Equity Elev. & Trading Co.
　　Whitman, ND," green and brown sponging, emb
　　ribs, 4¹/₂" h. **50.00**
Rolling Pin, wood handles **175.00**
Soap Dish, round, 5¹/₂" d **175.00**
Vegetable Dish, brown sponging, oval, 8³/₄" l **30.00**
Wash Bowl and Pitcher, brown and blue sponging,
　　brown stripe, 9¹/₂" d bowl **300.00**

INDEX

L.E. Smith glass, 186-187; 108
Leyendecker, J. C., 165
Libbey glass, 189
License plates, automobilia, 20
Life magazine, 201-202, 218-219
Lighters, 189-190; 120, 200, 231
Limited edition collectibles, 190-193
    Hallmark, 146-147
    Paperweights, 240
    Precious Moments collectibles, 270-271
    whiskey bottles, 388-389
Lincoln Logs, 69
Lindstrom, 361
Linemar, 291, 361
Linens, 193-194
Lionel, toy trains, 358
Little Golden Book look–alikes, 196-197
Little Golden Books, 194-195
Little Lulu, 50, 273
Little Orphan Annie, 33-34, 237, 273, 283, 379
Little Red Riding Hood, china items, 197-198
Lladro porcelains, 198
Lobby cards, 218
Lone Ranger, 66, 76, 134, 148, 214, 226, 267, 273, 316, 374
Look magazine, 201
Lotton, Charles, 198-199
Loveland pottery, 269
Lucent dinnerware, 210
Lum and Abner, 274
Lunch boxes, 199-200
    cartoon characters, 49-50
    television personalities/characters, 343-345

– M –

Machines
    business/office machines, 44
    calculators, 44-45
Maddux, 71, 107-108
Made in Japan, 200
Magazines, 200-201; 257, 260
Magilla Gorilla, 149
Major Bowes, 283
Mallow–Ware, 210
Man from U.N.C.L.E., 67
Manoil, 355
Manker pottery, 268
Maps, 136, 238
Marantz stereo, 153
Marblehead, art pottery, 15
Marbles, 201-202
Mar–Crest, 210
Marx, 358, 361-362
Masonic memorabilia, 124
Matchbox, 203-204
Matchcovers, 204-205
Mattel, 96, 226, 362
Max, Peter, 82, 275
Maynard, Ken, 76
McCoy pottery, 205-206; 51, 71, 83, 91, 107-108, 377
McDonald's memorabilia, 206-207; 220
McIntosh stereo, 154
McKee glass, 207-208; 54-55,   179-180
McKinnell pottery, 269

McNeill, Don, 282
Medical items, 209
Melmac, 209-210
Memphis furniture, 131
Messer pottery, 269
Metalcraft, 362
Metlox, 210-211; 56, 71, 82, 107-108, 377
Mickey Mouse, 3, 13, 33, 38, 61, 90-91, 112, 185, 274, 304, 379
Midgetoy, 362
Midwest Potteries, 217
Mighty Mouse, 50
Mignot, 355
Mikasa, 332
Militia Models, 355
Milk bottles, 211-212
Milk glass, 212-213
Mills Novelty, 256, 313-314
Miniatures, Sebastian Miniatures, 306
Mix, Tom, 34, 76-77, 148, 263, 379
Model kits, 214
Molds, food molds, 119
Monroe, Marilyn, 202; 267, 304, 316
Monster collectibles, 215
Morgantown glass, 215-216
Morrison pottery, 269
Mortens Studios, 91
Morton Potteries, 216-217; 377
Motorola, 284, 346
Mount Clemens, dinnerware, 88
Mouseketeers, 90
Movie memorabilia, 217-219
    autographs, 18-19
    Marilyn Monroe, 202
    non–sport trading cards, 226-227
    posters, 267-268
    Shirley Temple, 346-347
Moxie, 219-220
Mr. Magoo, 51, 66, 274, 317
Munsters, 134, 215
Murray, 243
Mush Mouse, 149
Musical instruments, 220-221
Music boxes, 220
    limited edition collectibles, 192
Music. *See* Records; Sheet music

– N –

Napkin rings, 222
Nash glass, 248
National Potteries, 71
National Youth Administration pottery, 270
Nazi items, 222-223
Neo–Modern furniture, 131
Newcomb College, art pottery, 15-16
New Martinsville/Viking glass, 223-224; 108
Newspapers, 224-225
Nicodemus, wall pockets, 377
Niloak, art pottery, 16, 377
Nipper, RCA Victor, 9
Nodders/bobbin' heads, 225-226; 27, 121, 232
Nomura, 362
Non–sport trading cards, 226-227
Noritake
    Azalea, 227-228

    china, 228-229
    limited edition collectibles, 192
    snack sets, 315
    Tree in the Meadow, 229
    wall pockets, 377
North Dakota pottery, 269-270
North Dakota School of Mines, art pottery, 16
Northwood, wall pockets, 378
Nutcrackers, 229-230
Nutting–like photographs, 231
Nutting, Wallace, 230-231
Nylint, 362

– O –

Occupied Japan, 231-232; 13, 74, 340, 352, 378
Ocean liner collectibles, 232-233
Ohio Art, 305, 362
Oklahoma pottery, 270
Olive Oyl, 51
Oneida, flatware, 115-116
O'Neill, Rose, 165
Ornaments
    Christmas, 56
    Hallmark, 146-147
    limited edition, 192-193
    Precious Moments collectibles, 271
Orrefors, stemware, 332
Overbeck, art pottery, 16
Owens Illinois glass, 180

– P –

Pacific Clay, 108, 268-269
Paden City glass, 233-234; 179
Paden City pottery, 234-235
Pails. *See* Sand pails
Paint By Number sets, 235; 329
Paintings, folk art, 117
Pairpoint, 235-236; 248
Paperback books, 239-240
Paper dolls, 236-237; 73
Paper ephemera, 237-239
Paperweights, 240
    advertising, 5
    aviation collectibles, 21
    British royalty commemoratives, 43
    Charles Lotton, 198-199
    dairy collectibles, 80
    Van Briggle pottery, 370
Parker pens, 246
Parkhurst trading cards, 155
Parrish, Maxfield, 241
Patches, Boy Scout, 40
Patriotic collectibles, 241-242
Paul Revere, art pottery, 16
Peanuts collectibles, 242-243; 112, 199, 220, 225-226, 249, 274, 316, 379
Pedal cars, 243-244
Pennants, 244; 27
Pennsbury pottery, 244-245
Pens/pencils, 245-246
Pepsi–Cola, 246-247; 98
Perfume bottles, 247-248
    Avon, 22

RINKER ENTERPRISES, INC.

HARRY L. RINKER
President

DANA N. MORYKAN
Senior Editor

DENA C. GEORGE Associate Editor	**KATHY WILLIAMSON** Associate Editor	**NANCY BUTT** Librarian
VIRGINIA REINBOLD Support Staff	**RICHARD SCHMELTZLE** Support Staff	**HARRY L. RINKER, JR.** Support Staff

ABOUT THE AUTHOR — HARRY L. RINKER

Harry L. Rinker is one of the most forthright, honest, and "tell–it–like–it–is" reporters in the antiques and collectibles field today. He is the King of Collectibles, the last of the great antiques and collectibles generalists.

Rinker is president of Rinker Enterprises, Inc., a firm specializing in providing consulting, editorial, educational, photographic, research, and writing services in the antiques and collectibles field. He also directs the Institute for the Study of Antiques & Collectibles, serving as the principal instructor for its seminars and conferences.

Rinker is a prolific antiques and collectibles writer. Other House of Collectibles titles by Rinker include *Dinnerware of the 20TH Century: The Top 500 Patterns, Silverware of the 20TH Century: The Top 250 Patterns,* and *Stemware of the 20TH Century: The Top 200 Patterns.* Rinker also is author of *Price Guide to Flea Market Treasures, Fourth Edition* and *Hopalong Cassidy: King of the Cowboy Merchandisers.* He is co–author with Dana N. Morykan of *Warman's Country, 3RD Edition* and *Garage Sale Manual & Price Guide* and with Norman Martinus of *Warman's Paper.*

Rinker on Collectibles, a weekly syndicated column, appears in trade and daily newspapers from coast to coast. Often highly opinionated and controversial, it is one of the most widely read columns in the antiques and collectibles trade.

Rinker is a frequent television and radio guest. He often refers to himself as the "national cheerleader for collectibles and collecting." His television credits include *Oprah, NBC–Today Show, ABC–TV Good Morning America, CNBC–TV Steals and Deals,* and *MPT Wall Street Week With Louis Rukeyser. Whatcha Got,* a ninety–second antiques and collectibles daily feature, is distributed to radio stations by the Minnesota News Network. Rinker also does weekly call–in radio shows for KFGO (Fargo, North Dakota) and WIBC (Indianapolis, Indiana).

Each year Rinker lectures and/or makes personal appearances in over a dozen cities across the United States, often sponsored by the Antiques and Collectibles Dealers Association, trade publications, and antiques mall or show promoters. In 1996 Rinker and James Tucker co–founded the National Association of Collectors.

Rinker is a dedicated accumulator, a collector of collections. He is continually adding new items to over 250 different collections. Among collectibles collectors, he is best known for his collections of Hopalong Cassidy memorabilia and jigsaw puzzles, the latter exceeding 5,000 examples.

Rinker and Connie A. Moore, his wife, live at Schtee Fens (Stone Fences), a modern passive solar house in eastern Pennsylvania.

"One great thing about spending time with Harry is that you come away with some great 'Harry' stories. People who have met him trade these stories like bubble gum cards. Each person tries to have the most outrageous story to tell. I brought back some good ones."

Connie Swain, Editor, Eastern Edition, *AntiqueWeek*

"He was brash, he was iconoclastic, he was funny, and above all, he was thought provoking."

Cheryl York–Cail, *Unravel the Gavel*

HOUSE OF COLLECTIBLES

THE OFFICIAL® IDENTIFICATION AND PRICE GUIDES TO

AMERICAN INDIAN ARROW-
HEADS
1st edition
John L. Stivers
876-37913-7 $17.50

ANTIQUE
AND MODERN FIREARMS
8th edition
Robert H. Balderson
876-37907-2 $17.00

ANTIQUE AND
MODERN TEDDY BEARS
1st edition
Kim Brewer and Carol-Lynn
Rossel Waugh
876-37792-4 $12.00

ANTIQUE CLOCKS
3rd edition
876-37513-1 $12.00

ANTIQUE JEWELRY (ID) 6th
edition
Arthur Guy Kaplan
876-37759-2 $21.00

ARTS AND CRAFTS
*The Early Modernist
Movement in American
Decorative Arts, 1894–
1923* (ID) 2nd edition
Bruce Johnson
876-37879-3 $12.95

AUTOMOBILIA
1st edition
David K. Bausch
676-60030-1 $19.95

THE BEATLES
Records and Memorabilia
1st edition
Perry Cox and Joe Lindsay,
with an
introduction by Jerry Osborne
876-37940-4 $15.00

BEER CANS
5th Edition
Bill Mugrage
876-37873-4 $12.50

BOTTLES
11th edition
Jim Megura
876-37843-2 $14.00

CIVIL WAR
COLLECTIBLES
1st edition
Richard Friz
876-37951-X $17.00

COLLECTIBLE TOYS (ID), 5th
edition
Richard Friz
876-37803-3 $15.00

COLLECTOR CARS
8th edition
Robert H. Balderson
676-60024-7 $17.00

COLLECTOR HANDGUNS
5th edition
Robert H. Balderson
676-60038-7 $17.00

COLLECTOR KNIVES
11th edition
C. Houston Price
876-37973-0 $17.00

COLLECTOR PLATES
6th edition
Rinker Enterprises
876-37968-4 $17.00

COMPACT DISCS
1st edition
Jerry Osborne
876-37923-4 $15.00

COUNTRY MUSIC RECORDS
1st edition
Jerry Osborne
676-60004-2 $15.00

ELVIS PRESLEY RECORDS
AND
MEMORABILIA
1st edition
Jerry Osborne
876-37939-0 $14.00

FINE ART
2nd edition
Rosemary and Michael
McKittrick
876-37909-9 $20.00

FRANK SINATRA RECORDS
AND CDs
1st edition
Vito R. Marino and Anthony C.
Furfero
876-37903-X $12.00

GLASSWARE
1st edition
Mark Pickvet
876-37953-6 $15.00

OLD BOOKS
2nd edition
Marie Tedford and
Pat Goudey
676-60041-7 $17.00

ORIENTAL RUGS
2nd edition
Joyce C. Ware
676-60023-9 $15.00

POSTCARDS (ID)
1st edition
Diane Allmen
876-37802-5 $9.95

POTTERY
AND PORCELAIN
8th edition
Harvey Duke
876-37893-9 $15.00

RECORDS
12th Edition
Jerry Osborne
676-60051-4 $24.00

ROCK AND ROLL—
MAGAZINES, POSTERS, AND
MEMORABILIA (ID), 1st edi-
tion
David K. Henkel
876-37851-3 $12.50

STAR TREK COLLECTIBLES
4th edition
Sue Cornwell
and Mike Kott
876-37994-3 $19.95

WATCHES
10th edition
Cooksey Shugart &
Tom Engle
876-37808-4 $18.00

THE OFFICIAL® BLACKBOOK PRICE GUIDES TO

U.S. COINS
36th Edition, 1998
Thomas E. Hudgeons, Jr.
676-60067-0 $6.99

U.S. PAPER MONEY
30th Edition, 1998
Thomas E. Hudgeons, Jr.
676-60070-0 $6.99

U.S. POSTAGE STAMPS
20th Edition, 1998
Thomas E. Hudgeons, Jr.
676-60064-6 $7.99

WORLD COINS
1st Edition, 1998
Thomas E. Hudgeons, Jr.
876-37945-5 $6.99

COIN COLLECTING

COIN COLLECTOR
STARTER KIT/ONE-MINUTE
COIN EXPERT
Scott A. Travers
676-60045-X $9.95

HOW TO MAKE MONEY IN
COINS RIGHT NOW
Scott A. Travers
876-37997-8 $12.95

ONE-MINUTE COIN EXPERT
*The Complete and Easy Guide
for Fun and Profit*
Second Edition
Scott A. Travers
676-60027-1 $5.99

THE OFFICIAL® GUIDE TO

GUNMARKS
3rd edition
Robert H. Balderson
676-60039-5 $15.00

THE OFFICIAL® DIRECTORY TO

U.S. FLEA MARKETS
5th edition
876-37978-1 $6.99

THE OFFICIAL® BECKETT PRICE GUIDES TO

FOOTBALL CARDS
16th edition, 1997
676-60020-4 $6.99

HOCKEY CARDS
6th edition, 1997
676-60022-0 $6.99

BASKETBALL CARDS
6th edition, 1997
676-60021-2 $6.99

BECKETT GREAT SPORTS HEROES

TROY AIKMAN
676-60035-2 $15.00

WAYNE GRETZKY
676-60032-8 $15.00

ANFERNEE HARDAWAY
676-60033-6 $15.00

MICHAEL JORDAN
876-37979-X $15.00

DAN MARINO
676-60034-4 $15.00

JOE MONTANA
876-37981-1 $15.00

SHAQUILLE O'NEAL
876-37980-3 $15.00

FRANK THOMAS
676-60029-8 $15.00